THE RANDOM HOUSE
THESAURUS

meghan
Fowler

From the **Ballantine Reference Library**
Published by Ballantine Books:

NEW WORDS DICTIONARY
Harold LeMay, Sid Lerner, and Marian Taylor

1000 MOST CHALLENGING WORDS
Norman W. Schur

1000 MOST IMPORTANT WORDS
Norman W. Schur

PRACTICAL ENGLISH: 1000 MOST EFFECTIVE WORDS
Norman W. Schur

THE RANDOM HOUSE BASIC DICTIONARY
French–English–French
Edited by Francesca L. V. Langbaum

THE RANDOM HOUSE BASIC DICTIONARY
German–English–German
Edited by Jenni Karding Moulton

THE RANDOM HOUSE BASIC DICTIONARY
Italian–English–Italian
Edited by Robert A. Hall, Jr.

THE RANDOM HOUSE BASIC DICTIONARY
Spanish–English–Spanish
Edited by Donald F. Sola

THE RANDOM HOUSE BASIC DICTIONARY OF
SYNONYMS AND ANTONYMS
Edited by Laurence Urdang

THE RANDOM HOUSE DICTIONARY
Edited by Jess Stein

TEST YOUR WORD POWER
Jerome B. Agel

THE WORD-A-DAY VOCABULARY BUILDER
Bergen Evans

THE RANDOM HOUSE THESAURUS
Edited by Jess Stein and Stuart Berg Flexner

RANDOM HOUSE WEBSTER'S DICTIONARY
Edited by Sol Steinmetz and Carol G. Braham

THE RANDOM HOUSE

THESAURUS

Edited by

JESS STEIN

and

STUART BERG FLEXNER

THE BALLANTINE REFERENCE LIBRARY

BALLANTINE BOOKS   NEW YORK

Copyright © 1984 by Random House, Inc.

Based on the Reader's Digest Family Word Finder, Copyright © 1975 The Reader's Digest Association, Inc. Copyright © 1975 The Reader's Digest Association (Canada) Ltd.

Library of Congress Catalog Card Number: 84-4914

ISBN 0-345-37778-8

This edition published by arrangement with Random House, Inc.

Manufactured in the United States of America

First Ballantine Books Edition: August 1992
Fourth Printing: August 1993

TO THE READER

The *Random House Thesaurus* was compiled to help you write and speak better by letting you find the most effective words to express yourself. It will lead you to the right word for every purpose or occasion, be it in personal letters and conversation; business and professional reports, letters, and talks; or student papers and compositions. In addition, if you use it frequently, or browse through it regularly, you will find that it will improve both the range and exactness of your vocabulary.

The word *thesaurus* came into English from Latin, where it meant "a storehouse of knowledge." It is, indeed, a storehouse of knowledge about words—the proper choice and use of words. Therefore, this thesaurus belongs on your desk or bookshelf right beside your dictionary, because these two reference books are the essential tools for anyone who wants to speak and write with clarity, effectiveness, and individuality.

The dictionary provides the meanings or definitions for given words, whereas the thesaurus provides you with words for given meanings. Thus, when you encounter a word that is new to you, or a word whose meaning you have forgotten or know only vaguely, a good dictionary, such as the *Random House Webster's College Dictionary,* is your best reference source. On the other hand, when you have a particular meaning or thought in mind but do not know, or cannot recall, the most effective word to express it, the thesaurus is your best guide. Together, the thesaurus and the dictionary offer you access to the complete range and unparalleled richness of the English language.

While almost everyone knows the value of using a dictionary, many people have been frustrated or discouraged by the complicated, time-consuming procedure required to use the index or the many cross references of the old-fashioned type of thesaurus. In recent years, however, editors, linguists, and lexicographers have perfected ways to organize the thesaurus in the familiar, easy-to-use alphabetical form. We have tried to make this book achieve that easy-to-use and effective form as fully as possible.

The Random House Thesaurus has been planned, edited, and designed for maximum usefulness, to help you find the right word or phrase—the one with just the right shade of meaning, the right overtone, the right level of usage—instantly.

To those unfamiliar with a thesaurus of synonyms and antonyms, it should be pointed out that only a very small number of words in the English language are completely identical in meaning, shade of meaning, and use. Most "syno-

To the Reader

nyms" are actually words that have similar or closely related meanings but are not perfect substitutes for each other under all circumstances. They often refer to different aspects or shades of meaning or uses of the same general concept, item, or idea. For example, among the synonyms of *road* are *boulevard, street, highway,* and *path,* though there are obviously significant differences between each of these terms. Even though they are not exact synonyms, each should be listed in a thesaurus, since one might be the exact word you are looking for.

As an added feature, we have included in this edition a selection of synonym studies following the thesaurus proper. These studies explore the subtle differences between various common words with a core meaning.

This project has had the benefit of many outstanding contributors who have worked with exceptional care and devotion. Eugene F. Shewmaker, Gloria Mihalyi Solomon, Robert L. Hurtgen, Dorothy Gerner Stein, Regina B. Wilson, and Keith Hollaman have contributed much to the final project. We would also like to express our appreciation to Eric Stein, Sharon Leong, and Rose M. Price. We have had the advantage of access to much of the material in *The Family Word Finder,* published by Reader's Digest, for which we are very grateful. The Random House dictionary staff have been generous with their help and guidance and have checked the manuscript for accuracy and ease of use.

JESS STEIN and
STUART BERG FLEXNER
Random House Reference Books

ORGANIZATION OF ENTRIES

Although anyone who opens this book at random should be able to use it immediately, the following notes may be useful:

1. All main entries are in **boldface** type and are arranged in one simple alphabetical list.
2. Each of these boldfaced main entries is followed by its part of speech. Standard abbreviations are used for this purpose: *n.* for noun, *v.* for verb, *adj.* for adjective, *adv.* for adverb, *prep.* for preposition, *conj.* for conjunction, and *interj.* for interjection. When a main entry word has more than one part of speech, each part of speech is listed separately.
3. When a main entry word has more than one meaning, each meaning is preceded by a boldfaced number and has its own separate list of synonyms.
4. Each meaning is introduced by one or more example sentences or phrases. This will help you identify the particular meaning and show you how the main entry word is used in context.
5. The synonyms listed under each meaning are generally arranged so that the most common ones, and the ones closest in meaning to the main entry word, come first. Within each list of synonyms there may be clusters of words set off by semicolons to group together separate shades of meaning or levels of use.
6. Italicized labels are included before some synonyms to show that a word or phrase has certain limitations in usage (such as *Informal* or *Slang*), that it is used primarily in a specific field of knowledge or endeavor (such as *Medical* or *Nautical*), or that it is still primarily regarded as foreign (such as *French* or *Latin*), though used in English.
7. When highly specialized synonyms are offered, they are usually preceded by "*(variously)*" to indicate that caution must be used to select the appropriate specialized word. Similarly, when very broadly applicable synonyms are offered, they are usually preceded by "*(loosely)*" to point out their highly general character.
8. At the end of many synonym lists there are lists of antonyms, introduced by the abbreviation *Ant.* Each of these antonym lists is preceded, when necessary, by a boldfaced number that matches the number of the related synonym list.

A

abandon v. 1 *The crew abandoned the sinking ship:* desert, forsake, leave, depart from, leave behind, withdraw from, evacuate; relinquish, run out on, turn one's back on. 2 *The scientists abandoned their research:* discontinue, give up, drop, stop, cease. —n. 3 *The children danced with abandon:* unrestraint, freedom; immoderation; recklessness, wantonness, impulsiveness, impetuosity, spontaneity; enthusiasm, gusto, exuberance.
Ant. 1 claim; keep. 2 continue, maintain. 3 restraint, control; moderation.

abandoned adj. 1 *an abandoned house:* deserted, forsaken, vacant, desolate, unoccupied; discarded, cast aside, left behind, marooned. 2 *The barbarians led an abandoned life:* debauched, dissipated, dissolute, profligate, reprobate, shameless, immoral, disreputable, wild, wicked, wanton, unprincipled.
Ant. 1 occupied. 2 virtuous, reputable, respectable, upright; pure, chaste.

abase v. *The Bible says that the proud shall be abased:* humble, bring low, cast down; *Informal* put down, bring down a peg, cut down to size; humiliate, disgrace, dishonor, defame, debase.
Ant. elevate, raise, exalt, uplift; honor, acclaim, praise.

abashed adj. *We were abashed at forgetting their anniversary:* embarrassed, ashamed, chagrined, mortified, dismayed, taken aback, nonplussed, disconcerted.
Ant. proud, pleased, elated, exalted; poised, undaunted, reassured.

abate v. *The wind abated:* decrease, diminish, lessen, subside, fade, dwindle, moderate, mitigate, weaken, wane, ebb, go down, taper off, lighten, soften, quiet, slow, slake off; ease, relieve, alleviate; dampen.
Ant. increase, intensify, heighten, grow; rise, strengthen; quicken, accelerate, speed up.

abbey n. *The monks live in an abbey:* monastery, friary, cloister, priory, hermitage; convent, nunnery.

abbreviate v. *The word "Mister" is abbreviated as "Mr." As time was short, we abbreviated our visit:* shorten, abridge, curtail, condense, reduce; cut, cut short.
Ant. lengthen, extend, stretch out, draw out; expand, enlarge, amplify, increase, add to, pad out; prolong, protract.

abbreviation n. *"Dr." is the abbreviation of "Doctor." This edition is an abbreviation of a longer work:* shortened form, short form, shortening, condensed form, contracted form, cut-down form; reduction, contraction, abridgment, condensation, digest, cutting.
Ant. full form, written-out form; lengthening, drawing out; expansion, enlargement.

abdicate v. *Edward VIII of England abdicated (his throne):* renounce, resign, vacate (a throne); relinquish, give up, surrender, quit, cede, yield.
Ant. accede (to a throne); claim, possess, assume, keep.

abdomen n. *He exercised to flatten his abdomen:* stomach, visceral cavity, epigastrium; belly, tummy; gut, breadbasket.

abduct v. *Kidnappers abducted the child:* kidnap, carry off, make off with, steal, seize.
Ant. return, bring back; relinquish.

aberration n. 1 *a lens with spherical aberration. The new rules were full of aberrations:* irregularity, deviation, abnormality, anomaly, incongruity, aberrance. 2 *His only aberration was an occasional lapse of memory:* quirk, peculiarity, oddity, strangeness; illusion, delusion, self-deception, hallucination.
Ant. 1, 2 normality, regularity.

abet v. *The criminal was aided and abetted by his brother:* encourage, support, sustain, back, sanction, promote; urge, urge on, goad, spur, incite, instigate; assist, help, aid.
Ant. discourage, dissuade, denounce; deter, stop, check, thwart, obstruct, balk.

abeyance n. *The project will be held in abeyance until spring:* postponement, suspension, intermission, deferral; pause, delay, cessation, recess, hiatus.
Ant. continuance, continuation.

abhor v. *We abhor violence:* detest, hate, loathe, dislike, despise, abominate; feel aversion toward, be revolted by, find repulsive, regard with repugnance, view with horror, eschew, can't stand.
Ant. love, adore, like, delight in, dote on, cherish, relish, treasure, desire, crave.

abide v. 1 *I can't abide loud noise:* bear, stand, tolerate, put up with, endure, stomach, brook; submit to, accept, stand for.

2 *Abide with me a while longer:* stay, remain, tarry, linger, stop; live, reside, dwell. *Ant.* 2 go, leave, quit, depart; flee.

abiding *adj. Abraham Lincoln had an abiding faith in the Union:* lasting, everlasting, enduring, unending, durable, firm, fast; changeless, unchanging, steadfast, constant, unshakable.

Ant. temporary, passing, momentary, impermanent; weak, shaky, changeable, fickle.

ability *n. A good salesperson has the ability to sell anything:* capability, capacity, power, facility, faculty, aptitude, potential, knack, competence, qualification; skill, talent, knowhow, expertise; genius, gift, mind for, bent.

Ant. inability, incapacity, inaptitude, incompetence, inadequacy.

abject *adj.* 1 *They lived in abject poverty:* hopeless, inescapable, complete, thorough; wretched, miserable. 2 *an abject coward:* spiritless, cringing, groveling; contemptible, despicable, vile, base, mean, low, ignoble, sordid.

Ant. 1 hopeful; dignified, honorable. 2 courageous, spirited, bold, staunch; domineering, arrogant; admirable, respected, esteemed, worthy.

abjure *v.* 1 *Pacifism abjures the use of force:* disclaim, disallow, repudiate, reject. 2 *The prisoners abjured their heresies and lived:* renounce, give up, forswear, recant.

Ant. maintain, uphold.

ablaze *adj.* 1 *The house was ablaze when the fire trucks arrived:* burning, blazing, on fire, afire, flaming, aflame, in flames; fiery, glowing. 2 *The students were ablaze with enthusiasm:* eager, excited, fervent, fervid, zealous, impassioned; feverish, flushed, ardent; turned-on.

able *adj.* 1 *an able lawyer:* skillful, proficient, capable, competent, expert, good, talented, highly qualified, effective, efficient, adroit, adept. 2 *He was barely able to walk. We are not able to grant your request:* capable, fit, competent; equal to, adequate, qualified.

Ant. 1 unskillful, incapable, incompetent, inept, inefficient, ineffective, amateurish; mediocre. 2 incapable, unfit, incompetent.

able-bodied *adj. We need four able-bodied people to move the piano:* physically fit, muscular, brawny, robust, strong, vigorous; beefy, strapping, rugged, hardy, sturdy.

Ant. weak, puny, feeble, frail.

ablution *n.* 1 *After ablutions in the river, the holy man prayed:* ceremonial washing, ritualistic washing; bathing, cleansing, purification. 2 *daily ablutions:* washing, bathing, cleaning, lavation; wash, bath.

abnegation *n. In a mood of abnegation, he gave up sweets:* self-denial, sacrifice, renunciation, relinquishment, giving up, eschewal; abstinence, temperance, continence. *Ant.* self-indulgence, indulgence, abandon; intemperance.

abnormal *adj. an abnormal fear of heights. An abnormal amount of snow fell in October:* unnatural, atypical, unusual, irregular, aberrant, uncommon, exceptional, extraordinary, unexpected, inordinate; strange, peculiar, rare, queer, odd, freakish, curious; monstrous, deformed.

Ant. normal, natural, typical, usual, ordinary, common; conventional, routine, regular, customary.

abnormality *n. A physical abnormality may be corrected by surgery:* deformity, malformation; aberration, aberrance, anomaly, deviation, perversion; oddity, curiosity, peculiarity.

abode *n. The hermit's abode was a cave:* residence, place of residence, dwelling place, dwelling; house, home, living quarters, domicile.

abolish *v. Prohibition was abolished in 1933:* eliminate, eradicate, exterminate, extirpate, terminate, end, put an end to, wipe out, stamp out, do away with, quash; repeal, revoke, annul, nullify, declare null and void, rescind, cancel; set aside, repudiate.

Ant. establish, institute, introduce; sustain, continue; revive, reinstate, renew, restore; authorize, legalize, enact.

abolition *n. The senator fought for abolition of the income tax:* elimination, ending, termination, eradication, abolishment; repeal, annulment, nullification, revocation, cancellation, rescinding.

Ant. establishment, institution, introduction, creation, inauguration; authorization, enactment; continuation; reinstatement, restoration.

abominable *adj.* 1 *an abominable crime:* detestable, despicable, contemptible, reprehensible, loathsome, abhorrent, disgusting, revolting, repulsive, repugnant; vile, base, wretched, heinous, villainous, infamous, atrocious, horrid, horrible. 2 *The weather was abominable:* very unpleasant, disagreeable, miserable, terrible, extremely bad, awful, *Informal* lousy.

Ant. 1 laudable, praiseworthy, commendable, admirable; satisfactory, gratifying. 2 pleasant, agreeable, enjoyable, pleasing, delightful, good, wonderful.

abomination *n.* 1 *The dirty streets are an abomination!:* abhorrence, horror, disgrace, defilement, annoyance. 2 *feelings of abomination for concentration camps:* revulsion, loathing, repugnance, disgust, detestation, hate, hatred, abhorrence.

Ant. 1 delight, joy, pleasure; benefit, blessing, boon. 2 love, liking, affection, fondness, relish; admiration, appreciation, respect, approval.

aboriginal *adj. The Indians were the aboriginal people of America:* native, indigenous, original; earliest, first, ancient, primary, prime.

Ant. alien, foreign; late, recent, successive, modern.

aborigine *n. The Australian aborigines hunt with spears:* original inhabitant, primitive inhabitant, indigenous person; native.

Ant. alien, foreigner, newcomer, late arrival.

abortive *adj. Efforts to raise the sunken ship proved abortive:* fruitless, useless, unsuccessful, unproductive, unavailing, futile, unfruitful.

Ant. successful, fruitful, productive.

abound *v. Our garden abounds with roses. Tulips abound in Holland:* teem, overflow, be filled, be well supplied, be rich in, swarm, proliferate; exist in great numbers, be plentiful, flourish, thrive.

Ant. lack, want, have too few, be deficient in; be in short supply.

about-face *n. The senator did an about-face on tax cuts:* reversal, turnaround, reverse, turnabout, switch, shift; disavowal, recantation, retraction.

aboveboard *adj. Her criticisms seemed fair and aboveboard:* candid, open, honest, truthful, sincere, frank, square-dealing, on the up and up; guileless, ingenuous, artless; unconcealed.

Ant. devious, evasive, underhand.

abrasion *n.* 1 *The abrasion on his knee soon healed:* scraped spot, scrape; scratch, lesion. 2 *Years of abrasion had worn the stones smooth:* scraping, grating, rubbing, friction; erosion, wearing away, wearing down.

abrasive *n.* 1 *Sandpaper is an abrasive:* scraping material, grinding material, scouring material; smoothing substance. *—adj.* 2 *abrasive remarks:* harsh, annoying, irritating; rasping, grating, caustic; nasty, hurtful, galling, chafing.

Ant. 2 mild, soothing, comforting, gentle, agreeable.

abreast *adv., adj. The soldiers marched three abreast:* side by side, in a line across, in rank.

Ant. one behind another, one after another.

abridge *v.* 1 *The book was abridged:* shorten, condense, reduce, digest, abbreviate, cut, cut down, pare down. 2 *No one can abridge your legal rights:* restrict, limit, diminish, lessen, reduce, decrease; deprive one of.

Ant. 1 expand, enlarge, lengthen; augment, add to. 2 increase, augment.

abridgment *n.* 1 *a new abridgment of Gibbon's Roman history:* shortened form, condensed form, condensation, digest, truncation. 2 *an abridgment of the mayor's power:* restriction, limitation, curtailment, reduction, lessening, decrease.

Ant. 1 lengthened version. 2 expansion, enlargement, increase, augmentation, extension.

abroad *adv.* 1 *On our trip abroad we visited England:* overseas, out of the country. 2 *Is it safe to be abroad at night?:* out of doors, outside, out of the house, out in the open air. 3 *A thousand rumors were abroad:* in circulation, at large, making the rounds; spread far and wide, rife, astir.

Ant. 1 near home; in one's native land. 2 indoors, inside, in, in the house.

abrogate *v. Congress must abrogate this unjust law:* abolish, cancel, terminate, put an end to, end, do away with, quash; repeal, revoke, rescind, annul, nullify, void, invalidate, set aside; retract, withdraw, repudiate.

Ant. institute, establish, enact, ratify; confirm, uphold, support

abrupt *adj.* 1 *The car came to an abrupt stop:* sudden, unexpected, unforeseen, unanticipated; hasty, quick, instantaneous, precipitate. 2 *Your abrupt reply hurt our feelings:* curt, brusque, blunt, brisk, short; discourteous, impolite, ungracious, rude. 3 *The cliff made an abrupt descent to the sea:* steep, sheer, sharp, precipitous.

Ant. 1 anticipated, expected, foreseen; gradual, unhurried, slow, easy. 2 courteous, polite, gracious, thoughtful, civil. 3 gradual.

abscond *v. The thief absconded with the jewels:* flee, take flight, fly, depart hastily, leave suddenly; take off, make off, steal away; escape, run away, run off; *Informal* skip.

absence *n.* 1 *The teacher noted the student's absence:* not being present, nonattendance, nonpresence, nonappearance, absenteeism. 2 *an absence of initiative:* lack, nonexistence; scarcity, deficiency, insufficiency, want, dearth.

Ant. 1 presence, attendance. 2 existence; abundance, sufficiency, plethora.

absent *adj.* 1 *Why were you absent from class?:* not present, nonpresent, nonattendant; missing, out, truant. 2 *He gave her an absent look:* inattentive, unthinking, heedless, oblivious, preoccupied, distracted; vacant, blank, vague. *—v.* 3 *Why did you ab-*

sent yourself from the meeting?: cause to be not present, fail to attend, not appear, stay away, keep away, play truant.

Ant. 1 present, in attendance. 2 attentive, thoughtful, aware, alert. 3 attend, appear at, show up.

absent-minded *adj. He's so absent-minded he's lost three hats:* forgetful, distracted, unheeding, unmindful, preoccupied, woolgathering, oblivious, daydreaming.

Ant. attentive, alert, heedful, observant.

absolute *adj.* 1 *an absolute monarch:* unrestricted, unrestrained, unlimited, unconditional; complete, supreme. 2 *His story was an absolute lie:* complete, pure, total, definite, thorough, unqualified, unadulterated, unmitigated, utter; consummate, outright; *Informal* out-and-out. 3 *We have absolute proof of his guilt:* positive, definite, conclusive, certain, sure, decisive; real, genuine, unquestionable, undeniable, unequivocal.

Ant. 1 restricted, conditional, limited, provisional, qualified. 2, 3 qualified, conditional, provisional, dubious; incomplete.

absolutely *adv. I am absolutely sure:* entirely, completely, wholly, utterly, definitely, positively; unconditionally. 2 *Good nutrition is absolutely essential:* positively, utterly, definitely, truly, really; undoubtedly, unquestionably, indubitably.

Ant. 1 somewhat, fairly. 2 probably, conditionally.

absolution *n. They came to the shrine, seeking absolution for their sins:* pardon, amnesty, forgiveness, deliverance, exculpation, remission.

Ant. blame, censure, condemnation.

absolve *v.* 1 *The priest absolved their sins:* pardon, forgive, shrive. 2 *The jury absolved him of the crime:* acquit, find not guilty, judge innocent, exonerate, clear. 3 *I was absolved of having to pay the debt:* release, free, set free, excuse from, exempt, discharge.

Ant. 1 accuse, blame; condemn. 2 convict, find guilty. 3 obligate, oblige, bind.

absorb *v.* 1 *The sponge absorbed all the water:* soak up, take up, suck up, drink in, sponge up. 2 *Can the students absorb this lesson?:* take in completely, assimilate, incorporate, digest, ingest. 3 *I was so absorbed in this book that I didn't hear you:* engross, immerse, occupy, preoccupy, engage, rivet, fix.

Ant. 1 exude, eject. 2 disperse, impart.

absorbent *adj. Blotting paper is extremely absorbent:* permeable, spongy, absorptive, porous, thirsty, pervious.

Ant. moistureproof, waterproof, water-repellent, impermeable.

absorbing *adj. Tom Sawyer is an absorbing book:* fascinating, interesting, engrossing, captivating, engaging.

abstain *v. Vegetarians abstain from eating meat:* refrain, desist, forbear, eschew, avoid, forgo; deny oneself, resist.

Ant. indulge in, yield to, give in to; abandon oneself to.

abstemious *adj. His abstemious habits allowed him few pleasures:* abstinent, ascetic, austere, temperate, abstentious.

Ant. self-indulgent, abandoned, uncontrolled, hedonistic, profligate, immoderate.

abstention *n. Vegetarians are known for their abstention from eating meat:* abstaining, refraining, desisting, holding back, forbearance, eschewing, eschewal, avoidance, refusal.

Ant. indulgence, abandon.

abstinence *n. I admire Quakers for their abstinence:* nonindulgence, self-denial, self-restraint, self-control, discipline, abstention; *(variously)* temperance, sobriety; continence, chastity.

Ant. indulgence, self-indulgence, abandon, excess.

abstract *adj.* 1 *Abstract ideas:* theoretical, theoretic, unapplied, general, generalized, imaginary, visionary, intangible, hypothetical, impractical; recondite, arcane, intellectual. —*n.* 2 *Please write an abstract of this article:* summary, synopsis, précis, brief, digest, extract, condensation. —*v.* 3 *to abstract salt from sea water:* extract, remove, withdraw, take out; separate, dissociate. 4 *Please abstract this article:* summarize, synopsize; digest, condense, abridge.

Ant. 1 concrete, specific, material; practical; factual, real, actual. 2 amplification, enlargement, expansion. 3 add; unite, combine.

abstruse *adj. Mathematics can be an abstruse subject:* hard to understand, obscure, incomprehensible, unfathomable, complex, complicated, puzzling, perplexing, arcane; subtle.

Ant. simple, direct, easy, obvious, clear, uncomplicated.

absurd *adj. It's absurd to believe the earth is flat. The clown wore an absurd costume:* unreasonable, illogical, irrational, preposterous; ridiculous, foolish, stupid, idiotic, asinine, comical, farcical; funny, laughable.

Ant. reasonable, logical, sensible, rational.

absurdity *n. His story was sheer absurdity. The absurdities of the monkeys amused us:* nonsense, unreasonableness, unbelievability, inanity, irrationality, ridiculousness;

falsehood, delusion; foolishness, buffoonery, comicalness, silliness.

Ant. truth; reasonableness; sagacity.

abundance *n. an abundance of food:* ample amount, great supply, full measure, profusion; excess, more than enough, plenty, surplus, glut, plenitude, plethora, surfeit; bounty, wealth, richness.

Ant. scarcity, lack, dearth, scantiness, paucity.

abundant *adj. an abundant water supply:* ample, sufficient, enough, plenty, more than enough, copious, bounteous, bountiful, lavish, replete, galore.

Ant. insufficient, scant, sparse, meager, scarce, skimpy, sparing.

abuse *v.* 1 *Good carpenters don't abuse their tools. Stop abusing that dog!:* misuse, use improperly, ill-use; mistreat, maltreat, illtreat; harm, hurt, injure. 2 *He abused everyone in a loud voice:* insult, speak ill of, berate, carp at, rail at, vilify; speak harshly to, reproach, criticize, censure, bawl out, upbraid; malign, ridicule, slur, denigrate; curse, slander; disparage, inveigh against. —*n.* 3 *an abuse of friendship:* misuse, unfair use, improper use, misapplication; exploitation, imposition. 4 *Child abuse is a punishable offense:* mistreatment, maltreatment, ill-use, cruelty; injury, harming, beating, assault. 5 *I'll listen to no more of your abuse!:* insulting language, insults, berating, railing, invective, tirade; reproach, criticism, tongue-lashing, scolding, upbraiding, diatribe, carping; disparagement, slander, ridicule, derision, vilification; defamation.

Ant. 1 protect, care for. 2 praise, speak well of, extol, laud. 5 praise, compliment, acclaim; flattery.

abusive *adj.* 1 *Please don't use such abusive language:* insulting, harsh, vituperative, mean; railing, offensive, obscene, foulmouthed, vile, rude, gross; derogatory, disparaging, defamatory, scurrilous, critical, censorious, slanderous, reviling, maligning. 2 *He was arrested for his abusive treatment of the dog:* cruel, improper; harmful, hurtful, injurious.

Ant. 1 laudatory, flattering, complimentary, extolling, courteous, respectful, polite. 2 kind; just.

abut *v. The two yards abut:* meet end to end, meet, join, adjoin, touch; border, be contiguous.

abysmal *adj. abysmal ignorance:* thorough, endless, unending, complete; boundless, profound, extreme, vast, stupendous, immense.

abyss *n. One slip and you'll fall into the*

abyss: bottomless pit, vast chasm, crevasse, fissure; void, depth.

Ant. elevation, height; mountain, hill.

academic *adj.* 1 *He remembered his academic years:* school, scholastic, educational; collegiate, university. 2 *an academic mind:* scholarly, studious; educated, erudite; pedantic, bookish. 3 *an academic high school:* general, liberal-arts, scholastic, collegepreparatory; nontechnical, nonvocational. 4 *How to talk to a Martian is an academic question:* theoretical, hypothetical, abstract, conjectural, suppositional; not practical.

Ant. 2 nonscholarly, nonstudious, unschooled, unlettered, unlearned. 3 technical, vocational, trade. 4 practical, realistic, immediate.

accede *v. The mayor acceded to the demands:* consent to, approve, agree to, accept, concur with; concede, yield to; abide by, comply with.

Ant. reject, refuse, disallow, decline; oppose, object to, resist, balk at.

accelerate *v.* 1 *The car suddenly accelerated:* to go faster, to move faster, speed up, pick up speed, quicken pace. 2 *Fertilizer will accelerate the growth of plants:* speed up, hurry, quicken, hasten, rush, step up, spur, expedite, further, promote.

Ant. 1, 2 slow, slow down, decelerate. 2 delay, retard, hinder, impede, hamper.

accent *n.* 1 *The word "woman" has its accent on the first syllable:* stress, emphasis; primary accent, primary stress. 2 *to speak with a German accent:* pronunciation, enunciation, articulation, manner of speaking, twang, drawl. 3 *The room was white with a few red accents:* hint, touch, embellishment, detail; ornament, trimming. —*v.* 4 *Accent the word on the first syllable:* stress, accentuate; give prominence to.

accept *v.* 1 *She accepted the invitation:* take something offered, receive willingly, receive with favor. 2 *I accept your apology. The police accepted his story as true:* agree to, consent to, grant as satisfactory, accede to, acknowledge. 3 *The boy accepted full responsibility:* assume, undertake, acknowledge, admit, avow.

Ant. 1, 2 refuse, reject, decline, spurn, turn down. 3 disown; deny, disavow.

acceptable *adj.* 1 *The lawyers found the contract acceptable:* capable of being accepted, agreeable, proper, suitable, admissible, satisfactory. 2 *His grades are acceptable:* adequate, suitable, passable, tolerable; barely satisfactory, *Informal* so-so.

Ant. 1, 2 unacceptable, unsatisfactory.

acceptance *n.* 1 *His acceptance of bribes led to his arrest:* accepting, taking, receiv-

ing; receipt. 2 *The employer gave his acceptance to the suggestions:* approval, consent, agreement, permission, acquiescence; *Informal* O.K. 3 *It took years for Einstein's theory to gain acceptance:* approval, approbation, belief, recognition, acknowledgment.
Ant. 1, 2 rejection, refusal; disapproval. 3 rejection; disavowal.

accepted *adj. Money orders are an accepted means of payment:* agreed upon, approved, acceptable, acknowledged, established; common, normal, usual, regular, customary.

access *n.* 1 *Who has access to the vault?:* admittance; entrance, entrée. 2 *Switzerland has access to the sea via the Rhine:* a means of reaching, an approach, passage, passageway, gateway; road, path, way, avenue.

accessible *adj.* 1 *Is the telephone accessible at all time?:* available, ready, at hand, on hand, handy, within reach; obtainable, attainable, reachable. 2 *The principal was always accessible to students:* available, approachable, reachable.
Ant. 1 unavailable, unobtainable, beyond reach. 2 unapproachable, unavailable, inaccessible.

accessory *n.* 1 *This belt makes a beautiful accessory to your dress:* accompaniment, adornment, decoration; complement, detail. 2 *He was convicted as an accessory in the robbery:* accomplice, confederate; associate, cohort; contributor, auxiliary.

accident *n.* 1 *Columbus discovered America by accident:* chance, fluke, happenstance; luck, good fortune. 2 *An ambulance rushed to the accident. a skiing accident:* collision, crash, wreck, smashup; mishap, misadventure; bit of bad luck.
Ant. 1 plan, intention, intent, design.

accidental *adj. Our meeting was purely accidental:* unplanned, unintentional, unpremeditated, uncalculated; unexpected, unanticipated, fortuitous; chance, inadvertent.
Ant. planned, intentional, intended, calculated; prepared, designed.

acclaim *v.* 1 *Critics acclaimed the new play:* praise, loudly approve, applaud, cheer, hail, laud, extol, sing the praises of, cheer, compliment; honor, celebrate. —*n.* 2 *The new opera was greeted with acclaim:* great praise, loud approval, applause, plaudits, kudos, bravos, cheering, rejoicing, enthusiasm.
Ant. 1 criticize, denounce, condemn, disapprove, *Informal* pan. 2 criticism, condemnation, disapproval.

acclamation *n. The queen received an acclamation from the crowd. He was elected*

president of the club by acclamation: ovation, burst of applause, cheering, shout of approval; acclaim; cheers, hurrahs, hosannas.
Ant. booing, hissing; disapproval, denunciation.

acclimate *v. You'll soon be acclimated to the cold weather:* get used to, accustom, adapt, adjust, accommodate, inure.

accolade *n. the highest accolade a writer can receive:* award, honor, tribute, prize; praise, compliment, commendation, acclaim.

accommodate *v.* 1 *Can you accommodate me with a loan?:* do a kindness for, do a favor for; oblige, help, aid, assist. 2 *This hotel can accommodate 500 guests:* have capacity for, furnish room for, house; entertain; hold, contain; lodge, put up. 3 *accommodate yourself to the situation:* adapt, adjust, fit, accustom; conform, modify; reconcile.
Ant. 1 inconvenience, disoblige.

accommodating *adj. She was very accommodating:* obliging, helpful, considerate, kind; polite, courteous; conciliatory, yielding.
Ant. inconsiderate; rude.

accommodation *n.* 1 *What kind of accommodations did you have on the ship?:* rooms, quarters, housing; arrangements. 2 *If we don't reach an accommodation there will be a strike:* compromise, settlement, adjustment; agreement, reconciliation.

accompany *v.* 1 *My daughter accompanied me on the trip:* go in company with, go along with, attend; conduct; escort, convoy, attend. 2 *Suffering accompanies war:* to occur with, go together with, go hand in hand with, go hand in glove with, follow.

accomplice *n. an accomplice in the robbery:* confederate, accessory, partner, collaborator, co-conspirator, partner-in-crime; cohort, ally, comrade; assistant, subordinate, helper, abettor.

accomplish *v.* 1 *Edison accomplished what he set out to do:* achieve, succeed at, carry out, do; perform, realize, execute, attain, fulfill. 2 *If you organize your work you'll accomplish more:* do, get done, finish, complete, achieve.
Ant. 1 fail, fall short. 2 leave undone.

accomplished *adj.* 1 *Space flight is an accomplished fact:* existing, realized, effected; established, accepted, proven, proved. 2 *an accomplished pianist:* expert, able, proficient, capable, fine, skilled, skillful; masterly, well-trained, finished, experienced; talented, gifted, brilliant, qualified.
Ant. 1 unrealized, unestablished, unproven. 2 unskilled, incompetent, inept,

inexpert; inexperienced; untalented, amateurish.

accomplishment *n.* 1 *All nations must work for the accomplishment of peace:* achievement, realization, attainment, triumph, victory, fulfillment, success, carrying out. 2 *Developing the supersonic jet was quite an accomplishment:* achievement, feat, success, attainment, exploit, triumph, victory. 3 *Playing the piano is one of her accomplishments:* achievement, feat, skill; talent, gift.

Ant. 1 failure. 2 failure, blunder. 3 lack, deficiency.

accord *v.* 1 *Our views accord on the new tax bill:* agree, concur; conform, correspond, match, jibe; be in tune. 2 *High honors were accorded him:* grant, present, give, bestow, award; allow, cede. —*n.* 3 *Our views are not in accord:* agreement, harmony, accordance, mutual understanding, concurrence, uniformity.

Ant. 1 differ, disagree, conflict, clash. 2 withhold, deny, refuse. 3 conflict, disagreement, dissidence, dissension.

accordingly *adv.* 1 *I'm an adult and expect to be treated accordingly:* in accordance with the fact, correspondingly, suitably. 2 *This furnace is new; accordingly, it should perform perfectly:* therefore, thus, so, hence, wherefore, whereupon, consequently, as a result.

Ant. 1 conversely.

accost *v.* *A beggar accosted me:* hail, call to; greet, address; confront, approach, buttonhole, waylay; solicit, make an appeal to.

account *n.* 1 *Give us a full account of your vacation:* description, report; story, history, record, narrative, narration; explanation, version. 2 *The student disobeyed and on this account is being expelled:* reason, cause, grounds, basis, consideration. 3 *These old letters are of no account:* importance, import, worth, significance, consequence, note; use, merit. 4 *household accounts:* financial record, financial statement, books, accounting. —*v.* 5 *He accounts himself lucky:* consider, regard, believe, think, judge, count, deem, hold, take to be; estimate, value. 6 *Can you account for your behavior?:* explain, justify, give a reason for.

accountable *adj.* *You will be held accountable:* liable, answerable, responsible, obligated.

Ant. exempt, innocent.

accountant *n.* *An accountant filled out my tax form:* certified public accountant, CPA; bookkeeper.

accredit *v.* 1 *The new college is fully accredited:* furnish with credentials, certify, li-

cense, authorize, sanction, officially recognize. 2 *The invention is accredited to Thomas Edison:* attribute, ascribe, assign, credit.

accretion *n.* *The coral reef was built up by accretion:* increase, addition, increment, augmentation, accumulation, accrual, growth.

Ant. loss, decrease, diminution, shrinkage.

accumulate *v.* *Snow accumulated on the ground. He accumulated a fortune:* gather, gather together, pile up, amass, collect, accrue, assemble; save up, store up, hoard.

Ant. scatter, disperse, distribute.

accumulation *n.* 1 *an accumulation of junk in the attic:* collection, assemblage, conglomeration; mass, heap, pile, hoard, store; pile-up, aggregation, accrual. 2 *The accumulation of rare books is his pastime:* collecting, amassing, gathering; acquiring, hoarding.

Ant. 2 distribution, dispersing, dispersal.

accuracy *n.* *Check your work for accuracy:* accurateness, correctness, freedom from error; exactness, precision; truth, truthfulness, verity.

Ant. error, inaccuracy, incorrectness; lies, lying, fallaciousness.

accurate *adj.* *The drawing is accurate in every detail. He is an accurate mathematician:* correct, without error, unerring, true, truthful, faithful, faultless, exact.

Ant. incorrect, wrong, inaccurate; inexact, faulty.

accusation *n.* *The accusation is untrue. The accusation is grand larceny:* charge, allegation, complaint, citation, indictment.

Ant. reply, answer, rebuttal.

accuse *v.* 1 *accuse someone of murder:* charge, lodge a complaint against, arraign, indict, cite. 2 *accused of laziness:* charge, reproach, take to task, call to account, upbraid; blame.

Ant. 1, 2 reply, answer, plea, rebut.

accustomed *adj.* 1 *Painting barns red is an accustomed practice:* usual, common, normal, regular, general, customary, established, conventional, commonplace, ordinary, familiar, everyday. 2 *Alaskans are accustomed to cold weather:* used to, acclimated, seasoned, acquainted with, in the habit of, given to, habituated, prone.

Ant. 1 unusual, uncommon, rare, strange, unfamiliar; singular, infrequent, peculiar, unconventional. 2 unused, unaccustomed.

acerbity *n.* 1 *to receive uninvited callers with acerbity:* ill-tempered manner, brusqueness, sarcastic irritability, sarcasm, irascibility, nastiness, sharpness. 2 *the acerbity of citrus* *fruit:* acidity, sourness, tartness, astringency, acridity.

Ant. 1 good nature, cordiality, good humor, affability.

ache *n.* 1 *A dentist can fix that ache:* pain, throb, twinge, pang, hurt. —*v.* 2 *The blow made my head ache:* hurt, feel pain, be sore, smart, throb. 3 *The child ached for a bicycle:* desire, want, crave, need, hunger, yearn, long for.

achieve *v.* 1 *to achieve a goal:* accomplish, attain, realize, reach, arrive at, fulfill; bring to pass, bring about, carry out, succeed in. 2 *Can anyone achieve perfect happiness?:* attain, obtain, realize, gain, earn, win.

Ant. 1 fail, fall short of. 2 lose.

achievement *n.* 1 *a stunning achievement:* accomplishment, attainment, fulfillment; exploit, feat, act, deed. 2 *Playing the piano is just one of his achievements:* accomplishment, attainment, acquirement.

Ant. 1 failure, defeat.

acid *adj.* 1 *These lemons are more acid than usual:* sour, tart, astringent, sharp, vinegary. 2 *an acid wit:* acerbic, acrimonious, sharp, biting, stinging, cutting, scathing, bitter, acrid, caustic, vitriolic.

Ant. 1 sweet, succulent; pleasant-tasting. 2 gentle, mild; pleasant; friendly, benign.

acknowledge *v.* 1 *to acknowledge defeat:* recognize, accept, admit, own, own up to, allow, concede, concur. 2 *The chair acknowledges the delegate from Ohio:* recognize, take notice of; call upon. 3 *Did he acknowledge your greeting?:* respond to, reply to; express appreciation for, thank for.

Ant. 1 disclaim, reject; deny, disavow. 2, 3 ignore, disregard, slight, reject; deny.

acknowledgment *n.* 1 *He gave her full acknowledgment for her help:* recognition, credit. 2 *his acknowledgment that he stole the money:* affirmation, admission, confession. 3 *Accept our grateful acknowledgment:* thanks, gratitude, appreciation; response, answer, reply.

Ant. 1, 2 denial, disavowal.

acme *n.* *the acme of her career:* height, peak, pinnacle, zenith, high point; crown, crest, apex, culmination.

Ant. depth, low point, bottom, nadir.

acolyte *n.* *Two acolytes attended the priest:* altar boy; novice, ministerial assistant.

acquaint *v.* 1 *Were you acquainted before?:* introduce, make known socially, meet. 2 *Let me acquaint you with the facts:* familiarize, apprise, disclose, reveal, advise, inform, enlighten, make aware.

Ant. 2 hide, conceal; withhold, hold back.

acquaintance *n.* 1 *He's just an acquaintance:* person slightly known, distant friend.

2 *We had a brief acquaintance with her:* friendship, association, dealings. 3 *The curriculum stresses acquaintance with the sciences:* familiarity, awareness, knowledge.

Ant. 1 stranger; good friend. 3 unfamiliarity, ignorance.

acquiesce *v.* *I don't like the idea, but will acquiesce to it:* consent, agree, assent, allow; bow to, yield; admit, concede, comply, concur.

Ant. resist, fight, contest, object, disagree, dissent, demur.

acquire *v.* *to acquire a fortune. to acquire a knowledge of French:* get, obtain, attain, gain, procure; achieve, win.

Ant. lose, be deprived of; relinquish.

acquisition *n.* 1 *the museum's most recent acquisition:* acquirement, procurement, possession, property. 2 *the acquisition of knowledge:* attainment, obtainment, acquirement, procurement.

acquisitive *adj.* *an acquisitive person:* covetous, grasping, greedy, avaricious.

Ant. altruistic; generous.

acquit *v.* 1 *The jury acquitted the defendant:* declare not guilty, declare innocent, clear; exonerate; exculpate, absolve, let off, reprieve, set free; exempt, excuse. 2 *to acquit oneself well in any situation:* conduct, behave, comport, act.

Ant. 1 convict, declare guilty; condemn.

acrid *adj.* 1 *acrid smoke:* caustic, harsh, sharp, bitter, burning, stinging, irritating, pungent; smelly, foul-smelling, malodorous. 2 *an acrid sense of humor:* harsh, sharp, biting, acid, nasty, vitriolic; sarcastic, ironic, satirical.

Ant. 1 sweet, pleasing. 2 gentle, sweet, benign.

acrimonious *adj.* *Don't be acrimonious about it:* sarcastic, spiteful, rancorous, bitter, ill-natured, nasty; venomous, vitriolic, caustic, cutting, biting.

Ant. pleasant, agreeable, good-humored, civil, polite.

acrimony *n.* *There was bitter acrimony between the candidates:* ill will, hard feelings, rancor, bitterness; animosity, hostility, spitefulness, antagonism, spite, scorn, animus.

Ant. good will, good feelings.

act *n.* 1 *a careless act:* deed, action, step, move; feat, exploit, accomplishment, achievement. 2 *caught in the act:* action, process of doing. 3 *an act of Congress:* official decision, law, edict, decree, enactment, legislation, bill, resolution, statute, order. 4 *the last act of Romeo and Juliet. His song and dance act was a sensation:* segment of a play, main division of a play; short performance, routine. 5 *Her sickness is an act to get sympathy:* pretense, pose, posture, fake, affectation, show. —*v.* 6 *Act now and save money during our sale:* do it, perform, do, function, execute, carry out; commit oneself. 7 *Act your age! Miss Smith will act as chair:* behave, conduct oneself, comport oneself; work, operate, function. 8 *When you see the gift, act surprised:* pretend to be, feign, fake, affect, simulate. 9 *to act the part of Hamlet:* perform, play, portray, enact.

Ant. 1 inactivity, inaction.

acting *adj.* 1 *She will serve as acting mayor:* temporary, substitute, provisional, officiating, interim. —*n.* 2 *Acting can be a difficult profession:* dramatics, thespianism, stage playing.

action *n.* 1 *The action of this crank turns the wheel:* work, effort; effect, influence; movement, motion. 2 *The fire department was called into action:* operation, activity, functioning, performing, performance. 3 *an unpopular action:* act, deed, step, move. 4 *We expect action on our complaint:* activity, work, effort, exertion, movement; committed attention, progress. 5 *The general has seen action in three wars:* combat, battle, fighting. 6 *a boring movie with no action:* movement, excitement, adventure.

Ant. 2 inaction, inactivity.

activate *v. These switches activate the elevator.* start, turn on, actuate, put into action, set going; drive, impel, motivate, energize.

Ant. deactivate, immobilize; stop, turn off.

active *adj.* 1 *an active teenager. the most active member of the team:* energetic, vigorous, lively, animated, peppy, spirited; busy, on the go, occupied, engaged, industrious, enterprising. 2 *Skiing is an active sport:* strenuous, energetic; vigorous. 3 *an active member of the club. an active volcano:* functioning, actively operative, acting. 4 *an active mind:* alert, quick, vigorous, lively; agile, spry, nimble, sprightly; industrious.

Ant. 1–4 inactive. 1 torpid, sluggish, idle. 2 sedentary. 3 nonfunctioning; dormant. 4 sluggish, slow, dull.

activity *n.* 1 *The room was full of activity:* action, movement; enterprise; commotion, hustle, bustle; vivacity, liveliness, animation. 2 *We need a little activity to keep warm:* exercise, exertion, movement. 3 *What activities interest you?:* undertaking, pursuit, enterprise, function, venture, endeavor, project.

Ant. 1 inactivity, torpor, dullness. 2 relaxation, rest.

actor *n.* 1 *A good actor can play any role:* performer, thespian, dramatic artist,

trouper, player. 2 *We are all actors in the drama of life:* participant, doer, functionary.

actual *adj.* 1 *an actual case:* real, existing, factual, true, genuine, bona fide, authentic. 2 *What is the actual location of the ship?:* real, physical, existent, existing; certain, sure; current, present, prevailing.

Ant. 1 fictional, fictitious, hypothetical, theoretical. 2 probable, conjectured.

actuality *n. In actuality he never liked her at all:* reality, fact, truth, point of fact.

actually *adv. The events depicted did not actually take place:* in fact, really, truly, genuinely, literally.

actuate *v.* 1 See ACTIVATE. 2 *actuated by greed:* motivate, prompt, cause, induce, stimulate, instigate, drive, impel, trigger; influence, inspire.

Ant. 1 See ACTIVATE.

acumen *n. His business acumen will help the company:* keenness, acuteness, smartness, astuteness; discernment, intelligence, wisdom, judgment; insight.

Ant. obtuseness, dullness, ignorance.

acute *adj.* 1 *an acute angle:* sharply pointed, sharp, peaked, needle-shaped. 2 *an acute headache. acute appendicitis:* severe, intense, fierce, powerful, very great, very bad, critical; excruciating, distressing, piercing, agonizing. 3 *acute intelligence:* keen, penetrating, piercing, sharp; discriminating, discerning, sensitive.

Ant. 1 obtuse, dull. 2 mild, moderate.

adage *n. "Live and let live" is an old adage:* saying, proverb, maxim, axiom, aphorism, epigram; dictum, truism, platitude, cliché, *Informal* old saw.

adamant *adj. He's adamant that we follow the rules:* insistent, unyielding, inflexible, fixed, set, firm, immovable, uncompromising, unbending, resolute, determined, obdurate.

Ant. yielding, flexible, pliant, compliant, compromising.

adapt *v.* 1 *The chameleon adapts to its surroundings by changing color:* adjust, conform, accommodate, assimilate, acculturate, attune to. 2 *The play is adapted from a novel:* reshape, shape, fashion, transform, rework, modify, change, alter.

adaptable *adj.* 1 *an adaptable person:* flexible, pliant, compliant, open-minded; obliging, accommodating, malleable. 2 *The new auditorium is adaptable for either theatrical or sports events:* usable, serviceable, applicable, accommodative; changeable, adjustable, alterable.

Ant. 1 inflexible, rigid.

adaptation *n.* 1 *The barn is undergoing adaptation to living quarters:* alteration, modification, remodeling, conversion; adjustment, change. 2 *The TV series is an adaptation of a movie:* altered version, modification, reworking, reshaping.

add *v.* 1 *Let's add up the cost of our purchases:* total, sum up, count up, figure up, compute, calculate, reckon. 2 *Add one more item to the list. May I add a point or two?:* include, attach, append, affix, join, tack on. **Ant.** 1 subtract, deduct. 2 remove, eliminate; take, take away.

addendum *n. The report has an addendum:* added section, supplement, addition, codicil.

addict *n.* 1 *Addicts must be identified and treated:* drug addict; *Slang* junkie, user. 2 *an opera addict:* devotee, fan, adherent, habitué; *Slang* nut, buff.

addition *n.* 1 *Addition is taught before subtraction:* mathematical summation, totaling, counting up, summing up, reckoning. 2 *The addition of a porch will increase the value of the house:* adding, including, joining, adjoining, annexing, appending, attaching; extending, increasing. 3 *The addition in cost over last year's bill is $200:* increase, increment; enlargement, extra, additive, expansion. 4 *an addition to the town library:* annex, wing, extension, appendage; adjunct, addendum.
Ant. 1–3 subtraction. 2 subtracting, removing, removal. 3 decrease, reduction.

additional *adj. The charge for delivery is additional:* extra, added, added on, supplementary.

addled *adj. The witness was addled by the cross-examination:* confused, mixed-up, muddled, befuddled, nonplussed.

address *n.* 1 *Please print your name and address:* street number, city, and state; mailing address, postal address, street address; place of residence, dwelling, place of business. 2 *The Presidential address will be broadcast:* speech, talk, oration. —*v.* 3 *Address this letter:* write for delivery to, put an address on. 4 *The general addressed his troops:* give a formal talk, talk to, speak to, orate, lecture.

adept *adj. She's adept at organizational work:* skilled, skillful, expert, accomplished, masterful; good, able, adroit, gifted.
Ant. unskilled, inept, clumsy, awkward.

adequate *adj. Our hotel room was adequate:* suitable, satisfactory, sufficient, passable, tolerable; enough, *Informal* so-so.
Ant. inadequate, unsuitable, unsatisfactory, insufficient.

adhere *v.* 1 *The decal doesn't adhere to the window:* stick, stick fast, hold, cling, cleave; glue; fix, fasten. 2 *He adhered to the faith of his youth:* be faithful, be loyal, be constant, keep, keep to, maintain, abide by.
Ant. 1 come unstuck, come loose. 2 break with, part from, leave.

adherence *n.* 1 *Put more glue on the wallpaper to increase its adherence:* adhesion, adhesiveness, stickiness. 2 *adherence to the rules:* strict observance, attachment, keeping to, obedience; loyalty, fealty, faithfulness, constancy, allegiance, devotion.
Ant. 2 disobedience, disloyalty, unfaithfulness, infidelity.

adherent *n.* 1 *a leader with many adherents:* follower, supporter, disciple; devotee, acolyte, pupil. —*adj.* 2 *Scrape off that adherent substance:* adhesive, sticky, sticking, gummy, viscous, viscid, clinging.
Ant. 1 opponent, detractor.

adhesive *adj.* 1 *Glue is an adhesive substance:* adherent, adhering, sticky, sticking, clinging; mucilaginous. —*n.* 2 *An adhesive will hold these cutouts in place:* sticky substance, adhering substance; glue, paste, rubber cement, cement, epoxy.
Ant. 2 solvent.

ad infinitum *He talks about his job ad infinitum:* ceaselessly, continuously, endlessly, unendingly, unceasingly; limitlessly, boundlessly.
Ant. occasionally, on occasion; never; seldom, infrequently, rarely.

adjacent *adj. Our farm is adjacent to yours:* next to, beside, right beside, abutting, bordering, next door to; contiguous with, conterminous.
Ant. far from, distant from; separated from.

adjoining *adj. adjoining rooms:* joining, joined, touching, connected, contiguous, next-door.

adjourn *v.* 1 *He adjourned the meeting:* recess, suspend, discontinue; close, end, dismiss, dissolve. 2 *They adjourned to the living room:* repair, remove, withdraw, move.
Ant. 1 convene, be in session; assemble, gather, continue. 2 remain, stay.

adjudge *v. The justices adjudged the case:* decide, determine, consider, adjudicate, settle, rule, rule on; decree, pronounce.

adjunct *n. Railroads can be an adjunct to military operations:* accessory, supplement, complement, auxiliary part, subsidiary, secondary feature.

adjust *v.* 1 *Please adjust the thermostat:* set, fix, regulate, change, order. 2 *My eyes haven't adjusted to the dark:* accustom, acclimate, accommodate, adapt; fix, alter, modify, regulate.

adjustment *n.* 1 *These eyeglasses need adjustment:* adjusting, alignment, straightening; fixing, regulating, modification, alteration; reconciliation, rectification. **2** *This knob on the TV set is the vertical adjustment:* control, regulator, adjusting device; setting. **3** *a period of adjustment:* settling in, settlement, acclimation, adapting.

adjutant *n. The general chose the major as his adjutant:* assisting staff officer, aide, assistant, right-hand man, right hand, aide-de-camp.

ad-lib *n.* **1** *The comedian's ad-libs were funny:* extemporaneous wisecrack, improvisation. *—v.* **2** *If you forget your speech, just ad-lib:* improvise, extemporize, speak extemporaneously, speak off the cuff, speak impromptu, *Slang* wing it.

administer *v.* **1** *to administer a large corporation:* manage, run, direct, govern, supervise, superintend, preside over. **2** *Administer the salve with a swab:* dispense, apply, give.

administration *n.* **1** *the administration of justice:* administering, application, execution, management; dispensation. **2** *an executive experienced in administration:* management, superintendence, leadership, overseeing, governing, government. **3** *The teachers are responsible for the administration:* officers, executives; governing body, management, managerial organization, government.

administrative *adj. an administrative problem:* executive, managerial, management, organizational.

admirable *adj. His honesty is admirable:* worthy of admiration, commendable, praiseworthy, laudable.
Ant. deplorable, reprehensible.

admiration *n. admiration for his courage:* high regard, high opinion, esteem; veneration, approval, respect.
Ant. low regard, disdain.

admire *v. I admire your courage:* view with approval, hold in high regard, hold in esteem, think highly of, esteem, praise, value, prize.
Ant. hold in low regard, view with disapproval, disdain.

admissible *adj. admissible evidence:* capable of being admitted, permitted, allowed, allowable, permissible, acceptable, admittable.
Ant. inadmissible, unacceptable.

admission *n.* **1** *Admission is limited to invited guests:* admittance, permission to enter, entry, entrance, entreé, access. **2** *Admission is $3.00:* price of admission, entrance fee; ticket; fee. **3** *an admission of*

guilt: acknowledgment, confession, profession, declaration.
Ant. **3** denial, disavowal.

admit *v.* **1** *Please admit the guests. Ten new lawyers were admitted to the bar:* let in, allow to enter, let enter, give access to, grant entrance; appoint, induct; receive. **2** *Did the thief admit his guilt?:* acknowledge, confess, profess, *Informal* own up.
Ant. **1** exclude, keep out. **2** deny, disavow.

admixture *n. an admixture of ingredients:* blend, amalgam, combination, composite, amalgamation, mixture, intermingling, commingling, commixture; conglomeration, jumble, potpourri.

admonish *v.* **1** *Admonish the guards to be on the alert:* warn, caution, put on guard; advise, enjoin. **2** *The preacher admonished him:* reprove, censure, reprimand, rebuke, reproach, remonstrate, chasten, scold, upbraid, criticize, take to task.
Ant. **2** praise, compliment, commend.

admonition *n. The judge gave the careless driver an admonition: drive slowly:* reprimand, mild reproof, scolding, reproach, rebuke; warning, chiding, cautionary reminder, advice.
Ant. compliment, commendation, pat on the back.

ado *n. much ado about nothing:* bustle, commotion, stir, bother, flurry, pother, fuss; to-do, turmoil, agitation, tumult, uproar, furor.

adolescent *n.* **1** *Most adolescents will finish high school:* teenager, teen, young teen, young man or woman, youth, schoolboy, schoolgirl. *—adj.* **2** *The script is adolescent:* for a teenager, befitting a teenager, not adult; immature, sophomoric, puerile, juvenile; callow; youthful; childish, babyish.
Ant. **1** adult; child. **2** grownup, mature.

adopt *v.* **1** *Many childless couples adopt children:* become the legal parent of, take as one's own child. **2** *The schools must adopt new methods of teaching:* formally approve, accept, take up, follow, embrace, espouse; utilize, employ, use.
Ant. **2** give up, cast aside, cast off; spurn, forswear, reject.

adorable *adj. The little girl was adorable. an adorable dress:* lovable, delightful, precious, darling; appealing, charming, captivating, fetching, irresistible.
Ant. unlovable, hard to like, despicable; unappealing.

adoration *n. the adoration of God:* worship, worshiping, glorification, exaltation, veneration, adulation, devotion; honor, idolization.
Ant. blasphemy, reviling, execration.

adore *v.* **1** *He adores his wife. I adore your*

new hat: love, hold dear, cherish; fancy, like, dote on; admire. 2 *O, come let us adore Him:* worship, glorify, exalt, revere, venerate.

Ant. 1 hate, abhor, loathe, despise. 2 blaspheme, revile, execrate, belittle.

adorn *v. A gold pin adorned her dress:* ornament, decorate, embellish, bedeck; beautify, set off to advantage.

adornment *n. The garden's greatest adornments were its rare orchids:* ornament, ornamentation, decoration, embellishment; finery, attire.

adrift *adj.* 1 *The boat was adrift on the tide:* drifting, afloat, unmoored, aweigh, unanchored. 2 *After college they were adrift for several years:* confused, lost, uncertain, perplexed, irresolute, unsettled.

Ant. 1 moored, anchored.

adroit *adj. A sculptor must have adroit hands. Politicians must be adroit speakers:* dexterous, nimble; deft, apt, proficient, skilled, skillful, expert, masterful; clever, artful, facile.

Ant. clumsy, awkward.

adulation *n. the adulation of a hero:* flattery, adoration, fawning, fulsome praise.

Ant. condemnation, denunciation, defamation, censure.

adult *n.* 1 *Many of the adults own homes:* grownup, man, woman. *—adj.* 2 *The clothing comes in adult sizes only:* mature, big, of age, full-grown, grownup.

Ant. 1, 2 baby, infant, adolescent. 1 child.

adulterate *v. to adulterate wine with water:* contaminate, thin, water, water down.

adultery *n. In many countries adultery is a punishable offense:* unfaithfulness, fornication, marital infidelity, illicit intercourse, cuckoldry, unchastity, extramarital relations.

Ant. fidelity, faithfulness, constancy.

advance *v.* 1 *The troops advanced. We will advance hard workers:* move forward, send forward, progress, move up, move onward; promote. 2 *The biologist advanced a new theory:* proffer, bring forward, offer, bring to notice. 3 *to advance our knowledge of the moon:* bring forward, further, increase, improve, add to. 4 *He advanced me $50 against next week's salary:* pay beforehand, give beforehand; pay on account, pay now. *—n.* 5 *The enemy advance must be stopped!:* forward movement, progress, onward movement. 6 *a major medical advance. His advance in the firm led him to president:* improvement, advancement, progress, furthering, promotion, growth, gain. 7 *The plumber wanted an advance of $50:* prepayment, down payment. 8 *Stop making advances to all the girls:* pass, amo-

rous overture, overture. *—adj.* 9 *The advance troops sighted the enemy:* forward, foremost, before all others, in front, up front. 10 *the advance sale of tickets:* preliminary, previous, prior, before the fact.

Ant. 1 retreat, go backward, regress, move back; demote. 2 withhold, suppress. 3 decrease, lessen, diminish. 5 retreat, withdrawal. 6 setback. 9 rear, hindmost.

advantage *n.* 1 *Being able to speak French is a great advantage:* asset, help, benefit, aid, blessing, boon, convenience. 2 *The taller team has an advantage:* edge, upper hand; superiority.

Ant. 1, 2 disadvantage. 1 hindrance, drawback, deterrent, curse. 2 handicap.

advantageous *adj.* 1 *You'll find it advantageous to learn Spanish:* helpful, beneficial, useful, valuable, profitable, of assistance, of service. 2 *an advantageous position:* superior, favorable, dominating, auspicious, fortunate.

Ant. 1 useless, detrimental; harmful. 2 inferior, unfavorable, unfortunate.

advent *n. The advent of the railroad opened up travel:* coming, arrival, onset, beginning, occurrence, appearance, appearing, opening up.

Ant. end, conclusion, demise.

adventure *n. the adventures of Marco Polo:* enterprise, undertaking, venture, escapade.

adventurer *n. There's a little bit of the adventurer in everyone:* daredevil, romantic, hero, heroine.

adventurous *adj.* 1 *an adventurous individual:* seeking excitement, eager for experience, daring, bold, venturesome; brave, courageous, valiant, intrepid. 2 *The trip promised to be adventurous:* challenging, risky, hazardous, dangerous, perilous.

Ant. 1 cautious, hesitant. 2 dull, boring, routine.

adversary *n. adversaries on the football field:* opponent, rival, competitor, foe, antagonist, enemy.

Ant. ally, accomplice; friend.

adverse *adj. adverse winds. adverse criticism:* unfavorable, contrary, opposing, unpropitious, detrimental, negative; hostile, antagonistic, inimical; pernicious.

Ant. favorable, helpful, beneficial; auspicious.

adversity *n. Be brave in the face of adversity:* unfavorable circumstances, misfortune, calamity, ill-fortune, bad luck, hardship, mishap; trouble, distress.

advertise *v. Don't advertise your shortcomings:* publicize, call attention to, give public notice of, proclaim, broadcast, tout, noise abroad.

Ant. hide, conceal, keep secret, keep under wraps.

advertisement *n. I saw your advertisement:* want ad, classified ad, announcement, flier, handbill, poster, placard, public notice, leaflet, circular, commercial.

advice *n. Get a lawyer's advice:* recommendation, counsel, suggestion, opinion, view; advisement, guidance.

advisable *adj. It's advisable to eat well:* recommendable; prudent, judicious, wise, smart; suitable, sound, proper, fitting.

advise *v.* 1 *I advise you to reconsider:* counsel, recommend, recommend to, suggest, suggest to, offer an opinion; commend, urge, encourage; caution, warn, admonish. 2 *We have been advised that the roads are icy:* inform, notify, apprise, report, give notice.

adviser, advisor *n.* 1 *chief medical adviser to the health department:* consultant, counselor; aide, surrogate, assistant. 2 *Each student has a faculty adviser:* counselor, guide, mentor, preceptor; director, coach; instructor.

advisory *adj. an advisory capacity:* informational, informative, consultatory, consultative, counseling; admonitory, cautionary, warning.

advocacy *n. advocacy of equal rights for women:* championship, campaigning for, pleading the case of, speaking out for, support, supporting, backing, advancement, furthering, promotion; recommendation, endorsement.

Ant. opposition; combatting.

advocate *v.* 1 *The committee is advocating revision of the law:* recommend, advise, propose; champion, urge, promote, plead the cause of, argue for, speak out for; encourage, favor, support, back, espouse. —*n.* 2 *an advocate of environmental protection:* champion, backer, supporter, proponent, promoter, spokesman for; defender, pleader, propagandist. 3 *He hired the best advocate he could find:* lawyer, attorney, legal adviser, counsel, counselor, attorney-at-law.

Ant. 1 oppose, combat. 2 opponent, adversary, enemy.

aegis *n. The concert was presented under the aegis of the Chamber of Commerce:* sponsorship, auspices, patronage, shelter, backing, support.

aerial *adj.* 1 *Seagulls glided overhead on aerial currents:* air, in the air, from the air, by air, airborne; by aircraft, of aircraft, flying, capable of flight. 2 *These aerial notions of yours are just daydreams:* dreamy, ethereal,

ephemeral, lofty, unsubstantial, unreal, fanciful, soaring, visionary, imaginary.

Ant. 2 down to earth, real, realistic, practical.

aesthetic. See ESTHETIC.

affable *adj. an affable companion:* amiable, genial, congenial, agreeable, friendly, cordial, gracious, sociable; good-natured, good-humored, pleasant, warm, easygoing.

Ant. unfriendly, disagreeable, unsociable, haughty; ill-humored, unpleasant, uncivil, rude, curt, surly.

affair *n.* 1 *What I do in my spare time is my own affair:* personal business, private matter, concern, business; personal problem. 2 *Running a household is a complex affair:* undertaking, activity, matter, operation; incident, occurrence, episode, event, happening. 3 *a gala affair:* celebration, festivity, party, social gathering, social function. 4 *The affair between the two movie stars caused a scandal:* love affair, romance, relationship, liaison, amour.

affect[1] *v.* 1 *The rain will affect our plans:* influence, be of importance to, impinge on, act on, produce an effect on; alter, change, modify; concern, relate to, pertain to. 2 *The speech deeply affected the audience:* have an emotional effect on, move, touch, stir.

affect[2] *v. He affects a British accent:* make a pretense of, feign, fake, put on, pretend to, assume, imitate, counterfeit.

affectation *n. His British accent is just an affectation:* false mannerism, pretense, pretension, sham, façade; airs, artificiality.

affected[1] *adj.* 1 *The affected workers said the layoff was unfair:* acted upon, concerned, pertinent, interested; influenced, changed. 2 *The story left him deeply affected:* moved, touched, stirred, impressed; grieved, sorry, sorrowful, troubled, upset.

Ant. 1, 2 unaffected. 1 unconcerned, uninterested. 2 unmoved, untouched.

affected[2] *adj. Wealth has made him so affected that I don't like him any more:* pretentious, pompous, conceited, vainglorious, vain; artificial, unnatural, mannered; assumed, contrived, studied.

Ant. natural, unpretentious, genuine.

affection *n. He feels great affection for her:* emotional attachment, love, fondness, tenderness, warmth.

Ant. hate, loathing, antipathy, enmity; dislike.

affectionate *adj. an affectionate child. an affectionate relationship:* loving, demonstrative; warm, tender, tender-hearted, fond, caring.

Ant. cold, cool, undemonstrative; callous.

affiance v. *The king affianced his daughter to a prince:* engage to marry, betroth, pledge.

affiliate v. 1 *Business people should affiliate with the Chamber of Commerce:* associate, connect; join, unite, ally, band together. —n. 2 *an affiliate of a large corporation:* close associate, legally connected associate, colleague; branch, chapter, part, arm, division, subdivision.

affiliation n. *The two hospitals have a close affiliation:* association, relationship, alliance, connection.

affinity n. 1 *an affinity for jazz:* natural liking, partiality, fancy, penchant, liking, fondness; leaning, bent, tendency, proclivity, propensity, inclination. 2 *the close affinity between lemons and limes:* family resemblance, similarity, likeness, parallelism; relation, connection, compatibility.
Ant. 1 aversion, repulsion, antipathy. 2 dissimilarity.

affirm v. 1 *We affirm these statements to be true:* declare, assert, aver, avow, maintain, proclaim; profess, hold, contend, claim. 2 *Congress affirmed the treaty:* confirm, sustain, ratify, validate, endorse, approve, uphold.
Ant. 1 deny, refute, repudiate, disavow. 2 reject, rescind, nullify, veto, disallow.

affirmation n. 1 *a formal affirmation:* strong assertion, avowal, declaration. 2 *The President is awaiting Congressional affirmation of his nominee:* confirmation, ratification, approval, consent, certification.
Ant. 1 denial, refutation, repudiation, disavowal, renunciation. 2 rejection, nullification, veto.

affirmative adj. 1 *an affirmative answer:* yes, assenting, positive, affirmatory; approving, concurring. 2 *The medical tests are affirmative:* positive, confirming, confirmatory, affirming. —n. 3 *Our debating team gave the arguments for the affirmative:* side in favor of a question; positive side, optimistic side.
Ant. 1–3 negative.

affix v. *Affix the sticker to your windshield:* attach, fasten, fix, add on; seal, stick, glue, paste.
Ant. detach, unfasten, take off.

afflict v. *Famine and war still afflict people:* distress, oppress, torment, plague, beset.
Ant. relieve; bless, delight.

affliction n. *to endure affliction:* distress, hardship, trouble, trial, tribulation, torment, adversity, misfortune, ordeal, calamity, pain, anguish, misery.
Ant. relief, comfort; blessing.

affluent adj. *an affluent society:* rich, wealthy, prosperous, well-to-do, moneyed, well-off.
Ant. poor, impoverished; destitute, indigent.

afford v. 1 *Can we afford a new car?:* have the money for, meet the expense of, manage, support. 2 *I can't afford to take chances with inferior equipment:* bear the consequences of, bear; risk, chance. 3 *The terrace affords a fine view:* give, provide, offer, supply, furnish, grant, yield.

affray n. *The police broke up the affray:* fight, brawl, row, donnybrook, fracas, free-for-all, altercation, row, melee.

affront v. 1 *Don't affront the judge:* offend, insult, cause umbrage to. —n. 2 *a personal affront:* offense, insult, slur, slight, indignity; rudeness, discourtesy; dishonor, disgrace, ignominy, humiliation, mortification; wrong, abuse, ill-treatment.
Ant. 1 pamper, flatter, humor, indulge; appease. 2 courtesy, compliment.

afraid adj. 1 *I'm afraid of lightning:* scared, fearful, frightened, terrified, terror-stricken; alarmed, anxious, anxiety-ridden, apprehensive, timorous, panic-stricken; fainthearted, cowardly. 2 *I'm afraid I can't come to your party:* regretful, sorry, apologetic.
Ant. 1 fearless; bold, audacious.

afresh adv. *Let's start afresh:* anew, again, over, once more.

aftermath n. *The picnic had an unfortunate aftermath—we all had poison ivy:* consequence, outcome, result; sequel, follow-up.

agape adv. 1 *He just stood there with his mouth agape:* wide open, gaping. 2 *The symphony left the audience agape:* wonderstruck, spellbound, dumbstruck, dumbfounded, amazed, astonished, awestruck, flabbergasted, agog.

age n. 1 *The child was three years of age. Our age is three score and ten:* period of existence, duration of life, life span; lifetime. 2 *wrinkled with age. You can't get a driver's license until you're of age:* old age, advanced age, seniority; adulthood. 3 *the last ice age:* era, epoch, period, phase, date; stage of time. 4 *It seemed an age before he arrived:* a long time, forever. —v. 5 *Children seem to age before our eyes. The tragedy aged him:* advance in age, grow older, mature, develop; make old. 6 *The cheese was aged for two years:* mature, ripen, mellow.
Ant. 2 youth, childhood, adolescence. 4 short time, instant, second.

aged adj. 1 *an aged and venerable man:* old, elderly, of advanced age, advanced in years, ancient. 2 *A little girl, aged 3:* of the age of,

as old as, having lived for. **3** *an aged cheddar cheese:* mature, ripe, ripened.
Ant. **1** young, youthful, juvenile.

agency *n.* **1** *an employment agency:* service organization, bureau, department. **2** *He was granted a pension through the agency of the king:* power, action, activity, operation; intervention, mediation, influence, means, instrument.

agenda *n. What's on your agenda today?:* list of things to be done, schedule, docket, program; items of business.

agent *n.* **1** *The actress has a good agent:* representative; emissary, envoy, deputy, advocate. **2** *Gravity is a natural agent:* force, power, agency, mover, effective principle; means, instrument, cause. **3** *She was an agent of mercy:* doer, perpetrator, performer, practitioner, worker, mover.

aggrandize *v. His being mayor aggrandized his standing in the community:* enlarge, increase, amplify, magnify, inflate, build up, expand, broaden, widen; strengthen, intensify.
Ant. decrease, diminish; deflate, collapse.

aggravate *v.* **1** *Don't scratch—you'll only aggravate the itch:* make worse, worsen, make more severe; intensify, inflame, irritate, increase, heighten. **2** *His bossy attitude aggravates me:* irritate, annoy, exasperate, anger, vex, rile, nettle.
Ant. **1** improve; soothe, relieve, assuage, alleviate, ease, lessen, mitigate. **2** please; soothe, calm.

aggregate *n. The plan was an aggregate of all our ideas:* composite, combination, accumulation, collection, amassing, bringing together, mixture, mix, blend.

aggression *n. an act of open aggression:* hostile behavior, hostility, fighting spirit, pugnacity, belligerence, combativeness; hostile act, assault, offense.
Ant. peacefulness; peace, pacification.

aggressive *adj.* **1** *aggressive nations:* hostile, belligerent, combative, pugnacious, tending to attack. **2** *An aggressive individual can go far in this firm:* self-assertive, forceful, competitive; enterprising, ambitious.
Ant. **1** peaceful, friendly; submissive. **2** retiring, quiet, shy.

aggrieved *adj. She felt aggrieved at the slight:* sorrowful, saddened, troubled, pained; sad, grieving, grief-stricken; offended, affronted, wronged, hurt, stung, wounded, ill-treated, distressed.

aghast *adj.* **1** *We were aghast at his failure:* astonished, amazed, stunned, astounded. **2** *She was aghast at the brutal fight:* filled

with horror, horrified, horror-struck, shocked, appalled.
Ant. **1** nonplussed. **2** pleased; unmoved, unaffected.

agile *adj. an agile dancer. an agile mind:* nimble, supple, limber, lithe, graceful; clever, alert, keen, active.
Ant. clumsy, awkward, heavy; inactive, torpid.

agitate *v. A mixer agitates the cement:* stir, stir up, shake, shake up, churn, mix. **2** *The speech agitated the crowd:* upset, excite, work up; provoke, disquiet, trouble, alarm.
Ant. **2** calm, calm down, soothe, pacify.

agitator *n. Agitators disrupted the meeting:* inciter, instigator, provoker; troublemaker, provocateur, rabble-rouser.

agnostic *n. The agnostic said he was not interested in religion:* nonbeliever, unbeliever; doubter, skeptic, freethinker; disbeliever.

agog *adj. The teenagers were agog at the sight of the movie star:* openmouthed, awestruck, enthralled, thrilled, excited.
Ant. indifferent, uninterested.

agonize *v. He agonized over the guilt he felt:* be in agony, suffer, anguish, be tormented, be tortured, be distressed; worry.
Ant. enjoy, exhilarate.

agony *n. the agony of war:* suffering, pain, torment, torture; anguish, distress, misery; sorrow, anxiety.
Ant. pleasure, joy; comfort.

agrarian *adj. an agrarian state:* agricultural, farming, crop-raising.
Ant. manufacturing, industrial.

agree *v.* **1** *to agree to the terms of a contract:* assent, consent, accede, go along with; think alike, side with, support, come to the same conclusion, grant, accept, allow. **2** *The two stories don't agree:* concur, accord, conform, correspond; jibe, match.
Ant. **1, 2** disagree, differ. **1** dissent, dispute, refute, oppose.

agreeable *adj.* **1** *an agreeable person:* pleasing, pleasant, congenial; to one's liking, to one's taste, acceptable. **2** *Are you agreeable to my plans?:* in accord, consenting, complying, amenable, concurring.
Ant. **1** disagreeable, unpleasant. **2** disapproving.

agreement *n.* **1** *friendly agreement:* mutual understanding, accord; concord, harmony, concert. **2** *The plans were in agreement with the zoning laws:* harmony, in keeping, compliance, conformity, accordance, affinity; analogy, correspondence. **3** *an agreement to rent the house:* promise, contract, compact, pact, arrangement, settlement, *Informal* deal.

Ant. 1, 2 disagreement, discord. 1 dissension. 2 inconsistency, difference, discrepancy.

agriculture *n. better methods of agriculture to feed the world's population:* farming, husbandry, crop-raising, cultivation, tillage, agronomy.

aground *adj., adv. The ship was aground:* stranded, grounded, foundered, beached. *Ant.* afloat.

aid *v.* 1 *to aid the poor:* help, assist, lend assistance, give a helping hand; give support to, sustain; contribute, give alms to. 2 *A dictionary can aid language learning:* foster, further, promote, advance; facilitate, make easy. —*n.* 3 *The climbers needed aid to get back down the mountain:* help, assistance, helping hand. 4 *to live on government aid:* relief, dole; charity, donation, contribution, assistance. 5 usually **aide.** *a political aide:* assistant, right-hand, subordinate, adjutant, auxiliary; helper, *Military* aide-de-camp.
Ant. 1 hurt, harm, injure; oppose, hinder. 2 hinder, obstruct, block; discourage, thwart, impede. 3 hindrance.

ail *v.* 1 *What's ailing you today?:* bother, annoy, trouble, distress, worry; afflict, sicken, make ill. 2 *My grandmother is ailing:* be sick, be ill, fail in health, be infirm. *Ant.* 1 make happy. 2 be in good health; thrive, flourish.

ailment *n. Back pains are a common ailment:* disorder, complaint, malady, discomfort, affliction; illness, sickness, disease.

aim *v.* 1 *Aim at the target:* point, direct, level, train on; take aim, sight, focus. 2 *We aim to please:* try, strive, aspire to, work toward, endeavor, seek, attempt; intend, mean, have in view. —*n.* 3 *The gunner's aim was on target:* aiming, line of sighting; marksmanship. 4 *His aim is to retire:* desire, wish, intention, intent; goal, ambition, target, object.

aimless *adj. an aimless discussion:* directionless, undirected, unorganized, unguided; pointless, purposeless, unfocused; haphazard, accidental, random.
Ant. well-organized, purposeful, systematic.

air *n.* 1 *The glider soared high in the air:* atmosphere, stratosphere, sky. 2 *Cold air blew in through the window:* wind, breeze, draft, air current; blast, puff, zephyr, breath of air. 3 *An air of mystery pervaded the house:* atmosphere, aura, mood, feeling, ambience; quality, manner, look, appearance. 4 **airs.** *Don't put on airs with me!:* affectations, affectedness, pretensions, pretense, artificial manners; haughtiness, hauteur.

5 *The child sang a delightful air:* tune, melody, song, strain. 6 *The candidates aired their views on television:* voice, express, declare, vent, tell; proclaim, make public, disclose, divulge, publicize, expose.
Ant. 6 suppress, hide, conceal.

airplane *n. The airplanes flew overhead:* plane, aircraft, heavier-than-air craft, *British* aeroplane.

airship *n. The airship floated over the trees:* lighter-than-air craft; *(variously)* dirigible, blimp, balloon.

airy *adj.* 1 *The halls were large and airy:* open to the air, well-ventilated, sunny, spacious. 2 *The goats hopped about in an airy way:* sprightly, lively, frolicsome; light-hearted, merry, cheerful. 3 *airy thoughts:* imaginary, fanciful, dreamy, ethereal; immaterial, unrealistic.
Ant. 1 airless, stifling. 2 ponderous, heavy, sluggish. 3 substantial, factual, realistic.

ajar *adv. The door was ajar:* partly open; open, agape, gaping.

akin *adj., adv.* 1 *Wolves and dogs are akin:* related by blood, related, kin, kindred; having a common ancestor; allied, affiliated. 2 *Her thoughts are akin to mine:* alike, like, identical; similar, resembling, parallel, corresponding, analogous; congenial.
Ant. 1, 2 unrelated, unconnected. 2 unlike, different, divergent, dissimilar.

alacrity *n.* 1 *to answer a call for help with alacrity:* willingness, enthusiasm, eagerness, fervor, zeal, avidity; alertness, promptness, dispatch. 2 *He moved with alacrity:* liveliness, briskness, sprightliness; agility, nimbleness.
Ant. 1 unwillingness, apathy, reluctance; disinclination. 2 slowness, sluggishness.

alarm *n.* 1 *Sound the alarm!:* warning, danger signal, alert. 2 *She responded with alarm to the news:* apprehension, trepidation, consternation, agitation, dismay, distress, perturbation; fear, fright, panic, terror. —*v.* 3 *The sight of smoke alarmed them:* unnerve, frighten, scare; dismay, disturb, make uneasy, make anxious, make nervous, agitate.
Ant. 1 all clear. 2 composure, self-possession, equanimity, calmness, serenity, tranquillity. 3 give courage; calm, assure.

alcoholic *adj.* 1 *alcoholic beverages:* intoxicating, inebriating, spirituous, hard; fermented, distilled. —*n.* 2 *He became an alcoholic and lost his job:* drunkard, drunk, dipsomaniac, inebriate; sot, rummy, tippler, imbiber; *Slang* lush, souse, boozer.
Ant. 1 nonalcoholic, nonintoxicating. 2 teetotaler, abstainer.

alcove *n. a dining alcove:* recess, niche, nook, bay.

alert *adj.* 1 *The baby was exceptionally alert:* aware, attentive, wide-awake, observant; active, quick, lively. 2 *The alert guard foiled the robbery:* watchful, vigilant, diligent, keen-eyed, wary. —*n.* 3 *an air raid alert:* alarm, siren; warning, signal. —*v.* 4 *The sign alerted us to the thin ice:* warn, forewarn, make aware of, notify, inform.
Ant. 1 unaware, oblivious; listless, sluggish, inactive, lethargic. 2 unwary, heedless, lackadaisical, dilatory.

alias *n. The robber traveled under an alias:* assumed name, pseudonym, nom de guerre.

alibi *n. The defendant had no alibi:* defense of being elsewhere; excuse, explanation, justification.

alien *n.* 1 *All aliens had to register with the government:* resident foreigner, foreigner, outlander; immigrant, newcomer. —*adj.* 2 *Orange trees are alien to Canada:* foreign, not native, strange; exotic. 3 *Cheating is alien to my nature:* contrary, opposed, contradictory, inconsistent, incompatible, different, dissimilar, incongruous; estranged.
Ant. 1 citizen, countryman; native. 2 native, indigenous. 3 compatible, consistent.

alienate *v. His belligerence alienated him from his friends:* estrange, separate, keep at a distance; turn away, set against.

alight *v. She alighted from the bus:* come down, get down, descend, climb down, get off, disembark

align *v.* 1 *She neatly aligned the flower pots:* arrange in line, line up; straighten, even up; put in a row. 2 *He aligned himself with the major political party:* join, ally, side, cast one's lot with; associate, affiliate.

alike *adj.* 1 *They are very much alike:* same, identical, uniform, equal, even, one and the same; corresponding, equivalent, synonymous, homogeneous, analogous. —*adv.* 2 *Good teachers treat all students alike:* equally, in the same way, similarly, evenly, uniformly.
Ant. 1 different, unlike, dissimilar. 2 differently, unequally, disparately, diversely.

alive *adj.* 1 *My brother is alive and in Mexico:* living, among the living, animate, breathing, subsisting, *Informal* alive and kicking. 2 *I am most alive early in the day:* full of life, vital, lively, active, vivacious, animated, vigorous, energetic; eager, alert, spirited. 3 *Our plans are still alive:* in existence, extant, in force; possible, viable.
Ant. 1 dead, deceased, expired, lifeless. 2 lifeless, unanimated, unaware. 3 inactive, inoperable.

all *adj.* 1 *We drank all the coffee:* the whole of,

the total of; the entire contents of, every part of. 2 *All the workers agree:* every one of, each of, each and every one of, every single one of; any of, any one of; the whole number of. 3 *In all fairness I have to warn you of his plans:* complete, total, full, entire, perfect, utmost. —*adv.* 4 *This shirt is all worn out:* completely, entirely, totally, utterly, wholly, altogether; very, exceedingly, fully. —*pron.* 5 *Is that all you can carry?:* everything, the whole quantity, the greatest number, the greatest amount, the total, the utmost possible.
Ant. 1, 2 none of. 5 nothing, none; some.

all-around *adj. an all-around ballplayer:* versatile, many-sided, multifaceted, well-rounded, all-round.

allay *v.* 1 *His words allayed my fears:* calm, quiet, put to rest, soothe; subdue, appease, pacify, mollify. 2 *This medicine will allay the pain:* relieve, ease, alleviate, lessen, assuage, reduce, diminish, mitigate, mollify; blunt, dull, moderate, subdue, quiet, quench.
Ant. 1 arouse, kindle, excite, provoke. 1, 2 make worse, aggravate, increase, intensify, heighten.

allegation *n. Your allegation must be proved:* assertion, declaration, claim, avowal, contention; charge, accusation.
Ant. retraction; denial, disavowal, refutation.

allege *v. The newspaper alleges that the mayor is corrupt:* claim, declare, state, assert, maintain, say, avow, contend.
Ant. retract; disclaim, deny, disavow.

allegiance *n. to pledge allegiance to the flag:* loyalty, faithfulness, fidelity, fealty, constancy; devotion, obedience.
Ant. disloyalty, betrayal, treachery, treason, traitorousness.

allegory *n. George Orwell's* Animal Farm *is an allegory about the Russian Revolution:* fable, parable.
Ant. true story, history.

alleviate *v. This medication will alleviate the soreness:* relieve, ease, allay, assuage; lessen, reduce, abate, diminish, lighten, soften, mitigate; moderate, slake, slacken, subdue, quench.
Ant. make worse, aggravate, increase, intensify, heighten, enhance.

alley *n. There was an alley behind the store:* narrow back street, byway; passageway, passage.

alliance *n.* 1 *England and France formed an alliance:* agreement, pact, compact, treaty, concordat. 2 *The American colonies joined in an alliance against the British:* association, partnership, affiliation, league, confederation, federation, coalition.

allied *adj.* 1 *the allied armies of the United States, Canada, Britain, and France:* joint, combined, united; associated; affiliated. 2 *Music and drama are allied arts:* related, kindred, akin; similar, resembling, alike.

Ant. 1 unallied, uncombined; individual. 2 alien, foreign, unrelated; different, dissimilar, unalike, disparate.

allocate *v. The town allocated funds for the school:* set aside, designate, earmark, allot, assign.

Ant. withhold, hold back, deny.

allot *v. to allot a parking space to each employee:* assign, allocate, earmark, give out; apportion, portion out, distribute, parcel out, dole out, provide.

Ant. withhold; deny, refuse.

allotment *n. Rationing will assure that each person gets a fair allotment:* share, portion, quota, measure, apportionment, allocation, ration, consignment.

all-out *adj. an all-out effort:* unstinted, unreserved, full-scale, total, complete, maximum, intensive, exhaustive, unlimited.

Ant. half-hearted, indifferent, perfunctory.

allow *v.* 1 *The teacher allowed us to leave early:* permit, let, give permission to, give leave to; authorize, sanction. 2 *Allow yourself an hour to get to the airport:* allot, allocate, give, provide.

Ant. 1 forbid, refuse, prohibit, disallow.

allowance *n.* 1 *an allowance of 50¢ a week:* allotment, ration, subsidy, stipend, grant, bounty; annuity, income, pension. 2 *Trade in your old car and get an allowance on the new one:* discount, deduction, reduction, concession.

alloy *n.* 1 *Brass is an alloy of copper and zinc:* fusion, compound, amalgam, synthesis, blend, composite. —*v.* 2 *Bronze is made by alloying tin with copper:* mix, admix, commix, combine, conglomerate, intermix.

all right *adj., adv.* 1 *She felt all right:* well, healthy, in good health; safe, uninjured, unharmed, *Informal* O.K. 2 *The cake turned out all right:* satisfactorily, acceptably, fair, *Informal* O.K. 3 *All right, I'll do as you wish:* yes, very well, *Informal* O.K.; certainly, absolutely.

Ant. 1 bad, poorly, in bad health. 2 badly, poorly, unsatisfactorily. 3 no; absolutely not.

allude *v. He frequently alluded to his childhood:* mention, refer, speak of, hint.

allure *v.* 1 *We were allured by her sophistication:* lure, attract, entice, lead on, bait, seduce; fascinate, beguile, charm, captivate. —*n.* 2 *The allure of foreign travel:* attrac-

tion, enticement, lure, temptation; fascination, charm, glamour.

Ant. 1 repel, alienate, *Slang* turn off.

allusion *n. The book makes a brief allusion to the war:* reference, mention; suggestion.

ally *n.* 1 *The United States was an ally of Great Britain in two world wars:* partner, associate, confederate, affiliate; colleague, confrere. —*v.* 2 *The people allied themselves in the fight:* unite, join together, join forces, band together, bind together.

Ant. 1 enemy, foe, adversary, opponent.

almighty *adj.* 1 *a supreme deity having almighty power:* unlimited, absolute, sovereign, supreme, infinite, omnipotent, all-powerful. —*n.* 2 **The Almighty.** See GOD.

almost *adv. She almost fell. It's almost ten miles from here:* nearly, very nearly, about, just about, practically, approximately, close to, not quite, well-nigh.

Ant. exactly, definitely.

alms *n. beggars demanding alms:* donation, gift, contribution, offering, handout; aid, charity.

aloft *adv. The glider soared aloft. They held their heads aloft:* in the air, above, overhead, in the sky, skyward; up, high up, on high.

Ant. down, low; below, beneath.

alone *adv., adj.* 1 *She's too young to go alone. The house stood alone on the hill:* by oneself, without others, unaccompanied, separately, singly, solitarily; single, solitary, isolated; unescorted, unattended, unchaperoned. 2 *a job for one person to do alone:* without help, unaided, unassisted, single-handedly, all by oneself, only, solely. 3 *Mount Everest stands alone in its magnificence:* unique, uniquely, singularly; unsurpassed, unequalled, unrivaled, unmatched, matchless, unparalleled, incomparable. 4 *She felt terribly alone:* lonely, lonesome, friendless; forsaken, deserted, isolated, desolate.

Ant. 1 accompanied, with others; attended, chaperoned. 2 with assistance, assisted, with help, helped, aided. 3 among others, equally, equalled.

aloof *adj.* 1 *an aloof manner:* cool, cold, detached, standoffish, distant, remote, reserved, unapproachable, unconcerned; haughty. 2 *The royal family stands aloof from politics:* apart, at a distance, above.

Ant. 1 warm, friendly, familiar, gregarious.

aloud *adv. Say it aloud:* not in a whisper; in a normal speaking voice, audibly.

Ant. whispered, in a whisper; inaudibly.

alpine *adj. the alpine country of Switzerland:* mountainous, lofty, elevated, alpen; alpestrine; snow-capped, snow-clad.

alter *v. A wig alters one's appearance:*

change, transform, make different, amend, modify, vary, recast.
Ant. keep, retain.

alteration *n. The store will close for alterations:* change, modification, remodeling; conversion; adjustment.

altercation *n. Their altercation destroyed their friendship:* dispute, argument, quarrel, spat, row, wrangling; disagreement; fight, bickering; fracas, scuffle, affray, brawl, melee.

alter ego *n. A close friend is sometimes called one's alter ego:* twin, other self, second self, counterpart; complement, match.

alternate *v.* 1 *We alternate in washing the supper dishes. The temperatures alternate from 120° at noon to 40° at night:* take turns, rotate; interchange; vary, change, alter. —*adj.* 2 *alternate red and white stripes:* every other, every second; alternating; consecutive, successive. 3 *Take an alternate route:* another, substitute, second, backup. —*n.* 4 *He attended the convention as an alternate:* substitute, surrogate, second, standby, backup; deputy, proxy.

alternative *n. He has no alternative but to go by plane:* choice, other choice, option, recourse; selection, substitute.

altitude *n. At that altitude most people have trouble breathing:* height, elevation; loftiness; prominence, eminence, sublimity.
Ant. depth.

altogether *adv.* 1 *an altogether magnificent performance:* completely, entirely, utterly, absolutely, totally, wholly, thoroughly, perfectly, on the whole. 2 *The bill came to $67 altogether:* in all, as a whole, in toto, in sum total; all inclusive. 3 *Altogether, I'm glad we're moving:* all told, all in all, on the whole, in sum.
Ant. 1 partially, partly. 2 in part. 3 partially, partly.

altruism *n. A man of great altruism, he spent his life helping the poor:* selflessness, unselfishness, beneficence; humanitarianism, benefaction, benevolence, humanity.
Ant. selfishness, misanthropy.

altruistic *adj. Her altruistic deeds helped many people:* unselfish; generous, benevolent; humanitarian; charitable, philanthropic.
Ant. selfish, self-seeking, egoistic, egocentric.

alumnus *v. He was an alumnus of the University:* male graduate, former student.

always *adv.* 1 *Work always begins at nine:* every time, on every occasion, without exception; regularly, invariably, consistently. 2 *Will you love me always?:* forever, forever and ever, for all time, eternally, everlast-

ingly, evermore; continually, unceasingly, incessantly.
Ant. 1 never; rarely.

amalgam *n. a curious amalgam of charm and aggressiveness:* mixture, blend, fusion, combination, amalgamation, union, admixture, composite, intermixture, alloy; joining, alliance.

amalgamate *v. Silver must be amalgamated with a harder material to make durable jewelry:* combine, blend, merge, fuse, mix; unite, unify, join together, consolidate.
Ant. separate, disunite.

amass *v. He amassed a fortune in business:* accumulate, gather, collect, acquire, assemble, compile, heap up.

amateur *n.* 1 *When it comes to golf, I'm an amateur:* nonprofessional, dabbler, hobbyist; beginner, novice, neophyte, tyro. —*adj.* 2 *an amateur theatrical group:* nonprofessional; unprofessional, unpolished, inexperienced.
Ant. 1, 2 professional, expert.

amatory *adj. amatory glances:* amorous, passionate, ardent, impassioned, romantic, loverlike, loving, adoring, tender, lovesick.

amaze *v. His progress in karate amazed me:* surprise, astonish, astound; flabbergast; dumbfound, stupefy.

amazement *n. Imagine my amazement when I found the diamond:* astonishment, surprise, shock, stupefaction; disbelief, incredulity; wonder, awe.
Ant. calmness, composure, indifference.

ambassador *n. the ambassador to Chad:* diplomat, representative, minister, envoy; agent, deputy, emissary, go-between, intermediary.

ambience *n. The restaurant had a nice ambience:* atmosphere, environment, surroundings, milieu; character, mood, tenor.

ambiguity *n. The ambiguities of his statement led us to suspect him of lying:* equivocation, vagueness, uncertainty, indefiniteness.
Ant. clarity, explicitness.

ambiguous *adj. an ambiguous word:* vague, unclear, enigmatic, indefinite, uncertain; having a double meaning.
Ant. explicit, direct, plain, unmistakable.

ambition *n.* 1 *An executive has to have a lot of ambition:* drive, desire, push, striving. 2 *Her ambition is to be a lawyer:* aspiration, goal, aim, intent; desire, dream, hope.
Ant. 1 indifference; indolence, sloth.

ambitious *adj.* 1 *Ambitious students make the best grades:* zealous, eager, intent, avid, determined. 2 *an ambitious undertaking:*

grandiose, enterprising, industrious; difficult, arduous.
Ant. 1 unambitious, unaspiring; apathetic. 2 modest, humble; easy, simple.

ambivalent *adj. I have ambivalent thoughts on the matter:* contradictory, conflicting, opposing; confused, undecided, mixed, wavering.
Ant. definite, positive.

amble *v. We ambled across the meadow:* stroll, walk leisurely, wander aimlessly, ramble, saunter.

ambulatory *adj. Your leg is healing well and you'll soon be ambulatory:* up and about, not confined to bed; walking, mobile, peripatetic.
Ant. bedridden; not walking.

ambush *n.* 1 *The robbers lay in ambush:* concealment, hiding, ambuscade, hiding place. —*v.* 2 *The soldiers ambushed the enemy patrol:* waylay, surprise, trap, entrap, lay for.

ameliorate *v.* 1 *to ameliorate foreign policy:* improve, better; correct, rectify; amend, revise, improve upon. 2 *The patient's condition has ameliorated:* improve, get better, progress, come along, mend, show improvement.
Ant. 1 ruin, botch, destroy. 2 deteriorate, decline, worsen.

amen *interj. The prayer ends with an "Amen!":* so be it, it is so, let it be so, would that it were so.

amenable *adj. Are you amenable to having the meeting?:* agreeable, willing to agree, cooperative; favorably disposed, open, open-minded, acquiescent, willing.

amend *v.* 1 *to amend the constitution:* change, revise, modify, alter, emend. 2 *amend your manners:* improve, better, polish; emend, correct, rectify, reform, mend.
Ant. 2 corrupt, damage, impair, blemish.

amendment *n.* 1 *the first ten amendments to the U.S. Constitution:* addition, adjunct. 2 *Amendments must be made to the blueprints:* revision, modification, change, alteration, emendation.

amends *n. Is there any way I can make amends?:* apology, vindication; redress, restitution, recompense, restoration, payment, requital, expiation; atonement, satisfaction.

amenity *n.* 1 *amenities. the social amenities:* good manners, politeness, courtesies, niceties; refinement. 2 *The host greeted his guests with amenity:* geniality, amiability, affability, graciousness, friendliness, civility.
Ant. 1 bad manners, impoliteness, discourtesy. 2 surliness, incivility.

amiable *adj. amiable neighbors:* friendly,

agreeable, amicable, congenial, good-natured, cordial, sociable, affable; genial, gracious.
Ant. unfriendly, hostile, disagreeable, sullen, surly, sour.

amicable *adj. to seek amicable means of settling a dispute:* friendly, peaceable, amiable, amenable, harmonious; cordial, civil, polite, courteous; sociable, neighborly.
Ant. unfriendly, hostile, antagonistic, contentious; unsociable.

amiss *adj.* 1 *I knew something was amiss:* wrong, awry, inappropriate; faulty, mistaken, incorrect, erroneous; false, fallacious; untoward. —*adv.* 2 *Did I speak amiss?:* wrongly, wrong, inappropriately, unsuitably, improperly, mistakenly, untowardly; incorrectly, erroneously, falsely, faultily, inaccurately.
Ant. 1 right, proper, *Informal* perfect, O.K.; in order. 2 properly, appropriately; correctly, truly.

amity *n. to live side by side in amity:* friendship, harmony, good will, cooperation, agreement, accord, concord; cordiality, fellowship.
Ant. enmity, hostility, animosity, ill will; disagreement, dissension, discord.

amnesty *n. The king granted amnesty to the rebels:* pardon, reprieve; forgiveness, absolution.

amorous *adj. an amorous glance:* loving, enamored, lovesick; ardent, passionate, impassioned; fond, tender.
Ant. unloving, uncaring, cold; hateful.

amorphous *adj. an amorphous haze:* shapeless, formless, undefined, undelineated, unshapen; vague, indeterminate, characterless.

amount *n.* 1 *What is the amount of my bill?:* total, sum, sum total, aggregate; extent, magnitude. 2 *a small amount of sugar:* quantity, measure.

amour *n. He's always bragging about his amours:* love affair, affair, romance, intrigue, liaison.

ample *adj.* 1 *ample funds:* enough, sufficient, adequate; substantial, plenty, abundant, plentiful, generous. 2 *ample muscles:* large, big, extensive, expansive; roomy, spacious, voluminous.
Ant. 1 insufficient, inadequate, scant, scanty, meager, skimpy. 2 small, little.

amplification *n.* 1 *The amplification of the project will take time:* enlargement, expansion, increasing, development, extension. 2 *Your story needs amplification:* elaboration, developing, augmentation, added detail, fleshing out.
Ant. 1 reduction, decreasing, curtailment,

contraction. 2 simplification, simplifying; condensing, abridging, cutting.

amplify v. 1 *We must amplify our effort:* increase, intensify, strengthen, heighten; expand, broaden, enlarge. 2 *Please amplify your remarks:* elaborate on, illustrate, expatiate on; expand, develop, add to, augment, fill out.

Ant. 1 reduce, decrease, curtail. 2 simplify, condense, abbreviate, abridge.

amplitude n. 1 *The amplitude of the universe is awesome:* magnitude, extent, size; vastness, largeness, bigness; spaciousness, capaciousness; dimension, breadth, width; bulk, volume. 2 *Leonardo da Vinci had a great amplitude of creative power:* range, scope, extent, sweep; expanse; fullness, abundance, profusion, plentitude, plethora.

Ant. 1 smallness. 2 limitation, restriction.

amply adv. *The troops were amply supplied:* adequately, sufficiently, thoroughly, completely, fully; abundantly, plentifully, profusely, copiously, liberally, unstintingly.

Ant. inadequately, insufficiently; scantily, meagerly.

amputate v. *The surgeon had to amputate:* cut off, sever, excise, remove.

amuck adv. *The escaped mongoose ran amuck:* wildly, insanely, uncontrollably, maniacally, in a frenzy, frenziedly, berserk.

amulet n. *The shaman wore an amulet:* charm, talisman, fetish, lucky piece.

amuse v. *We amused ourselves by playing games:* entertain, divert, occupy; engross, absorb; please, gladden, cheer, enliven.

Ant. bore; vex, annoy.

amusement n. 1 *Reading is my favorite amusement:* pastime, diversion, pleasure, distraction; entertainment, recreation; fun, play. 2 *He smiled with amusement:* merriment, pleasure, enjoyment.

Ant. 1 bore, boredom, tedium, ennui. 2 sadness; displeasure.

amusing adj. 1 *an amusing game:* entertaining, diverting, beguiling, engrossing, absorbing; pleasant, delightful, pleasurable, pleasing, cheering. 2 *His jokes were amusing:* funny, comical, humorous, witty, droll.

Ant. 1 boring, dull, tedious.

analgesic n. *Aspirin is an analgesic:* painkiller, anodyne; *(variously)* anesthetic, narcotic, opiate, drug.

Ant. irritant.

analogous adj. *The heart is analogous to a pump:* similar, like, comparable, akin, equivalent, correlative, corresponding.

Ant. dissimilar, unlike.

analogy n. *the analogy between the heart and a pump:* similarity, likeness, resemblance, similitude; correspondence, parallelism, correlation.

Ant. dissimilarity, difference.

analysis n. 1 *an analysis of how the crime was committed:* examination, investigation, inquiry, study, test. 2 *The analysis of the election results was interesting:* evaluation, interpretation, assay, appraisal; summary, review. 3 *The doctor recommended analysis:* psychoanalysis, psychotherapy, therapy.

analyst n. 1 *The patient was sent to an analyst:* psychoanalyst; *Slang* headshrinker, shrink. 2 *A coach has to be a good analyst of players' abilities:* judge, evaluator, appraiser; examiner, investigator.

analytic, analytical adj. *an analytic mind:* logical, rational, systematic, problem-solving; inquiring, searching, testing.

Ant. illogical, unsystematic, chaotic.

analyze v. 1 *The doctor analyzed the blood sample:* separate and examine the parts of. 2 *The mathematician analyzed the figures again:* examine, study, investigate, search, appraise; evaluate, judge, think through, reason out.

anarchist n. *Anarchists burned down the palace:* rebel, revolutionary, insurgent, terrorist, mutineer; syndicalist; nihilist.

Ant. loyalist, tory, conservative; disciplinarian.

anarchy n. *Any form of government is better than anarchy:* absence of government, disorder, lawlessness, chaos.

Ant. authority; government, organization.

anathema n. 1 *The traitor's name is anathema:* taboo, unmentionable. 2 *an anathema against heretics:* curse, malediction; ban, proscription; denunciation, condemnation.

Ant. 2 blessing, benediction.

anathematize v. *We declare him anathematized and condemned to eternal fire:* excommunicate, damn; condemn, accurse, execrate.

ancestor n. 1 *His ancestors were pioneers:* forefather, forebear; progenitor, procreator. 2 *The icebox is the ancestor of the refrigerator:* forerunner, predecessor, antecedent, precursor.

Ant. 1 descendant, progeny. 2 successor.

ancestry n. 1 *I'm of Spanish ancestry:* descent, extraction; origin, stock, heredity. 2 *My aunt has made much of her ancestry:* ancestors, lineage, progenitors; family, line, parentage, genealogy, pedigree, blood line, family tree.

Ant. 2 descendants, progeny.

anchor n. 1 *Drop the anchor when the engine stops: Informal* hook; ground tackle, mooring. 2 *The Bible is the anchor of our faith:*

mainstay, support, bulwark, basis, foundation. —v. 3 *They anchored the boat in the bay:* secure by anchor, moor. 4 *We anchored the hammock to the trees:* secure, fix, affix, fasten.

anchorage n. *The breakwater provided an anchorage for the boats:* harbor, roadstead, mooring, harborage, berth, dock, quay, jetty.

ancient adj. 1 *ancient times:* long past, remote, olden, old; early, primeval, prehistoric. 2 *an ancient Packard:* old, very old, aged, age-old; antique. 3 *That the woman's place is only in the home is an ancient idea:* out-of-date, old-fashioned, outmoded, antiquated, passé, bygone; obsolete, archaic. *Ant.* 1 recent, late. 2 new, young. 3 modern, fresh, up-to-date, newfangled.

ancillary adj. *The addendum is ancillary to the contract:* supplementary, auxiliary, accessory, adjunct; secondary, subordinate, subsidiary; dependent, subservient. *Ant.* main, major, primary; independent.

anecdote n. *humorous anecdotes:* story, tale, short narrative, brief account, reminiscence.

anemic adj. 1 *He felt weak because he was anemic:* deficient in hemoglobin, thin-blooded. 2 *an anemic-looking room:* pale, pallid, dull, colorless; weak, feeble. *Ant.* 2 bright, colorful; strong, powerful.

anesthesia n. *The anesthesia lasted several hours after the operation:* insensibility to sensations, loss of feeling, insentience, numbness; unconsciousness.

anesthetic n. *The doctor used a new anesthetic:* painkiller, analgesic, narcotic, opiate, drug. *Ant.* stimulant, analeptic.

anew adv. *Begin your research anew:* again, once more, over again; from scratch, in a new way.

angel n. 1 *The angel Gabriel is mentioned in the Bible:* messenger of God, heavenly spirit, celestial being; (*variously*) seraph, cherub, throne, domination, virtue, power, principality, archangel. 2 *I know an angel:* angelic person, treasure, saint. 3 *He's an angel of the new play on Broadway:* financial backer, patron, benefactor, sponsor, underwriter. *Ant.* 1 devil.

angelic adj. 1 *The music had an angelic quality:* ethereal, celestial, heavenly, divine, saintly. 2 *What an angelic child!:* angellike, good, innocent; beautiful, lovely, enrapturing, rapturous. *Ant.* 1, 2 demonic. 1 hellish, netherworld. 2 diabolical, fiendish.

anger n. 1 *My anger grew:* rage, outrage,

fury, wrath, ire, choler, pique, dander; indignation, exasperation, vexation, irritation, umbrage; enmity, acrimony; ill temper, hot temper. —v. 2 *I did not mean to anger you:* infuriate, enrage, outrage, madden, incense, pique, rile, gall, nettle, exasperate, vex, irritate, rankle; antagonize, cause ill feelings; *Informal* ruffle one's feathers, get one's dander up. *Ant.* 1 love, liking; good will, peacefulness, amiability; equanimity; forgiveness. 2 placate, appease, pacify, mollify, calm, soothe; please.

angle n. 1 *an angle of 90°:* Geometry space between two lines or planes that meet; divergence. 2 *The road makes a sharp angle:* bend, turn, corner, cusp. 3 *Try to look at the situation from my angle:* point of view, viewpoint, standpoint, position, side, outlook, perspective.

angry adj. *Rudeness makes me angry:* mad, furious, infuriated, enraged, outraged, raging, fuming, boiling, incensed, inflamed, irate, indignant, resentful, vexed, piqued, riled, nettled, galled, irritated, annoyed, displeased, acrimonious; ill-tempered, petulant, irascible, splenetic, huffy. *Ant.* loving, fond; calm, soothing, mild, complaisant, amiable; pleased, gratified, gratifying; good-natured, even-tempered; apologetic, forgiving, unresentful, placating.

anguish n. *The mother waited in anguish for her missing child:* distress, pain, agony, suffering, torment, misery; anxiety, grief, woe. *Ant.* comfort, solace, consolation.

angular adj. 1 *The mountain trail is angular:* sharp-cornered, bent, crooked, jagged. 2 *an angular face:* bony, gaunt, spare, lean, raw-boned, lanky, lank. *Ant.* 1 straight; rounded. 2 chubby, fleshy, rotund, plump.

animal n. 1 *Corals are compound animals:* living being, creature, organism. 2 *No animals are allowed in the restaurant:* nonhuman; (*variously*) wild animal, beast, farm animal, pet. 3 *Those hoodlums behaved like animals:* brute, beast.

animate v. 1 *All living forms are animated by the "life force":* make alive, vivify, vitalize, quicken. 2 *Her gaiety animated the entire group:* make lively, enliven, invigorate, energize. 3 *She was animated by the poem:* stimulate, arouse, stir, inspire, spur on, move. —adj. 4 *Do you think animate beings exist on Mars?:* alive, having life; moving. *Ant.* 1 make lifeless, devitalize. 2 depress, dishearten, dull. 3 discourage, dampen; inhibit, curb, check. **4** inanimate, dead, lifeless.

animated *adj. animated conversation:* lively, spirited, active, vivacious, vigorous, zestful, energetic, exciting, vibrant, dynamic, vivid, fervent, ebullient, zealous, passionate, buoyant, sprightly, brisk.
Ant. dull, deadly, lifeless, boring; depressed, dejected; inactive, spiritless, lethargic, torpid, slow, apathetic, dispirited.

animation *n. The children sparkled with animation:* liveliness, life, spirit, high spirit, vivacity, vitality, vital power, zest, vigor, vim, verve, exhilaration, eagerness, enthusiasm, ebullience; excitement, ardor, vibrancy, fire, alertness, brightness, alacrity, good cheer, sportiveness.
Ant. lifelessness, dullness, spiritlessness; lethargy, dejection, depression, low spirits.

animosity *n. the animosity between Alexander Hamilton and Aaron Burr:* ill will, antagonism, bitterness, dislike, unfriendliness, malice, malevolence, hatred, hate, hostility, enmity, antipathy, anger, rancor, acrimony.
Ant. good will, love, friendship, harmony, congeniality.

animus *n. I have no animus toward him; I just don't like being around him:* animosity, hatred, hostility, enmity, ill will, antagonism, dislike, ill feeling, rancor.
Ant. friendliness, affection, amicability, friendship.

annals *n. Never in the annals of crime has there been such a robbery:* yearly records, chronological records; chronicles, records, registers, archives; history.

annex *v.* **1** *The city annexed the area:* attach, add, incorporate, appropriate, expropriate; merge, connect, join, affix, append. —*n.* **2** *a new annex to the school:* addition, attachment, appendage.
Ant. **1** detach, separate, disconnect.

annihilate *v. The dictator sought to annihilate resistance:* wipe out, exterminate, liquidate, destroy completely, obliterate, extinguish, end, abolish, eradicate, erase, extirpate.

annotate *v. to annotate the plays of Shakespeare:* explicate, commentate, elucidate, interpret, expound; gloss, footnote.

annotation *n. The annotations were printed in italics:* note, footnote, gloss, marginalia; remark, comment, observation; commentary, elucidation, explication, exegesis.

announce *v.* **1** *The President announced his cabinet appointments:* publish, proclaim, declare; broadcast, give out, sound abroad; disclose, divulge, reveal. **2** *The clouds announced the coming storm:* herald, foretell, presage, augur, betoken, signify, signal.
Ant. **1, 2** suppress, secrete, hide, conceal, keep secret.

annoy *v. Your constant questions annoy me:* disturb, bother, pester, badger, harry, harass, hector, tease; trouble, worry, torment, plague, distract; irritate, exasperate, vex, gall, irk, nettle.
Ant. calm, soothe, comfort, please, gratify.

annul *v. The contract was annulled:* render null and void, nullify, negate, invalidate, cancel, void; revoke, rescind; abolish, undo.
Ant. validate.

annulment *n. a marriage annulment:* nullification, invalidation, cancellation, voiding; revocation, retraction, reversal; dissolution, undoing.
Ant. validation.

anoint *v.* **1** *She anointed herself with lotion:* put oil on, smear with oily liquid, pour oil on, oil. **2** *They anointed David king:* crown, ordain, consecrate by unction, make holy by anointing, sanctify by anointing.

anomalous *adj. An Eskimo would be an anomalous figure in Rio:* odd, strange, peculiar, incongruous, out of keeping; irregular, abnormal, atypical.
Ant. common, usual, unexceptional, ordinary, natural, normal, customary, normal.

anomaly *n. His mature behavior was an anomaly for someone so young:* irregularity, exception to the rule; oddity, rarity; abnormality, peculiarity, incongruity.
Ant. the norm, the rule.

anonymous *adj. an anonymous gift:* nameless, unnamed, bearing no name, unsigned; unidentified, unacknowledged, of unknown authorship.

answer *n.* **1** *Please send an answer to my letter:* reply, response, rejoinder. **2** *the correct answer:* solution, explanation, resolution. —*v.* **3** *Answer your sister's letter soon:* reply, respond, acknowledge, react to. **4** *I answered all the problems on the test:* give a solution to, solve, resolve. **5** (usually followed by **for**) *He must answer for his mistakes:* be responsible, be accountable, be liable; pay for, suffer for, make amends for, atone for. **6** *Her qualifications answer the requirements of the job:* meet, fill, fulfill, serve, suit; be sufficient, be adequate, be enough, pass muster, be satisfactory.
Ant. **1** question, query, inquiry, interrogation. **2** problem. **6** fail; differ.

answerable *adj. All adults are answerable for their behavior:* accountable, responsible, liable.
Ant. exempt, unaccountable, not responsible.

antagonism n. There was antagonism between the brothers: hostility, conflict, friction, discord; animosity, enmity, antipathy, rivalry, dissension; bitterness, rancor, resentment; hatred, dislike, aversion, detestation.
Ant. love, friendship, amity, accord, concord, harmony.

antagonist n. His antagonist won the debate: opponent, adversary, rival, competitor, disputant; enemy, foe.
Ant. ally, teammate; supporter, patron, defender.

antagonize v. His remarks antagonized the guests: alienate, estrange, repel, offend.
Ant. conciliate, placate, pacify, appease, mollify.

ante n. a two dollar ante in the poker game: stake, bet, beginning bet, wager.

antecedent adj. 1 The harpsichord was antecedent to the piano: precursory, preexistent, anterior, precedent, previous, prior. —n. 2 The horse and buggy was the antecedent of the automobile: precursor, forerunner, predecessor, precedent, ancestor. 3 antecedents. My antecedents were pioneers: ancestors, forefathers, forebears, family, predecessors, ancestry; pedigree, extraction, progeniture.
Ant. 1 subsequent, following, later, after. 2 successor, sequel; aftermath. 3 descendants, progeny.

antedate v. The American Revolution antedated the French Revolution: precede, come first, occur earlier than, predate, happen before, anticipate, antecede.
Ant. follow, succeed, come after.

antediluvian adj. antediluvian ideas: antiquated, antique, archaic, obsolete.

anterior adj. 1 the anterior wall of a building: front, in front, forward, placed before. 2 The Magna Carta is anterior to the U.S. Constitution: previous, precedent, prior, antecedent.
Ant. 1 posterior, rear, back. 2 subsequent, posterior.

anthology n. an anthology of Edgar Allan Poe's stories: collection, compendium, compilation, choice; treasury; selections, extracts, miscellany.

antic n. usually **antics**. The clown's lively antics made us laugh: pranks, tricks, monkeyshines, tomfoolery, clownishness, buffoonery; playful behavior, fanciful acts, shenanigans, skylarking, escapades.
Ant. seriousness, solemnity, gravity.

anticipate v. We anticipate a lot of snow this winter: expect, look for, await; count on, prepare oneself for; look forward to, long for; foresee, forecast, predict.

anticipation n. The children were filled with anticipation: expectation, expectancy, hope.

anticlimax n. The final act was an anticlimax: letdown, comedown, disappointment, dull ending.

antidote n. 1 an antidote to the snake bite: antipoison, countervenom, antitoxin, counteragent. 2 a good antidote for boredom: remedy, cure, countermeasure.

antipathy n. I feel antipathy toward aggressive people: dislike, aversion, distaste; disgust, repulsion, loathing, repugnance; antagonism, animosity, ill will, enmity, rancor, unfriendliness.
Ant. affinity, sympathy, attraction.

antiquated adj. antiquated ideas about etiquette: antique, old-fashioned, outmoded, passé, dated, out-of-date, outdated; obsolete, archaic.
Ant. modern, new, recent, fresh, up-to-date.

antique adj. 1 a collection of antique furniture: old, antiquated. —n. 2 a display of valuable antiques: relic, rarity, curio, memorabile.
Ant. 1 modern, new, recent, current.

antiquity n. 1 The vase is of great antiquity: ancientness, age, oldness. 2 antiquities. The British Museum displays many antiquities: relics, monuments, artifacts.
Ant. 1 modernity, newness.

antiseptic n. 1 Put an antiseptic on that cut: disinfectant, germicide, bactericide, prophylactic. —adj. 2 The operating room must be antiseptic: sterile, germ-free, aseptic.

antisocial adj. 1 Is he antisocial or just shy?: unfriendly, unsociable, unsocial, misanthropic. 2 antisocial behavior: hostile, antagonistic, belligerent; alienated, disruptive, rebellious.
Ant. 1 gregarious, friendly, sociable. 2 cooperative, well-adjusted.

antithesis n. Good is the antithesis of bad: direct opposite, reverse, inverse, converse, opposite extreme, contrary.

antonym n. An antonym is a word that is opposite in meaning to another: antithesis, opposite.

anxiety n. Our anxiety grew: uneasiness, unease, worry, distress, concern; suspense, disquiet; dread, fear, alarm.
Ant. relief; assurance.

anxious adj. 1 She was anxious about her friend's illness: uneasy, distressed, apprehensive, tense, worried, troubled, disquieted, concerned, anguished, fearful, alarmed. 2 The children are anxious to go: eager, impatient, desirous, itching, yearning; intent, keen, fervent, zealous.
Ant. 1 relieved, assured; calm, composed,

unruffled, unperturbed, nonchalant. **2** reluctant, averse, loath, disinclined.

anyhow *adv*. See ANYWAY.

anyway *adv*. **1** *It rained, but we went hiking anyway:* anyhow, nevertheless; nonetheless, just the same, regardless. **2** *It's too cool to go swimming anyway:* in any case, in any event, at any rate, anyhow.

apace *adv. He galloped apace to warn of the enemy's approach:* fast, quickly, rapidly, swiftly, speedily, posthaste, at top speed, flat-out, lickety-split.

Ant. slow, slowly, lackadaisically.

apart *adv.* **1** *The toy fell apart:* into pieces, into parts, asunder. **2** *The two stores are a block apart:* distant, one from another. **3** *One child sat apart from the others:* aside, to one side, by oneself, by itself, alone; isolated, separate.

Ant. **1** together. **3** in the midst of, surrounded.

apartment *n.* **1** *a three-room apartment:* set of rooms, suite, flat. **2** *There are sixteen units in the new apartment:* apartment building, multiple-dwelling building.

apathetic *adj. Today's students are not apathetic:* indifferent, unconcerned, uninterested, unresponsive, uncommitted, impassive, unmoved; unemotional, unfeeling, phlegmatic, spiritless.

Ant. concerned, responsive, committed, active; stirred, aroused, excited, passionate, vehement.

apathy *n. Public apathy can lead to bad government:* indifference, unconcern, lack of interest, passiveness, lethargy, lassitude; emotionlessness, coolness, impassivity.

Ant. concern, interest, responsiveness; excitement, passion, vehemence, enthusiasm, fervor.

ape *n.* **1** *Gorillas are the largest of the apes:* tailless monkey, primate. *—v.* **2** *He apes everything his brother does:* mimic, imitate, copy, parrot, emulate.

aperture *n. aperture in the roof:* opening, hole, orifice, slit, space; rift, rent, gap.

apex *n. The apex of a pyramid. Winning the Nobel prize was the apex of his career:* summit, highest point, pinnacle, peak, height, tip, zenith, crowning point, cap; acme, culmination.

Ant. bottom, base, foot; lowest point, low point, depth, nadir.

aphorism *n. "A man is known by the company he keeps" is an aphorism:* maxim, epigram, proverb, adage, axiom, apothegm, dictum, saying.

apiece *adv. The rings cost thirty dollars apiece:* each, individually, respectively.

Ant. together, all together, overall, collectively.

aplomb *n. A good officer can handle any situation with aplomb:* composure, poise, self-composure, calmness, equanimity, level-headedness, imperturbability; self-assurance, self-confidence, confidence, savoir faire, sang-froid.

Ant. awkwardness, confusion; embarrassment.

apocalyptic *adj. His apocalyptic views seemed to doom the human race:* prophetical, prophetic, oracular, revelational, revelatory, prescient.

apocryphal *adj. The story of George Washington's cutting down a cherry tree is apocryphal:* probably untrue, doubtful, questionable, dubious, unauthentic; mythical, unauthenticated, unverified, unsubstantiated; uncanonical, spurious.

Ant. undisputed, unquestionable; authentic, true, factual; verified, authenticated, substantiated; approved, official, sanctioned, canonical.

apogee *n. Verdi, at 80, was at the apogee of his powers:* farthest point, highest point, most distant point; apex, zenith, acme; top, crest, pinnacle, summit, peak.

Ant. nadir, bottom, lowest point.

apologetic *adj.* **1** *If you're truly apologetic, say you're sorry:* regretful, sorry, contrite, remorseful. **2** *Good students don't need to be apologetic about their grades:* making excuses, defensive, excusatory.

Ant. **2** proud.

apologize *v. He apologized for his behavior:* express regret, make apology, beg pardon, say one is sorry.

apology *n.* **1** *She made an apology:* expression of regret, begging pardon; acknowledgment of error. **2** *The writer's autobiography was an apology for the way he lived:* explanation, justification, defense, excuse.

apostate *n. Julian "the Apostate" attempted to replace Christianity with worship of the old gods:* heretic, dissenter, dissident, traitor, defector, deserter, turncoat, turnabout, nonconformist.

apostle *n.* **1** *Paul was an apostle of Christ:* missionary, evangelist, proselytizer, disciple, witness; envoy, emissary, messenger. **2** *Thomas Paine was an apostle of free speech:* advocate, supporter, proponent, exponent, propagator, propagandist.

Ant. **2** opponent, detractor.

apotheosis *n. the apotheosis of the self-made man:* immortalization, deification, exaltation, glorification, enshrinement, idealization, canonization, elevation; quintessence, embodiment, epitome, essence.

appall v. *I am appalled at your behavior:* horrify, dismay, shock, offend, outrage; disgust, repel, revolt; stun, alarm, abash.

Ant. please, gladden; comfort, console.

appalling adj. *The plight of the starving children is appalling:* dreadful, horrible, horrifying, terrible, dire, dismaying, horrid, frightful, ghastly, shocking, outrageous, intolerable; disgusting, sickening, revolting, repulsive, repellent; alarming, terrifying, frightening.

Ant. pleasing, pleasant; reassuring, comforting.

apparatus n. 1 *This apparatus desalinates sea water:* equipment, machinery, mechanism, machine, contraption, device, contrivance, gadget. 2 *the apparatus of government:* system, organization.

apparel n. *Pack all your apparel in one suitcase:* clothing, clothes, garments, dress, attire, *Slang* duds, togs.

apparent adj. 1 *The correct answer is apparent:* obvious, evident, self-evident, plain, patent, conspicuous, clear; understandable, unmistakable. 2 *It was an apparent heart attack:* probable, seeming, according to appearances, presumable, ostensible. 3 *The boat slowly became apparent through the fog:* visible, discernible, perceivable, perceptible.

Ant. 1 unclear, uncertain; hidden, veiled. 2 doubtful, unlikely. 3 invisible, indiscernible, imperceptible.

apparition n. 1 *Was it real or an apparition?:* ghost, phantom, specter, spirit, wraith, spook; manifestation, presence. 2 *Snow is an apparition in Florida:* unusual sight, strange spectacle.

appeal n. 1 *an appeal for funds:* plea, request, entreaty, petition, solicitation. 2 *The kitten's appeal was hard to resist:* attraction, charm, fascination, allure, charisma. —v. 3 *The besieged nation appealed for aid:* plead, entreat, implore, solicit, beseech, beg, supplicate. 4 *The idea appeals to me:* attract, interest, allure, entice, invite, fascinate.

Ant. 1 refusal, rejection, denial. 3 refuse, reject, deny. 4 repel, repulse, revolt, disgust.

appear v. 1 *Dark clouds appeared on the horizon:* come into view, become visible, show up, turn up, loom up; materialize, emerge. 2 *She appears older than she is:* look, seem, strike one as being. 3 *It appears that supper will be late:* be evident, be apparent, be obvious, be clear, be manifest, be patent. 4 *The ad will appear in tomorrow's paper:* be published, come out, be placed before the public; be on the stage, come before the public, perform.

Ant. 1 disappear, vanish. 3 be uncertain, be unclear; be doubtful.

appearance n. 1 *The sudden appearance of the bear terrified us. Everyone looked forward to the appearance of spring:* appearing, coming into view, showing up, turning up; arrival, coming, advent. 2 *a neat appearance:* look, aspect, image. 3 *He gave the appearance of being successful:* outward show, impression.

Ant. 1 disappearance, vanishing; departure, passing.

appease v. 1 *Nothing would appease the crying baby:* calm, pacify, quiet, soothe, mollify, compose, placate. 2 *The sandwich appeased my appetite:* satisfy, ease, allay, abate, assuage, alleviate, mitigate, relieve; slake, quench, quiet, dull.

Ant. 1, 2 aggravate, provoke, inflame, arouse. 1 disturb, upset.

appeasement n. 1 *appeasement of an enemy:* acceding to demands, conciliation, propitiation, accommodation; submission, giving in. 2 *Music is an appeasement to shattered nerves:* means of quieting, means of calming, easing; alleviation, allaying, abating, mollification, assuagement, mitigation, abatement.

Ant. aggravation, provocation.

appellation n. *Richard I was given the appellation "The Lion-Hearted":* name, title, designation, epithet, cognomen, sobriquet, nom de guerre.

append v. *The professor will append a glossary to his book:* add, affix, attach, tack on; suspend, hang on.

Ant. remove, take away, detach.

appendage n. 1 *The porch was added later as an appendage:* addition, attachment, extension; supplement, auxiliary, accessory. 2 *The insect had lost one of its appendages:* extremity, projecting part; *(variously)* branch, limb, arm, leg.

Ant. 1 main body.

appendix n. *The book's appendix included a list of dates in history:* supplement, codicil, back matter; addendum.

Ant. front matter, introductory material.

appertain v. *The responsibilities that appertain to parenthood:* belong to, be part of, pertain to, be characteristic of; relate to, apply to, concern; refer to, bear upon.

Ant. be unrelated, be irrelevant.

appetite n. *an enormous appetite for classical music:* desire, craving, yearning, passion, penchant, proclivity; relish, zest, gusto; hunger.

Ant. surfeit, fill; aversion, dislike, loathing, revulsion, repugnance.

appetizing adj. *The smell of the food was*

appetizing: mouth-watering, appealing, inviting, enticing, alluring, tantalizing; savory, palatable, succulent.

Ant. unappetizing; nauseating, repulsive; distasteful.

applaud v. 1 *Please don't applaud until everyone has performed:* clap. 2 *The mayor applauded the fire fighter's bravery:* praise, laud, commend, compliment; acclaim, hail, extol, sing the praises of.

Ant. 1 boo, hiss. 2 criticize, censure; disparage, decry, belittle.

applause n. 1 *The applause was deafening:* clapping, ovation. 2 *Her work deserves applause:* praise, accolades, plaudits, compliments, kudos.

Ant. 1 booing, hissing. 2 criticism, condemnation.

appliance n. *a kitchen appliance:* device, apparatus, machine, mechanism, contraption, contrivance.

applicable adj. *Your suggestion is not applicable to the problem:* relevant, pertinent, adaptable, germane, useful, suitable, fit, fitting, apropos.

Ant. inapplicable, inappropriate, unsuitable, irrelevant.

applicant n. *There were three applicants for the job:* candidate, aspirant, hopeful; job seeker.

application n. 1 *The burn needs an application of ointment:* spreading on, putting on. 2 *The application was effective against sunburn:* ointment, salve, unguent, lotion, balm, poultice, dressing, emollient. 3 *The application of French cooking terms to American cooking is open to debate:* relevance, pertinence, suitability. 4 *Have you made out your application for a passport?:* request, requisition, form; petition, claim. 5 *His application to his studies was rewarded:* attention, attentiveness, diligence, industry, dedication, commitment, assiduity.

Ant. 5 inattention, indolence.

apply v. 1 *Apply two coats of varnish to the wood:* put on, lay on, spread on. 2 *He applied what he had learned in class to the experiment:* use, utilize, employ, implement, bring to bear. 3 *The rules of safe driving apply to everyone:* be applicable, refer, pertain, have bearing upon, fit, suit. 4 *Job seekers should apply at the office:* make application, request, petition. 5 *It's difficult to apply oneself to a boring task:* devote, dedicate, direct, address.

Ant. 1 remove, take off. 3 be inapplicable, be irrelevant, be inappropriate.

appoint v. 1 *The President appointed a new cabinet member:* name, designate, commis-

sion, delegate; select. 2 *Let's appoint a time for our meeting:* designate, set, fix, determine, establish; decide on, choose, settle, arrange.

Ant. 1 dismiss, discharge.

appointment n. 1 *The cabinet appointments will be announced:* designation, assignment, commissioning; selection, nomination. 2 *the appointment of an ambassador:* assignment, position, office, post, job, station. 3 *What time is your lunch appointment?:* meeting, engagement, date. 4 **appointments.** *The room's appointments were in Early American style:* furnishings, furniture; accouterments.

Ant. 1 dismissal.

apportion v. *Apportion the food to soldiers:* allocate, allot, distribute proportionally, portion out, parcel out, mete out, ration; disperse.

Ant. collect, gather.

apposite adj. *His remarks were not apposite to the topic:* appropriate, suitable, fitting, apropos, applicable, pertinent, relevant, germane.

Ant. unsuitable, inappropriate, irrelevant.

appraisal n. 1 *What's your appraisal of the situation?:* evaluation, estimate, assessment. 2 *The bank must make an appraisal on the house:* monetary evaluation, estimated value, valuation; assessment.

appraise v. 1 *The gem is appraised at $25,000:* value, estimate to be worth, assay; assess. 2 *The personnel director appraises each applicant:* evaluate, judge, examine, inspect, review, *Informal* size up.

appreciable adj. *an appreciable difference:* noticeable, obvious, evident, substantial, significant, recognizable, perceptible, perceivable, discernible.

Ant. unnoticeable, imperceptible, unsubstantial.

appreciate v. 1 *I appreciate all you've done:* be grateful for, be thankful for, regard highly. 2 *They appreciate good wine:* realize the worth of, estimate justly; value, rate highly, hold in high regard, esteem, relish; like, admire, respect. 3 *Do you appreciate how complex the work is?:* realize, understand, comprehend, perceive, be conscious of, be aware of, be cognizant of.

Ant. 1 be ungrateful. 2 undervalue, underrate; belittle, disparage, scorn, disdain. 3 be unaware.

appreciation n. 1 *How can we express our appreciation?:* gratitude, gratefulness, thankfulness, thanks. 2 *an appreciation of good music:* understanding, comprehension, recognition of worth; admiration, liking. 3 *The appreciation of real estate values* *has been phenomenal:* increase in value; growth, rise.

Ant. 1 ingratitude. 2 ignorance, antipathy, aversion. 3 depreciation, devaluation; fall, decline.

apprehend *v.* 1 *The police expect to apprehend the kidnappers:* arrest, take into custody, take prisoner; catch, capture. 2 *The public doesn't fully apprehend the complexity of flight:* comprehend, understand, perceive, realize, recognize, know.

Ant. 1 release, free, let go. 2 be unaware of, be unconscious of.

apprehension *n.* 1 *He was filled with apprehension:* foreboding, uneasiness, misgiving, dread, anxiety, alarm, suspicion, mistrust; worry, concern, distress; presentiment of evil, premonition of trouble. 2 *the apprehension of the murderer:* arrest, capture, seizure. 3 *Quickness of apprehension is the mark of a good student:* comprehension, perception, understanding.

Ant. 1 confidence, assurance; trust; composure. 2 release, freeing; discharge. 3 incomprehension.

apprehensive *adj. The prospect of surgery would make anyone apprehensive:* uneasy, anxious, disquieted, distressed, worried, concerned, fearful, afraid; nervous, jittery; suspicious, distrustful.

Ant. confident, assured, calm, composed, unruffled, nonchalant.

apprentice *n. an apprentice to a master craftsman:* indentured assistant, learner, student, pupil; beginner, novice, tyro, neophyte.

Ant. expert, master, *Informal* pro.

apprise *v. Police should apprise arrested persons of their right to be represented by a lawyer:* inform, notify, advise, tell, make aware, disclose.

Ant. keep secret, keep quiet about.

approach *v.* 1 *The car approached the corner:* come, near, come near, draw near, come nearer to, come close, move toward. 2 *Few actors approach him in ability:* come close to, approximate; equal, match, compare. 3 *We have approached people about filling the job:* make overtures to, broach a subject to, make advances to, sound out. 4 *Approach each job with enthusiasm:* embark on, undertake, set about, enter upon, begin. —*n.* 5 *The dog's barking announced our approach:* drawing near, coming nearer. 6 *the approach to the castle:* access, way; road, passage. 7 *His approach to the problem is wrong:* way of handling, method of attack, attitude; method, procedure, modus operandi.

Ant. 1 leave, go; retreat, withdraw, go back. 4 finish, end. 5 leaving, withdrawal. 6 exit.

approbation *n. She received approbation for her good work:* praise, congratulation, compliment, good word; approval, acceptance, support, endorsement.

Ant. censure, condemnation, criticism.

appropriate *adj.* 1 *This suit is appropriate for a wedding:* suitable, proper, well-suited, fitting, befitting, correct, seemly, apt; apropos, pertinent, relevant. —*v.* 2 *to appropriate money for new schools:* allocate, set apart, allot, apportion, earmark. 3 *to appropriate land for a new highway:* take possession of, take, confiscate.

Ant. 1 inappropriate, unsuitable, unsuited, out of place. 2 withhold. 3 give, bestow, donate.

appropriation *n.* 1 *an appropriation for a new building:* allocation, money set aside, apportionment of funds, allotment. 2 *He was jailed for his appropriation of company funds:* taking for one's own use, taking, misappropriation; confiscation, usurpation.

Ant. 2 return, reimbursement, repayment.

approval *n.* 1 *He won his teacher's approval:* good opinion, regard, acceptance, respect, esteem, favor. 2 *Parental approval is necessary before signing up for the school trip:* permission, consent, concurrence, agreement, leave, sanction; authorization, mandate.

Ant. 1 disapproval, disfavor, displeasure, censure, criticism, reproof, reproach. 2 refusal, disapproval, denial.

approve *v.* 1 *Friends approve of her taste:* consider favorably, judge as good, regard as worthy, think highly of, have a good opinion of, receive with favor; esteem, appreciate, accept. 2 *No one can approve of cheating:* consent to, condone, countenance, assent to, accede to, uphold, go along with, subscribe to. 3 *The Senate approved the housing bill:* confirm, affirm, sustain, uphold, ratify, pass, authorize, sanction.

Ant. 1 disapprove. 2 repudiate, reject, object to. 3 reject, veto.

approximate *adj.* 1 *The approximate time is two o'clock:* very near, relative; nearly accurate, almost exact. —*v.* 2 *The color of the curtains approximates that of the rug:* almost match, approach, come close to, border on, nearly equal; closely resemble.

Ant. 1 exact, precise, correct; specific.

approximately *adv. The time is approximately ten o'clock:* just about, almost, around, more or less, very nearly, close to, in the vicinity of, in the neighborhood of.

Ant. exactly, precisely; specifically.

apropos *adj. The speech was not apropos for the occasion:* appropriate, fitting, befitting, suitable, well-suited, opportune, correct, seemly; pertinent, relevant, germane.
Ant. inappropriate, unsuitable, unsuited, unseemly, out of place, inopportune; irrelevant, unrelated.

apt *adj.* **1** *That dog is apt to bite:* likely, liable; inclined, prone, given to, predisposed. **2** *Alert children are apt students:* bright, clever, intelligent. **3** *The doctor made a few apt remarks about nutrition:* appropriate, suitable, well-suited, fitting, seemly, apropos; pertinent, germane.
Ant. **1** unlikely; disinclined. **3** inappropriate, unsuitable, ill-suited, unsuited, improper, unseemly; irrelevant.

aptitude *n. a natural aptitude for music:* ability, capacity, capability, talent, faculty, knack, flair, facility; inclination, predisposition, leaning, bent, propensity, penchant, predilection.
Ant. inaptitude, ineptitude; disinclination.

aquatic *adj.* **1** *Ducks are aquatic creatures:* at home in water, living in or near water, growing in water; marine *(salt water),* oceanic, pelagic *(open sea),* thalassic *(seagoing),* lacustrine *(lake-dwelling),* fluvial, fluviatile *(river and stream),* littoral, neritic *(offshore),* abyssal *(deepest parts of the ocean).* **2** *Water-skiing is a popular aquatic sport:* occurring on water, carried on in water.
Ant. **1** land, terrestrial.

aqueduct *n. aqueducts to transport water from the mountains:* conduit, channel, watercourse, duct, race.

aqueous *adj. The eye is filled with aqueous humor:* watery, liquid, moist, damp.

arable *adj. arable land:* cultivable, farmable, tillable; fertile.
Ant. uncultivable; barren, unfertile.

arbiter *n. an arbiter of good manners:* judge, referee, umpire, arbitrator; authority, connoisseur.

arbitrary *adj. an arbitrary decision:* subjective, personal, willful, random, summary; capricious, whimsical, inconsistent; imperious, autocratic.
Ant. objective, impersonal.

arbitrate *v.* **1** *The United Nations will arbitrate the international dispute:* decide, settle, mediate; judge, adjudge, adjudicate. **2** *The union agreed to arbitrate its differences with the company:* submit to arbitration, allow to be decided by an arbitrator.

arbitrator *n. If negotiations are deadlocked, an arbitrator must be called in:* mediator, arbiter, adjudicator, judge; *(loosely)* negotiator, intermediary, go-between.

arc *n. The rainbow formed a beautiful arc:* curve, arch, semicircle, crescent, bow.

arcade *n. The two buildings are connected by an arcade:* colonnade, archway, cloister, gallery, covered passageway, vaulted passage.

arcane *adj. an arcane subject:* mysterious, enigmatic, esoteric, abstruse, recondite, obscure.
Ant. clear, obvious, understood, known, well-known.

arch¹ *n.* **1** *the arch of the ceiling:* curved span, vault, dome. **2** *Her eyebrows have a high arch:* curvature, curve, arc, bow shape, bend. —*v.* **3** *The trees arched over the path:* span, curve, bend. **4** *The cat arched its back:* curve, bend.

arch² *adj.* **1** *the arch villain of the play:* chief, primary, principal, main, major. **2** *an arch look:* sly, wily, saucy; designing, cunning.
Ant. **1** minor, petty, lesser. **2** frank, open.

archaic *adj. Hitching posts are archaic:* antiquated, obsolete, obsolescent, gone out of use, out-of-date, old-fashioned, behind the times; ancient, antique.
Ant. modern, current; new, up-to-date.

archenemy *n. Sherlock Holmes's archenemy was Moriarty:* foe, adversary, antagonist, opponent.
Ant. friend, ally.

archetype *n. Satan is the archetype of evil-doers:* original, prototype, classic, model, exemplar, prime example.

architect *n.* **1** *Frank Lloyd Wright is my favorite architect:* building designer, master builder. **2** *Thomas Jefferson was the prime architect of the Constitution of the United States:* originator, creator, author, designer, planner, deviser, shaper.

archives *n. pl.* **1** *The original manuscript is in the university's archives:* depository, library, museum. **2** *The museum's Civil War archives are valuable:* documents, papers, records, memorabilia.

arctic *adj.* **1** *Permafrost occurs in arctic regions:* north of the Arctic Circle, near the North Pole; polar, far-northern. **2** *an arctic wind:* bitter, icy, frigid, ice-cold, freezing. —*n.* **3** *Arctic. Admiral Byrd explored the Arctic:* region north of the Arctic Circle, North Pole, north polar region.
Ant. **2** hot, warm, summery.

ardent *adj. an ardent patriot:* impassioned, passionate, zealous, fervent, fervid, fiery, vehement, emotional, enthusiastic, intense, fierce.
Ant. indifferent, half-hearted, unenthusiastic, apathetic.

ardor *n.* **1** *The artist began each painting with great ardor:* feeling, passion, fervor, intensity, gusto, zeal, excitement, enthusiasm, spirit, verve. 2 *Women spoke of Rudolph Valentino with ardor:* passion, rapture, love, warmth.

Ant. 1 indifference, disinterestedness, apathy.

arduous *adj. an arduous undertaking:* difficult, hard, laborious, wearisome, exhausting, burdensome, trying; vigorous, strenuous, energetic.

Ant. easy, simple, effortless.

area *n.* 1 *The plantation occupies a large area:* expanse, extent, stretch, space. 2 *a marshy area:* region, locality, territory, tract, district. 3 *She excels in the area of the arts:* field, sphere, realm, province.

arena *n.* 1 *a new sports arena:* coliseum, stadium, amphitheater, bowl, gymnasium, field; ring, stage. 2 *arena of international trade:* field, realm, area, province, domain, sphere; sector.

argot *n. the argot of pick-pockets:* criminal jargon, cant; *(loosely)* lingo, vernacular, idiom, slang.

argue *v.* 1 *The merchants argued that a parking lot was necessary:* contend, maintain, assert, hold, plead, expostulate. 2 *The children argued about whose turn it was:* have an argument, quarrel, dispute, bicker, wrangle.

Ant. 2 agree, concur.

argument *n.* 1 *Arguments about matters of taste:* quarrel, bickering, squabble, row, spat, tiff, imbroglio; disagreement, dispute, heated discussion. 2 *a powerful argument for turning the land into a park:* reason, line of reasoning, case.

Ant. 1 agreement, accord, concord. 2 rebuttal, refutation.

argumentative *adj. He's very argumentative:* quarrelsome, contentious, disputatious; fractious, querulous, contrary.

Ant. amenable, cordial.

aria *n. an aria from "Tosca":* solo, song, tune, melody, air; selection, number; canzonetta, aria cantabile.

arid *adj.* 1 *an arid land:* dry, dried-up, waterless, parched, drought-scourged, desertlike; barren. 2 *His life was never arid:* dull, tedious, colorless, uninteresting, unimaginative, jejune.

Ant. 1 well-watered; lush, verdant. 2 lively, interesting, exciting.

arise *v.* 1 *She arises at six every morning. I arose from the chair:* get out of bed, awake, wake, wake up; get up, rise, stand up. 2 *Smoke arose from the volcano:* rise, move upward, ascend, go up. 3 *Accidents arise from carelessness:* come into being, occur,

spring up, crop up, emanate, ensue; stem from, start, begin, result.

Ant. 1 retire, lie down, go to bed, recline; sit, sit down. 2 descend, fall.

aristocracy *n. members of the Spanish aristocracy:* nobility, peerage, patricians; gentry.

Ant. bourgeoisie, commoners, masses; proletariat, hoi polloi.

aristocrat *n. Club membership was once limited to aristocrats:* noble, nobleman, noblewoman, lord, peer, grandee; gentleman, gentlewoman, Brahmin, blue blood, patrician.

Ant. commoner, bourgeois, peasant.

aristocratic *adj. an aristocratic family:* noble, titled, lordly, royal, regal, courtly; blue-blooded, highborn, patrician, silk-stocking, upper-class.

Ant. common; bourgeois, middle-class, lower-class.

arm *n.* 1 *Put the bracelet on your arm:* upper limb, forearm, upper arm. 2 *The English Channel is an arm of the sea:* appendage, branch, projection. 3 *The Secret Service is an arm of the U.S. Treasury Department:* branch, division, department, section, sector. 4 **arms.** *The army deperately needs the shipment of arms:* firearms, guns, weapons; ordnance, weaponry. 5 *the royal arms:* coat of arms, heraldic emblem, insignia, crest. —*v.* 6 *The cowboys armed themselves to fight the rustlers:* take up arms, obtain arms; furnish with weapons. 7 *He armed himself for the night's work by collecting his books and papers:* prepare, make ready; equip, outfit; fortify, protect, brace.

Ant. 6 disarm.

armada *n. The armada was off the coast, ready for battle:* fleet, flotilla, squadron, escadrille.

armament *n. The battleship's armament included rocket launchers:* weapons, arms, guns, ordnance, weaponry.

armistice *n. Armistice was declared on November 11, 1918:* suspension of hostilities, ceasefire, truce; peace.

Ant. outbreak of war, hostilities.

armor *n.* 1 *Bulletproof cars are sheathed in armor:* protective covering, protection, shield, bulwark. 2 *Knights fought in armor:* suit of armor, coat of mail, mail.

armory *n. Many armories are now used to house reserve units:* arsenal, arms depot, ordnance depot.

army *n.* 1 *The Allied Army invaded Nazi-occupied France on June 6, 1944:* military force, military machine, military; land forces, land force, troops, soldiers, soldiery, fighting men. 2 *An army of ants swarmed* *over the hill:* host, horde, swarm, multitude, throng.

aroma *n. the aroma of cooking:* good smell, pleasant odor, scent, fragrance, bouquet.
  Ant. stench, stink.

aromatic *adj. an aromatic pipe tobacco:* fragrant, sweet-smelling, sweet-scented, scented, perfumed.
  Ant. unscented; bad-smelling, stinking, malodorous, rank.

arouse *v.* 1 *She aroused herself from her nap:* awaken, wake up, waken, rouse. 2 *Don't arouse my anger!:* summon up, call forth, excite, stimulate, provoke, incite, kindle, stir up, foment, quicken; pique, fan.
  Ant. 1 put to sleep, lull. 2 still, quench; dampen, dull, calm, quell, allay, assuage, pacify, placate, mollify.

arraign *v.* 1 *The suspect was arraigned:* indict, charge. 2 *The association met to arraign the member for unethical behavior:* accuse, charge, indict; call to account, denounce, censure, impute.
  Ant. 1 withdraw charges, excuse. 2 condone, approve, support.

arrange *v.* 1 *The books were arranged in alphabetical order:* group, array, set out; order, set in order, organize, sort, marshal, line up. 2 *The travel agent arranged the trip:* plan, schedule, prepare; provide, design; settle, agree to. 3 *The musician arranged the symphony to be performed by a marching band:* orchestrate, score, adapt.
  Ant. 1 disarrange, jumble.

arrangement *n.* 1 *flower arrangement. The arrangement of the files is uncomplicated:* grouping, arraying, distribution; ordering; order, organization, systematization, methodization. 2 Often **arrangements.** *funeral arrangements:* plans, preparations, measures, provisions; agreement, terms, compact. 3 *The orchestra played a special arrangement of "Silent Night":* orchestration, score, adaptation.
  Ant. 1 disorder, disorganization, disarray.

arrant *adj. an arrant knave:* thorough, thoroughgoing, utter, confirmed, outright, downright, unmitigated, out-and-out, extreme, notorious.
  Ant. partial, sometimes.

array *n.* 1 *an array of Christmas merchandise:* display, exhibition, arrangement, marshaling, order; collection, assortment, supply. 2 *The revelers were decked out in their best array:* finery, fine clothes, attire, clothing, apparel, garments, dress, garb. —*v.* 3 *Array the paintings so everyone can see them:* arrange, group, order, organize; set out, place, display, deploy, pose. 4 *ar-rayed in silk and lace:* clothe, attire, dress, adorn, bedeck, deck, outfit, robe, wrap.
  Ant. 1 disarray, hodgepodge.

arrears *n. He hasn't paid the arrears on his mortgage.* overdue debt, unpaid debt, outstanding debt; indebtedness, debit, balance due.

arrest *v.* 1 *The police arrested the suspect:* take into custody, apprehend, catch, capture, take prisoner, collar; *Slang* bust, nab, pinch. 2 *A speck on the horizon arrested the navigator's attention:* catch, fix, hold, seize, capture; engage, absorb. 3 *The new drug arrested the spread of the disease:* check, block, stay, halt, stop; delay, slow, retard, inhibit, hinder. —*n.* 4 *Fingerprints on the safe led to an arrest:* apprehension, capture, seizure, taking into custody, *Slang* bust.
  Ant. 1 release, free, set free. 3 encourage, quicken, speed up. 4 release.

arrival *n. The President's arrival was greeted with cheers:* arriving, coming, advent, appearance, entrance.
  Ant. departure, leaving, going.

arrive *v.* 1 *Fire fighters arrived quickly:* come, reach, get to, appear, show up, turn up. 2 *Good weather has arrived at last:* come, occur, happen, take place, come to pass, appear.
  Ant. 1, 2 depart, go, go away, leave.

arrogance *n. the arrogance of the king:* overbearing pride, haughtiness, presumption, loftiness, imperiousness; conceit, egoism, vainglory, self-importance, insolence.
  Ant. humility, modesty, self-deprecation, diffidence, meekness.

arrogant *adj. The boss was arrogant to all the employees:* overbearing, haughty, presumptuous, imperious, overweening, high-and-mighty; vain, conceited, egoistical, vainglorious, self-important; insolent, contemptuous, lordly, pompous, supercilious.
  Ant. unassuming, considerate, modest, diffident, deferential; meek.

arrogate *v. The President arrogated to himself the powers of Congress:* take over, claim, appropriate, preempt, usurp, assume.
  Ant. cede, relinquish, yield.

arsenal *n.* 1 *The gun collector's home looked like an arsenal. This arsenal produces gunpowder:* armory, arms depot, ordnance depot, military storehouse, magazine; arms factory, munitions factory. 2 *The police found an arsenal in the car:* cache of weapons, weapon collection, weapons, military stores.

art *n.* 1 *Music is my favorite form of art:* artistic activity, creative work, artistry. 2 *a fine collection of modern art:* works of art, objects of art. 3 *Caruso's art is demon-*

strated in this recording: artistry, genius, mastery, expertise, skill, facility, virtuosity. **4** *a bachelor of arts degree:* liberal arts, humanities. **5** *the art of flattery:* craft, technique, methods, principles; fine points, subtleties, finesse, knack.

Ant. **1** science. **3** lack of skill, ineptitude, incompetence.

artful *adj.* **1** *an artful excuse:* cunning, crafty, wily, foxy; scheming, designing, contriving, machinating; deceitful, deceptive, disingenuous, tricky. **2** *an artful lawyer:* skillful, sharp, astute, quick, adroit, deft, resourceful, ingenious, imaginative, nimble-minded, knowing, masterly, proficient.

Ant. **1** artless; candid, frank, straightforward; ingenuous, naïve. **2** ungifted, untalented, unadept, unskilled.

article *n.* **1** *Today's newspaper has an article about conservation:* piece, write-up, story, essay. **2** *Every article in the store is on sale:* item, thing, piece, object. **3** *We discussed every article of business on the agenda:* item, piece, point, particular, matter, detail.

articulate *adj.* **1** *The first human language consisted of articulate cries:* enunciated, intelligible, meaningful, speechlike. **2** *Porpoises communicate but are not truly articulate:* capable of speech. **3** *a highly articulate speaker:* eloquent, expressive, fluent, facile; clearly expressed. —*v.* **4** *Please articulate clearly:* enunciate, pronounce, enounce. **5** *A good debater must articulate ideas well:* express, state, voice; formulate, organize. **6** *The hand articulates with the forearm at the wrist:* hinge, connect, join, fit together. *Ant.* **1–3** inarticulate. **1** unintelligible, incomprehensible. **4** mumble, murmur.

articulation *n.* **1** *Clear articulation was emphasized in the speech class:* enunciation, pronunciation; diction, elocution. **2** *The knee forms a ball-and-socket articulation:* joint, juncture, connection, hinge.

artifice *n.* **1** *a magician's artifice:* trick, device, tactic, maneuver, contrivance; subterfuge, ruse. **2** *a master spy full of artifice:* cunning, craftiness, guile, wiliness, artfulness, intrigue, trickery, machination, scheming, deceit, deception, duplicity; ingenuity, inventiveness.

Ant. **2** frankness, candor, openness, artlessness, ingenuousness.

artificial *adj.* **1** *artificial flowers:* manmade, manufactured, synthetic; imitation, simulated, fake, counterfeit, sham; ersatz. **2** *an artificial smile:* insincere, feigned, pretended, phony, forced, affected, stilted.

Ant. **1** natural, real, genuine, authentic,

bona fide. **2** sincere, natural, honest; unaffected.

artillery *n. General Grant had numerical superiority in artillery:* cannon, big guns, mounted guns, ordnance.

artisan *n. The carpenter is a talented artisan:* craftsman, handicraftsman; skilled worker; master, master craftsman.

artist *n.* **1** *an operatic artist:* practitioner of a fine art. **2** *He's an artist in the kitchen:* master, expert, virtuoso.

Ant. **2** amateur, beginner, tyro, novice.

artistic *adj.* **1** *high artistic standards:* aesthetic. **2** *Picasso's artistic ability:* befitting an artist, of an artist, of art, in art. **3** *The flower arrangement is very artistic:* elegant, exquisite, attractive, handsome, tasteful, aesthetic, stylish.

Ant. **1** inartistic, unaesthetic. **3** tasteless, inelegant, unattractive.

artistry *n. Duke Ellington's artistry will long be admired:* artistic ability, mastery, talent, proficiency, virtuosity.

artless *adj.* **1** *as artless as a child:* frank, candid, open, honest, guileless, innocent, naïve, simple, straightforward; sincere, unpretentious, trusting, undesigning, openhearted, ingenuous, unsophisticated, unaffected, unself-conscious. **2** *artless beauty:* natural, unadorned, simple; primitive, crude. **3** *The painting was completely artless:* inartistic, lacking art; without artistic talent.

Ant. **1** cunning, crafty, deceitful, designing, artful, insincere, false; sophisticated, affected, self-conscious; suspicious, distrustful. **2** artificial, unnatural.

ascend *v.* **1** *The climbers ascended the mountain:* rise; climb, mount, scale. **2** *The queen ascended the throne when her father died:* succeed to, inherit.

Ant. **1** descend; fall.

ascendancy, ascendance *n. The Labour party gained ascendancy in Parliament:* power, control, domination, dominance, predominance, superiority, supremacy, preeminence, upper hand.

ascension *n. The climber's ascension of the mountain was difficult:* ascent, rising, mounting, climbing, scaling.

ascent *n.* **1** *The steeplejack made a careful ascent:* ascension, climb, climbing, scaling, mounting, rise, rising. **2** *The road made a sharp ascent:* upgrade, grade, incline, slope. **3** *His ascent from office boy to president:* advancement, advance, rise, progress, progression, climb.

Ant. **1–3** descent.

ascertain v. Can you ascertain the exact value of the jewels: find out, establish, determine; learn, discover, unearth, ferret out.

ascetic n. 1 Most of the early saints were ascetics: self-denier, abstainer, self-mortifier; hermit, recluse, eremite, anchorite, cenobite. —adj. 2 Trappist monks lead an ascetic existence: austere, self-denying, abstemious, Spartan.
Ant. 1 hedonist, sensualist, voluptuary, sybarite. 2 self-indulgent, indulgent, pampered, luxurious; dissolute, voluptuous, sybaritic.

ascribe v. Scholars ascribe the painting to Rubens: attribute, credit, accredit, assign.

ashamed adj. He was ashamed of his bad manners: feeling shame, mortified, embarrassed, chagrined, discomfited, abashed, shamefaced; guilt-stricken, conscience-stricken.
Ant. proud, arrogant, vain.

ashen adj. an ashen complexion: wan, pale, pallid, pasty, gray, leaden, blanched, anemic.
Ant. vivid, colorful.

ashore adv. The wreckage of the boat washed ashore: to shore, onto the shore, on shore, on land, on dry land.

asinine adj. It's asinine to build a house so close to the shore: stupid, foolish, ridiculous, absurd, senseless, idiotic, irrational.
Ant. smart, wise, intelligent, clever; sensible, reasonable.

ask v. 1 May we ask where you've been all this time? The driver asked directions: inquire, query, request an answer to; request information about, request information from; question, interrogate, quiz. 2 Ask the Johnsons to come to dinner: invite, request, bid, summon. 3 Don't ask for a raise: express a desire for, seek, request, apply, petition, solicit, appeal, entreat, beg. 4 The antique dealer is asking $25 for that old watch: state as a price, charge, request, seek.

askance adv. He looked askance at the crowd of young rowdies: skeptically, distrustfully, mistrustfully, suspiciously; disdainfully, disapprovingly.

askew adj. His tie was askew: crooked, awry, aslant.
Ant. straight, centered, even.

asleep adj., adv. The child was asleep before the story was finished: sleeping, slumbering; sound asleep, fast asleep; dozing, napping.
Ant. awake, wide awake.

aspect n. 1 a mysterious aspect: look, air, appearance. 2 the financial aspects of owning your own house: feature, point, side, facet, angle, consideration.

asperity n. With some asperity I rejected his help: crossness, crankiness, acerbity, acrimony, crabbedness, irritability, irascibility, sullenness, surliness, bitterness, testiness, snappishness.
Ant. affability, cheerfulness, geniality.

aspersion n. Don't cast aspersions on someone you don't know: slur, abuse, slander, deprecation, disparagement, defamation; reproach, censure, vilification.
Ant. praise, plaudit, compliment, commendation.

asphyxiate v. Carbon monoxide asphyxiates dozens of people every year: suffocate, smother; stifle, choke.

aspiration n. Her aspiration was to end poverty in the world: ambition, object, objective, end, endeavor, purpose, intent, intention; hope, desire, longing, wish, yearning, craving, hankering.

aspire v. He aspired to an acting career: desire, wish for, hope for, crave, covet, hanker after, thirst after, hunger over; seek, pursue, aim at.

assail v. A mugger assailed him on the street: attack, assault; set upon.

assailant n. The assailant was arrested: attacker, mugger, assaulter, assailer.

assassin n. John Wilkes Booth was Lincoln's assassin: killer, murderer, slayer.

assassinate v. President Kennedy was assassinated in 1963: kill, murder, slay.

assault n. 1 The army began the assault at midnight: attack, onslaught; (variously) raid, strike, foray, charge, offense, invasion. —v. 2 The king's troops assaulted the castle: attack, assail, set upon, fall upon; (variously) raid, strike, charge, invade, storm.
Ant. 1 defense, resistance. 2 defend, protect, resist.

assay v. 1 The teacher assayed to explain the meaning of the story: try, attempt, endeavor, undertake, essay. 2 Historians have not yet assayed the recent past: analyze, assess, evaluate, appraise, rate.

assemblage n. The zoo has a remarkable assemblage of animals: collection, gathering, assembly, aggregation, aggregate; amassment, accumulation; group, company, store, stock, flock, herd, pack, cluster, pile, heap.

assemble v. 1 The club members assembled: gather, convene, come together, congregate, meet; convoke, call together, summon. 2 Assemble your papers and file them: gather, collect, accumulate, bring together, group together, amass; muster, marshal, compile. 3 It took two hours to assemble the bicycle: put together, fit together, construct, fabricate; join, connect.

Ant. 1 disperse, disband, adjourn. 2 disperse, scatter, distribute. 3 disassemble, dismantle.

assembly *n. The assembly of doctors discussed medical research:* assemblage, gathering, company, convocation, group, body, conclave; crowd, throng; collection, aggregate, aggregation, cluster.
Ant. dispersion, dismissal, disunion, disruption.

assent *v.* 1 *The majority assented to my views:* agree, concur, accept, subscribe to, concede, approve, grant; acquiesce, consent. —*n.* 2 *with a nod of assent:* agreement, concurrence, consent, approval, compliance, acquiescence, accord, confirmation.
Ant. 1 dissent, disagree, differ, protest, object, refuse, spurn. 2 disagreement, dissent, dissension, disapproval, protest, objection; unacceptance.

assert *v. He asserts that garlic prevents rheumatism:* maintain, contend, avow, claim, uphold, declare, state, aver, argue, avouch.
Ant. deny, disavow, disclaim, refute.

assertion *n. the assertion that gout is caused by eating rich foods:* claim, contention, declaration, statement, avowal.
Ant. denial, disavowal, disclaimer.

assertive *adj. An officer must be assertive:* forceful, decisive, strong-willed, self-assured, self-assertive, emphatic; aggressive, outspoken.
Ant. retiring, reserved; hesitant, fearful.

assess *v.* 1 *The house was assessed at $150,000:* value for taxation, appraise, value. 2 *The club assessed each member $100:* levy a charge on, tax. 3 *The general assessed the situation:* judge, evaluate, appraise, look over, consider.

assessment *n.* 1 *a high assessment on the house:* value for taxation, appraisal. 2 *The city levied an assessment on each property owner:* tax, tariff, impost; fine, toll, charge, fee, dues. 3 *the critic's assessment of the book:* judgment, evaluation, appraisal, estimation.

asset *n.* 1 *A knowledge of French can be a great asset:* benefit, advantage, help, aid, service, plus. 2 **assets.** *This bank has assets of more than $1 billion:* financial resources, means, wealth; money and cashable possessions; *(loosely)* cash, property, effects, possessions, capital, money.
Ant. 1 liability, handicap, disadvantage, drawback. 2 liabilities, debts.

asseverate *v. The witness asseverated that he had met the defendant:* avow, state, avouch, assert, declare, aver, affirm, attest, swear, contend.

assiduous *adj. assiduous work to learn Rus-*

sian. an assiduous student: diligent, industrious, hardworking, laborious, unremitting, determined, persistent, persevering, earnest, steadfast, constant, tenacious, dogged, untiring, unflagging, indefatigable.
Ant. indolent, lazy; haphazard, casual, lax.

assign *v.* 1 *A locker was assigned to each student:* allot, allocate, consign, grant, give. 2 *The reporter was assigned to cover international news:* designate, name, appoint, commission, delegate, choose; charge. 3 *Let's assign a day for the next meeting:* name, fix, set, appoint, specify, designate, stipulate, determine.

assignation *n. Their assignation had to be kept secret:* tryst, rendezvous, meeting, appointment.

assignment *n.* 1 *The assignment was to write a book report:* homework, lesson, exercise; chore, task, job, duty. 2 *The ambassador's next assignment will be to India:* post, appointment, designation, commission. 3 *The foreman is responsible for the assignment of jobs:* distribution, apportionment, parceling out, allotment, allocation.

assimilate *v. Food is assimilated into our systems:* absorb, take in, digest, metabolize, incorporate, integrate.

assist *v. The nurse assisted the patient:* help, aid, work for, lend a hand.
Ant. hinder, hamper, impede, obstruct.

assistance *n.* 1 *The pilot needed the copilot's assistance:* help, aid, helping hand; cooperation, reinforcement. 2 *public assistance:* financial support, contribution, charity, alms, relief, subsidy.
Ant. 1 hindrance, obstruction.

assistant *n. The new assistant is a hard worker:* helper, subordinate, aide, subaltern, lieutenant, adjutant, sidekick, aid, helping hand.

associate *v.* 1 *Summer is associated with picnics:* identify, relate, link, connect, affiliate, ally, league, couple; pair, tie, yoke, combine. 2 *They associate with all the right people:* fraternize, be friends, consort, mingle, hobnob, hang out, rub elbows. —*n.* 3 *The doctor's associates agreed:* colleague, confrere, collaborator, co-worker, partner, confederate, intimate. 4 *My associates on the hike included three neighbors:* comrade, companion, fellow; friend, pal, buddy, chum. —*adj.* 5 *an associate member of the club:* subordinate; closely connected, affiliated, allied.
Ant. 1 dissociate, divorce. 2 avoid; alienate, estrange. 4 stranger.

association *n.* 1 *the local farmers' association:* organization, federation, confederation, confederacy, alliance, league, syndicate, coalition, society; body, group; company, corporation, partnership. 2 *Our association with the firm lasted 20 years. My association with them goes back to high school:* affiliation, connection, membership, relation, relationship, relations; friendship, acquaintance, familiarity, companionship, fellowship. 3 *In China fireworks have a strong association with New Year's:* identification, connection, linkage, bond, affiliation. 4 *a rare association of brains and brawn:* combination, mixture, blend, meld, mingling, union.

Ant. 2 disassociation, dissociation, separation.

assorted *adj. assorted candies:* mixed, various, varied, diverse, diversified, sundry, miscellaneous.

Ant. uniform, unvaried, homogeneous.

assortment *n. a wide assortment of merchandise:* variety, mixture, selection, diversity; motley, medley, hodgepodge; mélange; array, collection, stock, store.

Ant. uniformity, sameness, monotony.

assuage *v. Liniment will assuage the pain:* allay, ease, relieve, mitigate; lessen, mollify, alleviate, soothe, calm, quiet, temper.

Ant. intensify, aggravate, exacerbate, heighten, increase; provoke, arouse.

assume *v.* 1 *Scientists assume there is no life on Mars:* take for granted, suppose, presume, believe, think, guess, imagine, theorize, hypothesize, speculate, conjecture. 2 *The new buyer assumed the mortgage:* take on, take over, become responsible for, accept; enter upon, undertake. 3 *The Bolsheviks assumed power in the October Revolution:* seize, take, appropriate, usurp, commandeer, expropriate.

Ant. 1 know, prove. 2, 3 renounce, give up, give over, hand over, put aside, divest oneself of.

assumed *adj.* 1 *an assumed name:* pseudonymous, pseudonymic, fictitious, make-believe, made-up, phony, bogus, falsified, fake, false. 2 *the assumed time of his arrival:* supposed, presupposed, presumed.

Ant. 1 real, actual, true. 2 stated, known.

assuming *adj. assuming airs:* presumptuous, forward, presuming; overbearing, pushy, self-assertive; haughty, arrogant, insolent.

Ant. meek, retiring, modest, humble.

assumption *n.* 1 *a basic assumption of physics:* belief, supposition, presumption, presupposition; premise, theory, hypothesis, postulate. 2 *The new governor's assumption of office takes place Tuesday:* taking on, taking up, assuming; accepting,

acceptance. 3 *His assumption of power was the start of a dictatorship:* seizure, taking, appropriating, usurpation.

assurance *n.* 1 *He gave us his assurance that he would pay the bill:* pledge, promise, word of honor, vow, profession, guarantee. 2 *the natural assurance of a born leader:* self-assurance, assuredness, confidence, self-confidence, self-possession, sureness, poise.

Ant. 1 doubt, uncertainty, skepticism. 2 self-doubt, uncertainty, hesitancy.

assure *v.* 1 *The witness assured the judge that she was telling the truth:* vow to, promise, pledge to, give one's word to. 2 *One more touchdown will assure victory:* make sure, make certain, guarantee, ensure.

Ant. 1 deny, disavow, disclaim.

assured *adj.* 1 *Her next movie was an assured success:* guaranteed, certain, sure; dependable, settled, fixed, positive; indubitable. 2 *General Patton was an assured man:* self-assured, self-confident, self-possessed, confident.

Ant. 1 uncertain, questionable, doubtful, dubious. 2 timid, timorous, self-doubting, uncertain.

astern *adv. The tugboat drew astern of the ship:* to the stern, toward the stern, aft, abaft, to the rear, behind.

Ant. fore, afore, forward; ahead, in front.

astir *adj., adv. The campers were astir at dawn:* awake, roused, out of bed; up, up and about, afoot, moving about, on the move, active.

Ant. asleep, in bed; quiet, still.

astonish *v. The magician's trick will astonish you:* surprise, astound, amaze, overwhelm; startle, stun, shock, stupefy, daze, stagger, dumfound, flabbergast; perplex, bewilder, confound.

astonishing *adj. The small store had an astonishing selection of watches:* surprising, astounding, amazing, overwhelming; startling, breathtaking, staggering, striking, impressive, shocking, dazzling; perplexing, bewildering, confounding.

astonishment *n. Imagine our astonishment when we heard the news!:* amazement, surprise, shock; wonder, wonderment, awe; bewilderment, confusion, stupefaction.

astound *v. Alexander Graham Bell astounded the world with the telephone:* astonish, amaze, stun, startle, electrify, stupefy, dazzle, daze, dumfound, flabbergast, surprise.

astray *adj., adv. We were led astray by false clues:* off the course, off the mark, amiss, afield, into error.

astringent *adj.* 1 *Use an astringent lotion*

after shaving: invigorating, bracing, restorative, salutary, salubrious, curative; styptic.
2 *astringent remarks:* severe, austere; sharp, biting, stabbing, piercing.
Ant. 1 bland, mild.

astute *adj. an astute judge of character:* shrewd, smart, sagacious, keen, keen-minded, sharp, acute; able, intelligent, discerning, penetrating.
Ant. dull, unknowing, unintelligent, stupid, gullible, naïve.

asunder *adj., adv. The election debate tore the country asunder:* apart, into pieces, to shreds; in pieces, torn apart.

asylum *n.* 1 *The state maintains several asylums:* institution, home; *(variously)* sanitarium, sanatorium, mental hospital, mental institution, state hospital, insane asylum, madhouse; orphanage, children's home. 2 *The United States granted asylum to the political refugees:* refuge, haven, harbor; place of immunity.

atheism *n. The minister was shocked by the youth's atheism:* disbelief, unbelief, godlessness, irreligion, apostasy.
Ant. religion, belief.

atheist *n. I believe in God but my brother is an atheist:* disbeliever, unbeliever, nonbeliever, denier of God's existence, godless person, infidel.
Ant. believer.

athletic *adj.* 1 *Teddy Roosevelt built himself up into an athletic man:* strong, able-bodied, muscular, brawny, powerful, sturdy, strapping, robust, stalwart. 2 *In the old days sailors led athletic lives:* physically active, vigorous, hardy.
Ant. 1 frail, weak, puny; feeble, run down, out of shape. 2 sedentary, inactive.

athwart *adv., prep. Our position lay athwart the enemy's line of advance:* across, astride; crosswise, crossways, sidewise, sideways, at a right angle to.
Ant. parallel to.

atmosphere *n.* 1 *We must stop polluting the atmosphere:* gaseous envelope, air. 2 *the cheerful atmosphere of Christmas:* mood, spirit, feeling, feel, ambience, aura, tone; environment, surroundings.

atom *n. There was not an atom of truth in what he said:* particle, scrap, shred, grain, iota, bit, whit, jot, scintilla.

atone *v. to atone for one's sins:* repent, do penance for, make amends for, expiate; make reparation for, render satisfaction for, redeem, shrive.

atonement *n. The criminal promised atonement for his acts:* repentance, penance, amends, satisfaction, shrift, expiation, redress, recompense, redemption.

atrocious *adj.* 1 *an atrocious crime:* cruel, brutal, inhuman, heinous, monstrous, horrible, terrible, villainous, outrageous, infamous, vile, evil, savage, barbarous, vicious, hellish. 2 *an atrocious play:* bad, dreadful, terrible; tasteless, uncouth, tawdry, vile. 1 humane, kind, benevolent, merciful; virtuous, honorable; admirable. 2 good, fine, tasteful.

atrocity *n. The mercenaries committed one atrocity after another:* crime against humanity, savage deed, atrocious deed, outrage, villainy, enormity; barbarity, barbarism, brutality, inhumanity.

atrophy *n. Bedridden people should exercise to prevent atrophy of their muscles:* wasting away, withering, degeneration, deterioration, shriveling.
Ant. growth, development.

attach *v.* 1 *Attach the trailer to the car. Attach a stamp to the envelope:* fasten to, make fast, connect, couple; affix, fix, secure. 2 *The submarine was attached to the Pacific fleet:* assign, allocate, designate, detail; associate, affiliate, connect. 3 *The child was very attached to the new puppy:* be fond of, be devoted to, be in love with; feel affection for, be bound by love of.
Ant. 1 detach, unattach, unfasten, disconnect, unconnect, separate.

attaché *n. an attaché from the American Embassy:* diplomat, consul, envoy, emissary, minister, consul general, ambassador, vice consul, military attaché; aide, assistant, adjutant.

attachment *n.* 1 *The attachment of the engine to the train took a few minutes:* attaching, fastening, coupling, connection; affixing, securing. 2 *She has a great attachment to her sister:* love, devotion, affection, fondness; bond, affinity, friendship, liking, regard. 3 *The vacuum cleaner has four attachments:* accessory, supplement, addition, appendage; addendum, appendix.
Ant. 1 separation, unfastening. 2 antipathy; estrangement, alienation.

attack *v.* 1 *The Japanese attacked on December 7, 1941:* assault, assail, strike, take the offensive, begin hostilities against, set upon, fall upon. 2 *The book attacks the Navy for being unprepared:* censure, denounce, disparage, damn, blame, criticize. 3 *Attack each task with enthusiasm:* set about, undertake, go at, tackle. —*n.* 4 *The attack came at dawn:* offensive, offense, assault, invasion, onslaught, incursion. 5 *The newspaper's attack on the mayor's plans:* censure, impugnment, denigration, disparagement, criticism. 6 *His attack worried the doctors:* seizure, stroke, fit, paroxysm, spell.

Ant. 1 withdraw, retreat; defend, resist. 2 defend, support, uphold, vindicate. 4 retreat, withdrawal; defense, resistance. 5 defense, support, vindication.

attain *v. She attained success:* achieve, gain, win, earn, obtain; accomplish, acquire, reach, realize.

Ant. lose, forfeit; fail at, fall short of.

attainment *n.* 1 *the attainment of an engineering degree:* attaining, obtaining, gaining, getting, earning, acquirement, acquiring, procuring, procurement. 2 *a woman of great attainments:* achievement, accomplishment, success, acquirement; competence, skill, talent.

attempt *v.* 1 *We will attempt to climb the mountain:* try, strive, endeavor, undertake, seek, work at, make an effort, have a go at. —*n.* 2 *Hannibal's attempt to cross the Alps was successful:* effort, undertaking, try, endeavor.

attend *v.* 1 *All students must attend the class:* be present at, go to, appear at, show up. 2 *I'll attend to the work tomorrow. The nurse is attending the patient now:* take care of, tend to, look after; minister to, wait upon, care for, provide for. 3 *Each child must be attended by a parent:* accompany, conduct, escort, convoy, usher; oversee, superintend. 4 *Her illness was attended by weakness:* accompany, be associated with; follow. 5 *Attend to my words of warning:* heed, mind, listen to, harken to, consider, pay attention to, note, observe, mark.

Ant. 1 be absent, *Informal* cut, skip. 2 ignore, disregard, neglect. 4 be unrelated to. 5 ignore, disregard.

attendance *n.* 1 *Your attendance at the meeting is necessary:* presence, attending, being there, appearance. 2 *The attendance at the Super Bowl was more than 90,000:* number present, audience, crowd, assemblage.

Ant. 1 absence, nonattendance.

attendant *n.* 1 *The queen was surrounded by her attendants:* servant, underling, menial, lackey; aide, assistant; companion, escort, chaperon. —*adj.* 2 *Winter and its attendant hardships:* accompanying, associated, related; consequent.

attention *n.* 1 *Pay attention to the warning:* heed, regard, note, notice, mind, concern, consideration; alertness, vigilance, wariness. 2 *Give your full attention to the problem:* concentration, diligence, alertness, deliberation. 3 *The attention of the host pleased the guests:* courtesy, civility,

thoughtfulness, politeness, deference; service, care. 4 *He showered his attentions on his fiancée:* devotion, suit, court, wooing; gallantries.

Ant. 1–4 inattention, neglect, negligence, indifference, unconcern. 3 thoughtlessness, discourtesy.

attentive *adj.* 1 *an attentive audience:* heedful, mindful, intent, alert; listening, observant. 2 *an attentive hostess:* thoughtful, considerate, obliging, accommodating, courteous, deferential, diligent.

Ant. 1 inattentive, indifferent, heedless. 2 thoughtless, inconsiderate, unaccommodating; discourteous, negligent.

attenuate *v.* 1 *The silversmith attenuated the ingot into one long thread:* draw out, make thin, make fine, make slender, spin out. 2 *Aspirin attenuated the pain:* weaken, reduce, diminish, lessen, decrease. 2 increase, amplify, intensify, strengthen.

attest *v. The lawyer attested to the validity of the will. The success of the operation attests the surgeon's skill:* testify, swear to, verify, confirm, corroborate, vouch for, warrant, affirm; demonstrate, exhibit, show, display, give evidence, bear witness.

Ant. refute, deny; disprove, belie.

attic *n. The Christmas decorations were stored in the attic:* garret, loft; clerestory.

attire *v.* 1 *The mourners were attired in black:* dress, clothe, garb, robe, gown; array, bedeck, don. —*n.* 2 *wedding attire:* dress, garments, apparel, clothing, clothes, costume, outfit, wardrobe, habiliments, raiment; finery.

attitude *n.* 1 *a belligerent attitude:* disposition, outlook, point of view, perspective, manner, demeanor. 2 *The listeners stood in an attentive attitude:* posture, stance, pose.

attorney *n. the defendant's attorney:* lawyer, counsel, counselor, legal adviser, attorney at law, member of the bar, *British* barrister, solicitor, advocate.

attract *v.* 1 *Sugar attracts flies:* draw, lure, allure, entice; interest, appeal to, fascinate; captivate, charm. 2 *Try not to attract attention:* draw, induce, cause, bring about, evoke.

Ant. 1 repel, repulse.

attraction *n. Suspense novels hold a special attraction for me:* appeal, fascination, allure, lure, enticement, inducement; magnetism, charisma, charm, attractiveness.

Ant. repulsion, aversion, disinclination.

attractive *adj. The dress is very attractive:* appealing, pleasing, charming, delightful, enchanting; lovely, beautiful, pretty, handsome, becoming, fetching, tasteful; inviting, tempting, enticing, fascinating, alluring, captivating.

Ant. unappealing, repellent, repulsive, revolting; ugly, unbecoming.

attribute *v.* 1 *The accident was attributed to faulty brakes:* ascribe, credit, assign, account for, impute, blame on; cause by, derive from. —*n.* 2 *Generosity is one of her many attributes:* characteristic, trait, quality, virtue; aspect, facet, feature, property; accomplishment, acquirement, attainment; faculty, distinction, gift, talent.

attrition *n.* 1 *Attrition over thousands of years formed a cave in the rocks:* wearing down, wearing away, friction, abrasion, erosion. 2 *The staff will be reduced by natural attrition:* decrease, reduction, loss.

attune *v. Astronauts have to attune themselves to weightlessness in space:* adapt, accustom, adjust, acclimate.

atypical *adj. Seasickness is an atypical ailment among experienced sailors:* unusual, uncommon, untypical, nontypical; abnormal, unnatural, irregular, uncustomary.

Ant. typical, common, familiar, ordinary, customary, normal, natural, expected.

auburn *adj. auburn hair:* reddish-brown, golden-brown, tawny, chestnut-colored, nut brown; russet, rust-colored, copper-colored, henna.

audacious *adj.* 1 *an audacious leader:* bold, daring, adventurous, venturesome; fearless, unafraid, intrepid, dauntless, *Slang* gutsy. 2 *the audacious feats of the trapeze artists:* bold, daring, reckless, rash, risky, daredevil; heedless, foolhardy. 3 *audacious behavior:* impudent, impertinent, insolent, brazen, fresh, shameless; outrageous, unabashed, forward, saucy, cheeky; disrespectful, discourteous.

Ant. 1 unadventurous, fainthearted, timid. 2 careful, cautious. 3 ingratiating, deferential; polite, courteous, refined.

audacity *n.* 1 *Skydiving takes audacity and skill:* boldness, daring, nerve, spunk, grit, pluck, mettle, *Slang* guts; recklessness, rashness, foolhardiness. 2 *She had the audacity to walk out on her boss:* impudence, impertinence, insolence, brashness, effrontery, brazenness, brass, shamelessness, cheek, gall.

audible *adj. The music was barely audible:* loud enough to be heard, heard, perceptible, discernible.

Ant. inaudible, faint.

audience *n.* 1 *The audience applauded:* listeners, spectators, onlookers, assembly. 2 *Shakespeare has always had a large audience:* public, following, readership, market.

3 *an audience with the Pope:* interview, personal meeting, hearing; conference, consultation, talk.

audit *v.* 1 *Accountants audit the company's books:* examine, inspect, check; verify, review. —*n.* 2 *an audit of the firm's accounts:* examination, inspection, scrutinizing; verification, review.

audition *n.* 1 *The actor's audition landed him a role in the new play:* tryout, hearing, test performance. —*v.* 2 *The opera company is auditioning new singers:* try out, give a test performance.

auditor *n.* 1 *The auditor checked the firm's books:* financial examiner; *(loosely)* accountant, bookkeeper, comptroller. 2 *I'm just an auditor of the course:* one who listens, listener.

auditorium *n. The graduation exercises took place in the auditorium:* assembly hall, lecture hall, concert hall, meeting hall.

aught *n. Eight followed by three aughts is 8,000:* zero, naught; nothing, null, *Slang* goose egg, zip.

augment *v. The boy augmented his allowance by mowing lawns:* add to, increase, enlarge, expand, extend, boost; amplify, magnify, flesh out.

Ant. decrease, reduce, lower.

augur *n.* 1 *Roman augurs predicted the future:* oracle, prophet, seer; diviner, prognosticator, soothsayer. —*v.* 2 *Dark clouds augured the coming storm:* prophesy, predict, prognosticate, presage, be an omen of; be a sign of, signify, portend, forecast, foretell, herald, forewarn.

augury *n.* 1 *I don't believe in augury:* prophecy, divination, prognostication, soothsaying, fortunetelling. 2 *The rainbow was an augury of clear weather:* omen, portent, sign, token, warning, forewarning; herald, forerunner, precursor, harbinger.

august *adj. George Washington is an august figure in American history:* awe-inspiring, monumental, majestic, magnificent, impressive, imposing, sublime; noble, dignified, distinguished, eminent, illustrious, stately, solemn, exalted, glorious, superb, lofty, high-ranking.

Ant. unimpressive, unimposing, uninspiring; undistinguished, ignoble; paltry, insignificant.

aura *n. There was an aura of glamour about her:* atmosphere, ambience, feeling, feel, character, quality.

auspice *n.* 1 *an auspice of better weather to come:* indication, sign, portent, omen, warning. 2 **auspices.** *The concerts were offered under the auspices of the opera company:*

sponsorship, patronage, support, advocacy, aegis; charge, authority, control, protection.

auspicious *adj.* 1 *an auspicious beginning:* being a good omen, encouraging, favorable, promising, propitious. 2 *an auspicious occasion:* happy, felicitous; good, fortunate, lucky; timely.

Ant. 1,2 inauspicious. 1 ominous, discouraging, unfavorable, unpromising. 2 sad, unhappy, sorrowful, melancholy, joyless, dismal; unfortunate, unlucky.

austere *adj.* 1 *Grandfather was an austere man:* stern, strict, severe, forbidding. 2 *The Puritans led austere lives:* rigid, Spartan, ascetic, self-denying, abstemious; strict, simple, stark.

Ant. 1 permissive, lenient, indulgent; frivolous, joyful, merry, jolly, playful. 2 luxurious, easy; loose, dissolute, dissipated, debauched, depraved, wanton, abandoned.

authentic *adj.* 1 *an authentic Persian rug:* genuine, real, true, actual, bona fide, original. 2 *the authentic story of a doctor's life:* true, actual, real; factual, faithful; authoritative.

Ant. 1 imitation, counterfeit, simulated, fake, sham, phony, bogus. 2 inaccurate, unfaithful; fictitious, make-believe, untrustworthy; deceptive, misleading, fraudulent.

authenticate *v. The lawyer authenticated the will:* establish as genuine, document, verify, confirm, corroborate, validate, certify; guarantee, warrant, endorse.

Ant. invalidate, disprove, discredit, negate, repudiate; deny, refute.

author *n.* 1 *Mark Twain is the author of* Tom Sawyer: writer; *(variously)* novelist, short-story writer, poet, essayist, playwright. 2 *the authors of U.S. foreign policy:* creator, originator, maker, innovator, initiator, inventor, framer; producer, planner.

authoritarian *adj.* 1 *an authoritarian government:* favoring authority, repressing individual freedom; strict, harsh, severe, unyielding, inflexible; dogmatic, doctrinaire; dictatorial, tyrannical, fascist. —*n.* 2 *The sergeant was a strict authoritarian:* disciplinarian, rule follower; martinet, tyrant, little dictator.

Ant. 1 revolutionary, insurgent; lenient, permissive. 2 rebel, revolutionary, dissenter.

authoritative *adj.* 1 *an authoritative order from the general:* official, sanctioned, commanding obedience; administrative, ruling. 2 *There was an authoritative tone in her voice:* showing authority, commanding, imperative, decisive, imposing, peremptory; dogmatic, dictatorial, tyrannical. 3 *an au-*

thoritative book on the Civil War: trustworthy, reliable, dependable, definitive, factual, scholarly, learned.

Ant. 1 unofficial, unauthorized; facetious, frivolous. 2 subservient, servile; indecisive, meek, humble.

authority *n.* 1 *The sheriff's authority ends at the county line:* control, power, rule; dominion, strength, might, importance; prestige, esteem; jurisdiction, administration. 2 **authorities.** *Notify the authorities that the child is missing:* powers that be, government administration; officialdom, police. 3 *a leading agricultural authority:* expert, specialist, scholar; connoisseur; accepted source, trustworthy source.

authorize *v.* 1 *The law authorizes police officers to carry revolvers:* give authority to, empower, permit, allow, commission, license, entitle, enable, give leave. 2 *The bookkeeper has to authorize all payments:* give authority for, approve, sanction; certify, warrant, vouch for.

Ant. 1 enjoin, prohibit, forbid, proscribe; prevent, disallow.

autocracy *n.* 1 *Nazi Germany was an autocracy:* dictatorship, monocracy, totalitarian regime, autarchy, absolute monarchy; despotism, absolutism, tyranny, totalitarianism.

autocrat *n. My father was the autocrat in our house:* absolute ruler, ruler, dictator; tyrant, despot.

autocratic *adj. an autocratic ruler:* having absolute power, dictatorial, monarchical, tyrannical, despotic, authoritarian; oppressive, iron-handed.

Ant. limited, democratic, egalitarian.

automatic *adj.* 1 *an automatic dishwasher:* self-operating, self-acting, self-propelling; electric, mechanical, push-button, automated. 2 *Blinking is an automatic reaction:* involuntary, reflex, instinctive, unconscious, nonvolitional, uncontrolled, unwilled; mechanical, routine, habitual.

Ant. 1 manual. 2 voluntary, conscious; intentional, deliberate.

automation *n. We're living in the age of automation:* automatic machinery, machine-operated machinery, robotism.

automobile *n.* See CAR.

autonomous *adj. The school is an autonomous extension of the university:* self-governing, self-determined; self-sufficient, independent.

autonomy *n. Britain granted many of its colonies autonomy:* self-government, home rule, self-rule, self-determination; independence; sovereignty.

autumn *n. Autumn begins on September*

21st: fall, Indian summer, harvest time; autumnal equinox.

auxiliary *adj.* 1 *If the power fails, the hospital will use its auxiliary generator:* supplementary, ancillary, subordinate, secondary, subsidiary, accessory; reserve. —*n.* 2 *The helicopters serve as an auxiliary to the reconnaissance planes:* supplement, subsidiary, accessory; partner, companion, associate; helper, assistant; reserve, backup.

Ant. 1 main, chief, primary.

avail *n.* 1 *Efforts to save the ship were of no avail:* use, usefulness, advantage, purpose, service, benefit; help, aid. —*v.* 2 *Avail yourself of every opportunity:* use, utilize, profit from, take advantage of; benefit, help, aid, assist.

Ant. 2 overlook, neglect, ignore, pass up, spurn.

available *adj. The motel had available rooms. Is a doctor available?:* ready for use, ready for service, free, obtainable; accessible, at one's disposal, on hand, at hand, handy.

Ant. unavailable, taken; inaccessible.

avalanche *n.* 1 *The avalanche trapped the climbers:* snowslide; earthslide, rockslide. 2 *an avalanche of mail at Christmas:* overwhelming amount, barrage, bombardment, flood, deluge, torrent.

Ant. 2 paucity, scantiness; dearth.

avant-garde *n. Picasso was a member of the avant-garde:* artistic innovators, advance guard, vanguard; trailblazers, trendsetters, pioneers, tastemakers; leaders, originators.

avarice *n. His avarice led him into unethical business deals:* lust for money, greed, greediness; rapacity, venality, covetousness.

Ant. benevolence, munificence, unselfishness.

avenge *v. The parents avenged the kidnapping:* take vengeance for, wreak vengeance, revenge, retaliate, get even for, repay, exact satisfaction for.

Ant. excuse, forgive, overlook; tolerate.

avenue *n.* 1 *The avenue was lined with shops:* boulevard, thoroughfare, broad street; parkway, tree-lined road. 2 *the only avenue to freedom:* way, route, road, course, path; opportunity, chance, means, access.

Ant. 1 alley, lane.

aver *v. The witness averred he had seen the crime:* assert, declare, affirm, state, avow, maintain, swear, insist, contend, profess, proclaim, asseverate.

Ant. deny, disavow, disclaim, repudiate.

average *n.* 1 *The average of 2, 3, and 7 is 4. to graduate with a B average:* arithmeti-

cal mean, mean amount; *(loosely)* mean, median, medium, norm, midpoint. 2 *She bowls better than average:* the ordinary, the standard, the general, the usual, normal, the run of the mill, the rule. —*adj.* 3 *Our average speed was 40 miles an hour:* mean; *(loosely)* medium, median. 4 *It was an average movie. an average working day:* typical, ordinary, common, normal, usual, standard; fair, passable, so-so, mediocre, run-of-the-mill.

Ant. 4 unusual, uncommon, different, remarkable, exceptional, extraordinary; outstanding, superlative, excellent, wonderful, terrific; awful, bad, terrible, horrible, lousy.

averse *adj. I'm not averse to a glass of wine now and then:* opposed, loath, disinclined, unwilling, reluctant, ill-disposed, unfavorable, recalcitrant.

Ant. agreeable, amenable, inclined, disposed.

aversion *n. Cats have an aversion to getting wet:* dislike, unwillingness, reluctance, disinclination; distaste, prejudice against, abhorrence, loathing, hatred, disgust, repulsion.

Ant. inclination; desire, love, liking.

avert *v.* 1 *She averted her face:* turn aside, turn away. 2 *The quick arrival of fire fighters averted a major fire:* prevent, avoid, preclude, ward off, stave off, keep off, nip in the bud.

Ant. 2 allow, permit, let.

aviation *n. The Wright brothers were pioneers in aviation:* flying, flight; aeronautics, aerodynamics.

aviator *n. the most famous aviator of World War I:* pilot, flyer, airman.

avid *adj.* 1 *He's avid for success:* eager, hungry, desirous, keen, anxious; covetous, voracious, rapacious. 2 *an avid football fan:* devoted, enthusiastic, ardent, rabid, fanatic.

Ant. indifferent, apathetic 1 unconcerned, disdainful.

avocation *n. The doctor's avocation was painting:* sideline, secondary occupation; hobby, diversion, pastime, recreation.

Ant. vocation, occupation, work, business.

avoid *v. How did the burglars avoid the guards? Avoid fried foods:* evade, elude, escape, avert, skirt; keep away from, shun, steer clear of, refrain from, eschew, forsake.

Ant. meet, confront, incur, seek out, invite, solicit.

avoidance *n. Avoidance of exercise is unhealthy:* keeping away from, shunning, evasion, eluding, shirking.

Ant. pursuit, embrace; facing, confronting.

avouch *v. The authenticity of the painting*

was avouched by experts: declare, affirm, assert, aver, swear, certify, confirm; admit, confess, acknowledge.

Ant. deny, repudiate, disclaim, disavow.

avow *v. He avowed his love:* declare, announce, own, disclose, reveal, proclaim, profess; assert, state, swear, aver.

Ant. disavow, disclaim, deny; keep hidden, keep secret.

avowal *n. an avowal of guilt:* admission, confession, profession, declaration, acknowledgment; affirmation, assertion, averment.

Ant. disavowal, disclaimer, repudiation.

avowed *adj. an avowed vegetarian:* self-declared, professed, self-proclaimed, sworn; acknowledged, declared, admitted.

await *v. The audience awaited the speaker's arrival:* wait for, look forward to, anticipate, expect.

awake *v.* 1 *We awake at six:* wake, wake up, awaken. 2 *to awake the country to the need for better health care:* arouse, incite, inspire, stimulate, provoke, bestir; alert, make aware, make heedful. —*adj.* 3 *The campers lay awake:* not sleeping, wide-awake, open-eyed. 4 *A pilot must be awake to changes in the weather:* alert, attentive, watchful, vigilant, heedful, conscious.

Ant. 1 sleep, go to sleep; doze, nap. 3 asleep, sleeping, dozing, napping. 4 unaware, inattentive, unmindful, unconscious.

awaken *v.* 1 *The parents were awakened by the child:* wake, wake up, awake, rouse from sleep. 2 *The book awakened my interest in the Civil War:* arouse, call forth, stimulate, excite; fan.

Ant. 1 go to sleep, put to sleep. 2 dampen, subdue.

awakening *n.* 1 *an early awakening:* awaking, waking, waking up. 2 *a gradual awakening to the joys of music:* arousal, stimulation, stirring.

award *v.* 1 *They award the trophy to the winner:* accord, confer on, bestow, grant, give; assign, allot, allow; decree, appoint. —*n.* 2 *the Academy Awards:* prize, trophy; medal, decoration, citation.

Ant. 1 withhold, disallow, deny.

aware *adj. Are you aware of the dangers of cigarette smoking?:* conscious, cognizant, acquainted with, informed, apprised; mindful, alert to.

Ant. unaware, unacquainted with, uninformed about, ignorant, unmindful, oblivious.

awareness *n. an awareness of what the people want:* realization, familiarity, understanding, mindfulness, acquaintance, con-

sciousness, perception, acuteness; knowledge.

Ant. unawareness, unfamiliarity, obliviousness, ignorance.

awe *n.* 1 *Notre Dame Cathedral filled the tourists with awe:* wonder, reverence, veneration, solemnity, respect, adoration; amazement, astonishment. 2 *The approaching tornado struck awe in our hearts:* fright, fear, terror, panic, alarm; shock, horror. —*v.* 3 *I was awed by the sheer force of the hurricane:* strike with wonder, amaze, astonish, cow, intimidate; fill with reverence; frighten, terrify, fill with dread, panic.

Ant. 1 contempt, scorn, disdain; irreverence, disrespect. 2 scorn, disdain.

awesome *adj. The eruption of a volcano is an awesome sight:* solemn, inspiring, majestic, magnificent, wondrous, astonishing, amazing, awe-inspiring, overwhelming; fearsome, fearful, frightening, terrifying.

awful *adj.* 1 *What awful weather! an awful crime:* bad, dreadful, terrible, horrible, horrendous, deplorable, unpleasant, disagreeable; appalling, frightful, ghastly, horrifying, hideous, ugly, gruesome, monstrous, revolting, despicable, contemptible; mean, low, base. 2 *the awful expanse of the solar system:* awe-inspiring, awesome; wondrous, majestic, amazing, stupefying, fearsome, terrifying.

Ant. 1 good, fine, wonderful, terrific; attractive, beautiful, pretty; admirable.

awfully *adv. It's awfully cold today:* very, extremely, quite, exceptionally, terribly, dreadfully, excessively.

awkward *adj.* 1 *an awkward skier:* clumsy, uncoordinated, without grace, graceless, ungainly; inexpert, unskillful, inept, bungling. 2 *The ax was awkward to use:* unwieldy, unhandy, cumbersome, inconvenient, difficult, unmanageable. 3 *an awkward situation:* embarrassing, unpleasant, trying, difficult, uncomfortable, disconcerting, ticklish, touchy, delicate.

Ant. 1 graceful, well-coordinated; skillful, adept. 2 handy, convenient. 3 pleasing, pleasant, comfortable.

awry *adj., adv.* 1 *The picture is hanging awry:* askew, crooked, crookedly, unevenly, uneven. 2 *Something went awry:* wrong, amiss, askew, astray.

Ant. 1 straight, even, evenly. 2 right, perfectly.

axiom *n. The statement that "all men are created equal" is an axiom of democracy:* basic, principle, postulate, precept, fundamental law.

axiomatic *adj. It is axiomatic that absolute power corrupts absolutely:* assumed, accepted, generally understood, self-evident; indisputable, manifest, unquestioned, given.
   Ant. debatable, questionable, controversial.

axis *n.* **1** *The globe spun on its axis:* line of rotation, line of symmetry, center line; shaft, spindle, stem; pivot, pivotal point.

2 *Germany, Italy, and Japan formed an axis in World War II:* alliance, coalition, alignment, confederation.

aye *n. The ayes have it:* yes, yea; affirmative vote.
   Ant. nay, no; negative vote.

azure *n.* **1** *Azure goes well with blond hair:* sky blue, clear blue, cerulean, cobalt, lapis lazuli. —*adj.* **2** *azure skies:* clear blue, sky blue, cobalt, cerulean, lapis; cloudless.

B

---

babble *n.* **1** *The sales talk was pure babble:* drivel, twaddle, blabber, blab, gab, jabber, jabbering, prattle. **2** *The speaker shouted over the babble of the crowd:* murmur, clamor, hubbub, din. **3** *the babble of a brook:* murmur, murmuring, babbling, burble, gurgle. —*v.* **4** *The baby babbled happily:* gurgle, murmur, gibber, coo. **5** *Don't babble on the phone all day:* talk, talk idly, talk foolishly, prattle, jabber, chatter, chitchat, blabber, blather, prate, run off at the mouth. **6** *The brook babbled merrily:* murmur, gurgle.
   Ant. **2** silence, quietness. **4** articulate, enunciate.

babe *n. The mother cuddled the babe:* baby, infant, child, tot.

babel Sometimes **Babel.** *n. a babel of conflicting opinions:* tumult, confusion, turmoil, uproar, bedlam, clamor, hubbub, din.
   Ant. stillness, quiet, quietness.

baby *n.* **1** *The baby slept in its crib:* infant, babe, babe in arms, newborn child. **2** *Dr. Anderson is the baby of our club:* youngster; junior member, youngest member, newest member. **3** *Don't be such a baby!:* sniveler, crybaby, coward. —*v.* **4** *Her sisters always babied her:* pamper, indulge, spoil, humor. —*adj.* **5** *a baby bird: Her garden is full of baby marigolds:* young; small, diminutive, miniature, little.
   Ant. **1** adult; elder, oldster. **5** adult, mature; giant, large.

babyish *adj. babyish temper tantrums:* childish, infantile, immature, juvenile; babylike.

bacchanal *n. That party was a real bacchanal!:* drunken party, orgy, debauch, debauchery, carousal, revel, Saturnalia.

back *n.* **1** *Bend your back and touch your*

toes: rear part of the body; backbone, spine, spinal column, dorsum. **2** *the back of the bookcase. Move to the back of the bus:* rear, hind part, far end, afterpart; reverse side, far side. —*v.* **3** *Back the car out of the garage. Back away!:* move backward; retreat, retire, pull back, draw back, back off; reverse, revert, recede, ebb; rebound, recoil. **4** *Which candidate will you back?:* support, aid, endorse, sponsor, vouch for, advocate, promote, uphold, second; reinforce, corroborate, substantiate, confirm, attest, verify, take sides with; praise, protect; finance, subsidize, underwrite. —*adj.* **5** *The dog stood up on its back legs. the back porch:* rear, hindmost, hind; furthermost, rear; farthermost. **6** *a back road:* minor, unimportant; secluded, untraveled, rural, remote. **7** *back issues of a newspaper:* past, previous, earlier; out-of-date, obsolete, expired, bygone. **8** *He owed three months' back rent:* overdue, tardy, late, past; in arrears, not paid.
   Ant. **1** front; stomach. **2** front, head. **3** move forward, move ahead, approach, advance. **4** oppose, resist, block; repudiate. **5** front, fore. **6** main, urban. **7** future, late; up-to-date. **8** advance.

backbiting *adj.* **1** *The candidate resorted to backbiting attacks on his opponent:* belittling, deprecating, abusive, maligning, defamatory, disparaging, derogating, denigrating, vilifying, malicious. —*n.* **2** *Character assassination and backbiting were useful to him in his writing:* scurrility, vilification, vituperation, invective, gossip, aspersion, maliciousness, abuse, obloquy, cattiness, belittling, disparagement, backstabbing.

backbone *n.* **1** *Good posture results from holding the backbone straight:* spine, spinal column, vertebrae, back 2 *They lack the backbone to overcome defeat:* strength of character, fortitude, resolve, resoluteness, resolution, mettle, spunk, pluck, grit, guts, bravery, courage. 3 *The cotton industry was the backbone of the South:* mainstay; basis, foundation.

Ant. 2 spinelessness; cowardliness, cowardice.

backer *n. To win the election you'll need some powerful political backers:* supporter, champion, ally, follower; sponsor, underwriter, investor, financier.

backfire *v. Even the most carefully laid plans may backfire:* miscarry, go awry, come to nothing, fall through, boomerang, flop, fizzle.

background *n.* 1 *The painting showed trees in the background:* distance, rear, landscape. 2 *Lincoln came from an impoverished background. Her background qualifies her for the job:* environment, circumstances, upbringing, training, experience, education.

Ant. 1 foreground; fore.

backing *n.* 1 *The bill has the President's backing:* help, support, aid, assistance; endorsement, sanction, sponsorship, advocacy, encouragement. 2 *The plaster wall has a backing of wood:* back, core, reinforcement.

Ant. 1 opposition, resistance; repudiation. 2 front, covering, cover, exterior.

backlash *n. The threat of higher taxes triggered a backlash among voters:* negative reaction, resistance, recoil, counteraction, antagonism, hostility, opposition.

backlog *n. a backlog of work:* reserve supply, store, accumulation, amassment, excess, abundance, reservoir.

Ant. shortage, dearth, lack, scarcity.

backside *n. He fell on his backside:* posterior, rump, buttocks, derriere, behind, rear, rear end, sitter; duff, fanny, prat.

back talk *n. I don't want any back talk!:* sass, lip, guff, impudence, sassiness, insolence, impertinence.

backward Also **backwards.** *adv.* 1 *Take two steps backward:* toward the rear, rearward, back, in reverse. 2 *Can you somersault backward? Your shirt's on backward. You did the job backward:* with the back first, *(variously)* upside down, inside out, wrong side out, topsy-turvy, wrong, improperly. 3 *You can't turn the clock backward:* in reverse, toward the past, to the past. —*adj.* 4 *a sad backward glance:* turned toward the back, reversed, inverted. 5 *He's a little backward in his studies:* slow, slow-paced, retarded, behind, impeded, sluggish, slow-witted. 6 *Why do you act so*

backward with strangers?: shy, bashful, timid, withdrawn. 7 *the backward flow of the tide:* reverse, receding, retreating, withdrawing.

Ant. 1, 3, 7 forward. 5 advanced, ahead. 6 forward, bold, brazen, brash.

backwoods *n. I love the backwoods of Kentucky:* remote area, unpopulated area, country, rural area; wilds, woodland.

Ant. city, metropolitan area, urban area.

bacteria *n. Some bacteria are beneficial, as in cheesemaking:* germ, microbe, microorganism, *Slang* bug; bacillus, pathogen.

bad *adj.* 1 *a bad singer. The battery is bad:* not good, poor, inferior, awful, terrible, dreadful; substandard, below par, secondrate, lousy; faulty, defective, deficient, valueless, useless. 2 *Lying is a bad thing to do:* immoral, unethical, sinful, evil, wicked, naughty, corrupt, unprincipled; detestable, deplorable, reprehensible, base, mean, vile, nefarious, rotten. 3 *bad judgment. bad spelling:* erroneous, wrong, incorrect, imperfect, unsound, faulty, poor. 4 *Candy is bad for your teeth:* harmful, unhealthy, hurtful, detrimental, troublesome; risky, dangerous, hazardous. 5 *bad news. He's in a bad mood:* unpleasant, unwelcome, disagreeable, glum, grim, disheartening, dreadful; cross, angry, short-tempered, irascible, irritable. 6 *Don't feel bad about breaking the glass:* sorry, sad, regretful, remorseful, guilty, conscience-stricken. 7 *bad milk:* spoiled, rotten, sour, rancid, moldy, mildewed, contaminated, polluted, tainted. 8 *a bad smell:* disagreeable, unpleasant, sickening, odious, nasty, distasteful, foul, disgusting, nauseating, putrid, revolting, repulsive, vile, repugnant 9 *I feel bad enough to go to the hospital:* ill, sick, sickly, unwell, ailing, infirm, under the weather. 10 *a bad accident. a bad toothache:* severe, harsh, terrible, serious, grave, acute, dreadful; distressing, grievous, miserable. —*n.* 11 *Take the bad with the good:* harmful things, sad events, disappointment, misfortune. 12 *the bad that people do:* evil, wickedness, sin, offenses, wrongs; villainy, crimes.

Ant. 1–9, 11, 12 good. 1 fine, excellent, superior, first-rate. 2 virtuous, moral, ethical, right, exemplary. 3 correct, right; sound. 4 beneficial, healthful; harmless, safe. 5 pleasant, welcome, encouraging; happy, joyful. 7 fresh, sweet; uncontaminated. 8 agreeable, pleasant, fragrant, sweet. 9 well, healthy, fit. 10 minor; mild, light.

badge *n. The police officer wore her badge proudly. The war veteran considers his scar a badge of honor:* emblem, insignia, medallion, ensign, shield, seal, symbol, sign, mark, token.

badger *v. You can't badger me into going to the party!:* goad, bully, provoke, bait, pester, nag, hector, hound; tease, annoy, vex, nettle, trouble, plague.

badly *adv.* 1 *He did the work badly:* poorly, improperly, incorrectly, wretchedly, imperfectly, inadequately, wrong, unsatisfactorily, incompetently, carelessly, sloppily. 2 *He behaved badly:* immorally, unethically, wickedly, wrongly, corruptly, villainously, disreputably. 3 *The boy wants a new bicycle badly. The tooth hurts badly:* very much, greatly, exceedingly; intensely, severely, acutely, sorely.
Ant. 1 well, excellently, superbly; properly, correctly, competently, ably, satisfactorily. 2 morally, ethically, virtuously.

baffle *v.* 1 *The news baffled us:* confuse, bewilder, perplex, befuddle, stump, puzzle. 2 *The walls baffled the street noises:* stop, restrain, inhibit, thwart, bar, check; deaden, dull.

bag *n.* 1 *a bag of groceries:* sack, paper bag; packet, bundle. 2 See SUITCASE. 3 See PURSE.
—*v.* 4 *That suit bags on you:* sag, droop, hang loosely. 5 *The hunter bagged a deer:* shoot; capture, catch, trap; get, collect, obtain.

baggage *n.* 1 *Customs officers examined all baggage:* luggage, suitcases, bags. 2 *The king's army traveled with much baggage:* equipment, movables, gear, paraphernalia, accouterments, trappings; belongings, effects.

baggy *adj.* 1 *Circus clowns wear baggy pants:* sagging, droopy, loose-fitting, slack, limp. 2 *His eyes are baggy with fatigue:* paunchy, swollen, bloated, puffed.
Ant. 1 tight, tight-fitting, close-fitting.

bail *v. Bail the water out of the boat:* scoop, ladle, lade, dip.

bailiwick *n. The kitchen's my bailiwick:* domain, province, realm, department, sphere; *Slang* turf.

bait *n.* 1 *Worms are good bait for catfish:* lure. 2 *The store offered a gift as bait to get customers:* lure, allure, allurement, inducement, enticement, attraction, come-on.
—*v.* 3 *He baited his sister unmercifully:* tease, torment, antagonize, provoke, harass, hector; badger, worry.

balance *n.* 1 also **balances.** *Weigh it on the balance:* scales, scale. 2 *A counterweight keeps the machine in balance:* equilibrium, stability, equipoise, counterpoise; symmetry. 3 *The speech struck a balance between humor and seriousness:* equilibrium, proportion, harmony; middle ground. 4 *She*

has a great deal of emotional balance: stability, steadiness, poise, composure, equanimity, equilibrium, self-possession, level-headedness, judgment. 5 *On balance, his accomplishments outweigh his faults:* comparison, evaluation, consideration, appraisal. 6 *The balance on your account is $5.00. Leave the balance of the work until tomorrow:* amount owed, amount credited, sum minus payment; remainder, rest.
—*v.* 7 *Can you balance on one foot?:* keep steady, stabilize. 8 *The good balances the bad:* offset, counterbalance, counteract, neutralize, compensate for. 9 *We balanced the benefits against the costs:* compare, contrast, evaluate, weigh; consider. 10 *The company balances its accounts every month:* compute, calculate, sum up, total, tally, reckon.
Ant. 2 imbalance. 4 instability, uncertainty, shakiness. 8 outweigh.

balanced *adj. a balanced account of the affair:* fair, equitable, just, impartial, unprejudiced.
Ant. one-sided, prejudiced, biased, slanted.

balcony *n.* 1 *a wrought-iron balcony:* deck, veranda, terrace. 2 *the balcony of the theater:* mezzanine, loges, upper circle, upper floor.

bald *adj.* 1 *When he grew bald he bought a toupee:* baldheaded, baldpated; hairless, depilated. 2 *The mountain is bald above the tree line:* bare, treeless, denuded, barren. 3 *That is a bald falsehood!:* open, bare, undisguised, flagrant, unadorned, stark, outright, utter.
Ant. 1 hairy, hirsute. 3 hidden, disguised, devious.

balderdash *n. That story is balderdash:* nonsense, poppycock, tommyrot, stuff and nonsense, drivel, trash, rot, claptrap, bunk, bosh.

bale *n. cotton bales:* bound bundle, bundle, pack, packet, parcel.

baleful *adj. a baleful look:* sinister, ominous, threatening; evil, malignant, malign, malevolent, malicious, dire.
Ant. kindly, friendly, benevolent, benign.

balk *v.* 1 *The burro balked at climbing the path:* shirk, refuse, resist, hesitate. 2 *The kidnapping was balked by the police:* thwart, forestall, stymie, prevent, check, foil, block, obstruct.
Ant. 2 aid, help, assist, abet; further, advance, expedite, facilitate; permit.

balky *adj. That mule is balky:* contrary, stubborn, obstinate, ornery; unmanageable, refractory, disobedient, intractable.
Ant. obedient, submissive, cooperative, tractable.

ball[1] *n.* 1 *a ball of twine:* round mass, sphere,

spheroid, globe. 2 *The muskets were loaded with powder and ball:* shot, bullets.

ball² *n. The banquet was followed by a ball:* dance, dancing party, cotillion.

ballad *n.* 1 *He read one of the great Scottish ballads:* narrative poem, narrative verse. 2 *A folk singer sang ballads:* folk song, song, lay; ditty.

ballast *n. The ship carried sand as ballast:* stabilizing material, counterweight, counterpoise, weight, dead weight; balance, counterbalance.

balloon *n.* 1 *a child's balloon. weather balloon:* air-filled bag, gas-filled bag, inflatable bag. —*v.* 2 *His coat ballooned in the wind:* billow, swell out, puff out, fill with air, inflate, fill out, distend.
   Ant. 2 deflate, collapse.

ballot *n.* 1 *Three candidates are listed on the ballot:* ticket, slate. 2 *He won the nomination on the third ballot:* vote, round of voting, voting, poll, polling.

ballyhoo *n.* 1 *Ballyhoo preceded the movie's premiere:* promotion, publicity, advertising, hoopla, puffery, *Slang* hype. —*v.* 2 *The ads ballyhooed the movie:* publicize, promote, advertise, tout, *Slang* puff, hype.

balm *n.* 1 *Put some balm on that sunburn:* ointment, salve, unguent, emollient, lotion, cream. 2 *The music was balm for his jangled nerves:* solace, comforter, comfort, restorative, curative, palliative.
   Ant. 1 irritant, abrasive.

balmy *adj.* 1 *The weather turned balmy:* gentle, mild, fair, temperate, warm, pleasant. 2 *He was balmy to try swimming across the lake:* eccentric, weird, crazy.
   Ant. 1 harsh, raw; stormy, unseasonable.

baluster *n. The railing is supported by a series of balusters:* post, support, upright, column, pillar, pilaster.

bamboozle *v. The con man bamboozled him out of $500:* dupe, deceive, trick, cheat, swindle, cozen; delude, hoodwink, fool.

ban *v.* 1 *Bicycles are banned from the highway:* prohibit, bar, exclude, banish, forbid; proscribe, interdict. —*n.* 2 *a ban against parking on this street:* prohibition, forbiddance, proscription, interdict, exclusion, restriction, restraint.
   Ant. 1 allow, permit, authorize, countenance. 2 approval, permission.

banal *adj. a banal lecture:* stale, trite, unoriginal, hackneyed, pedestrian, unimaginative, stock, humdrum, conventional, stereotyped, tired, corny, cliché-ridden, vapid.
   Ant. original, novel, unique, fresh, innovative, provocative, imaginative.

band¹ *n.* 1 *A band of students confronted the*

dean: group, company, party, body, crowd, gang, party, pack, bunch, throng. 2 *The band played until midnight:* orchestra, ensemble, group. —*v.* 3 *We must band together:* unite, join; gather, group.

band² *n. Her hair was held in place by a velvet band:* strip, streak, strap, binding; ribbon, thong, swath.

bandage *n.* 1 *Wrap the bandage around your injured arm:* dressing, compress. —*v.* 2 *Disinfect the wound and then bandage it:* dress, bind.

bandanna *n. She wore a bandanna:* kerchief, neckerchief; handkerchief, scarf.

bandit *n. The stagecoach was held up by bandits:* outlaw, robber, desperado, highwayman, thief, brigand, burglar.

bane *n. Dirt was the bane of our existence:* plague, curse, scourge, torment, affliction, blight, poison, thorn in the side.
   Ant. blessing, treasure, prize, bright spot, joy, comfort, solace.

bang *n.* 1 *He closed the door with a bang:* report, boom, pop, burst, crash, explosion. 2 *The falling branch gave her a bang on the head:* blow, hit, knock, smack, clout, wallop, whack, thwack, thump, buffet. 3 *Slang. We got a bang out of seeing the movie star:* thrill, excitement, pleasure, enjoyment, *Slang* kick. —*v.* 4 *to bang a drum. Don't bang the door!:* strike noisily, beat; close loudly, slam.

bangle *n. a bangle on a charm bracelet:* fob, charm, ornament, bauble, trinket, knickknack, gewgaw, bibelot; chain; costume jewelry.

banish *v.* 1 *The king banished the traitor:* exile, expel, eject, outlaw, cast out, turn out, send away. 2 *Banish gloom from your thoughts:* ban, shut out, dismiss, exclude; cast out, eliminate, eradicate, oust, reject.
   Ant. 1, 2 invite, receive with open arms, welcome, harbor; foster, cherish.

bank¹ *n.* 1 *a high bank of earth:* embankment, mound, heap, pile; ridge, rise, hill, knoll. 2 *the bank of the river:* shore, side, edge, margin. 3 *The Grand Banks of Newfoundland:* shoal, reef, shallow, bar, shelf. —*v.* 4 *The plow banked the snow along the road:* pile up, heap, stack. 5 *The highway banks sharply:* slope, slant, tilt, tip.
   Ant. 1 ditch, trench. 3 deep water, depths. 4, 5 level, smooth out.

bank² *n. a bank of spotlights:* row, tier, rank, line, file, string, series, array.

bankrupt *adj. Severe losses left the company bankrupt:* ruined, failed, without funds, insolvent, broke, wiped out; penniless, depleted, *Slang* busted.
   Ant. solvent, sound; prosperous.

banner *n.* 1 *Welcoming banners hung from the balconies:* standard, flag, colors, ensign, pennant, burgee. —*adj.* 2 *Farmers had a banner year:* outstanding, most successful, notable, record, red-letter.

banquet *n.* 1 *a victory banquet:* feast, repast, dinner. —*v.* 2 *The guests banqueted until midnight:* feast, dine.

bantam *adj. The boy is a bantam edition of his father:* miniature, small, little, diminutive, pocket-sized, Lilliputian.
    Ant. large, blown-up, overgrown, giant.

banter *n.* 1 *We laughed at their banter:* kidding, joking, ribbing, joshing, jesting, waggery, badinage. —*v.* 2 *He stood bantering with friends:* kid, josh, rib, chaff, tease.

baptism *n.* 1 *the baptism of new members of the church:* sacrament of initiation; sprinkling, immersion; spiritual rebirth, purification. 2 *The battle was his baptism as a soldier:* initiation, rite of passage; introduction.

bar *n.* 1 *the bars of a cage:* pole, rod, stick, stake, rail, pale, paling, grating. 2 *a bar of soap:* block, ingot, cake. 3 *The boat ran aground on the bar:* sandbar, shoal, shallow, shelf, flat. 4 *We had a beer at a neighborhood bar. We opened a snack bar:* tavern, saloon, taproom, cocktail lounge, lounge; pub; serving counter; lunchroom. 5 *A bar of light fell across the room:* band, strip, stripe, ribbon, streak, beam. 6 *Nearsightedness is a bar to becoming a pilot:* obstacle, barrier, obstruction, impediment, stumbling block, hindrance, constraint, limitation. 7 *the bar of public opinion:* court, tribunal, forum. 8 *The song is 24 bars long:* measure. —*v.* 9 *Bar the barn door:* bolt, fasten, secure; block up, barricade. 10 *He has been barred from practicing medicine:* ban, prohibit, enjoin, restrain, prevent, forbid, blacklist, blackball, exclude, preclude. 11 *Reporters were barred from the courtroom:* exclude, shut out; banish, expel, evict, eject.
    Ant. 3 deep water, depths. 6 aid, advantage, boon. 10, 11 allow, permit; invite, welcome.

barb *n.* 1 *The fishhook has a barb at the tip:* spur, point, spike, bristle, cusp, barbule. 2 *We're tired of your nasty barbs:* disagreeable remark, sarcasm, insult, criticism, dig, jibe, cut.

barbarian *n.* 1 *the invading barbarians:* savage, alien, outlander. 2 *Young barbarians have defaced public buildings:* hoodlum, roughneck, ruffian, rowdy, tough, punk, hooligan; bully, lout. 3 *Barbarians in the audience jeered the new work:* anti-intellectual, lowbrow, philistine, vulgarian, ignoramus. —*adj.* 4 *barbarian invaders:* savage, alien. 5 *barbarian tastes:* uncultivated, uncultured, crude, philistine, uncouth, boorish.
    Ant. 1 native, citizen. 3 highbrow, intellectual, sophisticate. 5 cultivated, cultured, highbrow, intellectual; refined.

barbaric *adj.* 1 *The Huns were notorious for barbaric cruelty:* barbarian, uncivilized, barbarous, savage, wild. 2 *His behavior was barbaric:* coarse, uncouth, crude, vulgar, rude.
    Ant. 2 civilized, cultivated, polite.

barbarity *n. The pirates treated captives with barbarity:* savageness, cruelty, brutality, ruthlessness.

barbarous *adj.* 1 *It's barbarous to keep a dog cooped up like that:* cruel, brutal, mean, inhuman, vicious, barbaric. 2 *The letter was written in barbarous English:* coarse, crude, rough, vulgar.
    Ant. 1 humane, merciful.

bare *adj.* 1 *bare to the waist:* stripped, naked, nude, undressed, unclothed, disrobed, uncovered, unclad. 2 *bare walls. The cupboard was bare:* empty, vacant, unadorned, unembellished, austere, plain. 3 *The carpet was worn bare:* threadbare, bald, thin. 4 *the bare necessities:* just sufficient, just enough, scant, mere, meager. 5 *the bare facts of the case:* plain, undisguised, stark, bald, simple; fundamental, basic, unelaborated, unadorned, unembellished, unvarnished. —*v.* 6 *Bare your head when the flag is raised:* uncover, undress, unveil, undrape; unsheathe. 7 *The poet bared her heart to the world:* open, reveal, show, expose, unmask.
    Ant. 1 clothed, dressed, covered. 2 full, well-stocked; adorned, embellished, ornamented. 4 abundant, profuse, copious, plentiful, bounteous, ample. 6 cover, clothe, dress, veil. 7 hide, conceal, mask.

barefaced *adj. barefaced lies:* brazen, impudent, shameless; transparent, bald; bold, unabashed, brash, fresh, cheeky.

barely *adv. He was barely alive:* just, scarcely, hardly, slightly, scantly.
    Ant. fully, completely.

bargain *n.* 1 *We made a bargain to do the work:* agreement, compact, pledge, accord, understanding, arrangement, contract. 2 *At that price the house is a bargain:* good deal, good buy; *Slang* steal. —*v.* 3 *I refuse to bargain over the price:* negotiate, haggle, dicker, deal.

bark¹ *n.* 1 *the bark of a dog:* yelp, yip, yap, howl, howling, bay, cry. —*v.* 2 *The dog barks at strangers:* yelp, yip, yap, howl, bay. 3 *The captain barked a command:* shout, bellow, yell, roar, holler.

bark[2] *n.* **1** *a tree's bark:* covering, husk, sheathing, skin, casing, *Scientific* periderm. —*v.* **2** *He barked his shins:* scrape, skin, abrade.

barrage *n.* **1** *The cannons kept up a barrage:* bombardment, shelling, salvo, volley, cannonade, fusillade, curtain of fire. **2** *a barrage of questions:* volley, salvo, fusillade, torrent, burst, stream.

barrel *n. a barrel of apples:* cask, keg, hogshead, butt.

barren *adj.* **1** *a barren cow:* infertile, sterile, infecund, farrow. **2** *barren land:* infertile, unproductive, unfruitful; desolate, arid, dry. **3** *It's a barren topic:* unproductive, unfruitful, fruitless, unrewarding, futile; uninteresting, dull, uninformative, uninspiring. *Ant.* 1–3 productive, fertile. 2 lush, rich. 3 worthwhile, fruitful, profitable.

barricade *n.* **1** *The rebels fired from behind barricades:* barrier, rampart, bulwark, obstruction, impediment, obstacle. —*v.* **2** *The police barricaded the streets:* block, obstruct.

barrier *n.* **1** *The stallion leaped over the barrier:* obstruction, obstacle, barricade. **2** *Not knowing a foreign language is a barrier to travel abroad:* obstacle, impediment, handicap, difficulty, limitation. *Ant.* 1 opening, passage, passageway, way. 2 aid, advantage.

barter *v. to barter beaver pelts for food:* trade, swap, exchange.

basal *adj.* **1** *basal characteristics:* basic, fundamental, necessary, essential, intrinsic, prerequisite, indispensable, key. **2** *a series of basal readers for the lower grades:* elementary, primary, rudimentary, beginning; easy, simplified.

base[1] *n.* **1** *The lamp stands on a circular base:* support, pedestal, stand, bottom, foundation. **2** *the base of his argument:* foundation, basis, essence, principle, root, core, key, ground. **3** *The troops marched back to the base:* camp, station, post, installation, garrison. —*v.* **4** *This song is based on an old folk tune:* derive from, model on, found on. **5** *The company's headquarters is based in Paris:* station, locate, situate, establish, place. *Ant.* 1 top, summit; superstructure.

base[2] *adj.* **1** *Zinc is a base metal:* inferior, poor quality; impure, debased, adulterated. **2** *Cheating is a base practice:* mean, vile, low, contemptible, despicable, ignoble, wicked, dishonorable, dastardly, corrupt, nefarious, ignominious, unworthy, disgraceful, unprincipled, detestable, reprehensible, disreputable, abject. *Ant.* 1 precious, valuable, rare; pure, una-

dulterated. **2** virtuous, honorable, honest, upright, admirable.

baseless *adj. The story is baseless:* unfounded, groundless, without basis, unsupported, unsubstantiated. *Ant.* well-founded, substantiated, factual.

bashful *adj. too bashful to speak to strangers:* shy, timid, unconfident, timorous, modest, shrinking, sheepish. *Ant.* brash, bold, brazen, impudent, immodest, forward; confident, self-assured.

basic *adj.* **1** *a basic ingredient:* fundamental, vital, essential, intrinsic, key, core, primary. —*n.* **2** *Reading is one of the basics of education:* fundamental, essential, rudiment, foundation. *Ant.* 1 supporting, supplementary, complementary, secondary. 2 unessential.

basin *n.* **1** *a basin of warm water:* bowl, washbowl, pan, tub, washbasin, sink. **2** *Torrential rains caused flooding in the basin:* valley, dale, dell, glen, hollow.

basis Plural **bases** *n. Charity is the basis of her philosophy:* base, starting point, root, foundation, touchstone, bedrock, cornerstone.

bask *v.* **1** *They basked by the fire:* warm oneself, toast oneself, soak up warmth. **2** *He basked in admiration:* revel, wallow, luxuriate, delight, relish.

bastard *n.* **1** *The king sired three bastards:* illegitimate child, love child. —*adj.* **2** *He spoke a kind of bastard French:* impure, irregular, imperfect.

bastion *n.* **1** *Soldiers stormed the bastion:* fortress, fort, citadel; rampart. **2** *The university is a bastion of intellectual freedom:* bulwark, stronghold, citadel.

bat *n.* **1** *The player swung her bat:* club, mallet; baton, stick; staff, cudgel, shillelagh, truncheon. —*v.* **2** *We batted the shuttlecock across the net:* hit, strike, smack, cuff, whack, thwack.

batch *n. a batch of cookies:* group, bunch, lot, stock, collection, aggregate, quantity.

bath *n. a long, uninterrupted bath:* cleansing, ablution; shower, showerbath; wash, washing, sponge bath.

bathe *v. We bathed in a cool stream:* wash, cleanse, lave; dip, wet, douse.

bathos *n. The play is full of bathos:* sentimentality, sentimentalism, mawkishness, false pathos, maudlinism.

bathroom *n. The child wants to use the bathroom:* washroom, men's room, ladies' room, lavatory, toilet, commode, facility, powder room, restroom, *Slang* john, *Army* latrine.

baton *n. The drum majorettes twirled their batons:* staff, mace, scepter, wand; stick, nightstick, cudgel, truncheon, billy, billy club, bat.

batter v. 1 *Enemy fire battered the fort:* beat, buffet, pound, pummel. 2 *Police battered down the door:* pound, smash, break, beat. 3 *The old hat was battered beyond recognition:* beat up, mangle, knock out of shape.

battery n. 1 *a battery of tests:* group, set, series, block. 2 *assault and battery:* hitting, thrashing, beating, clubbing.

battle n. 1 *the Battle of Waterloo. the Battle of the Bulge:* combat, clash, skirmish, fight; contest, fray, engagement, bout. 2 *the battle for equal rights:* struggle, fight, contest; dispute, debate, confrontation, crusade. —v. 3 *The armies battled all night. He battled the decision in court:* war, fight, clash, engage; struggle, contend, contest; quarrel, argue, dispute.

Ant. 1 armistice, peace, truce.

battlefield n. *The armies met on the battlefield:* battleground, theater of war, field of battle, battle line, the front, front line.

bawdy adj. *The drinking song was bawdy but amusing:* earthy, lusty, risqué, ribald, indecent, coarse, gross, licentious, off-color, indecorous, indelicate.

brawl v. 1 *The babies were bawling in the nursery:* cry, wail, howl; weep. 2 *The captain bawled for the sergeant:* shout, bellow, yell, roar, cry out, call, call out.

bay¹ n. *The ship anchored in the bay:* cove, inlet, estuary; sound, gulf.

bay² n. *the dining bay:* alcove, nook, niche, recess, compartment.

bay³ n. 1 *the bay of hounds:* barking, howling, bellowing, cry, yelping, yapping. 2 *at bay. A bear at bay is very dangerous:* cornered, trapped. —v. 3 *The hound bayed mournfully:* howl, bellow, bark, yelp, yap, cry.

bazaar n. 1 *We bought this rug at the bazaar in Marrakesh:* market, marketplace, outdoor market, mart, shopping quarter, trade center, exchange. 2 *a church bazaar:* charity fair, charity sale; fair, carnival.

beach n. *The waves receded from the beach:* shore, seashore, strand, coast, littoral, water's edge.

beacon n. *a flashing beacon:* light, beam, signal.

bead n. *Beads of sweat covered his brow:* drop, droplet, globule, blob, pellet, spherule, speck.

beam n. 1 *a roof beam: (in technical use)* horizontal support; structural support, girder, rafter, joist, brace, stud, timber. 2 *a beam of light:* ray, streak, stream, gleam, glimmer. 3 *The ship was broad in the beam:* widest part, width, expanse,

breadth. —v. 4 *Television stations beamed the news to the country. A searchlight beamed in the distance:* transmit, emit, radiate, broadcast; gleam, glimmer, glitter, glow, shine. 5 *Her face beamed with happiness:* shine, glow, radiate.

bear v. 1 *These columns bear the weight of the roof. He bears responsibility well:* support, sustain, maintain, carry, shoulder, hold up under. 2 *Donkeys bore supplies up the mountain trail:* transport, carry, bring, haul, take, convey. 3 *She bore three children:* give birth to, bring forth, produce, deliver. 4 *Apple trees bear blossoms in spring:* produce, bring forth, yield. 5 *Bear these thoughts with you:* maintain, carry, keep in mind, harbor. 6 *She can't bear loud noises:* tolerate, abide, endure, stand, put up with. 7 *This information bears on the matter under discussion:* pertain, relate, apply, refer, appertain, concern, be pertinent to, affect, touch upon. 8 *This matter bears investigation:* warrant, invite, be susceptible to, allow, encourage. 9 *You bear a strong likeness to my sister:* exhibit, manifest, display, show, have, carry, possess. 10 *To get this door open you have to bear hard against it:* press, push, bear down.

Ant. 4 shed, lose.

beard n. 1 *a two-day growth of beard:* whiskers; bristles, stubble, five-o'clock shadow. —v. 2 *Daniel bearded the lion in its den:* corner, bring to bay, confront, face, defy, brave.

bearded adj. *Lincoln had a bearded face:* bewhiskered, whiskered, unshaven, hairy, hirsute; bushy, bristly.

Ant. clean-shaven, smooth-shaven.

bearing n. 1 *a regal bearing:* carriage, mien, manner, presence; demeanor. 2 *Your remarks have no bearing on our discussion:* relevance, pertinence, reference, application, applicability, connection, relation, relationship. 3 *These fruit trees are past bearing:* reproducing, reproduction, giving birth, procreation, propagation, producing, breeding. 4 **bearings.** *We lost our bearings in the darkness:* sense of direction, orientation, direction, way, course, position.

beast n. 1 *The lion is the king of beasts:* animal, creature, mammal, quadruped. 2 *You were a beast to insult her:* brute, savage, barbarian, cad, cur.

Ant. 2 gentleman, lady.

beastly adj. *The weather has been beastly. a beastly little man:* unpleasant, disagreeable, nasty, vile, loathsome, contemptible; cruel, monstrous, inhuman, bestial, brutish; bad, terrible, awful, dreadful, deplorable, *Slang* lousy.

Ant. pleasant, agreeable, admirable; good, fine, wonderful.

beat *v.* 1 *Listen to him beat that drum:* hit, strike, pound, wallop, whack, thwack, punch, slap, smite, clout, tap, rap, bang, hammer. 2 *They beat him to within an inch of his life:* thrash, pummel, batter, maul, trounce. 3 *She beat every opponent:* defeat, be victorious over, triumph over, win over, overcome, vanquish, best; trounce, drub. 4 *He beat all competition in the elections:* win out over, excel over, surpass, outdo, prevail over, overcome. 5 *Our hearts beat madly:* pulsate, pulse, throb, pound, palpitate, flutter, quiver. 6 *Beat the egg whites until they are stiff:* whip; stir vigorously, mix. —*n.* 7 *the beat of a gong:* blow, stroke, strike, hit, whack. 8 *The music had a familiar beat:* cadence, time, rhythm, meter, stress. 9 *The police officer was on his beat:* route, rounds, circuit, path; zone, territory, domain.

Ant. 3, 4 lose, suffer defeat, fail.

beatific *adj. The Madonna's beatific smile:* blissful, serene, sublime, exalted, transcendental, saintly; enraptured.

Ant. worldly; coarse, crude.

beatitude *n. an aura of beatitude:* bliss, blessedness, saintliness; exaltation, exaltedness, transcendence, ecstasy.

beau Plural **beaux** *n.* 1 *Will Helen marry her new beau?* boyfriend, sweetheart, young man, steady, fellow, suitor, admirer, swain; fiancé, betrothed. 2 *The young beau flirted with the ladies:* ladies' man, cavalier, dandy, fop, swell, playboy.

beautiful *adj.* 1 *a beautiful child. The music is beautiful:* pretty, handsome, good-looking, lovely, gorgeous, comely, seemly; pleasing, enjoyable, captivating. 2 *You did a beautiful job:* very good, excellent, first-rate, superb, wonderful, fine, splendid, great, stupendous, commendable.

Ant. 1 ugly, unattractive, hideous, grotesque; repulsive, revolting. 2 bad, awful, terrible, lousy, second-rate.

beautify *v. Planting flowers along the streets will beautify the town:* enhance, adorn, ornament, improve, grace, dress up.

Ant. spoil, mar, deface.

beauty *n.* 1 *a city of great beauty:* loveliness, handsomeness, good looks, pulchritude, attractiveness, resplendence, magnificence. 2 *one of the great beauties of our time:* beautiful woman, belle, goddess, Venus. 3 *The beauty of the plan is its simplicity:* advantage, asset, attraction, feature.

Ant. 1 ugliness, repulsiveness. 3 disadvantage, shortcoming, flaw.

beckon *v.* 1 *The leader beckoned us to fol-*

low: signal, motion, wave at, gesture, gesticulate. 2 *The sea beckoned the old sailor:* entice, lure, allure, draw, pull, call.

becloud *v. Don't try to becloud the issues:* obscure, confuse, obfuscate, hide, confound, muddle, camouflage, veil.

become *v.* 1 *My eyes become tired after reading:* get, begin to be, grow, come to be. 2 *Lavender becomes you:* suit, go with, flatter, complement, agree with, enhance; harmonize with, be consistent with.

Ant. 2 disagree with, detract from.

becoming *adj.* 1 *His behavior was very becoming:* suitable, appropriate, seemly, fitting, befitting, worthy. 2 *Blue is a becoming color on you:* flattering, enhancing, attractive, pretty; congenial, compatible.

Ant. unbecoming. 1 unsuitable, inappropriate, improper, unfitting, unbefitting. 2 ugly, unattractive.

bed *n.* 1 *The cowboy made a bed on the ground:* bedstead, place to sleep, bunk, pallet, berth. 2 *a bed of lettuce:* base, bottom, floor, foundation. 3 *a bed of anthracite coal:* layer, stratum, band, belt, zone; seam, deposit, lode. 4 *a bed of roses:* plot, patch.

bedazzle *v.* 1 *The bright lights bedazzled her:* daze, confuse, bewilder, befuddle, fluster. 2 *Her charm bedazzled all:* dazzle, confound, astound, stagger, flabbergast, overwhelm; enchant, captivate.

bedlam *n. The party was a bedlam:* scene of wild confusion, uproar, pandemonium, chaos, madhouse, turmoil.

bedraggled *adj. The bedraggled children looked hungry:* unkempt, untidy, messy, disordered, tattered, seedy, ragtag, draggletailed.

Ant. neat, well-groomed.

bedroom *n. The house has three bedrooms:* sleeping room, bedchamber, boudoir.

beehive *n.* 1 *The bees flew back to the beehive:* hive, apiary. 2 *a beehive of activity:* busy place.

beer *n. a bottle of beer:* (variously) lager, ale, stout, porter, malt liquor, dark, bitter, light, *Slang* brew.

befall *v. Bad luck may befall us:* happen, occur, come to pass, ensue, fall.

befitting *adj. A tuxedo is befitting the reception:* suitable, appropriate, fitting, fit, proper, seemly, right.

Ant. unsuitable, inappropriate, unfitting, improper, unseemly.

beforehand *adv. You should have told me beforehand:* earlier, sooner, before now, ahead of time, in advance.

Ant. afterwards, after.

befriend *v. to befriend a stranger:* make

friends with, get acquainted with; assist, help, protect.

Ant. alienate, estrange.

befuddle *v.* 1 *The new arrival was befuddled:* confuse, perplex, bewilder, puzzle, baffle, confound; daze, rattle, fluster, muddle. 2 *The wine had befuddled him:* addle, stupefy, make groggy, intoxicate, make tipsy.

Ant. 2 sober, clear one's head.

beg *v.* 1 *The poor man had to beg for a living:* seek charity, solicit, panhandle; mooch. 2 *The accused begged for understanding:* plead, entreat, implore, beseech, supplicate, petition, importune. 3 *Your reply begs the question:* evade, avoid, dodge, shirk, shun; parry, fend off, sidestep.

Ant. 1 give, contribute, donate. 2 demand, insist.

beget *v.* 1 *Fine calves were begotten from that bull:* father, sire, propagate, procreate. 2 *Evil deeds beget dire consequences:* bring about, result in, cause, effect, lead to, give rise to, engender.

Ant. 2 prevent, forestall, ward off.

beggar *n.* 1 *a street beggar:* almsman, mendicant, panhandler, tramp, moocher. —*v.* 2 *The hat was so funny it beggars description:* make inadequate, be beyond; challenge, baffle.

Ant. 1 giver, contributor, donor.

begin *v.* 1 *School begins on Monday:* start, commence, initiate, embark on. 2 *since the world began. He began a new business:* come into existence, start, commence, initiate, undertake; originate, establish, introduce, found, institute, launch, inaugurate.

Ant. 1, 2 end, finish, terminate, conclude.

beginner *n.* 1 *I'm just a beginner:* novice, neophyte, tyro, learner, apprentice. 2 *My grandmother was the beginner of this business:* founder, originator, initiator, creator, author, organizer.

Ant. 1 expert, master, old hand.

beginning *n.* 1 *This is only the beginning!:* start, commencement, starting point, onset, outset. 2 *The beginning of the scandal was an item in the paper:* origin, source, fountainhead, wellspring, springboard; embryo, inauguration, inception, seed, germ; introduction. —*adj.* 3 *a beginning chess player:* novice, neophyte, inexperienced, new.

Ant. 1, 2 end, ending, conclusion, finish, termination. 3 experienced, expert, master.

begone *v. Begone with you!:* go away, away, be off, get out, out, depart, beat it, scat, shoo.

Ant. come here, come.

begrudge *v. Why do you begrudge us our*

success?: grudge, resent, hold against; envy, be jealous of.

Ant. congratulate, be happy for.

beguile *v.* 1 *He was beguiled into thinking he could become a famous singer:* delude, lead astray, deceive, dupe, ensnare, lure, trick. 2 *Beguiled by the warm day, the students daydreamed:* lull, distract, enchant, charm, bewitch, divert, amuse.

Ant. 2 alert, alarm.

behave *v.* 1 *Why can't that child behave?:* conduct oneself properly, comport oneself well, act correctly, control oneself. 2 *You behave as if you'd been wronged:* act, conduct oneself, comport oneself.

Ant. 1 misbehave.

behavior *n.* 1 *Your behavior is admirable:* conduct, manner, attitude, comportment, deportment. 2 *The compass is showing strange behavior:* response, reaction, functioning, operation, performance. 3 *the behavior of lions in their natural habitat:* acts, deeds, actions, activity, conduct, habits.

behead *v. Anne Boleyn was beheaded:* decapitate, bring to the block; guillotine, decollate.

behest *n. at the attorney general's behest:* order, direction, command, instruction, mandate, say-so, injunction, bidding.

behold *v. Behold the king!:* look, look at, look upon, observe, note, see, gaze at, stare at, view, regard, watch, examine, inspect, notice, heed, contemplate.

Ant. overlook, disregard, ignore.

beholden *adj. I am beholden to you:* under obligation, obligated, obliged, indebted, in one's debt; answerable, accountable.

behoove *v. It would behoove you to take better care of your health:* be advantageous, benefit, be advisable; be fitting, befit, suit, be proper, be appropriate.

being *n.* 1 *A new world came into being:* existence, existing, occurrence, reality, actuality, life. 2 *My very being felt the need of love:* nature, soul, spirit, core, inner person. 3 *Can there be beings on other planets?:* living creature, creature, human being, human, person, fellow creature.

Ant. 1 nothingness, nonexistence.

belabor *v. Don't belabor the point:* hammer away at, dwell on, go on (and on) about, reiterate.

belated *adj. Our good wishes are belated but sincere:* late, tardy, past due, overdue, delayed, after the fact.

Ant. early, ahead of time.

belch *v.* 1 *After the feast the king belched:* burp, eruct. 2 *The volcano belched fire:* emit, discharge, spew, spout, eject, issue, send forth, gush, disgorge, vomit, vent. —*n.*

3 *The gluttonous king gave forth a belch:* burp, eructation. **4** *a belch of flame:* emission, discharge, spurt, spout, gush, eruption.

beleaguer *v.* **1** *Enemy troops beleaguered the city:* besiege, surround, blockade, assail. **2** *He beleaguered her with pleas for forgiveness:* harass, badger, pester, bother, annoy, hector, plague.

belfry *n.* *The boys climbed the belfry and rang the bells:* bell tower, campanile; *(loosely)* steeple, spire.

belie *v.* **1** *The facts belie your story:* disprove, refute, contradict, controvert, repudiate, show to be false, give the lie to. **2** *His smile belied his anger:* misrepresent, falsify; disguise, camouflage, mask, conceal.
Ant. **1** prove, verify, confirm, corroborate. **2** represent, disclose, indicate.

belief *n.* **1** *The belief is that Mars is uninhabited. It is my belief that it's going to rain:* conviction, firm notion, opinion, view, theory, persuasion; conclusion; presumption; feeling, impression, guess. **2** *I have complete belief in my friends:* confidence, trust, faith. **3** Often **beliefs**. *political beliefs:* conviction, persuasion, principle, way of thinking; morality, morals; faith, creed, dogma, doctrine, tenet, canon.
Ant. **2** distrust, mistrust.

believable *adj.* *The story is hardly believable:* plausible, credible, convincing, possible.
Ant. unbelievable, incredible, dubious, unconvincing, implausible.

believe *v.* **1** *Don't believe everything you hear:* trust, put faith in, credit, rely on, depend on; presume true, accept as true, be convinced by, be persuaded by. **2** *I believe it's going to rain:* presume, think, imagine, guess, surmise, judge, suppose, assume, consider, conjecture; theorize, deduce, infer; maintain, hold.
Ant. **1** doubt, question, distrust, mistrust, disbelieve.

belittle *v.* *Don't belittle her piano playing:* make light of, disparage, deride, scorn, disdain, sneer at, malign, cast aspersions on, deprecate; play down, minimize, underrate, undervalue, underestimate.
Ant. overpraise, praise, vaunt, magnify; make a fuss over.

bell *n.* *church bells. a fire bell:* tocsin, chime, carillon; peal of bells, peal, ringing, tintinnabulation.

belle *n.* *a Southern belle and her beau. the belle of the ball:* beautiful girl, beautiful woman, beauty; star, queen; charmer.

bellicose *adj.* See BELLIGERENT.

belligerence, belligerency *n.* *The two*

regarded each other with belligerence: warlike attitude, hostility, combativeness, pugnacity, antagonism, animosity.
Ant. peacefulness, friendliness.

belligerent *adj.* **1** *belligerent attitudes:* warlike, hostile, antagonistic, aggressive, combative, bellicose. **2** *belligerent feelings:* unfriendly, hostile, antagonistic, bellicose, pugnacious, contentious, irascible. —*n.* **3** *Switzerland was not a belligerent in World War II:* warring country, nation at war, combatant, adversary, aggressor, attacker.
Ant. **1, 2** peaceful, peaceable. **1** pacific; neutral. **2** friendly, amicable. **3** neutral, noncombatant.

bellow *v.* **1** *to bellow with rage:* roar, shout, yell, bawl, holler, scream, shriek, whoop. —*n.* **2** *a loud bellow of pain:* roar, shout, yell, shriek, scream, whoop.
Ant. **1, 2** whisper. **1** murmur, mutter.

bellwether *n.* *We need a bellwether to take the initiative:* leader, guide, lead; precursor, forerunner, guidepost.

belly *n.* **1** *Eating green apples gave me a pain in the belly:* stomach, tummy, abdomen, paunch, vitals, *Slang* gut, guts, midriff, breadbasket. **2** *He has no belly for adventure:* liking, desire, appetite, stomach. **3** *The luggage is in the belly of the plane:* bowels, depths, interior, insides.

belong *v.* **1** *These woods belong to the property that's for sale:* be part of, attach to, go with; pertain to, be connected with. **2** *This book belongs to the school:* be the property of, be owned by, be held by. **3** *We belong to the club:* be a member of, be included in; be associated with, be allied to.

belongings *n.* *Pack up your belongings:* possessions, effects, personal property, movables, goods; gear, things, stuff.

beloved *adj.* **1** *a beloved friend:* loved, cherished, dear, treasured, adored, darling; highly valued, esteemed, revered. —*n.* **2** *a long letter from his beloved:* sweetheart, loved one, love; *(variously)* steady, lover, boyfriend, beau, girlfriend, betrothed, fiancé, fiancée, spouse, husband, wife.

belt *n.* **1** *a red leather belt:* sash, band, cinch, waistband, cummerbund. **2** *A belt of trees encircled the field:* circle, band, strip, stripe, layer. **3** *the corn belt:* area, district, region, zone, country. —*v.* **4** *The coat is belted at the waist:* encircle by a belt, fasten with a belt, cinch, girdle, encircle.

bemoan *v.* *Stop bemoaning the loss of your watch:* grieve over, weep over, cry over, whine over, lament, bewail, mourn, regret, rue.

bemused *adj.* **1** *a bemused look:* preoccupied, absent-minded; thoughtful. **2** *The*

bench

wine left him somewhat bemused: confused, muddled, bewildered, fuzzy, dull-witted, dazed.

Ant. 1 angry, stern, unsympathetic. 2 clearheaded, perceptive.

bench *n.* 1 *a park bench:* seat, settee, pew. 2 *a carpenter's bench:* workbench, worktable, counter, table. 3 *The accused will be brought before the bench:* court, tribunal, seat of justice; judge's chair.

benchmark *n. Our work is the benchmark for all woodwork:* standard, yardstick, measure, gauge, criterion, touchstone, model, exemplar, paradigm; reference.

bend *v.* 1 *Don't bend that spoon. The road bends treacherously:* twist, make crooked, become crooked, warp, buckle; curve, arc, turn, wind. 2 *Bend at the knee when you ski downhill:* flex, crouch, stoop, lean. 3 *We will not bend to the will of a tyrant:* bow down, submit, yield, give in, defer, relent, succumb, be subjugated, surrender, capitulate. 4 *The welder bent to her work:* apply oneself, attend, put one's heart into. —*n.* 5 *a bend in the river:* curve, turn, crook, arc.

Ant. 1, 2 straighten; stiffen.

benediction *n. The bishop gave the benediction:* blessing, prayer, benison, consecration, invocation, closing prayer.

Ant. malediction, curse.

benefactor *n. The hospital is the gift of a generous benefactor:* supporter, patron, donor, sponsor, angel; contributor.

beneficial *adj. Exercise is beneficial:* helpful, advantageous, useful, valuable, favorable, profitable, productive; healthful, good for.

Ant. detrimental, detractive, disadvantageous; harmful.

beneficiary *n. Who is the beneficiary on the insurance policy?:* inheritor, legatee, heir, heiress; receiver, recipient.

benefit *n.* 1 *Your advice was of great benefit:* help, aid, service, use, avail, value, worth, advantage, asset, good. —*v.* 2 *I benefited from my father's advice:* help, aid, assist, be useful to, be an advantage to, do good for, advance, profit; be helped, gain, profit from.

Ant. 1 damage, harm, disservice, disadvantage, drawback. 2 harm, injure, impair, detract from, be bad for, worsen, hold back.

benevolence *n.* 1 *to smile with benevolence:* good will, kindliness, kindheartedness, kindness, compassion. 2 *The shelter depends on the public's benevolence:* generosity, charity, charitableness, bountifulness, liberality.

Ant. 1 ill will, unkindness, malevolence. 2 selfishness, greediness; stinginess, illiberality.

beset

benevolent *adj.* 1 *a benevolent feeling:* kindhearted, warmhearted, kind, compassionate, tender, benign, humane. 2 *a benevolent donation:* charitable, philanthropic, humanitarian; generous, liberal, bountiful.

Ant. 1 unkind, malevolent, malicious, malignant. 2 selfish, greedy; stingy, miserly.

benighted *adj. a benighted tribe living in the mountain's caves:* backward, unenlightened, primitive, uncivilized, uncultured, illiterate, unlettered, uneducated, uninformed, untaught.

Ant. cultured, educated, civilized.

benign *adj.* 1 *The benign uncle spoiled the child:* kind, kindly, kindhearted, tenderhearted, gentle, benevolent, humane. 2 *The decrease of the patient's fever was a benign sign:* good, favorable, salutary, auspicious, encouraging, propitious. 3 *a benign climate:* temperate, mild, balmy, pleasant, nice; healthful, harmless.

Ant. 1 unkind, hard-hearted, harsh, malicious, malevolent, hateful. 2 bad, unfavorable, discouraging, threatening, ominous. 3 harsh, severe.

bent *adj.* 1 *I can't use that bent pin:* angled, crooked, curved, arched, contorted; stooped, hunched, bowed. —*n.* 2 *a bent for music:* leaning, tendency, inclination, propensity, proclivity, predisposition; liking, fondness, partiality, predilection; talent, gift, flair, facility, ability, endowment, aptitude.

Ant. 1 unbent, straight. 2 disinclination, antipathy, hatred, abhorrence.

bequeath *v. to bequeath property to one's family:* will, leave, hand down, endow.

bequest *n. They left a bequest to each grandchild:* legacy, inheritance, endowment.

berate *v. The principal berated the student:* scold, upbraid, reprimand, rebuke, reprove, reproach, criticize, castigate, take to task, chew out.

Ant. praise, compliment, laud.

bereave *v. The refugees arrived bereft of their possessions:* deprive, strip, divest.

berserk *adj. The berserk robot threw rocks at everyone:* maniacal, frenzied, amok, wild; frantic, wild-eyed; deranged, insane.

Ant. calm, serene, pacific.

berth *n.* 1 *the upper berth of a Pullman car:* bunk, bed, sleeping place. 2 *The ship rested in its berth:* dock, pier, slip, anchorage; haven, resting place. 3 *I found a new berth with a shoe company:* job, position, situation, place, office, post, appointment.

beseech *v. I beseech you to forgive me:* beg, plead with, implore, entreat, supplicate.

beset *v.* 1 *beset by angry customers:* attack on all sides, besiege, surround, set upon; beleaguer, bedevil, plague. 2 *The crown* *was beset with rubies:* set, stud, array, deck, embellish.

besiege *v.* 1 *The troops besieged the fort:* lay siege to, surround and attack, beleaguer. 2 *besieged with requests for money:* beset, pester, badger, harass, bedevil.

besmirch *v.* *The report besmirched my name:* smear, taint, tarnish, stain, sully, blacken; dishonor, disgrace, discredit, defame.

Ant. respect, honor.

best *adj.* 1 *the best picture of the year:* most excellent, finest, choice, highest quality, topnotch, unsurpassed, unexcelled, unequaled; most desirable. 2 *It rained for the best part of a week:* largest, greatest, most. *—adv.* 3 *Which cleaner picks up dirt best? Which coat do you like best?:* most successfully, beyond all others; most, most of all, above all others. 4 *the person best able to do the job:* most fully, most. *—n.* 5 *The dog was the best of the breed:* finest, most excellent, choice, foremost, pick, cream. 6 *I'm not at my best today:* most pleasant, loveliest, most competent.

Ant. 1, 3, 6 worst. 2, 4 least.

bestial *adj.* *bestial treatment:* brutal, cruel, beastly, ruthless, barbaric, barbarous, inhumane.

Ant. humane; kind, merciful.

bestow *v.* 1 *The country bestowed a medal on the hero:* confer, present, give, award, render, mete; donate, consign, settle upon. 2 *Bestow more time to work:* apply, devote; use, utilize, spend.

Ant. 1 get, receive, earn, collect. 2 waste.

bet *v.* 1 *Over $1 million was bet on the Derby:* wager, gamble, make a bet, stake, venture, chance, hazard. *—n.* 2 *Put your bet down now:* wager, gamble, ante.

betray *v.* 1 *He betrayed his country:* be disloyal, be treacherous, be unfaithful, break faith with, sell out, inform against; doublecross, deceive, dupe; abandon. 2 *Her eyes betrayed her sadness:* reveal, disclose, divulge, show, tell, give away.

Ant. 1 be loyal, be faithful, be true. 2 preserve, conceal, mask.

betrayal *n.* 1 *the betrayal of Christ by Judas:* treachery, treason, disloyalty, unfaithfulness, falseness, breach of faith, bad faith, perfidy, double cross; deception, duplicity. 2 *the betrayal of a confidence:* revelation, disclosure, divulgence; violation.

Ant. 1 loyalty, faithfulness.

betroth *v.* *She is betrothed to John:* engage, affiance, promise, pledge.

betrothal *n.* *A feud prevented Romeo and Juliet's betrothal:* engagement, affiancing, troth, betrothing.

better *adj.* 1 *A down jacket is better than a wool one:* superior, finer, of higher quality; preferable, of greater value, more suitable, more desirable. 2 *the better part of the day:* greater, larger, longer. 3 *The patient is better today:* healthier, stronger, fitter; improved, recovering. *—adv.* 4 *You understand the problem better than I do:* in a superior way, more completely, more thoroughly. 5 *It takes better than an hour to get to work:* more, greater; longer, farther. *—v.* 6 *He tried to better himself:* improve, advance, further, raise, upgrade, elevate, enrich, cultivate, promote. 7 *to better the world's record:* surpass, exceed, outdo, top.

Ant. 1, 3, 4 worse, poorer. 1 inferior. 2 lesser, smaller; shorter. 3 sicker, weaker. 5 less, under.

betterment *n.* *to work for the betterment of humanity:* improvement, advancement, promotion, enrichment; correction, amendment, regeneration, reform.

Ant. debasement, degeneration, decline.

bevy *n.* 1 *a bevy of quail:* flock, flight; group, covey. 2 *a bevy of children:* company, crowd, assemblage, gathering, collection, group, horde, host, throng.

bewail *v.* *The boy bewailed the loss of his dog:* lament, mourn, grieve over, bemoan, moan over, cry over, weep over.

Ant. rejoice over, celebrate.

beware *v.* *Beware of the dog:* look out for, watch out for, take warning, guard against, take care, take precautions, be on the alert, be wary, take heed.

bewilder *v.* *bewildered by conflicting road signs:* confuse, puzzle, perplex, baffle, befuddle, muddle, nonplus, fluster.

Ant. enlighten, inform, instruct, edify.

bewilderment *n.* *Imagine my bewilderment when the plane landed in the wrong city!:* confusion, puzzlement, perplexity.

bewitch *v.* 1 *He was accused of having bewitched the cow:* put under a spell, cast a spell on. 2 *Shirley Temple bewitched a generation of moviegoers:* charm, enchant, entrance, captivate, fascinate.

Ant. 2 repulse; repel, disgust.

bias *n.* 1 *a bias against foreigners, a bias for Chopin:* prejudice, inclination, bent, predilection, propensity, proclivity; preconceived idea, preconception, narrow view, onesidedness, unfairness; bigotry, intolerance. 2 *The dress was cut on the bias:* angle, slant, diagonal line. *—v.* 3 *Don't let him bias you against her:* prejudice, predispose.

Ant. 1 fairness, impartiality, objectivity; tolerance.

Bible *n.* 1 *We studied the Bible in Sunday school:* the Holy Scriptures *(Hebrew and*

Christian); the Scriptures, Holy Writ, the Good Book, the Book, Gospel. **2 bible.** *To spell well, let a dictionary be your bible:* authority, guide; guidebook.

bicker *v. The children constantly bicker:* squabble, wrangle, quarrel, argue, spat, disagree.

Ant. agree, concur, accord.

bicycle *n. Don't ride a bicycle on the highway:* bike, two-wheeler, cycle.

bid *v.* **1** *The queen bids you join our party:* command, order, charge, call upon, instruct; invite, summon, ask, request. **2** *He bade us farewell:* tell, say, wish, greet. **3** *The antique dealer bid $200 for the rug:* offer, tender, propose; submit an offer. —*n.* **4** *What was the highest bid? Every senior will receive a bid to the prom:* offer, offering, bidding; invitation. **5** *Her bid for the presidency failed:* try, attempt, effort.

Ant. **1** forbid, prohibit, ban.

bidding *n.* **1** *The dog came at my bidding:* command, order, request, behest, direction, charge, instruction; summons, summoning, invitation, call. **2** *The bidding reached $500 for one antique chair:* offer, offers, tendering, proposal.

bide *v.* **1** *Bide with us awhile:* remain, stay, tarry, linger, abide. **2** *Mary could never bide children:* endure, put up with, tolerate, stand.

Ant. **1** go, depart, leave.

big *adj.* **1** *a big country. a big corn crop:* large, huge, enormous, vast, immense; sizable, substantial, abundant, prodigious. **2** *It's a big decision to make. Clark Gable was a big star in his day:* important, vital, major, momentous, weighty; prominent, leading, eminent, top, main. **3** *No one likes big talk:* pretentious, arrogant, pompous, boastful, bragging. **4** *a big heart. It takes a big person to admit mistakes:* generous, magnanimous, kind; noble, honorable, just, high-minded, great. **5** *You're a big boy now:* mature, grown, grown-up.

Ant. **1** little, small. **2** unimportant, inconsequential, minor. **3** modest, humble, unassuming, unpretentious, restrained. **4** petty, ignoble. **5** young, immature.

big-hearted *adj. a big-hearted contributor:* generous, liberal, open-handed, benevolent, unstinting, magnanimous, charitable, beneficent.

Ant. miserly, stingy.

bigoted *adj. Bigoted people never admit they're wrong:* prejudiced, intolerant, biased, closed-minded.

Ant. unprejudiced, tolerant, unbiased, open-minded.

bigotry *n. Every race has been the object of*

bigotry: prejudice, intolerance, bias, closed-mindedness; racism, unfairness.

Ant. tolerance, open-mindedness.

big shot *n. The board of directors is composed of big shots: Slang* wheel, big gun, bigwig, big cheese, VIP, high-muck-a-muck; dignitary, tycoon, name.

bilious *adj.* **1** *That hot dog gave me a bilious feeling:* sick, queasy, nauseous, sickening. **2** *The boss was in a bilious mood:* irritable, peevish, ill-tempered, ill-humored, angry, grumpy, cranky, crabby, grouchy, testy, snappish, short-tempered, cantankerous, huffy, out of sorts.

Ant. **2** happy, pleasant, good-tempered, genial, cordial, mild, agreeable.

bilge *n. His speech was full of the same old bilge:* nonsense, drivel, rubbish, stuff and nonsense, *Slang* bosh, hogwash, twaddle, bunk, malarkey, humbug, baloney.

bilk *v. We were bilked out of our inheritance:* swindle, cheat, defraud, dupe, bamboozle, fleece.

bill *n.* **1** *Did you pay the phone bill?:* statement, invoice, account, charge, tally. **2** *a dollar bill:* banknote, treasury note, treasury bill, greenback. **3** *How many bills are before Congress?:* piece of legislation, proposal; measure, act. **4** *Post no bills:* poster, placard, advertisement, bulletin; handbill, leaflet. **5** *The Palace used to have the best vaudeville bill. a bill of fare:* program, schedule, agenda, card, catalog, register, docket.

billet *n.* **1** *Find billets for the soldiers:* quarters, lodging, dwelling. —*v.* **2** *Headquarters said to billet the soldiers in the barn:* lodge, house, quarter, put up.

billfold *n.* See WALLET.

billow *n.* **1** *The boat was tossed by the billows:* wave, swell, breaker. **2** *a billow of steam:* wave, cloud. —*v.* **3** *The sails billowed in the wind:* swell, puff up, balloon, belly.

Ant. **1** trough. **3** deflate, collapse.

bind *v.* **1** *Bind those boxes together:* fasten, tie, tie up, truss, strap, rope, lash; join, attach, affix. **2** *The doctor bound the wound. The book was bound in leather:* bandage, swathe; cover, encase. **3** *The contract binds the company to pay royalties:* obligate, require, necessitate, oblige, force. **4** *She bound the hem of the dress:* border, edge, trim, fringe. **5** *This jacket binds under the arms:* confine, encumber; chafe.

Ant. **1** untie, unbind, unfasten. **2** unbandage; unwrap. **3** free, exempt.

binge *n. He went on a three-day binge:* drunken spree, spree, bender, fling, tear, toot; carousal, bacchanalia.

birth *n.* **1** *The birth occurred at 2 a.m.:* being

born; childbirth, delivery, parturition. 2 *of royal birth*: descent, ancestry, family, parentage, extraction, lineage, breeding, blood. 3 *the birth of jazz in New Orleans*: start, beginning, origin, inception, genesis. *Ant.* 1 death. 3 end, death.

bisect *v. The highway bisects the town*: cut in two, cut in half, divide, split; intersect, cross.

bit *n.* 1 *The glass broke into bits*: small piece, piece, fragment, smithereen. 2 *A bit of carrot fell on the floor*: small amount, trace, scrap, morsel, speck, dab, pinch, whit, smidgen, drop, dollop. 3 *Stay a bit longer*: short while, little while, short time, spell. *Ant.* 2 lot, mass, heap. 3 long time.

bite *v.* 1 *Be careful, that dog bites! A mosquito just bit me*: seize with the teeth, eat into, nip; sting. 2 *The tires bit into the snow*: take hold, dig, grip. —*n.* 3 *I just want a bite of pie*: small portion, small piece, mouthful, morsel. 4 *The dog gave the mail carrier a nasty bite. an insect bite*: tooth wound, nip; sting. 5 *the cold bite of the wind*: sting, stinging, nip.

biting *adj.* 1 *biting cold*: stinging, piercing, sharp, smarting, cutting, bitter. 2 *biting remarks*: sarcastic, sharp-tongued, cutting, stinging, caustic, withering, scathing. *Ant.* 2 pleasant, soothing, flattering, complimentary.

bitter *adj.* 1 *a bitter taste*: sour, acid, acerbic, acrid, tart, sharp, harsh, astringent. 2 *bitter cold*: stinging, smarting, piercing, sharp, biting, severe. 3 *a bitter blow to one's pride*: grievous, harsh, painful, distressing. 4 *a bitter argument*: resentful, sullen, spiteful, rancorous, scornful, mean, angry. *Ant.* 1 sweet, mild, flat, dull. 2 mild, gentle, balmy. 3 happy, joyful, delightful, pleasant. 4 friendly, amiable, genial.

bizarre *adj. to wear bizarre costumes at Halloween*: strange, fantastic, weird, freakish, grotesque, odd. *Ant.* subdued, ordinary.

blabber *n.* 1 *It was hard to concentrate with blabber on all sides*: chatter, jabber, prattle, babble, gab; *Slang* gabble, twaddle, blather. —*v.* 2 *They never get tired of blabbering*: *Slang* gab, prattle, prate, blab, yak.

blabbermouth *n. He's a blabbermouth so don't tell him anything*: gossip, scandalmonger, gossipmonger, rumormonger, tattletale, busybody, talebearer, informer, prattler, bigmouth.

black *adj.* 1 *a black cat*: coal-black, jet, raven, ebony, sable. 2 *It was a black night*: dark, murky, lightless, sunless, moonless. 3 Often **Black**. *Jackie Robinson was the first black major-league baseball player*: Negro,

colored, dark-skinned, African-American. 4 *a black outlook on the state of the world*: gloomy, grim, dismal, somber. 5 *a black look*: sullen, hostile, furious, angry, threatening. 6 *The villain had a black heart*: evil, wicked. —*n.* 7 *Black is the most somber color*: ebony, jet, raven, sable. 8 Often **Black**. *Martin Luther King, Jr., was the first American Black to win the Nobel Prize*: Negro, African-American, black person, colored person, person of color. *Ant.* 1 white, snow-white. 2 bright, light, lighted, well-lighted, lit. 4 optimistic, bright. 5 friendly, amicable, congenial. 6 good, virtuous, honorable. 7 white.

blackball *v. They blackballed him from the club*: ban, proscribe, blacklist, exclude, debar, turn down, reject, vote against. *Ant.* vote in, bid, welcome, invite.

blacken *v.* 1 *The commandos blackened their faces with charcoal*: make black, become black; darken, black. 2 *He blackened her name by spreading rumors*: defame, dishonor, defile, discredit, tarnish, sully, stain, smear, slander, libel. *Ant.* 1 lighten, whiten. 2 honor, praise.

blackguard *n. In the play, the blackguard was outwitted by the hero*: villain, scoundrel, knave, rogue, rascal, cad. *Ant.* hero; gentleman.

blacklist *v. Communists were blacklisted from working in the industry*: blackball, bar, debar, ban, preclude, exclude. *Ant.* accept, invite.

blackmail *n.* 1 *She demanded $10,000 blackmail*: hush money, extortion, shakedown, payoff. —*v.* 2 *He blackmailed the firm into paying him for keeping quiet*: extort, shake down, coerce, *Slang* squeeze.

blade *n.* 1 *The blade needs sharpening*: cutting edge, cutter; *(variously)* sword, knife, scalpel, razor; skate runner, sled runner. 2 *a blade of grass*: leaf, frond, needle, switch.

blah *n.* 1 *It was the same old blah you've heard before*: nonsense, bunkum, humbug, hooey, bosh, blather, eyewash, balderdash, twaddle, hot air, guff, claptrap. —*adj.* 2 *Everyone seems to feel blah today*: lifeless, listless, dull, dreary, unimaginative, humdrum. *Ant.* 2 vivacious, energetic, alive, dynamic.

blame *v.* 1 *The police blame the accident on the driver. I don't blame you for being angry*: hold responsible, accuse, charge; fault, reproach, condemn, criticize, disapprove. —*n.* 2 *Don't put all the blame on me*: responsibility, liability, guilt, onus, fault, culpability; accusation, charge, recrimination;

reproach, censure, rebuke, criticism, castigation, remonstrance.

Ant. 1 exonerate, vindicate, clear, forgive; praise, laud, commend, compliment, approve of. 2 exoneration, vindication; praise, commendation, compliment, credit, honor, glory, distinction.

blameless *adj. The jury found the contractor blameless. a blameless reputation:* not responsible, not at fault, not guilty, innocent; irreproachable, spotless, unsullied, unstained, unblemished.

Ant. responsible, at fault, guilty, culpable; sullied, tainted.

blanch *v. He blanched with fright:* whiten, turn pale; bleach, lighten.

bland *adj.* 1 *a bland movie:* uninteresting, unexciting, dull, uninspiring, unstimulating, tedious, tiresome, humdrum, vapid, nothing. 2 *bland spring days:* mild, balmy, calm, tranquil, quiet, temperate, unruffled, soothing, peaceful, peaceable.

Ant. 1 interesting, exciting, electrifying, thrilling, inspiring, stirring, rousing, overpowering, moving. 2 turbulent, tempestuous; harsh, severe, irritating, annoying.

blandishment Often **blandishments** *n. Her blandishments couldn't win us over:* flattery, cajolery, coaxing, wheedling, inveiglement, sweet talk.

Ant. threats, scolding, bullying, browbeating.

blank *adj.* 1 *a blank sheet of paper:* not written on, clean, unused, not filled out. 2 *a blank look:* vacant, empty, expressionless, unrecognizing; uninterested, thoughtless, dull, vacuous. 3 *She spent long blank days alone:* empty, idle, warding, valueless, inconsequential, insignificant, profitless, unprofitable. —*n.* 4 *Fill in the blanks:* empty space, space, void, gap; emptiness.

Ant. 1 marked, filled out, filled in. 2 thoughtful, interested, meaningful, expressive, alert. 3 full, busy; rewarding, valuable, worthwhile, useful, meaningful, profitable, fruitful, productive.

blanket *n.* 1 *Put a blanket on the bed:* comforter, coverlet, quilt. 2 *a blanket of snow:* covering, cover, coating, coat, mantle, carpet, film. —*v.* 3 *Confetti blanketed the ballroom floor:* cover, carpet, overlay.

blare *v. The loudspeaker blared:* sound loudly, blast, resound, scream, bellow, roar.

Ant. hum, murmur, whisper.

blarney *n. a line of blarney:* flattery, fawning, overpraise, honeyed words, sweet words; cajolery, wheedling, inveigling, coaxing; fanciful talk, exaggeration, hyperbole.

Ant. truth, frankness, directness.

blasé *adj. Don't be so blasé about your good fortune:* bored, unexcited, unenthusiastic, unconcerned, uninterested, indifferent, insouciant; world-weary, jaded, surfeited.

Ant. enthusiastic, excited, spirited.

blasphemous *adj. "God is dead" is a blasphemous statement:* irreverent, sacrilegious, irreligious, impious, ungodly, godless.

Ant. reverent, pious, godly.

blasphemy *n. Taking the name of the Lord in vain is blasphemy:* profanity, profanation, irreverence, sacrilege, impiety, impiousness.

Ant. prayer, praying; veneration, reverence.

blast *n.* 1 *a blast of wind:* gust, gale, surge, burst, rush, roar. 2 *the blast of the factory whistle:* loud noise, blare, scream, roar, bellow, bleat, shriek. 3 *The blast demolished the building:* explosion, detonation, report, burst, discharge. —*v.* 4 *Music blasted from the radio:* sound loudly, blare, scream, shriek, roar, bellow.

blatant *adj.* 1 *a blatant error in the bill:* obvious, clear, conspicuous, prominent, glaring, overt, flagrant. 2 *He's so blatant no one likes him:* obtrusive, offensive, crude, uncouth, gross, coarse, vulgar, brazen, unrefined, tasteless, unsubtle; noisy, blaring, clamorous, deafening, piercing.

Ant. inconspicuous, subtle. 1 hidden. 2 unobtrusive, agreeable, refined, dignified, delicate, tasteful, cultured, polished; quiet, subdued.

blaze *n.* 1 *the blaze of the bonfire:* fire, flame, flames, conflagration. 2 *the blaze of sunlight on the water:* glow, gleam, shimmer, glitter, flash, shine, glare, beam, ray; radiance, brilliance, brightness. 3 *a blaze of anger:* outburst, burst, flash, rush; explosion. —*v.* 4 *The fire blazed all night:* burn brightly, burn, flame. 5 *Her eyes blazed with happiness:* glow, gleam, shine, glisten, glitter, shimmer, be bright; flash, beam, flame, flare.

bleach *v. The sun bleached my hair:* whiten, blanch, lighten, fade.

Ant. blacken, darken; stain, dye.

bleak *adj.* 1 *a bleak country:* bare, barren, desolate. 2 *a bleak wintry day:* gloomy, dreary, dismal, grim, depressing, cheerless; distressing, somber. 3 *a bleak wind:* raw, cold, icy, piercing, biting, nipping, frosty, wintry.

Ant. 1 wooded, forested. 2 bright, cheerful, cheery, sunny; pleasant; promising. 3 mild, balmy, soft, warm, springlike.

blemish *n.* 1 *a blemish in the wood. a skin blemish:* flaw, imperfection, defect, disfig-

urement; blotch, blot, mark, *Slang* zit.
—*v.* 2 *The loss blemished the team's record:*
flaw, mar, spoil, tarnish, sully, taint, stain,
smirch; mark, blotch, blur, disfigure.
Ant. 1 decoration, ornament. 2 enhance;
reclaim, restore.

blend *v.* 1 *Blue and yellow blend to make
green:* mix, merge, combine, unite, mingle;
fuse, melt together, coalesce, amalgamate.
2 *The drapes blend with the rug:* harmonize,
go well, complement. —*n.* 3 *Mocha is a
blend of coffee and chocolate:* mixture, mix,
combination; merger, mingling, concoction;
compound, amalgam, fusion.
Ant. 1 separate, divide. 2 clash.

bless *v.* 1 *The bishop blessed the new chapel:*
consecrate, sanctify, hallow, give benediction; anoint, baptize. 2 *Fate blessed him with
talent:* favor, endow, bestow, grace, give.
3 *God bless you:* guard, protect, watch over,
support.
Ant. 1 curse, anathematize. 2 curse, condemn, disfavor.

blessed *adj.* 1 *He prayed to the Blessed Virgin:* revered, holy, hallowed, sacred, sanctified, consecrated, adored, venerated. 2 *a
blessed event:* joyous, joyful, happy, wonderful. 3 *I consider myself twice-blessed:* fortunate, favored, lucky.
Ant. 1 cursed, accursed. 2 unhappy, sad,
unfortunate, grievous.

blessing *n.* 1 *the blessing of the new temple.
Do you say a blessing before meals?:* consecration, sanctification, dedication, hallow-
ing, benediction; grace, prayer of thanks,
thanksgiving. 2 *the blessings of a happy
childhood:* advantage, benefit, good, good
fortune, favor, gift. 3 *The astronauts had
the blessing of their families:* approval, consent, concurrence, permission, leave, sanction, good wishes.
Ant. curse. 1 imprecation, malediction.
2 deprivation, misfortune, disadvantage,
drawback, damage. 3 disapproval, objection, condemnation, denunciation, disfavor.

blight *n.* 1 *A blight destroyed the crop:* plant
disease, pestilence; (*loosely*) dry rot, rot,
rust, fungus, mildew, decay. 2 *Greed is a
blight on humanity:* affliction, curse, plague,
scourge, corruption, pox. —*v.* 3 *Lack of education blighted his chances:* spoil, ruin,
wreck, kill, destroy; cripple, thwart, injure,
frustrate.
Ant. 2 blessing, good, favor, service, boon.
3 help, aid, improve, better, advance, further, foster, promote.

blind *adj.* 1 *Helen Keller was born deaf and
blind:* sightless, unable to see, without vision. 2 *Do not be blind to the suffering of
others:* ignorant, unaware, unknowing,

unobserving, unobservant, incognizant, unconscious of, unseeing; unmindful, unfeeling, unperceptive, indifferent, heedless.
3 *a blind rage:* uncontrolled, uncontrollable,
mindless, irrational. —*n.* 4 *The blinds keep
the sun out:* shade, sun shield. 5 *The nightclub was just a blind for the gambling ca-
sino:* cover, front, subterfuge, disguise;
dodge, ruse, pretext, deception.
Ant. 1 sighted, seeing. 2 aware, conscious,
observant, cognizant; mindful, sensitive, attentive, heedful. 3 controlled, controllable,
rational.

blink *v.* 1 *He bet me he could hold my gaze
without blinking:* wink, nictitate, bat the
eyes. 2 *The beacon blinked:* twinkle, flash,
flicker, sparkle, glimmer, shine, shimmer.

bliss *n.* *Being home was pure bliss:* happiness, joy, ecstasy, delight, rapture; luxury,
heaven, paradise.
Ant. misery, agony, anguish, torment, unhappiness.

blithe *adj.* 1 *a blithe personality:* joyous,
merry, happy, cheery, cheerful, sunny, glad,
gleeful; carefree, light-hearted, debonair,
sprightly, jaunty. 2 *a blithe disregard of
others:* heedless, careless, thoughtless, unmindful, insensitive, uncaring, unfeeling;
indifferent, unconcerned.
Ant. 1 sad, unhappy, sorrowful, depressed,
gloomy, cheerless, glum, morose, dour, melancholy. 2 thoughtful, considerate, concerned.

blizzard *n.* *The blizzard brought 2 feet of
snow:* snowstorm; blow, blast, gale, snowfall, winter storm.

bloat *v.* *The cow's stomach was bloated:* distend, swell, puff up, inflate, blow up, enlarge.
Ant. contract, shrivel.

bloc *n.* *The farm bloc influenced the election:*
faction, group, clique; alliance, coalition,
combine.

block *n.* 1 *concrete blocks:* brick, bar, cube,
square. 2 *The filibuster was a block to passage of the bill:* obstruction, barrier, obstacle, bar, impediment; hindrance. —*v.* 3
Snowdrifts blocked our progress: obstruct,
blockade, bar, stop up; hinder, impede,
check, halt, thwart. 4 *hats cleaned and
blocked:* shape, form, mold; reshape, reform.
Ant. 3 clear, unblock, open; advance, further, facilitate.

blockade *n.* *Ships could not get past the
blockade:* block, blockage, roadblock, barrier, barricade, obstruction, stoppage.

blockhead *n.* *Only a blockhead would buy
that stock:* fool, dunce, nitwit, nincompoop,

simpleton, booby, dolt, dummy; imbecile, moron.

blond, blonde *adj.* 1 *He has blond hair and blue eyes:* light-colored, yellowish, yellow, gold, golden, flaxen. 2 *The Nordic peoples tend to be blond:* fair, fair-skinned, light-complexioned, light, pale, fair-haired. —*n.* 3 *Blond is a fashionable color for furniture:* light tan, yellowish tan, whitish brown. 4 *Do Caucasians prefer blondes?:* blond-haired woman; person having fair skin and hair.
Ant. 1,2 brunette, brunet, dark.

blood *n.* 1 *The boxer had blood running down his face:* life fluid, vital fluid, gore. 2 *Tolerance is the very blood of democracy:* vital principle, vital force. 3 *He's a terror when his blood is up:* temper, passion, spirit. 4 *a woman of noble blood:* extraction, lineage, descent, ancestry, family, family line.

bloodshed *n.* *unconscionable bloodshed:* carnage, killing, slaying, spilling of blood, slaughter, massacre; manslaughter, murder, mass murder.

bloodthirsty *adj. a bloodthirsty killer:* murderous, homicidal, savage, inhuman, brutal, barbarous.

bloom *n.* 1 *This plant has one white bloom. The dogwood had a heavy bloom this spring:* blossom, flower, bud; flowerage, blossoming, florescence. 2 *the bloom of youth:* glow, flush, radiance, luster, shine, beauty, zest; flowering, flourishing. —*v.* 3 *The plant blooms in the spring:* flower, blossom, sprout, bear fruit, fructify. 4 *Musical talent blooms at an early age:* flourish, thrive, burgeon; develop, grow, flare.
Ant. 2 pallor, grayness, wanness; decay. 3 wither, die. 4 wither, fade, wane.

blooper *n. The speaker made a blooper:* mistake, error, blunder, slip, gaffe; *Slang* goof, booboo.

blossom *n.* 1 *orange blossoms:* flower, bloom. —*v.* 2 *Did the wisteria blossom this year?:* flower, bloom, burgeon. 3 *Their project was blossoming:* bloom, grow, develop; flourish, thrive.
Ant. 2 wither, die. 3 wither, fade.

blot *n.* 1 *an ink blot:* blotch, spot, splotch, smudge, smear, stain. 2 *The poor grade was a blot on her record:* blemish, flaw, blotch, taint, stain. —*v.* 3 *The ink blotted on the paper:* smear, smudge, splotch; spot, stain. 4 *Blot the ink with a blotter:* soak up, absorb, take up; dry.
Ant. 2 credit, distinction, honor.

blotch *n. The measles gave him red blotches:* spot, splotch, blot.

blow *n.* 1 *The fighter was punch-drunk from too many blows on the head:* hit, knock,

punch, smack, whack, clout, sock, wallop, bang, belt, cuff. 2 *The failure of our business was a terrible blow:* shock, upset, disappointment, reversal; tragedy, disaster, calamity, misfortune, affliction. 3 *The weather channel forecasts a big blow:* gale, squall, windstorm, storm, wind, gust of wind, blast. —*v.* 4 *The wind is blowing:* gust, puff. 5 *Blow on your hands to keep them warm:* exhale, breathe, indigo, aqua, 6 *Who's blowing a horn?:* sound, toot; honk, play. 7 *The left tire blew:* burst, explode, blow out.
Ant. 1 caress, pat. 2 comfort, relief, blessing. 3 calm.

blue *adj.* 1 *The sky is very blue today:* bluish, azure, cerulean, sky blue, cobalt blue, cobalt, Prussian blue, navy blue, navy, robin's-egg blue, powder blue, indigo, aqua, aquamarine, turquoise. 2 *homesick and blue:* depressed, dejected, sad, gloomy, despondent, downcast, downhearted, disconsolate, melancholy, doleful, down in the dumps, down in the mouth.
Ant. 2 elated, exultant, exhilarated, happy, joyful, glad, merry, jolly, in high spirits.

bluff¹ *adj.* 1 *Teddy Roosevelt had a bluff nature:* outspoken, plain-spoken, blunt, frank, open, unceremonious, candid, direct, straightforward, forthright, bold, headlong, abrupt, brusque, curt. —*n.* 2 *a bluff high above the river:* promontory, cliff, palisade, headland, bank.
Ant. 1 retiring, reticent, repressed, shy; indirect, roundabout, deceptive; mannered, tactful.

bluff² *v.* 1 *The poker player bluffed his opponents:* delude, humbug, mislead, fool, dupe; *Slang* fake out; fake, pretend. —*n.* 2 *The bully's claim to be a professional boxer was just a bluff:* pretense, fake, sham, fraud, lie, deception; idle boast, boast, bragging. 3 *He's just a big bluff:* bluffer, pretender, fraud; liar, boaster.
Ant. 2 truth, fact.

blunder *n.* 1 *a social blunder:* mistake, error, slip; impropriety, indiscretion, gaucherie, gaffe, *Slang* boner, goof. —*v.* 2 *The clerk blundered when totaling the bill:* make a mistake, be in error, be at fault, slip up. 3 *I blundered into the wrong room:* flounder, bumble, bungle; stumble, stagger.
Ant. 2 be correct, be accurate.

blunt *adj.* 1 *a blunt knife:* dull, dulled, unsharpened; thick, edgeless. 2 *to hurt people's feelings by being blunt:* frank, outspoken, candid, straightforward, explicit, to the point; curt, abrupt, brusque. —*v.* 3 *Lack of sleep blunted our thinking:* dull, numb, deaden, make insensitive, stupefy; moderate, mitigate, soften.

Ant. 1 sharp, keen, acute; pointed. 2 tactful, diplomatic, polite, courteous. 3 sharpen, hone, put an edge on, make keen.

blur *v.* 1 *Mist often blurs the view:* cloud, fog, make hazy, dim, obscure, veil. 2 *The damp paper caused the ink to blur:* smear, smudge, spread, run, blot. —*n.* 3 *The ink made a blur on the paper:* smudge, smear, blotch, blot. 4 *The evening was just a blur:* confusion, fog, haze.

blush *v.* 1 *I blush easily:* flush, redden, turn red. —*n.* 2 *at the first blush of dawn:* reddening, rosy tint, pinkish tinge.

Ant. 1 blanch, turn pale, pale.

bluster *v.* 1 *He blusters so much it's hard to believe him:* boast, swagger, rant, brag; threaten, storm, bully. —*n.* 2 *His bragging and bluster made him unpopular:* bluff, swagger, swaggering, bravado, bombast, boasting, ranting.

Ant. 1 be retiring, be reticent, be shy. 2 shyness, meekness, reticence.

board *n.* 1 *Saw this board in half:* plank, piece of lumber; slat, clapboard, panel, deal, batten. 2 *How much is room and board?:* meals, daily meals, food. 3 *The decision of the board:* board of directors, directors; council, tribunal. —*v.* 4 *The ranch boards vacationers:* lodge, house, quarter, put up; billet, bed; feed. 5 *The passengers boarded the plane:* get on, go onto, embark.

Ant. 5 leave, get off, disembark, deplane, detrain.

boast *v.* 1 *She boasted that she was the best swimmer in school:* brag, crow; talk big. 2 *The city boasted two new schools:* be proud of, speak proudly of, show off, exhibit; contain, possess.

boastful *adj. Discount their boastful claim:* conceited, cocky, vainglorious, full of swagger, pretentious, braggadocio; vaunting, exaggerated.

Ant. modest, self-disparaging, deprecating, self-belittling.

boat *n. The boat left the dock:* vessel, craft, ship.

bob¹ *v. The skiff bobbed in the water:* move up and down; bounce.

bob² *v. Women bobbed their hair in the 1920's:* crop, shorten, clip, shear, dock.

body *n.* 1 *When a body meets a body coming through the rye. a body of water:* person, being; thing, quantity, mass. 2 *a muscular body. the body of the airplane:* physique, figure, build, form; frame, main part; torso, trunk. 3 *The body is in the morgue:* corpse, remains, cadaver, *Slang* stiff. 4 *The body of the populace supported the mayor. a large*

body of people: majority, bulk, mass; group, throng, mob, multitude. 5 *a governing body:* assembly, confederation, federation, congress, council, faction, bloc, coalition; league, society. 6 *Flour will give the gravy body:* consistency, thickness, cohesion.

Ant. 2 soul, spirit; mind; limb, wing. 4 minority.

bog *n.* 1 *Walking is difficult in the bog:* marsh, marshland, swamp, swampland, wetlands; spongy ground. —*v.* 2 *The car was bogged down in the mud:* be stuck, mire.

Ant. 1 dry ground, firm ground.

bogus *adj. bogus diamonds:* counterfeit, fraudulent, spurious, artificial, synthetic, fake, imitation, simulated, faux, phony, sham, false, feigned, ersatz.

Ant. genuine, real, authentic, true, bona fide, actual.

Bohemian, Also **bohemian** *adj. The poet lived a bohemian life in Paris:* nonconformist, unconventional, unorthodox.

Ant. conformist, conventional, *Slang* square.

boil *v.* 1 *Boil the water:* simmer, seethe, brew; parboil, stew. 2 *The waves boiled around the ship:* bubble, froth, foam, churn, toss, simmer. 3 *to boil with anger:* rage, rave, seethe, fume, fulminate, rant, burn. —*n.* 4 *to lance a boil:* sore, abscess, fester, pustule, carbuncle.

Ant. 1 freeze; cool, gel 2 subside, calm.

boisterous *adj. The children became boisterous:* noisy, loud; disorderly, wild, rowdy, unruly, obstreperous.

Ant. quiet, still, calm; well-behaved, restrained.

bold *adj.* 1 *a very bold soldier. a bold plan:* brave, courageous, unafraid, fearless, valorous, stalwart, dauntless, lionhearted, intrepid, unshrinking; daring, audacious, adventuresome; imaginative, creative. 2 *bold remarks:* rude, impudent, fresh, insolent; brazen, impertinent, defiant, brash, forward; fiery, spirited. 3 *bold colors:* colorful, loud, eyecatching, hot, vivid, striking, flashy.

Ant. 1 cowardly, fainthearted, fearful, chickenhearted, yellow; mundane, modest, unimaginative. 2 meek, timid, bashful, shy. 3 pale, dull, conservative, cool.

bolster *v.* 1 *More timbers are needed to bolster the roof:* support, brace, prop up, buttress; sustain, shore up. 2 *More facts are needed to bolster your argument:* support, uphold, strengthen, reinforce, help, aid, assist. —*n.* 3 *Put the bolster on the couch:* cushion, pillow.

Ant. 2 diminish, lessen, weaken.

bolt *n.* 1 *Is the bolt on the door closed?:* sliding

bar, bar, catch, rod, latch. 2 *The engine is held in place by two bolts:* fastening rod, pin, dowel, rivet. 3 *He made a bolt for the door:* dash, rush, run, sprint; jump, leap. 4 *two bolts of cloth:* roll, length. 5 *a bolt of lightning:* thunderbolt, firebolt, shaft, stroke, flash. —*v.* 6 *Bolt the windows:* bar, latch, lock, fasten, secure. 7 *He bolted out of the room:* dash, rush, run, speed, hurry, scoot, flee, tear, sprint; jump, leap. 8 *Don't bolt your food:* eat rapidly, gulp, swallow whole, wolf.

Ant. 6 unbolt, unlatch, unbar, unlock, unfasten.

bomb *n.* 1 *The plane carries 5,000 pounds of bombs:* explosive device, explosive missile. 2 *(Slang) The play was a bomb:* failure, fiasco, flop, dud, bust. —*v.* 3 *The rebels bombed the factory:* set off a bomb in, drop a bomb on, throw a bomb at, bombard. 4 *(Slang) The movie bombed at the box office:* fail, flop, fizzle.

bombard *v.* 1 *Artillery bombarded the enemy port:* rain explosives upon, fire upon, pepper, shell. 2 *The company was bombarded with calls:* barrage, besiege, beset, pepper, assail; pester, hound.

bombastic *adj. bombastic claims:* grandiloquent, pompous, windy, inflated, verbose, wordy.

Ant. unpretentious, modest, simple, unaffected.

bona fide *adj. a bona fide $100 bill.* genuine, real, actual, true, authentic, legitimate.

Ant. counterfeit, fraudulent, spurious, forged; artificial, synthetic, imitation, fake, phony, sham, bogus.

bonanza *n. Our investment grew into a bonanza:* windfall, sudden profit, gold mine.

bond *n.* 1 Usually **bonds.** *The captive could not break the bonds:* bindings, fastenings; *(variously)* rope, cord, chains, shackles, manacles, handcuffs, irons, fetters. 2 *a strong bond between siblings:* affinity, allegiance, connection, attachment. 3 *One's word is one's bond:* guarantee, pledge, compact, promise.

bondage *n. Lincoln freed the slaves from bondage:* slavery, servitude, enslavement, vassalage, captivity; bonds, shackles, chains, fetters.

Ant. freedom, liberty, emancipation, liberation.

bonus *n. a Christmas bonus:* gift, premium, dividend; prize, reward, benefit, bounty.

Ant. fine, penalty.

book *n.* 1 *to read a book:* volume, written work, bound work, tome; opus, treatise. 2 *an autograph book:* notebook; album. —*v.* 3 *The travel agent booked our vacation cruise:* reserve, make reservations, engage, schedule, line up. 4 *The police booked him:* register, list, record, enter, write down, note, enroll; file, catalog; charge, accuse.

boom *n.* 1 *the boom of the explosion:* bang, roar, blast, thunder. 2 *a business boom:* prosperous period, successful period, good times; upsurge, upturn, boost, expansion, growth, development. —*v.* 3 *The drums boomed:* bang, rumble, roar, blast, thunder. 4 *The frontier town boomed:* thrive, flourish, prosper, grow, develop.

Ant. 2 depression, recession, bad times, slump, bust. 4 fail, slump.

boondocks *n. a small school in the boondocks:* backwater, backwoods, hinterland, backcountry, provinces; *Slang* boonies, sticks.

boor *n. a clumsy boor:* lout, oaf, churl, bumpkin, rustic; vulgarian, brute, philistine.

Ant. sophisticate, cosmopolitan.

boorish *adj. She considers him boorish:* crude, rude, coarse, vulgar, unrefined, uncouth, gauche; loutish, oafish; rustic, peasantlike.

Ant. polished, cultured, refined, cultivated; sophisticated, cosmopolitan.

boost *v.* 1 *Boost me up so I can look in the window:* lift, raise, heave, hoist, push. 2 *to boost production:* increase, raise, advance, add to, expand; advance, develop, improve. 3 *The Chamber of Commerce boosts local business:* promote, advance, further, support; speak well of, propound, praise, extol, acclaim, laud. —*n.* 4 *Give me a boost onto the horse:* lift, heave, hoist, push. 5 *a boost in sales:* increase, raise, growth, expansion, advance, rise, upsurge, upswing, upturn, upward trend. 6 *The charity bazaar got a boost in the newspaper:* favorable mention, good word, good review, free ad, *Informal* plug.

Ant. 1, 2 lower, push down. 2 decrease, reduce, lessen, cut, curtail. 3 hinder, hold back, criticize, *Informal* knock. 5 decrease, reduction, cutback, decline, falling off, deterioration. 6 *Informal* knock.

booth *n.* 1 *a phone booth.* compartment, enclosure, hutch. 2 *a booth at the fair:* stall, stand, counter.

booty *n. The pirates buried their booty:* loot, plunder, spoils, pillage; prize, winnings, *Slang* boodle.

border *n.* 1 *the border of the lake. The bedspread had a fringed border:* edge, rim, periphery, perimeter, extremity, verge, margin, skirt. 2 *the Mexican border:* frontier, boundary, line. —*v.* 3 *California borders the Pacific:* be next to, adjoin, flank, touch, neighbor on, abut, verge upon. 4 *The seam-*

stress *bordered the dress with flowers:* edge, trim, fringe, bind, rim, hem.

Ant. **1** interior, inside, middle, center.

borderline *adj. He's not insane, but he's borderline:* marginal, problematic; indefinite, unclear, uncertain, ambivalent, indeterminate, equivocal, undecided; vague, ambiguous.

Ant. decisive, clear, positive, definite.

bore[1] *v.* **1** *Long stories bore me:* be tedious to, tire, weary, fatigue, tax one's patience. *Slang* be a drag. —*n.* **2** *The speaker was a deadly bore:* dull person, tiresome thing, *Slang* drag.

Ant. **1** excite, interest, stimulate, delight. **2** life of the party.

bore[2] *v.* **1** *Engineers had to bore through solid rock:* drill, tunnel, gouge out, burrow. —*n.* **2** *Rifles have smaller bores than shotguns:* inside diameter, caliber.

Ant. **1** fill, plug.

boredom *n. long days of boredom:* dullness, tedium, ennui, monotony, tediousness.

Ant. excitement, stimulation.

boring *adj. Playing bridge can be boring:* dull, unexciting, uninteresting, tiresome, monotonous, tedious, wearisome, insipid.

Ant. exciting, interesting, stimulating, exhilarating.

born *adj.* **1** *Charles Dickens was born in 1812:* given birth to, brought forth, delivered. **2** *a born musician:* natural, intuitive; endowed from birth.

borrow *v.* **1** *May I borrow your car?:* use, take on loan, take and return. **2** *The playwright borrowed the plot from Shakespeare:* appropriate, take, get, obtain, acquire, use, usurp; filch, pirate, plagiarize, steal.

Ant. **1** lend; return.

bosom *n.* **1** *She clutched the child to her bosom:* breast, bust, chest. **2** *Conflicting emotions wrestled in his bosom:* heart, innermost being, inmost nature, core, breast. **3** *the bosom of one's family:* midst, inner circle, heart, nucleus, core. —*adj.* **4** *bosom buddies:* close, intimate, dear.

boss *n.* **1** *A good boss keeps workers happy:* employer, supervisor, foreman, superintendent, executive; chief, leader. —*v.* **2** *Don't boss me around!:* order, command.

Ant. **1** employee, worker, subordinate, underling.

botch *v.* **1** *The typist botched the job:* spoil, muff, bungle, make a mess of, ruin, do unskillfully, butcher; blunder, fail, fumble, flub, *Slang* louse up, foul up. —*n.* **2** *The cook made a botch of the dinner:* mess, bungle, failure, flop.

Ant. **1** master, perfect, do skillfully, triumph at. **2** success, triumph.

bother *v.* **1** *My cold still bothers me:* annoy, trouble, distress, inconvenience, worry, disturb, upset; pester, nag, harass, harry, vex, irk, irritate. **2** *She didn't bother to say she was sorry:* trouble, attempt, make an effort. —*n.* **3** *It's no bother at all:* inconvenience, trouble, difficulty, strain, load, encumbrance, nuisance; impediment, worry, aggravation, vexation; disturbance, commotion, tumult, stir, flurry, rumpus, racket.

Ant. **1** help, aid, comfort, solace. **3** convenience, help, aid; pleasure, delight, comfort.

bothersome *adj. Being without a car was bothersome:* troublesome, annoying, inconvenient, vexing, worrisome, disquieting.

Ant. convenient, helpful, comfortable.

bottle *n. a bottle of soda:* glass container, vessel; *(variously)* phial, vial, carafe, flask, flagon.

bottleneck *n. A bottleneck at the bridge stopped traffic:* jam, gridlock, obstacle, obstruction, blockage, congestion, stoppage.

bottom *n.* **1** *the bottom of the lamp:* base, foot, pedestal, foundation. **2** *at the bottom of the trunk:* lowest part, deepest part. **3** *Is that gum stuck to the bottom of your shoe?:* underside, underpart, lower side. **4** *The ship sank to the bottom:* ocean floor, riverbed, depths. **5** *She spanked the child on its bottom:* rump, backside, buttocks, seat, fundament; *Slang* fanny. **6** *Let's get to the bottom of this:* basis, root, heart, core, substance, essence, principle; gist, quintessence; source, origin, cause. —*adj.* **7** *the bottom step:* lowest, lower, deepest, deeper.

Ant. **1**–**4, 7** top. **1** crown, height; lid, cover. **4** surface. **7** uppermost, upper.

bough *n. A bough broke off the tree:* branch, limb.

boulevard *n. the main boulevard of the city:* avenue, wide street, tree-lined street, parkway, concourse.

bounce *v.* **1** *The ball bounced against the wall:* rebound, ricochet, carom, bound, recoil; bob, jounce, bump. —*n.* **2** *Hit the ball before the second bounce:* rebound, bound, hop. **3** *A good entertainer has to have a lot of bounce:* vitality, liveliness, pep, animation, vivacity, vigor, verve, energy.

bound[1] *adj.* **1** *Bound newspapers will be collected for the paper drive:* tied, tied up, fastened, secured, trussed. **2** *the bound books in the local library:* encased, wrapped, covered. **3** *The roses are bound to die in this frost:* sure, certain, fated, destined, doomed. **4** *The borrower is bound by contract:* required, obliged, restrained, limited; liable, forced; determined, resolved, resolute.

Ant. **1** unbound, untied, loose. **4** free, unrestrained.

bound^2 *n.* 1 *The hunting lodge is within the bounds of the estate. to overstep the bounds of good taste:* limit, boundary, border, confine, line; periphery, extremity, rim. 2 *the vast bounds of Yellowstone Park:* area, territory, region, compass, domain, district; realm, bailiwick. —*v.* 3 *A stone wall bounds the property:* surround, enclose, encircle, border; mark, define, limit, demarcate.

bound^3 *v.* 1 *The dog bounded out of the house:* leap, jump, vault, spring; gambol, flounce. —*n.* 2 *In one bound, the boy jumped the fence:* leap, jump, vault, spring.

boundary *n. the boundary between Kentucky and Indiana:* border, dividing line, line, demarcation; rim, edge, margin, periphery.

boundless *adj. boundless energy:* vast, immense; limitless, unlimited, unbounded, endless, inexhaustible, immeasurable, unending, perpetual.

Ant. limited, bounded; small, little.

bounteous *adj.* 1 *bounteous crops:* abundant, plentiful, plenteous, bountiful, copious, ample, prolific, lavish, large, abounding. 2 *bounteous donors:* generous, bountiful, munificent, unstinting, magnanimous, charitable, beneficent, liberal.

Ant. 1 sparse, spare, meager, scant, scanty, lean, modest, small, inadequate. 2 stingy, niggardly, sparing, stinting, frugal, parsimonious.

bountiful *adj.* See BOUNTEOUS.

bounty *n.* 1 *The poor had to depend on the parish's bounty:* generosity, benevolence, munificence, charitableness, charity, assistance, aid, help, giving, almsgiving. 2 *Every soldier was promised ten acres of land as a bounty:* grant, reward, recompense, bonus, tribute, favor, contribution.

Ant. 1 stinginess, closeness, niggardliness, miserliness.

bouquet *n.* 1 *a bouquet of roses:* bunch of flowers, garland, spray, nosegay; boutonniere. 2 *The wine has a marvelous bouquet:* aroma, scent, odor, fragrance.

bourgeois *n.* 1 *The princess married a bourgeois:* member of the middle class, commoner, burgher. —*adj.* 2 *bourgeois taste:* middle-class, conventional, ordinary, unimaginative, *Slang* square.

bout *n.* 1 *a championship bout:* fight, boxing match, match, battle, contest; conflict, struggle, fray. 2 *a bout of the flu:* spell, session, course, interval, period, term; siege.

bow^1 *v.* 1 *The duke bowed and kissed her hand. Bow your head when the flag passes:* bend, salaam, genuflect; *(of a female)* curtsy. 2 *He refused to bow to the wishes of the mayor:* yield, give in, submit, surrender,

capitulate, comply, acquiesce, concede, knuckle under, kowtow. —*n.* 3 *The conductor made a deep bow:* bend, salaam, *(of a female)* curtsy.

Ant. 2 contest, resist, stand fast.

bow^2 *n. the bow of the ship:* forward end, front, prow.

Ant. stern.

bowels *n.* 1 *He ran his sword through the bowels of the villain:* guts, intestines, entrails, innards, stomach, vitals. 2 *in the bowels of the earth:* depths, innermost part, interior, core, heart.

bowl *n.* 1 *What lovely salad bowls! a bowl of soup:* deep dish, vessel, container, receptacle; *(variously)* tureen, porringer, boat; bowlful, portion. 2 *The entire area was a dust bowl. the bathroom washbowl:* basin; hollow, depression, valley.

box^1 *n.* 1 *a box of candy:* carton, cardboard container, container, receptacle; crate. 2 *a box at the opera:* stall, compartment, booth.

box^2 *v.* 1 *Father used to box our ears:* cuff, slap, bat, hit, rap, whack, thwack, buffet. 2 *The champion was asked to box in an exhibition bout:* fight, spar, exchange blows, engage in fisticuffs. —*n.* 3 *a box on the ears:* cuff, slap, whack, thwack, hit, rap; buffet.

boy *n. We have two boys:* male child; lad, youth, stripling, youngster.

boycott *n.* 1 *a meat boycott to protest high prices:* refusal to buy, rejection, spurning, exclusion. —*v.* 2 *The people boycotted the store:* refuse to have dealings with, reject, spurn.

boyfriend *n. She had a new boyfriend every few weeks:* beau, fellow, young man, date, gentleman caller, swain, admirer, suitor, wooer, steady; lover, beloved, sweetheart, paramour, inamorato, man, flame.

boyish *adj. boyish good looks. a boyish prank:* youthful, boylike, juvenile, innocent; childish, childlike, immature, puerile; sophomoric.

Ant. adult, mature, sophisticated, worldly.

brace *n.* 1 *The table is shaky because the braces are loose:* reinforcement, support, prop, stanchion, stay, strut. 2 *a brace of squab:* pair, couple, duo. —*v.* 3 *Brace those sagging shelves:* reinforce, strengthen, steady, prop up, shore, shore up, bolster, buttress, support.

bracelet *n. a charm bracelet:* armlet, bangle.

bracing *adj. A cold shower is very bracing:* invigorating, stimulating, energizing, exhilarating, restorative, refreshing; strengthening, fortifying, reviving.

Ant. soporific, restful, weakening, debilitating.

bracket *n.* 1 *The shelf was supported by a bracket at each end:* support, brace, stay, strut, prop, stanchion. 2 *What tax bracket are you in?:* group, grouping, class, classification, category, range, division, rank, designation. —*v.* 3 *Bracket those shelves with two-by-fours:* support, brace; prop up, shore, shore up. 4 *All able-bodied men will be bracketed as 1-A in the military draft:* class, classify, group, categorize, designate.

brackish *adj. The water is brackish:* salty, saline, salt.

Ant. fresh, sweet.

brag *v.* 1 *He constantly brags about how well he plays golf:* boast, extol oneself, vaunt, crow, talk big, pat oneself on the back. —*n.* 2 *Really good bridge players don't have to make brags about it:* boast, boasting, boastfulness, bragging, self-praise, crowing.

Ant. 1 be humble, be self-deprecating, deprecate. 2 humility, humbleness, modesty, self-deprecation, self-criticism.

braggart *n. He's so proud that he's become a braggart:* bragger, boaster, *Slang* blowhard.

Ant. humble person, self-effacing person, modest person.

braid *v. She braided the girl's hair into two pigtails:* plait, weave, intertwine, entwine, twine, interlace.

brake *n.* 1 *four wheel brakes. Higher taxes will put a brake on inflation:* curb, restraint, control, rein, check. —*v.* 2 *Don't brake the car abruptly:* stop, halt, arrest, check; reduce speed, slow; curb, control.

Ant. 1 acceleration, stimulus; freedom. 2 start; accelerate, speed up.

branch *n.* 1 *a branch of the tree:* limb, bough. 2 *the west branch of the river:* leg, prong, channel, tributary; extension, offshoot. 3 *the local branch of the union. Theater is a branch of the arts:* section, part, component, arm, wing, division, subdivision; bureau, office, branch office, department, agency. —*v.* 3 *The highway branches into three local roads:* divide, separate, fork, bifurcate.

Ant. 2 main channel.

brand *n.* 1 *The ranch's brand is an X. The store removed the brands from the dresses:* branding iron; mark made by branding; label, mark, emblem, sign, trademark. 2 *Which brand of peanut butter is cheapest?:* brand name, make, manufacture. 3 *After the scandal he carried the brand of an informer:* stigma, stain, mark, disgrace, slur, taint, imputation. —*v.* 4 *The cowboys*

branded a hundred calves: mark with a branding iron, mark, sear, burn in. 5 *His criminal record branded him for life:* stigmatize, mark, taint, spot, blemish.

Ant. 3 laurel, honor.

brandish *v. The cavalry officer brandished his sword:* flourish, wave, shake, wield; flaunt, display.

brash *adj.* 1 *Buying the house was very brash:* rash, reckless, incautious, foolhardy, imprudent; impetuous, madcap, hasty. 2 *a brash young man:* impudent, impertinent, forward, cheeky, sassy, *Slang* fresh; bold, overconfident, *Slang* smart-alecky.

Ant. 1 cautious, prudent, careful, thoughtful. 2 respectful, deferential, reserved; uncertain, timid, timorous.

brassy *adj. The job requires someone who's a bit brassy:* brazen, bold, impudent, insolent, sassy, forward; shameless, unblushing, unabashed, brash, impertinent, arrogant, cocky.

Ant. shy, modest, retiring, reticent, self-effacing.

brat *n. That little brat needs spanking:* spoiled child, rude child, hoyden, whelp, rascal, imp.

bravado *n. Bravado hides fear:* show of courage, swaggering, swagger, braggadocio, bravura, boastfulness, bragging, big talk, bombast, cockiness, bluster.

Ant. nervousness; shame.

bravo *adj.* 1 *a brave fire fighter:* courageous, valiant, valorous, heroic, fearless, dauntless, undaunted, intrepid, unafraid, unflinching; plucky, spunky, game, *Slang* gutsy. —*v.* 2 *The Coast Guard braved the storm to reach the sinking ship:* dare, confront, challenge, face, defy, breast; bear, withstand, weather, brook, abide.

Ant. 1 cowardly, fearful, afraid, craven, fainthearted, *Slang* chicken, yellow; timid, timorous. 2 back away from, surrender to, *Informal* turn tail.

bravery *n. The officer showed great bravery:* courage, valor, heroism, fearlessness; boldness, daring, pluck, spunk.

Ant. cowardice, faintheartedness, timidity.

brawl *n. The movie included a scene with a barroom brawl:* fight, scuffle, fracas, fray, melee, row, ruckus, broil, uproar; quarrel, squabble, tiff, dispute.

brawn *n. the brawn of a weight lifter:* brawniness, muscles, muscular development; robustness, huskiness, beefiness.

Ant. scrawniness, thinness, skinniness, slenderness.

brawny *adj. Most wrestlers are brawny:* muscular, burly, husky, sturdy, strapping, mighty.

Ant. scrawny, gaunt, slender, slight, skinny, slim, fragile, delicate.

brazen *adj. a brazen lie:* brassy, impudent, shameless, bold, boldfaced, barefaced, brash, unabashed, immodest, audacious; open, arrogant, cheeky.

Ant. reserved, reticent, modest; underhand, secret.

breach *n.* 1 *a breach in the enemy's lines:* opening, break, rift, gap; crack, cleft, crevice, fissure. 2 *He'll sue for breach of contract. a breach of the peace:* violation, infringement, infraction, trespass, nonobservance, noncompliance, disregard.

Ant. 1 closure; stoppage. 2 adherence to, observance, compliance with; heed, regard.

breadth *n.* 1 *The breadth of a football field is 160 feet:* width, wideness, broadness, latitude. 2 *a mind of great breadth. The breadth of the mountain range:* broadness, scope, range, reach, compass, span, expanse, extent, extensiveness; size, area.

Ant. 1 length. 2 narrowness, confinement, circumscription.

break *v.* 1 *to break a vase. I broke my leg:* shatter, fragment, burst, crack, fracture, rupture, snap, split, *Slang* bust; smash. 2 Often **break off, break away.** *Break off a piece of licorice for me:* detach, separate, pull off, tear off, sever, disjoint, disconnect. 3 *The TV set is broken:* be inoperative, work improperly; ruin. 4 Usually **break off.** *The union broke off negotiations:* end, stop, cease, halt, suspend, interrupt, discontinue. 5 *Who's going to break the bad news to her?:* disclose, reveal, divulge, announce, proclaim, tell, inform, make public. 6 *When the storm breaks, run for the house:* erupt, burst out; happen, occur. 7 *Mustangs must be broken before they can be ridden. to break the cigarette habit:* tame, train, discipline, control, subdue, overcome. 8 *Paying for the house will break me:* bankrupt, ruin, wipe out, impoverish, make insolvent. 9 *The net broke the acrobat's fall:* take the force of, soften, cushion, lessen. 10 *This winter broke the record for snowfall:* surpass, exceed, better, top, outdo, outstrip, beat, eclipse. 11 *He broke out of jail:* escape, get away from, make a getaway, slip away; flee, run, run away, take flight. 12 *to break a law. to break a promise:* violate, be guilty of infraction of, infringe on, transgress against, disobey; be derelict in, shirk, renege on. —*n.* 13 *Water seeped through the break in the dam:* shattering, breaking, burst, snap, fracturing; breach, opening, rupture, fissure, rent, crack, fracture, gap, rift, split, cleft. 14 *Let's take a short break:* interruption, interlude, recess, interval, in-

termission, hiatus, rest, pause. 15 *The actress's big break came when she substituted for the star:* stroke of luck, opportunity, chance, opening.

Ant. 1 repair, fix; mend, heal. 2 connect, join, fasten, secure, attach. 3 repair, fix. 4 continue, prolong. 5 conceal, hide, secrete. 6 end, stop, cease, halt. 7 submit to, yield to. 12 obey, adhere to, comply with. 13 closing, stopping, blockage. 14 continuation, resumption.

breakable *adj. Those plates are breakable:* fragile, delicate, frail.

Ant. unbreakable.

breakdown *n.* 1 *The train had a breakdown. a nervous breakdown:* failure, collapse; mishap, *Slang* crackup. 2 *Give me a breakdown of what you need:* categorization, detailed list, item-by-item count; analysis.

breakup *n. the breakup of the ice in the spring:* separation, breaking, dispersal, disintegration.

breast *n.* 1 *He beat his breast in agony:* chest, bust, bosom. 2 *My breast was full of pride:* heart, innermost self, core.

breath *n.* 1 *You could see your breath:* exhaled air. 2 *The patient's breath faltered:* breathing, respiration; inhalation, exhalation. 3 *the breath of life:* spirit, vital spirit, vital spark, divine spark; animation, vitalization.

breathe *v.* 1 *Breathe that clear air!:* draw breath, draw in air, inhale and exhale, respire; gasp, pant, puff, huff. 2 *Don't breathe a word of it:* whisper, murmur; utter.

breathtaking *adj. breathtaking feats:* exciting, amazing, astonishing, startling, surprising.

breech *n.* 1 *"Breech" means "backside":* buttocks, rump, seat, behind, posterior, fundament; hindquarters, hind part. 2 **breeches.** *riding breeches:* knee breeches; *(loosely)* trousers, pants.

breed *v.* 1 *Mosquitoes breed in stagnant water:* reproduce, propagate, beget, multiply, procreate, produce offspring; proliferate. 2 *Familiarity breeds contempt:* foster, develop, promote; produce, spawn; give rise to, cause, lead to. —*n.* 3 *a breed of dog:* species, strain, race, stock; variety, type, kind.

Ant. 2 eradicate, erase; stifle, hinder, block; stop, stay.

breeding *n.* 1 *Cattle breeding is a big business. Draining ditches reduces mosquito breeding:* raising, producing, production, growing; reproduction, propagation, procreation, generation, germination. 2 *The horse has good breeding:* lineage, bloodline,

line, heredity, ancestry, parentage, pedigree, family tree, genealogy. 3 *people of good breeding:* manners, refinement, gentility, background, cultivation; upbringing.

breeze n. 1 *a warm breeze:* gentle wind, light wind, current of air, puff of wind, light gust, zephyr, waft. —v. 2 *We breezed through the test:* sweep, sail, flit, pass.

breezy adj. 1 *It's breezy on deck:* windy, windswept, gusty, blustery. 2 *a short breezy talk:* casual, buoyant, lively, animated, vivacious, cheerful, jaunty, brisk, peppy, sprightly, spirited.
Ant. 1 calm. 2 heavy, depressed, dull, sad, lifeless; serious.

brevity n. *Brevity is the soul of wit:* briefness, shortness, conciseness, pithiness, succinctness, terseness.
Ant. long-windedness; lengthiness.

brew v. 1 *Brew the tea. to brew beer:* boil, steep, seethe, cook; ferment, soak. 2 *She's brewing a surprise for your birthday:* concoct, contrive, plot, devise, plan, prepare, foment, *Informal* cook up; originate, initiate, hatch, formulate. —n. 3 *a delicious brew:* beverage, drink, concoction, mixture; *(variously)* beer, ale, stout, porter, malt liquor.

bribe n. 1 *Never accept a bribe:* payoff, hush money, illegal gift, graft. —v. 2 *He tried to bribe the police:* buy off, pay off, *Informal* grease the palm of.

bric-a-brac n. *Their home is filled with bric-a-brac:* baubles, trinkets, ornaments, bibelots, knickknacks, gimcracks, gewgaws, dustcatchers.

bridal adj. *a bridal gown:* bride's; wedding, marriage, matrimonial, nuptial.

bridge n. 1 *a bridge over the highway:* span, overpass; viaduct, catwalk. 2 *a strong bridge of friendship:* bond, tie, connection; association, alliance. —v. 3 *A plank bridged the stream:* span, cross, cross over, traverse, extend across, reach across.
Ant. 2 schism, split, break. 3 separate, divide, split.

bridle n. 1 *Grab the horse by the bridle:* head harness; *(loosely)* bit and brace, restraint, muzzle, check, curb. —v. 2 *Bridle the horses:* put on the head harness; harness. 3 *You must bridle your temper:* curb, check, restrain, control, suppress, repress, constrain, inhibit, arrest; muzzle, gag.
Ant. 2 unbridle, unharness. 3 voice, vent, let out, free.

brief adj. 1 *a brief stop:* short, short-lived, momentary, quick, hasty, fleeting, transient. 2 *a brief talk:* short, concise, succinct, terse, compact; abbreviated, condensed, abridged, compressed, limited, shortened,

curtailed. —v. 3 *The secretary of defense briefed the President:* inform, fill in on, give the details of, describe to, prepare. —n. 4 *The law journal printed the brief of the case:* legal summary; *(loosely)* argument, contention, case; précis, abstract, abridgment.
Ant. 1, 2 long, lengthy, extended, prolonged.

brigade n. 1 *an army brigade: (technically, two or more)* regiments, battalions, army groups, squadrons; *(loosely)* military unit, unit, legion, contingent, body of troops. 2 *a volunteer fire brigade:* company, corps, unit, force, squad, contingent.

brigand n. *Brigands held up stagecoaches:* outlaw, bandit, desperado, ruffian, cutthroat; *(variously)* highwayman, robber.

bright adj. 1 *bright lights. bright colors:* brilliant, blazing, dazzling, vivid, intense; gleaming, beaming, glittering, resplendent; illuminated, light-filled. 2 *a bright idea:* intelligent, smart, brainy, brilliant; shrewd, keen, clever, inventive, resourceful, ingenious, perceptive, discerning, acute, astute. 3 *the children's bright laughter:* merry, blithe, happy, joyous, joyful, cheerful; jolly, lively, exhilarating. 4 *a bright future:* promising, favorable, auspicious, propitious, hopeful, optimistic, rosy; successful, prosperous, happy, healthy; excellent, good.
Ant. dull. 1 dim, subdued, dark, drab, gloomy. 2 dumb, stupid, witless, simpleminded, foolish, rattlebrained, featherbrained, idiotic, asinine; thick, slow. 3 sad, glum, dreary, joyless, gloomy, forlorn, unhappy, cheerless, depressed, doleful, melancholy, downhearted. 4 unpromising, inauspicious, hopeless, pessimistic, grim.

brighten v. 1 *Brighten the kitchen by painting it yellow:* make brighter, lighten, enliven, perk up. 2 *Your visit brightened my day:* gladden, cheer, make happy, perk up, buoy up, enliven.
Ant. 1 darken, dull. 2 sadden, depress.

brilliance, brilliancy n. 1 *a diamond's pure white brilliance:* brightness, radiance, sparkle, glitter, luster, gleam, glow, shine, sheen, shimmer; resplendence, splendor; intensity, vividness. 2 *the brilliance of an Einstein:* intelligence, smartness, braininess, wisdom, sagacity, keenness; cleverness, inventiveness, ingenuity; perception, discernment, awareness, quickness, sharpness, acuity; genius, talent, gift; competence, masterfulness, excellence; greatness, illustriousness, grandeur, distinction.
Ant. 1 dullness, darkness, drabness. 2 stupidity, dumbness, idiocy, asininity, simple-mindedness, doltishness, oafish-

ness, folly, silliness; inanity, ineptitude, incompetence, mediocrity.

brilliant *adj.* 1 *brilliant jewels:* See BRIGHT, def. 1. 2 *a brilliant mind:* See BRIGHT, def. 2.

brim *n.* 1 *Fill the cup to the brim:* upper edge, brink, rim, border, margin, verge. —*v.* 2 *Her eyes brimmed with tears:* fill, fill up, well up, overflow.

brine *n. To make dill pickles, soak cucumbers in brine:* salt water, salt solution, saline solution, pickling solution; the sea, sea water.

bring *v.* 1 *Bring the dessert to the table:* carry, convey, bear, fetch, deliver, transport, take; accompany. 2 *April showers bring May flowers. The district attorney will bring charges:* bring about, induce, effect, institute, begin, start, initiate, usher in, result in. 3 *I can't bring myself to apologize:* compel, force, make, persuade.
Ant. 1 take away, send. 2 quash, prevent, suppress, squelch, nullify, abolish, void, revoke.

brink *n. the brink of the cliff:* edge, margin, rim, brim, verge, border; shore, bank; threshold.

brisk *adj.* 1 *a brisk pace:* quick, swift, lively, active, sprightly, spry, energetic, vigorous, snappy, peppy, alert, animated. 2 *a brisk fall day:* bracing, invigorating, refreshing, fresh, stimulating, stirring, rousing, exhilarating.
Ant. 1 sluggish, lethargic, unenergetic. 2 tiring, exhausting, fatiguing, wearisome.

brittle *adj. This chalk is too brittle:* breakable, fragile, frangible, crumbly, friable.

broach *v. We've never broached the subject of marriage:* mention, suggest, introduce, bring up, touch on, advance; institute.
Ant. repress, suppress, secrete; close, end.

broad *adj.* 1 *broad shoulders:* wide; outspread. 2 *the broad plains of the West:* expansive, extensive, extended, spacious, immense, large. 3 *a broad knowledge:* extensive, comprehensive, sweeping, general, far-reaching, wide, wide-ranging; nonspecific, undetailed. 4 *a broad hint. in broad daylight:* full, plain, open, clear, obvious.
Ant. narrow. 2, 3 limited, confined, circumscribed, restricted, small. 3 specific, detailed. 4 veiled, obscure, enigmatical.

broadcast *v.* 1 *The World Series is broadcast all over the world:* transmit, send out, beam, radio, televise, cable; distribute, spread. —*n.* 2 *The special broadcast will be on tonight:* program, show; announcement, statement.

broaden *v. The road was broadened into a highway. The company broadened its line by adding new items:* widen, enlarge, expand,

extend; increase, boost, build up, augment, develop.
Ant. narrow, contract, decrease; reduce.

broad-minded *adj. a flexible and broad-minded individual:* open-minded, tolerant, unprejudiced, unbiased, unbigoted, undogmatic, liberal, unprovincial, receptive.
Ant. narrow-minded, closed-minded, intolerant, biased, inflexible, dogmatic, provincial.

brochure *n. an advertising brochure:* pamphlet, leaflet, circular, flier, throwaway, booklet.

broil *v.* 1 *Don't fry the steaks; broil them:* cook by direct heat. 2 *This sun will broil you:* make very hot, burn, scorch, sear, cook, blister, bake, roast, fry.

broke *adj. The company went broke:* without funds, bankrupt, penniless, insolvent, wiped out, impoverished.
Ant. wealthy, rich, prosperous, solvent.

broken-hearted *adj. Both were broken-hearted when they split up:* heartbroken, sad, mournful, forlorn, dejected, depressed, despairing, disconsolate.
Ant. elated, light-hearted, merry, jolly.

bronze *adj. skin bronzed from the sun:* reddish-brown, copper-colored, chestnut, reddish-tan, tan, brownish.

brooch *n. The dress had a brooch on the lapel:* pin, clasp.

brood *n.* 1 *The hen guarded her brood:* hatchlings, chicks, young, offspring, litter, children. —*v.* 2 *The hen is brooding her eggs:* sit upon, incubate, hatch, cover. 3 *Don't brood over lost opportunities:* worry, fret, agonize, mope; dwell, mull.

brook[1] *n. There are trout in this brook:* stream, streamlet, creek, rivulet, rill, run.

brook[2] *v. I will not brook insolence!:* take, stand, abide, allow, accept, tolerate, bear, put up with, endure.
Ant. forbear, forbid, prohibit, disallow, rebuff, renounce.

broth *n. a cup of beef broth:* stock, clear soup, bouillon, consommé.

brothel *n. New Orleans was once notorious for its brothels:* whorehouse, house of prostitution, sporting house, bawdy house, house of ill repute, house of ill fame, house, bordello.

brother *n.* 1 *a sister and brother:* male sibling, blood brother. 2 *We are all brothers under the skin. brothers in arms:* fellow member, kinsman, peer; fellowman; comrade, companion; colleague. 3 *Trappist brothers:* monk, friar, monastic.
Ant. 1 sister, female sibling.

brow *n.* 1 *She wiped the sweat from her brow:*

forehead. 2 *the brow of a cliff:* edge, brink, brim, rim, periphery, verge, margin.

browbeat *v. The lawyer browbeat the witness:* bully, intimidate, cow, tyrannize; badger, harass, hector; terrorize.
Ant. coax, persuade, flatter, charm.

brown *adj. pot roast with brown gravy:* brownish, brunet, brunette, chocolate, cocoa, coffee, mahogany, walnut, nut brown, drab, khaki, chestnut, tawny, sorrel, hazel, bay, reddish-brown, terra-cotta, rust, russet, roan, bronze, buff, golden-brown, copper, auburn, light brown, dun, sand-colored, cinnamon, tan, fawn, beige.

browse *v.* 1 *Cows were browsing in the field:* graze, pasture, feed. 2 *I just browsed through the paper:* peruse, look through, look over, glance through, examine cursorily, skim, scan.

bruise *v.* 1 *I was cut and bruised. Don't bruise the tomatoes:* discolor, mark, mar, blemish; injure, wound, hurt, damage. 2 *The insult bruised her feelings:* offend, wound, hurt. —*n.* 3 *The blow caused a large bruise:* contusion, black mark, discoloration, blemish; injury, wound.

brunet, brunette *adj. She prefers brunet men:* dark-haired, brown-haired; brown-haired and brown-eyed, dark, olive-skinned.
Ant. blond, blonde, light-haired, light-skinned.

brunt *n. The Florida Keys bore the brunt of the hurricane:* full force, force, impact, thrust, main shock.

brush[1] *n.* 1 *Use this brush to paint your room:* bristled tool; *(variously)* paintbrush, whisk, clothes brush, hairbrush, nailbrush, scrub brush, toothbrush, shoe brush. 2 *She removed the dust with a brush of her hand:* brushing, sweep, whisk, flick, dusting; stroke. 3 *a brush with the law:* encounter, confrontation, skirmish, engagement, run-in. —*v.* 4 *Brush your teeth:* use a brush on; *(variously)* wash, clean, cleanse, scrub, groom, paint, shine. 5 *He brushed the papers aside. The spider web brushed my forehead:* sweep, whisk, flick; graze, touch, stroke, caress.

brush[2] *n. The rabbit disappeared into the brush:* underbrush, brushwood, undergrowth, bush, bushes, thicket, bracken, fern, copse, scrub, woodland, woodlands, bush country.

brush-off *n. He gave me the brush-off:* rejection, cold shoulder, rebuff, snub; cut.

brusque *adj. Being busy is no excuse for being brusque:* abrupt, curt, short, gruff; blunt, bluff, rude, impolite, ungracious, unceremonious.

Ant. civil, considerate, patient, courteous, gracious, cordial.

brutal *adj. a brutal pirate. a brutal crime:* cruel, vicious, savage, inhuman, barbaric, barbarous, ruthless, hardhearted, heartless, pitiless, merciless, bloody, brutish, bloodthirsty, atrocious, hellish.
Ant. humane, gentle, kind, softhearted, merciful, sympathetic, noble, refined.

brutality *n. extreme brutality toward prisoners:* cruelty, viciousness, savagery, savageness, ruthlessness, barbarity, brutishness.
Ant. humaneness, gentleness.

brute *n.* 1 *Hunger can turn people into brutes:* savage, barbarian, monster, swine. 2 *the difference between angels and brutes:* beast, wild animal, animal, dumb creature, beast of the field.
Ant. 1 angel.

bubble *n.* 1 *A bubble of paint ruined the smooth wall:* globule, droplet, blister, bleb. 2 **bubbles.** foam, froth, fizz, effervescence. —*v.* 3 *The water began to bubble:* boil, percolate, seethe; foam, froth, fizz, effervesce, gurgle, burble.

buccaneer *n. Buccaneers attacked treasure galleons:* pirate, privateer, freebooter, corsair.

bucket *n. The bucket leaks:* pail, tub, container, pitcher, vessel; bucketful, pailful.

buckle *n.* 1 *a belt with a silver buckle:* clasp, hasp, fastener. —*v.* 2 *Buckle the strap tighter:* clasp, fasten, secure, hook. 3 *The walls of the building buckled:* bend, belly out, bulge, warp, curl; collapse, cave in, crumple.
Ant. 2 unbuckle, unfasten, uncouple. 3 straighten.

bud *n.* 1 *the plant's first buds:* unopened flower; sprout. —*v.* 2 *The rosebushes are budding:* put forth shoots, sprout, open; begin to grow, begin to bloom, blossom, flower, develop.

buddy *n. He talked to some of his buddies:* friend, pal, *Brit.* mate, chum, comrade, companion, crony, fellow, intimate.
Ant. foe, enemy, adversary.

budge *v.* 1 *We couldn't budge the heavy rock:* stir, move, shift, dislodge, dislocate, push, slide, roll. 2 *Once she had made a decision, no one could budge her:* move, change, influence, persuade, sway, convince.
Ant. 1 stick, remain, stay.

budget *n.* 1 *the federal budget. the household budget:* financial plan, spending plan, financial statement; allowance, allotment, allocation, funds, moneys, means. —*v.* 2 *Smart people budget their income:* allocate, schedule, apportion, portion out, ration.

buff *n.* 1 *a jacket made of buff:* leather, buffalo hide. 2 *The children swam in the buff:*

nakedness, bare skin, *Informal* the raw. **3** *the buff that came with the bottle of shoe polish:* polisher; swab, dauber. **4** *an opera buff:* devotee, fan, enthusiast, connoisseur, mavin, *Slang* nut, freak. —*adj.* **5** *buff-colored hair:* yellowish-brown, tan, tawny; sandy, yellowish. —*v.* **6** *She buffed the wood until it shone:* polish, rub, burnish, smooth.

buffet *v. The boxer buffeted his opponent:* hit, strike, beat, wallop, cuff, slap, knock, baste, pound, thump, rap, thwack, pummel.

buffoon *n. the class buffoon:* clown, jester, joker, prankster, funnyman, zany, comedian, comic, wag; fool, harlequin, Punchinello.

bug *n.* **1** *The campers were plagued by bugs:* insect, *(in technical use)* Hemiptera, Heteroptera. **2** *the flu bug:* virus, germ. **3** *The plan contained too many bugs to be effective:* defect, flaw, fault. —*v.* **4** *Stop bugging me!:* bother, annoy, pester, nag, badger.

build *v.* **1** *The school is building a new gym. This factory builds cars:* construct, erect, make, put up, set up, put together, fabricate, fashion, manufacture, produce. **2** *My partner built this business. You must build up your strength:* increase, enlarge, develop, raise, improve; intensify, amplify, strengthen; establish, found, originate, launch, institute, begin, start. **3** *The army tries to build men and women:* form, shape, mold, create. —*n.* **4** *Your build is too small for football:* physique, form, figure, body, shape.
Ant. 1–3 demolish, tear down, dismantle, destroy. **2** decrease, diminish, reduce, lessen, lower, shrink; weaken, deplete, sap; cripple, injure; end, stop, finish, wind up, close, discontinue.

building *n. This building was a store:* structure, edifice.

bulge *n.* **1** *What's that bulge in the bag?:* lump, bump, protuberance, protrusion, projection, prominence, curve. —*v.* **2** *The Christmas stocking bulged with goodies:* swell, swell out, puff out, protrude, distend; stand out, stick out; bag, sag.
Ant. 1 hollow, cavity. 2 cave in, collapse.

bulk *n.* **1** *the sheer bulk of an elephant:* mass, massiveness, largeness, bigness, amplitude, magnitude, size, volume, weight, extent, quantity, hugeness. **2** *He left the bulk of his estate to his wife:* main part, major part, greater part, principal part, better part, lion's share, body, most, majority, preponderance, plurality.

bulky *adj. The package is too bulky to carry:* cumbersome, unwieldy, unhandy, un-

gainly, unmanageable, lumpish; large, big, huge, massive, immense.
Ant. handy, manageable, wieldy; small, little.

bull *n. The elephant herd contained three bulls:* male; *(variously)* male bovine, ox, male elephant, male whale, male seal, male elk, male moose.

bulldoze *v.* **1** *to bulldoze a path through the forest:* drive, thrust, push, force, shove; fell, level, flatten. **2** *We bulldozed the committee into agreeing with us:* browbeat, intimidate, cow, bully, hector, coerce.

bulletin *n. a news bulletin:* brief announcement, report, dispatch, communication, notification, note.

bully *n.* **1** *The bully terrorized the children:* tormentor, intimidator, browbeater, petty tyrant, despot, oppressor, tough. —*v.* **2** *He loved to bully his younger brother:* intimidate, browbeat, tyrannize, domineer, frighten, coerce.
Ant. 2 flatter, coax, cajole.

bulwark *n.* **1** *A bulwark surrounded the fort:* defensive wall, earthwork, embankment, rampart, parapet; barrier, guard. **2** *The town meeting was the bulwark of New England democracy:* support; mainstay; foundation; strength.

bum *n.* **1** *The bum begged from passersby:* tramp, hobo, derelict, vagrant, vagabond; loafer, idler, drifter. —*v.* **2** *Stop bumming cigarettes from me!:* beg, borrow, cadge, mooch, sponge.

bump *v.* **1** *The child bumped her head. The two cars bumped together:* hit, strike, knock, slam, bang, smack, rap; collide, crash into, smash into, run into. **2** *The old truck bumped along the road:* bounce, jolt, jounce, jostle. —*n.* **3** *a headache caused by a bump on the head:* blow, rap, knock, hit, whack, wallop, bang, crack; collision. **4** *His legs were covered with bumps. a bump in the road:* lump, swelling, node; hump, knob, protuberance, bulge, excrescence, gnarl, knot, nodule.
Ant. 2 glide, sail, flow, slide, slip.

bumptious *adj. a bumptious young man:* overbearing, aggressive, pushy, self-assertive, impudent, insolent, cocky, cocksure, overconfident, impertinent, brazen, forward, presumptuous, arrogant, haughty, conceited, swaggering, boastful.
Ant. shy, retiring, self-effacing, demure, timid, modest, bashful.

bun *n.* **1** *cinnamon buns:* roll, soft roll, sweet roll. **2** *She wore her hair in a bun:* coil, knot.

bunch *n.* **1** *a bunch of grapes. a bunch of newspapers:* cluster, clump; bundle, batch, collection, assortment, accumulation, heap, pile. **2** *a bunch of children:* group, band, flock, troop, pack, company, gang, gathering; assembly. —*v.* **3** *We bunched around the fire:* huddle, crowd, gather, cluster, group, mass, collect, draw together, congregate, pack.

bundle *n.* **1** *a shopper loaded down with bundles. A bundle of books was donated to the library:* package, parcel, packet; bale, sheaf, pack; heap, pile, bunch, batch, collection, assortment, accumulation, multitude; group, lot, quantity. —*v.* **2** *Newspapers were bundled on the truck:* tie together, wrap, bind, truss.

bungle *v.* *He bungled the job. I bungled in thinking $100 would be enough:* blunder, botch, mismanage, do badly, spoil, ruin, butcher, mess up, make a mess of; miscalculate, misreckon, misestimate, miscompute, misjudge.

bunk[1] *n.* *Passengers sleep in bunks:* berth, built-in bed, platform bed; bed, pallet, cot.

bunk[2] *n.* *His claim is a lot of bunk:* poppycock, baloney, hokum, tommyrot, rot, hogwash, claptrap, humbug, hooey, malarky, hot air, stuff and nonsense, bunkum, balderdash, blather; nonsense, bombast.

buoy *n.* **1** *The Coast Guard replaced the buoy in the channel:* floating marker, bellbuoy, float, beacon, bell. —*v.* **2** *A good joke will buoy our spirits:* lift, uplift, raise, boost, elevate; lighten, cheer, cheer up, gladden, brighten.
Ant. **2** lower, dash, depress, dull, darken, dampen.

buoyancy *n.* **1** *Life preservers have a great deal of buoyancy:* floatability; lightness, weightlessness. **2** *Her buoyancy made us all feel better:* good spirits, animation, vivacity, enthusiasm, good humor, cheerfulness, cheeriness, joyousness, sunniness, gaiety, lightheartedness.
Ant. **2** depression, dejection, low spirits, cheerlessness, gloominess, melancholy; lethargy.

buoyant *adj.* **1** *Holding your breath will keep you buoyant in the water:* afloat, floating, floatable; light, weightless. **2** *a buoyant personality:* animated, vivacious, enthusiastic, cheerful, happy, joyful, joyous, sunny, lighthearted; optimistic, hopeful, carefree; energetic, peppy, lively, sprightly.
Ant. **2** gloomy, glum, dour, sullen, sad, joyless, cheerless; depressed, dejected, morose, doleful, melancholy, despondent; pessimistic; forlorn, hopeless, despairing; lethargic.

burden *n.* **1** *a burden of several hundred pounds:* load, weight; cargo, freight, pack. **2** *the burden of raising two children alone:*

weight, load, strain, stress, care, responsibility, trouble, anxiety; hardship. —*v.* **3** *burdened with a heavy pack. I was burdened with someone else's problems:* weigh down, load with, load, overload; make responsible for, obligate, saddle with, trouble, encumber, tax; vex, afflict, handicap, oppress, hamper.
Ant. **2** freedom, ease. **3** lighten, free.

bureau *n.* **1** *Put the shirts in the bureau:* chest of drawers, dresser, chiffonier. **2** *the Weather Bureau:* agency, department, office, division, branch, service.

bureaucrat *n.* *the bureaucrats at City Hall:* civil servant, public servant, functionary, *Russian* apparatchik.

burgeon *v.* *The business is burgeoning. Spring has begun to burgeon:* thrive, flourish, expand, enlarge, grow, develop, wax, increase, proliferate; bloom, blossom, flower.

burglar *n.* *The burglar robbed eight houses:* housebreaker, prowler, robber, thief; second-story man.

burglary *n.* *The burglary took place at night:* breaking and entering, break-in, theft, robbery, housebreaking, burglarizing; stealing, larceny.

burial *n.* *The burial was held at a nonsectarian cemetery:* inhumation, interment, funeral.
Ant. exhumation, disinterment.

burlesque *n.* *a burlesque on absent-minded professors:* satire, parody, farce, takeoff, spoof, caricature, travesty.

burly *adj.* *a burly man:* strapping, hefty, brawny, beefy, stocky, thickset, big, large, strong.
Ant. puny, skinny, scrawny, gaunt.

burn *v.* **1** *The building burned to the ground:* be on fire, blaze, be ablaze, flame, be in flames, smoke, smolder; glow. **2** *Rake up the leaves and burn them:* ignite, kindle, fire; set on fire, set fire to, incinerate, consume with flames, reduce to ashes; char, scorch, sear, scald, singe. **3** *This car burns too much gas:* use as fuel, consume. **4** *The child burned with fever:* be hot, swelter, be flushed. **5** *The cut burns from the iodine. Holding the rope burned my hands:* pain, hurt, smart, sting; chafe, abrade, blister. **6** *I burn too easily to stay on the beach for long:* sunburn, tan, suntan. —*n.* **7** *The fire fighter suffered severe burns. The burn of the antiseptic made him wince. a rope burn:* (variously) first-degree burn, reddening, second-degree burn, blistering, blister, third-degree burn, charring; smart, sting, pain; abrasion, chafe, scrape, irritation.

8 *I smell the burn of rubber:* incineration, burning, fire, flames, smoke, smoldering, kindling.

Ant. 1, 2 extinguish, put out, go out, burn out. 4 be cold, shiver, chill. 5 assuage, soothe.

burning *adj.* 1 *a burning building:* flaming, aflame, afire, blazing, fiery, ignited, kindled, smoldering, smoking. 2 *a burning desire:* all-consuming, fervent, fervid, passionate, impassioned, ardent, eager, zealous, intense, heated. 3 *The hot mustard left a burning sensation on his tongue:* stinging, smarting, piercing, irritating, tingling; painful, caustic, biting, sharp, astringent, acrid.

Ant. 2 half-hearted, indifferent, lukewarm, mild, perfunctory, faint. 3 soothing, cooling.

burnish *v. The silver was burnished to a bright finish:* polish, wax, buff, shine, rub up.

Ant. abrade, scratch.

burrow *n.* 1 *the rabbit's burrow:* hole, furrow, dugout, den, lair. —*v.* 2 *The rabbit burrowed into the ground:* dig, tunnel, excavate, scoop out, hollow out.

bursar *n. Tuition checks are made out to the bursar:* treasurer, purser, cashier, cash keeper, paymaster.

burst *v.* 1 *The balloon burst. This dress is so tight the seams are bursting:* break, break open, shatter, fly apart, fragment; explode, blow up, rupture; pull apart, tear apart; sunder, rend. 2 *to burst into tears. He burst into the room:* erupt, break, break out, gush forth; rush, run, barge. —*n.* 3 *the burst of guns in the distance:* explosion, detonation, discharge, bang; breaking, shattering. 4 *a great burst of speed:* outburst, outpouring, eruption, torrent.

Ant. 1 put together, hold together, connect, join, unite, attach. 4 cessation, stopping.

bury *v.* 1 *a hero buried in Arlington Cemetery:* inter, entomb, inhume. 2 *The letter was buried under a pile of papers:* hide, conceal, cover, cover up; immerse, engulf.

Ant. 1 exhume, disinter. 2 unearth, discover, bring to light, reveal.

bush *n.* 1 *neatly trimmed bushes:* plant, shrub, shrubbery, hedge. 2 *The safari headed into the bush:* woods, woodlands, veld, barrens, forest, jungle, brush.

business *n.* 1 *What business are you in?:* job, profession, vocation, occupation, career, calling, pursuit; work, employment, line, field, activity, specialty; position, place, assignment, walk of life. 2 *a keen understanding of business:* commerce, industry, trade, merchandising; transaction. 3 *My father owns a small business:* firm, establish-

ment, concern; store, shop, factory, office; enterprise, venture, undertaking; corporation, company, partnership. 4 *Let's get down to business:* concern, affair, problem, question; matter, job, task, chore, situation, subject.

Ant. 1 avocation, hobby, entertainment.

businesslike *adj. to conduct a meeting in a businesslike manner:* orderly, organized, systematic, methodical, efficient, professional, correct; serious, careful, thorough, diligent.

Ant. disorderly, disorganized, unorganized, unsystematic, irregular; frivolous; inefficient, unprofessional, sloppy, slipshod.

bust *n. The sweater had a blue stripe across the bust:* bosom, breast, chest.

bustle *v.* 1 *The clerk bustled about:* scurry, hurry, rush, scamper, dash; flit, scuttle, flutter, fluster; stir, bestir, be active, —*n.* 2 *the bustle of the city:* commotion, flurry, tumult, hustle, hurly-burly, activity, hurry.

Ant. 1 move slowly, crawl, creep, procrastinate; loaf, relax, rest. 2 quiet, peacefulness, tranquillity.

busy *adj.* 1 *The secretary was busy all day:* occupied, active, engaged, employed, working, hard at work; laboring, toiling. 2 *This is one of my busy days:* active, strenuous, full.

Ant. 1, 2 idle, inactive, at leisure. 2 lazy, sluggish, slack.

busybody *n. That busybody wants to know everyone's business:* meddler, snoop, pry; gossip, scandalmonger, telltale, tattletale, blabbermouth, blabber.

butcher *v.* 1 *The barbarians butchered many of the villagers:* massacre, murder, kill, slaughter. 2 *The band butchered the march:* botch, ruin, mess up, bungle, goof, muff. —*n.* 3 *the Butcher of Buchenwald:* killer, murderer, mass-murderer, slaughterer, homicidal maniac.

butt¹ *n. Pork butt makes a good roast:* end, blunt end, bottom, shank; stub, stump.

Ant. front, top.

butt² *n. the butt of a joke:* target, victim, object, laughingstock, *Slang* goat.

butt³ *v. The rams butted each other: (with the head or horns)* push, shove, bump, knock, hit, strike, ram, thrust.

buttocks *n. The pants are tight across the buttocks:* posterior, rump, seat, rear, rear end, backside, bottom, derrière, *Informal* fanny, *Slang* behind, butt; fundament.

buttress *n.* 1 *The wall of the cathedral had a stone buttress:* support, brace, prop, stanchion. —*v.* 2 *You'd better buttress your ar-*

gument with more facts: prop up, brace, shore, shore up; reinforce, strengthen, bolster.

buxom *adj. Is she thin or buxom?:* (of *women*) plump, robust, well-developed, chesty, large-breasted, bosomy, voluptuous, *Yiddish* zaftig.
Ant. delicate, thin, slender, skinny.

buy *v.* 1 *to buy a new car:* purchase, pay for, invest in; acquire, procure, obtain, get. 2 *Honest politicians cannot be bought:* bribe, buy off, corrupt.
Ant. 1 sell; rent, lease.

buzz *n.* 1 *The audience made such a buzz, I couldn't hear the play:* murmur, whisper; buzzing, hum, humming sound. —*v.* 2 *Insects buzzed around the flowers:* hum, drone, whir.

bygone *adj. bygone days:* gone by, past, earlier, previous, former, of yore, olden.
Ant. future, coming.

bypass *v. Route 80 bypasses Cleveland:* go around, go by, circumvent, detour around; avert.
Ant. go through, bisect, cross.

bypath *n. We took the bypath through the woods:* lane, trail, dirt road, byway, footway, footpath, shortcut.

bystander *n. an innocent bystander:* onlooker, looker-on, spectator, witness; passerby.
Ant. participant, principal.

byword *n. "Haste makes waste" is my byword:* rule, dictum, principle, precept, truth; pet phrase, slogan, motto, maxim, axiom, watchword, catchword.

C

cab *n. hail a cab:* taxi, taxicab, hack.

cabal *n.* 1 *The government was toppled by a cabal:* junta, combination, band, ring, league. 2 *an anti-government cabal:* intrigue, conspiracy, plot, scheme, connivance.

cabalistic *adj. cabalistic interpretations of the Scriptures:* obscure, occult, mysterious, supernatural, abstruse, esoteric, arcane, secret, mystic; impenetrable, unknowable.
Ant. obvious, apparent, evident.

cabaret *n. Cabarets are full on New Year's Eve:* supper club, nightclub, bistro, café, *Informal* club.

cabin *n.* 1 *a cabin by the lake:* log cabin, hut, shack, shanty, hutch; lodge, cottage: 2 *the captain's cabin:* stateroom, quarters, room; compartment.
Ant. 1 mansion, palace, castle.

cabinet *n.* 1 *the president's cabinet:* council, group of counselors, official advisers, advisory board. 2 *Put the dishes in the cabinet:* cupboard, kitchen cabinet, china closet, china cabinet, breakfront, bureau; case, chest, chest of drawers, file.

cable *n.* 1 *the telephone cables beneath the streets. The tarpaulin was held in place by cables:* bundle of wires, electric wire, wires, wire line, line, wire rope; rope, cord, twisted strand; chain, mooring, hawser. 2 *Send a cable to our overseas office:* cablegram, overseas telegram, wire.

cache *n.* 1 *a cache of firearms:* store, stockpile, stock, secret repository, hoard. 2 *Pirates buried gold in a cache near here:* hiding place, hideaway, secret place.

cacophonous *adj. cacophonous sounds:* dissonant, inharmonious, discordant, unmusical, unmelodious; strident, jarring, disharmonious, nonmelodious.

cad *n. Only a cad would strike a woman:* dishonorable man, bounder, rotter, lout, churl, dastard, cur, heel, rat; villain, scoundrel, rascal, knave, rogue, caitiff.
Ant. gentleman, hero.

cadaver *n. The cadaver was taken to the morgue:* corpse, dead body, body, remains, deceased, *Slang* stiff.

cadaverous *adj. a cadaverous appearance:* corpselike, deathlike, deathly; ghastly, gaunt, pale, ashen, chalky, pallid.

cadence *n. The soldiers marched to the cadence of the drum:* rhythmic pattern, beat, tempo; swing, lilt, throb, pulse; accent, measure, meter.

café *n. a little sidewalk café:* restaurant, bistro, coffeehouse, tavern, bar and grill, cafeteria, diner, lunchroom; *Slang* eatery, beanery; nightclub, supper club, discotheque, cabaret; *Slang* nitery.

cage *n.* 1 *the lion in its cage:* barred enclosure, enclosure; pen, coop. —*v.* 2 *In modern zoos animals are not caged:* lock up, shut in, pen, pen in, coop up.

cagey adj. The cagey fox avoided the hunter's traps: wary, cautious, chary, careful, alert, watchful, heedful; wily, cunning, crafty, shifty, sly, foxy, shrewd.
  Ant. unwary, careless, heedless, unthinking, unguarded.

cajolery n. The mother used cajolery to get the child to eat spinach: wheedling, coaxing, inveigling, beguilement, Informal sweet talk, Slang soft soap; flattery, blandishment.
  Ant. threats, extortion, coercion, force.

cake n. 1 The cake had chocolate icing: (variously) layer cake, loaf cake, cupcake, gateau; (loosely) pastry, sweet rolls, buns, tortes, éclairs. 2 a cake of soap: block, bar; lump. —v. 3 The mud caked on the car: harden, solidify, coagulate, congeal, crust; compress.

calamitous adj. A drought would be calamitous: disastrous, catastrophic, ruinous, destructive, harmful; tragic, woeful, baleful.
  Ant. beneficial, advantageous, helpful, valuable.

calamity n. The flood was a calamity: disaster, catastrophe, tragedy, affliction, misfortune, downfall, blow, scourge; ill fortune, bad luck; misery, trouble, woe.
  Ant. benefit, blessing, help, boon, good fortune, good luck.

calculate v. 1 Did you calculate the tax?: compute, figure, reckon, determine; count, sum up, add up. 2 I calculate we'll be in San Diego in six hours: judge, estimate, figure, reckon, surmise. 3 The speech was calculated to ease world tensions: design, intend, plan, mean.

calculating adj. a cold, calculating man: scheming, designing, plotting, contriving; crafty, manipulative, cunning; shrewd, sly.
  Ant. open, candid, frank, direct, plain-spoken, sincere; naïve, artless, guileless, ingenuous, undesigning.

calculation n. 1 The scientist's calculations proved right: computation, figuring, reckoning. 2 By my calculations, we'll win the game by one point: estimation, reckoning.

calendar n. Write the appointment on your calendar: chart of days, weeks, and months; agenda, day book, diary, schedule, list, register, docket.

caliber n. 1 the caliber of a gun: bore, inside diameter. 2 character of the highest caliber: worth, merit, excellence, quality, competence; stature, reputation, repute, importance, prominence, distinction, estimation.

call v. 1 Did you hear someone call?: call out, cry out, cry, shout, yell, holler, hail, halloo. 2 Call the children in for supper. Call a meeting of the club: summon, ask, direct, in-

struct, charge; call together, convene, assemble, convoke. 3 The hospital calls on everyone for support: appeal to, ask, call upon, bid, request, petition, invoke, supplicate. 4 Friends came to call: visit, pay a visit, look in on, drop in, stop off, stop by. 5 The union called a strike: proclaim, declare, command. 6 The publisher decided to call the book The Golden Flower. The play was called a masterpiece: name, dub, christen, title, entitle, designate, style, label, characterize, describe as, know as, specify. 7 Call me tonight: telephone, phone, Informal buzz, ring. —n. 8 Did you hear a call?: outcry, crying out, cry, shout, yell; hail, halloo. 9 a call to arms: summons, order, command, demand, charge; bid, proclamation, declaration. 10 Let's make a call on the Johnsons: visit, stop. 11 The secretary took all calls: telephone call, phone call, telephone message. 12 You had no call to do that: right, need, cause, reason, grounds, justification, excuse.
  Ant. 1 be silent, be quiet; whisper, murmur. 2 excuse, dismiss. 5 call off, cancel.

calling n. 1 We could hear him calling to us: calling out, crying out, outcry, shouting, yelling, screaming, bellowing, hailing, hallooing. 2 Math is her calling: main interest, mission, first love, dedication, passion, enthusiasm, forte, specialty, métier; life's work, profession, vocation, line, field.
  Ant. 1 whispering, murmuring. 2 bane, nuisance, curse, aversion, anathema.

callous adj. 1 The farmer's hands were callous: callused, hard, hardened, tough, thick-skinned. 2 callous to the suffering of others: unfeeling, insensitive, hardened, inured, apathetic, dispassionate, unresponsive, indifferent.
  Ant. 1 tender, soft, thin-skinned. 2 sympathetic, sensitive, soft-hearted, caring, responsive.

callow adj. a callow youth: immature, inexperienced, unseasoned, untried, green, raw, uninitiated, uninformed, shallow, unsophisticated; crude.
  Ant. mature, grown-up, adult, experienced; sophisticated, polished.

calm adj. 1 The sea was calm: motionless, smooth, quiet, still, unruffled, undisturbed, placid, serene. 2 The defendant remained calm: unperturbed, unshaken, unruffled, unexcited, composed, self-possessed, unagitated, cool, cool-headed; passionless, imperturbable, untroubled, serene, peaceful. —n. 3 peace and calm. Her calm is amazing: calmness, quiet, quietness, tranquillity, serenity, stillness, smoothness; windlessness, stormlessness; composure, self-control, placidity, self-possession, imperturbability, *Slang* cool. —*v.* 4 *Calm yourself:* calm down, compose, collect, pacify, cool off, *Slang* simmer down. 5 *This ointment will calm the pain:* allay, assuage, soothe, quell, mollify, mitigate, relieve, alleviate, moderate, subdue, cause to subside, ease, lessen, diminish, reduce.

Ant. 1, 2 agitated, disturbed, ruffled, raging, fierce, wild. 1 turbulent, rough. 2 excited, aroused, passionate; perturbed, worried, upset, uncollected, discomposed, shaken, frantic, frenzied. 3 disturbance, agitation, violence, fierceness. 4 excite, agitate, disturb, arouse, work up. 5 irritate, aggravate, inflame.

calumny *n. The calumnies in his speech were aimed at his opponent:* slander, libel, defamation, vilification, depreciation, deprecation, disparagement, derogation, animadversion, revilement, denigration; slur, smear.

Ant. praise, acclaim, kudos.

camaraderie *n. the easy camaraderie of college days:* conviviality, good-fellowship, sociability, friendliness, affability, companionship, congeniality, comradeship, esprit de corps, bonhomie.

camouflage *n.* 1 *The camouflage prevented enemy planes from seeing them. His friendliness is camouflage to get us off our guard:* deceptive markings, deceptive covering, disguise; mask, masquerade, false appearance, front, cover, screen. —*v.* 2 *A chameleon camouflages itself by changing color:* cover with a disguise, disguise, mask, screen, cloak, conceal, hide, cover up, veil.

Ant. 2 expose, display, exhibit.

camp *n.* 1 *The hikers set up camp for the night. an army camp:* encampment, campground, temporary shelter, tents, tent, bivouac; army base, barracks. —*v.* 2 *Our family camped in Yellowstone Park:* encamp, pitch a tent; bivouac; rough it.

campaign *n.* 1 *The desert campaign was won with tanks:* military operation, operation, offensive, regional battle, battle series, action. 2 *a new sales campaign:* drive, effort, push, endeavor. —*v.* 3 *The President is campaigning for reelection:* electioneer, solicit votes, compete for office, run.

canal *n.* 1 *the Panama Canal:* artificial waterway, man-made waterway; channel, conduit, aqueduct; arm of the sea. 2 *the alimentary canal:* duct, tube, passage, channel.

cancel *v.* 1 *The general canceled all military leaves:* call off, set aside, quash, do away with, dispense with, abolish, revoke, rescind, retract, vitiate; annul, nullify, void. 2 *This show of kindness cancels the cruelty*

shown yesterday: offset, make up for, counterbalance, balance out, neutralize, erase.

Ant. 1, 2 confirm, affirm, reaffirm.

cancer *n.* 1 *Cigarette smoking can cause lung cancer:* malignant growth, malignancy, malignant tumor, carcinoma, sarcoma. 2 *The cancer of Hitlerism was widespread in Germany:* malignancy, plague, sickness, rot, scourge.

candid *adj.* 1 *To be candid, I don't think you're a great violinist:* frank, open, honest, truthful, blunt, forthright, plain-spoken, direct, plain, unvarnished; fair, just. 2 *candid photographs:* impromptu, spontaneous, unposed, informal, natural.

Ant. 1 diplomatic, flattering, fawning; mealy-mouthed. 2 formal, posed.

candidate *n. There are three candidates for the job. the Republicans' presidential candidate:* applicant, nominee, aspirant, eligible, possibility, hopeful, contender, contestant; office seeker, job seeker.

candlestick *n. Before the party, put fresh candles in the candlesticks:* candleholder, candelabrum, sconce, chandelier, girandole.

candor *n. a friend of great candor:* frankness, openness, honesty, truthfulness, straightforwardness, forthrightness, plainspokenness, directness; fairness, justness, impartiality.

Ant. diplomacy, flattery, evasiveness, deceit; insincerity, hypocrisy, unfairness, partiality, bias.

candy *n. Christmas candy:* sugar candy, confection, confectionary, dainty, sweet, sweets, sweetmeat; *(variously)* hard candy, filled candy, chocolate, kiss, bonbon, fudge, cream, jelly, toffee, taffy, caramel, nougat, fondant, comfit, candy bar, lollipop, all-day sucker, candy cane, peanut brittle, praline, gumdrop, jellybean.

cane *n.* 1 *He walks with a cane:* walking stick, stick, staff. —*v.* 2 *Schoolmasters used to cane students:* flog, thrash, whip, flail, switch.

canker *n.* 1 *The canker caused her lip to swell:* mouth sore; lesion, ulcer, sore. 2 *Crime is a canker on our way of life:* source of corruption, cancer, blight.

canny *adj. a canny politician:* artful, skillful, knowing, astute, shrewd, sharp, clever, cunning, crafty, foxy, wily, cagey; wary, careful, judicious, sagacious, perspicacious.

Ant. unskilled, inept, obtuse.

canon *n.* 1 *The canons of the Roman Catholic Church permit divorce only by dispensation:* doctrine, dogma, decree, edict. 2 *The canons of good behavior apply to everyone:* rule, principle, precept, code, standard, criterion.

canonical *adj. Only canonical texts will be used:* accepted, authorized, sanctioned, recognized, approved.

canopy *n. A canopy shaded the entrance:* awning; covering, cover, tester, hood.

cant *n.* 1 *His story was just a lot of cant:* hypocrisy, insincerity, pretense, sham. 2 *Thieves' cant is unintelligible to outsiders:* jargon, lingo, talk, slang, argot.

cantankerous *adj. The coach is in a cantankerous mood:* quarrelsome, argumentative, contentious, contrary, testy, touchy, peevish, huffy, ill-tempered, ill-humored, disagreeable, grouchy, grumpy, irascible, irritable, cranky, cross, surly, snappish, waspish, morose, sullen, short, crusty, choleric, splenetic.
Ant. agreeable, good-humored, good-natured, amiable, affable, genial, mellow; happy, jaunty, cheerful, lighthearted.

canteen *n.* 1 *a canteen of water:* flask, pocket flask, bottle. 2 *The sergeant bought a razor at the canteen:* commissary, post exchange, PX.

canvas *n.* 1 *Gym shoes are made of canvas:* sailcloth, tent cloth, duck. 2 *The artist set his canvas on the easel:* painting, picture.

canvass *v. After the canvass of voters, each party was forecasting victory:* poll, survey, evaluation, analysis, enumeration, inquiry, exploration, scrutiny.

canyon *n. A trail led down into the canyon:* gorge, gully, pass, ravine, gulch, coulee, draw, wash.

cap *n.* 1 *The nurse wore a pleated cap:* brimless hat; visored hat. 2 *Put the cap back on the bottle:* top, lid, cover, seal. —*v.* 3 *The Wright brothers capped their first flight with many longer ones:* better, surpass, exceed, outdo, top off.

capability *n. Someone of the highest capability:* ability, competency, competence, attainment, proficiency, skill, qualification; potential, potentiality, talent.
Ant. incompetence, ineptitude, inability.

capable *adj. a capable worker:* able, competent, skillful, skilled; accomplished, gifted, talented, adept, apt, adroit, effective.
Ant. incapable, incompetent, unqualified, unskilled, inept.

capacious *adj. a capacious handbag:* roomy, spacious, commodious, ample; extensive, expansive, broad, wide, voluminous; big, large, vast.
Ant. small, narrow, cramped.

capacity *n.* 1 *The water tank has a fifty-gallon capacity:* maximum contents, limit, extent, volume; room, space. 2 *the capacity to outproduce others:* ability, power, capability, faculty, facility, strength. 3 *a student*

of overwhelming capacity: ability, endowment, talent, gifts, faculty, aptitude, potential; intelligence, intellect, sagacity. 4 *In his capacity as Commander in Chief, the President is head of the armed forces:* role, function, position.
Ant. 2, 3 inability, incapacity.

cape *n.* 1 *The uniform includes a cape:* cloak, mantle; shawl, manta, pelisse, tabard, poncho, serape. 2 *Ships avoid the cape:* peninsula, point, promontory, headland, tongue, spit.

caper *v.* 1 *The fawns capered in the forest:* prance, gambol, frisk, cavort, romp, frolic; leap, jump, hop, skip, bound. —*n.* 2 *the students' latest caper:* lark, escapade, caprice, frolic; trick, prank, stunt.

capital *n.* 1 *London is the capital of England:* seat of government; chief city, first city. 2 *Print in capitals:* capital letter, upper-case letter, majuscule. 3 *Corporations need capital:* investment funds, working capital, resources, available means, money, cash, working assets. —*adj.* 4 *It was a capital idea!:* excellent, supreme, great, fine, super, first-rate.
Ant. 2 small letter, lower-case letter, minuscule. 4 bad, poor, inferior, awful, lousy, second-rate.

capitalize *v.* 1 *The investors capitalized the business at a million dollars:* bankroll, finance, fund, stake, put up the money. 2 *She capitalized on the resurgent market to sell her stocks:* take advantage of, profit by, make capital of, exploit, utilize, cash in on, avail oneself of, make the most of.

capitol *n. The Capitol is in Washington:* legislative building; statehouse, government house.

capitulate *v. Lee capitulated to Grant:* surrender, submit, give up, give in, yield, acquiesce, accede.
Ant. defeat, be victorious.

caprice *n. Is your decision just a caprice?:* whim, fancy, notion, impulse; eccentricity, idiosyncrasy, peculiarity; escapade, caper, stunt.

capricious *adj. a capricious man:* changeable, fickle, variable, impulsive, erratic, mercurial, indecisive, undecided, irresolute, uncertain; irresponsible, inconsistent, quirky.
Ant. consistent, unchangeable, unwavering, resolute, steadfast, certain, decided, decisive; serious.

capsize *v. The boat capsized:* overturn, turn over, keel over, tip over, flip over.
Ant. right, upright.

captain *n.* 1 *William Bligh was the captain of the* Bounty: commanding officer, master, skipper. 2 *Six first lieutenants were pro-*

moted to captain: company commander, commanding officer, commandant, chief officer. **3** *Robin Hood was the captain of a robber band:* leader, headman, chief, head.

captious *adj. a captious critic:* carping, nitpicking, hypercritical, faultfinding, caviling, niggling, querulous, deprecating, cutting, belittling; peevish, testy, petulant; contrary, fractious, cantankerous.
   Ant. flattering, laudatory, appreciative, fawning.

captivate *v. Her voice captivated the audience:* charm, enchant, bewitch, delight, enrapture, transport, win over, attract.
   Ant. repulse, repel, alienate; disgust.

captive *n.* **1** *Captives were kept in POW camps:* prisoner; internee; hostage. —*adj.* **2** *The captive fliers were released after the war:* imprisoned, confined, penned, caged, locked up; subjugated, enslaved.
   Ant. **1** captor; free person. **2** free, unconfined; freed, liberated.

capture *v.* **1** *The boys captured a hawk. The police captured the criminal:* seize, take, take prisoner, take captive, catch, snare, bag, lay hold of; arrest, apprehend, take into custody, *Slang* collar, nab, bust. —*n.* **2** *The capture of the white whale was Captain Ahab's obsession:* seizure, taking, capturing, taking prisoner, taking captive, catching.
   Ant. **1** release, free, let go. **2** release, freeing, liberation.

car *n.* **1** *The new car had disc brakes:* automobile, auto, motorcar, motor, machine, motor vehicle, *Slang* jalopy, heap, wheels, buggy, hot rod. **2** *The railroad bought 200 new cars:* railway car; *(variously)* coach, parlor car, sleeping car, Pullman car, sleeper, dining car, baggage car, freight car, boxcar, cattle car, coal car; streetcar, cable car, horsecar.

caravan *n. a caravan of old cars:* procession, parade, column, train, motorcade, cavalcade, line.

card *n.* **1** *Each player is dealt seven cards:* playing card. **2** *Amy mailed a card from France:* postcard, *(variously)* picture postcard, greeting card, birthday card, Christmas card, anniversary card, New Year's card, Easter card, Valentine's Day card, Valentine, get-well card. **3** *The sales representative left his card:* *(variously)* business card, calling card. **4** *The vaudeville card included two singers:* program, bill.

cardinal *adj.* **1** *Decorum was the cardinal rule in the office:* first, foremost, basic, prime, primary, fundamental, elementary, main, key, principal, most important, paramount, highest, greatest, dominant, preemi-

nent, uppermost. **2** *The king wore a cardinal robe:* deep red, cherry, blood-red, carmine, wine-colored, claret, scarlet.
   Ant. **1** subordinate, insignificant, unessential, irrelevant, extraneous.

care *n.* **1** *Handle with care. Answer the questions with care:* carefulness, caution, precaution, diligence, attention, heed, vigilance, thought; regard, concern, effort, pains, consideration, discrimination, solicitude, application, exactness. **2** *We don't have a care in the world:* concern, worry, responsibility, anxiety; bother, annoyance, vexation, tribulation, trouble, hardship, affliction, misery. **3** *under a doctor's care:* ministration, attention, supervision, custody, charge, keeping. —*v.* **4** *Do you care about money?:* be concerned, be interested in, be worried, mind, bother about, trouble about. **5** *The guests didn't care to stay:* want, wish, desire.
   Ant. **1** carelessness, negligence, recklessness, unconcern, thoughtlessness, indifference.

career *n. He made nursing his career:* profession, vocation, occupation, business, activity.
   Ant. hobby, avocation, sideline, diversion, relaxation.

carefree *adj. healthy and carefree:* free of care, without worry, without a worry in the world, untroubled, light-hearted, easygoing; in high spirits, jaunty, buoyant; happy, cheerful, gleeful.
   Ant. careworn, heavy-hearted, worried; joyless, cheerless, gloomy, dejected, disconsolate, despondent.

careful *adj.* **1** *Mother was careful to show no favoritism:* cautious, watchful, wary, chary, on guard, vigilant; diligent, mindful, regardful, heedful, scrupulous; circumspect, discreet, judicious. **2** *a careful handwriting:* precise, punctilious, exact, fastidious, particular, meticulous, fussy, painstaking, scrupulous.
   Ant. **1** careless, reckless, rash, lax, negligent, remiss, heedless, thoughtless, unthinking, unconcerned, improvident. **2** careless, sloppy, slipshod, slovenly; inexact, imprecise, inaccurate.

careless *adj.* **1** *a careless mistake. careless remarks:* thoughtless, unthinking, mindless, unmindful; lax, negligent, rash; inconsiderate. **2** *careless about personal appearance:* nonchalant, offhand, indifferent, heedless, unconcerned, forgetful, negligent, neglectful, lackadaisical, casual, lax. **3** See CAREFREE.
   Ant. **1** careful, cautious, wary, diligent,

mindful, concerned. **2** careful, fastidious, meticulous, fussy, painstaking, precise.

caress n. **1** *She gave each of the children a caress:* gentle touch, stroking, pat, petting. —v. **2** *He thoughtfully caressed his beard:* stroke, fondle, pet, pat, touch.
Ant. **1** hit, slap, cuff, box.

caretaker n. *the caretaker of the mansion:* custodian, keeper, overseer, curator, warden; superintendent, janitor, porter; watchman, gatekeeper.

cargo n. *The cargo was put in the hold:* freight, shipment, consignment, load, lading.

caricature n. **1** *The caricature of the president was amusing:* lampoon, takeoff, burlesque, parody, satire; distortion, absurdity, exaggeration. —v. **2** *The cartoonist caricatured rich senators:* lampoon, burlesque, parody, mock.

carnage n. *the carnage of war:* slaughter, butchery, blood bath, mass killing, massacre.

carnal adj. *carnal thoughts:* sexual, sensual, erotic, prurient, lustful, libidinous, fleshly, unchaste, lascivious, lecherous, venereal, wanton.
Ant. chaste, modest, pure.

carnival n. **1** *two circuses and a carnival:* small circus, traveling sideshow. **2** *a street carnival:* fair, festival, jamboree, celebration, jubilee, fete, gala, Mardi Gras.

carnivorous adj. *Lions are carnivorous:* meat-eating, flesh-eating.
Ant. herbivorous; vegetarian.

carol n. *Sing a carol:* Christmas carol, noel; hymn, canticle, paean, song of praise, song of joy.
Ant. dirge, lament.

carouse v. *The sailors caroused in the pub:* revel, make merry; drink, tipple, imbibe, *Informal* go on a binge.

carp v. *The man carped continually about the service:* complain, find fault, nag, cavil, criticize; belittle, knock, deprecate, disparage, reproach.
Ant. compliment, praise, laud.

carpet n. **1** *the living room carpet:* rug; matting, mat. **2** *a carpet of snow:* blanket, layer, covering.

carriage n. **1** *The queen rode in an ornate carriage:* coach, horse-drawn coach; buggy, rig; conveyance. **2** *a woman of erect carriage:* bearing, posture, comportment; demeanor, mien, poise, presence.

carrion n. *Vultures feed on carrion:* remains, corpse, cadaver, dead body, carcass, putrefying flesh.

carry v. **1** *The bellhops carried our luggage:* take, bring, tote, bear, fetch, haul, lug; move, transport, convey, conduct. **2** *The walls carry the weight of the roof:* support, sustain, maintain, bear, uphold, hold up, prop. **3** *All the papers carried the story:* communicate, disseminate, publish, run, print, broadcast. **4** *The shop carries name brands:* supply, stock, keep on hand, offer.
Ant. **3** withhold, reject, censor, keep secret.

cart n. **1** *The farmer sold corn from his roadside cart:* wagon, dumpcart, trap; dogcart, gig, dray, tipcart; go-cart, pushcart, handcart. —v. **2** *Trucks carted the garbage to the dump:* transport, haul, lug, tote, carry, bear, move; take, bring, fetch, convey.

carte blanche n. *The decorator was given carte blanche in decorating the house:* a free hand, free reign, full authority, unconditional power, blank check.

cartel n. *The cartel was accused of restraining trade:* monopoly, trust, consortium, combine.

carton n. *The books were packed in cartons:* box, cardboard box, container, cardboard container; packing case, case.

carve v. **1** *The statue was carved from marble. The boys carved their initials in the tree:* sculpture, sculpt, chisel, hew; shape, fashion, form, turn; incise. **2** *Who carved the Thanksgiving turkey?:* slice, cut up, dissever; hack, slash; cleave; split, divide, quarter, apportion, allot.

Casanova n. *He was known as a Casanova:* ladies' man, Lothario, Don Juan, Romeo, lover boy; admirer, suitor, wooer, lover, beau; womanizer, lady-killer, philanderer, chaser, wolf, roué, lecher.

cascade n. **1** *The water formed a cascade down the mountain:* waterfall, falls, cataract, Niagara. —v. **2** *The water cascaded over the cliff:* surge, pour, gush, plunge, rush, fall, tumble.
Ant. **2** trickle, dribble, drip.

case[1] n. **1** *In this case, no action is necessary. It was a case of love at first sight:* instance, incident, situation, episode; example, illustration, circumstance; matter, affair, concern. **2** *The case is before a jury:* lawsuit, suit, litigation, action; dispute, inquiry, hearing, proceeding. **3** *A doctor attended the case:* patient, sick person, victim; disease, injury.

case[2] n. **1** *a packing case. a jewel case:* box, crate, carton, chest; cabinet, display case, bin. **2** *The credit card was in a plastic case:* wrapper, cover, covering, sheath, jacket, envelope.

cash n. **1** *We paid cash:* money, currency, legal tender, paper money, bank notes, bills, coins, change; coin of the realm, cash on the barrelhead. —v. **2** *The store cashes checks:*

turn into money, give cash for, obtain cash for; redeem.

cashier n. *Please pay the cashier:* cash keeper; teller, bank teller; bursar.

cask n. *The wine was kept in casks:* vat, barrel, keg, hogshead; tub, butt, tun.

casket n. *Six pallbearers carried the casket:* coffin, sarcophagus, pall.

cast v. 1 *Never cast the first stone:* pitch, toss, fling, hurl, throw, sling; propel, launch, fire, shoot, catapult. 2 *The candles cast a warm glow:* shed, spread, diffuse, disseminate, disperse; broadcast, sow. 3 *The director cast leading actors in the play:* assign, pick, choose, give parts to. 4 *The statue was cast from bronze:* mold, form, shape, model, set. —n. 5 *The fisherman caught a trout on the first cast:* pitch, toss, throw; fling, hurl, heave. 6 *The play's cast was given a standing ovation:* performers, actors, company, troupe, players; list of characters, dramatis personae. 7 *The plaster was poured into a bronze cast:* mold, form, shape, pattern, casting, casing. 8 *Her face has a benign cast:* look, appearance, semblance.

castaway n. *the castaways of society:* outcast, pariah, offscouring; exile, expatriate; vagrant, vagabond, hobo, derelict, down-and-outer, *Slang* bum.

caste n. *Hindu society is based on a system of castes:* hereditary social class, lineage, rank, position, status, station.

castigate v. *He castigated the students for their behavior:* chastise, upbraid, rebuke, censure, reprimand, reproach, chasten, reprove, berate, scold, admonish, criticize, chide, bawl out, chew out, take to task; punish, discipline.
Ant. praise, laud, compliment, reward.

castle n. *Royalty lived in castles:* palace, mansion; hall, manor, chateau; fortified residence, stronghold, citadel, fortress.

casual adj. 1 *a casual meeting:* chance, unexpected, accidental, unplanned, unarranged, unpremeditated, unintentional. 2 *a casual interest in golf:* incidental, informal, undirected, offhand, vague, half-hearted; relaxed, easygoing, lackadaisical, nonchalant, indifferent. 3 *casual attire:* informal, nondressy, sporty; haphazard, random.
Ant. formal. 1 intentional, planned, arranged, deliberate, intentional. 2 serious, committed, concerned; systematic, professional; all-consuming, wholehearted, enthusiastic. 3 dressy.

casualty n. *They are casualties of bigotry:* injured, victim, wounded or dead person.

casuistry n. *If I can follow his casuistry, our defeat was really a victory:* sophistry, soph-

ism; equivocation, sophistication, fallacy, quibbling, hair-splitting, subtlety.

cat n. 1 *We have a dog and a cat:* feline, house cat, pussycat, pussy, puss, tabby, tabby cat, mouser; *(young)* kitten, kitty; *(male)* tomcat, tom. 2 *At the zoo, the bears are next to the cats: (loosely)* lions and tigers; *(variously)* lion, tiger, leopard, panther, cougar, lynx, ocelot, wildcat, bobcat.

cataclysm n. *The government could not withstand another cataclysm:* catastrophe, calamity, disaster, debacle, upheaval.
Ant. triumph, victory, success.

catalog, catalogue n. 1 *Let's order from the store's catalog:* list, listing, ventory, file, record; roll, roster, register, directory, syllabus. —v. 2 *Librarians catalog books alphabetically:* list, inventory, classify; enumerate, file, record, post, index, register.

catapult n. 1 *The catapult hurled the missile:* hurling engine, sling, slingshot. —v. 2 *The shove catapulted the boy into the room:* hurl, fling, throw, propel, heave, toss, shoot.

cataract n. 1 *the cataracts of the Colorado River:* rapids, falls, waterfall, cascade. 2 *a cataract of rain:* deluge, torrent, downpour.

catastrophe n. *The flood was a major catastrophe:* disaster, calamity, misfortune, mishap, tragedy; affliction, cataclysm, devastation.
Ant. benefit, good fortune, boon.

catcall n. *catcalls from the audience:* boo, hiss, hoot, whistle, jeer, gibe, heckling; *Slang* raspberry, Bronx cheer.
Ant. applause, cheering.

catch v. 1 *to catch a fish. The police caught the thief:* seize, capture, take captive, take, trap, snare, bag, hook; arrest, apprehend, take into custody; *Slang* collar, nab, bust. 2 *The runner caught her opponent at the finish line:* overtake, reach, get to, intercept. 3 *caught in the act:* discover, detect, come upon, discern, expose, spot, unmask. 4 *I was caught by false promises:* deceive, fool, dupe, take in, delude, mislead, hoodwink, bamboozle; lure, ensnare. 5 *A snowball caught the passerby in the shoulder:* strike, hit, bang, bump, buffet, whack, smack, smite. 6 *Children catch cold easily:* contract, get, come down with, become infected with, break out with. 7 *The child caught the group's fancy:* captivate, attract, enchant, bewitch, transport, delight, dazzle, enrapture. 8 *I caught something of his sadness from his voice:* sense, feel, discern, perceive, recognize. 9 *This belt buckle doesn't catch:* fasten, hook, latch, clasp, lock. —n. 10 *The fielder made a good catch:* catching, seizure, grab, grasp, snare. 11 *The fisherman's* *catch was two trout:* take, haul, bag, capture, yield, prize. **12** *The catch on the screen door is loose:* fastening, latch, hook, clasp, hasp, lock. **13** *There must be a catch:* hitch, snag, drawback, trick. **14** *a catch in his voice:* break, crack, rasping.

Ant. **1** free, release, let go, liberate. **4** undeceive, undupe, undelude. **5** miss. **6** avoid, evade. **7** repel, turn away. **9** unfasten, unhook, unlatch, unlock. **13** advantage, benefit.

catching *adj. Chicken pox is catching:* contagious, communicable, infectious, transmittable.

Ant. noncatching, noncontagious, uncommunicable, noninfectious, nontransmittable.

catchword *n. the catchwords used on television:* slogan, pet phrase, cliché, byword, watchword.

categorical *adj. a categorical denial:* absolute, unconditional, unqualified, unequivocal, unreserved, express, flat, emphatic, explicit.

Ant. conditional, qualified, equivocal, vague.

cater *v. They cater to their children:* humor, pamper, indulge, pander.

caterwaul *v. the caterwauling of the cats:* howl, wail, cry, scream, shriek, screech, yelp, squeal, bawl.

catharsis *n. Tragic drama provides catharsis for the audience:* purification, cleansing, purging, release, venting.

catholic *adj.* **1** *Catholic. a Catholic school:* Roman Catholic. **2** *a catholic ecumenical Christianity:* universal, world-wide, all-inclusive, all-embracing. **3** *She has catholic sympathies:* broad, comprehensive, universal, liberal.

Ant. **1** non-Catholic. **2** sectarian, parochial, provincial. **3** narrow, exclusive, limited.

cattle *n. herds of beef cattle:* livestock, stock, cows; *(male)* bulls, bullocks, steers, beefs, beeves, oxen; *(female)* cows, milk cows, dairy cattle; *(young)* calves.

catty *adj. That gossip always has something catty to say:* spiteful, malicious, malignant, malevolent.

caucus *n. The delegates held a caucus:* assembly, meeting, council, conference, parley, session.

causation *n. What was the causation of the universe?:* origin, genesis; cause, etiology, source, mainspring, reason, stimulus, determinant, invention, inspiration; author, originator, generator.

Ant. aftermath, effect, consequence, outcome.

cause *v.* **1** *Icy roads cause many accidents:*

bring about, lead to, give rise to, bring to pass, produce, effect, provoke; motivate, incite, stimulate. *—n.* **2** *Differences over money was the cause of the argument:* reason, source, root, prime mover; provocation, grounds, instigation, initiation, occasion, stimulus. **3** *the cause of liberty:* goal, aspiration, object, principle, ideal, belief, conviction, side.

Ant. **1** prevent, deter, inhibit, foil. **2** result, end result, consequence, outcome.

caustic *adj.* **1** *Acid is caustic:* burning, corrosive, corroding, erosive; astringent, stinging, biting, sharp. **2** *caustic remarks:* sarcastic, biting, stinging, cutting, scathing, harsh, acrimonious.

Ant. **2** flattering, complimentary; kind, gentle, gracious.

caution *n.* **1** *Proceed with caution:* care, carefulness, wariness, alertness, watchfulness, vigilance, precaution, heed, deliberation, guardedness. *—v.* **2** *The state trooper cautioned us about the icy roads:* warn, forewarn, alert, put on one's guard, advise.

Ant. **1** carelessness, recklessness, rashness, daring.

cautious *adj. Be cautious swimming in deep water:* careful, wary, alert, vigilant, attentive, guarded, prudent, circumspect, judicious.

Ant. careless, reckless, rash, foolhardy, daring, impetuous.

cavalcade *n. a cavalcade of movie stars:* parade, procession, column, troop; caravan.

cavalier *n.* **1** *The parade featured the king's cavaliers:* cavalryman, mounted soldier, horse soldier, horse, horseman; dragoon, hussar. **2** *Beau Brummel was the epitome of a cavalier:* gallant, courtier, courtly man, gentleman; beau, dandy, swell, fop; man about town, playboy, gay blade. *—adj.* **3** *Don Juan was known for his cavalier treatment of women's feelings:* disdainful, offhand, cursory, indifferent, nonchalant; arrogant.

Ant. **1** infantryman, foot soldier. **3** conscientious, diligent, caring, thoughtful.

cavalry *n. The cavalry led the attack:* mounted troops, horse soldiers, horse troops, mounted men; dragoons, hussars.

Ant. infantry, foot soldiers.

cave *n. Bears hibernate in caves:* underground chamber, cavern, grotto; hollow, den.

caveat *n. The senator's caveat went unheeded:* warning, caution, forewarning, admonition, admonishment, word to the wise.

cavern *n. Carlsbad Caverns:* large cave, large underground chamber.

cavernous *adj. a large house with cavern-*

ous rooms: vast, huge, yawning, gaping, cavelike; enormous, immense.

Ant. small, cramped.

cavil *v. My boss cavils at the least detail:* complain, find fault, faultfind, criticize, disparage, deprecate, belittle, deride.

Ant. praise, compliment, flatter.

cavity *n. The meteor left a cavity in the ground:* crater, concavity, depression, hole, basin, hollow, pit; dent, pocket, dip.

cavort *v. The ponies cavorted in the corral:* prance, frisk, frolic, gambol, bound, romp, play.

cease *v. The music ceased:* stop, halt, leave off, quit; conclude, end.

Ant. begin, commence, start.

ceaseless *adj. We had ceaseless rain:* endless, uninterrupted, incessant, continuous, unceasing, interminable, constant, neverending, unremitting.

Ant. transitory, intermittent, spasmodic.

cede *v. Mexico ceded New Mexico to the United States:* yield, grant, deliver up, hand over, surrender, tender, relinquish, transfer.

Ant. keep, retain.

celebrate *v.* 1 *They celebrated their fiftieth anniversary:* commemorate, observe; ceremonialize. 2 *Americans celebrate free enterprise:* proclaim, acclaim, praise, extol, honor, exalt, laud, cheer.

celebrated *adj. a celebrated poet:* famous, renowned, well-known, prominent, acclaimed, notable, eminent, illustrious, respected, honored.

Ant. unknown, little-known, undistinguished, insignificant.

celebration *n. a birthday celebration:* party, festivity, festival, feast, gala, fete, jubilee; commemoration, observance, ceremony, ceremonial.

celebrity *n.* 1 *Diamond Jim Brady was a celebrity in his day:* famous person, notable, luminary, name; person of note, *Slang* big shot. 2 *Babe Ruth gained celebrity by hitting home runs:* fame, renown, notoriety, notability, distinction, prominence, eminence.

Ant. 1 unknown, nobody. 2 obscurity, oblivion.

celerity *n. The order must be carried out with celerity:* haste, dispatch, speed, expedition, alacrity, expeditiousness.

celestial *adj.* 1 *The child had a celestial beauty:* heavenly, divine, angelic, seraphic, blissful, sublime, beatific, ethereal, otherworldly, unearthly. 2 *A celestial map shows the positions of the planets:* astral, astronomical, planetary, stellar; sky.

Ant. 1 earthy, earthly, worldly; hellish, infernal, satanic. 2 earthly, terrestrial.

celibacy *n. Priests take vows of celibacy:* chastity, virginity, continence, abstinence.

celibate *adj. to lead a celibate life:* unmarried, unwed, single; chaste, virginal, continent, abstinent.

Ant. married, wedded; unchaste, promiscuous, wanton.

cellar *n. The furnace is in the cellar. a storm cellar:* basement, downstairs; underground room, subterranean room; dugout.

Ant. attic, garret; upstairs.

cement *n.* 1 *a cement sidewalk. rubber cement: (loosely)* concrete; mortar; glue, paste. —*v.* 2 *Cement the parts together:* glue, paste, fix, seal, bind, secure.

cemetery *n. The cemetery has many old graves:* graveyard, burial ground, memorial park, churchyard, burying ground, necropolis, *Slang* boneyard.

censor *n.* 1 *The censors cut the second act of the play:* custodian of morals, examiner, guardian of the public morals, expurgator, bowdlerizer. —*v.* 2 *The dictator censors all news reports:* expurgate, blue-pencil, bowdlerize, blip, purge, suppress.

censure *n.* 1 *The sleeping sentry received a censure:* reprimand, reproof, rebuke, reproach, admonition, scolding, chiding, remonstrance; criticism, disapprobation. —*v.* 2 *The dean censured the students for cutting classes:* rebuke, reprimand, admonish, upbraid, reproach; denounce, condemn, berate, reprove, scold, *Slang* bawl out, rap on the knuckles.

Ant. praise 1 commendation, compliment. 2 commend, compliment, laud.

center Also **centre** *n.* 1 *the center of a target:* middle point, dead center, hub; middle, central part; core, heart, nucleus. 2 *Broadway is the theatrical center of the United States:* focal point, focus, main point, main place, hub, heart. —*v.* 3 *She centered her attention on the task at hand:* concentrate, direct, address, fix, focus.

Ant. 1 outside; perimeter, edge, rim.

central *adj.* 1 *the central part of the state:* middle, middlemost, interior, inner, inmost. 2 *The President is the central figure in government:* major, main, principal, most important, chief, key, primary, paramount, dominant, foremost, focal, pivotal.

Ant. 1 outer, exterior. 2 minor, subordinate, secondary.

centralize *v. The performing arts are centralized in New York:* focus, concentrate, center, center on, converge.

Ant. disperse, scatter, spread.

ceremonial *adj.* 1 *the king's ceremonial manner:* formal, ceremonious, ritualistic. 2 *the ceremonial music for the Easter ser-*

vice: used in ceremonies, liturgical. —*n.* 3 *the ceremonial of the mass:* ritual, rite, service, ceremony; formality, celebration.
Ant. 1 informal, relaxed, casual.

ceremonious *adj. The host's greetings were rather ceremonious:* formal, stiff, overly polite, proper, starched, rigid, methodical, punctilious; solemn, dignified, pompous.
Ant. unceremonious, informal, relaxed, casual, down-to-earth.

ceremony *n.* 1 *an inauguration ceremony:* rite, ritual, service, observance, ceremonial, celebration, function, formalities. 2 *Lack of ceremony caused chaos:* formality, formal behavior, decorum, protocol, propriety.
Ant. 2 informality.

certain *adj.* 1 *I'm certain I returned the book:* sure, positive, confident, convinced, satisfied, secure, assured. 2 *War seemed certain. That the diamonds are real is certain:* definite, inevitable, inescapable, bound to happen, settled, sure; conclusive, indubitable, unmistakable, unquestionable; indisputable, undeniable, incontrovertible; reliable, valid. 3 *a certain person:* specific, particular, individual, express.
Ant. 1 uncertain, doubtful, dubious. 2 doubtful, unlikely, questionable, unclear, unsettled, disputable.

certainty *n.* 1 *The forecast was given with certainty:* positiveness, confidence, assurance, surety; conviction, belief, faith; authoritativeness. 2 *It is a certainty that the highway will be built:* fact, reality, inevitability, inescapability, sure thing.
Ant. uncertainty. 1 indecision, unsureness; doubt.

certificate *n. a certificate of ownership:* document, certification, credential, permit, license, deed, authentication; diploma.

certify *v. Two witnesses must certify that this is your signature. Ask the bank to certify this check:* confirm, corroborate, attest, substantiate, validate, verify, witness, testify to, vouch, guarantee, authorize, notarize, authenticate.
Ant. repudiate, disavow, deny.

cessation *n. a cessation of hostilities:* stopping, stop, ceasing, halting, halt, desisting, quitting, ending, end, termination, leaving off; discontinuing, suspension, pause.
Ant. starting, start, beginning, commencement; continuance, continuation; resumption.

chafe *v.* 1 *The collar chafed his neck:* rub, scratch, scrape, rasp, abrade. 2 *The driver chafed at the slow traffic:* be irritated, be

exasperated, be annoyed, rankle, seethe, burn, fume.
Ant. 1 soothe, heal.

chaff *n.* 1 *to separate the wheat from the chaff:* husks, hulls, shells. —*v.* 2 *The kids chaff him about his big ears:* rib, kid, razz, josh, twit, rag, ride, ridicule.

chagrin *n. I resigned with chagrin:* shame, humiliation, embarrassment, mortification.
Ant. pride, glory.

chain *n.* 1 *a bicycle chain:* linked cable, metal links; fob. 2 Usually **chains.** *The prisoners were put in chains:* shackles, fetters, bonds, irons; manacles. 3 **chains.** *The Civil War freed the slaves from their chains:* bondage, subjugation, enslavement, slavery, servitude. 4 *a bizarre chain of events:* series, sequence, succession, string, train. —*v.* 5 *Chain the dog to the fence:* shackle, fetter, fasten, secure, tether.
Ant. 5 unchain, unshackle.

chairman *n. the chairman of the board:* presiding officer, head, director, supervisor; chairwoman, chairperson; chair; moderator, leader.

chalice *n. The priest poured wine into the chalice:* goblet, cup, vessel.

challenge *n.* 1 *The champion issued a challenge to other boxers:* summons, dare, bid, hostile invitation. 2 *Mt. Everest is the supreme challenge to a mountain climber:* test, trial. —*v.* 3 *The fathers challenged the sons to a race:* dare, summon, bid, invite to compete, fling down the gauntlet. 4 *I challenge the truth of your story:* question, impute, dispute, take exception to. 5 *The job challenged my skill:* test, try, tax.
Ant. 4 accept, agree with; concede, acquiesce.

chamber *n.* 1 *the chambers of Congress:* room, inner room, office; hall. 2 *The king retired to his chamber:* bedroom, boudoir; sitting room, parlor, drawing room. 3 *The Senate chamber approved the amendment:* legislative body; council, assembly, congress, diet, house.

champion *n.* 1 *the heavyweight boxing champion:* title holder; victor, winner, conqueror, vanquisher; master, paragon. 2 *a champion of peace:* upholder, advocate, defender, supporter, protector, promoter. —*v.* 3 *to champion the establishment of national parks:* fight for, uphold, support, back, defend, stand up for, promote, advocate.
Ant. 1 loser. 2 opponent, enemy. 3 oppose, hinder.

chance *n.* 1 *The two friends met by chance:* accident, happenstance; luck, destiny, fate. 2 *a chance of rain:* possibility, likelihood, probability. 3 *Will she get another chance?*: opportunity, try, attempt; occasion, possibility. 4 *Don't take chances*: risk, danger, hazard; gamble. —*v.* 5 *It chanced someone found the ring*: happen, occur, come to pass, come about, turn out, befall. 6 *Should we chance making it home before it snows?*: take a chance, risk, hazard, venture, gamble, try, attempt. —*adj.* 7 *a chance meeting*: accidental, unexpected, unlooked for, unplanned, unforeseen, unpremeditated, fortuitous.

Ant. 1 plan, design, intent. 2 unlikelihood, impossibility, improbability; certainty. 7 intentional, planned, premeditated; arranged.

chancy *adj.* *The prospect of making a profit is chancy*: risky, dubious, doubtful, uncertain, unpredictable, iffy.

Ant. sure, safe, certain.

change *v.* 1 *Rain made us change our plans. The caterpillar changed into a butterfly*: alter, modify, vary, recast; transmute, mutate, transform, turn, metamorphose. 2 *You'd better change that shirt for a larger one*: exchange, swap, trade, switch, replace. —*n.* 3 *After warm days, cold weather is quite a change. The owner made a lot of changes in the business*: difference, modification, switch, shift, variation, fluctuation; alteration, reform, reorganization, remodeling, restyling; transformation. 4 *Let's eat out for a change*: novelty, something different, switch; variety. 5 *Do you have change for a dollar?*: coins, small coins, silver.

Ant. 1 keep; stay, remain. 2 keep. 3 constancy; stability, invariability, unchangeableness. 5 bills, paper money.

changeable *adj.* *Your moods are changeable*: variable, varying, erratic, irregular, alternating, inconstant, fickle, volatile, fluctuating, mercurial, fitful, vacillating, uncertain, unstable, capricious; reversible, modifiable.

Ant. unchangeable, invariable, regular, undeviating, constant, steady, reliable, stable; immutable, irreversible.

channel *n.* 1 *the English Channel*: strait, passage, watercourse, narrows. 2 *Heavy rains wore a channel in the yard*: groove, furrow, trough, gash, cut. 3 *It takes a week by the normal channels*: route, course, avenue of communication. —*v.* 4 *Requests for transfers are channeled through the personnel office*: route, direct, send, convey.

chant *n.* 1 *They entertained us with chants and dancing*: song, hymn, melody, chanson; psalm, doxology, plainsong, canticle, offertory, Gregorian chant, chorale, Gloria Patri, elegy, ode. —*v.* 2 *The monks chanted softly as they filed in for vespers*: sing, croon, intone, vocalize, chorus.

chaos *n.* *to live in a state of chaos*: turmoil, upheaval, confusion, agitation, tumult, furor; disorder, disarray, disorganization, disarrangement, mess.

Ant. order, organization; calmness, quiet, peacefulness.

chaperon, chaperone *n.* 1 *The teenagers needed a chaperon for their party*: adult overseer, adult attendant; attendant, duenna. —*v.* 2 *Parents chaperoned the high-school dance*: oversee, shepherd; accompany, escort.

chaplain *n.* *an army chaplain*: priest, minister, rabbi, padre, reverend; pastor, parson, preacher.

chapter *n.* 1 *Read chapter 5 of the textbook. The Civil War was an important chapter in United States history*: part, section, division, portion; episode, period, phase, era. 2 *The fraternity has local chapters all over the country*: branch, affiliate, group, division.

char *v.* *The sparks charred the carpet*: singe, scorch, sear, burn.

character *n.* 1 *We should be judged by our character*: qualities, attributes, nature, being, makeup, individuality, distinctiveness. 2 *A person who cheats has little character*: honor, integrity, moral strength, morality, honesty. 3 *a suspicious character*: person, individual, being. 4 *He's a character!*: odd person, eccentric, original, *Slang* oddball. 5 *the main character in Shakespeare's* Hamlet: fictional person, person, persona; role, part; *(plural)* dramatis personae.

characteristic *adj.* 1 *Windy days are characteristic of March*: typical, representative, indicative, emblematic, distinguishing. —*n.* 2 *Tactfulness is a useful characteristic*: attribute, trait, quality, aspect, feature, property, mark; mannerism, peculiarity.

Ant. 1 uncharacteristic, atypical, unrepresentative.

characterization *n.* *The actress's characterization of Juliet was superb*: representing, representation, portrayal; depiction; description.

charge *v.* 1 *The hotel charges $100 a day*: fix as a price, put a value on, ask, require, price; request payment, levy. 2 *Did you charge the purchase?*: put on one's account, use credit, delay payment; debit. 3 *The air was charged with electricity*: load, fill, lade. 4 *The major charged his soldiers to stand firm*: command, order, direct, instruct, bid, call upon, enjoin. **5** *The investigator charged the fire to a faulty heater. He was charged with reckless driving:* attribute, ascribe, impute, assign; accuse, blame, indict, lodge a complaint against, prefer charges against. **6** *The cavalry charged the fort:* rush, attack, storm, assail, assault, make an onslaught. —*n.* **7** *a charge for admission:* fee, cost, price, assessment, rate, payment; payment due. **8** *the charge up San Juan Hill:* attack, assault, storming, onset. **9** *The children are in the charge of a nursemaid:* care, custody, keeping, guardianship; jurisdiction, superintendence, supervision; administration, control, management. **10** *a charge of theft:* allegation, accusation, complaint; arraignment, indictment. **11** *The judge made a brief charge to the jury:* direction, advice; instruction, injunction; order, command, bidding.

Ant. **2** pay, pay cash. **5** absolve, exculpate; vindicate, exonerate, acquit. **6** retreat, withdraw. **8** retreat, withdrawal. **10** absolution, vindication, exoneration; acquittal.

charisma *n. The charisma of a movie star:* charm, appeal, magnetism, fascination, allure, bewitchery, enchantment.

charitable *adj.* **1** *The Community Chest asks us to be charitable this year. a charitable organization:* generous, giving, bountiful, bounteous, munificent; philanthropic, almsgiving, eleemosynary, benevolent. **2** *A charitable person would forgive the boy:* forgiving, kindly, kind, kindhearted, benevolent, considerate, magnanimous.

Ant. **1** uncharitable, stingy, parsimonious. **2** unforgiving, unkind, malevolent, hardhearted.

charity *n.* **1** *The orphanage is supported by the charity. The Red Cross is my favorite charity:* philanthropy, contributions, donations, donating, alms, alms-giving, gift, offering, benefaction, fund-raising; charitable institution. **2** *faith, hope, and charity:* good will, altruism, love, compassion, sympathy, kindness, benevolence, benignity.

Ant. **2** malice, hate, hatred, selfishness.

charlatan *n. Fortune-tellers are charlatans:* fake, fraud, quack, impostor, cheat, swindler, mountebank.

charm *n.* **1** *The host of a TV show must have lots of charm:* power to please, fascination, enchantment, allure, attraction, magnetism. **2** *a magic charm:* spell, incantation, conjuration; sorcery, magic; lucky piece; amulet, talisman. —*v.* **3** *Everyone was charmed by the child:* please, give pleasure, delight, enrapture, enthrall; fascinate, attract, allure, entrance, enchant. **4** *They charmed us into*

buying a car: lure, cajole, win over, beguile, bewitch.

charming *adj. a charming personality:* attractive, pleasing, delightful, agreeable, winning, likable; entrancing, fascinating, engaging, bewitching, enchanting, fetching, magnetic.

Ant. unattractive, unpleasing, unpleasant, unlikable; repulsive, repellent.

chart *n.* **1** *He plotted the ship's course on the chart. The chart showed the decline in the company's sales:* map, navigator's map, mariner's map; diagram, graph, table; blueprint, scheme, plan. —*v.* **2** *She charted the plane's course. The committee charted the fund-raising drive:* map, map out, draw up, plot; draft, plan, design, outline, lay out.

charter *n.* **1** *to operate under federal charter:* permit, license, authority, franchise, contract, sanction. —*v.* **2** *The state chartered the university:* establish by charter, license, commission, authorize. **3** *We chartered a fishing boat:* rent, hire, lease, engage.

chary *adj. We were chary about endorsing the plan:* wary, suspicious, leery; cautious, careful, prudent, watchful, guarded, distrustful.

Ant. reckless, rash, heedless.

chase *v.* **1** *The police chased the thief:* pursue, go after, run after, try to overtake; hunt, stalk, follow. **2** *Mother chased the cat from the room:* drive, put to flight; oust, send away, drive away, rout, shoo. —*n.* **3** *Many hunters find the chase exciting:* hunt, hunting, quest, pursuit, pursuing.

Ant. **1** let escape; escape, flee.

chasm *n. The earthquake left a chasm in the earth:* abyss, fissure, rift, split, gorge, gap, crevasse, gulf, break, cleft, crack; pit, crater, cavity.

chaste *adj.* **1** *Be chaste in mind and body:* virginal, pure, continent. **2** *The couple was hardworking and chaste:* clean-living, decent, virtuous, sinless, untainted, uncorrupted. **3** *The author's chaste style is elegant:* pure, classic, restrained, austere, severe, precise; unadorned, unornamented, unembellished.

Ant. **1** unchaste, incontinent, lewd, wanton, promiscuous, licentious, ribald. **2** corrupt, unwholesome, dishonorable, immoral, tainted, sullied, blemished, tarnished. **3** ornate, flashy, gaudy, unrestrained.

chasten See CHASTISE.

chastise *v. The teacher chastised the child:* punish, discipline; whip, spank; reprimand, scold, upbraid, rebuke, reproach, reprove, censure, criticize, berate, take to task, call on the carpet.

Ant. reward, praise, compliment, commend.

chastity *n. Nuns take vows of chastity:* celibacy, purity, virginity, continence; singleness, bachelorhood, spinsterhood.

Ant. promiscuity, lewdness, wantonness, licentiousness.

chat *v.* 1 *Stop and chat a while:* talk, converse, chatter, gab, chitchat, prate, prattle, chew the rag, chew the fat. —*n.* 2 *Call me tomorrow and we'll have a chat:* talk, conversation; chitchat, confabulation.

chattel *n. The will says "all goods and chattels" are left to his brother:* personal possessions, personal effects, belongings, effects, movable property, movables.

chatter *v.* 1 *The guests chattered as they waited for dinner:* talk, talk idly, babble, jabber, prattle, gabble, chitchat, chitterchatter, patter. 2 *My teeth are chattering:* clatter, click. —*n.* 3 *The children's chatter was irritating:* jabber, babble; talk, talking, gossip, chitchat, chitterchatter, gabble, twaddle, blather, idle talk.

chatterbox *n. My seatmate on the plane was a chatterbox:* talker, jabberer, gabber, chatterer, babbler, prattler; *Slang* windbag; gossip, talebearer, tattletale, tattler.

chatty *adj. Mother was in a chatty mood:* talkative, talky, effusive, voluble, garrulous, gabby, loquacious.

Ant. close-mouthed, secretive, uncommunicative, taciturn.

chauvinism *n. The senator's chauvinism made him intolerant of other countries:* superpatriotism, ethnocentricity, blind patriotism, flag-waving, jingoism.

cheap *adj.* 1 *Chicken is not as cheap as it was:* inexpensive, low-priced, economical, reasonable. 2 *Talk is cheap:* effortless, costless, easy. 3 *The coat looks cheap:* shoddy, shabby, inferior, second-rate; flashy, gaudy, in bad taste, tacky, common, inelegant. 4 *Spreading gossip is a cheap thing to do:* petty, despicable, mean, base; vulgar. 5 *He's too cheap to pick up the check:* tight, stingy, miserly, penurious, tightfisted, close.

Ant. 1 expensive, costly, high-priced, overpriced. 3 superior, first-rate; in good taste, tasteful, elegant, chic, smart. 5 generous.

cheat *v.* 1 *Her uncle cheated her out of her inheritance:* swindle, defraud, trick, bilk, gyp, fleece; deceive, dupe, betray, hoodwink, bamboozle, cozen. 2 *Only a cad would cheat at cards:* practice fraud, practice trickery, break the rules. 3 *You can't cheat fate for long:* escape, thwart, foil, circumvent, outwit. —*n.* 4 *That cheat would defraud his own mother!:* swindler, con artist, deceiver; fraud, charlatan, mountebank.

check *v.* 1 *Inflation must be checked:* stop, bring to a standstill, halt; restrain, slow, hold back, curb, limit, inhibit, arrest, rein in, retard, thwart. 2 *Please check the broken light switch:* inspect, look at, test, examine. 3 *Check on the problem and report back to me:* investigate, take stock of, review, probe, inspect, survey, look over, examine. 4 *His alibi checks with the information:* agree, correspond, fit, tally, conform, jibe. —*n.* 5 *a system of checks and balances:* restraint, limit, limitation, restriction, control, curb, prohibition, constraint. 6 *The plumber made a careful check of the pipes:* inspection, examination; search, probe, investigation.

Ant. 1 begin, initiate, start; accelerate, speed up, let loose, foster, encourage, further. 2, 3 ignore, overlook, disregard. 4 disagree, contradict.

checkered *adj.* 1 *a red and white checkered tablecloth:* checked, particolored. 2 *a checkered career of failure and success:* varied, uneven, inconstant, irregular, vacillating, up-and-down.

Ant. 1 solid. 2 consistent, constant, steady, stable.

cheek *n.* 1 *Don't put too much rouge on your cheeks:* jowl, side of the face. 2 *I wouldn't have the cheek to go to a party uninvited:* impudence, impertinence, nerve, insolence, arrogance, effrontery, audacity, brazenness, brass, forwardness, brashness.

Ant. 2 shyness, bashfulness, timidity.

cheep *v.* 1 *Listen to the little chicks cheep!:* peep, chirp, chirrup; tweet, twitter. —*n.* 2 *the cheeps of the birds:* chirp, peep, chirrup, tweet, twitter.

cheer *n.* 1 *The touchdown brought loud cheers from the crowd:* approving shout, encouraging cry, acclamation, acclaim, hooray, huzzah, bravo. 2 *words of cheer:* assurance, reassurance, encouragement, comfort, hope; optimism. 3 *The party sparkled with cheer:* gaiety, merriment, joviality, gladness, high spirits, vivacity, buoyance, joyfulness, glee, geniality. —*v.* 4 *The fans cheered the team to victory:* root, hail, encourage, hurrah. 5 *A vase of roses cheered the room. Her words cheered the family:* brighten, enliven; gladden, assure, reassure, encourage, comfort, hearten, warm.

Ant. 1 boo, catcall, hiss, Bronx cheer, raspberry. 2 gloom, discouragement, pessimism. 3 gloom, sadness, despondency. 5 sadden; discourage, depress, dishearten.

cheerful *adj.* 1 *It's wonderful to see you so cheerful:* cheery, joyful, joyous, light-

83

hearted, happy, merry, high-spirited, in high humor, buoyant. 2 *Yellow is a cheerful color:* bright, lively, cheery, sunny.

Ant. 1 glum, gloomy, dour, dejected, depressed, downcast, downhearted, sad, doleful, despondent, joyless, miserable. 2 somber, depressing.

cheerless *adj. a cheerless mood. a cheerless fall day:* gloomy, dreary, glum, despondent, dolorous, downhearted, funereal, doleful, dejected, joyless, desolate, solemn, grim, morose, sad, unhappy; bleak, gray, sunless, dismal, depressing.

Ant. cheerful, joyful, light-hearted, happy, merry.

cherish *v. to cherish one's friends:* love, hold dear, treasure, value, prize, appreciate, honor, esteem; care for, take care of, sustain, succor.

Ant. scorn, disdain; desert, forsake, abandon.

chew *v. Chew your food slowly:* masticate; champ, gnaw, crunch, munch, nibble; ruminate.

chic *adj. a chic dress:* fashionable, stylish, smart, elegant; modish, *Slang,* ritzy, snazzy.

Ant. unfashionable, unstylish; dowdy, shabby.

chicanery *n. There was some chicanery in their business dealings:* deception, trickery, fraud, deceit, double-dealing, duplicity, subterfuge, hoodwinking; knavery.

chichi *adj. a chichi house:* showy, ostentatious, flashy, splashy, garish, vulgar; pompous, pretentious, grandiose, affected; precious, overnice, overrefined; prissy.

Ant. plain, simple, natural, unaffected.

chide *v. Mother chided me for being late:* admonish, reprimand, scold, chasten, rebuke, reproach, reprove, upbraid, berate; censure, denounce.

Ant. praise, commend, laud, compliment.

chief *n.* 1 *The chief of the delegation addressed the U.N.:* head, leader, director, chairman; boss, overseer; commander, master; ruler, chieftain, monarch. —*adj.* 2 *his chief concern:* major, main, prime, primary, first, number-one, foremost, cardinal, highest, greatest, paramount, uppermost, highest, supreme, principal, leading.

Ant. 1 subordinate, underling. 2 minor, least, last, subordinate, secondary, subsidiary.

chiefly *adv. Shakespeare thought of himself chiefly as a poet:* primarily, principally, mainly, first, most of all, especially.

Ant. least, least of all.

child *n. The child is only six:* youth, youngster, juvenile, kid, boy, lad, girl, lass, *Infor-*

mal tad; baby, infant, tot, tyke, toddler, moppet; son, daughter, offspring.

Ant. adult, grownup; parent.

childbirth *n. natural childbirth:* childbearing, giving birth, delivery, parturition.

childhood *n. a happy childhood:* youth, boyhood, girlhood; school days, adolescence.

Ant. adulthood, maturity.

childish *adj. His behavior is childish:* immature, childlike, infantile, puerile, juvenile, adolescent, babyish; naïve, simple.

Ant. mature, grown-up, adult, sophisticated.

chill *n.* 1 *There's a chill in the air:* chilliness, coolness; iciness, frostiness, frigidity; crispness, nip. 2 *I caught a chill from being in the rain:* cold; fever. —*adj.* also **chilly.** 3 *a chill wind:* chilling, cold, wintry, arctic, icy, frigid, penetrating, cool; biting, bitter, raw, nippy. 4 *a chill greeting:* icy, frigid, cold, aloof, unfriendly, indifferent, uncaring, stiff, forbidding.

Ant. 1 warmth, warmness. 3 warm, warming, hot, tropical, balmy, mild. 4 warm, friendly, cordial.

chime *n.* 1 *Our church's chimes are more than 200 years old:* set of bells, carillon. 2 *Listen to the chime of the bells:* peal, pealing, ring, ringing, toll, tollings, knell, tinkling, tintinnabulation. —*v.* 3 *The bells chimed:* peal, ring, sound, toll, knell, tintinnabulate; jingle, tinkle.

chimera *n. His chimera was that one day he would write a novel:* delusion, illusion; dream, fantasy, fancy, pipe dream, daydream; self-deception, self-deceit, figment of one's imagination.

china *n. Set the table with the good china:* dishes, cups and saucers, plates, tableware, chinaware; crockery.

chink[1] *n. a chink in the roof:* crack, rift, rent, cleft, breach, fissure, gap, gash, break.

chink[2] *v. The coins chinked in my pocket:* clink, jingle, jangle, clank, ring.

chintzy *adj.* 1 *The furniture was chintzy:* shabby, sleazy, tacky, dowdy, frowzy, frumpy. 2 *She's never chintzy when we eat out:* stingy, cheap, tight, miserly, close, grudging, niggardly, closefisted, stinting.

Ant. 1 stylish, elegant, classy, ritzy, fashionable.

chip *n.* 1 *Gather some wood chips for the fire. potato chips:* small piece, fragment, scrap, sliver, chunk, shaving, splinter, shred; slice, paring, cutting. 2 *This glass has a chip:* nick, gash. —*v.* 3 *I chipped the dish when I dropped it:* nick, gash. 4 *The sculptor chipped away at the block of marble:* hew, chop, cut, whittle, hack, chisel.

chipper *adj. You're looking chipper again:*

lively, animated, sprightly, cheerful, jaunty, peppy, pert, spry, high-spirited, energetic.
Ant. downhearted, sad, morose.

chirp *v.* 1 *Listen to the birds chirping:* chirrup, tweet, twitter, sing, cheep, peep. —*n.* 2 *The chirps of the crickets keep us awake:* chirrup, tweet, twitter, chitter, cheep, peeping, cheeping, chirr.

chivalrous *adj. Men can be chivalrous:* gallant, courtly; polite, mannerly.
Ant. ungallant, loutish, boorish, rude.

chivalry *n. Chivalry isn't dead:* knighthood; gallantry, courtliness, courtesy.
Ant. loutishness, boorishness, rudeness, discourtesy.

choice *n.* 1 *The worker left the job of his own choice. The child had no choice but to go to bed:* choosing, decision, deciding, discretion, opting, determination; alternative, option. 2 *My choice for dessert is ice cream:* selection, preference, pick. 3 *The store has a poor choice of dresses:* selection, variety, stock, supply, collection, assortment. —*adj.* 4 *choice fruits and vegetables:* select, well-chosen, superior, first-rate, first-class, best, prime, preferred; exceptional, superlative, extraordinary.
Ant. 1 coercion, order. 4 poor, inferior, second-rate, mediocre.

choke *v.* 1 *The strangler choked his victims. The rescuers were choking from the smoke:* strangle, garrote, throttle; smother, asphyxiate, suffocate; gag, stifle. 2 *Ice choked the river:* stop up, clog, obstruct, constrict, block, dam up.
Ant. 2 unclog, unstop, unblock, unplug.

choleric *adj. She grew more choleric with the years:* cranky, cantankerous, testy, peevish, irate, irascible, ill-tempered, waspish.
Ant. easygoing, serene.

choose *v.* 1 *What game did the girl choose?:* select, pick out, pick, take, decide on, settle on, single out, opt for. 2 *President Johnson chose not to run for a second term:* decide, determine, resolve, prefer, commit oneself, opt, elect, see fit.
Ant. 1 reject, decline, spurn, aside, forgo.

choosy *adj. She's choosy about food:* fussy, finicky, particular, fastidious, picky, discriminating.

chop *v.* 1 *to chop down a tree. Chop some wood for the fire:* cut, fell; sunder, hew, hack, split, cleave. 2 *Chop the carrots for the stew:* cut up, dice, mince, cube. —*n.* 3 *The lumberjack gave the tree one last chop:* stroke, whack, blow, hit, cut, hack. 4 *pork chops:* cutlet, rib slice, *French* côtelette.

chore *n.* 1 *household chores:* household task, domestic work, farm task, small job, task,

job, duty, work, errand. 2 *Filling out tax forms is a chore:* unpleasant task, difficult job, burden, tedious job, exacting task.

chortle *v.* 1 *Father used to chortle over the comics:* chuckle, snort merrily, laugh. —*n.* 2 *The child gave a merry chortle:* chuckle, merry snort, laugh, gleeful whoop.

chorus *n.* 1 *Sing the last chorus again:* refrain, antiphony, response. 2 *The chorus sang carols:* choir, singing group, glee club, choral society, vocal ensemble; line of dancers. 3 *The union members shouted their assent in chorus:* concert, unison, one voice; accord, concord, unanimity.

christen *v. The baby was christened in St. Patrick's Cathedral:* baptize, sprinkle, dip, immerse; name, designate.

chronic *adj. a chronic cough:* habitual, longstanding, continual, continuous, constant, persistent, persisting; recurring, recurrent.

chronicle *n.* 1 *a chronicle of war:* record, history, chronology; journal, diary, account, log, annals, story. —*v.* 2 *The historian chronicled the events of the decade:* record, set down, list, docket, log, note, report.

chronological *adj. List the historical events in chronological order:* consecutive, successive, progressive, dated, time-ordered, sequential.

chubby *adj. He's gotten quite chubby:* pudgy, stocky, plump, stout, portly, paunchy, tubby, fat, flabby, rotund.
Ant. lean, skinny, gaunt, thin, emaciated.

chuck *v.* 1 *He chucked the child under the chin:* pat, tap, pet, tickle. 2 *Chuck the suitcase onto the back seat:* toss, fling, sling, throw, heave, pitch.

chum *n. We were childhood chums:* friend, close friend, pal, buddy, bosom buddy, companion, comrade, cohort, intimate, confidant.
Ant. casual acquaintance; enemy.

chummy *adj. The two seemed very chummy:* friendly, close, intimate, familiar, congenial, affectionate, *Slang* palsy-walsy, buddy-buddy.
Ant. estranged, alienated; distant, aloof, cool.

chunk *n. chunks of ice in the river:* lump, hunk, piece, mass, batch, clod, block.

chunky *adj. "Chunky" is one way of saying "short and plump":* stocky, thickset, pudgy, stubby, squat, chubby, dumpy.
Ant. slender, gangling, lanky.

church *n.* 1 *St. Peter's in Rome is the largest Christian church:* house of worship, house of God, Lord's house, tabernacle, chapel, temple; cathedral, basilica, mosque, synagogue. 2 *Did you attend church Sunday?:* religious service; service, divine worship, devotions. **3** *I belong to the Episcopal Church:* religion, denomination, faith, affiliation, persuasion.

churlish *adj. I'm churlish before breakfast:* surly, grouchy, crabbed, bearish, crusty, ill-tempered, irascible, testy, irritable, waspish; uncivil, ill-mannered, unmannerly, rude, impolite.

Ant. pleasant, easygoing, good-humored, even-tempered; polite, courteous.

churn *v. Butter is made by churning cream. The sea was churning furiously:* beat, whip, shake, shake up, agitate; toss, heave, roll, roil, rage.

cinder *n. cinders in the furnace:* ember, ash; clinkers, scoria, slag.

cinema *n. Mary Pickford was one of the first stars of the cinema:* motion pictures, moving pictures, movies, films, flicks.

cipher *n.* **1** *One followed by two ciphers is 100:* zero, naught, aught; nothing, nil; *Slang* goose egg, zip. **2** *He was a cipher all his life:* nobody, nonentity, nullity, nothing. **3** *The spy's report was written in cipher:* code, secret writing; cryptograph; anagram, acrostic.

Ant. **1** infinity; something. **2** somebody, notable.

circle *n.* **1** *Gather around in a circle. There's a circle of haze around the moon:* ring, circuit; halo, corona, belt, girdle, circlet. **2** *He is not in my circle of friends. Sports are not within my circle of interests:* group, set, coterie, clique; sphere, field, realm, compass, range, theater, sweep. **3** *the circle of the seasons:* cycle, round, revolution, turn, swing, circuit, course, sequence, progression. —*v.* **4** *The fence circles the yard:* encircle, surround, ring, enclose, border, circuit; wind about, bound. **5** *The plane circled the airport. The children circled around and around:* revolve around, curve around, move around; revolve, pivot, reel, turn.

circuit *n.* **1** *The circuit of the earth around the sun:* circling, orbiting, revolving; revolution, course. **2** *It rained within a fifty mile circuit of town:* circumference, perimeter, area; border, bounds, limit, confine; extremity, edge, margin. **3** *The mail carrier makes the same circuit every day:* beat, route, round, course, territory, tour.

circuitous *adj. a circuitous path. circuitous reasoning:* circular, winding, roundabout, circumlocutory, indirect, meandering, rambling; serpentine, labyrinthine.

Ant. direct, straight.

circular *adj.* **1** *a circular table. a circular drive:* round, rounded, ring-shaped, curved. **2** *the circular motion of the merry-go-round:* turning, rotary, revolving, spinning, twirl-

ing, pivoting, coiling, swiveling, gyrating. —*n.* **3** *a circular advertising the sale:* handbill, bill, flier, leaflet, throwaway.

Ant. **1** square, rectangular; straight.

circulate *v.* **1** *Blood circulates in the veins and arteries. Waiters circulated among the guests:* flow, circle, move around, course; go around, move about; visit around. **2** *Pictures of the criminals were circulated:* distribute, disperse, pass around, give out; make public, spread, publicize, make known.

Ant. **2** keep secret, hide, conceal; suppress.

circulation *n.* **1** *the circulation of the blood:* flow, flowing, circling; rotation, motion. **2** *The five-dollar gold piece is no longer in circulation:* distribution, dissemination.

circumference *n. the circumference of the moon. the entire circumference of the island:* distance around, periphery, perimeter, boundary, extremity, edge, margin, rim, outline.

Ant. center, interior.

circumlocution *n. The speech was full of circumlocutions:* roundaboutness, roundabout expression, verbiage, garrulity, verbosity, rambling, digression.

Ant. directness, conciseness, terseness, succinctness.

circumscribe *v.* **1** *On this map, cities are circumscribed in red:* circle, encircle, delineate, surround, enclose. **2** *His illness circumscribed his activities:* limit, restrict, restrain, confine, constrain, impede, curb.

Ant. **2** expand, extend.

circumspect *adj. Be circumspect in making decisions:* careful, cautious, guarded, discreet, wary, prudent.

Ant. rash, reckless, foolhardy, audacious.

circumstance *n.* **1** *Bad weather is a circumstance we cannot control:* factor, occurrence, happening, phenomenon, condition, state of affairs, matter. **2** *The coronation was an occasion for pomp and circumstance:* ceremony, pageantry, ritual, formality.

circumstantial *adj.* **1** *circumstantial evidence:* presumed, inferred, inferential, conjectural, implied, deduced; incidental, provisional, secondary. **2** *a circumstantial account:* detailed, precise, explicit, full, complete, thorough, blow-by-blow.

Ant. **2** cursory, superficial.

circumvent *v. The pilot circumvented the storm:* circle, circumnavigate, go around, bypass, skirt; escape, avoid, elude, evade.

citadel *n. Soldiers defended the citadel:* fortress, fort, stronghold, bastion, fortification.

citation *n.* **1** *The book contains citations from famous authors:* quotation, quote, excerpt, passage, extract. **2** *citations for brav-ery:* commendation, official praise; medal, award, honor.

cite *v.* **1** *The lawyer cited a previous case to support her argument:* allude to, refer to, specify, quote, mention, note, bring forward, give as example. **2** *The corporal was cited for bravery:* commend, honor, mention, name.

citizen *n. citizens of the United States. citizens of Paris:* national, subject; inhabitant, resident, denizen, native.
Ant. alien, foreigner.

city *n.* **1** *The city is an exciting place:* big town, megalopolis, metropolis; incorporated town, municipality. **2** *The entire city celebrated:* population of a city, townspeople, inhabitants, residents, denizens.

civic *adj.* **1** *a civic duty:* citizen's, public. **2** *civic pride:* communal, community, local, public.

civil *adj.* **1** *civil rights:* citizen, citizen's, individual. **2** *The governors met to discuss civil problems:* community, communal, state, city, municipal, civic. **3** *Public education is under civil control:* communal, secular, lay, civic, public; nonmilitary. **4** *Be civil:* polite, courteous, well-mannered, respectful; cordial, neighborly, amiable, obliging, conciliatory.
Ant. **1** state. **3** religious; military. **4** uncivil, impolite, rude, discourteous; uncordial.

civilian *n. What does it feel like to be a civilian again?:* private citizen, nonmilitary person; nonuniformed person; lay person.
Ant. soldier, member of the military.

civility *n. He treated us with civility:* politeness, courtesy, courteousness, good manners, respect, tact; graciousness, cordiality, good temper.
Ant. impoliteness, discourtesy, bad manners, disrespect; unfriendliness, disagreeableness.

civilization *n.* **1** *We returned to civilization after two years in the jungle:* civilized life or society. **2** *ancient Greek civilization:* society; culture, enlightenment, refinement, sophistication.
Ant. **1, 2** barbarism, savagery.

civilize *v. to civilize the children:* educate, teach, enlighten, humanize.

clad *adj. The beggar was clad in rags:* clothed, dressed, attired, outfitted, garbed, arrayed.
Ant. undressed, unclothed, naked.

claim *v.* **1** *She claimed the ring was stolen:* assert, declare, maintain, avow, allege. **2** *Has anyone claimed the gloves you found?:* lay claim to, seek as due; call for, request,

take. —*n.* **3** *The defendant's claim of innocence:* assertion, avowal, declaration, profession, postulation. **4** *The doctor's work makes too many claims on her time. His claim to the property was valid:* demand, requirement; right, title, ownership.
Ant. **1** deny. **2** disclaim, renounce, repudiate, refuse, forgo, waive. **3** disavowal, denial.

clairvoyant *adj. Mediums are said to be clairvoyant:* telepathic, psychic, extrasensory, prescient, precognitive, oracular, telekinetic, psychokinetic, psychometric.

clammy *adj. My hands are clammy:* cold and damp, damp, sticky, slimy, pasty; sweaty, perspiring.

clamor *n.* **1** *the clamor of the traffic:* noise, din, hubbub, jangle, clangor; tumult, commotion, chaos, bedlam; shouting. **2** *a clamor of protest:* cry, outcry, shout, call, bellow, yell, howl. —*v.* **3** *The audience clamored for the star:* shout, cry out, call out, call, bellow, howl, yell.
Ant. **1–3** whisper, murmur. **1** silence, quiet.

clan *n.* **1** *a Scottish clan:* tribal family, family group, house, dynasty; line, lineage, strain. **2** *The same clan of actors always eats here:* circle, group, party, crowd, brotherhood.

clandestine *adj. The spy had a clandestine meeting:* secret, undercover, covert, secretive; private, confidential, unrevealed; stealthy, surreptitious; underhanded.
Ant. open, public, disclosed, revealed.

clang *v.* **1** *The bells clanged:* ring loudly, resound, peal, bong, gong, chime, toll, knell, jangle. —*n.* **2** *the clang of pots and pans:* clash, clashing, din, clangor, clank; resounding, peal, tolling, knell, bong, gong, jangle.

clank *n.* **1** *pots and pans clanking in the kitchen:* rattle, clang, clink, clangor, chink, jangle. —*v.* **2** *The snow chains clanked every time the car moved:* rattle, clang, clink, jangle, clatter.

clannish *adj. The older families in town are clannish:* cliquish, exclusive, aloof, distant, unfriendly.
Ant. friendly, warm.

clap *v.* **1** *The audience clapped:* applaud. **2** *The victorious players clapped each other on the back:* slap, smack, strike, whack, thump, hit, thwack; bump, buffet. **3** *A detective clapped the handcuffs on the suspect. He clapped the door shut:* set, thrust; slam, hurl, fling, push, shove. —*n.* **4** *a sudden clap on the shoulder:* slap, slam, rap, smack, swat, hit, whack, cuff, thump, thwack. **5** *a clap of thunder:* peal, burst, roar, crack, explosion.

claptrap   clean

Ant. **1** boo, hiss, give a Bronx cheer, give
the raspberry.

claptrap *n. an old-fashioned melodrama,
full of claptrap:* pretentiousness, humbug,
sham, staginess, quackery, hokum, blarney,
twaddle; flapdoodle, bosh.

clarify *v.* **1** *How do you clarify syrup?:* clear,
purify. **2** *His explanation clarified the mystery:* clear up, make clear, resolve, solve,
illuminate, explicate, make plain, make understandable.

Ant. **2** obscure, confuse.

clarion *adj. the clarion call of a bugle:* clear,
shrill, high-pitched, ringing, sharp, piercing, blaring; resonant, sonorous; stirring,
compelling.

Ant. muted, muffled, soft.

clarity *n.* **1** *He analyzed the situation with
clarity:* lucidity, intelligibility, comprehensi-
bility; precision, exactness, explicitness.
2 *The clarity of the water was amazing:*
clearness, transparency, purity.

Ant. **1** confusion; imprecision. **2** muddi-
ness, murkiness.

clash *v.* **1** *The garbage cans clashed:* crash,
clang, bang, clatter, crash. **2** *The armies
clashed on the plain:* battle, fight, contest,
contend, combat, skirmish, cross swords,
exchange blows. **3** *The lawyers clashed in
court:* argue, dispute, quarrel, wrangle,
squabble, lock horns. —*n.* **4** *the clash of
swords:* crash, crashing, clang, clatter,
clangor. **5** *The clash occurred at dawn:* battle, fight, combat, contest, fray, skirmish,
encounter. **6** *the clash of opinions:* conflict,
disagreement, difference, opposition.

Ant. **2** make peace. **3** agree, concur.
5 peace, truce. **6** concord, accord.

clasp *n.* **1** *The bracelet has a gold clasp:* fastening, fastener, catch, latch, hasp, buckle.
2 *The child held my hand in a tight clasp:*
hold, grip, embrace, hug, grasp. —*v.* **3**
Clasp the necklace with the catch: latch,
hook, lock, hasp, buckle, secure, fasten.
4 *The child clasped the doll tightly:* hold,
grip, grasp, hug, embrace, clutch.

Ant. **3** unclasp, unfasten, open. **4** let go,
release.

class *n.* **1** *Pine trees belong to the evergreen
class:* classification, category, group, type,
kind, sort, order, variety, division, genre,
species, genus. **2** *the senior class:* set of
pupils, graduating group, grade, form.
3 *a history class:* course, session; lesson.
4 *the middle class:* social stratum, social
rank, station, status. —*v.* **5** *Jackson Pollock
is classed as an abstract expressionist:* classify, group, categorize, designate, type,
codify, label, pigeonhole.

classic, classical *adj.* **1** *a classic biogra-

phy. Sneezing and a sore throat are classic
symptoms of a cold:* definitive, authoritative; absolute, accepted, traditional, archetypal, prototypal, exemplary; outstanding,
distinguished, consummate. **2** *Latin is a
classical language. Caesar was a hero of classical antiquity:* ancient Greek or Roman;
Greco-Roman. —*n.* **3** *a literary classic:* masterpiece, standard work; prototype, archetype, model, first-class example, paragon.

Ant. **1** bad, poor, inferior; unrepresentative, atypical.

classification *n.* **1** *The classification of
books in the library follows the Dewey Deci-
mal System:* grouping, categorization,
categorizing, arrangement, arranging, organization, ordering, codification, labeling,
systematization. **2** *Aspirin belongs to the
classification of nonprescription drugs:*
group, grouping, class, category; order,
rank, series, family, species, genus, kind,
sort, type.

classify *v. Eggs are classified according to
size:* organize, class, grade, type, rank, rate,
categorize, group, assort.

classy *adj. It was a classy affair:* smart, elegant, fashionable, high-class, stylish, chic,
genteel, refined, ultrasmart; *Slang* posh,
ritzy, swank, tony, spiffy.

clatter *v.* **1** *The shutters clattered in the
wind:* clash, clack, rattle, bang, crash, clang,
clank, clink, jangle. —*n.* **2** *the clatter of
machinery:* clattering, clack, clank, rattling,
crashing, clamor.

clause *n. the third clause of the contract:*
provision, proviso, stipulation, article, covenant.

claw *n.* **1** *the cat's claws:* talon, animal nail.
2 *The animal's claw was caught in the trap.
The boy gnawed on a lobster claw:* paw, foot;
pincer. —*v.* **3** *He clawed at the door:* tear,
maul, lacerate, scratch, scrape.

clean *adj.* **1** *a clean shirt. a clean room:* unsoiled, spotless, immaculate, unstained,
unspotted; cleaned, cleansed, washed,
scrubbed, bathed, scoured, laundered. **2**
The cabinetmaker did a clean job: flawless,
faultless, neat, fine, trim. **3** *clean air:* unpolluted, pure, clear, uncontaminated, undefiled. **4** *a clean life:* wholesome, honorable, upright, virtuous, moral, decent,
innocent, healthy, chaste, exemplary, untainted, unsullied, unblemished, unspotted.
—*v.* **5** *The curtains cleaned beautifully.
Clean your room:* cleanse, wash, scour,
scrub, launder, bathe, shampoo; sweep, vacuum, mop, dust; tidy, tidy up, neaten.

Ant. **1** dirty, filthy, soiled; unwashed, un-
bathed; messy, disorderly. **2** flawed, imperfect, faulty, crude, sloppy. **3** contaminated,

polluted. 4 unwholesome, immoral, indecent, stained, unhealthy, tainted, sullied, blemished. 5 soil, dirty; mess up.

cleanse v. 1 *Cleanse your face thoroughly:* clean, wash, bathe, launder, scrub, scour, shampoo. 2 *Her words cleansed my heart of guilt:* rid, free, expunge, expurgate, clear, absolve; unburden, deliver.
Ant. 1 soil, dirty. 2 burden, weigh down, fill.

clear adj. 1 *a clear sky. The water was clear as glass:* unclouded, cloudless, unobscured, fair, sunny; bright, brilliant, dazzling, sparkling; lucid, transparent, translucent, pellucid. 2 *The singing was loud and clear:* distinct, audible, intelligible, articulate. 3 *Your meaning was clear:* plain, obvious, unmistakable, evident, self-evident, manifest; comprehensible; undisguised, unambiguous; explicit, inescapable, apparent, certain, unequivocal, undeniable; express. 4 *clear thinking:* unconfused, unmuddled, alert, keen, discerning. 5 *The path was clear:* open, free, unobstructed, unimpeded, unblocked. —adv. 6 *I hear you loud and clear:* clearly, distinctly, plainly, audibly, articulately. —v. 7 *The skies cleared:* become unclouded, brighten, lighten; become fair. 8 *The snowplows cleared the streets:* unblock, open; free, remove obstacles from. 9 *The plane cleared the trees easily:* pass over, fly over; vault over, leap over. 10 *A witness cleared him of the crime:* vindicate, exculpate, exonerate, free, absolve, acquit.
Ant. 1 cloudy, clouded, obscured; murky, muddy, unclear. 2 inaudible, unclear, indistinct. 3 unclear, ambiguous, uncertain. 4 confused, muddled. 5 obstructed, blocked, closed. 6 unclearly, indistinctly. 7 cloud, darken. 8 obstruct, block, clog, close.

clear-cut adj. *a clear-cut explanation:* precise, distinct, definite, explicit, lucid, plain, express, detailed, unambiguous, crystal-clear, understandable.
Ant. hazy, vague, muddled, confused.

clearheaded adj. *Stay clearheaded on this job:* alert, clear-witted, sensible, realistic, practical.
Ant. unrealistic, impractical.

clearly adv. *We're clearly in the midst of a drought:* undoubtedly, beyond doubt, beyond question, unquestionably, decidedly, undeniably, certainly; plainly, evidently, unmistakably, noticeably, perceptibly, surely, obviously.

cleave¹ v. *His shirt cleaved to his back. Cleave to your principles:* cling, stick, hold fast, adhere; be faithful, be constant, be true, abide by.

Ant. separate, come loose; forsake, abandon.

cleave² v. 1 *He cleaved the tree:* split, divide, bisect, halve, rend, slice, part; cut, slash, hew, lay open. 2 *He cleaved the bones from the side of beef:* sever, cut off, sunder, chop off.
Ant. 1, 2 unite, join. 2 attach, affix.

cleft n. 1 *a cleft in the ice:* split, crack, crevice, crevasse, rift, fissure, rent, aperture, breach, gap, slit. —adj. 2 *a cleft branch:* divided, cloven, bisected, split, forked.

clemency n. 1 *the judge's clemency:* mercy, mercifulness, forbearance, forgivingness, magnanimity, leniency. 2 *the clemency of the weather:* mildness, moderation, softness, temperance.
Ant. 1 sternness, strictness; hard-heartedness. 2 harshness, severity.

clench v. 1 *He clenched his fists in anger:* close tightly, set firmly, tighten, tense. 2 *She clenched the arms of the chair:* grasp firmly, clasp, grip, hold fast.
Ant. 1 unclench, relax. 2 unclench, unclasp.

clergy n. *members of the clergy:* ministry, priesthood, pastorate, rabbinate, the cloth, clergymen, preachers, ministers, pastors, prelates, priests, rabbis.

clergyman n. *A clergyman should help others:* member of the clergy, minister, priest, reverend, rabbi, father, preacher, pastor, chaplain, man of the cloth.

clerical adj. 1 *clerical work:* of clerks, office; *(variously)* bookkeeping, filing, typing. 2 *clerical robes:* ecclesiastical, churchly, pastoral, ministerial, priestly, rabbinical.

clerk n. 1 *The clerk is an excellent typist:* clerical worker, office worker; *(variously)* file clerk, bookkeeper, typist. 2 *The store needs more clerks:* salesclerk, salesperson, salesman, saleswoman.

clever adj. 1 *a clever student:* smart, bright, sharp, astute, quick, quick-witted. 2 *a clever plan:* ingenious, imaginative, original, adroit, artful, shrewd.
Ant. 1 dull, stupid, inept. 2 clumsy, awkward, unimaginative.

cleverly adv. *The escape was cleverly executed:* ingeniously, imaginatively, craftily, artfully, adroitly, deftly, intelligently.
Ant. inexpertly, stupidly, awkwardly.

cliché n. *an old cliché:* hackneyed expression, saw, stereotype, banality, platitude, trite phrase.

click n. 1 *the click of a key in the door:* sharp sound, clack, clink, snap. —v. 2 *The lock clicked shut:* clack, clink, crack, snap.

client n. *The shop has many clients:* person

represented, advisee; patron, customer, purchaser, shopper.

cliff *n. the top of a cliff:* bluff, palisade, precipice, promontory.

climate *n.* 1 *a mild climate:* usual weather, weather pattern, weather. 2 *The climate of the meeting was tense:* general feeling, atmosphere, spirit, character, temper.

climax *n.* 1 *the climax of our trip:* highest point, high point, culmination, supreme moment, crowning point, height, peak. 2 *the climax of the play:* turning point, decisive point, critical point, moment of revelation, denouement.

Ant. 1 nadir. 2 anticlimax.

climb *v.* 1 *The cat climbed the tree:* ascend, clamber up, scramble up, scale, rise, go up, come up. —*n.* 2 *the climb to the mountain top:* ascent, climbing.

Ant. 1 descend, go down, come down. 2 descent.

clinch *v.* 1 *The touchdown clinched the game. I clinched the deal with a handshake:* make sure of winning, win; obtain, make sure, settle, cinch, secure; close, conclude, establish, fix, verify, confirm. 2 *Clinch the boards together:* nail, screw, clamp, bolt, fasten.

cling *v. Wet clothes cling to the body. Cling to your beliefs:* stick, hold, adhere, cleave; hang on to, hold on to, be faithful, be constant, be true.

Ant. separate; let go, forsake, abandon, relinquish.

clinic *n. a health clinic:* medical center, outpatients' ward; infirmary.

clink *n.* 1 *Keys clinked in his pocket:* jangle, clank, jingle, tinkle, clack. —*n.* 2 *the clink of glasses:* tinkle, ting, jingle, clank.

clip¹ *v.* 1 *Clip the shrubbery:* cut off, shorten, trim, crop. —*n.* 2 *The veterinarian gave the dog a close clip:* clipping, trim, crop, cropping, cut, bob, shearing, cutting.

clip² *v.* 1 *Clip the cards together:* clamp, fasten, couple, clinch. —*n.* 2 *a hair clip:* fastener, grip, clasp, clinch.

Ant. 1 unclip, unfasten, separate.

clique *n. The summer visitors form a clique:* coterie, circle, set, faction, crowd.

cloak *n.* 1 *an ermine cloak:* cape, mantle, robe. 2 *a cloak of secrecy:* cover, curtain, shield, concealment, veil, curtain. —*v.* 3 *The soldiers cloaked their fear:* hide, mask, veil, conceal, disguise.

Ant. 3 reveal, show, bare.

clobber *v. The champion clobbered the challenger:* wallop, whip, batter, beat up, hit, punch, strike, clout, beat the tar out of; *Slang* belt, slug, sock.

clod *n.* 1 *clods of dirt:* lump, clump, chunk,

glob. 2 *He's a clod:* boor, bumpkin, lout; dolt, oaf, ignoramus.

clog *v.* 1 *Leaves clogged the gutter:* stop up, stop, block, obstruct, choke. —*n.* 2 *There's a clog in the pipe:* stoppage, obstruction, block, blockage.

Ant. 1 unclog, unblock, clear.

cloister *n.* 1 *a life of prayer in a cloister:* monastery, abbey, friary; convent, nunnery. 2 *He waited in the cloister:* colonnade, gallery, arcade, ambulatory, walkway, promenade. —*v.* 3 *They cloistered themselves from the world:* sequester, shut away, seclude, closet.

cloistered *adj. to lead a cloistered life:* secluded, sheltered, withdrawn, recluse, sequestered, solitary; hidden, concealed.

close *v.* 1 *Close the door. Close the hole in the wall with plaster. Close the horse in the stall:* shut, secure; close up, stop up, fill, fill in, plug, plug up, block; shut in, confine. 2 *The surgeon closed the incision:* join, connect, unite, bring together. 3 *schools closed for the holiday:* end, conclude, stop, cease; adjourn, recess, suspend, discontinue. —*adj.* 4 *The house is close to the park. Winter is close:* near, nearby, next to, neighboring; imminent, at hand, impending, nigh. 5 *a close grip. Keep a close watch on the children:* tight, firm, secure, fast; alert, intent, careful, attentive, vigilant. 6 *close quarters. a close weave:* congested, crowded, populous; tight, cramped, confined, narrow, restricted; solid, impenetrable, impermeable. 7 *The air is very close:* stuffy, stagnant; muggy, humid; hot, warm. 8 *The brothers are very close:* friendly, intimate, loving, devoted; inseparable, allied. 9 *The color is close to what I want. a close race:* near, similar, akin, almost like, nearly. 10 *He's close with his money:* stingy, miserly, tight, tight-fisted, close-fisted, penurious, parsimonious, niggardly. —*n.* 11 *the close of the game:* end, finish, conclusion, completion, closing, ending, finale. —*adv.* 12 *Come close:* near, nearby, in proximity.

Ant. 1–3, 5, 6, 10 open. 1 unstop, unplug, unclog; release, let out. 2 widen; separate, part. 3 begin, start, commence. 4 far, distant. 5 loose, weak; careless. 6 spacious, uncrowded; open, loose. 7 fresh, cool. 8 unfriendly, distant, indifferent. 10 extravagant, generous, open-handed, free, liberal. 11 beginning, start, commencement. 12 far.

close-fisted *adj. as close-fisted as Scrooge:* stingy, miserly, niggardly, parsimonious, penurious, penny-pinching, tight-fisted.

Ant. generous, open-handed.

closely *adv. Listen closely:* carefully, attentively, heedfully, intently, vigilantly.
Ant. carelessly, inattentively.

close-mouthed *adj. She's close-mouthed about her personal affairs:* uncommunicative, reticent, taciturn, secretive.
Ant. open, talkative.

closure *n.* 1 *a container with a small closure:* stopper, cork; cover, lid. 2 *the closure of the doors:* closing, shutting; locking, barring. 3 *the closure of debate:* termination, conclusion, ending, stop, closing, cloture, stoppage.
Ant. 3 beginning, opening, start.

clot *n.* 1 *a blood clot:* embolism, occlusion, coagulation, gob, lump, thrombus. —*v.* 2 *Her blood doesn't clot properly:* coagulate, congeal, solidify.

cloth *n. two yards of cloth:* fabric, dry goods, piece goods, yard goods, goods, textile.

clothe *v.* 1 *I clothed myself for the party:* dress, attire, garb, array, cloak, deck, outfit, costume. 2 *A fog clothed the road:* cover, envelop, enwrap, shroud, cloak, veil.
Ant. 1 undress, disrobe, strip. 2 uncover, expose.

clothes *n. pl. We make our own clothes:* clothing, wearing apparel, apparel, garments, wardrobe, attire, *Slang* duds, togs.

clothing *n.* See CLOTHES.

cloud *v.* 1 *The sky clouded. Fog clouded the road.* grow cloudy, overcast, darken; obscure, blur, cover, veil, cloak, conceal, hide. 2 *A misunderstanding clouded his good name:* place under suspicion, discredit, tarnish, sully. 3 *Love can cloud your vision:* impair, distort, mar, disturb; confuse, muddle, blind.
Ant. 1 clear; show, reveal. 2 confirm, clear. 3 clear; restore.

cloudy *adj.* 1 *cloudy skies:* clouded, overclouded, overcast, dark, gray, leaden; hazy, murky, sunless. 2 *The reason is rather cloudy:* unclear, vague, confused, hazy, mysterious, obscure.
Ant. 1 uncloudy, clear, bright, fair, sunny. 2 clear, transparent, plain, obvious.

clown *n.* 1 *a circus clown. The boy plays the clown to get attention:* buffoon, jester, comic, comedian, fool, zany, joker, merry-andrew; wit, wag, card. —*v.* 2 *Don't clown around!:* joke, jest, cut up, fool around.

club *n.* 1 *The officer swung a club:* truncheon, bludgeon, stick, bat, billyclub, billy. 2 *a bridge club:* group, society, league, association; brotherhood, sisterhood, lodge. 3 *Dances were held at the club:* clubhouse; country club. —*v.* 4 *The farmer clubbed the snake:* beat, strike, hit, pummel, bat, bash, cudgel, bludgeon, flail.

clue *n. a clue to the mystery:* hint, cue, indication, mark, key, scent, inkling; guide, indicator, pointer; inference, suggestion.

clump *n.* 1 *clumps of daisies:* cluster, group, mass, bunch; thicket, grove, copse. 2 *clumps of soil:* lump, mass; knot, knob. 3 *The book fell with a clump:* thump, thud, clunk, plunk, bump. —*v.* 4 *The skiers clumped into the lodge:* stomp, stamp; plod, lumber.

clumsy *adj.* 1 *a clumsy waiter:* blundering, bungling, careless, butterfingered; inept, graceless, ungraceful, awkward. 2 *a clumsy package to carry. a clumsy piece of work:* cumbersome, unwieldy, unmanageable; awkward, crude, rough, inept, ill-contrived, careless.
Ant. 1 deft, handy, adroit; graceful. 2 handy; professional, expert.

cluster *n.* 1 *clusters of four-leaf clovers. People were standing in a cluster:* clump, bunch, mass; group, crowd, knot, band, throng, pack. —*v.* 2 *The campers clustered around the fire:* gather, group, crowd, bunch, collect, congregate, throng, converge.

clutch *v.* 1 *The girl clutched my hand tightly:* grasp, clasp, hold, grip; hug, embrace, squeeze. —*n.* 2 *The man held the money in a tight clutch:* grasp, hold, grip, clasp; hug, embrace.
Ant. 1 let go, loose.

clutter *v.* 1 *Children clutter rooms with toys:* strew, litter, pile, heap. —*n.* 2 *a clutter of dirty dishes. The clutter in this room is disgraceful:* pile, heap; mess, litter, hodgepodge, jumble, disorder, disarray.
Ant. 1 straighten, tidy, arrange, organize. 2 neatness, tidiness, order.

coach *n.* 1 *a coach pulled by white horses:* carriage; stagecoach, stage. 2 *The train has new coaches:* railroad passenger car; motor coach, bus, omnibus. 3 *a football coach. The professor was the boy's math coach:* trainer, athletic director; tutor, private teacher, preceptor, mentor. —*v.* 4 *I coach a baseball team:* train, instruct, tutor, teach, drill; advise, direct.

coagulate *v. The blood will coagulate:* clot, congeal; solidify; set, gel, jell, harden, thicken.

coalesce *v. The Liberal and Democratic parties coalesced to back one candidate:* unite, unify, combine, fuse, meld, join, join forces, come together, form an alliance, merge.
Ant. separate, divide, part; split.

coalition *n. a coalition of charities:* alliance, partnership, affiliation, federation, association, confederacy, combination; fusion, consolidation.

coarse *adj.* 1 *a coarse beard:* rough, rough-textured, scratchy, bristly, bristling. **2** *a coarse man:* crude, unrefined, rough, ungentlemanly, unladylike, ill-bred, uncouth, boorish, loutish, brutish, rude, ill-mannered; vulgar, indelicate, indecent, indecorous, gross, lewd, licentious, lascivious, ribald. *Ant.* **1** smooth, soft, silky. **2** refined, gentlemanly, ladylike, genteel, well-bred, cultivated, polished; polite, well-mannered, mannerly; decent, delicate, decorous.

coast *n.* **1** *Fishing was good along the coast:* seacoast, shore, littoral, strand, shoreline, seaboard. —*v.* **2** *The sled coasted down the slope:* glide, glissade, skim; slide. *Ant.* **1** interior, hinterland.

coat *n.* **1** *Wear a heavy coat:* topcoat, overcoat; raincoat; jacket, sports coat. **2** *The horse's coat was shiny:* hair, fur, hide, pelt. **3** *Apply two coats of paint:* coating, covering; layer. —*v.* **4** *Coat the table with varnish:* cover, spread, overlay, *(variously)* paint, enamel, lacquer, glaze, whitewash.

coating *n. a coating of snow:* coat, covering, layer, overlay, film, sheet, veneer.

coax *v. John coaxed his father to let him use the car:* wheedle, cajole; inveigle, talk into.
Ant. intimidate, threaten, bully, coerce.

cock *n.* **1** *The cock crowed:* cockerel, rooster; male bird. **2** *Turn the cock to increase the flow:* valve, faucet, handle, knob. —*v.* **3** *The puppy cocked its ear:* raise, stand up, perk up.
Ant. **1** hen; chick.

cockeyed *adj.* **1** *Her hat was cockeyed:* awry, aslant, askew, off-center; crooked, twisted, tilted, lopsided. **2** *one of his cockeyed ideas:* ridiculous, foolish, preposterous, insane, crazy; *Slang* goofy, wild, weird.
Ant. **1** straight, centered, even. **2** sensible, reasonable.

cocksure *adj. He was so cocksure, he could never admit a mistake:* cocky, overconfident, arrogant, brash, smug, overbearing, swaggering, self-assured.

coddle *v.* **1** *His parents coddled him:* pamper, spoil, indulge, baby, mollycoddle. **2** *The mother coddled the baby:* fondle, cuddle, caress.
Ant. **1** neglect; deny.

code *n.* **1** *The spy sent his message in code:* secret writing, secret language; cipher; cryptogram, cryptograph. **2** *the club's code of dress:* laws, rules, regulations, standards; statute, ordinance.

codicil *n. a codicil to the will:* added clause, addendum, rider; postscript, appendix.

codify *v. The computer will codify the data:* classify, catalog, categorize, systematize, arrange, organize, index, methodize.

coerce *v. Prisoners were coerced into con-*fessing: force, pressure, compel, make, intimidate, cow, bully, strong-arm.
Ant. coax, cajole.

coercion *n. The prisoner confessed under coercion:* force, pressure, compulsion, intimidation, threats, browbeating.
Ant. by choice, volition.

coffer *n.* **1** *a coffer of coins:* depository, chest, treasure chest, strongbox, case. **2 coffers.** *The nation's coffers are empty:* treasury, vaults, cash boxes.

coffin *n. The coffin was taken to the cemetery:* casket, pall, catafalque, sarcophagus.

cogent *adj. cogent reasons:* compelling, valid, persuasive, forceful, powerful, convincing, well-founded, sound, well-grounded.
Ant. unconvincing, unsound, dubious.

cogitate *v. I need to cogitate the problem:* think, ponder, contemplate, think about, reflect upon, deliberate on, mull over, consider thoroughly.

cognate *adj.* **1** *French and Italian are cognate:* related, kindred, relative, familial, affiliate. **2** *Jogging and bicycling are cognate exercises:* similar, like, alike, parallel.
Ant. **1, 2** unrelated. **2** unlike, unalike, dissimilar, different; unassociated, unaffiliated.

cognizance *n.* **1** *Take cognizance of the flowers:* notice, note, heed, recognition, awareness; regard. **2** *Cognizance of the facts was necessary:* knowledge, awareness, comprehension, perception, understanding.
Ant. **1** disregard, nonobservance. **2** ignorance, unfamiliarity, unawareness.

cognizant *adj. cognizant of one's surroundings:* aware, informed, knowing, familiar, acquainted, conversant; understanding, enlightened, conscious.
Ant. unaware, unfamiliar, unknowing, unacquainted, oblivious, unconscious.

cohere *v.* **1** *The snow wouldn't cohere into snowballs:* stick together, hold together, cling, bind, stick, hold, coalesce. **2** *Our views didn't cohere:* agree, coincide, correspond, match, tally, harmonize, concur, jibe, square.
Ant. **1** separate, scatter, disperse. **2** disagree, differ, diverge, be at odds.

coherence *n. the coherence of her argument:* consistency, cohesion, congruity, rationality; unity, harmony.
Ant. incoherence, inconsistency.

coherent *adj. a coherent story:* logical, intelligible, articulate, rational, lucid, connected, understandable; consistent, cohesive, congruous.
Ant. disjointed, disconnected, inconsistent, incongruous; confusing, incomprehensible.

cohesive adj. a cohesive substance: coherent, cohering, sticky, sticking.

cohort n. He sees his cohorts every night: companion, comrade, fellow, chum, pal, buddy, crony; associate; accomplice, follower.

coiffure n. The hairdresser created a dramatic new coiffure: hairdo, hairstyle, Slang coif.

coil v. 1 Vines coiled around the tree: wind, spiral, loop, twist, twine; encircle. —n. 2 a coil of rope: loop, spiral, ring, circle; curl, braid.

coin n. 1 five dollars in coin: change, silver. —v. 2 Who coined that phrase?: create, make up, originate, invent, concoct, think up.

coincide v. 1 The two paths coincide. Our birthdays coincide: meet, come together, converge; be concurrent, occur simultaneously. 2 Do the two stories coincide?: agree, concur, accord, correspond, match, tally, jibe, square.
Ant. 1 diverge, separate, part. 2 disagree, differ, contradict.

coincidence n. It was pure coincidence: chance, accident, happenstance.
Ant. design, plan, on purpose.

coincidental adj. 1 The meeting was coincidental: accidental, unplanned, chance, happenstance. 2 Her illness was coincidental with the bad news: simultaneous, contiguous, concomitant.

cold adj. 1 a glass of cold milk. The coffee is cold: cool, cooled, chilled, ice-cold, frigid; unheated, unwarmed. 2 cold weather: wintry, freezing, chilly, chill, cool, icy, frigid, glacial, arctic, brisk, crisp, snappy, nippy, bitter, severe, biting, bone-chilling. 3 You must be cold: chilled, chilly, cool, chilled to the bone, freezing. 4 a cold look: unemotional, passionless, frigid, unresponsive, unfeeling, unmoved; impervious, impassive, unexcitable, apathetic, unsympathetic, unconcerned; indifferent, uncaring, unloving; unfriendly; reserved, detached, aloof, haughty, disdainful, forbidding, steely; heartless, cold-hearted, cruel, inured, callous. 5 (Informal) The fighter was knocked cold: unconscious, insensible, insensate. —n. 6 Some people feel the cold more than others: coldness, coolness, chill.
Ant. 1–4 hot, warm. 1 steaming; heated, warmed. 2 sweltering, balmy, mild, summery. 3 sweltering, roasting. 4 passionate, ardent, fervent, responsive; animated, spirited; sympathetic, compassionate, concerned, caring, loving, friendly. 5 conscious. 6 heat, warmth.

cold-blooded adj. 1 a cold-blooded speech:

unfeeling, unemotional, passionless, unimpassioned; unsympathetic, implacable, unfriendly, reserved, formal, stiff; unconcerned, detached, uncaring, unmoved, passive, impassive; calculating, stony, cruel, callous. 2 a cold-blooded murder: brutal, inhuman, bloodthirsty, savage, fiendish, ruthless, merciless, unmerciful, diabolical.
Ant. 1 warm, emotional, heartfelt, passionate, impassioned; sympathetic, compassionate, friendly, responsive, concerned, caring, loving, kind. 2 humane, merciful.

coliseum n. a sports coliseum: stadium, arena, amphitheater, bowl; theater, exhibition hall.

collaborate v. 1 They collaborated on the song: work together, team up, create together, cooperate. 2 Few townspeople collaborated with the enemy: cooperate, collude, assist.

collaborator n. 1 Gilbert and Sullivan were collaborators: colleague, confederate, coworker, co-partner. 2 Following the liberation of Paris, many collaborators were executed: collaborationist, quisling, traitor.

collapse v. 1 The earthquake caused the building to collapse: cave in, fall, buckle, give way, crumple. 2 The negotiations collapsed: break down, fall through, flounder. 3 to collapse from smoke inhalation. to collapse with laughter: fall prostrate, become unconscious, Slang keel over; fall helpless, give way, break up. —n. 4 The collapse of the bridge forced the ferry into operation. the collapse of the government: fall, falling apart, disintegration; downfall, breakdown, failure. 5 Her collapse was brought on by overwork: breakdown, sudden illness, attack.
Ant. 2 succeed, triumph. 3 get well, recover.

collateral n. 1 The house was collateral for the loan: security, pledge, warranty, guarantee, surety. —adj. 2 The information was collateral to the main issue: secondary, incidental, auxiliary; supplementary, additional, supporting, supportive.
Ant. 2 primary, essential, fundamental, basic.

colleague n. She was highly respected by her colleagues: confrere, associate, fellow; coworker, fellow worker, teammate.
Ant. rival, competitor, opponent.

collect v. 1 A crowd collected to watch the fight: gather, assemble, congregate, cluster around, draw together, convene. 2 Dust collects on furniture: accumulate, amass, pile up. 3 The charity collected $1,000,000 this year: raise, obtain, solicit, amass, get, muster. 4 *The garbage is collected every Wednesday:* pick up, call for, gather up. 5 *Give me a few minutes to collect myself:* compose, calm, get hold of, pull together; prepare, muster, marshal.

Ant. 1–4 disperse, scatter.

collected *adj. The witness was remarkably collected:* self-controlled, self-possessed, composed, poised, calm, cool, steady; even-tempered; serene, tranquil, peaceful, unruffled, unperturbed, undisturbed, unemotional.

Ant. nervous, perturbed, disturbed, ruffled, distressed.

collection *n.* 1 *a strange collection of people. a collection of books:* group, gathering, assemblage, crowd, bunch, body; accumulation, assortment, array; heap, pile, cluster. 2 *a stamp collection. a collection of short stories:* assemblage, aggregation, compilation, store; anthology. 3 *The church collection was made before the hymn:* collecting, gathering, accumulating, receiving; soliciting; gift, offertory, oblation.

collective *adj. The team made a strong collective effort:* unified, joint, combined, cooperative, common, cumulative.

Ant. individual, separate.

collide *v.* 1 *The cars collided:* run into one another, crash, hit; strike against, bump into. 2 *Their political views collide:* disagree, conflict, clash, diverge.

Ant. 2 agree, coincide, accord, mesh, jibe.

collision *n.* 1 *a three-car collision:* crash, smash-up, accident; impact, clash, bump. 2 *the collision of the opposing armies:* battle, combat, fight, encounter, engagement.

colloquial *adj. colloquial language:* folksy, homespun, homey, chatty, vernacular, idiomatic, everyday, informal, conversational, familiar.

Ant. formal; literary.

colloquy *n. a colloquy between the ambassadors:* talk, dialogue, conference, discussion, parley, discourse, council.

collusion *n. He was in collusion with the enemy:* secret agreement, conspiracy, collaboration, intrigue, guilty association; treason; fraud.

colony *n.* 1 *a Dutch colony:* settlement, province, territory, dependency, possession, mandate. 2 *A colony of terns inhabits the island:* community, group, body, band, swarm, flock.

color *n.* 1 *bright colors:* coloring, coloration, tint, hue, shade, tone, tinge, cast; pigment, pigmentation, paint, dye, dyestuff. 2 *It was the color of his criticism that hurt her:* tone, spirit, mood, intent, intention, force, implication, insinuation, connotation, import.

—*v.* 3 *Let's color the walls green:* paint, stain, dye, tint, crayon, chalk, wash. 4 *Judges can't let personal feelings color decisions:* prejudice, influence, affect, bias, distort, taint. 5 *Her face colored when she was embarrassed:* redden, blush, flush, glow, become florid.

Ant. 2 denotation. 5 blanch, go white.

colorful *adj.* 1 *colorful wallpaper:* brightly colored, bright, vibrant, florid, loud; multicolored, many-colored. 2 *a colorful character:* interesting; unusual, distinctive, unique; vivid, dynamic, forceful.

Ant. 1 dull, drab, dreary, dark; faded, washed-out, pale. 2 dull, uninteresting, colorless.

colorless *adj.* 1 *Many washings had made the shirt colorless:* without color, natural, neutral; whitened, grayed, pale, bleached, faded, washed-out, dull. 2 *colorless skin:* pale, pallid, ashen, ashy, wan, blanched, white, sallow, pasty. 3 *a colorless personality:* dull, unexciting, lifeless, boring, unanimated; ordinary, commonplace, vapid, insipid.

Ant. 1 bright, lustrous, colorful. 2 ruddy. 3 colorful, exciting, interesting, lively, dynamic, strong.

colossal *adj. colossal strength. a colossal blunder:* extremely large, huge, immense, massive, enormous, gigantic, giant, mammoth, great, tremendous; prodigious, inordinate, imposing, awe-inspiring, monumental.

Ant. small, little; ordinary, average, so-so.

column *n.* 1 *white marble columns:* pillar, support, upright, post, pilaster. 2 *The accounting ledger had many columns:* vertical row, vertical list; row, line. 3 *a column of soldiers:* row, line, file; procession, formation, caravan, train.

comatose *adj.* 1 *The patient was comatose:* unconscious, insensible. 2 *The stock market was comatose all winter:* sluggish, lifeless, torpid, lethargic, listless, inactive, inert; indifferent, unresponsive.

Ant. 2 active, lively.

comb *n.* 1 *a comb and brush:* hair comb, fine-tooth comb; card, currycomb. 2 *The rooster had a red comb:* cockscomb, topknot; tuft, panache. —*v.* 3 *Comb your hair:* dress, groom, untangle; style, arrange; curry, card. 4 *Police combed the house:* search, hunt over, look through, scour.

combat *n.* 1 *The ship was sunk in combat:* military action, action, fighting, battle, engagement. 2 *We're engaged in a combat over the housing bill:* conflict, battle, clash, struggle, fight, confrontation. —*v.* 3 *to combat invaders. to combat disease:* fight, battle, do battle with, war against, wage war, go to war; grapple with, struggle with, resist, oppose. *Ant.* 1 peace; armistice, truce. 2 agreement, accord, concord.

combatant *n. How many combatants were killed?:* fighting man, soldier, serviceman; fighter. *Ant.* noncombatant; civilian.

combination *n.* 1 *The combination of yellow and blue forms green:* combining, mixture, mix, mixing, blend, union; compound, composite, synthesis, amalgam; assortment. 2 *The combination of 50 states forms the United States:* union, federation, confederation, confederacy; merger, alliance, association, coalition, league. *Ant.* 1, 2 division, separation.

combine *v. combine yellow and blue. They combined their resources:* unite, join, bring together, put together, merge, consolidate, pool, lump together; mix, blend, mingle, commingle, compound, amalgamate. *Ant.* separate, divide.

combustible *adj. Gasoline is highly combustible:* flammable, inflammable, incendiary, conflagrative, burnable.

combustion *n. spontaneous combustion:* burning, ignition, kindling, flaming.

come *v.* 1 *Come here!:* move toward, approach, draw near. 2 *When are the guests coming?:* arrive, reach a destination; appear, show up. 3 *Father's birthday comes in September:* take place, fall, occur, happen, come to pass; appear, materialize, arrive; advance, approach. 4 *The belt came unbuckled:* become; be. 5 *John Kennedy came from Boston. This radio comes from Japan:* be a resident, be a native; issue, arise, descend; germinate; be a product of, originate in, emanate. 6 *The curtains come just to the window sill:* reach, extend, stretch, range, spread. 7 *The blouse comes in all colors:* be made, be produced, be available. *Ant.* 1, 2 go, go away, depart.

comedian *n. a very funny comedian:* comic, joker, jokester, humorist, wag; clown, jester, buffoon, madcap, zany, prankster; comic actor.

comedy *n.* 1 *Shakespeare wrote many comedies:* play with a happy ending, farce, satire, light entertainment; travesty, burlesque. 2 *The situation left no room for comedy:* joking, jesting, humor, wit, banter; silliness, foolery, tomfoolery, cutting up, buffoonery, horseplay. *Ant.* 1 tragedy; melodrama. 2 seriousness, solemnity, sadness.

comely *adj.* 1 *a comely child:* pretty, fair, well-favored, attractive, bonny, winsome,

pleasing, engaging. 2 *The child's comely behavior:* seemly, becoming, suitable, tasteful, proper, decorous; appealing, pleasing, agreeable, engaging, charming; natural, simple, unaffected. *Ant.* 1 ugly, homely, unattractive, ill-favored. 2 unseemly, unbecoming, tactless, indecorous, improper; disagreeable, unpleasant; affected, pretentious.

come-on *n. The ad was a come-on to attract customers:* lure, enticement, allurement, seduction, bait, snare.

comfort *v.* 1 *to comfort a child:* console, solace, soothe, quiet, calm, reassure; hearten, encourage. —*n.* 2 *After the disaster, we found comfort in our friends:* solace, succor, reassurance; peace, calm, cheering up; help, relief. 3 *The child is a great comfort to me:* consolation, solace; source of serenity, source of encouragement. 4 *all the comforts of home:* creature comforts; ease, satisfaction, gratification, contentment, coziness. *Ant.* 1–4 discomfort, distress, trouble. 1 aggravate, annoy; sadden, depress, dishearten, discourage. 2–4 aggravation, irritation, annoyance; sadness, discouragement. 3 bane. 4 inconvenience.

comfortable *adj.* 1 *a comfortable house:* providing comfort, giving ease; pleasant, congenial, agreeable, satisfactory, adequate. 2 *I don't feel comfortable with strangers at ease,* easy, relaxed, serene, untroubled. *Ant.* uncomfortable. 1 unsatisfactory, unsuitable. 2 uneasy, nervous, tense, disturbed.

comic Also **comical** *adj. a comic state of affairs:* funny, humorous, laughable, amusing, ludicrous, absurd, mirthful, risible, whimsical, jocose, jocular, droll, witty. *Ant.* tragic; serious; pathetic, sad, depressing.

coming *n.* 1 *the coming of rain:* arrival, arriving, approach, approaching, nearing; advent, occurrence, emergence. —*adj.* 2 *the coming year:* next, forthcoming, subsequent; advancing, approaching; future, to come, on the way. *Ant.* 1 departure, withdrawal. 2 past, previous, prior.

command *v.* 1 *The king commanded the guards to fire:* order, direct, bid, charge, call upon, instruct; call for, summon, enjoin. 2 *General Patton commanded the 7th Army in World War II:* direct, lead, head, have charge of; rule, boss, govern; manage, supervise. —*n.* 3 *Who issued the command to fire?:* order, direction, directive, injunction, charge, instruction. 4 *The dictator assumed* *command of the country:* control, domination, rule, power, authority; charge, governing, leadership, supervision. **5** *a good command of French:* mastery, comprehension, understanding, grasp, knowledge.

Ant. **1** plead, beg; obey.

commandeer *v. The police commandeered a taxi to chase the robbers:* appropriate, expropriate, seize.

commander *n. General Eisenhower was commander of the Allied forces during World War II:* commanding officer, commander-in-chief; chief, head.

Ant. subordinate, follower.

commanding *adj.* **1** *You have a commanding manner:* authoritative, imposing, dynamic, gripping, arresting; striking; distinguished, stately. **2** *the commanding officer:* in command, directing, controlling, governing; chief, head, ranking, senior. **3** *a commanding view:* dominating, towering, prominent.

Ant. **1** unimposing, unimpressive. **2** subordinate, junior.

commemorate *v.* **1** *The monument commemorates local heroes:* memorialize, honor, pay tribute to, hallow. **2** *The bicentennial will commemorate the town's first 200 years:* celebrate, observe, hail, mark; solemnize, revere.

Ant. **1, 2** dishonor, degrade. **2** ignore, forget.

commence *v. Dancing will commence after dinner:* begin, start, get started.

Ant. end, conclude.

commencement *n.* **1** *the commencement of World War II:* beginning, start, inauguration, outset, onset. **2** *The dean gave a speech at commencement:* graduation, graduation ceremonies, commencement exercises.

Ant. **1** end, close.

commend *v.* **1** *Her teachers commended her to prospective employers:* recommend; laud, praise, extol, approve. **2** *He commended his business to his son:* entrust, give over, give, commit, consign, confer, convey, transfer.

Ant. **1** denounce, criticize, censure.

commendable *adj. a commendable trait:* to be commended, praiseworthy, admirable, laudable, honorable, notable, deserving.

Ant. discreditable, undeserving.

commensurate Also **commensurable** *adj. My salary is commensurate with my experience:* in accord, consistent, appropriate, compatible, corresponding, relative, equal, relative.

Ant. inconsistent, inappropriate; disproportionate, unequal.

comment *n.* **1** *The teacher wrote comments in the margin:* commentary, criticism, remark, observation, reflection. **2** *harsh comments from the critics:* remark, statement, commentary; word, utterance. —*v.* **3** *Would you care to comment?:* explain, clarify, expound, shed light; touch upon; talk about, make a statement.

commentary *n.* **1** *Write a commentary on the play:* explanatory essay, critique, explication, exposition, interpretation. **2** See COMMENT, defs. **1, 2**.

commentator *n. a TV sports commentator:* newscaster, news analyst; critic, reviewer.

commerce *n. overseas commerce:* business, trade, trading.

commercial *adj.* **1** *the commercial world:* business, trade, mercantile, profit-making. —*n.* **2** *TV commercials:* advertisement, ad.

commiserate *v. Friends commiserated with the bereaved:* express sorrow, sympathize with, grieve with, share one's sorrow.

commission *n.* **1** *the commission of a felony:* committing, committal, carrying out, act, perpetration, transacting. **2** *the commission to negotiate a treaty:* authority, authorization, power; duty, task, mission, assignment; office, role. **3** *a lieutenant's commission in the Army:* officer's rank, rank, appointment; certificate, written orders. **4** *the Housing Commission:* board, agency, committee; delegation. **5** *She earned a commission on every sale:* percentage, fee. —*v.* **6** *An architect was commissioned to design the building:* authorize, appoint, assign, name; delegate, charge, bid, direct; engage, employ, hire, contract. **7** *Annapolis graduates are commissioned as naval officers:* grant officer's rank, appoint; certify.

Ant. **1** noncommittal, nonperformance. **5** salary.

commit *v.* **1** *accused of committing robbery:* perform, carry out, do, transact, perpetrate, execute, effect, participate in. **2** *He was committed to an insane asylum:* consign, put in the custody of, give over, entrust, place, put; confine, institutionalize. **3** *The government committed itself to building new roads:* obligate, bind, make liable; engage, determine.

Ant. **2** release, free.

commitment *n.* **1** *a period of commitment in the penitentiary:* confinement, internment, institutionalizing, imprisonment, detention, incarceration. **2** *a commitment to pay:* obligation, liability, responsibility; bond, pledge, assurance, vow, word, promise; decision, determination.

Ant. 1 release, freeing. 2 disavowal, reneging.

commodious *adj. a commodious house:* roomy, spacious, capacious; large, ample. *Ant.* cramped; small.

commodity *n.* 1 *Wheat is a valuable commodity:* article of trade, article of commerce, merchandise, goods. 2 *A good reputation is a valuable commodity:* asset, possession, property, advantage. *Ant.* 2 liability, handicap, disadvantage.

common *adj.* 1 *common knowledge:* public, general, joint, shared, collective; widespread, universal. 2 *a common saying:* commonplace, ordinary, frequent, routine, regular; conventional, standard, established, familiar, everyday, well-known, widely known, popular, traditional, stock, prosaic. 3 *a common man:* ordinary, average, normal; undistinguished, unnoticed; middle-class, plebeian, bourgeois; unimportant, insignificant. 4 *Your common manners repulse her:* coarse, crude, crass, uncouth, boorish, loutish; brash, brazen, shameless; unrefined, uncultured, unpolished; tasteless, base, cheap, ill-bred, low-bred. *Ant.* 1 private, personal. 2 uncommon, unusual, rare, infrequent; unique, odd, exceptional, extraordinary; unknown, little-known. 3 exceptional, extraordinary; famous, renowned. 4 polished, refined, gentle; well-bred.

commonly *adv. Barbara was commonly known as Babs:* usually, ordinarily, generally, normally, customarily, regularly, routinely, traditionally, conventionally, habitually, frequently, by and large, in general, as a rule, for the most part, popularly, widely; familiarly, informally. *Ant.* rarely, seldom, infrequently; privately, secretly.

commonplace *adj.* 1 *Horses were commonplace sights in 1900:* common, ordinary, routine, everyday, familiar, regular, customary. 2 *The movie has a commonplace plot:* common, banal, run-of-the-mill, pedestrian, unimaginative, unoriginal; trite, hackneyed, stale, threadbare. *Ant.* 1, 2 uncommon, unusual, rare; unique, extraordinary, infrequent. 2 imaginative; original.

common sense *n. Use your common sense:* native reason, good sense, good judgment, basic intelligence.

commotion *n. What's all the commotion about?:* hullabaloo, fuss, bustle, stir, ado, to-do; tumult, furor, uproar, turmoil. *Ant.* tranquillity, calm; quiet, quietness.

communal *adj. communal property:* community, common, collective, joint, shared, public. *Ant.* private, personal.

commune *v. St. Francis was said to commune with the birds:* communicate, talk, converse, discourse.

communicable *adj. a communicable disease:* contagious, catching, infectious, transmittable, transmissible. *Ant.* uncommunicable, uncontagious.

communicate *v.* 1 *The radio stations communicated the storm warnings:* make known, announce, tell, notify, advise, pass on, convey, relate, proclaim, broadcast, publicize. 2 *The two friends hadn't communicated for years:* exchange information, express feelings; converse, speak together, talk; correspond. *Ant.* 1 keep secret, suppress, withhold.

communication *n.* 1 *There can be no friendship without communication:* exchanging information, expressing feelings; rapport; conversation, speaking, correspondence, writing. 2 *the latest communication from the ship:* report, message, news, information; intelligence, communiqué; correspondence, letter, dispatch, note; telephone call, telegram; radio message, broadcast.

communicative *adj. He's not very communicative:* talkative, free-spoken, loquacious, voluble; sociable, friendly; open, candid, forthright; informative, expressive, revealing. *Ant.* uncommunicative, reserved; secretive; uninformative.

communion *n.* 1 often **Communion.** *The family took Communion at midday Mass:* Holy Communion, the Eucharist. 2 *They had a perfect communion of thoughts:* sharing, harmony, agreement, affinity, sympathy. 3 *in communion with nature:* spiritual concentration, contemplation, rapport, communication.

communiqué *n. the latest communiqué from our ambassador:* bulletin, dispatch, message, communication, notice, letter, aviso, telegram.

community *n.* 1 *This is a good community to bring up children:* neighborhood, area, vicinity, environment, surroundings. 2 *the entire community. the scholarly community:* group, social group, interest group; populace, population, citizenry, public. 3 *a community of interest:* area, sphere, field, range, realm, scope. *Ant.* 3 dissimilarity, disparity.

commute *v. The governor commuted the convict's sentence:* change, reverse, adjust, alter; mitigate, diminish.

compact[1] *adj.* 1 *The hut was made of com-*

pact mud: compressed, pressed, tightly packed, dense. **2** *a compact but well-equipped kitchen:* small, little; snug. —*v.* **3** *Try to compact the sand into the mold:* pack closely, compress, press, pack, squeeze.

Ant. **1** loosely packed, loose. **2** spacious, roomy; large, big.

compact[2] *n. a compact to preserve the peace:* agreement, pact, treaty, contract; understanding, arrangement, alliance.

companion *n. Bad companions can lead us astray:* associate, friend, comrade, crony, chum, pal, buddy, mate; attendant, escort.

Ant. stranger; enemy, foe.

companionate *adj. a companionate marriage:* harmonious, suitable; providing companionship, compatible, nonsexual, platonic, nonphysical; companionable, friendly, agreeable; warm, affectionate, genial, warm-hearted.

Ant. discordant, inharmonious, incompatible.

companionship *n. The lonely long for companionship:* friendship, friendly relations, fellowship, sociability; friends, companions, comrades.

Ant. solitude; loneliness.

company *n.* **1** *Company is coming:* guest, guests, visitor, visitors, callers. **2** *I enjoy her company. I don't want any company around when I'm working:* presence, companionship, friendship, society; people, friends, companions. **3** *the advantages of working for a large company:* business concern, concern, firm, corporation. **4** *a company of men:* assembly, assemblage, gathering, group, band, throng, party.

comparable *adj. This is comparable to the best French cooking:* similar, like, equal, equivalent, as good as, on a par with; tantamount, commensurate; approximate, approaching, close, a match for.

Ant. incomparable, different, unlike; unequal.

compare *v.* **1** *Compare food costs with those of a year ago:* note the similarities of, note the differences of, contrast. **2** *Many compared Marilyn Monroe to Jean Harlow:* liken, equate, draw a parallel between, correlate. **3** *Canned soup can't compare to homemade:* match, equal, compete with, approach, bear comparison, hold a candle to, be in a class with.

comparison *n.* **1** *a comparison between the Alps and the Rocky Mountains:* comparative estimate, judgment, contrast. **2** *There was no comparison between the two:* similarity, comparability, likeness, resemblance, relation, correlation, parallel.

Ant. **2** difference, dissimilarity, discrepancy.

compartment *n. Put it in the glove compartment:* cubicle, niche, alcove, nook, pigeonhole, cubbyhole; section; booth, box, stall; berth, room, cabin.

compassion *n. a great compassion for the poor:* sympathy, empathy, commiseration, fellow feeling, pity, tenderness, tenderheartedness.

Ant. indifference, disdain; cold-heartedness, hard-heartedness.

compassionate *adj. a compassionate judge:* sympathetic, humane, merciful, kind-hearted, benevolent, charitable.

Ant. uncompassionate, unsympathetic, pitiless.

compatibility *n. They attributed their happy marriage to complete compatibility:* affinity, rapport, agreement, accord, likemindedness, congeniality.

Ant. incompatibility, disagreement, discord.

compatible *adj. The two weren't compatible:* in harmony, like-minded, mutually sympathetic; suitable, in accord, seemly, apt, appropriate.

Ant. incompatible, contradictory; unsuitable, inappropriate, inconsistent.

compel *v. Bad health compelled me to resign:* force, drive, necessitate, oblige, make.

compensate *v.* **1** *The firm compensated the injured worker:* recompense, reimburse, make restitution, make up, make compensation; pay, remunerate. **2** *The acting compensated for the play's weak script:* make up, offset, balance, make amends.

Ant. **2** emphasize, exaggerate.

compensation *n.* **1** *The injured were granted $10,000 in compensation:* recompense, reimbursement, restitution, redress; benefits, settlement. **2** *The job is hard but the compensation is good:* pay, payment, salary, wages, fee; profit, gratuity, gain.

Ant. **1, 2** loss, expenditure.

compete *v. Three teams will compete for the prize:* contend, vie, be rivals; fight, combat, battle.

competence *n. She showed exceptional competence:* ability, ableness, capability, competency, proficiency, skill, expertise.

Ant. incompetence, inability, inadequacy.

competent *adj. a competent electrician:* skilled, skillful, expert, proficient; qualified, trained, experienced; dependable, trustworthy.

Ant. incompetent, unskilled; unqualified, inexperienced, inadequate.

competition *n.* **1** *Competition between firms keeps prices down:* competing, rivalry, contention, struggle. 2 *Who will be the team's competition?:* opposition, rival, opponent. 3 *the figure-skating competition:* contest, event, match, tournament.

Ant. 1 cooperation, collaboration, teamwork.

competitive *adj. a competitive spirit:* competing, fighting, combative, striving, aggressive.

Ant. cooperative, noncombative.

competitor *n. the firm's largest competitor. The champion is fighting an unknown competitor:* rival, opposition; opponent, adversary, contestant, contender, fighter.

Ant. ally, partner.

compilation *n.* 1 *the compilation of data:* compiling, collecting, gathering, accumulating, marshaling, garnering, assembling. 2 *a compilation of recipes:* collection, compendium, accumulation.

Ant. 1 distribution, dispersal.

compile *v. Doctors compiled thousands of case histories:* collect, assemble, amass, gather, muster, marshal, bring together.

complacent *adj. He's too complacent since he got a raise:* content, contented, self-satisfied, smug; untroubled, unbothered.

Ant. discontent, discontented, troubled, uneasy.

complain *v. The tenants complained:* state a grievance, express dissatisfaction, find fault; carp, cavil, *Informal* gripe, kick, grouse.

Ant. compliment, praise, commend.

complaint *n.* 1 *My department handles customer complaints:* grievance, criticism, faultfinding, protest; *Informal* beef, gripe. 2 *Arthritis is a common complaint:* disorder, malady, infirmity, ailment.

Ant. 1 compliment, praise, commendation. 2 remedy.

complaisant *adj. Her complaisant manner made us feel welcome:* obliging, solicitous, agreeable, compliant, cordial, congenial, affable, warm, gracious, friendly; good-natured, good-humored, easygoing.

Ant. unobliging, contrary; disagreeable, unpleasant, unfriendly.

complement *n.* 1 *Travel can be a complement to one's education:* completion, rounding-out; supplement, companion. 2 *The farm was sold along with its complement of livestock:* full amount, full number, total; entirety; required number, necessary amount. —*v.* 3 *A flaming dessert complemented the dinner:* make complete, round out; serve as a companion, supplement.

complementary *adj. The costume calls for a complementary hair style:* integral, corre-

sponding, related, compatible, companion, matched.

Ant. incongruous, inconsistent; contradictory.

complete *adj.* 1 *a complete set of Shakespeare:* entire, whole, full; unabridged; intact, undivided. 2 *Our triumph was complete:* absolute, total, conclusive, fully realized; achieved, carried out. —*v.* 3 *The workers haven't completed the house:* make complete, make whole; finish, conclude; accomplish, achieve, fulfill; consummate. 4 *A good brandy completes a fine meal:* complement, round out; perfect, crown.

Ant. 1, 2 incomplete, partial. 2 inconclusive, imperfect, unfinished. 3 start, begin, commence. 4 spoil, ruin, mar.

completion *n.* 1 *the completion of the new road:* completing, finishing; concluding, ending. 2 *the completion of the school year:* conclusion, end, close, finish; expiration, fulfillment, consummation.

Ant. 1, 2 beginning, starting, commencing.

complex *adj.* 1 *complex problems:* complicated, intricate, involved; difficult, perplexing, enigmatic; composite, compound, variegated, knotty. —*n.* 2 *the military-industrial complex:* system, network, aggregate, conglomerate. 3 *an inferiority complex:* subconscious idea, fixed idea, psychological feeling; obsession, preoccupation.

Ant. 1 simple, uncomplicated, uninvolved, unconfused.

complexion *n.* 1 *a fair complexion:* skin coloring, coloring, pigmentation; color, hue, tone; skin texture. 2 *That puts a different complexion on the case:* appearance, aspect, look, outlook, guise, slant, character.

complexity *n. the complexity of the problem:* complication, intricacy, involvement; entanglement.

Ant. simplicity, clearness, clarity, obviousness.

compliance *n. compliance with the law. Yes-men are known for their compliance:* conformity, obedience; submission, deference; assent, acquiescence.

Ant. noncompliance, disobedience; rebelliousness, assertiveness.

complicate *v. Don't complicate the problem:* make complex, make difficult, involve, confound, confuse.

Ant. uncomplicate, simplify, clarify.

complication *n. an unexpected complication:* problem, difficulty; hitch, snag, obstacle, stumbling block.

compliment *n.* 1 *She received compliments on her speech:* praise, approving remark, commendation, kudos; honor, homage, congratulation. **2 compliments.** *Please give my compliments to your parents:* regards, respects, greetings, salutations. —*v.* 3 *We complimented her for a job well done:* pay a compliment to, praise; laud, applaud, commend.

Ant. 1 insult, condemnation, criticism, reproach. 3 criticize, denounce, disparage, censure, reproach.

complimentary *adj.* 1 *complimentary remarks:* commendatory, praising, laudatory, plauditory, extolling; congratulatory, adulatory. 2 *complimentary tickets:* free, gratis, without charge.

Ant. 1 uncomplimentary, disparaging, critical.

comply *v. You must comply with the rules:* conform, adhere, abide by, follow, obey, observe; meet, satisfy; submit, yield, defer; consent, acquiesce.

Ant. disobey, break, spurn, disregard; resist, oppose.

component *adj.* 1 *Iron and carbon are component elements of steel:* constituent, ingredient, composing; fundamental, essential. —*n.* 2 *a component of the stereo system:* part, constituent, element; ingredient; piece; item; detail, particular.

Ant. 1, 2 whole, compound.

comport *v. He comported himself with dignity:* conduct, carry; behave, acquit.

compose *v.* 1 *to compose a sonnet:* create, form, formulate, frame, shape, fashion, devise, write. 2 *England, Scotland, and Wales compose the island of Great Britain:* be part of, be a portion of; *(loosely)* make up, form, comprise. 3 *Compose yourself before answering:* calm, settle, collect, pull oneself together; relax.

composed *adj. The captain remained composed throughout the storm:* calm, peaceful, tranquil, quiet; cool, cool-headed, collected, poised, controlled, steady, level-headed, even-tempered, unperturbed, unexcited, unruffled, unemotional.

Ant. unpoised, uncontrolled; agitated, disturbed.

composite *adj. a composite drawing of the two faces:* combined, compound, blended.

Ant. uncombined, single.

composition *n.* 1 *The orchestra played a modern composition:* work, piece, creation; exercise. 2 *The composition of the report took two months:* composing, creating, creation, making, preparation, devising. 3 *The composition of the painting is very graceful:* structure, design, arrangement, form, organization.

composure *n. She retained her composure*

throughout the heckling: poise, aplomb, calmness; coolness, cool-headedness, self-control, self-possession, self-restraint, even-temperedness, equanimity, unexcitability, imperturbability.

Ant. nervousness, uneasiness; impatience, agitation, hot-headedness, instability.

compound *adj.* 1 *Bronze is a compound metal made of copper and tin:* combined, composite, mixed, blended. —*n.* 2 *Water is a compound of hydrogen and oxygen:* combination, composite, blend, mixture, union, fusion, amalgam. —*v.* 3 *The chemist compounded several elements to form the antidote:* combine, blend, mix, unite, fuse; formulate, prepare, concoct, synthesize. 4 *He compounded his mistake by arguing with the police officer:* add to, increase, heighten, reinforce.

Ant. 1 simple, pure, unmixed, unblended. 2 element. 3 separate. 4 lessen, ameliorate, mitigate, moderate.

comprehend *v. The child couldn't comprehend the advanced textbook:* understand, grasp, fathom, make out, absorb, assimilate, appreciate.

Ant. misapprehend, misinterpret, misconceive.

comprehension *n. She had no comprehension of the boy's problem:* understanding, conception, grasp, perception, insight; realization, awareness.

Ant. misunderstanding, misconception, incomprehension, unawareness.

comprehensive *adj. a comprehensive study of the 1930's:* all-inclusive, all-embracing, overall, extensive, general; exhaustive, complete, thorough.

Ant. limited, narrow, specialized; incomplete.

compress *v. Compress this clay into a small ball. Compress your speech into five minutes:* press, squeeze, compact, pack; condense, reduce, shorten, abbreviate, abridge.

Ant. stretch, spread, expand, enlarge.

comprise *v. Our country is comprised of 50 states. A full deck comprises 52 cards:* include, contain, be composed of, consist of; *(loosely)* constitute, make up, form, compose.

compromise *n.* 1 *A compromise was finally reached:* mutual concession, accommodation; conciliation, rapprochement; balance, happy medium. —*v.* 2 *Let's compromise:* make mutual concessions, adjust differences, meet halfway. 3 *The rumors compromised my good reputation:* endanger, jeopardize; discredit, make suspect.

Ant. 1 dispute, disagreement. 3 enhance, support, assure.

compulsion n. *It took a lot of compulsion to get Dad to wear a tuxedo:* coercion, pressure; obligation, requirement, demand; strong inducement, urging.

compulsive adj. *compulsive gamblers:* unable to resist, uncontrollable, obsessive, addicted, habitual.

compulsory adj. *The nation has compulsory education:* mandatory, obligatory, required, requisite, demanded.
Ant. voluntary, optional, discretionary, nonrequisite.

compunction n. *to have no compunctions about cheating:* pang of conscience, qualm, misgiving; regret, concern, contrition, unease, remorse, scruple.

compute v. *to compute a bill. Compute the distance of the moon from the earth:* add, add up, total, count up, tally; calculate, determine mathematically, ascertain, work out.
Ant. guess, suppose, estimate, approximate.

comrade n. *The boys have been comrades since kindergarten:* companion, friend, crony, confrere, intimate, pal, chum, buddy; colleague, fellow member, associate, confederate.
Ant. stranger; enemy, foe.

concave adj. *concave cheeks:* curving inward, sunken, hollow.
Ant. convex, rounded.

conceal v. *The robber concealed the weapon. You can't conceal the truth:* hide, cover, cover up, keep out of sight; keep secret, disguise, obscure.
Ant. reveal, disclose, divulge; expose, display, uncover.

concealment n. 1 *Concealment of evidence is against the law:* concealing, hiding, secreting. 2 *The thief remained in concealment:* hiding, hiding place, hideout, under cover.
Ant. 1 disclosure, revealing, revelation.

concede v. 1 *I concede your request is reasonable:* grant, agree, acquiesce, accept, recognize, allow; confess, admit. 2 *The chess player conceded the game:* give up, yield, abandon, relinquish, cede.
Ant. 1 deny, refute, reject; dissent, protest.

conceit n. *Her conceit is unbearable:* vanity, vainglory, egotism, self-love, self-esteem.
Ant. humility, modesty; self-deprecation.

conceited adj. *a conceited actor:* vain, overproud, arrogant, egotistical, self-important, swell-headed, vainglorious.
Ant. humble, modest, unassuming, self-effacing.

conceivable adj. *There is no conceivable way to raise a thousand dollars:* imaginable,

possible, perceivable, knowable, believable.
Ant. inconceivable, unthinkable; incredible.

conceive v. 1 *to conceive a plan:* think up, form, create, hatch, contrive, concoct, invent, dream up. 2 *I can't conceive of living without a telephone:* imagine, envision, envisage; understand, comprehend.

concentrate v. 1 *Please concentrate on the lesson:* focus, center, bring to bear; pay attention to, pay heed; be engrossed in, put one's mind to. 2 *Many retirement villages are concentrated on Florida's west coast:* mass, congregate, converge, assemble, gather, cluster, bunch, heap up.
Ant. 2 spread out, disperse, diffuse.

concentration n. 1 *Chess requires great concentration:* concentrating, close attention, mental application, deep thought, absorption. 2 *There's a concentration of colleges in the Boston area:* cluster, collection, accumulation, aggregation, gathering; centralization, convergence.
Ant. 1 inattention, inattentiveness; absent-mindedness. 2 scattering, dispersion, diffusion.

concept n. *a new scientific concept:* idea, conception, theory, hypothesis, supposition; impression, view; belief.

conception n. 1 *the conception of the plan:* conceiving, envisioning; forming, formation, devising; creating, originating; genesis, birth, invention, initiation, start, beginning. 2 *Have you any conception of how I feel?:* idea, concept; perception; understanding, apprehension, notion. 3 *Conception occurred in Europe but the baby was born in America:* becoming pregnant, fertilization, inception of pregnancy.
Ant. 1 completion; outcome, result.

concern v. 1 *Good government concerns every citizen:* affect, involve, relate to, pertain to, appertain to; apply to, interest. 2 *The boy's health concerned his parents:* worry, trouble, disturb, make anxious. —n. 3 *Earning a living was her first concern:* consideration, business, interest, matter, affair; duty, mission. 4 *The teacher began to feel concern about the child's absences. Show concern for others:* worry, anxiety, apprehension; disturbance; thoughtfulness, regard, solicitude, consideration. 5 *The two banking concerns merged:* firm, company, corporation, business; store.
Ant. 1 be irrelevant to. 4 unconcern, indifference; heedlessness, carelessness.

concerned adj. 1 *Good citizens must be concerned in civic affairs:* involved, committed, engaged, participating, active; caring, interested, attentive. 2 *concerned about the ap-*

proaching storm: worried, anxious, uneasy, disturbed, troubled.

Ant. 1 unconcerned, indifferent; uninterested; neglectful, remiss. 2 undisturbed, untroubled.

concert *n. We worked in concert to complete the work:* unity, harmony, accord, union, concord; teamwork, cooperation, association; unanimity, correspondence.

Ant. opposition; discord, disunity.

concerted *adj. a concerted effort to win the game:* united, joint, cooperative, agreed upon.

Ant. disunited, individual.

concession *n.* 1 *The lawyer's concession on that point will help your case:* admission, assent, acquiescence. 2 *The union made concessions at the bargaining table:* compromise, adjustment, modification; giving in. 3 *the hot-dog concession at the ball park:* franchise, lease, privilege.

Ant. 1 denial, disavowal.

conciliatory *adj. One conciliatory remark would make them friends:* peacemaking, reconciling, placatory, pacifying, appeasing.

Ant. antagonistic, hostile, unfriendly.

concise *adj. a concise summary of the book:* terse, succinct, pithy; brief, short.

Ant. rambling, wordy, verbose.

conclave *n. The members held a conclave before the public meeting:* private meeting, secret council, private gathering; meeting, council, conference.

conclude *v.* 1 *The pianist concluded the recital:* close, finish, end, complete; discontinue, stop. 2 *The negotiations were successfully concluded:* settle, decide, resolve, arrange; accomplish, carry out. 3 *They concluded that she wasn't coming:* decide, determine, judge; deduce, surmise, infer, gather.

Ant. 1 begin, commence, start; open; prolong, extend.

conclusion *n.* 1 *the conclusion of the play:* end, close, completion, finale, final part, denouement, resolution. 2 *the conclusion of a new union contract:* arrangement, settlement, resolution, agreement, completion. 3 *The astronomer's conclusion was erroneous:* finding, determination, decision, judgment, deduction, inference; result, outcome, resolution.

Ant. 1 beginning, commencement; opening.

conclusive *adj. Fingerprints were conclusive evidence:* decisive, definite, absolute, certain; undeniable, irrefutable, incontrovertible, unimpeachable; clear, manifest, obvious.

Ant. inconclusive, indecisive, uncertain; doubtful, dubious, questionable.

concoct *v. The cook concocted a stew. He'll concoct some excuse:* cook up, mix, formulate; make up, think up, invent, fabricate, devise, contrive.

concoction *n. The dessert was a concoction of custard and bread crumbs. The story was a fantastic concoction of lies:* mixture, blend, compound; creation, invention, fabrication.

concord *n. The two countries have lived in concord:* peace, harmony, agreement; goodwill, cordial relations, accord; friendship.

Ant. discord, conflict, strife, dissension, contention.

concourse *n. There was a tremendous concourse of people into the square:* flocking together, confluence, meeting, junction, flowing together; assembling, congregation, convergence, concentration.

Ant. separation, dispersal.

concrete *n.* 1 *The walk was paved with concrete: (loosely)* cement. *—adj.* 2 *The remark was a concrete example of rudeness:* real, tangible, factual, substantial; definite, precise, explicit, express, particular.

Ant. 2 theoretical, abstract, inexplicit.

concur *v. The two accounts concur:* agree, be in accord, correspond, coincide, conform, match.

Ant. disagree, differ, be at odds.

concurrence *n.* 1 *When the two reach concurrence they will sign a contract:* agreement, accord, concord, mutual consent; consensus, meeting of the minds; cooperation. 2 *The concurrence of the two events made for a fun-filled day:* simultaneous occurrence, coincidence, correspondence, conformity, coexistence.

Ant. 1 disagreement, difference, divergence.

concurrent *adj.* 1 *Our views are concurrent:* agreeing, in agreement, in accordance, harmonious; sympathetic, compatible; matching, congruous. 2 *New Year's Day and the Rose Bowl game are concurrent:* occurring at the same time, coinciding, simultaneous, coexisting.

Ant. 1 in disagreement, different; incompatible.

condemn *v. In 1915 women were condemned for wearing short skirts:* censure, disapprove, criticize, denounce, rebuke.

Ant. praise, compliment, commend, applaud.

condemnation *n. Cheating deserves our harshest condemnation:* censure, disapproval, criticism, reproach, reproof, rebuke, denunciation; punishment.

Ant. praise, commendation, approval; exoneration, vindication.

condensation *n. a condensation of the novel:* abridgment, condensed version, digest.

condense *v.* 1 *Moisture condensed into dew:* liquefy, precipitate. 2 *The editors condensed the manuscript:* abridge, shorten, reduce, cut, pare down, boil down. 3 *Condense the mixture by boiling:* thicken, concentrate, reduce; compress, compact.
Ant. 1 evaporate, vaporize. 2 expand, lengthen, beef up. 3 dilute.

condescend *v.* 1 *The director condescended to take advice from the stagehand:* humble oneself, deign, come down off one's high horse. 2 *Don't condescend to me!:* patronize, talk down to, look down on.

condescending *adj. a condescending manner:* patronizing, superior, disdainful.

condescension *n.* 1 *I admire the king's condescension toward his subjects:* assumption of equality, self-effacement, humbleness, humility, modesty, deference. 2 *The duke's condescension infuriates me:* haughtiness, disdain, hauteur, patronizing attitude; *Informal* high-and-mighty attitude, airs.
Ant. 1 arrogance, haughtiness.

condign *adj. condign punishment:* fitting, appropriate, suitable, fair, just, due, proper, warranted, deserved
Ant. unjust, unwarranted, inappropriate.

condition *n.* 1 *in good financial condition:* state, situation, circumstances, state of affairs, shape, position. 2 *The doctor says your condition is better, a heart condition:* state of health, physical fitness; ailment, malfunction, malady, complaint, problem. 3 *the conditions of the contract. We agreed to rent the house on condition the roof be repaired:* term, provision, proviso, stipulation, arrangement, agreement; prerequisite, requisite; restriction, limitation, reservation. —*v.* 4 *Jogging conditioned her for skiing:* prepare, ready, train, fit, tone up, accustom.

conditional *adj. a conditional truce:* provisional, tentative, qualified, limited; contingent, dependent.
Ant. unconditional, absolute; unlimited, unrestricted.

condolence *n. The widow received many letters of condolence:* sympathy, commiseration, solace, comfort, consolation.
Ant. congratulation, felicitation.

condone *v. Never condone bad behavior:* overlook, let pass, ignore, disregard, put up with; excuse, justify.
Ant. condemn, denounce; punish.

conducive *adj. Exercise is conducive to good health:* contributive, contributory, favorable, helpful, beneficial.
Ant. harmful, deleterious, damaging.

conduct *n.* 1 *disruptive conduct:* behavior, comportment, deportment; action, deeds. 2 *His conduct of the business was successful:* management, administration, direction, guidance, supervision, leadership. —*v.* 3 *The mayor conducted the visitors through town. to conduct a meeting:* guide, lead, escort, usher, convey; preside over, chair. 4 *The children conducted themselves well:* behave, comport, act. 5 *The oldest son conducts the family's affairs:* manage, administer, direct, guide, govern, supervise; perform, transact, execute, operate, look after.

conduit *n. The water flows through this conduit:* main, pipe, duct, tube, canal, channel, passage.

confederacy *n. The seaports formed a confederacy against pirates:* alliance, league, coalition, association, federation, confederation.

confederate *n. Tom Sawyer was Huck's confederate:* ally, colleague, partner, associate, collaborator, accomplice, fellow conspirator, cohort, helper.
Ant. opponent, rival, foe.

confederation *n. a confederation of many countries:* league, association, alliance, coalition, federation, confederacy, union.

confer *v.* 1 *Diplomas were conferred on the graduating class:* present to, bestow upon, award, give. 2 *The lawyers conferred on the case:* consult, discuss, hold a conference, deliberate together.
Ant. 1 withdraw, take away; withhold, deny.

conference *n. The teacher had a conference with each student. the annual conference of lawyers:* discussion, talk, consultation; meeting, convention, conclave.

confess *v. He confessed his love:* admit, acknowledge; reveal, disclose, divulge, make known; declare, avow.
Ant. repudiate, deny; hide, conceal.

confession *n.* 1 *the thief's confession:* admission, acknowledgment; revelation, disclosure, declaration, avowal. 2 *He made his confession at St. Patrick's:* priestly confession, confessional, *Archaic* shrift.
Ant. 1 denial, disavowal; concealment, hiding.

confidant, confidante *n. She is my closest confidante:* intimate, friend, trusty companion.

confide *v. Did she confide her plans to you?:* tell secretly, tell privately; reveal, disclose, make known, divulge.

Ant. keep one's own counsel, keep secret, keep mum.

confidence *n.* 1 *The bank has complete confidence in its tellers:* trust, faith; belief, reliance. 2 *He needs more confidence:* self-confidence, self-assurance, faith in oneself; certainty, certitude; courage, intrepidity. 3 *The friends exchanged confidences:* secret, intimacy, confidential matter.

Ant. 1 distrust, mistrust; doubt, misgiving. 2 self-doubt, timidity, shyness.

confident *adj.* 1 *The team is confident it will win:* convinced, certain, sure, positive; assured, optimistic. 2 *A champion must be very confident:* self-confident, self-assured, sure of oneself; intrepid, dauntless, bold.

Ant. 1 uncertain, unsure; apprehensive, pessimistic. 2 self-doubting, insecure; hesitant, nervous.

confidential *adj. confidential reports:* secret, private, not to be disclosed, top-secret, classified.

Ant. public, open; publicized.

confidentially *adv. She told me the news confidentially:* in confidence, in secret, privately, sub rosa.

Ant. openly, publicly.

confine *v.* 1 *Please confine your remarks to the topic under discussion:* limit, restrict, restrain, keep. 2 *The dog was confined by a fence:* keep in, shut in, shut up, coop up, hold, cage, pen, tie, bind; imprison, jail, incarcerate.

Ant. 2 release, free, loose.

confinement *n.* 1 *Expectant mothers used to spend a long time in confinement:* lying in, accouchement, childbirth. 2 *The prisoner is in confinement:* detention, custody, imprisonment, incarceration.

Ant. 2 release, freeing.

confines *n. pl. The missing child must be in the confines of the town:* limits, border, bounds, boundaries; edge, circumference.

confirm *v.* 1 *The witnesses confirmed the suspect's story:* corroborate, bear out, uphold, sustain, verify, substantiate. 2 *The hotel confirmed our reservations:* acknowledge, agree to, accept; make firm, validate, certify.

Ant. 1 contradict, refute, deny, disavow, contravene, controvert. 2 cancel; refuse.

confirmation *n.* 1 *The newspaper received confirmation of the story:* substantiation, verification, corroboration, authentication, validation, proof. 2 *The committee's choice requires confirmation by the club members:* approval, endorsement, ratification; assent, agreement.

Ant. 1 denial, repudiation, refutation. 2 rejection, disapproval.

confirmed *adj.* 1 *confirmed reports from the front:* corroborated, substantiated, authenticated, verified, proven true. 2 *a confirmed bachelor:* established, inveterate, chronic, set, fixed, dyed-in-the-wool.

Ant. 1 unconfirmed, unsubstantiated, unverified, unproven. 2 sometimes, occasional.

confiscate *v. The customs officer confiscated the smuggled goods:* seize, commandeer, appropriate, take, expropriate.

Ant. release, return.

conflagration *n. The conflagration destroyed several houses:* fire, blaze, inferno, holocaust.

conflict *v.* 1 *Our views conflict:* disagree, oppose, be contrary, clash. —*n.* 2 *armed conflict:* fight, combat, battle, struggle, clash, warfare; encounter, confrontation. 3 *the conflict between the brothers:* disagreement, difference, discord, dissent, dissension; antagonism, friction.

Ant. 1 agree, harmonize, coincide. 2 peace; truce, treaty. 3 harmony, accord, concord.

confluence *n. St. Louis is located at the confluence of the Mississippi and Missouri rivers:* convergence, coming together, junction, union, meeting, juncture, flowing together; assembling, concentration.

conform *v.* 1 *All must conform to the rules:* follow, comply with, obey, submit to, adhere to. 2 *The dress must conform to the pattern:* correspond to, agree with, tally with, fit, jibe with.

Ant. 1 disobey, oppose. 2 differ.

conformation *n. The horse had the conformation of a thoroughbred:* form, shape, configuration, build, figure, structure.

conformity *n. Live in conformity with your beliefs. There is too much conformity in these designs:* agreement, accord, compliance; uniformity, likeness, similarity.

Ant. disagreement, discord, opposition; difference, divergence.

confound *v. The symptoms confounded the doctor:* perplex, baffle, bewilder, puzzle; disconcert, unsettle, nonplus; amaze, astound, astonish, dumfound.

Ant. explain, solve, clarify.

confront *v. The boy confronted his accuser:* face, face up to, encounter; challenge, dare, brave, defy.

Ant. avoid, evade; yield to.

confrontation *n. a confrontation between opposing forces:* showdown, encounter, face-to-face meeting; conflict, battle, clash.

confuse *v.* 1 *The road signs confused us:* perplex, bewilder, baffle, puzzle; rattle, muddle, befuddle, mix up, confound. 2 *You confused me with my twin brother. This new* *clue confuses the case:* mix up, mistake; make perplexing, make baffling, muddle.

Ant. 2 explain, solve, clarify.

confusion n. 1 *Imagine our confusion when we found the car was gone:* bewilderment, stupefaction, bafflement, perplexity, puzzlement; discomposure, abashment. 2 *The room was in a state of confusion. a confusion of colors:* chaos, disorder, disarray, disorganization; muddle, jumble, hodgepodge; pandemonium, hullabaloo, commotion, ferment, bedlam.

Ant. 1 solution, clarification; composure, calm. 2 organization, orderliness, tidiness, neatness.

congeal v. *The gelatin will congeal quickly:* set, solidify, thicken; clot, coagulate; jell.

congenial adj. 1 *The friends had congenial tastes:* compatible, kindred, harmonious, like, agreeing, corresponding. 2 *a congenial disposition:* agreeable, pleasant, amenable, affable, genial, cordial.

Ant. 1 different, incompatible, opposite. 2 disagreeable, unpleasant, ungracious.

congenital adj. *Left-handedness is a congenital trait:* innate, inherent, inborn, inbred, intrinsic, hereditary, inherited.

congested adj. *The roads are becoming more congested:* crowded, filled, packed, jammed.

Ant. uncongested, uncrowded.

conglomeration n. *a conglomeration of potatoes and vegetables:* mixture, combination, aggregate, medley; jumble, hodge podge.

congratulate v. *I congratulate you on your anniversary:* give one's best wishes, salute, felicitate, compliment, rejoice with.

congratulations n. pl. *Let's telegraph our congratulations:* best wishes, well-wishing, felicitations.

congregate v. *A crowd congregated around the body:* assemble, gather, collect, cluster, mass, flock.

Ant. disperse, scatter.

congregation n. 1 *He spoke before a large congregation:* assembly, gathering, crowd, group, throng. 2 *The congregation welcomed its new minister:* church membership, parishioners, parish, brethren, laity.

congress n. 1 *a congress of heart specialists:* conference, convention, assembly, council, gathering; delegates, representatives. 2 usually **Congress.** *the United States Congress:* legislature, legislative body.

conjecture n. 1 *Do you know for sure or is it conjecture?:* guesswork, supposition, inference, deduction, surmise, guess, speculation, theory, hypothesis, assumption. —v. 2 *He conjectured that it would be a cold*

winter: suppose, think, surmise, theorize, imagine, infer, forecast, speculate, presume.

Ant. 1 fact, certainty. 2 know.

conjugal adj. *conjugal love:* marital, wedded, married; matrimonial, nuptial, connubial, spousal.

Ant. unmarried, unwedded.

conjunction n. *The conjunction of heavy rains and high winds caused flooding:* combination, union, joining, meeting, concurrence.

conjure v. *Wizards conjure the Devil:* call forth, make appear, summon, invoke; make disappear; practice sorcery, bewitch, charm, cast a spell.

connect v. 1 *Connect the two wires:* join, attach, fasten together; couple, combine, merge. 2 *Connect the two facts:* associate, relate, correlate.

Ant. 1 disconnect, detach, unfasten, separate.

connection n. 1 *The connection between the two parts is broken:* coupling, fastening, bond, linkage. 2 *There is no connection between the two incidents:* relation, relationship, interrelation, association; attachment, alliance. 3 *They have the same name but are not connections of ours. He's just a business connection:* relative, relation, family, kin; friend, associate, acquaintance, contact.

connive v. *They connived in the smuggling of goods:* conspire, plan, plot, collude, be in collusion with.

connoisseur n. *a connoisseur of fine wines:* expert, judge, authority.

connotation n. *The word "bitch" has bad connotations:* suggested meaning, implication, insinuation, significance, intimation, evocation.

Ant. denotation, literal meaning.

connote v. *The word "home" connotes contentment:* imply, suggest, intimate, bring to mind.

connubial adj. *connubial bliss:* conjugal, wedded, married, marital, matrimonial, nuptial.

Ant. unmarried, unwedded.

conquer v. 1 *The Allies conquered Germany in World War II:* defeat, vanquish, overcome, triumph over; beat, best; subdue, subjugate. 2 *You must conquer your fear:* overcome, master, prevail over, get the better of.

Ant. 1 be defeated, lose, surrender. 2 yield to, surrender to.

conqueror n. *The conqueror marched into the defeated country:* victor, vanquisher; winner; champion.

Ant. conquered, defeated, vanquished.

conquest n. 1 *the conquest of fear:* conquering, defeat, vanquishment, mastery, overcoming, subjugation. 2 *Her eloquence won her many conquests:* captive, adherent, follower; lover, adorer.

Ant. 1 surrender, submission, loss.

conscience *n. His conscience would not let him lie:* moral sense, sense of right and wrong, scruples.

conscientious *adj. a conscientious worker:* dutiful, scrupulous, responsible, honest, trustworthy; painstaking, careful, exact, particular, meticulous, fastidious.

Ant. unconscientious, unreliable; careless, negligent, irresponsible.

conscious *adj.* 1 *Is the patient conscious?:* sentient, sensible. 2 *Were you conscious of his hostility?:* aware, cognizant, knowledgeable, perceiving, noticing, alert to.

Ant. 1–3 unconscious. 2 unaware, oblivious.

consciousness *n.* 1 *The victim lost consciousness:* awareness, sensibility. 2 *That people are starving never entered his consciousness:* awareness, perception, mind, thoughts.

conscript *v.* 1 *The armed forces will conscript the able-bodied:* draft, induct, call up, mobilize; enlist, register, enroll. —*n.* 2 *All conscripts will report for duty:* draftee, inductee, selectee.

consecrate *v. The shrine was consecrated:* declare sacred, sanctify; hallow, bless.

Ant. desecrate, profane, defile.

consecutive *adj. in consecutive order:* successive, progressive, sequential, in turn.

Ant. random, haphazard.

consensus *n. a consensus of the voters:* general agreement, general opinion; common consent; concord, accord.

Ant. minority opinion; disagreement, discord.

consent *v.* 1 *I consented to his offer:* agree, concur, assent, accept, accede, acquiesce, concede. —*n.* 2 *We must have the council's consent:* agreement, concurrence, assent, approval, acceptance, permission, sanction, endorsement, acquiescence.

Ant. 1 dissent, refuse, decline; disagree, disapprove. 2 refusal, disapproval, dissent.

consequence *n.* 1 *As a consequence of his laziness, he was fired:* result, outcome, development, upshot; aftermath. 2 *an event of great consequence:* importance, import, significance, moment; distinction, prominence; seriousness, gravity; influence.

Ant. 1 source, cause, reason. 2 insignificance, unimportance, triviality.

conservation *n. energy conservation:* preservation, husbandry, careful use; protection, maintenance, upkeep.

Ant. waste, destruction.

conservative *adj.* 1 *conservative views. a conservative dresser:* nonliberal, traditional, right-wing, reactionary; cautious, moderate, undaring. —*n.* 2 *The conservatives voted against the new road:* opponent of change, right-winger, reactionary.

Ant. 1 radical, liberal, progressive; avant-garde, faddish. 2 radical, liberal, progressive.

conserve *v. to conserve electricity:* preserve, save, use sparingly, husband; maintain, care for.

Ant. waste, squander.

consider *v.* 1 *Consider the consequences:* think about, reflect on, contemplate, regard, weigh, appraise; examine, study; deliberate on, note; respect, honor, make allowances for. 2 *I considered the food excellent:* regard, judge, deem, think, believe.

Ant. 1 ignore, overlook, disregard.

considerable *adj. a considerable achievement:* substantial, large, great; ample; significant, notable, noteworthy, remarkable, impressive.

Ant. small, insignificant; unimportant, unremarkable.

considerably *adv. He had changed considerably:* substantially, significantly, noticeably; greatly; remarkably.

considerate *adj. It was very considerate of you:* thoughtful, kind, solicitous, attentive; concerned, obliging.

Ant. inconsiderate, thoughtless; selfish.

consideration *n.* 1 *Thank you for your consideration:* thought, regard, concern, deliberation, contemplation; judgment; study, examination. 2 *consideration of others:* thoughtfulness, regard, respect; tact; kindliness. 3 *Cost is a major consideration:* factor, concern, interest; inducement, motive, reason.

Ant. 2 thoughtlessness; selfishness.

consign *v. He consigned his property to charity:* transfer, entrust, commit, deposit with, convey, remit, remand; relegate, delegate.

Ant. retain, withhold.

consignment *n. the consignment of the property to the new owners:* transfer, committing, depositing, assignment, handing over, consigning; entrusting, relegation, delegation.

Ant. receiving; keeping, retention.

consist *v.* 1 *Fudge consists largely of chocolate and sugar:* to be composed of, be made up of, contain, include. 2 *Happiness consists in appreciating what you have:* lie, to be found in, reside.

consistency, consistence *n.* 1 *This sauce has a thin consistency:* texture, viscosity, thickness, stiffness, compactness; body, composition; makeup. 2 *There is no consistency in the furniture in this room:* harmony, unity, uniformity; agreement, correspondence, connection, compatibility.

Ant. inconsistency, disharmony, disagreement.

consistent *adj.* 1 *a consistent winner:* constant, steady, regular; unchanging, undeviating. 2 *Choose furniture that's consistent with the style of the house:* harmonious, in agreement, agreeing, compatible, congenial, correspondent, suitable.

Ant. 1 inconsistent, erratic, changing. 2 inconsistent, incompatible, incongruous, discordant, contrary.

consolation *n. Words are little consolation:* solace, comfort, succor, alleviation; condolence, sympathy.

console *v. She consoled the child:* comfort, succor, cheer, ease; commiserate with, express sympathy for.

Ant. distress, sadden, disquiet.

consolidate *v.* 1 *The two railroads were consolidated:* combine, unify, incorporate, unite, merge, join, integrate; compress, condense. 2 *Her victory consolidated her chance for the championship:* strengthen, solidify, make firm.

Ant. 1 separate. 2 weaken, make uncertain.

consort *n.* 1 *Prince Albert was the consort of Queen Victoria:* spouse, mate; companion, associate. —*v.* 2 *to consort with known criminals:* keep company, fraternize, mingle, mix, pair off, hang out.

Ant. 2 dissociate, separate, part, estrange.

conspicuous *adj.* 1 *That red hat is conspicuous. conspicuous violators of the law:* easily seen, easily noticed, highly visible, obvious, striking; clear, evident, manifest, patent, glaring, prominent, flagrant. 2 *a conspicuous achievement:* outstanding, remarkable, notable; illustrious, distinguished, glorious, memorable; prominent, well-known.

Ant. 1 inconspicuous, unnoticeable, unseen, unapparent. 2 inconspicuous, undistinguished, common, ordinary; modest, commonplace.

conspiracy *n. conspiracy against the king:* criminal plan, secret plan, plot, intrigue, collusion; sedition, treason.

conspirator *n. conspirators against the king:* plotter, schemer; traitor, subversive.

conspire *v.* 1 *They conspired to overthrow the king:* scheme, intrigue, collude, connive, plot treason. 2 *Rain and car trouble conspired to ruin our vacation:* combine, unite, concur.

constant *adj.* 1 *Keep the chemicals at a con-*

stant temperature: fixed, uniform, steady, even, unchanging, invariable, undeviating, stable. 2 *constant nagging:* incessant, unceasing, ceaseless, unrelenting, continual, interminable, persistent; uninterrupted. 3 *The dog was her constant companion:* loyal, devoted, faithful; trustworthy, steadfast, dependable; abiding, enduring.

Ant. 1 variable, fluctuating, changing; uneven, unstable. 2 occasional, intermittent, spasmodic, sporadic. 3 disloyal, unfaithful, faithless, false; undependable, fickle.

consternation *n. The swimmers' consternation stemmed from a report of sharks:* fear, panic, terror, horror; dismay, apprehension, trepidation.

Ant. composure, calmness, aplomb.

constitute *v.* 1 *What constitutes a balanced diet?:* form, compose, make up, make. 2 *A committee was constituted to investigate rising prices:* establish, create, set up, institute, found; appoint, commission, authorize, name.

constitution *n.* 1 *the fabric's open-weave constitution:* composition, construction, structure. 2 *He has a strong constitution:* physique, figure, body. 3 *to amend the Constitution:* governing charter, charter, basic laws.

constitutional *adj.* 1 *His limp is constitutional:* organic, physical; congenital, inborn, inherent, intrinsic. 2 *Freedom of speech is a Constitutional guarantee:* of the Constitution, chartered; fundamental. —*n.* 3 *a daily constitutional:* walk, stroll, ramble.

Ant. 1 external, extrinsic; accidental. 2 unconstitutional.

constrain *v.* 1 *His conscience constrained him to apologize:* force, compel, coerce, oblige, drive, necessitate. 2 *She constrained her impulse to flee:* restrain, curb, fight down, suppress, check, squelch.

constraint *n.* 1 *He returned the money under constraint of law:* force, obligation, coercion, pressure, compulsion, necessity. 2 *to speak with constraint:* restraint, reserve, inhibition, diffidence.

Ant. 1 desire, wish. 2 openness, frankness.

constrict *v. Doesn't that tight bracelet constrict your arm?:* squeeze, cramp, bind; contract, compress, shrink.

constriction *n. constriction in the patient's chest:* tightness, compression, narrowing, constraint; squeezing, cramping, pinching, binding; shrinking.

Ant. loosening; expansion, widening, dilation, distension.

construct *v. to construct a building. to construct a plan:* build, erect, make, fabricate;

create, formulate, form, frame, design, devise, fashion, shape.

Ant. demolish, raze, tear down.

construction *n.* 1 *the construction of the bridge:* constructing, building, putting together, erecting, fabrication; fashioning, creation. 2 *The construction will be used to store equipment:* building, structure, edifice. 3 *The construction of the new school is modern:* style, form; build, conformation; composition. 4 *The witness's construction of the crime is confusing:* rendition, version, explanation, interpretation.

Ant. 1 demolition, razing.

constructive *adj. constructive criticism:* helpful, practical, useful, valuable.

Ant. destructive; useless.

construe *v. I construe that remark as critical:* interpret, understand, take.

consul *n. the French consul:* diplomatic agent, representative, foreign officer; minister, envoy, emissary.

consult *v.* 1 *Did anyone consult the boss about this?:* ask advice of, seek counsel from, seek the opinion of. 2 *The lawyers consulted on the case:* confer, deliberate together, talk over, discuss together.

consultation *n. a consultation with a patient:* meeting, conference; council, discussion.

consume *v.* 1 *The car consumed very little gas:* use up, expend; deplete, exhaust. 2 *The children consumed all the hamburgers:* eat, devour, eat up; drink up. 3 *The building was consumed by fire:* destroy, lay waste. 4 *consumed with envy:* absorb, engross.

Ant. 1 provide, supply.

consumer *n.* 1 *Consumers want safer products:* user, customer, buyer. 2 *Worry is a consumer of energy:* user, spender; waster, squanderer.

Ant. 1 manufacturer, maker. 2 supplier, provider.

consummate *v.* 1 *to consummate a deal:* complete, fulfill, execute; realize, effect; bring about. —*adj.* 2 *He is a consummate pianist:* finished, complete, accomplished; thorough, utter, unmitigated, total.

Ant. 1 initiate, inaugurate. 2 unfinished, incomplete; partial, conditional.

consummation *n. the consummation of negotiations:* achievement, realization, attainment; completion, conclusion, close.

Ant. beginning, inception; failure.

consumption *n. increased consumption of oil:* use, using up, consuming, utilization.

Ant. conservation, preservation.

contact *n.* 1 *The rear wheels lost contact with the road:* touch, connection; meeting,

touching; union, abutment. 2 *The pilot lost contact with the control tower:* communication, connection, association. —*v.* 3 *The two wires contact:* touch, meet, connect. 4 *I contacted him by phone:* communicate with, reach, get in touch with.

contagious *adj. a contagious disease:* catching, infectious, communicable, transmittable.

Ant. noncontagious, noncatching.

contain *v.* 1 *The suitcase contained two suits. The story contained humorous passages:* hold; include, incorporate. 2 *Try to contain your anger:* control, suppress, restrain, curb, check.

Ant. 2 vent, release.

container *n. Is that container large enough?:* receptacle, holder; *(variously)* vessel, carton, box, bag, can. bottle, jar.

contaminate *v. The oil spill contaminated the gulf:* taint, pollute, foul; make impure, poison; corrupt, defile.

Ant. purify, clean, cleanse.

contamination *n. the contamination of the river:* polluting, fouling; poisoning, spoiling; impurity, pollution, uncleanness.

Ant. purity, cleanness.

contemplate *v.* 1 *The astronomer contemplated the stars:* regard, scan, stare at, gaze at, observe. 2 *Contemplate the problem before making a decision:* ponder, mull over, think about, consider fully, weigh, ruminate. 3 *Our neighbor contemplates a trip to Chicago:* anticipate, envision, imagine; plan, intend, look forward to.

Ant. 1, 2 disregard, overlook, ignore.

contemplation *n.* 1 *the tourists' contemplation of the Alps:* viewing, observation, seeing, looking, gazing. 2 *She reached her decision after much contemplation:* thought, thinking, reflection, pondering, deliberation, musing; rumination, reverie.

contemplative *adj. a contemplative tone in his writings:* thoughtful, reflective, meditative, ruminating; pensive, introspective, studious.

Ant. thoughtless, impetuous.

contemporary *adj.* 1 *contemporary furniture:* modern, up-to-date, current, present-day, recent; ultra-modern. 2 *Hitler was contemporary with Mussolini:* of the same time, coexistent, concurrent, simultaneous.

Ant. 1 antique, old-fashioned, out-of-date.

contempt *n. a contempt for traitors:* scorn, disdain; derision, ridicule; shame, humiliation, ignominy; disgust, distaste, repugnance, detestation, loathing, hatred, abhorrence.

Ant. honor, respect, esteem.

contemptible *adj. Gossip is contemptible:*

mean, vile, low, base, shameful; wretched, unworthy; disgusting, repugnant, revolting, despicable, detestable.
Ant. honorable, admirable, laudable; attractive, appealing.

contemptuous *adj. contemptuous of others:* scornful, disrespectful, disdainful, condescending, derisive.
Ant. deferential, gracious, admiring.

contend *v.* 1 *Three students contended for the prize:* fight, struggle, strive, contest, battle, grapple; compete, vie. 2 *She contended that the witness was lying:* assert, avow, aver, claim, hold, allege; argue, quarrel, dispute.
Ant. 1 yield, surrender.

content *adj.* 1 *Many people are content with a routine life:* satisfied, contented; happy, comfortable; untroubled, unconcerned, serene. —*v.* 2 *The cozy fire contented him:* satisfy, comfort, gratify, please. —*n.* 3 *The children ate to their heart's content:* satisfaction, contentment, gratification; comfort, peace, serenity.
Ant. 1–3 discontent. 1 dissatisfied, unsatisfied; troubled, worried; restless. 2 dissatisfy, displease; upset, annoy.

contented *adj. Are you contented with things as they are?:* satisfied, content, pleased, happy; comfortable, serene, at peace.
Ant. discontented, dissatisfied, displeased, uncomfortable, uneasy.

contentment *n. a smile of contentment:* satisfaction, content, contentedness, gratification, happiness, pleasure; peace, serenity, comfort.
Ant. discontent, dissatisfaction, unhappiness, discomfort.

contest *n.* 1 *a contest of wills. a beauty contest:* conflict, struggle, fight, battle, war; competition, match, tournament, tourney. —*v.* 2 *The soldiers contested their fort to the end:* fight for, battle for, struggle for; contend for, vie for. 3 *The referee's decision was contested:* dispute, argue against, challenge, object to.
Ant. 2 relinquish, surrender, yield. 3 accept, agree to.

context *n. Chapter three can be understood only in the context of the entire book:* framework, setting, frame of reference, surroundings; connection, relationship, milieu; meaning.

contiguous *adj. Their farms were contiguous:* adjoining, bordering, abutting, adjacent, touching.

continence *n. The minister advised continence:* self-restraint, forbearance, absti-

nence, moderation; *(variously)* chastity, temperance.
Ant. incontinence, wantonness, drunkenness.

contingency *n. Be prepared for any contingency:* emergency, unforeseen event, possibility.

contingent *adj. The picnic is contingent on the weather:* dependent, subject to, controlled by.
Ant. independent, unrelated.

continual *adj.* 1 *Traffic passed in a continual flow:* unceasing, continuous, constant, incessant, unremitting, never-ending, unending; uninterrupted. 2 *continual trips to the doctor:* frequent, habitual, constant, recurring, persistent.
Ant. 1 fitful, spasmodic, intermittent. 2 infrequent, rare, occasional; exceptional.

continuance *n. We hope for a continuance of prosperity:* continuation, continuing; persistence; extension, protraction, prolongation.
Ant. end, cessation.

continuation *n. This road is a continuation of the old highway:* continuance, continuing, extension.

continue *v.* 1 *The rain continued all day:* keep on, keep up, persist, persevere, last; resume. 2 *She will continue as principal of the school:* remain, stay, stay on.
Ant. 1 stop, cease, quit. 2 leave, resign, retire, quit.

continuous *adj.* 1 *a continuous line of cars:* unbroken, successive, consecutive; connected. 2 *continuous hot weather:* unremitting, constant, uninterrupted, incessant, continuing, ceaseless, steady; endless, everlasting, persistent; protracted, prolonged.
Ant. 1 intermittent. 2 spasmodic, sporadic, occasional; ending, ceasing.

contort *v. His face contorted with rage:* twist, distort; warp, be misshapen.

contour *n. The road follows the contour of the land:* outline, profile, shape, form, silhouette.

contraband *n. Customs agents checked for contraband:* prohibited articles, illegal imports, smuggled goods; unlawful trafficking.

contract *n.* 1 *a binding contract:* written agreement, compact, pact, covenant. —*v.* 2 *the muscles contract:* draw together, compress, tighten, constrict; shorten, narrow, shrink, dwindle. 3 *He contracted huge debts:* acquire, incur, get, assume, enter into. 4 *The firm contracted for the merchandise:* sign an agreement, agree; undertake, come to terms.

Ant. **2** expand, stretch, distend, swell, increase. **3** avoid, evade, shun, avert.

contraction *n. Cold causes a contraction in the metal:* constriction, compression, tightening, shrinkage, shriveling; decrease, reduction, lessening, shortening, narrowing, abbreviation.
Ant. expansion; stretching, swelling, enlargement.

contradict *v. The witness contradicted the defendant:* refute, confute, controvert; counter, dispute, be contrary to, gainsay; disprove, belie.
Ant. corroborate, confirm, verify, substantiate; affirm, sustain.

contradiction *n. One story is a contradiction of the other:* refutation, denial, disagreement, rebuttal, negation.
Ant. corroboration, confirmation, affirmation.

contradictory *adj. contradictory opinions:* conflicting, opposing, contrary, disagreeing, countervailing, discrepant; inconsistent.
Ant. similar, like, agreeing.

contrary *adj.* **1** *Lying is contrary to my beliefs:* opposed, opposite, contradictory, at variance; incompatible, antithetical, inimical, discordant. **2** *Don't be so contrary!:* unaccommodating, stubborn, obstinate, intractable, refractory, recalcitrant; hostile, antagonistic.
Ant. **1** consistent, accordant. **2** compliant, obliging, accommodating; good-natured, pleasant.

contrast *v.* **1** *This cold weather contrasts with last week's heat:* differentiate, set in opposition; differ, disagree with. —*n.* **2** *In contrast to our old house, the new one is a mansion!:* comparing differences; comparison, differentiation; difference, dissimilarity, variance.
Ant. **1** liken, resemble. **2** similarity, likeness, same, similitude.

contravene *v.* **1** *He had contravened one of the rules:* violate, breach, disobey, overstep; encroach upon. **2** *The proposal had to be contravened:* oppose, contradict, gainsay, repudiate, reject; resist, nullify, abrogate.
Ant. **1** observe, comply with, adhere to. **2** support, agree with.

contribute *v.* **1** *We contributed to the charity:* give, donate, present. **2** *Air pollution contributes to respiratory diseases:* advance, influence, lead to, help bring about, forward, be conducive to.
Ant. **1** take, receive. **2** curb, check, slow.

contribution *n. a five-dollar contribution:* donation, gift, bestowal, benefaction, offering; alms.

contrite *adj. His contrite manner made us forgive him:* conscience-stricken, regretful, repentant, rueful, penitent, remorseful; chastened, humbled.
Ant. unrepentant, unapologetic.

contrition *n. Did Judas feel contrition for his betrayal?:* self-reproach, regret, remorse, qualms of conscience, compunction; repentance, penitence, penance, atonement.

contrivance *n. This contrivance peels and cores apples:* device, contraption, gadget, implement; tool, machine, *Slang* gizmo, doodad, thingamajig.

contrive *v.* **1** *She contrived a bookcase out of bricks and boards:* devise, create, concoct, improvise; invent, design. **2** *The youth contrived to stow away:* scheme, plot, plan; manage, effect by stratagem.

control *v.* **1** *The president controls the company:* command, rule, regulate, manage, have charge of, supervise, steer; dominate, reign over. **2** *Control your temper:* restrain, restrict, repress, subdue, contain, curb, bridle. —*n.* **3** *The island was under the control of Great Britain:* command, management, regulation, direction, rule; dominion, domination, jurisdiction, authority; supervision, charge. **4** *Aspirin is an effective control for headaches:* curb, restraint, suppressant.
Ant. **2** let loose, give vent.

controversial *adj. a controversial matter:* widely discussed, causing debate; arguable, open to discussion, questionable, at issue.

controversy *n. a controversy over the plans for the new school:* discussion, dispute, contention; argument, quarrel, disagreement.

contusion *n. They only suffered a few contusions:* bruise, discoloration, black-and-blue mark; abrasion.

conundrum *n. Find the answer to the conundrum:* puzzle, riddle, enigma, mystery, paradox, brain-teaser.

convalescence *n. Rest helped the patient's convalescence:* recovery, recuperation, return to health.

convene *v. The club convenes every month. The chairman convened the meeting:* assemble, meet, gather; summon, convoke; call to order, begin.
Ant. adjourn, dissolve.

convenience *n.* **1** *the convenience of a refrigerator:* usefulness, service, benefit; handiness, accessibility. **2** *Energy is a modern convenience:* comfort, accommodation, facility; appliance. **3** *Shopping bags are provided for your convenience:* accommodation, use, ease. **4** *Call at your earliest convenience:* opportunity, chance, convenient time.

Ant. 1 inconvenience, nuisance. 3 inconvenience.

convenient *adj.* 1 *This lamp is convenient for reading:* suitable, useful, helpful, easy to use, handy. 2 *The parking lot is convenient to the office:* easily accessible, nearby, at hand.

Ant. 1 inconvenient, unsuitable, awkward. 2 inconvenient, inaccessible, distant.

convent *n. The religious girl joined a convent:* society of nuns, nunnery, cloister.

convention *n.* 1 *the Republican presidential convention:* assembly, congress, convocation, conclave, caucus; meeting, gathering. 2 *the conventions of society:* custom, social rule, code; precept, protocol, formality.

conventional *adj. White is the conventional color of a wedding gown:* traditional, customary; accepted, proper, normal, regular, routine, usual.

Ant. unconventional, unorthodox, uncommon.

converge *v. The Mississippi and Missouri rivers converge at St. Louis:* come together, meet, approach.

Ant. diverge, separate.

conversant *adj. Are you conversant with calculus?:* familiar, knowledgeable of, well-informed, proficient, erudite, skilled.

Ant. ignorant, unversed, unfamiliar.

conversation *n. a long conversation:* talk, dialogue, chat, chitchat, tête-à-tête.

converse[1] *v. We conversed for hours:* talk, speak together, chat, *Slang* gab, chew the fat, shoot the breeze, rap.

converse[2] *n. His views are the converse of mine:* opposite, reverse, contrary, antithesis.

Ant. identical, same.

conversion *n.* 1 *the conversion of an old school to an office building:* change, transformation, modification; metamorphosis, transmutation. 2 *Saint Patrick was responsible for Ireland's conversion to Christianity:* change, change of religion; change of heart.

convert *v.* 1 *The plant converts crude oil into gasoline:* change, transform, modify, turn. 2 *He converted to Judaism:* change one's religion, change one's belief; cause a change of opinion. —*n.* 3 *a convert to Buddhism:* converted person; proselyte.

convex *adj. a convex lens:* curved outward, rounded; protuberant, bulging.

Ant. concave; sunken.

convey *v.* 1 *The pipeline conveys natural gas to the Midwest:* carry, transport, conduct, bring, move, transmit. 2 *Please convey my best wishes to her:* communicate, make

known, impart, relate, give, tell. 3 *He conveyed the family farm to his son:* transfer, cede, deed, consign, grant; will, bequeath.

Ant. 3 retain, keep, hold on to.

conveyance *n.* 1 *the conveyance of lumber to building sites:* conveying, transport, transportation, carrying, transfer, carriage. 2 *What kind of conveyance does the dairy use?:* transportation, vehicle; *(variously)* bus, car, truck, van, wagon.

convict *v.* 1 *convicted of manslaughter:* find guilty; condemn. —*n.* 2 *The convicts complained about prison conditions:* prisoner, felon; *Slang* jailbird, con.

Ant. 1 acquit, find innocent.

conviction *n.* 1 *political convictions:* belief, view, viewpoint, opinion, judgment; principle, tenet, position. 2 *The audience was swayed by the speaker's conviction:* certainty, certitude; intensity, earnestness.

Ant. 2 doubt, uncertainty, misgiving.

convince *v. The speech convinced us to vote for her:* persuade, sway, win over; assure, satisfy.

convivial *adj. convivial people:* sociable, friendly, companionable, genial, affable, fun-loving, gregarious.

Ant. unsociable, reserved, solemn.

convocation *n. a convocation of experts:* convention, congress, conference, council, meeting.

convolution *n. the convolutions of a snake:* coiling, coil, twisting, twist, winding, undulation; contortion.

convulsion *n. an epileptic convulsion:* spasm, fit, seizure, paroxysm; outburst.

cool *adj.* 1 *a cool day:* somewhat cold, chill, chilly. 2 *She had a cool, unruffled manner:* calm, unexcited, composed, imperturbable, self-possessed; cool-headed, undisturbed; unemotional, dispassionate. 3 *a cool reception:* unfriendly, uncordial, distant, reserved, aloof, indifferent; cold, frosty. —*v.* 4 *Cool the soup:* make cool, become cool, chill.

Ant. 1 warm, warmish. 2 frenzied, frantic; impassioned, nervous, tense, agitated, troubled. 3 cordial, warm. 4 warm, heat.

cooperate *v. Please cooperate with us:* work together, participate, act jointly, join, share in, go along; pull together.

Ant. oppose, conflict.

cooperation *n. with the cooperation of all the employees:* cooperating, participation, joint action, pulling together.

Ant. opposition, dissension, discord.

coordinate *v.* 1 *Try to coordinate their work:* organize, order, systematize; correlate, match, mesh. —*adj.* 2 *the coordinate*

branches of the armed services: equal, equally important, correlative.
Ant. 2 unequal, disparate.

cope *v. to cope with one's problems:* contend, wrestle, face, struggle; manage, handle.

copious *adj. a copious supply:* profuse, plentiful, abundant, bountiful; extensive, ample, liberal, generous.
Ant. sparse, meager, scant.

copy *n.* 1 *a copy of the painting:* reproduction, facsimile; duplicate, carbon copy, replica; imitation, counterfeit, forgery, fake. 2 *The reporter's copy was due:* text, story, manuscript. —*v.* 3 *Copy this letter in triplicate:* make a copy of, reproduce, duplicate. 4 *Don't copy everything he does!:* emulate, imitate, mimic, ape.
Ant. 1 original.

coquette *n. That little coquette stole her boyfriend:* flirt, vamp, heartbreaker.

cord *n. Tie the box with cord:* twine, thin rope, heavy string.

cordial *adj. a cordial greeting:* friendly, genial, amiable, affable, warm; sincere, heartfelt.
Ant. unfriendly, cool, distant, aloof.

cordiality *n. She greeted her guests with cordiality:* friendliness, warmth, affability, amiability, geniality, agreeableness, amicability.
Ant. coldness, ill will.

core *n.* 1 *an apple core:* center, central part; innermost part, nucleus. 2 *Let's get to the core of the matter:* essence, essential part, gist, heart; substance, crux, nub.

corner *v.* 1 *to corner a suspect:* trap; back into a corner. —*n.* 2 *all four corners of the room:* angle; bend. 3 *He got himself into a corner with debts:* predicament, dilemma, plight, impasse, awkward position; *Slang* fix, jam, pickle.

corny *adj. He thinks the two-step is corny:* trite, banal, insipid, platitudinous, square, old-fashioned; unsophisticated, inane.

corporal *adj. corporal punishment:* bodily, physical.

corporeal *adj. our corporeal existence:* physical, bodily; mortal, worldly; nonspiritual, material.
Ant. spiritual.

corps *n.* 1 *the signal corps:* military branch; body of troops; combat unit. 2 *a corps of doctors:* team, crew, force, band.

corpse *n. The coroner examined the corpse:* dead body, body, cadaver, remains.

corpulent *adj. Our family is corpulent:* fat, obese, overweight, portly, stout, plump, chubby, pudgy.
Ant. emaciated, thin, slender, slim, lean, skinny, scrawny.

correct *v.* 1 *Please correct any misspellings. Glasses should correct your vision:* make right, remove the errors of, rectify, repair, remedy; improve; regulate, fix. 2 *His father corrected him when he misbehaved:* reprimand, admonish, rebuke, censure, reprove, take to task; punish, discipline, chastise. —*adj.* 3 *Each correct answer was worth ten points:* accurate, right, true. 4 *correct behavior:* proper, fitting, appropriate, suitable; seemly, acceptable.
Ant. 2 condone, praise, compliment, laud. 3 incorrect, wrong, inaccurate. 4 improper, inappropriate, unsuitable, unseemly.

correction *n. The navigator made a correction to bring the ship back on course:* rectification, improvement; alteration, change, modification, adjustment.

corrective *adj. corrective measures:* counter, counterbalancing; reformatory, rectifying; improving; therapeutic, remedial, compensatory.

correlate *v. correlate the testimony of the two witnesses:* relate, show relationship between, compare; connect, correspond, parallel.

correspond *v.* 1 *The two sisters correspond every week:* exchange letters, write, communicate. 2 *The report doesn't correspond with the facts:* agree, conform, concur, coincide, accord, match, fit, jibe, square.
Ant. 2 differ, disagree, diverge.

correspondence *n.* 1 *business correspondence:* mail, letters; dispatches, bulletins, communiqués. 2 *There is no correspondence between the two stories:* similarity, resemblance, analogy.

corridor *n. Each office opens onto the corridor:* hallway, hall, passageway; passage.

corroborate *v. Recent experiments corroborate the theory:* prove, verify, confirm, uphold, support, substantiate; certify, endorse.
Ant. disprove, contradict, refute.

corrode *v. Acid had corroded the pipes:* eat away, erode; rust, oxidize.

corrugated *adj. corrugated cardboard:* ridged, furrowed, crenelated, puckered, pleated; creased, wrinkled, crinkled.

corrupt *adj.* 1 *corrupt politicians:* dishonest, crooked, unscrupulous, fraudulent, unethical, unprincipled. 2 *Corrupt friends led me astray:* wicked, immoral, debased, low, sinful, evil. —*v.* 3 *Greed corrupts many people:* make immoral, debase, lead astray; poison; pervert, seduce.
Ant. 1 honest, upright, principled. 2 virtuous, moral, high-minded. 3 reform, uplift.

corruption *n.* 1 *Our police seem free of corruption:* dishonesty, graft, bribery, shady dealings. 2 *The Bible warns against corrup-*

tion: wickedness, depravity, evil ways, immorality, sinfulness, wrongdoing.

Ant. 1 honesty, integrity. 2 goodness, righteousness, morality.

corsair *n. The treasure ship was set upon by corsairs:* pirate, privateer, buccaneer, sea rover, freebooter; marauder, plunderer.

cortege *n. The cortege followed the hearse to the cemetery:* funeral procession, train, entourage, escort; company, attendants, column, caravan, motorcade, cavalcade.

cosmic *adj.* 1 *Cosmic space can't be understood:* of the universe, *(especially)* extraterrestrial, of outer space, interplanetary, interstellar. 2 *a matter of cosmic importance:* vast, immense, enormous, widespread, grandiose; infinite, universal.

Ant. 2 minor, small.

cosmopolitan *adj.* 1 *a cosmopolitan city:* sophisticated, worldly, worldly-wise, urbane; international. —*n.* 2 *a true cosmopolitan:* man of the world, woman of the world, sophisticate, cosmopolite, citizen of the world.

Ant. 1 provincial, insular, parochial. 2 provincial, rustic.

cosmos *n. There may be other intelligent life in the cosmos:* universe, interstellar system, earth and the heavens.

cost *n. What's the cost of a European vacation?:* price, charge, amount; expense, expenditure; bill, tab, fee; worth, value. 2 *The soldiers captured the hill at great cost:* loss, sacrifice; expense, price; pain, distress, suffering, harm, injury, damage. —*v.* 3 *This coat costs $3,000:* sell for, be priced at, amount to, come to, 4 *That mistake will cost you!:* harm, injure, hurt, damage; burden, cause to lose.

costly *adj.* 1 *The house is too costly:* expensive, high-priced, dear, steep. 2 *a costly mistake:* disastrous, catastrophic; harmful, damaging.

Ant. 1 cheap, inexpensive; reasonable.

costume *n. Today's costume should be shorts and a sport shirt:* dress, garb; outfit, attire, raiment, apparel, garments, clothing, clothes; uniform.

coterie *n. the literary coterie:* set, clique, circle, crowd, group, band, crew.

cottage *n. a rustic cottage:* simple house, bungalow; lodge, chalet.

Ant. palace, castle, mansion.

couch *n.* 1 *Sit beside me on the couch:* sofa, divan, davenport, settee; *(variously)* chesterfield, love seat. —*v.* 2 *He couched his demands in polite language:* express, voice, word, utter, state, phrase, frame.

council *n.* 1 *a council of leading educators:* convention, conference, congress, convocation, colloquy; gathering. 2 *the city council:* legislative body, assembly, governing body, representatives; cabinet, ministry; panel, committee.

counsel *n.* 1 *Seek an architect's counsel:* advice, opinion, guidance, recommendation, suggestion. 2 *on advice of counsel:* lawyer, legal adviser, counselor, counselor-at-law, attorney. —*v.* 3 *The teacher counseled us to study harder:* advise, recommend, suggest, advocate, urge, charge, instruct; warn, admonish, caution.

counselor Also **counsellor** *n.* 1 *Each student has a counselor. The queen met with her counselor:* adviser, instructor, tutor; cabinet member, minister. 2 *the counselor for the defense:* legal adviser, lawyer, attorney, counsel, counselor-at-law, advocate.

count *v.* 1 *Count from one to ten:* add one by one, enumerate, numerate. 2 *The old friend was counted as a member of the family:* include, consider; regard, look on. 3 *Count yourself lucky:* consider, regard, deem, hold, rate, reckon, estimate, judge. 4 *Every penny counts:* matter, be important, enter into consideration, add to the number. 5 *according to my count:* total, tally, calculation, reckoning, numeration.

countenance *n.* 1 *I'd recognize his countenance anywhere:* look, mien, aspect, visage; face, features. 2 *The mayor will give his countenance to the new tax:* approval, sanction, approbation, advocacy. —*v.* 3 *I won't countenance such behavior!:* permit, approve; sanction, condone; advocate, support, promote, uphold, champion.

Ant. 2 disapproval, opposition. 3 prohibit, condemn.

counter[1] *n.* 1 *Watches are at the jewelry counter:* table, stand, display case; bar, fountain, buffet. 2 *In Monopoly each player moves a counter around the board:* playing piece, piece, disk, man.

counter[2] *adv. & adj.* 1 *The results are counter to all predictions:* contrary, contradictory, at variance, opposite, opposed, against, in conflict. —*v.* 2 *The boxer countered with a left:* retaliate, strike back, fight back, hit back; oppose, offset, resist.

Ant. 1 in agreement, accordant with. 2 yield, surrender.

counteract *v. This medicine should counteract the fever:* act against, negate, neutralize, offset; fight, check, curb; alleviate, assuage; conflict with, counterattack.

Ant. aid, assist, reinforce; promote, further.

counterbalance *v. The virtues of the book counterbalanced its shortcomings:* offset, compensate for, make up for; balance, neutralize; counterweigh, countervail.

counterfeit *adj.* 1 *counterfeit money:* fake, phony, bogus, sham; imitation, simulated, artificial, ersatz; feigned, make-believe. —*n.* 2 *The painting is a counterfeit:* forgery, fake, phony, imitation.
Ant. 1 genuine, real.

countermand *v. The second order countermanded the first:* revoke, rescind, cancel, overrule, withdraw, retract, annual, nullify, reverse, set aside.
Ant. reinforce, reiterate.

counterpart *n. Canada's Prime Minister is the counterpart of the U.S. President:* equal, correspondent, correlative, match.
Ant. antithesis, opposite.

countless *adj. the countless stars in the sky:* innumerable, infinite, myriad, multitudinous, unlimited, limitless, untold, immeasurable, measureless, incalculable.
Ant. finite, limited.

country *n.* 1 *mountainous country:* terrain, land, area, region; countryside, landscape, scenery. 2 *a citizen of this country:* nation, state, kingdom, realm. 3 *The country will elect a new president:* nation, population, populace, inhabitants, citizens. 4 *His father's country was Czechoslovakia:* native country, native land, mother country, homeland, fatherland. 5 *She prefers the city to the country:* rural areas, countryside, hinterlands, farming area. —*adj.* 6 *a little country town out west:* rural, farming, provincial.
Ant. 5 city, town, metropolis. 6 urban, cosmopolitan, city.

countryman *n.* 1 *my fellow countrymen:* compatriot, fellow citizen, landsman. 2 *The city slicker tried to outwit the innocent countryman:* rustic, farmer, provincial; *Slang* yokel, hick, country bumpkin, rube.
Ant. 1 alien, foreigner. 2 townsman, urbanite, metropolitan, cosmopolitan.

coup de grace *An officer administered the coup de grace with a pistol:* deathblow, mercy stroke, decisive blow.

coup d'état *Army leaders ousted the president in a coup d'état:* rebellion, palace revolution; mutiny.

couple *n.* 1 *Arrange the chairs in couples:* pair, combination of two, doublet. 2 *a nice-looking couple:* twosome, pair, duo; husband and wife, engaged pair, dating pair, man and woman. —*v.* 3 *The caboose is coupled to the last freight car:* connect, join, link, fasten, hitch; bind, yoke.
Ant. 3 detach, disconnect, unfasten.

courage *n. He received a medal for courage:* bravery, valor, fearlessness; daring, boldness.
Ant. cowardice, pusillanimousness, timidity.

courageous *adj. a courageous act:* brave, valiant, fearless, intrepid, unafraid; valorous, heroic.
Ant. cowardly, craven.

courier *n. The courier carried the dispatch:* messenger, runner, bearer; go-between, envoy.

course *n.* 1 *The ship was off course:* route, direction, path; channel, passage, road. 2 *in the course of the discussion:* progression, development, sequence, flow. 3 *Your best course is to accept my offer:* procedure, action, conduct; method, policy. 4 *a college course:* class, lessons, lectures; course of study; curriculum, subject. 5 *The race was run on the turf course:* circuit, circle, round, run; racecourse, track. —*v.* 6 *The stream courses over the rocks:* run, flow, race, pour, surge, gush.

court *n.* 1 *the court of Queen Elizabeth I:* royal household, entourage, retinue; advisers, council, attendants. 2 *The king held court:* audience, hearing, assembly, session, meeting. 3 *The apartment house is built around a court:* courtyard, yard, enclosed area, atrium, quadrangle. 4 *The knight paid court to his fair lady:* courtship, homage, respects, courtesies; suit, wooing. 5 *The lawyer made her appearance before the court:* court of law, court of justice, bench, bar. —*v.* 6 *Some companies court only wealthy clients:* curry favor with, pander to; flatter, blandish; woo, pay suit to, pursue, run after. 7 *Don't court disaster:* invite, provoke, seek.
Ant. 6 avoid, shun; reject, turn down.

courteous *adj. a courteous youth:* polite, well-mannered, mannerly, respectful.
Ant. discourteous, impolite, rude, ill-mannered.

courtesy *n. Treat everyone with courtesy:* politeness, courteousness, good manners, respect.
Ant. discourtesy, impoliteness, bad manners, rudeness, disrespect.

courtly *adj. courtly manners:* refined, genteel, elegant, gallant, chivalrous, stately; aristocratic; polite, courteous.
Ant. unrefined, undignified, impolite; ill-mannered, discourteous, rude.

courtship *n. a courtship of nine years:* wooing, courting, keeping company.

cove *n. The boat was in the cove:* bay, inlet, lagoon, estuary.

covenant *n. the covenant the Jews made with God:* solemn agreement, pledge, vow, promise, bond.

cover *v.* 1 *Cover the table with a cloth:* put on, put over, overlay; clothe, sheathe. 2 *The tent covered us from the rain:* protect, shield, shelter. 3 *She covered her face with her hands:* hide, conceal; cloak, veil, screen. 4 *The book covers the years of Eisenhower's presidency:* deal with, include, involve; encompass; report, describe, chronicle, write up. 5 *We covered three states in two days:* travel through, pass through, traverse, cross. —*n.* 6 *The box had a carved wooden cover:* lid, top; covering; envelope, jacket, sheath. 7 *Do you want another cover on the bed?:* blanket, comforter, quilt, coverlet. 8 *We took cover under a tree:* shelter, shield; asylum, refuge, sanctuary; concealment, hiding place.

Ant. 1 uncover. 2 expose. 3 uncover, reveal, show, expose. 4 exclude, omit.

coverage *n.* 1 *This insurance provides coverage for accidents:* protection, indemnity; payment, reimbursement. 2 *the newspaper's coverage of the election:* reporting, description; publishing, broadcasting.

covering *n.* 1 *a waterproof covering:* cover, wrapper, wrapping, casing, envelope, sheath. —*adj.* 2 *Send a covering letter with your résumé.* descriptive, explanatory, introductory.

covert *adj.* *The FBI had a covert meeting with the kidnappers:* secret, clandestine, hidden, surreptitious.

Ant. overt, open, public.

covet *v. I covet the boss's job:* desire greedily, crave, lust after, yearn for, want, long for, aspire to, hanker after.

covetous *adj. You are covetous of others' wealth:* craving, desirous, lustful; greedy, avaricious, grasping; envious.

Ant. forswearing, abjuring.

cow *v. The boys were cowed by the class bully:* intimidate; frighten, terrorize, terrify; bully, bulldoze; dishearten, dismay, discourage.

coward *n. Only a coward would run away:* uncourageous person, dastard, caitiff, craven.

Ant. hero, daredevil.

cowardly *adj. a cowardly act:* uncourageous, fainthearted, timorous, craven, pusillanimous; *Slang* chicken; afraid, fearful.

Ant. brave, courageous, valiant, valorous, lionhearted; bold, daring, intrepid.

cowboy *n. The cowboys branded the calves:* cowpoke, broncobuster, cowpuncher, cowhand, buckaroo; *Spanish* gaucho, vaquero.

cower *v. The serfs cowered before the king:* cringe, draw back, shrink, recoil; quail, tremble.

Ant. swagger, strut, stand tall.

coy *adj. The child gets coy when asked to recite:* shy, modest, bashful, sheepish, overmodest; coquettish, kittenish.

Ant. brash, brazen, bold, impertinent, pert, saucy.

cozy *adj. a cozy evening by the fire:* snug, comfortable, relaxing; homey.

crack *v.* 1 *The whip cracked:* snap, pop, crackle; clap, thunder. 2 *The plate cracked:* split, fracture, cleave. 3 *Anyone can crack under pressure:* break, lose control, go to pieces. —*n.* 4 *a crack of rifle fire in the distance:* report, burst, snap, pop. 5 *The earthquake caused cracks in the earth:* split, fissure, rift, rent, cleft, slit, gash, crevice. 6 *Don't make any cracks about her hat:* wisecrack, joke, quip, gag, jest, gibe; insult, taunt.

crackpot *n.* 1 *All public figures have to deal with crackpots:* eccentric, crackbrain, lunatic, crank, *Slang* nut, screwball, weirdo. —*adj.* 2 *crackpot ideas:* crackbrained, foolish, eccentric, *Slang* weirdo, nutty.

Ant. 2 rational, sensible, sound.

crackup *n.* 1 *a crackup on the thruway:* collision, smashup, pileup, wreck, accident. 2 *The soldier suffered a crackup:* nervous breakdown, battle fatigue, combat fatigue, *Archaic* shellshock.

cradle *n.* 1 *The child slept in her cradle:* bed on rockers; *(loosely)* crib, bassinet. 2 *the cradle of democracy:* birthplace, source, origin, fountainhead, wellspring. —*v.* 3 *She cradled the infant:* rock, cuddle, snuggle, hug, clasp.

craft *n.* 1 *Making stained-glass requires great craft:* skill, ability, deftness, adroitness; expertise, know-how, technique. 2 *Weaving was the town's chief craft:* trade, business, occupation, vocation, industry; handicraft. 3 *Magicians use craft to hoodwink us:* craftiness, cunning, artifice; trickery, deception, guile, duplicity, deceit, perfidy. 4 *a small craft:* ship, boat, vessel; aircraft, airplane, plane.

Ant. 1 unskillfulness, maladroitness, incompetency, clumsiness. 3 openness, candor, sincerity.

crafty *adj. a crafty politician:* cunning, shrewd; wily, foxy, tricky, sly, guileful, artful; shifty, underhand, devious, deceptive, deceitful; scheming, designing, calculating.

Ant. honest, open, candid, frank, aboveboard; naive, innocent, ingenuous.

craggy *adj. the craggy coast of Maine:* rocky, stony, cragged, rugged, rockbound, jagged, rock-ribbed; steep, precipitous.

Ant. smooth, even, flat.

cram *v. I couldn't cram any more into the suitcase:* jam, pack, stuff, crowd, press, squeeze.

cramp *n.* 1 *a cramp in her leg:* muscular contraction, spasm, stitch, charley horse.

—v. 2 *Lack of education cramped his chances:* hamper, hold back, restrict, limit, hinder, restrain, frustrate, handicap.

Ant. 2 help, aid, increase.

cranky *adj. I'm cranky in the morning:* grouchy, cross, bearish, crabby, crotchety, ill-humored, irascible, cantankerous, peevish, waspish, testy.

Ant. good-natured, cheerful, agreeable.

crash *v.* 1 *The flowerpot crashed to the sidewalk:* fall heavily, strike noisily, smash, shatter. 2 *The cars crashed at the intersection:* collide; smash, bump, bang. 3 *Five boys tried to crash her party:* come uninvited, enter without a ticket; slip in, sneak in. —n. 4 *the crash of pots and pans in the kitchen:* clatter, bang, din, clangor; crack, boom; shattering, smashing; hitting, bumping. 5 *Several were injured in the crash:* collision, smashup, accident, pileup. 6 *the stock market crash of 1929:* financial collapse, failure; *(loosely)* depression, recession, slump, decline.

Ant. 4 murmur, whisper.

crass *adj. crass manners:* coarse, crude, vulgar, gross, unrefined, inelegant; uncaring, insensitive, boorish, unsympathetic, unfeeling.

Ant. refined, elegant; deferential, sympathetic, kind.

crave *v. He craves sweets:* pine for, sigh for, desire, long for, yearn for, hunger for, thirst for, hanker after, have a yen for.

Ant. spurn, scorn; detest, loathe, hate, abhor.

craven *adj. Refusing to fight was a craven thing to do:* cowardly, dastardly, pusillanimous; timorous, fearful, frightened, scared; *Slang* yellow, chicken; base, low.

Ant. brave, courageous, heroic, valorous, valiant; bold, daring.

crawl *v.* 1 *The caterpillar crawled across the rock:* creep, slither, squirm, wiggle, wriggle, writhe, worm; move on hands and knees. 2 *The traffic crawled:* go at a snail's pace, inch along.

Ant. 1 walk; run.

craze *v.* 1 *crazed with thirst:* make crazy, drive wild, make berserk, derange, unhinge. —n. 2 *Hula-Hoops were a craze:* fad, rage; mania, passion.

crazy *adj.* 1 *Not all crazy people are in asylums:* insane, mad, demented, deranged, maniacal, daft, unbalanced, unhinged; *Slang* cracked, nuts, nutty. 2 *a crazy hat:* bizarre, weird, strange; silly, absurd, outrageous. 3 *It was a crazy thing to do:* foolish, imprudent, unwise, foolhardy; senseless, stupid, silly, ridiculous, idiotic, absurd. 4 *I'm crazy about clothes:* mad, smitten with, taken with, wild; frantic, excited; infatuated, gaga.

Ant. 1 sane, mentally sound, rational, well-balanced. 2 sensible, practical; conservative, common. 3 smart, wise, prudent, sensible.

creak *v. The hinges creaked:* rasp, squeak, screech, screak.

crease *v.* 1 *Iron the creases out of this blouse:* fold, wrinkle, ridge, crinkle, rumple; corrugation, furrow. —v. 2 *Worry creased his brow:* wrinkle, pucker; crinkle, ruffle, crimple, corrugate, furrow; fold, pleat, crimp.

Ant. 2 smooth, flatten, straighten out.

create *v.* 1 *Chemists created waterproof glue:* originate, invent, devise, formulate; make, concoct, contrive, fashion, design; form, mold, erect, construct; conceive, bring into being, give birth to; cause, bring to pass. 2 *The government has created a new agency:* found, establish, set up, institute, form.

creation *n.* 1 *the largest mammal in creation:* the world, the universe, nature; all things, all living things. 2 *the creation of new playgrounds:* creating, making, institution, development, devising, establishment, founding, bringing into existence, formation; building, construction, fabrication, fashioning, erection. 3 *the designer's latest creation:* original work, invention, conception, concoction, handiwork.

creative *adj. She's full of creative ideas:* original, imaginative, ingenious, inventive, resourceful, fanciful.

creator *n.* 1 *the creators of the U.S. Constitution:* originator, author, framer, designer, architect, maker, inventor, founder, father. 2 **the Creator.** See GOD.

creature *n. all creatures great and small:* living being, living thing; animal, lower animal, beast, dumb animal.

credence *n. Don't give credence to rumors:* belief, confidence, trust, reliance, credibility, creditability; trustworthiness, reliability, dependableness; certainty, certitude.

Ant. doubt, mistrust, skepticism, distrust.

credentials *n. She has the proper credentials for the job:* letter of credence; official testimonials; certificate, diploma, reference, letter of recommendation; authorization, permit, license.

credible *adj. Is the story credible?:* believable, plausible, reasonable; conceivable, thinkable.

Ant. incredible, unbelievable, implausible.

credit *n.* 1 *The photographer was given credit in the program:* recognition, acknowledgment; honor, regard, commendation.

2 *We bought the sofa on credit:* installment plan, charge account, time. **3** *You have a credit of $10:* allowance, prepayment. *—v.* **4** *Edison is credited with the invention of the phonograph:* attribute, ascribe, assign, acknowledge, recognize; honor, acclaim. **5** *How could you credit such a wild story?:* believe, have faith in, rely on, *Informal* buy.
Ant. **2** cash. **3** debit. **5** doubt, disbelieve, distrust, question.

creditable *adj. a creditable job:* admirable, commendable, praiseworthy, laudable; reputable, estimable, respectable.

credo *n. His credo is "Work hard and save":* creed, set of beliefs, set of principles, doctrine, tenet, code.

credulous *adj. Anne is so credulous she'll believe anything:* easily convinced, gullible, trusting, believing; overtrustful, unsuspicious, unquestioning.
Ant. incredulous, unbelieving; suspicious, wary, cynical.

creed *n. The minister explained the church's creed:* religious belief, belief, profession of faith, doctrine, dogma, set of principles, set of beliefs, credo, tenets; canons, gospel.

creek *n. to wade in the creek:* stream, brook, rivulet, rill, run; millstream.

creep *v.* **1** *The snake crept along the wall:* crawl, slither, writhe, wriggle. **2** *The hunter crept close to the deer:* advance secretly, sneak, steal. **3** *The old car crept down the road:* move slowly, inch, crawl, go at a snail's pace.
Ant. **1** run. **3** race, rush, fly, tear.

cremate *v. His remains were cremated:* reduce to ashes, burn, incinerate; consume by fire.

crest *n.* **1** *The bird has a red crest:* tuft, topknot, comb. **2** *on the crest of the hill:* top, summit, pinnacle, highest point, peak; apex, height. **3** *the family crest:* coat of arms, arms, armorial bearings, escutcheon.
Ant. **2** bottom, base.

crestfallen *adj. The losers were crestfallen:* downhearted, downcast, dejected, depressed, discouraged, disheartened, dispirited, despondent, woebegone.
Ant. elated, exuberant, happy; encouraged, heartened.

crevice *n. a huge crevice:* fissure, crack, cleft, split, fracture, rift, rent, slit; chasm, crevasse.

crew *n.* **1** *a construction crew:* gang, squad, corps, force, team, party. **2** *a ship's crew:* work force, company of sailors, company, complement, hands, sailors, mariners, seamen. **3** *a motley crew:* band, pack, group, mob, throng, troop, horde.

crime *n.* **1** *the crime of embezzling:* unlawful act, lawbreaking; foul play, offense; *(variously)* capital crime, felony, misdemeanor, malfeasance. **2** *It's a crime to waste food:* wrong, misdeed; senseless act, outrage, abomination.
Ant. **2** good deed, virtue.

criminal *adj.* **1** *Robbery is a criminal act:* illegal, unlawful, lawbreaking, lawless, illicit. **2** *It's criminal to let a fine garden go to ruin:* wrong, senseless, outrageous, villainous, abominable. *—n.* **3** *The criminal was sent to prison:* guilty person; culprit, lawbreaker, outlaw, felon; wrongdoer, transgressor, offender.
Ant. **1** lawful, legal, licit. **2** right, commendable, admirable, praiseworthy.

cringe *v. The child cringed every time the father raised his voice:* cower, flinch, shrink, quail, recoil; dodge, duck; grovel.
Ant. strut, swagger.

crinkly *adj. crinkly paper:* wrinkly, wrinkled, crimped, crimpled, puckered; ruffled, curly, wavy, frizzy, frizzled.
Ant. smooth, flat, unwrinkled.

cripple *v.* **1** *The accident crippled her permanently:* make lame, disable, incapacitate; impair, maim. **2** *The snowstorm crippled rail transportation:* impair, disable, incapacitate; paralyze, stop, halt.
Ant. **2** help, assist, facilitate.

crisis *n. Negotiations are approaching a crisis:* turning point, climax, emergency, critical stage.

crisp *adj.* **1** *Potato chips are crisp:* crispy, crunchy. **2** *crisp conversation:* brisk, sharp, pointed, incisive, candid, terse; lively, sparkling. **3** *a crisp fall day:* brisk, pleasantly cool, chilly, nippy; bracing, refreshing, invigorating.
Ant. **1** soft. **2** dull, insipid. **3** warm, balmy.

criterion *n. What is the major criterion for judging a symphony?:* standard, gauge, yardstick, guidepost; rule, principle, norm; model, precedent, example, touchstone.

critic *n. I like painting, but I'm no art critic:* judge, connoisseur, authority, cognoscente; evaluator, analyst, professional reviewer. **2** *The senator will answer critics:* detractor, attacker, faultfinder, criticizer.

critical *adj.* **1** *Don't be so critical:* censorious, faultfinding, picky, fussy, caviling, nitpicking, disapproving. **2** *to develop one's critical abilities:* discriminating, analytical, diagnostic. **3** *This is a critical time in history:* decisive, crucial, grave, serious; sensitive, urgent, dangerous.
Ant. **1–3** uncritical. **1** complimentary, approving, laudatory. **3** settled, tranquil; safe.

criticize *v. He's always criticizing his*

brother: find fault with, reprove, reproach, censure; nag at, carp, cavil, pick.

Ant. compliment, praise, commend, laud.

critique *n. The students wrote a critique of a novel:* critical essay, criticism, critical commentary, analysis.

crony *n. Frank and his cronies get together every Thursday night:* friend, companion, pal, chum, comrade, buddy; cohort, accomplice.

crook *n.* 1 *a sharp crook in the road:* bend, curve, turn, twist, angle, curvature; hook. 2 *Only a crook would charge for work and not do it:* cheat, knave, criminal, robber, thief, bandit, swindler, embezzler; burglar, robber.

crooked *adj.* 1 *Straighten that crooked picture. a crooked road:* askew, awry, not straight; curved, twisted, twisting, winding, meandering, tortuous, sinuous, serpentine, zigzag; bent, bowed, hooked. 2 *crooked dealings:* dishonest, unscrupulous, criminal, unlawful; deceptive, fraudulent, underhanded, deceitful, shady.

Ant. 1 straight. 2 honest, legal, lawful, ethical, honorable, aboveboard.

crop *n.* 1 *this year's corn crop:* harvest, yield, production, gleaning. —*v.* 2 *His hair was cropped:* cut short, clip, shear, trim, cut, bob, prune.

cross *n.* 1 *The church has a cross on its steeple:* crux, rood, crucifix. 2 *Her illness is a cross she will have to bear:* burden, misfortune; affliction, distress, suffering, ordeal, adversity, trial. 3 *The mule is a cross between a female horse and a male donkey:* crossbreed, hybrid, half-breed. —*v.* 4 *Cross the eggs off the list:* delete, strike out, cancel, cross out. 5 *We crossed the river in a rowboat:* go across, traverse, go over, travel through; intersect, meet. 6 *They tried to cross a beagle with a Saint Bernard:* crossbreed, interbreed; cross-pollinate, cross-fertilize. —*adj.* 7 *The roof is supported by cross timbers:* intersecting, lying crosswise; athwart, transverse, oblique. 8 *Why is Mother so cross?:* angry, mad, ill-tempered, annoyed, in a bad mood, cranky, ill-humored, grouchy, snappish, out of sorts, irritable, waspish, irascible, crotchety.

Ant. 2 boon, benefit. 3 thoroughbred. 8 good-humored, good-tempered; agreeable.

crotchet *n. It was his crotchet to begin a meal with dessert:* quirk, eccentricity, idiosyncrasy, whim, peculiarity, caprice, whimsy.

crotchety *adj. Grandfather has grown crotchety:* cranky, contrary, grouchy.

crouch *v. The hunters crouched in the reeds:* bend, stoop, squat, hunker down.

crow *v.* 1 *The rooster crows at daybreak:* cock-a-doodle-doo. 2 *Stop crowing about your promotion:* gloat, boast, brag; exult.

crowd *n.* 1 *Shop early and avoid the crowd:* throng, multitude, horde, mob, crush, herd, host; gathering, assemblage. 2 *a fast crowd:* set, circle of friends, clique, claque, group, gang. —*v.* 3 *We crowded around the speaker:* congregate, flock, swarm, gather, assemble; cluster, mass, throng, huddle. 4 *The spectators crowded into the stadium:* shove, push, press, cram, jam, squeeze, swarm, surge.

crowded *adj. This store is always crowded:* jammed, jampacked, packed, full, filled, mobbed, congested, teeming, swarming, thronged.

Ant. empty; half-full.

crown *n.* 1 *the queen's crown:* coronet, tiara, diadem, circlet. 2 *The winner was given a crown of laurel leaves:* wreath, garland. 3 *a representative of the British Crown:* sovereignty, monarchy. 4 *the crown of a hat:* highest part, top, summit, pinnacle, peak, crest. —*v.* 5 *British kings are crowned in Westminster Abbey:* give royal power to, put a crown upon. 6 *Winning the award crowned the actor's career:* top, top off, climax, complete, cap.

Ant. 4 bottom, base, foot. 5 dethrone, depose.

crucial *adj. a crucial decision:* decisive, critical, determining, significant, momentous, weighty, important, urgent.

crude *adj.* 1 *crude sugar:* raw, unrefined, unprocessed; coarse. 2 *the crude sketches of the architect's plans:* uncompleted, incomplete, unfinished, rough, imperfect. 3 *a crude sense of humor:* vulgar, unrefined, coarse, tasteless, gross, uncouth.

Ant. 1 refined, processed. 2 final, finished, completed. 3 refined; subtle.

cruel *adj. a cruel tyrant:* inhuman, inhumane, sadistic, brutal, vicious, savage, merciless, unmerciful; heartless, pitiless; unfeeling, hardhearted, cold-blooded.

Ant. humane, benevolent, merciful, kind, warmhearted.

cruise *v. We cruised from Piraeus to Istanbul:* sail, ply the seas, voyage.

crumb *n. There were crumbs all over the table:* scrap, shred, bit, morsel, sliver, fragment.

crumble *v. After years of neglect the house began to crumble:* decay, disintegrate, fall apart, decompose.

crumple *v.* 1 *The fabric won't crumple when folded:* wrinkle, rumple, crease, crinkle.

2 *The staircase crumpled under his weight:* collapse, give way, cave in, fall, fall to pieces.

crunch *v. The squirrels crunched on the nuts:* chomp, gnaw, gnash, grind, munch; chew, masticate.

crusade *n.* 1 often **Crusade**. *The First Crusade began in 1096:* military expedition against non-Christians. 2 *a crusade to clean up the slums:* reform movement, idealistic campaign, movement, drive.

crush *v.* 1 *To make wine, first crush the grapes:* mash, squash, squeeze, press, pulverize. 2 *I crushed the child to me:* hug tightly, embrace, enfold, squeeze, press. 3 *The army crushed the uprising:* subdue, suppress, quash, squash, squelch, quell; overpower.

crusty *adj. Our crusty neighbor complains every time the dog barks:* peevish, gruff, testy, waspish, surly, ill-tempered, cranky, irascible, crabby.
Ant. agreeable, good-natured.

crux *n. the crux of the matter:* main point, decisive point, essence, essential, basis, heart, core, nub.

cry *v.* 1 *Many mourners were crying:* weep, shed tears; sob, bawl, blubber, snivel, whimper. 2 *He cried a warning:* cry out, call, call out, shout, yell, scream; roar, bellow, shriek, howl, screech; whoop, hurrah, huzzah. 3 *The prisoner cried for mercy.* beg, plead, implore, appeal. *—n* 4 *He gave a cry of alarm:* call, shout, yell, scream, yelp, screech, roar, bellow, shriek, howl; outcry, whoop, cheer, hurrah, huzzah. 5 *Hear our cry, O Lord!:* plea, entreaty, appeal, supplication, prayer; request.
Ant. 1 laugh, snicker, giggle. 2, 4 whisper, murmur, mutter.

cryptic *adj. The fortune-teller kept muttering cryptic warnings:* enigmatical, mysterious, obscure; vague; secret, mystical.

cuddle *v.* 1 *The little girl cuddled the rabbit:* hug tenderly, embrace, snuggle; caress, fondle, pet. 2 *The children cuddled up in the warm bed:* snuggle, nestle, draw close.

cudgel *n. The peddler carried a cudgel for protection:* club, shillelagh, staff, stick.

cue *n. Her wink was my cue to suggest we leave:* signal, sign, hint, tip.

cull *v. We culled enough of her paintings to make an interesting exhibition:* choose, select, pick out, gather, collect; winnow, sift, sort out, set apart.

culminate *v.* 1 *A fireworks display culminated the festivities:* top off, climax, cap, crown, complete. 2 *The disagreement culminated in a fight:* conclude, end, result, terminate, finish.

culpable *adj. The driver is culpable:* guilty, at fault; liable, blameworthy, to blame.
Ant. innocent, blameless.

culprit *n. Police apprehended the culprit:* guilty party, offender; lawbreaker, criminal, felon; malefactor, miscreant; evildoer, sinner, transgressor, wrongdoer.

cult *n.* 1 *He formed his own cult:* religious rites, religious observances; sect, religious group. 2 *the youth cult:* devotion, admiration; devotees, admirers, followers, disciples.

cultivate *v.* 1 *to cultivate the soil:* till, farm; plow, hoe; sow, plant, grow. 2 *She cultivated her mind:* develop, improve, enrich, enhance. 3 *Cultivate new friends:* acquire, develop, seek, court; run after.

cultivation *n.* 1 *Most of the land is devoted to cultivation:* agriculture, farming, agronomy, husbandry, gardening; tilling, planting, sowing. 2 *They are people of great cultivation:* culture, refinement, polish, good taste.

culture *n.* 1 *A child should be exposed to culture:* art, music, and literature; the arts. 2 *ancient Egyptian culture:* civilization.

cultured *adj.* 1 *One doesn't have to be cultured to enjoy good music:* well-educated, artistically knowledgeable. 2 *She learned cultured manners in a finishing school:* cultivated, sophisticated, refined, polished, genteel.
Ant. 1 uncultured, uncultivated. 2 uncultivated, unrefined, unpolished, coarse, crass, common.

cumbersome *adj. too cumbersome to carry:* unwieldy, clumsy, unmanageable, awkward, ungainly, bulky.

cunning *n.* 1 *The prime minister had great cunning:* craftiness, shrewdness; guile, artifice, wiliness, foxiness, artfulness; duplicity, deception, deceit. 2 *The inlaid desk had been made with great cunning:* cleverness, craft, skill, dexterity, adroitness, deftness, subtlety.
Ant. 1 sincerity, candor.

cupboard *n. There's a box of salt in the cupboard:* kitchen cabinet, cabinet; sideboard, china closet.

cupidity *n. His cupidity is boundless:* greed, avarice, covetousness, graspingness, acquisitiveness, greediness, selfishness, rapaciousness, avariciousness.

cur *n.* 1 *Put a muzzle on that cur:* mean dog, unfriendly dog; mongrel, mutt. 2 *Only a cur would treat a child like that!:* blackguard, scoundrel, villain, varlet, rascal, cad, rogue.

curb *n.* 1 *Park parallel to the curb:* curbstone; edge, rim, border, ledge, brink. 2 *to put a curb on spending:* restraint, restriction, check, bridle, rein, limit. —*v.* **3** *Try to curb your enthusiasm:* restrain, restrict, check, control, bridle, suppress; inhibit, limit, moderate.

curdle *v. The cream will begin to curdle:* clot, curd, thicken, coagulate, solidify, congeal; turn, ferment, sour, spoil.

cure *v.* **1** *Moving to Arizona cured her of asthma:* restore to health, make well, heal, rid of an illness. **2** *The hams were cured over a hickory fire:* preserve, smoke; dry, salt. —*n.* **3** *a cure for the common cold:* remedy; corrective, treatment, antidote.

curiosity *n.* **1** *She's full of curiosity:* inquisitiveness, questioning; prying; *Slang* nosiness. **2** *This unusual shell is quite a curiosity:* rarity, curio, novelty; oddity, freak.
    Ant. **1** indifference, apathy.

curious *adj.* **1** *Humans are naturally curious:* inquisitive, eager to learn, anxious to know, inquiring, questioning; nosy, snooping, prying. **2** *a curious way of talking:* unusual, odd, peculiar, strange, queer; quaint, singular, uncommon, unique.
    Ant. **1** incurious, indifferent, apathetic. **2** customary, common, usual, familiar.

curl *v.* **1** *Her mother curled her hair:* form into ringlets, coil, wave; frizz, frizzle, crimp. **2** *Smoke curled from the chimney:* coil, curve, swirl, wind, twist, twirl, spiral. —*n.* **3** *The girl had blond curls:* ringlet, lock. **4** *Curls of wood lay on the floor:* coil, spiral, twist, curlicue.

curmudgeon *n. The curmudgeon never smiled:* grouch, grumbler, crank, *Slang* grump, crab.

currency *n.* **1** *The pound sterling is the currency of Britain:* medium of exchange, legal tender, money; cash, bills, coin, coinage, bank notes, paper money, ready money. **2** *That style enjoyed currency in the 1920's:* popularity, vogue, prevalence.

current *adj.* **1** *current fashions:* present, present-day, up-to-date, contemporary, modern, in vogue. —*n.* **2** *a current of air:* flow, stream, tide; draft. **3** *a current of unrest among the people:* undercurrent, tendency, inclination, drift, trend; feeling, mood, atmosphere.
    Ant. **1** past, out-of-date; old-fashioned, obsolete, passé.

curse *n.* **1** *The witch put a curse on the princess:* evil spell; damnation, execration, malediction, imprecation. **2** *His curse made her blush:* swearing, oath; expletive, profanity, blasphemy, obscenity. **3** *Housework was the curse of my life:* burden, ordeal, affliction, misfortune, trouble, trial, tribulation, bane, annoyance, torment, vexation.

—*v.* **4** *He cursed everyone in sight:* swear at, swear, utter a profanity, utter a blasphemy, utter an obscenity, *Informal* cuss; damn, condemn, execrate. **5** *cursed with poor health:* afflict, burden, torment, vex, plague.
    Ant. **1** blessing, benediction. **3** joy, boon. **4** compliment, praise, laud; bless.

cursory *adj. a cursory glance:* quick, hasty, hurried, brief, passing, perfunctory; haphazard, casual, offhand, superficial, inattentive.
    Ant. careful, searching.

curt *adj. a curt reply:* abrupt, blunt, brusque, short, terse, snappy, gruff, rude.
    Ant. friendly, courteous, polite.

curtail *v. The trip was curtailed:* cut short, shorten; reduce, diminish, abridge, abbreviate.
    Ant. lengthen, extend, prolong, protract, expand.

curve *n.* **1** *This road is full of curves:* bend, turn, crook, arc, arch, bow, curvature, loop. —*v.* **2** *The ball curved to the right:* bend, hook, curl, wind, arch, twist, swerve, coil, spiral.

cushion *n.* **1** *The children sat on cushions:* pillow, pad, bolster. —*v.* **2** *to cushion a blow:* damp, dampen, stifle; muffle, deaden.

custodian *n.* **1** *The custodian locked the doors:* caretaker, janitor, superintendent, concierge, watchman. **2** *Who is the child's custodian?:* guardian, keeper, warden.

custody *n.* **1** *The mother was given custody of the child:* guardianship, charge, care, trusteeship; safekeeping, protection. **2** *The police took the suspect into custody:* detention, confinement; possession.

custom *n.* **1** *It is the custom for gentlemen to shake hands:* habitual practice, convention, usage, fashion, habit. **2** *customs We had to pay customs on the camera we bought abroad:* duty, import tax; tariff, levy.
    Ant. **1** rarity, curiosity.

customary *adj. her customary promptness:* usual, habitual, normal, regular, routine; typical, conventional, traditional, common.
    Ant. unusual, uncommon, rare, exceptional.

customer *n. The store has many customers:* patron, shopper, buyer, purchaser; client.

cut *v.* **1** *He cut his chin shaving. Cut the cake:* lacerate, incise, gash, slash, hack, nick, slit; slice, carve, sunder, rive. **2** *It's time to cut the lawn:* trim, clip, shear; mow, prune, crop. **3** *Cut the report to four pages:* condense, abridge, abbreviate, pare down, reduce, curtail, decrease; leave out, delete. **4** *We spoke to her, but she cut us:* snub, ignore, give one the cold shoulder. **5** *The*

road cuts through the forest: cross, intersect, bisect, go through, go across. —*n.*
6 *Put a bandage on that cut:* incision, gash, nick. **7** *The agent gets a 10 percent cut:* piece, portion, share, slice, part. **8** *a price cut:* reduction, decrease, diminution, lessening.
Ant. **3** expand, increase, lengthen. **8** increase, rise.

cute *adj. a cute baby:* pretty, dainty; adorable, darling, sweet, precious; beautiful, handsome, attractive, lovable.

cutting *adj.* **1** *a cutting wind:* piercing, sharp, harsh, stinging, nipping, biting.

2 *a cutting remark:* harsh, sharp, caustic, stinging, scathing, biting, sarcastic.
Ant. **1** balmy, soothing, pleasant. **2** flattering; soothing, kind, mild.

cycle *n. the cycle of the seasons:* series, progression, sequence, succession.

cynic *n. A cynic attributes selfish motives to all acts:* skeptic, scoffer, misanthrope, misogynist.

cynical *adj. a cynical outlook:* misanthropic, misogynic, skeptical, sneering, sardonic, scornful.

czar Also **tsar** *n. the czar of Russia:* emperor, ruler, caesar, king.

D

dab *v.* **1** *She dabbed some water on her face:* pat, apply gently. —*n.* **2** *a dab of butter.* pat, bit, smidgen, soupçon.

dabble *v.* **1** *We dabbled our feet in the brook:* splash, slosh, spatter. **2** *He dabbles in politics:* putter, do superficially, work on casually, toy with.

daily *adj. daily exercises:* each day, day in day out, day by day, from day to day; everyday, quotidian, circadian, per diem.

dainty *adj.* **1** *dainty hands:* delicate, refined, pretty. **2** *dainty eaters:* fussy, choosy, fastidious, particular.

dally *v.* **1** *Don't dally:* dawdle, dillydally; loiter, fritter away time. **2** *In the novel, the prince dallied with the servant girl:* flirt, toy, trifle.
Ant. **1** hurry, hasten.

dam *n.* **1** *a dam across the stream:* barrier, obstruction, hindrance. —*v.* **2** *to dam the floodwaters:* block, bar, barricade, obstruct, hold back, hold in, restrain.
Ant. **2** free, loose, release.

damage *n.* **1** *The flood caused great damage:* injury, harm, destruction, despoliation, loss. **2** *to pay damages for an accident:* cost, compensation. —*v.* **3** *The fire damaged our house:* injure, hurt, mar, impair, ravage; partially destroy.
Ant. **1** improvement. **3** improve; repair.

damn *v.* **1** *The reviewer damned the novel:* condemn, blast, criticize, censure, denounce, rail at. **2** *Should all sinners be damned?:* doom, condemn, sentence to hell.
Ant. **1** commend, praise, laud, applaud. **2** redeem.

damp *adj.* **1** *damp from the rain:* moist, wet, soggy, clammy. **2** *a cold, damp day:* wet, rainy, drizzly, foggy, misty. —*n.* **3** *The sad story put a damp on our happy feelings:* curb, check, discouragement, restraint. —*v.* **4** *His loss didn't damp his zest:* check, curb, restrain, inhibit; discourage, depress.
Ant. **1, 2** dry.

dampen *v. to dampen a sponge:* moisten, wet.

damsel *n. a damsel in distress:* young lady, girl, lass, maiden.

dance *v.* **1** *The couple danced a polka:* perform. **2** *We danced with glee at the good news:* leap, jump; cavort, prance, frolic, gambol. —*n.* **3** *They're having a dance at the club:* ball, party; prom, hop.

dandy *n.* **1** *Beau Brummel was a famous dandy:* fop, clotheshorse, beau, fashion plate, man of fashion; peacock. —*adj.* **2** *That's a dandy idea:* fine, great, excellent, superb; swell, terrific, super; first-rate.
Ant. **1** slob. **2** bad, terrible, awful.

danger *n. a life full of danger:* peril, risk, hazard, jeopardy, endangerment.
Ant. security, safety.

dangerous *adj. It's dangerous to skate on thin ice:* risky, perilous, hazardous, chancy, unsafe, precarious.
Ant. safe.

dangle *v. A handkerchief dangled from his pocket:* hang, suspend, swing, hang down, droop.

dank *adj. a dark, dank cave:* damp, moist, wet; humid, clammy, soggy.

dapper *adj. You look dapper today:* smart, neat, trim, spruce; stylish, jaunty, natty.

dappled *adj. a dappled horse:* spotted, mottled, flecked, variegated.

dare *v.* 1 *I don't dare correct him:* venture, have the courage or nerve. 2 *I dare you:* challenge, defy. *—n.* 3 *On a dare I jumped off the diving board:* challenge; taunt.

daring *n.* 1 *the daring of a stunt pilot:* boldness, courage, bravery; audacity, adventurousness. *—adj.* 2 *daring acts behind enemy lines:* bold, gallant, valiant, courageous, brave; adventurous, venturesome, dauntless, intrepid; plucky, game; audacious.
Ant. 1 cowardice, timidity. 2 cowardly, uncourageous.

dark *adj.* 1 *a dark night:* black, obscure, dim, shadowy; murky, inky; sunless; without light. 2 *dark eyes:* deeply colored, not pale. 3 *The war was a dark period:* gloomy, dismal, bleak, dreary, joyless, sorrowful, somber; disheartening, discouraging. 4 *Her dark expression showed her mood:* angry, somber, gloomy, forbidding, ominous, bleak; sinister, threatening. 5 *a dark meaning in the remark:* hidden, concealed, secret; obscure. *—n.* 6 *It was hard to find a seat in the dark:* darkness. 7 *Come home before dark:* nightfall, night, nighttime; evening, twilight.
Ant. 1–7 light. 1–4 bright. 1 luminous, lit, illuminated; radiant. 3 happy, joyful. 4 happy, joyful, cheerful. 5 clear, plain, transparent. 7 dawn, morning, daybreak.

darken *v.* 1 *We darkened the room:* dim, blacken, make darker, make dim. 2 *The argument darkened her mood:* cloud, sadden; make despondent, make gloomy.
Ant. 1 lighten, brighten.

darkness *n.* 1 *Darkness comes early in winter:* nighttime, night, dark; evening, twilight, dusk, nightfall. 2 *The room was in complete darkness:* dark, blackness; dimness, shade.

darling *n.* 1 *You're my darling:* beloved, dear, dearest, sweetheart, love. *—adj.* 2 *my darling child:* beloved, dear, dearest; precious, loved, lovable, adored, cherished; sweet, charming, enchanting, lovely. 3 *a darling hat:* cute, attractive; charming, enchanting, adorable.

dart *n.* 1 *We threw two darts at the target:* missile, projectile; small arrow. *—v.* 2 *He darted from the room:* dash, rush, bolt, run, race, sprint; spring, leap, bound.

dash *v.* 1 *She dashed the plate against the door:* hurl, throw, fling, slam, smash. 2 *He dashed out of the room:* dart, bolt, tear, race, rush, run, bound, speed. 3 *The rain dashed our plans for hiking:* ruin, spoil; thwart, frustrate, foil; discourage, disappoint, dampen. *—n.* 4 *He made a dash for the train:* dart, bolt, rush, run, sprint. 5 *the 100-yard dash:* sprint. 6 *a dash of vinegar:* pinch, bit, drop, touch, soupçon. 7 *She played with a great deal of fire and dash:* verve, vigor, spirit, flair, exuberance, animation, vivacity.

dashing *adj.* 1 *a dashing hero:* impetuous, daring, audacious, bold, swashbuckling, gallant, brave, courageous, fearless.

dastardly *adj. a dastardly villain:* cowardly, mean, sneaky, base, vile, despicable.
Ant. gallant, brave, courageous.

data *n. pl. The data was incomplete:* information, facts, figures; documents, evidence.

date *n.* 1 *Didn't we have a date for lunch today?:* appointment, engagement, rendezvous, agreement to meet. 2 *Who's your date for the dance?:* escort, companion, partner. *—v.* 3 *He's been dating Thelma for years:* escort, court, take out, keep company with.

dated *adj. Clothing styles become dated very quickly:* old-fashioned, unfashionable, out-of-date, outmoded, passé, antiquated, *Slang* old hat.

daub *v.* 1 *First daub the surface with paint:* coat, cover, smear, paint. 2 *The walls were daubed with finger marks:* smear, smudge, spot; stain. *—n.* 3 *daubs of mud:* blot, blotch, spot, splotch.

daunt *v. Nothing daunted the divers:* intimidate, dismay, faze, discourage, dishearten, deject, depress, unnerve; browbeat, cow, frighten, scare.
Ant. embolden, encourage, cheer.

dauntless *adj. The dauntless troops charged the enemy:* fearless, unafraid, bold, courageous, brave, valiant, valorous, heroic; resolute, stouthearted.
Ant. cowardly, fearful, apprehensive, fainthearted; irresolute.

dawdle *v. Don't dawdle!:* dally, dillydally, idle, loiter, loaf; delay; procrastinate; waste time.

dawn *n.* 1 *I woke at dawn:* daybreak, sunrise, sunup, daylight. 2 *the dawn of science:* beginning, commencement, birth, origin, start; emergence, early development. *—v.* 3 *A new age is dawning:* begin, appear, commence; develop, unfold, emerge. 4 *It dawned on me that I'd left the oven on:* occur, strike.

day *n.* 1 *She never goes out during the day:* time between sunrise and sunset, from dawn to dusk; period during daylight hours; period of 24 hours. 2 *What day is her birthday?:* date; particular day. 3 *The day of the horse and buggy is past:* heyday, period,

time, epoch, age. 4 *to work an 8-hour day:* workday, period of activity.
Ant. 1 night, nighttime.

daybreak *n. He was up at daybreak:* dawn, break of day; sunrise, sunup.

daydream *n.* 1 *She daydreamed about her vacation:* muse, imagine, fantasize; woolgather, dream. —*n.* 2 *His daydream is to retire to a tropical island:* fantasy, dream, reverie, pipe dream.

daylight *n.* 1 *Wear dark glasses in the daylight:* sunlight, sunshine; light of day. 2 *A farmer must finish the chores during daylight:* daytime, day; the period between sunrise and sunset, the period between dawn and dusk, the daylight hours. 3 *He feeds the livestock before daylight:* dawn, daybreak, crack of dawn, sunrise, sunup.

daze *v.* 1 *The blow dazed me:* stun, shock, stupefy; stagger, confuse, bewilder, disorient. 2 *The beauty of the Grand Canyon dazed us:* amaze, astound, astonish, dazzle, stun. —*n.* 3 *He walked around in a daze:* stupor, muddle, shock, bewilderment; astonishment, surprise.

dazzle *v.* 1 *The light dazzled us:* daze, blind, confuse, blind temporarily. 2 *The glamorous movie star dazzled us:* awe, overawe, overwhelm.

dead *adj.* 1 *The doctor pronounced him dead:* deceased, expired, perished, lifeless. 2 *Mercury is a dead planet:* lifeless, inorganic, devoid of life. 3 *a dead language:* defunct, extinct; no longer in use. 4 *The battery was dead:* inoperative, inactive; not working, out of operation. 5 *This town is dead after 10 P.M.:* dull, lackluster, unexciting; vapid, flat, insipid. 6 *dead center:* exact, precise. 7 *dead capital:* unproductive, ineffectual, unused, useless; unprofitable, stagnant. 8 *There was a dead silence:* total, complete, utter, absolute, thorough, entire. 9 *After a day of shopping, I'm dead:* exhausted, tired, spent; worn-out, *Slang* beat. —*n.* 10 *in the dead of winter:* midst, depth, middle; period of greatest darkness, cold, gloom. 11 **the dead.** *We must pray for the dead:* dead people; those who have died. —*adv.* 12 *She stopped dead in her tracks:* abruptly, suddenly. 13 *I am dead certain:* absolutely; completely, entirely, utterly.
Ant. 1 alive, living, live. 3 living. 4 working, operative, operating. 5 lively, exciting. 7 productive, effective, useful.

deaden *v. This pill will deaden the ache:* dull, diminish, moderate, mitigate; abate, lessen, weaken; assuage, alleviate; drug, anesthetize; muffle, mute.

deadlock *n. The negotiations reached a deadlock:* standoff, impasse, stalemate.

deadly *adj.* 1 *a deadly disease:* fatal, lethal, mortal, death-dealing; destructive. 2 *a deadly enemy:* dangerous, relentless, unrelenting, implacable. 3 *a deadly silence:* excessive, extreme, inordinate. 4 *The lecture is deadly—let's leave:* boring, dull, tedious, wearisome, tiresome. —*adv.* 5 *a deadly boring play:* completely, entirely, fully, thoroughly, totally; terribly, awfully.
Ant. 1 benign, harmless. 4 exciting.

deal *v.* 1 *I'll deal with that problem:* treat, handle, oversee; attend to, see to, take care of, cope with, dispose of. 2 *His book dealt with the life of George Washington:* concern, consider; have to do with. 3 *The store deals in antiques:* trade, market, buy and sell; do business. 4 *The challenger dealt the champion a blow:* give, deliver, administer. 5 *Deal the cards:* distribute, dispense, apportion, give out, mete out, parcel out, dole out. —*n.* 6 *He had four aces on the last deal:* distribution, apportionment; round, hand, single game. 7 *It's a deal:* bargain, agreement.

dealing *n.* 1 Usually **dealings.** *We have dealings with their firm:* relations, transactions, trade; business. 2 *a reputation for honest dealing:* treatment, practice; method of conduct.

dear *adj.* 1 *She's very dear to us:* precious, beloved, loved, cherished. 2 *Diamonds are very dear:* expensive, costly, valuable. —*n.* 3 *You're a dear to look after the children:* darling, sweetheart, love, angel, kind person.
Ant. 1 hated, disliked. 2 inexpensive, cheap, worthless.

dearth *n. a dearth of skilled workers:* scarcity, lack, shortage, paucity; deficiency.
Ant. abundance, plethora, plenty.

death *n. He mourned her death:* dying, demise, passing, departure, decease, expiration; loss of life.
Ant. life; birth; beginning.

deathless *adj. The soul is deathless:* immortal, eternal, perpetual, everlasting.
Ant. mortal; perishable.

deathly *adj.* 1 *a deathly fear of snakes:* extreme, terrible, intense, overwhelming. —*adv.* 2 *deathly ill:* extremely, very; unto death.

debacle *n. The battle turned into a debacle:* disaster, catastrophe, devastation; overthrow, rout; bankruptcy, dissolution.
Ant. success, victory, achievement, triumph.

debase *v. Don't debase yourself by accepting a bribe:* lower, degrade, defile, disgrace, dishonor; corrupt.
Ant. elevate, uplift, heighten.

debatable *adj. It's debatable whether I will go to Europe:* questionable, doubtful, dubious; undecided, uncertain, unsure; problematical, arguable, disputable.
Ant. certain, sure, settled, decided.

debate *n.* 1 *The teams will have a debate Saturday:* argument, discussion, dispute; formal discussion of opposing points of view. 2 *After much debate, I refused the offer:* deliberation, consideration, reflection, meditation, cogitation. —*v.* 3 *The senate debated the bill:* argue, dispute, discuss. 4 *I debated whether to accept the job:* deliberate, consider, ponder, cogitate.

debauched *adj. a debauched life:* depraved, corrupted, perverted, lascivious, lecherous, wanton, dissipated, dissolute, immoral, profligate.
Ant. pure, moral, virtuous.

debauchery *n. a life of debauchery:* excess, intemperance, immoderation, self-indulgence, dissipation.

debilitate *v. to be debilitated by illness:* weaken, devitalize, make feeble, wear out.
Ant. strengthen, invigorate, vitalize; restore.

debility *n. The flu left her with a feeling of debility:* weakness, infirmity, feebleness, invalidism.
Ant. vigor, vitality, energy.

debonair *adj.* 1 *a debonair gentleman:* charming, urbane, suave; elegant, sophisticated. 2 *a debonair walk:* carefree, lighthearted, jaunty, dapper, sprightly.
Ant. 1 rude, gauche. 2 gloomy.

debris *n. The explosion reduced the building to debris:* rubble, trash, rubbish, wreckage, litter, ruins; fragments, shards.

debt *n. I'll pay off all my debts:* liability, obligation, debit, bill, arrears.

debut Also **début** *n.* 1 *The actress made her debut:* first public appearance. 2 *She made her debut at the annual ball:* coming out, formal introduction into society.

decadence *n. a period of decadence:* decline, deterioration, decay; corruption, immorality, degeneracy.

decadent *adj. a decadent way of life:* corrupt, immoral, degenerate, debased, depraved, debauched, perverted, dissolute.

decamp *v.* 1 *The army decamped during the night:* depart from camp, break camp; move off, march off. 2 *The treasurer decamped with the payroll:* depart suddenly, leave quickly or secretly, run away, sneak off, take off.

decay *v.* 1 *The tree began to decay:* rot, decompose; spoil, putrefy. —*n.* 2 *The decay of the meat could have been prevented by re-* frigeration: decomposition, rot, rotting, putrefaction; spoiling.

deceased *adj.* See DEAD.

deceit *n. the deceit practiced against consumers:* deception, cheating, fraud, dishonesty, deceitfulness; double-dealing, duplicity, trickery, misrepresentation.
Ant. honesty, frankness, candor, truthfulness; fair dealing.

deceitful *adj. Saying one thing and doing the opposite is deceitful:* insincere, hypocritical; underhanded, false, dishonest, deceptive, treacherous; sneaky, duplicitous.

deceive *v. He deceived me:* mislead, delude, cheat.
Ant. enlighten; tell the truth to.

decency *n. Please have the decency to apologize:* propriety, decorum; respectability; modesty, appropriateness.
Ant. indecency.

decent *adj.* 1 *The workers want decent working conditions:* adequate, satisfactory, acceptable; suitable, fitting, appropriate; passable, fair; sufficient, reasonable. 2 *He was decent enough to say thank you:* courteous, accommodating, obliging, nice; correct, seemly.
Ant. 1 unsuitable, inappropriate, inadequate; unfair, intolerable. 2 gauche, crude; discourteous.

deception *n.* 1 *There was deception in your claims:* deceit, deceitfulness, deceptiveness, fraud, fraudulence; duplicity, double-dealing. 2 *The magician's act was done by deception:* trick, artifice, illusion.
Ant. 1 candor, honesty, truthfulness.

deceptive *adj. deceptive ads:* misleading, dishonest, deceitful, fraudulent.

decide *v.* 1 *We've decided to buy the house:* determine, resolve, settle; choose, elect, select; make up one's mind. 2 *The court decided the case:* settle, decree, rule; judge; make a decision.

decided *adj.* 1 *It was a decided win for our team:* clear-cut, unquestionable, unmistakable, definite, indisputable. 2 *She coped with the problems in a decided manner:* determined, decisive, definite, unhesitating, unwavering, resolute, deliberate; assertive, firm.
Ant. 1 dubious, doubtful, questionable. 2 indecisive, hesitating, irresolute.

decipher *v. to decipher the spy's messages:* decode, cryptanalyze; translate, interpret, deduce, puzzle out, solve, make out.

decision *n.* 1 *I came to a decision to move:* conclusion, judgment; resolution; determination; result after consideration. 2 *the court's decision:* ruling, verdict, finding, decree; pronouncement. 3 *an individual of de-*

cision: determination, decisiveness, resolve, purpose, purposefulness.
Ant. 3 indecision, uncertainty.

decisive *adj.* 1 *a decisive victory:* conclusive, undeniable, indisputable, final, convincing. 2 *a decisive person:* resolute, determined, positive, definite, absolute; firm.
Ant. 1 inconclusive, disputable, dubious. 2 indecisive, irresolute, hesitant.

deck *v. The women decked themselves in silk:* decorate, adorn; dress, clothe, garb, outfit, array, bedeck, ornament; trim; embellish, festoon; beautify, deck out.

declaration *n.* 1 *My declaration presented the facts as I knew them:* statement, affirmation; attestation, testimony, deposition; vowal, assertion. 2 *The Declaration of Independence:* announcement, proclamation; notification, notice; document.
Ant. 1 denial; disavowal.

declare *v.* 1 *The governor declared a state of emergency:* proclaim, pronounce, announce. 2 *They declared their willingness to compromise:* affirm; reveal, show, express, give evidence of.

decline *v.* 1 *I declined the invitation:* refuse, reject, spurn; fail to accept, turn down. 2 *The road declines sharply:* slope downward, incline downward, slope down. 3 *Her health has been declining. His popularity declined:* weaken, fail, flag, sink, deteriorate, worsen; wane, diminish, dwindle, decrease. —*n.* 4 *The path follows a sharp decline:* downgrade, declivity, drop; downward incline, downward slope. 5 *the decline of ancient Rome:* downfall, deterioration, decay. 6 *Business has gone into a decline:* slump, downswing, downward tendency.
Ant. 1 accept. 2 rise. 3 improve, increase, strengthen. 5, 6 rise, improvement.

decompose *v.* 1 *The dead tree decomposed:* rot, decay, putrefy, spoil. 2 *Salt decomposes into sodium and chlorine:* separate; break up, disintegrate, break down.

decor, décor *n. French Provincial decor:* decoration, ornamentation; style of decorating.

decorate *v.* 1 *We decorated the house for the holidays:* ornament, adorn, beautify, bedeck, deck, array; trim, garnish, embellish, festoon. 2 *The soldier was decorated for bravery:* honor; award a decoration to.

decoration *n.* 1 *Christmas decorations:* ornament, ornamentation, trimming, trim, embellishment, adornment, garnish. 2 *The admiral's uniform was covered with decorations:* medal, award, emblem, ribbon, badge.

decorous *adj. decorous behavior:* proper, correct, suitable, dignified, becoming,

seemly; decent, polite, mannerly, respectful.
Ant. improper, unbecoming, undignified.

decorum *n. to act with decorum:* propriety, politeness; tact, respectability, dignity.
Ant. impropriety, bad manners.

decoy *n.* 1 *The hunters used wooden ducks as decoys:* enticement, lure, snare, inducement. —*v.* 2 *He used a whistle to decoy the birds within range:* entice, lure, allure; attract by deceptive means.

decrease *v.* 1 *Water consumption decreased:* diminish, lessen, reduce, drop, subside, slacken, ease, abate, decline. —*n.* 2 *a big decrease in sales:* reduction, lessening, decline, fall-off.
Ant. 1, 2 increase. 2 growth, expansion.

decree *n.* 1 *The king issued a decree of amnesty:* order, command, proclamation, dictum, edict. —*v.* 2 *The king decreed an amnesty:* order, command, proclaim.

decrepit *adj. a decrepit building:* broken-down, dilapidated, rickety.

decry *v. She decried the lack of good work:* criticize, denounce, rail against, condemn; disparage, deprecate.
Ant. laud, commend, praise.

deduce *v. I deduced that she was an only child:* conclude, reason, gather, infer; comprehend, understand.

deduct *v. They deducted the cost of the broken window from his allowance:* subtract, take, withdraw; decrease by, take from.
Ant. add.

deduction *n.* 1 *It was the inspector's deduction that the crime was an inside job:* conclusion, inference, judgment, supposition, analysis, calculation; understanding, guess, speculation, consideration. 2 *a deduction of 10 percent for cash payment:* reduction, discount, concession, abatement, allowance, subtraction.
Ant. 2 increase, addition, increment.

deed *n.* 1 *good deeds:* act, action, feat, achievement, accomplishment. 2 *the deed to a house:* legal document showing ownership of property.

deem *v. I deem it advisable:* think, believe, judge, regard, consider, hold, view.

deep *adj.* 1 *deep water. a deep hole:* of great depth, far below the surface, extending far downward. 2 *a deep closet. deep into the woods:* far in or back, extending inward from front to back. 3 *in a deep sleep:* intense, profound. 4 *deep in thought:* absorbed, involved, immersed, engrossed; lost. 5 *a deep thinker:* intelligent, astute, sagacious, discerning, wise, profound, philosophical. 6 *deep blue:* dark, strong, intense; rich, vivid. 7 *a deep voice:* resonant, sonorous; low in pitch.

Ant. 1, 2 shallow. 3 light. 5 superficial. 6 light, pale. 7 high.

deeply *adv.* 1 *How deeply did the submarine dive?:* deep; far down. 2 *I was deeply moved by the testimony:* greatly, profoundly, intensely; passionately. 3 *He spoke deeply:* resonantly, sonorously; with a deep tone, at a low pitch. 4 *He's deeply in debt:* seriously, gravely; over one's head.

deface *v. He defaced the book by writing in it:* mar, damage, disfigure; spoil, bruise, mark, scar.

de facto *adv.* 1 *The queen ruled de facto:* actually, really; in fact. —*adj.* 2 *The queen was the de facto head of state:* actual, real, in existence.

defamation *n. defamation of character:* slander, libel; disparagement, vilification.

defamatory *adj. defamatory remarks:* libelous, slanderous; disparaging, derogatory, vilifying.

defame *v. We expect politicians to defame each other:* slander, libel; malign, disparage, discredit, denigrate, derogate, vilify.
Ant. praise, laud, extol.

defeat *v.* 1 *We defeated the enemy:* overcome, conquer, rout, vanquish, overpower, overwhelm, crush, trounce, prevail over. 2 *The problem defeated me:* confound, baffle, thwart, foil, frustrate; get the better of.
Ant. 1 lose, surrender, yield, submit.

defect *n.* 1 *The television had a defect:* fault, flaw, imperfection; blemish, stain; scar, crack. 2 *a defect of character:* deficiency, omission, shortcoming, fault; weakness, failing.
Ant. 2 strength, forte.

defective *adj. a defective machine:* faulty, imperfect, flawed, impaired; inadequate, insufficient, wanting; broken; out of order, inoperative.
Ant. perfect, adequate.

defend *v.* 1 *A family must defend its home:* protect, preserve; secure, shield, guard, safeguard; keep safe, watch over. 2 *We must always defend freedom:* uphold, sustain, support, maintain; advocate, champion.

defense *n.* 1 *the defense of our country:* protection, preservation, security, safeguard, guard; safekeeping, custody. 2 *We must strengthen our defenses:* fortification, barricade; means of defending. 3 *I want to speak in my defense:* upholding, justification, support, advocacy. 4 *The defense rests its case:* the defendant(s) and their counsel.
Ant. 4 prosecution.

defensible *adj. The attorney claimed the client's conduct was defensible:* justifiable,

warrantable; proper, valid, suitable, fit, permissible.
Ant. indefensible, unwarranted, unjustifiable.

defer[1] *v. You may defer payment:* delay, postpone, put off.
Ant. expedite.

defer[2] *v. The child always deferred to others:* yield, submit, capitulate, accede; give in; pay respect to.

deference *n. to show deference to one's parents:* consideration, respect, reverence, honor, esteem, regard; obedience.
Ant. disrespect, contempt; disobedience.

deferential *adj. deferential treatment of one's elders:* considerate, respectful, courteous, polite, reverential; obedient.

deferment Also **deferral** *n. deferment of payment:* postponement, delay; extension, stay.

defiance *n. He showed defiance by refusing to eat:* disobedience, rebelliousness, rebellion, obstinacy, hostility.

defiant *adj. a defiant attitude:* rebellious, disobedient, provocative; aggressive.
Ant. obedient, yielding, submissive.

deficiency *n.* 1 *a calcium deficiency:* shortage, insufficiency, inadequacy. 2 *mental deficiencies:* flaw, defect, imperfection, failing, frailty, shortcoming, weakness.
Ant. 1 sufficiency, adequacy, abundance.

deficient *adj.* 1 *a diet deficient in vitamins:* lacking, inadequate, insufficient. 2 *mentally deficient:* flawed, defective, substandard, weak.
Ant. 1 sufficient, adequate.

deficit *n. We ended the year with a deficit:* shortage, shortfall, deficiency.

defile *v.* 1 *Insults can defile a person's honor:* dirty, soil, befoul, besmirch, stain, taint, tarnish; dishonor, debase. 2 *The infidels defiled the shrine:* desecrate, profane.

define *v.* 1 *Define this word:* state the meaning of. 2 *This book defines the committee's functions:* specify, describe, state, delineate; explain.

definite *adj.* 1 *a definite time:* precise, exact, fixed, set. 2 *She was definite:* sure, positive, certain.
Ant. 1, 2 indefinite, undetermined, uncertain.

definitely *adv. John will definitely be here:* indubitably, absolutely, undeniably, surely, certainly, assuredly, positively; expressly, explicitly, decisively.

definitive *adj. a definitive method for success:* complete, reliable, conclusive; exact, decided.
Ant. incomplete, inconclusive; inexact.

deflect v. The shield deflected the bullet: divert, swerve; alter the course.

deform v. Strip mining deforms the land: mar, disfigure, contort, twist; mangle, maim.

deformity n. a deformity that makes walking difficult: deformation, malformation.

defraud v. He defrauded her of her savings: cheat, bilk, fleece, swindle, Slang con.

deft adj. a deft backhand: skillful, expert; dexterous, adroit, apt; sure.
Ant. unskillful, maladroit, inept; unsure.

defunct adj. The company is defunct: extinct, dead.

defy v. to defy convention: challenge, confront, oppose; disregard, disdain; resist, withstand.
Ant. encourage; support.

degenerate v. 1 The debate degenerated into a shouting match: deteriorate, disintegrate, worsen, decline, revert, sink; decay, rot. —adj. 2 degenerate behavior: debased, dissolute, depraved, decadent, perverted, profligate, debauched, immoral, corrupt, degraded.
Ant. 1 improve, progress, advance. 2 virtuous, moral, upright.

degradation n. In his degradation he drank heavily: humiliation, disgrace.

degrade v. 1 The sergeant was degraded to private: demote, lower, downgrade. 2 Don't degrade yourself by cheating: lower, debase, dishonor, disgrace.
Ant. 1, 2 promote, elevate. 2 dignify.

degree n. 1 He worked his way up a degree at a time: step, grade, mark, phase. 2 a high degree of intelligence: level, order, grade. 3 a temperature of more than 80 degrees: division, interval, unit.

deign v. I would not deign to comment: stoop, condescend, consent, deem.

deity n. The ancient Greeks had many deities: god, God, supreme being, goddess, divinity, divine being.

dejected adj. We were dejected by the refusal: depressed, downhearted, low, disheartened, despondent, down; sad, unhappy, discouraged, dispirited.
Ant. elated, encouraged.

delay v. 1 Delay action on the matter: postpone, suspend; shelve, table, put off. 2 A storm delayed the plane: hinder, slow, hold up, keep back. 3 Don't delay: procrastinate, dawdle, wait. —n. 4 Please finish without delay: loitering, tarrying, dawdling. 5 a delay of 48 hours: postponement, deferment, suspension, stay. 6 The delay was caused by an accident: stoppage, slowing; hindrance.
Ant. 1, 2, 3 expedite, hasten, speed.

delectable adj. The dinner was delectable: delightful, enjoyable, pleasurable, pleasant, gratifying; delicious.

delegate n. 1 We sent a delegate to the convention: representative, agent, deputy, proxy. —v. 2 We have delegated her to represent us: designate, name, authorize; appoint. 3 She delegated the work to her nephew: entrust, assign, give, transfer.

delete v. Delete the last paragraph: remove; cut; take out, omit, leave out.

deleterious adj. a deleterious habit: harmful, hurtful, detrimental; destructive, injurious.
Ant. beneficial, helpful, advantageous.

deliberate adj. 1 a deliberate lie: intentional, premeditated, planned, prearranged, purposeful, willful; calculated. 2 a deliberate opinion: careful, considered, prudent, thoughtful. 3 a deliberate pace: leisurely, slow, easy, unhurried; measured. —v. 4 He deliberated his decision: consider, weigh; contemplate, mull over, reason out. 5 The board deliberated for two days: confer, discuss; talk over.
Ant. 1, 2 impulsive, rash, impetuous. 3 fast, hurried.

delicacy n. 1 the delicacy of the imported cloth: fineness, exquisiteness; softness, smoothness, lightness. 2 The carving was executed with great delicacy: precision, perfection, accuracy; fine workmanship. 3 Pheasant is a delicacy: choice food. 4 a subject that must be approached with great delicacy: tact, taste, discrimination; sensitiveness. 5 the delicacy of his health: frailness, frailty, fragility.
Ant. 4 insensitiveness, inconsideration, rudeness.

delicate adj. 1 a gown of delicate silk: fine, dainty, exquisite. 2 The plate was so delicate I was afraid to wash it: fragile, frail, flimsy; dainty. 3 in delicate health: frail, feeble, weakened; infirm, sickly, ailing. 4 a tray of delicate tidbits: palatable, savory, delicious, appetizing. 5 a delicate blue: soft, muted, subdued. 6 She handled the situation in a delicate manner: tactful, tasteful, diplomatic, careful, sensitive. 7 a delicate subject: touchy, ticklish, sensitive; precarious.
Ant. 1 coarse, crude, rough. 2 strong. 3 strong, good. 4 unappetizing. 5 harsh, bright. 6 inconsiderate, insensitive, unrefined.

delicious adj. a delicious cake: delectable, tasty, luscious, mouth-watering, appetizing; delightful, charming.

delight n. 1 They got a good deal of delight from their children: pleasure, happiness, en-

joyment, joy. —*v.* 2 *Your visit delighted us:* please, gratify; charm, enchant, amuse. 3 *I delight in antique stores:* revel; take great pleasure in.
Ant. 2 displease; bother. 3 dislike.

delighted *adj. a delighted audience:* pleased, captivated, enthralled, enraptured; elated, ecstatic.
Ant. displeased, disgusted.

delightful *adj. a delightful party:* enjoyable, pleasing, pleasurable; charming, engaging, entertaining, amusing, enchanting.
Ant. unpleasant, distressing; disagreeable.

delinquent *adj.* 1 *He was delinquent in his duties:* neglectful, negligent, derelict, remiss. 2 *delinquent taxes:* overdue, late; in arrears. —*n.* 3 *juvenile delinquents:* misdoer, miscreant, wrongdoer; hoodlum.

delirious *adj.* 1 *She was delirious from the high fever:* incoherent; hallucinating, raving. 2 *The crowd became delirious when the hero appeared:* frantic, frenzied; excited, ecstatic.
Ant. 1 coherent, rational. 2 calm.

deliver *v.* 1 *to deliver groceries:* carry, bear, convey; surrender; give over, hand over. 2 *to deliver a speech:* give, utter, say, proclaim. 3 *to deliver a blow:* launch, throw, deal, strike. 4 *They were delivered from slavery:* save, rescue, liberate, free, release.
Ant. 4 enslave, oppress.

deliverance *n. The village owes its deliverance to the army:* liberation, release; rescue, salvation.

delivery *n. We awaited the delivery of the documents:* transfer, transmittal, transferral, transmission, handing over.

delude *v. I may be deluding myself:* mislead, deceive, fool, trick; dupe.

deluge *v.* 1 *the Deluge:* flood, inundation. 2 *a deluge of requests:* inundation, flood, barrage, torrent. —*v.* 3 *The overflowing river deluged the town:* overwhelm with a flood, inundate, drown, submerge, engulf; bury, flood.
Ant. 1 drought.

delusion *n. He had the delusion that he was a boy:* illusion, misbelief, misconception.

deluxe *v. a deluxe restaurant:* elegant, grand, fine, luxurious, choice, posh, *Slang* classy.

delve *v. We delved into the files:* search, probe, examine, explore.

demagogue *n. Demagogues exploit prejudices:* rabble-rouser, agitator, haranguer; hothead, firebrand.

demand *v.* 1 *She demanded a refund:* order, require; insist upon, lay claim to. 2 *The situation demands immediate attention:* need, require, call for. —*n.* 3 *The king's*

demand was carried out: command, order. 4 *a demand for experienced workers:* need, requirement.

demean *v. Don't demean yourself:* debase, lower, degrade, humiliate, disgrace, shame.
Ant. honor; glorify, elevate.

demeanor *n. a pleasing demeanor:* conduct, behavior, deportment, manner, comportment, bearing, presence.

demented *adj. He must be demented!:* insane, mad, lunatic, crazy, crazed, deranged.
Ant. sane, rational.

demise *n.* 1 *his untimely demise:* death, decease, passing, expiration. 2 *the demise of the empire:* end, fall, collapse.

democracy *n.* 1 *A true democracy allows free speech:* government by the people, representative government. 2 *the democracy of the courts:* fairness, equality.

demolish *v.* 1 *to demolish a building:* wreck, destroy, level, raze; tear down. 2 *The evidence demolished the attorney's case:* ruin, devastate.
Ant. 1 build, create. 2 strengthen.

demolition *n. the demolition of the old tower:* destruction, wrecking, razing, leveling.

demon *n.* 1 *to exorcise demons:* devil; evil spirit, malignant spirit. 2 *The demon held us prisoner in the tower:* fiend, monster.
Ant. 1, 2 angel.

demonic *adj. demonic energy:* fiendish, devilish; frantic, frenzied.

demonstrate *v.* 1 *She demonstrated the proper way to tie knots:* teach, show; illustrate, explain. 2 *to demonstrate great courage:* show, display, exhibit, manifest. 3 *The lawyer demonstrated that the witness was lying:* prove, show, establish; make evident. 4 *to demonstrate for better working conditions:* picket, parade, march, hold a protest meeting.

demonstration *n.* 1 *a demonstration of the manufacturing process:* exhibition, display, presentation, illustration. 2 *a demonstration of patriotism:* expression, manifestation, display. 3 *an anti-war demonstration:* parade, march, picketing; protest meeting, rally.

demonstrative *adj. The child was very demonstrative:* affectionate; effusive.

demoralize *v. Defeat demoralized the team:* discourage, dishearten, dispirit, undermine.
Ant. encourage, hearten.

demote *v. The corporal was demoted to private:* lower in rank, degrade; *Slang* bust.

demur *v.* 1 *A few demurred:* object, disagree; take exception. —*n.* 2 *to follow an order without demur:* hesitation, qualm, compunction; objection, protest.

demure *adj. a demure reply:* modest, prim, reserved; bashful.

Ant. brazen, brash, impudent.

demurrer *n. The resolution passed without demurrer:* objection, challenge, dissent, protest, question; scruple, qualm.

Ant. consent, agreement, acquiescence.

den *n. a fox's den. a den of thieves:* lair, shelter, retreat; haunt, hangout. 3 *Mother won't let any of us into her den:* study, library.

denial *n.* 1 *a denial of wrongdoing:* disowning, disavowal, disclaimer. 2 *his denial of the petition:* rejection, refusal.

Ant. 1 affirmation, acknowledgment, admission. 2 granting.

denigrate *v. He denigrates everything he doesn't understand:* defame, malign, slander, tear down, disparage, run down, blacken, call names, vilify, revile; soil, sully.

Ant. praise, commend, acclaim.

denizen *n. the denizens of the forest:* inhabitant, resident, dweller.

denomination *n.* 1 *The subjects fall under several denominations:* name, designation, category, class, grouping. 2 *He's a churchgoer, but I don't know what denomination:* sect, religious group, persuasion.

denote *v. The flashing red light denotes danger:* indicate, mark, signal, signify; mean, name.

denounce *v.* 1 *to denounce the book:* condemn, criticize, censure, vility. 2 *She was denounced as a thief:* accuse; inform against.

Ant. 1 commend, praise, extol, laud.

dense *adj.* 1 *a dense crowd. dense fog:* crowded, compressed, compact, concentrated, thick, impenetrable; heavy. 2 *He's so dense he'll never understand:* dumb, stupid, dull, dim-witted, thick.

Ant. 1 sparse, scattered, dispersed; thin, light. 2 bright, intelligent, quick, clever.

dent *n. The car is full of dents:* pit, nick, hollow, indentation.

denunciation *n. a denunciation of dishonest government:* condemnation, censure, denouncement; attack against.

Ant. defense, recommendation.

deny *v.* 1 *She denied making such a statement:* contradict, disavow, disaffirm, disclaim, refute. 2 *He denied me a chance to speak:* refuse, disallow; withhold from. 3 *Atheists deny the existence of God:* not recognize; declare untrue.

Ant. 1 confirm, admit. 2 grant. 3 acknowledge, recognize.

depart *v.* 1 *We must depart now:* go, leave; exit, go away, set out, go forth. 2 *He de-*

parted from the text to tell an anecdote: digress, turn aside, deviate.

Ant. 1 arrive; remain, stay.

department *n. the payroll department:* division, bureau, branch, section, unit; district, sector.

departure *n.* 1 *Our departure is tomorrow:* leaving, going, exit, exodus; going away. 2 *a departure from her previous work:* digression, divergence, deviation.

Ant. 1 arrival.

depend *v.* 1 *We depend on you to do the work well:* rely, count, place trust, have faith. 3 *The picnic depends on the weather:* hinge, rest, be determined by, be contingent upon.

dependable *adj. a dependable worker:* reliable, trustworthy, trusty, trusted; loyal, faithful, steadfast; sure.

Ant. untrustworthy, unreliable.

dependence *n.* 1 *She resented dependence on her children:* dependency 2 *Dependence on religion is growing:* reliance, trust, confidence.

dependent *adj.* 1 *Children are dependent on their parents:* needing help, needful of, reliant. 2 *Good health is dependent on proper nourishment:* determined by; contingent on; subject to.

Ant. 1 self-reliant, independent.

depict *v.* 1 *The painter depicted Napoleon at Waterloo:* paint, portray, draw, represent. 2 *The story depicts a cynical opportunist:* describe, dramatize, narrate, record, chronicle, relate, recount, detail.

deplete *v. The drought has depleted our supply of water:* exhaust, use up, lessen, reduce, decrease, consume.

Ant. increase, augment.

deplorable *adj.* 1 *a deplorable slum:* wretched, awful, miserable. 2 *His actions were deplorable:* deserving reproach, reprehensible, blameworthy.

deplore *v.* 1 *They deplored the death of the king:* lament, mourn, bemoan, bewail, grieve for. 2 *We deplore your manners:* censure, condemn; disapprove of.

deport *v.* 1 *The authorities deported us for illegal entry:* oust, expel; banish; exile. 2 *The children deported themselves in a mannerly way:* behave, act, carry; conduct.

deportment *n. If her deportment doesn't improve, the school may expel her:* conduct, behavior; comportment, demeanor.

depose *v. to depose a king:* dethrone; oust; remove from office.

deposit *v.* 1 *Deposit your books at the door:* put, place; set down. 2 *The soil was deposited on the banks:* accumulate, place; put down. 3 *We deposited $300 on a car:* give as security, give as partial payment; put down. **4** *I deposited $10 in my savings account:* place for safekeeping; put in the bank, commit to custody. —*n.* **5** *The flood left a large deposit of mud in the street:* accumulation, sediment, pile. **6** *a $10 deposit on a new coat:* down payment, partial payment.

deposition *n.* **1** *the deposition of Charles I:* the act of deposing. **2** *The witnesses gave their pretrial depositions:* testimony, declaration, statement.

depot *n.* **1** *a train depot:* terminal, terminus; station. **2** *a supply depot:* storage place, dump.

depraved *adj. a completely depraved person:* perverted, wicked, debased, debauched, degenerate.
Ant. moral, virtuous.

deprecate *v. The critic deprecated the exhibit:* condemn; object to, express strong disapproval of.
Ant. approve, favor.

depreciate *v.* **1** *Inflation depreciated the country's currency:* reduce the value of, diminish. **2** *He depreciates all efforts to help:* belittle, disparage, scorn, denigrate.
Ant. **1** appreciate.

depress *v.* **1** *Her news depressed me:* dispirit, sadden, dishearten, deject, lower in spirits. **2** *The new highway depressed business along the old road:* lessen, weaken, diminish, reduce, cut back. **3** *Depress the lever:* lower; press down.
Ant. **1** elate, gladden, hearten. **2** increase, strengthen.

depression *n.* **1** *a feeling of depression:* sadness, dejection, discouragement, downheartedness; despondency. **2** *a depression in the earth:* indentation, hollow, dimple. **3** *an economic depression:* decline, recession.
Ant. **1** cheerfulness, gladness; joyousness. **3** boom.

deprive *v. deprived of membership for nonpayment of dues:* dispossess, divest, strip; take from.

depth *n.* **1** *a depth of 300 feet:* downward measurement, perpendicular measurement. **2** *Her poem has remarkable depth:* profundity, deepness. **3** *the depth of his voice:* timbre, deepness.
Ant. **1** height.

deputy *n. We sent our deputy to the preliminary talks:* agent, assistant; representative, surrogate, proxy, second.

deranged *adj. a deranged person:* insane, irrational, unbalanced, demented; crazy.
Ant. sane, rational.

derelict *adj.* **1** *derelict in responsibilities:*

negligent, delinquent, remiss; careless. **2** *a derelict ship:* abandoned, deserted. —*n.* **3** *They run a home for derelicts:* bum, vagrant, tramp, hobo.

deride *v. They derided the new music:* ridicule, mock, scoff, scorn, sneer at.

derision *n. The loser was the target of derision:* ridicule, mockery, disdain, scorn, sneering.

derivation *n.* **1** *the derivation of plastic from chemicals:* deriving, acquiring, obtaining, getting. **2** *The waltz is of German derivation:* origin, source. **3** *the derivation of a word:* etymology; historical development.

derive *v.* **1** *She derives great satisfaction from sports:* gain, obtain, glean, enjoy. **2** *Many English words are derived from Latin:* descend; originate; stem from.

derogatory *adj. derogatory remarks:* belittling, disparaging, uncomplimentary, unfavorable.
Ant. flattering, complimentary.

descend *v.* **1** *The elevator descended slowly:* drop, come down, go down. **2** *The walk descends sharply:* incline, slope, slant. **3** *The house descended through the male heirs:* be inherited, pass, be handed down.
Ant. **1** ascend, climb.

descendant *n. The British royal family are descendants of Queen Victoria:* offspring, issue, progeny.
Ant. ancestor, forefather.

descent *n.* **1** *the descent of the balloon:* fall, drop, coming down. **2** *a gradual descent from the house to the lake:* slope, slant, decline. **3** *proud of her descent from a Confederate colonel:* ancestry, origin, lineage.
Ant. **1** ascent, rise.

describe *v.* **1** *They described their journey:* detail, narrate, relate, recount; illustrate, characterize, depict. **2** *Describe a circle with a piece of chalk:* draw, trace, outline, mark out.

description *n.* **1** *an accurate description of her appearance:* account, depiction, portrayal, characterization. **2** *dogs of every description:* kind, sort, type, ilk, variety.

desecrate *v. Vandals desecrated tombstones in the cemetery:* defile, violate, profane, dishonor.
Ant. honor, esteem.

desert[1] *n.* **1** *the Gobi Desert:* wasteland; arid region, barren wilderness. —*adj.* **2** *Desert land will never be valuable:* barren, desolate; infertile, arid; uncultivated, untilled.

desert[2] *v. She deserted her children:* abandon, forsake, leave.

deserts *n. pl. The thief got his just deserts:* due; payment, reward; punishment.

deserve *v. He deserves the award:* merit,

warrant; be worthy of, be entitled to, qualify for, be deserving of.

design v. 1 *She designed a new generator:* plan, conceive, fashion, devise; draw up plans for. 2 *This fund is designed to help students:* intend, set up. —n. 3 *the designs for the house:* sketch, drawing, plan, blueprint, diagram. 4 *The quilt has a sunburst design:* pattern, motif; form, arrangement. 5 *He has a design for becoming a millionaire:* plan, project, blueprint, intention, goal, target, objective, end, aim. 6 *designs against the government:* plan, scheme, plot; intrigue.

designate v. 1 *He designated where we were to meet:* specify, indicate, name, select. 2 *Martha was designated cochair:* appoint, choose, select, name, assign. 3 *The shopping center is designated York Plaza:* name, call, identify.

designing adj. *designing politicians:* scheming, conniving, crafty, cunning, wily, plotting.
    Ant. candid, frank, open.

desirable adj. 1 *a desirable neighborhood:* pleasing; worth having, in demand. 2 *Such changes are desirable:* advisable, advantageous, beneficial.
    Ant. 1 undesirable. 2 harmful, inadvisable, improper.

desire v. 1 *I desired nothing but sleep:* crave, want, long for; yearn for, hunger for, thirst for. 2 *We desire your early reply:* request, ask for. —n. 3 *the desire for fame:* longing, craving, yearning, thirst, hunger.
    Ant. 3 distaste, aversion, dislike.

desist v. *They agreed to desist from false advertising:* cease, stop; discontinue, suspend; refrain from.
    Ant. persist, continue.

desolate adj. 1 *The town was a desolate place:* deserted; bare, barren, bleak, forsaken, abandoned. 2 *She has been desolate since losing her job:* despondent, dejected, downcast, downhearted, depressed, sad; wretched, miserable. —v. 3 *Many towns were desolated by the hurricane:* ravage, devastate, destroy, demolish; lay waste. 4 *We were desolated by her death:* sadden, grieve, depress, distress; dishearten; discourage.
    Ant. 2 cheerful, happy, glad. 4 cheer, hearten, encourage.

desolation n. 1 *The desolation of the town was complete:* ruin, devastation, destruction. 2 *We couldn't stay in that desolation another day:* barrenness, emptiness, bleakness. 3 *Her desolation is greater now that the children are away:* loneliness, seclusion, solitude. 4 *That's too much desolation for

anyone to bear:* sadness, unhappiness, sorrow, depression, dejection; distress, misery.

despair n. 1 *He sank into despair:* hopelessness, despondency, gloom, depression. 2 *She has been the despair of her teachers:* ordeal, trial. —v. 3 *I despair of ever finding her again:* have no hope, lose heart, lose faith in.
    Ant. 1 hopefulness, cheerfulness. 2 delight, pride. 3 have faith in, have confidence in.

desperado n. *The desperado was wanted in seven states:* bandit, outlaw, brigand; fugitive; ruffian, gunman.

desperate adj. 1 *a desperate criminal:* dangerous, wild, frantic; daring, rash. 2 *a desperate illness:* grave, critical, dangerous, serious. 3 *She became so desperate she feared for her:* despairing, despondent, wretched; beyond hope. 4 *in desperate need of help:* extreme, great, urgent, critical, dire.

desperation n. *In desperation, he finally broke down:* despair, hopelessness, recklessness.

despicable adj. *despicable behavior:* contemptible, detestable, vile, mean, base, reprehensible.
    Ant. praiseworthy, laudable, worthy.

despise v. *I despise cruelty:* loathe, detest, abhor; contemn, disdain; look down on.
    Ant. admire, appreciate, respect.

despoil v. *Barbarians despoiled the town:* rob, plunder, ravage, pillage, loot.

despondent adj. *I get despondent when plans go awry:* discouraged, depressed, dejected, downhearted, disconsolate, downcast, disheartened.
    Ant. encouraged, joyful, happy, glad.

despot n. *to revolt against a despot:* tyrant, dictator, oppressor.

dessert n. *Does the meal include dessert?:* final course; (variously) pie, tart, cake, sweet, ice cream; fruit, nuts.

destination n. *My destination is Los Angeles:* journey's end; goal, plan, purpose, ambition, objective, aim, target, object.

destiny n. *Do you believe our destiny is predetermined?:* future, fate, fortune, lot; karma, kismet.

destitute adj. *to aid destitute families:* poor, poverty-stricken, needy, indigent, penniless, broke.
    Ant. rich, affluent, wealthy.

destroy v. *Fire destroyed several stores:* ruin, demolish, waste, ravage, devastate.
    Ant. preserve, conserve.

destruction n. *the destruction of landmarks:* destroying; demolition, wrecking, devastation.
    Ant. preservation, conservation.

destructive adj. a destructive storm: damaging, ruinous, injurious, devastating; harmful, hurtful.

Ant. beneficial, constructive; preservative.

detach v. They detached their trailer and set up camp: separate, disconnect, disengage, unhitch, unfasten.

Ant. attach, fasten, connect, engage.

detached adj. 1 The coupon is not valid if detached: separated, disconnected; unfastened, disengaged, unhitched, unconnected, uncoupled, severed. 2 A judge must be detached: impartial, neutral, unbiased, unprejudiced, disinterested, objective.

Ant. 1 attached, joined, connected. 2 partial, biased, prejudiced.

detachment n. 1 the detachment of cars from the train: separation, disconnection, disengagement; severing. 2 You need detachment to arrive at a just decision: impartiality, objectivity, neutrality. 3 an air of detachment: aloofness, indifference, coolness. 4 a detachment of guards: unit, special force.

detail n. 1 perfect in every detail: particular, item, fact, component, feature, aspect, respect. —v. 2 The workers detailed their grievances: itemize, enumerate, specify, delineate, designate; relate, recount. 3 She was detailed to act as courier: select; assign to a task, appoint.

Ant. 1 whole, aggregate, sum.

detain v. 1 Bad weather detained us: delay, stop; hinder, retard, slow. 2 The police detained the suspect: confine, hold, keep in custody; arrest.

detect v. We detected a note of pity in her voice: discover, uncover, notice, note, observe, perceive.

deter v. Bad weather didn't deter us: hinder, prevent, dissuade, daunt; stop, impede.

deteriorate v. The patient's condition has deteriorated: worsen, degenerate, decline; decay.

Ant. improve, ameliorate, advance.

determination n. 1 a determination I never regretted: decision, resolution, resolve; judgment, solution, conclusion. 2 The determination of our slogan was arrived at by a vote: determining, settling, resolving, fixing, deciding. 3 She has the determination to succeed at anything: resolution, resoluteness, perseverance, tenacity, persistence, stick-to-it-iveness.

Ant. 3 irresolution, indecision, doubt.

determine v. 1 I tried to determine the reason for her actions: ascertain, discover, learn, establish, find out. 2 Present decisions will determine the future: affect; decide, influence. 3 She determined to vaca-

tion in Canada: settle, decide, resolve, conclude.

deterrent n. Punishment is a deterrent to crime: restraint, curb, hindrance, check.

detest v. I detest snakes: abhor, despise, loathe, hate; dislike intensely, recoil from.

Ant. like, love, relish, cherish.

detestable adj. Selfishness is a detestable quality: hateful, abhorrent, loathsome, odious; repulsive, vile, revolting, disgusting.

Ant. likable, lovable, attractive.

detonate v. Workers detonated the dynamite: explode, set off, touch off; discharge, fire.

detract v. The peeling walls detract from the apartment: diminish, reduce, lower, lessen.

Ant. increase, heighten, enhance.

devalue v. The country devalued its currency: devaluate, depreciate; lower, cheapen, debase.

devastate v. The hurricane devastated the coast: waste, destroy, ravage, ruin, wreck, demolish, lay waste.

devastation n. The explosion caused complete devastation: ruin, ruination, destruction, demolition.

develop v. 1 The children developed their reading skills: expand, broaden, improve, advance; mature, grow, enlarge, amplify; elaborate on. 2 I developed a cold: acquire, contract, come to have. 3 It developed that they had an alibi: evolve, turn out, unfold, come to light.

development n. 1 the development of the human species: progress, growth, evolution, history. 2 the latest developments in medicine: event, advance; event, result.

deviate v. The witness deviated from the truth: part, stray, wander, depart; turn aside, swerve, veer.

device n. 1 a device that automatically closes windows: invention, contrivance, apparatus, contraption, gadget, mechanism. 2 He is full of devices for getting sympathy: plan, plot, scheme, trick, ploy, design, artifice; stratagem, ruse.

devil n. 1 the Devil. The preacher warned against the Devil: Satan, archfiend, prince of darkness, Lucifer, Beelzebub, spirit of evil. 2 those young devils: mischief-maker, hellion, scoundrel, rogue, villain, ruffian. 3 The poor devil never knew what hit him: wretch, creature, unfortunate, Informal fellow, guy.

devious adj. devious business methods: dishonest, deceitful, sneaky, tricky, wily, sly, treacherous, dishonorable.

Ant. forthright, aboveboard, honest.

devise v. to devise a plan: design, invent,

conceive, concoct, contrive, think up, formulate, construct.

devoid *adj.* *devoid of sympathy:* lacking, wanting, bereft of, without.
Ant. full, abounding, replete, abundant, overflowing.

devote *v.* *She devoted her life to helping others:* dedicate, give over to, direct, apply, utilize; give oneself up to; consecrate.

devoted *adj.* *devoted public servants:* dedicated, earnest, staunch, zealous, steadfast; ardent, loving; faithful, true, loyal.
Ant. undedicated, indifferent; unloving; unfaithful, disloyal.

devotion *n.* **1** *devotion to one's mother:* dedication, commitment; regard, reverence, love, concern for; loyalty, faithfulness, allegiance; zeal, ardor. **2** *His devotion led him to the priesthood:* devoutness, religious fervor, holiness, piety, reverence, godliness. **3** *(Usually plural) Devotions are held every Sunday morning:* act of religious worship, prayer service, religious observance.
Ant. **1** indifference, unconcern, disregard; unfaithfulness, disloyalty. **2** impiety, irreverence.

devour *v.* **1** *He devoured several sandwiches:* eat voraciously, consume greedily, gobble up, wolf down. **2** *She devours historical novels:* read eagerly and swiftly, read compulsively.

devout *adj.* *the more devout members of the congregation:* religious, pious, worshipful, reverent; ardent, fervent, earnest, passionate, zealous.
Ant. irreligious, impious, irreverent; indifferent.

dexterity *n.* *A surgeon must have dexterity:* manual skill, deftness, adroitness, handiness, nimbleness with the fingers.

dexterous *adj.* *dexterous fingers, a dexterous mind:* nimble, agile, adroit, deft; resourceful, active, quick.
Ant. clumsy, awkward.

diabolic Also **diabolical** *adj.* *a diabolical plan:* devilish, satanic, fiendish, wicked, evil, malevolent, demonic, villainous, monstrous.
Ant. angelic, saintly, pious.

diagnosis *n.* *the doctor's diagnosis, a diagnosis of the city's problems:* identification of a disease; determination, study, examination, analysis.

diagram *n.* *a diagram of the new airplane:* plan, drawing, sketch.

dialogue, dialog *n.* **1** *The owner consented to a dialogue with the strike leaders:* formal discussion, conference, talk, exchange of viewpoints. **2** *the dialogue of a play:* spoken discourse; verbal exchange, conversation; lines, speech.
Ant. **2** monologue, soliloquy.

diaphanous *adj.* *The fabric was diaphanous:* translucent, transparent, sheer, filmy, gossamer, gauzy.
Ant. opaque, thick, heavy.

diary *n.* *She writes in her diary every night:* daily journal, journal, daybook; log, chronicle.

diatribe *n.* *His diatribe gave full vent to all his resentments:* harangue, tirade, denunciation, stream of abuse, invective, vituperation.

dicker *v.* *to dicker for a new contract:* negotiate, bargain, haggle, drive a bargain.

dictate *v.* **1** *The conqueror dictated the surrender terms:* lay down, ordain, determine, order, direct, prescribe, impose, decree. —*n.* **2** *the dictates of the law:* requirement, stricture, rule, ruling, order, decree, dictum; bidding, urging.

dictator *n.* *Hitler was one of the most feared dictators in history:* despot, tyrant; *(variously)* czar, kaiser, duce, führer, caesar.

dictatorial *adj.* **1** *dictatorial powers:* absolute, unlimited, unrestricted, arbitrary. **2** *a dictatorial manner:* domineering, imperious, tyrannical, despotic, autocratic; peremptory, overbearing, arrogant.
Ant. **1** democratic, limited. **2** humble, considerate.

diction *n.* *Bad diction marred the speech:* enunciation, articulation; pronunciation; elocution.

dictum *n.* **1** *We must accept the boss's dictum:* dictate, edict, decree, pronouncement, order. **2** *There's an old dictum that blood is thicker than water:* saying, adage, maxim, axiom, proverb.

didactic *adj.* **1** *The talk was didactic but entertaining:* instructive, educational, edifying, tutorial. **2** *a didactic manner:* preachy, pedantic, pedagogic, donnish; moralizing.

die *v.* **1** *He died in the war:* perish, suffer death, expire, pass away, pass on, depart, meet death, *Slang* croak, kick the bucket. **2** *The chiming of the bells died:* wane, ebb, decline, recede, fade away, subside, fade, diminish. **3** *The car battery died:* fail, become inoperative; lose power; stop, break down, run down. **4** *I'm dying to see Jamaica:* yearn, be eager, be anxious, long, pine, be consumed with desire, ache.
Ant. **1** live, flourish. **2** increase, build, become strong.

diet *n.* **1** *a balanced diet:* nutritional regimen; eating habits, eating regimen. —*v.* **2** *You will have to diet to lose weight:* eat abstemiously, eat judiciously, follow prescribed eating habits, cut back on one's food, eat sparingly.

differ v. 1 *This photograph differs from the other:* contrast, stand apart from, deviate from, be unlike, be dissimilar, be disparate. 2 *I differ with you:* disagree, take issue, be of a different opinion, think differently; dissent, dispute.

Ant. 2 concur, agree.

difference n. 1 *the difference between asking and demanding:* distinction, dissimilarity, unlikeness, contrast; variation, disagreement, contrariety, deviation, divergence, contradiction; distinguishing characteristic. 2 *The difference in their ages is six years:* discrepancy, disparity. 3 *They haven't spoken since their difference last year:* dispute, argument, disagreement, falling out, quarrel, squabble.

Ant. 1 resemblance, similarity; agreement, uniformity, unity, sameness.

different adj. 1 *Her hat is different from yours:* unlike, dissimilar, distinct, disparate, divergent, contrasting. 2 *We put the cookies in three different boxes:* separate, distinct, individual. 3 *I heard the news from different sources:* several, various, sundry, divers, diversified, separate. 4 *He has a different outlook:* unconventional, unusual, uncommon, rare, unique, singular, distinctive, strange, peculiar.

Ant. 1 identical, same, like. 4 ordinary, common, usual, conventional.

differentiate v. 1 *to differentiate between white wines:* discriminate, distinguish, see the difference in. 2 *The trim differentiates the luxury model from the standard:* distinguish, set off, set apart, make different; separate.

difficult adj. 1 *a difficult task:* hard, laborious, strenuous, demanding, arduous, burdensome, exhausting, tedious, formidable, troublesome, exacting; complex, complicated, enigmatic, perplexing. 2 *a difficult child:* hard to deal with; unaccommodating; hard to manage, unruly, obstinate, stubborn, unmanageable, recalcitrant, obstreperous, unyielding, intractable, fractious. 3 *Times were difficult:* hard, grim, rough, full of hardship, tough, trying.

Ant. 1 simple, easy; uncomplicated. 2 cooperative, accommodating, manageable, tractable.

difficulty n. 1 *the difficulty of the job:* troublesomeness, arduousness, laboriousness, hard sledding; obstacle, impediment, obstruction, stumbling block; problem, dilemma, quandary. 2 *in financial difficulty:*

trouble, predicament, pickle, critical situation, crisis, straits.

Ant. 1 ease.

diffidence n. *His diffidence keeps him from arguing:* timidity, timidness, timorousness, shyness, meekness, retiring disposition, reserve; modesty, humbleness, unassertiveness, sheepishness.

Ant. boldness, assertiveness, aggressiveness.

diffuse adj. 1 *soft, diffuse light:* scattered, spread out, unconcentrated, dispersed. 2 *His talk was too diffuse:* discursive, rambling, disjointed, digressive, roundabout, wandering, meandering, cumlocutory.

Ant. 1 concentrated. 2 pithy, methodical, organized.

diffusion n. 1 *the diffusion of knowledge:* spread, dispersal, scattering. 2 *The diffusion of his speech was confusing:* circumlocution, indirection, roundaboutness, rambling, maundering, disjointedness, discursiveness.

Ant. 1 concentration, centralization.

dig v. 1 *We dug a tunnel:* excavate, scoop out, gouge, hollow out; unearth. 2 *Can you dig the material out of the archives?:* search, retrieve, extricate, find among, come up with. 3 *He dug his elbow into my ribs:* poke, drive, jab, thrust, prod. —n. 4 *a dig in the ribs:* poke, thrust, jab, prod. 5 *She couldn't resist a dig about my hat:* cutting remark, gibe, jeer, slur, verbal thrust, taunt.

digest v. 1 *Some foods are hard to digest:* assimilate; dissolve. 2 *It took her a while to digest the bad news:* grasp, comprehend, absorb, assimilate, understand. —n. 3 *a digest of a novel:* condensation, abridgment; summary, abstract.

dignified adj. *too dignified to do anything so silly:* full of dignity, decorous; circumspect, distinguished, proper, upright.

Ant. undignified.

dignity n. *She maintained her dignity:* dignified behavior, respectful deportment; self-possession, decorum; proud demeanor, augustness; high position, importance.

digress v. *Let me digress for a moment:* depart from the subject, stray, divagate, deviate, turn aside.

digression n. *His long digression made him forget his main point:* divergence, deviation, detour, straying, wandering, diversion.

dilapidated adj. *a dilapidated house:* rundown, decrepit, broken-down, tumbledown, falling to pieces, ramshackle, in disrepair, shabby, rickety.

dilate v. *This medicine will dilate the pupils:* expand, enlarge, distend, extend; widen.

Ant. constrict, contract, shrink.

dilatory *adj. She was dilatory about her homework:* inclined to delay, procrastinating, remiss, tardy, sluggish; lackadaisical, negligent.
   Ant. diligent, industrious, conscientious; punctual, prompt.

dilemma *n. His dilemma was whether he should tell us the truth:* plight, difficult choice, problem, quandary, predicament.

dilettante *n. a dilettante of the arts:* cultured hobbyist; dabbler, trifler.

diligent *adj. a diligent worker:* industrious, hardworking, persevering, earnest, untiring; painstaking; careful, thorough.
   Ant. dilatory, careless, laggard, indifferent.

dilute *v. 1 Dilute the ammonia with water:* thin, weaken, adulterate; water down. **2** *His love for the boy diluted his anger:* diminish, mitigate, temper, decrease, attenuate, reduce, diffuse. —*adj.* **3** *dilute whisky:* diluted, watered down, adulterated.
   Ant. **1** thicken, strengthen.

dim *adj.* **1** *The room was too dim for reading:* lacking light, not bright, unilluminated, darkened, dusky, murky; indistinct, obscured, clouded; blurry, blurred. **2** *I had a dim suspicion:* vague, intangible, faint, indefinite, indistinct, remote.
   Ant. **1** bright, radiant. **2** distinct, clear, definite, pronounced.

dimension *n.* Often **dimensions. 1** *the dimensions of the room:* measurements, size, length, width, height, thickness. **2** *No one realized the dimensions of our problem:* range, scope, magnitude, extent, importance.

diminish *v.* **1** *The cold spell diminished our wood supply:* reduce, lessen, shrink, abate, decrease, lower. **2** *Our friendship diminished:* lessen, shrink, dwindle, be reduced, shrivel, wane, decline, subside.
   Ant. enlarge, increase, enhance, expand.

diminutive *adj. Gulliver encountered a diminutive people:* tiny, little, small, short, slight, undersized, miniature, minute, lilliputian; teeny, wee.
   Ant. enormous, gigantic, oversized, huge, vast, colossal, mammoth.

dimwit *n. That dimwit knew nothing about the job:* dummy, blockhead, dunce, simpleton, nitwit, numskull, booby, dolt, dumbbell, knucklehead, pinhead.

din *n. There was such a din I didn't hear the phone:* clamor, uproar, hubbub, racket, clangor, babble.
   Ant. quiet, silence, stillness.

dine *v. She dines with friends every night:* eat, sup, feast, break bread, banquet; eat (or have) dinner, supper, lunch, breakfast.

dingy *adj. a dingy storeroom:* dirty and drab, murky, shabby, dreary, gloomy, dismal.
   Ant. bright; cheerful.

dint *n. by dint of hard work:* force, effort, struggle, strain, labor, exertion, endeavor, power, might, strength.

dip *v.* **1** *She dipped the blouse into the suds:* dunk, soak, submerge, immerse. **2** *He dipped the chowder into individual bowls:* scoop, dish, ladle, spoon. **3** *The moon dipped behind the trees:* droop, descend; slope, incline downward, sink. **4** *I've only dipped into politics:* dabble, study slightly, peruse, glance at.
   Ant. **3** rise, climb, ascend.

diplomacy *n.* **1** *international diplomacy:* conduct of international relations, statesmanship, foreign affairs, international politics. **2** *She used great diplomacy in handling the situation:* tact, discretion, prudence, subtlety.
   Ant. **2** tactlessness, crassness, clumsiness.

diplomat *n.* **1** *a U.S. diplomat assigned to London:* statesman, national representative, international affairs expert, negotiator; ambassador, consul, minister, envoy, attaché, emissary. **2** *We need a diplomat to deal with the problem:* tactful person, artful handler of people.

diplomatic *adj.* **1** *a diplomatic post in Paris:* ambassadorial, foreign-service, state-department. **2** *He's very diplomatic:* tactful, discreet, politic, sensitive, prudent.
   Ant. **2** tactless, rude, unthinking.

dire *adj.* **1** *dire consequences:* dreadful, awful, appalling, horrible, terrible, grave; calamitous, catastrophic, disastrous; urgent, desperate, extreme, crucial, critical. **2** *a dire prediction:* ill-boding, grim, ominous, portentous, dreadful, ill-omened, dismal, inauspicious.
   Ant. **1** happy, favorable. **2** favorable, auspicious.

direct *v.* **1** *He directs the community center. I was directed to cut the budget:* supervise, manage, oversee, head, serve as director for, conduct, administer, preside over; instruct, order, command, charge. **2** *She directed us to the shopping center:* point the way, show the way, usher, indicate, lead, guide. **3** *She directed her remarks to the speaker:* level at, aim, focus, address, designate. —*adj.* **4** *direct negotiations between the two leaders:* face-to-face, personal, first-hand, unmediated. **5** *direct questions:* straightforward, frank, candid, clear, explicit, point-blank; pointed, forthright.
   Ant. **4** indirect, roundabout. **5** indirect, sly, oblique.

direction *n.* **1** *The work will be under her*

direction: management, superintendence, supervision, guidance, leadership, charge; administration, command. 2 *In which direction is the beach?:* way, path, track, route. 3 *You're thinking in the right direction:* line of thought or action; inclination, tendency, bent, course, track. 4 *(Usually plural)* Follow *the directions carefully:* instruction, order; guidelines; recipe.

directly *adv.* 1 *She drove directly to school. He lives directly across the street from me:* straight, unswervingly, as the crow flies, in a beeline. 2 *The guests will arrive directly:* soon, presently, momentarily; forthwith, right away. 3 *I spoke directly to the manager:* face-to-face, in person, personally. 4 *Answer me directly:* openly, honestly, frankly, straightforwardly, candidly; in plain terms, unambiguously.

Ant. 3 indirectly. 4 equivocally, deceitfully, dishonestly.

director *n. the camp's recreation director:* supervisor, manager, superintendent, conductor, head, leader, organizer, overseer, administrator.

dirge *n. a dirge to honor the war dead:* funeral song, requiem, death song, death march, lament, threnody.

dirt *n.* 1 *The abandoned house was full of dirt:* mud, dust, filth; trash, refuse, garbage, rubbish, muck; grime, slime, sludge. 2 *good dirt for growing vegetables:* soil, earth, loam, humus. 3 *Those shops still peddle their dirt to the tourists:* smut, filth, pornography. 4 *Her column is filled with dirt about famous people:* gossip, rumor, scuttlebutt, scandal, sensational exposé.

dirty *adj.* 1 *a dirty face:* unclean, grimy, soiled, begrimed, muddied, filthy, unwashed, smudgy. 2 *dirty dealings:* unscrupulous, illegal, illicit; contemptible, devious, deceitful, shabby, sordid, dishonest, fraudulent, crooked, dishonorable, corrupt. 3 *dirty words:* obscene, vulgar; pornographic, indecent, prurient, smutty, lewd, filthy. 4 *I seem to get the dirty jobs:* unpleasant, disagreeable; hard, difficult. —*v.* 5 *We certainly dirtied this floor:* soil, make dirty; smear, smudge, muddy, stain, spot, begrime.

Ant. 1 clean, washed, spotless. 2 honest, aboveboard, honorable. 4 easy; pleasant. 5 clean.

disability *n.* 1 *His disability prevents him from working:* handicap, disablement, impairment, affliction, impediment. 2 *Not speaking French in Paris is a disability:* disadvantage, handicap, shortcoming, minus.

Ant. 2 advantage, plus.

disable *v. The plane was disabled:* incapacitate, render inoperable, damage, cripple, impair; handicap.

disabuse *v. Someone ought to disabuse him of those notions:* enlighten about, free from error, disillusion, disenchant, open the eyes of.

disadvantage *n.* 1 *His experience put me at a disadvantage:* weak position, handicap. 2 *What are the disadvantages of owning your own home?:* drawback, handicap, detriment, weak point, impediment, nuisance, burden.

Ant. 1 advantage. 2 advantage, merit, benefit.

disadvantaged *adj. disadvantaged countries:* underprivileged, underdeveloped, impoverished, emerging; deprived; handicapped.

disagree *v.* 1 *My total disagrees with yours. We disagree on politics:* differ, be unlike, be at variance, conflict, deviate, diverge; be of different opinion, think differently, be unreconciled. 2 *Too much sun disagrees with me:* be injurious, cause problems; discomfit, make ill, upset.

Ant. 1 agree, coincide.

disagreeable *adj.* 1 *The weather has been disagreeable:* unpleasant, nasty; repugnant, disgusting, repellent, repulsive; offensive; uninviting. 2 *She is always disagreeable:* unpleasant, ill-natured, uncongenial; ill-tempered, churlish, nasty, grouchy, cross, peevish, surly.

Ant. 1 agreeable, pleasant, delightful. 2 agreeable, pleasant, congenial, amiable.

disagreement *n.* 1 *There was disagreement between their stories:* difference, lack of agreement, discrepancy, disparity, lack of harmony, divergence, diversity; dissimilarity, dissimilitude, incompatibility. 2 *They haven't spoken since their disagreement:* quarrel, squabble, fight, argument, difference, falling-out, misunderstanding, dispute.

Ant. 1 agreement, unity, accord, harmony.

disappear *v. The sun disappeared behind the clouds:* vanish from sight, be lost to view; withdraw, retire, go, be gone, depart; flee, leave.

Ant. appear, materialize; arrive.

disappearance *n. the disappearance of the secret documents:* vanishing, sudden or unexplained loss, passing from sight.

Ant. appearance, materialization.

disappoint *v. You disappointed us:* fail to live up to the expectations of, let down; sadden, disillusion, dishearten; thwart, frustrate.

disappointment *n.* 1 *Rover has been a*

disappointment us a watchdog: letdown, failure, dissatisfaction, dud. **2** *She learned to accept disappointment:* thwarted expectation, unrealization, unfulfillment, frustration, setback, defeat, failure.

disapprove *v.* **1** *I disapprove of such behavior:* view with disfavor, frown upon, discountenance, object to, find unacceptable, condemn, regard as wrong, dislike, take exception to, look askance at; deplore. **2** *His request was disapproved:* refuse, turn down, disallow, veto, reject.
Ant. **1** approve, commend, applaud, sanction. **2** approve, allow, accept.

disarm *v.* *Children disarm me with smiles:* persuade, win over, sway, influence, prevail on, move, entice, charm.
Ant. alienate, irritate, repel.

disarming *adj. a disarming smile:* winning, winsome, charming, ingratiating, beguiling, irresistible, captivating, appealing, bewitching, seductive.
Ant. irritating, annoying, exasperating.

disarrange *v. My records were disarranged by the children:* scramble, disorder, mix up, displace, put out of order, disarray, jumble, disorganize, confuse; dishevel, ruffle.
Ant. arrange, order, systematize.

disarray *n. The room was in disarray:* disorder, messiness, upset, untidiness, confusion, chaos, shambles.

disaster *n. The fire was a disaster:* catastrophe, calamity, great mishap, cataclysm, tragedy, crushing reverse, ruination.
Ant. blessing, benefit, boon, windfall.

disastrous *adj. Investing in that stock was disastrous:* ruinous, catastrophic, calamitous, devastating, fatal, tragic.

disavow *v. He disavowed the rumors:* repudiate, deny, reject, abjure; retract, recant; disclaim knowledge of, deny responsibility for, disown, divorce oneself from, refuse to acknowledge.
Ant. acknowledge, admit; accept.

disbelief *n. My disbelief was obvious:* skepticism, lack of credence, doubt, unbelief, incredulity; distrust, mistrust.
Ant. belief, credulity, credence.

disburse *v. Salaries are disbursed by the paymaster:* pay out, allocate, give out in payment; distribute.

discard *v. Let's discard these old papers:* get rid of, throw away, throw out; remove; have done with, drop, shed, junk, dispose of, dispense with, dump, scrap.
Ant. retain, keep.

discern *v. She could discern a faint light:* detect, make out, perceive, see, observe, ascertain.

discerning *adj. He was discerning in his*

analysis of the problem: perceptive, acute, perspicacious, astute, penetrating, intelligent, wise, sage.
Ant. undiscerning, unperceptive.

discharge *v.* **1** *to discharge a rifle:* set off, shoot, fire, detonate, explode; send forth a missile from, eject; launch, propel, let fly. **2** *The boiler discharged steam:* emit, throw off, send forth, expel, exude, gush. **3** *His boss discharged him:* fire, dismiss, release, oust, let go, terminate, sack, can, axe, lay off, send packing, cashier. **4** *discharged from prison:* release, allow to go, let go, free, set free. —*n.* **5** *the discharge of the revolver:* firing, discharging, detonating, activating, exploding; detonation, explosion, blast, shot. **6** *an honorable discharge from the army:* release, release document, demobilization.

disciple *n. a disciple of yoga:* pupil, student, follower, devotee; adherent, believer, admirer; proselyte, convert.
Ant. master, teacher, guru.

disciplinarian *n. a strict disciplinarian:* one who maintains discipline, stickler for rules, taskmaster, martinet.

discipline *n.* **1** *the discipline at the military academy:* training, drill, schooling, indoctrination; enforcement of rules, rigor. **2** *Daily practice is a discipline observed by most musicians:* method, regulated activity, prescribed habit, regimen. —*v.* **3** *We disciplined students by keeping them after school:* punish, chastise, chasten.

disclaim *v. Don't disclaim responsibility:* disavow, deny, repudiate, renounce, decline, disown; forswear, abnegate.
Ant. claim, affirm, acknowledge, admit.

disclose *v.* **1** *The lawyer disclosed the details of the merger:* tell, reveal, divulge, make known, bare, make public, impart. **2** *Daylight disclosed a chain of mountains in the distance:* uncover, reveal, show, expose.
Ant. **1** conceal, hide, withhold. **2** cloak, cover, veil.

discolor *v. Water discolored the carpet:* stain, spot, tarnish, streak, bleach.

discomfort *n.* **1** *The dentist said there would be some discomfort:* ache, hurt, pain, soreness, irritation; hardship, uncomfortableness; vexation, annoyance, nuisance, distress. —*v.* **2** *We were discomforted by her cool manner:* make uneasy, embarrass, make uncomfortable; distress, disquiet.
Ant. **1** comfort, ease, pleasure.

discomposure *n. She betrayed no discomposure:* perturbation, agitation, uneasiness, confusion, embarrassment, anxiety, nervousness.
Ant. composure, poise, equanimity.

disconcerted *adj. We were disconcerted by the noise:* distracted, agitated, unsettled, confused; upset, annoyed, disturbed, troubled, perturbed.
Ant. unruffled, undistracted.

disconnected *adj. The plot was too disconnected:* confused, rambling, disorganized, incoherent, disjointed.
Ant. connected, organized, coherent.

disconsolate *adj. She is disconsolate over her job:* depressed, downcast, unhappy, sad, dejected, despondent, dispirited, discouraged, doleful.
Ant. happy, cheerful; hopeful, optimistic.

discontented *adj. discontented with life:* unhappy, dissatisfied, displeased, bored, fretful.
Ant. contented, satisfied, happy.

discontinue *v. to discontinue gymnastics class:* stop, interrupt, terminate, suspend, drop, cease, desist, give up, quit.
Ant. continue, extend.

discord *n. years of discord:* dispute, disagreement, conflict, quarreling, contention, differences, dissension, wrangling, friction.
Ant. harmony, accord, agreement, compatibility.

discount *n. Students get a discount at the bookstore:* reduction, deduction, cut rate, break, abatement.

discourage *v.* 1 *The failure discouraged me:* dishearten, deject, unnerve, dispirit, depress, dash one's hopes, dampen one's spirits. 2 *They discouraged us from going:* dissuade, deter, keep back, advise against.
Ant. 1 encourage, hearten, inspire, embolden. 2 encourage, urge.

discouragement *n.* 1 *Discouragement drains one of vitality:* dejection, despair, despondency, downheartedness, gloom, dismay, pessimism. 2 *Her frail health is a discouragement:* worry, damper, constraint, restraint, curb, hindrance, obstacle, impediment.
Ant. 1 encouragement, hopefulness, optimism, cheerfulness. 2 encouragement.

discourse *n.* 1 *They enjoyed hours of leisurely discourse:* conversation, talk, discussion, chat. 2 *a discourse on the evils of drugs:* lecture, address, speech, talk, sermon, discussion; essay, treatise.

discourteous *adj. a discourteous reply:* rude, impolite, ungracious, uncivil, uncourteous, ill-mannered, surly, disrespectful; impertinent, fresh, insolent, impudent.
Ant. courteous, civil, polite, gracious, respectful.

discover *v.* 1 *Astrophysicists discovered dark matter:* come upon, find, learn of, detect; uncover, unearth, locate; root out, find

out, ascertain. 2 *I discovered my error:* realize, notice, see, perceive, spot, discern, learn of, determine, find, detect, uncover, locate.

discredit *v.* 1 *She discredited his good name:* defame, dishonor, vilify, disparage, smirch, debase, degrade, demean, tarnish, taint, undermine, sully. 2 *The investigator discredited the claim:* prove false, disprove, reject; shake one's faith in, undermine belief in; dispute, challenge, question.
Ant. 1 praise, laud. 2 prove, support, verify.

discreet *adj. discreet inquiries:* prudent, tactful, sensitive, thoughtful, judicious, cautious, circumspect, diplomatic, polite.
Ant. indiscreet, rash, heedless, imprudent, impetuous.

discrepancy *n. a discrepancy between the two accounts:* difference, inconsistency, variance, disagreement, disparity, divergence.

discrete *adj. The corporation has six discrete departments:* separate, distinct, different, disconnected, independent, unassociated; several, various.
Ant. merged, combined, interdependent.

discretion *n.* 1 *Use your own discretion:* judgment, preference, choice, inclination, option. 2 *Show discretion in handling the situation:* judgment, judiciousness, sagacity, discernment, prudence, tact.
Ant. 2 indiscretion, thoughtlessness, recklessness, insensitivity, tactlessness.

discriminate *v. to discriminate between good and bad art:* differentiate, draw a distinction, distinguish, separate.

discrimination *n.* 1 *laws against religious discrimination:* bias, prejudice, bigotry, inequity, favoritism. 2 *You show fine discrimination in choosing wines:* discretion, discernment, judgment; taste, refinement.

discursive *adj. a discursive style of writing:* digressive, rambling, roundabout, wandering, meandering, circuitous.
Ant. direct, succinct.

discuss *v. to discuss yesterday's events:* talk about, talk over, speak of, exchange views on; debate.

discussion *n. a discussion of the proposed law:* talk, dialogue, discourse, debate, argument, disputation, deliberation.

disdain *v.* 1 *He disdained all offers of help:* look down upon, frown upon, spurn, snub, brush aside, consider beneath oneself. —*n.* 2 *I have only disdain for bigots:* scorn, contempt, abhorrence, dislike, disrespect, distaste.
Ant. 2 admiration, respect, esteem.

disease *n. Doctors now can treat this disease:* illness, sickness, physical disorder, ailment, malady, affliction.

disembark v. *The troops disembarked on the beach:* land, go ashore, debark; detrain, deplane.

Ant. embark, go aboard.

disfavor n. 1 *She incurred our disfavor:* disapproval, disapprobation, displeasure, dislike, disregard, dissatisfaction, disrespect; disgrace. 2 *We did ourselves a disfavor by inviting them:* disservice, ill turn.

Ant. 1 favor, approval, approbation, esteem. 2 favor, service.

disfigure v. *Was she disfigured by the accident?:* deform, deface, render unsightly, maim; scar, blemish; mutilate.

disgorge v. *The dog disgorged the bone from its throat:* dislodge, throw up, discharge, spout, vomit forth, spew, eject, expel.

disgrace n. 1 *a disgrace to his family. Bad schools bring disgrace on the town:* shame, reproach, dishonor, blot, smirch, blemish, stain, embarrassment; contempt, disrepute, discredit. —v. 2 *Don't disgrace yourself by passing out at the garden party:* embarrass, humiliate; dishonor, debase, bring reproach upon, shame.

Ant. 1 honor, credit, glory. 2 honor, distinguish.

disgraceful adj. *disgraceful manners:* shameful, dishonorable, scandalous, shocking, appalling, disreputable, outrageous, ignominious; unseemly; low, mean, inglorious, base.

Ant. honorable, worthy, seemly, becoming.

disgruntled adj. *Our cat becomes disgruntled when dinner is late:* sulky, grumpy, vexed, peevish, displeased, irritated, malcontent, sullen, petulant.

Ant. contented, pleased, satisfied.

disguise v. 1 *She came to the ball disguised as Marie Antoinette:* garb, mask, cloak; camouflage; counterfeit, feign. 2 *She tried to disguise her feelings:* conceal, hide, cover up, mask, veil. —n. 3 *His disguise did not conceal his identity:* cover, counterfeit appearance, deceptive covering, camouflage, guise, false appearance; cover-up, mask, screen, false front, sham, pretense.

disgust v. 1 *His crudeness disgusted us:* repel, revolt, be repulsive to, appall, put off, offend; sicken. —n. 2 *He couldn't hide his disgust:* revulsion, repugnance, loathing, distaste, abhorrence, repulsion, aversion, detestation, dislike.

Ant. 1 please, delight. 2 liking, fondness, love.

dish n. 1 *Put the potatoes in the dish:* plate, saucer; serving dish, platter, shallow bowl. 2 *Would you like a dish of peaches?:* dishful, portion, plateful, bowlful, serving, helping.

—v. 3 *Dish the berries into the bowl:* place, transfer, scoop, spoon, ladle; portion, serve, dispense.

dishearten v. *I was disheartened by my failure:* dispirit, dismay, discourage, deject, depress, dash, sadden.

Ant. encourage, uplift, hearten.

disheveled adj. *Her hair was disheveled:* unkempt, rumpled, disorderly, disarrayed, disarranged, mussed; messy, untidy, in disorder.

Ant. neat, tidy; kempt, groomed.

dishonest adj. 1 *a dishonest man:* corrupt, untrustworthy, false, lacking integrity, faithless, crooked, unscrupulous, deceitful, two-faced, fraudulent, underhanded. 2 *The lawyer made dishonest claims:* misleading, deceptive, false, fraudulent, untruthful.

Ant. 1 honest, upright, honorable, lawabiding. 2 honest, true.

dishonor n. 1 *You brought dishonor to the family:* shame, disgrace, discredit, ignominy, disrepute, infamy, humiliation, scandal. 2 *Refusing our offer was a dishonor to us:* slight, affront, insult, discourtesy. —v. 3 *Corruption dishonored the politician:* disgrace, shame, deprive of honor, discredit, blacken, tarnish, sully, debase, stigmatize; degrade, humiliate.

Ant. 1 honor, glory, renown, esteem, respect, admiration. 2 honor, compliment, courtesy.

disillusion v. *I hate to disillusion you:* undeceive, shatter one's illusions, disenchant, disabuse.

Ant. deceive, lead on.

disintegrate v. *The plane disintegrated in the air:* fall apart, break up, shatter, crumble.

disinterested adj. *a disinterested judge:* impartial, unbiased, neutral, unprejudiced, uninvolved.

Ant. partial, biased, prejudiced.

disjointed adj. 1 *The house was disjointed from the garage:* disconnected, detached, unconnected, unattached, split, divided. 2 *The movie was too disjointed:* rambling, confused, disconnected, disorganized, chaotic, discontinuous, incoherent, irrational, illogical.

Ant. 1 connected, attached. 2 coherent, logical.

dislike v. 1 *I dislike selfish people:* feel repugnance toward, regard with displeasure, have no taste for, object to; loathe, abhor, despise, hate, detest. —n. 2 *Her dislike of the child was obvious:* distaste, aversion, antipathy; loathing, repugnance, hatred, repulsion, revulsion, abhorrence, detestation, animosity, disdain, enmity, rancor.

Ant. 1 like, esteem. 2 liking, attraction, admiration.

dislodge *v. The bulldozer dislodged the rock:* dig out, remove, displace, eject, oust, uproot, extricate.

Ant. lodge, embed, root.

disloyal *adj. She felt disloyal for giving up her citizenship:* unfaithful, inconstant, untrue, undutiful; perfidious; seditious, treasonable, traitorous, subversive.

Ant. loyal, faithful, constant, steadfast.

disloyalty *n. He proved his disloyalty by betraying me:* faithlessness, unfaithfulness, perfidy, deceitfulness, falseness, breach of trust, inconstancy; treachery, treason, subversion.

Ant. loyalty, allegiance, fidelity, constancy.

dismal *adj. a dismal little room. his dismal attitude:* gloomy, cheerless, somber, bleak, dreary, drab; doleful, dolorous, despondent, sad, joyless, dejected, pessimistic, downcast, depressed, sorrowful, disheartened, desolate, disconsolate, woebegone, forlorn.

Ant. cheerful, bright, inviting; happy.

dismay *v.* 1 *Our sudden lack of money dismayed us:* alarm, frighten, distress, unnerve, horrify; dishearten, abash, discourage; disillusion, disappoint. —*n.* 2 *Imagine our dismay at the sight:* alarm, apprehension, anxiety; distress, concern, consternation, trepidation; terror, dread, fright, horror; disheartenment, discouragement. 3 *I couldn't hide my dismay:* disappointment, disillusionment, discouragement.

Ant. 1 cheer, reassure, relieve, encourage, hearten. 3 happiness, joy, relief.

dismiss *v.* 1 *The students were dismissed for lunch. Dismiss the meeting:* allow to leave, release, excuse, let go; dissolve, adjourn. 2 *He was dismissed for loafing on the job:* fire, discharge, sack, can, let go, terminate, send packing, cashier. 3 *I dismiss any suggestion of dishonesty:* put out of mind, reject, disregard; disclaim, repudiate.

Ant. 1 detain, recall. 2 hire, employ. 3 welcome, accept.

disobedient *adj. a disobedient boy:* insubordinate, rebellious, noncompliant, unmanageable, ungovernable, recalcitrant, intractable; contrary, stubborn, refractory; defiant, undutiful, unruly.

Ant. obedient, manageable, dutiful, wellbehaved.

disobey *v. to disobey the law:* disregard, defy, refuse to obey, rebel against; violate, overstep, transgress, fail to comply with.

Ant. obey, follow, abide by.

disorder *n.* 1 *I can't stand disorder:* disarray, mess, clutter, muddle, disorderliness, disorganization, confusion. 2 *a kidney dis-*

order: ailment, illness, sickness, affliction, disease, malady, complaint. 3 *The campus disorder was on tonight's news:* commotion, disturbance, riot, uproar, disturbance of peace.

Ant. 1 order, orderliness, organization, neatness.

disorderly *adj.* 1 *Help me straighten these disorderly files:* disordered, out of order, unsystematized, disorganized, unsystematic, pell-mell, unsorted, jumbled, confused, helter-skelter; messy, sloppy, disheveled, unkempt, slovenly. 2 *disorderly conduct:* unlawful, lawless, disruptive, wayward, constituting a nuisance; unruly, undisciplined, wild, obstreperous, rowdy.

Ant. 1 orderly, arranged, organized, methodical; neat, tidy.

disorganized *adj. The plan is too disorganized:* confused, jumbled, muddled, mixed-up, unsystematic, chaotic.

Ant. organized, systematic, systematized, methodized.

disown *v. He disowned his son:* disinherit, disclaim, repudiate, renounce, forsake, denounce, reject, refuse to acknowledge.

Ant. claim, accept, acknowledge.

disparage *v. Don't disparage me:* belittle, ridicule, discredit, put down, denigrate, underrate, depreciate.

Ant. praise, laud, extol, commend.

disparate *adj. Their views are usually disparate:* dissimilar, different, unlike, at odds, at variance, discordant.

Ant. similar, like, accordant.

disparity *n. a disparity between promises and actions:* inequality, discrepancy, dissimilarity, divergence, contrast, difference, inconsistency; disagreement, contradiction.

Ant. accord, unity.

dispassionate *adj. He described the problem in a dispassionate way:* unemotional, unexcited, unimpassioned, calm, serene, composed, unruffled, detached; impartial, unbiased, unprejudiced, impersonal, disinterested.

Ant. passionate, impassioned, emotional, excited; biased, prejudiced.

dispatch *v.* 1 *Dispatch the report to the commander:* send off, transmit, post, forward. 2 *The job was dispatched in record time:* finish, complete, execute quickly, carry out, dispose of. 3 *The injured horse was dispatched by its owner:* kill, finish off, put to death, slay, put an end to. —*n.* 4 *He sent a dispatch from Hong Kong:* message, report, missive, bulletin, official communication, flash; communiqué. 5 *Do it with dispatch:* promptness, haste, quickness, swiftness, speed, celerity, alacrity.

dispel v. *The attack dispelled the enemy troops. Let me dispel your doubts:* scatter, drive away, expel, repel, drive off; put an end to, resolve, allay, remove, banish.

dispensable adj. *Remove any dispensable items from the budget:* unnecessary, expendable, nonvital, disposable, unessential, nonessential, unimportant.

   Ant. indispensable, necessary, essential.

dispensation n. 1 *the dispensation of blankets to the needy:* distribution, dispensing, allocation, dealing out, meting out, dissemination, consignment, allotment, bestowal. 2 *a dispensation from the Pope:* permission, authorization, exemption.

disperse v. *A thunderstorm dispersed the picnickers:* drive off, scatter, dissipate, send off, rout; disband; distribute, spread throughout, diffuse.

   Ant. assemble, gather, collect, convene; concentrate.

dispirited adj. *The team was dispirited after the defeat:* dejected, downhearted, discouraged, downcast, disheartened, crestfallen, glum, sad, cheerless, depressed.

   Ant. cheerful, elated, joyful.

displace v. 1 *The automobile displaced the horse and buggy:* supplant, supersede, replace. 2 *The inhabitants were displaced by the flood:* dislocate, dislodge, move; shift, put in a wrong place.

display v. 1 *The officer displayed great courage:* exhibit, show, demonstrate, reveal. —n. 2 *The store has a large display of gems:* exhibition, exhibit, show; presentation.

   Ant. 1 cloak, hide, conceal.

displease v. *Loud talking displeases me:* annoy, irritate, irk, pique, provoke.

   Ant. please, gratify.

displeasure n. *The speech incurred our displeasure:* annoyance, vexation, irritation, wrath, indignation; dissatisfaction, dislike, disapproval.

   Ant. pleasure, satisfaction, approval.

disposal n. 1 *the disposal of trash:* disposition, riddance, discarding, dumping. 2 *The king's subjects are at his disposal:* command, control; direction, authority. 3 *I liked the disposal of the furniture:* arrangement, array, placement, disposition, distribution.

   Ant. 1 acquisition, accumulation, collection.

dispose v. 1 *I'm not disposed to go:* incline, motivate; be willing. 2 *My property was disposed of in a sale:* distribute, get rid of.

disposition n. 1 *a cheerful disposition:* nature, temperament, characteristic mood. 2 *She has a disposition to criticize:* tendency, inclination; predisposition. 3 *the dis-*

position of troops for battle: arrangement, grouping, placement, distribution.

disprove v. *Evidence has disproved that theory:* refute, discredit; controvert, prove to be false or wrong.

   Ant. prove, verify.

disputable adj. *The results are disputable:* questionable, debatable, doubtful, dubious.

dispute v. 1 *I dispute your claim:* doubt, question, challenge, call in question, impugn. 2 *The workers disputed with management:* argue, quarrel, wrangle, squabble, clash. —n. 3 *a dispute over wages:* controversy, debate, argument; quarrel, disagreement, squabble, clash.

disqualify v. *Lack of education will disqualify you for the job:* make unqualified, make unfit; pronounce unqualified, declare ineligible, deny participation.

disquieting adj. *a disquieting remark:* disturbing, upsetting, vexing, troubling; disconcerting, unsettling, distressing, perturbing.

disregard v. 1 *Disregard the mess:* overlook, ignore; pay no heed to, pay no attention to. —n. 2 *disregard of others:* lack of regard or respect, lack of attention, oversight.

   Ant. 1 heed; pay attention to, regard. 2 consideration.

disreputable adj. *disreputable business dealings:* shady, dishonorable, unprincipled; not reputable; shameful, disgraceful, not respectable.

   Ant. reputable, honorable, respectable.

disrespect n. *The disrespect she shows her parents is shocking:* contempt, dishonor, irreverence, disregard; impoliteness, rudeness, lack of respect.

   Ant. respect, esteem, regard.

disrespectful adj. *disrespectful behavior:* rude, impolite, discourteous, impertinent.

   Ant. respectful, courteous, polite.

disrupt v. 1 *The special TV report disrupted regular programming:* interrupt, interfere with. 2 *The war disrupted many lives:* upset; throw into disorder.

dissatisfied adj. *She was dissatisfied with the results:* displeased, unhappy, discontented.

   Ant. satisfied, pleased.

dissect v. 1 *In biology we had to dissect a frog:* cut apart, separate into pieces. 2 *Dissect the poem and find the author's meaning:* analyze, examine part by part, break down.

dissemble v. *He dissembled his disappointment with a joke:* hide, mask, disguise, camouflage, conceal.

   Ant. show, reveal.

disseminate *v. to disseminate the news:* scatter, spread, diffuse, disperse, circulate, broadcast.

dissent *v.* 1 *If members dissent, the bill won't be approved:* disagree, protest, object, oppose. —*n.* 2 *There is dissent among the leaders:* disagreement, difference, opposition, dissension, discord.
Ant. 1 agree, concur. 2 agreement, accord.

disservice *n. He did you a disservice:* wrong, injustice, injury, bad turn.
Ant. service, favor; good turn.

dissident *adj.* 1 *The dissident members booed:* disagreeing, dissenting, opposing. —*n.* 2 *The dissidents are protesting loudly:* dissenter, rebel, agitator.
Ant. 1 consenting, satisfied.

dissimilar *adj. They're so dissimilar you wouldn't believe they were sisters:* unlike, different, distinct, disparate.
Ant. alike, similar.

dissimulate *v. They dissimulated their true intentions:* hide, conceal, mask, disguise, camouflage.

dissipate *v.* 1 *He dissipated his inheritance:* squander, waste, misspend, fritter away. 2 *The fog dissipated when the sun came out:* disperse, dispel, scatter.

dissociate *v. He dissociated himself from his former companions:* separate, disconnect, break off with.

dissolute *adj. a dissolute man:* dissipated, loose, debauched, immoral; abandoned.
Ant. moral, temperate, sober.

dissolve *v.* 1 *Dissolve the chocolate in a pan:* melt, liquefy; soften, thaw. 2 *The decree dissolved their marriage:* end, terminate; abrogate, disband; annul, void. 3 *The rider dissolved into the mists:* vanish, disappear, fade; disintegrate, dissipate.
Ant. 1 congeal, harden, solidify.

dissonant *adj.* 1 *The violins sounded dissonant:* harsh, discordant, inharmonious, grating, unmelodious, cacophonous. 2 *dissonant opinions:* incompatible, inconsistent, irreconcilable, clashing, disagreeing, contradictory, warring.
Ant. 1 melodious, mellifluous, harmonious. 2 compatible, congenial.

dissuade *v. He dissuaded me from going:* discourage; persuade not to, urge not to.
Ant. persuade to, urge to.

distance *n.* 1 *The distance between the farms is 3 miles:* span, gap, interval, intervening space, stretch. 2 *There was some distance between them at the last meeting:* reservation, reserve, coldness, coolness, aloofness, stiffness.
Ant. 2 warmth, friendliness.

distant *adj.* 1 *distant lands:* far, far-off, re-

mote, faraway. 2 *She was so distant I thought she was angry:* unfriendly, cool, cold, aloof, standoffish, reserved.
Ant. 1 near, close. 2 friendly, cordial, warm.

distasteful *adj. Asking people for money is distasteful. The medicine is distasteful:* unpleasant, disagreeable, repugnant, loathsome, disgusting.
Ant. pleasant, pleasing; tasty.

distend *v. stomachs distended by malnutrition:* swell, bloat, expand, bulge, inflate, puff out.

distill *v.* 1 *The liquid distills when heated:* evaporate, condense, vaporize. 2 *Whiskey is distilled from fermented mash:* separate by evaporation and condensation, purify by distillation; extract.

distinct *adj.* 1 *Her business life is distinct from her social life:* separate, different, dissimilar, diverse, individual. 2 *The photograph showed a distinct image:* clear, lucid, plain; definite, clear-cut, unmistakable. 3 *It was our distinct pleasure:* unmitigated, explicit; extraordinary, supreme.
Ant. 1–3 indistinct. 1 similar, identical. 2 vague, obscure, indefinite, blurred.

distinction *n.* 1 *to make a distinction between red and green:* differentiation, separation, discernment, discrimination. 2 *What is the distinction between the two?:* difference, contrast. 3 *a painter of distinction:* eminence, notability, prominence, renown, importance, preeminence.

distinctive *adj. a distinctive way of speaking:* unique, different, characteristic, uncommon, individual, original, singular, special.
Ant. typical, common, ordinary.

distinguish *v.* 1 *His red hair distinguished him from his brothers:* differentiate, set apart; define, characterize. 2 *to distinguish between right and wrong:* discriminate, discern, decide; note differences. 3 *She distinguished herself as a lawyer:* make well known, make prominent.

distinguished *adj.* 1 *a distinguished playwright:* notable, renowned, famous, acclaimed, illustrious, prominent, eminent. 2 *The teachers looked distinguished:* dignified, elegant; grand, splendid.
Ant. 1, 2 undistinguished. 1 unknown. 2 inelegant, common.

distort *v.* 1 *to distort the news:* slant, misrepresent, give a one-sided meaning to. 2 *Pain distorted his face:* contort, deform; misshape, twist out of shape.

distract *v.* 1 *The clowns distracted the children:* divert, entertain, amuse; draw away the attention of. 2 *Fear distracted her:* disturb, trouble, perplex, agitate, worry; confuse, bewilder; torment, madden, craze.

distraction *n.* 1 *Music is my major distraction:* diversion, amusement, entertainment, pastime, recreation. 2 *I was worried to distraction:* desperation, frenzy, mental distress.

distraught *adj. The distraught mother waited for news:* distressed, agitated, anxious, frantic; beside oneself, troubled.
Ant. collected, calm, serene, composed.

distress *n.* 1 *His distress was obvious:* pain, torment, agony, anguish; need, want, suffering; trouble, danger. —*v.* 2 *The news distressed us greatly:* grieve, trouble, upset, disturb, torment.
Ant. 2 relieve, comfort; make happy.

distribute *v.* 1 *The agency will distribute the food:* apportion, disperse, parcel, allot; dispense, give out; deliver, circulate, disseminate. 2 *The lessons were distributed over 24 chapters:* separate, spread out, arrange, systematize, catalog, tabulate, methodize.
Ant. collect, gather.

distribution *n.* 1 *the distribution of news:* dissemination, dispersion, scattering, spreading, circulation. 2 *The distribution of schools has been criticized:* arrangement, grouping, disposition, sorting, organization. 3 *The distribution of property is stated in her will:* apportionment, allotment, allocation, division.

district *n. an election district:* neighborhood, ward, parish, precinct; area, region.

distrust *v.* 1 *I distrust him:* suspect, doubt, mistrust, question. —*n.* 2 *My distrust made our friendship difficult:* suspicion, doubt, mistrust, misgiving; lack of faith.
Ant. 1 trust; have confidence in, believe in. 2 confidence, trust.

disturb *v.* 1 *Don't disturb her:* interrupt, bother, intrude on, annoy. 2 *Only bad weather can disturb our plans:* unsettle, disarrange, disrupt, disorganize. 3 *Her attitude disturbed her friends:* worry, distress, trouble, upset, perturb.

disturbance *n.* 1 *You can work here without disturbance:* interruption, distraction, bother, annoyance. 2 *a disturbance at City Hall:* rioting, disorder, uproar, turmoil, tumult. 3 *The family's disturbance was evident:* worry, upset, perturbation, distress.
Ant. 1 serenity, quiet.

dive *v.* 1 *The parachutists dived from the plane:* fall, plunge, leap, jump. —*n.* 2 *The officer made a dive for the weapon:* lunge, plunge; jump, leap.

diverge *v.* 1 *The roads diverge:* separate, deviate, split off; swerve, deflect. 2 *Her poli-*

tics and mine diverge: differ, conflict, disagree, be at odds.
Ant. converge.

divergent *adj.* 1 *The two roads become divergent:* separate, drawing apart. 2 *Their divergent views:* different, disagreeing, conflicting.
Ant. 1 convergent. 2 agreeing, concurring, similar.

diverse *adj.* 1 *We have diverse ideas:* different, differing, dissimilar, disparate, contradictory, conflicting. 2 *diverse interests:* varied, sundry; eclectic.
Ant. identical, same.

diversify *v. Investors are careful to diversify their holdings:* vary; variegate; diffuse, divide up, spread out.

diversion *n.* 1 *The diversion of the stream changed the land:* turning aside, deflection. 2 *His only diversion is golf:* distraction, pastime, amusement; hobby, avocation.

diversity *n. diversity of opinions:* difference, variance, diversification, variety, assortment.
Ant. likeness, similarity, sameness.

divert *v.* 1 *Our plane was diverted to another airport:* deflect, sidetrack, turn aside. 2 *The children were diverted by the stories:* distract, amuse, entertain; draw to a different subject.

divide *v.* 1 *to divide the land into home sites:* separate, split, part, partition. 2 *We divided the property evenly:* distribute, share, allocate, apportion. 3 *The proposal divided the committee:* disunite, split, cause to take sides. 4 *Divide the shirts according to size:* classify, arrange, sort, separate.
Ant. 1 unite, join, attach. 3 unite.

divination *n.* 1 *He claimed the power of divination:* augury, soothsaying, prophecy, prescience. 2 *Her divinations have not been accurate:* prediction, premonition, conjecture, foreboding.

divine *adj.* 1 *a divine blessing:* heavenly, holy, sacred; celestial. 2 *What a divine chocolate cake!:* heavenly, excellent, wonderful, marvelous. —*v.* 3 *The oracle divined the future:* foretell, prophesy, predict, forecast; fathom, surmise, guess.

divinity *n.* 1 *They believed in the divinity of Zeus:* holiness, divine nature. 2 *He is a student of divinity:* religion, theology. 3 *The ancients believed in many divinities:* god, goddess, deity; divine being, celestial being.

division *n.* 1 *a division into three parts:* separation, splitting up. 2 *They put up a division between kitchen and dinette:* partition, divider, room separator, room divider. 3 *a division of the government:* part, branch, department, section, unit. 4 *a divi-*

sion of opinion: difference, disagreement, divergence, variance.

divorce *n.* 1 *a divorce between feelings and actions:* separation, split, rift. —*v.* 2 *to divorce fantasy from reality:* separate, disunite, dissociate, divide.

Ant. 1 unity. 2 unite, join.

divulge *v. Did he divulge the secret?:* disclose, reveal, tell, relate, make known.

Ant. conceal, keep secret.

dizzy *adj.* 1 *I feel dizzy after riding the merry-go-round:* shaky, giddy, reeling, unsteady, light-headed, vertiginous. 2 *The marchers kept up a dizzy pace:* rapid, quick, fleet, swift.

do *v.* 1 *Has she agreed to do the work?:* perform, execute, carry out, bring about, accomplish, achieve. 2 *They do the kitchen every day:* clean, put in order, arrange, organize. 3 *Do as you're told:* behave, act, conduct oneself. 4 *We used to do business on Grand Street:* conduct, proceed, carry on. 5 *Will this tablecloth do?:* suffice, serve; be satisfactory, be enough. 6 *She's doing well:* fare, get on, make out. 7 *Last summer we did ten countries in three weeks:* cover, travel through, visit.

docile *adj. a docile horse:* manageable, tractable, compliant, tame, obedient, complaisant.

Ant. ungovernable, untrainable.

dock[1] *n.* 1 *We went down to the dock to see the ships:* wharf, pier, quay, landing. —*v.* 2 *The tanker will dock in San Pedro:* berth, come into port. 3 *The two modules docked in outer space:* couple, hook up, link up, join.

dock[2] *v.* 1 *The tail of the colt was docked:* crop, cut short; cut off. 2 *They docked my salary:* deduct a part from; deduct from the wages of.

docket *n. a case on today's docket:* agenda, program, schedule, calendar, bill, slate, roster.

doctor *n.* 1 *You'd better see a doctor:* physician, medical practitioner; *(variously)* internist, general practitioner, GP, dentist, osteopath, pediatrician, podiatrist, ophthalmologist. —*v.* 2 *Doctor that cold:* treat, apply medication to, give medical treatment to.

doctrinaire *adj. He's so doctrinaire it's pointless to disagree:* dogmatic, inflexible, opinionated, authoritarian, imperious.

Ant. reasonable, flexible.

doctrine *n. The Church teaches the doctrine of free will:* principle, belief, philosophy, tenet, precept, dogma.

document *n.* 1 *a document containing the*

king's signature: official paper, record, instrument, legal form. —*v.* 2 *The lawyer will document the charges:* support, verify, certify, substantiate.

dodge *v.* 1 *He threw it at me, but I dodged:* duck, swerve, sidestep, turn aside. 2 *We dodged her queries:* evade, avoid, elude; equivocate, fend off. —*n.* 3 *I found a new dodge to avoid taxes:* trick, stratagem, wile, machination.

doer *n. Fred is a doer:* activist, go-getter, hustler, dynamo.

doff *v. I doffed my hat:* remove, take off, put off, shed; strip, undress, disrobe.

dog *n.* 1 *What kind of dog is that?:* canine; pup, puppy, mutt, mongrel, cur. 2 *He's a dirty dog:* scoundrel, villain, blackguard.

dogma *n. a religious dogma:* doctrine; teachings, set of beliefs, principles, convictions, credo, tenet.

dogmatic *adj.* 1 *She's so dogmatic you can't tell her anything:* opinionated, biased, prejudiced; imperious. 2 *a dogmatic statement of faith:* doctrinal, expressing dogma.

dole *n.* 1 *Many families are living on the dole since the strike:* welfare; allotment, apportionment, allocation, share. —*v.* 2 *He doled out many gifts to the needy:* give, hand out, distribute.

doll *n.* 1 *Children like dolls:* dolly, figurine, dummy; *(variously)* baby doll, rag doll, puppet, marionette. 2 *(Informal) What a little doll!:* pretty child; honey, sweetheart, darling.

dolorous *adj. It was a dolorous occasion:* mournful, sorrowful, grievous, woebegone; wretched, pathetic, pitiable; distressing, lamentable, doleful, unhappy.

Ant. cheerful, happy, lighthearted.

dolt *n. Some dolt mislaid my application:* idiot, jerk, clod, imbecile, fool, blockhead, bonehead, moron, nitwit, numskull.

domain *n.* 1 *Our domain extends for 20 miles in every direction:* estate, land, territory, property; dominion, kingdom, empire. 2 *The doctor works in the domain of public health:* sphere, area, field, province.

domestic *adj.* 1 *Marriage made them very domestic:* hearth-loving, given to the concerns of home. 2 *domestic animals:* domesticated, tame; 3 *Their new car is a domestic make:* native, not foreign, not imported, indigenous; native-grown, home-grown, homemade. —*n.* 4 *It takes a staff of domestics to run that big house:* servant, household help; *(variously)* maid, cook, butler, houseboy.

Ant. 2 wild, untame. 3 foreign, imported.

domicile n. *Her domicile is in Los Angeles:* residence, legal residence, dwelling, home.

dominant adj. 1 *The dominant party took control:* ruling, controlling, predominating, predominant, commanding; major, principal, chief. 2 *the dominant building in the city:* outstanding, most important, most prominent.

dominate v. 1 *She completely dominates her family:* rule, govern, control, domineer. 2 *A huge oak tree dominated the house:* tower over, dwarf.

domination n. *She has been under the domination of her father:* rule, control, authority, command, power, superiority.

domineering adj. *a domineering man:* dictatorial, despotic, imperious, authoritative, commanding, overbearing.

Ant. subservient, submissive; timid, shy.

dominion n. 1 *The king has sole dominion over this land:* rule, sovereignty, jurisdiction, authority, command. 2 *the law throughout the dominion:* domain, realm; territory, land, region.

don v. *We donned our best apparel:* wear, put on, dress in, get into.

donate v. *She donated a large sum to charity:* contribute, give, bestow, make a gift of.

donation n. *donations of clothing for the flood victims:* present, gift, contribution.

done adj. *The pie isn't done:* ready; cooked sufficiently, prepared; finished, completed.

Don Juan n. *He was a Don Juan:* lothario, Romeo, Casanova, pursuer, lady-killer; *Slang* skirt chaser, wolf.

donnybrook n. *The two teams got into a donnybrook:* brawl, fight, fray, affray, scuffle, free-for-all, fracas, melee.

donor n. *The charity needs more donors:* contributor, benefactor, giver.

doohickey n. *Is this the doohickey you want?:* thing, whatsis, whatchamacallit, doodad, object, device, gadget, gizmo, thingamajig, thingamabob.

doom n. 1 *She could only await her doom:* fate, lot, portion, destiny; end, destruction, ruin, death. 2 *the day of doom:* the Last Judgment, Judgment Day, doomsday, end of the world. —v. 3 *Many landmarks are doomed:* consign to ruin, consign to destruction.

doomsday n. *On doomsday, we will have to account for our sins:* Day of Judgment, end of the world, Judgment Day, the Last Judgment.

door n. *I stood in the door and greeted everyone:* doorway, entrance, entrance-way; entry, exit.

dope n. 1 *Put some dope on that mosquito bite:* preparation, medication, astringent, antiseptic, disinfectant. 2 *(Slang) He was accused of peddling dope:* narcotics, drugs, opiates; uppers, downers. 3 *(Slang) He gave me some dope on the fifth race:* tip, news; inside information. 4 *(Slang) The dope never knows when I'm kidding:* dummy, fool, jerk. —v. 5 *Louise was heavily doped before the operation:* drug, sedate, anesthetize.

dopey adj. 1 *This dopey dog!:* dumb, stupid, mindless, witless, blockheaded, idiotic, asinine. 2 *These pills make me feel dopey:* sluggish, lethargic, slow-witted, torpid.

dormant adj. *The volcano was dormant:* inactive, quiescent; idle, sleeping, hibernating.

Ant. active; awake.

dose n. *Double her dose of medicine:* measure, portion; quota, allotment, allowance, quantity.

dossier n. *The office keeps a dossier on every employee:* file, record, detailed report.

dot n. *a blue dress with white dots:* mark, speck, small spot; period, point.

dotage n. *He's in his dotage:* senility, feeblemindedness, second childhood.

Ant. youth, heyday, salad days.

dote v. *Grandparents dote on their grandchildren:* fuss over, lavish fondness on.

double adj. 1 *double pay for working on Sundays:* multiplied by two, twice as much, twice as great, again as much. 2 *The house has double windows:* paired, twin, two-part. 3 *a double meaning:* two-sided, dual, ambiguous; twofold. 4 *a double bed:* meant for two; accommodating two. —n. 5 *She is the double of her aunt:* twin, duplicate, replica; *Slang* spitting image, dead ringer. —v. 6 *I doubled my income:* make twice as great, multiply by two, increase twofold.

double-cross v. *He would double-cross his own mother:* betray, deceive, sell out.

double-talk n. *All I got was double-talk:* mumbo jumbo, gobbledygook, flimflam.

doubt v. 1 *She doubts that anyone is clairvoyant:* question, be skeptical, be doubtful. 2 *I doubt his word:* distrust, mistrust, suspect; lack confidence in. —n. 3 *Is there any doubt about it?:* uncertainty, indecision, question; misgiving, suspicion, apprehension.

Ant. 1 believe. 2 trust, believe. 3 trust, confidence, faith.

doubtful adj. 1 *She's still doubtful about her choice:* undecided, uncertain, unconvinced, unsettled; hesitating. 2 *of doubtful authenticity:* dubious, suspicious, suspect, questionable. **3** *The results are doubtful:* unclear, vague, inconclusive.

Ant. **1** decided, certain, positive. **2** indubitable, incontrovertible.

dour *adj. She has a dour expression:* sullen, morose, sour; solemn, forbidding.

Ant. happy, bright, cheerful.

douse *v. He doused his face in the sink:* drench, submerge, immerse, soak.

dovetail *v.* **1** *The sides of the drawer dovetail:* unite, join, fit together, connect by interlocking. **2** *If our schedules dovetail, I'll see you there:* coincide, match, jibe.

dowdy *adj. Why is he so dowdy?:* shabby, sloppy, slovenly, tacky.

Ant. well-dressed; neat, trim, tidy.

down *adj.* **1** *I've been down ever since I heard the news:* downcast, disheartened, dispirited, dejected, depressed, blue. —*v.* **2** *He downed the champion with a left hook:* fell, floor, drop, knock down, *Slang* deck. **3** *He downed a martini before dinner:* swallow, gulp; drink down.

Ant. **1** gladdened, glad, happy.

downcast *adj. Don't be downcast:* unhappy, sad, disconsolate, disheartened, depressed, dejected, blue, discouraged.

Ant. happy, glad, encouraged.

downfall *n.* **1** *the dictator's downfall:* fall, ruin, ruination, destruction, collapse. **2** *a heavy downfall:* downpour, shower, rainstorm, rain.

downhearted *adj. The loser is downhearted:* unhappy, depressed, sad, disheartened, dispirited, dejected, downcast.

Ant. happy, glad.

downpour *n. We got caught in a sudden downpour:* shower, cloudburst, rainstorm, rain.

downright *adj.* **1** *a downright lie:* absolute, total, utter, complete, out-and-out. **2** *Her downright answer startled us:* direct, straightforward, candid, open, frank, blunt; straight-from-the-shoulder. —*adv.* **3** *He was downright rude:* completely, thoroughly, unmistakably, unequivocally; utterly.

down-to-earth *adj. a down-to-earth approach to life:* realistic, pragmatic, matter-of-fact, sensible, practical, no-nonsense, unsentimental.

downturn *n. a downturn in the stock market:* decline, downward trend, dip, drop, deterioration, slide, skid, slump, depression.

Ant. upturn, boom.

doze *v.* **1** *She was dozing in the hammock:* nap, sleep lightly. —*n.* **2** *He took a little doze after lunch:* nap, snooze, light sleep, siesta, forty winks, catnap.

drab *adj. a drab little office:* dreary, gloomy, dull, dingy, dismal, cheerless.

Ant. bright, cheery, colorful.

draft *n.* **1** *the first draft of her novel:* outline, version. **2** *I feel a draft:* wind, breeze; current of air. **3** *He had to register for the draft:* conscription, military service. —*v.* **4** *He drafted a letter:* write, create a version of; outline, diagram, sketch. **8** *He was drafted by the army:* conscript, call for military service.

drag *v.* **1** *Drag the chair over here:* pull, haul; bring. **2** *The bride's train dragged behind her:* trail; be drawn, be pulled along. **3** *Traffic just drags:* crawl, creep along, inch along.

drain *v.* **1** *Drain the oil out of the crankcase:* draw, empty out. **2** *The river drains into the Pacific:* discharge, flow; debouch. **3** *He drained his parents of every cent they had:* empty, deplete, impoverish; use up. —*n.* **4** *the bathtub drain:* pipe, outlet; drainpipe. **5** *This car has really been a drain on my income:* sap, drag, strain; depletion.

drama *n.* **1** *a three-act drama:* play, theatrical piece, dramatic composition. **2** *She wants to study drama:* dramatic art, acting; the stage, the theater. **3** *the drama of a true-life adventure:* excitement, dramatic quality, vividness.

dramatic *adj.* **1** *dramatic talent:* theatrical; of the drama, for the theater. **2** *a dramatic confrontation:* emotional, striking, climactic, suspenseful.

drape *v. She draped a coat over her shoulders:* cover, wrap, swathe, enwrap, cloak, swaddle; adorn, dress, garb, deck, attire, array, bedeck, festoon.

drastic *adj. He's liable to do something drastic:* extreme, rash; dire, dreadful; dangerous.

draw *v.* **1** *How many horses draw the royal coach?:* pull, drag, haul, tow. **2** *to draw the winner's name from a hat:* extract, pull out, take out, draw out, pick. **3** *The food will draw flies:* attract, lure; allure, entice; evoke, elicit. **4** *The assignment is to draw a horse in motion:* sketch, limn, make a picture of. **5** *to draw a proper contract:* draft, write. **6** *She drew the wrong conclusion:* get, take, deduce, infer. **7** *The strands of rubber were drawn to test their strength:* stretch, attenuate, elongate; extend. **8** *He drew up his face in an expression of disgust:* contract, distort, wrinkle. —*n.* **9** *The young actor is a big draw at the movie theaters:* attraction, lure, enticement, inducement. **10** *The bake-off was a draw:* tie, stalemate; deadlock.

Ant. **1** push, shove. **7** contract.

drawback *n. Lack of funds was a drawback:*

obstacle, handicap, detriment, impediment, stumbling block, disadvantage.

drawing n. 1 *a drawing of the village green:* sketch, picture, study, illustration. 2 *The drawing for prizes will be held at 8 P.M.:* selection of winners, lottery.

dread v. 1 *I dread snakes:* fear, be afraid of, anticipate with horror, shrink from, cringe at. —n. 2 *a dread of being home alone:* fear, fright, terror, apprehension, anxiety, trepidation. —adj. 3 *the dread consequences:* frightening, alarming, terrifying, fearful, awful.

dreadful adj. *a dreadful accident:* awful, terrible, horrible, tragic; fearful, frightful, shocking, distressing.

dream n. 1 *I had another dream about a faraway place:* sleeping vision; nightmare. 2 *her dream of success:* daydream, fantasy, reverie, vision; desire, wish, goal, hope. 3 *That new car is a dream:* joy, pleasure, delight. —v. 4 *I dreamed I won a million dollars:* have a dream, have a sleeping vision. 5 *Stop dreaming and get to work!:* daydream, be lost in thought, pass time in reverie, muse. 6 *I wouldn't dream of doing it:* consider, think, give serious thought to. 7 *The delegates dreamed of peace:* desire, wish, hope for, have as a goal, look forward to.

dreary adj. *a dreary little room:* gloomy, depressing, cheerless, bleak, drab, dismal. *Ant.* cheerful, bright.

dregs n. pl. 1 *coffee dregs:* residue, sediment, settlings, grounds, deposit. 2 *the dregs of humanity:* lowest and worst part, riffraff.

drench v. *Take your raincoat or get drenched:* douse, saturate, wet, soak.

dress n. 1 *a new dress:* gown, frock; costume. 2 *The dress of the guards is unique:* clothing, clothes, costume, attire, apparel, garb. —v. 3 *Try to dress appropriately:* clothe oneself, attire, put on clothes. 4 *The store dressed its windows for Christmas:* trim, adorn, ornament, decorate; deck, embellish, garnish. 5 *She spends hours dressing her hair:* arrange, groom; comb. 6 *His wounds were dressed:* treat, bandage, apply a dressing to; cleanse, disinfect.

dribble v. 1 *Milk dribbled from the baby's mouth:* drip, drizzle, trickle. 2 *She dribbled the ball down the court:* bounce; kick.

drift v. 1 *The boat drifted down the river:* be carried by a current. 2 *The wind drifted the leaves across our yard:* pile up, amass, accumulate. —n. 3 *an easterly drift of winds:* direction, course, current, flow, stream; movement. 4 *The snow was in 10-foot drifts:* heap, pile, mass, accumulation.

5 *The drift of his question seemed to embarrass the speaker:* implication, meaning, gist, sense; object, aim, direction, intention.

drill n. 1 *Vocabulary is taught by daily drill:* practice, training, repetition, repeated exercises. —v. 2 *The teacher drilled the class in pronunciation:* instruct by repetition, train, exercise.

drink v. 1 *Do you drink tea or coffee?:* imbibe, ingest, partake of. 2 *We drank each other's health:* toast, salute, drink in honor of. —n. 3 *a cool drink:* beverage, liquid refreshment, libation. 4 *He took to drink:* alcohol, alcoholic liquor; alcoholism, drunkenness, heavy drinking. 5 *Give me a drink of your lemonade:* sip, gulp, swallow, swig, taste.

drip v. 1 *To drip water on the floor:* trickle, dribble; sprinkle, drizzle. —n. 2 *the drip of a leaky faucet:* trickle, dribble, dripping.

drive v. 1 *They drove the cattle along the Chisholm Trail:* move, advance; lead, guide, conduct; spur, urge along. 2 *The boss drives her workers hard:* press, urge, prod, goad; incite. 3 *Our troops are driving toward the enemy stronghold:* advance, press forward. 4 *We drive to the country on Sunday. She drives a car skillfully:* go by car, ride, go driving, motor; guide, steer; operate. 5 *His pride drove him to complete the job:* motivate, force, compel, coerce. 6 *Just what are you driving at?:* suggest, intend, insinuate. —n. 7 *a drive in the country:* ride, excursion; trip by car. 8 *the team's drive toward the goal:* push, advance, onward course. 9 *She has tremendous drive:* motivation, ambition.

drivel v. 1 *The baby sat driveling in its highchair:* drool, dribble, slobber, slaver. —n. 2 *We listened to a lot of drivel:* gibberish, nonsense, senseless talk.

driver n. 1 *He hired a car and driver:* chauffeur. 2 *The driver made sure the herd kept moving:* cowboy, drover, herdsman.

droll adj. *We found the play very droll:* humorous, whimsical, funny, laughable.

drone v. 1 *The air conditioner droned:* hum, buzz, whir. —n. 2 *The drone of the machines distracted me:* hum, buzz, whir, murmuring.

drool v. *The dog drooled over its dinner:* slobber, slaver, dribble, water at the mouth, salivate.

droop v. 1 *The branches drooped after the heavy rain:* sag, hand down, dangle; bend, bow. 2 *Our spirits drooped:* wither, sink, flag, diminish.

drop n. 1 *drops of water:* droplet, drip, driblet, globule, bead. 2 *Add some liquid—just* *a drop:* dash, dab, trace, sprinkling; smidgen. **3** *It's a 20-foot drop to the ground:* descent, fall; plunge; precipice. **4** *The drop in temperature was a relief:* decline, fall, lowering, decrease. —*v.* **5** *Water dropped from the ceiling:* drip, dribble, trickle. **6** *The sky diver dropped toward the earth:* fall, plunge, plummet, dive, descend. **7** *Let's drop the subject:* abandon, leave, bring to an end, terminate. **8** *Sales drop in the spring:* fall, lessen, dwindle, decline, diminish, slacken, sink. **9** *The boss dropped him from the staff:* discharge, dismiss, fire, *Informal* can, sack. **10** *The challenger dropped the champion in the fifth round:* fell, floor, knock down, *Slang* deck. **11** *Don't drop the "r" of "teller":* leave out, omit.

Ant. **3** rise. **4** rise, increase. **6** rise, soar. **7** take up, discuss, consider. **8** rise, increase. **9** hire. **11** include, pronounce.

drought Also **drouth** *n.* **1** *The drought caused famine:* period of dry weather, lack of rain. **2** *There's a drought of new ideas:* scarcity, paucity, lack, shortage, deficiency, dearth, insufficiency.

drown *v.* **1** *He drowned when the boat capsized:* asphyxiate, to go down for the third time, meet a watery end. **2** *The crops were drowned by the heavy rain:* inundate, flood, deluge, immerse, submerge; drench, soak. **3** *The audience's coughing drowned out the music:* overpower, overwhelm, overcome, engulf, swallow up.

drowsy *adj.* *The medicine made me drowsy:* sleepy; lethargic, languid, listless, sluggish; tired.

Ant. alert, lively; wide awake.

drub *v.* *I was drubbed for stealing the horse:* beat, whip, thrash, flog.

drudge *n.* *She's merely a drudge in her uncle's office:* menial, lackey; underling, subordinate, inferior.

drudgery *n. Doing these reports is drudgery:* distasteful work, toil, travail, grind.

drum *v.* **1** *The rain drums on the windowpane:* rap, tap, beat, tattoo. **2** *The sound of the surf drummed in our ears:* roll, roar, beat, rumble, reverberate, din. **3** *They will drum you out of the corps:* expel, discharge, dismiss, drive out. **4** *Respect for elders was drummed into us:* repeat persistently, reiterate, drive home, harp on.

drunk *adj.* **1** *He was drunk when he arrived:* intoxicated, inebriated, tipsy, under the influence; *Slang* soused, plastered, smashed, stewed, three sheets to the wind. —*n.* **2** *Her uncle was a drunk:* drunkard, lush, sot, rummy, souse, barfly; alcoholic, dip-

somaniac. **3** *a three-day drunk:* drinking spree, binge, *Slang* bender.

Ant. **1** sober.

dry *adj.* **1** *dry weather:* arid, rainless; free from moisture. **2** *I'm so dry, let's stop for a soda:* thirsty; dehydrated, parched. **3** *a dry speech:* uninteresting, dull, tedious, monotonous, boring. **4** *a dry wit:* deadpan, low-key; droll. —*v.* **5** *Dry the dishes:* blot, wipe; make dry.

Ant. **1** wet, damp, moist. **3** interesting, fascinating, entertaining.

dual *adj.* *a dual purpose:* twofold, double, two-part.

Ant. single, singular.

dubious *adj.* **1** *I was dubious about your ability:* doubtful, uncertain, unsure, skeptical. **2** *dubious friends:* shady; unreliable, untrustworthy, undependable.

Ant. **1** sure, positive, certain.

duck *v.* **1** *I ducked when I saw the rock falling:* swerve, veer, dodge, sidestep; crouch, stoop. **2** *She ducked the interviewers:* evade, avoid, elude, dodge.

ductile *adj.* *Gold is extremely ductile:* flexible, pliable, formable, malleable, elastic, pliant, stretchable, bendable, tensile, extensible.

Ant. rigid, firm, unbending.

dud *n. His new play was a dud:* failure, fiasco, debacle, disappointment, fizzle, botch; *Slang* flop, bust, bomb.

Ant. success, smash, triumph.

due *adj.* **1** *A hundred dollars is still due:* unpaid, owing, owed, outstanding; in arrears. **2** *the respect due a president:* suitable, fitting, rightful, deserved, merited, appropriate, proper. **3** *The plane is due at 4:15:* scheduled, expected to arrive. **4** *due cause for alarm:* sufficient, adequate, enough, ample.

Ant. **2** inappropriate, improper. **4** insufficient, inadequate, scanty, scant.

dull *adj.* **1** *This knife is dull:* blunt; not sharp, not keen. **2** *a dull student:* slow, dense, thick, obtuse, dim-witted, stupid. **3** *a dull business day:* slow, inactive, not brisk. **4** *a dull book:* boring, uninteresting, vacuous, unimaginative, prosaic. **5** *a dull blue:* muted, subdued, quiet. **6** *a dull sound:* muffled, indistinct, subdued, deadened.

Ant. **1** sharp. **2** intelligent, clever, bright. **3** active, busy. **4** interesting, exciting. **5** bright. **6** distinct, clear.

dullard *n. People took advantage of the dullard:* dunce, dolt, nitwit, half-wit, imbecile, dumbbell, dummy.

duly *adj.* **1** *The hostess was duly thanked:*

rightfully, properly, suitably, deservedly; correctly, appropriately. 2 *The witness duly arrived:* punctually; on time, at the proper time.

dumb *adj.* 1 *deaf and dumb children:* mute, incapable of speech. 2 *She's tired of being called dumb:* stupid, unintelligent; foolish, dull, dense, dim-witted.
Ant. 1 articulate. 2 smart, intelligent, bright.

dumbbell *n. That dumbbell forgot to lock the door:* dunce, ignoramus, blockhead, oaf, dummy, numskull, simpleton, moron, imbecile, idiot, dimwit; *Slang* lunkhead, noodlehead, lamebrain, birdbrain.

dumbfound Also **dumfound** *v. We were dumbfounded by the damage:* stun, astonish, amaze, flabbergast.

dummy *n.* 1 *the store's display window dummies:* mannequin, model, form, figure. 2 *Some dummy mixed up the letters:* blockhead, dolt, dumbbell, idiot, simpleton, chowderhead, knucklehead, dunderhead.

dump *v.* 1 *Dump your books on the table:* toss, drop heavily. 2 *The truck dumped three loads of gravel on the driveway:* unload, empty; dispose of, get rid of. —*n.* 3 *This furniture is ready for the dump:* rubbish heap, refuse pile, junkyard.

dunce *n. Who was the dunce that left the door open?:* dummy, idiot, moron, imbecile, simpleton, dimwit, nitwit, blockhead, numskull.

dunk *v. to dunk a doughnut in coffee:* douse, immerse, dip, plunge, submerge, souse, sop, duck, saturate, soak, steep, sloah.

duo *n. Mutt and Jeff make a funny duo:* pair, twosome, couple; combination.

dupe *n.* 1 *He was the dupe of racketeers:* pawn, patsy, fall guy, *Slang* sucker. —*v.* 2 *They duped her for $200:* trick, fool, mislead, deceive; humbug, bamboozle, hoodwink.

duplicate *n.* 1 *Can you tell the duplicate from the original?:* facsimile, reproduction, replica, imitation; copy. —*v.* 2 *No one can duplicate that fudge cake:* match, parallel, make again, copy.
Ant. 1 original.

duplicity *n. He had behaved with duplicity:* deceit, deceitfulness, fraud, dishonesty, falseness, deception.
Ant. honesty, candor.

durable *adj. a durable material:* enduring, lasting; sturdy, tough, strong, long-wearing.
Ant. fragile, weak, flimsy.

duration *n. for the duration of the strike:* extent, term, period, continuation.

duress *n. I confessed under duress:* force, constraint, threat, coercion; pressure.

dusk *n. At dusk the lights come on:* twilight, sunset, sundown, nightfall.

dusky *adj.* 1 *It's hard to see in the dusky light:* dim, veiled, cloudy, gloomy, murky. 2 *a dusky complexion:* dark, swarthy.
Ant. 1 bright, clear. 2 fair, light.

dutiful *adj. a dutiful child:* diligent, faithful, loyal; obedient, conscientious.
Ant. uncaring; disrespectful.

duty *n.* 1 *It was his duty to tell the police:* obligation, responsibility; business, province. 2 *One of her duties is to report absentees:* function, task, assignment, charge.

dwarf *n.* 1 *Snow White and the Seven Dwarfs:* pixie, elf, gnome, leprechaun, imp. —*adj.* 2 *dwarf marigolds:* diminutive, small, bantam, tiny, pygmy, miniature. —*v.* 3 *This trouble dwarfs all others:* overshadow, diminish.
Ant. 2 huge, gigantic.

dwell *v.* 1 *He dwells in the country:* reside, live, inhabit, abide. 2 *She dwelt on the similarities in the paintings:* linger over, harp on.

dwelling *n. a three-story dwelling:* house, home, residence, abode, domicile.

dwindle *v. Our food supply dwindled:* diminish, decrease, decline, lessen, shrink; wane, fade.
Ant. increase, grow; burgeon.

dye *n.* 1 *red dye:* color, coloring, tint. —*v.* 2 *Dye that skirt to match your blouse:* color, tint, stain.

dynamic *adj. a dynamic leader:* active, vigorous, vital, energetic, forceful; driving, powerful.

dynasty *n. The Bourbon dynasty ruled France:* ruling house, line, lineage, regnancy, regency, monarchy.

dyspeptic *adj. My uncle was dyspeptic:* bad-tempered, ill-natured, ill-humored, crotchety, irritable, irascible, choleric, touchy, sour-tempered, cantankerous, grouchy, crabby, grumpy.
Ant. good-natured, even-tempered, serene.

E

eager *adj.* 1 *We were eager to go on the picnic:* avid, keen, desirous, yearning, longing, impatient. 2 *an eager student:* earnest, enthusiastic, intent, intense, fervent, ardent; impassioned, passionate, zealous; industrious, hardworking, diligent, resolute; ambitious.
Ant. 2 indifferent, uninterested, apathetic, inattentive, unenterprising.

early *adv.* 1 *an appointment early in the week:* during the first part, near the beginning. 2 *The speaker arrived early:* ahead of time, in advance, beforehand; too soon, prematurely. *—adj.* 3 *He was early for the appointment:* ahead of time; beforehand, premature. 4 *an early Egyptian tomb:* ancient, very old; primitive, prehistoric, primordial.
Ant. 1, 4 late. 1 later. 2 late, tardily. 3 tardy.

earmark *n.* 1 *That had all the earmarks of an insult:* characteristic, feature, trait, quality, attribute, token, distinctive feature. *—v.* 2 *I've earmarked this for my vacation fund:* designate, allocate, assign, reserve.

earn *v.* 1 *She earns $65,000 a year:* make, receive, get, collect, draw, realize, clear, net. 2 *She earned the promotion:* deserve, merit, rate, warrant, be entitled to; attain, achieve, secure.
Ant. 1 spend.

earnest *adj.* 1 *an earnest chess player:* serious, intent, determined, resolute, purposeful, diligent, hardworking, persevering, industrious. 2 *an earnest young man:* sober, serious, grave, solemn, sedate. 3 *an earnest request for forgiveness:* sincere, honest, heartfelt; impassioned, intense, ardent, fervent, fervid; vehement; spirited, enthusiastic.
Ant. 1, 2 frivolous, trifling, flippant. 3 insincere, indifferent, halfhearted.

earnings *n. pl. Income taxes are based on one's earnings:* money earned, income, wages, salary, pay, payment, compensation, profits, receipts, proceeds.
Ant. costs, expenditures, outlay.

earth *n. a handful of earth:* soil, dirt, ground, land, topsoil; loam, clay, dust.

earthly *adj.* 1 *Are we too occupied with earthly matters?:* worldly, terrestrial, mundane; secular, nonspiritual, temporal, mate-

rial, materialistic; corporeal, physical, bodily. 2 *of no earthly value:* possible, practical; conceivable, imaginable, feasible.
Ant. 1 unearthly, celestial, heavenly, spiritual, divine; nonmaterialistic.

earthquake *n. the San Francisco earthquake:* quake, tremor, shock, seism, temblor.

earthy *adj. an earthy sense of humor:* coarse, lusty, bawdy, ribald; rough, unrefined.
Ant. genteel, refined, dainty.

ease *n.* 1 *The salve brought ease to my aching body:* comfort, relief, assuagement, solace. 2 *a life of ease:* comfort, leisure; relaxation, rest, quiet, serenity, tranquillity; security, peace of mind; prosperity, luxury, luxuriousness, abundance, plenty, affluence. 3 *Our team won with ease:* easiness, effortlessness, facility, readiness. 4 *The hostess greeted her guests with ease:* naturalness, relaxed manner, unaffectedness, unconstraint, aplomb, poise, composure, confidence. *—v.* 5 *The aspirin eased his headache. Your calm manner eased my fears:* relieve, assuage, mitigate, abate, allay, alleviate, mollify, palliate, lessen, lighten, diminish; quiet, still, calm. 6 *Ease the piano through the door:* move carefully, maneuver gently, handle with care, slip, slide.
Ant. 1 pain, discomfort. 2 hardship, difficulty, poverty, worry; turmoil, annoyance, toil, hard work. 3 difficulty, effort. 4 stiffness, tension, constraint; embarrassment, self-consciousness, awkwardness. 5 worsen, irritate, aggravate; make uneasy, make tense.

easily *adv.* 1 *The porpoise swam easily:* with ease, without difficulty, with facility, effortlessly. 2 *He is easily the school's best student:* beyond question, certainly, surely, far and away, by far, clearly, undoubtedly, undeniably.
Ant. 1 with difficulty; clumsily.

East, the *n. More Americans visit Europe than the East:* the Orient, the Far East, Asia; the Near East; Eastern Hemisphere.
Ant. the West, Western Hemisphere, the Occident.

easy *adj.* 1 *It was an easy job:* not difficult, not hard, easily done, effortless, simple. 2 *They led an easy life:* comfortable, untroubled, carefree; leisurely, relaxed, serene, tranquil, peaceful, calm; wealthy, luxurious, affluent. **3** *an easy manner:* relaxed, unaffected, natural, easygoing, informal, friendly, pleasant, open, unforced. **4** *an easy teacher:* not strict, lenient, not harsh, indulgent, accommodating; gullible, overly trusting, naïve. —*adv.* **5** *I won't rest easy until you're home:* without worry, without anxiety, serenely, peacefully, calmly.

Ant. **1** difficult, hard, arduous, laborious. **2** hard, difficult; impoverished, poor; troubled, anxious. **3** stiff, formal, forced, tense, anxious; constrained, self-conscious, secretive. **4** hard, strict, harsh, demanding, exacting, dictatorial, oppressive; suspicious.

easygoing *adj. Easygoing people seldom get ulcers:* calm, relaxed, carefree, happy-go-lucky, nonchalant, unexcitable; even-tempered, mild-tempered.

Ant. tense, compulsive, rigid, excitable, volatile, impatient.

eat *v. Did you eat? The children ate a hearty lunch:* feed, take nourishment, take sustenance, take a meal, break bread; *(variously)* breakfast, lunch, dine, sup; feast, gormandize; devour, ingest, bolt, gulp, wolf down, gobble.

Ant. fast, abstain; starve, go hungry

eavesdrop *v. We eavesdropped on their conversation:* listen surreptitiously, listen in, overhear.

ebb *v.* **1** *The tide ebbed:* recede, go out, flow away, flow back. **2** *His strength began to ebb:* decline, fade away, abate, subside, dwindle, diminish, decrease, weaken.

Ant. **1** flood, rise, swell. **2** increase, grow, build, advance.

eccentric *adj.* **1** *Comets move in eccentric orbits:* off center, not circular, parabolic, elliptical. **2** *eccentric behavior:* peculiar, odd, strange, queer, weird, bizarre, unusual, extraordinary, offbeat, outlandish, freakish; capricious, quixotic, curious, unconventional, erratic, irregular. —*n.* **3** *The old eccentric left a fortune to his cat:* character, odd person, crackpot; *Slang* oddball, screwball, kook, nut, flake, weirdo.

Ant. **1** concentric; circular. **2** common, ordinary, conventional, normal, natural.

ecclesiastic *n.* **1** *The dean of the divinity school has to be an ecclesiastic:* clergyman, cleric, churchman, minister, priest, rabbi, preacher, pastor, parson, chaplain, curate, prelate, rector, vicar, deacon. —*adj.* **2** See ECCLESIASTICAL.

ecclesiastical, ecclesiastic *adj. The bishop is responsible for ecclesiastical mat-*

ters: religious, churchly, clerical, parochial, pastoral.

Ant. secular, lay.

echo **1** *The bells echoed across the valley:* resound, reverberate, ring. **2** *Her speech echoed my own feelings:* match, parallel, reflect, mirror, repeat; ape, parrot.

Ant. **2** contradict, differ from, oppose.

eclipse *n.* **1** *a solar eclipse:* obscuration, darkening, veiling, masking, shadowing. **2** *The scandal caused an eclipse of his reputation:* diminishing, clouding, overshadowing, erasing. —*v.* **3** *The moon will eclipse the sun:* cast a shadow upon, obscure, darken, cover, mask, conceal. **4** *Her latest book eclipses her previous ones:* overshadow, dim, surpass, outdo, exceed.

Ant. **2** brightening, enhancement.

economic *adj.* **1** *the economic growth of the country:* material, monetary, productive. **2** *We bought a small car for economic reasons:* monetary, pecuniary, financial, budgetary. **3** See ECONOMICAL.

economical *adj. economical shoppers:* thrifty, economizing, economic, saving, frugal, not wasteful; sparing, scrimping; low-priced, cheap, reasonable.

Ant. extravagant, wasteful; expensive, high-priced.

economize *v. We must economize:* cut expenses, cut costs, be economical, avoid waste, be frugal, tighten one's belt; save, conserve, scrimp, use sparingly, husband.

Ant. be extravagant, squander, waste.

economy *n.* **1** *to practice economy:* thrifty management, thriftiness, thrift. **2** *the nation's economy:* material well-being, financial status, monetary resources, productive power, financial management.

Ant. **1** extravagance, wastefulness.

ecstatic *adj. ecstatic at the birth of a child:* joyful, overjoyed, happy, delighted, enraptured, elated, exalted, ebullient, excited.

Ant. unhappy, miserable, sorrowful, grief-stricken, saddened.

ecumenical *adj. an ecumenical conference:* universal, worldwide, global, international; comprehensive, all-inclusive.

eddy *n. The river is full of eddies:* countercurrent, whirlpool, maelstrom.

edge *n.* **1** *the edge of the property:* boundary line, border, outline, contour, periphery, margin, rim, limit; brink, verge. —*v.* **2** *The blouses were edged with ribbon:* border, trim, rim, bind, outline, hem. **3** *We began to edge toward the door:* move sideways, sidle, move little by little, slink.

Ant. **1** center, middle. **3** rush, run, speed.

edible *adj. Are those mushrooms edible?:*

eatable, suitable for eating, comestible, consumable.

Ant. inedible, uneatable.

edict *n. the dictator's edict:* decree, proclamation, pronouncement, pronunciamento, dictate, command, order, dictum, injunction; law, regulation, ruling.

edification *n. the edification of the young:* enlightenment, moral improvement; teaching, education, instruction, guidance.

edifice *n. a 50-story edifice:* building, structure.

edit *v. Edit the manuscript. edited for television:* revise, correct, polish, rephrase, adapt, abridge, blue-pencil, censor.

educate *v. to educate children:* teach, instruct, train, school; enlighten, inform.

education *n. a college education:* schooling, training, instruction, teaching, learning; enlightenment, edification; pedagogics, pedagogy.

eerie *adj. an eerie feeling:* fearful, frightening, ominous; creepy, mysterious, uncanny, strange, apprehensive.

efface *v. Time effaced the ancient inscription:* obliterate, eradicate, erase, expunge, destroy, annihilate.

effect *n.* 1 *the effect of the drought:* result, consequence, upshot, aftermath, outgrowth. 2 *The plea had no effect on the judge:* influence, force, effectiveness, efficacy, impact. 3 *The law went into effect yesterday:* operation, force, enforcement; function. 4 *In effect, her insult ended our friendship:* fact, actuality, reality; significance, meaning, purport, import, essence. 5 *(usually plural) They sold many of their effects:* personal property, possessions, things, goods, movables, chattels. —*v.* 6 *The new law effected a startling change:* produce, accomplish, bring about, cause, achieve, carry out, attain.

Ant. 1 cause; origin.

effective *adj.* 1 *an effective sales campaign:* effectual, efficient, productive, useful; capable, competent; successful, forceful, powerful, influential. 2 *The new law became effective:* operative, active, in effect. 3 *The book has a very effective closing:* cogent, convincing, compelling, persuasive; striking, powerful; moving, eloquent.

Ant. 1–3 ineffective. 1 ineffectual, unproductive, inadequate, 3 weak, unimpressive, disappointing, unsatisfactory.

effeminate *adj. effeminate manners:* womanish; unmanly, sissyish, sissified.

Ant. manly, masculine, virile.

effervescence *n.* 1 *The soda lost its effervescence:* bubbliness, bubbling, fizz, fizziness. 2 *She was full of effervescence:* liveli-

ness, ebullience, buoyancy, life, vitality, animation, spirit.

effervescent *adj.* 1 *Champagne is effervescent:* bubbling, bubbly, fizzy, sparkling. 2 *the effervescent youngsters:* lively, vivacious, ebullient, animated, merry, irrepressible.

Ant. 1 flat. 2 subdued, sedate, grave.

effete *adj. The aristocracy had grown effete:* decadent, degenerate; enervated, exhausted.

Ant. healthy, vigorous.

efficient *adj. an efficient worker:* effective, productive, proficient, businesslike, workmanlike, capable, competent, effectual.

Ant. inefficient, ineffectual, unproductive, unbusinesslike; wasteful.

effort *n.* 1 *with little effort:* exertion, power, force, energy, labor, work, struggle, stress, pains, trouble. 2 *an effort to provide better working conditions:* endeavor, attempt, try.

effortless *adj. They made the job look effortless:* easy, simple, painless.

Ant. hard, difficult.

effrontery *n. What effrontery to barge in uninvited!:* brazenness, brashness, impertinence, insolence, impudence, cheek, nerve, gall.

Ant. reserve, timidity; respect, diffidence.

effusive *adj. effusive praise:* lavish, profuse, unreserved, extravagant, copious; exuberant.

Ant. restrained, sparing, sparse.

egocentric *adj. an egocentric view of the world:* self-centered, egoistic, self-absorbed, narcissistic, wrapped up in oneself.

egoism *n. extreme egoism:* self-centeredness, self-importance, self-love, pride, vanity.

Ant. humility, modesty.

egotism *n. overwhelming egotism:* self-admiration, bragging, boastfulness, immodesty, conceit, vanity, smugness.

Ant. modesty, humility.

egregious *adj. an egregious mistake:* flagrant, glaring, outrageous, extreme, monstrous; grievous.

Ant. minor, unnoticeable.

egress *n.* 1 *The thieves made their egress through a rear door:* exit, departure, escape; discharge, issue, outflow. 2 *Is there an egress to a fire escape?:* way out, passage out, outlet, exit.

Ant. 1, 2 entrance.

eject *v.* 1 *The volcano ejected lava:* discharge, emit, spew, spit out, spout, disgorge, exude. 2 *The police ejected the demonstrators:* oust, expel, remove, *Slang* bounce; exile, banish.

elaborate *adj.* 1 *an elaborate lighting sys-*

tem: complex, involved, complicated, intricate. **2** *an elaborate costume:* ornate; ostentatious, gaudy, garish. —*v.* **3** *to elaborate on a statement:* expand, add details, clarify, embellish.
Ant. **1, 2** simple, plain.

elapse *v. Twenty years have elapsed:* pass, lapse, go by.

elastic *adj. an elastic waistband:* stretchable, flexible, resilient, supple; pliant, yielding.
Ant. stiff, inflexible, rigid.

elated *adj. elated at setting a new record:* overjoyed, jubilant, exalted, exhilarated, ecstatic, excited, delightful, pleased, gleeful, proud.
Ant. dejected, depressed, sad, unhappy.

elder *adj.* **1** *the elder son:* older, senior. —*n.* **2** *respect for one's elders:* senior, older adult.
Ant. younger, junior.

elderly *adj. an elderly man:* old, aged, past one's prime.
Ant. young, youthful.

elect *v.* **1** *to elect a president:* select by vote, vote into office, choose by ballot; choose, select. **2** *to elect painting as a career:* choose, select, decide on, opt for, settle on, espouse, embrace.
Ant. reject, abjure, renounce, dismiss.

election *n.* **1** *a municipal election:* voting, choosing by vote, vote, balloting, poll. **2** *The election to merge or not is up to the directors'* choice, selection, decision, option, determination.

elective *adj.* **1** *an elective position:* chosen by election, filled by election. **2** *an elective course in college:* optional, not required, voluntary, discretionary.
Ant. **1** appointed. **2** required, obligatory.

electrify *v. The trapeze act electrified the audience:* thrill, stir, excite, rouse, stimulate, galvanize; amaze, astound, astonish, daze, dazzle, take one's breath away.

eleemosynary *adj. The orphanage is an eleemosynary institution:* charitable, existing on donations; philanthropic.

elegance *n. the elegance of the hotel:* luxuriousness, sumptuousness, grandeur, richness; *Slang* class; refinement, grace.

elegant *adj.* **1** *an elegant lace cloth:* exquisite, fine, rich, sumptuous, luxurious; tasteful, refined, graceful, well-proportioned; beautiful, handsome. **2** *an elegant manner:* refined, genteel, well-bred, polished, cultivated, dignified, gracious; *Slang* classy; fashionable, stylish.
Ant. **1** inelegant; tawdry, crude, rough. **2** unrefined, coarse, low-bred, rude.

elegy *n. an elegy on the death of the king:*

poem of lamentation, lament for the dead, requiem, funeral song.

element *n.* **1** *Hydrogen is an element:* basic chemical substance, uncompounded substance. **2** *Cells are the elements of the human body:* basic unit, constituent, component, ingredient, building block, subdivision. **3** usually **elements.** *the elements of physics:* principles, basics, rudiments, foundations, essence, features.
Ant. **1** compound.

elementary *adj. a course in elementary math:* basic, basal, fundamental, rudimentary, elemental; simple, plain; primitive, primary, original; undeveloped, crude.
Ant. advanced, higher.

elevate *v.* **1** *A special device elevated the stage:* raise, upraise, raise aloft, lift up, uplift. **2** *The vice president was elevated to president:* raise, promote, advance; improve.
Ant. lower. **1** drop. **2** demote.

elevation *n.* **1** *The elevation is 7,500 feet:* height, altitude, height above sea level; prominence, lift. **2** *We picnicked on an elevation:* high place, rise, hill, mountain. **3** *the sergeant's elevation to lieutenant:* rise, promotion, advancement; bettering, cultivation.
Ant. **1** depth. **2** low ground, valley. **3** demotion.

elf *n. elves in an enchanted forest:* pixie, puck, brownie, sprite, leprechaun.

elicit *v. The remark elicited a flood of criticism:* bring forth, call forth, evoke, extract, exact, cause.

eligible *adj. Is she eligible for membership?:* qualified, acceptable, authorized, suitable, fitting, applicable.
Ant. ineligible, unacceptable.

eliminate *v. to eliminate poverty:* get rid of, banish, abolish, eradicate, exterminate, annihilate, stamp out; remove, exclude, reject, drop, leave out, omit; eject, expel, cast out.
Ant. obtain, get, establish; include.

elite *n. the elite of the students:* best, best group, select body, cream; upper class, high society, aristocracy, blue bloods, *French* haut monde; notables.
Ant. worst, dregs; lower class, rabble, hoi polloi, riffraff.

elocution *n.* **1** *the speaker's elocution:* articulation, pronunciation, diction. **2** *a course in elocution:* public speaking, oratory, diction, articulation, enunciation, pronunciation.

elongate *v. The table could be elongated:* lengthen, extend; draw out, prolong, protract.
Ant. shorten, contract.

eloquent *adj. an eloquent plea:* persuasive,

forceful, stirring, moving; passionate, impassioned; poetic.

elucidate v. *The footnotes elucidated the text:* clarify, explain, explicate, illuminate; expound, spell out.

Ant. confuse, obscure, muddle.

elude v. *He eluded his pursuers:* evade, avoid, escape, dodge, shun.

Ant. confront, encounter; challenge.

elusive adj. 1 *Antelope are elusive animals:* hard to catch; tricky, shifty, wily, foxy. 2 *an elusive concept:* difficult to comprehend; baffling, puzzling, hard to express.

emaciated adj. *emaciated after weeks without food:* thin, wasted, gaunt; skinny, lean, scrawny, skeletal, cadaverous.

Ant. robust, stout, fat, plump.

emanate v. *The command emanated from headquarters:* flow, issue, come from, spring, originate, stem.

emancipate v. *to emancipate slaves:* free, set free, liberate, release, manumit.

Ant. enslave, subjugate.

emasculate v. 1 *The SPCA has recommended emasculating male cats:* castrate, geld, alter. 2 *The law is emasculated by fining offenders only $5:* weaken, make less forceful, render impotent.

Ant. 2 strengthen, reinforce.

embargo n. *an embargo on foreign cars:* ban, prohibition, restriction, restraint of trade.

embark v. 1 *The passengers embarked:* board ship, go aboard; board; entrain, enplane. 2 *to embark on a business venture:* start, begin, undertake, launch, set out.

Ant. 1 disembark, go ashore; detrain. 2 end, terminate.

embarrass v. *embarrassed by a child's bad behavior:* mortify, shame, abash, chagrin; disconcert, upset, discompose.

embellish v. *Writing embellished with curlicues:* enhance, ornament, decorate, adorn, beautify, garnish, dress up.

embezzle v. *Don't embezzle money:* misappropriate; defraud, swindle, cheat; *Slang* fleece.

embitter v. *Being fired embittered me:* make bitter, make resentful, make rancorous, rankle, sour.

embody v. 1 *The poem embodies my love of nature:* express, represent, personify, exemplify, manifest. 2 *The testimony is embodied in the court record:* include, incorporate, contain; assimilate, merge.

embrace v. 1 *The two sisters embraced:* hug; grasp, clasp. 2 *Iceland embraced Christianity:* accept, espouse, adopt. 3 *The study embraced all aspects of the problem:* include,

involve, contain, incorporate, cover, encompass.

Ant. 2 spurn, reject, repudiate. 3 omit, exclude; ignore, disregard.

embroider v. *He embroidered his adventures as years passed:* embellish, elaborate, exaggerate, dress up; romanticize.

embryonic adj. *an embryonic plan:* undeveloped, beginning, rudimentary, incipient, immature; rough.

emend v. *The report must be emended:* correct, revise, improve, change.

emerge v. 1 *Life emerged from the sea:* rise, surface, issue, come forth, come into view. 2 *A solution emerged:* develop, arise, dawn, become apparent, surface, appear, come to light, turn up.

Ant. 1 submerge, sink. 2 disappear, hide.

emergency n. *Sound the alarm in case of emergency:* unforeseen danger, pressing necessity, contingency, exigency; crisis.

emigrate v. *The Russian emigrated to Canada:* move, migrate, remove; leave, depart.

Ant. immigrate.

émigré n. *Vienna was full of émigrés:* exile, emigrant, expatriate, refugee, immigrant.

eminence n. 1 *Toscanini's eminence as a conductor:* high position, elevated rank, repute, public esteem, preeminence, importance, standing, prominence, fame, celebrity, conspicuousness, greatness. 2 *an eminence overlooking the sea:* elevation, high place, height, prominence, promontory; hill, summit, rise, peak, bluff, cliff.

Ant. 2 lowland, declivity, valley.

eminent adj. 1 *an eminent statesman:* illustrious, preeminent, high-ranking, important, esteemed, distinguished, famous, renowned, prominent, well-known, outstanding, noted, great. 2 *The situation was handled with eminent restraint:* extraordinary, remarkable, outstanding, noteworthy.

Ant. 1 undistinguished; unknown. 2 unremarkable, ordinary.

emissary n. *the queen's emissary:* delegate, ambassador, envoy, representative, deputy, agent.

emission n. 1 *automobile exhaust emissions:* discharge, ejection, expulsion, excretion; *(variously)* smoke, fumes, pollutant, waste. 2 *the emission of radio signals:* sending out, emitting, transmission, issuance.

emit v. *The radiator emits little warmth:* send out, give forth, discharge, issue, secrete, dispatch, expel, excrete.

Ant. receive; retain, withhold.

emollient adj. 1 *The lotion had an emollient effect:* soothing, relieving, palliative, alleviative, healing; assuasive, calming, relaxing.

—*n.* **2** *an emollient for skin rash:* balm, salve, lotion, ointment; lubricant, oil.
Ant. **1** irritating, painful, aggravating.

emotion *n.* *The candidate spoke with emotion:* strong feeling, fullness of heart, passion, sentiment, zeal, ardor, fervor; *(variously)* love, hate, anger, jealousy, sorrow, sadness, fear, happiness, satisfaction, pride.
Ant. indifference, apathy.

emotional *adj.* **1** *an emotional occasion:* sentimental, moving, touching, heartwarming, thrilling. **2** *He's too emotional:* easily affected by emotion, temperamental, demonstrative, sentimental; passionate, fervent, ardent, zealous, impetuous; excitable, hysterical, high-strung.
Ant. **1, 2** unemotional. **2** unfeeling, indifferent, apathetic, undemonstrative, unsentimental, unexcitable.

emperor, empress *n.* *the emperor of Japan:* ruler, monarch, sovereign; *(variously)* caesar, czar, mikado, kaiser; *(fem.)* czarina, sultana.

emphasis *n.* **1** *The emphasis must be on cutting costs:* stress, prominent point, feature. **2** *Put the emphasis on the first syllable:* stress, accent, accentuation.

emphasize *v.* *The biography emphasized his boyhood:* stress, accent, feature, dwell on.
Ant. deemphasize, play down, underplay.

emphatic *adj.* **1** *an emphatic denial:* strong, vigorous, forceful, assertive, decisive, unqualified, unequivocal, insistent, categorical. **2** *an emphatic success:* definite, unmistakable, undeniable, striking, distinct, decided, telling, marked, pronounced, conspicuous.
Ant. **1** weak, qualified, equivocal. **2** uncertain.

empire *n.* *the British Empire:* sovereignty, dominion, realm, domain, commonwealth, imperium.

empirical *adj.* *empirical knowledge:* practical, experiential, pragmatic; firsthand.
Ant. theoretical, secondhand.

employ *v.* **1** *to employ workers:* hire, use, engage, retain, take on. **2** *She employs her time well:* use, utilize, make use of, apply, occupy. —*n.* **3** *in the employ of a large company:* service, employment; hire.
Ant. **1** discharge, dismiss, fire. **2** waste, fritter away.

employee *n.* *wage increases for all employees:* worker, wage earner, job holder, staff member.
Ant. employer.

employer *n.* *She was my employer for 20 years:* boss; proprietor, business owner;

business, firm, company, organization, outfit.
Ant. employee, worker, wage earner, staff member.

employment *n.* **1** *I'm looking for summer employment:* work, job, employ; service; occupation, business, profession, vocation, pursuit, trade, field, line; task, chore. **2** *the employment of great ingenuity:* utilization, exertion, use, employing, application, exercise.
Ant. **1** leisure, inactivity. **2** disuse, putting aside.

empower *v.* **1** *Police are empowered to make arrests:* authorize, sanction, invest, vest, license, permit, allow, enable; delegate. **2** *The workers empowered themselves:* make powerful, take control, become confident.
Ant. **1** disbar, forbid, enjoin. **2** lack confidence, be weak.

empty *adj.* **1** *an empty house:* vacant, unoccupied, uninhabited; bare, void. **2** *an empty life:* aimless, meaningless, purposeless, unfulfilled, idle. —*v.* **3** *The Mississippi empties into the Gulf of Mexico:* pour out, drain, dump, evacuate; discharge, flow.
Ant. **1** full; occupied, inhabited. **2** meaningful, purposeful, fulfilled, busy, full, rich. **3** fill.

emulate *v.* *Emulate Abraham Lincoln:* take as a model, follow the example of, follow, copy, imitate; mimic, ape.

enable *v.* *Education enables a person to get a better job:* make able, empower, qualify, allow, permit; aid, assist, facilitate, benefit.
Ant. prevent, bar, disqualify, prohibit; hinder, thwart.

enact *v.* *Congress enacted the bill:* pass into law, pass, legislate, authorize, approve.
Ant. reject, vote down, veto; annul, repeal.

enamor *v.* *John is enamored of power:* enrapture, infatuate, draw to, enthrall, charm, enchant, entrance, captivate, bewitch, fascinate.
Ant. repel, repulse, revolt, disgust.

enchant *v.* **1** *The sorcerer enchanted the forest:* cast a spell over, place under a spell, bewitch. **2** *We were enchanted with the child:* charm, delight, entrance, enthrall, captivate, enrapture, fascinate.
Ant. **2** repel, repulse, revolt, disgust.

enchantress *n.* **1** *The enchantress turned the prince into a frog:* sorceress, witch. **2** *a powerful enchantress:* seductress, temptress, vamp, charmer, femme fatale.

encircle *v.* *A fence encircles the compound:* circle, ring, surround, girdle, gird; enclose, fence.

enclose Also **inclose** *v.* **1** *A stone wall en-*

closed the estate: surround, ring, circle, encircle, fence in, wall in, close in. 2 *Please enclose a check:* include, insert, put in the same envelope.

encompass *v.* 1 *High mountains encompass the ski resort:* surround, encircle, circle, ring. 2 *The encyclopedia encompasses much information:* include, cover, embrace, contain, comprise, incorporate.
Ant. 2 exclude, leave out, omit.

encounter *v.* 1 *to encounter difficulties:* meet, chance upon; run into, experience, come upon. 2 *Napoleon encountered Wellington at Waterloo:* clash with, do battle with, confront, engage, face. —*n.* 3 *Many men were lost in the encounter:* battle, combat, fight, confrontation, bout, engagement.
Ant. 1 shun, elude, avoid.

encourage *v.* 1 *We encouraged the mayor to run again:* inspire, give confidence to, induce, hearten, rally, spur, exhort, reassure, hearten, cheer. 2 *Good health encourages clear thinking:* foster, promote, advance, further, assist, help, aid.
Ant. 1 discourage, dissuade; dishearten, dispirit. 2 retard, hinder, inhibit.

encouragement *n.* *A little encouragement is all some people need:* encouraging, praise, support, reassurance; boost, lift.
Ant. discouragement, criticism.

encroach *v.* *to encroach on a person's rights:* intrude, infringe, invade, impinge, violate, trespass, interfere.
Ant. safeguard, protect.

encumber *v.* *encumbered by a heavy pack:* burden, weigh down, load down, lade, saddle; hinder, impede.

end *n.* 1 *at the south end of town:* extremity, terminus; edge, limit, boundary. 2 *We stayed to the very end:* conclusion, ending, termination, close, finish, expiration, cessation, completion, finale. 3 *What will be the end of their deliberations?:* outcome, result, consequence, effect. 4 *Ends rarely justify the means:* aim, goal, purpose, object, objective, result. 5 *the end of civilization:* extinction, extermination, destruction, annihilation, termination, ruin; death. —*v.* 6 *The book ends on page 364:* conclude, halt, draw to a close, terminate, cease, finish, stop, leave off, close.
Ant. 1, 2, 3, 5 beginning, start, inauguration; inception, birth. 6 begin, start, commence.

endanger *v.* *Pollution endangers wildlife:* threaten, put in danger, imperil, jeopardize, preserve.

endear *v.* *Her good humor endeared her to*

us: make dear; create goodwill among, ingratiate with.
Ant. alienate, estrange.

endearment *n.* *letters full of endearments:* loving word, sweet talk; affectionate term.
Ant. curse, malediction.

endeavor *v.* 1 *Endeavor to be more considerate:* try, attempt, strive, undertake; aspire, aim, seek. —*n.* 2 *an honest endeavor to do the work:* attempt, effort, try, exertion, striving. 3 *a lifelong endeavor:* undertaking, enterprise, work, preoccupation, interest.

ending *n.* *a happy ending:* conclusion, end, close, finish, termination, cessation, completion, culmination.
Ant. beginning, start, inception.

endless *adj.* *their endless bickering:* without end, unending, uninterrupted, interminable, infinite, unlimited; perpetual, everlasting, never-ending, eternal; constant, continuous, continual, persistent.
Ant. limited, temporary, brief, passing, transient.

endorse Also **indorse** *v.* 1 *to endorse a candidate:* support, back, champion, approve, advocate, recommend, stand behind. 2 *Endorse the check:* sign, countersign; authorize, validate, certify.
Ant. 1 denounce, reject, repudiate.

endow *v.* 1 *Grandfather endowed each child with a trust fund:* bequeath, settle on, leave, will; confer, grant, bestow. 2 *Nature endowed her with wit:* supply, equip, provide, accord, grant, furnish; bless, grace, favor.
Ant. 2 divest, deprive, take.

endowment *n.* 1 *He left an endowment to each child:* legacy, bequest, grant, gift, donation. 2 *A natural bent for music is one of her endowments:* natural gift, talent, aptitude, attribute.

endurance *n.* *The marathon required great endurance:* stamina, durability, strength; fortitude, perseverance, persistence, staying power; permanence, stability.
Ant. frailty, weakness.

endure *v.* 1 *We endured tremendous losses:* sustain, bear, withstand, stand, experience, undergo, weather, suffer, bear up under; countenance, brook. 2 *Their love would endure:* last, persist, prevail, live on, continue.
Ant. 1 evade, avoid, sidestep, be defeated by. 2 perish, die, end, wither away.

enemy *n.* 1 *He has many enemies:* antagonist, detractor, opponent, adversary, foe, rival, competitor. 2 *The enemy was advancing:* opposing military force, hostile nation, belligerent state.
Ant. 1 friend, supporter. 2 ally, confederate.

energetic *adj.* *an energetic worker:* full of

energy, active, vigorous, lively, animated; forceful, dynamic, hard-working, industrious.

Ant. lethargic, sluggish, listless; phlegmatic.

energy *n. Her energy never seems to give out:* vitality, vigor, verve, pep, liveliness, animation, zest, enterprise.

Ant. lassitude, listlessness, sluggishness.

enervate *v. The hot weather enervated us:* exhaust, weary, weaken, debilitate, devitalize, sap one's energy, fatigue, tire.

Ant. energize, invigorate, vitalize.

enforce *v. The police must enforce the law:* carry out, administer, compel obedience to, implement, execute, apply.

Ant. ignore, disregard; waive.

engage *v.* 1 *They are engaged in many activities:* involve, occupy, engross, absorb; participate, partake. 2 *to engage another worker:* employ, hire, take on, retain, take into service. 3 *The couple married after being engaged a month:* betroth, affiance, pledge. 4 *The battleship engaged the enemy:* begin conflict with, encounter in battle, fight with, give battle to.

Ant. 2 fire, lay off, let go.

engagement *n.* 1 *a luncheon engagement:* appointment, date, meeting. 2 *The couple announced their engagement:* betrothal, troth, affiancing. 3 *She had a brief engagement as a singer:* employment, job, position, situation, billet. 4 *a major engagement with the enemy:* battle, fight, encounter, combat, action, bout.

engaging *adj. an engaging manner:* winning, winsome, charming, fetching, pleasing, likable, lovable, appealing, ingratiating.

Ant. disagreeable, unpleasant, unlikable, unlovable; repulsive, repellent.

engender *v. Respect can engender love:* cause, beget, breed, generate, produce, occasion, precipitate.

Ant. kill, end, crush.

engross *v. I was completely engrossed in the book:* absorb, preoccupy, involve, immerse, engage.

engulf *v. The flood engulfed the village:* swallow up, envelop, bury, overrun, inundate, submerge, immerse.

enhance *v. Health enhances pleasure:* intensify, heighten, make more attractive; elevate, lift.

Ant. lessen, minimize, detract from.

enigma *n. Why he switched political parties is an enigma:* puzzle, riddle, question, conundrum, mystery.

enigmatic, enigmatical *adj. an enigmatic smile:* mysterious, puzzling, indeci-

pherable, perplexing, inscrutable, elusive, ambiguous.

Ant. candid, frank, open; explicit, express.

enjoin *v.* 1 *The fire fighters enjoined the onlookers to stand clear:* advise, counsel, warn, admonish, command, bid, charge, direct, instruct; beg, ask, urge. 2 *The judge enjoined the strikers from picketing:* prohibit, forbid, restrain, ban, bar.

Ant. 2 permit, allow, let.

enjoy *v. She enjoyed the opera:* like, appreciate, take pleasure in, delight in, fancy, relish; savor.

Ant. dislike, hate, detest, despise.

enjoyable *adj. an enjoyable evening:* pleasant, pleasing, pleasurable, fun-filled, delightful, satisfying, gratifying.

Ant. unpleasant, disagreeable, unenjoyable, unpleasurable, unsatisfying.

enjoyment *n.* 1 *The resort provides for its guests' enjoyment:* pleasure, delight, satisfaction, gratification, joy, relish; fun, entertainment, amusement, good time. 2 *Every citizen is guaranteed the enjoyment of liberty:* benefit, advantage, blessing, right, exercise, possession.

Ant. 1 displeasure, dissatisfaction, dislike. 2 disadvantage, handicap.

enlarge *v.* 1 *The hotel is being enlarged:* make larger, expand, swell, extend, inflate, augment, add to, multiply; magnify, amplify; grow, develop. 2 *Please enlarge on your statement:* expand, amplify, elaborate, expound.

Ant. 1 shrink, contract, reduce, diminish, lessen.

enlighten *v. The tour of the battlefield enlightened the historian:* inform, instruct, educate, edify, clarify, apprise, advise.

Ant. mystify, perplex, puzzle, mislead, confuse.

enlist *v.* 1 *to enlist in the army:* join, join up; enroll, sign up, volunteer. 2 *Enlist every citizen in the clean-up campaign:* recruit, engage, obtain, gain the assistance of.

Ant. 1 resign, retire.

enliven *v. Games enlivened the party:* make lively, animate, pep up, cheer up, brighten, wake up.

Ant. dampen, cast a pall over, subdue, depress.

enmity *n. Strong enmity remains between them:* hostility, ill will, rancor, acrimony, animosity, bitterness, antipathy, malice, bad blood.

Ant. goodwill, amity, friendliness, love, affection.

ennui *n. An idle life causes ennui:* weariness,

boredom, tedium, languor, listlessness, lassitude.

Ant. excitement, interest.

enormity *n.* 1 *the enormity of the crime:* monstrousness, atrociousness, outrageousness, vileness, villainy, depravity, viciousness, wickedness, evilness, malignity. 2 *The enormity of the task overwhelmed them:* immensity, vastness, largeness, enormousness.

Ant. 1 inoffensiveness, innocuousness, harmlessness. 2 smallness, insignificance.

enormous *adj. an enormous room:* huge, vast, immense, colossal, gigantic, mammoth, gargantuan, massive.

Ant. small, little, tiny, minute, miniscule, teeny.

enough *adj.* 1 *Is there enough food for everyone?:* adequate, sufficient, ample, plenty, abundant, copious. —*pron.* 2 *Did you buy enough?:* sufficient amount, sufficiency, ample supply, full measure. —*adv.* 3 *I'm hungry enough to eat a bear:* adequately, sufficiently, amply, abundantly; tolerably, reasonably.

Ant. 1 inadequate, insufficient. 2 insufficiency, inadequacy. 3 inadequately, insufficiently.

enrage *v. Sloppy work enrages me:* infuriate, incense, make furious, anger, throw into a rage.

Ant. placate, pacify, appease, mollify.

enrapture *v. Her singing enraptured audiences:* enthrall, hold rapt, entrance, enchant, captivate, delight.

enrich *v.* 1 *Oil enriched the Arab nations:* make rich, make wealthy. 2 *enriched with vitamins and minerals:* elevate, improve; enhance, fortify, endow; embellish.

Ant. 1 impoverish.

enroll *v. to enroll new students:* register, sign up, enter; admit, accept; enlist, join, recruit.

Ant. dismiss, expel.

enrollment *n. Today is the day for enrollment in the swimming classes:* enrolling, registration, signing up; enlistment, admittance.

Ant. withdrawing, dropping out.

ensemble *n.* 1 *Mixing furniture styles in a room can make a striking ensemble:* totality, entirety, grouping, assembly, aggregate. 2 *She wears a different ensemble every day:* outfit, costume, attire. 3 *The entire ensemble of dancers took a bow:* company, troupe.

ensign *n. the ship's ensign:* flag, banner, standard, pennant, pennon, colors.

enslave *v. The tyrant enslaved the peasants:* make a slave of, enthrall, indenture; subjugate, capture, dominate.

Ant. free, emancipate, liberate.

ensue *v. After the rains, floods ensued:* follow, result, come to pass, derive.

Ant. herald, precede, introduce.

ensure Also **insure** *v.* 1 *Come early to ensure getting a good seat:* assure, be sure of, make sure; guarantee, warrant, secure. 2 *Will carrying a rabbit's foot ensure me from harm?:* protect, guard, safeguard, secure.

entail *v. The job entails selling:* require, necessitate, call for; include, involve, incorporate, occasion.

entangle *v.* 1 *entangled in the netting:* tangle, enmesh, ensnare, snare; snarl, intertwine, twist up. 2 *entangled in a web of lies:* tangle, catch, trap, involve, embroil; complicate; confuse, muddle.

Ant. 1 disentangle, free, extricate.

entente *n. an entente between nations:* understanding, rapprochement, agreement, accord, understanding; pact, treaty.

Ant. disagreement, conflict, dispute, discord.

enter *v.* 1 *The thief entered by a window:* come in, go in, proceed into, make an entrance, arrive, penetrate. 2 *to enter the diplomatic corps:* join, embark upon, become a member of; participate in, take part in. 3 *Enter your name for the contest:* enroll in, sign up for, register for, join; list, record, post, inscribe.

Ant. 1 exit, leave, depart, go. 2, 3 leave, withdraw from, resign from, retire from.

enterprise *n.* 1 *the firm's latest enterprise:* undertaking, venture, endeavor, project, operation, effort, task. 2 *We were pleased with the enterprise:* initiative, drive, aggressiveness, push, ingenuity, ambition, industry, energy, zeal, daring.

Ant. laziness, spiritlessness, indolence.

enterprising *adj. an enterprising student:* ambitious, aggressive, industrious, hardworking, energetic, venturesome, inventive, bold, zealous.

Ant. lazy, indolent, cautious.

entertain *v.* 1 *The magician entertained the children:* amuse, divert, give enjoyment to, regale. 2 *Diplomats entertain often:* have guests, give a party, play host. 3 *We cannot entertain such outrageous ideas:* consider, admit, contemplate, imagine, harbor.

Ant. 1 bore; disgust. 3 reject, ignore, disregard.

entertainment *n. The city offers all kinds of entertainment:* amusement, diversion, distraction, divertissement, fun, good time, pastime, pleasure, enjoyment, satisfaction.

enthrall, enthral *v. The acrobats enthralled the audience:* spellbind, fascinate;

enchant, captivate, charm, transfix, rivet, entrance, thrill.
Ant. bore, disinterest.

enthusiasm *n.* 1 *We are looking forward with enthusiasm to your visit:* eagerness, keenness, anticipation, ardor, relish, exuberance, elation. 2 *Her great enthusiasm is skiing:* interest, passion, love, devotion, craze; diversion, distraction.
Ant. 1 apathy, indifference, aloofness.

enthusiast *n. a baseball enthusiast:* fan, buff, devotee, aficionado.

enthusiastic *adj. an enthusiastic golfer. enthusiastic praise:* wholehearted, ardent, fervent, fervid, zealous, passionate; unqualified, unstinting.
Ant. blasé, lukewarm, unenthusiastic, disinterested, halfhearted.

entice *v. Can we entice you to come to the party?:* induce, tempt, lure, allure, attract; persuade, coax.
Ant. discourage, dissuade.

entire *adj.* 1 *The entire school turned out for the game:* whole, total, full, complete, all-inclusive. 2 *The vase was entire:* intact, unbroken, undamaged.
Ant. 1 partial, incomplete. 2 broken, damaged.

entirely *adv. He's entirely wrong:* completely, wholly, fully, totally, thoroughly, altogether, utterly, absolutely.
Ant. partially, somewhat, partly.

entitle *v. This coupon entitles you to a free lesson:* give the right to, authorize, make eligible, allow, permit.

entity *n. an unknown entity:* thing, object, article, body, substance, quantity.
Ant. nonentity, illusion, mirage, chimera.

entourage *n. The king traveled with an entourage:* retinue, attendants, cortege, escort, following, staff, court, associates.

entrance[1] *n.* 1 *the front entrance:* entry, entranceway, way in; access, approach, ingress. 2 *They were refused entrance:* permission to enter, entry, admittance, access. 3 *Her entrance caught everyone's attention:* entry, coming in, appearance.
Ant. exit, departure, egress.

entrance[2] *v. a toy to entrance any child:* delight, gladden, enrapture, spellbind, fascinate, captivate, charm, beguile.
Ant. bore, disinterest.

entrap *v. He says the police entrapped him:* tempt, entice, allure; capture, snare, catch, ensnare.

entreat *v. I entreat you to contribute:* beseech, implore, plead with, appeal to, exhort, request, beg, supplicate, petition.
Ant. command, direct, demand.

entreaty *n. the prisoner's entreaty for*

mercy: earnest request, plea, appeal, supplication, prayer, petition.
Ant. demand, ultimatum.

entrée, entree *n.* 1 *He has entrée into the best social circles:* admittance, admission, entry, entrance, access. 2 *The price includes entrée, dessert, and coffee:* main course, main dish.

entrench Also **intrench** *v. Most habits are entrenched during childhood:* fix, set, install; embed, implant, ingrain, plant, root.

entrust Also **intrust** *v. The manager is entrusted with full responsibility:* trust, put in trust of, charge with, give the custody of, commit, assign, delegate.

entry *n.* 1 *the entry to the estate:* entranceway, way, approach, ingress, access. 2 *Please wait in the entry:* entrance hall, foyer, doorway, vestibule. 3 *An ovation greeted her entry into the hall:* approach, entrance; admission, admittance, ingress. 4 *a diary entry:* record, registration; note, memo, minute, item, jotting.
Ant. 1 exit, egress. 3 exit, departure, leaving, leave-taking.

enumerate *v.* 1 *The teacher enumerated the spelling mistakes:* specify, numerate, cite, detail, recount. 2 *Enumerate the items to be sure none is missing:* count, count up, add, add up, sum up, total, tally, tabulate, number, list, tick off.

enunciate *v. to enunciate clearly:* pronounce, articulate, sound, speak.

envelop *v. Fog enveloped the town:* wrap, enwrap, cover, sheathe, engulf, encircle, blanket, shroud, veil; contain, encompass.

envelope *n. Put the letter in an envelope:* paper wrapper, wrapping, jacket, cover, covering.

enviable *adj. in an enviable position:* covetable; desirable, advantageous, agreeable, beneficial, fortunate.

envious *adj. Don't be envious of a friend's good fortune:* jealous, filled with envy, green with envy, covetous; resentful, spiteful.

environment *n. Mold grows best in a warm environment. a loving environment:* medium, habitat, element; surroundings, setting, locale, scene, milieu, atmosphere, ambience, background.

environs *n. pl. the city and its environs:* outskirts, suburbs, surrounding area, outlying area.
Ant. central city, inner city.

envisage *v. Envisage the Swiss Alps:* picture, imagine, visualize, conceive, envision, conceptualize, dream of.

envoy *n. The president sent a special envoy to*

France: representative, delegate, emissary, ambassador, agent, deputy, minister, attaché, legate.

envy *n.* 1 *It is hard to suppress envy:* jealousy, enviousness, resentfulness, resentment, grudging, covetousness. —*v.* 2 *It's hard not to envy someone who has everything:* feel envious toward, be jealous of, resent, begrudge.

ephemeral *adj. the ephemeral joys of youth:* brief, temporary, transient, short-lived, transitory, fleeting, evanescent, passing.
Ant. permanent, lasting, everlasting, perpetual.

epic *n.* 1 *The Aeneid is a great epic:* epic poem, historic poem, heroic poem; heroic adventure. —*adj.* 2 *Ulysses is an epic character:* heroic, majestic, noble; legendary, fabled.

epidemic *n.* 1 *Thousands died in the flu epidemic:* outbreak, plague, pestilence, scourge. —*adj.* 2 *an epidemic disease:* dangerously contagious, pandemic, rampant, widespread, far-reaching, pervasive, prevailing; catching, infectious.

epigram *n. Oscar Wilde was celebrated for his epigrams:* witty saying, bon mot, witticism, quip; maxim, apothegm, aphorism, adage.

epilogue *n. the book's epilogue:* final section, addendum, rider, codicil, afterword; concluding speech.
Ant. preface, prologue, introduction.

episode *n.* 1 *We'll forget this little episode:* event, occurrence, happening, incident, affair. 2 *a famous episode in the novel:* scene, passage, section, chapter; installment.

epistle *n.* 1 *St. Paul's Epistle to the Ephesians:* letter, missive, encyclical, written communication, message.

epithet *n.* 1 *"The Conqueror" was an epithet of William I of England:* appellation, designation, sobriquet, nickname. 2 *He screamed epithets at us:* curse, abusive word, insult, expletive.

epitome *n. She is the epitome of wit:* embodiment, exemplification, typification; ideal, height.

epoch *n. The Renaissance was an epoch of achievement:* period, age, era, time.

equable *adj.* 1 *an equable disposition:* even-tempered, easygoing, calm, serene, imperturbable, *Slang* unflappable; good-natured, agreeable, pleasant. 2 *Florida has an equable climate:* uniform, constant, unvaried, unchanging, even, steady, consistent.
Ant. 1 nervous, excitable, temperamental; disagreeable, unpleasant. 2 variable, changeable, uneven, inconsistent.

equal *adj.* 1 *of equal height:* the same, even,

like, uniform; identical; matched, equivalent, corresponding. —*n.* 2 *Their Minister of Foreign Affairs is the equal of our Secretary of State:* peer, match; equivalent, counterpart, opposite number. —*v.* 3 *The debits must equal the credits:* be the same as, be identical to, accord with, agree with, tally with, match, balance with.
Ant. 1 unequal, different, uneven, dissimilar, diverse. 3 be unequal, disagree, diverge.

equality *n.* 1 *Democracy must offer everyone equality:* equal opportunity, justice, impartiality, fair play. 2 *equality of pay for women:* parity, coequality, uniformity, equivalency, correspondence.
Ant. 1 inequality, injustice, unfairness. 2 inequality, dissimilarity, difference.

equanimity *n. We must keep our equanimity:* calmness, composure, self-possession, steadiness, poise, aplomb, imperturbability, presence of mind.
Ant. panic, hysteria, disquiet, discomposure.

equate *v. You can't equate money with happiness:* equal out, match, be equivalent to, equalize, average, balance; consider as, draw a parallel between, compare, liken.

equilibrium *n. The scale is in equilibrium:* balance, stability, equipoise.

equip *v. Equip yourself with a tent:* furnish, supply, outfit, provide, provision, stock.

equipment *n. fishing equipment:* apparatus, gear, paraphernalia, matériel, accoutrements, equipage, tackle, stuff.

equitable *adj. an equitable settlement:* fair, just, evenhanded, reasonable, proper.
Ant. inequitable, unfair, unjust, unreasonable.

equity *n.* 1 *The Court must judge with complete equity:* impartiality, fairmindedness, fairness, evenhandedness. 2 *The family has $35,000 equity in the house:* assets over liabilities, assets after mortgage, cash value; assets, investment.
Ant. 1 unfairness, partiality, bias, prejudice.

equivalent *adj.* 1 *A dime is equivalent to ten pennies:* equal, comparable, commensurate with, corresponding, correlative; even. —*n.* 2 *It cost the equivalent of a week's salary:* equal amount; peer, counterpart, parallel.
Ant. 1 unequal, incomparable.

equivocal *adj. an equivocal feeling:* ambivalent, ambiguous, imprecise, undecided, uncertain, doubtful.
Ant. precise, definite, specific, clear-cut.

equivocate *v. Please stop equivocating!:* evade, avoid the issue, hedge, stall, pussyfoot, mince words, straddle the fence.

era *n. the Christian era:* period, age, epoch, time.

eradicate *v. to eradicate crime:* eliminate, exterminate, erase, expunge, extirpate, destroy, wipe out, get rid of, abolish.
Ant. establish, implant, create.

erase *v. Erase the penciled notes:* wipe away, rub out, eradicate, expunge; remove, eliminate, delete.

erect *adj.* 1 *an erect posture:* upright, vertical, straight, unstooped; stiff, rigid. —*v.* 2 *The town will erect a monument:* construct, build, put up, raise.
Ant. 1 horizontal, stopped, bent. 2 raze, demolish, tear down.

erode *v. Acid erodes metal:* corrode, eat away; wear away.

erotic *adj. John Donne wrote several erotic poems:* wanton, suggestive, risqué; lascivious, lewd, lusty; sexual, sexy, sexually stimulating, carnal.

err *v.* 1 *to err in math:* make a mistake, be incorrect, be in error, miscalculate. 2 *to err is human:* lapse from virtue, transgress, sin, go astray, do wrong.

erratic *adj. erratic behavior:* inconsistent, unpredictable, unstable, changeable; odd, strange, peculiar, unusual; unnatural, wayward, abnormal.
Ant. consistent, unchanging, stable, predictable, dependable; normal, natural.

erroneous *adj. The conclusion is erroneous:* inaccurate, incorrect, untrue, wrong, fallacious, mistaken.
Ant. correct, accurate, true.

error *n. an error in addition:* mistake, inaccuracy, miscalculation, fault; misconception, misunderstanding, misapprehension, fallacy.

ersatz *adj. ersatz coffee:* synthetic, artificial, imitation, counterfeit, fake, phony.
Ant. real, genuine, authentic.

erstwhile *adj. an erstwhile friend:* former, past, bygone, *Informal* ex.
Ant. current, present.

erudite *adj. an erudite speaker:* learned, well-educated, literate, well-read; thoughtful, well-reasoned.
Ant. uninformed, uneducated, illiterate, unthinking.

erudition *n. an individual of formidable erudition:* learning, education, knowledge, learnedness, scholarship, literacy, schooling.

erupt *v. Lava erupted from the volcano:* burst forth, pour forth, belch forth, emit, vent, flow forth, gush.

eruption *n.* 1 *the eruption of lava from the volcano:* discharge, ejection, venting, bursting forth, outbreak, pouring forth, flare-up,

outpouring, belching forth, flowing forth, gushing. 2 *a skin eruption:* rash, inflammation, breaking out; dermatitis, eczema.

escalate *v.* 1 *Prices are escalating:* rise, increase, advance, ascend, elevate, mount. 2 *The enemy escalated the war:* intensify, step up, expand, amplify.
Ant. 1 lower, decrease, fall, descend. 2 deescalate, limit, narrow.

escapade *n. the students' latest escapade:* prank, caper, antic, mischief; lark, fling, spree; adventure.

escape *v.* 1 *The prisoner escaped:* break free, get away, make a getaway, make off, slip away, run away, flee, abscond, avoid capture. 2 *The skiers escaped the avalanche. to escape doing work:* get away safely, avert; avoid, skirt, shun. 3 *Gas is escaping from the pipe:* issue, emerge, emanate, be emitted; leak, seep, pour forth, flow, stream, gush. —*n.* 4 *How did the prisoners manage their escape?:* breakout, flight, getaway. 5 *Her escape from the fire was miraculous:* avoidance of danger, extrication, deliverance. 6 *Television is my favorite escape:* diversion, distraction, way of getting away from it all. 7 *an escape of gas from the tank:* emission, outflow, leakage, seepage, issuing forth, pouring forth, outburst.
Ant. 1 capture, apprehend. 4 capture, apprehension.

eschew *v. Eschew fattening foods:* abstain from, forgo, give up, avoid, shun.
Ant. seek, indulge in, welcome.

escort *n.* 1 *The king's escort totaled 50 men:* guard, retinue, cortege, entourage, attendants. 2 *an escort for the dance:* date, companion, conductor, chaperon. —*v.* 3 *Let me escort you to the door:* conduct, guide, lead the way, take, usher; squire, chaperon.

esoteric *adj.* 1 *Some fields of science seem hopelessly esoteric:* abstruse, recondite, arcane, mysterious, obscure; mystical, occult.
Ant. obvious, simple.

especial *adj.* See SPECIAL.

especially *adv.* 1 *The dress was made especially for her:* expressly, specifically, exclusively; particularly, primarily. 2 *The sunsets here are especially beautiful:* exceptionally, outstandingly, particularly, extraordinarily, unusually.

espouse *v. to espouse conservation:* adopt, take up, embrace; support, champion, advocate, promote, express belief in.
Ant. reject, abjure; denounce, block, thwart.

essay *n.* 1 *The assignment was to write an essay:* short composition, theme, paper; treatise, editorial, article, commentary, critique. 2 *His first essay at flying was a near* *disaster:* attempt, effort, try, venture. —*v.* 3 *Who will essay crossing the stream first?:* try, attempt, undertake, venture.

essence *n.* 1 *the very essence of justice:* basic quality, essential character, quintessence, nature, principle, life-blood, heart, soul; meaning, significance. 2 *essence of turpentine:* concentrate, tincture, elixir, spirits, extract. 3 *My favorite essence smells like gardenias:* perfume, scent, cologne, fragrance, toilet water.

essential *adj.* 1 *Water is essential to crops:* indispensable, necessary, needed, crucial, vital. 2 *The essential purpose of a vacation is to relax:* basic, fundamental; main, principal, important, inherent, intrinsic. —*n.* 3 *(sometimes pl.) Petroleum is an essential of modern industry. the essentials of French:* requisite, necessity, indispensable element, vital part; basics, fundamentals, principles. *Ant.* 1, 2 dispensable, unimportant, incidental, unnecessary, immaterial.

establish *v.* 1 *to establish a business:* institute, found, form, organize, create, begin, start, initiate. 2 *He established himself as an expert on stamps:* gain recognition for, install, settle. 3 *The evidence establishes their guilt:* prove, show, confirm, demonstrate, sustain, uphold, validate; justify, warrant. *Ant.* 1 close, dissolve, liquidate. 3 refute, deny, question.

establishment *n.* 1 *the establishment of a new school:* establishing, instituting, founding, formation, institution, organization, creation. 2 *The mill is the oldest establishment in town:* business, company, concern, firm, corporation, organization. *Ant.* 1 closing, dissolution, disbanding.

estate *n.* 1 *He left an estate of a million dollars:* assets at death, assets, wealth, property, holdings; inheritance, legacy, bequest, will. 2 *At 21 a boy reaches a man's estate:* state, station, condition, status, period of life; rank, class.

esteem *v.* 1 *Shakespeare is esteemed as the best English playwright:* venerate, revere, hold in high regard, value, honor; prize, treasure, admire, look up to. 2 *Experts esteem it prudent:* consider, regard, believe, think, hold, deem. —*n.* 3 *I have the highest esteem for your honesty:* regard, respect, estimate, admiration, veneration, reverence. *Ant.* 1 disdain, scorn, disparage, decry; belittle, underrate. 3 contempt, disdain, scorn.

estimable *adj. an estimable poet:* highly regarded, worthwhile, important, admired, treasured, prized, respected, revered, praiseworthy, admirable. *Ant.* scorned, disdained; unworthy, undeserving, inferior, bad.

estimate *v.* 1 *The expert estimated the ring's value at $3,000:* evaluate, judge, reckon, calculate, appraise, value, assess, assay. 2 *The archaeologist estimated that the vase was 3,500 years old:* think, believe, surmise, guess, conjecture, opine. —*n.* 3 *The estimate is that the painting is worth $2,500:* evaluation, estimation, assessment, appraisal, calculation, assay; opinion, judgment, thinking, view.

estimation *n. the estimation of the critics:* opinion, judgment, appraisal, estimate, view, belief, consideration, evaluation.

estrange *v. Political differences estranged the two friends:* alienate, drive apart, part, make hostile. *Ant.* unite, bind; reconcile.

estuary *n. anchored in the estuary:* tidal basin, inlet, arm of the sea; river mouth.

eternal *adj.* 1 *eternal life:* lasting forever, everlasting, infinite, endless, immortal. 2 *his eternal nagging:* continual, unending, never-ending, perpetual, ceaseless, constant, endless. *Ant.* 1 transient, transitory, fleeting, finite, mortal. 2 occasional, spasmodic, temporary, on-and-off.

eternity *n.* 1 *My love will exist throughout eternity:* forever, infinity, time without end, eons and eons. 2 *The minister spoke about eternity:* everlasting life, immortality, the hereafter, the next world, the afterworld, the world to come; Heaven, paradise. *Ant.* 1 instant, moment. 2 the here and now, mortality.

ethereal *adj. ethereal beauty:* sublime, celestial, aerial, unearthly, unworldly; elusive, rare. *Ant.* earthly, mundane, worldly.

ethical *adj. ethical conduct:* moral, virtuous, honorable, upright, proper, just, fair, aboveboard. *Ant.* unethical, shady, unfair, unscrupulous, immoral.

ethics *n. pl. (Sometimes sing.) Ethics would never allow me to betray a friend:* moral code, moral standards, moral principle, principles, morality, conscience.

etiquette *n. the rules of etiquette:* polite behavior, amenities, protocol, conventions, civilities, manners, usage, decorum, courtesy; good form. *Ant.* impropriety, boorishness, rudeness, indecorum.

eulogize *v. The deceased was eulogized by friends:* praise highly, laud, panegyrize, extol, exalt, celebrate, pay tribute to. *Ant.* malign, defame, vilify, condemn.

eulogy *n. a graveside eulogy:* oration of praise, praise of the dead, encomium, pane-

gyric; tribute, homage, laudation, paean.
Ant. condemnation, criticism; vilification, defamation.

euphemism *n.* *"Five-fingered discount" is a euphemism for "theft":* mild expression, inoffensive expression, delicate term, refined term; prudish phrase.

evacuate *v.* 1 *to evacuate a building:* leave, quit, vacate; abandon, desert, forsake. 2 *Police evacuated the burning hotel:* remove, move out, take out, order out.
Ant. 1 enter, go in.

evade *v.* *The thief evaded the police. He evaded all questions about his past:* avoid, dodge, elude, duck, shun, side-step, circumvent, equivocate.
Ant. face, confront; encounter.

evaluate *v.* *The teacher evaluated each student:* appraise, rate, assess, judge, estimate, size up, value, assay.

evaporate *v.* 1 *The water evaporated:* dry up, vaporize, melt away; dehydrate, desiccate. 2 *When the fight ended the crowd evaporated:* disappear, vanish, fade away, melt away.
Ant. 1 condense, reconstitute, construct. 2 appear, materialize, gather.

evasion *n.* *the witness's evasion of the question:* avoidance, dodging, eluding, ducking, sidestepping, circumventing.
Ant. confronting, facing up to.

evasive *adj.* *an evasive answer:* elusive, elusory, ambiguous, equivocal, equivocating, dodging, hedging, devious, shifty, deceptive, misleading.
Ant. candid, straightforward, frank, guileless.

even *adj.* 1 *Plant the bushes in an even row:* level, smooth; flat, plumb, straight; parallel, uniform. 2 *The plane flew at an even speed:* constant, steady, uniform, unvarying, unwavering. 3 *Pour even amounts of milk into each cup:* equal, identical, the same, uniform. 4 *an even disposition:* even-tempered, calm, steady, equable, unruffled, unexcitable; balanced, fair, just, impartial, unbiased.
—*v.* 5 *Even that picture on the wall:* straighten, make parallel, make flush; smooth, level; equal, equalize, balance.
Ant. 1–4 uneven. 1 undulating, rough, bumpy; crooked, slanted, irregular. 2 variable, changing, fluctuating. 3 unequal, different. 4 emotional, excitable, easily ruffled; biased, unfair, prejudiced.

evening *n.* *Evening is a peaceful time:* sundown, sunset, twilight, dusk, gloaming; day's end, close of day; eve, even, eventide, nightfall.
Ant. dawn, sunrise, sunup, daylight.

event *n.* 1 *a major event in her life:* occur-

rence, occasion, episode, happening, experience, incident. 2 *track and field events:* contest, competition, tournament, game, bout.

eventful *adj.* *an eventful year:* noteworthy, notable, memorable, momentous, epochal, important, weighty, critical, crucial.
Ant. trivial, unimportant, insignificant, inconsequential, irrelevant.

eventual *adj.* *my eventual retirement:* future, prospective, later; upcoming, ultimate, final; following, subsequent, consequent, ensuing.

eventually *adv.* *The house will have to be repainted eventually:* sometime, one day, ultimately, sooner or later, finally, in the long run.
Ant. immediately, at once.

everlasting *adj.* 1 *May she rest in everlasting peace:* eternal, immortal, perpetual, lasting, never-ending. 2 *The everlasting beauty of the sea:* long-lasting, timeless, imperishable, indestructible, undying, continual. 3 *everlasting complaints:* constant, endless, ceaseless, unceasing, incessant, continuous, interminable.
Ant. 1, 2 transitory, temporary, passing, fleeting, ephemeral. 3 intermittent, occasional.

everyday *adj.* 1 *my everyday job:* daily, day after day, quotidian. 2 *Wear your everyday clothes:* ordinary, commonplace, workaday, usual, customary, familiar, established, regular; conventional, run-of-the-mill; mundane, trite.
Ant. 1 occasional, infrequent, irregular.

everywhere *adv.* *Flags flew everywhere:* every place, far and wide; extensively, ubiquitously; all over, throughout.
Ant. nowhere, here and there.

evict *v.* *The landlord evicted the tenant:* turn out, dispossess, expel, eject, oust, kick out, throw out.

evidence *n.* *The fingerprints were the main evidence:* proof, substantiation, documentation, corroboration, confirmation; exhibit, testimony, indication, sign, token.

evident *adj.* *It was evident the play was a hit:* clear, plain, obvious, manifest, conspicuous, noticeable, certain, patent; visible, tangible.
Ant. unclear, doubtful, uncertain, questionable; secret, known, undiscovered.

evidently *adv.* *He evidently has a cold:* apparently, assumedly, to all appearances; obviously, clearly, certainly, doubtless, doubtlessly.

evil *adj.* 1 *an evil king:* bad, wicked, iniquitous, immoral, sinful, base, malevolent, villainous, nefarious, heinous, black-hearted.
—*n.* 2 *The minister preached against evil:*

sin, wickedness, immorality, wrongdoing, vice, dépravity, corruption.
Ant. 1 good, honorable, moral, virtuous, benign. 2 good, goodness, virtue, morality, righteousness.

evoke *v. The book evoked fond memories:* call forth, summon, invoke, conjure up, elicit, induce, produce, stimulate, provoke, arouse, rouse, waken.
Ant. repress, suppress, inhibit, stifle, curb, check.

evolution *n. the evolution of medical research:* development, unfolding, progression, maturation; change, metamorphosis.

evolve *v. The plan evolved slowly:* develop, grow, unfold, mature, ripen.

exacerbate *v. Criticizing him will only exacerbate the situation:* aggravate, intensify, worsen, fan the flames, add fuel to the flames.
Ant. relieve, soothe, alleviate, assuage, mollify.

exact *adj.* 1 *Please give your exact age:* accurate, specific, explicit, precise. 2 *Watchmaking is an exact skill:* meticulous, painstaking, exacting, careful, punctilious, systematic, methodical. —*v.* 3 *The kidnappers exacted ransom:* demand, extract, require, compel, extort.
Ant. 1 approximate, imprecise. 2 sloppy, careless, slovenly.

exacting *adj.* 1 *a exacting teacher:* demanding, meticulous, unsparing, strict, unbending, stern, severe, harsh, hard, no-nonsense. 2 *an exacting task:* demanding, hard, arduous, difficult, trying, strenuous.
Ant. 1 easygoing, nonchalant, soft, lenient, permissive. 2 easy, effortless, undemanding.

exactly *adv.* 1 *Where exactly is the pain?:* precisely, specifically, explicitly; accurately, correctly, literally. 2 *You may do exactly as you like:* just, entirely, absolutely, fully, wholly, precisely. 3 *Exactly, we agree:* quite so, that's right, indeed, certainly, definitely.
Ant. 1 approximately, more or less; inaccurately, incorrectly.

exaggerate *v. Don't exaggerate!:* overstate, amplify, hyperbolize, enlarge on, stretch, embroider, embellish.
Ant. understate, minimize.

exalt *v.* 1 *He was exalted by colleagues:* laud, extol, praise, honor, applaud, commend; glorify, venerate, worship. 2 *The performance truly exalted the audience:* uplift, inspire, ennoble, stimulate, exhilarate.
Ant. 1 damn, condemn, dishonor, demean, disparage, depreciate. 2 depress, dispirit, dishearten.

exaltation *n.* 1 *to welcome the returning heroes with exaltation:* tribute, praise, eulogizing, panegyric; honor, glory; worship, veneration, deification. 2 *her exaltation on hearing the good news:* elation, exultation, ecstasy, rapture, exhilaration, bliss.
Ant. 1 damnation, condemnation, depreciation, degradation, dishonor. 2 depression, dejection, gloom, misery.

exalted *adj.* 1 *Kings are the most exalted rulers:* high-ranking, august, lofty, illustrious; glorious, elevated, venerable, notable. 2 *The play put us in an exalted mood:* ecstatic, rapturous, inspired, elated, blissful, lofty.
Ant. 1 lowly, ignoble. 2 depressed, dejected, despondent, miserable.

examination *n.* 1 *a thorough examination of the house:* inspection, scrutiny, survey; investigation, review, study; physical checkup. 2 *The examination consisted of 50 questions:* exam, test, quiz.

examine *v.* 1 *Examine the merchandise carefully:* look over, inspect, scrutinize, view, observe. 2 *Examine the facts carefully:* study, inquire into, consider, investigate, review. 3 *The lawyer examined the witness:* quiz; question, query, interrogate.

example *n. The cathedral is an example of Gothic architecture:* sample, illustration, exemplification, specimen; paragon.

exasperate *v. The interruption exasperated the speaker:* annoy, rile, irk, anger, madden, incense, infuriate, enrage; rankle, ruffle, vex.
Ant. mollify, pacify, placate, appease, calm.

exceed *v.* 1 *Don't exceed the speed limit:* go beyond, go over, pass, overdo, outreach. 2 *Americans exceed in basketball:* excel, predominate, be superior, outrival, outrank.
Ant. 1 stay within, keep under. 2 fail, be inferior.

exceedingly *adv. exceedingly well behaved:* very, extremely, greatly, especially; enormously, outstandingly, impressively, preeminently, surpassingly, superlatively, extraordinarily, unusually, inordinately, amazingly.

excel *v. The Australians excel at tennis:* exceed, surpass, predominate, outdo, *Slang* take the cake.
Ant. fail, fall short, be inferior to.

excellence *n. This car is known for its excellence:* high quality, quality, superiority, perfection, merit, distinction.
Ant. inferiority, poor quality, imperfection, fault, shortcoming, failing.

excellent *adj. an excellent pianist:* outstanding, superior, superlative, exceptional, superb, choice, capital, terrific, wonderful, fine, topnotch, first-rate.

Ant. bad, poor, inferior, terrible, awful, second-rate, *Slang* lousy.

except *prep.* 1 *Put everything except the vase in the box:* excepting, excluding, exclusive of, but, save, saving. —*v.* 2 *The A students were excepted from the exam:* exempt, excuse, exclude, omit; bar, ban, remove, disallow, reject.

Ant. 1 including.

exception *n.* 1 *All the houses in the block are brick, with one exception:* exclusion, exemption, omission, debarment; separation, isolation; leaving out, disallowment; rejection, renunciation, repudiation. 2 *This case is an exception:* deviation, special case, anomaly, oddity, peculiarity, difference.

Ant. 1 inclusion.

exceptional *adj.* 1 *Snow in April is exceptional:* unusual, unique, uncommon, rare, irregular, atypical; anomalous, abnormal, unnatural, strange, aberrant, phenomenal, freakish. 2 *The movie was good but not exceptional:* outstanding, superior, excellent, noteworthy; wonderful, terrific, great, marvelous, special, extraordinary, remarkable.

Ant. 1 common, usual, normal, typical, natural, expected. 2 average, mediocre, so-so; bad, terrible, awful, second-rate, *Slang* lousy.

excerpt *n.* We read excerpts from the book: extract, selection, portion, section, piece, part; quoted passage.

excess *n.* 1 *an excess of energy:* surplus, overabundance, superabundance, undue amount, oversupply, profusion, glut. —*adj.* 2 *The excess furniture was in the cellar:* surplus, extra, excessive, overflow; remainder, residue.

Ant. 1 deficiency, shortage, scarcity, dearth, paucity, inadequacy, insufficiency. 2 insufficient, scanty, scarce.

excessive *adj. excessive spending:* excess, undue, too much, extreme, extravagant, inordinate, exaggerated.

Ant. insufficient, inadequate, meager, scanty, scant, skimpy, sparse.

exchange *v.* 1 *The trapper exchanged furs for food:* trade, swap, barter. —*n.* 2 *an exchange of greetings among friends:* interchange, reciprocity, trade, swap, switch, bandying.

Ant. 1 keep, hold on to.

excise *v. The surgeon excised the carbuncle:* remove, cut out, cut off, eradicate, extract, pluck out.

excite *v.* 1 *The news excited the nation:* thrill, electrify, rouse, arouse, move, stimu-

late, energize, kindle, fire, inflame; provoke, incite. 2 *The lecture excited our interest:* evoke, elicit, waken, awaken, stimulate, whet, pique.

Ant. 1 bore; soothe, calm. 2 diminish, deaden, kill, quench.

excitement *n. The trip was full of excitement:* thrill, adventure, *Slang* kicks; stimulation, interest, enthusiasm; action, furor, ferment, commotion, tumult, agitation, flurry, frenzy.

Ant. serenity, peace; inactivity, boredom.

exciting *adj. an exciting movie:* thrilling, electrifying, breathtaking, hair-raising, rousing, stirring, impelling, stimulating, dazzling.

Ant. unexciting, uninteresting, dull, boring, monotonous.

exclaim *v. "You're a liar!" she exclaimed:* cry out, call out, ejaculate; shout, yell.

exclamation *n. an exclamation of surprise:* ejaculation, outcry, cry, shout, yell, shriek; interjection, expletive.

exclude *v.* 1 *The association voted to exclude amateurs:* keep out, bar, ban, prevent entrance of, reject, prohibit, forbid, disallow; expel, oust, eject, throw out. 2 *The doctor excluded food poisoning as a cause:* rule out, omit, except, leave out; repudiate.

Ant. 1 invite, welcome; admit, accept, allow.

exclusion *n. The exclusion of women from the league was illegal:* keeping out, barring, debarment, rejection, prohibition, refusal; prevention, preclusion; eviction, removal, expelling, ouster, ejection, expulsion.

Ant. admittance, inclusion, acceptance.

exclusive *adj.* 1 *an exclusive club:* select, elect; restricted, restrictive; closed, private; clannish, cliquish; aloof, snobbish. 2 *the exclusive right to a house:* sole, single, private, unshared, undivided; complete, entire, full.

Ant. 2 nonexclusive, shared, partial.

excruciating *adj. excruciating pain:* extremely painful, unbearable, insufferable, unendurable, agonizing, racking, tormenting; acute, severe, extreme, fierce, intense.

Ant. mild, slight, gentle, trivial.

excursion *n. a weekend excursion:* outing, junket, trip; pleasure trip, short journey, jaunt; sally, expedition, sortie; *(variously)* drive, cruise, flight, walk, stroll.

excuse *v.* 1 *Excuse me:* forgive, pardon, make allowance for, bear with, indulge, accept one's apology. 2 *I can't excuse his rudeness:* apologize for, justify, explain, defend; pardon, absolve, acquit, exonerate, exculpate, clear; mitigate, overlook. 3 *She was excused from duty today:* release, exempt, free, let off, relieve of. —*n.* 4 *Ignorance is no*

excuse: justification, defense, acceptable explanation; absolution, exoneration, reason, alibi; plea for forgiveness.
Ant. 1, 2 censure, blame, chasten, punish; charge, accuse, convict, sentence. 3 subject to; obligate, oblige.

execute *v.* 1 *The plan was well executed:* carry out, effect, discharge, accomplish, achieve, effectuate, realize, carry through. 2 *Nathan Hale was executed as a spy:* put to death, inflict capital punishment on; kill, murder. 3 *The concerto was executed with great flair:* perform, render, play, act, enact.

execution *n.* 1 *the successful execution of our plans:* carrying out, effecting, accomplishment, performance, discharge, implementation, realization, achievement, completion. 2 *This guillotine was used for executions:* putting to death, infliction of capital punishment; killing, slaying. 3 *The pianist's execution was flawless:* performance, rendition, interpretation.

executive *n.* 1 *an executive with wide business experience:* administrator, administrative head, director, manager. —*adj.* 2 *She has executive potential:* administrative, managerial, directorial, supervisory, leadership.
Ant. 1 worker, subordinate, flunky, underling.

exemplary *adj.* 1 *exemplary behavior:* worthy of imitation, emulative, model; admirable, praiseworthy, commendable, laudable, noteworthy, ideal, meritorious. 2 *The costumes were exemplary of Renaissance dress:* typical, characteristic, illustrative, representative, sample.

exempt *v.* 1 *This note will exempt you from class:* except, excuse, free, release; grant immunity to. —*adj.* 2 *Church property is exempt from taxation:* not subject to, immune, excepted, excused, relieved, freed, absolved, not liable to, released from.
Ant. 1 subject, oblige, liable.

exemption *n.* 1 *an exemption from military service:* release, freedom, absolution, dispensation, exception, excuse. 2 *a tax exemption:* deduction, allowance; expense.
Ant. 1 responsibility, obligation, liability.

exercise *n.* 1 *Exercise stimulates the flow of blood:* workout, warm-up, physical activity; calisthenics, aerobics, isometrics, gymnastics, a daily dozen. 2 *the military exercises:* practice, training, schooling, drill. 3 *the exercise of caution. graduation exercises:* use, practice, employment, application; ceremony, performance, program. —*v.* 4 *To stay healthy, exercise:* work out, be physically active, do calisthenics. 5 *The President exercises the duties of Commander in*

Chief: carry out, perform, execute, discharge, employ, utilize, wield; apply, practice, exert, display, exhibit.
Ant. 1 inactivity, idleness. 3 ignoring, overlooking. 4 be sedentary, be inactive.

exert *v. Exert all your strength:* put forth, exercise, employ, wield, use, utilize, apply, expend, avail oneself of.

exertion *n. The task took a great deal of exertion:* effort, energy, strength, labor, toil, work, pains, trouble, industry, application, activity.
Ant. idleness, inertia; ease, leisure.

exhale *v. Take a deep breath, then exhale:* breathe out, respire, expire, breathe; pant, puff, huff.
Ant. inhale, breathe in.

exhaust *v.* 1 *They had exhausted their supplies:* use up, expend, deplete, spend, consume. 2 *The game exhausted me:* wear out, overtire, fatigue, drain, devitalize; weaken, debilitate.
Ant. 1 conserve, preserve, store, hoard. 2 invigorate, refresh, revive, enliven.

exhausted *adj.* 1 *The children were exhausted:* tired out, dead tired, fatigued, worn out, all in, done in; drained, spent; *Slang* beat, bushed. 2 *The food supply was exhausted:* used up, finished, spent, depleted, consumed, drained, expended.
Ant. 1 full of pep; invigorated, refreshed, revived. 2 conserved, preserved.

exhaustion *n.* 1 *The runner was ready to drop with exhaustion:* fatigue, weariness, tiredness, enervation. 2 *the exhaustion of the army's rations:* using up, spending, consumption; depletion, draining.
Ant. 1 energy, pep, vim, vigor. 2 conservation, preservation.

exhaustive *adj. The student did exhaustive research:* comprehensive, thorough, intensive, complete, all-embracing.
Ant. cursory, superficial.

exhibit *v.* 1 *Manufacturers are exhibiting their new cars:* display, show, present for inspection, make public, unveil. —*n.* 2 *an art exhibit:* exhibition, display, exposition, show, public showing.

exhibition *n. an exhibition of antique glassware:* exhibit, show, showing, public showing, display, demonstration.

exhilarate *v. The walk exhilarated us:* fill with high spirits, invigorate, hearten, lift, enliven, elate, gladden, cheer.
Ant. depress, sadden, deject.

exhilaration *n. The winning team was full of exhilaration:* high spirits, exaltation, elation, liveliness, delight, gladness, joyousness.
Ant. dejection, depression, gloom.

exhort v. *She exhorted women to rebel:* encourage, spur, goad, prod, give a pep talk to; urge, enjoin, persuade.
Ant. dissuade, discourage.

exile v. 1 *The king exiled the rebel leader:* banish, deport, expel, eject, oust, expatriate, drive out. —n. 2 *political exiles:* exiled person, banished person, refugee; outcast, pariah.

exist v. 1 *A few old whaling ships still exist:* be in existence, survive, endure, remain. 2 *Humans do not exist on Mars:* live, survive, maintain life. 3 *A life free from worry doesn't exist:* occur, happen, ensue, obtain.
Ant. 2 die, perish.

existence n. 1 *Do you believe in the existence of the Loch Ness monster?:* actuality, reality, presence; tangibility, materiality. 2 *the patient's very existence:* life, being, survival; subsistence.
Ant. 1 nonexistence. 2 death.

exit n. 1 *There is only one exit:* way out, egress, passage out. 2 *We made a hasty exit:* departure, withdrawal, retreat, exodus. —v. 3 *Please exit by the rear door:* leave, depart, go out, withdraw.
Ant. 1, 2 entrance. 3 enter, come in.

exodus n. *the exodus from Egypt:* departure, going forth, exit, flight, hegira, emigration, exile.

exonerate v. *The jury exonerated the accused:* clear, free, absolve, vindicate; find innocent, acquit.
Ant. condemn, blame, find guilty.

exorbitant adj. *exorbitant prices:* excessive, unreasonable, preposterous, outrageous, extreme, undue, out-of-line, inordinate; overpriced, extravagant.
Ant. cheap, reasonable, inexpensive.

exotic adj. 1 *Palm trees are exotic to Alaska:* foreign, not native, not indigenous, alien. 2 *She was famed for her exotic hats:* unusual, different, unique, intriguing, exceptional; colorful; outlandish.
Ant. 1 native. 2 commonplace, ordinary.

expand v. 1 *The business has expanded:* grow, increase, enlarge, heighten; widen, swell, fatten, inflate. 2 *The eagle expanded its wings:* stretch, spread, spread out, extend, open.
Ant. 1 decrease, shrink, contract. 2 close, fold.

expanse n. *the vast expanse of the Great Plains:* extent, area, space, sweep, stretch, reach, magnitude, compass.
Ant. limit, confine, enclosure.

expansion n. *an expansion of the business:* enlargement, enlarging, increase, augmentation, growth, extension, spreading; swelling, distention, dilation.

Ant. decrease, shrinkage, contraction, reduction.

expansive adj. 1 *an expansive personality:* open, effusive, extroverted, outgoing, affable; generous, bountiful. 2 *an expansive knowledge of the law:* extensive, broad, vast, comprehensive, wide-ranging, wide.
Ant. 1 reserved, restrained, introverted, shy, reticent. 2 limited, restricted.

expect v. 1 *The skiers expected snow:* look forward to, plan on, look for, anticipate, foresee, contemplate. 2 *The company expects promptness:* demand, require, trust, count on, hope for. 3 *I expect it will rain:* assume, presume, guess, suppose, believe, surmise, imagine, conjecture, *Informal* reckon.
Ant. 1 despair of; dread, fear.

expectation n. *an expectation of winning:* expectancy, anticipation, likelihood, prospect, chance, assurance, hope, reliance, belief, contemplation.
Ant. unlikelihood, despair, discouragement.

expedient adj. 1 *It's expedient to lecture from notes:* useful, helpful, worthwhile, advantageous, beneficial, practical, effective. 2 *In an expedient move, the legislators voted to raise their salaries:* self-serving, self-seeking, selfish, opportune. —n. 3 *The neon sign is a necessary expedient to business:* practical aid, help, advantage, benefit; resort, means, measure.
Ant. 1 inexpedient, impractical, ineffective; futile, vain, fruitless. 2 unselfish, altruistic.

expedite v. *to expedite work:* hasten, speed up, accelerate, quicken; promote, further, facilitate, advance.
Ant. slow, slow down, impede, hinder, obstruct.

expedition n. 1 *a scientific expedition:* trip, journey, voyage; mission, campaign. 2 *The expedition slept in tents:* travelers, voyagers; explorers.

expeditious adj. *The emergency demands expeditious action:* prompt, speedy, hasty, quick, fast, swift; immediate, instant, punctual; alert, awake, effective.
Ant. slow, leisurely, deliberate, inefficient, ineffective.

expel v. 1 *The whale expelled water from its blowhole:* force out, cast out, eject, discharge, excrete, evacuate, eliminate, void, dislodge, spew. 2 *He was expelled from the club:* eject, oust, throw out; dismiss, drum out; banish, exile, evict.
Ant. 2 admit, accept, invite.

expend v. 1 *to expend energy:* use up, spend, consume; drain, exhaust, empty, squander.

2 *to expend $100:* spend, pay out, pay, disburse, dispense.
Ant. 1, 2 conserve, save, preserve, hoard. 2 earn, receive, collect.

expendable *adj.* 1 *expendable funds:* spendable, available, disbursable. 2 *Some of the equipment is expendable:* able to be sacrificed, replaceable, dispensable, superfluous, extraneous, nonessential.

expenditure *n.* 1 *Expenditures should be less than income:* expenses, spending, disbursement, outlay; payment, cost. 2 *a great expenditure of energy:* spending, expending, application, use, consumption.
Ant. 1 receivables, receipts, income. 2 conservation, preservation, hoarding.

expense *n.* *the expense of remodeling:* cost, price, charge, outlay; item paid for; depletion; financial burden.
Ant. return, profit, gain.

expensive *adj.* *expensive clothes:* costly, high-priced, dear; extravagant, uneconomical.
Ant. cheap, inexpensive, economical.

experience *n.* 1 *Experience is the best teacher:* personal knowledge, personal involvement, doing, practice, seasoning, familiarity, exposure. 2 *a memorable experience:* event, episode, incident, adventure, happening, occurrence. —*v.* 3 *to experience hunger:* know, undergo, live through, encounter, meet, endure, suffer; feel, see.
Ant. 1 inexperience; theory. 3 escape, miss.

experienced *adj.* *an experienced bookkeeper:* practical, seasoned, qualified, veteran, expert; master; sophisticated, wise, worldly-wise.
Ant. inexperienced, unqualified; green, apprentice.

experiment *n.* 1 *As an experiment she substituted honey for sugar. chemical experiments:* test, trial, tentative procedure, tryout, venture; research, investigation, analysis, experimentation. —*v.* 2 *The chemist experimented with a new formula:* test, try out, explore; research, investigate, analyze, examine.

experimental *adj.* *experimental designs:* tentative, speculative, conjectural, conceptual, developmental, trial, test; new, radical.
Ant. traditional, proven; commonplace, routine.

expert *n.* 1 *a chess expert:* authority, specialist, master, professional, virtuoso, connoisseur, ace, veteran. —*adj.* 2 *expert flyers:* skilled, masterful, masterly, experienced, master, accomplished, knowledgeable, proficient, able, competent, capable.

Ant. 1 amateur, tyro, novice; dabbler. 2 unskilled, inexperienced, inept, incompetent.

expertise *n.* *She has a great deal of scientific expertise:* special skill, skill, know-how, specialization, professionalism.

expire *v.* 1 *The magazine subscription expired:* come to an end, run out, lapse, cease, discontinue, end, conclude. 2 *The heroine expired:* die, pass away, perish, decease, succumb.
Ant. 1 begin, start, commence. 2 live; be born.

explain *v.* 1 *Explain how an airplane flies:* describe, make clear, explicate. 2 *How do you explain such rude behavior?:* interpret, account for, fathom, justify, rationalize, give an explanation for.

explanation *n.* 1 *an explanation of the theory:* explication, account, elucidation, clarification. 2 *an explanation for his erratic behavior:* reason, accounting, answer, cause, motive, motivation; justification, rationale, excuse.

explicit *adj.* *She gave explicit directions:* specific, precise, exact, distinct, clear; candid, frank, direct, blunt.
Ant. vague, general, indefinite, inexact, obscure; indirect.

explode *v.* 1 *The gas main exploded:* blow up, burst violently; erupt, discharge violently; detonate. 2 *to explode with anger:* erupt, utter noisily, express noisily. 3 *New facts explode the theory that the moon was once part of the earth:* disprove, prove false; belie, refute, expose, discredit, repudiate, invalidate, burst.

exploit *n.* 1 *the hero's many exploits:* achievement, feat, accomplishment, heroic act, brave deed, adventure. —*v.* 2 *You must exploit every opportunity:* use to advantage, utilize, make use of, put to use, capitalize on, profit by. 3 *The company exploited its workers:* take advantage of, make selfish use of, take unfair advantage of.
Ant. 1 failure, defeat. 3 pamper, coddle, spoil.

explore *v.* 1 *Lewis and Clark explored the Northwest:* scout, travel over, survey, traverse. 2 *to explore ways to increase production:* look into, examine, research, investigate, search into, probe, inquire into.

explosion *n.* 1 *The explosion shook the town:* blowing up, detonation, blast; eruption, discharge. 2 *an explosion of anger:* burst, outburst, outbreak, eruption, paroxysm, fit.

explosive *n.* 1 *dynamite and other explosives:* blasting material; ammunition; pyrotechnics. —*adj.* 2 *an explosive gas:* liable to explode, capable of exploding, unstable, volatile. 3 *an explosive international situation:* dangerous, tense, volatile, precarious, touchy, ticklish, shaky.

exponent *n. He's an exponent of free trade:* advocate, supporter, champion, proponent, promoter, expounder, defender.
Ant. opponent, foe; critic.

expose *v.* 1 *In some Muslim countries women do not expose their faces in public:* bare, uncover, show, display, exhibit. 2 *The child exposed the plans for the surprise party:* disclose, reveal, divulge, let out; uncover, unearth. 3 *to expose students to good art and music:* familiarize with, put in contact with, acquaint with. 4 *The magazine exposed the politician as a crook:* disclose to be, reveal to be, show in one's real light.
Ant. 1 hide, conceal, mask, cover, shield. 2 conceal, keep secret.

exposé *n. The paper printed an exposé of local crime:* exposure, scandalous disclosure, divulgence, revelation.
Ant. cover-up, whitewash.

exposition *n.* 1 *The antique exposition will be held in the armory:* exhibition, exhibit, trade show, show; fair, world's fair, *Informal* expo. 2 *Provide a clear exposition of your views:* explanation, explication, elucidation, exegesis, commentary; presentation.

expostulate *v. I expostulated with him to reconsider:* remonstrate, inveigh against, enjoin, plead with, exhort, forewarn, counsel, caution, reason against.

exposure *n.* 1 *The exposure of dishonest dealings:* disclosure, divulging, revelation, bringing to light, exposé, unmasking, uncovering. 2 *Her skin was dry after exposure to the wind:* subjection, laying bare, making vulnerable. 3 *The room has a southern exposure:* outlook, vista, view.
Ant. 1 hiding, concealment, cover-up.

expound *v. The candidate expounded her views:* state in detail, hold forth, explain, elucidate; make clear, uphold.

express *v.* 1 *to express one's thoughts:* put into words, articulate, relate, communicate, state, speak, declare, describe, verbalize, voice. 2 *Her face expressed her disappointment:* reveal, divulge, show, exhibit, evidence, evince, convey, communicate. —*adj.* 3 *I gave express orders:* explicit, definite, specific, unequivocal, exact, clear, precise, direct, particular. 4 *the express train:* nonstop, stopping infrequently; fast, high-speed.
Ant. 2 hide, conceal, mask; supress, re-

press. 3 implicit, implied, indirect, vague, indefinite.

expression *n.* 1 *the poem's beauty of expression. the expression of views:* wording, phraseology, style, language; stating, saying, airing, venting, uttering, declaration, relating, communication. 2 *a colorful expression:* term, word, phrase, turn of phrase, idiom. 3 *She has a happy expression on her face:* look, aspect, mien, countenance.
Ant. 1 suppression, repression.

expressly *adv.* 1 *I expressly said I wouldn't go:* explicitly, definitely, pointedly, unequivocally, decidedly, clearly, plainly. 2 *We went to the Alps expressly to ski:* specifically, specially, precisely.
Ant. 1 implicitly, indirectly, vaguely.

expropriate *v. The government expropriated the property:* confiscate, appropriate, take, take over; seize, commandeer.

expulsion *n. expulsion from school. the expulsion of gas from an engine:* expelling, ejection, ousting, removal; exile, banishment, eviction, exclusion, debarment; discharge, elimination.
Ant. entering, entrance, inclusion; injection.

expurgate *v. The censor expurgated a passage from the book:* cut, cut out, remove, delete, excise, censor, bowdlerize, *Television* blip, bleep out.

exquisite *adj.* 1 *an exquisite china figurine:* delicate, fine, elegant; particularly beautiful, beautifully dainty, lovely. 2 *exquisite calligraphy:* superb, superlative, matchless, peerless, flawless, fine, choice, splendid. 3 *She had exquisite taste in clothes:* discriminating, impeccable, faultless, perfect, fastidious, meticulous.
Ant. 1 bulky, ugly. 2 sloppy, inferior, bad. 3 unrefined, indiscriminate, slovenly.

extant *adj. the earliest extant manuscript:* in existence, existing, existent, surviving, present, living.

extemporaneous *adj. She gave an extemporaneous talk on conservation:* impromptu, improvised, extemporary, ad-lib, extempore, unprepared.
Ant. well-rehearsed, prepared.

extend *v.* 1 *Extend the line to the edge of the paper. We extended the meeting 15 minutes:* draw out, lengthen, make longer, elongate; continue, protract, prolong. 2 *He extended his hand in greeting. The professor extended an invitation to students:* advance, submit, put out, stretch forth; offer, give, proffer, bestow, impart, grant. 3 *The course will extend my knowledge:* expand, enlarge, increase, augment.

Ant. 1 shorten, curtail, contract, shrink. 2 withdraw, take back. 3 decrease, limit, reduce.

extended *adj.* 1 *with extended arms:* spread out, stretched out, unfolded. 2 *an extended engagement:* prolonged, long, protracted, lengthened, drawn out.

Ant. 1 folded. 2 short, shortened, curtailed.

extension *n.* 1 *a two-day extension of our trip:* lengthening, continuation, increase, prolongation; delay, postponement. 2 *The shed was an extension of the house:* wing, annex, adjunct, addition, appendix; enlargement, expansion, continuation.

Ant. 1 shortening, curtailment.

extensive *adj.* 1 *an extensive desert:* wide, broad, large, vast, extended, great; lengthy, long, protracted. 2 *an extensive knowledge of history:* wide, broad, comprehensive, thorough.

Ant. 1 small, little. 2 restricted, specialized.

extent *n. The extent of the forest was unknown to the settlers. Laws limit the extent of personal freedom:* expanse, area; scope, range, compass, magnitude, size, sweep, reach, amount, degree; duration, time, length.

Ant. limitation, limits.

extenuating *adj. extenuating circumstance:* justifiable, mitigating, attenuating, qualifying, tempering, moderating.

Ant. aggravating, intensifying.

exterior *adj.* 1 *an exterior covering:* outside, outer, outermost, external, superficial. 2 *exterior events:* external, foreign; extrinsic, extraneous. —*n.* 3 *the exterior of a house:* outside, outer side, surface. 4 *a calm exterior:* outward appearance, manner, demeanor, bearing.

Ant. 1 internal, inner. 2 internal, intrinsic, inherent. 3 interior, inside.

exterminate *v. to exterminate cockroaches:* destroy, wipe out, kill, massacre, annihilate, eliminate, eradicate, abolish.

external *adj.* 1 *The external layer of skin is the epidermis:* outside, outer, outermost, exterior, surface, superficial. 2 *Insulate the house to keep out external heat:* from the outside, extraneous, extrinsic; foreign.

Ant. 1 internal, inner, innermost, inside. 2 internal; intrinsic.

extinct *adj.* 1 *The passenger pigeon is extinct:* defunct, dead, vanished, no longer in existence, died out. 2 *an extinct volcano:* no longer burning, quenched, extinguished.

Ant. 1 extant, surviving; flourishing, thriving. 2 active.

extinguish *v.* 1 *Firemen extinguished the blaze:* put out, douse, quench. 2 *The bad*

news extinguished hope: wipe out, destroy, end, kill, demolish, eradicate, crush, quash, dash.

Ant. 1 ignite, light, fire. 2 foster, build up; establish, confirm, support.

extol *v. He extolled their bravery:* praise, laud, commend, acclaim, celebrate, eulogize.

Ant. denounce, damn, curse, criticize.

extortion *n. The gangster was arrested for extortion:* blackmail, shakedown; coercion; forced payments, hush money, graft, ransom, tribute.

extra *adj.* 1 *The store hired extra clerks. Why did you buy extra eggs?:* additional, supplemental, more; spare, auxiliary; superfluous, surplus, unnecessary. —*n.* 2 *My car has all the extras:* accessory, additional feature, adjunct, attachment. —*adv.* 3 *The coffee is extra strong:* unusually, uncommonly, exceptionally, particularly, extraordinarily.

extract *v.* 1 *The dentist extracted her tooth:* pull out, take out, remove, extricate, pluck out. 2 *Extract some humor from every situation:* get, glean, derive, exact, wrest, bring out, elicit. 3 *to extract oil from shale:* separate, take out, squeeze out, press out, distill. 4 *The newspaper extracted several passages from the speech:* excerpt, cull, copy out; cite, quote. —*n.* 5 *vanilla extract:* concentrate, essence, distillate, juice. 6 *The book contains extracts from famous poems:* excerpt, selection, passage.

Ant. 1, 2 insert, implant; inject, infuse.

extraneous *adj. extraneous remarks:* irrelevant, unrelated, not germane, not pertinent, inappropriate, nonessential, immaterial, incidental.

Ant. relevant, pertinent, germane, appropriate, material, essential.

extraordinary *adj. What an extraordinary idea!:* unusual, uncommon, remarkable, phenomenal, unique, exceptional, notable; strange, odd, queer.

Ant. common, ordinary, unremarkable, customary.

extravagance *n.* 1 *Extravagance led us into bankruptcy:* excessive spending, overspending; waste, wastefulness, improvidence. 2 *She was misled by the extravagances of the travel brochure:* excess, excessiveness, unrestraint, immoderation.

Ant. 1 economy, frugality, stinginess, miserliness. 2 moderation, restraint.

extravagant *adj.* 1 *The car is too extravagant:* expensive, high-priced, costly, exorbitant. 2 *extravagant spenders:* profligate, overspending, spendthrift; wasteful, squandering, imprudent. 3 *The ad made extravagant claims:* excessive, unre-

strained, inordinate, outlandish; fabulous, unreal, high-flown.
Ant. **1** cheap, economical, low-priced. **2** thrifty, economical; frugal, stingy, miserly. **3** restrained, realistic; careful, cautious.

extreme *adj.* **1** *extreme cold:* severe, intense, great, excessive, extraordinary, unusual, inordinate. **2** *Her political views were extreme:* radical, advanced, outrageous. —*n.* **3** *She will go to any extreme for friends:* limit, extremity, boundary, height, depth, end; excess.
Ant. **1** moderate, mild, common, ordinary. **2** traditional, conservative.

extremely *adv.* *It's extremely warm:* very, quite, exceptionally, especially, extraordinarily, exceedingly, excessively, immoderately, intensely, remarkably, awfully.

extremity *n.* **1** *the western extremity of the ranch:* end, terminus, edge, tip; limit, boundary, border. **2** *He is good at drawing faces but not extremities:* hand, foot; arm, leg; finger, toe.

extricate *v.* *to extricate oneself from a trap:* free, release, get out, rescue, liberate; disentangle, disengage, wriggle out of.
Ant. catch, trap, snare, entangle.

extrovert *n.* *The extrovert loves to meet people:* outgoing person, gregarious person, sociable person; show-off.
Ant. introvert; loner.

exuberance *n.* *The children are full of exuberance:* enthusiasm, energy, vitality, liveliness, spirit, zeal, vigor, vivacity, animation.
Ant. despair, dejection; lethargy.

exuberant *adj.* *The crew gave an exuberant shout:* enthusiastic, lively, spirited, sprightly, animated, eager, excited, vigorous.
Ant. dejected, unenthusiastic, dispirited, lethargic.

exult *v.* *to exult on winning:* rejoice, be jubilant, be elated, be delighted, glory; *Informal* jump for joy.
Ant. be downcast, be blue, feel sad.

eye *n.* **1** *She shaded her eyes from the sun:* (*variously*) eyeball, iris, pupil; *Informal* orb, peeper. **2** *Are your eyes good enough without glasses? an artist's eye:* eyesight, vision, sight; perception, discrimination, taste. —*v.* **3** *She eyed the stranger with amusement:* look at, gaze at, view, scan, observe, regard, study, inspect, scrutinize, stare at, watch, behold.

eyewitness *n.* *Her testimony was supported by eyewitnesses:* looker-on, bystander, onlooker, observer, beholder, witness.

F

fable *n.* *the fable about the fox and the grapes:* parable, tale, allegory, myth.

fabled *adj.* *the fabled Loch Ness monster:* fanciful, imaginary, fictitious; legendary, mythical, mythological, fabulous, storied.
Ant. real, authentic, factual.

fabric *n.* **1** *Wash this fabric in cold water:* cloth, textile, material, dry goods, yard goods, stuff. **2** *the fabric of a nation:* framework, structure, makeup, organization; substance; texture, foundation.

fabricate *v.* **1** *All the furniture is fabricated on the premises:* build, form, construct, assemble, manufacture, produce. **2** *She fabricated a good excuse:* invent, concoct, make up, devise, contrive, falsify, feign.
Ant. **1** destroy, raze, dismember.

fabrication *n.* **1** *the fabrication of airplane parts:* building, construction, constructing, manufacture, assemblage, production.

2 *His alibi was a fabrication:* falsehood, invention, lie, untruth, fiction, forgery.
Ant. **2** truth, fact, actuality.

fabulous *adj.* **1** *fabulous adventures:* amazing, extraordinary, astonishing, astounding, incredible. **2** *a fabulous party:* marvelous, wonderful, great, spectacular, stupendous. **3** *the fabulous unicorn:* fabled, legendary, mythical, mythological, storied, imaginary, invented.
Ant. **1** ordinary, routine. **2** ordinary, fair. **3** real, natural, historical, actual.

façade *n.* **1** *the façade of the building:* front, face. **2** *to wear a façade of confidence:* false appearance, pretense, false front, mask, veneer.

face *n.* **1** *She powdered her face:* visage, facial features; *Slang* mug, pan. **2** *Put on a happy face:* expression, look, countenance, air. **3** *Pioneers changed the face of the prairie:* appearance, look, semblance. **4** *to save* *face:* reputation, good name, dignity, repute, image, prestige. 5 *I scratched the face of my belt buckle:* front surface, obverse, principal side, façade, forepart. 6 *I didn't have the face to go back on stage:* nerve, boldness, daring, pluck, spunk, bravado; cheek, front, gall, effrontery, impudence. —*v.* 7 *The opponents faced each other across the chessboard:* encounter, confront, meet face to face.

Ant. 5 back, reverse. 6 shyness, timidity.

facet *n.* 1 *the many facets in the diamond:* surface, plane, cut. 2 *Generosity is one facet of character:* aspect, side, part.

facetious *adj. facetious remarks:* humorous, funny, amusing, jocular, joking, jesting, clever, comic, playful.

Ant. solemn, serious, sober.

facile *adj.* 1 *a facile worker:* skillful, adroit, handy, quick, adept, effortless. 2 *I don't trust facile talk:* glib, slick, superficial, shallow, smooth, artful, clever.

Ant. 1 clumsy, awkward, plodding, slow. 2 careful, thoughtful.

facilitate *v. The machine facilitates work:* expedite, speed up, make easier, assist the progress of; promote, further, advance, foster.

Ant. hinder, hamper, complicate, slow.

facility *n.* 1 *She speaks German with facility:* ease, fluency, skill, proficiency, effortlessness, knack, deftness, competence. 2 *modern facilities:* appliance, convenience, aid; resource, means.

Ant. 1 ineptness, clumsiness, effort, pains, labor.

facsimile *n. a facsimile of the original:* copy, reproduction, replica, duplicate, likeness.

fact *n. The lawyer tried to establish the facts:* occurrence, event, act, particular, specific; reality, actuality, truth.

Ant. fiction, supposition, opinion, lie, invention.

faction *n.* 1 *the liberal faction of the party:* group, side, subdivision, section; clique, set, circle, coterie; bloc, splinter group. 2 *The convention broke up in bitter faction:* discord, dissension, conflict, disagreement, strife, division, schism, split; disruption.

Ant. 2 agreement, accord, harmony.

factious *adj. to bring factious elements of the committee into agreement:* contentious, divisive, quarrelsome, bickering, disputatious, disagreeing, dissentious; insubordinate, belligerent, warring; alienated, estranged, disaffected.

Ant. consenting, agreeing, assenting, acquiescing.

factor *n. Money was the main factor in my* *decision:* consideration, circumstance, element, part, component, influence.

factual *adj. a factual account:* full of facts, literal; actual, authentic, correct, exact, faithful, true, accurate.

Ant. fanciful, imaginary, fictional.

faculty *n.* 1 *the faculty of the university:* teaching staff, teaching body, professors, teachers. 2 *He has a faculty for putting people at ease:* knack, capacity, capability, ability, skill, gift, talent, quality, power, aptitude. 3 *the faculty of speech:* power, capability, function, endowment. 4 **faculties.** *The old man still has all his faculties:* wits, reason, mental powers.

Ant. 2 inability, incapacity; weakness, failing.

fad *n. Miniskirts were a fad in the 1960's:* craze, rage, fashion, mania, vogue.

fade *v.* 1 *The rug has faded. The light faded as the sun went down:* pale, dim, bleach, lose color, lose brightness, dim, whiten. 2 *Her strength seemed to fade:* decline, dwindle, fail, diminish, wither, lessen, ebb, droop, wane, disappear, recede, melt away, dissipate.

Ant. 1 brighten. 2 rise, increase, grow; endure, abide.

fail *v.* 1 *Our best-laid plans may fail:* not succeed, be unsuccessful; come to nothing, fall through, turn out badly, be defeated, flop. 2 *I failed math:* flunk, get less than a passing grade. 3 *Our friends failed us:* disappoint, let down, forsake, desert. 4 *His energy failed after his illness:* decline, dwindle, fade away, waste away, wane, become weaker, deteriorate, flag, droop, give out, ebb. 5 *Bad investments caused the company to fail:* go bankrupt, go under, become insolvent.

Ant. 1 succeed. 2 pass. 4 grow, strengthen, flourish, gain.

failure *n. Her failure surprised us:* failing, lack of success, vain attempt, ill success. 2 *failure to pay one's debts:* neglecting, dereliction, nonperformance, remissness, delinquency, default, nonobservance. 3 *the failure of the bank:* bankruptcy, insolvency, ruin, collapse. 4 *The party was a failure:* nonsuccess, disappointment, washout; botch, muddle, mess, mishap, *Slang* flop, dud. 5 *the failure of her eyesight:* decline, loss, deterioration, deteriorating, breakdown.

Ant. 1 success; fulfillment. 3 success, prosperity. 4 success. 5 strengthening, improvement.

faint *adj.* 1 *The music was too faint to hear. a faint trace of lipstick on the glass:* soft, inaudible, remote, low, weak, muted; dim, pale, faded, delicate, obscure, inconspicuous. 2 *He needed more than faint encouragement:* feeble, weak, slight, small, meager, little. 3 *She felt faint:* dizzy, light-headed, vertiginous, giddy; feeble, weak. 4 *Faint heart ne'er won fair lady:* timorous, timid, fearful, lacking courage, cowardly. —*v.* 5 *The actor fainted:* swoon, black out, pass out, lose consciousness.

Ant. 1 bright, conspicuous; loud, blaring, glaring. 2 strong, vigorous. 4 brave, bold, courageous.

fainthearted *adj. a fainthearted attempt:* irresolute, halfhearted, indifferent; lacking courage, cowardly, timid.

Ant. brave, courageous, bold.

fair *adj.* 1 *The lottery was fair:* unprejudiced, impartial, equitable, evenhanded; just, unbiased, objective, legitimate; honest, reasonable, square, upright, honorable, aboveboard; according to the rules, proper, justified, on the up and up. 2 *He's only a fair hitter:* average, moderate, pretty good, so-so, mediocre, passable, adequate, tolerable, medium, ordinary, run-of-the-mill. 3 *The day was fair:* cloudless, unclouded, sunny, fine, bright. 4 *She has fair hair:* light-colored, pale, blond; fair-skinned. 5 *The old song was about a fair maiden:* attractive, lovely, pretty, comely, well-favored, beautiful. —*adv.* 6 *He was accused of not playing fair:* justly, truthfully, honestly, honorably, legally, ethically.

Ant. 1 unfair, prejudiced, partial, inequitable, dishonest. 2 exceptional; poor, bad. 3 cloudy, stormy, dark, threatening. 4 dark. 5 ugly, homely. 6 unfairly, dishonestly.

fairly *adv.* 1 *The case will be decided fairly:* justly, honorably, honestly; equitably, even-handedly, impartially; objectively, legitimately, properly. 2 *He's fairly bright:* rather, tolerably, passably, moderately, reasonably. 3 *The children fairly raced out of school:* actually, really, fully, completely, absolutely, positively.

Ant. 1 unfairly, unjustly, inequitably, dishonestly. 2 extremely, very, exceptionally.

faith *n.* 1 *I have faith in your integrity:* belief, confidence, trust, certitude, reliance, credence, conviction. 2 *the Catholic faith:* religion, creed, persuasion, denomination, sect, church. 3 *Keep faith by paying your debts:* pledge, word of honor, promise; fidelity, constancy, loyalty.

Ant. 1 doubt, uncertainty, skepticism, disbelief; mistrust, misgiving, distrust.

faithful *adj.* 1 *a faithful employee:* loyal, devoted, steadfast, conscientious, staunch, true, constant, reliable, trustworthy, dependable, unswerving, trusty, honest.

2 *a faithful account of the accident:* exact, truthful, factual, accurate.

Ant. 1 faithless; disloyal, false; fickle, inconstant, unfaithful, untrue, untrustworthy. 2 inexact, inaccurate.

fake *v.* 1 *He faked an illness to stay out of school:* pretend, feign, simulate, falsify, hoax, sham. 2 *She was arrested for faking famous paintings:* counterfeit, forge, falsify. —*n.* 3 *The pearls were fakes:* counterfeit, imitation, forgery, sham, make-believe; trick, hoax, fabrication, imposture, delusion, ruse. 4 *The traveling psychics were fakes:* imposter, poseur, fraud, pretender, faker, phony, charlatan, humbug. —*adj.* 5 *I wore a fake mustache to the party:* false, bogus, counterfeit, phony, spurious, sham, forged, simulated, artificial, make-believe.

Ant. 5 real, authentic, actual.

fall *v.* 1 *He fell down the stairs:* drop, tumble, topple, come down suddenly, collapse, crash down. 2 *The cost of meat fell:* decline, come down, decrease, diminish, depreciate. 3 *Her dress falls in pleats from the waist:* extend down, slope, cascade; descend, drop. 4 *The town fell to the enemy:* surrender, be captured, be overthrown, be defeated, be taken, capitulate, succumb; be wounded, be slain, die. 5 *How many of the righteous have fallen?:* transgress, give in to temptation, go astray, sin. 6 *My birthday falls on Sunday:* occur, happen, take place, come around. —*n.* 7 *The net broke the acrobat's fall:* plunge, drop, spill, tumble, plummet. 8 *a fall in stock prices:* drop, decline, decrease, reduction, slump, depreciation. 9 *falls. We could see the falls downriver:* waterfall, cascade, cataract. 10 *School starts in the fall:* autumn, harvest time. 11 *the fall of an honest individual:* ruin, loss of innocence, going astray, lapse into sin, downfall. 12 *the fall of the Roman Empire:* surrender, capitulation, overthrow, capture; downfall, collapse, defeat.

Ant. 1–2 rise, ascend. 2 soar, increase. 7 rise, ascent. 8 rise, climb, increase, advance.

fallacy *n.* 1 *It's a fallacy that everyone needs the same amount of sleep:* misconception, error, false notion, misapprehension. 2 *the fallacy in an argument:* fault, flaw, inconsistency, erroneous reasoning, mistake, catch.

Ant. 1 truism, fact, certainty. 2 logic, proof, truth.

fallible *adj. Human judgment is fallible:* imperfect, liable to error; human, mortal.

Ant. infallible, perfect; divine.

false *adj.* 1 *a false impression:* faulty, incorrect, untrue, wrong, fallacious, erroneous, mistaken, inaccurate; misleading, deceptive, deceiving. **2** *a false friend:* disloyal, faithless, unfaithful, untruthful, devious, hypocritical, dishonest, treacherous, perfidious, inconstant, deceitful. **3** *false diamonds:* artificial, bogus, counterfeit, fake, make-believe, imitation, faux, ersatz, forged, spurious, feigned, sham, phony.

Ant. **1** true, correct, right, accurate. **2** loyal, true, faithful, sincere, steadfast, honest. **3** real, genuine, authentic.

falsehood *n.* **1** *Don't resort to falsehoods:* lie, untruth, fabrication, fiction, story, fib, whopper, white lie. **2** *Con artists are known for cheating and falsehood:* lying, untruthfulness, falseness, dishonesty, deceptiveness, deception, misrepresentation, deceit, mendacity, perjury, double-dealing, hypocrisy, duplicity, insincerity.

Ant. **1** truth, fact. **2** veracity, honesty, honor.

falsify *v. The police falsified their report:* alter fraudulently, misrepresent, fake, distort, doctor.

falter *v.* **1** *I never faltered in my loyalty:* hesitate, waver, vacillate; demur, shrink. **2** *The drunk faltered toward the door:* stumble, teeter, stagger, totter, reel; shamble, shuffle, dodder.

Ant. **1** persevere, persist.

fame *n. Pablo Picasso achieved great fame as a painter:* eminence, prominence, repute, renown, celebrity, public esteem, glory, popularity, notoriety, preeminence, distinction, note.

Ant. obscurity, oblivion; disgrace, dishonor, disrepute.

familiar *adj.* **1** *a familiar saying:* often encountered, well-known, known, frequent, habitual; commonplace, ordinary, everyday, common, proverbial, customary, conventional, accepted, stock, traditional. **2** *Are you familiar with the subject?:* acquainted, conversant, informed about, versed in, apprised of; experienced at, skilled in, proficient at. **3** *Passengers on the cruise became quite familiar:* friendly, informal, close, intimate, chummy; forward, impertinent, disrespectful.

Ant. **1** unfamiliar, unknown, uncommon, unusual, unconventional, rare. **2** unfamiliar, ignorant, unversed, unacquainted, uninformed. **3** distant, formal, aloof.

familiarity *n.* **1** *She has some familiarity with Latin:* knowledge, acquaintance, comprehension, understanding, proficiency, conversance, experience. **2** *She brags about her familiarity with the duchess:* closeness, intimacy, friendship, association, chumminess. **3** *He received us with familiarity:* in-

formality, ease, casualness, unconstraint, unreserve; impertinence, disrespect, impudence, forwardness.

Ant. **1** unfamiliarity, ignorance, inexperience. **3** formality, constraint, reserve; propriety, respect.

familiarize *v. The newcomers had to familiarize themselves with the town:* acquaint, accustom, make conversant, instruct, edify, inform, enlighten; acclimatize, habituate.

family *n.* **1** *Do you want a large family?:* issue, offspring, progeny, brood. **2** *Our family had a reunion in Chicago:* relatives, kin, kinsmen, kith and kin, kinfolk, relations. **3** *The Hapsburg family ruled Austria:* house, lineage, ancestry, line, dynasty; clan, tribe, genealogy, race, stock; forebears, parentage; **4** *the Indo-European family of languages:* group, division, class, classification, kind, order, set, category.

famine *n.* **1** *Crop shortages are causing famine:* starvation, famishment, extreme hunger. **2** *a famine of executive talent:* shortage, want, deficiency, paucity, dearth, lack, scarcity, scantiness, insufficiency, short supply.

Ant. **1, 2** abundance, surfeit, sufficiency, glut.

famous *adj. a famous movie star:* well-known, noted, celebrated, prominent, renowned, far-famed; eminent, illustrious, notable, distinguished.

Ant. obscure, unknown, unsung, obscure, forgotten.

fan *n. a devoted football fan:* enthusiast, aficionado, follower, supporter, rooter, partisan, booster, fanatic, addict, buff; *Slang* nut, freak, bug.

fanatic *n. The political fanatics refuse to negotiate:* zealot, enthusiast, extremist, hothead, militant, true believer.

fanaticism *n. His religious fanaticism led him to execute heretics:* zealotry, fervor, intemperance, obsession, monomania, extremism, militantism, dogmatism.

Ant. cynicism, skepticism; indifference.

fanciful *adj.* **1** *fanciful ideas:* whimsical, flighty, imaginative, capricious, fantastic, unusual, unpredictable. **2** *Children's stories are filled with fanciful characters:* unreal, imaginary, fabulous, fantastic, chimerical, mythical.

Ant. **1** unimaginative, conventional, sensible; prosaic, predictable. **2** real, realistic.

fancy *n.* **1** *It suited my fancy to have a costume party:* imagination, whimsy, caprice, fantasy. **2** *She had some fancy that she'd get rich:* illusion, fantasy, daydream, reverie, conceit, notion, idea, dream. **3** *a fancy for rich desserts:* leaning, liking, longing, fondness, predilection, inclination, relish, pen-

chant, partiality, preference, desire, yen.
—*adj.* 4 *stationery with a fancy border.
fancy foods:* showy, ornamental, decorative,
ornate, intricately wrought, elaborate; fine,
special, superior, specially selected, deluxe.
—*v.* 5 *Can you fancy that?:* imagine, picture, conceive of. 6 *I fancy you'll get the
promotion:* suspect, suppose, think, assume, imagine, presume, suspect. 7 *I fancy
the chocolate cake:* like, have a mind to, be
bent upon, want, favor, be fond of, crave,
yearn for, *Informal* hanker after; relish,
enjoy.
  Ant. 3 dislike, distaste, aversion. 4 plain,
undecorated; common.

fantastic *adj.* 1 *He had a fantastic notion
that his cat could talk:* weird, odd, bizarre,
wild, extravagant, absurd, crazy, mad, ridiculous, preposterous, outlandish, grotesque, implausible, unbelievable; strange,
irrational, farfetched; romantic, visionary,
imaginary, chimerical, fanciful, illusory.
2 *a fantastic amount of praise:* great, extravagant, extreme, huge, enormous, tremendous. 3 *This is a fantastic dessert!:* marvelous, wonderful, sensational, fabulous,
terrific, great, superb.
  Ant. 1 reasonable, sensible, rational.
2 moderate, limited. 3 ordinary; poor.

fantasy *n.* 1 *We all commit brave deeds in
fantasy.* fancy, imagination, realm of
dreams, mind, make-believe. 2 *Some of the
old fantasies about the space age are coming
true:* fancy, illusion, daydream, imagining,
dream, reverie; visionary idea, notion, fiction, vision.
  Ant. 1, 2 reality, actuality, fact.

far *adv.* 1 *Our land extends far beyond the
fence:* a long way, distantly, deeply, to a
distant point, yonder, afar. 2 *The weather
was far worse than expected:* much, to a
great degree, greatly, a great deal, considerably. —*adj.* 3 *We travel to far places:* distant, far-off, far-away, remote.
  Ant. 2 little. 3 near, nearby, close.

farce *n.* 1 *Her new farce got very good reviews:* satirical comedy, broad comedy, burlesque, parody, low comedy. 2 *Freedom of
the press is a farce under a dictatorship:*
sham, mockery, travesty, pretense, absurdity, parody.
  Ant. 1 tragedy. 2 reality.

fare *n.* 1 *The bus fare has gone up:* charge,
passage money, ticket price, fee, cost of
transportation. 2 *The fare served on the
cruise was excellent:* food, food and drink,
provisions, victuals, diet, comestibles,
menu. —*v.* 3 *He has fared well in business:*
manage, get on, do, make out, perform.

far-fetched *adj. What a far-fetched theory!:*

improbable, unlikely, implausible, doubtful, dubious; preposterous, unconvincing,
strained.
  Ant. likely, probable, plausible.

farm *v. He farms 400 acres:* cultivate, have
under cultivation; till the soil, plant, practice husbandry; *(variously)* plow, harvest,
reap, sow.

farmer *n. a tobacco farmer:* grower, planter,
cultivator of land, agriculturist, agrarian,
agronomist, tiller of the soil.

farsighted *adj.* 1 *Farsighted people usually
need glasses for reading:* hyperopic. 2 *A
farsighted leader would have avoided war:*
foresighted, farseeing, foreseeing, provident, wise, prudent, acute, shrewd.
  Ant. 1 nearsighted, myopic. 2 shortsighted, improvident, injudicious.

farther *adv.* 1 *I'm farther into the book than
you are:* further, to a greater distance, past
the point that; to a greater extent, deeper.
—*adj.* 2 *at the farther end of the room:*
more distant, more remote, further. 3 *The
trip is farther than I thought:* longer, length-
ier.
  Ant. 2 closer, nearer. 3 shorter.

fascinate *v. The magician fascinated the
children. The snake was fascinated by the
charmer's music:* charm, captivate, beguile,
entrance, enchant, grip the attention of, engross, delight, enthrall, allure, spellbind, absorb.
  Ant. bore, repel.

fascinating *adj. a fascinating novel:* gripping, engrossing, enthralling, absorbing,
riveting; charming, captivating, enchanting, beguiling, entrancing, alluring, interesting, spellbinding.
  Ant. boring, uninteresting, dull; repellent.

fascism *n. Fascism caused many people to
flee the country:* right-wing dictatorship;
Nazism; totalitarianism, police state.
  Ant. socialism, democracy.

fashion *n.* 1 *the latest fashion:* style, custom,
mode, trend, usage, prevailing taste, vogue,
craze, fad, rage. —*v.* 2 *She fashioned a necklace from paper clips:* shape, create, make,
form, contrive, design, frame, devise, fabricate, construct; compose, produce.

fashionable *adj. a fashionable restaurant:*
in fashion, stylish, in style, smart, in vogue,
all the rage, chic.
  Ant. unfashionable, old-fashioned, dated.

fast *adj.* 1 *Cheetahs are very fast animals. a
fast pace:* swift, quick, fleet; rapid; brisk,
hasty, hurried; accelerated; speedy, expeditious. 2 *a fast crowd:* wild, reckless, extravagant, dissipated, profligate, intemperate,
wanton, dissolute, immoral, loose, debauched. 3 *fast friends:* steadfast, firm, con-

stant, unwavering, steady, unswerving; loyal, devoted, staunch, true, lasting, faithful. 4 *The cargo was made fast in the hold:* secure, fastened, firm, steady, firmly fixed; resistant, stationary, taut, tight. —*adv.* 5 *The stamp ought to stick fast:* firmly, fixedly, tightly, securely, tenaciously, solidly. 6 *The child was fast asleep:* soundly, fully, completely. 7 *Don't drive so fast:* swiftly, rapidly, speedily, quickly; hastily, hurriedly.

Ant. 1 slow. 2 respectable, moral, sober, virtuous. 3 wavering, inconstant; disloyal, unfaithful. 4 loose, insecure. 7 slowly, slow.

fasten *v.* 1 *Fasten it to the wall. Fasten the ends together:* attach, tie, fix, make fast, secure, anchor, affix; *(variously)* tether, moor, pin, bolt, screw, rivet, weld, bind, stick, clamp, cement, solder; unite, join, connect, adhere; close, hook, button, couple, clasp, clip, snap. 2 *She fastened her gaze on us:* fix, direct, focus, hold.

Ant. 1 unfasten; loosen; separate, undo, remove, detach, disconnect.

fastidious *adj. a fastidious eater:* fussy, particular, persnickety, picky, finicky; meticulous, proper, choosy, exacting, precise; delicate, dainty, refined.

Ant. neglectful, lax; uncritical, indulgent.

fat *n.* 1 *I try not to eat much fat:* grease, animal fat, adipose tissue. —*adj.* 2 *He's too fat and needs to diet:* stout, heavy, plump, chubby, overweight, obese, fleshy, pudgy, rotund, portly, beefy, corpulent. 3 *The doctor warned against fat foods:* fatty, greasy, oily, containing fat.

Ant. 2 lean, skinny, gaunt, scrawny, thin, slender, slim. 3 lean.

fatal *adj.* 1 *a fatal illness:* terminal, deadly, mortal, lethal. 2 *Disagreement was fatal to the project:* ruinous, lethal, destructive, calamitous, disastrous, catastrophic.

Ant. 1 harmless, nonlethal. 2 constructive, beneficial, helpful.

fatality *n. A number of fatalities resulted from the fire:* death, casualty, violent death.

fate *n.* 1 *By a twist of fate, Thomas Jefferson and John Adams both died on July 4, 1826:* destiny, predestination, predetermination; providence, will of heaven. 2 *Always losing seemed to be his fate:* fortune, lot, destiny, karma, portion, kismet. 3 *The fate of the proposed bill is uncertain:* future, outcome, upshot, chances.

Ant. 1 will, choice, decision.

fateful *adj. Meeting you was a fateful moment in my life:* momentous, important, critical, decisive, determinative, crucial,

significant; ominous, portentous; fatal, disastrous.

Ant. unimportant, ordinary, insignificant.

father *n.* 1 *He resembles his father:* male parent, sire, *(variously)* dad, daddy, papa, pater, pop, *Slang* old man. 2 *They work the land as their fathers did:* forefather, ancestor, forebear, progenitor. 3 *Alexander Graham Bell was the father of the telephone:* inventor, creator, architect, designer, begetter, originator, founder, author, maker. 4 *I studied with the fathers at St. Joseph's Academy:* priest, padre, abbé, pastor, curé, parson, preacher, dignitary of the church. —*v.* 5 *A son owes a debt to the man who fathered him:* sire, beget, engender, procreate. 6 *The plan was fathered by a local banker:* found, originate, create, begin, hatch, author, design.

fatherland *n. After the war he returned to his fatherland:* homeland, native land, native country, mother country, motherland.

fatherly *adj. fatherly advice:* paternal, fatherlike, parental; benevolent, benign, kindly, affectionate; sympathetic, forbearing, protective.

fathom *v. Can anyone fathom the meaning of that story?:* penetrate, figure out, comprehend, understand; probe, divine, discover, get to the bottom of.

fatigue *n.* 1 *Fatigue overcame the sleepy child:* tiredness, exhaustion, weariness, lassitude, listlessness, languor, drowsiness, overtiredness. —*v.* 2 *Climbing the hill fatigued us:* exhaust, tire, overtire, weary, wear out, drain; *Informal* bush.

Ant. 1 energy, vigor, indefatigability. 2 refresh, restore, rejuvenate, renew.

fatuous *adj. The swain wore a fatuous grin:* foolish, inane, silly, vapid, vacuous, puerile, ridiculous.

Ant. sensible, prudent, wise, clever.

fault *n.* 1 *His only fault is that he lacks ambition:* shortcoming, defect, deficiency, insufficiency, imperfection, flaw, failing weakness, drawback; stain, blemish. 2 *I would be wise to confess your fault:* error, blunder, wrong, mistake, misdeed, transgression, sin, offense, wrongdoing, crime. 3 *Whose fault is it?:* responsibility, guilt, answerability, accountability, culpability, blame. —*v.* 4 *You can't fault me for trying:* blame, impugn, censure, criticize, reprove

Ant. 1 merit, virtue, strength. 3 credit. 4 credit, praise.

faultfinder *n. He's a constant faultfinder:* quibbler, carper, complainer, caviler, derogator, detractor, nitpicker, curmudgeon.

faultless *adj. Her piano playing was fault less:* perfect, without blemish, flawless

without fault, irreproachable, unblemished, impeccable; correct, accurate.

Ant. faulty, imperfect, defective; inaccurate, erroneous.

faulty *adj.* *I'd better get that faulty muffler fixed:* defective, impaired, imperfect, out of order, amiss, inadequate, deficient; incorrect, mistaken, erroneous, wrong, false.

Ant. sound, perfect, faultless; correct, accurate.

faux pas *n.* *Insulting the guest was a terrible faux pas:* breach of etiquette, mistake, blunder, gaffe, indiscretion, impropriety.

favor *n.* 1 *Would you do me a favor?:* good turn, kind act, service, accommodation; largesse, courtesy. 2 *to win the boss's favor:* approval, goodwill, esteem, good opinion; support, patronage, advocacy. —*v.* 3 *How many board members favor the merger?:* approve, be in favor of, support, endorse, be for; like, commend, esteem, countenance, encourage, uphold. 4 *The teacher favors serious students:* prefer, have a preference for, fancy, be partial to; pamper, humor, indulge. 5 *She favors her grandmother:* look like, resemble, take after, be the image of.

Ant. 1 injury, disservice, harm. 2 ill will, disfavor, antipathy, animosity, enmity; disapproval. 3 oppose, be against, disapprove. 4 dislike, object to.

favorable *adj.* 1 *The boat race depends on favorable winds:* advantageous, good, helpful, beneficial. 2 *The credit bureau gave me a favorable report:* approving, commendatory, salutary, good; friendly, kind, benign, amicable, sympathetic. 3 *Indications are favorable for spring planting:* promising, propitious, opportune, auspicious, good, conducive.

Ant. 1–3 unfavorable. 2 disapproving, unfriendly, unsympathetic. 3 unpromising, inauspicious.

favorite *n.* 1 *The oldest boy was her favorite:* preferred one, choice; pet, fancy, darling, apple of one's eye. 2 *the favorite in the election:* probable winner, one favored to win, front-runner. —*adj.* 3 *I can't find my favorite pen:* best-liked, preferred, choice.

favoritism *n.* *A wise teacher never shows favoritism:* partiality, bias, partisanship.

fawn *v.* *The bellhop fawned over the rich guest:* be servile, be obsequious, toady, pander, bow and scrape.

Ant. be insulting, ignore.

faze *v.* *Nothing fazes us:* disconcert, daunt, disturb, upset, bother, perturb, embarrass, abash, confound, fluster.

fear *n.* 1 *fear of the dark:* dread, fright, foreboding, terror, panic, horror, affright, apprehension, alarm, trepidation, consternation,

disquietude, quaking, perturbation, anxiety, worry, concern, fearfulness, cowardice. 2 *Snakes are my biggest fear:* phobia, apprehension, source of anxiety, dread; nightmare, bugaboo, bugbear, bogey; worry, concern, care. —*v.* 3 *I fear his wrath:* be afraid of, dread, be frightened of, be apprehensive of, take fright, be scared of, tremble at. 5 *The children were taught to fear God:* feel awe for, revere, respect deeply, honor humbly, venerate, reverence, esteem.

Ant. 1 fearlessness, bravery, courage; confidence, security.

fearful *adj.* 1 *a fearful bolt of lightning:* frightening, frightful, dreadful, terrible, alarming, formidable, appalling, terrifying, distressing, shocking, horrible, horrid, eerie, awful. 2 *We were fearful of offending someone:* afraid, frightened, apprehensive, alarmed, anxious, worried, scared, full of fear, uneasy, concerned, nervous. 3 *a fearful child:* frightened, tremulous, nervous, intimidated, anxious, skittish, panicky, scared, apprehensive.

Ant. 1 reassuring, pleasant, benign. 2 unafraid, confident. 3 fearless, brave, courageous, dauntless, intrepid.

fearless *adj.* *a fearless leader:* dauntless, bold, undaunted, unafraid, intrepid, brave, courageous, without fear, unflinching; daring, venturesome, adventurous, valiant, valorous, heroic, stout-hearted, doughty, lionhearted.

Ant. fearful, cowardly, timorous, afraid, apprehensive, terrified.

feasible *adj.* *It's not feasible to make the trip in one day:* possible, conceivable, achievable, attainable; viable, reasonable.

Ant. unachievable, impossible.

feast *n.* 1 *a feast fit for a king:* banquet, sumptuous repast, large dinner, elegant meal; rich supply, surplus, bounty. 2 *When is the feast of San Gennaro?:* holiday, festival, feast day, celebration, fete, saint's day. —*v.* 3 *The nobility feasted on venison:* eat richly, dine, have a feast, banquet, gorge, eat one's fill.

Ant. 1 fast, famine. 2 fast day.

feat *n.* *feats of strength:* deed, act, action; achievement, accomplishment, exploit, attainment; adventure, enterprise, triumph.

feature *n.* 1 **features.** *The veil obscured her features:* parts of the face, visage, aspect, lineaments, physiognomy. 2 *The landscaping is the dominant feature of the estate:* attribute, quality, trait, characteristic, mark, property, character, important part. 3 *The high-wire act is the feature of the circus:* highlight, main item, special attraction, specialty, drawing card. —*v.* 4 *The* *show featured a ventriloquist:* represent prominently, display, spotlight, headline, highlight, star, present. 5 *Informal Can you feature her playing a nun?:* imagine, see, picture, envision, fancy.

federation *n. a federation of workers:* union, united group, league, confederation, confederacy, alliance, association, coalition, brotherhood, sisterhood.

fee *n. the doctor's fee:* charge, payment for professional services, compensation, price, commission, honorarium, remuneration.

feeble *adj.* 1 *He's too feeble to do the work:* weak, weakened, infirm, sickly, fragile, debilitated, frail, enervated, powerless. 2 *feeble attempts to be funny:* ineffective, spiritless, frail, meager, faint, weak, flimsy, slight, lame, ineffectual, inadequate.
Ant. 1 robust, strong, sturdy; hale, healthy. 2 effective, forceful, strong.

feed *v.* 1 *to feed a large group:* provide food for; feast, cater, wine and dine. 2 *Pigs will feed on just about anything:* eat, take nourishment, consume, take food, devour. 3 *Applause feeds the ego:* nourish, nurture, fuel, encourage, maintain, strengthen, sustain, foster. —*n.* 4 *a bag of cattle feed:* foodstuff, nourishment, food for animals, provisions, fodder, victuals, provender, viands, comestibles.
Ant. 1 starve. 3 starve, stifle.

feel *v.* 1 *I love to feel silk against my skin:* touch, examine by touching, have the feeling of; handle, finger. 2 *He feels the cold more than most. I feel great guilt about what happened:* experience, sense, perceive, suffer from; understand, comprehend, know. 3 *She felt for the light switch in the dark:* grope, fumble, probe. 4 *I feel that you should resign:* be of the opinion that, believe, think, be convinced; sense, have an impression. 5 *It's hard to feel for someone so selfish:* have sympathy, sympathize with, have compassion, be moved by, be touched by, be stirred by. —*n.* 6 *Don't you like the feel of this material?:* feeling, sensation, touch, texture.

feeling *n.* 1 *He has no feeling in his left hand:* sense of touch, sensation, tactile sense, sensibility. 2 *a feeling of joy:* emotion, sense, thrill, reaction, response, sentiment; aura, atmosphere. 3 *She has great feeling for the suffering of others. He played the piece with great feeling:* sympathy, compassion, sensitivity; passion, emotion, ardor; affection, sentiment, fervor, vehemence, verve, enthusiasm, gusto, spirit. 4 *My feeling is that we should postpone the meeting:* opinion, view, attitude, impres-

sion, instinct, intuition, inclination, sentiment.
Ant. 1 numbness, insensibility, insensateness. 3 insensitivity, unconcern, apathy.

feelings *n. pl. to care about the feelings of others:* sensibilities, susceptibilities, emotions, passions, sensitivities; pride, self-esteem.

feign *v. She feigned surprise:* simulate, affect, assume, pretend, fake, make believe, sham.

feint *n. The boxers made a few feints at each other:* feigned attack, pass, bluff, move; pretense, ruse, ploy, trick, subterfuge.

felicitation *n. Please accept our felicitations on your marriage:* congratulations, best wishes, good wishes, blessings; greetings, salutations.

felicitous *adj.* 1 *a felicitous occasion:* happy, joyful, joyous, fortunate, propitious. 2 *a felicitous last line to the poem:* apt, appropriate, suitable, relevant, pertinent, germane, fitting, well-chosen, pleasing, effective.

fellow *n.* 1 *He's a nice fellow:* boy, man, chap, *Slang* guy. 2 *The boy joined his fellows on the playing field:* companion, associate, friend, comrade, chum, co-worker, compatriot, colleague, pal.

fellowship *n. We enjoy the fellowship of co-workers:* companionship, comradeship, cordiality, friendship, sociability, familiarity, amity, affability; society, association, fraternity, brotherhood.
Ant. unfriendliness; antagonism, hostility.

female *adj.* 1 *She is their oldest female child:* girl, woman; offspring-bearing, childbearing. 2 *Sewing was considered a female occupation:* feminine, womanly, ladylike, womanlike, distaff. —*n.* 3 *Females constitute a slight majority of the population:* woman, girl. 4 *This litter produced 2 males and 7 females:* female animal, offspring-bearing animal; *(variously)* mare, dam, sow, heifer, cow, bitch, tabby, hen.
Ant. male. 2 masculine, manly. 3 man, boy.

feminine *adj. Gentleness was considered a feminine trait:* womanly, female, girlish, ladylike; gentle, soft; dainty, delicate.
Ant. masculine, male, manly, mannish, unfeminine.

femininity *n. The Gibson girl epitomized American femininity:* womanliness, female quality, girlishness, femaleness, feminineness; softness, gentleness.
Ant. masculinity, manliness, mannishness.

fence *n.* 1 *We built a fence around the yard:* barrier, protective enclosure, rail, barricade. —*v.* 2 *to fence in a yard:* enclose with a fence, surround, encompass, grid, pen, en-circle.

fend v. 1 *The governor fended off reporters:* ward off, push away, keep off; repel, repulse, parry. 2 *You must fend for yourself:* manage, provide, shift, do, take care of, support.

ferment n. *The campus was in a state of ferment:* unrest, disquiet, disruption, agitation, turmoil, turbulence, tumult, commotion.

Ant. calmness, quiet.

ferocious adj. *a ferocious animal:* savage, bestial, brutish, ravening, predatory, fierce; merciless, ruthless, murderous, enraged, bloodthirsty, brutal, cold-blooded, deadly.

Ant. tame, domesticated; mild, calm.

fertile adj. 1 *fertile ground. The old mare was still fertile:* productive, fruitful, fructuous, fecund, rich; generative, reproductive, capable of bearing offspring, prolific. 2 *a fertile mind:* productive, prolific, resourceful, inventive, creative; original, ingenious.

Ant. 1 infertile, barren, unproductive; impotent, sterile. 2 unproductive, unimaginative, uncreative.

fervent adj. *a fervent plea for clemency:* earnest, impassioned, fervid, passionate, ardent, devout, zealous, eager, spirited, heartfelt, fiery, enthusiastic.

Ant. apathetic, impassive, unfeeling.

fervor n. *They prayed with fervor:* ardor, passion, intensity, earnestness; vehemence, zeal, animation, gusto, fire, enthusiasm, zest.

Ant. apathy, detachment, dispassion.

fester v. 1 *The wound festered:* suppurate, become infected, inflame, ulcerate; rot, putrefy. 2 *Her resentment had festered for many years:* rankle, smolder, intensify, grow, chafe, nettle, rile, vex.

festival n. *a May festival:* feast, celebration, holiday, carnival, fete, jubilee, gala.

fetch v. 1 *Dogs enjoy fetching sticks:* get and bring back, go for, retrieve; get, obtain, bring. 2 *The painting should fetch a good price:* sell for, bring, yield, realize, *Informal* go for.

fete n. *They held a lavish fete at their country house:* party, feast, celebration, gala; garden party, banquet, carnival.

fetid adj. *The room reeks of fetid cigar smoke:* stinking, malodorous, rank, foul, ill-smelling, noisome, rotten, putrid; gamy, tainted, rank, rancid; musty, moldy.

Ant. fragrant, aromatic, perfumed; fresh.

fetish n. 1 *A rabbit's foot carried for good luck is a fetish:* charm, talisman, magic object; superstition; idol, amulet. 2 *Don't*

make a fetish of housecleaning: preoccupation, obsession, mania, idée fixe.

fetter n. 1 *The guards put fetters on the prisoners:* foot shackle, ankle irons; bond, chain, manacle, handcuff. —v. 2 *Fetter the horse to keep it from straying:* shackle, hobble, tether, tie, manacle, handcuff, chain. 3 *He was fettered by lack of self-confidence:* hamper, hinder, hold back, restrain, encumber.

Ant. 2, 3 free, unfetter, release. 3 encourage, promote.

feud n. 1 *a feud between the two families:* vendetta, quarrel, conflict, disagreement, bickering, argument; hostility, animosity, enmity, hard feelings, bad blood. —v. 2 *They have been feuding for years:* quarrel, dispute, disagree, argue, bicker; wrangle.

feverish adj. 1 *Flu made him feverish:* fevered, febrile, flushed, parched. 2 *a feverish desire to begin the race:* ardent, fanatic, impatient, eager, passionate, fervent, impassioned; frenzied, excited.

Ant. 2 cool; calm, unruffled, nonchalant.

few adj. 1 *Few countries can survive without trade:* not many, hardly any; scant, sparse, skimpy, rare, scarce; occasional, infrequent, limited, meager, inconsiderable, insignificant; unusual. —n. 2 *I still have a few:* small number, some, several, handful.

Ant. 1 many, numerous, plentiful, bounteous.

fiasco n. *My attempt was a fiasco:* complete failure, disaster; debacle; *Slang* flop, fizzle.

Ant. success, triumph.

fiat n. *The emperor's fiat forbade gambling:* command, decree, law, act, rule, edict, commandment, order, ruling.

fib n. 1 *That compliment was a fib:* white lie; untruth, falsification, fiction, fabrication, invention. —v. 2 *I fibbed and told him he looked great:* lie, tell a white lie, stretch the truth.

fickle adj. *You're so fickle about what you like:* changeable, unpredictable, vacillating, inconstant, inconsistent, mercurial; capricious, erratic, fitful, spasmodic, fluctuating, variable.

Ant. constant, faithful, steadfast, resolute, changeless, reliable.

fiction n. 1 *Hemingway was a master of fiction:* imaginative literary work, prose narration; *(variously)* novel, novella, short story, tale, play; invention, imagination. 2 *That story about her rich grandfather was certainly a fiction:* falsehood, fabrication, fib, tall tale, lie.

Ant. 1 nonfiction. 2 fact, truth.

fictitious adj. *The spy used a fictitious name:* false, untrue, assumed, feigned, in-

vented, counterfeit, forged, bogus, spurious, fake, phony, made-up.
Ant. real, true, genuine, authentic.

fidelity *n.* **1** *I trust your fidelity completely:* devotion, loyalty, faithfulness, constancy, trustworthiness, integrity, honesty, truthfulness, allegiance, staunchness. **2** *The portrait had great fidelity:* accuracy, exactness, faithfulness, correspondency, adherence to fact; precision; reliability.
Ant. faithlessness, unfaithfulness, perfidy, falsity, disloyalty, treachery, infidelity.

fidgety *adj. The children got fidgety:* restless, restive, impatient; jumpy, squirmy, *Slang* antsy; nervous, jittery.

field *n.* **1** *The horses were in the field:* meadow, grassland, pasture, clearing. **2** *a playing field:* arena, turf, court, course, diamond. **3** *troops in the field:* battlefield, battleground, front, front lines. **4** *a leader in the field of medicine:* realm, domain, province, area, sphere; occupation, profession, line. **5** *one's field of vision:* scope, range, area, extent, reach, expanse, circle.

fiend *n.* **1** *People used to blame misfortune on fiends:* evil spirit, demon, incubus, succubus; devil, Satan, prince of darkness. **2** *the fiend who murdered the child:* villain, scoundrel, monster, brute, beast, barbarian.

fierce *adj.* **1** *The bear is one of the fiercest of animals:* savage, ferocious, fearful, bloodthirsty, violent, brutal, merciless; enraged, raging, furious, voracious; horrible, terrible. **2** *The wind was fierce:* powerful, strong, violent, vehement, intense, overpowering, extreme, overwhelming; unbridled; passionate, fiery, fervent, fervid.
Ant. **1** docile, gentle, harmless; submissive, sweet. **2** mild, peaceful, calm.

fiery *adj.* **1** *a fiery furnace:* full of fire, flaming, burning; intensely hot, blazing, alight, ablaze, afire; glowing, red-hot. **2** *The doctor felt the patient's fiery cheek:* feverish, fevered, burning, febrile, inflamed. **3** *a fiery speech:* ardent, passionate, fervent, fervid, impassioned; high-strung, impetutous, spirited, enthusiastic; zealous, vehement. **4** *You'd better control that fiery temper:* hotheaded, hot-tempered, easily angered, excitable, impetuous; angry, violent.
Ant. **2** cool, cold, icy, frigid. **3** indifferent, passionless, unimpassioned; dispassionate.

fight *n.* **1** *The two gangs had a fight:* skirmish, fray, melee, encounter, confrontation, contest, tussle, scuffle, fracas, bout; battle, combat, clash of arms, war, battle royal. **2** *The mayor has plenty of fight:* spirit, pluck, toughness, combativeness, mettle, gameness; belligerency, pugnacity, bellicosity. **3** *She had an awful fight with the*

IRS: dispute, contention, quarrel, feud, wrangling, tussle, bickering, squabble; brawl, scrap, row, brush, spat, tiff. **4** *A fight was arranged for the young boxer:* bout, match, prizefight. —*v.* **5** *David fought Goliath:* battle, do battle with, join battle with, take up arms against, cross swords with, combat, struggle with, engage, battle; go to war, wage war, exchange blows, scuffle, brawl, skirmish, tussle, scrap, box. **6** *She fought back the tears:* resist, struggle against, oppose, repulse. **7** *I separate the children when they start fighting:* argue, dispute, feud, wrangle, bicker, squabble.
Ant. **1** pacification, reconciliation, appeasement, compromise.

fighter *n.* **1** *Will both fighters last 15 rounds?:* boxer, pugilist, prizefighter. **2** *The army decorated him as a brave fighter:* warrior, soldier, military man, combatant, fighting man; belligerent.

figment *n. a figment of my imagination:* product, creation, fancy, fantasy, invention, concoction.
Ant. fact, reality, actuality.

figurative *adj. She used the word in its figurative sense:* metaphorical, not literal, symbolic, allegorical.
Ant. literal, exact; prosaic.

figure *n.* **1** *The figure for "one" is "1":* numerical symbol, digit, number, cipher, numeral. **2** *He named a figure more than we could pay:* price, amount, rate, cost, sum. **3** *figures. I was good at figures:* arithmetic, sums, calculations, computations. **4** *The clothes concealed his figure:* form, shape, outline, silhouette, body, physique, build; cut, cast; configuration. **5** *Michelangelo was one of the great figures of art:* personage, person, notable, eminence, presence, man, woman. **6** *The scarf had a spiral figure:* pattern, design, device, motif, emblem; sign, symbol; diagram, illustration, drawing. —*v.* **7** *Figure the total:* calculate, compute, add up, sum, reckon, total, tot up. **8** *The wallpaper was figured with rosebuds:* embellish, adorn, ornament, pattern. **9** *Informal I figure it must be close to three miles:* reckon, think, suppose, conjecture; presume, believe, judge, imagine, guess. **10** *Real historical events figure in the novel:* have a part, play a part, appear; be prominent, appear.

filch *v.* **1** *He filched apples from the fruit stand:* steal, purloin, pilfer, swipe, cop, hook. **2** *The professor caught me filching from another student's paper:* appropriate, pirate, copy, lift, plagiarize, crib.

file *n.* **1** *departmental files:* collection of documents, data; records, archives, dossier. **2** *A file of customers was waiting:* line, queue, rank, row. —v. 3 *Please file these letters:* store, put away, catalog, index, place on file; record, list. 4 *Did you file for disability insurance?:* apply, submit a claim, petition, put in, request. 5 *The students filed into the hall:* walk in line, march in a file, advance.

fill v. 1 *Fill the bottle with turpentine:* fill up; pervade, permeate, charge; saturate, impregnate, infuse, suffuse; load, lade, pack; crowd, cram; feed fully, gorge, sate, satiate. 2 *Has that job been filled?:* occupy, take, assign, fulfill, supply; do, execute, carry out. 3 *Does Ed need help filling those orders?:* make up, supply, provide; stock. 4 *This fills an urgent need:* satisfy, meet, supply, answer, take care of. 5 *Breathe in until your lungs fill with air:* expand, inflate, dilate, distend. —n. 6 *Have you had your fill of fruit?:* full amount, sufficiency, surfeit. *Ant.* 1 drain; empty, exhaust, vacate.

film n. 1 *a film of oil on the water:* thin layer, coat, coating, sheet; cloud, haze, mist. 2 *Who stars in the latest film?:* motion picture, movie, moving pictures, cinema, *Slang* flick. —v. 3 *Her eyes filmed over as she thought of the past:* haze, mist. 5 *They're filming a detective drama:* make a movie of, shoot.

filter n. 1 *The water passes through a filter before it is piped to our homes:* strainer, sieve, screen, purifying device. —v. 2 *Sunlight filtered through the venetian blinds:* seep, dribble, leak, trickle; ooze, drain, exude, effuse.

filth n. 1 *The sidewalks were full of filth:* foul matter, dirt, trash; ordure, sewage, muck, slime; contamination, pollution, impurity; dung, excrement, feces, excreta; slop, refuse, garbage; mud, sludge. 2 *They're trying to shut down those shops that sell filth:* pornography, obscenity, smut; indecency, lewdness; foul language.

final adj. 1 *our final meeting for the year:* last, closing, concluding; rear, rearmost, ending, terminating, terminal; extreme, ultimate. 2 *She said "No, and that's final":* decisive, conclusive, definitive; complete, thorough, finished, exhaustive; irrevocable, unappealable. *Ant.* 1 opening, first, initial.

finale n. *The finale of the pageant was a spectacular fireworks display:* last part, conclusion, close, end, finish, windup, culmination.

finally adv. *Finally, the report gave the yearly figures:* in the end, lastly, at the last, in conclusion, ultimately; eventually; conclusively, definitively, once and for all.

finance n. 1 *an executive who knows finance:* money management, banking, investment, fiscal matters, economics, accounts. —v. 2 *How will you finance a new car?:* pay for, raise money for, underwrite.

financier n. *The library got a large contribution from a local financier:* expert in money matters, broker, banker, investor, underwriter; backer, angel; capitalist.

find v. 1 *She found a diamond ring on the bus:* discover, come upon, stumble upon, come across, chance upon. 2 *Eli Whitney found a new way to remove seeds from cotton:* uncover, discover, hit upon, track down, ferret out; detect, learn, ascertain, determine. 3 *We were surprised to find you at the party:* discern, spot, see, meet. 4 *They all helped me find the ring I lost:* regain, recover, get back, retrieve, locate. 5 *She found peace of mind:* acquire, gain, attain, achieve, get, win. 6 *The jury found for the plaintiff:* declare a verdict, determine, pronounce; decide, rule, decree, judge, award. —n. 7 *That mahogany table was a real find:* bargain, good buy, bonanza; catch, acquisition. *Ant.* 1 lose, mislay, misplace.

fine[1] adj. 1 *fine foods:* high-quality, choice, top-grade, exceptional, first-class, superior; splendid, admirable, excellent, exquisite, magnificent. 2 *fine hair:* thin, slender; silky, delicate; flimsy, gossamer, diaphanous, sheer, transparent. 3 *fine sand:* powdery, pulverized, powdered, ground, refined. 4 *a fine edge on the knife:* keen, sharp; precise, perfect; skillful, accomplished. 5 *fine china:* delicate, fragile, exquisite, dainty. 6 *fine manners:* elegant, refined, fastidious, well-bred, exquisite. 7 *fine weather:* clear, bright; sunny, rainless, cloudless, fair. 8 *There's a fine distinction between "wealthy" and "rich":* subtle, nice, slight. 9 *They have two fine children:* handsome, attractive, comely, good-looking, well-favored, beautiful, pretty, lovely. —adv. 10 *Pat is doing fine in business:* very well, excellently. *Ant.* 2, 3 thick, coarse. 4 dull, blunt. 6 crude. 7 cloudy, foul. 8 broad, clear, obvious. 9 ill-favored. 10 poorly, badly.

fine[2] n. 1 *The fine for overtime parking is $50:* penalty, assessment, damages, forfeit. —v. 2 *The judge fined her $50:* penalize, assess, charge.

finesse n. *The situation was handled with great finesse:* delicacy, tact, discretion, savoir-faire, artfulness; wile, ruse, artifice, cunning, guile.

finger n. 1 *How do you get a child to stop sucking its finger?:* organ of touch, digit; *(variously)* thumb, forefinger, middle finger, ring finger, little finger; pointer; *Slang* feeler. —*v.* 2 *The grocer asked us not to finger the tomatoes:* handle, touch, feel, caress, manipulate; poke, punch, squeeze; *Informal* paw.

finicky *adj. He's finicky about what he eats:* particular, fussy; meticulous, precise, exacting, picky, fastidious.

Ant. sloppy, careless.

finish *v.* 1 *We finished dinner at 7:* end, conclude, complete; terminate, discontinue; stop, cease; accomplish, achieve, consummate, close, settle. 2 *Finish these potato chips:* use up, dispatch; consume, devour. 3 *What can we use to finish off these bugs?:* eradicate, exterminate, destroy, kill, get rid of; defeat, overcome. 4 *Finish the table with a walnut stain:* surface, veneer, face, glaze, gild; lacquer, varnish, coat. —*n.* 5 *At the finish no one applauded:* conclusion, end, close, termination, completion; finale, ending, curtain; final event, windup, last, last stage. 6 *The furniture has a glossy finish:* surface, coating, veneer, lacquer; polishing.

Ant. 1 begin, start, commence. 5 beginning, commencement, inauguration.

finite *adj. The number is immense, but finite:* measurable, limited, bounded, countable, circumscribed, confined, restricted; not infinite; not everlasting.

Ant. infinite, unlimited, boundless, measureless; endless.

fire *n.* 1 *A fire broke out in the house:* conflagration, blaze, flame, bonfire; spark, inferno, holocaust. 2 *a speech full of fire:* ardor, vigor; power, intensity, force, inspiration, vehemence, spirit, passion, fervor; enthusiasm, eagerness, vivacity, verve, vim; brilliance, luster, radiance. 3 *The soldiers held their fire:* discharge of firearms, firing; salvo, fusillade, volley, broadside, enfilade. —*v.* 4 *The guns began firing:* shoot, discharge, open fire, bombard, shell. 5 *The speech fired the heart of every patriot:* arouse, stimulate, rouse, spark, inspire, animate, excite, inflame, incite, stir, quicken. 6 *He was fired for incompetence:* dismiss, let go, oust, cashier; *Slang* sack, can.

firm[1] *adj.* 1 *The gelatin must set until firm:* stiff, hard, rigid; unbending, unyielding, solid, compressed, compact. 2 *The price was firm:* settled, fixed, definite, established, confirmed. 3 *Put another nail in the frame to make it firm:* steady, stable, fast, secure; immovable; taut, tight, rigid. 4 *Mother was firm in her resolve not to move:* resolute, steadfast, determined, unwavering, resolved, unflinching, unfaltering; decided, constant, definite, obstinate, inflexible.

Ant. 1 loose, flabby; soft, flaccid. 3 shaky, unsteady, unstable. 4 wavering, irresolute.

firm[2] *n. I've worked for the firm since high school:* company, concern, organization, business, establishment, house, corporation.

firmament *n. the starry firmament:* sky, heavens, canopy of heaven; space, outer space.

first *adj.* 1 *This painting received first prize:* foremost, leading, chief, principal, main, prime, ranking, highest; preeminent, supreme, paramount. 2 *Norsemen may have been the first European settlers in the New World:* earliest, original, eldest; primitive, primal, primeval, primordial, aboriginal; beginning, maiden. 3 *the first principles of math:* basic, fundamental, elementary, rudimentary, primary, introductory, beginning. —*n.* 4 *We were friends from the first:* beginning, commencement, start, outset. —*adv.* 5 *She asked first if we were free Tuesday evening:* before anything else, to begin with, at the outset, initially.

Ant. 1 subordinate, lesser. 2 later, subsequent.

first-rate *adj. She wrote a first-rate report:* excellent, very good, first-class, superior, outstanding, topnotch.

Ant. run-of-the-mill, mediocre, ordinary, indifferent.

fiscal *adj. fiscal responsibility:* financial, monetary, pecuniary, budgetary, economic.

fish *v.* 1 *We fished off the pier:* angle, cast; hook, net, troll, trawl, seine. 2 *She opened her purse and began fishing for change:* search, hunt, grope, rummage, cast about.

fishy *adj. Informal There's something fishy about his background:* doubtful, dubious, suspicious, suspect, questionable; peculiar, strange, odd, queer.

fit[1] *adj.* 1 *Is this water fit to drink? Do as you think fit:* suitable, good, adapted; appropriate; right, proper, meet, seemly, fitting, befitting, decorous; pertinent, relevant, applicable. 2 *Is he fit for the job?:* qualified, competent, trained, able; capable, prepared. 3 *She looks fitter than I've ever seen her:* healthy, hale, hardy, well, in good physical condition, strong. 4 *She's not fit to associate with decent folk:* worthy, deserving, suitable, good enough, sufficiently virtuous. —*v.* 5 *The house fits nicely in that wooded environment:* be suitable for, agree, harmonize, accord; conform, be adapted to, match. 6 *After she fits the dress it should be ready in a week:* adjust, adapt; shape, alter; correct, rectify.

Ant. 1 unfit, ill-suited, unsuitable. 2 ill-fitted, inadequate, improper, unseemly.

fit² *n.* **1** *Fido was subject to fits:* seizure, convulsion, spell. **2** *She had a fit of coughing:* spell, acute attack, spasm, paroxysm, outbreak. **3** *in a fit of pique:* outburst, explosion, burst.

fitful *adj.* *The rain was fitful all day:* irregular, intermittent, periodic, sporadic, spasmodic, now-and-then; unsteady, changeable, fluctuating, random, variable.
Ant. constant, steady, regular, uniform; changeless, unchanging.

fitting *adj.* *The head of state was given a fitting welcome:* suitable, proper, decorous, seemly, appropriate, befitting, congruous.
Ant. unfitting, unsuitable, ill-suited.

fix *v.* **1** *to fix the antenna to the roof:* secure, fasten, attach, affix, make fast, connect. **2** *He fixed the price at $50:* set, settle, determine, decide, establish, stabilize. **3** *Is something added to fix the cement?:* harden, solidify, set, congeal. **4** *Investigators fixed the blame on the alarm:* place, put, impose, affix. **5** *You'd better fix that leak:* repair, mend, patch, correct, set right; adjust, regulate. **6** *to fix dinner:* prepare, make; put together, assemble. —*n.* **7** *If you ruin this job you'll be in a real fix:* predicament, embarrassing situation, plight, difficulty, dilemma, awkward spot, *Slang* spot, pickle, bind.

fixation *n.* *a fixation about people staring at her:* obsession, preoccupation, fixed idea; delusion, complex, monomania.

fixed *adj.* **1** *a series of fixed fortifications:* stationary, immovable, fast; firm, stable; fastened, set, rooted; motionless, still, rigid. **2** *The price is fixed. a fixed stare:* not varying, not fluctuating, constant, steady; intent, steadily persistent, resolute; unbending, inflexible, firm, unwavering.
Ant. **1** moving, mobile. **2** unstable, unsteady, inconstant, varying.

fizzle *v.* **1** *The wet match fizzled:* sputter, hiss; bubble, fizz. **2** *Informal The plan fizzled for lack of interest:* come to nothing, fail, abort, fall through, *Slang* flop.

flabbergast *v.* *The news flabbergasted us:* amaze, confound, astound, astonish, shock, stun, stupefy, dumbfound.

flabby *adj.* **1** *Muscles can become flabby:* limp, flaccid, soft, yielding, slack. **2** *Your excuses are flabby:* feeble, enervated, spiritless, lame, flimsy.
Ant. **1** firm, hard, solid; tough, strong.

flag *n.* **1** *the country's flag:* banner, emblem, standard, ensign, pennant, colors; *(in the U.S.)* Stars and Stripes, Old Glory, Stars and Bars; *(in Great Britain)* Union Jack. —*v.* **2** *My energy flagged after climbing all those steps:* decline, wilt, languish; abate,

slump, subside, sag, fade, sink, ebb, wane, fail.

flagrant *adj.* *a flagrant abuse of authority:* shockingly shameless, brazen, blatant, flaunting, glaring, gross, obvious, barefaced; conspicuous; outrageous, monstrous.

flair *n.* *She has a flair for designing hats:* knack, talent, aptitude, gift, feel, faculty, capacity; style, taste; panache.

flake *n.* **1** *flakes of snow:* flat thin piece, scale, sheet, bit, fleck, shaving, patch. —*v.* **2** *This paint has started to flake:* peel off, peel, scale off, chip off, chip, crumble.

flamboyant *adj.* **1** *a room decorated in flamboyant reds and purples:* ornate, gaudy, garish, florid; showy, flashy, ostentatious. **2** *a flamboyant actress:* dashing, colorful, exciting, sensational, theatrical.

flame *n.* **1** *the flame of a match:* flare, blaze, fire, light, conflagration; spark, glare, glow, flash. **2** *the flame of ambition:* ardor, passion, fervor, intensity, fervency, zeal; enthusiasm; warmth, affection. **3** *Informal an old flame:* sweetheart, girlfriend; beau, lover, swain, boyfriend. —*v.* **4** *The gasoline flamed:* burst into flames, fire, kindle, light, ignite, blaze; glare, shine, flash, flush, blush.

flaming *adj.* **1** *The flaming wreckage burned for hours:* blazing, burning, fiery, afire, ablaze, alight; bright, brilliant, shining. **2** *I was in a flaming rage:* violent, ardent, intense, vehement, fervid, fervent, passionate; conspicuous, flagrant, glaring.

flammable *adj.* *Cleaning fluid is highly flammable:* inflammable, combustible, igneous, combustive, incendiary.
Ant. nonflammable, fireproof.

flank *adj.* **1** *He slapped the horse on the flank:* side, haunch, loin, hip. **2** *the army's left flank:* side, wing, edge, border. —*v.* **3** *Trees flanked the avenue:* line, border, skirt; edge, fringe.

flap *v.* **1** *That shutter flaps in the wind:* wave about, swing loosely, flop, flutter; shake, vibrate, oscillate. —*n.* **2** *We heard the flap of the screen door:* flop, flapping, flutter. **3** *a tent flap:* hanging piece, lap, fly, tab; skirt, apron.

flare *v.* **1** *The log made the fire flare:* flame, blaze, gleam, coruscate, glare, glow, incandesce, ignite, flash. **2** *Tempers flared:* erupt, explode, break out, boil over. **3** *His nostrils flared:* widen, broaden, spread, expand, distend, stretch, dilate.

flash *n.* **1** *a flash of lightning:* burst, streak, blaze, glare, gleam, flare, flame; radiance, coruscation. **2** *flashes of humor:* instance, occurrence, spark, glimmer, touch. **3** *I'll be back in a flash:* instant, moment, jiffy, minute, second, split second, trice. —*v.* **4** *The* *light was flashing:* blink, go on and off, flicker; sparkle, glitter; shine, blaze, glare, scintillate.

flashy *adj. flashy clothes:* dazzling, flamboyant, showy; sporty; pretentious, gaudy, garish, loud, ostentatious.

Ant. plain, modest, simple, unaffected.

flat *adj.* 1 *The land is absolutely flat:* level, horizontal, smooth; plane, planar, flush. 2 *They slept lying flat on the floor:* recumbent, prostrate, prone, supine; leveled. 3 *a flat denial:* unqualified, unequivocal, thorough, out-and-out, definite, absolute, complete, total, clear, direct. 4 *The ginger ale went flat:* lacking effervescence; stale; tasteless, insipid, flavorless; dull, vapid. —*n.* 5 Often **flats**. *The hunters waded into the flats:* level land, flat ground, lowlands; open country; shallow, shoal, marsh. 6 *The car has a flat:* deflated tire, blown-out tire, puncture. —*adv.* 7 *Lie down flat and breathe deeply:* horizontally, levelly, prostrate. 8 *He ran the mile in four minutes flat:* exactly, precisely.

Ant. 1 uneven, rugged, broken; vertical, upright, perpendicular. 4 bubbly, effervescent, fizzy; flavorful, tasty.

flatten *v.* 1 *Flatten the dough with your hands:* make flat, smooth, level; plane, even; press down, compress; deflate. 2 *The champion flattened all opponents:* knock down, floor, fell, *Slang* deck.

flatter *v. Everyone flattered me shamelessly:* overpraise, compliment, praise lavishly, gratify by praise; court, cajole, blandish; curry favor with, toady; soft-soap.

flattery *n. Flattery wins false friends:* excessive compliment, false praise, *Slang* snow job; sycophancy, toadying, fawning; wheedling, cajolery, blandishment, soft soap, jollying.

flaunt *v. They flaunt their power:* show off, parade, exhibit, brandish, vaunt, make a show of, advertise, broadcast, strut.

Ant. conceal, hide, mask.

flavor *n.* 1 *The shop sells ice cream in 30 different flavors:* characteristic taste, savor; tang, piquancy; flavoring. 2 *The novelist has captured the flavor of life in cities:* quality, distinctive character, attribute, essence, spirit; tenor, aura, ambience, tone.

flaw *n.* 1 *There was one flaw in our plan:* defect, blemish, fault, imperfection, weakness, fallacy, shortcoming; error, mistake; deformity, injury, defacement, disfigurement; failing, foible, vice. —*v.* 2 *The artist's garish use of color flawed the painting:* mar, impair, harm; weaken, detract from, make defective, deface, injure, disfigure.

flawless *adj. a flawless rendition of the sym-*

phony: faultless, errorless, impeccable, perfect; without blemish.

Ant. defective, flawed, marred.

flay *v.* 1 *Eskimos flay the caribou they kill and use the hides for garments:* skin, peel, bark; strip, fleece. 2 *The headmaster flayed the boys:* chastise severely, castigate, excoriate, censure harshly; assail, scold, rebuke, upbraid, punish; whip, cane, beat.

fleck *n.* 1 *The cat has flecks of orange and black:* spot, patch, mark, speck, flake, freckle, dot, speckle; drop, jot, particle. —*v.* 2 *The wallpaper was flecked with gold:* speckle, spot, flake, spatter, dapple, bespeckle, dot, besprinkle; streak, stipple, mottle.

fledgling *n. As a pilot, I'm still a fledgling:* novice, beginner, tyro, *Informal* greenhorn.

flee *v.* 1 *He fled the kidnappers:* escape from, run away from, get away from, make a getaway, take flight, abscond, skip, fly the coop, make off, hasten off, speed off. 2 *Why do you flee from responsibility?:* evade, avoid, shun, elude, dodge.

fleet *n.* 1 *the Third Fleet:* naval force, navy, naval division, *Archaic* armada; flotilla, squadron. —*adj.* 2 *Antelopes are among the fleetest animals:* swift, rapid, speedy, fast, swift-footed, fast of foot; hurried, quick, hasty; brief, short, transitory.

Ant. 2 slow, laggard, tardy.

fleeting *adj. We caught a fleeting glimpse of the president:* brief, passing, momentary; evanescent, short-lived, quick; transitory, ephemeral, unenduring.

flesh *n.* 1 *the flesh of the upper arm:* muscular tissue, soft tissue, muscle and fat, brawn; meat. 2 *The flesh is weak:* body, physical nature, flesh and blood, materiality; muscular energy, animal force; carnality, sensuality, bodily desire. 3 *the way of all flesh:* mankind, humanity, human race, man, people, living creatures. 4 *the flesh of a peach:* pulp, meat, edible part. —*v.* 5 *Three good meals a day should flesh you out:* fatten, fill out, make plump, become plump. 6 *Playwrights often fail to flesh out characters:* fill out, characterize fully, realize, individualize, particularize, give depth to.

fleshy *adj. Renoir painted fleshy women:* plump, corpulent, obese, fat, overweight, chubby, portly, well-padded, tubby, roly-poly.

Ant. thin, skinny, scrawny, lean.

flexible *adj.* 1 *The springs were of flexible steel:* easily bent, elastic, resilient, springy, extensible, bendable, ductile, plastic, tractable, pliable, pliant; supple, limber, lithe. 2 *We need a policy that is flexible:* adaptable, changeable, yielding, responsive; docile, submissive, amiable, genial.

Ant. 1 inflexible, stiff, rigid. 2 unyielding, absolute.

flicker *v.* 1 *The candle flickered:* flutter; glow, glisten, glitter, shimmer; flare, blaze, flash; sparkle, quiver, quaver. —*n.* 2 *There was a brief flicker and the light went out:* unsteady light, glitter, flare, gleam, spark, flash. 3 *a flicker of hope:* small amount, vestige, modicum, scintilla, spark, glimmer, trace.

flight *n.* 1 *Some birds are incapable of flight. a cross-country flight:* air travel, flying, soaring; aeronautics, plane trip; space travel. 2 *a flight of ducks:* flock, flying group, squadron, wing. 3 *the flight of time:* rush, swift movement, quick passage. 4 *The thief took flight:* hasty departure, running away, fleeing, escape; exodus, hegira.

flighty *adj. He was too flighty to get much out of college:* frivolous, fickle, impractical, capricious, changeable, mercurial; scatterbrained.

flimsy *adj.* 1 *These shirts are too flimsy:* unsubstantial, thin, slight, frail, fragile, delicate; diaphanous, sheer, filmy, gossamer; shoddy, ill-made, jerry-built. 2 *a flimsy alibi:* feeble, weak, inadequate; poor, worthless; trivial, trifling, petty, frivolous; shallow, superficial.

Ant. 1 sturdy, strong; well-made. 2 sound, substantial, solid.

flinch *v.* 1 *She flinched as she touched the hot stove:* wince, draw back; shrink, recoil, cringe, cower. —*n.* 2 *He gave a flinch of pain:* start, blench, wince, jerk, grimace.

fling *v.* 1 *She flung her coat on the chair:* throw, hurl, heave, pitch, toss, cast, dash, propel, sling. —*n.* 2 *Next weekend let's have a fling:* spree, Slang ball, lark. 3 *He had a fling at acting:* attempt, trial, go, try.

flip *v.* 1 *Let's flip a quarter to see who goes first:* toss, flick. 2 *He flipped through the pages of the book:* turn, thumb, turn over. —*n.* 3 *a flip of the thumb:* tap, flick, fillip; toss, throw, spin.

flippant *adj. flippant remarks:* impudent, brash, impertinent, disrespectful, saucy, insolent, *Informal* cheeky, flip; trifling, frivolous.

Ant. respectful, considerate.

flirt *v.* 1 *He flirts at every party:* toy, play at love, dally, trifle in love, tease, *Slang* make eyes at. 2 *She flirted with the idea:* toy, play, trifle; entertain. —*n.* 3 *You can't take a flirt too seriously:* flirter, tease, heartbreaker; *(fem.)* coquette.

flit *v. The bees were flitting from flower to*

flower: dart, skim, move swiftly, flicker, flitter, flutter; fly rapidly, hasten, scurry.

float *v. Float on your back:* rest on water; be poised in air; drift, hover, waft, bob, be buoyant, be buoyed up; levitate; buoy up, keep afloat.

Ant. sink, submerge.

flock *n.* 1 *a flock of sheep:* herd, pack, bunch, group, troop, drove, band, company, bevy; collection, aggregation; brood (of young birds), school (of fish), swarm (of insects), pride (of lions), pod (of seals or whales), covey (of game birds), gaggle (of geese). 2 *a flock of customers:* crowd, mob, gang, throng; gathering, assemblage; congregation. —*v.* 3 *Birds of a feather flock together:* run, gather, assemble, swarm, cluster, congregate, herd; crowd, throng, huddle.

flog *v. The quartermaster flogged the sailor:* whip, lash, thrash, beat, horsewhip, scourge, flail, cane.

flood *n.* 1 *During the flood many people were stranded:* inundation, overflow; deluge, cloudburst, downpour. 2 *a flood of tears:* torrent, stream, flow, outpouring, cascade, gush. —*v.* 3 *The rains flooded the farmlands:* inundate, deluge, submerge, wash over, flow over. 4 *The market has been flooded with electronic gadgets:* oversupply, overwhelm, glut, saturate, inundate, deluge.

Ant. 1 drought. 2 scarcity, lack, shortage.

floor *n.* 1 *The glass shattered on the floor:* bottom surface, bottom, flooring, base. 2 *an apartment on the 4th floor:* story, level; tier, deck. 3 *The government has put a floor under certain farm prices:* base rate, base, minimum. —*v.* 4 *The challenger was floored with a right hook:* knock down, fell, level, Slang deck.

flop *v.* 1 *The puppy flopped around on the slippery floor:* move clumsily or heavily; fall heavily, tumble, topple, drop, plop. 2 *The play flopped:* fail, close, fold, lay an egg. —*n.* 3 *The dinner party was a flop:* failure, fiasco, disaster, disappointment, Slang bust, bomb, turkey.

Ant. 2 succeed, triumph, flourish. 3 success, triumph, hit.

florid *adj.* 1 *a florid complexion:* ruddy, rosy, reddish, high-colored, rubicund; flushed. 2 *a long florid speech:* flowery, showy, elaborate, ornate; ostentatious, embellished, flamboyant, high-flown, grandiloquent.

Ant. 1 pallid, pale, bloodless. 2 prosaic, matter-of-fact.

flotsam *n. The flotsam was from the missing ship:* floating wreckage, floating goods, debris; castoffs; odds and ends, refuse, junk.

flounce[1] *v. She turned and flounced off the*

stage: sashay, strut, fling oneself, storm; skip, prance, gambol.

flounce[2] *n.* 1 *Her dress had many flounces:* ruffle, frill; valance, fringe, trimming. —*v.* 2 *The gown was flounced with pink lace:* trim, ruffle, frill, ornament, fringe, edge.

flounder *v.* 1 *The fawn floundered in the mud:* struggle, proceed clumsily, stumble, stagger; wallow, lurch, totter; limp, hobble. 2 *When she forgot her speech she floundered hopelessly:* falter, waver, hesitate, halt; miss one's way, wander aimlessly.

flourish *v.* 1 *Business flourished:* prosper, thrive, grow, succeed, fare well, be successful; bloom, flower, burgeon. 2 *Flourishing their swords, the troops attacked:* brandish, wave in the air, swing, wield, swish. —*n.* 3 *The armies met with a flourish of swords:* waving, shaking, brandishing, wielding; ostentatious display, show, parade; swagger, strut, pomp, dash. 4 *He signed his name with a flourish:* embellishment, curlicue, decoration; grace note, appoggiatura, cadenza. 5 *The senator speaks with a lot of flourish:* bravado, braggadocio, boasting, vaunting; rant, grandiloquence, magniloquence. 6 *a flourish of trumpets:* trumpet call, fanfare, fanfaronade.

Ant. 1 decline, fail, fade.

flout *v. to flout convention:* scorn, show contempt for, scoff at, spurn, jeer at, defy, disdain, mock.

Ant. revere; respect, esteem.

flow *v.* 1 *The river flows east:* course, move in a stream, run, pour, stream, cascade; rush, gush, well out, issue; discharge, drain; surge, deluge, swirl; seep; glide, sweep, drift. —*n.* 2 *The flow of melted snow cascaded down the mountain:* stream, course, torrent, flood; current, tide. 3 *a steady flow of ideas:* outpouring, stream, cascade, outflow; emanation, spurt, spout, gush; train, succession, sequence, progression.

flower *n.* 1 *He sent her flowers:* blossom, bloom, posy; nosegay, bouquet, floral tribute. 2 *the flower of the nation's youth:* best, pick, choicest part, cream; elite, aristocracy. —*v.* 3 *Peonies flower in spring. Mozart's genius flowered at an early age:* bloom, produce blossoms, produce flowers, blossom, be in flower; burgeon, develop, mature, ripen, flourish.

Ant. 2 dregs, residue.

flowery *adj. flowery language:* ornate, ornamental, embellished, fancy, euphuistic, florid; rhetorical, grandiloquent, magniloquent.

fluctuate *v.* 1 *With prices fluctuating, it's hard to budget:* rise and fall, change often,

vary irregularly, shift; wobble, veer; ebb and flow. 2 *to fluctuate between optimism and despair:* waver, vacillate, oscillate, undulate, swing, be unsettled, falter, shift, alternate, vary.

fluent *adj. Edna is fluent in Spanish:* able to speak readily; glib, smooth-spoken, eloquent, articulate; effortless, facile, wellversed.

Ant. hesitant, halting.

fluffy *adj. fluffy pillows:* feathery, downy; fuzzy, fleecy.

fluid *n.* 1 *cleaning fluid:* liquid, solution. —*adj.* 2 *The doctor prescribed a fluid diet:* liquid, liquefied, of fluids. 3 *Keep your plans fluid:* flexible, adaptable, adjustable; changeable, indefinite; unstable, unsettled, shifting.

Ant. 1, 2 solid. 3 fixed, settled, definite.

fluke *n. His winning was a fluke:* accident, unlikely event, quirk of fate, chance, mischance, stroke of luck.

flurry *n.* 1 *A flurry shook the branches:* sudden wind, gust, windy blast, squall; shower, light snowfall. 2 *There was quite a flurry when the president visited:* bustle, commotion, fuss, ado, stir, pother; nervous hurry, agitation, turbulence, tumult, disturbance, perturbation, confusion.

flush *n.* 1 *The child's face had an attractive flush:* blush, rosiness, rosy glow; bloom, tinge of color, tint; redness, ruddiness. 2 *A flush of water will clean the walk:* cleansing flow, gush, wash, rinse, spray, deluge. 3 *in a flush of anger:* rush of emotion, impulse; flutter, quiver; thrill, shock. 4 *the flush of youth:* bloom, glow, glowing, freshness. —*v.* 5 *They flushed with pleasure:* blush, redden, color, glow. 6 *Once a year the city flushes the sewers:* cleanse by flooding, wash out, flood, rinse, drench. 7 *The team was flushed with victory:* animate, elate, puff up; thrill, excite.

fluster *v.* 1 *I was flustered when company arrived unexpectedly:* disconcert, ruffle, make nervous, perturb, upset, agitate, startle, discompose, discomfit, befuddle, muddle, confuse; daze, throw off balance. —*n.* 2 *The president's visit caused a great deal of fluster:* nervous excitement, confusion, flutter, agitation, turmoil, commotion, flurry, dither.

flutter *v.* 1 *The flag fluttered in the breeze:* wave, toss about, flap; throb, tremble, shake, pulsate; bob, wobble, quiver; palpitate. 2 *The butterfly fluttered from leaf to leaf:* flit, flitter; wing. —*n.* 3 *There was a flutter of wings as the gull rose:* agitation, vibration, flapping; quiver, tremble, tremor.

flux *n.* 1 *the mighty flux of a river:* flow,

current, course, flood, stream, tide; motion. 2 *Our plans are in a state of flux:* continuous change, fluctuation, alteration, modification; unrest; shifting, transition.

fly *v.* 1 *The plane flies at the speed of sound:* travel through the air; pilot a plane; wing, take wing, take off; soar, glide, sail, coast, swoop. 2 *The king's banner was flying above the tent:* wave, flutter, undulate, flap, display in the air. 3 *The days really flew by:* move quickly, pass rapidly, go suddenly. 4 *He had to fly from the emperor's wrath:* flee, run away, make one's escape, take flight; hasten, hurry.

fly-by-night *adj. a fly-by-night scheme:* undependable, untrustworthy, unreliable, irresponsible; disreputable, shady, shifty, crooked, dishonest.
Ant. honest, dependable, trustworthy, honorable.

foam *n. The glass of beer was mostly foam:* froth, head, fizz, effervescence, bubbling; spume; suds, lather.

focus *n.* 1 *The café was the focus of social life:* center, hub; meeting place, gathering place, rendezvous; heart, core. —*v. Focus your attention on the blackboard:* bring into focus, adjust, center; converge, bring to a point; concentrate; fix, center, direct, aim, bring to bear.

fodder *n. Alfalfa is a fodder for cattle:* feed, food, silage, forage.

foe *n. Our foes made peace with us:* enemy, adversary, opponent, antagonist; rival, competitor, contender, disputant, combatant.
Ant. friend, ally, confederate.

fog *n.* 1 *The fog closed in:* thick mist, haze, smog, murkiness. 2 *My brain was in a fog:* daze, haze, stupor, trance. —*v.* 3 *Lack of sleep fogged his mind:* bewilder, muddle, daze, confuse, dim, cloud, darken.
Ant. 2 clarity, comprehension. 3 clear, clarify.

foggy *adj.* 1 *a foggy morning:* misty, hazy, clouded, murky, smoggy. 2 *He has only a foggy notion of it:* unclear, confused, vague, fuzzy, cloudy, dim, obscure, indistinct, shadowy.
Ant. 2 distinct, accurate, clear.

foible *n. Is vanity a sin or merely a foible?:* minor fault, weakness, shortcoming, frailty, failing, deficiency; quirk, whimsy.
Ant. strength, virtue, perfection.

foil¹ *v. The revolt was foiled:* frustrate, balk, thwart; prevent, check, nip.
Ant. advance, further, forward; incite, instigate.

foil² *n.* 1 *The picture frame is covered with gold foil:* leaf, flake, lamina, sheet, film.

2 *Her humor is a perfect foil for his seriousness:* contrast, antithesis, complement, counterpart, backdrop.

foist *v. Don't let them foist used merchandise on you:* pass off, palm off, impose, unload.

fold¹ *v.* 1 *Fold the napkins:* double, crease, pleat, corrugate; tuck, pucker; wrinkle, rumple, crumple; crinkle, crimp, curl. 2 *Fold the scarf in tissue paper:* wrap, wrap up, envelop, enfold, encase. 3 *She folded the child in her arms:* embrace, clasp, enfold, entwine. —*n.* 4 *It was concealed in a fold of her dress:* gather, tuck, pleat, crimp, crinkle, pucker. 5 *The map split along the fold:* crease, folding, bend.
Ant. 1 unfold. 2 unwrap.

fold² *n.* 1 *a sheep fold:* pen, enclosure, corral, yard; barnyard, stockade, compound. 2 *the preacher and members of the fold:* religious life; the church, congregation, flock, parish, sect; group, community.

foliage *n. The fall foliage was lovely:* leaves, foliation, leatage.

folks *n.pl.* 1 *Folks are talking about us:* people, the public, everyone. 2 *My folks will be here for Christmas:* parents, family, family members, relatives, kinsfolk, kinfolk, kith and kin, blood relations.

folklore *n. American folklore:* legends, lore, folk tales, fables, myths.

follow *v.* 1 *Who will follow when I retire?:* succeed, come next, come after; replace, take the place of. 2 *The citizens agreed to follow their civic leaders:* accept as authority, emulate, imitate, copy, take after. 3 *Follow instructions:* obey, heed, act in accordance with, comply with, observe, mind, conform to, be guided by; notice, watch, note. 4 *The detectives followed the gang to their hideout:* pursue, chase, go after; track, trail, *Informal* shadow, tail; attend, accompany. 5 *Everyone ought to have some ideals to follow:* emulate, cherish, strive after, aim at; cultivate. 6 *Could you follow what she was saying?:* understand, grasp, comprehend, catch, keep up with.
Ant. 1 precede. 2 forsake, desert, abandon. 3 disobey, ignore, flout.

follower *n.* 1 *They eluded followers by crossing the river:* pursuer, chaser; *Slang* tail, shadow. 2 *Mahatma Gandhi had many followers:* disciple, adherent, apostle, proselyte; devotee, admirer, fan, partisan, supporter, advocate; pupil, protégé. 3 *The queen's retinue included 30 followers:* attendant, servant, retainer; hanger-on, toady, sycophant.
Ant. 2 leader, teacher, guru; rival, opponent, detractor.

following *adj.* 1 *the following afternoon:*

next, succeeding, subsequent, ensuing; successive, consecutive. 2 *The President has issued the following statement:* ensuing, subsequent, below, now to be mentioned, coming next.

folly *n. It would be folly to try to lift that piano:* foolishness, senselessness, idiocy, brainlessness, inanity, asininity; fatuousness, silliness, irrationality; imprudence; mistake, indiscretion; frivolity, absurdity, tomfoolery, nonsense.

Ant. wisdom, prudence, levelheadedness.

foment *v. to foment a quarrel:* stir up, incite, foster, promote, instigate, provoke; urge, stimulate, foster; rouse, arouse, kindle, spur, goad, agitate.

Ant. suppress, quench; check, curb, restrain.

fond *adj.* 1 *I'm fond of desserts:* have a liking for, enamored, crazy about. 2 *He gave her fond looks:* loving, tender, affectionate, amorous; passionate, impassioned, ardent, enamored, infatuated, desirous. 3 *She has fond hopes of becoming a movie star:* cherished, held dear, preserved, harbored; naive, somewhat foolish.

Ant. 1 averse, indifferent. 2 unconcerned, unloving, hateful.

fondle *v. to fondle a kitten:* caress, stroke, pet; cuddle, hug, embrace, nestle.

fondness *n.* 1 *Our fondness for them is reciprocated:* tenderness, affection, attachment, devotion, love; amorousness, desire, passion, ardor. 2 *a fondness for rich desserts:* partiality, predilection, penchant, preference, inclination, propensity, desire, fancy, liking.

Ant. 1 antagonism, hostility, hatred, loathing. 2 dislike, aversion, revulsion.

food *n.* 1 *to buy food for an army:* foodstuffs, provisions, rations, comestibles, victuals, viands, eatables, edibles; nourishment, sustenance; *Slang* grub, chow. 2 *food for livestock:* fodder, forage, feed, silage.

fool *n.* 1 *Only a fool would do that:* stupid person, idiot, dolt, blockhead, bonehead, simpleton, lunkhead, nitwit, dummy, imbecile, moron, nincompoop, numskull, ignoramus, ass, dunce, ninny, oaf. 2 *The king laughed at his fool:* jester, clown, buffoon; merry-andrew, harlequin. —*v.* 3 *The con artists fooled him:* trick, deceive, make a fool of, dupe, hoodwink, hoax, beguile, bamboozle, humbug, diddle. 4 *You seem to be fooling:* joke, jest; pretend, feign, make believe, tease.

Ant. 1 genius, wise one, sage, scholar.

foolhardy *adj. a foolhardy venture:* rash, reckless, incautious, imprudent; daredevil,

madcap, headstrong, brash; heedless, careless, thoughtless.

Ant. wary, cautious, prudent, careful; calculating, shrewd.

foolish *adj. That was a foolish thing to say:* unwise, imprudent, ill-considered, ill-advised, incautious, irresponsible; absurd, inane, fatuous, witless, senseless; stupid, half-witted, brainless, silly, moronic, asinine, idiotic, imbecilic; preposterous, ridiculous.

Ant. intelligent, smart; quick-witted, wise, sage; prudent, circumspect, perspicacious; clever, sharp.

foolishness *n. Because of such foolishness they're deeply in debt:* imprudence, folly, irresponsibility; absurdity, preposterousness, ridiculousness, asininity; witlessness, brainlessness, silliness, stupidity, fatuousness, idiocy, lunacy, imbecility.

foot *n.* 1 *She dropped the book on her foot:* lower extremity; *Slang* tootsy, dog; (of animals) hoof, paw, trotter, pad. 2 *the foot of the stairs:* base, lower part, bottom, foundation.

footloose *adj. Now that our children are grown we're footloose:* free, unattached, uncommitted, unencumbered, fancy-free, carefree.

fop *n. In olden days he would have been called a fop:* dandy, Beau Brummel, swell, fashion plate.

foppish *adj. He wears foppish clothes:* dandyish, showy, ostentatious, dandified; vain, affected, finical.

Ant. modest, unaffected; dowdy, slovenly, tacky.

forage *n.* 1 *Do the cattle have enough forage?:* fodder, feed, silage; food, provisions. —*v.* 2 *to forage for something to eat:* search, rummage, seek, hunt, explore, scavenge, raid, plunder, ravage.

foray *n.* 1 *The Vikings made regular forays on coastal towns:* raid, sudden attack, incursion, sally. —*v.* 2 *The soldiers forayed into the surrounding countryside:* plunder, pillage, ravage, raid.

forbear *v.* 1 *Forbear from saying such cruel things:* refrain, desist, abstain, do without, hold back, give up; eschew, forgo, leave off, stop, cease, quit. 2 *I wanted to scream, but I had to forbear:* restrain oneself, hold back; be patient, be tolerant, tolerate; suffer, endure, bear.

forbearance *n. It takes forbearance to overlook faults:* patience, leniency, resignation, tolerance, self-restraint, endurance; mercy, mercifulness, clemency, pity, pardon; abstinence, temperance.

Ant. anger, impatience, intolerance.

forbid v. *I forbid you to go:* prohibit, not allow, order not to, enjoin, proscribe; ban, bar, disallow; preclude.
Ant. permit, allow, let, approve.

forbidding adj. *The forest looked forbidding:* disagreeable, unpleasant, dour, unfriendly; dangerous-looking, sinister, ominous, grim, threatening; ugly, repellent, horrible, repulsive, abhorrent, hideous.
Ant. attractive, alluring, inviting.

force n. **1** *the force of her personality:* energy, power, potency, strength; vitality, effectiveness; attraction, magnetism, charisma. **2** *to weigh the force of each word:* significance, meaning, value, import, signification; effect, impact. **3** *Push with as much force as you can:* power, might, strength; pressure, energy, momentum, stress. **4** *The police used force to hold back the crowd:* coercion, constraint, duress, compulsion, violence. **5** *the work force:* group, body, team, unit, division, crew, detachment. —v. **6** *Bad weather forced us to call off the picnic:* oblige, compel, make, necessitate, require, constraint, enjoin, impel, drive, induce. **7** *We forced water into the pipe:* thrust, propel, push, press, drive; impel, impose. **8** *The police tried to force the truth from the suspect:* obtain by force, wrest, squeeze, pry, wrench, drag; coerce, extort.
Ant. **1** weakness, frailty; inefficiency.

forced adj. **1** *The bridge had been built with forced labor:* enforced, compelled, coerced, involuntary, compulsory, slave. **2** *a forced smile:* strained, labored, artificial, insincere; mannered, affected.
Ant. **2** easy, natural, simple.

forceful adj. *a brief but forceful speech:* powerful, strong, dynamic, intense, vigorous, potent, impressive, effective, vivid.
Ant. feeble, weak.

fore adj. *the fore part of the ship:* front, forward, frontal, headmost, anterior.
Ant. rear, aft, posterior, back, hindmost.

forebear Also **forbear** n. *Our forebears came from Europe:* ancestor, progenitor, antecedent.

foreboding n. *We had a foreboding of disaster:* premonition, presentiment, prescience; omen, augury, portent; dread, misgiving.

forecast v. **1** *to forecast an upturn in the stock market:* predict, prognosticate, project; prophesy, augur, foresee; envision, foretell, presage. —n. **2** *The forecast for tonight is rain:* prediction, prognostication, prognosis, outlook; projection.

forefather n. *He wants to visit the land of his forefathers:* ancestor, forebear, progenitor, primogenitor, antecedent; forerunner, precursor; procreator, author, father.
Ant. descendant, progeny, issue.

forefront n. *The young singer is coming to the forefront:* lead, head, vanguard, position of prominence, fore; public attention, fame.

foreign adj. **1** *a foreign car:* from another land, alien, not domestic, not native; imported, introduced; strange, exotic, outlandish; distant, remote; unfamiliar, unknown. **2** *Spite is foreign to her nature:* extraneous, extrinsic, unconnected, unrelated; uncharacteristic, inappropriate, inconsistent, incongruous, incompatible; irrelevant, inapplicable.
Ant. **1** domestic, native. **2** intrinsic, characteristic; suited.

foreigner n. *Many foreigners visit our country:* alien, outlander, nonnative; immigrant, émigré, outsider.
Ant. native, citizen, aborigine.

foreknowledge n. *to have foreknowledge of the stock market crash:* prior knowledge, advance notice; precognition, prescience, anticipation, premonition.

foreman n. *a foreman in a shoe factory:* manager, overseer, supervisor, crew leader, chief workman, boss, superintendent; spokesman, chairman, presiding juror.

foremost adj. *our foremost tourist attractions:* principal, leading, main, preeminent, chief, paramount; vital, essential.

forerunner n. **1** *the forerunner of modern baseball:* precursor, predecessor, prototype; ancestor, forebear. **2** *a forerunner of spring:* herald, harbinger, foretoken, portent, precursor, forewarning.

foresee v. *to foresee success:* anticipate, expect, envision; prophesy, foretell, predict, prognosticate; be clairvoyant, be prescient, augur, presage, divine.

foresight n. **1** *to have foresight in predicting future events:* clairvoyance, prescience, power of foreseeing, prevision, precognition. **2** *a tragic lack of foresight:* preparedness, farsightedness, forethought, anticipation, provision for the future, discretion, precaution.
Ant. **1** hindsight. **2** carelessness, neglect.

forestall v. *to forestall a strike:* prevent, thwart, ward off, avert, avoid, block, preclude.

forest n. *a pine forest:* woods, wood, timberland, wooded area, woodland; stand, grove, thicket, copse; wilderness, jungle.

foretell v. *to foretell the future:* predict, prophesy, foresee, prognosticate, divine, augur, forecast; presage, portend.

forethought n. **1** *One needs forethought to succeed:* careful planning, prudence, carefulness, sagacity, heed. **2** *to answer without forethought:* deliberation, prior thought, consideration, premeditation.

Ant. **2** impulsiveness, spontaneity.

forever *adv.* **1** *I'll love you forever:* eternally, for all time, always, everlastingly, to the end of time, ever. **2** *He's forever asking to borrow something:* continually, perpetually, constantly, always; ceaselessly, unceasingly, incessantly.

Ant. never, occasionally.

forewarn *v.* *to be forewarned of the enemy's approach:* caution, alert, put on guard, give warning, tip off, prewarn, give advance notice.

foreword *n.* *the foreword to a book:* preface, introduction, introductory statement, preliminary remarks, preamble, prologue.

forfeit *n.* **1** *to pay a forfeit:* penalty, fine, assessment, forfeiture. —*v.* **2** *She forfeited the tennis match:* lose because of some offense, surrender, yield, default.

forge *n.* **1** *a blacksmith's forge:* furnace, hearth; smithy, ironworks. —*v.* **2** *The smith forged the horseshoe:* hammer out, shape, form, fabricate, make, manufacture, fashion. **3** *My signature was forged:* sign falsely, imitate fraudulently, counterfeit, falsify, simulate.

forgery *n.* *The museum discovered that the vase was a forgery:* counterfeit, imitation, copy; fraud, fake.

forget *v.* **1** *He forgot your name:* fail to recollect, not remember, be unable to recall; neglect, slight, disregard. **2** *Don't forget the plane tickets:* leave behind, fail to take, omit unintentionally; think no more of, dispense with, let bygones be bygones.

Ant. **1** remember, recollect, recall, retain.

forgetful *adj.* *She's forgetful, so remind her again:* apt to forget, absentminded; heedless, neglectful, unmindful, negligent.

Ant. retentive, careful, mindful.

forgive *v.* *We must forgive our enemies:* pardon, excuse, absolve, reprieve, let bygones be bygones.

Ant. blame, condemn, censure.

forgo Also **forego** *v.* *I'll have to forgo that new suit:* do without, relinquish, renounce; abstain from, refrain from, eschew, skip.

fork *n.* **1** *When you get to the fork in the road, bear right:* division, branching, branch, bifurcation, divergence, separation; bend, elbow. —*v.* **2** *The river forks before it reaches town:* diverge, divide, bifurcate, branch, branch out, split.

forlorn *adj.* **1** *She is lonely and forlorn:* unhappy, depressed, dejected, despondent, dispirited; brokenhearted, disconsolate, miserable, despairing. **2** *We stayed at a for-*

lorn little inn: forsaken, deserted, solitary; desolate, dreary, dismal; lonesome, lonely, destitute, abandoned, forgotten.

Ant. **1** happy, cheerful, elated, hopeful.

form *n.* **1** *The cookies were in the form of squares:* shape, outline, figure, contour; figuration, configuration; conformation; structure, format, design, style, plan. **2** *This coat fits your form:* body, figure, shape, anatomy, build, physique. **3** *When the cement has hardened, the form is removed:* mold, cast, frame, framework. **4** *Ice is water in another form:* appearance, phase, manifestation, arrangement, image, guise. **5** *The ant is a form of insect:* type, variety, kind, sort; genus, species, genre, class. **6** *You paint well, but your work lacks form:* order, system, structure, harmony, arrangement, proportion, symmetry. **7** *the traditional form of the marriage service:* method, order, format, rule, habit, practice, formality, ceremony, rite, ritual; formula, style, mode. **8** *It's not good form to talk about oneself:* social behavior, manners, deportment, practice, conduct, custom, usage, propriety, decorum; etiquette. **9** *If she's in form, she can win the match easily:* trim, fettle, fitness, shape, top condition. —*v.* **10** *Form the plaster with your hands:* fashion, shape, mold; carve, sculpt, cut, chisel, model; hew, cast, stamp; construct, structure, fabricate, forge, build; make, create, devise, put together, manufacture; found, establish. **11** *The sofa is formed of three sections:* compose, comprise, make up, constitute. **12** *He formed the habit of peering over his glasses:* develop, acquire, contract.

formal *adj.* **1** *Showing a white flag is a formal gesture of surrender:* ceremonial, conventional, ritualistic, prescribed, regular, customary, *Latin* pro forma. **2** *Your signature on the lease will make our agreement formal:* definite, settled, fixed; explicit, positive; proper, in due form, authoritative; legal, lawful. **3** *Her Highness is gracious but quite formal:* reserved, decorous, proper, aloof, distant, standoffish, straitlaced, stiff, rigid, solemn, ceremonious.

Ant. **1, 3** informal, casual, spontaneous, unceremonious.

formality *n.* **1** *He bowed with mock formality:* observance of form, conventionality, propriety, decorum, etiquette. **2** *Once the terms had been agreed to, signing the treaty was a formality:* ritual, rite, custom, convention, rule of procedure, ceremony.

Ant. **1** informality.

formation *n.* **1** *A formation of planes thundered overhead:* ordered group, configuration, arrangement; structure, composition, makeup. 2 *the formation of a new business:* creation, establishment, organization, genesis; manufacture, fabrication, building.

former *adj.* 1 *in former days:* past, prior, bygone; ancient, olden, of yore. 2 *Speaking of Alice and Sarah, the former married an archaeologist:* first-mentioned, before-mentioned, first-named; aforementioned, aforesaid. 3 *her former husband:* previous, earlier, prior; antecedent, foregoing; erstwhile, *Informal* ex.
Ant. 1 modern, coming, future. 2 latter, succeeding, following. 3 subsequent; present.

formerly *adv. She was formerly head of a large store:* once, at one time, in times past, previously; hitherto, lately.

formidable *adj. A charging rhinoceros is formidable:* awesome, imposing, impressive; fearful, terrifying, dreadful, menacing; threatening, forbidding; overwhelming; difficult, demanding, dangerous.

formula *n. What's your formula for success?:* prescription, recipe, blueprint; guideline, rule, principle, precept.

forsake *v.* 1 *He swore never to forsake us:* desert, abandon, leave, cast off. 2 *to forsake old habits:* renounce, forswear, abjure, give up, have done with, repudiate, abandon; relinquish, reject, discard, disclaim, disavow, deny.

forswear *v. The witness forswore his previous testimony:* retract, repudiate, recant, gainsay, disavow, disclaim; disown, reject, renounce, contravene.
Ant. affirm, confirm.

tort *n. Soldiers stormed the fort:* fortress, fortification, stronghold; bulwark, bastion, citadel; garrison, base, station, camp.

forte *n. Math is her forte:* strong point, specialty, strength, bent, skill, proficiency.

forth *adv.* 1 *from this day forth:* forward, onward, outward. 2 *He brought forth an idea that we liked:* to notice, before one's attention.

forthcoming *adj. a forthcoming play:* about to appear, upcoming, coming, approaching; imminent, impending; available, obtainable, accessible, at hand, handy, on tap.

forthright *adj.* 1 *I'll give you a forthright answer:* frank, open, blunt, outspoken, candid, direct, plainspoken, straightforward. —*adv.* 2 *Tell me forthright what you think:* straightforwardly, straight, straight out, frankly, openly, bluntly, candidly, truthfully.

forthwith *adv. We left forthwith:* immediately, without delay, at once, instantly, straightaway, quickly, promptly.

fortification *n. There were fortifications*

along the border: fortress, fort, citadel, garrison, bastion, bulwark, rampart, stronghold; breastwork, earthwork.

fortify *v.* 1 *The medieval town was fortified with a high wall:* strengthen against attack, defend with fortifications, protect, secure, shield. 2 *wooden beams fortified with steel:* strengthen, reinforce, brace, buttress; harden, stiffen. 3 *He drank a brandy to fortify himself:* sustain, make strong, build up, support, strengthen, brace; hearten, cheer, reassure; encourage. 4 *The bread is fortified with vitamins:* enrich, add nutrients to.
Ant. 2 weaken, impair. 3 demoralize, dishearten, unnerve.

fortitude *n. It takes fortitude to overcome difficulties:* endurance, courage, strength of mind, moral strength, resoluteness, mettle; spunk, backbone; resolution, determination, pluck, tenacity; valor, bravery.
Ant. cowardice, weakness, faintheartedness.

fortress *n. The enemy besieged the fortress:* fort, citadel, stronghold, fortification, bastion, bulwark.

fortuitous *adj. a fortuitous meeting:* chance, accidental, unexpected; undesigned, unpremeditated, inadvertent, unintended; incidental; lucky, happy, fortunate.
Ant. prearranged, planned, intentional.

fortunate *adj.* 1 *I'm fortunate to have a tolerant coach:* lucky, having good fortune, blessed, favored. 2 *It was a fortunate day for the victors:* bringing good luck, auspicious, propitious, favorable, advantageous, opportune, promising.
Ant. 1 unlucky, unfortunate. 2 ill-starred, disastrous, calamitous.

fortune *n.* 1 *Gold prospectors could make a fortune:* immense amount of money, wealth, riches; bonanza, windfall, godsend. 2 *Let's leave it to fortune:* fate, destiny, luck, chance, providence.
Ant. 2 design, intent, purpose.

fortuneteller *n. A fortuneteller told her she would succeed:* clairvoyant, seer, crystal gazer, palmist, medium, magician; soothsayer, oracle, prophet, augur.

forum *n.* 1 *The issues will be discussed at the town forum:* public meeting place, public arena, assembly place. 2 *There is a forum on drug addiction tonight:* open discussion, symposium, seminar, colloquium.

forward Also **forwards** *adv.* 1 *The cars moved forward:* ahead, onward, in front, toward the front, forth; toward the future. —*adj.* 2 *the forward motion of the car:* moving ahead, advancing, onward; frontal, fore; progressive, forward-looking, up-to-date. 3 *His behavior was rather forward:*

bold, brash, impudent, presumptuous, presuming, fresh, impertinent, cheeky, insolent, brazen, shameless. —v. 4 *Please forward our mail:* send forward, readdress, send on, relay. 5 *to forward a project:* advance, promote, further; assist, back, champion.

Ant. 1 backward, to the rear. 2 backward, regressive. 3 retiring, modest. 5 hinder, impede, obstruct, block.

foster v. 1 *His parents fostered his love of reading:* encourage, promote, further, forward, aid, nurture; advocate, support, back. 2 *They have fostered several orphans:* rear, bring up, raise; care for, tend, take in, sustain; harbor, protect.

Ant. 1 oppose, resist, curb, inhibit.

foul adj. 1 *a foul odor:* disgusting, loathsome, obnoxious, putrid, putrescent, stinking, smelly, malodorous; hateful, odious, revolting, repulsive. 2 *Take off those foul clothes and wash them:* dirty, soiled, filthy, nasty, unclean; begrimed, besmeared, sullied; grimy, grubby; squalid, sordid. 3 *foul weather:* stormy, blustery, wet, rainy, drizzly, misty; foggy, cloudy. 4 *foul language:* coarse, vulgar, indecent, obscene; profane, scurrilous, blasphemous; gross; abusive, insulting. 5 *a foul crime:* heinous, abominable, infamous, notorious; disgraceful, contemptible, detestable; vile, wicked, evil, monstrous, nefarious, villainous, atrocious. 6 *Masses of seaweed fouled the anchor:* tangle, clog, entangle, ensnare.

Ant. 1 fair, fragrant, pleasing. 2 clean. 3 fair, clear. 4 mild, modest, pure. 5 admirable, pleasant; honorable. 6 clear, untangle.

found v. 1 *His father founded the business:* establish, institute, organize, bring about, set up, originate, create, start. 2 *Her arguments were founded on fact:* base, rest, sustain, ground.

foundation n. 1 *The builders poured a foundation of cement:* base, substructure, understructure, underpinning, bottom. 2 *The charges of fraud were without foundation:* basis, base, justification, cause, reason; source, origin, premise, underlying principle. 3 *The foundation provides money for medical research:* institution; charity, philanthropy, endowment.

founder v. 1 *The ship foundered during a storm:* sink, go down; swamp; capsize, run aground. 2 *The company foundered during the recession:* fail, come to grief, go under.

fountain n. 1 *The park's fountains were spectacular:* stream of water; gush, flow, spout. 2 *Ancient Greece was a fountain of*

wisdom: origin, source; font, wellspring, fountainhead.

foxy adj. *He's too foxy to trust:* cunning, crafty, clever, artful, wily, tricky, sharp, shrewd; sly, devious, underhand; deceitful, deceptive; designing, conniving, scheming.

Ant. candid, open, artless, guileless, ingenuous, naive.

foyer n. *Wait in the foyer:* antechamber, vestibule, anteroom, waiting room, hall; lobby.

fractious adj. *Don't be fractious when I ask you to do something:* cross, irritable, peevish, ill-tempered, grouchy, snappish, irascible; huffy, petulant, quarrelsome; unruly, rebellious, contrary, manageable.

Ant. complaisant, good-humored, agreeable, good-natured.

fracture n. 1 *a fracture in the lower leg:* break, rupture, cleavage; breach, separation, division; split, rift, crack. —v. 2 *The dispute fractured their friendship:* break, split, shatter; disrupt, rend, cleave.

fragile adj. 1 *These wine glasses are fragile:* easily broken, frangible, breakable; delicate, dainty, flimsy, brittle, crumbly, soft, friable. 2 *in fragile health:* frail, infirm, delicate, feeble, weak, unsubstantial.

Ant. 1 strong, sturdy, resilient, durable.

fragment n. 1 *a fragment of ancient pottery:* part broken off, piece, segment, section, remnant; chip, shard, bit, morsel, shred. —v. 2 *to fragment the opposition:* disunite, break apart, splinter, shatter; divide, separate; cut up; crumble, disintegrate.

Ant. 2 unite, bring together, combine.

fragmentary adj. *a fragmentary account:* incomplete, unfinished, piecemeal, disconnected; choppy, segmented, disjointed, scattered; partial.

fragrance n. *the fragrance of lilacs:* fragrant odor, perfume, scent, aroma; bouquet.

Ant. stench, stink, offensive odor.

fragrant adj. *The roses made the whole house fragrant:* sweet-scented, sweet-smelling, odorous, odoriferous, aromatic, perfumed.

Ant. fetid, malodorous, stinking.

frail adj. 1 *The load was held by one frail rope:* easily broken or destroyed, fragile, frangible, brittle, breakable, crumbly; flimsy, unsubstantial, delicate. 2 *Her health has been frail:* slight, weak, delicate, feeble, fragile; infirm, decrepit.

Ant. 1 strong, stout, sturdy. 2 healthy, sound, hale, robust.

frailty n. *A liking for flattery was one of his frailties:* weakness of character, fault, sin, vice, failing, defect, flaw, weak point, fallibility.

Ant. strength, virtue.

frame n. 1 *a picture frame:* mounting, case, housing; border, setting, edging, rim. 2 *the frame of the house:* framework, skeleton, framing. 3 *a man of large frame:* physique, build, figure, shape, anatomy; constitution, construction. 4 *a happy frame of mind:* attitude; state, mood, humor, temperament. —v. 5 *A new set of bylaws was framed:* devise, conceive, contrive, invent, plan; draft, sketch, concoct, formulate, design; organize.

frank adj. *frank criticism:* candid, plainspoken, direct, outspoken, straightforward, free, forthright, open, honest, undisguised; unambiguous, unequivocal; patent, explicit. *Ant.* evasive, indirect, disingenuous.

frantic adj. *There was frantic activity before the visitors arrived:* excited, agitated, hectic; frenzied, frenetic; overwrought, beside oneself, distraught, nervous; impassioned, raving, ungovernable; crazy, mad, insane, deranged, beserk. *Ant.* calm, unruffled, composed.

fraternity n. 1 *the fraternity of workers:* brotherliness, brotherhood, kinship, interrelation. 2 *a literary fraternity:* club, society, circle; league, alliance, federation, confederacy, coalition; clique, coterie, clan, brotherhood.

fraud n. 1 *The fraud involved the sale of nonexistent land:* swindling, cheating, trickery, deceit, deception, dishonesty, misrepresentation, duplicity, double-dealing, chicanery; imposture, sham, hoax, swindle, humbug. 2 *As an actress, she's an absolute fraud:* impostor, charlatan, mountebank, sham, fake, counterfeit, pretender; quack, swindler, cheat, con artist. *Ant.* 1 fairness, honesty, integrity.

fraudulent adj. *fraudulent business practices:* dishonest, deceptive, underhanded, tricky, unprincipled, dishonorable, crooked, cheating; spurious, sham, bogus, false, counterfeit.

fraught adj. *a trip fraught with danger:* filled, full, laden, abounding, loaded, teeming, replete. *Ant.* devoid, lacking, wanting.

fray¹ n. 1 *The entire neighborhood was caught up in the fray:* quarrel, fight, dispute, disagreement, squabble, bickering; altercation, tussle, scuffle; brawl, melee. 2 *More troops were sent into the fray:* battle, conflict, contest, fight, combat, warfare; skirmish, engagement.

fray² v. *The collar has frayed:* ravel, tatter, become threadbare; chafe, rub.

freak n. 1 *The carnival advertised a two-headed freak:* monstrosity, monster, oddity, curiosity, aberration, mutation, abnormality. 2 *All this rain is a freak of the weather:* quirk, vagary, irregularity, anomaly; —adj. 3 *a freak accident:* odd, strange, queer, unusual, erratic, bizarre.

free adj. 1 *a free nation:* self-governing, autonomous, independent. 2 *The slaves became free:* emancipated, freed, liberated, enfranchised, manumitted, delivered, released; unshackled, unfettered, unbound, unconfined, unconstrained, unbridled, unhampered, unmuzzled, unrestrained, unchained; unattached, uncommitted. 3 *imports free of all duty:* exempt from, not liable to, excused from, absolved of; unaffected by, devoid of. 4 *You are free to go now:* allowed, permitted, at liberty. 5 *a free ticket:* complimentary, without cost, gratis, on the house, gratuitous. 6 *Tie the free end of the rope:* loose, unattached; not in use; unoccupied, available. 7 *They're free with their money:* generous, liberal, openhanded, lavish, prodigal, bountiful. 8 *The halls should be kept free of furniture:* clear, devoid, unobstructed, unimpeded, unblocked, unclogged. —adv. 9 *The door was swinging free in the wind:* freely, loosely; idly, carelessly. 10 *to be admitted free:* without charge, at no cost, gratis. —v. 11 *They freed the prisoners:* set free, liberate, set at liberty, release, let go; emancipate, manumit; discharge, unchain, uncage, unleash, unshackle, unfasten. 12 *to free people from hunger:* release, disengage, extricate, rid of. *Ant.* 1 occupied, dependent. 2 enslave; capture. 6 engaged, busy, occupied. 7 stingy, niggardly, close. 8 clogged, obstructed. 11 imprison, jail, intern, incarcerate, restrain.

freedom n. 1 *The country will gain its freedom:* political independence, autonomy, self-determination, sovereignty; emancipation, manumission; liberation. 2 *This larger coat gives me more freedom:* ease of movement, elbow room; latitude, scope, sweep, margin, play. 3 *You can speak with complete freedom:* openness, frankness, unrestraint, abandon, candor, bluntness, directness. *Ant.* 1 dependence; bondage, servitude, slavery; imprisonment, captivity.

free-for-all n. *The argument ended in a free-for-all:* brawl, fight, affray, fray, melee, fracas, row, scrap, donnybrook.

freeze v. 1 *The water will freeze:* become solid, solidify, turn to ice, harden; chill, cool; congeal. 2 *The skiers were frozen:* benumb, chill, stiffen with cold. 3 *We froze in terror:* become immobile, become paralyzed, stop; halt. —n. 4 *There will be a freeze tonight:* frost, chill, below-freezing temperature.

5 *There's a freeze on wages:* control, ceiling, restriction.

frenzy *n. a frenzy of rage:* fit, seizure, outburst, furor, delirium; fury, hysteria; mental agitation, turmoil; mad rush.
   Ant. calm, composure, equanimity.

frequency *n. Do the pains occur with any frequency?:* regularity, repetition, recurrence, reiteration, iteration, persistence.

frequent *adj.* 1 *We take frequent walks:* occurring often, at short intervals, numerous; recurrent, habitual, reiterative. 2 *We were frequent guests in their home:* regular, habitual; ordinary, common, familiar, customary, usual. —*v.* 3 *We frequent art galleries:* go to frequently, attend regularly, go often to, visit repeatedly.
   Ant. 1 rare, occasional; few. 3 shun, avoid, eschew.

frequently *adv. We frequently have dinner together:* often, many times, repeatedly; recurrently; usually, habitually, customarily, generally.
   Ant. rarely, seldom, hardly ever, infrequently.

fresh *adj.* 1 *fresh bread:* newly made, not stale, recent; unfaded, unspoiled, in good condition, unwithered, unwilted, not deteriorated, unworn, unused. 2 *There is a lot of fresh material in the play:* new, original, creative, inventive; unusual, untried, unique; recent, late, up-to-date. 3 *She was still fresh after working all day:* alert, lively, energetic, not fatigued, unwearied; refreshed, rested. 4 *a fresh complexion:* wholesome, clear, youthful-looking; rosy, gleaming, glowing. 5 *Open the window and let in some fresh air:* pure, refreshing, cool; chill, bracing, brisk. 6 *She was sent to her room for being fresh:* impudent, rude, cheeky, saucy, sassy, insolent, forward, presumptuous, smart-alecky, flippant, brassy; meddlesome.
   Ant. 1 stale, old. 2 trite, ordinary, hackneyed, shopworn. 3 weary, fatigued, exhausted. 4 sickly, wan, pallid. 5 stale, musty. 6 well-mannered, courteous, respectful.

fret *v. Fretting about it won't help:* worry, brood, agonize, stew, chafe; be peevish, be angry, be vexed, be irritated; mope, lament, pout, sulk.

fretful *adj. He's always fretful when the paper doesn't arrive:* peevish, irritable, cranky, grouchy, crotchety, sulky, cross, ill-tempered, contrary, petulant.
   Ant. good-natured, cheerful, agreeable, congenial.

friction *n.* 1 *It was worn away by friction:* rubbing, abrasion, grating, chafing. 2 *There was friction between the two dele-*

gates: conflict, opposition, discord, dissidence, disagreement, antagonism, animosity, hostility, bad feeling.

friend *n.* 1 *to have lunch with a friend:* acquaintance, comrade, companion, chum, buddy, pal, crony. 2 *a special performance for friends of the orchestra:* patron, supporter, benefactor; advocate, defender.
   Ant. foe, enemy, opponent, adversary.

friendly *adj.* 1 *a friendly greeting:* kindly, kind, well-disposed; amiable, neighborly, amicable; familiar, cordial, genial, gracious, chummy, companionable, convivial. 2 *friendly nations:* allied, not hostile, on good terms. 3 *A friendly wind helped the boat across the finish line:* favorable, helpful, auspicious, propitious, advantageous, beneficial, oportune.
   Ant. 2 belligerent, hostile. 3 unfavorable, inauspicious.

friendship *n. We maintained our friendship for years:* acquaintanceship; fellowship, relationship of friends; companionship, comradeship, friendly relations.
   Ant. enmity, animosity, antipathy, antagonism.

fright *n. The child ran in fright:* fear, alarm, terror, panic; scare, dread, apprehension, affright, horror.
   Ant. bravery, boldness, courage.

frighten *v. The lightning frightened me:* alarm, scare, make afraid, terrify; shock, horrify, startle; intimidate, daunt.
   Ant. calm, soothe, comfort, reassure.

frightful *adj.* 1 *Frightful howls pierced the air:* horrible, horrid, terrible, awful, fearful, shocking, appalling, dreadful, alarming, fearsome; ghastly, macabre, gruesome, sinister. 2 *The most frightful dog came bounding out at us:* offensive, loathsome, nasty, hideous, disgusting, detestable; revolting, repulsive, repellent. 3 *Informal He's a frightful snob:* very great, terrific, terrible, extreme, awful, dreadful, insufferable.
   Ant. 1 calming, soothing. 2 beautiful, attractive.

frigid *adj.* 1 *The winter was frigid:* cold, bitter cold, freezing, icy; gelid, glacial; cool, chilly. 2 *She was polite, but her manner was frigid:* stiff, unresponsive, distant, aloof; formal, rigid, austere, cold, cool, icy.
   Ant. 1 hot, sweltering, stifling. 2 cordial, friendly, warm; passionate, impassioned.

frill *n.* 1 *The child liked the frills on her dress:* ruffle, gathering, flounce, fringe, edging. 2 *The room had some added frills:* ornament, decoration, added touch, frippery, embellishment; superfluity, falderal.

fringe *n.* 1 *a shawl with a six-inch fringe:* edging, trimming, ornamental bordering, border, tassel, skirting, hem; margin, edge, periphery, limit, frontier. —*v.* **2** *Flowers fringed the pool:* border, edge, skirt; surround, rim, outline; decorate, embellish.

frisk *v. The dog frisked about on the lawn:* romp, frolic, caper, gambol, cavort, bound, disport, sport, jump about; skip, leap, jump, spring, hop.

frisky *adj. I'm still frisky at the age of 80:* lively, animated, spirited, nimble, spry, sportive, playful, frolicsome, in high spirits, peppy, waggish.

fritter *v. We frittered away our inheritance:* squander, waste, spend foolishly, dissipate, run through.
Ant. conserve, save.

frivolous *adj.* **1** *It may seem frivolous to you, but it's important to me:* impractical, trifling, trivial, worthless, unimportant, insignificant, pointless, silly, petty, paltry; piddling, flimsy, minor; careless; vain, extravagant. **2** *a frivolous gesture:* superficial, unserious, silly, flippant, insouciant, careless, heedless; foolish, fatuous; inane, silly, nonsensical.
Ant. **1** important, vital. **2** sensible, serious, earnest.

frolic *n.* **1** *The clowns were full of frolic:* fun, gaiety, merriment, merrymaking, mirth, amusement; sport, play, festivity, entertainment; tomfoolery, buffoonery; jollity, joviality; antic, gambol, romp, lark, escapade. —*v.* **2** *Children were frolicking on the lawn:* romp, frisk, skip, gambol, cavort, sport, play merrily.

front *n.* **1** *the front of the house:* face, forward part; façade, frontage. **2** *Go to the front of the line:* head, lead, top, beginning; fore. **3** *She maintained a calm front:* external appearance, semblance, demeanor, mien, bearing, presence; mask, pretense, façade. —*adj.* **4** *the front row:* located in front, fore, anterior; first, beginning, initial.
Ant. **1, 2, 4** back, rear.

frontier *n.* **1** *Soldiers guard the frontier:* border, boundary; limits, verge, edge, perimeter, extreme. **2** *Pioneers settled the frontier:* outlying area, remote districts, far country, backwoods, outskirts.

frost *n.* **1** *We may have a frost tonight:* below-freezing weather, cold spell, chill; frozen moisture, ice crystals; hoarfrost, rime. **2** *Did you detect a slight frost in her reply?:* frigidity, iciness, chill, chilliness, coldness, unfriendliness, aloofness, coolness.

froth *n.* **1** *Wind whipped the waves into a froth:* foam, spume, fume; fizz, bubbles; lather, suds. **2** *Critics dismissed the play as froth:* trivia, frippery, frivolity, triviality.

frown *v.* **1** *When she frowns, she's very*

angry: wrinkle the forehead, scowl, knit the brow, glower, look stern. **2** *I frown on that kind of behavior:* disapprove of, view with disfavor, look disapprovingly on, take a dim view of, discountenance. —*n.* **3** *With a frown he examined his son's report card:* frowning look, scowl, glower, black look.
Ant. **1** smile. **2** approve, support, favor, countenance.

frozen *adj.* **1** *The ship remained frozen in the ice. Keep the meat frozen until ready to cook:* icebound, obstructed, clogged, immobilized; refrigerated, chilled, cooled, iced, gelid, solidified by cold. **2** *My toes feel frozen:* benumbed, numb, cold; chill, chilly; icy, frostbitten.
Ant. **1** thawed, melted. **2** warm, hot.

frugal *adj.* **1** *To save money you'll need to be more frugal:* economical, thrifty, unwasteful, sparing; parsimonious, penny-pinching, stingy, niggardly. **2** *It was a frugal dinner, but nourishing:* scant, slim, sparing, skimpy.
Ant. **1** extravagant, wasteful, spendthrift. **2** luxurious, lavish.

fruit *n.* **1** *the fruits of the earth:* produce, product, crop, yield, production, harvest. **2** *the fruits of his labor:* result, product, consequence, outgrowth, effect, outcome; return, profit, benefit, remuneration, earnings; award, reward.

fruitful *adj.* **1** *Cherry trees in the city are seldom fruitful:* productive, fecund, prolific, yielding, fertile. **2** *The information proved fruitful:* profitable, productive, advantageous, effective, successful.
Ant. **1** unfruitful, barren, infertile. **2** fruitless, useless.

fruition *n. The plan should reach fruition next year:* fulfillment, achievement, realization, attainment; actualization; maturity, ripeness.

fruitless *adj. Further investigations proved fruitless:* unfruitful, pointless, purposeless, useless, unsuccessful, unavailing, vain, futile; unrewarding, unprofitable.
Ant. useful, profitable, fruitful, worthwhile, productive.

frustrate *v.* **1** *Steady rains frustrated our efforts to garden:* hinder, defeat, thwart, foil, inhibit, check, impede, forestall, balk, obstruct, prevent. **2** *Giving the child work he can't do will only frustrate him:* discourage, upset, dispirit, disappoint, disconcert, dishearten.
Ant. **1** foster, promote, further, forward, advance. **2** encourage, hearten, gratify.

frustration *n. All our efforts ended in frus-*

tration: failure, futility, nonfulfillment, thwarting, hindrance, balking, inhibition, bafflement, obstruction; disappointment.

fry *v. Fry the potatoes in hot fat:* sauté, brown, grill; pan-fry, French fry, deep fry, stir fry.

fuel *n.* 1 *Switch from coal to a cleaner fuel:* combustible material; *(variously)* wood, coal, oil, natural gas; gas, gasoline, petroleum. 2 *The news provided me with fuel for my speech:* material, ammunition, inspiration; sustenance, means, wherewithal; motivation, stimulus. —*v.* 3 *Fuel the furnace once a day:* provide with fuel, replenish with fuel, fill up, charge, recharge, stoke; activate, incite, inflame.

fugitive *n.* 1 *The fugitive was wanted in several countries:* runaway, deserter, outlaw; refugee, escapee; exile; rover, wanderer, itinerant. —*adj.* 2 *fugitive slaves:* escaped, fleeing, runaway.

fulfill *v.* 1 *Her dream is yet to be fulfilled:* carry out, accomplish, achieve, realize, effect, implement, bring about. 2 *You must fulfill your obligations:* perform, do, abide by, keep, discharge, comply with, adhere to, be faithful to, observe, follow, heed. 3 *to fulfill the requirements for graduating:* satisfy, suit, meet; make good, answer.
　Ant. 1 neglect, ignore, overlook, disregard. 3 fall short of, fail to meet.

fulfillment Also **fulfilment** *n.* 1 *the fulfillment of her dreams:* realization, accomplishment, attainment, achievement; completion; culmination; finishing touch. 2 *What fulfillment is there in the job?:* satisfaction, contentment, gratification; contentedness.

full *adj.* 1 *a full cup. full of energy:* filled, heaping, brimming; replete, abounding, fraught, crammed, packed, loaded, chockfull; teeming, saturated; sated, surfeited, stuffed. 2 *a full supply of firewood:* complete, entire, whole, thorough, maximum, intact. 3 *a full skirt:* ample, capacious, wide, broad, voluminous; comprehensive, all-inclusive; large, big; round, rotund; rich, resonant. —*adv.* 4 *He knew full well what I meant:* very, quite, perfectly; precisely.
　Ant. 1 empty, vacant. 2 partial, incomplete.

full-fledged *adj. She was a full-fledged CPA:* complete, mature, full-blown, full-grown; trained, qualified, experienced, schooled.

fully *adv.* 1 *Are you fully aware of what may happen?:* completely, entirely, wholly, totally, altogether, quite; perfectly, in all respects, utterly. 2 *Is he fully supplied with*

materials?: sufficiently, amply; abundantly, plentifully, copiously.

fumble *v. She fumbled the opportunity:* mishandle, bungle, botch, mess up, muff, bumble, muddle, bobble.

fume *n.* 1 *the fumes from a cigar:* smoke, haze, exhalation; vapor, billow, waft; unpleasant odor, reek, stench. —*v.* 2 *When I hung up the phone, I was fuming:* display anger, rage, seethe, lose one's temper, steamed up, rant, rave, foam, boil.

fun *n. We had fun at the pool:* enjoyment, gaiety, pleasure, amusement, merriment, diversion; entertainment, recreation; joking, jest, playfulness, jollity, mirth, good humor, joviality; game, sport, play, lark, good time.
　Ant. misery, melancholy, gloom, tedium.

function *n.* 1 *The function of the kidneys is to purify the blood:* purpose, role, activity, operation, job, business, task, duty; objective. 2 *It was a large function with dignitaries in attendance:* social gathering, fete, gala, affair; party, entertainment, reception, ceremony. —*v.* 3 *This couch also functions as a bed:* serve, act, perform, do duty; operate, work, purpose.

functional *adj. Is that oil lamp functional?:* working, operative, operable, functioning; useful, serviceable, practical, utilitarian.

fund *n.* 1 *a vacation fund:* sum of money, accumulated amount, savings, accumulation, pool, pot; foundation, endowment, investment. 2 *She's a fund of information:* store, supply, stock; repository, reservoir, well, fount, spring; storehouse, hoard, reserve. —*v.* 3 *The government will fund the project:* finance, pay for, underwrite; support, endow.

fundamental *adj.* 1 *the fundamental principles of law:* basic, underlying, essential, necessary, first, elementary; key, crucial, vital, central; major, principal, main, chief. —*n.* 2 *the fundamentals of math:* principle, basic, primary rule, ABC's, essential, requisite, element, basis, foundation, cornerstone; groundwork.
　Ant. 1 advanced; subordinate, lesser.

funds *n. pl. Bankrupts have no funds:* money, cash, wherewithal, means, resources, assets, capital; *Informal* dough.

funnel *n.* 1 *The steamship has four large funnels:* smokestack; chimney, smoke pipe, stovepipe, ventilator, flue, air shaft. —*v.* 2 *They funnel their income into investments:* pour, concentrate, channel, focus, direct.

funny *adj.* 1 *It's a very funny story:* comical, amusing, humorous, diverting, laughable, hilarious; absurd, ridiculous, ludicrous; witty, droll, comic, jocular, jocose. 2 *That's* *a funny way to speak of a relative:* odd, strange, unusual, weird, curious, bizarre, peculiar, offbeat.

Ant. 1 humorless; solemn, grave; mournful, melancholy.

furious *adj.* 1 *She's furious at being ignored:* enrage, irate, angry, mad, hot under the collar, infuriated, raging, wrathful, fuming. 2 *a furious gale:* fierce, intense, violent, vehement, raging, rampant; fiery, passionate.

Ant. 1 pleased, placated. 2 mild, calm.

furnish *v.* 1 *We will furnish you with supplies:* provide, equip, supply, stock, endow, vest; render; provision; give, bestow on. 2 *The house was furnished:* equip, appoint, outfit, fit out, array, fit up.

furor *n. The new book caused quite a furor:* commotion, uproar, excitement, reaction; noise; rage, fury, fit of anger, passion, frenzy, madness, agitation, raving; fervor, fanaticism.

furrow *n.* 1 *a series of furrows across the field:* trench, channel, depression, cut, rut, groove, ditch, track. 2 *the furrows on his brow:* crease, deep line, crow's foot. —*v.* 3 *Years of worry had furrowed her face:* wrinkle, line, pucker.

further *adv.* 1 *a block further down the street:* farther, yonder, at a greater distance, farther on. 2 *Let me say further that I support all your ideas:* more, additionally; again, yet, too, likewise, also; besides, furthermore, moreover. —*adj.* 3 *the further house:* more distant, farther, farther on. 4 *Where can I get further information?:* additional, supplementary, more, other; new, fresh. —*v.* 5 *His support furthered my career:* forward, aid, assist, help, advance, foster, promote, favor, contribute to, strengthen; hasten.

Ant. 1, 3 nearer, closer. 5 hinder, frustrate, thwart, impede.

furtherance *n. the furtherance of our cause:* advancement, advance, promotion, aid, help, assistance; advocacy, championship.

Ant. hindrance, defeat.

furthermore *adv. Furthermore she's devoid of talent:* also, moreover, besides, in addition, too, additionally, as well, likewise.

furtive *adj. furtive glances:* secret, secretive, surreptitious, stealthy, clandestine, covert; masked, veiled, cloaked; private, secluded, confidential, mysterious, undercover; conspiratorial; sly, shifty, underhand, sneaky; elusive, evasive.

Ant. straightforward, aboveboard; unconcealed, public.

fury *n.* 1 *He was in a complete fury:* rage, unrestrained anger, frenzy, wrath, ire; outburst, fit, tantrum; acrimony. 2 *Florida felt the full fury of the storm:* might, force, violence, fierceness, vehemence, ferocity, intensity, severity. 3 *The prima donna was rumored to be a real fury:* spitfire, she-devil, hellcat; shrew, termagant, virago, vixen.

Ant. 1 calm, serenity, tranquillity, composure.

fuse *v.* 1 *The heat caused the silverware to fuse:* smelt, meld, blend by melting together, weld. 2 *to fuse dissenting elements into a united party:* consolidate, merge, blend, meld, join, link, weld, combine; solidify, federate, amalgamate, confederate; assimilate, coalesce.

Ant. 2 separate, disunite.

fusillade *n. The ships exchanged fusillades:* barrage, broadside, salvo, volley, bombardment, cannonade, enfilade; shower, spray, hail.

fusion *n. Success depends on the fusion of many talents:* combination, blending, blend, union, merging, amalgamation, synthesis, unification; federation, confederacy, confederation, league, alliance, association, coalescence, coalition.

fuss *n.* 1 *Let's have a simple wedding with as little fuss as possible:* bustle, ado, anxious activity, stir, flutter, flurry, pother, bother; commotion, disturbance, confusion; ceremony, ceremoniousness; pomp; fret, stew, worry, agitation. 2 *The children had a fuss about toys:* quarrel, argument, dispute, spat, tiff. —*v.* 3 *Too nervous to sit still, he got up to fuss in the kitchen:* stir about, bustle, busy oneself, potter, putter, pother. 4 *Don't waste energy fussing over such a minor matter:* fume, fret, worry; carp, cavil, quibble; trouble, take pains, labor.

Ant. 1 peace, tranquillity, simplicity.

fussy *adj. I'm very fussy when it comes to food:* particular, hard to please, exacting, demanding; meticulous, nitpicking, finicky; painstaking, fastidious, scrupulous.

futile *adj. His efforts were futile:* useless, fruitless, vain, worthless, valueless, unprofitable; ineffective, unsuccessful, unavailing.

Ant. fruitful, successful; profitable, useful.

future *n.* 1 *In the future you'd better get permission first:* time to come, time from now on; hereafter. 2 *Does the job have any future?:* prospect, chance for advancement, opportunity; expectation; hope. —*adj.* 3 *future plans:* from now on, in prospect, to come, prospective, eventual, projected, anticipated, hereafter; following, subsequent, ensuing, succeeding; later, latter, after.

Ant. 1 past, time gone by. 3 past, former, previous.

G

gab *v.* 1 *We gabbed for hours:* chat, chatter, talk idly, babble, jabber, chitchat, blab, prattle, gossip; *Informal* shoot the breeze, chew the fat. —*n.* 2 *the gift of gab:* small talk, glib speech, chatter; conversation; blarney, gossip, chitchat; idle talk, prattle.

gadget *n. a new gadget:* contrivance, device, tool, contraption; *Slang* doohickey, doodad, thingamajig, thingamabob.

gag *v.* 1 *The robbers gagged him with a towel:* stop up the mouth of, silence, muffle, hush; suppress, muzzle. 2 *The smell of sulfur makes me gag:* retch, be sick, be nauseated, choke. —*n.* 3 *We fell for that old gag:* joke, practical joke, hoax, jest; horseplay, foolery.

gaiety Also **gayety** *n. The room seemed to reverberate with gaiety:* gay spirits, cheerfulness, joyousness, jollity, mirth, high spirits, liveliness, animation; festive spirits, frolic, amusement, merrymaking, merriment, fun.
Ant. sadness, melancholy, gloominess, despondency.

gain *v.* 1 *to gain experience:* acquire, obtain, secure, achieve, attain, get; gather. 2 *I gained five pounds:* acquire, put on, add, build up. 3 *We finally gained our destination:* attain, reach, arrive at; overtake, close with. 4 *The doctors say she continues to gain:* improve, recover, make progress. —*n.* 5 Often **gains** *The taxes will be high on this year's gains:* earnings, winnings, profit, compensation, wages, salary, bonus, income, revenue, remuneration, dividend; proceeds, yield. 6 *The gain in volume is nearly 10 percent:* increase, increment, addition; advantage, improvement, attainment.
Ant. 1 lose, forfeit. 4 fail, decline. 5 loss.

gainfully *adv. to be gainfully employed:* profitably, lucratively, productively, remuneratively; usefully.

gait *n. the even gait of a good horse:* walk, stride, step, pace; carriage, bearing.

gala *adj.* 1 *It's a gala occasion:* festive, celebratory, ceremonial, gay; splendid, grand, magnificent, majestic; glamorous, star-studded. —*n.* 2 *At the gala all the stars appeared:* celebration, festive occasion, festival, party, festivity, fete, benefit.

gale *n.* 1 *We reached port in a gale:* strong wind, windstorm, blow; gust, squall, tem-

pest. 2 *gales of laughter:* uproar, outburst, outbreak, eruption, flurry, fit, tumult.

gall¹ *n.* 1 *He has a lot of gall:* impudence, effrontery, audacity, brazenness; brass, nerve, cheek; insolence. 2 *Of their former friendship nothing is left but gall:* bitterness, bile, rancor, venom, animosity, acrimony.

gall² *v. It galls me that she does nothing and gets all the credit:* annoy, irritate, irk, provoke, gripe, vex, miff, exasperate, rile, anger, ruffle, enrage, nettle; affront, offend; sting.
Ant. delight, please, amuse.

gallant *adj.* 1 *Custer's army made a gallant stand:* brave, valiant, heroic; noble, chivalrous, courageous, daring, bold, high-spirited, valorous; game, resolute. 2 *a gallant young man:* chivalrous, cavalier, courtly, attentive, dashing; mannerly, courteous, polite, gentlemanly, well-bred; considerate, thoughtful, obliging. —*n.* 3 *The town's gallants meet at the coffee house:* cavalier, dandy, blood, gay blade.
Ant. 1 cowardly, ignoble. 2 impolite, discourteous, ill-mannered, rude.

gallantry *n.* 1 *The soldier was rewarded for gallantry:* bravery, heroism, valor, dashing, courage, courageousness, fearlessness, daring, mettle. 2 *His gallantry made him an ideal escort:* attentiveness, courtliness, chivalry, good manners, politeness, good breeding.
Ant. 1 cowardliness, cowardice. 2 loutishness, discourteousness, rudeness.

gallery *n.* 1 *The monastery garden was surrounded by a gallery:* covered walk, roofed promenade, arcade, portico, colonnade, cloister, passage, passageway, corridor, ambulatory. 2 *The actors loved playing to the gallery:* balcony, mezzanine; grandstand, bleachers. 3 *The gallery is having a show of new American art:* art gallery, picture gallery, exhibition hall, salon; art museum.

gallop *n.* 1 *They rode at a gallop:* fast gait; rapid ride, run, fast clip; jog, trot, sprint. —*v.* 2 *The horse galloped away:* run, race; ride at a fast gait, ride at full speed; dash, speed, bolt.
Ant. 1 slow gait. 2 amble, walk; crawl, creep, saunter.

galore *adv. We've had rainfall galore this*

year: in abundance, in great quantity, aplenty, to spare.

galvanize *v. The alarm galvanized the police into action:* arouse, rouse, stimulate, stir, move, electrify, quicken; vitalize, inspire, thrill, spur on, rally.

Ant. lull, soothe, pacify.

gambit *n. Pretending to be sick was only a gambit:* maneuver, ploy, stratagem, scheme, trick, ruse, artifice; opening move, initial play.

gamble *v.* 1 *He gambles at dice:* bet, wager, play for money; take a flyer, try one's luck. 2 *I'll gamble on her honesty:* take a chance, risk, hazard, chance; trust in, have faith in. —*n.* 3 *Opening a restaurant would be a gamble:* risk, hazard, uncertainty, speculation.

gambol *v. The lambs gamboled in the field:* romp playfully, skip about, frolic, frisk, sport, cut capers, cavort, disport, prance, rollick; leap, bound, spring.

game *n.* 1 *a child's game:* play, amusement, diversion, pastime, sport, entertainment, recreation, distraction. 2 *Who won the football game?:* match, contest, athletic contest, competition. —*adj.* 3 *a game fighter:* resolute, determined, plucky, unflinching, willing, dauntless, intrepid, spunky, daring. 4 *a game leg:* lame, crippled, limping; crooked, hobbling.

Ant. 1 work, toil, labor; job. 3 irresolute; fearful.

gamut *n. Her acting covers the gamut from comedy to tragedy:* full range, complete scale, entire sequence, compass, sweep, scope, reach, purview.

gang *n.* 1 *Most of our old neighborhood gang have left town:* crowd, group, band; clique, circle of friends, coterie; friends, comrades, chums, companions; *Informal* buddies, pals, cronies; associates, neighbors; co-workers, fellow workers, crew. 2 *a gang of highwaymen:* band, mob, company, troop, party, pack, contingent, body; ring. 3 *The gang of workers finished the rail line:* crew, squad, shift, team, relay; troop, company.

gap *n.* 1 *a gap in the wall:* opening, breach, empty space, hole, aperture; crack, crevice, fissure, break, slit, slot, rent, gash, cavity. 2 *There was a gap in the conversation:* interval, pause, void, interim, lacuna, hiatus; break, interruption. 3 *the Cumberland Gap:* mountain pass; valley, canyon, ravine, gulch, gully. 4 *How much of a gap is there in their ages?:* difference, disparity, divergence.

gape *v.* 1 *The audience gaped:* stare open-mouthed, stare in wonder, stare stupidly, regard with awe, gawk, stare, peer, ogle,

gaze. 2 *He gaped for breath:* open the mouth wide, gasp; yawn. 3 *The shirt gapes where the button came off:* part, separate, split, cleave, open wide, spread out.

garb *n. nurse's garb:* uniform, outfit, apparel, attire, dress, costume, clothing, clothes, garments, togs; habiliments, habit, vesture, vestment; gown, robe, gear.

garbage *n.* 1 *Put the garbage in the compost heap:* refuse, kitchen scraps; rubbish, trash; waste; swill, offal, carrion. 2 *Informal Why do you carry all that garbage around in your pockets?:* junk, useless things, odds and ends; rubbish, litter, debris.

garble *v. The instructions were garbled:* confuse, jumble, mix up, be unclear, misunderstand.

garden *n.* 1 *Don't plant your garden in sandy soil:* garden plot; *(variously)* flower garden, vegetable garden, kitchen garden, herb garden, truck garden, rock garden. 2 *The historic house and garden are closed:* small park, botanical garden, zoological park, natural park. 3 *The settlers made a garden out of the desert:* fertile region, agricultural region; paradise, Eden, green oasis.

gargantuan *adj. They bought a gargantuan house:* gigantic, enormous, immense, huge, great, unbelievably big; vast, colossal, tremendous, mammoth, stupendous, monstrous.

Ant. small, little, tiny, compact.

garish *adj. a garish dress:* gaudy, loud, flashy, showy, blatant, bright; too colorful, extremely ornate, ostentatious, pretentious.

Ant. sedate, conservative, modest; plain, simple.

garland *n. a garland of flowers:* wreath, festoon, diadem, crown, circlet, coronet, headband.

garment Often **garments** *n. winter garments:* article of clothing; apparel, attire, garb, dress, costume, raiment, togs, outfit.

garnish *v.* 1 *The chef garnished the chops with sprigs of mint:* embellish, decorate, adorn, ornament, trim, beautify, deck, bedeck, array, deck out. —*n.* 2 *The ham was given a garnish of parsley:* decoration, embellishment, adornment, ornament, trim, trimming, festoon.

garret *n. The poet lived in a garret:* attic, loft; topmost floor, floor under the eaves.

Ant. basement, cellar.

garrison *n.* 1 *The garrison faced starvation during the siege:* soldiers stationed at a fort, detachment; *(variously)* division, brigade, regiment, squadron, platoon, battery, escadrille. 2 *The army built a garrison to defend the town:* fort, fortification; military camp, military base. —*v.* 3 *The 49th Cavalry was* *garrisoned at Fort Big Horn:* place on duty, station, assign to, bivouac.

garrulous *adj. He's so garrulous you can't get a word in edgewise:* talkative, effusive, loquacious; windy, long-winded; gabby, voluble; babbling; gossipy.

Ant. reticent, taciturn, reserved, close-mouthed.

gash *n.* 1 *a long gash in the tent:* cut, slash, gaping wound, incision; split, cleft, slit, crack, fissure, rent. —*v.* 2 *The glass gashed her arm:* cut deeply, slash, incise, lacerate, slice; split, slit, cleave, rend.

gasp *v.* 1 *to gasp for air:* struggle *(for breath)* with open mouth, inhale frantically, suck in *(air)*, breathe convulsively; pant, wheeze, puff, catch the breath. 2 *The victim gasped the name of the assailant:* exclaim in short breaths, speak breathlessly, blurt, cry hurriedly. —*n.* 3 *Her words came in gasps:* sudden short breath, convulsive breathing, sharp inhalation, gulp.

gate *n.* 1 *Close that gate:* enclosure door, entrance to a pen, opening through a fence; portal, gateway. 2 *We bought our tickets at the gate:* entrance door; box office, ticket booth.

gather *v.* 1 *Storm clouds gathered. Gather together:* assemble, get together, bring together, marshal, muster, accumulate, collect, amass, mass, group, cluster, come together, bunch; heap up, stockpile. 2 *I gather that you're not happy:* infer, deduce, assume, be led to believe, conclude; learn, understand. —*n.* 3 *The dress had tiny gathers at each shoulder:* fold, pucker, pleat, ruffle.

Ant. 1 disperse, dissipate; separate.

gathering *n. a social gathering:* assembly, meeting, party, conference, convocation, convention; company, crowd, throng, assemblage, accumulation, aggregation, pack, bunch, horde, collection, concentration, convergence.

gauche *adj. He's so gauche he addressed the president as "Old Buddy":* uncouth, socially awkward, unpolished, inelegant, overly informal, unrefined, uncultured, boorish, oafish, ill-bred; blundering, clumsy, bungling, maladroit.

Ant. polished, suave, urbane, gracious, formal, refined.

gaudy *adj. gaudy clothes:* garish, flashy, loud, showy, tasteless; colorful, eye-catching, ostentatious, pretentious; brilliant. dazzling, vivid, intense.

Ant. sedate, conservative, unpretentious; subtle; dull, lackluster.

gauge Also **gage** *v.* 1 *Can you gauge the distance to that hill?:* estimate, judge, appraise, guess; evaluate, adjudge, rate, as-

sess. —*n.* 2 *This gauge registers the pressure:* measuring device, measure; standard, criterion, yardstick.

gaunt *adj. Illness has left him gaunt:* very thin, emaciated, scrawny, haggard; skinny, bony, lean, lank, slender, slim, scraggy, spindly, raw-boned, cadaverous, wasted, skeletal.

Ant. plump, fat, chubby, portly, obese, rotund.

gawk *v. Stop gawking at the celebrities:* stare stupidly, gape, rubberneck.

gawky *adj. The gawky child was poor at sports:* awkward, ungainly, clumsy, graceless, gawkish.

Ant. graceful.

gay *adj.* 1 *a gay, fun-loving person:* cheerful, cherry, happy, lighthearted, merry, joyful; sunny, vivacious, sparkling, in good spirits, buoyant, effervescent, smiling, animated, spirited. 2 *What a gay hat!:* bright, colorful, showy, brilliant, vivid, eye-catching.

Ant. 1 grave, somber, solemn, cheerless, joyless; morose, grim, melancholy. 2 dull, somber, colorless, drab, lackluster.

gaze *v.* 1 *to gaze into the distance:* look intently, look fixedly, stare; watch, eye, study, peruse; gape, ogle, peer, scrutinize, survey, inspect, examine; glance, scan, regard. —*n.* 2 *a gaze of admiration:* stare, steady look, scrutiny.

gear *n.* 1 *This large gear turns the small one:* toothed wheel, cogwheel; flywheel, cam. 2 *diving gear:* equipment, paraphernalia, outfit, things, accessories, apparatus, trappings; implements, instruments, rig, contrivances; personal effects, belongings; apparel, clothing, clothes, attire, dress, garments, togs.

gem *n.* 1 *diamonds and other gems:* jewel, precious stone; semiprecious stone. 2 *She's a gem to go to this trouble:* jewel, prize, treasure; wonder, marvel, dear, sweetheart.

genealogy *n. She can trace her genealogy back to the Pilgrims:* family tree, ancestry, lineage, list of forebears, family descent, parentage, extraction, pedigree; stock; line.

general *adj.* 1 *I have a general idea of how a car works:* comprehensive, overall, basic, sweeping, blanket; vague, imprecise, inexact. 2 *The suggestion met with general approval:* widespread, popular, prevalent, prevailing, broad. 3 *His general mood is pleasant enough:* usual, customary, regular, habitual, normal, typical, accustomed; everyday, conventional, frequent.

Ant. 1 specific, concrete; exact, precise. 3 exceptional, rare, uncommon, unusual, infrequent.

generality *n.* 1 *Stop speaking in generali-*

ties: sweeping statement, generalization; abstract thought, vague notion, inexact presentation. **2** *The generality of her knowledge is awesome:* universality, reach, far-flung scale; miscellaneousness; indiscriminateness. **3** *It's a generality that people want to improve their lot:* general rule, widespread principle, universal thing; obvious statement, truism, cliché, platitude.

Ant. **2** specialization.

generally *adv.* **1** *Dinner is generally at 7 P.M.:* usually, ordinarily, in general, as a rule, for the most part, in most cases, typically, mainly, habitually; often. **2** *Generally speaking, women live longer than men:* without particularizing, without noting the exceptions; for the most part, in the main, on the whole, largely, mainly, chiefly, mostly.

Ant. **1** rarely, occasionally, infrequently.

generate *v.* **1** *to generate electricity. to generate enthusiasm:* produce, make, form, engender, induce, institute, fabricate, frame, fashion, develop, occasion. **2** *The human race was generated by Lucy:* spawn; procreate, create; breed, reproduce, engender, propagate; proliferate, fructify, fecundate.

generation *n.* **1** *Their generation populated the earth:* progeny, issue, offspring; family, tribe, race, clan, house, line, strain, stock; kin. **2** *the generation of fruit flies:* reproduction, propagation, procreation, breeding; fertilization, impregnation. **3** *the generation of ideas:* creation, production, formation, causation; development.

generous *adj.* **1** *a generous benefactor:* openhanded, bighearted, ungrudging; lavish, liberal, munificent, bountiful, unrestricted, unstinting, unstinted; effusive; charitable, beneficent, philanthropic. **2** *generous portions:* plentiful, ample, large, copious, plenteous, abundant, liberal. **3** *a generous spirit:* unselfish, humane, humanitarian, benevolent, altruistic; accommodating, obliging; bighearted.

Ant. **1** stingy, tight, tightfisted, cheap, niggardly, miserly, parsimonious. **2** small, picayune, scanty. **3** mean, petty.

genesis *n.* *A news item was the genesis of her story:* origin, beginning, commencement, creation, birth, inception, begetting, engendering.

Ant. end, conclusion, finish.

genial *adj.* *a genial manner:* cordial, friendly, good-natured, congenial, amiable, affable, agreeable, pleasant, convivial, companionable, sociable, courteous, civil, warm, happy, expansive, kind, cheerful, in good spirits.

Ant. unfriendly, unpleasant, uncongenial,

ungracious, cool, cold; rude, discourteous, uncivil.

genius *n.* **1** *a scientific genius:* mental giant, mastermind, brilliant intellect, prodigy; *Slang* brain, whiz. **2** *You have a genius for painting:* natural talent, creative power, faculty, gift, knack, natural endowment, aptitude, penchant, proclivity, bent, propensity, flair, predilection, turn of mind; insight, perception, imagination, ingenuity; intelligence.

Ant. **1** idiot, imbecile, half-wit, moron; simpleton, dunce, dolt; numskull, blockhead, nitwit. **2** ineptitude.

genre *n.* *Shakespeare's* Macbeth *is an example of the tragic genre of drama:* style, category, kind, class, sort, type, classification, variety, school.

genteel *adj.* **1** *a genteel demeanor:* refined, well-bred, courteous, polite, civil, ladylike, gentlemanly, courtly, polished, cultivated; aristocratic, patrician. **2** *a genteel gathering:* elegant, stylish, elite; silk-stocking; *Slang* hoity-toity, swank, ritzy, high-toned.

Ant. **1** unrefined, unpolished; impolite, discourteous, boorish, plebeian, ill-bred.

gentility *n.* *The brothers were admired for their gentility:* refinement, polish, breeding, mannerliness, decorum, propriety, cultivation, civility.

Ant. coarseness, vulgarity, boorishness.

gentle *adj.* **1** *a gentle woman:* kindly, kind, peaceful, compassionate, tender, mild, benign, merciful. **2** *a gentle breeze:* mild, soft, light, slight; quiet, calm, placid; moderate, temperate. **3** *Is that horse gentle enough to ride?:* docile, tame, manageable, tractable; domesticated, broken, subdued; peaceful, calm.

Ant. **1** cruel, unkind, heartless, hardhearted. **2** rough, harsh, powerful, strong, violent. **3** wild, fierce, intractable; unmanageable.

gentleman *n.* **1** *A gentleman would never use such language!:* well-mannered man, honorable man, refined man, civilized man, man of social position, man of good family, man of good breeding, aristocrat, patrician; *Slang* gent, swell. **2** *Are you the gentleman who called?:* man, fellow, chap, *Slang* guy; *(of a male)* person, individual, one.

Ant. **1** brute, lout, churl, boor, scoundrel.

gentry *n.* *the English gentry:* aristocrats, aristocracy, upper class, nobility, blue bloods, gentlefolk, country gentlemen.

Ant. working class, bourgeoisie, commoners, hoi polloi.

genuine *adj.* **1** *genuine gold:* real, authentic, true, bona-fide, actual, honest, legitimate.

2 *genuine enthusiasm:* sincere, true, unaffected, earnest; frank, candid, open, honest, heartfelt, ingenuous, artless, guileless.

Ant. 1 fake, false, phony, bogus, counterfeit, imitation, ersatz, fraudulent, simulated. 2 insincere, hypocritical, pretended, fake, false, phony.

germ *n.* 1 *to spread germs:* microbe, virus, microorganism, bacterium, bacillus, *Informal* bug. 2 *the germ of an idea:* beginning, first stage, spark, rudiment; origin, root, seed, embryo.

Ant. 2 result; end, consummation.

germane *adj. That's not germane to our discussion:* pertinent, relevant, appropriate, applicable, connected, relative, material, related, to the point, to the purpose.

Ant. irrelevant, inappropriate, unrelated, immaterial, unconnected, extraneous.

germinate *v. The seeds will germinate:* sprout, put out shoots, spring up; develop, burgeon, bud, flower, bloom, blossom.

Ant. wither, die.

gestation *n. The period of human gestation is 9 months:* pregnancy, maturation; development, evolution, incubation.

gesticulate *v. We gesticulated for the car to stop:* gesture; signal, motion, beckon.

gesture *n.* 1 *His gestures seemed unrelated to his speech:* bodily movement, hand and arm movement, gesticulation, signal, sign, motion; *(variously)* shrug, nod, wave, nudge, wink. 2 *He said he would help, but I'm sure it was only a gesture:* formality, courtesy, demonstration.

get *v.* 1 *Get a copy of the book. You'll get the award:* obtain, acquire, attain, receive, procure, fetch, pick up, come by, secure, glean; achieve, win, gain, earn, realize, bag, reap, take. 2 *New Orleans gets hot in the summer:* become, get to be, grow, turn, wax. 3 *What time should I get lunch?:* have done, have, make ready, fix, prepare. 4 *I tried to get you on the phone. What time does the bus get to Chicago?:* reach, communicate with, contact; arrive, come to, get in to. 5 *He didn't get the point:* understand, comprehend, grasp, learn, perceive; hear, catch; take in, fathom, follow. 6 *It gets me why she decided to sell the house:* baffle, bewilder, perplex, puzzle, confound, confuse, mystify; upset, annoy, irritate, disconcert, *Slang* beat. 7 *Get the governor to serve as honorary chairman:* persuade, induce, influence, prevail upon, enlist, sway, win over, move, prompt. 8 *The goblins will get you if you don't watch out:* seize, grab, capture, take, snatch, grasp, ensnare, entrap. 9 *The*

teacher got chicken pox: catch, contract, be afflicted with, come down with.

Ant. 1 give; lose. 5 misunderstand. 7 dissuade. 8 let go, release, free. 9 cure.

ghastly *adj.* 1 *a ghastly complexion:* ghostlike, ghostly, deathlike, corpselike, cadaverous; deathly pale, pallid, ashen, colorless, wan, pasty. 2 *a ghastly accident. a ghastly shade of green:* hideous, revolting, gruesome, grisly, repellent, repulsive, loathsome, ugly; dreadful, horrible, horrendous, horrid; terrifying, frightful, terrible, appalling.

Ant. 1 ruddy, robust, healthy. 2 attractive, appealing, lovely, enticing.

ghost *n. A ghost is believed to haunt the house:* spirit of a dead person, disembodied spirit, departed spirit; phantom, apparition, phantasm, wraith, specter, banshee, sprite, phantasma.

ghostly *adj. a ghostly light:* ghostlike, spectral, wraithlike, phantasmal, phantomlike, unearthly, supernatural; *Slang* spooky.

Ant. earthly, natural.

giant *n. Our basketball team didn't have a chance against those giants:* tall person, tall thing, colossus, behemoth, titan.

Ant. dwarf, midget; half-pint, shrimp.

gibberish *n. The message was pure gibberish:* meaningless talk, senseless writing, nonsense, babble, gobbledegook, drivel, foolish talk; *Informal* balderdash, stuff and nonsense, bosh, twaddle, fiddle-faddle, double-talk.

gibe Also **jibe** *n.* 1 *She bore her sister's gibes through childhood:* taunt, taunting, jeer, criticism, sarcastic remark, sarcasm, cutting remark, scoff, sneer, ridicule, mockery, derision; *Slang* knock. —*v.* 2 *The children gibed at her:* jeer, taunt, poke fun, make fun of, scoff, mock, ridicule, laugh at, deride, sneer.

Ant. 1, 2 compliment, praise. 2 applaud; salute.

giddy *adj.* 1 *The medicine made her feel giddy:* dizzy, lightheaded; faint, fainting, vertiginous. 2 *the giddy height of the 90th floor:* causing dizziness, dizzying; awesome, overpowering. 3 *a giddy child:* flighty, frivolous, capricious, fickle, changeable, impulsive; silly, fanciful, whimsical, harebrained, muddled, befuddled.

Ant. 1 steady. 3 serious, earnest.

gift *n.* 1 *He claimed the stolen money was a gift:* present; donation, benefaction; bonus, grant, handout, largess, contribution, offering; legacy, bequest. 2 *To be able to paint well is a gift:* special ability, talent, natural endowment, aptitude, flair, genius, knack, faculty, capability, facility; attribute, quality, forte, bent.

gifted *adj.* 1 *a gifted pianist:* talented, naturally endowed; ingenious, inventive, able, adept, resourceful; proficient, accomplished, skilled, capable, expert, master, masterly, polished. 2 *a school for gifted children:* especially intelligent, unusually smart, bright, brilliant, having a high IQ.
Ant. 1 talentless; unskilled, inept. 2 retarded; dull, slow.

gigantic *adj. China is a gigantic country:* very large, huge, vast, enormous, immense, giant, colossal, mammoth, jumbo, elephantine; large-scale, prodigious; gargantuan, herculean, titanic.
Ant. small, little, tiny; *Slang* teeny-weeny, itty-bitty; dwarfish, pigmy.

giggle *v.* 1 *Why do teenagers giggle so much?:* laugh in a silly way, laugh nervously, titter, twitter, simper, snicker, snigger. —*n.* 2 *a nervous giggle:* silly laugh, titter, snigger, snicker, simper, tee-hee.

gild *v.* 1 *to gild a mirror:* coat with goldleaf, paint gold, gold-plate. 2 *She gilds the truth:* embellish, exaggerate, twist; slant, stretch.

gimcrack *n. a shelf full of gimcracks:* knickknack, bauble, gewgaw, trinket, ornament, curio, bagatelle, kickshaw, whatnot.

gimmick *n. The gimmick is that you have to buy the cars before you open a dealership:* scheme, stunt, ruse, wile, subterfuge, ploy; wrinkle, dodge; device, contrivance, gadget.

gingerly *adv. We walked gingerly over the slick floor:* very carefully, cautiously, warily, guardedly, charily, watchfully, circumspectly; suspiciously, hesitantly, timidly, delicately.
Ant. boldly, confidently; rashly, brashly.

gird *v.* 1 *The warriors girded their loins:* encircle with a belt, girdle, strap, belt, girt. 2 *Enemy troops girded the city:* surround, encircle, ring, encompass, hem in, circumscribe, circle; enclose, confine, wall in, hedge in. 3 *Gird yourself for bad news:* brace, steel, strengthen, prepare; harden, stiffen.

girdle *n.* 1 *More women used to wear girdles:* corselet, corset, foundation garment, waist cincher, bodice; stays. 2 *The king wore a girdle of red velvet:* waistband, sash, cummerbund; circlet, girth, cincture, surcingle. 3 *A girdle of trees enclosed the park:* ring, belt, circle, band, hedge.

girl *n.* 1 *The school is for girls. our oldest girl:* young female, schoolgirl, miss, lass, lassie, colleen; daughter, female child; maiden, maid, virgin, damsel. 2 *Freddy took his girl to the dance:* girlfriend, sweetheart; fiancée,

betrothed, affianced; lady love, darling, angel.

girlish *adj. She has a girlish laugh:* girl-like, maidenlike, youthful.
Ant. matronly, mature, womanly.

girth *n.* 1 *The girth of the tree was 100 inches:* circumference, perimeter, length around. 2 *Tighten the girth:* saddle girth, saddle band, cinch.

gist *n. What was the gist of the essay?:* essence, main idea, essential part, sense, significance, substance, sum and substance, implication, theme, drift; core, crux, heart, pith, purport.

give *v.* 1 *What can I give you for your birthday?:* present to, make a gift of, bestow, offer; donate, grant, accord, hand over; award, confer; commit, entrust. 2 *Most people give to charity. She gave her brother the bulk of her estate:* contribute, donate, bestow, consign, apportion, allot, dispense, distribute, subscribe, assign; endow, bequeath, leave. 3 *Give your hat to the checkroom attendant:* place in someone's care, give over, hand over, entrust. 4 *Give me one good reason. She gave a cry that brought us running:* show, provide, present, issue, convey, afford; utter, emit, offer, articulate. 5 *Would you give me that magazine on the table?:* hand to, accommodate with, provide with, supply with, equip with, present, furnish, deliver, hand over; proffer, tender, offer. 6 *The shop will give $10 for your old golf bag. She gave the porter a tip:* pay, compensate, recompense, remunerate, allow; tip, buy; confer, hand over, dispense, distribute, present; *Slang* fork over. 7 *She gave them notice that she was quitting:* notify, announce, let know, communicate, impart; present, issue, render. 8 *The assignment gave us a chance to prove our talents:* permit, allow, grant, enable; present, offer, accord, provide, supply, furnish, proffer, afford, confer, impart. 9 *He gave himself to the job with enthusiasm:* apply, devote; surrender, attach, lose oneself in. 10 *The branch gave under the weight of the snow:* give way, break down, collapse; slacken, loosen, relax, bend. 11 *Our picture window gives onto the patio:* open on; lead on to, afford an entrance; look out on, provide a vista. —*n.* 12 *A good mattress shouldn't have much give:* flexibility, resilience; bounce, springiness.
Ant. 1–8 receive, get, take, accept; keep, retain, withhold. 11 shut off, block, screen, conceal.

glacial *adj. a glacial wind. a glacial stare:* cold, chill, freezing, frigid, bone-chilling, polar, arctic, icy, frozen, congealed, frosty, wintry; hostile, unfriendly, disdainful, contemptuous.

Ant. hot, warm, balmy; friendly, cordial.

glad *adj.* 1 *We were glad you could visit:* happy, delighted, pleased, joyful, joyous, cheerful, exhilarated, rejoiced; *Slang* tickled. 2 *glad news:* happy, delightful, pleasing, joyous, joyful, exhilarating, cheerful, gratifying, cheering.

Ant. 1 sad, unhappy, sorry, sorrowful, displeased, disappointed. 2 depressing, sad, unhappy, unpleasant.

gladden *v. The children gladdened our hearts:* cheer, cheer up, please, hearten, delight, gratify, make happy; animate, raise the spirits of, enliven.

Ant. depress, sadden.

glamorous Also **glamourous** *adj. a glamorous movie star:* fascinating, charming, bewitching, enchanting, dazzling, captivating, alluring; attractive; exciting, magnetic, charismatic.

Ant. unglamorous, unexciting, colorless.

glamour Also **glamor** *n. Is there glamour in the advertising business?:* fascination, excitement, adventure, romance, allure, charm, enchantment.

glance *v.* 1 *He glanced at the paper:* look quickly, see briefly, scan, glimpse, regard hastily; peek, peep. 2 *The ball glanced off the wall. It glanced my shoulder:* rebound, ricochet, careen, bounce; graze, brush, skim, touch. —*n.* 3 *Take a glance at this report:* quick look, brief look, glimpse; peek.

Ant. 1 study, scrutinize, peruse.

glare *n.* 1 *the glare of headlights:* harsh light, gleam, glint, flash, flare, glitter; glaze, flame; brightness, luminosity, radiance, gloss, sheen, shimmer, sparkle. 2 *He ignored my glare and went on telling the story:* angry look, reproving look, black look, dirty look, threatening look; piercing stare, glower, scowl. —*v.* 3 *The sunlight glared on the ice:* shine harshly, reflect brightly, glitter, flare, gleam, glimmer, sparkle, glisten, shimmer, glow, flash, blaze. 4 *He glared at the student:* stare angrily, look fiercely, scowl, look blackly, glower.

glaring *adj.* 1 *glaring lights:* harsh, bright, strong, brilliant, intense, blinding, dazzling, piercing. 2 *a glaring error:* conspicuous, obvious, blatant, flagrant, unconcealed, unmistakable, egregious, undisguised; outrageous, gross.

Ant. 1 soft, subdued. 2 hidden, inconspicuous; subtle.

glaze *v.* 1 *My eyes began to glaze:* become glassy, film over, blur, grow dim. —*n.* 2 *The glaze is baked on the pottery:* glossy

coating, glazing, gloss, finish, enamel, varnish.

gleam *n.* 1 *a searchlight's gleam:* beam, ray, glow; glitter, glimmer; spark, sparkle, flash. 2 *A waxing will give the table a fine gleam:* sheen, luster, gloss; gleaming, radiance, glitter. 3 *a gleam of hope:* trace, ray, inkling, glimpse, bit, drop, jot, iota, hint, glimmer, flicker. —*v.* 4 *The lights gleamed in the distance:* shine, glow, flash, glare, flare, shimmer, glitter, glisten, glimmer, sparkle, scintillate, twinkle.

glean *v. to glean data from books:* gather, discover, collect, pick up, cull, accumulate, amass, harvest.

glee *n. to shout with glee:* merriment, gaiety, joy, joyfulness, joyousness, exhilaration, exultation, delight, gladness; hilarity, mirth, laughter; playfulness, sportiveness.

Ant. sadness, gloom, dejection, melancholy.

gleeful *adj. a gleeful shout:* happy, elated, glad, delighted, merry, joyful, joyous, exultant, cheerful, exhilarated; mirthful, jovial.

Ant. sad, gloomy, dejected, melancholy.

glen *n. the glens of Scotland:* narrow valley, dell, dale, vale, hollow.

Ant. height, peak, mountain, hill.

glib *adj. a glib answer:* facile, flippant, quick, ready, smooth, smooth-tongued, nimble of speech; insincere, devious; slippery.

Ant. well-considered, sincere, deliberate; hesitant, halting.

glide *v.* 1 *The hawk glided toward the mountain:* soar, float, coast, sail, drift, flow. 2 *The dancers glided over the floor:* move smoothly, move effortlessly, slide, skim; slip; skate. 3 *The years glide by:* slip, pass quickly, roll, run; proceed, issue.

Ant. 1 fall, plummet. 2 lurch, stagger, stumble, trip, shuffle.

glimmer *n.* 1 *a candle's glimmer:* faint gleam, glow, flicker, shimmer, glimmering, twinkle; ray, scintilla. 2 *a glimmer of hope:* trace, gleam, flickering, drop, speck, bit, hint, glimpse. —*v.* 3 *The lights glimmered in the distance:* shine, flicker, twinkle, flash, gleam, sparkle, glitter, glisten, shimmer, glow, flare, beam.

glimpse *n.* 1 *We had only a glimpse of the deer:* fleeting look, quick look, brief look, brief sight, momentary view, glance; peep, peek. —*v.* 2 *We glimpsed the diplomats as the motorcade passed:* see fleetingly, see briefly, catch sight of, catch a glimpse of, see, spot, peep at, peek at.

Ant. 2 survey, scrutinize, inspect.

glisten *v. The street glistened in the rain:* shine, sparkle, glitter, scintillate, shimmer, glow, glimmer, gleam, glint, twinkle, flicker.

glitter *v.* 1 *The diamond glittered:* sparkle, shine, glisten, gleam, glow, glimmer, flash, twinkle. —*n.* 2 *Cleaning will restore the gem's glitter:* luster, shine, sheen, gleam, glow, sparkle, radiance, brilliance. 3 *the glitter of opening night:* glamour, splendor, grandeur, pomp, show, excitement, thrill.
Ant. 2 dullness. 3 drabness, dullness, dreariness.

gloat *v. Good winners don't gloat:* crow over, vaunt, brag, glory over, preen oneself, relish maliciously.
Ant. belittle, disparage, deprecate, deride, scoff at.

global *adj. global war:* worldwide, world, universal, planetary, intercontinental, international; general, widespread, comprehensive, unlimited.
Ant. local, regional, sectional; limited, confined.

globe *n.* 1 *The earth is not a true globe:* sphere, spherical body, spheroid, spherule, orb, globule. 2 *Her travels took her all over the globe:* planet, world, Earth.

gloom *n.* 1 *A candle dispelled the gloom:* darkness, dark, blackness, dimness, murkiness, shadows, shade. 2 *Don't let defeat fill you with gloom:* depression, low spirits, despondency, dejection, sadness, melancholy, unhappiness, moroseness, heavy-heartedness, despair, hopelessness, forlornness, sorrow, grief.
Ant. 1 light, brightness. 2 joy, glee, delight, happiness, gladness, merriment, mirth, jollity.

gloomy *adj.* 1 *a gloomy day:* dark, dim, dreary, murky, somber; cloudy, overcast, sunless. 2 *a gloomy mood:* sad, unhappy, downcast, dejected, melancholy, despondent, depressed, cheerless, glum, doleful, disheartened, heavy-hearted, downhearted, morose, desolate, somber, *Slang* down in the mouth, down in the dumps; discouraged, pessimistic, sorrowful, forlorn.
Ant. 1 bright, sunny, brilliant. 2 happy, glad, cheerful, joyful, jolly; merry, jovial, lighthearted.

glorify *v. to glorify God. to glorify the past:* give glory to, pay homage to, exalt, venerate, revere, deify, apotheosize, canonize, worship, consecrate, sanctify, beatify; ennoble, dignify, immortalize, praise, laud, extol, honor, sing the praises of; glamorize, romanticize.
Ant. desecrate, profane, blaspheme, defile, dishonor, degrade.

glorious *adj.* 1 *What a glorious day!:* gorgeous, beautiful, wonderful, marvelous, splendid, fine, great, grand, excellent, superb, delightful, divine; sparkling, brilliant, dazzling. 2 *a glorious piece of music:* sublime, noble, magnificent, grand, majestic, august, imposing; distinguished, renowned, illustrious, notable, praiseworthy.
Ant. 1 awful, horrible, horrid, unpleasant, *Slang* lousy. 2 minor, trivial, trifling; undistinguished.

glory *n.* 1 *Sing glory to God:* adoration, worship, homage, veneration; praise, admiration. 2 *to win glory in battle:* honor, renown, fame, illustriousness, esteem, distinction, notability. 3 *the glory of the Grand Canyon:* grandeur, splendor, magnificence, majesty, gloriousness, resplendence, sublimity, stateliness, nobility, dignity, excellence. —*v.* 4 *His mother gloried in his success:* take pride, revel, take delight; be boastful, boast, vaunt.
Ant. 1 blasphemy, profanity. 2 dishonor, disgrace, shame, infamy, ignominy. 3 ugliness, meanness, triviality.

gloss *n.* 1 *a high gloss:* luster, shine, sheen, polish, glaze; gleam, brightness, glossiness. —*v.* 2 *He glossed over his mistakes:* treat lightly, explain away, rationalize, excuse, disguise, veil, cloak.
Ant. 2 exaggerate, overemphasize, face.

glow *n.* 1 *the glow of embers:* soft light, gleam, afterglow, glimmer, shimmer, flicker; soft heat, warmth. 2 *a glow in her cheeks:* color, warmth, brightness, reddening; flush, bloom, blush; radiance. —*v.* 3 *The fire glowed for hours:* burn softly, smolder; shine, gleam, glitter, shimmer, glisten, twinkle, flicker. 4 *The boy glowed with pride:* fill, flush, blush, thrill, tingle; feel intensely, be animated.
Ant. 2 paleness, pallor, grayness.

glower *v. She glowered at the student:* scowl, look angrily, look fierce, glare, stare, frown, look black; pout, sulk.
Ant. smile, grin.

glowing *adj.* 1 *The children had glowing cheeks. glowing shades of red:* ruddy, flushed, red; bright, vivid, luminescent, florid. 2 *a glowing review of the movie:* enthusiastic, rave, raving; fervent, ardent, ecstatic; sensational, exciting, passionate, rhapsodic.
Ant. 1 pale, pallid, white, wan, ashen; dull, drab. 2 unenthusiastic, cool, scathing, stinging, vitriolic.

glut *v.* 1 *to glut oneself on Thanksgiving turkey:* stuff, gorge, cram, fill, overfeed, overeat, satiate, eat one's fill. 2 *to glut the market with cheap radios:* oversupply, flood, deluge, overload, saturate; sate, surfeit; choke, clog, obstruct. —*n.* 3 *a glut on the* *market:* oversupply, overabundance, surplus, excess, superfluity, surfeit.

Ant. 1 starve. 2 undersupply. 3 scarcity, shortage, dearth, lack.

glutton *n. The gluttons cleared the table:* voracious eater, overeater, trencherman, gourmand, gormandizer, gorger, *Slang* pig, chowhound.

gluttony *n. High blood pressure can be the result of gluttony:* excessive eating, overeating, voracity, voraciousness, gormandizing, gourmandism; *Slang* eating like a pig.

gnarled *adj. a gnarled oak tree:* knotty, knotted, full of knots, nodular, covered with gnarls, snaggy, wrinkled, rugged; twisted, crooked.

Ant. smooth, sleek, unwrinkled.

gnaw *v. The boy gnawed an apple:* munch, eat away at, chew, nibble, chomp.

gnome *n. a fairy tale full of gnomes:* dwarf, troll, shriveled little old man; elf, goblin; pixy, leprechaun.

go *v.* 1 *What time will you go? On your mark, get set, go!:* move toward, set out for, begin, proceed, be off, advance, make headway, wend, repair; press onward, sally forth. 2 *Please go now:* leave, depart, go away, take one's departure, withdraw, retire, decamp, move out, move away, *Slang* scram, beat it, vamoose, blow, split; flee, fly, take flight. 3 *Does this road go to the city?:* lead, extend, reach, stretch to, spread to. 4 *Is the machine going now?:* work, operate, function, run, be operative, perform; be in motion. 5 *Time goes fast:* pass, pass by, go by, elapse, lapse, flow, glide by, slip away. 6 *Most of my money goes for rent:* be used, be applied on, be given; be awarded, be contributed. 7 *How did things go today?:* turn out, work out, fare, come to pass, transpire; result, end, terminate. 8 *Where do these cups go? That hat doesn't go with your coat:* fit, have a place, belong; be compatible, be suited to, agree, harmonize, blend. —*n.* 9 *a man with a lot of go:* ambition, drive, energy, vigor, vim, vitality, initiative, steam, spirit, verve, pep, enterprise. 10 *Let me have a go at it:* try, attempt, turn, chance, whirl; effort, experiment.

Ant. 1 stay, remain; arrive, end. 2 come. 4 stop. 8 mismatch, be incompatible, be unsuited. 9 laziness, lethargy.

goad *n.* 1 *Fear of failure can be a goad to hard work:* incentive, stimulus, stimulant, motivation, driving motive, spur; instigation. —*v.* 2 *I goaded him to ask for a raise:* prod, incite, spur, push, pressure, drive, stir up, arouse, *Slang* egg on; impel, propel, press.

Ant. 1 detriment, curb.

goal *n. Her goal is to own her own business:* aim, objective, ambition, purpose, object, intent, intention, design, end, target.

goat *n. When something goes wrong, I'm always the goat:* scapegoat, victim, fall guy, whipping boy, butt, laughingstock.

gobble *v. We gobbled our lunch and ran back to the office:* gulp, gulp down, bolt, bolt down, eat quickly, cram down, wolf.

gobbledygook *n. The speech was full of gobbledygook:* jargon, gibberish, balderdash, double-talk, bosh, nonsense, buncombe, bunk, rubbish, tommyrot, hocuspocus, fiddle-faddle.

go-between *n. Our go-betweens will settle the details:* intermediary, middleman, representative, emissary; arbiter, arbitrator, mediator, interceder, envoy, second.

goblin *n. Eat your spinach or the goblins will get you!:* wicked elf, evil sprite, bogeyman, bogey, demon, gremlin, ogre.

God *n.* 1 *God created the heavens and the earth:* Lord, Our Father, God Almighty, the Almighty, the Supreme Being, the Deity, the Creator; the Godhead, the Omnipotent, the Omniscient, the All-Merciful; *Slang* the Man Upstairs. 2 *usually* **god.** *the Greek god of war:* deity, divine being, ruling spirit, divinity.

Ant. 1 the Devil, Prince of Darkness, the Foul Fiend; Satan, Mephistopheles, Lucifer, Beelzebub; *Slang* Old Nick. 2 mortal, human, human being.

godforsaken *adj. The town was a godforsaken place:* desolate, deserted, remote; neglected; bleak, wretched, lonely.

godless *adj. He repented his godless life:* evil, wicked, depraved; atheistic, agnostic, irreligious, sacrilegious, ungodly, impious, profane; heathen, unsanctified, unrighteous.

Ant. godly, God-fearing, pious, religious, holy.

godly *adj. a wise and godly man:* devout, pious, reverent, reverential, religious, righteous, devoted, God-loving, God-fearing, believing; saintly, holy; moral, good.

Ant. ungodly, atheistic, irreligious, sacrilegious, impious; evil, wicked, depraved.

gold *n.* 1 *The prospectors found gold: (variously)* gold dust, nugget; bullion, ingot, bar, *Chemistry* aurum. 2 *The colors are green and gold:* bright yellow, yellow, gilt. 3 *He has a heart of gold:* goodness, kindness, purity; goodwill, humanity.

golden *adj.* 1 *golden hair:* bright-yellow, gold-colored, gold, aureate, blond; gilt, gilded. 2 *a golden opportunity:* advantageous, opportune, favorable, timely, promising, auspicious, propitious. 3 *These were*

my golden years: most joyous, happiest, great, glorious, best, blest, delightful, flourishing, halcyon; most precious, priceless, richest.
Ant. 2 unfavorable, inauspicious, unpromising. 3 worst, saddest, most wretched; lean.

good *adj.* 1 *a good teacher. good deeds:* virtuous, honorable, morally excellent, upright; honest, reliable, conscientious; moral, praiseworthy, exemplary; religious, pious, devout, pure, innocent, unsullied, untainted; humane, considerate, benevolent, kindhearted, kind, kindly, obliging. 2 *Have you been good?:* dutiful, obedient, proper, well-mannered, well-behaved. 3 *Faulkner's novels are good:* excellent, fine, great, wonderful, splendid, first-rate; worthy, worthwhile; valuable, admirable, commendable. 4 *a good typist:* skilled, skillful, capable, efficient, proficient, adroit, topnotch, first-rate, excellent, first-class, ace. 5 *Milk is good for you. It's a good day for swimming:* beneficial, healthful, healthy, salutary, advantageous; suitable, favorable, right, proper, fitting, useful; becoming, deserving. 6 *Have a good time. a good personality:* enjoyable, pleasant, agreeable; cheerful, lively, sunny, genial, convivial, sociable. 7 *Wear your good suit:* best; newest; most dressy, most stylish; expensive; valuable, precious. 8 *I would cash the check if I could be sure it was good:* valid, bona fide, sound; real, genuine, authentic. 9 *The farm is a good mile from here. She spends a good amount of time playing bridge:* full, complete, entire; considerable, substantial, sizable, ample; adequate, sufficient. —*n.* 10 *We all have some good in us:* goodness, virtue, merit, worth, value, excellence, kindness. 11 *for the good of the team:* benefit, advantage, gain, prosperity, success, welfare, interest, well-being; service, favor, good turn.
Ant. 1–6, 8, 10 bad. 1 evil, wicked, dishonorable, immoral, dishonest, unreliable; corrupt; mean, cruel, unkind. 2 naughty, mischievous. 3 awful, second-rate, worthless. 4 unskilled, incompetent, inefficient, awful, *Slang* lousy. 5 disadvantageous; unsuitable, inappropriate. 6 awful, *Slang* lousy; unpleasant, disagreeable. 7 worst, oldest. 8 phony, counterfeit, fraudulent, bogus; worthless. 9 scant, small, insubstantial. 10 evil, wickedness, badness, sinfulness, meanness. 11 detriment.

good-by Also **good-bye** *interj.* 1 *Good-by and write as soon as you can:* farewell, so long, bye, bye-bye, bye-now, till we meet again, be seeing you, see you later; French

au revoir; *Spanish* adios, *Italian* ciao, arrivederci; *German* auf Wiedersehen; *Japanese* sayonara. —*n.* 2 *a final good-by:* farewell, parting, leave-taking, departure, separation, send-off.
Ant. 1 hello, hi. 2 meeting, greeting.

good-humored *adj. a good-humored reply:* cheery, amiable, good-natured, cheerful, genial, pleasant, kindly, affable, mild, easygoing.
Ant. irritable, cranky, crotchety, surly.

good-looking *adj. Fashion models are good-looking:* handsome, clean-cut, nice-looking, well-favored, attractive; beautiful, lovely, pretty, comely, fair, pulchritudinous, eye-catching, sexy, ravishing.
Ant. homely, ugly, unattractive.

good-natured *adj. good-natured child:* amiable, affable, friendly, pleasant, cheerful, agreeable, easygoing, genial, good-humored, good-tempered, obliging, accommodating, warm-hearted.
Ant. cranky, cantankerous, cross, peevish.

goodness *n.* 1 *an individual of exceeding goodness:* moral excellence, honor, honesty, merit, wholesomeness, virtue, virtuousness, purity, innocence, benevolence, kindness, kindliness, generosity; piety; devotion. —*interj.* 2 *Goodness, what a big cake!:* gracious, goodness gracious, mercy, heavens, heavens to Betsy, sakes alive, landsakes, land alive; *Slang* wow, gee.
Ant. 1 badness, evil, wickedness, sinfulness, immorality, unwholesomeness, corruption.

goods *n. pl.* 1 *We put our goods on the moving van:* possessions, property, effects, worldly goods, movables, movable effects, chattels; furnishings, things. 2 *All the store's goods are on sale:* merchandise, stock, inventory, wares; articles of trade, commodities. 3 *dry goods:* cloth, fabric, material, woven goods; textiles, dry goods, piece goods, fabrics.

gore *n. There's much gore in bullfighting:* bloodshed, butchery, slaughter, carnage; blood, dried blood, clotted blood.

gorge *n.* 1 *The waterfall was at the end of the gorge:* steep valley, canyon, chasm, ravine, cleft, gully, gulch, defile; crevasse, gap, pass. 2 *The dog had a bone caught in its gorge:* throat, gullet, craw. 3 *It makes my gorge rise:* disgust, revulsion, repugnance, repulsion; anger, wrath, blood, ire, animosity, hatred. —*v.* 4 *The children gorged themselves on candy:* stuff, fill, glut, sate, fill, cram, satiate; overeat, overindulge, eat greedily, gormandize, gluttonize; gulp, gobble, bolt.

gorgeous *adj. a gorgeous coat:* beautiful,

attractive, good-looking, lovely, exquisite, stunning, ravishing.

Ant. ugly, hideous, unattractive, repulsive.

gory *adj.* 1 *The hunter's knife was gory:* bloody, bloodstained, bloodsoaked. 2 *The gory tale gave me nightmares:* bloody, scary, bloodcurdling, frightening, terrifying, horrifying.

gospel *n.* 1 Often **Gospel** *to preach the gospel. a translation of the Gospels:* the tidings of salvation proclaimed by Jesus Christ, the good news; any of the first four books of the New Testament: Matthew, Mark, Luke, or John. 2 *Her opinions are gospel to me:* the truth, ultimate truth, the final word, the last word; doctrine, creed, credo.

gossip *n.* 1 *a career ruined by gossip:* rumor, hearsay, whispering behind one's back, newsmongering, scandal; idle talk, prattle, twaddle. 2 Also **gossiper** *He's such a gossip you don't dare tell him anything:* talebearer, idle talker, rumormonger, scandalmonger, gossipmonger, newsmonger, blabbermouth, chatterbox, busybody. —*v.* 3 *Don't gossip about my friends:* spread rumors, talk idly, prattle, prate, blab.

gourmand *n.* *A gourmand likes good food and plenty of it:* trencherman, gormandizer, glutton, big eater; *Slang* chowhound.

gourmet *n.* *A gourmet wants the best food, not the most:* epicure, gastronome, gastronomer, connoisseur.

govern *v.* 1 *Canada is governed by a prime minister:* administer, manage, rule, direct, head, lead, guide, steer, run, supervise, oversee, exercise authority over. 2 *You'd better learn to govern your tongue:* control, restrain, check, hold in check, curb, bridle, keep under control; discipline, command, rule, dominate, boss. 3 *What governed your decision?:* guide, influence, sway, lead, steer, form, rule.

government *n.* 1 *Society could not exist without government:* governing system, rule, administration, authority, law, management, control, regulation, command, direction, guidance, supervision; state, dominion, reins of government. 2 *the prime minister and his government:* governing body, administration, regime.

gown *n.* *a white satin gown:* formal dress, long dress, fancy dress, party dress; dress, frock; nightgown, nightdress; academic garb, robe.

grab *v.* 1 *He grabbed his hat and ran:* seize, snatch, grasp, lay hold of; clutch, grip, hold, clasp; capture, catch, nab, collar, bag. —*n.* 2 *The boy made a grab at the frog:* sudden grasp, snatch, lunge, pass.

grace *n.* 1 *to walk with grace:* gracefulness, supple ease, lissomeness, willowiness, fluidity; beauty, pulchritude. 2 *the graces of a good hostess:* charming quality, endowment, accomplishment, skill; charm, refinement, culture, cultivation, elegance, manners, decorum, etiquette, propriety, tact, taste. 3 *Pray for grace:* God's favor, God's love, divine goodness; holiness, sanctity, saintliness; moral strength, virtue. 4 *by the king's grace:* mercy, clemency, lenience, charity, indulgence, mercifulness. 5 *Drivers have 30 days' grace to renew licenses:* extra time, exemption, reprieve, dispensation. —*v.* 6 *Flowers graced the paths in the park:* adorn, decorate, beautify, ornament, embellish, garnish, spruce up, dress up, enhance.

Ant. 1 clumsiness, awkwardness, gawkiness. 2 bad manners, tactlessness, tastelessness. 4 disfavor, enmity; harshness, cruelty.

graceful *adj.* *a graceful dancer:* easy-moving, supple, limber, lithe, willowy, lithesome, lissome, light-footed; sylphlike.

Ant. clumsy, awkward, ungainly, ungraceful, lumbering, stiff.

gracious *adj.* 1 *a gracious hostess:* kindly, courteous, cordial, amiable, hospitable, obliging, pleasant; kind, friendly, kindhearted, charitable, humane, benevolent, benign, merciful, lenient, clement.

Ant. 1 ungracious, unpleasant, ill-natured, unfriendly, cold, discourteous, brusque, curt; cruel, mean.

grade *n.* 1 *The truck moved slowly up the steep grade:* incline, slope, gradient, ramp; hill, bank. 2 *pearls of the highest grade. a naval lieutenant junior grade:* rank, degree, level, standing, place; order, class, status, station, position; stage, step; quality, value. 3 *The student got a grade of B:* mark; rating, standing. —*v.* 4 *to grade eggs:* classify, sort; rank, order, graduate, value, rate. 5 *to grade exams:* mark, give a grade to, rate. 6 *to grade a road:* level, even, smooth, flatten.

gradual *adj. a gradual improvement:* steady, progressive, regular, continuous, successive, incremental, slow, gentle, step-by-step, little-by-little.

Ant. sudden, abrupt, instantaneous, overnight.

graduate *n.* 1 *a graduate of the Sorbonne:* alumnus, alumna, recipient of a diploma, holder of a degree. —*v.* 2 *to graduate from college:* receive a diploma, receive a degree; award a diploma to, confer a degree on, grant a degree to. 3 *a measuring cup gradu-*

ated in ounces: mark with gradations, mark off, calibrate, grade, measure out.

graft¹ *n.* **1** *The graft on the apple tree is thriving:* inserted shoot, implant, implantation; splice; slip. —*v.* **2** *The surgeon grafted skin onto his burned arm:* implant, transplant; inset, infix, join.

graft² *n. to abolish graft in government:* corruption, bribery, payoffs, bribes, kickback, spoils.

grain *n.* **1** *Farmers raise millions of bushels of grain:* edible seed plants, cereal; *(variously)* wheat, rye, barley, oats, corn, maize, millet. **2** *grains of sand:* particle, granule; bit, pellet. **4** *There isn't a grain of truth in his assertion:* bit, speck, particle, trace, iota, jot, scintilla, whit, tittle, crumb, modicum.

grand *adj.* **1** *What could be more grand than Buckingham Palace?:* magnificent, majestic, stately, monumental, august, imposing, elegant, impressive, striking, splendid, superb, glorious; noble, imperial, palatial, royal; luxurious, sumptuous, opulent; showy; large, big, huge, mammoth. **2** *The queen received her in a grand manner:* stately, majestic, regal, noble, august, lofty, dignified, lordly, royal, kingly, queenly, princely; grandiose, arrogant, pompous, haughty. **3** *That's a grand idea:* good, splendid, excellent, wonderful, fine, great, terrific, marvelous, fabulous, superb, sensational, first-rate; *Slang* swell, keen, super, out of this world. **4** *Grand Marshal of the Army:* main, chief, head, principal, supreme. **5** *the grand total:* complete, full, all-embracing, all-inclusive, comprehensive.

Ant. **1** paltry, measly, small, little, meager; unimposing, insignificant; inferior. **2** undignified, common, low-class. **3** bad, poor, worthless, second-rate; *Slang* rotten, terrible, awful, lousy.

grandeur *n. the grandeur of the royal palace:* magnificence, majesty, splendor, stateliness, impressiveness, resplendence, nobility, glory, pomp, augustness, dignity.

Ant. paltriness, smallness; insignificance, inferiority.

grandiloquent *adj. a grandiloquent speech:* high-flown, high-sounding, flowery, florid, grandiose, pompous, bombastic, inflated, turgid, magniloquent, rhetorical.

Ant. simple, direct, unaffected, plain-spoken.

grandiose *adj. a grandiose idea:* high-flown, flamboyant, theatrical, pretentious, pompous, extravagant, *Slang* highfalutin.

grant *v.* **1** *to grant permission. The government will grant land to settlers:* give, allow, consent to, permit; bestow, accord, confer, allocate, present, donate, assign, award.

2 *Will you grant that I was right?:* concede, admit, allow, consent, vouchsafe, yield. —*n.* **3** *a grant of land from the government:* allotment, presentation, gift, donation, award, endowment, benefaction, bestowal; allowance, concession.

Ant. **1** refuse, deny, withhold.

graphic *adj. a graphic description of the accident:* vivid, realistic, lifelike, illustrative, pictorial; forcible, striking; explicit, descriptive.

Ant. unrealistic, hazy, vague, abstract.

grapple *v. to grapple with a problem:* struggle, contend, combat, fight, wrestle, take on, encounter, face, tackle, meet, confront, try to overcome.

Ant. avoid, evade, sidestep, run away from.

grasp *v.* **1** *She grasped the letter tightly:* seize, grab, snatch, catch, take hold of, lay hold of; hold, clutch, clasp, grip. **2** *I couldn't grasp the explanation:* comprehend, understand, get, fathom, follow, master. – *n.* **3** *Take a firm grasp on the rope:* grip, hold, clasp, clutch. **4** *The prize is within our grasp:* reach, power; compass, scope, range, sweep, sway. **5** *the students' grasp of algebra:* comprehension, understanding, perception, knowledge, mastery.

Ant. **1** release, let go.

grate¹ *n.* **1** *Build a fire in the grate:* fireplace, hearth, firebox. **2** *The city installed grates over the storm drains:* grating, grill, screen, bars, lattice, latticework.

grate² *v.* **1** *The fender grated against the curb:* scrape, rasp, grind, rub, scratch, abrade. **2** *Her gossip grates on my nerves:* chafe, jar, irritate, annoy, rankle, irk, exasperate.

Ant. **1** slide, glide. **2** calm, soothe, pacify, quiet.

grateful *adj. We were grateful for your letter:* thankful, full of gratitude, appreciative, gratified; obliged, obligated, under beholden, indebted.

Ant. ungrateful, unappreciative.

gratification *n.* **1** *Collecting stamps gives me tremendous gratification:* satisfaction, pleasure, enjoyment, comfort, solace; contentment, delight, joy, relish. **2** *the gratification of one's appetite:* gratifying, satisfying, indulgence; soothing, pleasing.

Ant. **1** frustration, dissatisfaction. **2** curbing, restraint; denial.

gratify *v.* **1** *Winning the tournament gratified her:* satisfy, give pleasure to, please, delight, gladden. **2** *Do you have some candy to gratify my sweet tooth?:* satisfy, indulge, favor; appease, soothe; flatter, compliment.

Ant. 1 frustrate, disappoint, dissatisfy. 2 control, curb, deny.

grating¹ *n. The entrance was blocked by a grating:* framework of bars, gate of bars, grate, grille, grid.

grating² *adj.* 1 *a grating sound:* rasping, scraping, raspy, creaky, squeaky, harsh, shrill, piercing, strident, discordant, jarring. 2 *His incessant chatter can be grating:* annoying, irritating, abrasive, exasperating, vexatious.

Ant. 1 melodic, dulcet, mellifluous. 2 agreeable; calming, soothing.

gratitude *n. How can I express my gratitude?:* gratefulness, appreciation, thanks, acknowledgment, recognition.

Ant. ingratitude, ungratefulness.

gratuitous *adj. a gratuitous insult:* uncalled for, unwarranted, unjustified, unfounded; unproven, baseless, presumptive, irrelevant.

Ant. justified, warranted, well-founded, relevant.

grave¹ *n. The funeral procession arrived at the grave:* excavation for burial, burial place, place of interment, last resting place; tomb, sepulcher, mausoleum, vault, crypt, catacomb, cenotaph.

grave² *adj.* 1 *His sister was carefree, but he was grave:* solemn, sedate, serious, subdued, quiet, dignified, sober, staid; somber, dour, frowning. 2 *a matter of grave concern:* serious, critical, crucial, urgent, pressing, acute, vital, momentous, of great consequence, significant, weighty.

Ant. 1 carefree, gay, joyous, merry, boisterous, devil-may-care. 2 trivial, unimportant, inconsequential, insignificant.

graveyard *n. There are a hundred tombstones in this graveyard:* cemetery, burying ground, memorial park, churchyard, necropolis, charnel, ossuary.

gravitate *v.* 1 *The sediment gravitates to the bottom:* settle, sink, descend, fall. 2 *We gravitate toward people who are kind:* be drawn, be attracted, have a proclivity for; lean toward, converge, tend.

gravity *n.* 1 *The surgeon spoke with the utmost gravity:* seriousness, solemnity, solemness, earnestness, thoughtfulness, sobriety, sedateness, staidness; gloominess, somberness, grimness. 2 *The situation has reached a point of extreme gravity:* seriousness, urgency, concern, crucial nature, danger, emergency; importance, import, significance, consequence.

Ant. 1 frivolousness, frivolity, flippancy; gaiety, merriment, glee. 2 unimportance, insignificance, pettiness.

gray Also **grey** *adj.* 1 *gray hair. His face was drawn and gray:* pearl-gray, grayish, silver, silvery, slate, dun, drab, dove-colored, mouse-colored; ashen, ashy, pale. 2 *a gray winter day:* gloomy, dismal, somber, cheerless, depressing, dark, overcast, sunless, cloudy.

Ant. 2 bright, clear, sunny.

graze *v. The child grazed her knee:* scrape, scratch, skin, abrade; touch lightly, brush, skim.

grease *n.* 1 *bacon grease. Put some grease on that squeaky hinge:* fat, drippings, lard, tallow; oil, lubricant. —*v.* 2 *to grease engine parts:* lubricate, oil, apply grease to; anoint.

greasy *adj.* 1 *a greasy plate:* grease-covered, oily, oleaginous; slippery, slick, slithery. 2 *This bacon is too greasy:* lardy, fat, fatty.

great *adj.* 1 *a building of great size. Great crowds of people came to the sale:* vast, immense, enormous, huge, large, big, tremendous, gigantic, colossal, stupendous, mammoth, prodigious, voluminous, monstrous, gargantuan; many, countless, multitudinous, abundant, boundless, inexhaustible, manifold. 2 *He felt great happiness:* extreme, pronounced, considerable, strong, high, inordinate, prodigious. 3 *a great day in history:* important, of much consequence, significant, momentous; grave, serious, critical, crucial. 4 *one of the great books of all time. This cake is great!:* outstanding, remarkable, superb, superior, superlative, magnificent, notable, prominent, distinguished, noted, renowned, illustrious, celebrated, esteemed; good, excellent, marvelous; grand, splendid, wonderful, fabulous, fantastic, terrific, sensational; *Slang* swell, super, out of this world; proficient, skillful, crack. 5 *Our minister is a great man:* fine, noble, of lofty character, humane, loving, generous, kind, gracious. —*adv.* 6 *Business is going great:* very well, well, fine, excellently, superbly, splendidly, wonderfully.

Ant. 1 small, little, puny; insignificant, paltry, trivial, measly. 2 mild, some. 3 unimportant, inconsequential, insignificant. 4 bad, worse, inferior, wretched, terrible, awful, *Slang* lousy. 5 ignoble, wicked, hateful, unkind. 6 badly, poorly.

greatly *adv. His health has greatly improved:* very much, tremendously, immensely, enormously, vastly, abundantly, considerably, remarkably, markedly, notably.

Ant. little, insignificantly, mildly, somewhat.

greed *n. Greed led us to cheat our partner:* greediness, avarice, avariciousness, covetousness, selfishness, cupidity, rapacity, rapaciousness.

Ant. generosity, altruism, unselfishness.

greedy *adj.* 1 *Greedy men cannot be trusted:* money-hungry, avaricious, grasping, acquisitive, covetous, selfish, mercenary. 2 *The greedy animals crowded around the trough:* ravenous, gluttonous, voracious, insatiable, famished, hungry. 3 *a student greedy for knowledge:* eager, avid, keenly desirous, ardent, fervent, burning, thirsting, hungry, craving.

Ant. 1 generous, altruistic, unselfish.

green *adj.* 1 *These green walls are hideous!:* green-colored, *(variously)* yellow-green, chartreuse, lime, lime-green, olive, olive-green, greenish, verdant, pea-green, forest-green, kelly-green, jade, emerald, sea-green, aquamarine, blue-green. 2 *The apples are too green to pick. green lumber:* unripe, immature, underdeveloped, undeveloped; young, tender, unfledged, crude; raw, unseasoned, not dried, not cured. 3 *green recruits:* inexperienced, callow, raw, untrained, unpolished, unsophisticated, unversed, immature; unskilled, inexpert, uninformed; gullible, credulous.

Ant. 2 ripe, mature, matured, aged, seasoned. 3 experienced, mature, seasoned, skilled.

greet *v.* 1 *The host greeted the guests:* welcome, bid welcome, salute, hail, receive. 2 *The class greeted my suggestion with boos:* meet, receive, welcome, accept.

greeting *n.* 1 *The greeting of all the guests took an hour:* welcoming, welcome, saluting, salutation, salute; reception. 2 Often **greetings** *When you see Jane, give her my greetings:* salutation, hello, regards, respects, remembrance, felicitations, well wishing, compliments, best, good wishes.

gregarious *adj.* *A gregarious person loves parties:* sociable, social, outgoing, convivial, extroverted, affable, friendly; talkative.

Ant. unsociable, introverted, retiring, shy.

grief *n.* *No one could console them in their grief:* grieving, sorrow, sadness, heartbreak, heartache, misery, agony, woe, suffering, anguish, distress, despondency, despair, desolation.

Ant. joy, happiness, gaiety, gladness, glee.

grievance *n.* *The workers had a long list of grievances:* complaint; injustice, wrong, hurt, affliction, hardship, injury.

grieve *v.* 1 *The nation grieved for its dead:* feel grief, mourn, weep, lament, sorrow, be sad, wail, shed tears, cry, bemoan. 2 *The loss of the pet grieved the child:* sadden, make sorrowful, distress; pain, break the heart, discomfort, deject, depress.

Ant. 1 rejoice, delight in, be happy about. 2 delight, gladden, cheer.

grievous *adj.* 1 *His death was a grievous loss:* tragic, sad, heartbreaking, woeful, distressing, lamentable. 2 *grievous crimes. a grievous injury:* very bad, grave, severe, serious, acute; appalling, atrocious, heinous, shocking, outrageous, monstrous; deplorable, intolerable, unbearable, distressing, burdensome, destructive, calamitous.

Ant. 1 delightful, welcome, joyous, happy. 2 trivial, trifling; unimportant, insignificant; mild.

grill *n.* 1 *Cook the hotdogs on the grill:* griddle, gridiron, grid, grating, crossbars. —*v.* 2 *Let's grill the steaks over charcoal:* broil, fry, sear, cook. 3 *Informal The police grilled the suspect:* interrogate, question, pump, quiz.

grim *adj.* 1 *She looked grim all morning:* somber, gloomy, austere; sullen, grumpy, sulky, scowling, morose, stern, severe, harsh, hard, relentless, merciless, cruel, heartless, implacable, determined, resolute. 2 *The subject is too grim to joke about:* horrible, sinister, grisly, frightful, horrid, hideous, gruesome, dreadful; repellent, repulsive, repugnant, loathsome, appalling, revolting, shocking; squalid, ugly.

Ant. 1 happy, cheerful; lenient, benign, merciful, sympathetic, amiable, congenial. 2 pleasant, pleasing.

grimace *n.* *She made a grimace when I mentioned his name:* face, wry face, expression of distaste.

grime *n. to wash the grime out of clothes:* oily grit, dirt, dust, soil, soot, filth.

grin *n.* 1 *A big grin broke out on his face:* smile, gleaming smile, simper, smirk. —*v.* 2 *She grinned with pleasure:* smile, beam, grin from ear to ear; smirk, simper.

grind *v.* 1 *The wheat will be ground into flour:* pulverize, powder, granulate, crush, triturate, mill. 2 *to grind the knives:* sharpen, whet, file, rasp; scrape, abrade. 3 *The child grinds his teeth:* grate, rasp, gnash, grit. —*n.* 4 *Informal Writing this report was a real grind:* chore, drudgery, dull task, laborious work, hard job.

Ant. 2 dull. 4 easy job, enjoyable task, *Slang* piece of cake.

grip *n.* 1 *He held the letter securely in his grip:* grasp, clutch, clasp, hold. 2 *in the grip of a strong emotion. She has a good grip of mathematics:* grasp, control, hold, clutches, domination; understanding, comprehension, perception. 3 *The sword has a gold grip:* handle, hilt. 4 *Grandmother traveled with two grips:* valise, suitcase, bag, traveling bag, satchel, gladstone. —*v.* 5 *He gripped the hammer and started work:* grasp, seize firmly, clutch, clench, hold fast, hold tight; seize hold of, catch hold of.

7 *The book gripped the readers' interest:* hold, retain, take hold on, spellbind, rivet.

gripe *n.* **1** *The manager wouldn't listen to the workers' gripes:* grievance, complaint; faultfinding, whining, grousing, grumbling; *Slang* beef, squawk. —*v.* *The waitress griped about the small tip:* complain, grumble, mutter, whine, grouse, cavil, *Slang* beef, squawk, bellyache.

grisly *adj. a grisly crime:* gruesome, horrible, horrid, hideous, ghastly, frightful, dreadful, shocking, gory, abhorrent, repugnant, repellent, revolting, repulsive, loathsome.
Ant. pleasant, pleasing, innocuous, attractive.

grit *n.* **1** *Wipe the grit off the window sill:* soot, dirt, dust, filth, muck. **2** *She has a lot of grit:* spunk, pluck, fortitude, courage, guts, mettle, determination, tenacity, resolution, spirit, stamina.
Ant. **2** faintheartedness, cowardice, timidity.

groan *v.* **1** *The patient groaned. The class groaned when the teacher assigned homework:* moan, whimper; grumble, complain, murmur, wail, lament; howl. **2** *The gate groaned on its hinges:* creak, squeak, screech. —*n.* **3** *With a groan he realized he had lost:* moan, whimper, whine, sorrowful, murmur, wail, lament. **4** *the groan of the branches under the weight of the snow:* moan, creak, crack, squeak.

groggy *adj. I'm always groggy when I wake up:* lethargic, sluggish, befuddled, bewildered, dazed, unsteady, stunned, dizzy, staggering, shaky, *Slang* woozy.
Ant. alert, aware, on one's toes.

groom *n.* **1** *The groom led the horse to the barn:* stableboy, hostler; footman. **3** *the bride and groom:* bridegroom; newly married man; husband, spouse. —*v.* **4** *The cowboy groomed his horse:* curry, currycomb, brush, comb, rub down. **5** *The girl spent hours grooming herself:* clean up, wash, make tidy, make neat, spruce up, primp, preen, comb; dress. **6** *The mayor is being groomed for governor:* prepare, prime, train, educate, develop.

groove *n.* **1** *The groove on the desk is for pencils:* rut, furrow, gutter, channel, trench, flute; cut, scoring, score, corrugation. **2** *to get out of one's groove and do something different:* rut, fixed routine, set ways; procedure, rule, practice, custom.
Ant. **1** ridge, bump.

grope *v. I groped for the light switch:* feel about, fumble, probe; fish for, paw, finger; move blindly, feel one's way; search blindly.

gross *adj.* **1** *the firm's gross profit:* total,

whole, entire, aggregate; total before deductions, before expenses, before taxes. **2** *gross negligence:* flagrant, downright, sheer, complete, total, plain, glaring, obvious, manifest; egregious, outrageous, unequivocal. **3** *gross remarks:* coarse, crude, vulgar, indelicate, improper, uncouth, offensive; lewd, smutty, foul-mouthed, indecent, obscene. **4** *The man was so gross he could hardly get through the door:* fat, obese, overweight, heavy; big, large, bulky, huge, immense, enormous, monstrous, gigantic, massive. —*n.* **5** *What is the gross of your earnings?:* sum total, total, total amount, whole, aggregate; total before deductions. —*v.* **6** *The movie grossed 200 million dollars:* earn, take in, make a gross profit of.
Ant. **1, 5** net; total after deductions, total after expenses. **3** refined, decent, proper, inoffensive, chaste. **4** thin, slim; small, little. **6** loose.

grotesque *adj.* **1** *grotesque statues from prehistoric times:* distorted, deformed, oddshaped, misshapen, contorted; fantastic, weird, bizarre, outlandish, odd, eccentric. **2** *grotesque humor:* outlandish, absurd, distorted, fantastic, wild, extravagant, weird, bizarre, preposterous.
Ant. **1** well-proportioned, classic. **2** routine, average, normal, unimaginative.

grouch *n.* **1** *Why did you have to be a grouch?:* complainer, grumbler, curmudgeon, sulky person, pouter, ill-humored person, sullen person, mope, crab. —*v.* **2** *to grouch about the bad weather:* complain, gripe, grumble, mutter, whine, grouse, rail; *Slang* beef, bellyache; sulk, fret, pout, mope.

ground *n.* **1** *It's good to be back on the ground:* the earth, firm land, terra firma; dry land. **2** *The ground must be plowed:* earth, soil, dirt, sod. **3** Sometimes **grounds** *high ground. I'll show you around the grounds:* tract of land, land, terrain; territory, realm, province, district, bailiwick, domain; property, premises, estate, lawns, gardens. **4** Usually **grounds** *grounds for divorce:* basis, cause, reason, motive; purpose, rationale, object, principle, occasion, considerations, arguments, inducement. **5 grounds** *coffee grounds:* sediment, dregs; settlings, deposit. —*v.* **6** *The ship grounded on a sandbar:* run aground, beach, strand, founder. **7** *Your accusation must be grounded on facts:* base, establish, support, found, set. **8** *to be well grounded in mathematics:* instruct, train, teach, familiarize with, educate, indoctrinate, practice, prepare.

groundless *adj. The accusation is groundless:* without basis, baseless, unjustified, unjustifiable, unfounded, unsupported, without cause, gratuitous.

Ant. well-founded, justified, proven, provable, supported.

groundwork *n.* 1 *The Magna Carta laid the groundwork for our freedom:* foundation, basis, base, ground, grounds, cornerstone, keystone, origin, source; fundamentals. 2 *It will take a lot of groundwork to start a new business:* preparation, planning, spadework, preliminary steps; learning, training.

group *n.* 1 *a group of students:* assemblage, aggregation, gathering, collection, crowd, band, throng, party, company, cluster, bunch, pack, troop. 2 *Children and the elderly are two groups who watch TV regularly:* class, classification, variety, branch, division, subdivision, section; set, faction, clique, circle, coterie; association, league, brotherhood, fraternity. —*v.* 3 *Group the shoes by size:* sort, organize, range, marshal, align, arrange, cluster, classify, class, catalog, place. 4 *At every party the same people group together:* associate, fraternize, mingle, cluster, marshal, consort.

Ant. 1, 2 individual. 3 separate.

grouse *v. He's always grousing:* complain, grumble, fret, gripe, fuss, mutter; *Slang* bellyache, kick.

Ant. praise, extol, laud, commend.

grove *n. a picnic in a quiet grove:* thicket, copse, coppice, woodland, small wood, bosk; orchard.

grovel *v. to grovel before one's superiors:* humble oneself, be servile, behave abjectly, cower, cringe; fawn, toady, crawl, kowtow, truckle, bow and scrape.

Ant. be proud, be haughty; browbeat.

grow *v.* 1 *My, how that child has grown!:* become larger, grow taller, spring up, shoot up, fill out; expand, increase, swell, widen, spread, extend; magnify, amplify. 2 *Trees won't grow in this climate:* develop, mature, ripen; germinate, vegetate, sprout, bud, blossom, flower, bloom. 3 *good soil to grow wheat:* cultivate, raise, produce, propagate, breed; sow, plant, till, farm. 4 *The report shows how our business has grown:* progress, develop, advance, enlarge, increase, expand, rise. 5 *The patient grew weaker:* become, come to be. 6 *Playing with the orchestra helped me grow as a musician:* mature, develop; get practice.

Ant. 1, 4 shrink, decrease, lessen, dwindle. 2 die, fail. 4 decline, wane.

growl *v.* 1 *The dog growled:* snarl, bark menacingly. 2 *The boss won't growl at you for asking for a raise:* snap, speak harshly, reply gruffly, complain, grumble, grouse, gripe, fret; mutter, murmur, grunt.

grown-up *n.* 1 *a movie for grown-ups:* adult, mature person, man, woman. —*adj.* 2 *When she was grown-up she would be a doctor:* adult, mature, full-grown, of age, big.

growth *n.* 1 *It's awesome to watch the growth of a child:* natural development, development; advancement, advance, progress, improvement; maturity. 2 *the growth of our business:* expansion, increase, development, extension, increment, enlargement, spread; progress, advancement, advance, rise. 3 *Is this wheat just one season's growth?:* crop, harvest, production, cultivation, produce. 4 *The doctor removed a small growth from her arm:* mass of tissue, lump; tumor; excrescence.

Ant. 2 decrease, decline, dwindling, shrinking; stagnation.

grubby *adj. He wore a grubby T-shirt:* dirty, grimy; sloppy, slovenly, unkempt, messy, seedy, filthy, shabby, tacky.

Ant. neat, well-groomed; clean, spick-and-span.

grudge *n.* 1 *Do you still bear me a grudge?:* ill will, resentment, hard feelings, malice, spite, rancor, pique, dislike, animosity. —*v.* 2 *I don't grudge her her good fortune:* begrudge, envy, resent.

Ant. 1 appreciation, thankfulness, goodwill.

grueling *adj. a grueling job:* tiring, exhausting, fatiguing; hard, punishing, torturous.

Ant. easy, soft, *Slang* cushy; enjoyable, pleasant.

gruesome *adj. a gruesome murder story:* horrible, horrifying, hideous, horrid, horrendous, grisly, gory, frightful, spine-chilling, bloodcurdling, revolting, repulsive, loathsome, grim, fearful, terrible.

Ant. pleasant, cheerful, delightful, appealing, sentimental.

gruff *adj.* 1 *The sergeant always gave a gruff answer:* surly, brusque, curt, short, stern, uncivil, discourteous, ungracious, snarling, grouchy, sour, crabbed, caustic, waspish, ill-humored, ill-natured, ill-tempered, sullen, bristling, crusty. 2 *A slight cold had given me a gruff voice:* hoarse, husky, rough, harsh, raspy, cracked, croaky.

Ant. 1 pleasant, sweet, good-humored; gracious. 2 mellifluous, rich.

grumble *v. He wouldn't do anything without grumbling first:* grouse, fret, murmur discontentedly, mutter, complain, grouch, gripe.

grumpy *adj. I'm grumpy when I first wake up:* surly, ill-tempered, crabby, cranky, grouchy, sullen, sulky, irritable, ill-humored, cantankerous, peevish, pettish, testy, in a bad mood, crusty.

Ant. in a good mood, in good humor, cheerful, sweet.

guarantee *n.* 1 *The car has a one-year guarantee:* warranty, written assurance of durability; surety, guaranty; pledge, assurance, word; security, bond, bail. 2 *Beauty is no guarantee of happiness:* assurance, promise. —*v.* 3 *The manufacturer guaranteed the furnace for five years:* give a guarantee on, warrant; vouch for; assure, endorse, insure, underwrite. 4 *The travel brochure guarantees you'll have the time of your life. A train ticket doesn't guarantee you a seat:* promise, pledge, give one's word, vouch for, assure, affirm, avow, swear, be responsible for, make certain, become surety for, bind oneself.

guaranty *n.* 1 *He gave his guaranty that I would repay the loan:* warrant, warranty, pledge, guarantee, formal assurance; security, surety, endorsement, promise. 2 *The bank can't give the loan without some kind of guaranty:* collateral, security, pledge; bail, bond; deposit.

guard *v.* 1 *Wear a hat to guard your face against the sun:* protect, safeguard, shield, defend; watch over, keep safe, preserve, secure. 2 *Policemen guarded the prisoner:* keep watch over, keep from escaping. —*n.* 3 *The guard won't let anyone through the gate:* sentinel, sentry, watchman, guardsman; body of defenders, garrison, patrol, picket, watch; convoy, escort; protector, bodyguard.

Ant. 1 endanger, threaten; imperil.

guarded *adj. Her answers were guarded:* cautious, chary, wary, careful, discreet, circumspect, prudent, hesitant, tentative.

Ant. careless, daring, rash, foolhardy.

guardian *n.* 1 *The churches are the guardians of the faith:* protector, preserver, keeper, custodian, defender, caretaker, shepherd, conservator, watchdog, champion, attendant. 2 *parent or guardian:* legal custodian.

Ant. 1 enemy, foe. 2 ward, protégé.

guess *v.* 1 *Did he guess your weight correctly?:* judge, estimate, correctly answer, divine, figure out; speculate, conjecture, hypothesize. 2 *I guess we'll go to Florida this year:* think, suppose, believe, assume, suspect, venture; gather, deduce, surmise, imagine; judge, reckon, estimate, predict, theorize. —*n.* 3 *My guess is that the job will take four hours:* estimate, supposition, assumption, speculation, opinion, belief, view, hypothesis, conjecture, presumption, sur-

mise, prediction, suspicion; theory, guesswork.

guest *n.* 1 *How many guests are coming?:* invitee, visitor, caller, company. 2 *The motel can accommodate 400 guests: (variously)* roomer, boarder, lodger, diner; patron, customer, client, paying customer.

guffaw *n. He let out a guffaw:* burst of laughter, peal of laughter, hearty laugh, roar of mirth.

guidance *n.* 1 *I sought guidance on the choice of a career:* counsel, advice, information, instruction, intelligence, enlightenment, pointer, tip, suggestion, clue, hint. 2 *Funds will be spent under the committee's guidance:* direction, leadership, management, supervision, auspices.

guide *v.* 1 *to guide someone through the jungle:* lead, pilot, steer, show the way to, direct, conduct; escort, usher, convoy, shepherd. 2 *My father guided this business to success:* maneuver, manipulate, manage, handle, direct, conduct, command, steer, lead, pilot; rule, govern, preside over, oversee. —*n.* 3 *Their guide was a seasoned scout:* pilot, escort, conductor, leader, director, usher; shepherd, attendant, chaperon. 4 *Let your conscience be your guide:* counselor, adviser, mentor, teacher, model, example, rule; signpost, marker, beacon.

Ant. 1 misguide, mislead.

guild *n. the musicians' guild:* professional organization, association, society, league, brotherhood, sisterhood, alliance, company, corporation, federation, coalition; union.

guile *n. He's full of guile:* trickery, trickiness, cunning, craftiness, artifice, wiliness, artfulness, strategy, sharp practice; deceit, treachery, duplicity, deception, dishonesty.

Ant. candor, frankness, honesty, truthfulness.

guileless *adj. as guileless as an innocent child:* straightforward, candid, frank, open, natural, honest, sincere, truthful; artless, ingenuous, naive, innocent, unaffected, unself-conscious.

Ant. deceitful, tricky, deceptive, treacherous.

guilt *n.* 1 *to establish the suspect's guilt:* guiltiness, criminality, culpability; wrongdoing, misconduct, misdoing, misbehavior, transgression; sinfulness, sin, vice; trespass, dereliction. 2 *Nothing could erase the guilt from his conscience:* guilty feeling, shame, disgrace, humiliation, dishonor, stigma.

Ant. 1 innocence, blamelessness, virtue. 2 pride, honor.

guilty *adj.* 1 *The jury found the defendant guilty:* justly charged, having committed a crime, culpable, blamable, blameworthy.

2 *guilty acts:* criminal; immoral, sinful, wrong, corrupt, erring, offensive. 3 *a guilty look:* sheepish, hangdog; contrite, regretful, ashamed, conscience-stricken.

Ant. 1–3 innocent. 1 blameless. 2 moral, virtuous. 3 proud, noble.

guise *n. The king traveled in the guise of a monk:* dress, attire, garb, costume, habit, clothing, apparel, clothes; disguise, pretense.

gulf *n.* 1 *the Gulf of Mexico:* large bay, estuary, arm of the sea; inlet, cove, lagoon. 2 *The earthquake left a gulf in the field. the gulf between the two friends:* chasm, abyss, crevasse, opening, rent, cleft; rift, split.

gullible *adj. Gullible people will believe anything:* easily fooled, easily deceived, easily cheated, easily duped; overtrusting, credulous, naive.

Ant. cynical, suspicious, untrusting.

gully *n.* 1 *When the snow melts the gully is flooded:* ravine, gulch, gap, small valley, gorge. 2 *The road had a gully on each side:* ditch, drainage ditch, gutter, furrow, trench.

gulp *v. The boy gulped down his lunch:* swallow in large mouthfuls, swallow eagerly, swallow greedily, swill, guzzle, wolf, bolt. *Ant.* sip; nibble.

gumption *n. It takes a lot of gumption to succeed:* initiative, spirit, drive, resourcefulness, courage, hustle, spunk.

gun *n.* 1 *The policeman drew his gun:* firearm; (*variously*) revolver, pistol, automatic, .45, .38, .22, six-shooter, Colt, derringer, rifle, shotgun, carbine, Winchester; machine gun; *Slang,* shooting rod, piece. 2 *an antitank gun:* cannon, fieldpiece, artillery piece.

gurgle *v.* 1 *The cider gurgled from the jug:* flow noisily, bubble, burble, babble.

—*n.* 2 *the gurgle of the brook:* gurgling, bubbling, babble, murmur, sputter.

gush *v.* 1 *Oil gushed from the well:* flow forth, pour out, spurt, spout, stream, well, rush forth, issue, run. —*n.* 2 *a gush of water:* sudden outflow, outpouring, spurt, torrent, stream, jet, spout, squirt, rush, outburst. 3 *Do we have to listen to that gush about your high-school days?:* foolish talk, boring talk, mawkishness, sentimentalism, emotionalism; nonsense, twaddle, drivel, rubbish, chatter.

Ant. 1 drip, trickle, ooze. 2 drip, trickle.

gust *n.* 1 *a gust of wind:* puff, blast, draft, breeze, wind; zephyr, squall, blow. 2 *a gust of laughter:* burst, outburst, outbreak, sudden rush, paroxysm, fit.

gusto *n. The man ate with gusto:* hearty enjoyment, zest, enthusiasm, fervor, exhilaration, zeal, delight.

gut *n.* 1 *He complained of a pain in his gut:* intestines, entrails, viscera; lower alimentary canal, bowels, *Slang* breadbasket. 2 *Slang You're getting a big gut:* stomach, abdomen; paunch, belly; bay window, beer belly, spare tire. 3 **guts** *Slang It really took guts to speak up:* courage, bravery, boldness, spunk; daring, nerve, backbone.

guttural *adj. a guttural voice:* throaty, husky, deep, low; harsh, raspy.

Ant. nasal, high-pitched, squeaky.

gyp *v.* 1 *He gypped me out of $50:* cheat, swindle, defraud, bamboozle, hoodwink, bilk, rook. —*n.* 2 *That deal was a real gyp:* fraud, flimflam, deception, cheat, con game, fake, phony, humbug; *Slang* con, scam.

gyrate *v. The figure skater gyrated faster and faster:* spin around, rotate, revolve, circle, twirl, whirl, turn around, wheel, spiral, swirl, pirouette.

H

habit *n.* 1 *Where did the habit of shaking hands originate?:* practice, behavior pattern, custom, convention, routine; characteristic tendency, trait, proclivity, inclination; observance, mannerism. 2 *the bad habit of biting your fingernails:* practice, acquired behavior, habitual action, fixed practice; leaning, inclination, predisposition, predilection, propensity. 3 *Each order of nuns wears its own special habit:* dress, attire,

costume, garb, apparel, raiment, clothes, clothing, outfit, uniform, robe, habiliments.

habitat *n.* 1 *The plains were the habitat of the buffalo:* native environment, natural home, area of distribution; terrain, territory, range, environment, haunt, locale, region. 2 *Our habitat was a crude cabin:* dwelling, place of abode, abode, domicile, home, housing, quarters; *Slang* digs.

habitation *n. These tenements are not fit*

for habitation: occupancy, tenancy, occupation, dwelling, lodging, residence.

habitual *adj.* 1 *She sat in her habitual place:* customary, usual, accustomed, regular, normal, established, traditional; routine, confirmed; continual, incessant. 2 *a habitual liar:* chronic, confirmed, inveterate, constant, addicted, frequent, repeated, periodic, recurrent, established.
Ant. 1 rare, uncommon, unusual, exceptional, unexpected. 2 infrequent, irregular, unconfirmed.

habituate *v. Working on the farm habituated us to rising early:* accustom, make used to, inculcate; inure, instill, imbue, adapt, season, drill.

habitué *n. a habitué of the city's museums:* frequenter, regular patron, frequent visitor, constant customer; *Informal* regular.

hack¹ *v. He hacked at the logs with his hatchet:* cut roughly, cut, cut up, chop, hew, chip, lacerate, gash, slice, cleave, slash; *Slang* whack.

hack² *n.* 1 *a license to drive a hack:* taxicab, taxi, cab. 2 *Grandfather recalled hiring a hack to take him to his wedding:* hackney coach, horse-drawn carriage, coach. 3 *Grandmother owned her own carriage and had a hack to pull it:* common horse, carriage horse, hackney; hired horse, cart horse, workhorse. 4 *Money turned a talented writer into a hack:* scribbler, penny-a-liner, grubstreet writer.

hackneyed *adj. The play had a hackneyed plot:* commonplace, routine, common, stale, trite, banal, inane, insipid, vapid, stereotyped, clichéd, threadbare, pedestrian, stock, worn-out, conventional, humdrum, unimaginative, jejune.
Ant. original, fresh, novel, imaginative, unusual, uncommon.

hag *n. Years of misfortune transformed the young girl into a hag:* harridan, crone, harpy, virago, shrew, witch, beldam, *Slang* battle-ax.

haggard *adj. The sailor was haggard from his long voyage:* tired-looking, hollow-eyed, gaunt, careworn; exhausted, spent, weary, fatigued, tired, drooping, toilworn, wasted.
Ant. energetic, vigorous, well-rested; hale, hale and hearty.

haggle *v.* 1 *to haggle over the price:* dicker, bargain, barter. 2 *We haggle over who should wash the dishes:* squabble, quibble, bicker, wrangle, quarrel.

hail *v.* 1 *A friend hailed me from across the street:* call to, shout at, cry out to; greet, accost, salute; welcome, receive, make welcome. 2 *We hailed the returning heroes:* acclaim, cheer, applaud, honor, extol, commend. —*n.* 3 *We heard a hail from a ship:* shout, call, calling out; hello, salutation, salute.

hair *n.* 1 *beautiful red hair:* head of hair, tresses, locks; curls, ringlets, bangs; *Slang* mop, mane. 2 *The car missed me by a hair:* narrow margin, iota, hair's-breadth.

hairy *adj. a hairy dog:* hirsute, shaggy, bushy, woolly, furry, fleecy.

hale *adj. He looks hale despite his recent illness:* healthy, hardy, well, robust, able-bodied, sound, vigorous, energetic, sturdy, fit, strapping, in the pink, in shape.
Ant. weak, sickly, frail, debilitated.

half *n.* 1 *Pay half now and the rest later:* one half, one of two equal parts, fifty percent; part, fraction, portion, some. —*adj.* 2 *His testimony was full of half-truths:* one-half, halved; partial, incomplete; imperfect, limited, deficient, meager, slight, scanty, skimpy; moderate. —*adv.* 3 *You're only half trying:* partially, partly, in part, inadequately, insufficiently, slightly, barely, moderately, tolerably.
Ant. 1 whole, total, sum total, all, entirety. 2 whole, complete, full. 3 entirely, fully, totally.

half-hearted *adj. a half-hearted smile:* unenthusiastic, indifferent, lackluster, perfunctory, cool, spiritless, faint, lukewarm; unaspiring, irresolute, lackadaisical, lethargic, apathetic.
Ant. wholehearted, enthusiastic, zealous, avid, animated, warm.

halfway *adv.* 1 *The house is halfway up the hill:* midway, half the distance, in the middle. 2 *We were halfway convinced to go:* partially, partly, in part, to a degree, in some measure, to some extent; nearly, almost; somewhat, rather, moderately. —*adj.* 3 *Chicago is the halfway point on the journey:* middle, midway, intermediate, medium, medial, midmost, middlemost, equidistant.

half-wit *n. Who was the half-wit who left the door open?:* fool, dunce, dummy, blockhead, dolt, ninny, nitwit, numskull, nincompoop, dimwit; feeble-minded person, moron, imbecile, idiot, mental defective, mental deficient.

hall *n.* 1 *the far end of the hall:* hallway, corridor, passageway, passage; gallery, arcade. 2 *Leave your umbrella in the hall:* entrance hall, entry, lobby, foyer, vestibule; anteroom, antechamber. 3 *Symphony Hall:* concert hall, auditorium, assembly room, meeting place, amphitheater; dining hall, banquet hall.

hallowed *adj. The graveyard is hallowed*

ground: sacred, consecrated, dedicated; holy, blessed, sanctified.

hallucination *n. You didn't see a ghost, it was just a hallucination:* delusion, fantasy, illusion, apparition, phantasmagoria, chimera, aberration.

halo *n.* 1 *Saints are painted with halos over their heads:* aureole, nimbus, corona, radiance; aurora. 2 *One feels a kind of halo surrounding the pure:* atmosphere of glory, magnificence, splendor, resplendence, radiance, luminousness, illustriousness; majesty, dignity, grandeur; holiness, sanctity, sublimity, spiritual aura, solemnity.

halt *v.* 1 *The hikers halted at the stream:* stop, pull up, draw up, wait, rest, pause, tarry; suspend, interrupt; terminate, quit, cease, discontinue, leave off. 2 *Officials are working to halt inflation:* stop, end, bring to a standstill, defeat, extinguish, vanquish, suppress, subdue, quell, quash; curb, check, hinder, impede, restrict, restrain, balk, thwart, stem, stall, stay, abate, foil, hold in check, bridle, block, inhibit. —*n.* 3 *The proceedings came to a halt around noon:* stop, cessation, standstill, discontinuance, suspension, termination, close, end; intermission, recess, pause, rest, interruption, delay. —*interj.* 4 *Halt! Who goes there?:* stop, stand still, don't move.

Ant. 1 continue, proceed; begin, start. 2 forward, aid, abet, bolster, boost. 3 beginning, start; resumption, continuation.

halve *v. Halve the apple:* cut in half, split in two, divide equally, bisect.

Ant. double.

hamlet *n. a hamlet of 200 people:* small village, village, crossroads; *Slang* whistlestop, hick town.

Ant. metropolis, city, megalopolis.

hammer *n.* 1 *a hammer and screwdriver: (variously)* claw hammer, ballpeen hammer, tack hammer; mallet, sledge hammer. —*v.* 2 *Hammer a hook in the wall:* nail; hit, pound, strike, pummel, whack, punch, bang, drive.

hamper *v. Rain is hampering our work:* hinder, impede, hold up, inhibit, thwart, prevent, frustrate, balk, stall, restrain, restrict, retard, curb, check, block, obstruct.

Ant. help, aid, assist, further, facilitate, expedite, speed.

hand *n.* 1 *Aren't your hands cold?:* palm, fist; *Slang* paw, mitt, meat-hook. 2 *The rancher hired three new hands:* laborer, hired hand, hired man, man, worker, workman, workingman, employee, helper. 3 *Give me a hand with this ladder:* help, assistance, aid, support, lift. 4 usually **hands.** *His fate is in the governor's hands:* care, keeping, charge, custody, control, possession, power, management, guidance. 5 *Aunt Edna writes a beautiful hand:* handwriting, penmanship, script, longhand. 6 *Give the girl a great big hand:* round of applause, burst of applause. —*v.* 7 *Hand me the newspaper, please:* give, pass, hand over, present, turn over to.

Ant. 2 employer, boss, foreman, overseer.

handful *n. Only a handful of people attended:* small number, smattering, sprinkling, scattering; small quantity, scant amount, modicum.

Ant. horde, mob, crowd, throng.

handicap *n.* 1 *Her lack of a college degree is a handicap:* drawback, disadvantage, detriment, impediment, limitation, obstacle, stumbling block, difficulty. 2 *It takes determination to learn to live with a handicap:* physical disability; *(variously)* lameness, loss of a limb, blindness, deafness, speech disability. —*v.* 3 *Being frail will handicap you in sports:* hinder, hold back, hamper, restrict, limit, place at a disadvantage, restrain, curb.

Ant. 1 advantage, benefit, asset, edge. 3 benefit, assist, aid.

handle *n.* 1 *a door handle:* hold, grasp, pull, knob, grip. —*v.* 2 *Don't handle the tomatoes:* hold; finger, knead, pinch, poke, touch, feel; stroke; *Slang* paw. 3 *The pilot really knows how to handle an airplane:* control, steer, guide, maneuver, pilot; operate, run, manipulate, use, manage, command. 4 *Can you handle this job?:* manage, deal with; command, control, manipulate, conduct, treat. 5 *The store handles a complete line of clothing:* sell, offer for sale, carry, deal in, trade in, market, merchandise.

handsome *adj.* 1 *a handsome child. What a handsome room!:* good-looking, attractive, fine-looking, comely, lovely, exquisite, stunning, beautiful, pretty, bonny, fair; tasteful, elegant, stately; well-formed, well-proportioned. 2 *The waiter received a handsome tip:* generous, liberal, ample, considerable, sizable.

Ant. 1 ugly, unattractive, homely, unsightly. 2 stingy, niggardly, miserly; small, meager, skimpy.

handy *adj.* 1 *Keep the flashlight handy:* accessible, close at hand, at hand, within reach, easily accessible, available, near, convenient. 2 *I'm handy at fixing things:* skillful, skilled, adroit, dexterous, deft, competent, capable, adept.

Ant. 1 inaccessible, unavailable, inconvenient. 2 clumsy, inept, unskilled.

hang *v.* 1 *The picture hangs over the mantle:* suspend, fasten from above, append, attach, affix; dangle, swing freely, be pendent, depend. **2** *The outlaw was hanged:* lynch, execute by hanging; *Slang* string up. **3** *Her career hangs on passing the bar exam:* depend, be dependent, be contingent, rest, turn upon, hinge, be subject to, revolve around. **4** *He hung his head in shame:* let droop, dangle, bow, lower, drop, incline, bend forward, sag.

hangdog *adj. a hangdog expression:* abject, defeated, intimidated, humiliated, browbeaten, wretched, resigned, hopeless; ashamed, embarrassed, guilty-looking, crestfallen, shamefaced.
Ant. confident, assured, bold.

hankering *n. to have a hankering for chocolate:* longing, craving, desire, yearning, yen, hunger, urge, itch, aching, pining.

haphazard *adj. to work in a haphazard way:* unmethodical, disorganized, unsystematic, unorganized, disordered, disorderly, random; careless, unthinking, indiscriminate, casual, chance, slapdash, fitful, sporadic; aimless, purposeless, accidental.
Ant. organized, methodical, systematic, orderly, ordered; careful, purposeful, intentional.

hapless *adj. It was a hapless day when that murderer was born!:* unlucky, unfortunate, jinxed, ill-starred, ill-fated; unhappy, forlorn, hopeless, wretched, woeful.
Ant. fortunate, lucky.

happen *v.* **1** *When did the accident happen?:* take place, occur, come about, come to pass, ensue, transpire, befall, eventuate; arise, crop up, come into existence. **2** *What will happen to her now?:* become of, befall, be one's fate; be experienced by, be suffered by.

happening *n. an unfortunate happening:* event, occurrence, incident, incidence, episode, affair, experience, occasion, happenstance, advent, accident.

happiness *n.* **1** *Imagine our happiness at having all the children home for Christmas!:* gladness, joy, delight; contentment, content, pleasure, enjoyment, satisfaction; rejoicing, elation, jubilation, bliss, rapture, ecstasy, gaiety, exultation; merriment, cheerfulness, glee. **2** *Her work is her greatest happiness:* pleasure, satisfaction, gratification, blessing, comfort.
Ant. **1** unhappiness, sadness, sorrow, grief, despondency, misery. **2** bane, annoyance; calamity, misfortune.

happy *adj.* **1** *I'm so happy! a happy occasion:* glad, pleased, delighted, content, contented, gratified, tickled, tickled pink; cheerful, in high spirits, elated, overjoyed, blissful, rapturous, ecstatic, gleeful, flushed with pleasure, in seventh heaven; pleasant, pleasing,

delightful, gratifying, joyful. **2** *a happy coincidence:* fortunate, lucky, auspicious, favorable, felicitous, opportune, fitting, fit, advantageous, agreeable.
Ant. **1** sad, unhappy, sorry, sorrowful, despondent, forlorn, miserable, glum, melancholy, downcast, joyless. **2** unfortunate, unlucky, inauspicious.

happy-go-lucky *adj. a happy-go-lucky attitude:* carefree, easygoing, untroubled, unconcerned, free and easy, unworried, lighthearted, nonchalant, irresponsible.
Ant. cautious, prudent, careful, discreet.

harass *v.* **1** *The traveller was harassed by punks:* attack repeatedly, raid frequently, assault continually, beset, besiege. **2** *If you'll stop harassing me I can finish this work:* torment, pester, badger, worry; disturb, annoy, bother, bedevil, plague, hound; tease, heckle, hector; persecute, browbeat, bully.

harbinger *n. a harbinger of spring:* herald, precursor, forerunner, indication, announcer, signaler, proclaimer; first sign, omen, portent, token.

harbor *n.* **1** *The ship was towed into harbor:* port, protected anchorage; *(variously)* bay, lagoon, inlet, basin; destination, goal. **2** *The library was a harbor from the city's noise:* haven, refuge, asylum, retreat, shelter, sanctuary, hideaway. —*v.* **3** *harboring an escaped convict:* give refuge to, shelter, hide; protect, care for, keep safe; quarter, house, lodge, keep. **4** *to harbor a grudge:* nurture, foster, hold, maintain, retain; brood over, muse over.

hard *adj.* **1** *hard candy:* firm, solid, hardened, rocklike, stony; rigid, stiff, unmalleable, inflexible, unpliable. **2** *a hard rain. a hard blow:* strong, powerful, forceful, heavy, intense, fierce, severe, violent. **3** *a hard question. a hard book to read:* difficult, arduous, laborious, strenuous, tough, exacting, formidable, troublesome, burdensome, wearisome; baffling, confusing, puzzling, perplexing, bewildering; complex, complicated, intricate, impenetrable, thorny, knotty. **4** *a hard worker:* industrious, energetic, vigorous, enterprising, assiduous, diligent, persevering, persistent, indefatigable, untiring, unflagging; zealous, eager, conscientious, willing. **5** *a hard master:* strict, stern, severe, unyielding, stubborn, uncompromising; oppressive, hardhearted, cruel, unrelenting, merciless, pitiless, unremitting; callous, impervious, ruthless, hardened, insensitive; inhuman, brutal. **6** *a hard winter. Many families had a hard time during the Depression:* severe, harsh, rough, difficult; unpleasant, disagreeable, distressing, burdensome; lamentable, sad, melancholy. **7** *We exchanged hard words:* hostile, belligerent, unfriendly, antagonistic, bellicose; mean, bitter, vicious, rancorous, venomous, malicious, acrimonious, vindictive, spiteful, unkind, critical, insulting. *—adv.* **8** *The ice is frozen hard:* solidly, firm, firmly, tight, tightly, rigid, stiff, closely. **9** *Hit the ball hard:* forcefully, forcibly, powerfully, strongly, heavily, fiercely, severely, violently, intensely, vigorously. **10** *to work hard:* industriously, vigorously, rigorously, energetically, arduously, furiously, intensely, relentlessly, unsparingly, diligently, persistently, untiringly, determinedly, assiduously, unflaggingly, conscientiously, resolutely, eagerly. **11** *She took the news very hard:* emotionally, to heart, with much sorrow, distressfully, severely, agonizingly; angrily.

Ant. 1–2, 5, 6, 8 soft. 3, 5, 6 easy. 1 flexible, pliable. 2 weak, light, mild. 3 simple. 4 lazy, lax, careless. 5 lenient. 6 mild, pleasant, agreeable, enjoyable. 7 friendly, loving, kind. 9 softly, weakly, gently, lightly. 11 calmly, mildly.

hard-and-fast *adj. hard-and-fast rules:* set, strict, inflexible, irrevocable, unyielding, uncompromising, rigorous, unremitting, mandatory, unalterable, unbending.

Ant. flexible, lax, lenient.

hardheaded *adj.* **1** *a hardheaded negotiator:* practical, objective, shrewd, pragmatic, realistic; unemotional, impersonal, tough-minded. **2** *He's so hardheaded he won't listen to reason:* stubborn, obstinate, contrary, intractable, balky, unbending, inflexible, immovable, unyielding, pigheaded.

Ant. 1 idealistic, impractical, theoretical. 2 flexible, agreeable, amenable.

hardhearted *adj. A hardhearted person has no sympathy for others:* cruel, cruel-hearted, unfeeling, mean, heartless, merciless, unsparing, unforgiving, uncaring, insensitive, unsympathetic, cold-blooded, unpitying, pitiless, hard, callous, thick-skinned, inhuman.

Ant. kind, loving, compassionate, sympathetic, softhearted, warmhearted, understanding, warm, humane, tender, forgiving.

hardly *adv.* **1** *It's hardly possible. It hardly ever happens:* scarcely, barely, only, just, almost not; rarely, uncommonly, infrequently, not often. **2** *That was hardly the way to greet a friend!:* by no means, not by any means, certainly not, in no way.

Ant. 1 easily, more than; often, frequently, usually. 2 by all means, certainly, truly.

hard-nosed *adj. He's hard-nosed about his*

decision: stubborn, hardheaded, unyielding, inflexible, uncompromising, rigid, unbending; businesslike, unsentimental.

Ant. open-minded, flexible, reasonable.

hardship *n.* **1** *to endure great hardship:* suffering, affliction, misfortune, adversity, ordeal; misery, sorrow, travail, woe, wretchedness, agony. **2** *Having another mouth to feed would be a great hardship:* privation, burden, difficulty, load, problem.

Ant. 1 comfort, happiness; good fortune. 2 help, blessing, boon.

hardy *adj. One has to be hardy to be a lumberjack:* robust, sturdy, hearty, strapping, able-bodied, strong, vigorous; healthy, fit, physically fit, hale.

Ant. frail, weak, feeble, sickly.

harebrained *adj. a harebrained scheme:* foolish, dimwitted, rattlebrained, scatterbrained, simple-minded, half-witted, silly, asinine, senseless, empty-headed, featherbrained.

Ant. prudent, intelligent, sensible.

harm *n.* **1** *bodily harm. The drought did a lot of harm to the crops:* injury, hurt, damage; impairment, detriment, mischief, adversity, hardship, misfortune, ill, destruction, scourge, calamity, havoc, devastation. **2** *What's the harm in having a little fun?:* wrong, wickedness, evil, sin, sinfulness, iniquity, immorality, vice, villainy. *—v.* **3** *Don't harm your eyes by reading in dim light:* impair, injure, hurt, wound, maim, ruin, cripple, abuse, maltreat, damage.

Ant. 1 good, benefit, help, aid. 2 goodness. 3 benefit, help, aid, assist; improve.

harmful *adj. This medicine has harmful side effects:* injurious, dangerous, deleterious, hurtful, destructive, ruinous, damaging; unwholesome, unhealthy, unhealthful, detrimental, bad, pernicious, baneful.

Ant. beneficial, helpful; wholesome, healthful, healthy; harmless, safe.

harmless *adj. Most snakes are harmless:* safe, not dangerous, benign; inoffensive, gentle, mild, innocent, innocuous, unobjectionable.

Ant. harmful, dangerous, unsafe, destructive, unhealthy, injurious.

harmonious *adj.* **1** *harmonious sounds. The room was decorated in harmonious shades of blue and green:* melodious, sweet-sounding, mellifluous, euphonious, sweet, dulcet; agreeable, matching, compatible, harmonizing, coordinated, consistent, unified, synchronized. **2** *The two friends were harmonious:* like-minded, in agreement, in harmony, cordial, in accord, compatible, congenial, agreeable, amiable, friendly.

Ant. 1 harsh, grating, unmelodious, cacophonous; clashing, incompatible, uncoordinated, inconsistent. **2** incompatible, unalike, discordant, dissident, unfriendly.

harmony *n.* **1** *The decorator chose the rugs and drapes for their harmony:* pleasing consistency, coordination, compatibility, agreement, concord, correlation, matching, balance; symmetry, order, proportion, unity. **2** *We worked together in harmony:* agreement, accord, concord, unanimity, likemindedness, conformity, unity; amicability, amity, congeniality, compatibility, friendship, cooperation, peace.

Ant. **1** incongruity, inconsistency; conflict. **2** disagreement, enmity, opposition, conflict, contention, discord.

harrowing *adj. a harrowing experience:* distressing, disturbing, tormenting, traumatic, upsetting; frightening, fearful, alarming, chilling, terrifying, threatening, dangerous.

harry *v.* **1** *Pirates harried the coastal towns:* attack repeatedly, raid frequently, beset; raid, plunder, sack, pillage. **2** *He could finish the job quicker if you wouldn't harry him:* trouble, torment, distress, disturb, bother, worry; harass, pester, badger, annoy, plague, hound, distract; tease, hector, heckle, intimidate, bully.

harsh *adj.* **1** *a harsh voice. harsh light:* piercing, jarring, grating, shrill, rasping, raspy, strident, scratchy, discordant, squawky; glaring, overbright. **2** *harsh treatment. harsh words:* cruel, pitiless, merciless, mean, severe, stern, unkind, abusive, heartless, hardhearted, brutal; bitter, caustic, hard, sharp.

Ant. **1** soft, gentle, mild, pleasant, pleasing, soothing. **2** kind, gentle, loving.

harvest *n.* **1** *Neighboring farmers helped with the harvest:* harvesting, reaping, crop gathering. **2** *the apple harvest:* crop, yield, season's growth, produce. **3** *the harvest of 30 years of research:* result, product, fruit; reward, benefit, proceeds, gain, return, yield, gleaning, reaping. —*v.* **4** *Harvest the fruit before the first frost:* gather, reap, pick, mow, cut; collect, amass, accumulate.

Ant. **4** plant, sow, seed.

hassle *n.* **1** *There was a hassle over who should pay:* squabble, quarrel, dispute, row, argument; fight, struggle, tussle, conflict. —*v.* **2** *The street vendor was hassled by the police:* harass, harry, persecute, hound, badger.

haste *n. The work must be completed with all possible haste:* speed, speediness, swiftness, quickness, celerity, rapidity, dispatch.

Ant. slowness, procrastination, sluggishness.

hasten *v.* **1** *She hastened to her appoint-*

ment: hurry, rush, speed, race, hustle, dash, scurry, fly, hurry up. **2** *A computer would hasten the work:* accelerate, speed up, expedite, quicken, precipitate.

Ant. **1** creep, crawl; plod, shuffle. **2** slow, delay, decelerate.

hastily *adv.* **1** *I dressed hastily:* quickly, speedily, fast, hurriedly, posthaste, apace; *Slang* pronto, on the double. **2** *Don't make important decisions hastily:* too quickly, rashly, recklessly, impetuously, impulsively, thoughtlessly, carelessly, heedlessly.

Ant. **1** slowly. **2** deliberately, carefully, thoughtfully.

hasty *adj.* **1** *A hasty search turned up the missing earring:* fast, quick, hurried, rapid, speedy, swift, prompt; cursory, brief, rushed, fleeting, superficial. **2** *hasty decisions:* unduly quick, rash, impetuous, impulsive, reckless, hurried, headlong, heedless, precipitate.

Ant. **1** slow, leisurely, long, protracted, meticulous, thorough. **2** deliberate, careful, thoughtful.

hatch *v. to hatch a plan:* think up, devise, concoct, plot, plan, contrive, make up, formulate, conceive, design, create, invent, originate, fashion, dream up; bring forth, produce.

hate *v.* **1** *They have hated each other since high school. I hate mice!:* dislike, despise, detest; abhor, loathe, abominate, recoil from, shrink from, be repelled by. **2** *Mother hated to move from such a nice town:* be sorry, be reluctant, be averse to, shrink from, not care to, would rather not, dread. —*n.* **3** *A wronged person is often full of hate:* hatred, dislike, disliking, aversion, loathing, abomination, abhorrence; enmity, hostility, detestation, rancor, malice, antipathy, animosity, animus, malevolence, resentment, vindictiveness, revengefulness, acrimony.

Ant. **1–3** love, like. **1** cherish, dote on. **2** enjoy, relish, fancy, prefer. **3** amity, goodwill.

hateful *adj.* **1** *Cheating is a hateful thing to do:* offensive, disgusting, detestable, repugnant, loathsome, despicable, contemptible, deplorable, abhorrent, odious, abominable, monstrous; ugly, nasty, vile, unpleasant, mean, wicked. **2** *a hateful look:* full of hate, expressing hate, forbidding, scornful, contemptuous.

Ant. **1** commendable, pleasing, charming, wonderful, good. **2** friendly, loving, affectionate, kind.

hatred *n.* **1** *His hatred of people has made him a recluse:* dislike, aversion, hate, loathing, abhorrence, distaste, detestation, repugnance, revulsion. **2** *Such hatred can only lead to bloodshed:* hostility, enmity, malice, rancor, animosity, antagonism, antipathy, animus; malevolence, ill will, venom, resentment, vindictiveness, revengefulness, acrimony, bad blood.

Ant. **1, 2** love, fondness, liking. **2** amity, goodwill, kindness.

haughty *adj. Her high position made her haughty:* arrogant, overly proud, disdainful, overbearing, lordly, aloof, officious; snobbish, condescending, patronizing.

Ant. humble, modest.

haul *v.* **1** *Haul the fish into the boat. The truck hauled the garbage away:* pull, drag, draw; carry, transport, move, convey, cart, bring, take. —*n.* **2** *The robbers got away with a $10,000 haul. The fisherman had a huge haul:* take, catch, yield, gain, takings; profit, booty, spoils, swag.

haunt *v.* **1** *As a girl, she used to haunt the local theater:* frequent, go to repeatedly; hover about, linger around; *Slang* hang around. **2** *Memories of her childhood haunted her:* obsess, weigh on, prey on, beset, obsess, preoccupy; trouble, torment, disturb, worry, plague. —*n.* **3** Often **haunts** *The snack bar was one of the students' haunts:* hangout, gathering place, meeting place, rendezvous, stamping grounds.

haven *n. The ship sought a haven in the storm:* shelter, refuge, retreat, sanctuary, asylum, hideaway, hideout; harbor, port.

havoc *n. The tornado wreaked havoc on the town:* damage, destruction, devastation, ruin; disaster, catastrophe, cataclysm, ruination; chaos, disorder.

hazard *n.* **1** *the hazards of white-water canoeing:* danger, risk, peril, endangerment; pitfall, jeopardy. —*v.* **2** *if I may hazard a guess. I'll hazard a dollar on the game:* venture, chance, dare, risk, submit, volunteer, offer, proffer; speculate, conjecture, hypothesize; gamble, bet, wager, stake.

hazardous *adj.* **1** *These stairs are hazardous:* dangerous, unsafe, perilous, risky. **2** *Prospecting is a hazardous way to earn a living:* chancy, precarious, unsure, uncertain, unreliable, insecure, speculative, shaky, iffy.

Ant. **1** safe. **2** sure, certain, reliable.

hazy *adj.* **1** *a hazy fall day:* misty, foggy, smoggy, smoky; overcast, cloudy; dim, murky; bleared, bleary, blurry, filmy, faint. **2** *a hazy idea:* vague, general, indefinite, ill-defined, uncertain, unclear, nebulous; faint, obscure, ambiguous, dim; confused, muddled.

Ant. **1** clear, bright. **2** clear, detailed, explicit.

head *n.* **1** *a good head for arithmetic:* mind, brain, mentality, intellect. **2** *She's head of the organization:* leader, chief, director, boss, administrator; *(variously in business)* chairman of the board, chairman, chief executive officer, chief executive, president, manager, superintendent, foreman, supervisor; *(variously in government)* dictator, king, queen, monarch, sovereign, ruler, czar, potentate, suzerain, president, prime minister, premier. **3** *at the head of the line:* front, first place, forward part, front rank, forefront, lead, place of honor. **4** *the head of the river:* source, origin, beginning; fountainhead, spring, wellspring, fountain. **5** *to bring matters to a head:* climax, crisis, peak, extremity, conclusion, culmination, end. **6** *the head of a pin. the head of a spear:* upper end, top, peak, tip, apex, crown, crest, vertex, acme, zenith, summit, pinnacle. —*adj.* **7** *the head bookkeeper:* chief, ranking, principal, main, foremost, first, highest, leading, supreme, superior, prime, premier, preeminent, paramount; governing, commanding, ruling, controlling. **8** *the head car of the cavalcade:* first, lead, leading, front, fore, foremost; highest, top, topmost, uppermost. —*v.* **9** *Didn't Teddy Roosevelt head the charge up San Juan Hill?:* lead, go at the head of, go first, precede, lead the way, take the lead, start, begin, initiate, inaugurate, launch. **10** *She was chosen to head the firm:* be head of, direct, supervise, manage, take charge of, administer, superintend, lead, boss, command, govern, rule, have authority over, preside over, be at the helm. **11** *Head the boat toward shore. Let's head for home:* steer, aim, turn, pilot, guide, direct; move toward, go in the direction of, go, proceed, make for, hie.

Ant. **2** subordinate; cog, underling, worker. **3** end, foot, last place. **4** mouth. **6** bottom, foot. **8** last, end, trailing, hindmost. **9** follow, go behind, be last; end, finish, conclude.

headstrong *adj. a headstrong youth:* willful, impulsive, rash, reckless, imprudent; hotheaded, intractable, ungovernable, refractory, uncontrollable, defiant, unmanageable, unruly; stubborn, obstinate, bullheaded, pigheaded, obdurate.

Ant. subservient, obedient, submissive; cautious, methodical.

heady *adj. Being offered the job was heady news:* exciting, exhilarating, intoxicating, thrilling, stirring.

Ant. depressing, disappointing.

heal *v.* **1** *This will help heal the wound. The*

doctor claimed to have healed a hundred similar cases: cure, make well, get well, heal over, heal up, knit, mend; return to health, recover, recuperate, improve, convalesce. **2** *We healed our differences:* reconcile, conciliate, settle, rectify, right, set right, restore good relations; soothe, relieve.

health *n.* **1** *How is your health?:* physical condition, general condition. **2** *Don't jeopardize your health:* good health, healthfulness, freedom from disease, fitness; wellbeing, hardiness, vitality, stamina.
Ant. **2** sickness, disease, ailment; debility, infirmity, frailty.

healthful *adj. a healthful diet:* healthy, good for one's health, conducive to health, healthgiving, salubrious, salutary; beneficial, nourishing; hygienic.
Ant. unhealthy, detrimental, deleterious.

healthy *adj. All the children are healthy:* in good health, enjoying good health; hale, hearty, sound, hardy, vigorous, in fine fettle.
Ant. sick, ill, infirm, unhealthy, ailing; unsound.

heap *n.* **1** *a heap of dirty clothes:* pile, stack, mass, mound, cluster, batch, bunch; accumulation, collection, gathering, assemblage; jumble, mess. **2** *"It takes a heap o' living to make a house a home":* large amount, lot, lots, great deal, abundance, profusion, multitude, plenty, considerable amount. —*v.* **3** *Rake the leaves and heap them by the garage:* pile, pile up, group, bunch, amass, mass, gather. **4** *The boss heaps work on me:* load, load up, pile, supply abundantly, give in profusion, fill, inundate, flood, deluge, engulf.
Ant. **2** little, dab, touch. **3** scatter, disperse.

hear *v.* **1** *A large audience heard the concert:* listen to, be among the listeners at; attend. **2** *I hear you're moving:* understand, find out, be informed, be told, receive news, be led to believe, be made aware of, receive information, learn, gather, discover, ascertain. **3** *Hear our plea, O Lord!:* listen to, heed, favor, approve, receive, hearken to, accede to, hold with, grant, admit, acknowledge; give assent, be favorably disposed to. **4** *The judge will hear the case:* judge, try.

hearsay *n. It's only hearsay:* rumor, gossip, report, talk, idle talk.

heart *n.* **1** *She has a warm heart:* feelings, emotion, sentiment, nature, disposition, nature. **2** *The child won our hearts:* sympathy, compassion, affection, fondness, love; tolerance, indulgence, forgiveness, clemency. **3** *I hadn't the heart to argue:* courage, enthusiasm, firmness, resoluteness, fortitude, pluck, spunk, resolution; bravery, valor,

boldness, audacity, audaciousness. **4** *the heart of the problem:* essence, core, root, source, base, crux, nub, soul, nucleus, center, kernel, pith, meat, quintessence; essentials, fundamentals, principles, foundation. **5** *in the heart of town:* center, central part, middle, hub, inner part, interior.
Ant. **2** hatred, enmity. **3** timidity, cowardice, fear. **4** side issue, irrelevancy. **5** outskirts, periphery.

heartfelt *adj. our heartfelt sympathy:* sincere, honest, profound, fervent, ardent, genuine, earnest, deep, wholehearted, intense.
Ant. feigned, insincere.

heartless *adj. That was a heartless thing to do:* cruel, cruelhearted, hardhearted, callous, unfeeling, insensitive, unkind, uncaring, unsympathetic, pitiless, mean, inhuman.
Ant. kind, generous, humane, compassionate, merciful.

hearty *adj.* **1** *a hearty welcome. hearty laughter:* sincere, genuine, wholehearted, cordial, warm; effusive, thorough, unrestrained, unreserved; vigorous, enthusiastic, zestful, heartfelt. **2** *The mountain climbers are all hearty:* healthy, well, physically fit, hale, sound, vigorous, strong, robust.
Ant. **1** halfhearted, lukewarm, mild, reserved. **2** sickly, ill, unhealthy, delicate, frail, feeble.

heat *n.* **1** *the heat of August:* hotness, warmness, warmth, high temperature; hot weather, warm weather. **2** *in the heat of anger:* passion, fervor, fervency, excitement, intensity; height, climax. —*v.* **3** *Heat the water:* make hot, warm, bring to a boil, warm up, heat up.
Ant. **1** cold, coldness, cold temperature. **2** calmness. **3** cool, chill; freeze.

heated *adj. a heated argument:* vehement, impassioned, passionate, fervent, excited, fierce, emotional, intense; stormy, tempestuous, raging, hot, fiery, violent, furious, angry, bitter.
Ant. dispassionate, calm, mild; friendly, sociable.

heathen *n. a missionary among the heathen:* infidel, idolator, non-believer, unbeliever; pagan, savage, barbarian; atheist, agnostic.
Ant. true believer, believer.

heave *v.* **1** *Heave this box onto the shelf:* hoist, haul up, pull up, drag up, draw up, lift, raise, boost. **2** *Heave the rocks into the ravine:* throw, pitch, fling, hurl, cast, chuck, sling, propel. **3** *I heaved a sigh of relief:* utter wearily, emit, exhale, eject; discharge, puff; groan, moan, sob; *Informal* retch, vomit, regurgitate, puke. **4** *His chest heaved as he gasped for breath:* expand and contract, surge; expand, swell, thrust up, bulge; draw a deep breath, pant.

heaven *n.* 1 Often **Heaven** *May her soul rest in Heaven:* paradise, afterworld, afterlife, next world, life everlasting, eternal bliss, the kingdom of Heaven, the heavenly kingdom, the City of God. 2 **the heavens** *to scan the heavens through a telescope:* the sky, the firmament; space, outer space. 3 *Our weekend in the country was heaven:* complete happiness, bliss, supreme happiness, paradise, ecstasy, perfection, utopia. *Ant.* 1 hell, hades, purgatory, the underworld, the abyss, limbo. 3 hell, agony, misery.

heavy *adj.* 1 *What a heavy suitcase!:* weighty; burdensome, hefty. 2 *heavy rains. heavy seas. a heavy smoker:* abundant, profuse, copious, extensive, excessive, intemperate, immoderate, unstinting, considerable; violent, strong, fierce, savage, raging, turbulent, seething, unrelenting, unremitting, intense. 3 *a heavy blow to my pride:* burdensome, harrowing, harsh, distressing, damaging, injurious, detrimental, destructive, crushing. 4 *a heavy heart:* sorrowful, sad, melancholy, full of care, pained, distressed, doleful, burdened; cheerless, joyless, forlorn, desolate, disconsolate, mournful, grieving, crestfallen, grief-stricken. 5 *The job carries heavy responsibilities. Philosophy is too heavy for me:* serious, solemn, important, imposing, notable, profound, deep, complex. 6 *He's so heavy he needs extra-large shirts. Heavy lines on the map indicate main roads:* fat, obese, stout, portly, plump, corpulent, overweight, hefty; thick, broad, dense, rough. *Ant.* light. 1 lightweight. 2 moderate, mild, soft, gentle, calm. 4 happy, cheerful, joyful. 5 trivial, frivolous; entertaining. 6 thin, skinny.

heckle *v. to heckle a speaker:* jeer at, badger, bait, needle, mock, hector, taunt; hoot, shout down, boo, hiss.

hectic *adj. Moving day was rather hectic:* frenetic, frantic, tumultuous, furious, feverish, frenzied, chaotic. *Ant.* calm, tranquil, relaxing, orderly.

hedge *n.* 1 *The new owner planted a hedge:* hedgerow, row of bushes; border, ring. 2 *a hedge against inflation:* protection, guard, insurance. —*v.* 3 *We hedged the yard with lilacs:* enclose, surround, border, bound, edge, encircle, outline, fence, ring, shut in, hem, hem in; delineate, demarcate, mark off. 4 *Answer the question—don't hedge:* equivocate, evade, temporize, duck, dodge, beg the question; *Informal* waffle, pussyfoot.

hedonist *n. "Eat, drink, and be merry" is the code of a hedonist:* pleasure seeker, libertine, profligate, voluptuary, dissipater, debauchee, sensualist, Sybarite. *Ant.* puritan; moralist.

heed *v.* 1 *Heed the doctor's advice:* follow, mind, obey, concur, comply with, be ruled by, observe, respect; listen to, consider, pay attention to, take note of, take to heart. —*n.* 2 *I warned him, but he paid me no heed:* attention, notice, regard, mind, mindfulness, care, attentiveness, carefulness, prudence, precaution. *Ant.* 1 ignore, disregard, neglect. 2 inattention, disregard, carelessness, neglect.

heedless *adj. Heedless people have the most accidents:* careless, thoughtless, unmindful, neglectful, unthinking, inattentive, oblivious, unobserving, unobservant, unwary, unconcerned, unaware, unheeding; lax, improvident, imprudent, incautious, rash, foolhardy, reckless. *Ant.* careful, cautious, wary, prudent; attentive, heedful, thoughtful, watchful, vigilant.

hefty *adj. Many football players are hefty:* husky, heavy, beefy, strapping, stout, strong, weighty, bulky, burly, robust, massive, hearty, muscular, stalwart. *Ant.* puny, skinny, weak, fragile.

height *n.* 1 *a height of sixty feet:* altitude, elevation, upward extent; tallness, highness, loftiness. 2 *the house on the height:* hilltop, vantage point, promontory, eminence; mountain, hill, highland, palisade, cliff, bluff, rise, pinnacle, summit, peak. 3 *the height of rudeness:* extremity, utmost degree, ultimate, maximum, peak; pinnacle, high point, summit, zenith, acme, apex, apogee; supremacy, consummation, flowering, heyday. *Ant.* 1 depth. 2 valley, ravine, abyss; lowland. 3 depth, low point, nadir.

heinous *adj. a heinous crime:* atrocious, abominable, abhorrent, repugnant, repulsive, reprehensible, despicable, horrid, shocking, monstrous, inhuman, detestable, loathsome, foul, hideous, contemptible, outrageous; disgusting, revolting, vile, sickening, villainous, iniquitous, terrible, grisly, outrageous; sinful, wicked, evil. *Ant.* beneficial, admirable, laudable, praiseworthy.

hell *n.* 1 Often **Hell** *The preacher warned us about punishment in Hell:* abode of the damned, infernal regions, bottomless pit, the abyss, the underworld, the nether world, below, home of lost souls, hellfire; *(variously)* hades, inferno, perdition. 2 *Her* *life has been hell:* torment, anguish, agony, wretchedness, suffering, misery.

Ant. 1, 2 heaven, paradise. 2 bliss, joy, happiness.

help *v.* 1 *Ted helped his brother. Please help the needy:* assist, give assistance to, aid, lend a hand, give a helping hand, collaborate with; serve; support, back, champion, uphold, promote, encourage; minister to, succor, give to, contribute to. 2 *Help me—I can't swim!:* save, rescue, aid, come to the aid of, extricate 3 *The shots helped my hay fever:* relieve, alleviate, soothe, mitigate, ease, remedy, improve, ameliorate, allay, correct, make healthy, make whole. *—n.* 4 *The movers need help lifting the piano. The senator needs help to be reelected. to give help to the poor:* assistance, aid, helping hand, cooperation, service; support, backing, encouragement; contribution, gift, protection, friendship, support; guidance, advice, care, welfare. 5 *The cafe needs kitchen help:* employees, workers, workmen, laborers, hands, hired hands, assistants, helpers, hired helpers; *(variously)* farmhand, domestic, servant, menial, retainer; staff, crew, work force. 6 *Aspirin may be a help for that headache:* cure, remedy, corrective, preventive, restorative, aid, relief, balm, salve.

Ant. 1 hinder, impede; oppose, fight. 3 aggravate, irritate. 4 hindrance, obstruction, opposition, discouragement. 6 bane, aggravation, irritant.

helper *n. I'm the carpenter's helper:* assistant, aide, right-hand man, right hand, man Friday, girl Friday, helping hand; auxiliary, subordinate; apprentice; partner, colleague, associate, accomplice, confederate, co-worker, confrere.

helpful *adj. helpful suggestions:* beneficial, useful, constructive, advantageous, usable, practical, serviceable; valuable.

Ant. useless, worthless; harmful, injurious.

henchman *n. the mobster's henchmen:* lieutenant, retainer; bodyguard, strong-arm man, hatchet man; hireling, flunky, lackey, hanger-on; thug.

herald *n.* 1 *The herald announced the king's approach:* messenger, crier, proclaimer, courier. 2 *Shakespeare called the lark the "herald of the morn":* forerunner, harbinger, precursor, envoy, foregoer, usher; omen, sign, token, indication, symbol, forecast, portent. *—v.* 3 *Robins heralded spring's approach:* announce, proclaim, report, foretell, presage, give tidings of, usher in; inform.

herculean Sometimes **Herculean** *adj.* 1 *a herculean wrestler:* strong, powerful,

mighty, muscular, strapping, burly, brawny, hefty; hard, tough. 2 *a herculean task:* strenuous, laborious, backbreaking, arduous, burdensome, difficult, onerous, prodigious, formidable.

Ant. 1 weak, frail, delicate. 2 easy, effortless.

herd *n.* 1 *a herd of buffalo:* pack, drove, flock, bunch, group, cluster, gathering. 2 *There was a herd of bargain hunters at the sale:* crowd, mob, throng, horde, swarm, drove, bunch, gang, band, pack, host, swarm, flock, cluster, army, group, assembly, company, body, multitude, conclave. *—v.* 3 *The drovers herded the cattle into the pens:* drive, guide, goad, spur; bring together, collect, muster, round up, assemble, gather, crowd, huddle, bunch, group.

hereafter *adj.* 1 *Hereafter I'll take your advice:* after this, from now on, in the future, henceforth, from this time forth; at a later date, at a later time. *—n.* 2 *The pious expect their reward in the hereafter:* afterlife, afterworld, next world, life after death, future life, life beyond, world to come, heaven, heavenly kingdom, paradise.

Ant. 1 heretofore, before this, before now, before, in the past. 2 mortal life, here, here and now.

hereditary *adj.* 1 *Is baldness hereditary?:* inherited, inheritable; inbred, inborn, congenital. 2 *a hereditary fortune:* inherited, handed-down, ancestral.

Ant. 1, 2 acquired.

heresy *n. Pope Leo X excommunicated Martin Luther for heresy:* heretical beliefs, apostasy, heterodoxy, unorthodoxy, unsound doctrine, fallacy, unorthodox belief, unorthodox opinion, nonconformity, irreligion, dissension, iconoclasm, dissent.

Ant. orthodoxy, catholicity; convention, conformity, traditionalism.

heritage *n. Fair play is part of our heritage:* tradition, birthright, inheritance, portion, patrimony; estate, family possession, legacy.

hermit *n. The hermit came to town once a year:* recluse, solitudinarian, solitary; religious recluse, anchorite, cenobite.

hero, heroine *n.* 1 *a war hero:* brave person, champion, fearless fighter; great person, noble person, chivalrous person, gallant; adventurer; legendary person, idealized person, idol, star. 2 *The hero gets the girl at the end of the movie:* leading man, protagonist, male lead, main actor, male star.

heroic *adj.* 1 *heroic deeds:* brave, courageous, valiant, valorous, dauntless, fearless, lionhearted, stouthearted, intrepid, resolute,

unflinching; bold, daring; noble, gallant.
2 *The opera* Lohengrin *is in the heroic style:*
classic, grand, epic, elevated, dignified, exalted; extravagant, grandiose, exaggerated, bombastic.

Ant. 1 cowardly, fainthearted, ignoble; mean, base. 2 simple, unadorned; lowbrow.

heroism *n. Davy Crockett's heroism is well-known:* bravery, courage, courageousness, valor, lionheartedness, boldness, daring.

Ant. cowardice, timidity; meanness, baseness.

hesitant *adj. Why were you so hesitant about asking for help?:* hesitating, reluctant, faltering, lacking confidence; undecided, indecisive, uncertain, halting, unsure, irresolute, wavering, vacillating.

Ant. eager, willing, keen; determined, steadfast, firm; confident, decisive.

hesitate *v.* 1 *The driver hesitated at the intersection:* pause, stop briefly, halt, falter; be undecided, be irresolute, waver, vacillate. 2 *I hesitate to pay so much for a suit:* shy at, be unwilling, be reluctant, balk.

heterogeneous *adj. It was a heterogeneous group of rich and poor, old and young:* mixed, varied, diversified, diverse, assorted, miscellaneous, motley, disparate, divergent.

Ant. homogeneous, uniform.

hiatus *n. There was a hiatus of two years before I went back to college:* lapse, interval, interim; break, gap, void, blank, interruption, lacuna.

hide *v.* 1 *Hide your money in your shoe:* conceal, secrete, keep out of sight, cache, seclude. 2 *The robbers hid in a cave:* lie concealed, hide out, conceal oneself, keep oneself out of sight, lie low, go into hiding, *Slang* go underground. 3 *I can't hide my feelings:* conceal, obscure, cover, veil, cloak; repress, suppress; mask, disguise.

Ant. 1, 3 reveal, show, expose, exhibit, parade, flaunt. 2 find. 3 divulge, disclose, bare, admit, confess.

hideous *adj. What hideous wallpaper! a hideous crime:* ugly, grotesque, dreadful, horrid, repulsive, repugnant, awful, abhorrent, abominable, frightful, ghastly, revolting, appalling, shocking, repellent, gruesome, horrendous, horrible; monstrous, loathsome, sickening, vile, odious.

Ant. beautiful, lovely, attractive, pleasing, appealing.

high *adj.* 1 *a high building:* tall, lofty, towering, soaring. 2 *traveling at high speed. Prices are high:* great, extreme, excessive, inordinate, unreasonable, undue, immoderate; extravagant, exorbitant. 3 *He holds a high position. One must have high ideals:*

important, serious, elevated, lofty, top, eminent, exalted, significant, prominent, august, superior, leading; prime, primary, foremost, chief, main, principal, capital, predominant, uppermost; peerless, ascendant, grand, excellent, noble. 4 *a high voice:* high-pitched, soprano, in the upper register; shrill, sharp, strident, piercing. 5 *high spirits:* elated, exuberant, exhilarated, exultant; merry, joyful, cheerful, lighthearted, playful, jubilant, gleeful, jovial. —*adv.* 6 *The plane was flying high:* at great altitude, at great height, way up, far up, aloft.

Ant. low. 1 short. 2 moderate, average, reasonable, routine, reduced. 3 lowly, unimportant, insignificant; common, routine, average. 4 low-pitched, base, alto; deep, husky. 5 sad, gloomy, joyless, depressed, dejected.

highbrow *n.* 1 *The lecture seemed to be for highbrows:* intellectual, scholar, mastermind, thinker. — *adj.* 2 *highbrow tastes:* intellectual, scholarly, erudite, cultured, cultivated, bookish; snobbish, elitist.

Ant. 1 lowbrow, ignoramus, Philistine. 2 untutored, uncultivated.

high-flown *adj. high-flown ideas. a high-flown speech:* lofty, grandiose; presumptuous; pretentious, extravagant, inflated, pompous, florid, flowery, high-sounding, exaggerated, flamboyant; bombastic, magniloquent, turgid, orotund, grandiloquent.

Ant. down-to-earth, practical, realistic; straightforward, terse, concise.

highlight *n.* 1 *The highlight of our trip was the visit to the White House:* climax, outstanding part, main feature, memorable part, high point, peak, most interesting aspect. —*v.* 2 *The senator's speech highlighted the need for reduced tariffs:* emphasize, stress, accent, feature, give prominence to, point up, underline.

Ant. 1 low point; disappointment. 2 play down, slight, overlook.

high-minded *adj. A high-minded person wouldn't lie:* honorable, ethical, principled, sincere, just, scrupulous, conscientious, virtuous, uncorrupt; idealistic, lofty.

Ant. unprincipled, dishonorable, unethical, corrupt; mean, low.

high-strung *adj. Thoroughbred horses are high-strung:* nervous, excitable, skittish, temperamental, jumpy, edgy, wrought-up, impatient.

Ant. calm, placid, even-tempered.

highway *n. The new highway will reduce the driving time to our cabin:* main road, thruway, expressway, freeway, speedway, turnpike; interstate, parkway, main artery, divided highway, four-lane road; paved road. *Ant.* byway, back road, side road.

hike *v.* 1 *We hiked to the reservoir:* tramp, trek, walk. —*n.* 2 *After the hike to the river the soldiers camped for the night:* march, tramp, journey by foot, walk. 4 *a hike in prices:* increase, rise, raise.

hilarious *adj.* 1 *He told hilarious stories:* very funny, laugh-provoking, comical, uproarious, hysterical, riotous, rollicking. 2 *Everyone at the party had a hilarious time:* lively, jubilant, jovial, jolly, joyous, mirthful, high-spirited, exuberant, exhilarated, joyful, merry, rollicking; boisterous, noisy, vociferous.
Ant. 1 sad, serious. 2 gloomy, depressed; sedate.

hill *n.* *The park is on a hill:* hilltop, knoll, foothill, rise, hillock, hummock, promontory, butte, bluff, cliff, highland, height, elevation, prominence.
Ant. valley, canyon, gorge, gully, ravine, hollow.

hinder *v.* *Heavy snow hindered the bus's progress:* delay, slow down, hold up, hold back, detain, stay, arrest, stall, check, curb, hamper, retard, deter, impede, restrain, inhibit, make difficult; stymie, thwart, hobble.
Ant. help, aid, advance, benefit, expedite, accelerate, speed, hasten, quicken.

hindrance *n.* *Lack of education could be a hindrance to your career:* impediment, obstacle, obstruction, handicap, restriction, limitation, interference, constraint, restraint, snag, curb; barrier, blockade.
Ant. help, aid, benefit, assistance, spur, boon.

hinge *v.* *The whole business hinges on the boss's decision:* depend, hang, revolve around, rest, turn; result from, arise from.

hint *n.* 1 *Give me a hint. There was a hint of anger in her voice:* clue, inkling, notion, idea, tip, pointer; suggestion, indication, insinuation, implication; innuendo, allusion, intimation, impression. 2 *There was a hint of garlic in the salad:* trace, touch, tinge, smattering, bit, suspicion, *French* soupçon. —*v.* 3 *She hinted that it was time we left:* suggest, intimate, imply, signify, indicate.
Ant. 2 profusion, plethora; excess, surplus. 3 declare, announce.

hire *v.* 1 *The store hired two clerks:* employ, engage, give employment to, take on, retain, secure, obtain. 2 *We hired a boat and went fishing:* rent, charter, lease, let, engage.
Ant. 1 fire, discharge, dismiss, let go.

hireling *n.* *The gangster sent hirelings to do the dirty work:* menial, minion, flunky, lackey; henchman, thug.

hirsute *adj.* *Neanderthals are often pictured as hirsute:* hairy; unshaven, unshorn, bearded, bewhiskered, whiskered; bushy, woolly, shaggy.
Ant. hairless, smooth-shaven; bald, close-cropped.

historic *adj.* *Plymouth Rock is a historic spot:* important in history; well-known, notable, outstanding, renowned, memorable, celebrated.

historical *adj.* *The book is based on historical events:* in history, of history, authentic, actual, documented, factual, attested, recorded, chronicled, supported by historical evidence.
Ant. present-day, contemporary; fictional, fictitious.

history *n.* 1 *Today's history is being made in Washington, London, and Moscow:* important events, major events, world events, national events, local events; political change, military action, human progress, development, growth, change; an interesting past, actual events. 2 *a history of western Canada:* narration of past events, factual story of the past, chronicle, account, record, saga, epic, annals; portrayal, recapitulation. 3 *way back in history:* the past, former times, bygone days, olden times, days of old, days of yore, yesteryear, yesterday.
Ant. 2 fiction, fantasy. 3 the present, today, now; the future.

histrionics *n.* *The play was filled with histrionics:* dramatics, theatrics, melodramatics; temper tantrum, ranting and raving, tirade, outburst, bluster, bombast.

hit *v.* 1 *The boxer hit his opponent. The golfer hit the ball:* strike, deal a blow, sock, smash, slug, knock, jab, wallop, punch, smack, slam, clout, belt, slap, whack, thwack, baste, lambaste, bash; pelt, punch; club, bat, cudgel. 2 *The truck hit the car at the intersection:* collide with, smash into, bump, strike together. 3 *The arrow hit the target. This car can hit 120 miles an hour:* strike, go straight to; attain, reach, achieve, realize, effect. 4 *The bad news hit everyone hard:* affect, touch, move, impress; upset, hurt, devastate, abash; arouse, rouse, incite, provoke, quicken, stir, inflame. 5 *Our troops will hit the enemy at dawn. The senator's speech hit at government spending:* attack, strike, strike out at, assault, assail, mount an offensive; denounce, criticize, censure, revile, reproach. —*n.* 6 *a hit on the head:* blow, impact, bump, knock, strike, rap, tap, whack, thwack, cuff, bang, wallop, clout, smash, belt, sock; smash, paste, jab, punch, smack, slap. 7 *The new play is a hit:* success, popular success; triumph, *Slang* smash.

Ant. 1 caress. 3 miss; fail. 5 surrender; defend, champion, praise, acclaim, applaud. 7 flop, failure.

hitch *v.* 1 *Hitch the mule to the plow:* tie, tether, make fast, couple, attach, fasten, connect, bracket, yoke, secure; put in harness, harness. —*n.* 2 *The horse was tied with a hitch to the post:* knot, loop; coupling, connection, fastening, tying. 3 *The program went off without a hitch:* mishap, mischance, mistake, complication, problem, catch, snag; trouble; delay, halt, hindrance, stop, interruption.

Ant. 1 unhitch, untie, unfasten.

hither *adv. Come hither:* here, over here, to this place, to the speaker, forward, on, near, nearer, close, closer.

Ant. thither, yon, there; away, farther.

hitherto *adv. Hitherto I have always liked your work:* till now, until now, up to now, thus far, before this, heretofore, hereto, ere now, to the present time.

Ant. henceforth, hereafter, in future, after this, subsequently.

hoard *n.* 1 *We kept a hoard of canned goods at the cabin:* stockpile, cache, store, supply, reserve; gathering, accumulation, collection, quantity. —*v.* 2 *In World War II, some people hoarded sugar:* stockpile, store away, lay away, lay up, cache; amass, accumulate, collect.

hoarse *adj. Her voice was hoarse:* husky, harsh, rasping, raspy, scratchy, croaky, rough, gruff, cracked, throaty, gravelly, guttural.

Ant. clear, melodious, mellifluous.

hoary *adj.* 1 *His hair and beard were hoary. fields hoary with snow:* gray with age, white with age; white, whitened, grizzled, grizzly, gray, grayed. 2 *That's a hoary tale:* old, ancient, aged; antique, dated, *Slang* old hat.

Ant. 2 new, modern, up-to-date.

hoax *n.* 1 *Telling the boy he could catch whales was just a hoax:* mischievous deception, humorous deception, absurd story, exaggerated tale; false alarm; trick, prank, chicanery, deception, fake, fraud, cheat. —*v.* 2 *They were hoaxed into believing Martians had landed:* hoodwink, deceive, delude, take in, fool, trick, mislead; defraud, swindle, cheat, dupe, cozen, gull.

Ant. 1 truth, true story, fact.

hobble *v.* 1 *Hobble the horse so it won't run away:* fetter, shackle. 2 *He hobbled around on crutches after the accident:* limp, walk lamely; shuffle, stumble, shamble, stagger. 3 *Bad luck hobbled me most of my life:* hold back, hinder, restrict, encumber, hamper,

thwart, impede, constrain, restrain, check, block, stymie.

Ant. 2 run, prance, walk briskly. 3 help, aid, benefit, advance, further.

hobby *n. Stamp collecting is my hobby:* diversion, pastime, leisure-time activity, relaxation, sideline, amusement, avocation.

Ant. work, job, vocation.

hocus-pocus *n.* 1 *The magician said some kind of hocus-pocus. The children enjoyed the magician's hocus-pocus:* magic formula, magic words, incantation, mumbo jumbo; magic tricks, magic, sleight of hand, legerdemain, prestidigitation. 2 *There's too much hocus-pocus in local politics:* deception, trickery, deceit, dishonesty, humbug, sham, fakery; subterfuge, hanky-panky; bosh, hogwash, poppycock, tommyrot.

hodgepodge Also **hotchpotch** *n. The garden is a hodgepodge of bushes and weeds:* jumble, mess, confusion, muddle, miscellany, conglomeration, medley, mélange, patchwork, mix, potpourri.

hoi polloi *n. He's too proud to mix with the hoi polloi:* the common people, the proletariat, the working class; the lower orders, the masses, the crowd, the mob, the multitude, the lower classes, the rank and file, riffraff, rabble.

Ant. aristocrats, blue bloods, the upper class, high society.

hoist *v. Hoist the flag:* raise, raise up, pull up, run up, lift, elevate, heave, bear up, bear aloft.

Ant. lower.

hold *v.* 1 *Hold the money tightly. The mother held the baby. A pile of sandbags held the bridge:* keep in the hand, grasp, clutch, grip, clasp; keep in the arms, embrace, enfold; carry, bear, support, uphold, brace, prop, shore. 2 *The glue didn't hold. This rope won't hold:* stick, cling, adhere, cleave; remain tied, stay fixed; unite, clinch, stay. 3 *This box holds a pound of candy:* have a capacity of, contain, accommodate, take in, include, enclose. 4 *Please hold your applause until the end. The police are holding the suspect:* restrain, contain, defer, postpone, repress, suppress, suspend, withhold, hold back, hold in check, check, curb, stay, keep, restrict; detain, confine. 5 *The airline is holding two tickets for you:* keep, retain, reserve, set aside. 6 *He's too lazy to hold a job:* keep, maintain, hold down; have, possess, occupy. 7 *The club will hold its monthly meeting Tuesday:* conduct, carry on, have, engage in, join in. 8 *We hold these truths to be self-evident. I will hold you responsible:* maintain, assert, affirm, declare, profess, deem, consider, regard, think, believe, count, reckon, suppose, presume, assume, understand, surmise, conclude, deduct; bind, obligate, enforce. —*n.* **9** *Take a firm hold on this line:* grasp, grip, clasp, clutch; embrace. **10** *Doesn't this suitcase have a hold?* The mountain climber couldn't find a hold: handle, knob, strap, grasp, hilt, shaft; foothold, toehold, handhold, advantage; leverage, purchase. **11** *Her brother has always had a strong hold over her:* influence, control, sway, domination, dominance, mastery, rule, power, ascendancy.

Ant. **1** let go, let loose. **2** come undone, come unstuck; come untied, loosen, break. **4** grant, tender, offer, release. **7** cancel, call off; postpone. **8** disavow, deny, repudiate, reject, abjure, forswear.

hole *n.* **1** *a hole in the fence:* opening, aperture, breach, break, gap, rent, slit, crack; puncture, perforation. **2** *The bomb left a big hole in the ground:* hollow place, depression, cavity, concavity, indentation, excavation, pocket; crater; den, lair, burrow. **3** *The police discovered several holes in her alibi:* fault, defect, fallacy, flaw, discrepancy, inconsistency.

Ant. **2** protuberance, convexity, mound.

holiday *n.* **1** *Easter is a holiday:* holy day; feast day. **2** *Is Labor Day still a holiday?:* celebration, jubilee, fiesta, festival, fete; vacation, vacation day, day of rest. —*adj.* **3** *in a holiday mood:* festive, celebrating, gala, merrymaking, joyous, joyful, cherry, cheerful.

Ant. **2** workday. **3** serious, somber, sad.

holiness *n.* *the holiness of the shrine:* sanctity, sacredness, blessedness, godliness, saintliness.

Ant. worldliness, secularity.

hollow *adj.* **1** *These chocolate Santas are hollow:* unfilled, not solid, vacant. **2** *hollow cheeks:* concave, curving inward, sunken, cavernous, depressed. **3** *His voice was hollow:* dull, expressionless, unresonant, nonresonant. **4** *a hollow victory:* meaningless, unavailing, empty, pointless, fruitless, profitless, useless, futile, unprofitable, valueless; unsatisfactory, disappointing. —*n.* **5** *More gravel is needed to fill the hollow in the driveway:* depression, concavity, cavity, hole, indentation, dip, sink; dent, dimple. **6** *Let's have a picnic down in the hollow:* valley, dale, dell, vale, glen.

Ant. **1** solid, filled. **2** convex, protruding, rounded. **3** vibrant, resonant; expressive. **4** worthwhile, profitable; meaningful, significant; satisfying, gratifying. **5** protuberance, bump, hump.

holocaust *n.* **1** *Firemen saved some buildings from the holocaust:* conflagration,

deadly fire; devastating blaze; inferno. **2** *Millions of Jews perished in the Nazi holocaust:* devastation, havoc, ravage; vast slaughter, massacre, carnage, killing, annihilation, genocide, mass murder, butchery.

holy *adj.* **1** *The Bible and the Koran are holy books:* of divine character, of divine origin, divine, divinely inspired, pertaining to God, from God, sacred; spiritual, religious. **2** *Francis of Assisi was a holy man:* saintly, godly, dedicated to God, devoted to God, spiritual; moral, righteous, guileless, undefiled, virtuous; devout, pious, religious, reverent. **3** *holy ground:* consecrated, hallowed, sacred, sanctified; solemn, venerated; worshiped, adored, revered.

Ant. unholy. **1, 2** secular, worldly, profane; sacrilegious, blasphemous, impious; sinful, wicked. **3** unconsecrated, unsanctified, unhallowed.

homage *n.* *This statue was erected in homage to war heroes:* honor, respect, reverence, veneration; praise, tribute, exaltation, glorification, devotion; deference, obeisance; worship, adoration, adulation.

Ant. dishonor, disrespect, irreverence.

home *n.* **1** *a home in Florida:* house, residence, place of residence, dwelling, dwelling place, domicile, abode, place of abode. **2** *Alaska is the home of the Kodiak bear:* habitat, habitation, native land, native region, natural environment. **3** *a home for the aged:* institution, residence; *(variously)* nursing home, sanatorium, orphanage, asylum.

homely *adj.* **1** *Cinderella's stepsisters were homely:* plain-looking, plain, unattractive, uncomely, rather ugly. **2** *homely manners. What a warm, homely room!:* plain, simple, unassuming, unpretentious, unaffected, ordinary, everyday, natural, artless, unsophisticated; homelike, homey, cozy, comfortable.

Ant. **1** beautiful, gorgeous, pretty, handsome, lovely, good-looking. **2** elegant, grand; pretentious, affected, ostentatious, sophisticated.

homespun *adj.* *The rugs had a homespun look to them:* homemade, hand-loomed, hand-woven, hand-wrought; simple, plain, unpretentious, unaffected, natural, homely, folksy, down-home.

homicide *n.* *He was charged with homicide:* murder, manslaughter, slaying.

homogeneous *adj.* *It was a homogeneous crowd:* of the same kind, of a piece; uniform, unmixed, unvarying, unadulterated; consistent, constant, similar.

Ant. heterogeneous, mixed, varied, variegated, diverse, divers.

honest *adj.* 1 *an honest judge. honest dealings:* law-abiding, ethical, truthful, upright, fair, just, honorable, virtuous, principled, conscientious, scrupulous, faithful, tried and true, aboveboard, on the level, on the up-and-up; legal, legitimate, lawful. 2 *an honest answer. an honest day's work:* true, truthful, straightforward, candid, blunt, forthright, trustworthy, dependable, reliable; valid, genuine, authentic, bona fide. 3 *an honest face. honest praise:* sincere, open, frank, candid, guileless, ingenuous, innocent, artless, undisguised.

Ant. dishonest. 1 unethical, untruthful, unfair, dishonorable, unprincipled, unscrupulous, unfaithful; illegal, illegitimate, unlawful, crooked. 2 false, lying, untruthful, deceitful, unreliable, untrustworthy; fake, counterfeit. 3 guilty, insincere, deceitful, hypocritical.

honesty *n. Are you questioning my honesty?:* truthfulness, integrity, trustworthiness, probity, veracity, sincerity, honor, faithfulness, morality, fairness, just dealing, square dealing.

Ant. dishonesty, deceitfulness, deception, untruthfulness, falseness, lying, duplicity, insincerity, guile.

honor *n.* 1 *I value my honor:* honesty, principle, honorableness, decency, trustworthiness, sincerity, faithfulness, honesty, integrity, virtue, fairness, justness, truthfulness, truth, veracity. 2 *I was taught to show honor to my elders. My grandfather won honor in the war:* respect, esteem, regard, deference, reverence, homage, veneration, admiration, tribute, adoration, worship, glorification; glory, acclaim, renown, distinction, prestige, repute, commendation, praise, recognition, eminence, illustriousness. 3 *It's an honor to meet you:* privilege, compliment, pleasure, favor. —*v.* 4 *Honor thy father and mother:* esteem, revere, venerate, respect; value, regard, admire, praise, laud, extol, commend, exalt, glorify, worship, show deference to, pay homage to; venerate, adore. 5 *The mayor will honor us with a visit:* confer honor upon, favor, compliment, dignify, glorify. 6 *Which credit cards does this restaurant honor?:* take, accept, credit, acknowledge; *(of a check or draft)* make payment on, pay, redeem, cash, credit, make good.

Ant. 1–5 dishonor. 1 bad character, dishonesty, insincerity. 2 disrespect, contempt, disdain, scorn, shame, disgrace; infamy, bad name. 3 insult, disfavor. 4 hold in contempt, disrespect, disdain, scorn, shame, discredit, slight, disobey. 5 insult, affront. 6 refuse, reject.

hoodlum *n. a gang of hoodlums:* gangster, mobster, gunman, crook, criminal, desperado; thug, tough, hooligan, ruffian, rowdy.

hoodwink *v. We were hoodwinked into investing in a nonexistent oil well:* deceive, trick, dupe, cheat, swindle, mislead, defraud, victimize; bamboozle; fool, hoax.

hook *n.* 1 *The driveway makes a hook around an old tree:* bend, curve, crook, angle, arc, crescent, arch, bow. —*v.* 2 *Hook the screen door when you come in:* fasten, latch. 3 *The creek hooks past the barn:* bend, curve, wind, angle, arc, arch, loop, curl. 4 *The fishermen were hooking bass:* catch, take, bag, nab, seize, grab; capture.

Ant. 1 straight line, beeline. 2 unhook, unlatch. 3 go straight, make a straight line.

hoot *v.* 1 *The owl hooted. The train hooted:* screech, shriek, scream, howl, shrill, whoop; moan, whistle, blow, honk. 2 *The crowd hooted its disapproval:* howl, shout, cry out, sing out, bellow, bawl, screech, scream, roar, whoop, yowl; boo, jeer, hiss, razz, scoff at, mock, cry down, sneer at, taunt.

Ant. 2 hail, cheer, applaud, *Slang* root for.

hop *v.* 1 *The rabbit hopped across the field. The frog hopped the mud puddle:* jump, spring, leap, bound, vault, skip; gambol, frisk, caper, romp; jump over, leap over, spring over, vault, bound over. —*n.* 2 *With one hop the frog was back in the pond:* jump, spring, leap, bound, skip.

hope *n.* 1 *hope for the future:* faith, confidence, assurance, reassurance, encouragement; optimism, expectation, great expectations, anticipation. 2 *My fondest hope is to retire to Florida:* desire, wish, aspiration, ambition, dream, daydream, fancy. 3 *Our only hope is that the Coast Guard heard our SOS:* chance, possibility, prospect; chance for survival, possible way out, help, rescue, salvation. —*v.* 4 *I hope you're feeling better. The Johnsons hope to buy a house next year:* trust, feel sure, be confident, desire, wish, aspire, look forward to, count on, expect, anticipate, reckon on, long for, dream of, have one's heart set on. 5 *The doctors are doing all they can; now we can only hope:* be hopeful, have faith, hope for the best; trust; look on the bright side, take heart.

Ant. 1 dread, despair, distrust, doubt. 4 doubt, deem unlikely, despair of. 5 dread, expect the worst.

hopeful *adj.* 1 *The team is hopeful that it will win:* full of hope, expectant, anticipative, optimistic, trusting. 2 *The patient's good appetite was a hopeful sign:* promising, favorable, propitious, auspicious, heartening, reassuring, encouraging.

Ant. 1, 2 hopeless. 1 despairing, despondent, pessimistic. **2** discouraging, depressing, unpromising, unfavorable, inauspicious, disheartening, unencouraging.

hopeless *adj.* **1** *It's a hopeless situation:* without hope, past remedy, incurable, irreversible, irreparable, irretrievable, impossible, beyond help, lost, futile. **2** *The wrestler felt hopeless when he saw how big his opponent was:* without hope, pessimistic, despairing, dejected, abject, despondent, disconsolate, downcast, depressed, downhearted; sad, forlorn, heartbroken, heavyhearted, sick at heart, sorrow-stricken, grief-stricken.

Ant. **1, 2** hopeful. **1** promising, encouraging, favorable, promising, heartening, rosy. **2** full of hope, confident, assured, encouraged, heartened.

horde *n. hordes of grasshoppers:* multitude, host, pack, crowd, throng, mob, bunch, drove, swarm, assemblage, assembly, gang, company, gathering; tribe, legion, band, troop.

horizontal *adj.* **1** *a horizontal line:* parallel to the horizon, level, parallel to the ground; flat, plane, plumb, flush. **2** *After I wrenched my back I had to stay horizontal for a week:* recumbent, prone, supine, reclining, prostrate, lying down, *Informal* flat on one's back.

Ant. **1** vertical. **2** upright, on one's feet.

horn *n.* **1** *the horns of a goat:* antler, cornu; tusk; excrescence, spike, point. **2** *The tuba is the largest horn in the band: (brass instrument: variously)* cornet, trumpet, trombone, tuba, bugle, baritone, sousaphone, euphonium, mellophone, French horn, alto horn; *(woodwind instrument: variously)* saxophone, clarinet, oboe, English horn, bassoon.

horrendous *adj. Don't tell the children such horrendous stories:* horrible, horrid, terrible, dreadful, appalling, frightful; revolting, repulsive, hideous, shocking, horrifying, ghastly, gory.

Ant. pleasing, pleasant, agreeable.

horrible *adj. The accident was a horrible sight. What a horrible thing to say!:* gruesome, revolting, repulsive, sickening, awful, disgusting, terrible, vile, hideous, grisly, nauseating; detestable, disagreeable, unpleasant, foul, nasty, horrid, obnoxious, abominable, appalling, dreadful, atrocious, monstrous, shocking, frightful, unspeakable, despicable.

Ant. pleasing, pleasant, agreeable, attractive, appealing, delightful, wonderful, lovely.

horrify *v. Try not to horrify them with such stories:* terrify, frighten, affright, petrify;

disgust, sicken, repel, revolt, nauseate; dishearten, disconcert, dismay.

Ant. please, delight; gladden, reassure, calm, soothe.

horror *n.* **1** *a horror of snakes:* fear, terror, dread, alarm, trepidation, dismay; aversion, loathing, abhorrence, detestation, hatred, distaste, disgust, dislike, repugnance, revulsion, repulsion. **2** *the horrors of war:* cruelty, outrage, inhumanity, atrocity; misery, woe, suffering, anguish, torment, affliction.

Ant. **1** liking, affinity, love, attraction. **2** pleasure, delight, joy, benefit.

hors d'oeuvre *n. Hors d'oeuvres were served on the patio:* appetizer, canapé, tidbit; *(variously)* little sandwich, finger sandwich, dip, relish tray.

horse *n. Saddle the horse: (young)* foal, yearling, pony; *(female)* filly, mare, broodmare; *(male)* colt, stallion, sire, stud, gelding; *(variously)* steed, charger, mount, equine, racehorse, trotter, pacer, mustang, cow pony, pinto, quarter horse, bronco, thoroughbred, draft horse, palfrey; *Slang* plug.

horseman *n.* **1** *The mountie was a good horseman:* rider, horseback rider, equestrian; *(variously)* horse breeder, trainer, groom, stable owner, stable keeper, stableboy, hostler, ostler. **2** *a detachment of horsemen:* cavalryman, horse soldier, mounted trooper, dragoon, horse marine, lancer, hussar.

hose *n. a pair of hose:* stockings, hosiery; socks.

hospitable *adj.* **1** *Be hospitable to guests:* gracious, cordial, genial, friendly, warm, welcoming, convivial. **2** *Be hospitable to new ideas:* receptive, accessible, open, openminded, approachable, responsive, tolerant.

Ant. **1, 2** inhospitable. **2** close-minded, unreceptive.

hospital *n.* **1** *a doctor at the local hospital:* medical center, clinic, polyclinic, medical pavilion. **2** *a hospital for the mentally disturbed:* sanatorium; *(variously)* asylum, home, state hospital.

hospitality *n. an evening of warm hospitality:* welcome, hospitableness, friendliness, congeniality, cordiality, geniality, sociability, neighborliness, warmheartedness.

host¹, hostess *n.* **1** *Fred was host at the banquet. a cordial hostess:* master of ceremonies, mistress of ceremonies; party giver, welcomer. **2** *Your host hopes your stay at the hotel will be pleasant:* hotel manager, hotel keeper, innkeeper, hotelier, hosteler; restaurant manager, receptionist, maitre d', headwaiter, head waitress.

Ant. **1, 2** guest. **2** customer, patron.

host² *n. A host of barbarians attacked the*

city: multitude, horde, swarm, drove, throng, band, group, party, body, company, mob, crowd.

hostile *adj.* 1 *hostile troops:* enemy, belligerent, bellicose, opposing, fighting, battling, contending, clashing, warring, at war; dissident, at odds. 2 *hostile words:* belligerent, angry, antagonistic, contentious, quarrelsome, bristling, disagreeing; malicious, vicious, malevolent, spiteful, malignant, malign; unfriendly, unkind, ill-disposed, disagreeable, cranky, cantankerous.

Ant. 1 friendly, peaceful. 2 friendly, amiable, amicable, cordial, congenial, sympathetic.

hostility *n.* 1 (*usually* **hostilities**) *Hostilities broke out:* war, warfare, state of war, warring, fighting, fight, conflict, combat, battling; dispute, contention, altercation, dissidence, disagreement. 2 *I can't understand the hostility to us:* belligerence, animosity, antagonism, antipathy, enmity, opposition; anger, malice, malevolence, bitterness, spleen, unfriendliness, ill will, hatred, hate.

Ant. 1 peace. 2 good will, amity, love, friendship, cordiality.

hot *adj.* 1 *hot weather. hot coffee:* very warm, uncomfortably warm, warm, sweltering, sultry, torrid; at high temperature, heated; simmering, steaming, burning, boiling, broiling, scalding, scorching, blistering, searing, baking, roasting, sizzling, piping hot, smoldering; molten, red-hot, white-hot. 2 *Put hot sauce on the barbecue:* piquant, peppery, highly seasoned, sharp, nippy, pungent 3 *a hot argument about politics:* intense, violent, furious, raging, vehement, fierce, fiery, ardent, passionate, fervid, tempestuous, emotional, animated, wrought-up. 4 *Informal the hottest new style of the year:* popular, most popular, successful, sought after, fast-selling.

Ant. 1 cold, chilly, chilled, cool, cooled, frigid, freezing. 2 mild, bland. 3 peaceful; unemotional, dispassionate.

hound *n.* 1 *The old hound has been chasing the cat again:* hunting dog; dog, canine; *Slang* pooch, mutt, poochie, doggy; (*young*) pup, puppy, whelp. —*v.* 2 *The bill collector hounded the debtor:* chase, pursue, track, trail, stalk; nag, keep after, hector, harass, pester, harry, bedevil, badger, worry.

Ant. 2 escape, evade, elude.

hour *n. When is your lunch hour?:* time, particular time, fixed time; period, interval.

house *n.* 1 *a new house:* home, dwelling, dwelling place, residence, abode, domicile; shelter, habitation. 2 *You woke up the whole house!:* household, family. 3 *the House of Hapsburg:* royal family, noble family, line,

dynasty, clan; lineage, ancestry, descent, family tree, ancestors, strain. 4 *a house of worship:* building, meeting place, gathering place; (*variously*) church, temple, theater, opera house, concert hall, auditorium, hippodrome, hall. 5 *John works for a brokerage house:* business firm, company, concern, firm, business, organization, establishment, corporation. —*v.* 6 *Many volunteered to house the flood victims:* lodge, shelter, quarter, board, billet, put up, accommodate.

housing *n.* 1 *families in need of housing:* house, home, dwelling, domicile; abode, shelter, lodging, quarters, accommodations, residence, habitation. 2 *a metal housing:* case, covering, casing, shield, sheath, jacket, envelope.

hovel *n. How can I live in that hovel?:* wretched dwelling, ramshackle building; *Slang* dump, hole; shanty, shack.

Ant. mansion, palace, showplace, castle.

hover *v.* 1 *The hawk hovered overhead:* pause in flight, hang suspended, poise, float; flutter, flit, flitter. 2 *I can't stand anyone hovering near me:* linger about, hang about, hang around, wait near at hand, attend. 3 *to hover between life and death:* waver, hang, falter, seesaw, fluctuate, vacillate.

howl *v.* 1 *The dog howled all night:* yelp, bay, cry, bark. 2 *to howl with pain:* cry out, yell, shout, bellow, roar, clamor, shriek, scream, hoot, yowl, yelp, wail. —*n.* 3 *the mournful howl of a wolf. a howl of protest:* cry, bay, yelp, bark, whine; outcry, clamor, uproar, yell, shout, bellow, roar, shriek, scream, yowl, hoot, wail.

Ant. 2, 3 whisper, murmur, mutter.

hub *n. Chicago is the hub of the midwest:* center, axis, pivot, core, focal point, heart, focus, middle.

hubbub *n. What was all that hubbub about?:* uproar, pandemonium, tumult, fuss, hullabaloo, disturbance, stir, commotion, turmoil, ferment, fuss, agitation; racket, noise, clamor, din, babble.

Ant. quiet, serenity, calm; stillness, hush.

huddle *v.* 1 *We huddled around the campfire:* crowd together, throng, cluster, gather closely, flock together, press together, converge, collect, bunch, herd. 2 *The kittens huddled together:* curl up, snuggle, nestle, cuddle. —*n.* 3 *The executives had a quick huddle before the meeting:* gathering, conference, discussion, think session.

Ant. 1 disperse, scatter.

hue *n. pale hues of green:* color, coloration, shade, tint, tone; cast, tinge.

hue and cry *n. A great hue and cry went up:* clamor, hullabaloo, uproar, outcry, bellow, roar, yell, shout, yowl, shriek; cry of alarm, alarm.

huff n. *We left the party in a huff:* ill humor, fit of anger, fit of pique, fury, rage; resentment, vexation, annoyance, petulance, snit.

huffy adj. *She's huffy when she doesn't get her way:* easily offended, touchy, sensitive; angry, irate, waspish, quarrelsome, ill-humored, resentful, petulant, churlish, snappish, testy, irritable, peevish, grumpy, cross, curt, out of sorts, sulky, surly, sullen, resentful, moping, disgruntled.

Ant. good-humored, cheerful, sunny, friendly.

hug v. 1 *They hugged the child:* embrace, hold, clasp, press to the bosom, hold close, cuddle, snuggle, nestle; cling together. 2 *The road hugs the river:* keep close to, cling to, follow closely, parallel closely, hover near.

huge adj. *Mammoth Cave is huge:* extremely large, immense, enormous, vast, extensive, colossal, gigantic, mammoth; monstrous, elephantine, jumbo, gargantuan, leviathan, herculean; massive, great, monumental; extravagant, prodigious.

Ant. small, little, tiny; petty, puny, insignificant.

hulking adj. *a great hulking figure:* bulky, heavy, massive, powerful, big, husky, massive; cumbersome, ponderous.

hull n. 1 *peanut hulls. a freighter's hull:* husk, shell, skin, pod, coating, shuck, peel, rind, case; epidermis, carapace, integument; body of a ship. —v. 2 *Hull a cupful of peas:* shell, husk, shuck.

hum v. 1 *Do you know this tune I'm humming?:* croon, drone, intone. 2 *The motor hummed:* whir, purr, drone, thrum, murmur, vibrate; buzz. —n. 3 *the steady hum of the motor:* whirring, whir, drone, droning, purring, purr, vibration; buzzing, buzz; murmur, faint sound.

human adj. 1 *To err is human. the human race:* characteristic of humankind, like people, of people, mortal, hominid, anthropoid. 2 *to act in a human way:* sympathetic, compassionate, humane, merciful, personal, humanitarian. —n. 3 *Wolves usually will not attack humans:* human being, person, man or woman; Homo sapiens.

Ant. 1 nonhuman; god; animal. 2 inhuman, beastly, brutish, cruel.

humane adj. *Helping the homeless is a humane thing to do:* kind, kindly, compassionate, sympathetic, benevolent, merciful, pitying, human, humanitarian, bighearted, magnanimous, unselfish.

Ant. inhumane, cruel, inhuman, uncivi-

lized, merciless, unmerciful, pitiless, ruthless; unkind, unsympathetic.

humanity n. 1 *crimes against humanity:* the human race, humankind, mankind, man, Homo sapiens; mortals, human beings, people, men and women. 2 *Our humanity unites us:* humanness, human nature, mortality. 3 *There is a great humanity in all of Thoreau's writing:* kindness, kindliness, compassion, sympathy, gentleness, benevolence, warmheartedness, fellow feeling, goodwill, magnanimity, mercy, love.

Ant. 2–3 inhumanity. 3 unkindness, cruelty, brutality, ruthlessness.

humble adj. 1 *She's famous but humble:* modest, unassuming, unpretentious, unpresuming, self-effacing; demure, meek; subservient, obsequious, deferential, respectful. 2 *Our summer cottage is a humble house:* poor, modest, shabby, inferior; plain, simple, common, ordinary, inglorious, insignificant, inconsequential, unimportant. —v. 3 *Management was humbled by the revolt:* bring down, put down, subdue, chasten, bring low; humiliate, abash, put to shame, embarrass, mortify, shame; conquer, crush; derogate, dishonor, demean, lower, debase.

Ant. 1 proud, arrogant, haughty, immodest, pretentious, vain, overbearing, snobbish, conceited, assuming. 2 rich, wealthy, sumptuous, elegant; superior, distinguished, illustrious, important, significant; high, high-ranking, aristocratic. 3 exalt, elevate, aggrandize; glorify.

humbug n. 1 *a humbug to sell worthless land:* deception, deceit, trick, trickery, fraud, cheat, flimflam, swindle, gyp, artifice; forgery, fake, counterfeit, imposture, dodge; sham, spoof, hoax, fiction. 2 *Speeches are full of humbug:* pretense, pretentiousness, pretension, sham, hypocrisy, flummery, lying, lies, falsehood; nonsense, poppycock; *Informal* bunk, bunkum, balderdash, claptrap, hokum. 3 *The humbug tried to pass as a lawyer:* fraud, quack, fake, faker, impostor, charlatan, mountebank; cheater, liar, fibber, perjurer, hypocrite. —interj. 4 *Bah! Humbug!:* nonsense, rubbish, balderdash, *Slang* phooey.

Ant. 2 truth, truthfulness.

humdrum adj. *another humdrum day:* dull, boring, monotonous, run-of-the-mill, uninteresting, routine, everyday, mundane, tiresome; lifeless, insipid, trite, trivial, banal, commonplace, hackneyed, mediocre, pedestrian, indifferent; unexciting, uneventful, unvarying, common, ordinary, conventional, unexceptional.

Ant. stimulating, exciting, provocative, entertaining, interesting; exceptional, extraordinary.

humid *adj. It's humid today:* muggy, sticky, sultry, steamy; damp, moist, dank.
Ant. arid, dry, parched.

humiliate *v. I was humiliated when I couldn't remember her name:* embarrass, make ashamed, shame, mortify, chagrin, abash, humble; disgrace, dishonor, chasten, crush, debase, degrade.
Ant. honor, make proud, exalt.

humiliation *n. He blushed in humiliation:* embarrassment, shame, mortification, chagrin; disgrace, dishonor, degradation, debasement.
Ant. pride, honor, exaltation.

humility *n. With humility she thanked others for their help:* modesty, humbleness, unpretentiousness, self-abasement; diffidence, demureness; meekness, shyness, timidity, bashfulness.
Ant. pride, arrogance, haughtiness, pretentiousness, vanity, pomposity, disdain, snobbishness, conceit, superiority.

humor *n.* 1 *the humor of the situation:* funniness, comedy, ridiculousness, ludicrousness, jocularity, jocoseness, jocosity. 2 *The book is full of humor:* jokes, joking, wit, wittiness, witticisms, gags, wisecracks, jests, jesting, tomfoolery, raillery, buffoonery, waggery; comedy, slapstick, burlesque, farce, parody, travesty, satire, whimsy, wordplay, puns. 3 *Dad's always in a good humor:* mood, temper, disposition, spirits, frame of mind. *—v.* 4 *You have to humor me:* indulge, pamper, flatter, spoil, baby, go along with; appease, soothe, placate, mollify, cajole.
Ant. 1, 2 seriousness, gravity, solemnity; sadness, sorrow, melancholy. 4 stand up to, oppose, fight.

humorous *adj. The play was humorous:* funny, comic, comical, witty, droll, mirthful, laughable, amusing, sidesplitting, ribtickling, waggish, whimsical, jocular, jocose, farcical, satirical; ludicrous, ridiculous, nonsensical.
Ant. grave, serious, solemn; sad, melancholy.

hump *n. The dromedary camel has one hump:* protuberance on the back, hunch; bulge, lump, bump, mound, prominence, rise, swelling, projection, excrescence; knob, knurl.

hunch *n.* 1 *I have a hunch Jack will be there:* intuition, feeling, foreboding, premonition, presentiment; idea, suspicion, inkling, clue. *—v.* 2 *We hunched our shoulders against the wind:* bend, hump, arch, tense.

hunger *n.* 1 *This meal ought to satisfy your*

hunger. *Hunger is a major problem in the drought-stricken area:* desire for food, hungriness, appetite, ravenousness, voracity; famine, starvation, malnutrition, lack of food. 2 *the hunger for power:* craving, greed, greediness, desire, lust, itch, yearning, yen, appetite, thirst, hankering; fondness, liking, love. *—v.* 3 *to hunger after knowledge:* long for, desire, crave, burn for, wish, want, thirst after, lust after, yearn for.
Ant. 1 satiety, fullness; overeating. 2 repulsion, revulsion, disgust, repugnance, loathing, abhorrence, aversion, hatred.

hunk *n. a hunk of bread:* chunk, piece, block, lump; wad, gob, glob; portion, mass.

hunt *v.* 1 *to hunt pheasant:* shoot, go after, chase, track, stalk, trail, seek. 2 *Police are hunting an escaped convict:* pursue, chase, track, trail, trace, stalk; look for, search for, seek, try to find, look high and low for, go in quest of, follow.

hurdle *n.* 1 *The racer cleared the last hurdle before the finish line:* barrier, obstacle; *(in steeplechase racing)* fence, hedge, wall. 2 *The exam is a student's last hurdle before graduation:* obstacle, barrier, difficulty, hindrance, impediment, obstruction, roadblock. *—v.* 3 *The horse hurdled the fence:* jump, leap, vault, bound, spring over.

hurl *v. to hurl the discus:* throw, fling, cast, sling, pitch, heave, chuck, toss, project, let fly; propel, launch, discharge, fire off.

hurried *adj. a hurried assessment of the problem:* hasty, fast, speedy, rushed; precipitate, headlong, cursory, superficial, slapdash, careless.
Ant. leisurely, slow, studied, thorough, deliberate.

hurry *v.* 1 *Hurry home before dark:* go quickly, come quickly, move fast, hasten, make haste, speed, speed up, accelerate, rush, hustle, get a move on; bolt, dart, dash, make time, make tracks, step on it, get hopping, get cracking, lose no time. 2 *Don't hurry the cook or he'll spoil dinner:* urge on, goad, prod, pressure; rush, speed up, accelerate. *—n.* 3 *There was much hurry at the last minute:* rush, haste, hustle and bustle, flurry, hurry-scurry, commotion, ado.
Ant. 1 delay, slow down; procrastinate, dawdle, dally. 2 delay, slow, slow down, detain.

hurt *v.* 1 *My feet hurt:* pain, ache, smart, sting, burn; torment, distress, agonize, torture. 2 *I hurt myself in the accident. Don't put that hot cup on the table; it will hurt the finish:* injure, harm, disable, maim, cripple, lame, mangle, mutilate, impair, damage, bruise, cut, scratch, scar, mar, mark, disfigure, deface. 3 *A sloppy appearance hurt* *his chances of getting a job:* hamper, impair, hinder, hold back, impede, retard, limit, inhibit, weaken, check, thwart, foil, block, forestall; decrease, lessen, reduce, diminish, lower. **4** *It hurts me when you talk that way:* offend, sting, aggrieve, grieve, distress, trouble. —*adj.* **5** *a hurt knee:* injured, bruised, cut, scratched; scarred, marked; disabled, crippled, lame; mangled, mutilated, damaged; painful, aching, smarting. **6** *She's hurt because she wasn't recognized:* offended, resentful, wounded, piqued, miffed, crushed; distressed, crestfallen, dismayed, aggrieved; mortified, chagrined; heartbroken, heartsick, dejected. —*n.* **7** *This salve will make the hurt go away:* pain, soreness, ache, pang, sting, discomfort. **8** *I never got over my hurt at being rejected:* pain, discomfort, mortification, embarrassment, chagrin, distress, misery, dismay, dejection, grief, heartbreak.

Ant. **1** relieve, alleviate, assuage, soothe. **2** heal, cure; repair, fix, restore. **3** help, aid, benefit; increase. **5** healed, cured; repaired, fixed, restored. **6** consoled, placated, complimented. **8** happiness, joy, delight; pride, satisfaction.

hurtle *v.* *The motorcycle hurtled along the road:* speed, fly, race, plunge, rush, shoot, tear, scoot; run, hie, gallop, lunge, scurry; bolt, dash, dart, bound.

Ant. crawl, creep.

husband *n.* **1** *Her husband is a stockbroker:* spouse, hubby, mate; *Slang* old man; groom, bridegroom; married man. —*v.* **2** *The nation must husband its resources:* conserve, preserve, use sparingly, manage wisely; save, retain, save up, maintain; accumulate, amass.

Ant. **1** bachelor. **2** waste, squander.

hush *interj.* **1** *Hush! Someone's coming!:* be quiet, be still, be silent, quiet down, silence, quiet; *Informal* shut up, shush, pipe down. —*v.* **2** *The mother hushed the baby:* quiet, shush, silence, still; soothe, calm. —*n.* **3** *There was such a hush in the empty house it was eerie:* silence, stillness; quiet, quietude, quietness, peacefulness.

Ant. **3** racket, din, noise, clamor.

husky *adj.* **1** *a husky child:* big, strong, robust, muscular, brawny, sturdy, strapping, stocky, burly, hefty, thickset, solid, powerful, athletic; stout, beefy, overweight, plump. **2** *The teacher's voice is husky:* hoarse, harsh, rough, rasping, grating, guttural, throaty, croaking, cracked, thick.

Ant. **1** puny, weak; thin, slim. **2** shrill.

hustle *v.* **1** *You'd better hustle:* hurry, hasten, make haste, rush, speed up, move quickly; bolt, dart, dash, scoot, make time,

step on it, lose no time. **2** *They hustled us out of the bar:* push, shove, nudge, elbow, prod, jostle, shoulder, bounce, throw, toss. —*n.* **3** *Before dinner there's always a hustle in the kitchen:* energetic action, bustle, stir, hurry, rush, flurry, fuss, tumult, turmoil, commotion, scramble, ado.

Ant. **1** procrastinate, dawdle, dally. **3** calmness, composure; peace, quiet.

hut *n.* *The shepherd lived in a hut:* shack, shanty, shelter, hutch; shed, lean-to, cabin, cottage.

Ant. mansion, palace, castle, manor.

hutch *n.* *a rabbit hutch:* pen, coop, cage, enclosure, shed; sty, cote, stall, crib.

hybrid *n.* *Mules are a hybrid. The play was a hybrid of suspense and humor:* crossbreed, cross, half-breed; mixture, composite, amalgam.

Ant. thoroughbred.

hygienic *adj.* *Public fountains are not hygienic:* clean, sanitary, germ-free, prophylactic, sterile, disinfected; pure, unpolluted, uncontaminated, disease-free, aseptic; healthful, healthy, salutary, salubrious, wholesome.

Ant. unsanitary, contaminated, dirty, polluted; unhealthy.

hymn *n.* *The church service ended with a hymn:* song in praise of God, anthem, psalm, paean, devotional song; song of praise.

hypocrisy *n.* *He showed hypocrisy by saying one thing and doing another:* insincerity, falsity, two-facedness, duplicity, phoniness; dishonesty, deceit.

Ant. sincerity, frankness, candor, forthrightness.

hypocrite *n.* *That hypocrite said he liked her hat, then laughed behind her back:* insincere person, false person, two-faced person, pretender, *Slang* phony; deceiver.

hypocritical *adj.* *It's hypocritical to praise bad work:* insincere, two-faced, dishonest, deceitful, deceptive.

Ant. sincere, unfeigned, honest; forthright.

hypothesis *n.* *the hypothesis that whales are as intelligent as humans:* theory, thesis, premise, assumption, postulate, proposition, proposal, conjecture, speculation, supposition.

hypothetical *adj.* *The medical students were asked how they would treat a hypothetical case:* supposed, assumed, theoretical, conjectural, possible, imaginary, postulated.

Ant. real, actual, confirmed, established, substantiated, verified.

hysteria *n.* *to calm one's hysteria:* emotional

outburst, hysterics, delirium, frenzy; uncontrolled fear, panic, uncontrolled weeping.

hysterical *adj.* **1** *They grew hysterical when they couldn't find the child:* overcome with fear, distraught, beside oneself, uncontrolla-

ble, frenzied, crazed, raving, overwrought; *Informal* carried away, crazy. **2** *a hysterical joke:* wildly funny, uproarious; comical, laughable, farcical, ludicrous.

Ant. **1** calm, composed, self-possessed.

I

iconoclast *n. an iconoclast who has nothing to do with religion:* dissenter, rebel, nonconformist; radical, revolutionary.

Ant. conformist, assenter.

icy *adj.* **1** *The roads are icy. an icy wind:* frozen over, glazed, slippery; cold, frigid, frozen, freezing, wintry, arctic, raw; frosty, gelid. **2** *an icy stare:* hostile, unfriendly, cold, forbidding, frigid, frosty; impassive, haughty, coldhearted.

Ant. **2** warm, friendly, sympathetic, cordial.

idea *n.* **1** *What is your idea of success?:* concept, mental picture, notion, thought, conception, insight, perception; view, feeling, understanding, sentiment, impression, outlook, conviction, belief. **2** *We need some idea of the cost:* hint, inkling, clue, indication, impression, approximation, suggestion, notion.

ideal *n.* **1** *the ideals of a free nation:* aim, objective, optimal goal, ultimate end, highest goal; level of perfection, highest attainment. **2** *She is the ideal of many actors:* model, inspiration, standard, perfect model, epitome, exemplar, last word, ultimate, criterion, paradigm, archetype; objective, dream, chief hope. —*adj.* **3** *an ideal place for children to play:* perfect, absolutely suitable, exemplary, optimal, excellent, faultless.

idealism *n. Nothing could shake our idealism:* belief in noble goals, persistent hopefulness, optimism, meliorism; wishful thinking, romanticism, utopianism.

Ant. pragmatism, cynicism.

idealist *n.* **1** *The idealists try to aid humanity:* persistent optimist, perfectionist. **2** *There are few idealists in politics:* utopian, visionary, romantic, dreamer.

Ant. **1, 2** pragmatist, skeptic, cynic.

identical *adj. identical chairs:* twin, duplicate, exactly alike, uniform, matched, indistinguishable, interchangeable.

Ant. different, disparate, unlike, dissimilar.

identification *n.* **1** *Identification of the jewels was made by the owner:* establishment of identity; verification, confirmation. **2** *his identification with organized crime:* relationship, connection, association, affiliation. **3** *A driver's license is adequate identification:* certificate of identity, credentials; *(variously)* passport, identity book, identifying badge.

identify *v.* **1** *You can identify me by my red hair:* recognize, know, distinguish, determine, know, tell the identity of. **2** *The world identifies Lincoln with emancipation:* associate, think of in connection, consider the same, regard as representative of.

identity *n.* **1** *Fingerprints established his identity:* name, individuality, delineation. **2** *an identity of political philosophy:* exact similarity, duplication, correspondence; oneness, accord, harmony, unanimity. **3** *In a large city I feel a loss of identity:* individuality, distinctness, self, personality, self-perspective, differentiation, personal uniqueness, social role.

Ant. **2** difference, separateness, contrariety.

ideology *n. Communist ideology:* set of beliefs, body of concepts, principles, ideals, doctrine, theory, dogma, political philosophy.

idiocy *n.* **1** *Idiocy can be congenital:* cretinism, mongolism. **2** *It would be idiocy to antagonize her:* folly, senselessness, stupidity, foolhardiness; fatuity, inanity, asininity, insanity, madness, lunacy.

idiom *n. a translation from French into the Spanish idiom:* language, mode of expression, characteristic style, parlance, speech; colloquialism, localism, dialect, vernacular, jargon, lingo; phrase.

idiosyncrasy *n. Wearing unusual eyeglasses is one of her idiosyncrasies:* peculiar trait, quirk, unusual characteristic, peculiarity, oddity, mannerism, eccentricity, distinction; personal mark.

idiot *n.* 1 *An idiot has a mental age of three or four years:* feebleminded person, mental defective, cretin. 2 *Some idiot forgot to mail the contract:* foolish person, fool, simpleton, halfwit, dope, moron, dolt, ninny, blockhead, nitwit, dimwit, nincompoop, jerk, dummy, dumbbell, dunce, numskull.

idiotic *adj. Not seeing a doctor was idiotic!:* stupid, emptyheaded, absurd, asinine, moronic, feebleminded, imbecilic, ridiculous, rattlebrained, doltish, foolish, foolhardy, irrational, senseless; *Informal* nutty, crazy.

Ant. intelligent, sensible, thoughtful, wise.

idle *adj.* 1 *Hundreds of employees were idle:* unemployed, lacking work, doing nothing, unoccupied, out of work, jobless, inactive. 2 *The fuel shortage left many airplanes idle:* unused, not operating, doing nothing, gathering dust, inactive. 3 *Spring makes me feel idle:* lazy, indolent, sluggish, slothful, languid, enervated, lethargic, listless. 4 *idle gossip:* baseless, worthless, empty, unsubstantiated; petty, trifling, trivial, useless, unproductive; fruitless, futile, pointless, aimless, unimportant. —*v.* 5 *We idled the summer away:* fritter, spend in idleness, pass lazily, while, wait out, loaf, laze.

Ant. 1 employed, working, occupied, busy. 2 operative, functioning, working, active. 3 energetic, industrious, wide-awake. 4 important, meaningful, worthwhile, advantageous, productive, purposeful.

idol *n.* 1 *The temple was filled with golden idols:* religious effigy, icon, graven image; statue, effigy. 2 *a matinee idol:* popular hero, popular figure, darling, public favorite; inspiration, adored person, hero, guiding light.

idolize *v. The boy idolized his father:* adore, venerate, revere, worship, deify; admire, honor, dote upon.

Ant. despise, scorn, disdain.

idyllic *adj. The grazing cows made an idyllic picture:* peaceful, rustic, pastoral, arcadian, charmingly simple, unspoiled.

iffy *adj. The outcome is iffy:* doubtful, unsettled, uncertain, dubious, unresolved, speculative, problematical, unsure, questionable, chancy, risky, unpredictable.

Ant. certain, sure, settled.

ignite *v.* 1 *A dropped match ignited the straw:* set on fire, set fire to, fire, kindle, light, touch off. 2 *Wood must be dry to ignite:* catch fire, catch on fire, burn, take fire, flame.

Ant. 1 stifle, extinguish, quench, douse.

ignoble *adj. an ignoble deed:* despicable, infamous, heinous, shameful, dishonorable,

base, contemptible, nefarious, vile, dastardly, low, foul, mean, depraved, cowardly, pusillanimous, craven, disgraceful, debased, discreditable, unworthy.

Ant. noble, glorious, distinguished, honorable, exalted, worthy, praiseworthy.

ignominious *adj. The army's retreat was ignominious:* humiliating, shameful, inglorious, disgraceful, degrading, sorry, dishonorable, discreditable, disreputable.

Ant. honorable, reputable, admirable, estimable, worthy.

ignoramus *n. Jim is no ignoramus:* simpleton, fool, dunce, low-brow, numskull, nitwit.

ignorance *n. Combating ignorance is a national priority. Ignorance of the law is no excuse:* illiteracy, lack of knowledge or education, lack of learning; unawareness, obliviousness, unenlightenment, unacquaintance, unfamiliarity.

Ant. knowledge, education, wisdom, learning, comprehension, understanding.

ignorant *adj.* 1 *Without schooling we would all be ignorant:* uneducated, unlearned, illiterate, lacking knowledge, unschooled, unlettered, unenlightened, untaught, untrained; naive, unworldly. 2 *The parent was ignorant of the child's fears:* uninformed, unknowing, unaware, unperceptive, unknowledgeable. 3 *an ignorant remark:* unintelligent, irresponsible, insensitive, foolish, uninformed; asinine, dumb, stupid.

Ant. 1 educated, learned, well-informed, wise, literate, cultured. 2 aware, conscious, informed, knowledgeable. 3 perceptive, astute, knowledgeable, wise, brilliant, sage.

ignore *v. to ignore a rude remark:* take no notice of, disregard, pay no attention to, pay no heed to, brush aside; neglect, slight, give the cold shoulder to, snub, overlook.

Ant. heed, notice, regard, recognize.

ill *adj.* 1 *The patient is still ill:* sick, sickly, unwell, ailing, unsound, diseased, unhealthy, indisposed. 2 *The perpetrator of this ill deed will be apprehended:* evil, harmful, wicked, vile, foul, malicious, unkind, vengeful. 3 *an ill omen:* unfavorable, boding bad luck, sinister, unpropitious, inauspicious, threatening, foreboding, ominous. —*n.* 4 **ills.** *to cure the ills of humanity:* affliction, ailment, disease, complaint, malady, infirmity; woe, trouble, sorrow, misfortune. 5 *They remain forgiving, despite the ill done them:* wickedness, evil, mischief, cruelty, abuse, ill-treatment, harm, damage. —*adv.* 6 *The country can ill afford to wage war:* not well, scarcely, hardly; by no means, nowise, noway.

Ant. 1 well, hale, healthy, vigorous. 5

ill-advised

ill-advised *adj. Your attempts at acting are ill-advised:* ill-considered, imprudent, unwise, injudicious, shortsighted, misguided; foolish.

ill-at-ease *adj. Speaking in public makes her ill-at-ease:* uneasy, uncomfortable, disquieted, nervous, troubled, perturbed, discomfited, on edge, discomposed; self-conscious, embarrassed, nonplused, abashed, disconcerted.
Ant. self-assured, self-confident, poised.

illegal *adj. Parking in this spot is illegal:* unlawful, against the law, not legal, prohibited, forbidden, banned, illicit, illegitimate; criminal, felonious, actionable, outlawed.
Ant. legal, licit, lawful, permissible.

illegible *adj. This document is illegible:* unreadable, impossible to read, indecipherable, undecipherable, unintelligible; hard to make out.
Ant. legible, readable, clear.

illegitimate *adj.* **1** *to make illegitimate use of public funds:* illegal, improper, not legitimate, unwarranted, unlawful, illicit, unauthorized, unsanctioned, prohibited. **2** *the king's illegitimate son:* bastard, natural, baseborn, misbegotten.
Ant. **1** legitimate, lawful, legal. **2** legitimate

ill-fated *adj. the ill-fated ocean liner* Titanic: unfortunate, ill-omened, ill-starred, doomed, luckless, unlucky, hapless, jinxed.

illicit *adj. the illicit drug trade:* unlawful, not legal, illegal, against the law, illegitimate, impermissible, criminal, felonious, lawless, prohibited, unauthorized.
Ant. licit, lawful, legal, legitimate, permissible.

illiterate *adj.* **1** *Too many people are illiterate:* unable to read and write, unlettered; ignorant, uneducated, unlearned. **2** *That illiterate report was a disgrace:* badly written, ungrammatical, childish, incoherent. **3** *I am illiterate about art:* ignorant, unknowledgeable, uninstructed, untutored, unversed, uninformed, unenlightened.
Ant. literate, educated, informed, knowledgeable.

ill-mannered *adj. an ill-mannered reply:* rude, impolite, discourteous, disrespectful, uncivil, ungracious, ill-bred; boorish, offensive, loutish.
Ant. gracious, well-mannered, courteous, respectful.

ill-natured *adj. Ill-natured patients demand most of my time:* ill-humored, unfriendly, quarrelsome, antagonistic, cross, peevish,

illustration

contentious, grouchy, cranky, irritable, cantankerous, crotchety, surly.
Ant. congenial, agreeable, amiable.

illness *n. an undiagnosed illness:* sickness, malady, disorder, disease, ailment, infirmity, complaint, ill health.
Ant. health, wholesomeness, salubriousness.

illogical *adj. Your conclusion is illogical:* inconsistent, unreasonable, fallacious, contradictory, incongruent, incongruous; unsound.
Ant. logical, reasonable.

ill-suited *adj. That speech was ill-suited for the occasion:* inappropriate, unsuitable, unsuited, ill-matched, mismatched, unbecoming, unbefitting, ill-adapted, inconsistent, incompatible.
Ant. apt, suitable, appropriate.

ill-tempered *adj. an ill-tempered neighbor:* peevish, cross, petulant, waspish, cantankerous, crotchety, ill-humored, ill-natured, cranky, testy, irritable, grouchy.
Ant. amiable, amenable, pleasant.

illuminate *v.* **1** *Torches illuminated the grounds:* light up, light, illumine, brighten. **2** *Footnotes illuminated the difficult passages of the book:* clarify, explain, make clear, throw light on, elucidate, give insight into.
Ant. **1** darken, cloud, obscure.

illumination *n.* **1** *The room needs better illumination:* lights, lighting, light fixtures, lighting equipment; source of light. **2** *We sought illumination by reading the great philosophers:* enlightenment, knowledge, perception, revelation, insight, wisdom; information, instruction, edification, education.

illusion *n.* **1** *Mirrors give an illusion of more space in a room:* semblance, misleading visual impression, deceiving appearance; impression, vision, false image, mirage; chimera, hallucination, apparition, phantasm, delusion, deception. **2** *the illusions of youth:* false idea, mistaken idea, delusion, misconception, misimpression, misapprehension, fancy.

illusory *adj. The illusory peace soon erupted into war:* unreal, illusive, deceptive, false, spurious, misleading; imaginary, fanciful, hallucinatory, sham, counterfeit; apparent, seeming.

illustrate *v.* **1** *The company's growth illustrates its success:* make clear, explain, elucidate, illuminate, define, clarify; demonstrate, show. **2** *The artist illustrated the book:* provide with illustrations; portray, delineate; represent, picture.

illustration *n.* **1** *The magazine has illustrations in color:* picture, photograph, drawing,

237

image. 2 *The speaker gave an illustration of poor nutrition:* example, instance, specimen, exemplification.

illustrious *adj.* 1 *an illustrious artist:* notable, famous, famed, eminent, renowned, celebrated, prominent, widely admired; distinguished, honored, acclaimed. 2 *an illustrious career:* distinguished, brilliant, splendid, glorious, magnificent; exemplary, peerless.

ill-will *n. She bore him no ill will:* malice, antipathy, hostility, enmity, animosity, rancor, spleen, antagonism, animus, malevolence, hatred, bad blood.

Ant. goodwill, cordiality, friendliness.

image *n.* 1 *The collection contains many images of farm life:* representation, likeness, facsimile, copy, picture, pictorialization; effigy, portrait, figure, delineation, depiction. 2 *the image of the trees in a lake:* reflection, mirroring, likeness; countenance, visage. 3 *The girl is the image of her mother:* copy, duplicate, reproduction, replica, double, facsimile, incarnation. 4 *The writer used the image of corn silk to describe the girl's hair:* simile; metaphor; symbol; concept, idea, mental picture. 5 *The devout worshiped images:* idol, icon, statue, effigy, graven image.

imaginary *adj.* 1 *All characters in the book are imaginary:* unreal, invented, made-up, fictitious, fancied; illusory, fantastic, fabulous, mythical. —*n.* 2 *to confuse the imaginary with the real:* fanciful, fiction, illusion, delusion, make-believe.

Ant. 1 real, actual, true, factual.

imagination *n.* 1 *to develop a child's imagination:* inventiveness, fancy, invention; creativity, creative thought. 2 *With a little imagination we should find a solution:* resourcefulness, ingenuity, inventiveness, creativeness; enterprise, cunning, astuteness.

imaginative *adj. the artist's imaginative use of color:* original, creative, innovative, inventive; ingenious; unusual, out of the ordinary.

Ant. unimaginative, literal, uninventive, ordinary, commonplace, unoriginal, uncreative, prosaic.

imagine *v.* 1 *Try to imagine being on the moon:* envision, picture, pretend, conceive, project, visualize, envisage, fantasize. 2 *I imagine you are tired from the journey:* presume, assume, suppose, should think, guess, conjecture, infer, judge, surmise; take for granted; suspect, fancy.

imbecile *n. He was an imbecile to sail in this storm:* fool, idiot, nitwit, jerk, dumbbell,

dummy, dope, simpleton, moron, dunce, nincompoop, ninny, blockhead, dolt.

imbibe *v. Our family imbibes gallons of iced tea:* consume, drink, quaff, ingest, swallow; *Informal* tipple, toss down.

imbue *v.* 1 *to imbue children with patriotism:* inspire, fill, endow, instill, inculcate, infuse, ingrain. 2 *Sunset imbued the skies with beautiful pastels:* tinge, tint, color, tincture, steep, suffuse.

imitate *v.* 1 *Don't imitate others:* follow the pattern of, copy, fashion oneself after, mirror, take as a model, simulate, emulate. 2 *The comedian imitated W. C. Fields:* mimic, impersonate, do a takeoff on, ape, parrot.

imitation *n.* 1 *The fabric isn't real silk, only an imitation:* simulation, copy, counterfeit, fake, reproduction, facsimile, duplication. 2 *I can do imitations of the president:* impersonation, impression, mimicry, takeoff, representation, aping. —*adj.* 3 *The coat is imitation fur:* simulated, fake, ersatz, phony, mock, sham; synthetic, artificial, manmade.

Ant. 3 real, true, genuine.

immaculate *adj.* 1 *The house was immaculate:* spotless, spic and span, impeccably clean; unstained, unsoiled, stainless, untarnished, unsullied. 2 *The senator's record is immaculate:* above reproach, faultless, clean, virtuous, perfect, unimpeachable, flawless, unsullied; sinless, saintly, chaste, virginal.

Ant. 1 dirty, filthy, unclean. 2 corrupt, defiled, tainted, tarnished, sullied.

immaterial *adj.* 1 *Our opinion is immaterial:* of no importance, not relevant, irrelevant, inconsequential, insignificant, extraneous, unimportant, of no moment, having no bearing. 2 *the immaterial world:* spiritual, incorporeal, bodiless, insubstantial, intangible, unearthly, extramundane, ethereal, spectral, extrasensory, mystical.

Ant. 1 relevant, significant, germane, important. 2 material, physical, tangible, corporeal, earthly.

immature *adj.* 1 *The caterpillar is the immature stage of the butterfly:* embryonic, unripe, young, youthful, rudimentary, unformed, half-grown, undeveloped, unfinished. 2 *an emotionally immature adult:* childish, juvenile, puerile, infantile, babyish.

Ant. 1 mature, adult, ripe, full-fledged.

immediate *adj.* 1 *Please send an immediate answer:* prompt, undelayed, instant, instantaneous, express, swift, speedy, hasty, punctual. 2 *in the immediate neighborhood:*

near, adjacent, close, local, nearby, nearest, proximate, contiguous, nigh; recent.
Ant. 1 leisurely, unhurried, slow; late, tardy. 2 distant, far, remote.

immense *adj. an immense quantity of food:* vast, enormous, monstrous, stupendous, extensive, great, tremendous, huge, gigantic, prodigious, mammoth, colossal.
Ant. small, tiny.

immerse *v.* 1 *Immerse the cloth in the dye:* submerge, dip, lower, dunk, duck, douse, sink, plunge. 2 *She is immersed in scientific research:* involve deeply, absorb, occupy, engross, preoccupy with.

immigrate *v. Many refugees immigrated to Canada:* migrate, move to, relocate in; settle, colonize.
Ant. emigrate; leave, depart from.

imminent *adj. My departure is imminent. in imminent danger:* impending, approaching, close at hand, near, immediate; threatening, looming, menacing.

immobile *adj. A back injury kept me immobile:* incapacitated, laid up, motionless, fixed, stationary, unmoving, still, immobilized.
Ant. mobile, on the move.

immoderate *adj. immoderate praise:* excessive, extravagant, prodigious, unreasonable, unbridled, inordinate, uncalled for, extreme, exorbitant, undue, unrestrained.
Ant. moderate; restrained; reasonable, cautious.

immodest *adj.* 1 *an immodest bathing suit:* indecorous, overly revealing, indecent, indelicate, shameless; suggestive, risqué, wanton, unchaste. 2 *He made immodest claims about his work:* vain, exaggerated, inflated, pompous, conceited, brazen, self-centered, self-aggrandizing, bombastic, boastful, pretentious.
Ant. 1 modest, decorous; chaste. 2 modest, humble, restrained.

immoral *adj. Cheating is immoral. The court banned immoral movies:* unethical, unprincipled, corrupt, evil, wrong, wicked, iniquitous, sinful; dissipated, dissolute; lewd, prurient, obscene, indecent; pornographic.
Ant. moral, virtuous, honorable, ethical; chaste, inoffensive.

immortal *adj.* 1 *The gods are immortal. the immortal works of Beethoven:* undying, not mortal, eternal, everlasting, divine, deathless; lasting, enduring, abiding. —*n.* 2 **Immortals** *In Greek mythology the Immortals dwell on Mount Olympus:* gods, deities. 3 *Chaucer is a literary immortal:* monumental figure, titan, giant, all-time great.

Ant. 1 mortal; transitory, fleeting, ephemeral, short-lived, passing.

immovable *adj.* 1 *an immovable rock:* unmovable, fixed, set, fast, secure, immobile, stationary. 2 *He was immovable in forbidding me to go:* unyielding, unchangeable, stubborn, obdurate, fixed, inflexible, inexorable, adamant, resolute, dogged.
Ant. 1 movable, portable, transportable. 2 flexible, open-minded; irresolute, changeable.

immune *adj.* 1 *immune to measles:* resistant, unsusceptible, protected, safe, invulnerable, not in danger of. 2 *Income from certain bonds may be immune from taxation:* exempt, free; not liable to, not subject to.
Ant. 1 vulnerable, susceptible. 2 subject, liable.

immutable *adj. Platinum is one of the most immutable of metals:* unchanging, unchangeable, changeless; unvarying, unalterable, incontrovertible; permanent, lasting, enduring, stable; firm, fixed, constant, inflexible.
Ant. changeable, unstable, alterable, variable.

impact *n.* 1 *The impact of the car cracked the fence:* collision, crash, smash, blow, force, jolt. 2 *the full impact of the news:* effect, brunt, influence, burden, shock, thrust; implication, repercussion.

impair *v. The water shortage impaired firefighting capacity:* hinder, damage, mar, hurt, cripple, lessen, weaken, decrease, detract from, reduce.
Ant. improve, better, enhance, facilitate, increase.

impart *v.* 1 *He imparted the news of his trip:* make known, tell, communicate, relate, report, reveal, disclose, divulge. 2 *The draperies impart a certain elegance to the room:* confer on, bestow on, give, lend, render, contribute, dispense, accord, afford.

impartial *adj. Try to remain impartial:* unbiased, fair, objective, nonpartisan, disinterested, dispassionate, detached, open-minded, evenhanded, neutral, unprejudiced, fair-minded.
Ant. partial, prejudiced, biased, unfair.

impasse *n. The two groups reached an impasse:* deadlock, stalemate, dilemma, standoff.

impassioned *adj. an impassioned speech:* ardent, intense, fervent, excited, passionate, earnest, eager, zealous, fiery, stirring, rousing, forceful.
Ant. dispassionate, apathetic, indifferent, detached.

impassive *adj. an impassive manner:* emotionless, unemotional, unmoved, dispassionate, aloof, stoical, untouched, calm, cool, reserved, unperturbed, unimpressible, impervious, stolid, apathetic, phlegmatic, indifferent.

Ant. responsive, emotional, passionate, excited.

impatient *adj. I'm impatient for vacation to begin:* restless, nervous, edgy, irritated, agitated, excitable, restive; eagerly desirous, feverish, passionate, hurried, anxious; peevish, irritable, irascible, testy, annoyed, touchy.

Ant. patient; composed, calm, serene, placid.

impeach *v.* 1 *to impeach the president:* accuse, indict, arraign, charge, incriminate. 2 *Don't impeach my honesty:* question, call into question, challenge, attack, impugn, discredit, slur, slander.

impeccable *adj. impeccable taste:* flawless, faultless, immaculate, perfect, excellent, above criticism, unimpeachable.

Ant. deficient, defective; faulty, flawed.

impede *v. A lumber shortage impeded construction:* delay, slow, block, interfere with, interrupt, check, obstruct, hinder, thwart, inhibit, stall, stymie, hamper.

Ant. assist, advance, further, help, aid.

impediment *n. Lack of confidence is an impediment to success. a speech impediment:* delay, block, blockage, barrier, stumbling block, obstruction, hindrance, interference, handicap, obstacle, drawback, detraction; defect, deformity.

Ant. advantage, help, aid.

impel *v. Financial woes impel us to cut spending:* force, require, drive, push, compel, urge, necessitate, prompt, prod, induce, constrain, stimulate, motivate, goad, incite.

impending *adj. an impending storm:* approaching, immediate, coming, due momentarily, imminent, near, oncoming, forthcoming; looming; threatening, menacing.

impenetrable *adj.* 1 *an impenetrable barrier:* impervious, inviolable, unenterable, impassable, invulnerable, inaccessible; solid, dense. 2 *The motive for the crime was impenetrable:* incomprehensible, mysterious, unfathomable, inscrutable, inexplicable, obscure, puzzling.

Ant. 1 penetrable, accessible, passable. 2 understandable, explicable, clear, obvious.

imperative *adj. It is imperative that we reach the doctor:* urgent, vitally important, essential, of the utmost necessity, requisite, necessary; mandatory, compulsory, obligatory, unavoidable.

Ant. unnecessary, unimportant; avoidable; nonobligatory.

imperceptible *adj. The difference between the two is imperceptible:* undetectable, unnoticeable, not readily apparent; inconsiderable, subtle, minimal, unappreciable, minute, small, insignificant, unperceivable; slight, minor.

Ant. manifest, obvious, clear, perceptible, noticeable, distinct.

imperfection *n.* 1 *The coat had a minor imperfection:* defect, flaw, blemish, fault; shortcoming, weakness. 2 *the imperfection of the plan:* faultiness, imperfectness, inadequacy, insufficiency, incompleteness.

Ant. 2 perfection, completeness, faultlessness.

imperial *adj. an imperial executive:* highhanded, imperious, dictatorial, despotic, authoritarian, domineering, lordly, overbearing, tyrannical, autocratic.

imperil *v. Lack of attention to safety may imperil your life:* endanger, risk, jeopardize, hazard, chance, expose to danger.

Ant. protect, shield, guard, safeguard.

impermanent *adj. Youthful beauty is impermanent:* fleeting, temporary, transitory, unenduring, evanescent, ephemeral, passing, transient.

Ant. permanent, immortal, fixed.

impersonal *adj. These suggestions are impersonal, not directed toward anyone in particular:* impartial, objective, dispassionate, detached, disinterested.

Ant. personal, specific.

impersonate *v.* 1 *Narcotics agents sometimes impersonate drug addicts:* pose as, dress up as, take the role of, represent oneself as, masquerade as, pass oneself off as. 2 *Bert Lahr impersonated a lion in* The Wizard of Oz: portray, play the part of, imitate, represent, personify, copy.

impertinent *adj.* 1 *an impertinent youth:* rude, unmannerly, disrespectful, insolent, impudent, presumptuous, arrogant, brazen, brassy, insulting, discourteous; *Informal* fresh. 2 *My testimony was impertinent to the case:* irrelevant, extraneous, immaterial, not germane, beside the point, unrelated, inappropriate.

Ant. 1 polite, respectful, mannerly, deferential. 2 pertinent, relevant, germane, important.

impervious *adj.* 1 *The firemen wore masks that were impervious to smoke:* impenetrable, impermeable, inaccessible, invulnerable. 2 *She seemed impervious to the ravages of age:* immune to, protected against; untouched by, unmarked by, unmoved by, unaffected by, invulnerable.

Ant. 1 susceptible, vulnerable. 2 exposed, susceptible, prone.

impetuous *adj. Inviting everyone was impetuous:* rash, impulsive, hasty, headlong, precipitate, unpremeditated.

Ant. cautious, wary.

impetus *n. Children need an impetus to study:* stimulus, stimulation, spur, moving force, motive, propulsion, drive, momentum, force, push, incentive, motivation.

impinge *v. I hate to impinge on your privacy:* encroach, intrude, infringe, trespass, obtrude.

impious *adj. impious thoughts:* sacrilegious, blasphemous, irreverent, ungodly, profane, irreligious, godless, apostate, immoral.

Ant. devout, reverent, pious, godly.

impish *adj. an impish ploy:* mischievous, puckish, playfully naughty, roguish, rascally, prankish.

implacable *adj. an implacable enemy:* irreconcilable, unappeasable, inexorable, inflexible, intractable, relentless, unrelenting.

implausible *adj. an implausible excuse:* unlikely, improbable, incredible, unbelievable, illogical, unreasonable, doubtful, inconceivable, preposterous, ridiculous, far-fetched.

Ant. plausible, credible, believable, likely.

implement *n.* 1 *gardening implements:* tool, utensil, instrument, device, apparatus, appliance, article, equipment —*v.* 2 *to implement child-care programs:* put into effect, begin, activate, start, set in motion, carry out, fulfill, accomplish, realize.

implicate *v. The suspect implicated two others:* involve, associate, connect, embroil, in criminate.

Ant. exclude, eliminate, rule out.

implication *n.* 1 *the political implications of the speech:* ramification, suggestion, effect, overtone, intimation, insinuation, inference, significance. 2 *We were judged guilty by implication:* association, connection, involvement, entanglement.

implicit *adj.* 1 *Victory was implicit in the early election returns:* implied, hinted, suggested, tacitly expressed; inferred, deducible, understood. 2 *We had implicit faith in the captain's judgment:* innate, inherent, unquestioning, absolute, complete, profound, unreserved, total.

implore *v. He implored the king for mercy:* beg, beseech, entreat, plead with, supplicate.

Ant. order, demand, command.

imply *v. Her frown implied that something was wrong:* indicate, suggest, hint, intimate, connote; presume; signify, mean, denote, evidence.

impolite *adj. It's impolite to wear a hat indoors:* discourteous, ill-bred, unmannerly, rude, unrefined, uncivil, disrespectful.

Ant. polite, courteous, civil, respectful.

import *n. the import of the situation:* significance, importance, meaning, burden, implication, moment.

importance *n.* 1 *the importance of loving care to a child:* value, significance, import, weight, relevance, worth, consequence. 2 *a visitor of great importance:* rank, position, influence, esteem, repute, stature, eminence.

Ant. 1 unimportance, triviality, insignificance.

important *adj.* 1 *an important message:* meaningful, consequential, significant, weighty, momentous, serious, notable. 2 *Picasso is an important painter:* leading, major, preeminent, prominent, influential, esteemed.

Ant. 1 unimportant, inconsequential, insignificant, minor, unnecessary, nonessential, trivial. 2 unimportant, insignificant, minor.

impose *v.* 1 *The mayor imposed a curfew:* institute, lay on, place on, set. 2 *Don't try to impose your wishes on us:* force, inflict, prescribe, apply, foist, thrust upon.

Ant. lift, remove.

imposing *adj. an imposing structure:* impressive, majestic, grand, outstanding, striking, monumental, awe-inspiring, commanding.

Ant. unimposing, unimpressive, insignificant.

impossible *adj.* 1 *It's impossible to speed in this traffic:* out of the question, not possible, unachievable, unattainable. 2 *an impossible problem:* intractable, stubborn, unyielding, unmanageable; intolerable, insufferable, unbearable; unsolvable, insoluble.

Ant. 1 possible, feasible.

impostor *n. The doctor was denounced as an impostor:* pretender, mountebank, fraud, masquerader, charlatan, counterfeit, sham; *Slang* phony, quack.

impotent *adj. Without a leader the government was impotent:* unable to function; ineffective, powerless, weak, helpless, paralyzed.

Ant. potent, powerful, forceful.

impoverished *adj.* 1 *impoverished drought victims:* poor, destitute, sorely wanting, without resources; impecunious, indigent, poverty-stricken. 2 *impoverished farmland:* exhausted, worn out, used up, depleted, bereft, barren, drained, unproductive.

Ant. 1 rich, affluent, wealthy, well-off. 2 fertile, rich, productive.

impractical *adj. an impractical dreamer:*

unrealistic, unwise, lacking foresight, starry-eyed, romantic.

Ant. sensible, practical, pragmatic.

impregnable *adj. an impregnable defense:* invincible, unconquerable, invulnerable, unassailable; strong, mighty, potent.

Ant. vulnerable, frail, flimsy, weak.

impregnate *v.* 1 *to impregnate lab animals by artificial insemination:* make pregnant, cause to conceive, get with young, inseminate, fertilize. 2 *Impregnate the cloth with cleaning fluid:* saturate, soak, imbue, drench, infuse, suffuse.

impress *v. The painter impressed the critics as an important new talent:* affect, influence, sway, move, stir, touch, excite, fix in the mind; overwhelm, overpower.

impression *n.* 1 *I made a bad impression on the boss:* effect, impact, feeling; reception, imprint. 2 *I had the impression you were ready to leave:* feeling, opinion, belief, understanding, idea, notion, hunch, conviction. 3 *deep impressions in the mud:* imprint, mark, outline, track, indentation; stamp, mold.

impressionable *adj. The early years of life are the most impressionable:* easily influenced, receptive, susceptible to impressions, sentient; suggestible, gullible, vulnerable.

impressive *adj. an impressive sight:* imposing, thrilling, awe-inspiring, magnificent, moving, soul-stirring, exciting, grand, majestic, striking, august, outstanding, memorable, unforgettable.

Ant. unimpressive, unimposing, ordinary, uninspiring, unmemorable.

imprison *v. The bank robber was imprisoned:* confine, incarcerate, jail.

Ant. free, release.

improbable *adj. an improbable explanation:* not probable, unlikely, doubtful, unreasonable, implausible, illogical.

Ant. probable, likely, reasonable, plausible.

impromptu *adj. an impromptu speech:* improvised, unprepared, extemporaneous, unrehearsed, unexpected, sudden, offhand, unpremeditated, makeshift, spontaneous; *Slang* off the top of one's head.

Ant. planned, prepared, rehearsed, premeditated.

improper *adj. improper dress:* not suitable, unsuitable, inappropriate, unfit, out of place, ill-suited; indecent, lewd.

Ant. proper, correct, fitting, apropos.

improve *v.* 1 *Improve your penmanship. The patient improved:* make better, help, better, correct, repair, enhance; recuperate, take a turn for the better. 2 *People can improve their lives by doing volunteer work:* enrich,

enhance, make productive, cultivate, develop.

Ant. 1, 2 worsen; injure, harm, damage.

improvement *n.* 1 *the improvement of social conditions:* betterment, progress, gain. 2 *Putting a new roof on the house is a valuable improvement:* enhancement, reconstruction, additive, emendation, reform; refinement, betterment, advance, advancement, step forward.

improvident *adj. The improvident heir quickly spent the family fortune:* thriftless, spendthrift, extravagant, wasteful, prodigal, imprudent; shortsighted, reckless, negligent.

Ant. provident, cautious, thrifty, prudent, farsighted.

improvise *v. We improvised bookcases out of orange crates:* perform without preparation; invent offhand, make up, extemporize, ad-lib; create.

improvised *adj. an improvised speech:* impromptu, ad-lib, offhand, extemporaneous, extempore, unrehearsed, off-the-cuff, spontaneous, spur-of-the-moment, extemporized.

Ant. rehearsed, prepared, polished.

imprudent *adj. It's imprudent to drive with worn tires:* incautious, unwise, inadvisable, ill-advised, ill-considered, thoughtless, untoward, foolish, foolhardy; unthinking, mindless.

Ant. prudent, wise, judicious, cautious, careful.

impudent *adj. The impudent child antagonized teachers:* rude, brash, disrespectful, insolent, discourteous, impolite, brazen, impertinent, forward, nervy, fresh, cheeky.

Ant. respectful, courteous, polite, deferential.

impulsive *adj. What an impulsive act!:* rash, capricious, whimsical, devil-may-care, unpredictable; spur-of-the-moment, impromptu, unpremeditated, unplanned, spontaneous, impetuous, incautious.

Ant. deliberate, premeditated, considered, circumspect, calculating, planned.

impure *adj.* 1 *impure air:* dirty, unclean, defiled, polluted; filthy, foul, sullied, tainted, contaminated, noxious, adulterated. 2 *The minister chastised him for using impure language:* immoral, indelicate, coarse, smutty, unchaste, dirty, lustful, lecherous, prurient, obscene, lewd, indecent.

Ant. 1 pure, clean, unpolluted, untainted, uncontaminated, wholesome, unadulterated. 2 chaste, wholesome, decent, decorous, clean.

impurity *n. The impurity of the water made it unfit to drink:* pollution, uncleanness, contamination, unwholesomeness, defilement, dirtiness, filth; adulterant, contaminant, pollutant; foreign matter; adulteration, taint.

Ant. purity, cleanness.

impute *v. The critics imputed the failure of the play to poor direction:* charge, ascribe, credit, attribute, assign, set down to.

inaccessible *adj. The island is inaccessible except by boat:* unapproachable, unreachable; beyond access, unattainable, unobtainable.

Ant. accessible, attainable, obtainable.

inaccuracy *n.* 1 *The inaccuracy of the report was disgraceful:* inexactness, faultiness, incorrectness, fallaciousness, imprecision. 2 *The novel was full of historical inaccuracies:* error, mistake, slip, fallacy, blunder; *Slang* boo-boo, goof.

Ant. 1 accuracy, correctness, exactness, precision.

inaccurate *adj. an inaccurate description:* incorrect, faulty, erroneous, wrong, false, fallacious, imprecise, inexact.

Ant. accurate, correct, true, exact.

inactive *adj.* 1 *Those machines have been inactive for days:* idle, inoperative, inert, quiet, still, dormant, out of service, unused. 2 *The inactive life of the tropics began to bore me:* idle, torpid, languid, easygoing, low-key, indolent, lazy, slothful, sedentary. *Ant.* 1 active, operative, operating. 2 active, bustling, busy, industrious.

inadequate *adj.* 1 *The fuel supply is inadequate:* not adequate, deficient, insufficient, lacking, meager, wanting, short, scanty. 2 *He's inadequate for the job:* incompetent, incapable, unqualified, unfit, inept, unfitted.

Ant. 1 adequate, sufficient, enough. 2 adequate, qualified.

inadvertent *adj. an inadvertent omission:* unintentional, unintended, accidental, unthinking, involuntary, unpremeditated.

Ant. deliberate, premeditated, intentional, conscious.

inadvisable *adj. It would be inadvisable to approach him while he's angry:* unwise, imprudent, ill-advised, inopportune, risky, inexpedient.

Ant. advisable, wise, prudent, politic, expedient.

inalienable *adj. an inalienable right:* inviolable, unassailable, absolute, unimpeachable, unforfeitable, sacrosanct, inherent; protected.

inane *adj. an inane remark:* foolish, senseless, vapid, silly, vacuous, shallow, pointless, asinine, insipid, empty, ridiculous; unthinking, dumb, stupid, idiotic, meaningless.

Ant. meaningful, sensible, thoughtful, intelligent, wise, sage, profound.

inapplicable *adj. Your idea is inapplicable:* not applicable, irrelevant, unsuited, unsuitable, not pertinent, inappropriate, not germane.

Ant. applicable, suitable, suited, relevant, germane, pertinent.

inappropriate *adj. Wearing shorts to church is inappropriate:* unsuitable, unsuited, improper, out of place, ill-timed, indecorous, infelicitous.

Ant. appropriate, fitting, proper, suitable, meet.

inarticulate *adj.* 1 *an inarticulate sound:* incoherent, unintelligible, mumbled, blurred, garbled, indistinct. 2 *Fear made me totally inarticulate:* incapable of speech, mute, dumb, tongue-tied, speechless, wordless; hesitant in speech, poorly spoken.

Ant. 1 articulate, clear, intelligible. 2 articulate, glib.

inattentive *adj. An inattentive driver is a menace:* not attentive, careless, negligent, unmindful, unobservant, heedless, unaware.

Ant. attentive, careful, aware.

inaugurate *v.* 1 *The city inaugurated the clean-air campaign with a parade:* begin, launch, set in action, undertake, initiate, institute, embark upon, usher in; start, *Informal* kick off. 2 *to inaugurate a new president:* induct formally into office, invest with office; induct, install.

Ant. 1 terminate, end, conclude, finish.

inauspicious *adj. an inauspicious time:* ill-omened, unpropitious, unfavorable, unlucky, unpromising, unfortunate, infelicitous, unlucky.

Ant. auspicious, favorable, propitious, fortunate, promising.

inborn *adj. an inborn love for music:* inherent, innate, inbred, congenital, natural, native, intuitive, instinctive, inherited, intrinsic.

Ant. acquired, nurtured, learned.

incalculable *adj.* 1 *The number of galaxies in the universe is incalculable:* beyond counting, too numerous to count, inestimable, countless, immeasurable, uncountable, innumerable, infinite. 2 *The future is incalculable:* unknowable, unforeseeable, uncertain, unpredictable.

Ant. 1 measurable, countable; limited, finite. 2 predictable, foreseeable, knowable.

incapable *adj. Incapable management ruined the company:* unskilled, inept, incompetent, unfit, unqualified, inadequate, inefficient, ineffective; unable, powerless, impotent.

Ant. capable, able, competent, qualified; efficient, effective.

incapacitate *v. A bad back incapacitated me:* disable, render incapable, make powerless, cripple, handicap, enfeeble, lay up.

incarcerate *v. to incarcerate criminals:* imprison, jail, confine, lock up, impound, intern, commit.

Ant. free, release.

incautious *adj. an incautious remark:* rash, brash, reckless, headstrong, impetuous, hotheaded; imprudent, thoughtless, unwary, injudicious, unthinking, careless, heedless, over-hasty.

Ant. calm, cool; wary, cautious; prudent.

incense *v. The unruly class incensed the teacher:* enrage, inflame, anger, infuriate, madden, make indignant, provoke.

incentive *n. Profit sharing is a good incentive for employees:* motivation, spur, motive, stimulus, inducement, lure, enticement.

inception *n. the inception of an idea:* commencement, beginning, origin, start, birth, onset, inauguration; outset.

Ant. termination, end, completion, finish, conclusion.

incessant *adj. incessant complaining:* constant, ceaseless, continuous, continual, unceasing, unremitting, unending, perpetual, everlasting, interminable, unbroken, unrelenting, uninterrupted.

Ant. intermittent, sporadic, occasional; rare, infrequent.

incidence *n. the incidence of childhood diseases:* frequency, rate, occurrence, commonness, scope, extent.

incident *n. The incident has been forgotten:* event, episode, affair, occurrence, happening; small disturbance, clash.

incidental *adj.* 1 *incidental costs:* secondary, extraneous, accessory, minor, subordinate; unexpected, unlooked-for. —*n.* 2 **incidentals.** *Take along a small valise for incidentals:* minor items; accessories, extras; odds and ends.

Ant. 1 essential, fundamental, basic.

incidentally *adv. Incidentally, the Joneses may come along:* by the way; connected with that, by the by, apropos, speaking of that, parenthetically, while we're on the subject.

incipient *adj. an incipient actress:* beginning, nascent, rudimentary, developing, promising, budding, embryonic, fledgling.

Ant. finished, full-blown; accomplished.

incisive *adj.* 1 *an incisive command:* sharp, crisp, brisk, curt, trenchant, express, summary. 2 *incisive humor:* penetrating, analytic, acute, sharp, precise; perceptive, probing, penetrating, trenchant.

incite *v. to incite people to rebellion:* rouse, stimulate, induce, arouse, urge on, inflame, provoke, foment, instigate, excite, agitate, fire up, impel.

incivility *n. She apologized for her incivility:* rudeness, disrespect, discourtesy, impoliteness, impudence, tactlessness.

Ant. decorum, propriety, seemliness.

inclement *adj. inclement weather:* stormy, cloudy, rainy, snowy, misty, overcast; harsh, raw, severe, foul, nasty.

Ant. clement, mild, clear.

inclination *n.* 1 *an inclination to loaf:* tendency, propensity, penchant, leaning, proneness, predilection, proclivity, predisposition; fondness, bent, liking. 2 *a steep inclination in the road:* slant, rise, dip, slope, acclivity, sloping, grade; bend, bending, incline.

Ant. 1 dislike, antipathy, disinclination.

incline *v.* 1 *The family inclines to rise early:* tend, prefer, enjoy, like, lean toward; be apt, be likely, have a propensity. 2 *The roof inclines over the porch:* slope, slant, tilt, decline, cant, pitch, lean. 3 *Incline your body from the waist:* bend forward, lean, bend, tilt, bow. —*n.* 4 *The house is perched on an incline:* slope, hill, gradient, pitch, inclined plane, acclivity.

Ant. 1 dislike, hate, be disinclined.

include *v. The meal includes appetizer, main course, dessert, and coffee:* contain, comprise, embrace, cover, incorporate, encompass, comprehend, involve, entail.

Ant. exclude, preclude; omit, leave out.

inclusive *adj. All prices are inclusive of tax:* including, incorporating, embracing, comprehending, taking in; comprehensive, overall, general, sweeping, all-encompassing.

incoherent *adj. His talk was incoherent:* disjointed, unintelligible, rambling, confused, irrational, illogical, inconsistent, muddled.

Ant. coherent, intelligible, logical, connected, rational.

income *n. I receive income from stock dividends:* revenue, earnings, livelihood, wages, salary.

Ant. expense, disbursement, outlay.

incomparable *adj. the incomparable beauty of Lake Louise:* peerless, matchless, unequaled, unrivaled, inimitable, beyond compare.

Ant. ordinary, mediocre, average, run-of-the-mill.

incompatible *adj.* 1 *They were too incompatible to work together:* inharmonious, uncongenial, lacking rapport, mismatched. 2 *Her deep voice is incompatible with her* *fragile appearance:* inconsistent, contrary, incongruous, jarring, discordant, at odds, contradictory, unsuited.

Ant. compatible, consistent, harmonious.

incompetent *adj. an incompetent typist:* inept, unskilled, ineffectual, ineffective, inefficient, unfit, incapable, inexpert, unqualified.

Ant. competent, apt, expert, efficient.

incomplete *adj. My set of china is still incomplete:* unfinished, lacking a part, partial, fragmentary; wanting, deficient.

Ant. complete, finished, whole.

incomprehensible *adj. Physics is incomprehensible to me:* baffling, bewildering, beyond understanding, beyond comprehension, unintelligible, confusing, inscrutable, unfathomable, abstruse, impenetrable.

Ant. comprehensible, understandable, clear.

inconceivable *adj. It's inconceivable that it snowed in July:* unthinkable, unbelievable, incredible, beyond belief; highly unlikely, unimaginable, improbable, impossible to comprehend.

Ant. conceivable, believable, credible, plausible, reasonable, likely, probable.

inconclusive *adj. The results are inconclusive:* undetermined, indeterminate, unresolved, unsettled, indefinite, open, up in the air, indecisive, still doubtful, unconvincing.

Ant. conclusive, decisive.

incongruous *adj.* 1 *Shorts look incongruous on a ski slope:* inappropriate, odd, outlandish, out of keeping, out of place, unsuitable, not harmonious. 2 *His incongruous testimony damaged his credibility:* conflicting, contrary, contradictory, inconsistent, irreconcilable, discrepant, disagreeing.

Ant. 1 congruous, fitting, suitable, appropriate, consistent.

inconsequential *adj. It's too inconsequential to worry about:* trivial, trifling, of no moment, valueless, slight, unimportant, of no consequence, insignificant, negligible, nugatory, piddling, petty.

Ant. consequential, important, momentous, significant.

inconsiderate *adj. It was inconsiderate to play music so loud:* thoughtless, rude, insensitive, uncaring, unkind, uncharitable; unthinking, remiss, tactless.

Ant. considerate, thoughtful; kind.

inconsistent *adj.* 1 *His deeds are inconsistent with his beliefs:* incompatible, dissonant, inharmonious, contrary, contradictory, not in agreement, incongruous, irreconcilable. 2 *Her inconsistent opinions confuse me:* erratic, constantly changing, changeable;

fickle, unpredictable, variable, vacillating, changeful.

Ant. 2 consistent, unchangeable; reliable, steady.

inconspicuous *adj. She tried to be inconspicuous:* unnoticed, unnoticeable, unobtrusive, unostentatious, attracting little attention, unassuming; unapparent, dim, muted, faint.

Ant. conspicuous, noticeable; striking, prominent.

incontrovertible *adj. The testimony was incontrovertible:* undeniable, indisputable, irrefutable, unquestionable, past dispute, unarguable.

Ant. disputable, questionable, debatable.

inconvenient *adj. It's inconvenient to work on the weekend:* unhandy, inopportune, untimely, bothersome, troublesome, awkward, annoying.

Ant. convenient, opportune, timely.

incorporate *v. The committee incorporated her findings in its report:* include, embody, work in; consolidate, fuse, introduce into, assimilate.

incorrect *adj. incorrect answers:* wrong, inexact, erroneous, untrue, false, mistaken, fallacious, inaccurate.

Ant. correct, right, accurate, true.

incorrigible *adj. an incorrigible thief:* uncontrollable, unmanageable, unruly; hopeless, past changing, beyond help, intractable; hardened, hard-core.

Ant. correctable, manageable, tractable.

incorruptible *adj. The incorruptible judge refused even a free cup of coffee:* upright, honest, beyond corruption, irreproachable, above temptation, faultless, unbribable.

Ant. corruptible, bribable, dishonest.

increase *v.* 1 *to increase one's knowledge:* make greater or larger, enlarge, expand, add to, augment; advance, enhance. 2 *The membership increased 50 percent:* enlarge, swell, expand, grow, multiply.

Ant. decrease, diminish, lessen, reduce, contract, decline, lower.

incredible *adj. an incredible story:* unbelievable, remarkable, awesome, inconceivable, preposterous, farfetched, amazing, astounding, astonishing, extraordinary.

Ant. credible, believable, unremarkable; ordinary, common.

incredulous *adj. The judge was incredulous when the defendant told a bizarre alibi:* dubious, skeptical, not believing, disbelieving, doubtful, suspicious; showing disbelief.

Ant. credulous, gullible, believing, trusting.

increment *n. a $100 increment in rent:* increase, gain, addition, augmentation, growth, supplement, enlargement, accretion, raise.

incur v. to incur debts: become liable for, assume, bring on, acquire, become subject to; arouse, incite, provoke, bring on oneself.

incurable adj. an incurable disease. an incurable optimist: beyond cure, having no remedy, irremediable; incorrigible, relentless, unflagging, inveterate, dyed-in-the-wool, hopeless.
Ant. curable, correctable, remediable.

incursion n. a military incursion over neighboring borders: invasion, foray, sortie, attack; assault, encroachment, infiltration, raid; forcible entering, push; advance.

indebted adj. 1 The store is indebted to the bank: under obligation, in debt, burdened with debt. 2 We are indebted to you for your support: obligated, bound, beholden, deeply appreciative, grateful, full of thanks.
Ant. 1 free and clear. 2 unobligated, unbeholden; ungrateful, unthankful.

indecent adj. 1 Talking business at the funeral seemed indecent: unseemly, improper, lacking common decency, rude, offensive, vulgar, in bad taste. 2 The indecent film was banned: immoral, immodest, obscene, pornographic, lewd, prurient, dirty, filthy, smutty.
Ant. 1, 2 decent. 1 proper, seemly, appropriate. 2 chaste, pure, modest, virtuous, moral.

indecisive adj. 1 The result was indecisive: not decisive, inconclusive, unsettled, indeterminate, doubtful, dubious, disputable, debatable; unclear, confusing. 2 An indecisive person makes a poor leader: irresolute, vacillating, hesitant, hesitating, wavering, uncertain, wishy-washy.
Ant. 1 decisive, conclusive, clear, certain. 2 decisive, resolute.

indecorous adj. indecorous behavior: immodest, unbecoming, unseemly, unfitting, improper, unsuitable, inappropriate, not in good taste, gross.
Ant. decorous, demure; proper, suitable.

indeed adv. The garden is indeed beautiful: in fact, truly, without question, certainly, for sure, veritably, in truth, undeniably, really, to be sure, positively, to tell the truth, in point of fact.

indefatigable adj. an indefatigable worker: tireless, inexhaustible, persevering, diligent, dogged, energetic, unflagging, untiring.

indefensible adj. an indefensible waste of money: inexcusable, beyond justification, unjustifiable, unpardonable, without reason, untenable.

Ant. defensible, justifiable, excusable, tenable.

indefinite adj. 1 The store will be closed for an indefinite period: undetermined, indeterminate, unknown, inexact. 2 an indefinite answer: unsettled, uncertain, indistinct, vague; dim, ill-defined, amorphous, indecisive, doubtful, tentative, ambiguous, unsure.
Ant. 1 definite, certain, known. 2 definite, certain, unambiguous.

indelible adj. The book left an indelible impression on me. an indelible stain: permanent, unforgettable, lasting, memorable; permanently fixed, fast, ineradicable, unerasable.

indelicate adj. 1 indelicate manners: coarse, crude, rude, unrefined. 2 an indelicate story: offensive, lacking good taste, indiscreet; off-color, immodest, indecent, vulgar, suggestive, lewd, risqué, obscene, coarse.
Ant. 1 delicate, refined, polite, polished. 2 decent, chaste.

indemnify v. The company indemnified me for the theft of my car: reimburse, repay, pay back, compensate, remunerate, recompense, make restitution, make good, rectify, make amends.

indentation n. The chef made indentations in the pie crust: cut, notch, incision, cavity, furrow, score; recess, concavity, niche, pocket, dent, pit, gouge, depression, nick.
Ant. bump, protruberance, projection.

independence n. The American colonies won their independence from England: emancipation, liberty, freedom; self-determination, self-government, self-reliance, autonomy.
Ant. dependence; subordination, dependency.

independent adj. 1 an independent thinker: self-reliant, on one's own, autonomous, self-directing, individualistic, uncoerced; unconstrained. 2 The United States became an independent country in 1776: free, self-governing, autonomous; self-determining. 3 The medical college is independent of the university: separate, not associated with, unattached to, distinct from, apart from, unconnected with, unallied.
Ant. 1 dependent; influenced, controlled, directed; subordinate.

indescribable adj. The beauty of the Grand Canyon is indescribable: beyond description, inexpressible, beyond words; overwhelming, unutterable.

indestructible adj. These plastic dishes are indestructible: unbreakable, damage-resistant, infrangible; enduring, permanent, everlasting, imperishable.

Ant. destructible, breakable, fragile.

indeterminate *adj. an indeterminate time:* unspecified, undetermined, unstipulated, uncertain, unfixed; unclear, obscure, vague, undefined; ambiguous, indefinite.

Ant. specified, definite, clear, certain, fixed.

indicate *v.* 1 *Her pallor indicates anemia:* be a sign of, be symptomatic of, show, designate, denote, imply, point to, suggest; evince, bespeak, reveal, signify, stand for. 2 *Indicate where the pain is:* point out, point to, specify. 3 *A barometer indicates air pressure:* show, make known, register, reveal, tell, establish, record.

indication *n. There was no indication that he would quit:* sign, hint, intimation, signal, manifestation, token, warning, evidence, mark, clue, suggestion, hint, portent, omen, mention.

indict *v. The grand jury indicted him:* arraign, accuse, charge, impute, cite; find an indictment against.

indifference *n.* 1 *cold indifference:* unconcern, absence of feeling, lack of interest, disinterest, neglect, inattention, impassiveness, impassivity, nonchalance, aloofness, insensibility, insensitivity, disdain, apathy, coldness. 2 *Religion is a matter of indifference to us:* unimportance, triviality, no import, insignificance.

Ant. 1 concern, warmth, attention, eagerness, caring. 2 importance, significance.

indifferent *adj.* 1 *The writer was indifferent to criticism:* unconcerned, not caring, impervious, uninterested, insusceptible, detached, unmindful, unmoved, cool. 2 *the actor's indifferent performance:* perfunctory, mediocre, undistinguished, uninspired, ordinary, so-so, rote, commonplace, middling, fair, passable, average; secondrate, rather poor.

Ant. 1 avid, eager; sensitive, susceptible, responsive, enthusiastic. 2 notable, remarkable, exceptional, superior, excellent.

indigenous *adj. Cotton is indigenous to the southern United States:* native, growing naturally, aboriginal, originating in, endemic, home-grown, domestic.

Ant. naturalized; exotic; foreign, alien.

indigent *adj. Many indigent people need government aid:* needy, destitute, poor, poverty-stricken, impoverished, penniless, moneyless.

Ant. wealthy, moneyed, rich, affluent.

indignant *adj. She was indignant at the criticism:* incensed, offended, angry, mad, infuriated, displeased, piqued, peeved, resentful, irate, riled, fuming; miffed, huffy, put out.

Ant. pleased, delighted.

indignation *n. Reports of political wrongdoing aroused public indignation:* resentment, displeasure, righteous anger, vexation, irritation, ire, choler, rage, wrath, fury, uproar.

Ant. calm, composure, complacency; approval.

indignity *n. The prisoners suffered many indignities:* abuse, insult, mistreatment, affront, humiliation.

Ant. dignity, honor, respect, courtesy.

indirect *adj.* 1 *an indirect route:* devious, roundabout, winding, rambling, circuitous, meandering, oblique, zigzag, digressive. 2 *an indirect outcome of the meeting:* incidental, unintentional, unintended; ancillary, secondary, derivative. 3 *an indirect answer:* evasive, oblique, digressive, circuitous; vague, hedging.

Ant. 1 direct, straight. 2 direct, primary. 3 direct, forthright, straightforward.

indiscreet *adj. Repeating a confidence is indiscreet:* imprudent, injudicious, improvident, unseemly; foolhardy, foolish, thoughtless, inconsiderate, unwise, careless; tactless, untactful, undiplomatic.

Ant. discreet, judicious, prudent; politic, tactful.

indiscriminate *adj.* 1 *an indiscriminate choice of friends:* undiscriminating, unchoosy, random, unselective, promiscuous, haphazard. 2 *an indiscriminate collection of artwork:* haphazard, random, unsystematic, disorganized, slapdash, jumbled, motley, aimless, chaotic; *Informal* higgledy-piggledy, hodgepodge.

indispensable *adj. A good worker is indispensable:* essential, crucial, vital, imperative, absolutely necessary, required, obligatory, mandatory, fundamental, basic.

Ant. dispensable, expendable, disposable.

indisposed *adj. I'm indisposed with a fever:* ailing, sickly, ill, laid up, slightly sick, taken ill, unwell.

Ant. healthy, hardy, hale, well.

indisputable *adj. She was the indisputable leader:* undeniable, irrefutable, incontestable, indubitable, incontrovertible, unquestionable; evident, obvious, unmistakable, definite, conclusive.

Ant. dubious, questionable, doubtful, iffy.

indistinct *adj. The sound was indistinct. The point of the book was indistinct:* muffled, vague, not distinct, unintelligible, unclear, weak, faint; obscure, ill-defined, indefinite, murky, nebulous, blurred, muddy;

uncertain, enigmatic, puzzling, hidden, indeterminate, ambiguous; confused.
Ant. distinct, clear, definite.

indistinguishable *adj.* 1 *One twin is indistinguishable from the other:* identical with, not distinguishable; a carbon copy of, *Informal* the spitting image of. 2 *The sign was indistinguishable in the fog:* indiscernible, unclear, imperceptible, indistinct, obscure.
Ant. 1 distinguishable, separate, different. 2 noticeable, apparent, distinct, clear.

individual *adj.* 1 *Students can apply for individual tutoring:* special, especial, separate, particular, exclusive, personal, private, independent, one's own, personalized. 2 *She has an individual way of dressing:* special, distinctive, unusual, original, personal, different, uncommon, unconventional, singular, characteristic, distinct, unique. —*n.* 3 *Everyone should be recognized as an individual:* person, somebody, single human being, distinct person, unique entity, autonomous being.
Ant. 1 general, group, collective. 2 conventional, ordinary, common, indistinct.

individuality *n. Individuality makes one interesting:* independent nature, uniqueness, distinction, particularity, singularity; unique character.

indolent *adj. The indolent worker was fired:* lazy, slothful, habitually idle, inactive, shiftless, sluggish, lethargic, listless.
Ant. industrious; busy; diligent, conscientious, energetic.

indomitable *adj. an indomitable spirit:* invincible, indefatigable, unconquerable, unyielding, staunch, steadfast, unwavering, resolute, dogged, unflinching, fearless, dauntless, unshrinking, intrepid, stalwart, courageous, undaunted.
Ant. yielding, weak, wavering, faltering, flinching, shrinking, cowardly.

indorse *v.* See ENDORSE.

indubitably *adv. Indubitably she will show up:* unquestionably, certainly, surely, without doubt, undoubtedly, for sure, for certain, doubtless, of course, with no question.

induce *v.* 1 *I was induced to vote for the bill:* coax, persuade, influence, spur, prevail upon, bring round, encourage, sway, win over, prevail on. 2 *Alcohol can induce drowsiness:* bring on, give rise to, lead to, occasion, cause, bring about, produce; motivate, effect, instigate, activate, provoke.
Ant. 1 dissuade, prevent, deter. 2 deter, stop, curb, suppress.

inducement *n. The biscuit was an inducement for the dog to perform:* incentive, enticement, allurement, spur, bait, stimulus,

motive, cause, reason, persuasion, instigation, attraction.
Ant. deterrent, discouragement.

induct *v. We inducted new members into our club:* initiate, instate, install, inaugurate, invest; conscript, enlist, draft.

indulge *v. The nurse indulged the child. He indulged his fondness for candy:* cater to, oblige, gratify, accommodate, give way to, yield to, pamper, coddle, pander to, humor, spoil.

indulgence *n.* 1 *Rich desserts are an indulgence:* luxury, self-indulgence, extravagance, excess, self-gratification, immoderation; dissipation, profligacy, debauchery. 2 *The pilot asked for the passengers' indulgence during the delay:* sufferance, understanding, tolerance, forgiveness, forbearance, patience, lenience, permissiveness, kindness, graciousness.

indulgent *adj. an indulgent parent:* lenient, tolerant, forbearing, humoring, forgiving, permissive, easygoing, complaisant, pampering, patient, yielding, obliging, benign, kind.
Ant. strict, stern, severe, harsh, unmerciful, demanding.

industrious *adj. an industrious employee:* hardworking, zealous, diligent, assiduous, busy, active, energetic.
Ant. idle, lazy, shiftless, indolent.

industry *n.* 1 *heavy industry:* business, commerce, manufacturing, trade. 2 *The clerk was rewarded for industry:* hard work, zeal, diligence, labor, assiduity, enterprise, energy, toil, assiduousness.

inebriated *adj. Both were too inebriated to drive:* drunk, under the influence, intoxicated, besotted, tipsy, *Slang* plastered, tight, high, loaded, three sheets to the wind, bombed, stoned, smashed, zonked, wasted.
Ant. sober.

ineffective *adj. an ineffective administrator:* of little use, futile, vain, inefficient, inept, unsatisfactory, unproductive; weak, inadequate, useless.
Ant. effective; efficient; useful, successful, satisfactory, capable, productive.

inefficient *adj. an inefficient system:* ineffective, ineffectual, unproductive, inadequate, wasteful, futile, pointless.
Ant. efficient, capable, effectual.

ineligible *adj. I was ineligible for the team:* unqualified, disqualified, not eligible, unentitled, unfit, unacceptable, unsuitable.
Ant. eligible, suitable, fit.

inept *adj.* 1 *an inept mechanic:* inefficient, incompetent, unskilled, unqualified, bungling, ineffective; awkward, clumsy. 2 *The speaker's inept comparison bewildered the* *audience:* out of place, pointless, inane, inappropriate, unsuitable, unfitting, foolish, senseless.

Ant. 1 efficient, skillful, competent, effective, adroit, able. 2 apt, appropriate, sensible.

inequality *n.* 1 *Women are fighting inequality in the business world:* unfairness, lack of equality, prejudice. 2 *the inequality of the two products:* difference, diversity, variableness, dissimilarity, unequalness, dissimilitude, disparity, divergence, unlikeness.

Ant. 1, 2 equality. 2 sameness, similarity, similitude, likeness.

inert *adj. He lay inert on the ground:* motionless, static, immobile, stationary, inactive, still, inanimate.

inevitable *adj. Traffic delays are inevitable:* inescapable, unavoidable, unpreventable; destined, predetermined, certain, sure to happen.

Ant. escapable, avoidable, preventable.

inexcusable *adj. Her rudeness was inexcusable:* unpardonable, unforgivable, indefensible, unjustifiable.

Ant. excusable, forgivable, justifiable, defensible.

inexorable *adj. The judge was inexorable:* unyielding, relentless, firm, inflexible, unbending, immovable, adamant, obdurate, uncompromising.

Ant. sympathetic, indulgent, compassionate.

inexpensive *adj. inexpensive meals:* low-priced, not expensive, popular-priced, reasonable, cheap, economical.

Ant. expensive, costly, high-priced.

inexperienced *adj. The crew was inexperienced:* unseasoned, unpracticed, uninitiated, untried, green; unaccustomed, unacquainted; unsophisticated, naive.

Ant. experienced, practiced, seasoned, accustomed; sophisticated, worldly, worldly-wise.

inexplicable *adj. The flying saucer sighting was inexplicable:* unexplainable, inscrutable, insolvable; unaccountable; mysterious, mystifying, baffling, puzzling, enigmatical.

Ant. explicable, explainable, understandable.

infallible *adj. The designer has an infallible eye for color. an infallible plan:* faultless, flawless, unerring, incapable of error, unfailing, perfect, foolproof, surefire.

Ant. fallible, questionable, dubious, untrustworthy, doubtful, unreliable, unsure.

infamous *adj. Bluebeard is infamous. infamous behavior:* notorious, disreputable, villainous, nefarious, outrageous, dishonorable, vile, scandalous, shameful; foul,

heinous, monstrous, evil, wicked, disgraceful, base, odious, detestable, abhorrent, abominable, low, iniquitous; corrupt, scurrilous, immoral, sinful.

Ant. illustrious; splendid, sublime, honorable, noble, good.

infamy *n. The attack on Pearl Harbor is "a day that will live in infamy":* dishonor, shame, disgrace, ignominy, disrepute, discredit; scandal; evil, wickedness, villainy, corruption, notoriety.

infant *n. infants in arms:* baby, babe, child, newborn, toddler, nursling.

infantile *adj. Temper tantrums are infantile:* babyish, childish, childlike, juvenile, infantlike.

Ant. mature, adult, grown-up.

infatuated *adj. I am infatuated with her:* enamored, enchanted, bewitched by, spellbound by, having a crush on, smitten by, obsessed by, entranced by, captivated by, enraptured by, enthralled by.

infectious *adj.* 1 *an infectious disease:* contagious, catching, communicable, virulent, catchable. 2 *The children's gaiety was infectious:* catching, contagious; irresistible, captivating.

Ant. 1 noncontagious, noncommunicable.

infer *v. She inferred that he was lying:* deduce, reckon, reason, guess, conjecture, speculate, gather, consider probable, suppose, surmise, presume.

inferior *adj.* 1 *Brass is inferior to gold. A private is inferior to a sergeant:* of lower quality than, less valuable than; lower in rank than, of less importance than, subordinate, subservient, secondary, junior, subsidiary. 2 *inferior food:* poor, substandard, low-quality, low-grade, second-rate; indifferent, mediocre, *Informal* not up to snuff.

Ant. 1 superior; senior. 2 superior, first-rate, prime, excellent.

infernal *adj.* 1 *the infernal world of Satan:* hellish, Hadean, Stygian, lower, nether. 2 *He has an infernal temper:* damnable, hellish, devilish, horrible, fiendish, diabolical, demoniacal, awful, terrible, vicious, malicious, atrocious, vile, abominable, horrendous.

Ant. 1 angelic, heavenly.

infertile *adj. The soil was infertile:* barren, unfruitful, sterile, unproductive, nonproductive, fallow, fruitless, impotent, unprolific, infecund.

Ant. fertile, fruitful, productive, fecund.

infidel *n. a missionary to the infidels:* unbeliever, heathen, pagan, idolater, nonbeliever; atheist, agnostic; savage, barbarian.

Ant. believer.

infidelity *n.* 1 *Infidelity was the cause of the divorce:* adultery, unfaithfulness; betrayal, perfidy, disloyalty. 2 *Infidelity to the organization's tenets will not be tolerated:* nonobservance, nonadherence, breach, disregard, transgression, violation, infraction.
Ant. fidelity, faithfulness, loyalty.

infinite *adj. The universe seems infinite. infinite patience.* boundless, limitless, unlimited; illimitable, unbounded, endless, without end; enormous, great, immense, tremendous; immeasurable, vast, measureless.
Ant. small, little, limited; finite, limited.

infinitesimal *adj. an infinitesimal amount:* tiny, insignificant, microscopic, imperceptible, small, diminutive, minute, wee; inappreciable, negligible.
Ant. enormous, vast, huge, large.

infinity *n. from now throughout infinity:* boundless time, eternity, eternal time, infinitude, endlessness, forever, perpetuity, everlastingness.

infirm *adj. I was too infirm to work:* weak, feeble, frail, weakened, unsound, ailing, decrepit, enfeebled, ailing, sickly, ill, debilitated, strengthless.
Ant. hale; strong, healthy, sound.

inflame *v. The agitator tried to inflame the mob:* excite, arouse, provoke, rouse, fire, excite the passions of, incite, stir up, agitate; rile, incense, enrage, madden.
Ant. calm, pacify, quiet, suppress.

inflammable *adj.* 1 *inflammable liquids:* flammable, combustible, ignitable, incendiary. 2 *an inflammable temper:* fiery, volatile, excitable, easily roused, incendiary, precipitate, overhasty.
Ant. 1 nonflammable, uninflammable. 2 placid, calm, easy, even.

inflammatory *adj. inflammatory remarks:* fiery, incendiary, rabble-rousing, enraging, inciting, rabid, arousing, intemperate, rebellious, mutinous, demagogic; combustible, inflammable.
Ant. soothing, calming, pacifying.

inflexible *adj.* 1 *Marble is an inflexible material:* unbending, unyielding, rigid, hard, firm, not flexible, fixed, taut, stiff, unmalleable. 2 *The committee was inflexible in its opposition to our request:* unchangeable, rigid, unyielding, unbending, obstinate, obdurate, intractable, stubborn, pigheaded, mulish, determined, adamant, resolute, uncompromising, implacable, unwavering, immovable; stringent, firm, immutable.
Ant. 1 flexible, elastic, resilient, supple, pliable, pliant, malleable, ductile. 2 flexible, changeable, compromising, irresolute, undetermined.

inflict *v. The hurricane inflicted severe damage on the island:* visit upon, impose, administer, bring to bear, perpetrate, wreak.

influence *n.* 1 *Special-interest groups have too much influence on government:* weight, sway, power, effect, pressure, hold; authority, domination, dominion, control, prestige; *Slang* clout. —*v.* 2 *He influenced me to accept the job:* induce, persuade, act upon, move, prompt, provoke, stir, inspire, incite, arouse, sway, incline, dispose, guide; bring pressure to bear on.

influential *adj. The senator was influential in changing the law:* effective, instrumental, consequential, effectual, powerful, important, significant, momentous, potent; leading, moving, inspiring, activating.
Ant. uninfluential, weak, unpersuasive, ineffectual, powerless, unimportant.

influx *n. an influx of warm air:* inflow, inundation, flowing in, inpouring, ingress, entry, arrival, converging.
Ant. outflow, outpouring, exodus.

inform *v.* 1 *Inform the prisoner of his rights:* tell, apprise, notify, let know, give notice to, advise, make known to, report to, acquaint, send word to, disclose to, communicate to, declare to, enlighten, edify, serve notice on, announce to, indicate to. 2 *Who informed on the killer?:* furnish incriminating evidence, report an offense, tell on, tattle; *Slang* snitch, squeal, fink.

informal *adj. The party will be informal:* casual, without formality, unceremonious, familiar, unofficial, not formal, easygoing, offhand.
Ant. ceremonious, formal, official.

information *n. Information can be found at the library:* data, news, report, facts, evidence, bulletin, communiqué, tidings, account; notice, intelligence, enlightenment; briefing, notification.

informer *n. The informer's identity was kept secret:* police informant, betrayer, tattler; *Slang* stool pigeon, squealer, snitcher, fink, stoolie, rat, canary.

infraction *n. a speeding infraction:* violation, breaking of a law, lawbreaking, infringement, breach, transgression, disobedience, unobservance, nonobservance; insubordination.

infrequent *adj. Her asthma attacks are infrequent:* occasional, rare, seldom, not regular, few and far between, sporadic, uncommon, unusual, unique, few, spasmodic, fitful.
Ant. frequent, usual, customary, ordinary, common, habitual.

infringe *v.* 1 *to infringe an author's copyright:* violate, transgress, break, commit an infraction of, disobey, commit a breach of. 2 *Don't infringe on my territory:* trespass, encroach, intrude, invade, overstep.

infuriate *v. His rudeness infuriated me:* anger, make angry, inflame, madden, enrage, rile, incense, provoke, make furious, vex, offend, aggravate, irritate.

infuse *v. Infuse your work with some enthusiasm!:* instill, inspire, imbue, pour into, impart to, introduce into, implant, inculcate, introject.

ingenious *adj. an ingenious escape:* clever, cunning, artful, inventive, masterful, deft, adroit, shrewd, crafty, resourceful, original. *Ant.* unoriginal, pedestrian, unimaginative, uninventive.

ingenuity *n. She showed ingenuity in solving the problem:* cleverness, inventiveness, resourcefulness, imagination, ingeniousness, imaginativeness, flair, cunning, shrewdness.

inglorious *adj. an inglorious deed:* disgraceful, dishonorable, shameful, ignominious, ignoble, contemptible, scandalous, shocking, outrageous. *Ant.* admirable, commendable, praiseworthy.

ingrained *adj. an ingrained fear of heights:* inborn, inbred, inherent, innate, deepseated, constitutional, intrinsic, inveterate.

ingratiating *adj.* 1 *an ingratiating manner:* winning, engaging, captivating, likable, magnetic, attractive, appealing, persuasive, charming, amiable, pleasing, affable. 2 *His smile is sickeningly ingratiating:* unctuous, gushing, fulsome, smarmy, obsequious; self-serving, presumptuous. *Ant.* 1 forbidding, austere, unattractive, unappealing, abrasive.

ingredient *n. Hard work is a vital ingredient of success:* element, part, component, constituent; factor, aspect.

inhabit *v. Does anyone inhabit the island?:* reside in, live in, dwell in, occupy; people, populate, settle.

inhabitant *n. the inhabitants of an island:* resident, native, dweller, occupant, inhabiter, denizen, inmate, tenant, occupier; citizen, settler.

inhale *v. to inhale deeply:* breathe in, draw into the lungs; snuff, sniff, respire. *Ant.* exhale, expire.

inherent *adj. Freedom of religion is an inherent part of the Bill of Rights:* essential, innate, inseparable, hereditary, native, intrinsic, inborn, inveterate, natural, inbred, constitutional, inalienable. *Ant.* foreign, alien, extrinsic.

inherit *v. to inherit a fortune:* fall heir to, come into, be bequeathed, be willed, be left, become heir to.

inheritance *n. A large inheritance:* legacy, bequest, bequeathal, estate, heritage, endowment; birthright, patrimony.

inhibit *v. The medicine inhibited the spread of the disease:* hold back, arrest, hinder, impede, restrain, suppress, check, block, control, curb, constrain, restrict; forbid, prohibit, bar. *Ant.* allow, let, permit; encourage, abet.

inhibition Often **inhibitions**. *n. I had no inhibitions about disagreeing with my boss:* mental reservation, guardedness, self-consciousness, mental block, holding back, reserve, restriction, constraint, restraint, impediment, obstruction, blockage, check.

inhospitable *adj. Our welcome was most inhospitable:* aloof, unfriendly, unsociable, cool, distant, standoffish; unkind, uncongenial, ungracious, discourteous, inconsiderate. *Ant.* cordial, genial, congenial.

inhuman *adj. inhuman treatment:* cruel, unfeeling, merciless, pitiless, heartless, brutal, barbaric, cold-blooded, savage, hardhearted, brutish. *Ant.* human, humane; benevolent, kind, compassionate, tender.

inhumanity *n. War is an example of inhumanity:* cruelty, savagery, brutality, ruthlessness, barbarity, brutishness, coldbloodedness, heartlessness. *Ant.* humaneness, kindness.

inimitable *adj. the painter's inimitable style:* matchless, unmatched, incomparable, unique, unparalleled, unequaled, unsurpassed, nonpareil, unrivaled, unexcelled. *Ant.* common, ordinary, imitable.

iniquity *n.* 1 *the iniquity of false testimony:* unfairness, gross injustice, dishonesty, violation of one's rights, immorality, inequity, unjustness. 2 *Iniquities should not go unpunished:* wickedness, wrongdoing, evil, evildoing, sin, transgression, infamy, villainy; abomination, sinfulness, depravity, corruption, immorality, vice. *Ant.* 1 justice, fairness, integrity. 2 virtue, honesty, goodness, morality.

initial *adj. The initial move must be to get the board's approval:* first, starting, beginning, opening, commencing, introductory, inaugural; original, germinal, primal. *Ant.* last, ultimate, final, concluding.

initiate *v.* 1 *to initiate a fund-raising drive:* begin, start, set going, open, enter upon, commence, launch, originate, institute, found, kick off, inaugurate, establish. 2 *The Rotarians initiated 12 new members:* induct, admit with special rites, inaugurate, install, take in, invest. **3** *A year in Italy initiated her into the art world:* introduce, familiarize with, acquaint with; accustom to.

Ant. **1** consummate; conclude, finish, end, complete. **2** reject, expel.

initiation *n. the initiation of hostilities:* commencement, initiating, opening, beginning, genesis, inception, outset, onset, start, starting, beginning, introduction, inauguration. *Ant.* end, finish, completion, termination, close.

initiative *n.* **1** *The mayor took the initiative in closing the park:* lead, first move, beginning step, introductory act. **2** *a woman of great initiative:* enterprise, leadership, forcefulness, dynamism, originality, creativity, power to begin, *Slang* get-up-and-go.

inject *v. Try to inject some life into the party:* insert, put, interject, introduce, infuse, imbue, instill.

injure *v. The boy injured his shoulder. A scandal injured my reputation:* harm, do injury to, wound, damage, do harm to, cause harm to, afflict, hurt, mar; bruise, deface; wrong, abuse, maltreat, offend, misuse, sting, sully, stain, malign, debase, spoil, blemish.

Ant. heal; aid, help, assist, benefit.

injurious *adj. Smoking is injurious to the lungs:* hurtful, damaging, harmful, detrimental, destructive, deleterious.

Ant. beneficial, helpful, advantageous, salutary.

injury *n. a head injury. The harsh review was an injury to the singer's pride:* hurt, harm, wound, damage, affliction; blow, injustice, indignity, affront; detraction, impairment, disservice.

injustice *n. a campaign against injustice:* unjustness, unfairness, inequality, bias, prejudice, inequity; unjust act, wrong, disservice, injury, wrongdoing, unfair treatment, tyranny.

Ant. justice, equity, fairness, fair play, impartiality.

inkling *n. Did you have any inkling they were coming?:* idea, vague idea, hint, indication, tip, clue, suggestion, glimmer, notion; intimation.

inn *n. We'll find a cozy inn to stay in:* public house, lodge, hotel, motel, lodging house, country hotel, pension, hospice, hostelry, tavern.

innate *adj. an innate genius for music:* native, natural, inborn, inherent, inbred, instinctive, intuitive, natural, intrinsic, congenital, constitutional, inherited, hereditary, indigenous.

Ant. acquired, learned, cultivated.

inner *adj.* **1** *the inner part of the forest:* interior, inward, inside, internal, central, middle. **2** *to seek inner peace:* spiritual, psychological, mental, psychic, emotional.

Ant. **1** outer, exterior, external, outermost.

innermost *adj. her innermost thoughts:* most personal, most intimate, most private, deep-rooted; farthest inward, deepest, inmost.

Ant. surface, superficial.

innocence *n.* **1** *the defendant's innocence:* guiltlessness, freedom from moral wrong, inculpability, blamelessness, sinlessness, incorruption; chastity, purity. **2** *the innocence of a child:* simplicity, artlessness, ingenuousness, guilelessness, freshness.

Ant. **1** guilt; sinfulness, impurity, corruption. **2** artfulness, guile, cunning, wiliness, disingenuousness, worldliness.

innocent *adj.* **1** *The jury found the defendant innocent:* guiltless, inculpable, blameless, faultless, free from moral wrong, sinless, unimpeachable. **2** *Jill is an innocent soul:* guileless, unsuspicious, naive, unworldly, unsophisticated, artless, ingenuous, childlike; honest, uncorrupt, uncorrupted, spotless, unblemished, undefiled, unstained, unsullied, virtuous, pure; virginal, chaste. **3** *an innocent question:* meaning no harm, harmless, unmalicious, innocuous, inoffensive, unoffending. *—n.* **4** *The fox's trick was to play the innocent:* naïf, unsophisticated person, artless one, *(fem.)* ingénue.

Ant. **1** guilty, culpable, responsible; immoral, sinful, unlawful, wicked, evil, impure. **2** worldly, sophisticated, scheming; corrupt, sullied. **3** harmful, malicious, offensive.

innocuous *adj. innocuous gossip:* harmless, not damaging, not injurious, innocent, inoffensive; meaningless, vapid, insipid, pointless, empty, trite, banal.

Ant. harmful, damaging, injurious, offensive, malicious.

innovation *n. the innovation of space flight:* introduction, establishment, inauguration, commencement; departure from the old, drastic change; novelty, latest thing.

innuendo *n. The gossip column was full of innuendos:* insinuation, intimation, oblique hint, veiled allusion, sly suggestion, implication, inference, imputation.

innumerable *adj. the innumerable stars in the sky:* countless, myriad, numberless, multitudinous, unnumbered.

inoffensive *adj. The odor is strong but inoffensive:* harmless, unobjectionable, unoffending, innocuous.

Ant. offensive, harmful, objectionable, offending.

inopportune *adj. an inopportune time:* inconvenient, untimely, ill-timed, inappropriate, unpropitious, unsuitable, unseasonable; awkward, troublesome; unfavorable, disadvantageous, inauspicious, unfortunate, ill-advised.

Ant. opportune, timely, convenient, appropriate, suitable, favorable.

inordinate *adj. an inordinate amount of money:* excessive, immoderate, extravagant, disproportionate, undue, unreasonable, unconscionable, exorbitant, extreme, intemperate, unnecessary, needless, uncalled-for, irrational; outrageous, disgraceful, shocking.

Ant. moderate; reasonable, sensible.

inquire *v.* 1 *The pilot inquired about the weather conditions:* ask, query, seek information, question, make inquiry. 2 *The reporter inquired into the rumors of fraud:* investigate, probe, study, look into, search, track down, *Informal* check out.

Ant. 1 reply, answer, respond.

inquiry Also **enquiry** *n. The murder inquiry was handled by the police:* investigation, examination, questioning, probe, study, research, analysis; query, question, interrogation.

inquisitive *adj.* 1 *She's bright and inquisitive:* eager for knowledge, intellectually curious, inquiring, questioning. 2 *an inquisitive gossip:* prying, interfering, meddling, overcurious, intrusive, meddlesome, snooping; *Informal* snoopy, nosy.

Ant. 1 incurious, uninterested, apathetic.

insane *adj.* 1 *The psychiatrists declared the killer insane. to be insane with jealousy:* mentally deranged, not sane, not of sound mind, mad, crazed, crazy, lunatic, unsound, demented, maniacal, out of one's mind; raving, frenzied, wild, berserk. 2 *It's insane to fly in this weather:* idiotic, senseless, unreasonable, foolish, dumb, imbecilic, crazy; imprudent, absurd, ridiculous; bizarre, eccentric.

Ant. 1, 2 sane; sensible, wise, prudent, reasonable.

insanity *n.* 1 *Insanity ran in the family:* mental illness, madness, mental disorder, derangement, lunacy. 2 *Few people dispute the insanity of nuclear war:* idiocy, senselessness, foolishness, absurdity, stupidity, madness, craziness, folly, unreasonableness.

Ant. sanity.

insatiable *adj. an insatiable appetite:* unap-

peasable, voracious, ravenous, gluttonous, unsatisfiable, implacable.

Ant. satiable, appeasable, satisfiable.

inscrutable *adj. The Sphinx of Greek mythology was inscrutable:* unknowable, incomprehensible, indecipherable, not easily understood, unfathomable; mysterious, mystifying, perplexing, baffling, inexplicable, enigmatic; hidden, concealed, veiled.

Ant. obvious, clear, manifest, evident, patent; comprehensible, understandable; explicable.

insecure *adj.* 1 *The battalion's position was insecure:* unsafe, endangered, in danger, vulnerable, exposed, unprotected, risky, perilous, precarious. 2 *She is insecure about her ability to do the job:* uncertain, doubtful, beset by doubt, not confident, unsure, in a state of uncertainty, full of misgivings.

Ant. 1 secure, safe, invulnerable, protected, secure, confident, certain, assured.

insecurity *n.* 1 *a feeling of insecurity:* lack of assurance, lack of confidence, uncertainty, self-doubt, doubt, doubtfulness, apprehensiveness. 2 Often **insecurities** *The insecurities of the venture kept investors away:* peril, hazard, danger, risk.

Ant. 1 security, assurance, confidence. 2 safeness, sureness, certainty.

insensitive *adj. insensitive to the feelings of others:* unaware of, not sensitive, indifferent, unconcerned, uncompassionate; hardened, unfeeling, callous, thick-skinned, cold; not capable of feeling, impervious, impassive, numb.

Ant. sensitive, compassionate, susceptible, open, thin-skinned.

inseparable *adj. The two friends are inseparable:* constantly together, always in each other's company, attached; incapable of being parted, indivisible.

Ant. separable, unattached.

insert *v. Insert the key in the lock. I inserted a comment in the margin:* place in, put in, set in, imbed, inject, inset, implant, put between, wedge in, push in, introduce, interpose, interject, enter, add.

Ant. extract, disengage, withdraw, remove.

inside *n.* 1 *the inside of the cabinet:* interior, inner part, inner space, interior part, inner surface, inner side. —*adj.* 2 *The lead horse was on the inside track:* inner, innermost, inmost, inward; internal, interior. 3 *to have inside information:* private, confidential, secret, intimate, internal.

Ant. 1 outside, exterior. 2 outside, outer, exterior, outermost, external. 3 public, open.

insidious *adj. an insidious plan:* treacherous, deceitful, guileful, crafty, tricky, sly, wily, cunning, foxy, artful, contriving, underhanded, perfidious, crooked, shady, designing; sneaky; falsehearted, disingenuous; undercover, furtive, clandestine, covert, concealed, disguised; pernicious, deleterious.

Ant. forthright, ingenuous, open, honest, innocuous, harmless.

insight *n. The teacher had unusual insight into children's emotions:* perception, understanding, apprehension, innate knowledge, discernment, intuition, cognition, perspicacity, perceptiveness, comprehension.

insignia *n. Sew the insignia onto the uniform:* emblem, badge, badge of office, mark, decoration, patch, sign.

insignificant *adj. The problem was insignificant:* unimportant, petty, negligible, trivial, of no consequence, inconsequential, having little meaning, paltry, nugatory, of no moment, small, trifling, picayune, meaningless, meager, irrelevant, immaterial, nonessential, niggling, beneath consideration, piddling.

Ant. significant, important, momentous, meaningful, essential; relevant, material.

insincere *adj. an insincere offer:* hypocritical, dishonest, deceitful, disingenuous, two-faced, untruthful, untrue, false, guileful, disingenuous, fraudulent, devious, lying, evasive, equivocal, double-dealing.

Ant. sincere, honest, candid, truthful.

insinuate *v.* 1 *The article insinuated that the fighter was bribed:* imply, suggest, hint slyly, intimate. 2 *Social climbers insinuate themselves into groups:* ingratiate, worm one's way, gently incorporate, introduce subtly, wheedle, inject, insert.

insipid *adj.* 1 *an insipid play:* uninteresting, pointless, dull, characterless, banal, bland, boring, trite, vapid, inane, drab, prosaic, jejune, lifeless, zestless, commonplace. 2 *The soup was insipid:* tasteless, savorless, vapid, unappetizing.

Ant. 1 interesting, provocative, stimulating, piquant. 2 pungent, savory, flavorful, tasty, appetizing.

insist *v.* 1 *She insisted she heard someone in the house:* maintain, contend, claim, hold, assert, aver, take a firm stand, persist. 2 *The doctor insisted that I stop smoking:* demand, advise firmly, urge, lay down the law, require, command, be emphatic, admonish.

Ant. 1 deny. 2 ask, request.

insolence *n. She refused to put up with the child's insolence:* insulting rudeness, impertinence, disrespect, disobedience; overbearing contempt, overweening pride, lordliness, arrogance, disdain, haughtiness,

imperiousness, superciliousness, presumption, impoliteness, brazenness, effrontery, gall, impudence.

Ant. deference, politeness, humility, mannerliness.

insolent *adj. An insolent child needs discipline:* disrespectful, insulting, impertinent, rude, discourteous, impolite, impudent, unmannerly, audacious, brazen, nervy, arrogant, presumptuous, defiant, fresh, haughty, supercilious, disdainful, contemptuous.

Ant. respectful, deferential; courteous, polite, civil.

insolvent *adj. We were insolvent and had to declare bankruptcy:* penniless, unable to pay one's debts, destitute, ruined, bankrupt, impoverished; *Informal* broke.

Ant. solvent, wealthy, rich.

insouciant *adj. Your insouciant air always lifts my spirits:* lighthearted, happy-go-lucky, carefree, easygoing, buoyant, untroubled, jaunty, breezy, devil-may-care, whimsical, capricious.

Ant. troubled, careworn, perturbed, uneasy.

inspect *v. Inspect the tires. Will the auditor inspect the books?:* examine, scrutinize, look over carefully, look carefully at; investigate, observe, eye; scan, study, survey, probe.

inspiration *n.* 1 *The painter's inspiration came from nature:* incentive, stimulus, influence, incitement, motivation, motive, prompting, spur, encouragement. 2 *He had a sudden inspiration:* flash, creative thought, idea, flight of fancy, revelation.

inspire *v.* 1 *Shakespeare has inspired generations of playwrights:* stimulate to creation, be an ideal for, fill with life or strength, influence, impel, motivate, prompt, occasion, encourage, embolden, fire, hearten, quicken; cause. 2 *A fair employer inspires loyalty:* arouse, rouse, enkindle, engender, encourage, stimulate, prompt, induce, stir, excite, give rise to, provoke, cause, occasion.

Ant. stifle, squelch, discourage.

instability *n. Instability makes one a poor job risk:* unstableness, lack of stability, insecurity, inconstancy, vacillation, unsteadiness, irresolution, indecision, wavering, changeability, changeableness, inconsistency.

Ant. stability, security, constancy.

install Also **instal** *v.* 1 *The building installed a new boiler:* place in service, lodge, establish, station, set in place, locate, position, situate, move in. 2 *The club installed new officers:* introduce into office, induct, invest, instate, receive, initiate, inaugurate; seat, crown, ordain.

installment *n.* **1** *How many installments did it take to pay off the loan? The first installment of the book was exciting:* payment, successive portion; section, fragment, part, unit, division, segment, issue. **2** *The installment of the phone didn't take long:* installing, installation, establishment, stationing, placing, locating.

instance *n. I can't think of an instance when she was unfair:* example, illustration, case, time, occasion, sample.

instant *n.* **1** *It was over in an instant:* split second, moment, minute; twinkling, jiffy, flash, trice. **2** *the instant we met:* specific moment, very minute, second. —*adj.* **3** *an instant reply:* immediate, quick, prompt, instantaneous; sudden.

Ant. **1** eon, age, eternity. **3** delayed, slow.

instantaneous *adj. The explosion was instantaneous:* immediate, sudden, happening in an instant, imperceptibly fast, prompt, direct; quick as a flash, speedy, swift.

Ant. delayed; slow, gradual.

instantly *adv. I want the job done instantly!:* at once; without delay, instantaneously, immediately, promptly, directly, quickly; right now.

Ant. later, in the future; at one's leisure.

instigate *v. to instigate a rebellion:* provoke, urge; incite, start, begin, initiate, spur, goad, rouse, prompt, stimulate, foment, stir up, kindle, set in motion.

Ant. repress, quell, quash, restrain, stop, suppress.

instill Also **instil** *v. to instill a love of music in children:* impart, introduce gradually, inculcate, teach, implant, inspire, induce; sow the seeds of.

instinct *n.* **1** *Instinct led the pigeons back to the roost:* inbred behavior, natural tendency, native aptitude, inborn drive; blind knowledge, intuition. **2** *an instinct for saying the right thing:* aptitude, gift, genius, faculty, intuition, knack, natural inclination, proclivity, predisposition.

instinctive *adj. The will to survive is instinctive:* innate, inherent, inborn, inbred, intuitive, natural, native; involuntary, spontaneous, automatic, impulsive.

Ant. learned, acquired, voluntary.

institute *v.* **1** *to institute a new agency:* establish, begin, found, originate, set up, bring into being, organize; start, initiate, inaugurate, introduce, put into effect, undertake, commence. —*n.* **2** *the Institute for Chinese Studies:* institution, school, college,

academy; establishment; association, organization, society, foundation.

Ant. **1** abolish, terminate, conclude, close, finish, complete.

institution *n.* **1** *The institution of slavery was once widespread:* custom, established practice, convention; rite, ritual, habit, usage, fixture. **2** *a financial institution:* company, organization, establishment, association, organized society, foundation. **3** *Our city boasts many excellent institutions:* institute, school, academy, college, university, seminary. **4** *He should be locked up in an institution:* lunatic asylum, madhouse, mental hospital, *Slang* nuthouse, bughouse; prison.

instruct *v.* **1** *A private tutor instructed the athlete:* teach, tutor, educate, school, train, indoctrinate, guide, coach. **2** *Instruct the passengers on customs regulations:* notify, apprise, brief, advise, acquaint, inform, enlighten.

instruction *n.* **1** *the instruction of students:* instructing, teaching, education, training, tutoring, tutelage, indoctrination. **2** Usually **instructions** *The instructions for assembling the toy are clear:* direction, information, guideline, explanation, advice; lesson.

instructor *n. a French instructor:* teacher, pedagogue, coach, professor, tutor, trainer, lecturer, schoolteacher; mentor, counsel, guide.

instrument *n.* **1** *surgical instruments:* implement, tool, device, appliance, apparatus, equipment, contrivance, machine, mechanism; gadget. **2** *A police force is an instrument for keeping law and order:* agency, means, medium, vehicle, tool; instrumentality; expedient.

instrumental *adj. He was instrumental in solving the problem:* helpful, useful, effective, effectual, contributory, valuable, conducive, assisting; decisive, crucial, vital, essential.

Ant. ineffectual, useless; insignificant, negligible.

insubordinate *adj. insubordinate children:* disobedient, refractory, insolent, defiant, intractable, recalcitrant, unruly, rebellious, fractious, disorderly, ungovernable.

Ant. obedient, submissive, obsequious.

insubstantial *adj.* **1** *The experience seemed as insubstantial as a dream:* unreal, immaterial, intangible, bodiless; baseless, groundless; imaginary, apparitional; ethereal. **2** *The chair is too insubstantial to hold an adult:* slight, frail, flimsy, weak, delicate, fragile; unsound, unstable. **3** *The donation was insubstantial:* modest, trifling, paltry, small, inconsiderable, trivial, piddling.

Ant. 1–3 substantial. 1 real, material, tangible. 2 sturdy, strong, stable. 3 large, great, considerable.

insufferable *adj. an insufferable bore:* unendurable, intolerable, unbearable; dreadful, detestable, disgusting.

Ant. tolerable, bearable; pleasant, pleasing, ingratiating.

insufficient *adj. insufficient funds:* inadequate, deficient, wanting, not enough; unsatisfactory.

Ant. sufficient, adequate, enough; satisfactory.

insult *v.* 1 *The student purposely insulted the teacher:* treat with contempt, be rude to, offend, treat insolently, scorn, deride, be discourteous to. —*n.* 2 *His patronizing words were an insult:* affront, slight, offense, indignity, rudeness, discourtesy, outrage; cheek, impudence.

Ant. compliment.

insulting *adj. The criticism was unnecessarily insulting:* rude, discourteous, impolite, disrespectful, uncivil, insolent, offensive.

insurgent *n.* 1 *Insurgents overthrew the government:* rebel, mutineer, insurrectionist, renegade, revolter, revolutionist. —*adj.* 2 *Insurgent activities will be dealt with harshly:* revolutionary, rebellious, mutinous, dissident; insubordinate, disobedient.

Ant. 1 loyalist. 2 obedient, loyal.

insurmountable *adj. The difficulties seem insurmountable:* incapable of being overcome, too great, hopeless; unconquerable, unbeatable.

Ant. surmountable.

insurrection *n. a prison insurrection:* revolt, rebellion, revolution, mutiny, uprising.

intact *adj. The vase was still intact:* undamaged, in one piece, whole, unbroken, complete; untouched, unimpaired, unharmed, unhurt, uninjured.

Ant. damaged, injured; broken.

intangible *adj.* 1 *Love is intangible:* incapable of being touched, immaterial, abstract, ethereal, insubstantial, impalpable, imperceptible. 2 *An intangible feeling of disaster filled the room:* vague, elusive, fleeting, evanescent, transient, fugitive, imperceptible, shadowy. —*n.* 3 *The plan is full of intangibles:* abstraction, imponderable, unpredictable happening, unforeseen turn of events.

Ant. 1, 2 tangible, palpable, material, physical.

integral *adj.* 1 *The hedge forms an integral part of the landscaping:* essential, necessary, indispensable; component, constituent, inherent, basic, requisite. 2 *The couple*

felt their life was integral without children: fulfilled, fulfilling, whole, entire, full, complete, intact, finished, rounded, well-rounded.

Ant. 1 unessential, unimportant, unnecessary. 2 lacking, incomplete, deficient.

integrate *v.* 1 *Integrate the reports into one long memo:* blend, combine, amalgamate, merge, unify, fuse, unite. 2 *The city integrated all public facilities:* make available to every race; open for use by all; desegregate.

Ant. 1 separate, divide. 2 segregate.

integration *n.* 1 *the integration of all our ideas into one plan:* combination, combining, blending, fusion, synthesis, union. 2 *racial integration:* desegregation, assimilation.

Ant. 1 separation. 2 segregation, separation, apartheid.

integrity *n.* 1 *His integrity is unquestioned:* honesty, probity, moral stature, principle, character; virtue, decency, morality. 2 *The integrity of a building depends upon a sound foundation:* soundness; unimpaired condition, reliability, completeness; wholeness, strength, unity, coherence, cohesion.

Ant. 1 duplicity, corruption, dishonesty, immorality. 2 flimsiness, fragility, unsoundness.

intellect *n.* 1 *Our intellect separates us from the beasts:* intelligence, mentality, mental power, power of thinking, reasoning faculty, cognitive power, *Informal* brains; sense, mind. 2 *I'm not much of an intellect:* thinker, intellectual, *Slang* brain.

Ant. 1 emotion, instinct; muscle. 2 idiot, moron.

intellectual *adj.* 1 *intellectual achievements:* cerebral, of the mind, using the intellect, mental; abstract; academic, scholarly. 2 *an intellectual student:* intelligent, scholarly, studious; *Informal* bookish, brainy; rational. —*n.* 3 *This can be understood only by an intellectual:* intellect, person interested in ideas; thinker, academic, scholar; sage, highbrow; *Slang* brain, longhair, egghead.

Ant. 1 physical; emotional. 2 unlearned, ignorant, stupid. 3 lowbrow, idiot, moron.

intelligence *n.* 1 *Her intelligence enlivened the discussion:* intellect, mental power, comprehension, understanding, mental skill, power of reasoning, wisdom, sagacity, perspicacity, *Informal* brains. 2 *Intelligence of a secret attack came over the wireless:* information, news, knowledge, advice, notice, report, notification.

Ant. 1 ignorance, stupidity.

intelligent *adj. an intelligent person. an intelligent question:* thoughtful, thinking, bright, smart, clearheaded, sensible, sage, wise, perspicacious, perceptive, brilliant, keen, quick, sagacious, quick-witted, prudent, astute; canny, sharp, shrewd, *Slang* brainy.

Ant. unintelligent; foolish, stupid, ignorant, dumb.

intelligentsia *n. The dictator jailed the intelligentsia:* educated class, intellectuals, academic community.

intelligible *adj. I wish his books were more intelligible:* understandable, clear, comprehensible, coherent, lucid, apparent, evident, obvious, unambiguous.

intend *v. What do you intend to do today?:* plan, aim, contemplate, have in mind, mean, propose, aspire, expect, wish, project.

intense *adj.* 1 *intense heat:* extreme, very great, concentrated, acute, sharp, strong, powerful, forceful, considerable, forcible, potent, violent, keen. 2 *an intense love of art:* fervent, passionate, ardent, strong, powerful, deep, vehement, burning, deeply felt.

Ant. 1 weak, mild, moderate, gentle. 2 casual, indifferent, weak, mild.

intensify *v. Lying down only intensified the pain:* increase, heighten, quicken, aggravate, escalate, make more intense, sharpen, strengthen, magnify, redouble.

Ant. reduce, lessen, diminish, mitigate, allay; alleviate, lighten, relieve.

intensity *n.* 1 *the intensity of the light:* magnitude, power, strength, depth, severity. 2 *The play's intensity left the audience drained:* passion, emotion, ardor, fervor, vehemence; energy, vigor, strength, power, force, earnestness, zeal, forcefulness.

intent *n.* 1 *I had no intent to kill:* intention, design, purpose, plan, determination, premeditation; aim, end. 2 *The intent of the speech escaped no one:* meaning, significance, purport, import, burden, drift; gist, substance. —*adj.* 3 *an intent gaze:* steady, steadfast, intense, fixed, piercing; concentrated, preoccupied, absorbed. 4 *She was intent on winning:* set, bent, insistent, resolved, determined.

Ant. 3 unsteady, wandering; casual, indifferent.

intention *n. His intention is to spend a month in Spain:* plan, aim, intent, objective, design, purpose, goal, resolution, object, resolve, end, determination.

intentional *adj. an intentional insult:* deliberate, intended, done on purpose, planned, designed, premeditated, calculated.

Ant. accidental, inadvertent, unintentional.

intercede *v.* 1 *Relatives interceded in behalf of the disowned son:* support or help, lend a helping hand, use one's influence; speak up,

plead. 2 *A neutral nation volunteered to intercede in the interest of achieving peace:* arbitrate, mediate, play intermediary, serve as go-between, intervene.

interchangeable *adj. "Hot dog" and "frank" are interchangeable terms:* switchable, tradable, exchangeable; equivalent, similar, synonymous, corresponding, parallel, analogous.

intercourse *n.* 1 *The war stopped commercial intercourse between the nations:* communications, dealings, trade, traffic, relations, correspondence, commerce; conversation, talk, communion, parley. 2 *Pregnancy is a result of intercourse:* sexual relations, copulation, coitus; coupling.

interest *n.* 1 *Often* **interests** *His interests include reading and tennis:* preferred activity, absorption, pursuit, avocation, pastime, hobby. 2 *The speech aroused little interest:* notice, attention, concern, curiosity, regard. 3 *Sometimes* **interests** *A good leader should act in the interests of the people:* behalf, benefit, service, advantage, good. 4 *The family has an interest in a chain of hardware stores:* share, portion, stake, part, investment, holding, partial ownership. 5 *The loan was made at 6 percent interest:* profit, yield, gain. —*v.* 6 *Geology interests me:* absorb, engage the attention of, preoccupy, excite the curiosity of, divert, attract; concern, involve.

Ant. 2 unconcern, indifference. 6 bore.

interesting *adj. The magazine was interesting:* absorbing, stimulating, arresting, striking; attractive, appealing, entertaining, engaging, fascinating, riveting.

Ant. uninteresting, dull, boring.

interfere *v.* 1 *The television interferes with my concentration:* conflict, hinder, obstruct, counter, be an obstacle to, frustrate. 2 *Don't interfere!:* meddle, intervene, interpose, step in, intrude, intercede; *Slang* butt in.

Ant. 1 aid, help, assist.

interim *n.* 1 *The meeting isn't until noon, so in the interim I can work:* intervening time, interval, interlude, meantime. —*adj.* 2 *an interim government:* temporary, provisional, stopgap, *Latin* pro tempore.

Ant. 2 permanent.

interior *adj.* 1 *the interior walls of the cabin:* internal, inmost, inner, innermost, inside, inward. —*n.* 2 *the interior of the house:* internal part, inside, inner space.

Ant. 1 exterior; outer, outward, outside, external. 2 exterior, outside.

interject *v. The speaker interjected a funny story into the lecture:* insert, put in, interrupt with, interpose, inject, introduce.

Ant. extract, remove, withdraw.

interloper n. *The host had the interloper thrown out:* intruder, outsider, trespasser; gatecrasher; meddler, interferer.

interlude n. *a pleasant interlude:* interval, intervening period, intermission, recess, pause, break, breathing spell; episode, event, incident.

intermediary n. *I served as intermediary in the dispute:* mediator, arbitrator, middleman, intermediate, go-between; referee, adjudicator.

intermediate adj. 1 *the intermediate part of the journey:* middle, midway, intermediary, halfway, mid, intervening. 2 *This piano piece is of intermediate difficulty:* medium, moderate, average, middling; fair, mediocre.

interment n. *The interment was at the national cemetery:* burial, burial ceremony, entombment; funeral.

interminable adj. *The speech seemed interminable:* endless, unending, ceaseless; tediously long; perpetual, continuous, incessant.
Ant. brief, short, fleeting.

intermingle v. *The ingredients intermingled into a delightful dish:* mix, combine, commingle, blend, intermix, fuse, unite, merge.
Ant. break up, separate.

intermission n. *We worked without intermission. The play has two intermissions:* pause, stoppage, halt, interlude, stop, rest, break, recess.

intermittent adj. *intermittent rain:* recurrent, spasmodic, occasional, periodic, discontinuous, sporadic, on and off, fitful, irregular.
Ant. steady, unceasing, continuous.

internal adj. 1 *an internal injury:* interior, inner, inmost. 2 *The nation's internal affairs:* domestic; governmental, administrative, state, sovereign.
Ant. 1 outer, exterior, external, outside. 2 foreign.

international adj. *international trade:* between nations; worldwide, universal.
Ant. national, domestic.

interpolate v. *She interpolated some personal remarks in the middle of her speech:* insert, inject, put in, add, introduce, interlard, interject, insinuate, intervene, intersperse.

interpret v. 1 *The teacher interpreted the poem for the class:* explain, make clear, clarify, explicate, elucidate. 2 *I interpreted her smile as approval:* understand, construe, take, accept, see, read, account for. 3 *Please interpret the comments of our foreign guest:* translate; restate, paraphrase, reword, render.

interrogate v. *The police interrogated the witness:* question, probe, examine, ask, query.
Ant. answer, respond.

interrupt v. 1 *The radio program was interrupted for a news flash:* stop, break off, halt temporarily, break in on, disturb, interfere with, obstruct the course of. 2 *Sea walls interrupt the long beach:* block partially, disconnect, intersect, sever.
Ant. 1 continue, resume.

interruption n. *The storm caused an interruption of rail service:* halt, pause, stop, obstruction, hindrance, disconnection, interference; break, gap, hiatus, lacuna, intermission, rift, interlude.
Ant. continuance, resumption.

intersect v. 1 *A beam of light intersected the darkness:* cut across, cross, traverse, crosscut, pass across, bisect, divide. 2 *The roads intersect:* cross, interconnect, crisscross, meet, come together.

intersection n. *The collision occurred at the intersection:* junction, crossroads, crossing, interchange.

interval n. 1 *An interval of a year passed:* intervening period, interim, pause, rest, recess, break, interlude, intermission. 2 *An interval of 40 yards separated two houses:* space, opening, gap, separation.

intervene v. 1 *Much had happened during the years that intervened:* occur, pass, take place, come to pass, befall. 2 *The referee intervened:* step in, break in, interpose, intrude, interfere, intercede, come between.

intestines n. pl. *Most digestion takes place in the intestines:* alimentary canal; insides, entrails, viscera, bowels, *Informal* guts.

intimacy n. *The two old friends spoke with great intimacy:* closeness, familiarity, caring, tenderness, fondness, affection; lovemaking, sexual relations, sexual intercourse; friendliness, chumminess, camaraderie, fraternity.
Ant. aloofness, alienation, estrangement, indifference.

intimate[1] adj. 1 *our most intimate friends:* close, cherished, dear, familiar, personal. 2 *Some feelings are too intimate to discuss:* personal, innermost, confidential, private. 3 *an intimate knowledge of the law:* detailed, deep, thorough, profound; personal, direct, first-hand, close. —n. 4 *Many artists were among Gertrude Stein's intimates:* close friend, close associate, confidant, familiar; *Informal* chum, crony, pal, buddy.
Ant. 1 distant, remote. 3 superficial, limited, slight. 4 stranger, outsider.

intimate² *v. The report intimated that more was involved than met the eye:* hint, suggest, imply, indicate, insinuate.
Ant. declare, assert, proclaim.

intimation *n. There are intimations that the director may be replaced:* hint, suggestion, inkling, clue, innuendo, indication, allusion, insinuation; sign, portent.

intimidate *v. The gang tried to intimidate the merchant:* terrorize, terrify, cow, frighten, alarm, bully, browbeat; coerce.

intolerable *adj. The noise is intolerable:* unendurable, unbearable, insupportable; excruciating, torturous, agonizing; abominable, loathsome, abhorrent; unreasonable, excessive, outrageous.
Ant. tolerable, bearable, endurable; reasonable.

intolerance *n. racial intolerance:* bigotry, bias, prejudice, narrow-mindedness, lack of forbearance; xenophobia, chauvinism, racism.
Ant. tolerance, compassion.

intolerant *adj. Don't be intolerant of other religions:* not tolerant, bigoted, prejudiced, narrow-minded, closed-minded, hostile, jealous, mistrustful.
Ant. tolerant, open-minded.

intone *v. The audience intoned the pledge of allegiance:* chant, drawl, singsong, hum, croon, vocalize, intonate; say, speak, utter, voice, murmur, pronounce, enunciate, articulate.

in toto *adv. The report was published in toto:* as a whole, entire, uncondensed, uncut, unabridged, entirely, completely, totally.
Ant. abridged, condensed, cut, in part.

intoxicated *adj. 1 He was intoxicated after only one glass of wine:* drunk, inebriated, drunken, *Informal* high, tight, tipsy, *Slang* smashed, loaded, bombed, oiled, stoned, plastered, zonked, stewed. *2 We were intoxicated by the beauty of the night:* transported, rapt, enthralled, infatuated, elated, exalted, entranced, enchanted, exhilarated.
Ant. 1 sober.

intractable *adj. The intractable child refused to obey:* stubborn, perverse, headstrong, ornery, obstinate, willful, unmanageable, obdurate, incorrigible, mulish, unruly, fractious, refractory, ungovernable, uncontrollable.
Ant. obedient, docile, submissive, compliant.

intrepid *adj. Intrepid commandos led the raid:* fearless, bold, valiant, brave, courageous, audacious, heroic, valorous, dauntless, resolute, doughty, daring, adventurous, undismayed.
Ant. cowardly, timid, fearful.

intricate *adj. an intricate problem:* complicated, complex, sophisticated, involved; full of detail or difficulties.
Ant. simple, straightforward.

intrigue *v. 1 Fairy tales intrigue most children:* interest greatly, fascinate, attract, absorb, enthrall, arouse the curiosity of, capture the imagination of. —*n. 2 Politics is full of intrigue:* scheming, machination, secret plotting, secret dealings; knavery, sharp practice, manipulation, plot, scheme, conspiracy. *3 King Arthur discovered the intrigue between Guinevere and Lancelot:* love affair, romance, amour.
Ant. 1 bore. 3 sincerity, candor, honesty.

intrinsic *adj. The play has little intrinsic value:* essential, innate, inherent, basic, fundamental, underlying, inborn, inbred, native, natural.
Ant. extrinsic, incidental; added, extraneous.

introduce *v. 1 Introduce me to your friends:* give an introduction, make acquainted, make known, present. *2 A trip to the museum introduced the class to art:* bring knowledge to, acquaint, inform, expose, familiarize, make familiar, initiate. *3 to introduce an alternative to the plan:* propose, advance, offer, put forward, present; originate, create, bring into notice. *4 The MC introduced the program:* start, begin, lead off, *Informal* kick off. *5 Saint Patrick introduced Christianity to the Irish:* bring in, show, make familiar, import, bring into practice, institute, establish. *6 Shakespeare introduced comic relief in his tragedies:* put in, insert, infuse, add, interject, interpose.

introduction *n. 1 the factory's introduction of automation:* introducing, instituting, institution, bringing in. *2 Make the introductions while I take the coats:* presentation, acquaintanceship, meeting of strangers. *3 the book's introduction:* preface, prefatory material, preamble, foreword, opening part, prelude, preliminary speech, opening remarks, prologue.
Ant. 1 elimination, removal, withdrawal; completion, end. 4 epilogue, afterword.

introductory *adj. an introductory price:* serving to introduce, preliminary, acquainting, initial, beginning, prefatory, precursory, *Informal* get-acquainted.
Ant. final, last, terminal.

introspection *n. After months of introspection he decided to become a priest:* self-analysis, self-examination, soul-searching, heart-searching, self-contemplation, meditation, brooding, self-questioning, deliberation, rumination, reflection.

intrude v. Don't intrude in a family dispute: enter uninvited, thrust oneself in, obtrude, interfere, intervene, interlope, trespass, encroach, meddle, Slang butt in.

intuition n. Intuition told me he would not show up: innate knowledge, instinct; precognition, insight, sixth sense; Informal hunch.
Ant. reasoning, deduction.

intuitive adj. an intuitive sense of music: innate, instinctive, natural, native, inborn, inbred.
Ant. acquired, learned.

inundate v. 1 Floodwaters inundated the valley: engulf, overflow, overspread, submerge, flood, deluge, drown. 2 I was inundated with questions: swamp, flood, saturate, overcome; load down, overburden, overwhelm.

inure v. We're inured to cold weather: accustom, habituate, make used to; harden, toughen, season, desensitize, discipline, adapt, acclimatize, acclimate.

invade v. 1 Germany invaded France in World War II: enter forcefully, swarm over, enter as an enemy, march into, strike at, assault, assail, attack. 2 Tourists invaded the city: overrun, engulf, flood, descend upon, overspread, spread throughout, permeate, infest. 3 The state must not invade the freedom of the church: intrude on, infringe upon, encroach on, trespass, violate.
Ant. 1, 2 abandon, vacate, evacuate. 3 respect, honor.

invalid[1] n. 1 The invalid is confined to a wheelchair: ill person, disabled person, enfeebled person, stricken person. —adj. 2 my invalid mother: infirm, enfeebled, disabled, sick, sickly, ailing, unwell, incapacitated.
Ant. 2 strong, well, healthy, vigorous.

invalid[2] adj. This document is invalid. an invalid argument: not valid, void, useless, worthless; unconvincing, illogical, fallacious, unsound, false.
Ant. valid, sound, legal; forceful, logical.

invalidate v. Inaccuracies invalidated the speaker's position: make invalid or worthless, nullify, vitiate, annul, abrogate, repeal, countermand, cancel, weaken, discredit, undercut, undermine, refute.
Ant. validate; strengthen, enhance.

invaluable adj. Those invaluable ancient scrolls belong in a museum: priceless, very precious, of great worth, very valuable; rare, choice.
Ant. worthless, valueless.

invariable adj. I respected her invariable

fairness: constant, unfailing, uniform, unwavering, unvarying, unchanging, changeless, undeviating, unchangeable, consistent.
Ant. variable, changing, changeable, varying.

invasion n. 1 a military invasion: incursion, aggression, assault, attack, raid, foray, sortie, onslaught. 2 an invasion of privacy: encroachment, breach, intrusion, infringement; overstepping, usurpation.
Ant. 2 respect, honoring.

invective n. Invective poured from the speaker's mouth: bitter language, harsh words, verbal abuse, venom, vilification, insult, contumely, diatribe, sarcasm; vituperation, denunciation, revilement, rant, railing.
Ant. praise, commendation.

inveigh v. He inveighed against unfair labor practices: denounce, criticize, castigate, rail, harangue, reproach, upbraid, revile, scold, censure.
Ant. commend, praise, approve.

inveigle v. They inveigled her into appearing at the benefit: entice, beguile, tempt, allure, seduce, wheedle, coax, flatter, cajole.

invent v. 1 Alexander Graham Bell invented the telephone: originate, create, develop, contrive, conceive, devise, fashion, formulate; Informal think up, come up with. 2 He invented some story as an excuse: make up, concoct, fabricate, contrive, coin; Informal cook up.
Ant. 1 copy, imitate, reproduce.

invention n. 1 the invention of the telephone: inventing, creation, origination, discovery. 2 The electric can opener is a clever invention: contrivance, gadget; implement, device, apparatus, machine, contraption. 3 The alibi was pure invention: fabrication, sham, fake, forgery, concoction, fiction, lie.

inverse adj. Double-check by adding the figures in inverse order: reversed, back to front, backward, right-to-left, bottom-to-top, opposite.

invest v. to invest time in community service: devote, give, allot, apportion, set aside, appoint. 2 Congress is invested with the power to declare war: endow, supply, enable.
Ant. 1, 2 withhold, deny.

investigate v. The police are investigating the murder: inquire into, explore, examine closely, study, scrutinize, research, probe, search into; question, query, ask about; sift, analyze, inspect.

investigation n. The investigation may take months: inquiry, investigating, examination, search, study, scrutiny, probe, survey, review, research, fact-finding; analysis, inspection.

investment *n.* 1 *She became rich through wise investments:* investing, allotment of funds, capital spending, stock acquisition; financial transaction. 2 *Each partner's investment was $5,000:* money invested, contribution, offering, share; risk, venture, stake, ante.

inveterate *adj.* 1 *an inveterate romantic:* confirmed, steadfast, constant, habitual, established, ingrained, deep-seated, diehard, incurable. 2 *an inveterate back problem:* established, continuous, recurrent, chronic, long-standing.
Ant. 1 incipient; reformed. 2 superficial, passing.

invidious *adj.* *an invidious comparison:* insulting, causing envy or hard feelings, offensive, slighting; malevolent, resentful, malicious, vicious, spiteful.
Ant. fair, just; flattering.

invigorating *adj.* *an invigorating walk:* refreshing, restorative, enlivening, animating, energizing, bracing, stimulating, rejuvenating.
Ant. tiring, weakening.

invincible *adj.* *an invincible defense:* unconquerable, indomitable, impregnable, insurmountable, invulnerable, unbeatable, undefeatable.
Ant. conquerable, vulnerable.

invisible *adj.* *a story about an invisible man:* not visible, not perceptible to the eye, imperceptible, undiscernible, unapparent, unseeable, unseen; covert, concealed, obscure, hidden.
Ant. visible, apparent, plain.

invitation *n.* 1 *Have the party invitations been sent out?:* request for someone's presence, summons, offer; call, bid, bidding. 2 *Gloomy thoughts are an invitation to depression:* inducement, lure, enticement, allurement, temptation, call.

invite *v.* 1 *Invite the family to stay for the weekend:* request the presence of, summon courteously; urge, call, bid. 2 *The hotel invited suggestions from the guests:* request politely, ask formally; encourage, welcome, solicit. 3 *Don't invite disaster:* tempt, induce, attract, entice, lure, encourage.
Ant. 2, 3 repel, forbid, discourage.

inviting *adj.* *an inviting idea:* tempting, attractive, appealing, intriguing, alluring, enticing, charming; warm, welcoming.
Ant. uninviting, forbidding, repellent.

invocation *n.* *The priest read a solemn invocation:* entreaty to a supernatural power, prayer, appeal, supplication, petition, plea.

invoke *v.* 1 *The sinner invoked the Lord's forgiveness:* entreat, call upon, petition, implore, appeal for, supplicate, pray for; beg, beseech, importune, ask for. 2 *The president invoked the veto:* put into effect, resort to, use, implement, employ, apply. 3 *The medium tried to invoke the spirits of the departed:* summon by incantation, call forth, conjure.

involuntary *adj.* 1 *an involuntary confession:* forced, coerced, unwilling, compulsory, against one's will. 2 *She gave an involuntary shiver:* spontaneous, reflex, unconscious, instinctive, automatic, inadvertent.
Ant. willing, voluntary, intentional.

involve *v.* 1 *The plan involves the cooperation of young and old:* include, contain, be a matter of, comprise; entail, imply. 2 *Treaty obligations involved the country in the war:* cause to be associated, implicate, embroil, entangle. 3 *The senator is involved in a national health insurance bill:* absorb fully, preoccupy, engage.
Ant. 2 extricate, disentangle. 3 disengage.

invulnerable *adj.* *The fortress seemed invulnerable:* unconquerable, unassailable, invincible, unbeatable, undefeatable, impregnable, undestroyable, imperishable.
Ant. vulnerable, defenseless, unprotected.

inward *Also* **inwards** *adv.* 1 *The door opens inward:* toward the inside, toward the interior, interiorly. 2 *Nostalgia turned his reflections inward:* toward one's private thoughts, into the mind or soul, inwardly. —*adj.* 3 *The explorers discovered an inward passageway. She has achieved inward peace:* directed toward the inside, ingoing, leading inside, interior; personal, private, mental, spiritual, inner.
Ant. 1, 2 outward, outside. 3 outer, exterior.

iota *n.* *There's not an iota of truth to the story:* particle, jot, smidgin, whit, shred, atom, scintilla, bit, spot, speck.

irascible *adj.* *an irascible old curmudgeon:* easily angered, touchy, cantankerous, waspish, bad-tempered, ill-humored, hot-tempered, irritable, intractable, ornery, cross, testy, cranky, grumpy, grouchy, peevish.
Ant. good-natured, mild, placid, easygoing.

irate *adj.* *The long wait made her irate:* angry, angered, furious, rabid, enraged, infuriated; burned up, irritated, annoyed, livid, riled, indignant, mad.
Ant. good-humored, pleased, tranquil.

ire *n.* *The crime stirred the community's ire:* anger, rage, outrage, fury, wrath, indignation, resentment, choler.
Ant. goodwill, patience, forgiveness.

iridescent *adj. The jewel was iridescent in the light:* changeable in color, glowing, shiny, many hued, rainbowlike, opalescent, prismatic.

Ant. colorless, dull, lusterless.

irk *v. Late arrivals irked the performers:* annoy, irritate, vex, gall; pester, provoke.

Ant. please, delight, overjoy.

ironclad *adj. an ironclad contract:* inflexible, unalterable, irrevocable, irreversible, unchangeable, immutable, fixed, unchanging, strict.

Ant. variable, changeable, revocable.

ironic Also **ironical** *adj.* 1 *My praise of that awful play was ironic:* mocking, sarcastic, filled with irony, sardonic, facetious; derisive, biting, cutting, sneering. 2 *It's ironic that the rain was followed by a drought:* incongruous, inconsistent, contradictory, surprising, unexpected, curious, strange, odd, weird; *Informal* funny.

Ant. 1 sincere, straightforward, direct. 2 natural, expected.

irony *n.* 1 *Her humor is filled with irony:* indirection, double meaning, facetiousness, sarcasm, mockery. 2 *What irony to be offered three jobs after having none for so long!:* incongruity, contrariness, absurdity, unexpected outcome.

Ant. 1 sincerity, straightforwardness, directness.

irrational *adj.* 1 *Fish are irrational creatures:* incapable of logical thought, unthinking, unreasoning. 2 *Your fears are irrational:* unsound, illogical, unreasonable, unfounded, baseless; nonsensical, absurd, foolish, ill-advised.

Ant. 1, 2 rational. 2 reasonable, sensible, logical.

irreconcilable *adj. Their differences are irreconcilable:* beyond reconciliation, unadjustable, unbridgeable, implacably hostile, unappeasable; incompatible, opposed.

Ant. reconcilable, appeasable.

irrefutable *adj. The argument is irrefutable:* undeniable, not refutable, incontrovertible, indisputable.

Ant. refutable, disputable, moot.

irregular *adj.* 1 *irregular teeth:* uneven, crooked, out of line, unaligned; not smooth, rough, broken, bumpy; asymmetrical. 2 *That behavior is highly irregular:* nonconforming, unconventional, unusual, uncharacteristic; improper, unsuitable, inappropriate, unfitting; eccentric, peculiar, queer, odd, abnormal, aberrant, anomalous; unsystematic, unmethodical, haphazard.

Ant. 1 regular, even, uniform. 2 regular,

normal, usual, customary; proper, established; methodical, orderly, systematic.

irrelevant *adj. The statement was irrelevant:* unconnected, unrelated, beside the point, immaterial, nonpertinent, not apropos, extraneous, foreign, not germane.

Ant. relevant, pertinent, germane.

irreligious *adj. Communists were assumed to be irreligious:* not religious, not holding religious beliefs, unbelieving, godless, atheistic, agnostic, impious; profane, sacrilegious, ungodly.

Ant. religious, pious, devout.

irreparable *adj. irreparable damage:* beyond repair, uncorrectable, irreversible, beyond redress, irremediable, unfixable.

Ant. reparable, reversible, remediable.

irrepressible *adj. irrepressible enthusiasm:* unrestrainable, uncontrollable, unsquelchable, unquenchable, undamped; bubbling, ebullient, vibrant, boisterous, full of life.

Ant. repressible, restrainable; damped, squelched.

irreproachable *adj. The judge's fairness is irreproachable:* beyond reproach or criticism, above reproof, without fault, flawless, blameless, faultless, impeccable.

Ant. reproachable, flawed, faulty.

irresistible *adj.* 1 *an irresistible urge:* overwhelming, not resistible, not withstandable, overpowering. 2 *The candy was irresistible:* extremely tempting, enticing, alluring, not to be resisted, tantalizing, seductive, enchanting, highly desirable.

Ant. 1 resistible, weak.

irresolute *adj. He has an irresolute nature:* indecisive, wavering, hesitating, hesitant, faltering, undecided, uncertain, unsure, changeable, vacillating, weak, unsteady, unresolved.

Ant. resolute, determined, decisive.

irresponsible *adj. an irresponsible decision:* careless, not responsible, undependable, unreliable, indifferent, untrustworthy, thoughtless; imprudent, reckless, rash, ill-considered, injudicious, overhasty, foolish.

Ant. responsible, thoughtful, trustworthy, dependable.

irreverent *adj. Talking in church is irreverent:* disrespectful, lacking reverence, impious; irreligious, profane, blasphemous; impudent, brazen, shameless, disparaging, slighting; skeptical, debunking.

irrevocable *adj. The decision is irrevocable:* final, conclusive, not subject to reversal, unchangeable, not commutable, irreversible, unalterable.

Ant. reversible, changeable, alterable.

irritable *adj. The heat made everyone irritable:* ill-humored, easily irritated, easily annoyed, ill-tempered, irascible, touchy, testy, peevish, grouchy, grumpy, waspish, impatient, snappish, fretful.

Ant. easygoing, good-natured, genial, affable.

irritate *v.* 1 *The child's whining irritated the nurse:* annoy, vex, anger, make angry, make impatient, peeve, exasperate, irk. 2 *Woolen clothing will irritate the rash:* make painful, aggravate, worsen, inflame, make sore; chafe.

Ant. 1 gratify, please, delight. 2 soothe, ease.

isolate *v. Researchers have isolated the virus:* separate, segregate, set apart; seclude, sequester.

Ant. unite, combine, mix.

issue *n.* 1 *Who handles the issue of supplies?:* giving out, granting; sending out, issuance, distributing, dispensation. 2 *Taxation was the main issue:* problem, question, matter for discussion, point of debate, matter to be settled, matter in dispute. 3 *The peace negotiations had a happy issue:* result, consequence, outcome; yield, product. 4 *The king's issue inherited the throne:* offspring, progeny, children, descendants, heirs; posterity. 5 *the issue of water from the cracked pipe:* outpouring, gush, discharge, outflow, effluence, eruption. —*v.* 6 *Lava issued from the volcano:* pour forth, go out, emanate, flow out, spout, gush, erupt, emerge. 7 *The post office issued the new stamp:* put in circulation, circulate, distribute, give out, dispense, allot.

Ant. 3 cause. 4 parent, sire. 7 withdraw, withhold.

itch *v.* 1 *Poison ivy makes the skin itch:* have an itch, feel the need to scratch, prickle, tickle, crawl, creep. 2 *The girl itched to see the world:* long, yearn, hanker, have a yen, crave, desire, pine, ache. —*n.* 3 *I have an itch on my back:* prickling sensation, tingling, itchiness, prickliness. 4 *Most people have an itch for romance:* strong wish, desire, yearning, urge, yen, hankering, craving, hunger, thirst.

item *n.* 1 *There are ten items on my list:* notation, entry, detail, particular; unit, thing, matter, subject, point. 2 *There is an item on the kidnapping in today's paper:* report, news article, notice, piece, story, account, feature.

itemize *v. Please itemize the purchases:* list individually, particularize, detail, enumerate, specify.

itinerant *adj. itinerant minstrels:* wandering, wayfaring, peripatetic, roving, roaming, migrant, traveling, nomadic, footloose, vagabond, transient.

itinerary *n. Leave an itinerary so we can reach you:* travel plan, schedule, detailed plan, course, route; log, travel record, journal.

J

jab *v.* 1 *Don't jab me in the side!:* poke, nudge, tap, bump, prod, dig, stab, strike, hit. —*n.* 2 *a series of left jabs:* short punch, quick thrust, cut, poke, stab, dig, swing; hit, blow, belt.

jabber *v.* 1 *He was jabbering about nothing:* babble, chatter, talk idly, prattle, prate, blather, drivel, gab, blab, gibber. —*n.* 2 *The endless jabber was infuriating:* jabbering, gibberish, drivel, idle talk, prattle, chatter, blabber, babble, prating, blather, gab, chitter-chatter, twattle, gossip, chitchat.

jacket *n.* 1 *a blue jacket:* short coat, *(variously)* sport coat, blazer, smoking jacket, dinner jacket. 2 *a book jacket:* outer covering, wrapper, wrapping, cover, envelope, casing, case.

jaded *adj.* 1 *the same old jaded plot:* shopworn, worn-out, tired, overused, stale; fatigued, exhausted, weary, tired out. 2 *I was jaded and unimpressible:* blasé, bored, surfeited, cloyed, satiated, sated, overindulged.

jagged *adj. a jagged tooth:* rough, irregular, uneven, indented, crenulated, ragged on the edges, broken; serrated, notched, sawtoothed, ridged, zigzag; angular, craggy, rugged.

Ant. smooth, even, level, straight.

jail *n.* 1 *She was sentenced to jail:* prison, penal institution, penitentiary, house of correction; *Slang* pen, hoosegow, jug, can, clink, cooler, slammer, stir. —*v.* 2 *I was jailed for theft:* imprison, incarcerate, confine, lock up.

Ant. 2 release, free, parole.

jam v. 1 *He jammed his clothes into the suit-case:* cram, crowd, stuff, pack; squeeze, ram, wedge. 2 *The accident jammed the road for three hours:* obstruct, congest, stall, stop; become stuck. —n. 4 *a traffic jam:* crowd, tie-up, multitude, throng, mob, horde, pack, flock, herd, swarm, host, drove, army; crush, shove, push, press. 5 *She's in an awful jam:* fix, trouble, mess, predicament, plight, dilemma.

jangle v. 1 *Bracelets jangled on her wrist:* rattle, clang, clatter, clank; jingle, ring, reverberate; clash, crash. —n. 2 *the jangle of an alarm bell:* rattle, clang, clatter, clank, clangor, harsh ringing.

jar v. 1 *The news jarred me:* disquiet, perturb, unsettle, upset, trouble, disconcert, distract, discompose, startle, shock, stun, take aback, confuse, fluster. 2 *The earthquake jarred the city:* shake, rock, jiggle, jolt, agitate, joggle. —n. 3 *The jar of the explosion was felt for miles:* concussion, reverberation, jolt, impact, shock.

jargon n. 1 *military jargon:* specialized language, idiom, parlance, phraseology, vocabulary, vernacular, argot, lingo, cant. 2 *The report was full of jargon:* meaningless writing or talk, nonsense, gibberish, prattle, drivel, blather, twaddle, rubbish, tommyrot; *Slang* balderdash, hogwash, bosh, poppycock, gobbledygook, hooey.

jaunt n. *a weekend jaunt:* short trip, excursion, junket, trip, tour, outing; ramble, stroll.

jaunty adj. *a jaunty young man:* lighthearted, high-spirited, buoyant, bouncy, lively, sprightly, vivacious, breezy, blithe, carefree; sporty, debonair.
Ant. staid, sober, sedate, lifeless.

jealous adj. 1 *We were jealous of their wealth:* envious, resentful, green-eyed, grudging. 2 *She was jealous of her boyfriend:* possessive, suspicious, mistrustful, mistrusting, wary, regardful, protective, watchful.
Ant. 2 trusting; indifferent, uncaring.

jeer v. 1 *They jeered the speaker:* deride, sneer, mock, revile, taunt, ridicule, harass, poke fun at, heckle, hector, scoff; hiss, boo. —n. 2 *jeers from the crowd:* derision, taunt, mockery, yell of contempt, hoot, abuse, scoffing.
Ant. 1 applaud, cheer. 2 adulation, applause.

jeopardy n. *Don't put yourself in jeopardy:* danger, peril, exposure, vulnerability, hazard, endangerment, liability, risk.
Ant. security, safety.

jerk n. 1 *Give the rope a firm jerk:* pull, tug, yank; shake, twitch, quiver. 2 *Slang Don't*

be a jerk: idiot, fool, dupe, dope, dunce, dummy, klutz. —v. 3 *He jerked on my lapel. His hands jerk when he's irritated:* pull, tug, pluck, yank, wrench; shake, twitch, quiver, tremble.

jest n. 1 *We laughed at the jests:* facetious remark, joke, jape, gibe, quip, wisecrack, crack, gag, bon mot. —v. 2 *It's too serious to jest about:* crack jokes, joke, quip, banter, play the fool, wisecrack.

jester n. *royal jesters:* clown, fool, zany, buffoon, joker, wag, madcap, *Informal* card; comedian, comic, quipster.

jet n. 1 *jets of water:* stream, fountain, spurt, spray, spout, squirt, flush, gush. —v. 2 *Oil jetted out of the well:* spout, spurt, stream, shoot, spray, squirt, issue, discharge, gush.

jettison v. *The crew jettisoned the cargo:* throw overboard, cast off; eliminate, discard, throw out, dump.

jewel n. 1 *The jewels were in the safe:* precious stone, gem, stone. 2 *She wore the finest jewels:* ornament, piece of jewelry, bangle, bauble, (variously) necklace, bracelet, earring, ring, tiara, lavaliere, locket, pendant, brooch. 3 *The house was a jewel:* treasure, prize, gem, one in a thousand, first-rater, find, honey; masterpiece.

jewelry n. *Her jewelry was insured:* jewels, gems, precious stones, adornments, personal ornaments, regalia; gewgaws, bangles, costume jewelry.

jibe v. *Our totals don't jibe:* agree, conform, accord, fit, harmonize, tally, correspond, match, square, coincide, concur, mesh, fit together.
Ant. conflict, differ, disagree.

jiffy n. *Lunch will be ready in a jiffy:* moment, minute, instant, trice, flash, second, twinkling, wink of the eye.

jiggle v. *Please stop jiggling!:* shake, wiggle, joggle, wriggle, fidget, twitch, jerk.

jingle v. 1 *The keys jingled in my pocket:* jangle, ring, clank, clink, clatter, tinkle. —n. 2 *the jingle of bells:* ringing, clang, tinkle, tintinnabulation, jangle.

jingoism n. *The jingoism of some politicians is self-serving:* chauvinism, nationalism, superpatriotism, flag-waving, blind patriotism, ultranationalism.

jinx n. *It was as if there were a jinx on the house:* evil spell, hex, curse; nemesis, bête noire, bugbear.

jitters n.pl. *Job interviews give me the jitters:* nervousness, shakes, shivers, fidgets; anxiety, tenseness, jumpiness, shakiness, uneasiness, quivering.
Ant. calm, composure, serenity.

job n. 1 *It was my job to see that orders were*

filled: work, task, responsibility, assignment, duty, business, mission, chore, function, role, activity. **2** *a job as a paramedical:* employment, position, situation, appointment; place, spot, opening; occupation, career, business, office; profession, calling, trade, craft. **3** *They were paid according to the jobs they completed:* unit of work, assignment, contract, commission; piecework.

jocular *adj. His jocular manner eases tensions:* humorous, given to joking, sportive, witty, joking, jesting, merry, mirthful, funny, prankish, amusing.

Ant. grave, sober, solemn.

jog *v.* **1** *The cart jogged down the road:* bounce, jar, rock, jiggle, jounce, shake, jostle, joggle; trot. **2** *The name jogged my memory:* nudge, stir, activate, actuate, stimulate, prompt.

join *v.* **1** *Join these two pieces:* bring together, connect, fasten, tie, marry, couple, bind, fuse, unite, splice, merge, mix, combine, pool, link, affix, attach; cement, glue, paste. **2** *Two groups joined to overthrow the government:* unite, ally, combine, merge, consolidate; federate, amalgamate, associate, confederate, syndicate; cooperate. **3** *We joined Greenpeace:* become a member of, associate oneself with, sign up with, enroll in, enlist in, enter, subscribe to.

Ant. **1** separate, sever, detach, disengage, disconnect. **3** resign, quit.

joint *adj. a joint effort:* mutual, common, shared, collaborative, collective, cooperative, combined, united, unified, associated, consolidated.

Ant. individual, solitary, lone.

joke *n.* **1** *a very funny joke:* jest, playful trick or remark, practical joke, gag, funny story, witticism, pun, quip, wisecrack. **2** *He was the joke of the town:* object of ridicule, butt, laughing stock; buffoon, clown. **3** *The job was so easy it was a joke:* cinch, pushover, nothing, child's play, farce. —*v.* **4** *Don't joke at a time like this:* jest, clown, crack jokes, play the fool, josh, wisecrack. **5** *They joked about his ineptitude:* poke fun at, ridicule, gibe at, laugh at, snicker.

joker *n. I was the class joker:* clown, jester, comedian, funnyman, wit, wag, jokester, zany.

jolly *adj. She's my jolliest aunt:* merry, mirthful, cheerful, funny, gleeful, jocular, fun-loving, jovial, merry, high-spirited, playful.

Ant. solemn, grave, serious; morose, dour.

jolt *v.* **1** *The news jolted me. The bumpy road caused the car to jolt:* startle, disturb, perturb, upset, take aback; shake, jar, shock, stun, *Informal* throw; jerk, bump, bounce, joggle, jostle. —*n.* **2** *The news was a jolt.*

We felt the jolts of the car: shock, jar, start, shaking, bounce, jounce, twitch, jerk, bump, lurch, jiggle, quiver.

josh *v. Her friends joshed her:* tease, ridicule, twit, poke fun at, chaff, haze; *Slang* rib, kid.

Ant. praise, flatter, compliment.

jostle *v. The students jostled each other on the stairs:* shove, bump, push roughly, hit against, run against, shoulder, elbow, push.

jot *n. It didn't upset me a jot:* the least bit, one little bit, one iota, speck, whit, bit, dot, trace, smidgen, particle, modicum, scintilla.

journal *n. She kept a journal of her trip:* daily record, diary, register, chronology, record; daybook, notebook, chronicle, history, memoir; ledger, account book.

journey *n.* **1** *My journeys took me to Paris:* trip, tour, junket, expedition, excursion, outing, jaunt, wandering, roving. —*v.* **2** *We journeyed around the world:* travel, tour, take a trip, trek, ramble, roam, wander.

jovial *adj. a kind, jovial sort:* cheerful, merry, mirthful, cheery, jolly, jocular, sunny, sportive, playful, fun-loving, laughing, humorous.

Ant. dour, morose, gloomy, melancholy.

joy *n.* **1** *She was filled with joy:* delight, happiness, gladness, exultation, satisfaction, rapture, ecstasy, elation, cheerfulness, glee, gaiety, exhilaration, jubilation, enjoyment, pleasure, contentment. **2** *Children are the joys of life:* cause of gladness, source of pride or satisfaction, treasure, prize, pride, jewel.

Ant. **1** sorrow, despair, unhappiness, grief. **2** bane, trouble, affliction.

joyful *adj. I was joyful to see my brother again:* delighted, jubilant, happy, glad, pleased, exultant, cheerful, elated, full of joy, ecstatic, overjoyed, enraptured.

joyous *adj. a joyous occasion:* happy, glad, joyful, festive, rapturous, merry, cheerful, gleeful; gratifying, pleasurable, heartening, heartwarming, delightful.

Ant. sad, unhappy, joyless.

jubilant *adj. The winner was jubilant:* joyful, overjoyed, ecstatic, in high spirits, exultant, rejoicing, rapturous, delirious, exuberant, elated, exhilarated; joyous, merry, glad, delighted, happy, gleeful, pleased, gratified, cheery, *Informal* tickled pink.

Ant. doleful, sorrowful, despondent, sad, melancholy.

judge *n.* **1** *the judge of the baking contest:* justice, magistrate; official, arbitrator, arbiter, adjudicator; critic, reviewer, censor; referee, umpire. **2** *a good judge of character:* assessor, appraiser, evaluator, connoisseur, authority. —*v.* **3** *I've judged many cases in my court:* rule on, settle, pass sentence, pronounce judgment on, administer justice, adjudge, adjudicate, arbitrate, sit in judgment on, determine, decide, find, conduct, try, hear. **4** *I judge the time to be about noon:* ascertain, find, resolve, determine, discern, distinguish; estimate, surmise, guess, conjecture, suppose, believe, assume, imagine, fancy; consider, regard, deem, conclude; infer, deduce; *Informal* reckon. **5** *He was always judging people according to their clothes:* appraise, rate, rank, assess, value, weigh, size up, analyze.

judgment Also *chiefly British* **judgement** *n.* **1** *In the jury's judgment you were guilty:* decision, finding, ruling, verdict; decree, adjudication, arbitration. **2** *poor judgment in picking friends:* discretion, taste, discernment, discrimination; perceptiveness, perception, sense, shrewdness, acumen. **3** *It was my judgment that the play would be a success:* opinion, appraisal, belief, conclusion, deduction, estimate, valuation, assessment, view.

judicial *adj.* **1** *the judicial process:* judiciary, jurisdictional, juristic, legal, official. **2** *a judicial bearing:* befitting a judge, judgelike, magistral, magisterial, majestic, imposing, distinguished.

judicious *adj.* *Be judicious in the way you handle the interview:* sensible, wise, sagacious, sage, perspicacious, sound of judgment, just, discriminating, discerning, astute, knowing, reasonable, acute; diplomatic, tactful, thoughtful, reflective, prudent.

   Ant. injudicious, imprudent, thoughtless, unreasonable.

jug *n.* *a jug of wine:* vessel, pitcher, ewer, jar, urn, crock, flagon.

juicy *adj.* **1** *These oranges are juicy:* juice-filled, succulent, luscious. **2** *a juicy scandal:* intriguing, exciting, thrilling, spicy, sensational, lurid, tantalizing, provocative.

jumble *v.* **1** *Someone jumbled the files:* mix up, throw together, strew about; pile up, heap, bunch. —*n.* **2** *The room was a jumble of clothes and soda bottles:* confusion, mixture, disarray, snarl, tangle, muddle, accumulation, mélange, miscellany; mess, chaos, clutter, hodgepodge.

   Ant. **1** order. **2** order, system, arrangement.

jumbo *adj.* *a jumbo steak:* huge, immense, gigantic, oversized, mammoth, colossal, stupendous, giant, enormous, monumental, monstrous, mighty, vast.

   Ant. small, tiny, minute, wee.

jump *v.* **1** *We jumped over the fence:* leap, hop, skip, vault, hurtle, spring, bounce, bound. **2** *She jumped when he came up be-*

hind her: start, flinch, blench, recoil. **3** *to jump from one topic to another:* skip, pass, digress, switch, change abruptly. —*n.* **4** *One jump and you'll be over the fence:* bound, leap, vault, skip, hop, spring. **5** *In May there was a jump in sales:* sudden rise, upturn; surge, swift increase, upsurge, advance.

jumpy *adj.* *Being alone at night makes me jumpy:* jittery, nervous, skittish, fidgety, trembling, twitching, twitchy, fretful, apprehensive, anxious, uneasy; panicky, frightened.

   Ant. calm, unruffled, composed, serene.

junction *n.* *the junction of two main roads:* juncture, convergence, linkup, joining place, concurrence, confluence, joining, connecting point; crossroads, interchange.

juncture *n.* **1** *At that juncture, I decided to leave:* point of time, occasion, moment, interval, point. **2** *the juncture of the two walls:* junction, joining, joint, connection, seam, closure, point of contact, meeting, intersection; convergence, confluence.

junior *adj.* **1** *the junior Mr. Smith:* younger, minor. **2** *the junior member of the committee:* lesser, subordinate, lower, secondary; more recent, newer.

   Ant. senior, elder, older.

junk *n.* **1** *We took all the junk out of the basement:* rubbish, litter, discarded material, clutter, trash, debris, refuse, waste, odds and ends, cast-offs; scrap, *Slang* garbage. —*v.* **2** *We junked the old TV set:* discard, throw away, dispose of, scrap, dump, throw out.

jurisdiction *n.* **1** *The city had no jurisdiction over the county:* judicial right, lawful power, authority, legal right, control, dominion, rule. **2** *The sheriff's jurisdiction was only within the county:* extent of authority, precinct, bailiwick, dominion, domain, legal bounds.

jurist *n.* *Earl Warren was a famous jurist:* justice, judge, magistrate, legal authority; lawyer, attorney-at-law, attorney, counselor, counsel, advocate.

just *adj.* **1** *A just person listens to both sides:* fair, equitable, even-handed, fair-minded, impartial, unbiased, unbigoted, unprejudiced; trustworthy, honest, uncorrupt, decent, blameless, ethical, principled, honorable. **2** *just beliefs:* reasonable, sensible, sound, balanced, logical, well-grounded, well-founded. **3** *Five years imprisonment was a just sentence:* deserved, fair, justified, equitable, justifiable, worthy, merited, due; suitable, appropriate, fitting, proper, befitting; logical, reasonable, adequate, acceptable. —*adv.* **4** *She was just here:* a brief time ago, a moment ago, a little while ago; not long ago, recently, lately, only now. **5** *The roast is just right:* exactly, precisely, in all respects, completely, fully, entirely, perfectly, absolutely, quite. **6** *I just managed to come in second:* by a narrow margin, narrowly, barely, only just, hardly, scarcely. **7** *You are just a slob:* only, nothing but, merely, but, no more than, simply, at most.

Ant. **1–3** unjust. **1, 2** corrupt; dishonest, prejudiced, unfair, unreasonable, inequitable. **3** undeserved, inappropriate.

justice *n.* **1** *In the name of justice, all people should be equal:* righteousness, probity, right, fairness, fair play, rightness, justness, truth, honesty, integrity, probity, virtue. **2** *I had justice on my side:* legality, right, legitimacy, lawfulness, the law, justifica-

tion. **3** *Is there no justice after a crime like this?:* due punishment, reparation, penalty, chastisement, correction, atonement, amends, redress, satisfaction, just deserts.

Ant. **1–3** dishonesty, favoritism, inequity, injustice, unfairness, unreasonableness.

justify *v.* *Does the end justify the means?:* vindicate, excuse, prove right, warrant, support, validate, uphold, sanction.

jut *v.* *The pier jutted out over the bay:* extend, protrude, project, stick out, bulge.

juvenile *adj.* **1** *a juvenile audience. The man acted in a very juvenile manner:* young, youthful, adolescent, junior; immature, childish, infantile, puerile, callow, sophomoric, unsophisticated. —*n.* **2** *two adults and a juvenile:* minor, youth, youngster, stripling, teenager, child, infant.

Ant. **1** adult, mature, grown-up; manly, womanly. **2** adult.

K

keen *adj.* **1** *The blade had a keen edge:* sharp, fine, finely honed. **2** *a keen mind:* sharp, shrewd, astute, acute, penetrating, incisive, alert, quick-witted, clever; discerning, perspicacious, discriminating; eager, intense, earnest, avid, zealous.

Ant. **1** blunt, dull.

keep *v.* **1** *I kept the family name:* retain, hold, possess, preserve, maintain, conserve. **2** *Keep your clothes in this closet:* hold, store, place, deposit, accumulate, heap, stack, pile. **3** *She kept her niece for a week:* care for, take care of, look after, mind; have as a guest; guard, watch over, safeguard. **4** *Can you afford to keep a car?:* support, provide for, sustain, pay for, maintain. **5** *The parade kept traffic from moving:* hold, hold back, restrain; encumber, stall, retard, impede, inhibit, arrest, constrain, prevent; obstruct, block, hinder, bar, hamper, detain, delay, hold up, deter. **6** *We kept at our studies:* continue, carry on, keep up, persist in; stay, stick, remain, persevere, be steadfast. **7** *We keep the religious holidays:* observe, hold, pay heed to, celebrate, honor, commemorate. —*n.* **8** *He paid for his keep:* room and board, food and lodgings, sustenance; support, maintenance.

Ant. **1** discard, abandon, give up. **5** re-

lease, free; expedite, hurry. **7** ignore, disregard.

keeper *n.* *She was the keeper of the art collection. Am I my brother's keeper?:* curator, caretaker, guardian, warden, custodian, conservator; protector, guardian.

keg *n.* *kegs of beer:* barrel, cask, drum, butt, vat, tank, tun, tub, hogshead.

kernel *n.* *The nut has a small kernel. There's a kernel of truth in the statement:* seed, grain, pit, stone, pip, nut; core, center, nub, gist; pith, nucleus, center.

kettle *n.* *The water boiled in the kettle:* teakettle, teapot, pot, cauldron.

key *n.* **1** *Use your key to open the door:* (variously) latchkey, master key, passkey, skeleton key, house key. **2** *the key to the mystery:* crucial determinant, solution, explanation, answer, meaning, interpretation, resolution; cue, clue. **3** *the key of E:* tonality; scale, mode.

keystone *n.* *a keystone of the law:* basis, base, principle, cornerstone, foundation, linchpin, central idea, cardinal point, main thing.

kick *v.* **1** *to kick a ball:* strike with the foot, punt, boot. **2** *kick out. The landlord kicked us out of our apartment:* eject, throw out, turn out, send packing, show the door, boot out. **3** *Informal What have you got to kick* *about?:* complain, fuss, protest, grouch, object, find fault, grouse, gripe, beef. —*n.* 4 *Give the ball a hard kick:* a hit with the foot, boot. 5 *the kick of a shotgun:* recoil, kickback, rebound, reaction. 6 *Slang Sailing gave her a kick:* thrill, pleasure, excitement, fun, enjoyment; satisfaction, gratification. 7 *Informal My kick was that I wasn't making enough money:* complaint, protestation, grievance, objection, protest, gripe, beef.

kickback *n. He wanted a kickback for approving the contract:* bribe, commission, recompense, graft, payoff; *Slang* payola.

kid *n.* 1 *The kids were kept in the small corral:* young goat, yearling; goatskin. 2 *Informal The kids went to the movies:* child, little one, youngster, tot, moppet, shaver, tyke; juvenile, adolescent, teenager; baby, infant. —*v.* 3 *They kid him because he grew a beard:* tease, make fun of, mock, laugh at, make sport of, josh, rag, rib, ride; ridicule, delude, trick, deceive.

Ant. 2 adult, grown-up.

kill *v.* 1 *The prisoners killed a guard:* murder, slay, slaughter, assassinate; mortally wound, injure fatally, take the life of, dispatch, exterminate, execute; *Slang* knock off, rub out, waste. 2 *Failures kill ambition:* extinguish, defeat, destroy, ruin, halt, quell, stifle, squelch.

killing *n.* 1 *The killing made headlines:* murder, slaying, homicide, manslaughter; annihilation, elimination, extermination. —*adj.* 2 *I dealt the killing blow:* lethal, mortal, deadly, fatal, death-dealing.

killjoy *n. She was a real killjoy:* spoilsport, sourpuss, grouch, malcontent, worrywart, grumbler; *Slang* party-pooper, wet blanket.

kin *n. All our kin were there:* family, relatives, kinfolk, relations, kith and kin, flesh and blood, kinsmen.

kind[1] *adj. our kind benefactor:* kindly, benign, good-hearted, tenderhearted, tender, gentle, compassionate, merciful, charitable, warmhearted, sympathetic, understanding, considerate, thoughtful; obliging, gracious, accommodating, amicable, friendly, gentle.

Ant. unkind, cruel, mean.

kind[2] *n. What kind of dessert do you like?:* sort, type, class, brand, make, variety, style, description; nature, designation.

kindhearted *adj. kindhearted deeds:* kind, kindly, good-hearted, tenderhearted, compassionate, charitable, good, warmhearted, sympathetic, generous, humanitarian, humane, gentle, gracious, merciful, accommodating, helpful; understanding, thoughtful, considerate.

Ant. hardhearted, coldhearted, heartless, unkind, cruel, mean.

kindle *v.* 1 *He kindled the logs in the fireplace:* enkindle, ignite, set on fire, set fire to, light. 2 *The orphan kindled our nurturing instincts:* stir, arouse, rouse, inspire, call forth, fire, stimulate, provoke, incite, inflame, excite.

Ant. extinguish, quench, dampen.

kindly *adj.* 1 *a kindly philanthropist:* kind, generous, warmhearted, tender, compassionate, gentle, charitable, merciful, sympathetic, benevolent, humanitarian, bighearted, humane, friendly, understanding, considerate, neighborly; cordial, good-humored, amicable. —*adv.* 2 *The nurse acted kindly toward patients:* benignly, warmheartedly, warmly, tenderly, compassionately, gently, charitably, mercifully, sympathetically, humanely, bigheartedly, understandingly, considerately, good-naturedly, neighborly, amiably, cordially, good-humoredly.

Ant. 1 unkindly, malevolent, malign, malicious, unsympathetic; mean, cruel. 2 unkindly, malevolently, malignly, maliciously; unsympathetically, meanly, cruelly.

kindness *n.* 1 *the kindness of friends:* kindliness, benevolence, beneficence, mercy, charity, charitableness, humanity, humanitarianism, humaneness, goodness, goodness of heart, sympathy, compassion, consideration, understanding, patience, tolerance, graciousness; goodwill, friendly feelings. 2 *I've never forgotten her kindnesses:* kind act, kindly gesture, good turn, generosity, gift, favor, kind help, aid, good treatment.

Ant. 1 unkindness, malevolence, cruelty, meanness. 2 unkind act, evil deed.

kindred *adj. We were kindred spirits:* like, allied, closely related, similar, corresponding, alike, matching, resembling, harmonious, agreeing, congenial, sympathetic; related, akin, familial.

Ant. alien, unrelated, uncongenial, different.

king *n. the King of France:* monarch, ruler, sovereign, liege, His Majesty, crowned head, royal personage.

kingly *adj. He received the visitors with kingly grace:* majestic, kinglike, imperial, royal, regal, monarchal, noble; splendid, magnificent, stately, august, autocratic, imperious, lordly, despotic, tyrannical.

kink *n.* 1 *Brush the kinks from the horse's mane:* twist, tangle, coil, crimp, crinkle, frizz, knot, frizzle. 2 *I had a kink in my leg:* pang, twinge, spasm, stiffness, knot, cramp; charley horse. 3 *There were many kinks in* *our plan:* complication, hitch, defect, difficulty, flaw, imperfection, loose end.

kinky *adj.* 1 *The rain made my hair kinky:* knotted, tangled, twisted, matted, frizzled, wiry, crinkled, frizzy. 2 *Her stories were a bit kinky:* odd, eccentric, peculiar, bizarre, strange, queer, perverse, idiosyncratic; freakish, abnormal, aberrant, unnatural.
　Ant. 2 orthodox, normal, ordinary.

kinsman *n. kinsmen from Europe:* relative, relation, kin; countryman, landsman, fellow citizen.

kismet *n. It was my kismet to be a soldier:* destiny, fate, portion, lot, predestination, inevitability.

kit *n. Get the kit from the truck:* set of tools, instruments, implements, utensils; equipment, tools, supplies, devices, gear, tackle, outfit, necessaries, provisions; things, paraphernalia, trappings, impediments, rig.

knack *n. She had a knack for math:* talent, facility, gift, aptitude, genius, faculty, flair, natural endowment, proficiency, capability, capacity, forte, bent, inclination.

knave *n. The knave cheated her:* rascal, scoundrel, blackguard, rogue, charlatan, swindler, scalawag, scamp, rapscallion, cad, rotter, bounder, good-for-nothing; *Slang* rat, cur, dog.

knickknack *n. They had knickknacks on the shelves:* small object, trifle, bagatelle, bauble, trinket, gewgaw, gimcrack, bric-a-brac.

knife *n. a knife for whittling:* cutting tool, blade; *(variously)* pocketknife, penknife, jackknife, paring knife, switchblade, bowie knife, hunting knife, bread knife, butcher knife, table knife, carving knife, scalpel, palette knife, putty knife, pruning knife, stiletto, dirk, dagger.

knit *v.* 1 *I knitted scarves:* weave, do needlework; twist, intertwine, plait, braid, crochet. 2 *Common interests knitted the group together:* draw, draw together, join, connect, unite, unify, bind, link. 3 *He knitted his brow:* wrinkle, knot, crease, furrow.

knob *n.* 1 *We replaced the knobs on the doors:* rounded handle, handhold, hold, grip. 2 *Smooth out the knobs on the wood:* lump, hump, bump, knot, knurl, knur, nub, node, protuberance, protrusion, bulge, swell, projection, prominence.

knock *v.* 1 *We knocked at the door:* rap, tap, hit, strike; bang, thump, thud; pound, pummel, batter, strike. 2 *The assailant knocked me to the ground:* hit, strike, smite, slap, pummel, pound, beat, push, jostle. 3 *Informal The critics knocked her last play:* criticize, find fault with, belittle, disparage, deprecate, cavil, lambaste, decry, condemn.
　—*n.* 4 *Amnesia can be caused by a knock on*

the head: stroke, hit, thump, thwack, bang, tap, rap, blow, smack, whack, smash, bump, blow, crack; sock, clout.

knot *n.* 1 *The rope was tied in a knot:* interlacement, twist, loop. 2 *a sweater decorated with knots of embroidery:* rosette, loop, frog, epaulet. 3 *A knot of people waited at the entrance:* cluster, bunch, clump; gathering, circle, group, assemblage, collection; bundle, pack, lump, heap, pile, mass. 4 *The blow left a knot on my head:* hump, bump, knurl. 5 *She wore her hair in a knot:* bun, chignon, top-knot, tuft.

knotty *adj.* 1 *knotty wood:* knobby, full of knots, gnarled, rough, rough-grained, coarse, coarse-grained, bumpy, knurly, knurled. 2 *a knotty problem:* difficult, tricky, complex, complicated, hard, tough, perplexing, puzzling, involved, intricate, baffling.
　Ant. 1 smooth. 2 simple, obvious, easy.

know *v.* 1 *I knew the job would be difficult:* be certain, be sure, apprehend, realize, discern, be positive, be confident, feel certain, be assured, have knowledge, have information about, be informed, recognize, perceive, see, understand, be aware of; be intelligent, be wise. 2 *He knew the layout of the room:* have knowledge of, have in one's head, be acquainted with, be familiar with, know inside out, know backwards and forwards, know by heart. 3 *We know many people in Chicago:* be acquainted with, be familiar with, enjoy the friendship of, be on good terms with, be close to, be on intimate terms with; have dealings with. 4 *One should always know one's enemies:* identify, be able to distinguish, discern, make out, perceive; recognize.
　Ant. 1 be ignorant, overlook, misunderstand. 3 be unacquainted with, be unfamiliar with.

know-how *n. She had know-how in computer programming:* expertise, skill, ability, proficiency, competence, mastery, capability, adeptness, skillfulness, experience.
　Ant. incompetence, inexperience, unfamiliarity.

knowing *adj.* 1 *a very knowing scholar:* sagacious, wise, intelligent, intellectual, knowledgeable, bright, widely read, educated, learned, well-informed, astute, shrewd, smart, sharp, aware, perceptive, perspicacious; understanding, comprehending, discerning. 2 *She gave us a knowing look:* meaningful, significant, expressive, revealing; conscious, aware, perceptive.
　Ant. 1 unknowing, unintelligent, uncomprehending. 2 blank, dull, empty.

knowledge n. 1 *I was amazed at the breadth of her knowledge:* learning, scholarship, education, intelligence, schooling, cultivation, information. 2 *The populace received knowledge that the war was over:* communication, information, data, news, tidings, intelligence; report, announcement, notice, notification. 3 *Amnesia left me with no knowledge of my past:* awareness, realization, consciousness, perception, cognizance, recognition, familiarity, memory, comprehension.
Ant. 1 ignorance, misunderstanding, unawareness.

knowledgeable adj. *I'm knowledgeable about current events:* well-informed, abreast of, conversant with, acquainted with, versed in, familiar with.

known adj. *She was a known star of stage and screen:* recognized, acknowledged, familiar, popular, celebrated, famous, prominent, well-known, noted; obvious, evident, manifest, self-evident, distinct, definite.
Ant. unknown, unfamiliar, unrecognized.

knurled adj. *a knurled walking stick:* knotted, gnarled, bumpy, lumpy, knurly, knobby, knotty, nubbly, gnarly.

kowtow v. *The mayor expected everyone to kowtow:* stoop, bend, genuflect, curtsy, bow, salaam; bow and scrape, grovel, toady, truckle; cower, fall on one's knees, prostrate oneself, bend the knee.

kudos n. Informal *His novel brought him kudos from the critics:* praise, laudation, honor, acclaim, commendation, esteem, glory, prestige; awards, prizes.

L

label n. 1 *The sale items had special labels:* tag, ticket, sticker, slip, sign, stamp, mark; name, brand, identification, designation, classification, appellation, earmark. —v. 2 *I was labeled a traitor:* mark, note, tag, ticket; name, classify, describe, designate, characterize, brand.

labor n. 1 *Much labor went into the project:* industriousness, laboriousness, plodding, toil, work, manual labor, travail, drudgery. 2 *She went into labor two weeks early:* birth pangs, birth throes; parturition, childbirth, accouchement. —v. 3 *We labored in the mines for 30 years:* work, drudge, toil, sweat, slave; occupy oneself with, busy oneself with, employ one's time. 4 *to labor under a delusion:* suffer, be the victim of, be affected by, be troubled by, be burdened by.
Ant. 1 rest, repose, relaxation, leisure. 3 rest, relax.

labored adj. 1 *She moved in a labored manner:* ponderous, heavy, stiff, wooden; difficult, strained, forced, laborious, halting. 2 *Your so-called witticisms are labored:* strained, studied, forced, contrived, unnatural, overdone, unspontaneous, self-conscious.
Ant. 1 easy, natural.

laborer n. *a laborer in a steel mill:* workman, worker, blue-collar worker, laboring man, workingman, workhand, toiler, manual worker; hand, hired hand.

laborious adj. *a laborious task:* strenuous, burdensome, onerous, toilsome, arduous, difficult, hard, troublesome, demanding; fatiguing, wearying, wearing.
Ant. easy, effortless, undemanding.

labyrinth n. *The second floor was a labyrinth of offices:* maze, network, convolution, perplexity, complexity, intricacy; snarl, tangle, web, knot.

lacerate v. *The broken glass lacerated her arm:* slash, cut, gash, puncture, wound, stab, slice; hurt, inflict pain, torment, distress.

lack n. 1 *a lack of food:* want, absence, deficiency, need; privation, deprivation; scarcity, scantness, dearth, shortage; omission. —v. 2 *We lacked the money to get the business started:* be short of, fall short of, want, be deficient in, be inadequate, be insufficient, be missing.
Ant. 1 sufficiency, adequacy; abundance, plentifulness, excess, surplus, plethora.

lackadaisical adj. *a lackadaisical worker:* indifferent, listless, lifeless, spiritless, uninspired, unambitious, unaspiring, unmotivated, languid, lethargic, phlegmatic; apathetic; uninterested, indifferent, unconcerned.
Ant. spirited, inspired, ambitious, intense, diligent.

lackey n. *the king's lackeys:* attendant, servant, helper, retainer, hireling, minion, hanger-on, toady, underling, menial, flunky.

lackluster adj. *a lackluster performance:* drab, dull, lifeless, pallid, lusterless, leaden, dreary, colorless, bland, uninteresting, ordinary, humdrum, boring.

   Ant. exciting, brilliant, scintillating.

laconic adj. *His speeches were laconic:* short, concise, brief, succinct, terse, compact, condensed, pithy, concentrated, sparing of words, to the point; curt, blunt.

   Ant. wordy, loquacious, garrulous, verbose.

lacuna n. *There was a lacuna in her life story:* gap, hiatus, break, blank, interstice, interval, interruption, interim, void, omission, hole, opening, gulf, breach, discontinuity, pause, suspension.

lacy adj. *lacy patterns of frost:* lacelike, gossamer, filigree, webby, filigreed, netlike, reticulate, latticelike, diaphanous, gauzy; fine, delicate, sheer.

lad n. *He's an enterprising lad:* boy, youth, juvenile, youngster, young man, schoolboy; stripling, kid, young fellow, young chap.

lady n. 1 *In the old days a lady didn't smoke:* well-bred woman, respectable woman, woman of refinement, woman of good family, gentlewoman; wife, spouse. 2 *The ladies entered first:* woman, matron, female.

ladylike adj. *That wasn't a ladylike thing to say: (of a woman)* well-bred, well-mannered, polite, courteous, mannerly, genteel, decorous, refined, dignified, well brought up, proper, respectable, civil.

   Ant. unladylike, ill-bred, ill-mannered, impolite, discourteous.

lag v. 1 *The toddler always lags behind:* trail, drag, linger, loiter, dawdle, tarry, delay, be slow; procrastinate, dally, take one's time, be late. —n. 2 *Bad weather caused a lag in the scheduled activities:* delay, slackening, falling behind, slowing down, hold-up.

   Ant. 1 lead, go ahead, hurry along. 2 speeding up, advance.

laggard n. *The sergeant shouted angrily at the laggards:* straggler, lingerer, dallier, dawdler, idler, sluggard, loafer, dilly-dallier, slowpoke.

   Ant. go-getter, live wire, dynamo.

laissez-faire n. *the government's policy of laissez-faire toward industry:* nonintervention, noninterference, let-alone policy; unconcern, indifference; live and let live.

lambaste v. 1 *The home team lambasted the visitors:* beat, thrash, trounce, whip, pummel, lick, pelt; defeat, subdue, vanquish, overwhelm, wallop, drub; *Informal* shellac, clobber. 2 *She lambasted me for being late:* scold, berate, castigate, repri-

mand, dress down, rebuke, cuss out, denounce; *Informal* bawl out.

   Ant. 2 praise, commend, extol, laud.

lame adj. 1 *The accident left him lame:* crippled, disabled, limping, halt, hobbled; game, deformed; feeble, faltering, weak, halting. 2 *a lame excuse:* weak, feeble, inadequate, sorry, insufficient, flimsy, unconvincing, ineffectual, unsatisfactory.

lament v. 1 *We lamented the death of our friend:* mourn, weep, bewail; deplore, show concern for, express pity for, regret. —n. 2 *We could hear her laments:* lamentation, sob, plaint, cry, moan, wail, keening, wail, whimper; mourning; dirge, song of lamentation, death song, funeral music, requiem.

lamentable adj. 1 *a lamentable accident:* deplorable, dreadful, terrible, regrettable, woeful, grievous, unfortunate, distressing, shameful, disheartening. 2 *the lamentable plight of the refugees:* heartbreaking, distressing, wretched, miserable, pitiable, piteous, pathetic.

   Ant. 2 happy, fortunate, felicitous.

lampoon n. 1 *a lampoon of the current political scene:* satire, burlesque, parody, mockery, spoof, travesty. —v. 2 *to lampoon the current administration:* satirize, parody, ridicule, burlesque, caricature.

land n. 1 *to be back on dry land:* ground, earth, dry land, terra firma. 2 *This land is good for vegetables. We own land in Vermont:* ground, soil, earth, dirt; real estate, realty, property; grounds, acres. 3 *the land my father came from:* country, nation, state; region, territory, terrain, area, district; fatherland, motherland, homeland, native land, native soil, the old country. —v. 4 *The plane landed in Chicago:* come in for a landing, descend, come down, alight, light, settle down; set down. 5 *The ship landed on Saturday:* dock, put into port, make port, anchor, drop anchor, tie up; debark, disembark. 6 *I landed six new accounts:* lay hold of, catch, gain, secure, get, capture, snare, net.

landmark n. *The court's decision is a landmark:* milestone, high point, turning point, watershed; signpost, guidepost, benchmark; monument, historic building.

lane n. *There was a narrow lane through the village:* path, passageway, footpath, way, road, roadway, alley, alleyway, passage, bypath; course, route, trail, access, approach.

language n. 1 *He spoke the language of his country:* speech, tongue, vocabulary, idiom, vernacular, mother tongue, native tongue; *Informal* lingo; dialect, patois, jargon;

slang, colloquialism, cant, argot, *Slang* jive. 2 *The student had problems with language:* oral communication, self-expression, reading and writing, verbal intercourse; elocution, public speaking; words. 3 *the language of the law:* vocabulary, wording, phraseology, speech, prose, parlance, expression, idiom, rhetoric, use of words; diction, idiom, mode of expression.

languid *adj. The illness made me feel languid:* faint, feeble, weak, weary, drooping, sickly, debilitated, fatigued, exhausted, worn-out, spent; lackadaisical, languorous, sluggish, listless, lifeless, lethargic, spiritless.
Ant. strong, energetic, vigorous, robust.

languish *v. We languished in the tropical climate:* decline, droop, flag, diminish, fade, wilt, wither, deteriorate, wane, ebb; waste away, become ill.
Ant. thrive, prosper, flourish.

languor *n. the languor of life in the tropics:* listlessness, torpor, lassitude, sluggishness, torpidity, lethargy, languidness, leisureness.
Ant. vitality, vigor, verve, zest.

lanky *adj. a lanky basketball player:* tall and thin, lean, bony, scrawny, skinny, rawboned, gaunt, spare, gangling.
Ant. burly, plump, rotund, chubby, stout, fat.

lap *v.* 1 *The kittens lapped up the milk:* lick, lick up, tongue; drink, sip. 2 *We heard the waves lapping at the shore:* ripple, slosh, wash, splash, plash; murmur, gurgle.

lapse *n.* 1 *a lapse of manners:* breach, disregard, dereliction, error, slight mistake, omission, slip, oversight, fault, flaw, negligence, infraction, loss, failure, failing, shortcoming. 2 *to lapse into ill health:* decline, descent, drop, relapse, regression, wane, slump, deterioration, degeneration. 3 *After a lapse of two years the business reopened:* interval, interim, interlude; intermission, interruption, pause, recess; break, hiatus, gap. —*v.* 4 *He lapsed into a coma:* fall, slip, decline, subside, sink, relapse, recede, deteriorate, degenerate, wither, drop. 5 *The warranty lapsed two months ago:* expire, run out, terminate, stop, cease. 6 *Only five minutes had lapsed before she returned:* pass by, elapse, slip by, slip away, go by.

larceny *n. The thief was charged with larceny:* stealing, theft, robbery, burglary; embezzlement, extortion, cheating, swindling, fraud.

large *adj. a large house. a large allowance. a large build:* big, huge, great, massive, immense, enormous, gigantic, spacious, capacious, vast, roomy, expansive, sizable; substantial, considerable, ample, goodly, liberal, copious; extensive, wide, broad, boundless, high; strapping, heavy, rotund, obese, fat, portly, plump, outsized, monstrous, colossal, gargantuan; kingsized, man-sized.
Ant. small, little, tiny, diminutive; inconsiderable, paltry, scanty, sparse, trifling, trivial; slight, slender, slim, thin.

largely *adv. I owe my success largely to hard work:* mostly, mainly, chiefly, for the most part, by and large, primarily, principally, generally, predominantly, substantially.

large-scale *adj. a large-scale war:* extensive, wide-ranging, far-flung, all-out, all-encompassing; big, huge, great, vast, gigantic, stupendous, monstrous, tremendous.
Ant. small-scale, limited, restricted.

largess Also **largesse** *n. She was known for her largess:* generosity, benefaction, kindness, benevolence, bounty, philanthropy; donation, gift, assistance, aid, help, charity, mercy, benignity; payment, remuneration, gratuity.

lascivious *adj. lascivious conduct:* indecent, lewd, immoral, lustful, prurient; vulgar, gross, coarse, indelicate, salacious, dirty, dirty-minded, impure, immodest, lecherous, lurid; wanton, licentious, depraved.

lash *n.* 1 *The pirate captain beat the crew with a lash:* whip, scourge, cat-o'-nine-tails; strap, thong. 2 *The criminal was sentenced to 50 lashes:* whip, blow, stroke, hit. —*v.* 3 *The wagon driver lashed the horses:* whip, whip up, flog, thrash, flail; horsewhip. 4 *Rain lashed against the windowpane:* beat, strike, smack, hit, knock, buffet, pound, hammer. 5 *The sergeant lashed the troops for their sloppy dress:* tongue-lash, berate, castigate, rail against, revile, curse, upbraid, scold.
Ant. 5 praise, compliment, commend, laud.

lass *n. the young lasses of Ireland:* girl, young woman, damsel, schoolgirl, maiden, maid, female, miss, virgin; colleen, lassie.

lassitude *n. Her lassitude was caused by overwork:* weariness, sluggishness, fatigue, tiredness, exhaustion, lack of energy, lethargy, listlessness, indolence, faintness, torpor, drowsiness, languor, languidness.
Ant. vigor, energy, verve, vitality, vim, pep.

last[1] *adj.* 1 *the last word. the last one on line:* final, conclusive, closing, concluding, terminal, ultimate; rearmost, hindmost, at the end, tailing. —*adv.* 2 *Our horse came in last in the race:* after all others, behind, in back of, in the rear, trailing, in last place. 3 *She told us her secret at last:* finally, ultimately, eventually. —*n.* 4 *You were the last on the* *list:* final one, concluding person or thing; rearmost one. **5** *At the last, you will not be able to repent!:* end, conclusion, crucial time, closing, ending, finish, finale; end of the world, doomsday, Day of Judgment.

Ant. **1** first, initial. **2** first, in front. **4** first.

last² *v. This coat will last for years:* continue, go on, persist, exist, survive, endure, remain, carry on, hold out, hold on, maintain, keep, persevere, abide, subsist, live; wear, stand up, hold up.

Ant. end, stop, expire, cease; wear out, give out.

lasting *adj. a lasting peace:* enduring, abiding, continuing, durable, permanent, never-ending, long-lived, protracted; of long duration; firm, steadfast, constant, perpetual, unceasing, indestructible; established, fixed, persistent.

Ant. fleeting, passing, transitory, short-lived, ephemeral, momentary.

lastly *adv. Lastly, let me stress the importance of everyone's cooperation:* finally, in conclusion, at last, after all.

Ant. firstly, at the outset, in the beginning.

latch *n.* **1** *The latch on the door is secure:* lock, catch, bolt, bar, fastening; hasp, clamp, buckle. —*v.* **2** *Latch the gate:* lock, bolt, fasten, hook, secure, make fast.

Ant. **2** unlatch, unfasten.

late *adj.* **1** *He was always late. The project is late:* tardy, overdue, unpunctual, dilatory, behind time; slow, delayed, postponed, put off, held up. **2** *I was a late addition to the crew:* recent, new, fresh. **3** *the late president:* lately dead, recently deceased; departed, passed on. —*adv.* **4** *We arrived late:* behind time, after time, tardily, dilatorily.

Ant. **1** early, punctual, prompt, ahead of time. **2** old, seasoned. **3** still living, existing. **4** early, ahead of time, beforehand.

lately *adv. Lately I've taken to skiing:* recently, of late, not long ago, a short time ago.

latent *adj. a latent volcano:* dormant, sleeping, quiescent, inactive; potential, undeveloped, unrealized, unaroused, not manifest, hidden, unexpressed.

Ant. activated, developed; manifest, apparent, evident, obvious.

later *adv.* **1** *The others will join us later:* afterward, at a subsequent time, in a while, thereafter, in time, presently, subsequently, after a while; next, following, from that moment, in the course of time. —*adj.* **2** *The later arrivals stood in back:* subsequent, ensuing, successive, following, succeeding. **3** *The later works are the composer's best:*

mature; more recent, most recent; toward the end, latter.

Ant. **2** earlier, prior.

lateral *adj. in a lateral direction:* side, sideways, sidewise, sideward, sidelong; flanking, flanked; slanting, sloping, oblique.

lather *n.* **1** *This shampoo makes a lot of lather:* foam, froth, suds, spume. —*v.* **2** *Lather your hair before rinsing:* soap, soap up; make froth, make foam.

latter *adj.* **1** *Of the two examples, I prefer the latter:* second-mentioned, most recent, latest, later; successive, succeeding, subsequent; last-mentioned, last. **2** *the latter part of the day:* later, final, last, end, ending, terminal.

Ant. **1** former, previous; first. **2** first, beginning, opening.

laudable *adj. a laudable deed:* praiseworthy, admirable, commendable, meritorious, exemplary, noble, excellent.

Ant. contemptible, base, unworthy, blameworthy, ignoble.

laudatory *adj. a laudatory letter of reference:* praising, complimentary, approving, favorable, commendatory, panegyrical, flattering, acclamatory, admiring.

Ant. critical, censorious, scornful.

laugh *v.* **1** *The clown made the children laugh:* chuckle, giggle, roar with laughter, chortle, guffaw, snicker, titter, snigger, cackle, split one's sides, howl. —*n.* **2** *The comedian drew laughs from the audience:* guffaw, giggle, chortle, roar, cackle, peal of laughter, snicker, snigger, horselaugh, bellylaugh, ha-ha.

Ant. **1** scowl, cry.

laughable *adj. The situation was laughable:* hilarious, funny, amusing, risible, droll, witty, comic, comical, farcical, sidesplitting, rib-tickling; ludicrous, ridiculous, silly, stupid, preposterous, outlandish, foolish, absurd.

Ant. solemn, serious, grave, somber.

launch *v.* **1** *The shipyard launched the freighter:* float, set afloat, send down the skids, set into the water. **2** *The firm launched a new product:* inaugurate, begin, initiate, start, introduce, unveil; embark upon, venture upon; institute, found, establish. **3** *to launch a rocket:* shoot, discharge, hurl, propel, project, cast forth, throw, eject, impel, send off, fire off, fire.

Ant. **1** beach, ground; dock. **2** withdraw.

laurels *n. She won her laurels as a scientist:* glory, fame, renown, honor, award, reward, praise, kudos, acclaim, distinction, illustriousness, commendation, recognition, accolade, citation.

lavish *adj.* 1 *lavish praise:* free, profuse, plenteous, plentiful, abundant, extravagant, generous, effusive, bounteous, bountiful, copious; sumptuous, opulent, luxuriant, lush, plush, excessive, profligate, immoderate, munificent, exuberant. —*v.* 2 *The prince lavished money on his yachts:* squander, spend freely, waste, dissipate, bestow generously, fritter away.

Ant. 1 meager, sparing, scanty, stingy, niggardly.

law *n.* 1 *a federal law:* rule, governing principle, regulation, commandment, dictate, decree, enactment, edict, order, statute, ordinance, canon, bylaw, act, bill. 2 *There was no law in many parts of the Old West:* system of laws, collection of rules, code; lawful behavior, orderliness, legal process, due process of law; legality, writ. 3 *Newton's laws of motion:* principle, standard, criterion, axiom, postulate, dogma, precept, fundamental, working rule, formulation, theorem; absolute, invariable. 4 *Will you go into law or medicine?:* jurisprudence, the practice of law, legal profession.

Ant. 2 chaos, anarchy, disorder.

lawful *adj.* 1 *lawful activities:* legal, sanctioned by law, legally permitted, authorized, legitimate, legalized, legitimized, within the law, licit, allowed, permissible. 2 *the lawful owner:* rightful, proper, acknowledged by law, legally entitled, legitimate, legally recognized, titled, due.

Ant. 1 unlawful, illegal, illicit.

lawless *adj.* 1 *the lawless activities of the cattle thieves:* unlawful, contrary to law, lawbreaking, illegal, illegitimate. 2 *a lawless crowd:* disorderly, rebellious, mutinous, unruly, uncontrollable, ungoverned, insurgent, refractory, riotous. 3 *The town was lawless until the marshal arrived:* heedless of law, ungoverned, chaotic, unrestrained, unbridled, freewheeling, wide open.

Ant. 1 lawful, law-abiding, licit, legitimate. 2 restrained, disciplined, orderly. 3 lawabiding.

lawn *n. The lawn needs mowing:* grass, yard, grassy ground, sward, grassy plot, turf, grounds.

lawyer *n. the lawyer for the accused:* attorney, attorney-at-law, counselor, counsel, advocate, legal advisor, jurist, counselor-at-law; *British* solicitor, barrister.

lax *adj.* 1 *The student was lax in studying:* negligent, neglectful, irresponsible, heedless, careless, unheeding, slipshod, remiss, derelict, indifferent, unconscientious, undutiful, indifferent, casual, unconcerned, thoughtless; permissive, lenient. 2 *The lax instructions left us confused:* careless,

vague, hazy, nebulous, ill-defined, imprecise, inexact.

Ant. 1 scrupulous, strict, rigid, conscientious; severe, stern, stringent. 2 exact, precise, specific.

lay[1] *v.* 1 *Lay the packages on the table:* put, place, set down, set, rest, deposit. 2 *The tornado laid the house flat:* prostrate, knock down, level, fell, knock over. 3 *The nominating committee laid its slate before the board:* present, offer, proffer, place, put. 4 *I'll lay you odds he will be late:* wager, bet, gamble, hazard; give odds. 5 *A turtle lays many eggs:* produce, bear, deposit, oviposit. 6 *The tiles were laid in a geometric pattern:* place, arrange, set, align, lay out, assemble. 7 *to lay too much emphasis on grades:* place, put, assign, allot, allocate, give; attribute, impute. 8 *The first act was laid at a country estate:* set, locate, place, depict, situate, stage, station. 9 *The prisoners laid an escape plan:* arrange, formulate, form, make, devise, concoct, plan. 10 *The town laid an assessment on property owners:* levy, charge, impose, exact, assess. —*n.* 11 *Survey the lay of the land:* position, situation, arrangement, disposition, orientation, configuration, conformation.

Ant. 1, 2 raise, lift. 3 withhold, withdraw.

lay[2] *adj.* 1 *She serves as a lay teacher at the convent school:* nonecclesiastical, profane, secular, nonclerical, laic, laical. 2 *The patient's lay diagnosis was close to the doctor's:* nonprofessional, unprofessional, amateur, nonspecialist.

Ant. 1 ecclesiastical, clerical, church. 2 professional, expert, specialized.

layer *n. a layer of fog. The cake has three layers:* thickness, fold, sheet, coat, stratum, seam, tier, slab, zone, level, story, ply.

layoff *n. Widespread layoffs affected much of the industry:* dismissal, discharge, firing, termination, sacking, furloughing; unemployment.

layout *n. The layout for the ad was approved:* design, plan, blueprint, diagram, sketch, drawing; arrangement, pattern, structure, form.

lazy *adj.* 1 *I'm too lazy to clean house:* unwilling to work, shiftless, indolent, slothful, listless, unindustrious. 2 *a hot, lazy day:* sluggish, lethargic, torpid, languid, slowmoving; easygoing, sleepy, drowsy.

Ant. 1 industrious, diligent. 2 active, brisk.

lead *v.* 1 *The tug will lead the liner into the harbor:* guide, draw, direct, command, conduct, convey, shepherd; precede, go before. 2 *The candidate's integrity led the voters to support her:* influence, persuade, attract, induce, allure, lure, tempt, seduce, draw, entice. 3 *The path leads to the river:* proceed, advance, go, extend. 4 *The dean will lead the meeting:* direct, moderate, conduct, manage, preside over, control, head, command. 5 *That nation leads in industrial output:* excell, rank first, outstrip, outdo, surpass, come first, pioneer. 6 *The drum major led the parade:* go first, head, be in advance, top. 7 *She leads a full life:* pass, conduct, pursue, experience, live, have. 8 *The accident led to many lawsuits:* result in, produce, issue in, bring on. —*n.* 9 *The black horse took the lead:* precedence, advance, first place, foremost position, advantage. 10 *The police haven't a single lead:* clue, hint, guide. 11 *Most of the legislators followed the lead of the governor:* model, example, direction, indication, leadership. 12 *A versatile actor is needed for the lead:* leading role, star part; protagonist, hero, principal performer; leading man, leading woman.

Ant. 1 tail, trail. 2 disincline. 5 lag, trail.

leader *n. the leader of the fund raising drive:* head, director, conductor, chief, supervisor, commander, manager, captain, foreman, boss; frontrunner, pacesetter, pacemaker, pioneer, pathfinder, trailblazer.

Ant. follower, adherent, disciple.

leadership *n.* 1 *the leadership of the country:* administration, directorship, managership, governorship, stewardship, guardianship, superintendency, guidance; supremacy, primacy; helm, wheel, reins. 2 *The child showed leadership:* ability to lead, managerial skill, command, preeminence.

leading *adj.* 1 *Monet was the leading French Impressionist:* foremost, most influential, most important, most significant, supreme, chief, prominent, notable, great, ranking, prime, preeminent, principal, dominant, main, top, paramount, outstanding, stellar. 2 *The leading group in the parade:* leadoff, foremost, advance, first, prime, initial, advance. 3 *my leading motive for writing the book:* principal, primary, guiding, directing, controlling, governing, ruling, motivating, prime, underlying, basic, essential, quintessential.

Ant. 1–3 secondary. 1 subordinate, inferior, minor, lesser. 2 hindmost. 3 incidental, superficial.

leaf *n.* 1 *the leaves of plants:* frond, cotyledon, blade, needle, bract, foliole. 2 *The old book's leaves are crumbling:* page, sheet, leaflet, folio. 3 *gold leaf:* foil, lamination, sheet of metal, lamella.

leaflet *n. a leaflet advertising a nearby restaurant:* pamphlet, handbill, flyer, folder, brochure, booklet; circular; broadside, tract; broadsheet.

league *n. Several nations formed a defense league:* alliance, association, group, collaboration, partnership, confederacy, confederation, federation, coalition, union, fraternity, society.

leak *n.* 1 *a leak in a water main:* opening, hole, puncture, perforation, rupture, break, breach, rent, rip. 2 *The leak was so slow we barely noticed it:* leaking, leakage, draining, drain, seepage, escape. —*v.* 3 *The roof leaks. The pipe leans:* admit leakage, be permeable, take in; discharge, vent, dribble, let enter. 4 *An informant leaked the news to the press:* divulge, reveal, disclose, give away, confide.

Ant. 4 conceal, hide, suppress.

lean[1] *v.* 1 *The exhausted runner leaned against the fence:* rest, rest one's weight, support oneself, prop oneself, recline. 2 *The tree leans in the wind:* bend, incline, tilt, slant, tip, list, slope. 3 *You can always lean on me:* rely, depend, have faith in, seek solace in, resort to, take assurance from, set store by, trust in, count on. 4 *Today, we lean toward casual clothes:* tend, incline, have a propensity for, be partial to, prefer.

lean[2] *adj.* 1 *He was lean and pale:* not fat, thin, spare, skinny, slender, willowy, svelte, slim, skeletal, spindly, lanky, rawboned, scraggy; emaciated, gaunt, scrawny. 2 *The firm realized lean profits:* meager, scant, scanty, small, spare, sparse, modest.

Ant. 1 brawny, plump, portly. 2 abundant, plentiful, ample.

leap *v.* 1 *We leaped over the wall:* jump, spring, bound, hop, hurtle, vault; bounce, gambol, prance, caper, frisk, frolic, skip, romp, cavort. 2 *Don't leap to any conclusions:* rush, hasten, jump, come hastily. —*n.* 3 *I cleared the fence in one leap:* bound, jump, spring, hurtle, hop, vault.

learn *v.* 1 *to learn to swim:* master, pick up, acquire knowledge of; receive instructions in, become able. 2 *to learn the answer:* find out, determine, discover, detect, unearth, ascertain. 3 *When did you learn of Mary's divorce?:* hear, find out about, become apprised, become familiar with, become informed. 4 *The actor had trouble learning the part:* memorize, commit to memory.

Ant. 1 teach, instruct. 4 forget.

learned *adj. a learned rabbi:* informed, educated, schooled, accomplished, scholarly, well-educated, cultivated, literate, knowledgeable.

Ant. uneducated, unlearned, ignorant.

learning *n. a university professor of immense learning:* education, scholarship, knowledge, schooling, culture, information, understanding, comprehension, cultivation. *Ant.* ignorance, uncomprehension.

leash *n.* 1 *the dog's leash:* lead, curb, rein, bridle, line, tether, choker. —*v.* 2 *Leash the dog. Leash your anger:* restrain, fasten, control, ruin, curb, harness; suppress, contain, stifle.

Ant. 2 unleash; release, vent.

leave *v.* 1 *Leave the room. The circus left town this morning:* go away from, separate from, quit, retire from, be off, depart, set out, go, exit, decamp, fly, flee, *Slang* shove off, take off, split. 2 *Leave that window open:* let stay, let remain, keep, maintain, retain. 3 *The boy left school in the middle of the year:* abandon, forsake, depart from; surrender, relinquish, desert, leave behind, yield, give up. 4 *Leave the diagnosis to the doctor:* yield, entrust, allot, consign, give over, resign, cede, forgo, release, surrender, commit, assign. 5 *The cigarette left a bad taste in my mouth:* result in, produce, deposit, generate, cause. 6 *He leaves a wife and three children:* leave behind, be survived by. 7 *We left our money to charity:* bequeath, bequest, legate, will; commit, assign, consign, apportion, endow. —*n.* 8 *The senator asked leave to speak:* permission, consent, allowance, indulgence, sanction, approval, endorsement; understanding, tolerance, concession. 9 *I took my leave after thanking the host:* parting, departure, farewell, going, leave-taking. 10 *She's on maternity leave:* furlough, sabbatical, respite, liberty, recess, time off, vacation.

Ant. 1 arrive, come, appear. 3 persist, gain, hold; stay, continue. 5 remove, erase, eradicate. 8 rejection, refusal, denial, prohibition. 9 arrival.

lecherous *adj. His lecherous behavior scandalized us:* lustful, lewd, libidinous, lascivious, salacious, prurient, licentious.

lechery *n. Don Juan led a life of lechery:* carnality, lust, lustfulness, promiscuity, lewdness, prurience, lasciviousness.

Ant. purity, chasteness, celibacy.

lecture *n.* 1 *a classroom lecture:* talk, address, speech, discourse, oral presentation, disquisition; oration; sermon. 2 *Mother gave us a lecture on keeping our rooms neat:* rebuke, reprimand, admonitory speech, harangue, admonishment, moralizing talk, warning, remonstrance, talking-to, dressing down, reproof, reproach, chiding. —*v.* 3 *to lecture on ancient history:* talk, give a talk, speak, expound, discourse. 4 *The doctor lectured her about smoking:* reprove, rebuke, call down, take to task, harangue, rail at, scold, admonish, criticize at length, censure, chide, upbraid; preach, sermonize.

Ant. 4 praise, compliment, laud.

ledge *n. a rocky ledge:* shelf, projection, ridge, outcropping, sill, step, foothold, shoulder.

leer *n.* 1 *His leer frightened her:* lewd look, lustful look, lascivious stare; sly glance, evil look, insulting stare. —*v.* 2 *The sailors leered at every passing girl:* stare suggestively, give the eye to, look knowingly, ogle; smirk.

leery *adj. Be leery of get-rich-quick schemes:* wary, suspicious, distrustful, circumspect, cautious, doubtful, skeptical, chary, mistrustful; hesitant, unsure, undecided.

Ant. trusting, credulous, unsuspecting.

leeway *n. Our schedule leaves no leeway for delays:* flexibility, latitude, margin for error, allowance, reserve.

leftover *n.* 1 *Save the leftovers for the dogs:* residue, excess, remainder, surplus, residual, oddments, overage; remaining food, remaining odds and ends, leavings. —*adj.* 2 *Use the leftover roast for hash:* remaining, residual, surplus, excess; unused; uneaten.

leg *n.* 1 *Stand on one leg:* lower extremity, limb; *Slang* underpinning, shank, gam; *(bones)* femur, fibula, tibia. 2 *One leg of the chair is cracked:* prop, support, upright, brace; post, column, pillar. 3 *the last leg of the journey:* portion, segment, part, stage, section.

legacy *n.* 1 *He left a large legacy:* bequest, gift; inheritance, estate. 2 *The Ionic style of architecture is a legacy from ancient Greece:* heritage, tradition; remaining portion, carry-over; heirloom, birthright; hand-me-down.

legal *adj.* 1 *a legal question:* of law; juridical, jurisprudential, juristic; judicial, adjudicatory; courtroom. 2 *a legal claim for redress:* permitted by law, lawful, permissible, sanctioned, licit, legitimate.

Ant. 2 illegal, unlawful, illegitimate, illicit.

legation *n. The nation's legation is housed near the UN:* diplomatic mission, consulate, delegation, ministry, embassy, chancellery.

legendary *adj.* 1 *a hero's legendary feats:* famous, familiar to all, famed, known by tradition, storied, proverbial, worthy of legend, celebrated. 2 *King Arthur is a legendary figure:* fabled, mythic, mythical, figuring in legends; fanciful, imaginary, fictitious, unauthenticated.

Ant. 1 unknown. 2 historical.

legerdemain *n.* 1 *the magician's legerdemain:* sleight of hand, prestidigitation, deftness, adroitness; juggling. 2 *a piece of political legerdemain:* deception, trickery, artfulness, cunning, adroit manipulation, maneuvering.

legible *adj. fancy but legible handwriting:* readable, easily read, decipherable, understandable, comprehensible, clear.

Ant. illegible, undecipherable, unreadable.

legion *n.* 1 *The ancient Roman legion had from 3,000 to 6,000 foot soldiers:* military force, army, division, brigade, corps. 2 *a legion of devoted followers:* multitude, great number, throng, swarm, mob, drove, horde.

legislation *n.* 1 *Legislation is the duty of Congress:* lawmaking, making law, passage of law. 2 *equal rights legislation:* legislative law, ordinance, enactment, bill, statute, act, measure, ruling.

legislator *n. Legislators are answerable to their constituents:* lawmaker, member of a legislature, representative, delegate, senator, representative, congressman, congresswoman, parliamentarian, councilman, assemblyman, alderman.

legislature *n. the state legislature:* lawmaking body; senate, parliament, congress, assembly, council, diet; house, chamber.

legitimacy *n. The legitimacy of their claim is in question:* legality, validity, lawfulness, rightfulness, correctness, appropriateness, authenticity.

Ant. illegitimacy, illegality, unlawfulness.

legitimate *adj.* 1 *Who is the legitimate heir?:* lawful, rightful, true, legal, licit. 2 *Their grievances are legitimate:* genuine, justified, authentic, logical, well-founded, just, valid; reasonable, fair; proper, appropriate.

Ant. 1 unlawful, illegal; fraudulent, false. 2 unfounded, unjustified, unfair.

leisure *n. a pleasant way to spend one's leisure:* free time, spare time, time off, idle hours, periods of relaxation; respite, rest, recess, diversion.

Ant. duty, work, occupation, employment.

leisurely *adj.* 1 *a leisurely stroll:* relaxed, restful, unhurried, without haste, slow-moving, casual. *—adv.* 2 *We walked leisurely:* unhurriedly, slowly, lingeringly, without haste.

Ant. 1 hasty, rushed, fast. 2 hurriedly, quickly, rapidly, fast.

lend *v.* 1 *Lend me five dollars:* loan, allow to use temporarily, trust one for. 2 *A fireplace lends coziness to a room:* impart, give, invest, supply, contribute. 3 *She lent her support to the plan:* contribute, give freely, put at another's disposal.

Ant. 1 borrow. 3 refuse, withhold.

length *n.* 1 *the length of the field:* reach, span, distance from end to end, extent, measure. 2 *The lot is 200 feet in length:* longer

dimension, longer side, lengthiest part. 3 *The length of the movie is two hours:* duration, extent, time; period, term, elapsed time. 4 *a length of string:* piece, segment, section, stretch.

Ant. 2 width, breadth, depth.

lengthen *v. to lengthen an essay:* extend, elongate, stretch, protract, draw out, drag out, prolong, expand, increase; add to.

Ant. shorten, abbreviate, decrease.

lengthy *adj. a lengthy speech:* long, overlong, of great length, extended, prolonged, protracted, elongated, extensive; drawn out, interminable, endless.

Ant. short, brief.

lenient *adj. The judge was lenient:* merciful, kind, clement, gentle, sparing, tender-hearted, indulgent, tolerant, forbearing, mild, soft, kind-hearted, soft-hearted, compassionate, sympathetic, benevolent; liberal, permissive, patient, forgiving.

Ant. harsh, stern, exacting, rigid, strict, cruel.

less *adj.* 1 *The movie had less success than expected:* smaller, not as great, more limited, slighter, not so significant. *—n.* 2 *People have been imprisoned for less:* a smaller amount, lesser action.

Ant. 1 more; greater, larger.

lessen *v. Talking lessened the tension:* decrease, decline, diminish, abate, dwindle, reduce; subside, lower, slacken, wind down, ease, wane, ebb; alleviate, mitigate.

Ant. increase, raise, heighten.

lesser *adj.* 1 *one of the composer's lesser works:* smaller, less important, secondary, slighter, minor. *—adv.* 2 *Of the two actors, he is the lesser known:* to a smaller degree, less.

Ant. 1 major, larger, primary. 2 greater.

lesson *n.* 1 *The test will cover lesson 8:* assignment, student's task, study, instruction, homework, drill, learning session. 2 *Her determination was a lesson to all:* example, model, exemplar, guide; moral, message, warning, admonition, caution; rebuke, punishment.

let *v.* 1 *Let me carry the bags:* permit, allow; authorize, approve, give assent to; sanction; enable, grant, empower, suffer, leave, tolerate; admit, concede. 2 *to let a house for the summer:* rent, lease, charter, sublease, sublet.

Ant. 1 forbid, prohibit.

letdown *n. I may have expected too much, but meeting her was a letdown:* disappointment, anticlimax, disenchantment; discontent, dissatisfaction, disillusionment; frustration, setback.

Ant. gratification, satisfaction.

lethal *adj. Sleeping pills can be lethal:* deadly, fatal, mortal, mortally toxic; dangerous, destructive; poisonous, venomous.

Ant. harmless, wholesome, healthful.

lethargic *adj. The hot, humid climate made us lethargic:* lazy, drowsy, sleepy, soporific, languid, indolent, idle, sluggish, slothful, listless.

Ant. energetic, vigorous, active; energized, stimulated.

lethargy *n. My lethargy made work impossible:* languor, lassitude, drowsiness, sluggishness, laziness, listlessness.

Ant. vigor, liveliness, eagerness.

letter *n.* 1 *to mail a letter:* epistle, missive; note, message, memorandum; love letter, billet-doux. 2 *to obey the letter of the law:* actual terms, specific details, literal wording, strict meaning, exact sense. 3 *letters a man of letters:* literary accomplishment, learning, erudition, scholarly attainment.

letup *n. She worked without letup:* stopping, slackening, cessation, pause, abatement, respite, lull; interlude, interval.

level *adj.* 1 *The floor is perfectly level:* flat, even, horizontal; flush, plane; uniform, consistent; smooth, unwrinkled; on an even keel, parallel to the horizon. 2 *Supply is level with demand:* even, on a line, aligned; equivalent to, comparable to, on a par with. —*n.* 3 *The water rose to the level of the porch:* height, elevation, vertical plane. 4 *She's at a third grade math level:* stage, rank, position, achievement. 5 *The shoe department is on the second level. They discovered fossils in the lowest level of rock:* floor, story, elevation; layer, bed, stratum, zone, vein. —*v.* 6 *to level a road:* grade, make even, even out, plane, flatten, smooth. 7 *A tornado leveled the town:* flatten, raze, knock down, topple, lay low, wreck, tear down, devastate. 8 *He leveled his gun at the target:* aim, direct, point.

Ant. 1 slanted, tilted, uneven, bumpy; vertical. 7 raise, erect; build, construct.

level-headed *adj. We need a leader who's level-headed:* sensible, prudent, steady, dependable, practical, sound; composed, cool-headed, self-controlled, poised, even-tempered.

Ant. foolish, thoughtless.

levy *n.* 1 *a levy on cigarette sales:* duty, excise, tax, assessment, fee, toll, tariff. —*v.* 2 *The court levied a fine on the defendant:* impose, demand, exact, assess, charge; collect. 3 *In 200 BC the Syrians levied war against Egypt:* wage, start, carry on, make, pursue.

lewd *adj. a lewd remark:* obscene, indecent, vulgar, lustful, lecherous, bawdy, ribald,

risqué, lascivious, wanton, licentious, prurient.

Ant. chaste, modest; proper, prim, pure.

lexicon *n. That word isn't in my lexicon:* wordbook, vocabulary, dictionary, thesaurus, glossary, wordlist, concordance, wordstock.

liability *n.* 1 *Heavy liabilities forced us into bankruptcy:* debt, obligation, indebtedness, debit; duty, responsibility. 2 *Shyness is a liability in politics:* disadvantage, drawback, burden, handicap, minus, impediment, hindrance, encumbrance.

Ant. 1, 2 asset. 2 plus, advantage, boon.

liable *adj.* 1 *Joggers are liable to knee injuries:* vulnerable, susceptible, open, exposed, subject; likely, apt, inclined, prone. 2 *He's liable for his wife's debts:* legally responsible, answerable, accountable, chargeable, obligated.

Ant. 1 immune; unlikely, disinclined.

liaison *n.* 1 *The negotiator acted as liaison between labor and management:* contact, connection, association, communication; alliance, bond, link; coordination, cooperation, interchange; go-between. 2 *The countess had a secret liaison with a cabinet minister:* love affair, illicit romance, amour, intrigue.

liar *n. a compulsive liar:* falsifier, prevaricator, fabricator, perjurer; fibber, storyteller.

libel *n.* 1 *a suit against the newspaper for libel:* printed slander, defamation, malicious falsehood; smear, aspersion, slur, vilification, unjust accusation. —*v.* 2 *The candidate charged that his opponent libeled him:* vilify, malign unjustly, slur, discredit, slander, defame, blacken.

liberal *adj.* 1 *liberal politicians:* progressive, reformist, freethinking; civil libertarian. 2 *Try to keep a liberal attitude and listen to both sides:* fair-minded, open-minded, broad-minded, tolerant, forbearing, unbigoted, unprejudiced, unbiased, impartial; enlightened, humanitarian. 3 *liberal donations to the hospital:* generous, lavish, openhanded, unsparing, bounteous, bountiful, handsome, munificent, unstinting, ample. 4 *a liberal interpretation of the rules:* lenient, broad, unrigorous, flexible, tolerant, not literal. —*n.* 5 *Liberals did not like the conservative policies:* progressive, reformer.

Ant. 1 conservative, reactionary, rightwing. 2 intolerant, narrow, bigoted, biased, prejudiced. 3 skimpy, small. 4 strict, inflexible, rigid, literal. 5 conservative, reactionary, right-winger.

liberate *v. to liberate the slaves. Liberate yourself from preconceived ideas:* set free, deliver, release, disencumber, emancipate,

manumit, redeem; rescue, extricate, let loose, unshackle, let out.
Ant. enslave.

libertine *n.* 1 *Casanova was a libertine:* debauchee, rake, voluptuary, lecher, roué, sensualist, seducer; moral iconoclast, womanizer. —*adj.* 2 *libertine excesses:* immoral, dissolute, unchaste, licentious, lewd, wanton, lascivious, lecherous, profligate.
Ant. 1 prude, puritan. 2 moral, virtuous, chaste.

liberty *n.* 1 *The Constitution guards our liberty:* freedom, self-determination, independence, autonomy; right, privilege. 2 *to give slaves their liberty:* freedom, manumission, emancipation, liberation. 3 *The crew had a week's liberty:* leave, furlough, vacation, free time, shore leave. 4 *Employees have liberty to use the gym:* freedom, permission, leave, sanction, license. 5 **liberties** *He takes too many liberties with his elders:* license, impropriety, undue intimacy.
Ant. 1 tyranny, despotism; coercion. 2 slavery, subjugation, enslavement.

license *n.* 1 *a driver's license:* authorization, charter, leave, permit, right, sanction, warrant, grant, franchise. 2 *Too much license was taken in translating the book:* liberty, latitude, deviation from custom, laxity, looseness; audacity, brazenness, presumptuousness; abused freedom, too much liberty, irresponsibility, recklessness, presumption; lawlessness, unruliness, disorder. —*v.* 3 *The county licensed local fishermen:* authorize, issue a license to, certify, warrant, empower, accredit.
Ant. 2 strictness, restraint, constraint, moderation. 3 prohibit, forbid; disallow.

licentious *adj.* *The licentious play was closed by the police:* lewd, lecherous, lascivious, immoral, libidinous, debauched, wanton, loose, promiscuous, dissolute, depraved.
Ant. chaste, pure, proper, prudish.

lick *v.* 1 *She licked her lips:* pass the tongue over, touch with the tongue; tongue; lap, collect with the tongue. 2 *Informal The Yankees licked the Dodgers in the World Series:* defeat, beat, conquer, vanquish, overcome, overpower, drub, rout, master, trounce, clobber. 3 *The father licked the boy for lying:* spank, beat, whip, thrash, hit, wallop. —*n.* 4 *John got a few licks in before the fight was broken up:* slap, blow, punch, hit, sock; verbal blow, sally, crack. 5 *You haven't done a lick of work:* bit, speck, particle, modicum, dab, jot, shred, iota, stroke, trace, scintilla.
Ant. 3, 4 caress, pet.

lid *n. Cover the pot with a lid. There was no*

lid on the amount one could bet: top, cover, cap; limit, ceiling, maximum.

lie[1] *n.* 1 *The testimony was a pack of lies:* falsehood, prevarication, falsification, untruth, fib, fiction, invention, fabrication, story. —*v.* 2 *He lied to the jury:* prevaricate, falsify, speak falsely, fabricate, tell untruths, fib, stretch the truth.
Ant. 1 truth, fact, gospel.

lie[2] *v.* 1 *Lie here until you feel better:* recline, rest, repose, be supine, be prone; sprawl, loll, lounge, stretch out. 2 *The village lies north of here. The responsibility lies with the driver:* be placed, be located, be found, exist, abide, rest, belong.
Ant. 1 rise, arise, stand.

life *n.* 1 *the many forms of life on earth:* living thing, living being, creature, organism, being. 2 *Many lives were lost in the explosion:* human, human being, person, individual, soul. 3 *The mayfly has a life of 24 hours:* lifetime, life span, life expectancy; longevity, duration. 4 *a life of great accomplishment. a quiet life:* career, lifework, path, course; existence, mode of living. 5 *the author's two-volume life of Michelangelo:* biography, autobiography, life story, memoir. 6 *She's full of life:* liveliness, vitality, animation, spirit, energy, zest, vivacity.
Ant. 6 dullness, sluggishness, torpor, vapidity.

lifeless *adj.* 1 *The animal lay lifeless in the road:* dead, without life, deceased; inert, inactive, inanimate. 2 *a dull, lifeless movie:* lacking vitality, dull, spiritless, sluggish, boring; stiff, lackluster.
Ant. 1 living, alive. 2 vital, dynamic, spirited.

lift *v.* 1 *Please lift the packages onto the counter:* hoist, heave, move upward, raise, elevate, raise up, upraise, boost. 2 *The government lifted the ban on travel:* cancel, revoke, rescind, put an end to, remove. 3 *The letter lifted our hopes:* elevate, uplift, raise. 4 *The fog lifted:* rise, disperse, dissipate, disappear, float away, move upward. —*n.* 5 *With one great lift, we moved the rock:* heave, hoist, boost, uplift, raising; ascent, upward movement, climb, rise, ascendance. 6 *Her praise gave the staff a lift:* rising of spirits; encouragement, reassurance, boost, inspiration.
Ant. 1 lower, drop. 2 establish, impose. 3 lower, depress, dash. 4 descend, fall. 6 letdown.

light[1] *n.* 1 *Light filled the room:* radiance, illumination, luminosity, brightness, blaze, glare, glow, luster, sparkle, brilliance, effulgence. 2 *Switch on a light: (variously)* lamp, lantern, beacon, torch, candle. 3 *to* *analyze the problem in a new light:* approach, aspect, manner, viewpoint, attitude, slant. 4 *New facts throw some light on the matter:* understanding, information, enlightenment, insight, illumination. 5 *Do you have a light for my pipe?:* means of ignition; match, lighter; flame. 6 *Helen Keller was a light to all handicapped people:* model, exemplar, paragon, paradigm, shining example, guiding light. —*adj.* 7 *The room is not light enough for reading:* bright, well lighted, illuminated; luminous, radiant, brilliant. 8 *a light yellow:* pale, light-toned, light-hued, fair; blond, blondish. —*v.* 9 *Light a fire:* ignite, set burning, set fire to, fire, catch fire, kindle. 10 *to light one's way:* illuminate, give light to, brighten. 11 *A smile lit up his face:* brighten, make cheerful, lighten, make radiant. 12 *Light some lamps:* turn on, switch on, put on.

Ant. 1 dark, darkness; shade, dimness. 4 obscurity, mystery. 7 dark, dim, gloomy, dusky. 8 dark, deep. 9 extinguish, put out, douse, quench. 11 darken, cloud.

light² *adj.* 1 *The suitcase is surprisingly light:* lightweight, underweight, not heavy. 2 *a light rain:* soft, moderate, faint, gentle; small, inconsequential, barely perceptible, inconsiderable, slight. 3 *a light movie:* lighthearted, amusing, carefree, frivolous, sprightly, blithe, nonintellectual, trifling; trivial, slight. 4 *a light dinner:* small, frugal, modest, not rich, meager, not heavy. 5 *Light exercise is healthy during convalescence:* easy, simple, moderate, untaxing, undemanding.

Ant. 1, 2, 4 heavy. 1 burdensome, weighty. 2 strong, substantial. 3 serious, deep, profound. 4 rich. 5 strenuous, taxing.

light³ *v.* 1 *The passengers lighted from the train:* alight, descend, get down, get off. 2 *The butterfly lit on a leaf:* come to rest, alight, stop, land, perch, settle.

Ant. 1 ascend, climb, get on.

lighten¹ *v.* *More lamps will lighten the gloomy room:* brighten, light up, illuminate, make bright, become light; shine, blaze, flare, flash, gleam.

Ant. darken.

lighten² *v.* 1 *to lighten the load:* make lighter, reduce, unload, ease, unburden. 2 *Extra help lightened the work:* ease, lessen, reduce, mitigate, alleviate, relieve, assuage, allay, abate, moderate. 3 *The good news lightened our mood:* lift, gladden, enliven, buoy, uplift.

Ant. 1 weight. 2 increase, intensify, aggravate. 3 depress, sadden, weigh down.

lighthearted *adj.* *They were lighthearted on the last day of school:* cheerful, carefree,

merry, joyous, jolly, joyful, glad, sunny, free and easy, untroubled, blithe, sprightly, lively.

Ant. heavyhearted, sad, depressed, despondent, melancholy, glum.

lightly *adv.* 1 *She tapped lightly on the door:* gently, weakly, faintly, softly. 2 *The cake is lightly sprinkled with sugar:* thinly, slightly, sparingly, sparsely, moderately. 3 *Respect is not won lightly:* easily, readily, without effort. 4 *She stepped lightly over the rocks:* nimbly, airily; quickly, swiftly, gracefully, lithely. 5 *Responsibility must not be taken lightly:* carelessly, thoughtlessly, unconcernedly, frivolously, indifferently, slightingly, blithely, flippantly.

Ant. 1 heavily, forcefully. 2 heavily, thickly, abundantly. 4 heavily, awkwardly, ponderously. 5 seriously, earnestly.

likable Also **likeable** *adj. a likable personality:* pleasing, attractive, charming, winsome, pleasant, agreeable, engaging, appealing, nice.

Ant. unlikable, unpleasant, hateful, repellent, repulsive.

like¹ *adj. The brothers have like personalities:* identical, similar, akin, much the same, comparable, corresponding; matched, analogous, equivalent, equal, uniform, parallel.

Ant. unlike, dissimilar, different, divergent.

like² *v.* 1 *They like music:* enjoy, take pleasure in, find agreeable, relish, fancy, be partial to, dote, savor, relish. 2 *Students like the new dean:* esteem, admire, find agreeable, have a friendly feeling for, be fond of, approve, favor. 3 *Would you like to join us?:* care, think fit, feel inclined, wish, have a mind, choose.

Ant. 1–3 dislike. 1, 2 hate, detest, loathe, abominate.

likelihood *n. There is a likelihood of rain today:* prospect, probability, possibility, good chance, potentiality.

Ant. improbability, unlikelihood.

likely *adj.* 1 *An accident is likely to happen at that intersection:* inclined, apt, probable, liable, destined. 2 *Your story is a likely one:* plausible, credible, believable, reasonable, rational, seemingly truthful. 3 *The park is a likely spot for the picnic:* suitable, fit, proper, befitting, appropriate; promising, able, apt. —*adv.* 4 *We will most likely be late:* probably, in all probability.

Ant. 1 unlikely. 2, 3 doubtful, dubious, questionable.

likeness *n.* 1 *This sketch is a likeness of my father:* portrait, picture, representation, image, study, depiction, rendition, portrayal; replica, facsimile. 2 *There is a likeness between the brothers:* resemblance, similarity, similitude, agreement, correspondence, analogy, affinity.

Ant. 2 dissimilarity, difference, disparity.

liking *n. to have a liking for animals:* affinity, preference, inclination, proclivity, partiality, affection, fancy, fondness, penchant, leaning, predilection, soft spot, bent, weakness.

Ant. dislike, disinclination; abhorrence, loathing, aversion.

limb *n. the limb of a tree:* appendage, part, extension; branch, projection, bough, outgrowth; wing, arm, leg.

limber *adj. a limber dancer:* flexible, pliant, bending, pliable, lithe, agile, lithesome, supple, lissome.

Ant. stiff, inflexible, wooden.

limit *n.* 1 *They reached the limit of their endurance:* end, furthest bound, greatest extent, breaking point, ultimate. 2 Often **limits** *These stakes mark the limits of the property:* edge, border, boundary; rim, frontier, margin, periphery, perimeter. 3 *the speed limit:* limitation, restriction, maximum, greatest allowed, ceiling, top; restraint, check, curb; quota. —*v.* 4 *to limit spending:* restrict, restrain, curb, check, keep within bounds, inhibit.

limited *adj. Each branch of government has limited powers:* defined, delimited, confined, restrained, controlled, circumscribed, specified, fixed; narrow, cramped, restricted, minimal.

Ant. unlimited, unbounded, unrestricted, limitless.

limitless *adj. The country's resources are not limitless:* endless, unlimited, unending, boundless, infinite, without limit.

Ant. limited, circumscribed, restricted.

limp[1] *n.* 1 *He had a pronounced limp:* lameness, halting walk, halt, lame movement, falter, hobble. —*v.* 2 *The player limped off the field:* hobble, falter, halt.

limp[2] *adj. I was limp with exhaustion:* slack, loose, droopy, drooping, floppy, flaccid, lax, soft, weak.

Ant. stiff, rigid.

limpid *adj. a limpid stream:* lucid, clear, transparent, translucent, pure, pellucid, crystalline.

Ant. muddy, cloudy, opaque.

line *n.* 1 *Draw a line under the word:* underscore, long mark, score, stripe, dash, streak, slash; demarcation, border, outline, contour. 2 *Her face bore lines of worry:* wrinkle, mark, crease, furrow, crow's foot. 3 *Is there a long line at the box office?:* queue, file, rank, procession. 4 *Drop us a line during your travels:* note, message, letter, postcard, card. 5 *Any deviation from the party line*

brought swift reprimands: policy, stance, position, ideology, doctrine, idea, intention, scheme. 6 *The calf comes from a long line of prize cattle:* lineage, stock, genealogy, race, family, house, strain, ancestry. 7 *the rail line:* transit company, transportation service, transit route. 8 *Public relations is my line:* occupation, business, profession, vocation, calling, pursuit, trade, craft. 9 *a fishing line:* cord, strand, thread, fishline; cable, rope; towline. 10 **lines** *The play follows traditional lines:* pattern, convention, principle, example, routine. —*v.* 11 *Line the pages for the graph:* rule, mark with lines, score, draw. 12 *People were lined up in front of the theater:* queue up, align, array, form in a line, rank, file.

lineage *n. a family of ancient lineage:* extraction, line, stock, pedigree, blood, descent, heredity, genealogy, ancestry, parentage.

linger *v.* 1 *The guests lingered until 2 A.M.:* stay, remain, tarry, delay departure, dawdle, loiter; *Informal* hang around. 2 *He lingered on for weeks:* last, survive, hang on, die slowly, cling to life.

Ant. 1 leave hastily, depart.

liniment *n. The liniment eased the ache:* ointment, lotion, balm, unguent, emollient, salve.

link *n.* 1 *a bracelet of silver links:* section of a chain, connective, bond, ring, loop, joint. 2 *a link with the past:* tie, bond, connection, interconnection, junction, association, relation, relationship. —*v.* 3 *Fingerprints linked the suspect to the crime:* connect, tie, couple; combine, bind, fuse, unite; bracket, associate, relate; implicate, involve.

lionize *v. Shakespeare is lionized by all drama lovers:* acclaim, admire, exalt, praise, glorify, revere, celebrate, eulogize, enshrine, immortalize.

Ant. belittle, deprecate, disparage, deride.

liquidate *v.* 1 *Liquidate your debts:* settle, pay, discharge, dispose of, clear, pay off, wipe out, abolish, erase. 2 *She liquidated her restaurant business:* close out, settle the affairs of, wind up, conclude, terminate. 3 *The dictator liquidated all opponents:* assassinate, kill, murder, eradicate; demolish, destroy, do away with.

liquor *n. You must be 21 to buy liquor:* alcoholic beverage, alcoholic drink, spirits, intoxicants, inebriants, distilled spirits; *(variously)* whiskey, Scotch, bourbon, rye, gin, rum, vodka, brandy; *Slang* booze, hooch.

lissome *adj. The dancer moved with lissome grace:* lithe, limber, supple, flexible, pliant, lithesome, nimble, agile.

Ant. stiff, wooden; clumsy, awkward.

list[1] *n.* 1 *The club has a list of all its members:*

written series, register, roster, roll, muster, inventory, slate; index, enumeration, table, catalog. —v. 2 *List what you need from the grocery:* write in a series, record, write down, catalog, tabulate.

list² n. 1 *The ship has a list to the port side:* tilt, leaning, lean, inclination, slant, slope. —v. 2 *The freighter listed as the cargo shifted:* tilt, lean, incline, slope, slant, tip.

listen v. *Please listen carefully:* attend, hark, heed, hearken, hear, give heed, keep one's ears open; *Informal,* bend an ear; eavesdrop, listen in, overhear.

Ant. be deaf to, turn a deaf ear to; pay no heed to.

listless *adj. I feel listless on rainy days:* sluggish, lazy, indolent, dull, spiritless, lethargic, soporific, enervated, sluggish; mopish, languid, dreamy, drowsy.

Ant. lively, energetic, wide-awake, alert.

litany n. 1 *The priest led the congregation in a litany:* ceremonial prayer, prescribed prayer, formal prayer, invocation with responses, prayer of supplication. 2 *She gave us a long litany of her woes:* recital, account, catalog, list, enumeration, rendition.

literacy n. *True literacy is something more than just the ability to read and write:* learning, erudition, eruditeness, learnedness, enlightenment, culture, intellectuality.

Ant. illiteracy, ignorance.

literal *adj.* 1 *a literal translation:* faithful, exact, precise, word-for-word, verbatim, strict, accurate, direct; without exaggeration, reliable, dependable, authoritative, meticulous, scrupulous. 2 *He's so literal he never knows when I'm kidding:* matter-of-fact, prosaic, unimaginative, taking everything at face value.

Ant. 1 free, liberal, general. 2 figurative; imaginative.

literary *adj. a literary club:* of literature, of writings, of belles lettres, of books; fond of books, addicted to reading, bookish; artistic, poetic; intellectual, literate, lettered, belonging to the literati.

Ant. uneducated, unlettered, unenlightened.

literate *adj.* 1 *Every adult should be literate:* able to read and write, proficient in reading and writing. 2 *a highly literate individual:* educated, learned, schooled, well-read, cultured, lettered.

literature n. 1 *a classic of American literature:* literary work of lasting value, artistic writing, letters. 2 *the literature on colonial furniture:* writings, works, books, publications, papers, scholarship.

lithe *adj. strong and lithe:* limber, supple,

flexible, pliable, lissome, agile, nimble, graceful.

Ant. rigid, stiff; clumsy, awkward.

litigation n. *They resorted to litigation to settle their dispute:* lawsuit, legal proceedings, suit, prosecution, legal action, filing of charges, judicial process.

litter n. 1 *Don't leave litter on the campsite:* scattered rubbish, rubbish, trash, refuse, debris; junk, mess, heap, pile. 2 *a litter of five pups:* group of animals born at one birth; issue. —v. 3 *The desk was littered with papers and coffee cups:* strew with rubbish, clutter with trash, strew, clutter; heap, pile, jumble.

Ant. 3 clean up, organize, arrange, tidy up.

little *adj.* 1 *a little house in the woods:* small, diminutive, bantam, pint-sized, pocket-sized, miniature, wee, tiny, minute; under-sized, dwarfish, stunted; pygmy. 2 *We have little hope for her recovery. There is little milk left in the pitcher:* small, scant, meager; skimpy, hardly any, not much, scarcely any; insufficient, deficient. 3 *We spent a little time in Italy:* brief, short, passing; short-lived, momentary. 4 *She had a little cold:* trivial, mild, slight, inconsequential, negligible, insignificant, unimportant, trifling, faint, piddling, paltry. 5 *people with little minds:* narrow, petty, short-sighted, opinionated, inferior, mediocre. —*adv.* 6 *I little thought he would take me seriously. The children visit us little now:* not at all, never, by no means, not in a thousand years; not much, slightly, scarcely, hardly, not often, seldom. —n. 7 *Just put a little on each plate:* small amount, small quantity; minimum; drop, crumb, iota, jot, whit, bit, dash, pinch, trifle, modicum; trace, hint, suggestion.

Ant. 1 big, large, great, immense, huge, enormous, colossal, giant. 2, 3 much, abundant, ample. 4 major, important, serious, considerable, significant. 6 certainly, surely, assuredly. 7 lot, much, many.

livable Also **liveable** *adj.* 1 *The house is very livable:* habitable; homey, snug, cozy, comfortable. 2 *A few luxuries make life more livable:* worth living, worthwhile; agreeable, comfortable, enjoyable, pleasant, satisfying, gratifying; bearable, tolerable, endurable.

Ant. 1 uninhabitable. 2 unbearable, intolerable, unendurable, disagreeable.

live¹ v. 1 *Is he still living?:* be alive, have life, draw breath, breathe; exist, come into existence. 2 *She lived to the age of 93. Tennyson's poetry will live forever:* remain alive, survive, endure, prevail; abide; stand, be permanent. 3 *to live on one's salary:* subsist, support oneself, provide for one's needs, maintain life, get along, make ends meet, make one's living. 4 *The castaways lived on fish and coconuts:* subsist, feed, be nourished, survive. 5 *I've always wanted to live in Alaska:* reside, be in residence, dwell, abide, make one's home, stay, settle.

Ant. 1, 2 die, pass away, decease, expire, perish. 4 starve to death, starve.

live² *adj.* 1 *a dozen live monkeys:* alive, living, quick; existent. 2 *Housing is still a live issue:* pertinent, active, prevalent, prevailing; current, up-to-date, still in use, going on, at hand.

Ant. 1 dead, deceased.

livelihood *n. to earn a livelihood. Farming has been the family's livelihood:* living, adequate income, support, maintenance, sustenance, source of income; occupation, vocation, business, line of work, trade, profession, job.

Ant. avocation, hobby, recreation.

lively *adj. He's 85 and still lively. a lively tune:* spirited, brisk, sprightly, vivacious, animated, energetic, full of life, buoyant; vigorous, alert, peppy, perky.

Ant. slow, sluggish, listless.

liven *v. I livened the party with some magic tricks:* enliven, animate, invigorate, inspirit, energize, buoy; perk up, pep up; cheer, gladden, brighten, exhilarate.

Ant. depress, dispirit, devitalize.

livid *adj.* 1 *a livid mark on the arm:* black-and-blue, discolored, purple; bruised. 2 *Her insult made me livid:* enraged, irate, incensed, inflamed, furious, infuriated, raging, fuming, mad, angry, outraged.

Ant. 2 delighted, blissful, overjoyed, happy, pleased.

living *adj.* 1 *every living creature:* alive, live, existing, existent, quick; animate, incarnate, corporeal, organic. 2 *English and French are living languages:* presently in use, active, operative, existent, extant, of present interest, surviving, enduring, persisting. —*n.* 3 *the joy of living:* existing, existence, life, being, subsisting, animation. 4 *reckless living:* way of life, mode of living, life-style. 5 *What do you do for a living?:* income, sustenance, livelihood, means of support; occupation, vocation, business, trade, profession, line of work, job, work.

Ant. 1, 2 dead, deceased, defunct, lifeless. 1 inanimate, inorganic. 3 dying, expiring. 5 avocation, hobby, entertainment, recreation.

load *n.* 1 *a load of gravel. a ten-ton load:* quantity carried; cargo, shipment, freight, lading, haul; capacity, contents. 2 *That's a load off my mind!:* burden, weight, pressure;

care, trouble, worry, oppression, affliction, tribulation; misfortune, unhappiness. —*v.* 3 *The men loaded the truck:* fill, lade, pile, pack, heap, burden. 4 *loaded down with responsibilities:* weigh down, burden, afflict, trouble; hamper, encumber, strain, hinder.

Ant. 3 unload, empty. 4 free.

loaf *v. Don't loaf—get to work!:* waste time, idle, do nothing, take it easy, laze about, dally, loll, lounge around, be lazy, malinger.

Ant. work, toil, labor.

loafer *n. That loafer won't look for a job!:* lazy person, idler, malingerer, laggard, wastrel, lazybones.

Ant. hard worker, worker, laborer.

loan *n.* 1 *She asked for the loan of our binoculars:* permission to borrow, lending; advance, giving credit. 2 *The bank arranged a loan:* sum of money lent, thing lent, thing borrowed; credit, mortgage, advance. —*v.* 3 *Can you loan me $10?:* lend, permit to borrow, advance; mortgage, credit.

Ant. 3 pay back, give back, return.

loathe *v. He loathes modern art:* detest, hate, despise, dislike, find disgusting, abominate, abhor, deplore, be unable to bear, scorn, disdain, recoil from, view with horror.

Ant. love, adore; admire, relish, dote on, enjoy; desire, crave.

lobby *n.* 1 *Wait in the lobby:* vestibule, entrance hall, foyer, reception hall, anteroom, waiting room, reception room, antechamber. —*v.* 2 *The group has been lobbying for gun controls for years:* politick, urge legislative action, solicit legislative votes, exert influence.

local *adj. a local celebrity:* citywide, regional, sectional, provincial, neighborhood; native, homegrown; geographically restricted, limited, confined, narrow, insular, parochial; nearby, adjoining.

Ant. international, national; foreign, exotic.

locale *n. The play's locale is London:* setting, location, locality, site, spot, area, zone, vicinity, region, neighborhood, section, province, precinct.

locality *n. The two factories are in the same locality:* neighborhood, area, district, section, province, precinct, zone, quarter, vicinity, region, location; locale, place, site, spot.

locate *v.* 1 *to locate a missing man:* find, discover the whereabouts of, track down, search out, unearth, uncover, pinpoint, discern, detect, come upon, meet with, lay one's hands on. 2 *The house is located on Main Street:* situate; place, establish, set down, put, fix, station, post. 3 *After Dad retires he's going to locate in California:* settle, reside, take up residence, dwell, live, establish one's home, move to.

Ant. 1 hide, conceal. 2 dislodge, displace. 3 leave, quit, vacate.

location *n. No one knows the location of the treasure:* whereabouts, position, site, spot, place; neighborhood, district.

lock¹ *n.* 1 *The door needs a stronger lock:* fastening device, securing device, fastening. —*v.* 2 *Lock the office door when you leave:* fasten, secure. 3 *The convicts were locked in their cells:* secure, lock up, keep under lock and key; confine. 4 *The men locked arms and sang the school song:* join, entwine, link, interlink, intertwine; clinch, grip, hold, grasp, clasp, hold, embrace.

Ant. 2 unlock, unbolt, unfasten; open. 3 free, release, let go.

lock² *n. a lock of hair:* tress, ringlet, curl, tuft, coil, bang.

locution *n. a midwestern locution:* expression, regionalism, term, idiom, saying, wording, phrase, phrasing, usage, turn of phrase, set phrase.

lodge *n.* 1 *We lived in a lodge:* cabin, cottage; hut, shelter; resort, camp. —*v.* 2 *We lodged in motels. The guest house can lodge five persons:* stay, put up, room; furnish with lodgings, house, bed, quarter, shelter, harbor. 3 *The dime lodged in a crack:* catch, become fixed, be positioned. 4 *to lodge a complaint:* submit, file, register, enter formally.

lodging *n. Do you have lodging for tonight?:* place to stay, accommodation, a room, sleeping accommodations.

loft *n.* 1 *The artist rented a loft. a choir loft:* attic room, attic, garret, top floor; balcony, clerestory, gallery. —*v.* 2 *The batter lofted the ball into the bleachers:* throw high, lob, hit high.

Ant. 1 basement, cellar.

lofty *adj.* 1 *lofty towers:* soaring, towering, tall, high, elevated. 2 *a lofty rank:* exalted, imposing, stately, elevated, dignified, majestic, noble; high, important, superior, distinguished, illustrious, eminent, preeminent, glorious, grand, great. 3 *a lofty attitude:* proud, haughty, arrogant, lordly, disdainful, scornful, aloof, distant, remote, cold, high-and-mighty, imperious, self-important, conceited.

Ant. 1 low, short. 2 lowly, ignoble, low. 3 modest, unassuming, humble; friendly, cordial, warm.

logic *n.* 1 *Lawyers should be versed in logic:* science of reasoning, reasoning, organized thinking, argument, deduction, analysis. 2 *There is no logic in that argument:* good sense, sound judgment, organized reasoning, reason, coherence.

logical *adj.* 1 *The plan was presented in a*

logical manner: consistent, well-organized, cogent, coherent, rational, sound, reasonable, intelligent; relevant, pertinent; analytical. 2 *He is the logical choice:* reasonable, likely, most likely, plausible, intelligent, sensible.

Ant. 1 illogical, inconsistent, unorganized, irrational, unreasonable. 2 illogical, unlikely, implausible.

loiter *v. A suspicious character was loitering in the hall:* linger idly about, hang around, hover around; tarry, dillydally, dally, dawdle, procrastinate.

loll *v. to loll around the house. Don't loll in your chair:* lounge, loaf, idle, take it easy, relax; recline, slouch, slump, sprawl.

lone *adj. a lone bandit:* sole, single, solitary, individual, alone, only, unaccompanied; isolated, singular.

lonely *adj.* 1 *We spent many lonely days on the island:* by oneself, solitary, without company, unaccompanied, companionless; secluded, withdrawn, reclusive. 2 *a lonely shut-in:* lonesome, depressed by solitude, lacking companionship, friendless, forsaken. 3 *The cabin was in a lonely spot:* isolated, secluded, remote, desolate, deserted, unfrequented.

Ant. 2 popular. 3 crowded, populous, bustling.

lonesome *adj. The outcast was very lonesome:* lonely, companionless, alone, friendless.

Ant. popular.

long¹ *adj.* 1 *a long wait:* lengthy, extended, prolonged, protracted, drawn-out, interminable. 2 *a long line:* lengthy, extended, extensive, elongated, protracted, far-reaching. —*adv.* 3 *all winter long:* during the time, throughout the period. 5 *The river is 1,000 miles long:* in length, from end to end.

Ant. 1, 2 short, brief. 1 momentary, fleeting.

long² *v. to long for the good old days:* yearn, crave, hunger, thirst, hanker, pine, have a desire, have a yen for, hope, want, wish, aspire, covet.

Ant. spurn, scorn, disdain, renounce.

longing *n.* 1 *She had a longing to see her hometown:* strong desire, yearning, craving, hungering, wish; hankering, yen. —*adj.* 2 *The child gave a longing look at the cake:* desirous, yearning, craving, hankering, hungering, wishful, pining, languishing, ardent.

Ant. 1 disinterest, unconcern, apathy. 2 disinterested, indifferent, unconcerned, apathetic.

longstanding *adj. a longstanding friendship:* long-lived, long-lasting, enduring, long, lasting, durable, long-established, abiding, persisting.

Ant. short, passing, short-lived, transitory.

look *v.* 1 *Look at the geese up there. Look at all the facts:* see, watch, fix the eyes on, regard, contemplate, stare, glance, scan, peek, behold, give attention to, study, survey, examine. 2 *Mother looks angry:* appear, seem, show, present evidence, exhibit, manifest, strike one as being. 3 *The house looks toward the lake:* face, front, have a view of, be directed. —*n.* 4 *Let's have a look at the new car:* glance, glimpse, peek, once-over, survey, scrutiny, visual search, stare, sight, gaze. 5 *He had a happy look on his face:* appearance, countenance, presence, mien, expression, demeanor, air, guise, cast, bearing.

Ant. 1 close one's eyes to, overlook, ignore, disregard.

lookout *n.* 1 *Keep a lookout for bears:* alertness, watchfulness, readiness, vigilance, guardedness, vigil, awareness, mindfulness, heed, precaution. 2 *We posted lookouts around the camp:* sentinel, guard, sentry; observer, spotter.

loom *v. The mountains loomed in front of us:* tower, whorl, ascend; come into view, emerge, rise, appear.

Ant. vanish, fade away.

loop *n.* 1 *the loops in embroidery:* circle, spiral, whorl, convolution, twirl, coil; eye, eyelet, ring, ringlet; bend, twist, curve. —*v.* 2 *Loop the rope over the post:* wind around, bend, twist, curve, encircle, circle, coil, curl.

loose *adj., adv.* 1 *Her hair hung loose. The dog ran loose in the yard:* unbound, untied, unfastened, free, freed, freely; untethered, unchained, unfettered, unyoked, unleashed, uncaged, unimprisoned; unattached, unconnected, unjoined. 2 *He likes to wear his coats loose:* slack, free, not fitting tightly, not binding, not tight, not fastened. —*adj.* 3 *loose living:* wanton, profligate, abandoned, dissipated, debauched, wild, fast, dissolute, licentious, lewd, unchaste. —*v.* 4 *Loose the hounds. They loosed the prisoners' bonds:* untie, untether, unbind, unfasten, loosen, unloose, undo; free, set free, release, let go, slacken.

Ant. 1 tied, secured, fastened, tethered, restrained, leashed. 2 tight. 3 abstemious, chaste, disciplined. 4 tie, bind, fasten, fetter; capture, imprison.

loot *n.* 1 *the pirate's loot:* spoils, plunder, booty, take, stolen goods; *Slang* boodle. —*v.* 2 *Vikings looted coastal towns:* plunder, pillage, ravage, sack, raid, rob.

lopsided *adj. The table was lopsided:* off-balance, askew, asymmetric, unbalanced, irregular, uneven, disproportionate, crooked; leaning, inclined, slanting, listing, tilting, slanted.

Ant. symmetrical, balanced, even, straight.

loquacious *adj. a loquacious speaker:* talkative, talky, garrulous, wordy, verbose, windy, long-winded; chatty.

Ant. reserved, taciturn, reticent.

lordly *adj.* 1 *a lordly feast:* fit for a lord, grand, majestic, regal, magnificent, sumptuous, stately, imposing, noble, august, exalted. 2 *a lordly manner:* haughty, arrogant, lofty, proud, disdainful, scornful, aloof, remote, cold, imperious, conceited, self-important; domineering, dictatorial.

Ant. 1 plebeian, humble, modest. 2 modest, unassuming, humble; servile.

lose *v.* 1 *I lost my wallet. She lost her balance:* suffer loss of, incur the loss of; misplace, mislay; miss, be thrown off. 2 *Don't lose your way. We lost all track of time:* stray from, miss, confuse; forget, ignore, fail to heed. 3 *We lost the game:* be defeated in, be the loser, fail to win, suffer defeat in, fail.

Ant. 1 keep, retain, preserve; find, recover. 2 find. 3 win.

loss *n.* 1 *the loss of a ship:* wreck, wrecking, destruction, ruin, annihilation; extermination, extinction, eradication; abolition, dissolution, removal. 2 *Can the company bear the loss of a million dollars?:* forfeiture, deprivation, privation, bereavement, expenditure, amount lost, number lost. 3 *How did he take the loss of the fight?:* losing, defeat, undoing, vanquishment. 4 *the loss of a purse:* losing, misplacing, mislaying, being without.

Ant. 1 saving, preservation. 2 gain, acquisition. 3 winning, win. 4 finding, recovery.

lost *adj.* 1 *a lost ring. a lost dog:* missing, mislaid, misplaced, gone out of one's possession; strayed, stray, absent, lacking. 2 *the lost hikers:* gone astray, unable to find one's way, off-course. 3 *How many planes were lost in the battle?:* destroyed, wrecked, demolished, ruined, abolished, annihilated, exterminated, eradicated; killed, perished. 4 *to make up for lost time:* wasted, misapplied, squandered, misdirected; misused. 5 *She was lost in thought:* absorbed, preoccupied, engrossed.

Ant. 1 found, recovered. 3 saved, preserved.

lot *n.* 1 *It was her lot in life:* fate, allotted portion, share; apportionment, allowance, ration, measure, allotment. 2 *a lot to build a house on:* parcel of land, plot, property, tract, piece of ground. 3 *We like ice cream,* *so give everyone a lot:* great deal, much, many, *Informal* lots, oceans, oodles.

lothario *n. The women knew he was just a lothario:* lover, rake, Don Juan, Romeo, Casanova, seducer, roué, libertine, philanderer, womanizer, lady-killer, skirt-chaser, *Slang* wolf, lover-boy.

lotion *n. This lotion should help your chapped hands:* ointment, balm, liniment, unction, wash, unguent, salve, skin cream.

loud *adj.* 1 *Who's making loud noises?:* noisy, earsplitting, deafening, clamorous, resounding, stentorian, booming, thundering. 2 *What a loud shirt!:* garish, gaudy, splashy, flashy; bright, vivid, colorful; showy, ostentatious.

Ant. 1 soft, subdued. 2 sedate, somber, colorless, conservative.

lounge *v. The passengers lounged in deck chairs:* idle, take it easy, do nothing, relax, lie around, dawdle, dally; recline, stretch out, laze, loll, slump, slouch.

lousy *adj. Informal That was a lousy thing to do. It was a lousy movie:* mean, nasty, crummy, unethical, unkind, contemptible; dreadful, inferior, bad, terrible, rotten, awful.

lout *n. That lout never thanks anyone:* boor, churl, clod, oaf, dunce, dullard, dummy, rustic, bumpkin.

Ant. gentleman, sophisticate.

lovable Also **loveable** *adj. a lovable child:* adorable, endearing, engaging, winning, enchanting, captivating, charming, delightful; cute, sweet, cuddly, darling.

Ant. hateful, detestable, obnoxious, loathsome, repugnant, revolting.

love *n.* 1 *The couple swore undying love. She felt a great love for her parents:* passion, passionate affection, amorousness, ardor, amour; devotion, adoration, fondness, tenderness, affection, affectionate regard, warm feeling, esteem, admiration; friendship, brotherhood, affinity, sympathy, solicitude. 2 *a love of good food:* strong liking, fondness, devotion, relish, taste, predilection, attachment, penchant, leaning, partiality, inclination. 3 *His love is out of town this weekend. The theater was her first love:* beloved, loved one, inamorata, truelove, paramour, lover, mistress, flame, sweetheart, darling, dear, dearest, precious, angel, sweetie, honey; boyfriend, beau, fellow, man; girlfriend, girl, woman; fondness, attachment, choice. —*v.* 4 *Romeo loved Juliet. Love thy neighbor:* have a passionate affection for, feel amorous toward, be infatuated with, be enamored of, be devoted to, adore, be fond of, lose one's heart to, hold dear, regard affectionately, feel warmly to-

ward, admire, esteem, treasure, cherish; sympathize with, feel goodwill toward, feel solicitude for. 5 *I love opera:* like immensely, be fond of, relish, delight in, fancy, take pleasure in, enjoy, appreciate, savor, bask in, rejoice in, revel in, have a penchant for, have a partiality for, have an inclination toward, have a weakness for.

Ant. 1–3 hate, hatred, dislike, aversion, abhorrence, repugnance, disgust, loathing. 1 animosity, antipathy, antagonism, hostility, malice, ill will. 4, 5 hate, dislike, abhor, loathe, detest.

lovely *adj. a lovely idea! a lovely person. a lovely time:* attractive, handsome, comely, beautiful, exquisite; delightful, charming, enjoyable, agreeable, pleasing, pleasant; captivating, alluring, engaging, endearing; good, fine.

Ant. ugly, hideous, unattractive; detestable, obnoxious, offensive, loathsome, revolting, repelling; awful, bad.

lover *n.* 1 *the starlet's latest lover:* paramour, mistress; beloved, loved one, inamorata, truelove, love, sweetheart; dear, darling, sweetie, honey; boyfriend, beau, fellow; suitor, wooer, admirer, man; girlfriend, girl, woman. 2 *art lovers:* devotee, enthusiast, aficionado, follower; fan, buff, fanatic.

loving *adj. a loving look. a loving nature:* affectionate, fond, tender, amorous, ardent, passionate, enamored, amatory, devoted, doting; warm, sympathetic, caring, kind, friendly, warm-hearted.

Ant. unloving, hateful, disgusting, contemptuous, angry, hostile; indifferent, detached, cold.

low *adj.* 1 *low clouds. a low chair:* near the ground, not far above the horizon, lowlying; unelevated; near the floor, low-slung; lower. 2 *a line of low hills. a low, two-story building:* short, having little elevation, squat; small, little. 3 *The low areas were flooded:* low-lying, unelevated, coastal; sunken. 4 *I've been feeling low:* unhappy, depressed, dejected, disheartened, despondent, downcast, down, melancholy, gloomy, dispirited, glum, lethargic; blue, down in the mouth. 5 *a low number. He works for low pay:* small, little; lowly, humble, insignificant, unimportant, low ranking, paltry, trifling, inferior. 6 *How could anyone do such a low thing?:* mean, base, vile, despicable, ignominious, dishonorable, contemptible, cruel, outrageous, scandalous, disrespectful, nefarious, corrupt, unethical, wicked, evil, cowardly, dastardly; degraded, depraved, sordid, squalid, gross, coarse, vulgar. 7 *Speak in a low voice:* subdued, hushed, muffled, muted, quiet; whispered, murmured, faint, soft, gentle, low-pitched.

Ant. 1–5, 7 high. 2 tall, lofty, soaring, towering. 3 elevated. 4 happy, elated, cheerful. 5 superior, consequential, significant, important; high ranking; above average. 6 wonderful, admirable, commendable, honorable, worthy; courteous; brave. 7 loud; high-pitched.

lower *v.* 1 *Lower that shelf. The deer lowered its head:* make lower, drop, let down, take down, put down, depress; submerge, immerse, duck, sink. 2 *We must lower our expenses:* decrease, reduce, diminish, curtail, pare, cut, prune. 3 *Please lower your voice. Can you lower those bright lights?:* tone down, soften, subdue, make less intense, dim, damp, muffle, mute, repress. —*adj.* 4 *Importers want lower tariffs:* reduced, decreased, diminished, lessened, curtailed, pared.

Ant. 1–3 raise. 1 elevate, lift up, hoist. 2 increase, boost. 4 higher, increased.

low-key *adj. The décor was very low-key:* subdued, toned-down, restrained, subtle, understated, relaxed, low-pressure, muted, soft, muffled, softened.

Ant. blatant, obvious, bold, obtrusive.

lowly *adj. He rose from lowly origins to become President:* humble, modest, unassuming, unpretentious, obscure, lowborn, plebeian, ignoble.

Ant. exalted, elevated, lofty.

low-priced *adj. low-priced tickets:* cheap, inexpensive, reasonable, moderate, dirt-cheap, economical, budget, nominal.

Ant. expensive, high-priced, costly, exorbitant.

loyal *adj. a loyal supporter:* faithful, steadfast, true, constant, reliable, trusty, trustworthy, devoted, dependable, unwavering, unswerving, staunch, firm, true-blue.

Ant. disloyal, faithless, unfaithful, perfidious, untrustworthy.

loyalty *n. Her loyalty never wavered:* faithfulness, fidelity, steadfastness, constancy, trustworthiness, devotion, staunchness, allegiance, adherence, fealty.

Ant. disloyalty, faithlessness, perfidiousness, perfidy, treachery.

lucid *adj.* 1 *a lucid sky:* shining, bright, clear, transparent, crystalline, brilliant, radiant, luminous, sparkling, dazzling. 2 *a lucid account of what happened:* clear, easily understood, intelligible, understandable, articulate, comprehensible; precise, straightforward, accurate, well-organized, to the point. 3 *The patient has some lucid moments:* clearheaded, clear-thinking, rational; responsive.

Ant. 1 dark, gloomy, obscure, opaque. 2 incomprehensible, unclear, ambiguous, garbled. 3 confused, irrational; unresponsive.

luck *n.* 1 *As luck would have it, we arrived as they were leaving:* fortune, fate, lot, destiny, karma, kismet; chance, happenstance. 2 *Did you have any luck finding a job?:* good luck, good fortune; success.

lucky *adj.* 1 *I'm just lucky:* fortunate, blest with good luck, favored, blessed. 2 *This is your lucky day!:* fortunate, opportune, providential, auspicious, propitious, favorable, bringing good luck.

Ant. 1, 2 unlucky, unfortunate, ill-favored. 2 inauspicious, unfavorable; sinister, ominous.

lucrative *adj. a lucrative position:* profitable, moneymaking, high-paying, high-income; beneficial, fruitful.

Ant. unprofitable, low-paying.

ludicrous *adj. a ludicrous situation:* ridiculous, absurd, outlandish, preposterous; amusing, laughable, comic, comical, funny.

Ant. sensible; tragic, solemn, serious, sad.

lukewarm *adj.* 1 *lukewarm water:* tepid, warm, room-temperature, blood-temperature. 2 *The reception we got was lukewarm:* halfhearted, unenthusiastic, detached, indifferent, uninterested, perfunctory, lackadaisical.

Ant. 2 impassioned, enthusiastic, wholehearted.

lull *v.* 1 *She lulled the child to sleep:* soothe, quiet, calm, pacify, hush, still, quell. —*n.* 2 *the lull before the storm:* hush, quiet, stillness, quiet interval, pause, break, halt, respite, recess, breather, breathing spell; calm, tranquility.

Ant. 1 excite, arouse, rouse. 2 tumult, turbulence, violence.

lumber *v. He lumbered into the water:* waddle, trudge, move clumsily, move heavily, plod, clump, shuffle.

luminary *n. Many luminaries attended the opera:* celebrity, famous person, eminent person, personage, dignitary, notable.

luminescent *adj. Fireflies are luminescent:* glowing, luminous, gleaming, glimmering, shimmering; glistening, twinkling, flickering.

Ant. incandescent.

luminous *adj. The watch has a luminous dial:* luminescent, radiant, irradiated, glowing, lustrous, shining; bright, brilliant.

lump *n.* 1 *a lump of dirt:* gob, chunk, clod, clump, cake, hunk. 2 *How did you get that lump on your head?:* bump, swelling, protuberance, knot; node, nodule, knurl; tumor, growth. —*v.* 3 *Lump all our money to-*

gether: heap, pile, mass, gather, bunch, group, compile, assemble, collect; combine, merge, pool.
Ant. **2** depression, hollow, indentation, dent. **3** scatter, disperse; separate.

lunacy *n.* **1** *Certain forms of lunacy are caused by chemical imbalances:* insanity, insaneness, madness, mental derangement, dementia, mania, psychopathic condition. **2** *It's sheer lunacy to drive so fast:* folly, foolishness, foolhardiness, imprudence, absurdity, senselessness, craziness; stupidity, asininity.
Ant. **1** sanity, reason. **2** good sense, prudence.

lunatic *n.* **1** *The lunatic was committed to an asylum:* madman, maniac, insane person, deranged person; psychopath, *Slang* loony. —*adj.* **2** *Such lunatic behavior is a menace to society:* insane, crazy, mad, deranged, demented; maniacal, unhinged, unbalanced, irrational; of unsound mind, mentally ill, senseless, loony; psychotic, psychopathic.
Ant. **2** sane, rational.

lunge *n.* **1** *He made a lunge at me:* charge, rush, lurch, dash, thrust; jab, stab, swing. —*v.* **2** *The cat lunged at the toy:* thrust, jab, strike, hit at; attack, charge, pounce.

lurch *v.* *She lurched forward and then fell:* pitch, tilt, swerve; jerk, lunge, plunge; stagger, stumble, sway, reel, totter, teeter.

lure *n.* **1** *Cheese is a lure for mice:* bait; decoy. **2** *The sale was just a lure to get customers into the store:* enticement, allurement, inducement, allure, attraction, temptation; cajolery, bribe. —*v.* **3** *The decoys lured the ducks to the pond:* entice, allure, attract, tempt, beguile, induce.
Ant. **1** repellent. **3** repel, deter.

lurid *adj.* **1** *lurid colors:* fiery, bright-red, flaming, bloody, sanguine, scarlet, carmine; glaring, glowing, shining. **2** *a lurid tale of crime in the big city:* sensational, graphic, vivid; shocking, grim, gory.
Ant. **1** pale, pastel.

lurk *v.* *The thief lurked in the shadows:* skulk, slink, prowl, lie concealed, hide, lie in ambush; go furtively.

luscious *adj.* *luscious strawberries:* delicious, mouth-watering, succulent, sweet and juicy, delectable, appetizing, flavorful, tasty, savory, toothsome.
Ant. bland, flavorless, tasteless.

lush *adj.* **1** *a lush growth of ivy:* luxuriant, profuse, flourishing, dense, prolific, abundant, rich. **2** *a lush hotel:* luxurious, grand, sumptuous, elegant, elaborate, ornate, splendid, fancy; *Slang* posh.
Ant. **1** sparse, thin, meager, scanty. **2** plain, simple, Spartan.

lust *n.* **1** *a lust for power. Lust is one of the seven deadly sins:* passion, craving; fleshly desire, sexuality, libidinousness, lasciviousness, lewdness, carnality, lechery. —*v.* **2** *to lust after money. Phaedra lusted after Hippolytus:* desire intensely, crave, have a passion for, covet, hunger for; seek sexually, be lascivious, be libidinous, be lecherous.
Ant. **1** unconcern, apathy. **2** be indifferent; spurn, disdain, scorn.

luster *n.* **1** *the luster of silver:* shine, gleam, sheen, gloss, burnish, brightness, brilliance, resplendence, radiance, glimmer, glitter, dazzle. **2** *Winning the prize added more luster to his name:* glory, distinction, illustriousness, fame, prestige, honor.
Ant. **2** ignominy, dishonor, shame, disrepute.

lustrous *adj.* *The coat was a lustrous silk:* bright, luminous, radiant, glistening, burnished, dazzling, glossy, shining, gleaming, polished, glowing.
Ant. drab, dull, lusterless.

lusty *adj.* *Robin Hood led a group of lusty men:* hearty, hale, full of life, vigorous, robust, virile, healthy; exuberant, wholehearted, unrestrained, uninhibited, irrepressible.
Ant. lethargic, listless; feeble, weak, frail.

luxuriant *adj.* **1** *a luxuriant growth of orchids:* lush, flourishing, dense, profuse, abundant, teeming. **2** *luxuriant scrollwork:* elaborate, ornate, fancy, elegant, extravagant, luxurious, grand, sumptuous; florid.
Ant. **1** sparse, thin, meager, scanty. **2** plain, simple.

luxurious *adj.* **1** *The house is full of luxurious appointments:* expensive, costly, rich, elegant, sumptuous; enjoyable, comfortable, pleasurable, gratifying. **2** *luxurious living:* costly, extremely comfortable, wealthy; loving luxury, indulgent, overindulged.
Ant. **2** ascetic, austere, Spartan, frugal, economical.

luxury *n.* **1** *She lived in luxury:* luxuriousness, material abundance, extreme comfort; wealth, riches; extravagance, indulgence. **2** *A long hot bath can be pure luxury:* delight, enjoyment, pleasure, satisfaction, gratification, bliss, heaven, paradise.
Ant. **1** poverty, deprivation, austerity. **2** deprivation, hardship, infliction.

lyric Also **lyrical** *adj.* **1** *The composer has a lyric gift:* songlike, melodious, musical, tuneful, melodic, lilting, sweet-sounding, mellifluous, mellifluent; poetic. —*n.* **2** Often **lyrics** *the lyrics of a song:* words of a song; poem.

M

macabre *adj. a macabre story of headless ghosts:* gruesome, grisly, grim, ghastly, frightful, frightening; eerie, weird, unearthly, ghostly, ghostlike.

Machiavellian *adj. a Machiavellian plan:* scheming, designing, self-serving, treacherous, unscrupulous, cunning, crafty, devious, deceitful.

machination *n. machinations to gain control of a business:* scheme, intrigue, crafty plan, plot, artifice, device, stratagem, maneuver, contrivance, ruse, dodge.

machinery *n.* 1 *The machinery is being overhauled:* mechanical equipment, mechanism, apparatus, gear, contrivances. 2 *the machinery of school authority:* system, organization, structure, setup, makeup; instrumentality, agency.

macrocosm *n. We're a speck in the macrocosm:* cosmos, universe, the great world; creation, nature.
Ant. microcosm.

mad *adj.* 1 *Haughtiness makes me mad:* angry, furious, irate, enraged, infuriated, incensed, miffed, fuming, boiling, seeing red, wrought up, riled up. 2 *a mad scientist:* insane, crazy, demented, lunatic, crazed, deranged, maniacal, unbalanced; *Slang* nuts, nutty, cracked. 3 *She's mad about tennis. He's been mad about her for months:* enthusiastic, wild, excited, fanatic, devoted to, impassioned; infatuated, in love with.
Ant. 2 sane, rational. 3 unexcited, nonchalant; disdainful.

madcap *adj. madcap ways:* wild, unruly, undisciplined, erratic, reckless, thoughtless, impulsive, rash, impractical, foolish.
Ant. cautious, prudent, practical.

madden *v. His indecision is enough to madden a saint:* enrage, anger, vex, infuriate, upset, exasperate, provoke, incense, outrage, gall; craze, derange, unbalance, unhinge.
Ant. calm, soothe, placate, mollify.

made *adj. How was this chair made?:* manufactured, fabricated, produced, constructed, built, assembled, formed; composed, developed.

madhouse *n.* 1 *Two inmates escaped from the madhouse:* insane asylum, lunatic asylum, mental hospital, mental institution, psychopathic hospital, state hospital; *Slang* loony bin. 2 *I can't work—this place is a madhouse:* bedlam, scene of pandemonium.

maelstrom *n. The canoe was caught in the maelstrom:* whirlpool, rapids, vortex, swirl, eddy, undertow, riptide.

magazine *n.* 1 *to sell subscriptions to a magazine:* periodical, journal; *(variously)* weekly, monthly, quarterly. 2 *There was an explosion in the ship's magazine:* powder magazine, powder room, munitions room; arsenal, military depot.

magenta *n. The evening sky was magenta:* reddish purple, purplish rose, fuchsia; maroon, vermilion; crimson, carmine.

magic *n.* 1 *Some Haitians still practice magic:* black magic, voodoo, voodooism, hoodoo, sorcery, occultism, witchcraft; spell, conjuration, divination. 2 *a wizard's feats of magic:* prestidigitation, legerdemain, sleight of hand. 3 *There was a magic in her presence:* magnetism, fascination, charisma, charm, enchantment, lure, allurement, entrancement.

magician *n.* 1 *Merlin was the magician of King Arthur's court:* wizard, sorcerer, necromancer, shaman, witch doctor, medicine man. 2 *Harry Houdini was a famous magician in vaudeville:* prestidigitator, sleight-of-hand artist, expert in legerdemain, illusionist, escape artist.

magistrate *n. They were married by a magistrate:* justice of the peace, *Informal* j.p.; judicial officer, civil officer, prefect, police judge.

magnanimous *adj. a truly magnanimous gift:* forgiving, generous, largehearted, liberal; charitable, beneficent, philanthropic, unselfish.
Ant. vindictive, resentful, petty.

magnetic *adj.* 1 *the magnetic field:* of a magnet, of magnetism. 2 *a magnetic personality:* attractive, fascinating, captivating, charismatic, enchanting, alluring, entrancing, charming, irresistible.
Ant. 1 antimagnetic. 2 repellent, repulsive.

magnetism *n.* 1 *Magnetism makes a compass needle point north:* magnetic force, magnetic attraction. 2 *the magnetism of her personality:* attraction, fascination, captivation, charisma, appeal, enchantment, charm, enticement, allure, allurement, lure. *Ant.* 1 repulsion.

magnificent *adj. a magnificent opera:* splendid, superb, grand, glorious, extraordinary, wonderful, fine, elegant, exquisite, majestic, imposing, impressive, resplendent.
Ant. modest, ordinary, undistinguished, poor, trivial, paltry, bad; *Slang* awful, lousy.

magnify *v.* 1 *This microscope magnifies the object 500 times:* enlarge optically; *Informal* blow up. 2 *to magnify one's problems:* enlarge, expand, amplify, inflate, heighten, maximize, exaggerate, overstate, enlarge upon, overrate.
Ant. 1, 2 reduce. 2 diminish, lessen, minimize; understate, underplay; belittle, deprecate.

magniloquence *n. The senator's speech was full of magniloquence:* bombast, pomposity, grandiloquence, grandiosity, highsoundingness.

magnitude *n.* 1 *a building of great magnitude:* size, extent, expanse, mass, bulk, amplitude, volume, measure; bigness, hugeness, enormity, largeness, vastness, immensity. 2 *a scientist of considerable magnitude:* eminence, distinction, renown, repute, fame; importance, consequence, significance.
Ant. 1 smallness, diminutiveness. 2 insignificance, unimportance, triviality.

maid *n. It takes two maids to keep up that big house:* housemaid, maidservant, female servant, domestic, hired woman.

maiden *n.* 1 *a young maiden:* girl, lass, maid, virgin, miss, lassie, colleen, damsel. *—adj.* 2 *my maiden aunt:* unmarried; chaste, virginal. 3 *The* Titanic *sank on its maiden voyage:* first, initial, inaugural, original.
Ant. 1 matron, dowager. 2 married, wedded.

mail *n.* 1 *Did we get any mail this morning?:* *(variously)* letters, postcards, packages. 2 *The mail has been slow lately:* mail delivery, postal service, post-office service. *—v.* 3 *Mail the check today:* put in the mail, post, dispatch, send by mail.

maim *v. The explosion maimed several bystanders:* mangle, mutilate, injure; rend, tear, rip, gash; disable, cripple, lame, deface, disfigure.

main *adj. The main thing is to keep costs low:* leading, principal, central, chief, primary, foremost, prime, predominant, paramount, preeminent, supreme; vital, essential, necessary, indispensable, requisite, important,

critical, crucial, urgent, pressing, consequential; special, particular.
Ant. subordinate, secondary; unimportant, insignificant, minor, nonessential.

mainly *adv. The book is mainly about horses:* chiefly, principally, mostly, primarily, predominantly, for the most part, in the main, on the whole.
Ant. subordinately; partially, minimally.

mainstay *n. He was the mainstay of his parents:* chief support, backbone, principal reliance; pillar, bulwark, buttress, prop.

maintain *v.* 1 *They maintained their friendship for years:* keep, keep up, keep alive, continue, sustain, preserve, conserve, uphold. 2 *How can they maintain such a large house?:* take care of, support, provide for, keep, keep up, care for. 3 *Each driver maintained that the accident was the other's fault:* declare, affirm, assert, insist, contend; hold, avow, aver, allege, claim.
Ant. 1 end, terminate, discontinue, abolish. 3 disavow.

majestic Also **majestical** *adj. the majestic Alps:* stately, grand, imposing, impressive, magnificent, splendid, glorious, sublime, noble, lofty, elegant; regal; distinguished, famous, illustrious; renowned.
Ant. modest, ordinary, unimposing, tawdry, paltry.

majesty *n. The majesty of the occasion thrilled us all:* grandeur, splendor, magnificence, dignity, distinction, loftiness, stateliness, glory, pomp, gloriousness, impressiveness, elegance, mobility, solemnity, sublimity.

major *adj.* 1 *the major part of the job:* greater, larger, main, principal, chief. 2 *a major poet. a major problem:* leading, primary, foremost, predominant, principal, chief, main, prime, paramount, outstanding, preeminent, ranking, important, serious, significant, consequential; vital, critical, crucial, urgent, pressing.
Ant. 1 lesser, smaller. 2 minor, lesser, secondary; insignificant, unimportant, trivial, inconsequential.

majority *n. The majority voted to strike:* mass, bulk, greater part, preponderance, greater than half the total, greater number, more than half.
Ant. minority, lesser part.

make *v.* 1 *This shirt is made of cotton:* manufacture, construct, produce, fashion, form, fabricate, create, compose, devise, build. 2 *Don't make trouble. He made a speech:* cause, produce, bring about, effect, engender, beget; deliver, utter, speak, pronounce. 3 *I won't go and you can't make me!:* compel, force, oblige, require, impel. 4 *Laws are*

made to be obeyed: establish, draw up, pass, enact, legislate. 5 *Hurry or you won't make the train:* reach, attain, arrive at; meet, arrive in time for, catch. —*n.* 6 *When buying a coat, look closely at its make:* kind, brand, mark; structure, construction, composition, makeup, fashioning.
Ant. 1 destroy, demolish. 2 end, conclude; abolish. 3 beg, plead, entreat. 4 repeal, revoke, nullify, abolish.

make-believe *adj.* 1 *Halloween is a time of make-believe ghosts and goblins:* imagined, imaginary, unreal, fantastic, simulated, pretended, invented, fictitious, artificial, made-up, feigned; phony, false, fake, spurious, counterfeit, sham. —*n.* 2 *the make-believe of fairy tales:* pretense, fantasy, invention, fabrication, fiction; fake, counterfeit, sham, falsification, charade.

malady *n. She was afflicted by one malady after another:* ailment, sickness, illness, disorder, disease, complaint, affliction, infirmity.

malcontent *adj.* 1 *a malcontent worker:* habitually unsatisfied, dissatisfied, discontented, hard to please, faultfinding; glum, morose, sullen, grumpy, grouchy; dejected, downcast, despondent. —*n.* 2 *Do you have a real grievance or are you just a malcontent?:* complainer, faultfinder, grumbler, grouch; insurgent, rebel.
Ant. 1 contented, content, satisfied, happy, easygoing.

male *adj.* 1 *two male babies:* masculine, of the sex that fathers young; manly, manlike. —*n.* 2 *Males are generally taller than females:* a male person or animal; man, youth, boy.
Ant. 1, 2 female, woman. 1 feminine.

malediction *n. She uttered a malediction against the rival clan:* curse, damnation, imprecation, execration.
Ant. benediction, blessing; eulogy, compliment.

malevolent *adj. a malevolent plot to destroy the world:* malicious, spiteful, ill-intentioned, malignant, sinister, acrimonious, venomous, resentful, vicious, rancorous, revengeful, invidious.
Ant. benevolent, magnanimous, kind, gracious.

malformed *adj. The tree has a malformed trunk:* misshapen, deformed, distorted, contorted, twisted, irregular, grotesque.

malice *n. I have no malice toward anyone:* ill will, evil intent, malevolence, maliciousness, hatred, spitefulness, spite, grudge, rancor, resentment, animosity, acrimony, enmity, hate, bitterness; evil disposition, hardheartedness.

Ant. benevolence, goodwill, friendliness, kindness.

malicious *adj. a malicious rumor:* vicious, spiteful, malevolent, malignant, vindictive, revengeful, resentful, rancorous, invidious, acrimonious.
Ant. benevolent, benign, friendly, amicable, kindhearted.

malign *v.* 1 *to malign one's opponent:* slander, defame, speak ill of, revile, belittle, disparage, denigrate, deprecate, vilify. —*adj.* 2 *a malign look:* evil, bad, harmful, injurious, detrimental, baneful, ominous, sinister, black, malignant, malevolent, threatening, menacing, malicious, hateful.
Ant. 1 praise, extol, compliment, commend. 2 benign, benevolent, friendly, warmhearted.

malignant *adj.* 1 *a malignant tumor:* deadly, pernicious, virulent; fatal, toxic, poisonous. 2 *malignant gossip:* malicious, malevolent, vindictive, resentful, revengeful, spiteful, rancorous, vicious, invidious, venomous, hostile.
Ant. 1 nonmalignant, benign. 2 friendly, kind, kindhearted.

mall *n.* 1 *The concert was in the park's mall:* promenade, esplanade; square, plaza, quadrangle, yard, parade ground, arcade, colonnade. 2 *We went shopping at the mall:* shopping mall, shopping plaza, shopping center.

malleable *adj.* 1 *Tin is a malleable metal:* easily shaped, easily wrought; ductile, tractable, plastic, pliant, flexible. 2 *Young children are malleable:* impressionable, easily influenced, tractable, teachable, manageable, adaptable, flexible, pliable.
Ant. 1 rigid, stiff, hard, inflexible. 2 intractable, recalcitrant.

mammoth —*adj. The Great Pyramids are mammoth structures:* enormous, huge, immense, massive, gigantic, colossal, very large, monumental, prodigious, gargantuan, elephantine, stupendous, tremendous.
Ant. small, little, minute.

man *n.* 1 *Man cannot live by bread alone:* mankind, the human race, men and women, human beings, humankind, people, humanity, Homo sapiens. 2 *Every man must follow his own beliefs:* individual, person, human being, human, one; anyone, somebody, someone. 3 *The average man is taller than the average woman:* male, masculine person; gentleman, chap, fellow; *Slang* guy, gent. 4 *man and wife:* married man, husband. 5 *Hire a man to take care of the garden:* handyman, workman, hired hand, hand, laborer, day laborer; employee, worker; manservant, male servant; assistant, helper, right-hand man. —v. 6 *Man the lifeboats!*: attend, staff, take up one's position in, take one's place at, get to one's post; supply with hands, furnish with men.

Ant. 3 woman, female. 4 bachelor.

manacle *n.* 1 Usually **manacles** *The sheriff put manacles on the prisoner's hands:* handcuffs, hand-fetters; irons, shackles, chains, bonds. —v. 2 *The sheriff manacled the thief:* handcuff, fetter, put in chains, put in irons, shackle.

Ant. 2 unfetter, unchain; free.

manage *v.* 1 *The prime minister manages the government:* run, direct, oversee, superintend, have charge of, take care of, look after, supervise, head, administer, conduct, preside over, govern, control, guide, steer, pilot. 2 *How will you manage without a job?*: survive, get on, fare, weather the storm. 3 *We don't have much time to do the job, but we'll manage it:* succeed, accomplish, deal with, cope with, work out.

management *n.* 1 *The plan failed due to bad management:* administration, supervision, direction, overseeing, superintendence; operation, regulation, conduct, control, handling, care; planning, organization; strategy, tactics, manipulation; dealing, transaction. 2 *Management has vetoed your suggestion:* executives, administrators, the administration, supervisors, directors, bosses.

Ant. 2 labor; staff, employees, workers.

manager *n.* 1 *a store manager:* boss, supervisor, foreman, superintendent, overseer; executive director, administrator; agent. 2 *a good manager:* planner, organizer, manipulator, negotiator.

Ant. 1 employee, worker, laborer.

mandatory *adj.* *Attendance is mandatory:* compulsory, required, requisite, obligatory, incumbent on, not optional, binding; essential, imperative, necessary.

maneuver *n.* 1 *army maneuvers:* troop movement, troop deployment; movement of warships, planes, armored vehicles, etc.; training exercise. 2 *the opposition's maneuver to gain control of the government:* scheme, stratagem, gambit, move, tactic, plot, artifice, device, contrivance, machination, trick, intrigue. —v. 3 *Maneuver the car into that parking spot:* deploy, move; manipulate, steer, pilot, guide. 4 *The vice-president is maneuvering to displace the president:* contrive, scheme, plot, devise a way, intrigue.

mangle *v.* *The shirt was mangled in the laundry:* mutilate, maim, disfigure; lacerate, tear, injure, damage, lame, impair.

manhood *n.* 1 *He had to support his family before he achieved manhood:* adulthood, maturity, legal age, majority, mature age. 2 *an insult to his manhood:* virility, manliness, manfulness, masculinity, maleness.

mania *n.* 1 *Hitler's mania is cited as a cause of World War II:* madness, derangement, insanity, lunacy, fanaticism, dementia; frenzy, raving, hysteria, delusion, aberration. 2 *a mania for collecting seashells:* passion, craze, enthusiasm, obsession, fascination, compulsion, fixation.

Ant. 1 sanity, rationality; self-control, stability, levelheadedness.

maniac *n.* *Some maniac set the fire:* madman, lunatic, crazy person, insane person, deranged person; *Slang* nut; psychopath; reckless person, half-wit.

manifest *adj.* 1 *Her displeasure was manifest:* obvious, clear, evident, self-evident, plain, apparent, patent, visible, noticeable, unmistakable, unconcealed. —v. 2 *I manifested my disgust with a scowl:* indicate, show, exhibit, reveal, express, disclose, evince, display, make visible, bare, expose.

Ant. 1 hidden, concealed, masked; unseen. 2 hide, conceal, mask, cloak, camouflage.

manifestation *n.* *The rally was a manifestation of support for the candidate:* indication, symptom, evidence; demonstration, example, instance, display, illustration, expression.

manifesto *n.* *The rebels issued a manifesto on their aims:* proclamation, declaration, pronouncement, announcement, statement, pronunciamento, notice, notification.

manifold *adj.* *She has manifold responsibilities:* many, numerous, multiple, myriad, innumerable; varied, diversified, diverse.

Ant. few, limited; simple.

manipulate *v.* 1 *The magician manipulated the cards and the ace vanished:* handle, finger; feel, pinch, stroke, pat, massage, squeeze. 2 *Do you know how to manipulate this machine?*: operate, work, use, handle, control; wield, drive. 3 *They tried to manipulate the financial records:* tamper with, change fraudulently, influence deviously; deceive, defraud.

mankind *n.* *Is mankind in danger of extinction?*: the human race, humankind, Homo sapiens, the human species, man, men and women, humanity, mortals, people.

manly *adj.* 1 *a manly voice:* masculine, male, malelike, virile. 2 *a manly physique. Each soldier must do his duty in a manly fashion:* strong, robust, husky, sturdy, muscular, athletic, powerful; brave, courageous, resolute, stouthearted, fearless, staunch, heroic.

Ant. 1 unmanly, effeminate, womanish,

childlike, childish. **2** frail; cowardly, faint-hearted, irresolute.

man-made *adj. a man-made lake:* artificial, manufactured, fabricated, synthetic, hand-crafted; mock, sham, simulated.

manner *n.* **1** *duck cooked in the Chinese manner:* way, style, mode, fashion, method, custom, practice; guise, appearance, character. **2** *Her manner seemed uneasy:* behavior, conduct; bearing, air, deportment, demeanor. **3** *What manner of bird is that?:* kind, type, sort, variety; class, genre, species, category, breed, strain, brand, make, form.

mannerism *n. an annoying mannerism:* habit, habitual gesture, eccentricity, idiosyncrasy; affectation, affected gesture.

mannerly *adj. We reward mannerly conduct:* polite, well-mannered, courteous, well-behaved; courtly, gentlemanly, gallant.
Ant. unmannerly, discourteous, rude, impolite, ill-mannered.

manners *n. pl.* **1** *bad manners:* social behavior, behavior, decorum, deportment. **2** *Don't they teach any manners at that school?:* good manners, politeness, etiquette, courtesy; refinement, gentility, gallantry.
Ant. **2** rudeness, impoliteness, bad manners.

mansion *n. The mansion is the town's showplace:* stately residence, impressive house, imposing dwelling; manor, manor house, villa, château.
Ant. hovel, shack, cabin, cottage.

manslaughter *n. The driver was charged with manslaughter:* accidental murder, unpremeditated killing, killing without malice aforethought; *(loosely)* murder, killing, homicide.

mantle *n.* **1** *She wore a velvet mantle over her gown:* cloak, cape, tunic; scarf. **2** *A mantle of fog settled over the city:* covering, cover, veil, cloak, curtain, blanket, screen, cloud, film.

manual *adj.* **1** *The car has a manual transmission:* hand-operated, nonautomatic. **2** *manual labor:* physical, done by hand. —*n.* **3** *a manual of home repairs:* handbook, guidebook, instruction book; textbook, primer, workbook.
Ant. **1** automatic. **2** mental, intellectual.

manufacture *v.* **1** *The company manufactures toys:* produce, make, fabricate, fashion, devise, frame; assemble, construct, build. **2** *to manufacture an excuse:* invent, fabricate, make up, concoct, create, think up.
Ant. **1** destroy, demolish.

many *adj.* **1** *I've told you many times:* numerous, innumerable, countless, myriad, various. —*n.* **2** *Many are called but few are chosen:* a considerable number, a lot, heaps, piles, scores, dozens, numbers; a profusion, an abundance.
Ant. **1** few, infrequent, once or twice. **2** few, hardly any; none.

mar *v.* **1** *A scratch marred the table:* disfigure, blemish, deface, damage, scar, mark. **2** *A series of sour notes marred her singing:* taint, blemish, impair, hurt, detract from, make imperfect.
Ant. **1** embellish, decorate. **2** improve, enhance.

marauder *n. The marauders raided several coastal towns:* plunderer, pillager, ravager, looter, despoiler; pirate, buccaneer, privateer, corsair, freebooter; roving outlaw band.

march *v.* **1** *to march in the parade. March right upstairs and change those wet clothes!:* parade, walk in step, walk in a procession; go, go directly, proceed. —*n.* **2** *a ten-mile march:* hike, tramp, group walk; parade, procession. **3** *the march of civilization:* progress, progression, development, advance, advancement, rise, growth.

mare *n. The mare had a colt:* female horse, broodmare.

margin *n.* **1** *the margins of a book:* border, boundary, edge, rim, verge, hem, fringe, skirt. **2** *no margin for error:* leeway, extra amount, allowance.
Ant. **1** center, middle, interior.

marine *adj.* **1** *marine biology:* oceanic, sea, saltwater; of the sea, aquatic, oceanographic, pelagic. **2** *a specialist in marine law:* maritime, of ships, naval, nautical.
Ant. **1** terrestrial, land; fresh-water.

mariner *n. The old mariner had sailed the seas for 40 years:* sailor, deck hand, seaman, seafarer, seafaring man; *Slang* salt; navigator, pilot, helmsman.
Ant. landlubber.

marital *adj. marital bliss:* wedded, married, of marriage, matrimonial, conjugal, spousal, nuptial, connubial.
Ant. single, unmarried, unwed.

maritime *adj.* **1** *maritime history:* marine, naval, nautical, of ships, of the sea, seagoing, seafaring; oceanic, aquatic. **2** *Canada's Maritime Provinces:* coastal, bordering on the sea; engaged in sea trade, making a living from the sea.
Ant. **1** land, terrestrial; fresh-water. **2** inland.

mark *n.* **1** *What made those marks on the wall?:* spot, streak, line, stain; scratch, scar, cut, nick, dent, pock, pit, notch, score; bruise, blemish. **2** *This vase bears the mark of a famous potter. Everyone stood as a* *mark of respect:* hallmark, sign, symbol, stamp, label, badge, emblem, brand, colophon; token, symbol, indication, evidence. 3 *The student received passing marks:* grade; rating. 4 *Your words were way off the mark:* target, objective, intent, point, track, bull's-eye; standard, criterion. —*v.* 5 *That wet glass will mark the table:* spot, streak, stain; scratch, scar, cut, nick, dent, score; bruise, blemish; mar, injure; make a line on, write on. 6 *The teacher marked the examination papers:* grade, correct. 7 *Well-kept houses mark a good neighborhood:* indicate, reveal, disclose, show, point out, denote, signify; characterize, typify, symbolize, evidence, betoken, be a sign of, distinguish; label, stamp, brand. 8 *Mark my words!:* heed, attend, pay attention to, mind, note, regard.

Ant. 8 ignore, overlook, disregard.

marked *adj. a woman of marked intelligence:* outstanding, conspicuous, striking, noticeable, obvious, prominent; exceptional, uncommon, noteworthy, extraordinary, unique, singular, remarkable, particular, definite, decided.

Ant. ordinary, undistinguished, routine, mediocre.

market *n.* 1 *a fruit market:* marketplace, wholesale market; stand; grocer's shop, grocery; meat market, butcher shop. —*v.* 2 *The inventor is trying to market a new product:* sell, vend, merchandise, retail.

marksman *n. a true marksman:* sharpshooter, good shot, crack shot, dead shot, sure shot.

maroon¹ *v. They were marooned on a small island:* strand, leave behind, put ashore; abandon, desert.

maroon² *adj. a maroon sweater:* brownish red, wine, magenta, plum.

marriage *n.* 1 *their forty years of marriage:* matrimony, marital state, wedlock, holy wedlock, conjugal union, connubial state, nuptial state. 2 *The marriage will take place in June:* wedding, marriage ceremony, nuptials, tying the knot.

Ant. 1 divorce; single life.

marry *v.* 1 *They will marry in June:* wed, get married to, espouse, exchange wedding vows with, lead to the altar, bestow one's hand upon, take for a husband, take for a wife; *Slang* get spliced, tie the knot. 2 *The minister has married over 400 couples:* wed, join in marriage, join in wedlock, unite in holy wedlock.

Ant. 1 divorce.

marsh *n. Ducks landed in the marsh:* swamp, bog, fen, bottoms, slough; marshland, wetland.

marshal *n.* 1 *U.S. marshals. a fire marshal:* law officer; sheriff, police chief; fire chief. 2 *the marshal of the Rose Bowl parade:* master of ceremonies, honorary leader, ceremonial head; chief, leader, director, supervisor, manager. 3 *the marshal of the armies:* field marshal, commander, general. —*v.* 4 *to marshal troops for battle:* gather, collect, muster, assemble, mobilize; arrange, order, group, deploy, array, align, line up.

mart *n. a merchandise mart:* trade center, trading center, exchange; marketplace, market; trade fair, trade show, exposition, show.

martial *adj.* 1 *martial law. a martial bearing:* military; soldierly, soldierlike. 2 *The country maintains a martial attitude:* warlike, belligerent, militant, combative, bellicose, contentious; military-minded.

Ant. 1 civilian, civil. 2 peaceful, conciliatory.

martinet *n. The boss is a real martinet:* taskmaster, disciplinarian, authoritarian, tyrant, despot, dictator.

martyr *n. early Christian martyrs:* person willing to die or suffer for a cause; person killed for his beliefs; one who undergoes great suffering; one venerated for dying or suffering.

martyrdom *n. the martyrdom of St. Sebastian:* the suffering of a martyr, death of a martyr; suffering, agony, anguish, torment, torture, ordeal, affliction.

marvel *n.* 1 *That speech was a marvel of tact:* miracle, wonder, phenomenon, wonderful example; rarity. —*v.* 2 *The tourists marveled at Lake Louise:* be awed, be overwhelmed, be struck with wonder, be amazed, be astonished, be stupefied, gape.

Ant. 1 commonplace.

marvelous Also **marvellous** *adj. It was a marvelous party:* wonderful, splendid, lovely, superb, outstanding, great, fine, first-rate, fabulous, heavenly, divine, extraordinary, stupendous, sensational, phenomenal, magnificent, remarkable.

Ant. terrible, awful, lousy.

masculine *adj. a masculine physique:* manly, male, virile; strong, robust, sturdy, husky, powerful, muscular, strapping, athletic; brave, courageous, resolute, daring, stouthearted, fearless, valiant, staunch, indomitable, self-reliant.

mash *v. Mash the potatoes:* puree, reduce to pulp; crush, pulverize, squash, smash.

mask *n.* 1 *a Halloween mask. Each diver has to wear a mask:* false face; face covering, face guard. 2 *The jokes were a mask to hide the sadness:* cover, cover-up, screen, cloak, veil; disguise, camouflage. —*v.* 3 *The bank* *robbers masked their faces:* cover, put a mask over, obscure, hide, disguise. **4** *She tried to mask her feelings:* hide, conceal, cover, screen, veil, keep secret; camouflage, disguise.

Ant. **2** revelation, manifestation, show, exhibition. **3** unmask. **4** reveal, disclose, divulge, show, display.

masquerade *n.* **1** *a Halloween masquerade:* costume party, masked ball, masque, mask. **2** *My laughter is just a masquerade:* cover, cover-up, mask, screen, veil; camouflage, pretense, subterfuge, guise, artifice, ruse. —*v.* **3** *He's been masquerading as a real doctor!:* go under the guise of, pass oneself off as, pretend to be, pose as, falsely claim to be; go disguised as.

Ant. **2** revelation, disclosure, display, manifestation.

mass[1] *n.* **1** *Einstein studied the relation of energy and mass:* (loosely) matter, material; weight. **2** *a solid mass of rock:* block, lump, chunk, hunk, clot, cake. **3** *a mass of clothing. a mass of people:* pile, heap, stack, batch, clump, bundle, pack, bunch; accumulation, collection, assemblage, gathering, group, body, aggregate, crowd, throng, mob, horde. **4** *the mass of public opinion:* greater part, preponderance, majority, plurality, bulk, main body. —*v.* **5** *Protesters massed in front of the city hall:* collect, amass, gather, assemble, congregate, accumulate; pile, heap, stack.

Ant. **4** minority, **5** disperse, scatter.

mass[3] *n.* Often **Mass** *Sunday Mass:* celebration of the sacrament, Communion service, Holy Communion, holy sacrament, Eucharist.

massacre *n. the massacre of captured troops:* mass slaughter, mass murder, killing, butchery; carnage, bloodbath.

massage *n.* **1** *A brisk massage restores the body's vigor:* rubdown; rubbing, kneading, stroking, manipulation. —*v.* **2** *He massaged his jaw thoughtfully:* rub, knead, chafe, stroke, manipulate, finger.

masses *n. pl. The masses are the true makers of history:* the common people, the crowd, the mob, the multitude, the populace, the many, hoi polloi, the common herd, the great unwashed; the working class, the proletariat, the lower classes, proles, plebeians, plebes, the riffraff, rabble.

Ant. the élite, the aristocracy, the gentry, the upper class, bluebloods, high society, the intelligentsia, the cognoscenti.

massive *adj. a massive rock formation:* immense, huge, gigantic, enormous, mammoth, colossal, great, gargantuan, elephan-

tine, monumental, vast, extensive; heavy, ponderous, weighty, bulky.

Ant. small, little, diminutive; petty, trivial; slight, frail.

master *n.* **1** *The dog obeyed its master:* owner, lord; conqueror, ruler. **2** *the master of a house:* head, boss, chief, leader, dominant person, authority, director, supervisor, overseer, superintendent. **3** *Grandfather was a master at silversmithing:* expert, master hand, skilled artist, craftsman, wizard; *Slang* whiz. —*adj.* **4** *the master bedroom:* main, chief, principal, most important, predominant, choice, best. **5** *a master craftsman:* expert, skilled, masterly, proficient, first-rate, practiced, accomplished, finished, talented. —*v.* **6** *You must master your temper:* conquer, subdue, overcome, control, govern, manage, dominate, tame, curb. **7** *to master mathematics:* learn thoroughly, be adept in, be skilled at, be proficient in, excel at.

Ant. **1** slave; servant. **3, 5** amateur, novice, tyro. **5** amateurish, incompetent, inept, unaccomplished.

masterful *adj.* **1** *a masterful performance:* masterly, skillful, expert, accomplished, finished, superb, excellent. **2** *a masterful presence:* strong-willed, resolute, forceful; commanding, domineering.

Ant. **1** amateurish, incompetent, inept, unaccomplished, clumsy. **2** weak, wishy-washy, meek, spineless.

mastermind *v.* **1** *Who masterminded the robbery?:* plan, organize, conceive, engineer, direct. —*n.* **2** *She's the mastermind of our new policy:* organizer, engineer, initiator, moving force, director. **3** *It will take a mastermind to solve this problem:* genius, mental giant, brilliant intellect, wizard; expert, specialist, master, master hand.

Ant. **3** idiot, simpleton; amateur, incompetent.

masterpiece *n. Rembrandt's paintings are masterpieces:* great work of art, masterwork, classic; prize, jewel, treasure.

mastery *n.* **1** *The sergeant had complete mastery over his men:* control, command, domination, dominance, leadership, sway, rule. **2** *a mastery of Japanese:* expert knowledge, expert skill, proficiency, deftness, acquirement, attainment.

Ant. **1** subservience, submission. **2** incompetence, ineptness.

match *n.* **1** *The shirt and tie are a good match. Can you find the match to this glove?:* matching pair, corresponding twosome; mate, duplicate, double, twin, companion. **2** *Bill is no match for his brother:* equal, equivalent, peer; parallel, counterpart.

3 *Who won the tennis match?:* game, contest, competition, tournament, meet, event. —*v.* **4** *The drapes match the rug:* harmonize, correspond, be alike, suit, fit, go well with; combine, agree.

Ant. **1** mismatch. **4** clash with, be a mismatch.

matchless *adj. a matchless painting:* incomparable, unmatched, unparalleled, unequaled, unrivaled; peerless, unsurpassed, unexcelled, superlative, preeminent, foremost; rare, priceless, inestimable.

Ant. equaled, surpassed, excelled; average, mediocre, ordinary.

mate *n.* **1** *Where's the mate to this sock?:* one of a pair, duplicate, match, twin, counterpart, companion, equivalent. **2** *The zoo is looking for a mate for its female panda:* one of a pair of mated animals; spouse, partner, consort, helpmate; husband, wife. —*v.* **3** *Some animals will not mate in captivity:* pair off; couple, copulate, cohabit.

material *n.* **1** *The material in the earth's crust is very old:* matter, substance, stuff, constituents, elements. **2** Often **materials** *building materials:* supplies, stores, stocks; equipment, machinery, tools. **3** *Mother bought some material to make a dress:* fabric, textile, drygoods; piece goods, yard goods, cloth. **4** *The reporter is collecting material for an article:* facts, figures, data, observations, impressions. —*adj.* **5** *the material universe:* physical, tangible, substantive, materialistic, concrete; bodily, corporeal. **6** *You made a material contribution to the work:* significant, important, substantial, consequential, essential, vital, indispensable; relevant, pertinent, germane, direct; momentous.

Ant. **5** nonmaterial, intangible; spiritual. **6** insignificant, unimportant, unsubstantial, inconsequential, unessential, superficial; irrelevant.

materialism *n. crass materialism:* love of possessions, love of material things, pursuit of wealth; acquisitiveness, covetousness.

Ant. asceticism; idealism.

materialize *v. The ghost materialized once a year:* appear, emerge, become visible, turn up, come forth, issue, manifest oneself.

Ant. disappear, vanish, evaporate, dissolve.

materially *adv.* **1** *Were things materially different in the old days?:* significantly, substantially, essentially, considerably, seriously. **2** *Materially, they are quite successful:* financially, monetarily, concerning material things; in substance, palpably.

Ant. **1** insignificantly, unsubstantially, superficially. **2** spiritually; intellectually.

matériel *n. matériel for the troops:* military supplies, gear, equipment, materials; supplies, stores, provisions.

maternal *adj.* **1** *maternal pride:* motherly, motherlike; doting, fond; shielding, protective. **2** *my maternal grandmother:* related through one's mother, on one's mother's side of the family.

Ant. **2** paternal.

mathematical Also **mathematic** *adj.* **1** *a mathematical genius:* of mathematics; computational. **2** *They worked with mathematical precision:* precise, exact, accurate, unerring, scientific, meticulous, scrupulous, strict, punctilious, rigorous.

matriarch *n. the matriarch of our family:* female head, female chieftain, female ruler, female leader, materfamilias.

matriculate *v. to matriculate at the university:* enroll, register; sign up, enter.

matrimonial *adj. matrimonial bliss:* married, wedded, nuptial, conjugal, marital, connubial, husbandly, wifely.

matrimony *n. young couples entering matrimony:* marriage, marital state, holy wedlock, connubial state, nuptial state.

Ant. divorce; single life.

matron *n.* **1** *Most of the members are matrons:* married woman, middle-aged woman, stately woman, dowager. **2** *a prison matron:* female supervisor, overseer, superintendent; directress, forelady, forewoman.

Ant. **1** girl, maid, maiden, miss, young woman.

matter *n.* **1** *The physical world is composed of matter:* material, substance, stuff, elements; object, thing. **2** *a controversial matter:* subject, theme, topic. **3** *There's that little matter of the money you borrowed:* affair, business, situation, transaction, episode, occurrence, adventure, event, happening. **4** *It is no matter that he didn't phone:* importance, consequence, significance, import, moment, difference. **5** *What's the matter?:* trouble, difficulty, cause of distress; dilemma, quandary, obstacle, impediment. —*v.* **6** *It matters very much:* be of importance, be of consequence, count, be of concern, be noteworthy.

Ant. **1** spirit, soul; mind, intellect. **4** insignificance, unimportance. **6** be unimportant, be inconsequential.

matter-of-fact *adj. a matter-of-fact appraisal of the situation:* practical, straightforward, realistic, factual, down-to-earth, sensible; hardheaded, unsentimental, pragmatic, candid.

Ant. theoretical; impassioned, emotional.

mature *adj.* **1** *a mature man:* grown,

matured, fully developed, grown-up, full-grown; of age, adult; middle-aged, experienced, seasoned. 2 *When the plan is mature we will proceed:* completed, ready, finished, full-fledged. —*v.* 3 *Girls mature earlier than boys:* maturate, reach maturity, come of age, become adult, grow up, develop; ripen, bloom.

Ant. 1 immature, unripe, underaged; young, juvenile. 2 incomplete, unperfected, unfinished.

maturity *n.* 1 *The body reaches maturity earlier than the mind:* adulthood, maturation, manhood, womanhood, full growth, full development; legal age, age of consent, majority; ripeness, completion, culmination. 2 *a student with a great deal of maturity:* experience, seasoning; levelheadedness, composure, mature judgment, matureness, responsibility.

Ant. 1 immaturity, youthfulness. 2 irresponsibility, hot-headedness.

maudlin *adj.* *The book has a maudlin plot:* overemotional, sentimental, mawkish, teary, gushy, mushy.

Ant. realistic, matter-of-fact, unsentimental.

maul *v.* *He was badly mauled in the fight:* manhandle, batter, beat, beat up, rough up, pummel, thrash; bruise, mangle.

maunder *v.* *My thoughts tend to maunder:* wander, ramble, drift, saunter, meander, stray; dawdle, loaf, dillydally.

mauve *adj.* *mauve irises:* light purple, bluish purple, lilac, lavender, puce, violet.

maverick *n.* 1 *The cowboys rounded up the mavericks:* unbranded calf, yearling; unbranded cow; motherless calf. 2 *a political maverick:* nonconformist, independent, individualist, loner; dissenter, dissident.

mawkish *adj.* *Mother gets mawkish when she speaks of her childhood:* sentimental, maudlin, emotional, tearful, teary, *Informal* mushy, gushy.

Ant. unsentimental, unemotional, matter-of-fact.

maxim *n.* *"A stitch in time saves nine" is a popular maxim:* adage, aphorism, axiom, proverb, apothegm; platitude, truism, saw, saying; motto, guiding principle, rule.

maximum *adj.* *at maximum speed:* greatest possible, optimum, greatest, utmost, top, highest.

Ant. minimum, minimal, least possible.

maybe *adv.* *Maybe we'll see you tomorrow:* possibly, perhaps, perchance, mayhap; feasibly, conceivably.

maze *n.* *a maze of offices:* labyrinth, complex, network, tangle.

meager *adj.* *a meager supply of food:* scanty, scant, little, skimpy, scrimpy, sparse, slender, slim; spare, scarce.

Ant. ample, abundant, plentiful, copious.

meal *n.* *the midday meal. a Chinese meal:* repast, spread, feast, banquet, refreshment, nourishment; food, cuisine, cooking, fare, victuals.

mean[1] *v.* 1 *Father didn't mean to be a clerk all his life:* intend, have in mind; plan, want, wish, resolve, determine upon, aim at, have in view. 2 *Dark clouds usually mean rain:* signify, tell of; indicate, point to, imply, suggest, hint at, betoken. 3 *Did she mean it?:* say truly, speak sincerely, express genuinely.

Ant. 2 hide, conceal, mask. 3 pretend, feign.

mean[2] *adj.* 1 *The shoes were of mean quality. She has some mean job at the local factory:* low, low-grade, poor, inferior, cheap; squalid, wretched, miserable, sordid; menial, low-ranking, petty, paltry, insignificant, inconsequential, small, picayune. 2 *How could anyone be so mean?:* malicious, vicious, malevolent, villainous, base, low, small-minded, contemptible, vile; nasty, disagreeable, cruel, hardhearted, merciless, pitiless, inhumane, unfeeling, unsympathetic, uncaring, unfair.

Ant. 1 superior, excellent, first-rate; important, consequential. 2 kind, goodhearted, sweet, humane, sympathetic, compassionate.

mean[3] *n.* 1 *Can't we strike a mean and find a house that's not too big or too small?:* average, norm, median, balance, midway point. —*adj.* 2 *the mean income of American families:* average; standard, medium.

Ant. 2 extreme; highest, lowest.

meander *v.* *The path meanders up the hill. The tourists meandered through the town:* wind, circle, loop, zigzag, twist, snake, spiral; wander, ramble, rove.

Ant. go directly, make a beeline.

meaning *n.* *Look up the meaning of the word in the dictionary. Did that speech have any meaning at all?:* denotation, sense, signification; significance, substance, content, essence, gist, pith, meat; implication, drift, suggestion, intimation, indication, hint; intention, intent, purpose, thrust, force, goal, point, value, worth.

Ant. meaninglessness, insignificance, absurdity.

meaningful *adj.* 1 *a meaningful look:* pointed, significant, purposeful, eloquent, expressive, designing, explicit. 2 *a meaningful job:* worthwhile, useful, significant, consequential, serious; gratifying, satisfying.

Ant. 1, 2 meaningless, superficial. 2 useless, insignificant, unimportant, trivial.

meaningless *adj.* 1 *Sanskrit is completely meaningless to me:* unintelligible, incomprehensible, incoherent, impenetrable, undecipherable; puzzling, baffling, mystifying, perplexing. 2 *She feels that her life is meaningless:* without meaning, without purpose, worthless, useless, aimless, insignificant, inconsequential, unimportant, unessential, trivial, senseless.

Ant. 1, 2 meaningful. 1 intelligible, comprehensible, understandable. 2 purposeful, worthwhile, useful, significant.

means *n.pl.* 1 *We don't have the means to travel. a person of means:* money, resources, wherewithal, funds, dollars, income, revenue; wealth, riches, substance, affluence. 2 *Taking a plane is the quickest means of getting there:* way, method; resort, course, process.

meantime *n. I'll call you Sunday, but in the meantime say nothing:* interim, interval, the intervening time.

meanwhile *adv. Meanwhile, across town, things were humming:* at the same time, simultaneously, concurrently; during the intervening period, in the interim, meantime.

measurable *adj. The distance to the farthest star is measurable:* computable, reckonable, capable of being measured, mensurable, determinable.

Ant. immeasurable, indeterminate.

measure *v.* 1 *Measure the windows before buying the curtains. The tablecloth measures 18 by 20 feet:* ascertain the dimensions of, find the size of, size, to be the size of, be long, be wide. 2 *It's hard to measure the importance of good manners:* evaluate, value, assess, appraise, gauge, judge. —*n.* 3 *Flood victims received a full measure of aid:* share, allotment, quantity, amount, portion, quota; extent, degree, range, scope. 4 *What measures were taken to prevent fires?:* course, means, step, act, method, resort, proceeding, procedure, plan.

measured *adj.* 1 *a measured mile:* predetermined; precise, exact. 2 *The dignitaries advanced with a measured tread:* uniform, steady, regular. 3 *Her reply was stated in measured phrases:* studied, deliberate, premeditated, calculated, well-planned, carefully thought-out.

Ant. 2 haphazard, irregular, random. 3 spontaneous, reckless, unplanned.

measurement *n.* 1 *The measurement of intelligence is difficult:* measuring, mensuration; evaluation, assessment, appraisal, estimation. 2 *What are the measurements of the rug?:* dimension, size, breadth, depth, length, height, width, area; capacity, volume, content; mass, weight; magnitude, amplitude.

meat *n.* 1 *Veal is a meat:* edible animal flesh, animal tissue or organs. 2 *The travelers were given meat and drink:* food, nourishment, victuals, sustenance, edibles, comestibles, fare, provender. 3 *the meat of an argument:* gist, point, essence, substance, core, heart, nucleus.

mechanical *adj.* 1 *a mechanical device:* run by machinery, having to do with machinery; machine-driven, automatic, self-acting. 2 *His gratitude seemed rather mechanical:* perfunctory, routine, unfeeling, impersonal; automatic, instinctive, involuntary.

Ant. 1 manual. 2 genuine, sincere, heartfelt, warm; voluntary, conscious.

mechanism *n. a simple mechanism:* apparatus, tool, instrument, implement, contrivance, appliance, machine; works, machinery, motor.

medal *n. The hero received many medals:* citation, decoration, medallion, ribbon, award of honor; trophy, award; honor, laurel.

meddle *v. Don't meddle in this affair:* interfere, intervene, intrude, concern oneself unasked, mix in.

meddlesome *adj. If I offered advice, she'd think I was meddlesome:* intrusive, officious, presumptuous, obtrusive, meddling, interfering.

Ant. reserved; standoffish.

mediate *v. The lawyer tried to mediate between the two:* arbitrate, negotiate, intervene, intercede, settle a dispute, effect an agreement; umpire, referee.

mediation *n. The dispute was settled by mediation:* arbitration, compromise, conciliation, coming to terms; negotiation.

mediator *n. The counselor will act as mediator:* arbitrator, negotiator, reconciler, go-between, intermediary.

medical *adj. Some herbs have medical value:* relating to medicine, medicinal, medicative, curative, healing, therapeutic, restorative, health-bringing.

medicine *n. What kind of medicine are you taking?:* curative agent, medication; drug, pill, remedy, nostrum; balm, salve.

Ant. poison, toxin, bane.

mediocre *adj. His work is mediocre:* ordinary, run-of-the-mill, undistinguished, commonplace, pedestrian, indifferent, passable, tolerable, so-so, fair, average; unimportant, inconsequential, insignificant; rather poor, second-rate.

Ant. extraordinary, distinguished, superior, excellent, superb.

mediocrity *n. the mediocrity of hack writing:* commonplaceness, ordinariness, unimportance, insignificance; low-quality, inferiority.
Ant. distinction, importance, significance; excellence, superiority, brilliance.

meditate *v. Set aside enough time to meditate:* think, reflect, think quietly, ruminate, muse, contemplate, ponder, mull over.
Ant. act, do.

medium *n.* 1 *Fish live in an aqueous medium:* environment; surroundings, atmosphere; setting, milieu. 2 *a medium between good and bad:* middle ground, midcourse, middle way; compromise, mean, balance. 3 *Television can be an excellent medium for education:* agency, means, way, mode, form, channel, instrument, vehicle, tool. 4 *The medium supposedly called forth her long dead uncle:* spiritualist, psychic, clairvoyant, fortuneteller, crystal gazer. —*adj.* 5 *He's of medium height:* average, normal, ordinary, moderate.
Ant. 2 extreme. 5 extraordinary, uncommon, distinctive, unusual.

medley *n. a medley of march tunes:* miscellany, mixture, assortment, potpourri, mélange, pastiche, patchwork; jumble, hodgepodge.

meek *adj. The boss mistreated his meek assistant:* submissive, deferential, docile, yielding, compliant, spineless, weak-kneed; humble, mild, gentle, unassuming, unassertive, retiring.
Ant. domineering, bossy, overbearing, self-assertive; rebellious, insubordinate; arrogant, proud.

meet *v.* 1 *I'd like you to meet my brother:* be introduced to, become acquainted with. 2 *I met an old friend today. to meet with danger:* come across, encounter, run into, light upon; confront, face, come into the presence of. 3 *The club meets every week:* assemble, convene, gather, congregate, come together. 4 *to meet one's financial obligations:* fulfill, comply with, satisfy, abide by, adhere to, carry out, perform, discharge, heed, acknowledge, respect. 5 *Turn left where the highway meets the dirt road:* cross, intersect, unite with; adjoin, abut, border.
Ant. 2 avoid, elude, miss. 3 adjourn; disperse. 4 fail, renege. 5 diverge.

meeting *n.* 1 *our meeting at the restaurant:* encounter, confrontation; date, engagement, rendezvous, tryst. 2 *Call the meeting to order:* gathering, assembly, group, conclave, council, congress, caucus; conference, convention, get-together.

melancholy *n.* 1 *a feeling of melancholy:* melancholia; depression, gloom, dejection, despondency, disconsolateness, forlornness, moodiness, low spirits, doldrums. —*adj.* 2 *Hamlet was a melancholy man:* suffering from melancholia; depressed, dejected, despondent, disconsolate, forlorn, moody, doleful, downhearted, heavyhearted, dispirited, downcast, morose, languishing.
Ant. 1 exhilaration, joy, delight, cheer, happiness. 2 exhilarated, joyful, lighthearted, happy, merry.

meld *v. Meld the ingredients into a smooth paste:* merge, mix, blend, fuse, combine, consolidate, unite, amalgamate, incorporate, join; jumble, scramble.
Ant. separate, divide.

melee *n. Rival fans started a melee:* fistfight, brawl, row, free-for-all, fracas, fray, set-to, tussle, altercation, riot.

mellifluous *adj. mellifluous bells:* sweetsounding, sweet-toned, euphonious, musical, harmonious, sweet, dulcet, melodious, resonant, full-toned.
Ant. harsh, discordant, grating, unmusical.

mellow *adj.* 1 *a good mellow cheese:* ripe, mature, matured, full-flavored, full-bodied; soft, rich —*v.* 2 *Age mellowed me:* mature; make more understanding, make compassionate, make more tolerant, soften.
Ant. 1 unripe, immature, green. 2 harden, make callous, make unfeeling.

melodious *adj. a melodious voice:* sweettoned, mellifluous, musical, sweet, dulcet; soft, smooth; clear, rich, full-toned, resonant.
Ant. harsh, discordant, grating, raucous.

melodramatic *adj. The play was melodramatic:* exaggerated, flamboyant, overly theatrical, sensational, stagy; sentimental, overemotional, overwrought, mawkish, maudlin, histrionic.
Ant. realistic, matter-of-fact; understated.

melody *n.* 1 *I'll hum the melody:* tune, air, strain, theme; song, ditty. 2 *The composer depends on melody:* tunefulness, melodiousness, musicality, melodic invention; euphony, harmoniousness, mellifluence.
Ant. 2 dissonance; discordance.

melt *v.* 1 *The snow melted quickly:* dissolve, liquefy, thaw. 2 *The crowd melted away:* dissipate, scatter, dispel, dwindle, fade, disappear, evaporate, vanish. 3 *His tears melted her heart:* touch, soften, disarm, make gentle, arouse pity; appease, mollify.
Ant. 1 freeze, congeal, harden. 2 gather, grow. 4 harden.

member n. a member of the committee: constituent, person who belongs to a group; component, element, part, piece, section, segment, portion, ingredient.

membership n. 1 We offer all bowlers membership in the league: fellowship, affiliation, league, fraternal union, connection. 2 The membership of the club is now 500: roster, personnel, body of members, number of members; community, company, association; society, fraternity, brotherhood, club, fellowship.

membrane n. a thin membrane: web, covering tissue; film, sheet, coating, skin, sheath, lining, envelope; integument, pellicle.

memento n. The photo was a memento of his visit: souvenir, token, keepsake, reminder, remembrance, memorabilia, remembrancer; relic.

memoir n. The duchess's memoirs caused a sensation: autobiography, diary, journal, reminiscences, biography, life story.

memorable adj. a memorable poem: unforgettable, noteworthy, impressive, illustrious, famous, celebrated, distinguished, eminent, important, significant, historic, outstanding, remarkable, striking.
    Ant. unmemorable, forgettable, unimpressive, undistinguished, unimportant, insignificant; commonplace, ordinary, prosaic, run-of-the-mill.

memorandum n. We received a memorandum about the meeting: memo, reminder, minute, note, brief report.

memorial n. 1 a memorial to the town's war dead: monument, testimonial. 2 Friends gathered at a memorial for the late statesman: tribute, homage, commemorative service, memorial service. —adj. 3 a memorial plaque: commemorative, monumental, testimonial.

memory n. 1 Can certain foods improve memory?: recall, ability to remember, power of recollection, mental retention. 2 Mother has lovely memories of her youth: recollection, reminiscence, remembrance, memento, souvenir, keepsake, reminder.
    Ant. 1 forgetfulness; amnesia.

menace n. 1 Icebergs are a menace to shipping: threat, danger, peril, hazard, endangerment, imperilment, pitfall, cause for alarm. —v. 2 Pollution can menace a person's health. The hoodlum menaced the local merchants: endanger, imperil, be a hazard to, jeopardize; intimidate, threaten, terrorize, bully, browbeat.
    Ant. 1 benefit, boon, advantage. 2 benefit, aid, promote, further; protect, guard.

mend v. 1 to mend a coat. The broken bone

is starting to mend: repair, fix, restore, patch, darn; heal, knit; cure, remedy. 2 to mend one's ways: correct, reform, improve, better, amend, rectify, revise.
    Ant. 1 tear; break, fracture.

mendacity n. There's too much mendacity in the world: lying, falsehood, falsity, untruthfulness, misrepresentation; deceit, deception, duplicity, insincerity.
    Ant. truth, truthfulness, veracity, honesty, sincerity.

menial adj. 1 Menial behavior disgusts me: lowly, degrading, humble, ignoble, abject; servile, subservient, obsequious, fawning, groveling, truckling, cringing, sycophantic. —n. 2 The king was surrounded by menials: servant, flunky, lackey, underling, subordinate; sycophant, toady.
    Ant. 1 noble, dignified; proud, haughty. 2 master, lord, superior.

mental adj. 1 mental arithmetic: of the mind, in the mind, done with the mind; intellectual, intelligent, cerebral, rational; psychic, psychological, abstract, subjective. 2 a mental patient: mentally ill, mentally disturbed, psychotic, neurotic; insane, lunatic.

mentality n. She has the mentality of a much older child: intellect, mental ability, intelligence, mental power, mind, brains; judgment, understanding, discernment, perspicacity, acumen, wisdom, sagacity.

mention v. 1 I hate to mention this, but—: allude to, speak of briefly, refer to, touch upon; name, specify, cite, disclose, make known, divulge; hint at, intimate, imply, insinuate; state, remark, say, report, recount, narrate. —n. 2 No mention was made of her illness: suggestion, indication, hint, insinuation, inkling, reference, remark, statement, comment, announcement, notice, report.
    Ant. 1 omit, be silent about. 2 silence, suppression.

mentor n. Students benefit from the guidance of a mentor: adviser, counselor, preceptor; teacher, instructor, professor, tutor; monitor, proctor.

mercenary adj. 1 mercenary impulses: selfish, greedy, venal; monetary, money-motivated, for gain, for pay; acquisitive, grasping, avaricious, covetous. —n. 2 Much of the fighting was done by mercenaries: hired soldier, paid soldier in a foreign army, soldier fighting for spoils; hireling.
    Ant. 1 idealistic, altruistic; generous, benevolent.

merchandise n. 1 The store has the best merchandise: manufactured goods, goods, wares, stock, stock in trade. —v. 2 There's no use in manufacturing an item unless you *can merchandise it:* sell, market, distribute; deal in, buy and sell, carry on commerce in, do business in, traffic in.

merchant *n. a diamond merchant:* salesman, saleswoman, dealer, wholesaler, trader; shopkeeper, retailer, storekeeper, peddler, hawker.

merciful *adj. a merciful judge:* compassionate, humane, exercising mercy, lenient, clement, sparing, forgiving, pitying, kindhearted, understanding, benificent.
Ant. merciless, cruel, inhumane, hardhearted, pitiless.

merciless *adj. a merciless killer:* pitiless, ruthless, unmerciful, inhumane, hardhearted, cold-blooded, unrelenting; cruel, harsh, severe, fierce, unsparing, heartless, unpitying, callous, ferocious.
Ant. merciful, humane, kindhearted, lenient.

mercurial *adj. He's too mercurial to trust:* impulsive, changeable, inconstant, erratic, fickle, unpredictable, volatile, fluctuating, variable, impetuous.
Ant. unchanging, stable, phlegmatic.

mercy *n. He begged for mercy:* compassion, forbearance, benevolence, clemency, sympathy, humaneness, humanity, tolerance, fellow feeling, forgiveness, leniency, lenience.
Ant. pitilessness, cruelty, harshness, severity, implacability, inhumanity.

mere *adj. It's a mere trinket:* inconsiderable, insignificant, trifling, paltry, negligible, unappreciable; nothing else but, nothing more than; bare, scant, bald.

merge *v. The two companies merged:* combine, amalgamate, consolidate, fuse, converge, blend, integrate, join, unite, confederate, associate, band together, unify.
Ant. separate, diverge, part.

merit *n. 1 There is great merit in the plan:* value, worth, worthiness, virtue, advantage, benefit, justification; ability, excellence, distinction. *—v. 2 The suggestion merits consideration:* deserve, be entitled to, rate, be worthy of, have a right to, warrant.
Ant. 1 fault, defect, weakness.

meritorious *adj. meritorious service:* commendable, laudable, praiseworthy, deserving of reward or commendation, worthy, excellent, exemplary, admirable.
Ant. unexceptional, unworthy, undeserving.

merriment *n. You never saw such merriment at a party!:* mirth, laughter, gaiety, jollity, hilarity, fun; glee, cheer, celebration, joviality, jocularity, merrymaking.
Ant. cheerlessness, distress, misery.

merry *adj. We joined the merry crowd:* jolly, cheerful, happy, cheery, gleeful, jovial, joyous, mirthful, jocular, fun-loving, lighthearted, jocund, jolly, high-spirited, laughing.
Ant. sad, unhappy, gloomy, dejected.

mesh *n. 1 The net was made of a fine mesh:* netting, network, grille, reticulation, openwork, screen, sieve, grid, webbing, latticework, grillwork, lacework. *—v. 2 The gears meshed:* engaged, interlock, interweave, connect, dovetail, fit together; coordinate, interact.

mesmerize *v. She mesmerized her audiences:* spellbind, bewitch, fascinate, entrance, transport, charm, enthrall; hypnotize.

mess *n. 1 Pick up that mess of dirty clothes:* clutter, unsightly accumulation, jumble, litter, hodgepodge, confused mass; untidy condition, disorder, disarray. 2 *How did you get into a mess like this?:* predicament, difficulty, plight, muddle, confusion, quandary, fix, strait, scrape, trouble; dilemma, crisis.

message *n. 1 I received a message that she would be late:* notice, report, word, statement, news, communication, memorandum, communiqué, intelligence, tidings. 2 *The play has a serious message:* point, theme, central idea, meaning, moral.

messenger *n. The messenger brought your note today:* carrier, bearer, runner, deliverer, delivery boy, delivery man, courier.

messy *adj. 1 a messy desk:* disordered, cluttered, untidy, littered, sloppy, chaotic, disarranged, jumbled; bedraggled, sloppy, disheveled, unkempt. 2 *a messy situation:* awkward, difficult, unpleasant, embarrassing, uncomfortable, tricky.
Ant. 1 neat, tidy, clean. 2 pleasant, comfortable.

metamorphosis *n. 1 the stages in the metamorphosis of a mosquito:* transformation, change of form, mutation, transmutation, structural evolution, transfiguration, modification, conversion, transmogrification. 2 *He underwent a complete metamorphosis after his failure:* change, transformation, alteration, permutation.

metaphor *n. In poetry the rose is often a metaphor for love:* image, figurative expression, poetic equivalent, symbol, figure of speech, simile, trope, metonymy, analogy, equivalence.

metaphysical *adj. metaphysical questions:* philosophical, speculative, abstract, unanswerable, intellectual; universal, eternal, fundamental, basic; ontological, cosmological, epistemological, existential; esoteric, mystical, intangible, vague; lofty, abstruse, oversubtle, recondite.

Ant. physical, mundane; tangible, down-to-earth.

meteoric *adj. a meteoric rise to success:* fleetingly bright, blazing; rapid, fast, swift, sudden, instant.

Ant. slow, gradual, inconspicuous.

method *n.* 1 *What guitar method did you study?:* system, technique, procedure, approach, process, way, course, means, program, formula; style, mode, manner. 2 *There's a method in my madness:* purpose, plan, design; order, scheme, system.

methodical Also **methodic** *adj. a methodical worker:* systematic, deliberate, precise, orderly, exact, tidy, regular, careful, meticulous; logical, analytical.

Ant. unmethodical, haphazard, casual, disordered, chaotic, jumbled.

meticulous *adj. a meticulous housekeeper:* fastidious, scrupulous, exact, exacting, careful, painstaking, precise, finicky, fussy, particular.

Ant. careless, sloppy, negligent.

métier *n. The law was his métier:* vocation, calling, occupation, employment, profession, trade, work, job, lifework, craft, specialty, pursuit, business, field, line, area.

mettle *n. a leader of mettle:* courage, nerve, grit, pluck, valor, spunk, fearlessness, fortitude, bravery, determination, resolution, boldness, temerity.

microscopic *adj.* 1 *The flu virus is microscopic:* so small as to be invisible without a microscope, infinitesimal, immeasurably small; of a microscope. 2 *I can't read this microscopic print:* very little, tiny, minute, diminutive, extremely small, teeny.

Ant. large, huge, immense.

middle *adj.* 1 *the middle section:* central, mid, midway, halfway, midmost, medial, middlemost; median, intermediate. —*n.* 2 *the middle of the room:* center, midpoint, central part; core, heartland, heart, hub, nucleus.

Ant. 1 beginning, end. 2 edge, periphery.

middleman *n. The middleman arranged the deal:* intermediary, agent, broker, go-between, jobber, distributor, wholesaler.

middling *adj. I had only middling success:* average, mediocre, fair, passable, moderate, so-so, medium, tolerable, indifferent, run-of-the-mill.

midst *n. in the midst of the forest:* heart, middle, center, interior, hub, thick, depths, core, eye; most critical time, most important part; halfway through, midway in.

mien *n. a dancer of refined mien:* bearing, air, demeanor, manner, behavior, carriage,

presence, deportment, attitude, appearance, aspect, countenance, visage, look.

might *n. The battle was a test of might:* power, force, strength, prowess, forcefulness, toughness, sturdiness, muscle.

Ant. weakness, feebleness.

mighty *adj.* 1 *a mighty warrior:* powerful, strong, robust, indomitable, stalwart, overpowering, forceful, courageous, brave, bold, valorous, valiant. 2 *a mighty iceberg came into view:* huge, enormous, immense, massive, extremely large, titanic, colossal, gigantic, vast, prodigious, gargantuan, stupendous, towering. —*adv.* 3 *That's mighty nice of you:* very, exceedingly; really, truly.

Ant. 1 feeble, weak. 2 small, tiny, negligible, unimpressive.

migrate *v.* 1 *to migrate to the United States:* emigrate, immigrate; relocate, resettle. 2 *Many birds migrate south every winter:* move periodically or seasonally, travel, go elsewhere, move.

mild *adj.* 1 *a mild disposition:* gentle, calm, serene, placid, good-tempered, docile, tranquil, moderate, pacific, pleasant, complaisant, forbearing. 2 *a mild day:* temperate, moderate, warm, balmy, springlike, pleasant. 3 *a mild soap:* not strong, weak, soothing; soft, delicate, emollient, not severe.

Ant. 1–3 harsh. 1 fierce, unpleasant; stormy, turbulent; biting, violent. 2 stormy, intemperate, cold. 3 strong, astringent, powerful.

milestone *n.* 1 *The ancient road was dotted with milestones:* road marker, signpost, milepost. 2 *Their moving west was a milestone in her life:* significant event, crucial occurrence, turning point; decisive achievement, memorable moment.

milieu *n. a sophisticated milieu:* environment, ambience, setting, background, surroundings, scene.

militant *adj. a militant attitude:* combative, aggressive, belligerent, contentious, uncompromising, assertive, pugnacious, disputatious; warlike, fighting, bellicose.

Ant. moderate, peaceable, pacific, pacifist.

military *adj.* 1 *military might:* armed, martial, warmaking, combative. 2 *a military demeanor:* soldierly, well-disciplined, crisp, martial. —*n.* 4 *The military took over the government:* army, armed forces, soldiers, standing army, militia, troops; generals, military establishment.

milksop *n. I've never known such a milksop:* coward, mollycoddle, sissy; milquetoast, namby-pamby, pantywaist, mama's boy, crybaby; wimp.

mill *v. The crowd was milling around the*

station: roam, meander, wander; converge, move aimlessly, swarm, teem.

mimic *v.* 1 *to mimic the teacher:* ape, imitate, impersonate, parrot; mirror, echo. —*n.* 2 *You're an incredible mimic:* imitator, mime, impressionist, copycat.

mince *v.* 1 *Mince the garlic:* dice, chop fine, cut into small pieces; shred, grate. 2 *I can't stand the way you mince around here:* pose, posture, put on airs, affect delicacy, affect primness. 3 *I never mince words:* moderate, mitigate, refine, soften, qualify, gloss over.

mind *n.* 1 *She has a good mind for math:* brain, intellect, mental capacity, brains, reason, judgment, comprehension, understanding, sense, intelligence, perception. 2 *Have you lost your mind!:* mental balance, sanity, reason, rationality, sense, wits. 3 *To my mind he's extremely offensive:* judgment, opinion, point of view, outlook, way of thinking. 4 *My mind is made up:* opinion, conclusion, consideration, judgment; intention, thought, notion, impression, sentiment, conception; propensity, inclination. 5 *The scrapbook brought our childhood to mind:* remembrance, memory, consciousness, recall, recollection, retrospection, reminiscence, contemplation. 6 *Spring makes it hard to keep one's mind on work:* attention, concentration, thought, thinking, focus. —*v.* 7 *Good drivers mind the speed limit:* obey, heed, pay attention to, observe, follow, comply with; bow to, acquiesce to, adhere to; be careful concerning, be wary of, note, be conscious of, watch, take notice of. 8 *My son can mind the store:* tend, attend to, look after, take care of. 9 *I don't mind your being late:* object to, resent, feel offended about, disapprove of, have an aversion to, detest, hate.

Ant. 1 body. 2 insanity, irrationality. 7 overlook, ignore, disregard.

mindful *adj. Be mindful of the danger:* alert to, regardful, cognizant, heedful, conscious, thoughtful, careful, watchful, aware, cautious, observant, wary; engrossed in, preoccupied with.

Ant. heedless, oblivious, unaware, thoughtless.

mindless *adj.* 1 *mindless behavior:* witless, asinine, stupid, unthinking, unreasoning, simple-minded, doltish, imbecilic, idiotic, insane. 2 *She is mindless of the feelings of others:* insensitive, careless, thoughtless, unattuned, oblivious, heedless, indifferent, unaware, inattentive, unheeding, neglectful.

Ant. 1 intelligent, reasonable, sane. 2 mindful, sensitive, considerate, aware, attentive.

mine *n.* 1 *a coal mine:* pit, excavation, tun-

nel, shaft, quarry. 2 *Her mine of anecdotes is inexhaustible:* supply, stock, store, fund, hoard, wealth, abundance. 3 *The soldiers mined the enemy fort:* burrow under, tunnel under; lay explosives under, booby-trap.

mingle *v.* 1 *The sounds mingle in a curious melody:* blend, mix, combine, intermingle, merge, intertwine, intersperse. 2 *A good host mingles with guests:* socialize, join, mix, associate, circulate.

Ant. 1 separate, divide.

miniature *adj. miniature paintings:* smallscale, diminutive, tiny, little, pocket-size, Lilliputian, pygmy, minuscule.

Ant. large, full-size, oversize, big, gigantic.

minimal *adj. He does a minimal amount of work:* minimum, least possible, lowest acceptable, smallest permissible, nominal, unappreciable, token.

Ant. maximal, maximum.

minimum *n.* 1 *These new floors require a minimum of care:* least possible amount, smallest amount possible, least possible degree, modicum, lowest quantity. —*adj.* 2 *a minimum wage:* lowest amount allowed; least, smallest, least possible; basic, base.

Ant. 1, 2 maximum, largest, greatest.

minister *n.* 1 *The minister began the sermon:* clergyman, preacher, pastor, chaplain, cleric, priest, parson, ecclesiastic, father, vicar, reverend, rabbi. 2 *She was appointed Minister of Agriculture:* chief government administrator, secretary, cabinet member. —*v.* 3 *He ministered to his wife's every need:* attend to, be solicitous of, serve, answer, oblige, tend, care for; pander to, cater to.

minor *adj.* 1 *minor injuries:* small, insignificant, slight, light, unimportant, petty, inconsiderable, trivial, trifling, picayune, inconsequential; lesser, secondary, subordinate. —*n.* 2 *They can't serve drinks to minors:* child, youngster, teenager, youth, adolescent.

Ant. 1 major; important, significant. 2 adult, grown-up.

minstrel *n. a wandering minstrel:* troubadour, singer, itinerant musician, bard, poet, serenader.

minute[1] *n. This will only take a minute:* moment, second, instant, shake, jiffy, twinkling, a short time; sixty seconds, sixtieth part of an hour.

Ant. forever, ages, eons.

minute[2] *adj.* 1 *The scratch was too minute to see:* little, extremely small, tiny, diminutive, miniature, Lilliputian, fine, scant, microscopic; negligible, inappreciable, trifling, insignificant, petty. 2 *The doctor made a*

minute study of the illness: exhaustive, meticulous, close, detailed, scrupulous, careful, strict, exact.
Ant. 1 huge, vast, enormous. 2 general, rough, superficial.

minutiae *n. pl. He concerns himself with minutiae:* trivia, trivialities, minor details, trifles, subleties, particulars.

miracle *n.* 1 *Atheists don't believe in miracles:* divine act, supernatural happening; mystery. 2 *Picasso's work is a creative miracle:* marvel, wonder, phenomenon, prodigy, sensation.

miraculous *adj.* 1 *St. John the Divine had a miraculous vision:* divine, supernatural, supernormal; wonderworking, magical; mysterious, inexplicable. 2 *The wounded man made a miraculous recovery:* extraordinary, exceptional, remarkable, spectacular; amazing, astonishing, astounding; unbelievable, incredible; phenomenal.
Ant. 1, 2 ordinary, normal. 1 human, natural, mundane. 2 routine, unexceptional.

mirage *n. The oasis was only a mirage:* optical illusion, illusion, phantasm, unreality, imagined image, fancy, hallucination, delusion, wishful thinking, fantasy.

mirror *n.* 1 *She's admiring herself in the mirror:* reflecting glass, looking glass, glass. 2 *She's the very mirror of virtue:* model, exemplar, paragon, standard, epitome, paradigm, image.

mirth *n. a party full of mirth:* merriment, amusement, jollity, hilarity, gaiety, joviality, glee, laughter, cheerfulness, levity, jocularity; drollery, merrymaking.
Ant. sadness, dejection, depression, melancholy.

misadventure *n. I had one misadventure after another:* mishap, misfortune, reverse, failure, disaster, calamity, catastrophe, unfortunate accident, debacle, mischance.

misanthropic *adj. a misanthropic personality:* antisocial, unfriendly, distrustful, unneighborly, inhospitable, morose, surly, discourteous, unaccommodating, unresponsive, cold, distant.
Ant. personable, amiable, sociable, cordial; humanitarian.

misapprehension *n. We shared a misapprehension about the work:* misunderstanding, misconception, false impression, misjudgment, mixup, misconstruction, mistake.

misappropriate *v. He was indicted for misappropriating public funds:* misuse, embezzle, defraud, steal, misapply, misemploy, cheat.

misbehave *v. If you misbehave you're going home!:* disobey, behave improperly, deport

oneself badly, do wrong, transgress, show poor manners.
Ant. behave, toe the line.

misbehavior *n. Her misbehavior was an embarrassment to her parents:* bad behavior, bad conduct, misconduct, impropriety, lapse, transgression, misdeed, bad manners, unmanageableness, obstreperousness.
Ant. good conduct, mannerliness.

miscarriage *n.* 1 *a miscarriage of justice:* failure, failing, unrealization, collapse, nonsuccess, default, nonfulfillment, *Informal* botch; frustration. 2 *She had two miscarriages:* premature stillbirth, spontaneous abortion.

miscellaneous *adj. The shop is filled with miscellaneous goods:* varied, assorted, mixed, various, motley, diversified, diverse, of every description, sundry.

miscellany *n. The little volume is a miscellany of quotes and bits of poetry:* collection, mixture, medley, compilation, anthology, potpourri, pastiche, omnium-gatherum, assortment; conglomeration.

mischief *n.* 1 *The child has a lot of mischief in him:* naughtiness, rascality, devilment, prankishness, playfulness, capriciousness. 2 *We fear he is up to serious mischief:* wrongdoing, malice, villainy, wrong; injury, evil, depravity.

mischievous *adj.* 1 *a mischievous child:* naughty, impish, prankish, teasing, playfully annoying, roguish, devilish, sportive. 2 *Her mischievous interference caused a lot of unhappiness:* wicked, vicious, spiteful, malicious, malign, malignant, uncalled for, annoying, vexing, injurious, destructive, harmful.

misconception *n. a misconception about cancer:* erroneous idea, mistaken notion, fallacious notion, misunderstanding.

misconduct *n. Because of his misconduct, he was asked to leave:* transgression, wrongdoing, misbehavior, impropriety, misdeed.

misconstrue *v. You misconstrued my words:* misinterpret, take in a wrong sense, construe wrongly, misreckon, mistake, misunderstand.
Ant. understand, apprehend.

misdeed *n. His misdeeds were the scandal of the town:* transgression, sin, offense, misconduct, peccadillo, misbehavior, wrong, trespass.

miser *n. The miser wouldn't contribute a penny:* pennypincher, Scrooge, skinflint, tightwad, pinchpenny; *Slang* cheapskate.
Ant. spendthrift, profligate.

miserable *adj.* 1 *Their living conditions are miserable:* wretched, very poor, deplorable, lamentable, sorry, pathetic, unbearable, sor-

did, mean, pitiable, second-rate, unfortunate, inferior; contemptible, despicable. 2 *The loss of my dog made me miserable:* forlorn, unhappy, heartbroken, crestfallen, disconsolate, brokenhearted, sorrowful, desolate, crushed, despondent, dejected, heartsick, depressed, cheerless, chapfallen, sad. 3 *It was a miserable performance:* sorry, deplorable, inept, abysmal, atrocious, appalling, abject; contemptible, despicable.
Ant. 1 comfortable, good. 2 happy, joyous, cheerful. 3 admirable, laudable.

miserly *adj.* *She's so miserly she won't give anything to anyone:* parsimonious, stingy, tight, tight-fisted, penurious, penny-pinching, closehanded, closefisted, cheap.
Ant. generous, extravagant, prodigal, profligate.

misery *n.* 1 *the misery of war:* sorrow, affliction, distress, suffering, wretchedness, hardship, ordeal, trial, tribulation, privation. 2 *I can't shake this feeling of misery:* wretchedness, desolation, unhappiness, sorrow, sadness, agony, woe, melancholy, anguish, despair, depression, dejection, despondency.
Ant. 1 luxury, ease, comfort. 2 happiness, joy, pleasure, enjoyment.

misfortune *n.* 1 *a time of misfortune:* trouble, hard luck, ill fortune, hard times, calamity, adversity, hardship. 2 *Her injury was a misfortune for the whole team:* blow, calamity, mishap, catastrophe, disaster, unfortunate accident, trouble, reverse, affliction, setback, downfall, tragedy, loss.
Ant. 1 good luck, good fortune.

misgiving *n.* Usually **misgivings** *We had misgivings about the trip:* anxiety, fear, doubt, apprehension, foreboding, lack of confidence, worry, suspicion, qualm, uncertainty, dread, alarm, doubtfulness.
Ant. confidence, trust, certainty.

misguided *adj.* *a misguided attempt:* mistaken, misled, in error, faulty, misdirected, ill-advised, erroneous, led astray, misinformed; unwise, imprudent.

mishap *n.* *We finished the voyage without a mishap:* misadventure, accident, reverse, setback.

misinform *v.* *He misinformed me about the cost:* mislead, misdirect, give incorrect information to, deceive, lead astray.

misjudge *v.* *I misjudged her abilities:* judge wrongly, underestimate, overestimate, misconstrue, misinterpret; judge unfairly, mistake, err about.

mislead *v.* *I was misled by the confidence man's respectable appearance:* misguide, deceive, misinform, lead into error, lead astray; delude, deceive, take in, betray, fool.

mismanage *v.* *I mismanaged the entire affair:* botch, mishandle, bungle, mess up.

misplace *v.* 1 *I've misplaced my umbrella:* mislay, lose. 2 *Don't misplace your confidence by trusting him:* place unwisely, entrust wrongly.

misrepresentation *n.* *a misrepresentation of the facts:* misstatement, distortion, falsification, falsifying, altering, incorrect picture, twisting, exaggeration.

miss[1] *v.* 1 *The batter missed the ball:* fail to hit, fail to reach; fall short, fail to attain, miss the mark, fail to light upon; fail to receive, fail to obtain. 2 *We missed the start of the movie:* fail to be present at, fail to meet; be late for, be absent from. 3 *She missed her only chance:* let slip, let go, fail to take advantage of, forego, disregard, overlook, neglect. 4 *to miss a deadline:* fail to perform, fail to meet, fail to accomplish. 5 *When did you first miss the jewels?:* notice the loss of, note the absence of. 6 *The child misses its mother:* want, long for, feel the loss of, feel the absence of, yearn for. 7 *I just missed burning my hand:* avoid, avert, escape. 8 *I missed what you said because of the noise:* fail to perceive, fail to hear, fail to understand, fail to see, lose. 9 *The cleaner missed the spot on the collar:* overlook, pass by, disregard, neglect, pass over, gloss over; bypass, overshoot. —*n.* 10 *After three misses I gave up trying to hit the target:* failure, failure to hit, failure to reach, false step, default, error, slip, miscue, blunder, omission, oversight, mistake.
Ant. 1 hit, reach, strike, attain, obtain. 2 meet, make. 3 seize, grasp. 4 meet, fulfill, make. 8 hear, understand. 10 hit, success.

miss[2] *n.* *a witty young miss:* unmarried woman, maid, maiden, girl, young lady, lass, colleen, schoolgirl.

missile *n.* *The missile hit the target:* projectile, shell, object or weapon that is thrown or shot; (*variously*) stone, spear, javelin, lance, harpoon, arrow, dart, bullet, ball, shaft; guided missile, rocket.

mission *n.* 1 *I was sent on a diplomatic mission:* assignment, undertaking, enterprise, quest, task, commission, job; military operation. 2 *The head of the Irish mission is on home leave:* delegation, legation, diplomatic representative; missionary post, ministry. 3 *He believed that his mission was medicine:* calling, pursuit, life's object, principal task.

misspent *adj.* *a misspent youth:* misapplied, wasted, spent foolishly, thrown away, squandered; depraved, dissolute, debauched.
Ant. productive, fruitful.

misstate v. *He was accused of misstating the facts:* state wrongly, state falsely, misreport, misrepresent, misquote, distort; garble, confuse.

misstep n. *They never forgave her for that one misstep:* error, transgression, offense, indiscretion, lapse, slip.

mistake n. 1 *Anyone can make a mistake:* error, misstep, wrong action, slip, blunder, miscalculation, slip of the tongue, gaffe, oversight. —v. 2 *Did you mistake the margarine for butter?:* confuse, identify incorrectly, take one for another, misidentify. 3 *Unfortunately she mistook his intentions:* misunderstand, misinterpret, misconstrue, misjudge.

mistaken adj. *Your argument is mistaken:* wrong, erroneous, in error, false, fallacious, incorrect, inaccurate, faulty; unfounded, unsound, unjustified, untrue, groundless.
Ant. accurate, true, correct, right, logical.

mistreat v. *The general was accused of mistreating prisoners:* maltreat, ill-treat, ill-use, abuse, oppress, misuse, treat unjustly, harm, wrong, brutalize, torment, injure.

mistress n. 1 *She is the mistress of the manor:* female head, matron, lady, headwoman, housewife, female owner. 2 *Does his wife know he has a mistress?:* lover, paramour, concubine, kept woman, inamorata, girlfriend.

mistrust n. 1 *a mistrust of new ideas:* distrust, skepticism, misgiving, qualm, doubt, wariness, chariness, apprehension. —v. 2 *Aunt Alice mistrusted any man who wore a mustache:* distrust, suspect, disbelieve, have doubts about.
Ant. 1 faith, confidence, trust. 2 trust, believe.

misty adj. *The park was misty:* clouded by mist, vaporous, dewy, foggy, steamy; hazy; nebulous, indistinct; filmy, opaque.
Ant. clear, unclouded.

misunderstand v. *I misunderstood her meaning:* misconstrue, misinterpret, misconceive, misapprehend, mistake, confuse.
Ant. understand, apprehend, perceive.

misunderstanding n. 1 *a misunderstanding of the lesson:* mistake as to meaning, failure to understand, misapprehension, misconception, false impression, miscomprehension. 2 *The brothers had a heated misunderstanding:* quarrel, disagreement, dispute, difference, rift, spat, dissension, squabble, altercation.

misuse n. 1 *Writing ad copy was a misuse of creative talent:* misemployment, wrong use, misappropriation, misapplication, waste, improper utilization, squandering, abuse, ill treatment, maltreatment, mistreatment.

—v. 2 *You misuse many words:* use improperly, misapply, use wrongly, misemploy. 3 *Don't misuse friends:* ill-treat, ill-use, wrong, mistreat, take advantage of, exploit.

mitigate v. *How can we mitigate their pain?:* lessen, relieve, moderate, alleviate, soften, assuage, allay, soothe, weaken, ameliorate, ease, reduce, lighten, diminish, temper.
Ant. increase, augment, heighten, enhance.

mix v. 1 *Mix flour and water:* combine, blend, unite, incorporate, mingle, compound, fuse, intersperse, merge, coalesce; incorporate. 2 *The captain never mixes with the enlisted men:* fraternize, associate, socialize, join. —n. 3 *The guests seemed an odd mix:* mixture, combination, mingling, assembly.

mixed adj. 1 *They are a people of mixed blood:* mingled, composite, combined, blended; hybrid, mongrel. 2 *It's a mixed collection:* diversified, variegated, motley, miscellaneous. 3 *That story shouldn't be told in a mixed crowd:* male-and-female, coed. 4 *My reaction was mixed:* indecisive, ambivalent, inconclusive.
Ant. 1 unmixed, pure, unblended. 2 homogeneous.

mixture n. *His painting is a grotesque mixture of styles:* combination, blend, admixture, union, fusion, amalgamation, mix, alloy, amalgam, composite, compound, medley; hodgepodge, jumble, mélange, potpourri.

moan n. 1 *the patient's moans:* groan, wail; lament, plaint, sob, lamentation. —v. 2 *He moaned when he read the bill:* groan; bemoan, lament, wail, keen.

mob n. 1 *The police tried to control the mob:* riotous throng, disorderly crowd; rabble, horde, crush of people, gathering, assembly. 2 *Politicians gear their appeals to the mob:* common people, masses, rank and file, hoi polloi, populace, proletariat, plebeians, rabble, multitude. —v. 3 *The kids mobbed the star when he left the theater:* surround noisily, swarm around, flock to, converge on, crowd around.

mobile adj. 1 *I converted my truck into a mobile snack bar:* movable, portable, transportable, traveling. 2 *Americans are a restless, mobile people:* moving readily, motile, active; rootless, wandering, nomadic, footloose.

mobilize v. *to mobilize troops:* muster, call up, summon, activate, assemble for action, organize, marshal, call to arms.
Ant. immobilize, disband.

mock v. *She mocked his awkwardness:* ridicule, make fun of, scorn, deride, revile, jeer at, taunt, make sport of, scoff at, sneer at, poke fun at; imitate, ape, burlesque, parody, caricature, mimic.

Ant. praise, honor, laud.

mockery n. **1** *Mockery is the only outlet for jealousy:* ridicule, sarcasm, derision, scoffing, jeering, scorn, raillery; mimicry, contemptuous imitation, burlesque. **2** *Bribery made a mockery of the contest:* sham, joke, farce; burlesque, travesty.

mode n. **1** *Your mode of doing business is offensive:* manner, way, fashion, method, practice, means, system, approach, procedure, process, style, technique. **2** *the modern mode:* style, custom, fashion, manner, taste, way, trend, vogue.

model n. **1** *a model of the proposed building:* replica, miniature representation, prototype; pattern, simulacrum, copy, dummy, mock-up. **2** *She's a model of perfection:* archetype, paragon, standard, ideal, exemplar. **3** *Who was the model for Goya's Olympia?:* source, subject, real-life version, prototype; mannequin. —*adj.* **4** *We looked at the model homes:* demonstrational, representative, simulated. **5** *He's a model father:* perfect, worthy of imitation, ideal, exemplary. —*v.* **6** *She models herself after her mother:* fashion, form, mold, design, shape, cast, build, outline, fashion, give form to. **7** *Will you model this coat for me?:* display, show, wear as a demonstration.

Ant. **5** imperfect, flawed, unworthy.

moderate adj. **1** *We did a moderate amount of business:* middling, modest, ordinary, mediocre, passable, fair. **2** *a moderate approach:* reasonable, temperate, mild, rational, unruffled, calm, cool, measured, careful. —*v.* **3** *He should moderate his voice:* temper, control, soften, tone down, make less severe, lessen, subdue, tame, restrain. **4** *to moderate a debate:* act as moderator, preside over, act as chairman; regulate, direct, manage, oversee, conduct.

Ant. **1** immoderate, excessive, inordinate, unusual. **2** unreasonable, extreme, radical. **3** intensify, heighten, increase.

moderation n. *moderation in all things. a moderation of the pain:* temperance, restraint, avoidance of extremes, forbearance, temperateness, frugality; lessening, abating, allaying, alleviation, diminution, relaxation, mitigation.

Ant. excess, intemperance; increase.

modern adj. *a modern hotel. modern ideas:* new, contemporary, present-day, up-to-date, modernized, of our time; recent, current, in vogue, modish, fashionable.

Ant. old, obsolete, antiquated; former, old-fashioned.

modernize v. *to modernize the kitchen:* ren-

ovate, refurbish, revamp, regenerate, update, do over, redo, redesign, bring up to date.

modest adj. **1** *He's famous yet still modest:* unassuming, humble, self-effacing, unpretentious, free from vanity. **2** *a modest meal:* simple, plain, unpretentious, limited, unostentatious; quiet, unobtrusive. **3** *I made a modest donation:* moderate, nominal, small; medium-priced, inexpensive. **4** *She's too modest to dance alone:* reserved, bashful, shy, self-conscious, timid, demure, blushing, timorous; proper, strait-laced, prim, prudish.

Ant. **1** immodest, vain, boastful, pretentious, egotistic. **3** generous, magnanimous. **4** shameless, brazen, immodest, indecent, improper.

modesty n. **1** *I respect modesty, but not coyness:* humility, humbleness, reserve, self-effacement. **2** *The modesty of their home belies their wealth:* simplicity, unpretentiousness, plainness, lack of ostentation, inexpensiveness, reasonableness. **3** *Her modesty kept her from wearing a miniskirt:* reserve, bashfulness, shyness, timidity, demureness, timorousness; propriety, prudery.

Ant. **1** boastfulness, conceit, arrogance, vanity, egotism. **2** extravagance, pretentiousness, showiness, ostentation. **3** immodesty, indecency, impropriety.

modicum n. *She had a modicum of wine:* minimum, drop, jot, sliver, smidgen, small quantity, mite, bit, pinch, small amount, dash, little bit, dab, tinge, sprinkling, touch, speck, fraction, handful, crumb, morsel, whit.

modify v. **1** *They modified the plan:* alter, change, adjust, transform, convert, refashion, rework, redo, reshape, revise, adapt. **2** *You'll have to modify your demands:* reduce, moderate, modulate, temper, tone down, lower, soften; qualify, limit, restrict, control, adjust.

modish adj. *modish clothes:* fashionable, chic, stylish, faddish, voguish, smart, current, up-to-the-minute, trendy.

Ant. passé, old-fashioned, dated.

modulate v. *Please modulate your voice:* reduce, regulate, turn down, tone down, moderate, lower, soften, temper; change, vary the inflection; shift harmonically.

mogul n. *a movie mogul:* magnate, tycoon; czar, potentate, lord, baron; *Slang* big shot.

moist adj. *a moist cloth:* damp, watery, slightly wet, wet; muggy, humid, dank, clammy, rainy, drizzly, dripping, vaporous; tearful.

Ant. dry, arid.

moisture n. a lot of moisture in the air: dampness, moistness, wetness, damp, wet; humidity, mugginess, dankness, dew, evaporation, vapor; perspiration, sweat; mist, drizzle.

mold[1] n. 1 a copper mold: cast, form, shaper; matrix, die. 2 the angular mold of the sculpture: shape, contour, line, formation, form, structure, construction, cut, conformation, outline, configuration. 3 People of that mold are easy to like: quality, type, ilk, sort, kind, character, stamp; make, brand. —v. 4 to mold a rabbit out of clay: model, shape, form, cast, fashion, knead, sculpt, construct; render, transform, develop.

mold[2] n. a green mold: fungus, mildew, blight, rust, lichen.

molest v. That big kid is always molesting the children: bother, harass, vex, annoy, pester, harry, torment, plague, hector; abuse, harm, attack, ill-treat, hurt, assault; sexually abuse.

mollify v. Try to mollify her anger: appease, calm, moderate, placate, lessen, mitigate, allay, reduce, make less violent, decrease, pacify, soothe, tone down, quiet, lighten, abate, ease, assuage, curb, check, dull. *Ant.* exacerbate, increase.

mollycoddle v. 1 They mollycoddle that boy!: spoil, pamper, overindulge, baby, cater to, indulge. —n. 2 As a child he was a mollycoddle: milquetoast, milksop, sissy, coward, weakling, mama's boy, crybaby.

molten adj. molten lava: liquefied, melted, smelted, fusible; red-hot.

moment n. 1 I'll be with you in a moment: minute, instant, twinkling, second, jiffy, flash. 2 At this moment I can't say: point in time, the present time, instant, particular time, juncture. 3 a decision of great moment: consequence, import, importance, significance, weight; gravity, concern, interest, weightiness. *Ant.* 3 insignificance, unimportance, inconsequence, unconcern.

momentary adj. 1 It was only a momentary feeling: temporary, transitory, passing, fleeting, brief, short, short-lived, transient, ephemeral. 2 We feared a momentary attack: sudden, imminent, instant, expected at any moment, immediate. *Ant.* 1 permanent, lasting, long-lived.

momentous adj. a momentous occasion: important, significant, critical, decisive, crucial, influential, fateful, far-reaching, consequential; grave, serious, substantial, weighty. *Ant.* unimportant, insignificant, trivial, inconsequential.

momentum n. The rocket was losing momentum: force, impetus, energy, moment, thrust, push, go, drive, propulsion, velocity, vigor, speed.

monarch n. The monarch abdicated: hereditary sovereign, crowned head, majesty, prince; (variously) king, potentate, emperor, czar, kaiser; pharaoh, shah, khan, chieftain, doge, emir, rajah, (fem.) queen, princess; empress, czarina, kaiserin, rani.

monastery n. The monks never leave the monastery: place of contemplation, retreat, cloister, convent, abbey, nunnery, priory, friary; community of monks, community of nuns.

monastic adj. the monastic life: of monks, of monasteries; contemplative, solitary, monkish, cloistered, unworldly, sequestered, celibate, ascetic, reclusive.

monetary adj. monetary problems: in money, pecuniary, financial, budgetary; fiscal.

money n. 1 Beads are used as money in some cultures: currency, cash, funds, revenue, paper money, coin, coinage, specie, hard cash, capital; Informal wherewithal, Slang dough, bread, long green; medium of exchange, legal tender. 2 They live as though they have money: wealth, affluence, hereditary wealth, riches, great income.

moneyed Also **monied** adj. a moneyed clientele: wealthy, affluent, rich, prosperous, well-to-do, well-off, well-heeled.

mongrel adj. 1 a mongrel dog: of mixed breed, half-breed, crossbred, hybrid; bastard, anomalous. —n. 2 The mongrel is a good watchdog: mutt, cur, an animal of mixed breed, hybrid, half-breed, crossbreed. *Ant.* 1, 2 purebred, thoroughbred. 1 pedigreed.

monitor n. 1 Mary served as monitor at the exam: proctor, disciplinarian, overseer, Informal watchdog. 2 Watch the program on the monitor: television set, studio television receiver; scanner, pickup, screen; warning device, sensor. —v. 3 He monitored the debate: listen to; watch attentively, observe critically; censor. 4 I'm monitoring the exam: supervise, oversee, tend, take charge of, guide, direct; police.

monk n. The monk took a vow of silence: brother, holy man, religious recluse, friar, abbé, abbot, monastic; recluse.

monkey n. 1 She made a monkey of me on the tennis court: fool, dupe, laughingstock, butt, buffoon. —v. 2 I monkeyed with the machine until I broke it: meddle, tamper, trifle, fool, fiddle, tinker.

monologue Also **monolog** n. a long monologue about her grandchild: soliloquy,

speech, oration, address, lecture, disquisition; sermon.
Ant. dialogue, conversation.

monopolize *v.* 1 *The firm tried to monopolize the industry:* have a monopoly of, obtain exclusive possession of, corner, own, take over. 2 *He monopolized the conversation:* appropriate, dominate, arrogate, take over, preempt.
Ant. 2 share.

monopoly *n. We achieved a monopoly over the entire industry:* exclusive possession, corner; trust, cartel, syndicate; control, domination.

monotonous *adj. a monotonous job:* unvaried, boring, dull, dreary, repetitious, tedious, routine, uninteresting.
Ant. varied, diversified, interesting.

monotony *n. The monotony of the work was unbearable:* tedium, dullness, boredom, predictability, sameness.
Ant. variety, excitement, diversity, stimulation.

monster *n.* 1 *A two-headed calf is a monster:* deviant, variant, freak, freak of nature; phenomenon, anomaly, abnormality, monstrosity; mythical or legendary being, semihuman creature. 2 *Cancer is a monster:* dangerous creation, destructive force, uncontrollable force, threat. 3 *The assassin was a monster:* fiend, demon, beast, brute; villain, scoundrel, cutthroat, savage, barbarian. —*adj.* 4 *a monster truck:* very large, giant, mammoth, huge, tremendous, oversized; imposing, impressive, overwhelming.
Ant. 1 commonplace. 2 boon, blessing. 3 paragon, saint. 4 dwarf, midget, pygmy; small, little.

monstrous *adj.* 1 *a monstrous shark:* huge, enormous, immense, gigantic, mighty, gargantuan, giant, tremendous, colossal, mammoth, hulking, prodigious; ghastly, revolting, gruesome, grisly, hideous, horrible. 2 *What a monstrous lie!:* outrageous, flagrant, egregious; fiendish, evil, villainous, odious, atrocious; shocking, scandalous; outright, obvious.

monument *n.* 1 *a monument to our war dead:* memorial, testament, testimonial, remembrance, witness, token, commemoration, reminder. 2 *A monument was placed over the grave:* memorial, stone, tombstone, gravestone; obelisk, cenotaph, monolith.

monumental *adj.* 1 *The Sphinx is an example of Egyptian monumental art:* monolithic, statuary; gigantic, colossal, massive, heavy, huge, larger than life. 2 *Lincoln's monumental Gettysburg Address:* historic, classic, immortal, enduring, memorable, lasting, awesome, stupendous, unprece-

dented. 3 *a monumental mistake:* egregious, colossal, immense, decisive; fatal, horrendous, catastrophic.
Ant. 1 small, delicate, dainty, miniature. 2 unimportant, insignificant, worthless.

mood *n. I'm just in one of my moods:* humor, disposition, state of mind, temper, temperament, frame of mind, mental state, feeling, spirit, emotional state; state of dejection, melancholy, gloominess, doldrums; state of irritation, vexation.

moody *adj.* 1 *Such a moody person can depress everyone:* melancholy, gloomy, pessimistic, despondent, morose, brooding, unhappy; irritable, irascible, ill-humored, surly, peevish. 2 *I'm too moody to know what I'll feel like doing next week:* changeable, fickle, variable, unpredictable, inconsistent, notional, temperamental, capricious, erratic.
Ant. 1 happy, joyful, cheerful. 2 constant, consistent, steady.

moor[1] *v. Let's moor at the next dock:* tie up, dock, anchor, berth; fix firmly, affix, fasten, tether, tie down, attach, make fast, lash.
Ant. untie, unfasten; cast off.

moor[2] *the moors of Scotland:* moorland, heath, wold, down, fell, upland; marsh, fen.

moot *adj. a moot question:* debatable, questionable, unsettled, disputed, disputable, arguable; problematical, undecided, unresolved, open, conjectural.
Ant. indisputable, self-evident, axiomatic.

mope *v. Stop moping!:* sulk, languish, be dejected, fret, worry, be gloomy, brood, pine, be downcast; grouse, grumble.

moral *adj.* 1 *a moral judgment:* ethical, of right and wrong, of proper conduct. 2 *It was not moral to accept the money:* ethical, right, proper, virtuous, honorable, principled, just, fair, aboveboard; honest, high-minded. 3 *a moral lecture:* of morals, didactic, sermonizing, preaching, moralizing. —*n.* 4 *Every story you tell has a moral:* lesson, message, moral teaching.
Ant. 2 immoral, wrong, sinful, unjust, unfair, dishonest, unethical, unprincipled.

morale *n. The team's morale is good:* spirit, disposition, mental attitude, mood, confidence, resolution, esprit de corps.

morality *n.* 1 *I'm concerned with the morality of the situation:* ethical values, ethics, right or wrong. 2 *He has no morality:* goodness, righteousness, virtue, honor, fairness, integrity; code of ethics, set of values.
Ant. 2 immorality, wickedness.

morbid *adj. Cheer up, don't be so morbid! The love of cemeteries is morbid:* depressed, gloomy, glum, sad, morose, brooding, despondent, somber, grim, pessimistic; unwholesome, preoccupied with death, mentally unhealthy.

Ant. cheerful, optimistic.

more *adj.* 1 *Are there more cookies?:* extra, additional, other, added, supplemental, supplementary, further; spare, reserve. —*adv.* 2 *He is more energetic than his sister:* to a greater extent or degree. 3 *If I have to work more tonight, I'll collapse:* further, longer, additionally.

Ant. 1, 2 less. 1 fewer.

moreover *adv. Bicycling is good exercise; moreover, it doesn't pollute the air:* further, besides, also, more than that, what's more, furthermore, in addition.

mores *n. pl. Other countries have different mores:* customs, conventions, practices, standards, traditions, observances, code, usages, rules, rituals, forms; morals, etiquette, proprieties.

moribund *adj. Many old customs are moribund:* dying, waning, stagnating, dying out, near death, fading out.

morning *n.* 1 *to get up in the morning:* morn, daybreak, dawn, sunrise, break of day, daylight, sunup, crack of dawn. 2 *sometime this morning:* forenoon, before 12 A.M.

Ant. 1, 2 afternoon, evening; dusk, sunset.

moron *n. What a moron I was to buy this junk:* fool, dope, nitwit, ninny, dunce, dummy, dolt, oaf, numskull, idiot, dimwit, imbecile, half-wit, muttonhead, blockhead, dumbbell, nincompoop, boob, sap, jackass.

Ant. genius, brain, mastermind.

morose *adj. I feel morose after that sad story:* depressed, crestfallen, sad, melancholy, downcast, moody, glum, dour, *Informal* blue, gloomy, despondent, mournful, solemn; sullen, sulky, surly, testy, waspish, grumpy, cranky, ill-tempered, irascible.

Ant. cheerful, happy; good-natured, amiable, friendly.

morsel *n. Taste just a morsel of this cake:* nibble, tidbit, taste, bite, swallow, crumb, sliver, sip, small amount, dollop, mouthful; bit, touch, little piece, trace, whit, fragment, particle, drop.

mortal *adj.* 1 *All things mortal pass swiftly:* human, earthly, corporeal, mundane. 2 *a mortal wound:* fatal, lethal, deadly. 3 *We were in mortal terror:* extreme, severe, intense, enormous, deep, grave, living. —*n.* 4 *We are mere mortals:* human being, person, creature, individual.

Ant. 1 immortal, undying, everlasting, eternal, divine.

mortality *n.* 1 *Mortality is obvious in time of war:* transience, impermanence, evanescence, transitoriness. 2 *The mortality from the earthquake was devastating:* human loss, loss of life, fatality, death toll.

Ant. 1 immortality, permanence; divinity.

mortify *v.* 1 *Forgetting her name mortified me:* shame, embarrass, appall, chagrin, discomfit, abash, disconcert. 2 *to mortify the flesh:* deny, discipline, self-discipline, be abstinent, practice continence; do penance.

Ant. 1 gratify, satisfy, make proud. 2 indulge, satisfy.

most *adj.* 1 *Of the three, Susan has the most freckles:* the greatest in number, degree, or quantity; maximum; in the majority. —*n.* 2 *Give the winner the most:* largest amount, maximum; the majority. —*adv.* 3 *That's the most beautiful cake I ever saw:* in the greatest degree, to the greatest extent, in the highest degree.

mostly *adv. The guests are mostly my friends:* primarily, chiefly, for the most part, predominantly, largely, mainly; especially, above all, specially, particularly, principally; as a rule, most often, generally.

mother *n.* 1 *A mother can be a child's best friend:* female parent, *Informal* mom, mama, momma, mommy, mum, mummy. 2 *Necessity is the mother of invention:* origin, source, wellspring, stimulus, inspiration. —*v.* 3 *She mothered two children:* bear, give birth to, bring forth, beget, produce, conceive. 4 *He mothers his friends:* care for, rear, raise, tend, mind, nurse, nurture, protect, indulge.

motherly *adj. The teacher is very motherly to students:* maternal, parental, nurturing; kind, loving, gentle, sheltering, protective, indulgent, devoted.

motif *n. My apartment will have a French Provincial motif:* style, theme, treatment, idea, shape, form, design, pattern, figure; refrain, thread.

motion *n.* 1 *Put the car in motion. the constant motion of the waves:* movement, mobility, moving, drift, passage, stir, flow, stream, flux, action. 2 *He directed traffic with hand motions:* gesture, signal, sign, move, action, movement, gesticulation, cue. 3 *I made a motion to dispense with the minutes of the last meeting:* formal proposal, suggestion, request, proposition, recommendation. —*v.* 4 *She motioned us to be quiet:* signal, beckon, nod, gesture, gesticulate.

Ant. 1 rest, repose, immobility.

motionless *adj. When the curtain rises, the dancers are motionless:* still, stationary, inert, immobile, unmoving, at rest, fixed, at

a standstill, static; transfixed, riveted, frozen.
Ant. mobile, active, moving.

motivate *v. What motivated you to go?:* impel, induce, stimulate, stir, move, arouse, provoke, influence, goad, prompt, persuade.
Ant. discourage, dissuade, disincline.

motivation *n. Our motivation was strong:* motive, impulse, impetus, cause, driving force, causation, provocation.

motive *n. What was the motive for the crime?:* reason, purpose, object, motivation, intention, grounds, rationale; incentive, provocation, enticement, stimulus, prompting, incitement; goal, aim, end.

motley *adj.* 1 *a motley group:* varied, heterogeneous, disparate, mixed, assorted, miscellaneous, variegated, diversified, incongruous. 2 *a motley fabric:* varicolored, multicolored, polychrome, dappled, piebald, particolored, mottled.
Ant. 1 uniform, homogeneous. 2 monochromatic, solid, plain.

motto *n. The state motto is "Let justice be served":* slogan, watchword; maxim, proverb, precept, byword, rule, principle, aphorism, saying, adage, catchword, dictum.

mound *n. an ancient burial mound:* knoll, hillock, hill, mount, hummock, mogul; pile, ridge, embankment, earthwork; stack, heap.
Ant. dip, valley, dell.

mount *v.* 1 *The speaker mounted the podium:* ascend, climb, go up, scale. 2 *The death toll mounted:* rise, ascend, increase, intensify, grow, swell. 3 *I mounted the camel and rode away:* climb up on, get astride, get upon, straddle. 4 *to mount guns on warships:* mount a diamond in a setting: install, fit, rig; put in position on, set into, affix, fix, set. —*n.* 5 *She urged her mount on:* riding animal; horse, saddle horse, steed, charger.
Ant. 1 descend. 2 fall, decline, lessen, decrease, diminish. 3 dismount.

mountain *n. The mountain was scaled for the first time:* peak, eminence, high hill, elevation, height, butte, mount, alp.

mountebank *n.* 1 *The mountebank sold colored water as medicine:* quack, quacksalver, medicine man, huckster. 2 *We were taken in by a clever mountebank:* confidence man, charlatan, fraud, swindler, cheat, con artist, phony.

mourn *v.* 1 *She's still mourning his death:* grieve, grieve for, express grief, lament, weep over, sorrow, bewail, weep, keen. 2 *I really mourn the loss of that old sweater:* regret, rue, deplore, bemoan.
Ant. 1 rejoice, exult, laugh.

mourning *n. a period of mourning:* grief,

grieving, lamentation, lamenting, sorrowing.
Ant. rejoicing, merrymaking.

mousy *adj. a mousy wallflower:* timid, shy, fearful, timorous, self-conscious; dull, colorless, drab; unobtrusive, inconspicuous.
Ant. brazen, brassy, bold, conspicuous, flamboyant.

mouth *n.* 1 *Open your mouth:* jaws, oral cavity. 2 *the mouth of a jar:* opening, aperture. 3 *the mouth of a river:* inlet, estuary, outlet, portal. —*v.* 4 *All he does is mouth truisms. She mouthed the words as the record played:* pronounce, speak, declare, say, voice, propound; feign speech, feign singing, lip-synchronize.

move *v.* 1 *Please move out of the way:* shift, stir, budge, change position, change place; proceed, advance, go; transpose, remove, transport, switch, bear, convey. 2 *She moved to Chicago:* transfer, relocate, change residence; shift, transplant. 3 *The clock doesn't move:* go, have motion, function, operate. 4 *Curiosity moved me to open the box:* cause, influence, induce, lead, impel, get, prompt, incite, drive, inspire, provoke, persuade, stimulate, motivate. 5 *I was moved by his tears:* touch, affect; arouse, rouse, stir, sway, interest, impress. 6 *I move that we accept the proposal:* propose, suggest, recommend, request, ask. —*n.* 7 *One move and I'll shoot!:* movement, motion, gesture, stirring, budging. 8 *Selling your car was a good move:* action, act, maneuver, ploy, stroke, step. 9 *It's your move:* turn, opportunity.
Ant. 1 stop, stay. 4 prevent. 5 untouched, unmoved, unimpressed.

movement *n.* 1 *The rowboat shook with every movement:* motion, change of position, locomotion, stirring, progress, agitation, action. 2 *My movement was not in time with the music:* bodily rhythm, motion, steps, gestures. 3 *The army's movements were kept secret:* activity, operation, maneuver. 4 *We're starting a movement to clean up the city:* drive, crusade, undertaking, program, effort. 5 *the first movement of Beethoven's Fifth Symphony:* section, part, division. 6 *This watch has a 21-jewel movement:* mechanism, action, works.
Ant. 1 inertia, stasis, quiescence.

movie *n. That movie is being shown on TV:* motion picture, film, cinema, show, picture show, picture, feature, *Slang* flick.

moving *adj.* 1 *It has no moving parts:* movable, capable of moving, mobile. 2 *What's the moving force behind the team?:* motivating, spurring, inspiring, stimulating. 3 *The* *song was so moving it made me cry:* touching, heart-rending, affecting, stirring, poignant.

Ant. **1** stationary, unmoving, still. **3** unaffecting, unimpressive.

much *adj.* **1** *We have much work ahead of us:* abundant, ample, plenteous, considerable, appreciable, copious, plentiful, plenty of, a lot of. —*n.* **2** *He hasn't done much:* appreciable amount, great deal; lots, loads, heaps. —*adv.* **3** *The professor is much revered:* greatly, to a great degree. **4** *You look much the same:* somewhat, rather, nearly, approximately, about, almost. **5** *Do you go there much?:* often, frequently, regularly, many times.

Ant. **1** little; scarce, few.

muck *n. The pipes were clogged with muck:* mud, dirt, filth, dung, sewage, slop, garbage, slime, sludge, mire, ooze; *Informal* guck, gunk.

muddle *v.* **1** *I muddled the recipe:* confuse, mix up; ruin, botch, bungle, mess up. **2** *I was muddled from the medication:* stupefy, mentally confuse, mix up, daze, confound, rattle, bewilder. —*n.* **3** *Our affairs are in a terrible muddle:* confused state, pother, haze, fog, daze; jumble, mess, disorder, disarray, chaos, clutter.

muffle *v.* **1** *Muffle yourself against the cold:* wrap, cloak, swathe, cover, enclose; conceal, mask, veil, envelop, shroud. **2** *He muffled his laughter:* suppress, stifle, silence, block off, blot out, quiet, hush, still, mute, quell, dull, deaden, dampen, soften.

muggy *adj. muggy weather:* humid, clammy, sultry, vaporous, steaming, steamy, oppressive, stuffy, sweaty, sticky, close, sweltering.

mull *v.* Usually **mull over** *I'll mull over your idea:* ponder, consider, reflect on, deliberate, think about, study.

multifarious *adj. multifarious duties:* varied, diverse, diversified, various, divers, variegated, manifold, miscellaneous, sundry, mixed; numerous, many, several.

multiply *v.* **1** *The mice multiplied till we had six:* procreate, propagate, reproduce, proliferate, breed, beget, generate. **2** *Her anxieties multiplied:* increase, enlarge, intensify, extend, spread, heighten.

Ant. **2** decrease, diminish, lessen, wane.

multitude *n. The multitude cheered. a multitude of problems:* crowd, throng, mob, horde; mass, array, host, great number, flock, slew, crush, pack, myriad.

mum *adj. Keep mum:* silent, still, quiet, wordless, closemouthed, mute, tight-lipped.

mumble *v. He mumbled his words:* mutter, murmur, utter indistinctly, speak inarticulately.

Ant. articulate, enunciate.

mundane *adj. the mundane affairs of life:* ordinary, prosaic, commonplace; worldly, terrestrial, earthly, down-to-earth, day-to-day, routine, humdrum, everyday, pedestrian.

Ant. heavenly, celestial, spiritual.

municipal *adj. a municipal auditorium:* civic, community, city; administrative, public.

munificence *n. The munificence of the patrons kept the symphony alive:* generosity, bountifulness, liberality, benevolence, largesse, bounteousness, philanthropy, charitableness, patronage.

Ant. parsimoniousness, stinginess, miserliness.

munificent *adj. a munificent gift:* generous, liberal, freehanded, benevolent, beneficent, bountiful, magnanimous, bounteous; lavish, profuse, extravagant.

Ant. stingy, mean, niggardly.

murder *n.* **1** *Matricide is the murder of one's mother:* homicide, assassination, manslaughter, killing. —*adj.* **2** *Informal This heat is murder!:* unbearable, intolerable, oppressive, agonizing; very difficult, impossible, formidable. —*v.* **3** *He murdered his rival:* kill, slay, assassinate, slaughter, cut down, *Slang* knock off, waste. **4** *You really murder the language:* use incorrectly, abuse, mangle, misuse, corrupt.

murderer *n. The murderer was executed:* killer, assassin, slayer, homicide.

murky *adj. murky light:* dark, dim, gloomy; hazy, misty, foggy, cloudy, dusky, gray, overcast, sunless, obscure, dreary, dismal, cheerless.

Ant. bright, clear, unobscured.

murmur *n. the murmur of a brook:* purl, low sound, soft utterance, whisper, undertone, rustle, swish, purr, hum, lapping, drone, mumble; mutter, grumble, lament, whimper, sigh.

muscle *n. It'll take a lot of muscle to move this piano:* power, brawn, strength, prowess, might, force, energy, vigor, stamina.

muscular *adj. a muscular bodybuilder:* strong, husky, powerful, brawny, strapping, well-developed, athletic.

muse *v. to muse over the past:* meditate, consider, ponder, deliberate, mull, speculate, ruminate, contemplate, cogitate, reflect; think reflectively, say reflectively.

mushroom *v. The village mushroomed into*

a metropolis: grow, expand quickly, spread, proliferate, burgeon, shoot up, spring up.

music *n.* 1 *Shall we have some music during dinner?:* harmonious sound, euphony, harmony, song, tune, melody; melodiousness, tunefulness, lyricism. 2 *He passed out the music to the orchestra:* score, sheet music.

musical *adj. a musical sound:* melodious, melodic, euphonious, harmonious, tuneful, mellifluent, pleasant-sounding.
Ant. unmusical, discordant, cacophonous.

muss *v. Don't muss the bed:* rumple, disturb, crumple, tousle, disorder, disarrange, ruffle, jumble, dishevel, mess.
Ant. straighten, arrange, tidy.

muster *n.* 1 *There will be a muster of volunteers:* assemblage, gathering, assembly, meeting, rally. —*v.* 2 *Muster the troops:* assemble, mobilize, round up, convene, call together, marshal, gather.

musty *adj.* 1 *The curtains were musty:* mildewed, moldy; stale, dusty; damp, dank. 2 *a musty joke:* hackneyed, stale, worn-out, old, antiquated, familiar.
Ant. 2 new, fresh, original.

mutation *n. This rose is a mutation:* change, alteration, permutation, variation, hybrid, metamorphosis, transformation, deviation, modification; anomaly, mutant.

mute *adj.* 1 *In the movie the mad scientist's assistant was mute:* dumb, speechless, voiceless, aphasiac. 2 *He's mute on the subject of religion:* noncommittal, silent, mum, reticent, close-mouthed, tight-lipped, uncommunicative; quiet, speechless, inarticulate. 3 *My name has a mute "e" in it:* unsounded, silent, unarticulated, unuttered, unpronounced.
Ant. 2 expansive, loquacious. 3 pronounced, articulated.

mutilate *v. The assassins mutilated their victims:* maim, mangle, lacerate, cripple, deform, disfigure, lame; amputate, truncate, dismember.

mutiny *n.* 1 *Troops put down the mutiny:* uprising, revolt, insurrection, rebellion, insurgency, coup. —*v.* 2 *The ship's crew planned to mutiny:* revolt, rebel, rise up, defy authority.

mutter *v. She muttered to herself:* mumble, grumble, murmur; grunt, growl, whisper; complain, gripe.

mutual *adj.* 1 *He is a mutual friend:* shared by two parties, common, coincident, joint, communal, related. 2 *The feeling is mutual:* reciprocated, reciprocal, shared, interchanged, returned.
Ant. 2 unreciprocated, unshared.

muzzle *v.* 1 *to muzzle a dog:* harness, gag, bridle; curb, check, rein in. 2 *He tried to muzzle the opposition:* silence, quiet, still, suppress, stifle, gag.

myriad *adj. Myriad fish swim the seas:* innumerable, multitudinous, countless, boundless, measureless, incalculable, immeasurable, untold, limitless, manifold, uncounted, endless.
Ant. few.

mysterious *adj. There is something mysterious about her:* strange, puzzling, enigmatic, secret, inscrutable, obscure, hidden, covert, baffling, impenetrable, perplexing, secretive, inexplicable, unfathomable, unknown, supernatural.
Ant. clear, plain, apparent, manifest.

mystery *n.* 1 *The mysteries of their religion uplifted them:* sacred rites, things unexplainable, mysticism, occult, sacramental rite, symbolism, holy of holies. 2 *to solve a mystery:* puzzle, problem, secret, riddle, conundrum, enigma. 3 *Mystery makes one interesting:* enigmatic manner, mysterious quality, elusiveness, mystification, secrecy, vagueness.

mystical Also **mystic** *adj. the mystical element of a play:* mysterious, inscrutable, obscure, unknowable, enigmatic, esoteric, cabalistic, symbolic, hidden, occult, cryptic; otherworldly, transcendental, ethereal, metaphysical.

mystify *v. Why I like it mystifies me:* bewilder, elude, confound, perplex, puzzle, baffle.

myth *n.* 1 *the classical myths:* story, legend, tale, fairy tale, fable, allegory. 2 *Her trip to California was a myth:* fiction, made-up story, falsehood, lie, fib, tall tale, canard, story. 3 *the myth that the earth was flat:* illusion, delusion, falsehood, error.
Ant. 2 truth, fact, actuality.

mythical Also **mythic** *adj.* 1 *The painting showed mythical subjects:* legendary, fabled, about myths, mythological. 2 *a mythical horse:* imaginary, fantasized, fictitious, fabricated, unreal, pretended.
Ant. 2 real, actual, real-life.

mythological Also **mythologic** *adj. a poem's mythological allusions:* drawn from mythology; legendary, mythical, mythic; unreal, fabulous, imaginary, fictitious, fantastic, imagined, illusory.

N

nab *v. The police nabbed the robber:* arrest, capture, apprehend, catch, seize, grab, snare, lay hold of.
Ant. release, let go, set free.

nadir *n. Flunking math was the nadir of my student days:* lowest point, low point, apogee; zero, nothing, bottom.
Ant. peak, zenith, high point.

nag *v.* 1 *Stop nagging!:* pester, badger, harp, hector, upbraid, scold; irritate, annoy, plague, bedevil. —*n.* 2 *What a frightful nag!:* scold, shrew, virago, termagant.

naive Also **naïve** *adj.* 1 *a naive question:* innocent, unaffected, unsophisticated, childlike, unspoiled, artless, ingenuous, guileless, unworldly. 2 *Don't be so naive:* gullible, foolish, simple, credulous, unsuspecting, unsuspicious, unwary.
Ant. 1 sophisticated, disingenuous. 2 sly, suspicious.

naiveté Also **naïveté, naivety** *n. His naiveté was obvious:* innocence, artlessness, ingenuousness, simplicity, unaffectedness, inexperience, childishness.
Ant. sophistication, worldliness, experience.

naked *adj.* 1 *Naked bathing is not allowed on this beach:* nude, unclad, undressed, unclothed, disrobed, bared, *Informal* in the buff, in the altogether. 2 *We picnicked on the naked sand:* uncovered, bare, exposed, wide-open. 3 *the naked truth:* plain, unvarnished, frank, blatant, bald, manifest, unqualified.
Ant. 1 dressed, clothed, clad, covered. 3 embellished, exaggerated.

namby-pamby *adj. Don't be so namby-pamby!:* wishy-washy, indecisive, weak, vapid; prim, prissy, mincing.
Ant. decisive, forceful, dynamic.

name *n.* 1 *The scientific name of the woodchuck is* Marmota monax: appellation, cognomen, designation; denomination, term. —*v.* 2 *What will you name the baby?:* call, christen, baptize, designate. 3 *When will they name a successor?:* choose, delegate, appoint, nominate, commission, ordain, authorize, select, specify.

nameless *adj.* 1 *The new company is as yet nameless:* unnamed, having no name, without a name, untitled. 2 *a nameless poet:* unknown, anonymous; obscure, unheard-of.
Ant. 2 famous, well-known, renowned.

nap *v.* 1 *The baby naps every afternoon:* doze, take a short sleep, drowse, slumber, have a catnap, doze off, drift off, drop off, rest, catch forty winks. —*n.* 2 *That nap really refreshed me:* short sleep, catnap, doze, siesta, *Informal* forty winks.

narcotic *n. The doctor prescribed a narcotic to ease the pain:* drug, opiate, soporific, painkiller, sedative, tranquilizer.

narrate *v. to narrate the story of Cinderella:* tell a story, retell, repeat, recount, relate; chronicle, give an account of, describe, recite, render.

narration *n. The narration was accompanied by slides:* storytelling, relating, speaking, telling, recounting, description, recitation; voice-over.

narrative *n.* 1 *The narrative of her life was fascinating:* story, tale, chronicle, account, report, recital. —*adj.* 2 *a narrative painting:* telling a story, involving storytelling, anecdotal, having a plot, episodic, historical.

narrow *adj.* 1 *a narrow waist:* slim, not wide, slender, attenuated, tapered. 2 *How can anyone work in such narrow confines?:* small, close, cramped, tight, restricted, confined, squeezed, compressed, constricted. 3 *You have a narrow mind:* bigoted, biased, opinionated, provincial, illiberal, dogmatic, parochial, shallow, intolerant, set.
Ant. 1 broad, wide. 2 spacious, ample. 3 open, liberal, receptive.

narrow-minded *adj. a narrow-minded bureaucrat:* provincial, bigoted, opinionated, small-minded, parochial, hidebound, petty.
Ant. broad-minded, inquisitive, tolerant.

nasty *adj.* 1 *What's that nasty smell?:* foul, odious, awful, nauseating, repellent. 2 *That was a nasty thing to do:* vicious, mean, abominable, hateful, vile, horrible. 3 *Firing people is a nasty job:* unpleasant, distasteful, disagreeable.
Ant. 1, 3 pleasant, enjoyable, nice. 2 kind, sweet, admirable, honorable.

native *adj.* 1 *our native land:* of one's place of birth, of one's homeland, natal, home, paternal. 2 *native ability:* inherent, inborn, innate, inbred, inherited, hereditary, intrinsic, congenital, natural, ingrained, instinctive. 3 *The house was built of native materi-*

als: local, national, indigenous, domestic, homegrown. —*n.* **4** *The natives were friendly to guests:* aborigine, original inhabitant; primitive, savage. **5** *a native of New York:* one born in a specific place, lifelong inhabitant, long-time resident; citizen, countryman, countrywoman.

Ant. **1** adopted. **2** acquired, learned. **3** imported, foreign. **5** foreigner, alien.

natural *adj.* **1** *to study natural history:* of nature, earthly, terrestrial. **2** *a natural phenomenon:* naturally occurring, formed naturally, native, made by nature. **3** *to have natural talent:* instinctive, inborn, inherent, god-given, intuitive; characteristic, essential, regular. **4** *The actress hasn't one natural gesture:* unaffected, spontaneous, genuine, straightforward, unstudied, unmannered, unpretentious.

Ant. **2** unnatural, artificial. **4** affected, assumed, feigned, calculated.

nature *n.* **1** *to leave the city and rediscover nature:* the natural world, physical world, creation, earth. **2** *A cat is by nature very clean:* instinct, constitution, disposition, bent, humor, mood; birth, character, essence; trait, characteristic, peculiarity, feature. **3** *What is the nature of your business?:* kind, variety, sort, type, category; style, stamp, particularity.

naughty *adj.* **1** *a naughty child.* bad, devilish, disobedient, misbehaving, mischievous, recalcitrant, fractious, unmanageable, disrespectful. **2** *His jokes are naughty:* off-color, bawdy, vulgar, dirty, ribald, risqué.

nausea *n.* **1** *The pitching of the ship filled me with nausea:* sickness, upset stomach, queasiness; retching, vomiting, heaving. **2** *I felt nothing but nausea for that kind of politicking:* disgust, revulsion, repulsion, loathing.

nauseate *v. The food nauseated me:* sicken, make sick, upset, turn one's stomach, make sick to the stomach; disgust, repulse, revolt, repel.

nauseated *adj. Several people became nauseated after eating:* sick to the stomach, sick, queasy, ill; disgusted, revolted, repelled, upset.

nauseous *adj. Rotten eggs are nauseous:* sickening, nauseating, disgusting, repulsive, revolting, repellent, abhorrent.

nautical *adj. a nautical map:* seagoing, of the sea, marine, oceanic, maritime; boating, yachting, naval.

navigate *v.* **1** *We navigated the channel in record time:* cross, sail across, sail, cruise, sail over, ride across, fly. **2** *I was trained to navigate by the air corps:* chart a course, plot a course; sail, maneuver.

navigation *n. My course didn't include night navigation:* art of sailing, seamanship, piloting, sailing, navigating, traveling, boating, cruising, voyaging.

navy *n. The navy defends the seas:* warships, naval forces, fleet, armada, flotilla, task force.

near *adv.* **1** *She came near:* close, close by, hereabouts, at close quarters, alongside. —*adj.* **2** *A storm is near:* close, imminent, impending, looming, approaching, threatening. —*prep.* **3** *Are you near the end?:* close to, proximate to, in the vicinity of, not far from. —*v.* **4** *The boat neared the dock:* approach, come close to, move toward, come up to, draw near, advance toward.

nearly *adv. I'm nearly ready:* about, almost, nigh, approximately, all but; roughly, just about, practically.

neat *adj.* **1** *a neat desk:* orderly, straight, tidy, shipshape, organized, uncluttered; clean. **2** *a neat mind:* efficient, purposive, controlled, methodical, systematic, accurate. **3** *Slang What a neat idea!:* great, exciting, striking, imaginative, ingenious, original.

Ant. **1** messy, disorderly, untidy, disorganized, cluttered. **3** awful, terrible, lousy.

nebulous *adj. Our plans are still nebulous:* vague, hazy, unclear, obscure, cloudy, indistinct, ambiguous, uncertain, indefinite, indeterminate, uncertain.

Ant. distinct, definite.

necessarily *adv. Clouds don't necessarily mean rain:* automatically, inexorably, inevitably, accordingly, compulsorily, by necessity, of course, perforce.

necessary *adj. Take whatever tools are necessary:* required, obligatory, needed, requisite, compulsory, indispensable, essential, called for, fitting, imperative.

Ant. unnecessary, dispensable, nonessential.

necessitate *v. The extra guests necessitated taking two cars:* require, make necessary, oblige, impel, constrain, create a need for.

necessity *n.* **1** *Often* **necessities** *Take only the necessities for the trip:* something needed, essential, indispensable, requisite. **2** *What's the necessity of leaving?:* urgency, demand, pressure, need.

need *n.* **1** *My daughter looks after my needs:* want, requisite, requirement, necessity, essential. **2** *They can't find work and are in dire need:* poverty, want, neediness, penury, indigence, destitution, pennilessness; distress, straits. —*v.* **3** *The boy needs a heavy* *coat:* require, lack, want, find necessary, have need of, necessitate.

Ant. 2 wealth, affluence.

needless *adj. a needless expense:* unnecessary, unneeded, unessential, uncalled-for, superfluous, dispensable; unavailing, pointless.

Ant. essential, obligatory, required, needful; useful.

needy *adj. to help needy families:* poor, destitute, indigent, impoverished, poverty-stricken, in want.

Ant. rich, affluent, wealthy, well-to-do, well-off.

ne'er-do-well *n. That ne'er-do-well isn't looking for a job:* idler, loafer, good-for-nothing, wastrel, no-account.

nefarious *adj. nefarious deeds:* evil, vile, infamous, wicked, foul, base, low, iniquitous, despicable, detestable; depraved; villainous, heinous; shameful, disgraceful, dishonorable.

Ant. good, honorable, noble; admirable, praiseworthy, laudable.

negate *v. This letter negates what you told me:* nullify, invalidate, void, reverse; quash, deny, abrogate, revoke, retract, disavow; rebut, refute, contradict; set aside, veto, repeal; disclaim, repudiate.

Ant. affirm, confirm, corroborate, reinforce, support.

negative *adj.* 1 *The answer was negative:* indicating "no," disapproving, refusing, declining, rejecting, opposing, opposed; objecting, demurring. 2 *a negative attitude:* antagonistic, uncooperative, contrary, skeptical; reluctant, unwilling, unenthusiastic; gloomy, pessimistic, fatalistic.

Ant. 1 affirmative, positive, assenting; approving; concurring. 2 positive.

neglect *v.* 1 *I've been neglecting my bills:* ignore, disregard, overlook, take no notice of, take no note of; let slide, slight, pass over, omit, lose sight of, be remiss, be inattentive; shirk; abandon. —*n.* 2 *Neglect of his studies caused him to fail:* inattention, disregard, neglectfulness, laxity, negligence, remissness, dereliction, noncompliance; indifference, carelessness, slovenliness, omission, unfulfillment.

Ant. 1 attend to, take care of, perform, notice. 2 attention, care, respect.

neglectful *adj. He's neglectful of his family:* negligent, thoughtless, heedless, forgetful, unmindful, unheeding, inattentive, unobservant, oblivious, derelict, indifferent; improvident.

Ant. attentive, thoughtful, considerate.

negligent *adj. I was charged with negligent driving:* neglectful, careless, indifferent, in-

considerate, thoughtless; unthinking, unmindful, unheeding, heedless, remiss, inattentive, unwatchful.

Ant. careful, thoughtful, considerate, mindful, heedful.

negligible *adj. a negligible amount:* unimportant, trifling, slight, inconsequential, insignificant, trivial, paltry, small.

negotiate *v.* 1 *to negotiate a settlement:* confer over, discuss, transact, bargain for, agree to arbitration, come to terms, settle; haggle, barter. 2 *I'll need help to negotiate these steps:* cope with, handle, deal with, manage.

neigh *v. The horse neighed:* whinny, nicker.

neighbor *n.* 1 *good neighbors:* person who lives nearby; adjoining country. —*v.* 2 *Canada neighbors the U.S.:* border, border on, adjoin, abut; meet, be near, verge upon.

neighborhood *n.* 1 *a residential neighborhood:* district, quarter, place, area, locale, vicinity, community, section, ward, precinct. 2 *debts in the neighborhood of a thousand dollars:* range, approximate amount.

neighboring *adj. a neighboring town:* nearby, adjacent, adjoining, close by; contiguous, abutting, bordering, near, near at hand; surrounding.

Ant. distant, faraway, remote.

neighborly *adj. The townsfolk were quite neighborly:* friendly, amiable, kindly, hospitable, warmhearted, considerate, helpful, cordial, gracious, obliging.

Ant. unfriendly, remote, hostile.

nemesis *n. Billy the Kid finally met his nemesis:* undoing, destruction, overthrow, ruin, downfall, *Informal* Waterloo.

neophyte *n. The neophyte learned very fast:* beginner, tyro, apprentice, trainee, novice, newcomer, tenderfoot, rookie, greenhorn, student.

Ant. veteran, old hand, expert.

nerve *n.* 1 *It takes a lot of nerve to work as a steeplejack:* courage, boldness, fearlessness, pluck, determination, coolness, steadiness, tenacity, bravery, resoluteness, *Informal* guts, spirit; confidence, self-assurance. 2 *She had some nerve to say that!:* gall, insolence, presumption, impertinence, impudence, effrontery, *Slang* brass, crust, cheek, brazenness.

Ant. 1 cowardice, faintheartedness.

nervous *adj. a nervous job applicant:* jumpy, jittery, high-strung, touchy; ruffled, disturbed, uneasy, skittish, fidgety, trembling, tense; anxious, fearful, apprehensive, timorous, alarmed.

Ant. calm, tranquil; confident, bold.

nestle *v. The kitten nestled in the child's arms:* lie snug, snuggle, lie, lie close; embrace, clasp, enfold, fondle, nuzzle, cuddle, bundle, coddle.

net¹ n. 1 a net for the tennis court: mesh, netting, meshwork, network, latticework; lattice; screen, grid; snare, trap. —v. 2 The fishing fleet netted tons of fish: capture with a net, ensnare, snare, enmesh, trap; entangle; seize, catch, get hold of, take captive, capture.

net² v. The business nets $10,000 a day: realize in profit, gain, earn, clear a profit of; accumulate, collect, bring in, obtain, take in.

nether adj. the nether regions of Hell: lower, lowest, below, under, inferior, subjacent, downward; bottom, bottommost, nethermost.

Ant. upper, higher, above.

nettle v. Loud music nettles her: annoy, irritate, exasperate, gall, provoke, bother, perturb, harass, get on one's nerves.

neurotic adj. a neurotic fear of the dark: unhealthy, nervous, anxious; psychoneurotic, disturbed, abnormal, unstable, overwrought, emotionally disordered; obsessive, intense.

neutral adj. 1 Ireland was a neutral nation in World War II: nonbelligerent, noncombatant, nonparticipating; noninterventionist, nonpartisan, noninterfering. 2 I'm neutral on the subject: impartial, disinterested, unbiased; indifferent, unconcerned, uninvolved; of two minds. 3 a neutral color: indefinite, in-between, medium, intermediate, normal, average.

Ant. 1 belligerent, participating. 2 partial, interested, biased, predisposed; decided.

neutralize v. A good defense will neutralize the attack: render ineffective, balance, counterbalance, counterpoise, counteract, nullify, negate, offset; check, block, stymie, cancel, stop, halt, impede, prevent; overcome, suppress.

never adv. I'll never speak to her again: at no time, nevermore, not ever, under no circumstances, on no occasion, not at all.

Ant. always, forever, eternally, evermore.

never-ending adj. never-ending rain: everlasting, unceasing, incessant, interminable, nonstop, continual, continuous, unremitting, persistent, constant, steady.

nevertheless adv. He seems honest; nevertheless I don't quite trust him: nonetheless, on the other hand, in spite of that, yet, but, regardless, however, notwithstanding, even so, just the same, for all that, contrarily, contrariwise, be that as it may.

new adj. 1 a new car: recently acquired, of recent make, brand-new, just out; up-to-date, modern, current, newly issued; novel, original, recent. 2 a new experience: untried,

unseasoned, unessayed, unaccustomed, unfamiliar; unused, unventured; uncharted, unexplored. 3 I feel like new: restored, reinvigorated, renewed, renovated, revivified, reborn, recreated, old-fashioned; changed, altered.

Ant. 1 old, ancient, antique; stale, hackneyed, outmoded, old-fashioned. 2 familiar.

newcomer n. They are newcomers to our town: recent arrival, stranger, outsider; immigrant; novice, tyro, neophyte.

newly adv. a newly painted chair: freshly, recently, lately, anew, afresh, of late, not long ago.

news n. pl. Did you hear the news?: information, intelligence, tidings, bulletin, communiqué, announcement, disclosure, report, release; dispatch, lowdown, revelation, rumor, talk, gossip, scandal.

nib n. 1 the nib of a pen: point, tip, peak, end; apex, vertex, top, pinnacle; extreme, extremity.

nibble v. 1 She nibbled a cookie: eat sparingly, bite, eat in small bites, gnaw; munch, peck at. —n. 2 Try a nibble of this cheese: bite, taste, small piece, morsel, speck.

nice adj. 1 That was a nice party: good, fine, pleasant, agreeable, pleasurable; lovely, wonderful, great, swell. 2 a nice person: friendly, sympathetic, warmhearted, good, kind, agreeable, amiable, congenial, pleasant; charming, attractive, delightful, gracious; understanding, compassionate; pleasing; cheerful, likeable. 3 Nice people don't go there: proper, refined, well brought up, virtuous, respectable, genteel, well-bred, ladylike, seemly. 4 The cabinetmaker does nice work: careful, painstaking, scrupulous, precise, meticulous, skillful; sensitive, exact; correct, accurate, methodical; strict, rigorous; subtle, delicate; fastidious, finicky, fussy.

Ant. 1 dreadful, miserable, awful; unpleasant. 2 unfriendly, mean. 3 coarse, vulgar, ill-bred. 4 sloppy, rough, careless, haphazard, undiscriminating.

nicely adv. Your arrival was nicely timed: carefully, accurately, faultlessly, exactly, precisely; fortunately, opportunely; attractively, neatly; pleasantly.

Ant. carelessly, haphazardly; unfortunately.

nicety n. 1 She understands the niceties of opera: subtlety, delicacy, fine point, subtle detail, small distinction; good taste, tastefulness, culture, cultivation, refinement, refined feeling, finesse, elegance, tact. 2 Notice the nicety of the cabinetmaker's work: meticulousness, attention to detail, delicacy, exactness, precision, care, accuracy.

Ant. 2 roughness, crudeness, sloppiness, slovenliness.

niche *n.* 1 *The statue was placed in a niche on the stairway:* recess, alcove, nook, cranny, cubbyhole; cavity, hollow. 2 *She found her niche in foreign service:* proper place, calling, suitable occupation, congenial job, vocation, trade.

nick *n.* 1 *This vase has a nick on the base:* cut, scratch, mar, chip, dent; wound, incision, scar; cleft, depression, gash, gouge. —*v.* 2 *He nicked his chin shaving:* cut, notch, lacerate, gash; dent, indent; mark.

nickname *n. My nickname is "Bo":* sobriquet, agnomen, familiar name, cognomen, diminutive; appellation, epithet; childhood name, pet name, baby name, school name.

niggardly *adj.* 1 *Don't be so niggardly with the mayonnaise:* stingy, miserly, parsimonious, closefisted, tight, cheap, stinting, ungenerous, illiberal, grudging, sparing, close, penurious; frugal, saving, thrifty. 2 *That was a niggardly gift for an old friend:* insufficient, paltry, poor, sorry, second-rate, meager, scanty, measly; cheap, tawdry, shabby.

Ant. 1, 2 bountiful, liberal, generous, profuse, lavish, bounteous, plentiful.

niggling *adj. It's a niggling amount:* small, trifling, picayune, minor, piddling; nit-picking, fussy, finicky; insignificant, inconsequential, negligible, nugatory.

Ant. considerable, sizable, consequential.

nigh *adv.* 1 *Evening draws nigh:* near, close, within sight. 2 *She's nigh onto 80 years old:* almost, nearly, practically, verging on. —*adj.* 3 *The time is nigh:* close, close at hand, at hand, near; close by, handy; in the vicinity.

Ant. 3 far, distant, remote.

night *n. The guard is on duty during the night:* nighttime, dark, darkness; evening, eventide, nightfall, sundown, dusk.

nightfall *n. We worked till nightfall:* twilight, dusk, day's end, evening, evenfall, eventide, sunset, sundown, moonrise.

Ant. dawn, daybreak, daylight.

nightly *adv. The restaurant is open nightly:* every night, nights, night after night; at night, by night.

Ant. daily, every day; diurnally.

nightmare *n. The child had a nightmare:* bad dream; frightening vision, hallucination.

nightstick *n. The officer twirled his nightstick:* baton, cudgel, billy club, truncheon, shillelagh, bludgeon.

nihilism *n. Her rejection of all philosophies amounted to nihilism:* disbelief in anything, skepticism, universal doubt, agnosticism;

amorality, anarchism, lawlessness, irresponsibility, license, chaos.

nil *n. My interest in the plan is nil:* nonexistent, none, naught, null, nothing, nothing whatever, none whatever, zero.

nimble *adj. I was nimble enough to jump the fence. a nimble mind:* agile, spry, supple; animated, swift, quick, mercurial, lively, sprightly, fleet, rapid; deft, skillful, dexterous.

Ant. clumsy, plodding, awkward, heavy; lethargic.

nincompoop *n. That nincompoop put the papers in the wrong file:* ninny, dunce, harebrain, featherbrain, scatterbrain, simpleton, blockhead, bonehead, knucklehead, fool, skull; dimwit, dolt, nitwit, half-wit; moron, idiot, imbecile; dope, dummy, lunkhead.

nip *v.* 1 *Nip the end of the wire with the pliers:* pinch, tweak, squeeze; clutch, seize, grab, grasp, clamp, grip, snatch. 2 *Don't nip the buds off the plant:* cut off, lop, snip, cut, clip, crop; cut short, curtail, shorten; sever. 3 *The government nipped the rebellion in the bud:* check, cut off, curtail, put an end to, quash, crush; thwart, frustrate. 4 *A sharp wind nipped our cheeks:* freeze, chill; pierce, bite, cut.

nitwit *n. The nitwit forgot to give her the message:* fool, blockhead, dummy, dolt, dunce, dimwit, nincompoop, lamebrain; bonehead, pinhead, birdbrain, numskull.

nobility *n.* 1 *The nobility favored the abdication:* noble class, aristocracy, ruling class, peerage, lords; royalty. 2 *nobility of character:* greatness, exaltedness, dignity, loftiness, stateliness, distinction, grandness, prestige; preeminence, supremacy, majesty, splendor, magnificence.

Ant. 1 lower classes, peasantry, plebeians. 2 lowness, meanness, ignobility.

noble *adj. of noble birth:* highborn, patrician, gentle, high-ranking, aristocratic, blueblooded; princely, royal. 2 *a noble character:* lofty, selfless, magnanimous, excellent, exemplary, moral, virtuous, meritorious, incorruptible, trustworthy, honorable, estimable, worthy, reputable, high-principled, honest, ethical. 3 *Noble mansions line the river:* stately, grand, majestic, lordly, imposing, splendid, magnificent, superb, glorious, sublime; dignified, distinguished; lofty, regal, imperial. —*n.* 4 *The nobles feared an uprising:* aristocrat, nobleman, patrician, peer, lord.

Ant. 1 lowborn, lowly, humble, plebeian. 2 ignoble, base. 3 modest, paltry, plain. 4 peasant, commoner, serf.

nocturnal *adj. Some animals are nocturnal*

feeders. night, nighttime, of the night; dark, obscure.

Ant. diurnal, by day.

nod *v.* 1 *She nodded to her friends:* incline the head, bow one's head. 2 *He nodded his assent:* express with a nod; signal, beckon, motion, gesture. 3 *We nodded as the speech dragged on:* doze, fall asleep, drop off, drowse, be torpid or languid.

node *n.* 1 *The stalk is covered with nodes:* knot, burl, joint; bud. 2 *He had some nodes removed from his vocal cords:* lump, bump, nodule, prominence, protuberance, swelling, knob, tumescence, excrescence.

nodule *n.* *The roots of the plant are covered with nodules:* knob, outgrowth, protuberance, growth, bump, lump, node, knot, projection, protrusion, prominence; swelling, bulge.

noise *n.* *Those planes make an awful noise:* sound, din, racket, clamor, uproar, clatter, bedlam, babel, blare, wail, boom, blast, bang, rumble, thunder, hubbub, discharge, report, reverberation, echo; dissonance, cacophony; roar, vociferation; caterwauling; shouting, brawling, gabbling.

Ant. quiet, silence, stillness; harmony, melody.

noisome *adj.* 1 *a noisome odor:* smelly, malodorous, stinking, fetid, reeking, rank, rotten, putrid. 2 *a noisome substance.* harmful, noxious, injurious, hurtful, unhealthy, deleterious, toxic, baneful, poisonous.

Ant. 2 wholesome, beneficial, healthful.

noisy *adj.* *a crowded, noisy street:* loud, clamorous, deafening, earsplitting, blaring, strident, boisterous, thunderous, resounding; grating, jarring, harsh-sounding; dissonant, discordant; clangorous; shrill, piercing, cacophonous.

Ant. quiet, silent, hushed, still; melodious.

nomad *n.* *Many Lapps were nomads:* wanderer, itinerant, mover; rambler, roamer, migrant, traveler, rover, vagabond; stray, refugee.

nomadic *adj.* *The Bedouins are a nomadic people:* traveling, wandering, roaming, roving, migratory, migrant, itinerant; vagabond, footloose, vagrant.

nom de plume *n.* *Samuel Clemens' nom de plume was "Mark Twain":* pen name, pseudonym.

nomenclature *n.* *the nomenclature of botany:* terminology, phraseology, vocabulary, terms; naming, appellation, designation, taxonomy.

nominal *adj.* 1 *The king is the nominal head of state, but the prime minister runs the country:* titular, ostensible, in name only, so-called; theoretical, official; purported,

professed. 2 *There will be a nominal charge:* small, low, minimum, moderate; unsubstantial, insignificant.

Ant. 1 actual, real, true. 2 considerable, substantial.

nominate *v.* *I nominate Bill for club president:* name as a candidate, propose, suggest, put forward.

nomination *n.* *She has a chance of winning the nomination:* choice of a candidate, selection, election, designation; submission of a name; appointment; accession, inauguration, investiture.

nonbeliever *n.* *The church tried to reach out to nonbelievers:* doubter, unbeliever, skeptic, cynic, freethinker; agnostic, atheist; heathen, pagan, infidel.

Ant. follower, devotee, disciple, believer; fanatic.

nonchalant *adj.* *How can you be so nonchalant?:* unconcerned, blasé, imperturbable, unexcited, unemotional, unmoved, unaffected, unstirred, unruffled, cool, collected; offhand, casual, indifferent, uninterested, phlegmatic, lethargic.

Ant. concerned, moved, affected; anxious, agitated.

noncommittal *adj.* *She gave me a noncommittal answer:* indefinite, equivocal, indecisive, vague, evasive; reserved, guarded, cautious, circumspect; tentative, ambiguous, temporizing.

Ant. definite, decisive, conclusive.

noncompliant *adj.* *My noncompliant attitude threatened my career:* nonconforming, unorthodox, unconventional, iconoclastic, dissenting, disagreeing, noncooperating, differing, dissident; rebellious, resistive, unruly.

Ant. complaisant, obedient, compliant.

nonconformist *n.* *The Pilgrims were religious nonconformists:* dissenter, dissident; individualist, free spirit, liberated person; heretic, rebel, revolutionary, radical, iconoclast; eccentric, original; insurgent, maverick; freethinker, bohemian.

nondescript *adj.* *a nondescript face:* undistinctive, ordinary, unexceptional, characterless; unimpressive, colorless, amorphous, undistinguished.

Ant. distinctive, unusual; vivid, unique.

nonentity *n.* *He's a nonentity in this firm:* nobody, unimportant person, mediocrity, small-fry, nothing, zero.

Ant. somebody, VIP.

nonessential *adj.* 1 *a nonessential expense:* unessential, unnecessary, extraneous, irrelevant; incidental, secondary; unconnected, beside the point, inappropriate; insignificant, trivial, inconsequential.

—n. 2 *The new budget cuts out all nonessentials:* unessential thing, unnecessary item, incidental; luxury.

Ant. 1 vital, essential, important; significant.

nonpareil *adj. a woman of nonpareil wit:* unequaled, unique, unsurpassed, unmatched, unrivaled, one-of-a-kind; exceptional, extraordinary.

nonpartisan *adj. Government agencies should be nonpartisan:* unaffiliated, nonpolitical, politically independent; unbiased, unprejudiced; impartial; uninfluenced, uninvolved, disinterested, objective.

Ant. partisan; biased, prejudiced.

nonplus *v. The child was nonplussed by the camera:* confuse, muddle, baffle, bother, disconcert, discountenance; disturb, upset, dismay, embarrass, faze; perplex, puzzle, bewilder, stump, mystify; flabbergast, astound, dumbfound, astonish.

nonsectarian *adj. a nonsectarian club:* interdenominational, interchurch, undenominational, nondenominational, ecumenical.

Ant. sectarian, denominational.

nonsense *n. Don't talk nonsense!:* foolishness, folly, ridiculousness, absurdity, stupidity, silliness, childishness; fooling, tomfoolery, joking, shenanigans, horseplay, high jinks, antics; meaninglessness, frivolity; prattle, babble, chatter, blather, drivel, gibberish, twaddle, bunk, rubbish, hogwash, fiddle-faddle, piffle, claptrap, balderdash, bosh.

Ant. sense, wisdom; fact, truth; seriousness, reason.

nonstop *adj. He's a nonstop talker:* continuous, endless; uninterrupted, unbroken; constant, incessant, never-ending, interminable, round-the-clock.

Ant. sporadic; interrupted.

nook *n. a breakfast nook:* recess, niche, alcove, cranny, corner; cubbyhole, cavity, snug place, retreat, refuge, haven, lair; hiding place, den, hideaway.

noon *n. We ate lunch at noon:* midday, twelve noon, 12 M.; noonday, high noon, noontime.

norm *n. This graph charts the norm:* standard, average, rule; pattern, model, gauge, criterion.

normal *adj. His growth is normal for that age:* standard, average, usual, ordinary; expected, natural, regular; conforming, consistent; typical, representative, conventional; constant, steady, unchanging; in good order, well-regulated, fit, sound, healthy; unchanging, uniform; reasonable, rational; middling, mediocre.

Ant. abnormal, unusual, exceptional, irregular; peculiar, singular, uncommon.

north *adj.* 1 *the north wind:* coming from the north, northerly; moving toward the north, northward; northern; polar, arctic. —*adv.* 2 *We headed north:* toward the north, northward; northerly.

nostalgia *n. Those old recordings arouse nostalgia:* longing for the past, bittersweet memory; homesickness, longing for home.

nostrum *n. an old nostrum for treating a cough:* remedy, medicine, formula, medicament, potion; cure, cure-all, panacea; patent medicine.

nosy Also **nosey** *adj. Don't be so nosy:* inquisitive, curious, prying, snooping, *Informal* snoopy.

notable *adj.* 1 *There is a notable difference:* conspicuous, marked, pronounced, noticeable, remarkable, striking. 2 *a notable doctor:* renowned, reputable, distinguished, famed, famous, celebrated, prominent, eminent, well-known. —*n.* 3 *The convention attracted many notables:* celebrity, dignitary, luminary, name, *Informal* VIP, bigwig.

Ant. 1 vague, imperceptible. 2 unknown, obscure, little known.

notably *adv. The audience was notably small:* strikingly, markedly, noticeably, conspicuously; distinctly, unmistakably.

notation *n. Make a notation on your calendar:* note, memorandum, entry.

notch *n.* 1 *He had a notch on his six-shooter for each victim:* nick, cut, score, scoring. 2 *This restaurant is a notch above the others:* degree, level, grade, *Slang* cut.

note *n.* 1 *Make a note to get more milk:* memorandum, notation. 2 *Drop Thelma a note and thank her:* brief letter, message, epistle, communication; dispatch, communiqué; memorandum, *Informal* line. 3 *She paid the bill in $50 notes:* bank note, bill, paper money; voucher, draft. 4 *Take note of the lavish decorations:* regard, notice. 5 *Several persons of note were at the party:* importance, consequence, distinction, prominence, eminence, fame, renown, celebrity. —*v.* 6 *Note the name and address in your book:* make a note of, mark down, set down, center, write down, make an entry of. 7 *We noted his reluctance to testify:* notice, perceive, be aware of, be conscious of.

Ant. 7 ignore, disregard, overlook.

noted *adj. a noted surgeon:* famous, renowned, eminent, celebrated, well-known, distinguished, prominent, reputable.

Ant. unknown, obscure, undistinguished.

noteworthy *adj. The book is noteworthy:*

distinguished, outstanding, significant, important, remarkable; exceptional, singular.
Ant. trivial, inconsequential.

nothing n. 1 *There is nothing for dinner. Her latest play is nothing:* naught, no thing; rubbish; trifle, trinket; trivia, inconsequentials. 2 *The score was nine to nothing:* zero, naught, none, cipher, nix, *Slang,* zilch, zip, love.

notice n. 1 *The plan is not worth our notice:* attention, regard, cognizance, heed. 2 *Did you receive a notice about the sale?:* information, mention, notification, intelligence, knowledge; declaration, communication, disclosure; poster, handbill, circular, leaflet; pamphlet, brochure; advertisement, announcement. 3 *She gave two weeks' notice when she quit:* warning, advisement, notification. 4 *The paper gave the play a bad notice:* review, critique, appraisal, rating. —v. 5 *Did you notice her new ring?:* see, catch sight of, observe, take notice of, mark, *Ant.* 1 oversight, neglect. 5 ignore, overlook.

noticeable adj. *a noticeable difference:* definite, clear, plain, distinct, evident, obvious, conspicuous, unmistakable; striking, noteworthy, appreciable, observable, manifest.

notify v. *They notified us of a rent increase:* inform, acquaint, let know, send word, advise, tell, apprise, warn.

notion n. 1 *I have no notion of what you meant:* idea, concept, suspicion, intimation, conception. 2 *That's an odd notion:* belief, view, opinion; whim, quirk, fancy; conceit, humor, eccentricity.

notoriety n. *She sought fame, but achieved only notoriety:* disrepute, ill repute, disgrace, dishonor, infamy, ignominy, scandal.
Ant. honor, esteem, good standing.

notorious adj. *a notorious jewel thief:* infamous, widely known, renowned, notable, celebrated.

nourish v. *They needed good food to nourish their bodies:* nurture, feed, sustain.
Ant. starve.

nourishment n. *She's beginning to take a little nourishment:* food, sustenance; nutriment, viands, victuals, comestibles, food and drink, meat, bread.

novel adj. *That's a novel way to do your hair:* unusual, original, new, different, innovative, uncommon, singular, unique.
Ant. usual, customary, ordinary, common, traditional.

novelty n. 1 *There's little novelty in his writing:* originality, newness, uniqueness, innovation, surprise. 2 *The shop sells novelties to tourists:* trinket, gewgaw, gimcrack, baga-

telle, bauble, knick-knack; souvenir, memento.

novice n. *I'm a novice in the trade:* beginner, tyro, learner, apprentice, newcomer; amateur; pupil, student.
Ant. master, old hand, professional.

noxious adj. *noxious fumes:* harmful, poisonous, injurious, baneful, hurtful; lethal, deadly, virulent; putrid, putrescent, noisome, foul-smelling, revolting, disgusting.
Ant. wholesome, beneficial; salubrious.

nuance n. *nuances of feeling:* subtle change, variation, nice distinction, nicety, shade, subtlety, refinement, modulation, fineness.

nucleus n. *Golfers make up the nucleus of the group:* core, nub, heart, kernel, center, pith.
Ant. exterior, outer shell.

nude adj. *a nude statue:* naked, bare, bared, unclad, undressed, stripped, exposed, unclothed; unadorned, uncovered; without a stitch; in one's birthday suit.
Ant. clothed, covered, dressed, clad.

nudge v. *She nudged me at all the funny lines:* elbow, poke, jab; bump, jostle, jolt, push, shove.

nugatory adj. *of nugatory value:* inconsequential, trifling, piddling, paltry; worthless, useless, valueless, profitless.
Ant. valuable, useful; profitable.

nuisance n. *That noisy fan is a nuisance:* annoyance, bother, pest, irritation, aggravation; inconvenience, worry, scourge, handicap, misfortune; plague, pestilence, blight, trouble, torment, burden.
Ant. pleasure, delight, satisfaction, blessing.

null adj. *The contract is null:* invalid, inoperative, void, nonexistent, null and void; no good.
Ant. valid, lawful, binding.

nullify v. *Such an antiquated law should be nullified:* repeal, abrogate, void, cancel, annul, abolish; set aside, revoke, rescind, invalidate.
Ant. enact, legislate, ratify, confirm.

numb adj. *My hands are numb from the cold:* unfeeling, insensate, benumbed, insensible; deadened, anesthetized, frozen.

number n. 1 *Assign a number to each box:* numeral, figure, integer, cipher, digit; amount, quantity. 2 *a large number of people:* quantity, multitude, company, group, crowd, mob, bunch, herd, swarm; abundance, indeterminate number; a good many. —v. 3 *Number the pages in sequence:* give a number to, enumerate; total.
Ant. 2 scarcity, paucity; want, lack.

numberless adj. *Numberless children were*

at the amusement park: countless, innumerable, numerous, multitudinous, myriad, uncountable, uncounted, unnumbered.

Ant. few, scarcely any, a couple of.

numeral *n. the numerals on a clock:* number, cipher, digit, integer.

numerous *adj. We received numerous gifts:* many, in profusion, abundant, myriad, a multitude of, multitudinous.

Ant. few, scarcely any, not many.

numskull Also **numbskull** *n. Slang The numskull didn't even know the alphabet!:* dunce, ninny, blockhead, dolt, half-wit, knucklehead, dummy, dimwit, nitwit, idiot, imbecile, chowderhead, muttonhead, fool, simpleton, dope, lunkhead, nincompoop.

nuptial *adj. a nuptial ceremony:* matrimonial, marital; conjugal, connubial; wedding.

nuptials *n.pl. The nuptials were held in the bride's home:* wedding, marriage, marriage ceremony, change of vows.

nurse *n. 1 The children were left with their nurse: (variously)* trained nurse, practical nurse, registered nurse, private nurse, public health nurse; governess, nanny, nursemaid. —*v. 2 I nursed him back to health:* attend, care for, minister to, attend to; doctor, treat, remedy. **3** *The cat nursed her kittens:* suckle, feed at the breast, give suck to. **4** *He's been nursing a grudge for weeks:* keep in mind, harbor, nurture; encourage, foster.

nurture *v. 1 The book told us how to nurture the puppy:* feed, nourish; tend, sustain, strengthen. **2** *to nurture a child's mind:* develop, prepare, cultivate, school, educate, teach, instruct; bring up, rear, raise.

Ant. **2** neglect, slight; disregard, ignore.

nut *n. 1 a bowl of nuts:* edible kernel, nutmeat; seed, stone, pit. **2** *I'm a nut about model airplanes:* enthusiast, fanatic, devotee, zealot, fan, buff, aficionado. **3** *That nut should be locked up!:* eccentric, crackpot, screwball, oddball; madman, lunatic, maniac, psychopath.

nutriment *n. a synthetic nutriment for space trips:* food, nourishment, foodstuff; nutrition, nutrient, sustenance, provisions, provender, feed, forage, fodder, fare.

nutrition *n. A balanced diet gives one proper nutrition:* food, nourishment, nutriment, sustenance.

nutritious *adj. The diet is nutritious:* nourishing, nutritive; wholesome, sustaining.

nuts *adj. You must be nuts to lend him money:* crazy, insane; *British* mad, unbalanced, cracked, demented; *Slang* dotty, loony, bananas.

nutty *adj. a nutty scheme to make wire shoelaces:* foolish, crackbrained, inane, lunatic, harebrained, silly; *Slang* loony, dotty.

nuzzle *v. She nuzzled the baby:* cuddle, coddle, snuggle, nestle, caress, embrace, fondle; pet, kiss.

O

oaf *n. That oaf built it backwards!:* dolt, lout, fool, numskull, blockhead, dunce, simpleton, ninny, nitwit, clod, ignoramus, nincompoop, moron, idiot, imbecile, half-wit, sap, dope, dummy.

Ant. genius, intellectual, sage.

oasis *n. 1 an oasis in the desert:* watering place, water hole; fertile area, green spot. **2** *The library was an oasis of quiet:* haven, refuge, sanctum, sanctuary, retreat, shelter.

Ant. **1** desert, arid region.

oath *n. 1 Every U.S. President takes an oath to uphold the Constitution:* vow, avowal, pledge, affirmation, attestation; declaration. **2** *He let out a stream of oaths when he hit his thumb with the hammer:* curse, curse word, profanity, blasphemy, obscenity, expletive, *Informal* cuss word, swear word.

Ant. **2** benediction, blessing; prayer.

obdurate *adj. 1 She was obdurate in refusing to eat:* stubborn, obstinate, unyielding, inflexible, adamant, immovable; headstrong, pigheaded, mulish, bullheaded; unmanageable, uncontrollable, ungovernable. **2** *The tyrant was obdurate in his treatment of prisoners:* unmoved, unfeeling, harsh, merciless, unmerciful, unpitying, pitiless, unsympathetic, uncompassionate, unsparing, hardened, cruel, hardhearted.

Ant. **1** obedient, compliant, manageable, tractable. **2** compassionate, sympathetic, merciful, relenting, softhearted.

obedience *n. The dog was taught obedience:* compliance, dutifulness, submissiveness, submission, subservience, docility, obeisance, deference, yielding, subjection; allegiance; conformability, compliance, accordance.

obedient *adj. an obedient child:* obeying, dutiful, compliant, submissive, yielding, docile; faithful, loyal, devoted; respectful, obeisant, tractable.

Ant. disobedient, disobeying, insubordinate, rebellious; recalcitrant, intractable, unruly, obstinate.

obeisance *n. Kings expect obeisance from subjects:* bow, curtsy, kneeling, genuflection, prostration; homage, deference, respect, veneration, reverence; obedience, humility, humbleness, self-abasement; fealty, allegiance.

Ant. disrespect, irreverence; disloyalty.

obese *adj. Obese people often have low rates of metabolism:* fat, overweight, corpulent, heavy, stout, tubby, pudgy, plump, chubby, portly.

Ant. skinny, thin, slim, slender, scrawny, gaunt.

obey *v. to obey the law:* comply with, be ruled by, follow orders, submit to, respect, observe, abide by, conform to, be governed by, mind, heed.

Ant. disobey, defy, revolt, rebel, resist.

object *v.* 1 *Mother objects to smoking:* be averse, take exception, disapprove of, oppose, protest, look askance at, frown on; dislike, abhor, abominate; criticize, denounce, find fault with. —*n.* 2 *a bright moving object:* thing, article, body, form, phenomenon; device, gadget, contrivance. 3 *You have been the object of much criticism:* subject, target, recipient, victim, butt, quarry. 4 *What is the object of your research?:* aim, goal, purpose, point, intent, intention, objective, end, target, mission; significance, sense, meaning, motive, incentive, inducement.

Ant. 1 approve, welcome; concur, consent, acquiesce, accede; applaud, laud, admire.

objection *n.* 1 *Father's objection was that the trip was too expensive:* complaint, criticism, opposing reason, counterargument, protest. 2 *I kept the dog despite my sister's objection:* disapproval, opposition, disagreement, reservation, disapprobation.

Ant. 2 approval, consent, agreement.

objectionable *adj. objectionable behavior:* unacceptable, intolerable, disagreeable, unpleasant, displeasing, inappropriate, unseemly; offensive, obnoxious, vile, odious, revolting, disgusting, abhorrent, loathsome, despicable, distasteful.

Ant. acceptable, agreeable, pleasant, pleasing, appropriate, seemly.

objective *adj.* 1 *objective criticism:* impartial, unprejudiced, detached, impersonal, unbiased, fair, just, open-minded, disinter-

ested. —*n.* 2 *Her objective is to get a college education:* aim, goal, purpose, object, intent, intention, design, end, mission.

Ant. 1 subjective, personal, biased, prejudiced.

obligation *n.* 1 *an obligation to support one's parents:* duty, responsibility, a favor owed, debt, liability, constraint, accountability. 2 *The manufacturer has not fulfilled the terms of his obligation:* agreement, contract, compact, bond, commitment, pledge, promise, oath, word, understanding.

obligatory *adj. Paying taxes is obligatory:* compulsory, mandatory, binding, required, enforced, requisite, necessary.

Ant. noncompulsory, voluntary.

oblige *v.* 1 *The will obliges the heirs to live in the family mansion:* obligate, require, demand of, necessitate; make, impel, compel, force, coerce. 2 *The pianist obliged the guests with a selection:* accommodate, favor, do a favor for; aid, assist, serve.

Ant. 1 free, liberate, release. 2 disoblige, inconvenience.

obliging *adj. an obliging clerk:* accommodating, helpful, cooperative, solicitous; considerate, friendly, amiable, agreeable; complaisant, courteous, gracious.

Ant. disobliging, unaccommodating, uncooperative, unhelpful; discourteous, surly.

oblique *adj.* 1 *an oblique line:* diagonal, slanting, slanted, inclined, sloping, tilted, aslant. 2 *an oblique reference to the queen:* indirect, masked, veiled, sly, devious, furtive, implied, hinted, suggested, allusive.

Ant. 1 vertical; horizontal. 2 direct, open, forthright, blunt, obvious.

obliterate *v.* 1 *The hurricane obliterated the town:* annihilate, eradicate, destroy, raze, level, wipe out. 2 *Obliterate the incident from your mind:* erase, expunge, wipe out, delete, abolish; write over, strike over, blot out.

Ant. 1 construct, create, raise up. 2 write; keep.

oblivion *n.* 1 *The writer is now relegated to oblivion:* obscurity, limbo, a forgotten state, disregard, insignificance. 2 *Nonreligious people believe that death brings complete oblivion:* nothingness, nonexistence, the void; forgetfulness, obliviousness, unconcern, unconsciousness, insensibility.

Ant. 1 fame, celebrity, immortality. 2 being, existence, life.

oblivious *adj. We were oblivious to the noise:* unaware of, unconscious of, undiscerning, insensible, unobservant; unmindful, disregardful, heedless, of, unconcerned.

Ant. aware, conscious, heedful.

obnoxious *adj. She's charming, but he's obnoxious:* offensive, objectionable, disagreeable, unpleasant, nasty, repugnant, odious, revolting, disgusting, despicable, abhorrent, repellent, detestable; unseemly, inappropriate, insufferable.
Ant. agreeable, pleasing, charming, likable, enchanting; appropriate, seemly, in good taste.

obscene *adj. The court must decide whether the movie is obscene:* indecent, morally offensive, pornographic; prurient, lewd, vulgar, scatological, dirty, filthy.
Ant. decent, modest, chaste, clean.

obscenity *n. The speech was full of obscenities:* vulgarity, profanity, obscene expression, taboo word, four-letter word, dirty word.

obscure *adj.* **1** *The point of the speech was obscure:* unclear, hidden, vague, uncertain, indefinite, inscrutable, unfathomable, puzzling, perplexing, enigmatic, confusing, confused. **2** *an obscure little town:* unknown, little known, nameless, unheard of, forgotten, unnoted, insignificant, inconsequential, unimportant, inconspicuous. **3** *An obscure figure could be seen through the fog:* indistinct, faint, dim, shadowy, murky; unlighted, unilluminated. *—v.* **4** *The building obscured the hills behind:* hide, conceal, cover, block; blur, cloud, befog; shroud, curtain, cloak, screen; mask, disguise; darken.
Ant. **1** clear, plain, transparent, obvious, evident, manifest, explicit. **2** well-known, famous, prominent; important, major. **3** distinct, well-defined. **4** reveal, disclose, show.

obsequious *adj. an obsequious underling:* servile, fawning, toadying, sycophantic, subservient, deferential, slavish, cringing, cowering.
Ant. domineering, overbearing, lordly, arrogant, brash, assertive, forceful.

observance *n.* **1** *Observance of the rules is important:* obeying, following, compliance, adherence, attention, heeding, observation. **2** *a religious observance:* ceremonial, commemoration, celebration, memorialization; ceremony, ritual, rite, custom, practice, formality.
Ant. **1** nonobservance, disobeying, noncompliance.

observant *adj. Be observant for danger:* watchful, vigilant, alert, on the lookout, careful; mindful, attentive, aware, heedful.
Ant. unobservant, inattentive, oblivious; unmindful, heedless.

observation *n.* **1** *the observation of distant stars. No clue escaped the detective's observation:* observing, watching, viewing, seeing, beholding, eyeing, inspection, detection, examination, surveillance, scrutiny, survey; notice, attention, watchfulness. **2** *I wrote down his observations. The speaker made some witty observations:* finding, description, diagnosis; remark, comment, statement, reflection, view, opinion, judgment, assertion.

observe *v.* **1** *We observed the ship leaving the harbor. Did you observe anything suspicious?:* see, watch, view, behold, peer at, catch sight of, stare at, make out, inspect, survey, glimpse, espy, spot, ogle, eye; notice, detect, perceive, mark, heed. **2** *She observed that we were late:* remark, comment, state, say, mention. **3** *Observe the rules:* obey, comply with, conform to, follow, heed, abide by, adhere to, keep, be guided by, defer to, carry out, respect. **4** *How many holidays do we observe?:* celebrate, commemorate, honor; sanctify, consecrate, solemnize; recognize, acknowledge.
Ant. **3** disobey, disregard, neglect. **4** profane.

obsessed *adj. He was obsessed with winning the race:* possessed, beset, dominated, controlled, having a fixation, haunted, overwhelmingly desirous, overwhelmingly fearful.

obsession *n. Cars are an obsession with him:* overwhelming fear, all-encompassing desire, fixation, fixed idea, mania, phobia, neurotic conviction, ruling passion, monomania; preoccupation, infatuation, craze.

obsolescent *adj. Propeller planes are obsolescent:* becoming obsolete, becoming out-of-date, disappearing, passing out of use, dying out.

obsolete *adj. Bloomers are obsolete:* out-of-date, out of fashion, out of use; old-fashioned, outdated, passé, outmoded, antiquated, bygone.
Ant. new, modern, modern, up-to-date, fashionable, in vogue.

obstacle *n. A stone fence was the last obstacle. Lack of education is an obstacle to success:* barrier, barricade, hurdle; impediment, obstruction, hindrance, stumbling block, limitation, restriction; stoppage, check, bar, block, snag, catch, problem, difficulty.
Ant. help, aid, benefit, furtherance.

obstinate *adj. We were too obstinate to leave when the flood began:* stubborn, obdurate, unyielding, unbending, inflexible, self-willed, headstrong, mulish, pigheaded.
Ant. compliant, yielding, pliant, flexible.

obstreperous *adj. An obstreperous child requires discipline:* unruly, uncontrolled, disobedient, unmanageable, ungovernable, uncontrollable; noisy, loud, boisterous.

Ant. obedient, well-behaved, manageable, tractable, docile; quiet.

obstruct *v.* 1 *A rock obstructed the road:* barricade, block, blockade, bar, shut off, stop, dam up, choke off, close, plug up; hide. 2 *Lack of funds obstructed the project:* delay, hinder, impede, curb, stall, check, hobble, restrict, limit; arrest, frustrate, thwart, throttle.

Ant. 1 unblock, clear, open. 2 help, aid, benefit, further, advance, spur, accelerate.

obstruction *n. There's an obstruction in the drainpipe:* obstacle, barrier, blockage, block, stoppage, barricade, impediment, hindrance.

Ant. clearing, opening; freeing, unblocking.

obtain *v.* 1 *How does one obtain a hunting license?:* acquire, get, attain, secure, procure, come by; receive, earn, achieve. 2 *The same rules obtain for everyone:* be in force, hold, prevail, exist, be the case.

Ant. 1 lose, relinquish, surrender.

obtrusive *adj.* 1 *It's hard to be polite to obtrusive people:* interfering, intruding, intrusive, meddlesome, meddling, prying; forward, presumptuous, impertinent, familiar. 2 *The red chair is too obtrusive:* prominent, conspicuous, outstanding, sticking out; protruding, projecting, bulging, protuberant.

Ant. 1, 2 unobtrusive. 2 inconspicuous.

obtuse *adj.* 1 *an obtuse angle:* not sharp, not pointed; blunt, blunted, dull. 2 *She's so obtuse she never gets the joke:* dull, slow, slow-witted, thick, stupid, simple; uncomprehending, insensitive, imperceptive.

Ant. 1 acute; sharp, pointed. 2 intelligent, bright, clever, quick-witted, sharp.

obvious *adj. Her displeasure was obvious:* evident, self-evident, clear, plain, unmistakable, discernible, distinct, palpable, conspicuous, apparent, patent, manifest, undeniable, striking; visible, perceptible, unconcealed, unhidden, undisguised, in plain sight.

Ant. concealed, hidden, obscure, unclear, indistinct, inconspicuous, unapparent, invisible.

occasion *n.* 1 *The country's bicentennial was quite an occasion:* event, special event, important event, occurrence, happening, episode, situation, incident, advent, experience, adventure; affair, celebration. 2 *I want to take this occasion to thank you:* particular

time, opportunity, instance, circumstance, chance, opening. 3 *There was no occasion for such behavior:* reason, cause, justification, provocation, motive, motivation, ground, grounds, base, basis, explanation, rationale. —*v.* 4 *The remark occasioned a burst of applause:* cause, elicit, prompt, lead to, provoke, inspire.

occasional *adj. The weather was good except for an occasional shower:* sporadic, fitful, spasmodic, intermittent, random, irregular, scattered, infrequent, incidental.

Ant. constant, continual, continuous, incessant.

occasionally *adv. They occasionally stop by to see us:* at times, sometimes, from time to time, every now and then, once in a while; intermittently, sporadically, irregularly, fitfully.

Ant. constantly, continually, continuously, incessantly; often, frequently, habitually, generally, usually.

occult *adj. occult powers:* supernatural, magic, mystic, mystical; secret, mysterious, cabalistic, unrevealed.

occupancy *n. The hotel rates are for double occupancy:* tenancy, occupation, lodgment, habitation, habitancy, inhabitancy; possession, use.

occupant *n. The new occupants of the house will move in tomorrow:* dweller, householder, resident, tenant, inhabitant, occupier; lessee, renter, roomer, lodger.

occupation *n.* 1 *He gave his occupation as bus driver:* job, trade, business, line of work, line, profession, work; vocation, craft; employment, livelihood, living; calling, pursuit. 2 *the World War II German occupation of France:* military occupation, military control, subjugation, subjection, seizure, conquest.

occupy *v.* 1 *Business occupies my mind most of the time:* fill, engage, employ, busy, engross, absorb, concern. 2 *Enemy troops occupied the country:* take possession of, have control, hold, conquer, subjugate. 3 *The Smiths occupy the house on the corner. Is anyone occupying this seat?:* dwell in, reside in, lodge in, room in; sit in, use; be in, be on, be situated in.

Ant. 2 liberate, free. 3 vacate, leave; relinquish, give up.

occur *v.* 1 *When did the accident occur?:* happen, take place, come about, come to pass, befall, transpire, ensue. 2 *Tuberculosis occurs most often in damp climates:* appear, arise, turn up, emerge, develop, materialize, manifest itself, be met with. 3 *It didn't* *occur to me that you would object:* enter one's mind, cross one's mind, suggest itself.

occurrence *n. It was a strange occurrence:* happening, event, incident, instance, episode, business, transaction, situation, affair, occasion; emergence, unfolding, development, manifestation.

ocean *n. The ship crossed the ocean:* sea, high sea, deep, briny deep, main, water.

odd *adj.* 1 *What an odd shell!:* unusual, strange, queer, uncommon, unique, out of the ordinary, rare, peculiar, singular, curious, bizarre, freakish, outlandish. 2 *What shall I do with this odd sock?:* being one of a pair, unmatched, single; leftover, surplus, remaining. 3 *The youth did odd jobs:* various, sundry, miscellaneous; occasional, casual, irregular, sporadic, spasmodic.

Ant. 1 common, ordinary, usual, customary, typical, normal, unexceptional. 3 regular, steady, permanent, full time.

oddity *n. An egg with two yolks is an oddity:* rarity, phenomenon, curiosity, freak; strangeness, singularity, peculiarity, uniqueness, unusualness, freakishness; queerness, eccentricity, unnaturalness, abnormality.

odious *adj. The Nazi concentration camps were the most odious places in history:* evil, vile, abominable, despicable, contemptible, detestable, heinous, repulsive, repugnant, revolting, disgusting, loathsome, infamous; offensive, nasty, foul, sickening, monstrous, hideous.

Ant. attractive, delightful, charming, pleasing, pleasant.

odor *n. the odor of freshly roasted coffee. What's that awful odor?:* smell, aroma; scent, fragrance, perfume, essence, bouquet; stench, stink.

off-color *adj. off-color jokes:* risqué, racy, spicy, indelicate, earthy, blue, suggestive, naughty, improper, indecent.

offend *v.* 1 *I apologized for having offended her:* affront, displease, insult, wound, disgust, anger, vex, aggravate, nettle, miff. 2 *She prayed that she would never offend:* sin, err, transgress, misbehave, fall from grace.

Ant. 1 please, delight; soothe, calm.

offense *n.* 1 *For what offense was he arrested?:* crime, misdeed, breach of conduct, infraction, violation; sin, transgression, lapse, slip, shortcoming; outrage, enormity, atrocity. 2 *I meant no offense:* insult, affront, disrespect, rudeness, harm, indignity. 3 *Our football team has the best offense:* offensive, attack, assault, aggression; offensive unit.

Ant. 1 innocence. 3 defense, resistance.

offensive *adj.* 1 *His language was offensive:* insulting, disrespectful, rude, abusive, unmannerly; objectionable, obnoxious, disgusting, unpleasant, disagreeable, distasteful; revolting, nasty, horrid, hideous, repulsive, loathsome, repugnant, abhorrent, detestable, sickening, nauseating. 2 *offensive troops:* attacking, attack, assault, assaulting, assailing; belligerent, aggressive. —*n.* 3 *The team took the offensive:* offense, attack, assault, aggression.

Ant. 1 polite, courteous, respectful; civil, pleasing, pleasant, agreeable. 2 defensive, defending. 3 defense, defensive.

offer *v.* 1 *She offered us some cookies:* proffer, tender, present, bestow on, bestow. 2 *May I offer a suggestion?:* propose, submit, render, advance, suggest, put forth, put forward, propound, volunteer, hold out, extend. —*n.* 3 *Shall I accept the offer to help?:* proposition, proposal, offering; bid, invitation, overture, suggestion.

Ant. 1, 2 withhold, deny; accept, take, receive. 3 acceptance; refusal, denial.

offhand Also **offhanded** *adj.* 1 *an offhand remark:* impromptu, extemporaneous, adlib, off-the-cuff, improvised, unpremeditated, unstudied, unprepared, unplanned, unrehearsed, spontaneous, chance, casual. 2 *He works in an offhand manner:* casual, careless, thoughtless, haphazard, nonchalant, cavalier.

Ant. 1 prepared, premeditated, studied. 2 responsible, careful, thoughtful.

office *n.* 1 *She was elected to the office of mayor:* position, post, job, capacity, function, occupation, commission, appointment. 2 usually **offices** *Did he appreciate your good offices?:* favor, service, help, assistance; duty, trust, function, task.

officer *n.* 1 *company officers:* official, executive, head, administrator, officeholder, director. 2 *a traffic officer:* policeman, police officer, officer of the law, law officer; patrolman, constable, cop.

official *n.* 1 *a company official. a public official:* officeholder, officer, executive, director, manager, administrator; functionary, dignitary, agent; administrative head. —*adj.* 2 *official duties. an official inquiry:* formal, administrative, vested; authorized, approved, sanctioned, authoritative, certified, accredited, licensed.

Ant. 1 underling, employee. 2 unofficial, unauthorized; informal.

officiate *v. The judge officiated at the wedding:* preside, head, superintend, be in charge of; moderate, emcee, chair, lead, regulate, supervise.

officious *adj. It's hard to be a manager with-*

out being officious: obtrusive, intrusive, interfering, meddlesome, meddling, prying; overbearing, domineering, self-important, self-assertive, pompous, patronizing.

offset *v. Inflation offset the pay raise:* counteract, countervail, counterweight, counterbalance, balance; cancel out, neutralize, equalize.

offspring *n. The couple's offspring are wrangling over the estate:* children, progeny, descendants, posterity, issue; child, descendant, young, brood, litter.

often *adv. It rains often this time of year:* frequently, regularly, repeatedly, habitually, much, time and again; generally, usually, customarily, commonly, ofttimes.
Ant. never; rarely, seldom, infrequently, occasionally, hardly ever.

ogle *v. The children ogled the cookies:* gaze at with desire; stare at, gape at, gawk at, eye, give the eye, give the once-over.

ogre *Fem.* **ogress** *n.* 1 *stories about fearful ogres:* man-eating giant, monster, fiend, brute; bugbear, bogeyman. 2 *The new supervisor is a real ogre:* tyrant, martinet, dictator, despot, slave driver.

oily *adj. His oily manner repelled us:* unctuous, smarmy, ingratiating, servile, fawning.

ointment *n. an ointment for burns:* unguent, balm, salve, emollient, liniment, lotion.

old *adj.* 1 *She's forty years old:* of age 2 *He's an old man now. What an old car!:* elderly, aged; antiquated, ancient, vintage, timeworn, antique, old-fashioned, out-of-date, outdated. 3 *She and I are old friends:* of long standing, long established, time-honored, traditional, age-old; of the past, from the past, bygone. 4 *old clothes:* worn-out, outworn, decrepit, dilapidated, used, time-worn; crumbling, tumbledown; familiar, hackneyed.
Ant. 2–4 new, recent, current, late. 2 young, immature. 4 brand-new, modern, modish, fashionable.

old-fashioned *adj.* 1 *an old-fashioned phone:* out-of-date, out of fashion, outmoded, unfashionable, behind the times, out of style, antiquated, antique, outdated. 2 *old-fashioned values:* traditional; time-honored, long-standing.
Ant. 1 modern, up-to-date, fashionable, in vogue, up-to-the-minute, chic.

omen *n. a good omen:* augury, sign, token, portent, auspice; indication, harbinger, herald, precursor, presage; foreboding, warning.

ominous *adj. ominous black clouds:* threatening, menacing, foreboding, sinister, disquieting, portentous, unpromising, unpropitious, unfavorable, inauspicious, ill-omened.
Ant. promising, favorable, propitious, auspicious.

omission *n. The omission was an oversight:* leaving out, exclusion, noninclusion, exception; something omitted, exclusion, neglected item.
Ant. inclusion; addition.

omit *v.* 1 *Be sure not to omit anyone's name:* leave out, exclude, except, preclude; delete, drop, excerpt, cut. 2 *You omitted telling me:* neglect, fail, overlook, ignore, bypass.
Ant. 1 include, put in, add. 2 remember.

omnipotent *adj. an omnipotent deity:* all-powerful, almighty, supreme.

omniscient *adj. No one is omniscient:* all-knowing, all-seeing, having infinite knowledge, all-wise.
Ant. ignorant, unknowing, unaware.

once *adv.* 1 *Once dinosaurs walked the earth:* formerly, at one time, previously, in times past, once upon a time, in other days, years ago; heretofore, hitherto. 2 *We've been to Europe once:* one time, on one occasion.
Ant. 1 in future, in time to come, hereafter. 2 never; repeatedly, frequently, often.

oncoming *adj. an oncoming train:* approaching, advancing, onrushing, nearing, bearing down.
Ant. receding, retreating.

one *adj.* 1 *I put one piece on each plate. I'm the one who can do it:* single, individual, a, an, sole, lone, solitary; only, singular, unique; entire, whole, complete. —*pron.* 2 *One never knows:* a person, an individual, a man, a human being, a creature, somebody, someone, you, a body, a mortal, a thing.

onerous *adj. an onerous task:* oppressive, burdensome, arduous, not easy to bear; distressing, painful, wearisome, exhausting, demanding, grievous.
Ant. easy, simple; trivial, trifling.

ongoing *adj. ongoing care:* continuing, proceeding, forward-moving, uninterrupted, unremitting, unending; lasting, enduring.
Ant. temporary, sporadic, provisional.

onlooker *n. Onlookers crowded the sidewalk:* spectator, observer, eyewitness, watcher, bystander.

only *adv.* 1 *Only Jennifer was left:* alone, by oneself, by itself, solely, exclusively, individually, singly. 2 *We see them only on Fridays:* merely, just, simply, purely; barely, at least. —*adj.* 3 *She's the only woman to be mayor of this town:* lone, sole, solitary, individual, single, singular, exclusive, unique, alone, one and only.
Ant. 3 many, several, numerous.

onrush *n. Residents fled the onrush of the*

flood: onset, torrent, attack, assault, charge, avalanche, cascade, wave, tide, flow, current, surge.

onset *n.* 1 *at the onset of the century:* start, beginning, outset, commencement, inauguration, initiation, outbreak; inception, genesis, birth, founding. 2 *The bombardment began the final onset:* attack, assault, onslaught, offensive, offense, raid, push, sally, charge, incursion, invasion.

Ant. 1 end, close, conclusion. 2 defense, resistance.

onslaught *n. an enemy onslaught:* attack, assault, charge, push, raid, foray, sally, offensive, offensive, invasion, incursion, aggression.

Ant. defense, resistance.

onus *n. the onus of proving the suspect's guilt:* burden, responsibility, obligation; weight, load, strain, liability, duty.

onward *adv.* Also **onwards** 1 *The ship sailed onward:* forward, ahead, toward the front, toward a goal, along, on the way. —*adj.* 2 *the ship's onward movement:* forward, frontward, advancing, progressive, ongoing.

Ant. 1, 2 backward. 1 backwards; aback.

ooze *v.* 1 *Water oozed from the pipe:* seep, exude, trickle, dribble, drip, leak, bleed, sweat. —*n.* 2 *The lake bed was covered with ooze:* mud, slime, sludge, silt, muck, mire, alluvium; secretion, seepage, leakage.

Ant. 1 gush, stream, cascade, pour.

opaque *adj.* 1 *Varnish is transparent, paint is opaque:* nontransparent, nontranslucent, impenetrable to light. 2 *The report was opaque:* hard to understand, unclear, impenetrable, obscure, abstruse, unintelligible, unfathomable.

Ant. 1, 2 clear. 1 transparent, translucent. 2 lucid, intelligible, comprehensible.

open *adj.* 1 *an open window. an open boat. with open arms:* not shut, unshut, not closed, unclosed, ajar; uncovered, unenclosed, unfastened, unlocked; extended, unfolded. 2 *the open sea. open country:* expansive, wide, unbounded, unfenced, unobstructed, uncluttered; uncrowded, uninhabited. 3 *The store is open till 5:* doing business, open for business, open to the public, accessible. 4 *She's a very open person:* open-hearted, forthright, sincere, natural, straightforward, honest, candid, outgoing, frank, direct. 5 *an open mind:* impartial, objective, unprejudiced, unbiased, unbigoted, disinterested; receptive, responsive. —*v.* 6 *Please open the door. Open the book to page 78:* unclose, set ajar, move aside, unlock, unfasten, unbar; unfold, expand, lay open; clear, unblock. 7 *We'll open the meet-*

ing at 8. begin, commence, start initiate, launch, embark upon; institute, found, undertake, establish. 8 *What time does the building open?:* open to the public, become available for use, permit access, receive customers, start business.

Ant. 1, 3 closed. 6–8 close. 1 shut; covered, enclosed, fastened, locked. 2 shut in, obstructed, crowded. 5 prejudiced, biased, bigoted; stubborn, obdurate. 6 shut; lock, fasten, bar; fold. 7 end, conclude, finish.

open-handed *adj. The museum needs open-handed patrons:* generous, magnanimous, bountiful, liberal, lavish.

Ant. stingy, closefisted, miserly.

opening *n.* 1 *an opening in the screen:* hole, break, breach, gap, aperture, rent, rift, slit, crack, fissure, gash, slot, tear, vent, chink. 2 *The opening of the highway is scheduled for next year. The book's opening is dull:* inauguration, initiation, launching, installation; beginning, start, commencement; first part, prelude, overture, introduction. 3 *We have an opening for a file clerk:* job opening, vacancy, place; opportunity, possibility, chance, occasion.

Ant. 1 obstruction, blockage. 2 closing, end, conclusion, finish, finale.

open-mouthed *adj. We stared in openmouthed wonder:* dumbfounded, wide-eyed, astonished, amazed, flabbergasted, agape, surprised, confounded, thunderstruck, spellbound, awed, awestruck, stupefied.

Ant. bored, indifferent, apathetic.

operate *v.* 1 *Do you know how this toaster operates? to operate a business:* work, go, function, run, behave, perform; manage, oversee, be in charge of. 2 *The doctor wants to operate:* perform surgery, perform an operation.

operation *n.* 1 *a printing press in operation. My time is devoted to the operation of the business:* action, performance, operating, running, working; conduct, procedure, activity, pursuit; supervision, management, overseeing. 2 *The plan is now in operation:* action, effect, force, exertion; agency, instrumentality. 3 *The heart operation was a complete success:* surgery.

opiate *n. an opiate to deaden the pain:* sedative, hypnotic, narcotic, soporific, tranquilizer, somnifacient, anodyne, depressant, painkiller, palliative.

Ant. stimulant, pep pill.

opine *v. He opined that we were in for a cold winter:* think, say, state, suggest, volunteer, conjecture, surmise, allow, reckon, offer, guess, imagine, speculate, conclude, presume, believe.

opinion n. It's just my opinion: belief, estimate, estimation, assessment, evaluation, judgment, view, impression; conviction, persuasion, notion, conclusion, surmise, thinking, conjecture, speculation.

opinionated adj. He's too opinionated to consider other people's views: closed-minded, stubborn, bullheaded, obstinate, obdurate, headstrong, inflexible, unyielding, pigheaded, dogmatic, uncompromising.

Ant. open-minded, broad-minded; receptive, responsive.

opponent n. The candidate criticized her opponent's record: opposition, rival, competitor, adversary, contender; foe, enemy, disputant.

Ant. ally, colleague, teammate, helper, accomplice, cohort; friend, supporter.

opportune adj. Now would be an opportune time to buy a house: timely, well-timed, advantageous, favorable, appropriate, suitable, fitting, apt, seasonable, proper, propitious, auspicious, convenient, fortunate, felicitous.

Ant. inopportune, unfavorable, inappropriate, unsuitable, unseasonable, inconvenient, untimely.

opportunity n. an opportunity to learn French. I'd like to take this opportunity to thank everyone: chance, good chance, favorable time, time; occasion, moment, means, situation, opening.

oppose v. We opposed the project: act in opposition to, speak against, fight, combat, battle, contest, contend against, resist, be set against, take a stand against.

Ant. support, aid, help, champion, advance, advocate.

opposite adj. 1 the opposite side of the street. What's on the opposite side of this coin?: facing, opposed, other; reverse, converse. 2 We have opposite views: opposing, opposed, conflicting, differing, contradictory, contrary; antithetical, adverse; counter.

Ant. 1 same. 2 like, identical, similar, agreeing, corresponding, parallel.

opposition n. 1 I don't understand your opposition to the plan: resistance, contention against, disagreement, disapproval, rejection, aversion, antagonism, hostility, enmity. 2 The opposition won: opponent, competitor, rival, adversary, contender, antagonist, foe, enemy, other side.

Ant. 1 support, backing, approval, help, assistance, promotion. 2 supporter, backer; ally, colleague.

oppress v. 1 She was oppressed by woes: trouble, worry, burden, weigh down; depress, dispirit, dishearten, deject; sadden, pain, grieve, sorrow. 2 The tyrant oppressed the people: tyrannize, persecute, treat harshly, abuse, maltreat.

Ant. 1 unburden, relieve; cheer, hearten, encourage.

oppressive adj. 1 The dictator was extremely oppressive: tyrannical, despotic, repressive; cruel, harsh, severe, hardhearted. 2 Obligations are often oppressive. oppressive heat: burdensome, onerous, wearing, trying, troublesome, worrisome, vexing, depressing, discouraging; painful, grievous; uncomfortable, distressing.

Ant. 1 humane, kind, compassionate, benevolent. 2 soothing, relieving; joyful, pleasant, pleasing, comfortable.

opt v. I opt for the blue sedan: choose, select, pick, decide on, elect, vote for, prefer, take, settle on, incline toward, tend toward.

Ant. reject, turn down, decide against.

optimism n. cheery optimism: confidence, hopeful outlook, hoping for the best, hopefulness, bright outlook, encouragement, cheerfulness, trust in the future.

Ant. pessimism, cynicism.

optimistic adj. 1 She's optimistic about the company's future: confident, disposed to take a favorable view, viewed favorably, hopeful, heartened, enthusiastic, encouraged, happily expectant. 2 There are optimistic signs for peace: promising, auspicious, propitious, favorable, encouraging, heartening, full of promise.

Ant. 1, 2 pessimistic. 1 cynical; despairing, depressed, discouraged, glum. 2 unpromising, inauspicious, unfavorable, discouraging.

optimum n. 1 Conditions are at the optimum: ideal, peak, height, best point, most desirable, perfect degree, crest, zenith, perfection, acme. —adj. 2 The experiment was conducted under optimum conditions: ideal, best, perfect, most favorable; prime, choice, select, first-rate, first-class, flawless, faultless.

option n. 1 She has the option of entering graduate school or starting her career: choice, selection, election; preference, liking, predilection, pleasure, will. 2 The publisher has an option on the author's next book: first claim, right to buy, right of first refusal, privilege.

Ant. 1 coercion; requirement, obligation, necessity.

optional adj. Air conditioning is optional: left to one's choice, individually decided, elective, voluntary, nonobligatory, not required, volitional, unforced, discretionary;

available at additional cost; open; allowable.

Ant. mandatory, obligatory, required, compulsory.

opulence *n.* 1 *the opulence of the pharaohs:* great wealth, riches, affluence, prosperity; luxuries, lavishness. 2 *The opulence of the food overwhelmed us:* abundance, profusion, copiousness, plenty, plentitude, bounty; elegance, lavishness, richness, sumptuousness.

Ant. 1 poverty, indigence, privation. 2 scarcity, scarceness, paucity, scantiness, dearth.

oracle *n. The oracle prophesied famine:* prophet, seer, augur, soothsayer, clairvoyant, wizard, diviner; predictor, forecaster.

oral *adj.* 1 *Each student had to give an oral report:* spoken, vocal, uttered, articulated, voiced. 2 *an oral vaccine:* treating the mouth, of the mouth; swallowed, ingested.
Ant. 1 written; silent.

oration *n. a funeral oration:* address, speech, eulogy, talk; discourse, disquisition, declamation, monologue, sermon, lecture, panegyric.

orator *n. William Jennings Bryan was one of our best known orators:* speaker, elocutionist, rhetorician, declaimer, public speaker, speechmaker, lecturer; preacher, sermonizer.

oratory *n. The senator was known for oratory:* rhetoric, eloquence, declamation; grandiloquence, bombast, art of public speaking, speechmaking, speechifying, preaching.

orbit *n.* 1 *The satellite was launched into orbit:* course, track, trajectory, path, circuit, route. —*v.* 2 *The earth orbits the sun:* circle, revolve around, travel around.

orchestra *n. The orchestra played a symphony:* company of musicians, ensemble, band, chamber orchestra, symphony orchestra, philharmonic.

ordain *v.* 1 *He was ordained a priest:* confer holy orders upon, name, invest, frock, consecrate; appoint, commission, elect. 2 *The king ordained that all forests belonged to the crown:* decree, rule, pronounce, prescribe, determine, adjudge, order, dictate, command.
Ant. 1 unfrock, defrock. 2 revoke, rescind, annul, cancel; repeal, nullify, overrule.

ordeal *n. the ordeal of war:* nightmare, trial, harsh experience, trying experience, oppression, worry, trouble, burden, care, strain, stress, tribulation, misery, torment, distress, agony, suffering, anguish, afflic-

tion, pain; unhappiness, sorrow, grief, tragedy.
Ant. delight, joy, happiness, ease.

order *n.* 1 *Loyal troops obeyed the duke's orders:* command, dictate, decree, pronouncement, instruction, bidding, dictum. 2 *in alphabetical order:* arrangement, organization, classification, system, categorization, codification, grouping, neatness, tidiness, orderliness; form, structure, pattern, framework. 3 *to maintain order:* quiet, law and order, peace and quiet, silence, harmony, tranquillity; control, discipline. 4 *Fish are a lower order than birds. Her talent is of the highest order:* classification, class, category, division, kind, species, family, caste, station, sort, type; quality, caliber, standing, rank, status, degree, grade. 5 *a religious order:* society, sisterhood, brotherhood; organization, fraternity, sorority, guild, body, society, association, group, club, lodge, confederacy, company, federation. —*v.* 6 *She ordered the dog to sit:* command, bid, direct, instruct, charge, decree, dictate, enjoin. 7 *Let's order dessert:* request, call for, ask for, engage, reserve, contract for, agree to, authorize the purchase of.
Ant. 1 request, plea, entreaty; supplication. 2, 3 disorder, confusion. 6 plead, entreat, supplicate, beg.

orderly *adj.* 1 *Keep your closets orderly:* neat, tidy, shipshape, uncluttered, systematic, organized, methodical, classified. 2 *an orderly manner:* disciplined, restrained, controlled, well-behaved, quiet, well-mannered, proper, law-abiding.
Ant. 1, 2 disorderly. 1 messy, disorganized, cluttered. 2 undisciplined, chaotic, uncontrolled.

ordinance *n. a city ordinance:* law, rule, ruling, regulation, statute; decree, edict, canon, dictum, act, mandate.

ordinarily *adv. Ordinarily we eat at 7:* usually, generally, normally, customarily, commonly, as a rule, as a matter of course, routinely, in most instances, habitually, regularly.
Ant. rarely, infrequently, hardly ever.

ordinary *adj.* 1 *an ordinary day:* common, commonplace, usual, average, customary, standard, normal, everyday, routine, familiar, typical, conventional, traditional, unexceptional, run-of-the-mill. 2 *The movie is quite ordinary:* undistinguished, commonplace, mediocre, unimpressive, uninspired, unimaginative, pedestrian, run-of-the-mill, so-so; humdrum; unimportant, insignificant.
Ant. 1, 2 extraordinary, exceptional, unusual, uncommon, unique, unconven-

tional. 2 superior, impressive, imaginative, inspired; important, significant.

ordnance *n. the army's new ordnance:* artillery, cannon, field pieces; military weapons and equipment, arms, munitions, war matériel, armaments.

organic *adj.* 1 *organic compounds. organic gardening:* containing carbon; of living things, living, alive, animate; natural, nonsynthetic. 2 *an organic health problem:* of an organ, physiological, physical, anatomical, constitutional. 3 *Frank Lloyd Wright was praised for his organic architecture:* unified, ordered, harmonious, well-organized, designed.

Ant. 1–2 inorganic.

organism *n.* 1 *The amoeba is a simple organism:* living thing, creature, animal, plant, organic structure; bacterium, microorganism, cell. 2 *The army is a complex organism:* organized body, organization, system, whole, entity.

organization *n.* 1 *The organization of the business took two years:* formulation, forming, formation; assembly, coordination, arranging, structuring, constitution, making. 2 *the painting's organization of the shapes and colors:* arrangement, design, pattern, composition, grouping, ordering, harmony. 3 *a professional organization:* association, society, fraternity, federation, union, club, league, alliance, corps; business, establishment, firm, company, corporation, outfit.

Ant. 1 dissolution, disbanding, breakup. 2 disorganization.

organize *v.* 1 *Let's organize a debating society:* form, establish, originate, found, create, set up. 2 *I'm trying to organize these files:* arrange, systematize, make orderly, order, neaten, tidy; classify, coordinate, group.

Ant. 1 dissolve, disband. 2 disorganize, confuse, mess up.

orgy *n. It was a quiet party, not an orgy!:* wild revelry, wild party, wanton celebration, drunken festivities, debauch, saturnalia, bacchanalia, bacchanal.

orient *n.* 1 **the Orient** *We visited two countries in the Orient:* Asia; eastern Asia, the Eastern Hemisphere, the Far East. —*v.* 2 *to orient students to campus life:* accustom, familiarize, acclimate, make feel at home. 3 *You can orient yourself by remembering that the hill is due north:* locate, situate, set, find.

Ant. 1 the Occident; Europe, the Americas; the Western Hemisphere. 3 disorient, lose, confuse.

orientation *n.* 1 *New employees go through a period of orientation:* familiarization, acclimation, adjustment. 2 *The hikers lost their orientation:* sense of direction, direction; alignment, location, situation.

Ant. 1 confusion, bewilderment, perplexity.

orifice *n. the whale's breathing orifice:* opening, hole, cavity, aperture, slot, slit, gap, cleft, vent, entrance, passage, fissure; mouth, oral cavity; hollow, pocket, pit, socket.

origin *n.* 1 *The reporter traced the story back to its origin:* source, cause, basis, base, foundation, derivation, generator, originator, creator, producer, prime mover, spring, fountainhead. 2 *the origins of jazz:* beginning, birth, genesis, inception, commencement; emergence, evolution, early development, rise. 3 *of Scandinavian origin:* extraction, descent, ancestry, parentage, family, lineage, stock, strain, line; birth, nativity.

Ant. 1 end, finish, conclusion. 2 death, extinction.

original *adj.* 1 *the original capital of the United States. The original idea was good:* first, initial, earliest; basic, fundamental, essential, underlying, formative, germinal; aboriginal, primordial, primary, primal. 2 *an original design:* having originality, imaginative, creative, inventive, ingenious; novel, new, unique, unusual, different, extraordinary, singular; uncommon, atypical, unconventional, unorthodox. —*n.* 3 *This plans is the original.* prototype, earliest model, pattern, example, first copy.

Ant. 1 last, latest, final. 2 unoriginal, commonplace, usual, typical, conventional, ordinary, standard; banal, trite, old, derivative, borrowed, copied. 3 copy, reproduction.

originality *n. The design shows originality:* imagination, creativity, inventiveness, ingenuity, individuality, freshness, newness, uniqueness, unconventionality.

Ant. unoriginality, conventionality, banality, triteness, predictability.

originally *adv.* 1 *We are originally from Springfield:* by origin; by derivation, by birth. 2 *The dress was originally $40:* at first, initially, at the outset, in the beginning. 3 *The apartment is decorated quite originally:* imaginatively, creatively, inventively, uniquely, differently, unusually, unconventionally.

Ant. 2 finally, in the end. 3 conventionally, routinely, unimaginatively, predictably.

originate *v.* 1 *The creek originates in a spring:* begin, start, commence, emanate; arise, germinate, flow, issue, crop up, sprout, emerge, stem. 2 *She originated a new printing process:* create, invent, devise,

initiate, inaugurate, formulate, fabricate, conceive, design; found, establish, develop.
Ant. 1 end, conclude, terminate. 2 copy, imitate.

ornament *n.* 1 *ornaments for the Christmas tree:* decoration, adornment, trimming, embellishment, trim, frills, garnish; ornamentation, elaboration. —*v.* 2 *to ornament a dress with lace:* adorn, decorate, bedeck, festoon, trim, garnish, embellish, beautify.

ornate *adj. an ornate picture frame:* elaborate, lavish, fancy; showy, flowery, flashy, flamboyant, ostentatious; decorated, adorned, embellished.
Ant. simple, plain, unadorned, unembellished.

orthodox *adj.* 1 *orthodox beliefs:* traditional, established, accepted; official, approved. 2 *orthodox thinking:* conventional, traditional, customary, conformable, usual, routine, fixed, established, regular, ordinary, usual; narrow, circumscribed, limited.
Ant. 1, 2 unorthodox. 1 heretical, radical, heterodox, unconformable. 2 unconventional, unique, original, eccentric, nonconformist, independent.

oscillate *v.* 1 *The pendulum oscillated:* swing, alternate; pulsate, vibrate, pulse, seesaw. 2 *He's been oscillating between the two views:* waver, vacillate, fluctuate, vary, hem and haw, shilly-shally.

ostensible *adj. the ostensible head of the company:* titular, nominal, apparent, implied, presumable, outward, seeming, declared, professed, perceivable; pretended, assumed, feigned.
Ant. real, true, actual.

ostentatious *adj. The car is too ostentatious:* flaunting wealth, fond of display, showing off; grandiose, high-flown; conspicuous, pretentious, flamboyant, flashy, showy, gaudy, garish, loud.
Ant. modest, reserved, conservative, inconspicuous; simple, plain.

ostracize *v. After the scandal her old friends ostracized her:* shun, snub, avoid, refuse to associate with, reject, exclude, shut out.
Ant. welcome, accept, acknowledge.

other *adj.* 1 *I'll take one other suit on the trip:* additional, more, further, added, extra, supplementary. 2 *Doesn't this come in other colors? the other side of the story:* different, additional, more, dissimilar, unlike, contrasted, differentiated; opposite, contrary, alternate, remaining.

otherwise *adv.* 1 *Leave now; otherwise you'll be late:* if not, or else; on the other hand. 2 *I think otherwise:* differently, in opposition, in disagreement, contrarily, contrariwise. 3 *He's too pale; otherwise he's nice looking:* in other respects, excluding this, barring this, excepting this, apart from this.
Ant. 2 similarly, alike, correspondingly.

oust *v. The umpire ousted me from the game:* expel, eject, evict, remove, put out, throw out; dismiss, discharge, cashier, fire, unseat, sack.
Ant. admit, welcome; hire, employ, appoint.

ouster *n. the ouster of the prime minister:* ejection, overthrow, expulsion, dismissal, firing, discharge, eviction, removal, dislodgment.

outbreak *n. an outbreak of violence:* outburst, burst, eruption, explosion, outpouring, display; sudden appearance, rapid spread.
Ant. waning, ebbing, decrease, decline.

outburst *n. an outburst of anger:* burst, eruption, outbreak, explosion, outpouring, display, fulmination.
Ant. suppression, repression, stifling.

outcast *n.* 1 *The one-time star became an outcast:* exile, deportee, man *or* person without a country; pariah, castaway, outlaw, fugitive. —*adj.* 2 *The Salvation Army was a haven for outcast souls:* rejected, discarded, expelled, castaway, ousted, banished.

outcome *n. What was the outcome of your interview?:* result, consequence, effect, upshot, end; outgrowth.

outcry *n. the sentry's outcry. There was a great outcry among consumers when prices rose:* crying out, cry, cry of alarm, cry of distress, cry of protest; shout, scream, shriek, caterwauling, screech, yell, roar, bellow, whoop, yowl, yelp; clamor, uproar, commotion, noise, hue and cry, hullabaloo.
Ant. whisper, murmur; silence, calm.

outdo *v. No one can outdo her:* excel, surpass, best, outshine, exceed, better, top, beat, outstrip, outplay; defeat, worst, outwit.

outer *adj. the outer surface. the outer suburbs:* exterior, external, outward, outside, without; farther, farther out, remote, outlying, peripheral.
Ant. inner, interior, internal, inside, within; close-in, adjacent.

outfit *n.* 1 *a new outfit for Easter. a scuba diving outfit:* ensemble, costume, set of clothing; equipment, gear, paraphernalia, trappings, *Slang* rig. —*v.* 2 *The expedition was outfitted with the latest equipment:* equip, supply, furnish; dress, clothe, array.

outgoing *adj.* 1 *outgoing mail:* outbound, going out, outward bound; leaving, departing. 2 *A hostess should be outgoing:*

friendly, gregarious, convivial, genial, social, sociable, extroverted, warm, warmhearted.

Ant. 1 incoming, inbound, arriving. 2 austere, distant, reserved, withdrawn.

outgrowth *n. The investigation is an outgrowth of numerous complaints:* result, consequence, upshot, product, culmination, sequel, aftereffect, aftermath, offshoot.

outing *n. an outing at the beach:* excursion, expedition, trip, pleasure trip.

outlandish *adj. an outlandish hat:* preposterous, outrageous, odd, bizarre, fantastic, freakish, eccentric, queer, strange, curious, peculiar, unusual, unconventional, unheard-of, unparalleled.

Ant. commonplace, ordinary, routine, normal, standard, run-of-the-mill.

outlast *v. A good suit will outlast a cheap one:* outwear, outstay, survive, endure, prevail, persist, continue, hold out.

outlaw *n. 1 A posse tracked down the outlaws:* criminal, fugitive, felon, bandit, desperado; outcast. *—v.* 2 *to outlaw the sale of fireworks:* make unlawful, forbid, prohibit, ban, bar, proscribe, deny, disallow.

Ant. 2 legalize, permit, allow.

outlay *n. an outlay of several thousand dollars:* expenditure, spending; amount spent, payment, disbursement, expense.

Ant. profit, gain, income.

outlet *n. 1 Switzerland has no outlet to the sea:* opening, egress, passage, channel, way, avenue; exit; duct, conduit. 2 *The child needs an outlet for all that energy:* vent, means of expression, escape.

Ant. 1 entrance, ingress, entry.

outline *n. 1 We saw the outline of the deer against the trees:* profile, silhouette, contour, delineation, lineation; perimeter, periphery. 2 *Just tell me the outline of the story:* synopsis, summary, brief report, sketch, digest, abstract, review. *—v.* 3 *Outline the figure in red paint:* draw a line around, trace, delineate; diagram, sketch out, plot.

outlook *n. 1 The outlook from the mountain is breathtaking:* view, vista, sight, panorama, scene, picture. 2 *Your outlook is pessimistic:* attitude, frame of mind, point of view, viewpoint, view, perspective. 3 *The business outlook is good:* prospect, expectation, anticipation, forecast, assumption, presumption; probability.

outlying *adj. an outlying area of the town:* outer, exterior, peripheral; remote, distant, far-off, suburban, exurban.

Ant. central, inner; nearby, neighboring, adjacent.

output *n. The company has doubled its output:* production, yield, productivity, product, turnout.

outrage *n. 1 Bombing the church was an outrage:* atrocity, inhumane act, wanton violence, barbarity, iniquity, enormity, monstrosity, evil, wrong, desecration, profanation. 2 *Such a lie is an outrage:* insult, affront, indignity, expression of contempt, disrespect. *—v.* 3 *The remark outraged the audience:* anger, incense, enrage, infuriate, madden, exasperate; insult, affront, offend, shock.

Ant. 3 calm, soothe, pacify.

outrageous *adj. 1 an outrageous crime:* atrocious, vile, base, heinous, iniquitous, monstrous, barbarous, inhumane, inhuman, brutal, despicable, wicked, nefarious, horrifying, odious, reprehensible, unspeakable. 2 *an outrageous remark:* offensive, abusive, shameless, shocking, scandalous, disgraceful, insulting, insolent, rude, disrespectful, infuriating, maddening, exasperating. 3 *The cost was outrageous:* monstrous, extreme, unreasonable, preposterous, flagrant, unwarranted, unconscionable, exorbitant, immense, excessive, enormous.

Ant. 3 reasonable, moderate, minor, trivial, paltry.

outright *adj. 1 an outright lie:* utter, complete, total, downright, unmitigated, unconditional, absolute, sheer, thorough, thoroughgoing, out-and-out. *—adv.* 2 *She was outright rude:* utterly, altogether, completely, absolutely, downright, thoroughly, entirely; openly, visibly.

Ant. 1 partial, qualified, conditional. 2 somewhat.

outside *n. 1 the outside of a house. The outside of the candy is chocolate:* exterior, surface, outer side, façade, face; covering, case, sheath, skin, coating. *—adj.* 2 *outside walls:* outer, exterior, external, outward, outermost, outdoor. 3 *There's an outside chance:* remote, distant, faint, slight.

Ant. 1, 2 inside, interior. 2 inner, innermost, internal.

outspoken *adj. She's so outspoken she's hurt the feelings of all her friends:* plainspoken, blunt, frank, honest, direct, straightforward, forthright, candid.

Ant. tactful, diplomatic; reticent, guarded.

outstanding *adj. 1 an outstanding painting:* foremost, eminent, prominent, famed, celebrated, distinguished, famous, renowned; remarkable, memorable, unforgettable, notable, noteworthy; exemplary, exceptional, extraordinary, marvelous, magnificent, great. **2** *The outstanding bills must be paid:* unpaid, unsettled, due, in arrears, uncollected, payable, owing.

Ant. **1** routine, ordinary, everyday, run-of-the-mill. **2** paid, settled, collected.

outward *adj. His outward appearance was calm but he was seething inside:* external, exterior, outer, outside, surface, superficial; visible, perceivable, perceptible, apparent, ostensible.

Ant. inward, internal, inner, inmost, innermost.

outwardly *adv. She was outwardly pleased:* to all appearances, apparently, evidently, seemingly, ostensibly, on the face of it.

Ant. inwardly, secretly.

outweigh *v.* **1** *The boxer outweighed his opponent by ten pounds:* weigh more than, be heavier than. **2** *The good points outweigh the bad points:* exceed, surpass, predominate, overshadow, eclipse, be more important than.

outwit *v. She outwitted the robbers:* outsmart, outfox, outmaneuver, trick, fool, dupe; foil, thwart.

oval *adj. an oval rug:* egg-shaped, ovoid, elliptical; curved, rounded, almond-shaped.

ovation *n. The singer was greeted with a standing ovation:* enthusiastic applause, cheers, cheering, acclamation, acclaim, hurrah.

Ant. jeering, catcalls, booing.

over *adv.* **1** *Please check this contract over:* all through, all over. **2** *This work will have to be done over:* again, once more, anew, afresh; repeatedly, often. **3** *Will there be any left over?:* remaining, in addition, in excess, into the bargain, to boot; too, also; extra. —*adj.* **4** *Is the meeting over?:* finished, ended, concluded, done, terminated, completed, settled; lapsed, elapsed, expired, no more, gone, past, bygone.

Ant. **2** once, only once. **3** under, short, deficient. **4** begun, started, commenced; in progress.

overabundance *n. There is an overabundance of tomatoes:* abundance, superabundance, excess, surplus, oversupply, superfluity, profusion, plethora, glut.

Ant. shortage, scarcity, dearth, scantiness.

overall *adj. The overall situation is encouraging:* total, general, complete, entire, comprehensive; long-range, long-term.

overbearing *adj. He's so overbearing no one likes him:* arrogant, high-handed, self-assertive, self-important, lordly, high-and-mighty, know-it-all, disdainful, domineering, dictatorial, autocratic, tyrannical, despotic; haughty, pompous, conceited.

Ant. modest, unassuming, humble, meek, shy; deferential, subservient; gracious.

overcast *adj. The forecast is for overcast skies:* cloudy, sunless, gray, dull, dreary, gloomy; threatening, lowering, hazy.

Ant. cloudless, unclouded, clear, sunny.

overcome *v. Someday we shall overcome racial intolerance. She was overcome with grief:* conquer, best, get the better of, master, surmount, vanquish, defeat, beat; overwhelm, overpower, subdue, prevail over, triumph over, transcend, survive.

overdo *v.* **1** *Exercise is fine, but don't overdo it:* do to excess, carry too far, not know when to stop; overtax oneself by; indulge oneself in. **2** *A simple "thank you" is enough; don't overdo it:* exaggerate, overstate, hyperbolize, stretch a point; magnify, expand, amplify, embroider, gild.

Ant. **2** understate, minimize, slight.

overdue *adj. Payment is long overdue:* past due, belated, late, tardy, behind time, behindhand, delayed, dilatory.

Ant. early, ahead of time, beforehand, premature.

overflow *v.* **1** *The bathtub overflowed:* flow over, run over, be filled to overflowing, slop over; inundate, flood. —*n.* **2** *There is an overflow of cheap ballpoint pens on the market:* overabundance, superabundance, surplus, excess, superfluity, profusion. oversupply, flood, glut.

Ant. **2** lack, scarcity, shortage, dearth.

overhaul *v.* **1** *The racing car overhauled the leader:* overtake, pass, catch up with, catch. **2** *to overhaul a motor:* renovate, revamp, rebuild, reconstruct, remodel, recondition.

overhead *adv.* **1** *Look overhead!:* over one's head, up, up above, above. —*adj.* **2** *Turn on the overhead light:* ceiling, roof; overhanging; uppermost. —*n.* **3** *To increase profits we must reduce overhead:* operating expenses, general expenses.

overjoyed *adj. She seemed overjoyed to see us:* delighted, deliriously happy, jubilant, elated, joyous, gratified, enthralled, exultant, thrilled, ecstatic.

Ant. disappointed, unhappy, sad, dejected, downcast.

overlook *v.* **1** *How could you overlook paying the rent?:* forget, neglect, not trouble oneself about, omit, leave out, miss, slight. **2** *She overlooks my faults:* ignore, disregard, regard indulgently; excuse, forgive. **3** *The house overlooks the river:* have a view of, look over, look out on.

Ant. **1** remember, pay attention to, keep in mind.

overly *adv. The review seemed overly critical:* excessively, needlessly, exceedingly, too, immoderately, inordinately, unreasonably, unfairly, unduly, disproportionately, to a fault.

Ant. insufficiently, inadequately; moderately, mildly.

overpower *v.* 1 *The speaker was overpowered with emotion:* overcome, overwhelm, affect strongly, move, sway, influence. 2 *He overpowered his assailant:* subdue, overcome, get the better of, best, get the upper hand over, overwhelm, vanquish, defeat, worst, beat, triumph over, crush, quell.

Ant. 2 surrender, give up, capitulate.

overrate *v. The critics overrated that show:* overpraise, overestimate, overesteem, rate too highly, overvalue, make too much of, attach too much importance to.

Ant. underrate, underestimate, undervalue.

overrule *v.* 1 *The judge overruled the counsel's objection:* disallow, rule against, reject, override, set aside, deny, veto, refuse, invalidate, countermand, overturn, revoke, cancel, annul, nullify. 2 *He wanted to raise the dues, but we overruled him:* prevail over, outvote, outweigh.

Ant. 1 allow, permit, approve, grant, sustain, support.

overrun *v.* 1 *The Vandals overran the Roman Empire. Weeds overran the garden:* swarm over, surge over, overspread, over whelm, invade; invade, swoop down on; sack, pillage, plunder, loot, engulf, inundate, overgrow, choke. *—n.* 2 *The overrun on the new bomber cost the government millions:* overproduction, surplus; additional cost, extra charge, higher price.

overseas Also **oversea** *adv.* 1 *We fought overseas in the war:* abroad, across the sea, beyond the sea; in foreign service. *—adj.* 2 *oversea shipments:* across the sea, beyond the sea; transoceanic, ultramarine.

oversee *v. My assistant will oversee the work:* supervise, superintend, have charge of, handle, attend to, see to, keep an eye on; administer, manage, direct, run, boss, command, govern, rule, guide, preside over, carry on, regulate.

overshadow *v.* 1 *Heavy clouds overshadowed the mountain:* cast a shadow over, shade, darken; obscure, cover, screen, mask, shroud, veil. 2 *His father overshadowed him:* outshine, eclipse, tower over, render insignificant by comparison, steal the limelight from.

oversight *n. Was it merely an oversight?:* omission, mistake, blunder, heedless mistake, careless error, slight; negligence, neglect, neglectfulness, carelessness, inattention, thoughtlessness, heedlessness.

Ant. care, attention, heed; diligence, vigilance, meticulousness, scrupulousness.

overstate *v. Don't overstate the importance of the work:* exaggerate, overdo, embellish, embroider, oversell, enlarge, inflate, magnify, stretch, enlarge on.

Ant. understate, undervalue, underplay, soft-pedal.

overt *adj. There was overt hostility between the two:* obvious, noticeable, visible, observable, open, unconcealed, perceptible, perceivable, palpable, evident, manifest, undisguised.

Ant. covert, unnoticeable, concealed, masked, undisclosed, disguised.

overtake *v. The champion overtook the lead runner:* come abreast of, catch up with, catch, gain on, run down; pass, go by.

Ant. fall back from, lose ground to.

overthrow *v.* 1 *to overthrow the regime:* topple, bring down, overcome, overpower, defeat, undo, do away with. *—n.* 2 *the overthrow of a dictator:* toppling, bringing down, casting out of power, undoing, downfall, defeat, abolition; revolution, rebellion.

Ant. 1 preserve, conserve, uphold, support, perpetuate; defend. 2 preservation, perpetuation; defense.

overtone *n. There were overtones of distrust in his voice:* suggestion, intimation, insinuation, hint, implication, connotation, indication, innuendo.

overture *n.* 1 *the opera's overture:* prelude, introduction, prologue; beginning. 2 *The losing army made a peace overture:* opening move, preliminary offer, receptive sign, invitation, approach, bid, offering, advance, tender, suggestion, proposal, proposition.

Ant. 1 finale, close; coda. 2 rejection, spurning.

overturn *v.* 1 *The waves overturned the boat:* capsize, knock over, upset, upend, topple, turn upside down. 2 *The mob overturned the monarchy:* defeat, vanquish, overthrow, overcome, overpower, overwhelm, turn out.

overweening *adj. overweening pride:* overbearing, haughty, disdainful, arrogant, highhanded, patronizing, egotistical, domineering, presumptuous, cocky, bossy, self-important.

overweight *adj. An overweight person should reduce:* obese, fat, corpulent, pudgy, chubby, plump, chunky, well-padded, fleshy, roly-poly, portly, tubby.

Ant. underweight, skinny, bony, gaunt, emaciated.

overwhelm *v.* 1 *Invading armies over-*

whelmed the town: overrun, overpower, overcome; defeat, vanquish, conquer, beat; swamp, engulf, inundate; devastate, crush. 2 The music overwhelmed me: confound, bowl over; overcome; impress, affect, move, stir, overpower.

Ant. 1 surrender, capitulate; rescue, save. 2 leave indifferent.

overwrought *adj.* He was overwrought after the argument: overexcited, excited, agitated, wrought up, worked up, carried away, riled, disturbed, wild, frenzied, wild-eyed; uneasy, perturbed, nervous.

Ant. calm, unruffled, serene, unexcited, untroubled, composed.

owe *v.* They owe the bank $10,000. You owe your parents respect: be in debt, be indebted to, be obligated, have a loan from; be under obligation to, be bound in gratitude, be beholden to.

Ant. repay, reimburse, liquidate, compensate.

own *adj.* 1 Bring your own tennis racket. What I do is my own business!: belonging to oneself, belonging to itself; personal, private, individual. —*v.* 2 Has she owned a car before?: possess, be the owner of, have; keep, maintain, hold. 3 She would never own up to a mistake: admit, acknowledge, confess to, concede, disclose, tell; assent, concur, acquiesce.

Ant. 1 another's. 3 deny, disown, disclaim, repudiate.

owner *n.* The house is for sale by its owner: possessor, proprietor, proprietress, holder, titleholder.

P

pace *n.* 1 The horse moved at an easy pace: stride, gait, tread, slow gait, walk, amble, saunter; step. 2 The work progressed at a slow pace: rate, speed, velocity, clip, motion, flow. —*v.* 3 She paced the floor: walk nervously back and forth across; walk, go at a slow gait, amble, stroll, saunter.

pacify *v.* The king pacified the mob with promises of reform: appease, calm, quiet, allay, soothe, placate, propitiate, mollify; restore to peace, conciliate, reconcile, settle differences.

Ant. make hostile, anger, enrage, agitate, provoke; begin hostilities.

pack *n.* 1 a pack of gum. That's a pack of lies!: package, packet, parcel, bundle, kit; batch, bunch, set, lot, heap, cluster, clump; collection. 2 a pack of thieves. a pack of wolves: crowd, throng, group, horde, mob, multitude; swarm, flock, herd, drove, covey, passel, bevy, gaggle. —*v.* 3 Spectators packed the stadium. Pack these books together: fill, load, jam, cram, stuff; bundle, bunch, batch, group; tie, bind, truss.

Ant. 3 unpack, empty; unwrap, untie.

package *n.* 1 a package of detergent. Do you have the package this came in?: pack, parcel, packet; bundle, box, carton, container, wrappings. —*v.* 2 Now they package the lettuce in cellophane: wrap, wrap up, pack, encase.

packet *n.* a packet of letters: parcel, package, pack, bundle, sheaf, bale, roll.

pact *n.* Seven countries signed the trade pact: treaty, international agreement, agreement, compact, contract; bond, covenant, alliance, understanding.

pad *n.* 1 Get a pad to lie on: cushion, cushioning, padding; mattress, mat, bolster. 2 Each student should have a pencil and pad: tablet, writing tablet, desk pad, memo pad. —*v.* 3 The movers padded the furniture with canvas: cushion, protect; upholster; stuff, fill. 4 The author padded the book with long quotations: fill out, expand, enlarge, amplify, stretch out, inflate, flatten, puff out.

pagan *n.* The pagans worshiped the god of rain: one who is not a Christian, Jew or Muslim; heathen, infidel, idolator, idol worshiper; nonbeliever, unbeliever.

Ant. Christian, Jew, Muslim; true believer, believer.

pageant *n.* The pageant commemorates the founding of the town: spectacle, elaborate performance, show, exhibition, display, extravaganza; ceremony, ritual, pomp; procession, parade.

pageantry *n.* the pageantry of a coronation: display, pomp, pageant, ceremony, spectacle; grandeur, magnificence, splendor, glitter, show, extravagance.

pain *n.* 1 I have a pain in my shoulder: ache,

aching, soreness, hurt, hurting, smarting, pang, throb, twinge, stitch, discomfort. 2 *the pain of war:* suffering, distress, anguish, agony, torment, ordeal, misery, grief, woe, heartache, heartbreak, sorrow, affliction, wretchedness, unhappiness. —*v.* 3 *Does your ankle pain you?:* hurt, ache, smart, throb, sting, discomfort. 4 *The child's constant tantrums pained his mother:* distress, agonize, torment, make miserable, trouble, worry, disturb, grieve, sadden; displease, annoy, vex, harass, rile, exasperate.

Ant. 1 comfort, relief. 2 delight, joy, pleasure, enjoyment, happiness; comfort, solace. 3 relieve, ease. 4 delight, please, gladden, gratify.

painful *adj.* 1 *a painful earache:* aching, very sore, agonizing, excruciating, throbbing, smarting, stinging, sharp, piercing, torturous, racking, distressful. 2 *It was my painful duty to inform the next of kin:* unpleasant, distressing, disagreeable, distasteful, difficult, trying, grueling, disturbing, disquieting; grievous, sad, sorrowful.

Ant. 1 painless; soothing, comforting, relieving. 2 pleasant, delightful, agreeable, happy.

painstaking *adj. painstaking research:* careful, thorough, thoroughgoing, conscientious, scrupulous, meticulous; precise, exacting, fussy, finicky, diligent, assiduous.

Ant. careless, haphazard, slapdash, negligent, thoughtless.

painter *n. This loft would make an ideal studio for a painter:* artist, old master, portrait painter, oil painter, watercolorist, landscapist, miniaturist; house painter.

pair *n.* 1 *a pair of shoes. The farmer hitched the pair of oxen to the wagon:* two matched items, set of two; team, brace, yoke, span. 2 *They make a good-looking pair:* couple, duo, twosome; match, combination. —*v.* 3 *Pair the socks and put them in the drawer:* match, match up, mate, pair off; couple, combine, unite.

pal *n. George and I were pals:* buddy, chum, comrade, companion, crony, friend, intimate, confidant.

palace *n. Buckingham Palace:* royal residence, castle; *(variously)* mansion, stately residence.

palatial *adj. a palatial home:* luxurious, opulent, sumptuous, stately, noble, splendid, regal, monumental, imposing, grandiose, elegant.

Ant. simple, humble, modest.

pale *adj.* 1 *She looks pale:* colorless, white, pasty, ashen, wan, pallid, sallow, anemic,

cadaverous, deathly, ghostlike, ghastly. 2 *a pale green:* light, light-colored, light-toned, bleached. —*v.* 3 *She paled when we told her the news:* become pale, blanch, whiten.

Ant. 1 ruddy, rosy-cheeked, rosy, florid, flushed. 2 dark, deep, vivid. 3 flush, blush.

pall[1] *n. The smoke cast a pall over the town. The bad news cast a pall over the party:* dark covering, shadow, dimness; gloom, melancholy, depression, moroseness, cheerlessness, desolation.

Ant. light, brightness; joviality, gaiety, joy, cheer, merriment, high spirits.

pall[2] *v. This game is beginning to pall:* become boring, become dull, be tiresome; weary, sicken, cloy; sate, satiate.

Ant. interest, excite, delight.

pallid *adj.* 1 *She was weak and pallid:* pale, anemic looking, sallow, wan, ashen, ghostly, pasty, colorless, ashy, waxen. 2 *The evening's entertainment was pallid:* dull, insipid, unimaginative, uninteresting, lifeless, boring, bland, vapid.

Ant. 1 rosy, glowing. 2 lively, exciting, imaginative.

pallor *n. His pallor indicates some serious malady:* paleness, colorlessness, whiteness, pastiness, ashen color, wanness, ghostliness, gray complexion.

Ant. ruddy complexion, ruddiness, flush.

palpable *adj. There is a palpable difference:* tangible, obvious, plain, clear, noticeable, visible, discernible, manifest, perceivable, perceptible, recognizable, definite, distinct, unmistakable.

Ant. unnoticeable, undiscernible, imperceptible.

palpitate *v. My heart is palpitating:* throb, pound, pulsate, beat quickly, pulse rapidly, flutter, quiver, quaver; vibrate, tremble, shiver.

paltry *adj. He worked his way up from a paltry job:* petty, trifling, trivial, piddling, unimportant, insignificant, inconsequential, inferior, poor.

Ant. important, significant, consequential, essential, major, valuable.

pamper *v. She pampers her child:* spoil, indulge, cater to, humor, mollycoddle.

Ant. deny, slight; mistreat; tyrannize, domineer.

pamphlet *n. This pamphlet tells how to care for your car:* booklet, brochure; *(loosely)* leaflet, circular, tract, monograph.

panacea *n. There is no panacea for the world's problems:* cure-all, universal cure, nostrum, elixir, sovereign remedy; easy solution, final answer.

pandemonium *n. Pandemonium broke*

out: tumult, turmoil, chaos, bedlam, disorder, wild confusion, commotion; uproar, clamor, racket, din, disturbance.

Ant. order, peace, quiet, calm.

panegyric *n. The retiree received a panegyric from the chairman:* eulogy, laudation, praise, homage, tribute, extolment, compliment, testimonial.

Ant. condemnation, denunciation, reproach, diatribe.

panel *n.* 1 *a wall panel:* surface section; compartment, partition, piece, pane, insert, divider. 2 *A panel of artists will judge the contest:* committee, board, group, expert group, advisory group, jury; discussion group, round table.

pang *n. a pang of regret:* twinge, ache, pain, throb, smart, stitch, sting, distress, discomfort; agony, anguish, suffering.

Ant. pleasure, delight, enjoyment, happiness; comfort, relief.

panic *n.* 1 *Panic swept the swimmers as they saw the shark:* terror, overwhelming fear, alarm, hysteria, scare, fright; horror, dread, apprehension, trepidation, nervousness, consternation, confusion. *—v.* 2 *In case of fire, don't panic:* give way to panic, succumb to fear, become hysterical.

panorama *n. The lookout tower gave us a panorama of the valley:* sweeping view, scenic view, scene, vista, prospect, picture, perspective, survey, overview, bird's-eye view, overall picture.

panoramic *adj. a panoramic view of the valley:* sweeping, extensive, all-embracing, all-encompassing, far-ranging, all-inclusive, bird's-eye, overall.

pant *v.* 1 *I was sweating and panting:* breathe hard, gasp for breath, gasp, huff, puff, blow, wheeze. 2 *All his life he panted for wealth and luxury:* long for, yearn for, lust after, hunger for, crave, covet, want, wish for, aspire to.

pants *n. pl.* 1 *This jacket will match those pants nicely:* trousers, pair of trousers, slacks, breeches; *Informal* britches, jeans. 2 *The child could put on his own undershirt and pants but needed help with his outer garments:* underpants, drawers, underdrawers, undershorts, shorts, panties.

pantywaist *n. He was such a pantywaist everyone took advantage of him:* weakling, milksop, sissy, Milquetoast, mama's boy, namby-pamby, crybaby, mollycoddle; coward; *Slang* wimp.

pap *n.* 1 *Mothers used to feed infants pap:* mush, mash, gruel, soft food; Pablum. 2 *Informal How can anyone write such pap?:* childish nonsense, drivel, trivia, rubbish, rot, twaddle, junk, bosh.

papal *adj. the church's new papal decree:* of the pope, pontifical, apostolic.

paper *n.* 1 *Bring a pen and paper to class: (variously)* writing paper, notepaper, stationery, letter paper, bond, carbon paper, onionskin; construction paper; tissue paper, tracing paper; wrapping paper, gift wrap; printing paper, newsprint; wallpaper. 2 *This paper gives you title to the property:* document, instrument, certificate, deed, writing. 3 *What does the paper say about tomorrow's weather?:* newspaper, journal, tabloid; daily, weekly, monthly; periodical, trade paper. 4 *Each student must write a term paper:* composition, essay, theme, report.

par *n.* 1 *Our income and expenses are on a par:* equal footing, parity, equality, equilibrium; balance, sameness. 2 *I'm not feeling up to par today:* average, normal, usual, standard, the norm.

parable *n. the parable of the loaves and the fishes:* allegory, story, tale, morality tale, fable, allegorical story, legend, homily.

parade *n.* 1 *the St. Patrick's Day parade:* procession, march, review; cavalcade, caravan, motorcade, cortege; progression, train, string. 2 *I've never seen such a parade of jewelry as at the party:* show, display, array, spectacle, flaunting. *—v.* 3 *They love to parade their wealth:* show off, make a show of, display, make a display of, vaunt, flaunt.

Ant. hiding, concealing. 3 hide, conceal.

paradise *n.* 1 *Adam and Eve dwelt in paradise. Hawaii is an island paradise:* Eden, Garden of Eden; utopia, Shangri-la, heaven. 2 *On a hot day a dip in the pool is sheer paradise:* delight, bliss, joy, enjoyment, ecstasy, rapture, heaven, happiness.

Ant. 2 misery, hell, agony, torture.

paradox *n. It's a paradox, but the older she gets the more active she is:* self-contradiction, self-contradictory statement; incongruity, anomaly, inconsistency; oddity; enigma, puzzle, riddle.

paragon *n. a paragon of virtue:* model, example, exemplar, archetype, idea, symbol, pattern, standard, criterion.

parallel *adj.* 1 *Parallel lines never meet:* running side by side, coextensive, equidistant, concurrent, abreast. 2 *Stamp collecting and coin collecting are parallel hobbies:* similar, alike, analogous, comparative, collateral, corresponding, akin, correlative; equivalent. *—n.* 3 *the parallel between the French Revolution and the American Revolution:* comparison, analogy, likeness, correlation, relation, connection, parallelism, correspondence, resemblance, similarity. 4 *The navy's seaman is the parallel of the army's* *private:* counterpart, equivalent, equal, corollary, correlative. —*v.* 5 *The stream parallels the road:* run parallel to, follow; run abreast of. 6 *Your educational background parallels mine:* be equivalent to, be similar to, be alike, be comparable to, correspond to, be analogous to, match.

Ant. 1 nonparallel. 2 dissimilar, unlike, disparate. 3 dissimilarity, difference, disparity. 4 opposite, reverse, counter.

paralyze *v. I was paralyzed with fright:* immobilize, benumb, incapacitate, stupefy, petrify, freeze.

paramount *adj. Quality is of paramount importance:* main, chief, foremost, utmost, greatest, highest, predominant, dominant, preponderant, supreme, leading, premier, principal; superior, peerless, leading, cardinal, outstanding.

Ant. secondary, least, negligible, insignificant, unimportant, minor.

paramour *n. He's the paramour of a wealthy actress:* lover; mistress, kept woman, girl friend, lady friend, inamorata, courtesan, concubine; boyfriend, kept man, lover boy, gigolo, inamorato, sugar daddy.

parapet *n. The defenders of the castle fought from behind parapets:* defensive wall, breastwork, earthwork; rampart, bulwark, barricade, battlement

paraphernalia *n. Bring along your fishing paraphernalia:* equipment, gear, outfit, implements, accoutrements, rig, stuff, apparatus, things, utensils, tackle, material; personal effects, effects, belongings, furnishings.

paraphrase *v. Just paraphrase what he said:* restate, reword, rephrase, state in one's own words.

Ant. quote, state verbatim.

parcel *n.* 1 *Send this parcel via airmail:* package, packet, bundle, pack, bale. 2 *a parcel of land:* lot, tract, plot. —*v.* 3 *The estate was parceled out to the heirs:* apportion, distribute, divide, allot, allocate, disperse, dispense, dole out.

Ant. 3 collect, gather, amass, accumulate.

parch *v. The lack of rain had parched the land:* dry out, dry up, dessicate, sun-dry, dehydrate; scorch, char, sear, singe, bake.

Ant. water, flood, inundate.

parchment *n. Ancient manuscripts were written on parchment:* sheepskin, goatskin, papyrus, vellum.

pardon *n.* 1 *May God grant you pardon for your sins:* forgiveness, forbearance, indulgence; absolution, mercy, deliverance, release, exculpation, amnesty. —*v.* 2 *Pardon the interruption:* forgive, excuse, forbear, indulge. 3 *The convict was pardoned:* absolve, vindicate, exonerate, exculpate, grant amnesty; remit the penalty of, reprieve, set free, release.

Ant. 1 punishment, retribution, vengeance, condemnation. 3 condemn, doom.

pare *v.* 1 *Pare the apple:* peel, skin, strip, trim. 2 *The firm must pare costs:* cut, cut down on, cut back, shave, trim, prune; reduce, decrease, lessen, diminish, lower, curtail.

Ant. 2 increase, raise, boost.

parent *n. to be a good parent. The Wright brothers' airplane is the parent of the jet:* mother, father; dam, sire, begetter, procreator; creator, originator, producer; ancestor, progenitor, predecessor, precursor, forerunner, antecedent.

parentage *n. The birth certificate left no doubt as to her parentage:* ancestry, antecedents, forbears, genealogy, ancestors; lineage, descent, heredity, origin, extraction, strain, pedigree, derivation, family tree.

parenthetical *adj. Your essay has too many parenthetical remarks:* in parentheses; incidental, interposed, inserted, intervening, aside, casual, extraneous.

pariah *n. After the scandal he became a pariah:* outcast, undesirable, untouchable, exile, expatriate, man without a country.

parish *n.* 1 *How are the parochial schools in this parish?:* church district, archdiocese, diocese, shire, canton; district, precinct, section, county, community. 2 *The priest asked the parish to pray for peace:* congregation, parishioners, pastorate, fold, flock, church members, brethren.

parley *n. The leaders will have a parley to discuss peace:* discussion, conference, conclave, summit, meeting, council, talk, conversation, palaver.

parlor *n. The parlor was used only when visitors came:* sitting room, front room, living room, drawing room; salon, reception room, saloon.

parochial *adj.* 1 *parochial schools:* parish, church, religious. 2 *The candidate's views are too parochial for a national leader:* local, regional, sectional; provincial, insular, countrified, small-town; narrow-minded, limited, narrow, restricted, petty.

Ant. 1 public; lay. 2 international, national; sophisticated, broad-minded, liberal.

parody *n.* 1 *a parody of* Hamlet: burlesque, takeoff, ludicrous imitation, caricature, lampoon, satire, travesty. —*v.* 2 *The comedian parodied the senator's drawl:* burlesque, caricature, mimic, lampoon, satirize.

parrot *v. She parrots every view her husband has:* repeat mindlessly, echo, reiterate, chorus; imitate, mimic, ape.

parry v. She parried all questions about her personal life: fend off, ward off, stave off; dodge, elude, sidestep, duck, circumvent.
Ant. face, confront.

parsimonious adj. Because they were parsimonious they never needed financial help: frugal, saving, thrifty, economical, sparing, penny-pinching; miserly, tight, tightfisted, close, closefisted, stingy.
Ant. extravagant, spendthrift, wasteful; generous, openhanded.

part n. 1 The U.S. government is made up of three parts. This looks like part of a broken cup: section, portion, division, subdivision, sector, branch, department, unit, component, element, member, region; piece, segment, fragment, fraction, scrap, shred, bit, sliver, chip, shard, sherd, snippet, cutting, slice, item. 2 The actress took the part of Joan of Arc: role, character; guise, disguise. 3 What was your part in the proceedings?: role, function, capacity, share, place, assignment, job, chore, task, duty. —v. 4 The curtain parted. The rope parted: separate, disengage, open, divide; detach, disconnect, split, slit, sunder, sever, rend, tear. 5 It's time to part: depart, go, leave, take one's leave, go one's way; take one's farewell, say good-bye, end a relationship, break off, call it quits.
Ant. 1 whole, entirety, totality. 4 unite, combine, join. 5 stay, remain, abide.

partake v. All the children will partake in the festivities: share, take part, participate, engage in, join in.
Ant. be excluded; refrain from, eschew.

partial adj. 1 a partial list: incomplete, limited, fragmentary, unfinished, uncompleted. 2 He's too partial to be a fair judge: partisan, biased, prejudiced, predisposed, slanted, subjective, one-sided; inequitable.
Ant. 1 complete, entire, total, final. 2 impartial, unbiased, objective, disinterested, unprejudiced.

partiality n. 1 The referee's partiality toward the home team was obvious: bias, prejudice, predisposition, predilection, partisanship, favoritism. 2 I have a partiality for ice cream: fondness, liking, weakness, love, affinity, propensity, penchant, fancy, proclivity; choice, preference.
Ant. 1 impartiality, objectivity, disinterest; fairness. 2 dislike, disinclination, distaste, aversion, antipathy.

partially adv. The work is partially finished: partly, in part, partway, incompletely, fractionally, somewhat.
Ant. completely, entirely, totally.

participate v. to participate in the tennis tournament: take part, engage in, join in, be a participant, perform, play a part, partake, share.
Ant. be excluded; forswear, forgo.

particle n. a particle of rock. There's not a particle of truth in that statement: small piece, small fragment, bit, speck, grain, shred, scrap, crumb, smidgen, morsel, jot, iota, atom; trace, snippet, whit, scintilla, mite.

particular adj. 1 On that particular day I was in Houston. Golf is our particular passion: specific, exact, explicit, express, special, especial, fixed, concrete, individual; definite, distinct, single, personal. 2 She's so particular that no one can please her: hard to please, critical, demanding, exacting, picky, fussy, finicky; strict, fastidious, meticulous, painstaking, scrupulous, punctilious. —n. Usually **particulars** 3 The lawyer must know all the particulars: detail, specific, item, fact, circumstance, event.
Ant. 1 unspecified, indefinite. 2 uncritical, undemanding, careless, haphazard, inexact.

particularly adv. 1 The coffee is particularly good today: especially, exceptionally, unusually, extraordinarily, markedly, notably, prominently. 2 We particularly asked that you be there: in particular, explicitly, expressly, especially, specially.

partisan n. 1 The hometown partisans cheered the local team: supporter, follower, adherent, sympathizer, champion, advocate, enthusiast, fan, devotee, rooter, booster. —adj. 2 partisan politics: favoring one political party, predisposed toward one group, favoring a cause, partial, biased, prejudiced, slanted.
Ant. 1 detractor, critic, opponent. 2 nonpartisan, bipartisan, impartial, disinterested, objective, open-minded.

partition n. 1 the partition of the town into two voting precincts: division, dividing, separation, splitting, parting; demarcation, segregation. 2 Put up partitions to separate the areas: dividing wall, non-supporting wall; wall, divider, screen; barrier, fence. —v. 3 The dormitory was partitioned into cubicles: divide, subdivide, separate, split up; distribute, disperse, dispense, apportion, allot, allocate.

partly adv. The back door is partly open: partially, in part, partway, fractionally, somewhat, incompletely, not wholly, to a limited extent; relatively, after a fashion.
Ant. fully, completely, entirely, totally.

partner n. The business is owned by two partners: co-owner, co-partner; colleague, fellow worker, collaborator, accomplice, confederate, teammate; friend, comrade, ally, companion, buddy, chum, pal.

party n. 1 a birthday party: social function, social gathering, gathering of friends, celebration, festivity, fete, get-together, affair. 2 a political party. a rescue party: alliance, federation, confederacy, league, coalition, faction; group, crew, team, band, body, company, squad, unit. 3 Both parties are to appear before the judge: participant, participator, perpetrator.

pass v. 1 She never passes without stopping to say hello. The guard allowed the visitor to pass: go by, go past, go beyond, go ahead, move onward, proceed. 2 Time passes quickly on vacation. Wait for the rain to pass: go, go by, go away, proceed, pass away, be over, end, terminate, die, fade away, blow over, run its course, disappear, dissolve, evaporate, depart, leave. 3 Mother passes her time reading: spend, expend, use, consume, employ, engage, busy, occupy, fill, take up. 4 Dick has already passed his father in height: surpass, exceed, go by, go beyond, go ahead, best, excel, outshine, eclipse, overshadow, outstrip, outdo. 5 Did you pass the chemistry course? To become a sergeant a policeman must pass certain requirements: receive a satisfactory grade in, complete successfully, satisfy, qualify, meet, finish. 6 Congress is expected to pass the bill: enact, legislate, establish by law, vote approval on, approve, authorize, legalize. 7 Please pass the salt. The quarterback passed the ball downfield: hand, hand over, convey, transfer, transmit, deliver, throw, toss, hit, kick. —n. 8 the Brenner Pass: mountain pass, gap, gorge, canyon, ravine, gulch; passageway, pathway, trail, lane, course, route, channel. 9 The soldier had a weekend pass. Retired players get season passes to all the games: permission to be absent, permission to leave, furlough; free ticket, complimentary ticket; right of passage, permit. 10 Things have come to a pretty pass!: state of affairs, situation, juncture, predicament, complication, difficulty, plight, strait, quandary.

Ant. 1, 2 stop, halt; wait. 2 begin, start, commence; continue. 3 waste, squander. 5 fail, flunk. 6 vote down, defeat, reject.

passable adj. 1 Are the roads passable in this snow?: traversable, fit for travel, clear, open, unobstructed. 2 This suit is worn, but passable. The movie wasn't great, but it was passable: presentable, respectable, acceptable, adequate, not bad, so-so, better than nothing, fair, middling, mediocre, tolerable.

Ant. 1 impassable, impenetrable, blocked, obstructed. 2 unacceptable, insufficient; exceptional, extraordinary.

passage n. 1 He quoted a long passage from the book: section, portion, piece, selection; paragraph, sentence, verse, chapter. 2 The hunters needed a guide for their passage through the jungle: progression, passing, movement; trip, journey, voyage, junket, trek, transit. 3 Passage of the bill depends on public support: passing into law, enactment, legislation, ratification, approval, acceptance; affirmation, confirmation. 4 Is there a passage through the mountains? The house has an underground passage: pass, passageway, way, course, route, path, road; corridor, hallway, hall, tunnel, canal, channel; access, approach.

Ant. 3 defeat, rejection. 4 barrier, obstacle, obstruction.

passageway n. Don't leave your umbrella in the passageway: corridor, hallway, hall; passage, tunnel; access, entrance, entryway, exit; path, walk; gangway, companionway.

passé adj. That idea is passé: out of fashion, old-fashioned, out-of-date, outdated, outmoded, antiquated; stale, hoary; lapsed, disused, past.

Ant. modern, new, novel, current, up-to-date, newfangled.

passion n. 1 He could never put any passion into his singing: emotion, feeling, warmth, heart, ardor, fervor, fire, intensity, sentiment, enthusiasm, earnestness, gusto, vehemence. 2 a crime of passion: lust, sexual desire, carnal love, fleshly desire; amorousness, love. 3 Skiing is my passion: obsession, craze, mania, rage, craving, urge, desire, hunger, thirst; idol, beloved, loved one, flame, inamorata.

Ant. 1 apathy, indifference, coldness, coolness.

passionate adj. a passionate debate. a passionate kiss: impassioned, fervent, fervid, ardent, emotional, earnest, intense, fiery, fierce, raging, tempestuous, excited, enthusiastic, heated, vehement; loving, amorous, desirous, lustful, sensuous, carnal, erotic, sexy.

Ant. dispassionate, cool, apathetic, indifferent.

passive adj. The townspeople remained passive throughout the occupation: submissive, inactive, unassertive, apathetic, impassive, compliant, acquiescent, yielding, inert, docile, pliable, tractable, spiritless, unresisting.

Ant. active, domineering, forceful, aggressive, assertive; energetic.

past adj. 1 The time for action is past. Forget past mistakes: gone by, passed away; elapsed, expired, ended, finished, gone, departed; bygone, ancient, historical, former,

previous, earlier, prior. —n. 2 *The old man loved to talk about the past:* days gone by, days of yore, days of old, yesteryear, former times, times gone by; ancient times, antiquity, events gone by.
Ant. 1 future, coming; present, now. 2 future, time to come, tomorrow; present, today.

pastel *adj. pastel colors:* pale, faint, soft, light, muted.
Ant. bright, deep, vibrant.

pastime *n. Stamp collecting is a pastime:* diversion, hobby, avocation, spare-time activity, relaxation, distraction, amusement, entertainment.
Ant. business, work, occupation, employment, job.

pastor *n. The pastor preached a lively sermon:* minister, priest, cleric, preacher, parson, rector, clergyman, vicar, dean, curé; padre, father, chaplain.

pastoral *adj.* 1 *a pastoral tale:* rustic, rural, portraying country life, depicting the life of shepherds; arcadian, idyllic. 2 *The new minister will take up his pastoral duties next month:* ministerial, ecclesiastical, clerical; priestly, episcopal, sacerdotal.
Ant. 1 sophisticated, cosmopolitan; urban, city. 2 secular, lay.

pasty *adj.* 1 *Breakfast was a pasty mess of boiled oatmeal:* like paste, gluey, mucilaginous, gummy, sticky, doughy; starchy, glutinous. 2 *a pasty complexion:* pale, ashen, ashy, wan, sallow, colorless, pallid, chalky, white, ghostlike, gray.
Ant. 1 dry, powdery. 2 ruddy, rosy, florid, rubicund.

pat *v.* 1 *The children wanted to pat the bunny:* pet, stroke, caress, fondle. —n. 2 *She gave the pillow several pats:* light blow, gentle stroke, tap, small spank; hit, thwack, slap, thump, rap. 3 *Put a pat of butter on each plate:* little slab, small square, cake, dab, daub. —*adj.* 4 *a pat answer:* contrived, rehearsed, glib, facile, ready, easy, smooth. 5 *There are no pat solutions to the problem:* perfect, ideal, exact, precise; appropriate, fitting, pertinent, suitable, apt; easy, simple.
Ant. 4 impromptu, spontaneous; sincere, thoughtful. 5 imperfect, inexact; irrelevant, unsuitable.

patchwork *n. He gave us a patchwork of quotations:* jumble, medley, potpourri, pastiche, mélange, miscellany, hodgepodge, mixture, hash.

patent *adj.* 1 *patent medicine:* protected by patent, trademarked; nonprescription. 2 *a patent falsehood:* obvious, manifest, self-evident, open, overt, transparent, palpable, decided, downright, unmistakable,

conspicuous, rank, flagrant, glaring, clear, bald, undisguised, unconcealed.
Ant. 1 unpatented; prescription. 2 imperceptible, subtle, concealed, disguised.

paternal *adj. paternal affection:* fatherly, fatherlike, of a father, from the father's side of the family, patriarchal; of a parent, parental; tender, kind, solicitous; concerned, watchful, vigilant.

path *n. We followed the path to the mill. the path to success:* walk, lane, pathway, trail, footpath; course, route, way, process, means.

pathetic *adj. The orphan's plight was pathetic:* pitiful, moving, affecting, touching, poignant, plaintive, distressing, arousing sympathy, pitiable, lamentable; sorrowful, sad, doleful, miserable, woeful, wretched.

pathos *n. The book had so much pathos I wept all through it:* pathetic quality, poignancy, plaintiveness, sadness, sentimentalism, sentimentality, pitiableness, anguish, heartache, misery.
Ant. amusement, humor, fun.

patience *n.* 1 *Have patience, the train will come:* calm endurance, forbearance, uncomplaining nature, sufferance, tolerance, restraint, imperturbability, equanimity; self-control, poise. 2 *It takes patience to learn Japanese:* persistence, perseverance, diligence, tenacity, determination, resolution, stick-to-itiveness.
Ant. 1, 2 impatience. 1 restlessness, exasperation, irritation, nervousness. 2 irresolution.

patient *n.* 1 *The doctor has several patients waiting:* person under medical care, case; sick person. —*adj.* 2 *Just be patient, you're next:* persevering, enduring, uncomplaining, forbearing, serene, composed; determined, tenacious, resolute, unwavering, dogged.

patio *n. Breakfast was served on the patio:* terrace, porch, veranda, piazza, deck.

patrician *n.* 1 *Only patricians sit in the House of Lords:* aristocrat, noble, nobleman, peer, lord. —*adj.* 2 *He still retains his patrician manners:* aristocratic, noble, lordly; imposing, stately, dignified, genteel, well-bred, upper-class, highborn.
Ant. 1 peasant, commoner, working man. 2 plebeian, proletarian, working-class, lower-class, lowborn; bourgeois, philistine.

patrimony *n. His patrimony was exhausted in less than two years:* inheritance, estate, legacy, endowment, bequeathal; birthright, heritage.

patron *n.* 1 *Patrons thronged the store:* customer, client, buyer, shopper; frequenter, habitué, spectator. 2 *a patron of the arts:*

sponsor, supporter, backer, benefactor, benefactress, financier, philanthropist; advocate, champion, well-wisher, friend.

patronage *n.* 1 *The restaurant appreciates your patronage:* business, trade, buying, purchasing, commerce, custom, dealing; clientele, customers, patrons, clients. 2 *The fund depends on the patronage of the alumni:* financial support, support, sponsorship, charity, benefaction, philanthropy, backing, help, aid, assistance; auspices, protection. 3 *The governor controls patronage in this state:* political favors, political appointments, spoils.

patronize *v.* 1 *I'll never patronize that store again:* do business with; trade with, deal with, shop at, buy from, frequent, be a habitué of, be a client of. 2 *Don't patronize me, I'm not a child!:* treat in a condescending way, act superior toward, assume a lofty attitude toward, act disdainfully toward.
Ant. 2 flatter, toady to, be subservient to.

patter *v.* 1 *The rain pattered on the window:* pat, beat, pound, tap, rap, drum, thrum, spatter. —*n.* 2 *the patter of raindrops:* pattering, pitter-patter, pad, tap, tapping, drumming; beat.

pattern *n.* 1 *a checkered pattern:* design, design, motif; form, shape. 2 *A good seamstress can make a dress without a pattern:* guide, design, plan, draft, model; original, prototype; standard, criterion, example, exemplar, sample, specimen, illustration. —*v.* 3 *The youth patterned his life on Martin Luther King's:* model, fashion, shape, mold, form; imitate, emulate, copy, follow.

paucity *n. There was a paucity of food:* scarcity, dearth, lack, shortage, scarceness, scantiness, deficiency, sparsity, meagerness, puniness, insufficiency.
Ant. surfeit, excess, surplus, abundance.

paunch *n.* 1 *The baby raccoons clung to their mother's paunch:* stomach, abdomen, midsection, *Informal* tummy. 2 *Excercise would reduce that paunch:* potbelly, belly, *Slang* bay window, breadbasket, gut, spare tire.

pauper *n. After paying these bills I'll be a pauper!:* poor person, indigent, insolvent; charity case, beggar.
Ant. rich person, millionaire.

pause *n.* 1 *After a brief pause the speaker continued:* stop, halt, rest, break, cessation, interval, hiatus, time out, letup, gap, suspension, interlude, intermission. —*v.* 2 *The joggers paused to catch their breath:* stop briefly, halt, rest, let up, take time out, break off; hesitate, deliberate.
Ant. 1 continuation, progress, advancement. 2 continue, proceed, advance.

pave *v. They're paving the road:* surface, resurface, face; cement, tar, asphalt, blacktop, macadamize.

pavilion *n.* 1 *The reception was held in a pavilion on the lawn:* tentlike building, light open structure; exhibition hall, exposition building; *(variously)* summerhouse, gazebo, pergola, kiosk, bandshell. 2 *the maternity pavilion:* hospital building, hospital section, ward, wing.

pawn[1] *v. I pawned my typewriter to pay the bill:* give as security, pledge, raise money on, borrow on, *Slang* hock.
Ant. redeem, take out of hock.

pawn[2] *n. You are merely the pawn of the racketeers:* instrument, agent, puppet, tool, dupe, cat's-paw; lackey, flunky.
Ant. leader, chief, head, boss, *Slang* kingpin.

pay *v.* 1 *They paid the cashier. Please pay this bill:* give money owed to, give money for; pay in full, remit, settle, square accounts, honor, liquidate. 2 *It doesn't pay to waste time:* be advantageous, be useful, benefit, serve. 3 *How much does that job pay?:* offer as compensation, offer as wages, bring in, reimburse; profit, yield, return. 4 *I paid her a compliment:* give, grant, render, extend, proffer, present. —*n.* 5 *How much is your pay?:* wages, salary, earnings, paycheck, income; compensation, recompense, fee, reimbursement, stipend.
Ant. 1 collect; owe, be in debt. 2 be disadvantageous, be futile. 4 withhold, suppress, repress; receive.

payable *adj. The bill is payable upon receipt:* due, owed, owing, outstanding, receivable, in arrears.

payment *n.* 1 *Payment may be by check. The bookkeeper is in charge of payments:* paying, remittance, settlement, liquidation; outlay, expenditure, disbursement, spending. 2 *a payment on the mortgage. What do you want in payment for that old car?:* installment, partial payment, premium; remuneration, compensation, recompense, reimbursement, fee; pay, salary, allowance, contribution.
Ant. 1 nonpayment; income, profit.

peace *n.* 1 *The country enjoyed 30 years of peace:* harmony, accord, concord, amity, entente, pacification; armistice, truce. 2 *the peace of the countryside:* calm, serenity, tranquillity; repose, content, composure.
Ant. 1 conflict, war, hostilities. 2 turmoil, disorder, chaos.

peaceful *adj.* 1 *I want my children to live in a peaceful world:* free from war, nonwarring, peacetime; peaceable, peace-loving, pacifistic, nonbelligerent. 2 *Labor and man-*

agement reached a peaceful settlement: amicable, friendly, nonviolent, harmonious, agreeable. 3 *It's so peaceful in the woods:* quiet, still, tranquil, serene, calm, placid, untroubled.

Ant. 1 warring, wartime; belligerent, warlike. 2 violent, strife-torn, bitter, antagonistic.

peacemaker *n. Can a peacemaker prevent war?* conciliator, intermediary, negotiator, mediator, pacificator, arbitrator, adjudicator; peacekeeper, peacemonger.

peak *n.* 1 *a mountain peak:* summit, pinnacle, tip, top, apex, crown, crest; apogee. 2 *the peak of the rush hour:* culmination, climax, maximum point, highest degree, acme, zenith, crest. —*v.* 3 *The floodwaters should peak by midnight:* reach a maximum, crest, climax, culminate.

Ant. 1 base, bottom, foot. 2 nadir.

peaked *adj. The patient looked peaked:* pale, pallid, wan, sallow, ashen, white; sickly, ill, weak, infirm, debilitated; thin, lean, spare, scrawny, gaunt, emaciated; haggard, drawn.

Ant. hearty, hale, healthy; robust, husky, strapping; ruddy, rosy-cheeked.

peal *n.* 1 *the peal of church bells. a peal of thunder:* ringing, ring, reverberation, resounding, clang, clangor, toll, knell, din, tintinnabulation; clap, crash, crack, boom, rumble. —*v.* 2 *All the bells in town pealed at noon:* ring, reverberate, resound, clang, toll, tintinnabulate.

peck[1] *v.* 1 *The bird pecked at the bread crumbs:* strike with the beak, pick up with the beak; tap, strike. 2 *The child just pecked at the food:* pick at, nibble. —*n.* 3 *Her husband gave her a peck on the cheek:* light kiss, absent-minded kiss, *Slang* buss, smack.

Ant. 2 devour, wolf down, gulp, bolt.

peck[2] *n. I'm in a peck of trouble:* a great deal, lots, heaps, a slew, scads, gobs, oodles, mess.

Ant. little.

peculiar *adj.* 1 *Every bell has its own peculiar sound:* particular, individual, distinctive, distinct, distinguishing, characteristic, typical, unique, singular, exclusive, special, specific. 2 *What a peculiar hat!:* odd, queer, strange, unusual, abnormal, curious, quaint, freakish, weird; eccentric, bizarre.

Ant. 1 common, universal, indistinctive. 2 commonplace, ordinary, conventional, familiar.

peculiarity *n.* 1 *The large fantail is a peculiarity of the peacock:* distinguishing quality, uniqueness, characteristic, quality, singularity, distinction, mark. 2 *Wearing only blue clothing is one of her peculiarities:* ec-

centricity, idiosyncrasy, odd trait; oddity, freakishness, weirdness, queerness, bizarreness, abnormality.

Ant. 1 universality, common quality, general thing. 2 conventionality, normalcy.

pedagogic *adj. pedagogic methods:* educational, tutorial, professorial, instructional; pedantic, didactic, donnish.

pedagogue Also **pedagog** *n. A lover of learning, he wanted to be a pedagogue:* teacher, schoolteacher, schoolmaster, schoolmistress, schoolmarm, educator, instructor, professor, academic.

pedant *n. Is she a brilliant scholar or just a pedant?:* bookworm, plodding scholar; doctrinaire scholar; methodologist, purist, dogmatist.

pedantic *adj. a pedantic answer:* ostentatiously learned, pompous, academic, scholastic, didactic, doctrinaire, bookish, stilted, dogmatic; nitpicking, fussy, finicky, overparticular.

pedestrian *adj. His newest play is a pedestrian affair:* unimaginative, mediocre, commonplace, ordinary, prosaic, run-of-the-mill, mediocre.

Ant. imaginative, interesting, fascinating; outstanding, remarkable, noteworthy.

pedigree *n. The poodle had an impressive pedigree:* record of ancestry, family tree, genealogical table; line of descent, descent, lineage, ancestry, family, parentage, line, bloodline.

peep[1] *v.* 1 *The girl peeped around the door:* peek, look surreptitiously, steal a look, look from hiding; peer, give a quick look, glimpse, skim. 2 *The sun peeped out from behind the clouds:* peer out, come partially into view, come forth. —*n.* 3 *The hunters got a peep at the deer:* quick look, glimpse, glance, peek.

Ant. 1 scrutinize, contemplate. 2 disappear. 3 good look.

peep[2] *n. the peeps of the baby chicks. One more peep out of you and you'll get a spanking!:* peeping, cheep, chirp, tweet, twitter, chirrup; word, whisper, mutter, whimper, murmur.

peer[1] *v.* 1 *She peered out the window:* look, gaze, stare, gape, peep, peek, squint. 2 *The moon peered out from behind a cloud:* appear, come into view, emerge.

peer[2] *n.* 1 *The defendant was tried by a jury of his peers:* equal, compeer; fellow citizen. 2 *the peers of the realm:* nobleman, noble, lord; aristocrat.

peerless *adj. Paganini played with peerless artistry:* unsurpassed, matchless, unmatched, unexcelled, unequaled, incomparable, unrivaled, inimitable; surpassing, consummate, preeminent, faultless, flawless.

Ant. commonplace, ordinary, routine; inferior, second-rate.

peeve *v.* 1 *What peeves me is the way she takes friends for granted:* annoy, provoke, gall, irritate, exasperate, irk, vex, nettle, aggravate, rile. —*n.* 2 *My pet peeve is discourteous people:* dislike, aggravation, annoyance, irritation, vexation, exasperation; complaint, grievance, gripe.

Ant. 1 please, delight, captivate. 2 pleasure, delight, like.

peevish *adj. Father gets peevish when he's kept waiting:* cross, irritable, testy, grumpy, grouchy, ill-humored, petulant, snappish, cantankerous, cranky, crabby, huffy; ill-natured, bad-tempered, quarrelsome.

pejorative *adj. In its pejorative sense, "light" means "weak":* belittling, disparaging, uncomplimentary, deprecatory, detracting, derogatory, depreciatory, demeaning, downgrading, degrading, debasing, disapproving.

Ant. complimentary, approving, favorable.

pell-mell *adv. The work was thrown together pell-mell:* helter-skelter, slapdash, recklessly, impetuously, rashly, hastily, precipitately, hurriedly, heedlessly, carelessly.

Ant. neatly, methodically; calmly, serenely.

pelt[1] *v. The boxers pelted each other in the middle of the ring:* hit, strike, batter, pummel, pound, punch, buffet, whack, thwack, thrash, rap, pepper; sock, belt.

pelt[2] *n. The goat had a grayish pelt:* animal skin, skin, hide, fur; coat, fleece.

pen *n. How many sheep are in the pen?:* enclosure, fold, pound, corral, paddock, compound, stockade; cage, coop, sty, crib, hutch, stall.

penal *adj. Devil's Island was a famous penal colony:* of punishment, disciplinary, punitive, corrective, punishing, castigatory, retributive; of jails, of prisoners.

penalty *n. The sign read "No trespassing under penalty of $50 fine":* punishment, forfeiture, retribution, infliction, assessment, suffering; fine, forfeit; handicap.

Ant. reward, prize.

penance *n. The faithful did penance for their sins:* repentance, expiation, atonement, contrition, mortification, penitence, propitiation.

penchant *n. He had a penchant for rich desserts:* fondness, partiality, liking, strong inclination, fancy, preference, predilection, proclivity, propensity, leaning, attraction, taste, relish, tendency, affinity, predisposi-

tion; flair, bent, readiness, knack, gift.

Ant. dislike, aversion; disinclination.

pendent Also **pendant** *adj. The necklace was a gold band with pendent diamonds:* hanging, suspended, dangling, pendulous, swinging.

pending *adj. Final disposition of the case is still pending:* awaiting, undetermined, undecided, unsettled, unresolved, unfinished, up in the air, imminent, in the offing.

pendulous *adj. The pendulous vines made the jungle impassable:* hanging, suspended, dangling, pendent; drooping, sagging.

penetrate *v.* 1 *The nail easily penetrated the soft wood:* pierce, puncture, cut into, bore, prick, perforate; cut through, pass through. 2 *The foul odor penetrated the house:* pervade, permeate; enter, invade, infiltrate. 3 *Were you able to penetrate the author's symbolism?:* understand, comprehend, fathom, get, figure out, see through, catch.

penetrating *adj.* 1 *a penetrating odor:* piercing, sharp, stinging, caustic, biting, acrid, strong, pungent, harsh; pervading, pervasive. 2 *The book is a penetrating study of the labor movement:* keen, perceptive, discerning, shrewd, astute, intelligent, smart, clever, trenchant.

Ant. 1 mild, sweet. 2 unperceptive, superficial, shallow.

penetration *n.* 1 *The heavier the arrow the greater its penetration into the target:* power of penetrating, foray, passage, invasion, intrusion; perforation, piercing, boring, puncturing. 2 *She showed great penetration in analyzing the problem:* insight, keenness, sharpness, perception, discernment, perspicacity, astuteness, intelligence, cleverness, quickness.

Ant. 2 obtuseness, superficiality, shallowness.

penitence *n. If a sinner feels penitence, he can be forgiven:* repentance, remorse, regret, sorrow, humiliation, contrition; penance, attrition, expiation, atonement.

penitent *adj.* 1 *Those who were penitent obtained absolution:* penitential, repentant, contrite, atoning, remorseful, sorry, conscience-stricken, regretful. —*n.* 2 *The penitents were saying their prayers at early Mass:* a penitent person; devotee, pilgrim.

Ant. 1 impenitent, unrepentant.

penitentiary *n. The murderer was sentenced to the penitentiary:* federal prison, state prison; *(loosely)* prison, jail, penal institution, house of correction, house of detention; *Slang* pen, joint, slammer, stir, big house.

pennant *n. A pennant was flying from the mast:* flag, banner, streamer, ensign, standard, colors, jack, pennon, burgee, bunting, ensignia.

penniless *adj. Bad investments left me penniless:* moneyless, destitute, poverty-stricken, impoverished, indigent, needy; insolvent, ruined, wiped out; *Slang* broke.

Ant. rich, wealthy, moneyed, well-heeled.

pensive *adj. a pensive mood:* sadly thoughtful, reflective, meditative, contemplative, introspective, musing, dreaming, daydreaming, dreamy; sad, wistful, melancholy, solemn, somber.

Ant. frivolous, joyous, cheerful, carefree, lighthearted.

pent-up *adj. The children need to work off their pent-up energy:* repressed, suppressed, restrained, stifled, checked, stored-up.

penury *n. She lived in penury during her last years:* poverty, impoverishment, indigence, privation, destitution; financial ruin, insolvency.

Ant. wealth, prosperity, luxury, affluence.

people *n. pl.* 1 *Will people ever live 200 years?:* human beings, humans, mortals, men and women, individuals, humankind, Homo sapiens, mankind, humanity. 2 *The people of the city want better schools. My people came from Ireland:* citizens, citizenry, inhabitants, population, populace; family, ancestors, relatives, kin, kinfolk, folks. 3 *A politician must appeal to the people:* the public, the common people, the rank and file, the masses, the multitude, the man in the street, John Q. Public; the common run; the working class, the mob, the rabble, the herd, the crowd, the great unwashed, the hoi polloi.

Ant. 3 nobility, aristocracy, gentry, blue bloods, silk-stockings.

pep *n. She's always full of pep:* vigor, vim, vitality, verve, energy, snap, zip, go, get-up-and-go; animation, vivacity, spirit, enthusiasm, life, ginger.

peppery *adj. This soup is too peppery:* highly seasoned, spicy, hot, piquant, fiery, pungent, sharp.

Ant. bland, mild, insipid.

peppy *adj. The band played a peppy tune:* brisk, lively, spirited, energetic, vigorous, dynamic, animated, vivacious, sparkling, snappy.

Ant. listless, lethargic, sluggish, slow, dull.

perceive *v.* 1 *We perceived a faint aroma of dill:* notice, be aware of, detect, note, discern, make out, recognize, distinguish, apprehend, discover; observe, see, hear, smell, taste, feel, sense. 2 *She gradually perceived that her parents had been right:* understand,

comprehend, apprehend, grasp, realize, know, conclude, deduce.

Ant. 1 overlook, ignore, miss.

perceptible *adj. The difference is barely perceptible:* perceivable, discernible, noticeable, apparent, detectable, observable, visible, discoverable, ascertainable; evident, manifest, tangible, notable; unconcealed, unhidden.

Ant. imperceptible, indiscernible, unnoticeable, unapparent, undetectable; concealed, hidden.

perception *n. A good driver must have a good perception of distance:* discernment, awareness, sense, faculty, apprehension, conception, recognition, comprehension, consciousness, detection; discrimination, judgment, understanding, grasp.

perceptive *adj. She is very perceptive about the moods of others:* full of insight, sensitive, aware, discerning, penetrating; intelligent, keen, sharp, astute, acute, sensible, quick.

Ant. insensitive, obtuse, callous, indifferent.

perch *n.* 1 *The bird sat on its perch:* roost, roosting place, resting place, rest, seat. —*v.* 2 *The boy perched in the tree and called to his friends:* sit, roost, rest, settle; light, alight, land.

perdition *n. Sinners may suffer eternal perdition:* damnation, condemnation, loss of heavenly salvation, loss of one's soul; everlasting punishment, hellfire, Hell.

peremptory *adj.* 1 *a peremptory decision:* final, irrevocable, irreversible, incontrovertible, unquestionable, decisive, unequivocal; unavoidable, obligatory, imperative. 2 *She's much too peremptory to cooperate with others:* domineering, authoritative, dictatorial, assertive, aggressive, high-handed; opinionated, dogmatic.

Ant. 1, 2 indecisive. 2 submissive, unassertive, passive, docile, compliant.

perennial *adj. He seems to have a perennial grin on his face:* perpetual, everlasting, permanent, constant, incessant, unceasing, ceaseless, continual, continuous, unremitting, persistent; fixed, changeless, unchanging, lasting, enduring, undying, unfailing, long-lived.

Ant. temporary, occasional, sporadic, intermittent, periodic.

perfect *adj.* 1 *Can you draw a perfect circle?:* exact, accurate, precise, true, correct in every detail, flawless, unerring, strict, scrupulous, faithful. 2 *in perfect health. The child has been a perfect angel:* faultless, flawless, without defect, unblemished, unimpaired, undamaged; complete, whole,

entire, unbroken, finished, absolute, thorough, unqualified, unmitigated, impeccable, ideal, blameless, untainted, immaculate.
—*v.* 3 *The scientist perfected a method of desalting seawater:* bring to perfection, develop, complete, achieve, accomplish, effect, realize, fulfill.
Ant. 1, 2 imperfect. 2 faulty, flawed, defective, impaired, ruined, spoiled, damaged, deficient, qualified; inferior, poor, bad, *Informal* awful, *Slang* lousy.

perfection *n.* 1 *The roast was cooked to perfection:* perfectness, excellence, faultlessness, flawlessness, superiority, ideal state; exactness, accurateness, precision. 2 *The perfection of the jet engine took many years:* development, completion, achieving, accomplishment, realization, fulfillment.

perfectly *adv.* 1 *The cake was baked perfectly:* to perfection, superbly, wonderfully, flawlessly, faultlessly, without fault, without defect, without·blemish. 2 *She's perfectly capable of taking care of herself:* entirely, thoroughly, completely, totally, fully, wholly, altogether, quite, utterly, absolutely, supremely, preeminently, consummately, to the nth degree; positively, purely.
Ant. 1 imperfectly, faultily; poorly, badly. 2 not; partially; mistakenly, erroneously, inaccurately.

perfidious *adj. Benedict Arnold's perfidious act:* treacherous, traitorous, treasonous, deceitful, false, disloyal, unfaithful, faithless, treasonable, dishonorable, untrustworthy, unscrupulous; dishonest, corrupt, untruthful, double-dealing, two-faced.

perforate *v. The nail perforated the tire:* pierce, prick, puncture, penetrate, punch, drill, stick; slit, gash, slash.

perform *v.* 1 *A skilled worker can perform the task easily:* do, accomplish, carry out, execute, effect, fulfill, discharge, dispose of. 2 *The actors performed* Twelfth Night: play, present, render; act, enact, take part in.
Ant. 1 neglect, forsake.

performance *n.* 1 *He failed in the performance of his duty:* discharge, accomplishment, execution, performing, doing, exercise, fulfillment, realization, achievement, dispatch, effectuation; completion. 2 *The theater gives two performances a day:* show, presentation, production, exhibition.

perfume *n. Who's wearing that spicy perfume?:* fragrance, scent, essence, cologne; aroma, smell, odor, bouquet.
Ant. stench, stink.

perfunctory *adj. That was a perfunctory "hello" she gave us:* indifferent, disinterested, offhand, careless, unconcerned, cursory, inattentive, lax, superficial, routine, mechanical, halfhearted, lukewarm, spiritless, negligent.
Ant. thoughtful, diligent, attentive, warmhearted, effusive, ardent.

perhaps *adv. Perhaps we could go:* maybe, possibly, conceivably, perchance, imaginably.
Ant. definitely, certainly, surely.

peril *n. Do you understand the perils?:* risk, danger, hazard, jeopardy, pitfall, threat, cause for alarm; uncertainty, unsafety.
Ant. safety, security, certainty, surety; invulnerability.

perilous *adj. The floodwaters were perilous to cross:* risky, hazardous, dangerous, unsafe; uncertain, unsure, chancy, vulnerable, precarious.

perimeter *n. Trees were planted on the perimeter of the garden:* periphery, border, borderline, circumference, bounds, margin, edge.
Ant. center, middle, heart.

period *n.* 1 *The lunch period is from twelve to one. Dinosaurs roamed the earth in an earlier period:* time, span of time, interval, interlude, duration; era, epoch, age, eon. 2 *The confession put a period to the investigation:* end, stop, close, finish, termination, halt, cessation.

periodic Also **periodical** *adj. She makes periodic visits to her mother:* repeated, recurring, recurrent, frequent, regular, at fixed intervals; cyclic, seasonal.

periodical *n. The library subscribes to scores of periodicals:* publication; *(variously)* newspaper, paper, magazine, newsletter, journal, bulletin, review, daily, weekly, monthly, quarterly, annual.

peripatetic *adj. a peripatetic painter:* wandering, itinerant, traveling, roving, migrant, rambling; walking, ambulating, tramping, roaming, migratory, nomadic.

periphery *n. on the periphery of the town:* outskirts, fringes; boundary, edge; perimeter, circumference, border.
Ant. center, middle, hub, heart.

perish *v. Dozens perished in the storm. The ancient Aztec culture has perished:* die, pass away; become extinct, vanish, disappear, be destroyed.
Ant. be born, arise; thrive, flourish.

perishable *adj. perishable foods:* subject to decay, subject to spoiling, decomposable; unstable; short-lived, transitory, ephemeral.
Ant. nonperishable, durable, long-lasting, long-lived.

permanent *adj. a permanent monument. Are these dyes permanent?:* lasting, perpetual, everlasting, eternal, undying, never-ending, unending, immortal, deathless, abiding, indestructible, imperishable; unalterable, changeless, immutable; long-lasting, durable, unfading, constant, stable. *Ant.* temporary, short-lived, variable, changing.

permeate *v. That cigar smoke permeates the house:* penetrate, soak through; pervade, saturate, diffuse throughout, infuse, fill, imbue.

permissible *adj. Is smoking permissible?:* permitted, allowed, admissible, granted; authorized, lawful, legal.
Ant. forbidden, prohibited, banned; unlawful, illegal.

permission *n. May I have permission to use the car?:* leave, consent, assent, approval, acquiescence, compliance, approbation; authorization, sanction, dispensation, indulgence.
Ant. refusal, denial, prohibition, ban.

permissive *adj. Should parents be strict or permissive?:* indulgent, lenient, assenting, consenting, acquiescent, tolerant, easygoing, forbearing.
Ant. strict, rigid, authoritarian, proscriptive.

permit *v.* 1 *Permit me to ask a question. The rules do not permit players to step out of bounds:* let, allow, give permission, consent to, tolerate, bear with, approve, condone, OK; authorize, sanction, endorse, license. —*n.* 2 *Do you have a driver's permit?:* license, official permission, authorization, authority, sanction.

pernicious *adj. a pernicious disease:* harmful, injurious, serious, destructive, damaging, deleterious, detrimental, dangerous, disastrous, baneful, lethal, deadly, fatal, mortal, toxic.
Ant. harmless, innocuous; beneficial, advantageous, wholesome.

perpetrate *v. to perpetrate a crime:* commit, perform, carry out, execute, do, enact, transact, pursue.

perpetual *adj. the perpetual care of the park. I'm tired of your perpetual nagging:* lasting forever, permanent, everlasting, eternal, enduring; constant, endless, never-ending, continuous, ceaseless, incessant, unceasing, interminable, uninterrupted, unremitting, continual.
Ant. temporary, short-lived, transitory.

perpetuity *n. The fund was endowed in perpetuity:* eternity, forever, permanence, time without end, all time, endlessness.

perplex *v. Mathematics perplexes me:* puzzle, baffle, confuse, bewilder, confound, muddle, befuddle, stump, mystify.

perquisite *n. The perquisites of the job included a car:* benefit, privilege, right, fringe benefit, *Slang* perk, gift, present, reward, recompense.

persecute *v. They were persecuted for their religious beliefs:* harass, harry, oppress, tyrannize, harrow, hector, hound; torment, maltreat, abuse.
Ant. pamper, indulge, humor.

persevere *v. To succeed you must persevere:* persist, be steadfast, be determined, be resolved, be resolute; work hard, keep at it, stick to one's guns.
Ant. be irresolute, waver, falter, give in.

persist *v.* 1 *She persisted in her efforts to get a college education:* persevere, work unflaggingly, be tenacious, not give up, be steadfast, be determined, be resolute, keep at it. 2 *The flowers persisted even in the driest weather:* last, endure, survive, continue.
Ant. 1 be irresolute, waver, vacillate; give up, stop, cease. 2 die, wither.

persistent *adj.* 1 *With persistent efforts we can finish on time:* stubborn, determined, obstinate, tenacious, relentless, persisting, dogged, persevering, steadfast, resolute, unfailing, unswerving. 2 *Her persistent criticism made everyone angry:* constant, unrelenting, unceasing, incessant, continual, continuous, endless, sustained, interminable, unremitting.

person *n. There will be 12 persons at our table:* individual, human being, human, being, creature, mortal, soul, body.

personable *adj. a personable hostess:* having a pleasing personality, likable, friendly, outgoing, amiable, cordial, charming, attractive, pleasant, cordial, amicable.
Ant. unpleasant, surly, ill-natured.

personage *n. the personages of the entertainment world:* luminary, dignitary, VIP, notable, nabob, celebrity, public figure, leading light, popular hero; *Slang* bigwig, big shot, big name.
Ant. nobody, unknown, nonentity.

personal *adj. the president's personal papers:* private, own, intimate, confidential, secret, particular, privy; inward, subjective.

personality *n.* 1 *an agreeable personality:* outward character, disposition, temperament, makeup, nature; identity, individuality. 2 *An entertainer has to have a lot of personality:* charm, personal attraction, friendliness, agreeableness, amiability, affability; magnetism, charisma.

personify *v. The Venus de Milo personified the ideal of female beauty:* embody, represent, exemplify, incorporate, express, symbolize; externalize.

personnel n. *All personnel will receive a bonus:* employees, workers, staff, staff members, work force, crew, manpower.

perspective n. 1 *From the top of the hill you can get a perspective of the entire park:* panoramic view, bird's-eye view, overview, vista, scene, view, outlook, prospect. 2 *I've been so close to the problem I have no perspective on it:* broad view, overview, comprehensive point of view, viewpoint, sense of proportion.

persuade v. *Can't we persuade you to join us?:* induce, influence, move, get, prevail upon, motivate, convince, win over, bring round, talk into, sway, coax, wheedle, cajole, inveigle; lure, tempt, entice.
Ant. dissuade, discourage, deter, inhibit.

persuasive adj. *a persuasive speaker:* convincing, compelling, forceful, believable, plausible, credible; effective, winning.

pert adj. 1 *Don't be pert to your elders:* impudent, impertinent, insolent, brash, flippant, flip, fresh, saucy, cheeky, brazen, brassy, smart-alecky. 2 *She walked with pert little steps:* lively, sprightly, brisk, perky, spry, chipper; alert, wide-awake.
Ant. 1 shy, bashful, meek, modest; respectful, diffident.

pertinent adj. *His remarks were pertinent to the discussion:* relevant, to the point, germane, material, appropriate, fitting, befitting, apt, applicable, suitable, apropos, meet; related, concerned, connected.
Ant. irrelevant, immaterial, inappropriate, unfitting, unrelated, unconnected.

perturb v. *The teacher was perturbed by the student's lack of interest:* disturb, trouble, worry, disquiet, upset; bother, fluster, disconcert.

perusal n. *a perusal of the document:* reading, examination, scrutiny, review, runthrough, inspection, study, scanning, scrutinizing.

pervade v. *The aroma of coffee pervaded the house:* permeate, spread through, diffuse throughout, suffuse, fill, infuse, imbue.

perverse adj. *She takes a perverse delight in disagreeing with everyone:* contrary, stubborn, obstinate, wrongheaded, ornery; headstrong, willful, wayward.
Ant. agreeable, good-natured, obliging, amiable.

pervert v. *The dictator perverts the very idea of democracy:* distort, warp, contort, abuse, misuse, corrupt, misapply, falsify; desecrate, corrupt, degrade, debase, deprave.

perverted adj. *a perverted sense of right and wrong:* distorted, twisted, warped, unbalanced; false, faulty, fallacious, unsound; degraded, depraved, debased, corrupt, un-

natural, abnormal, deviant.
Ant. sound, valid, balanced; natural, normal.

pesky adj. *The pesky mosquitoes attacked in droves:* annoying, exasperating, irksome, bothersome, vexatious, troublesome; aggravating, infuriating, maddening, disturbing; disagreeable, distasteful.

pessimism n. *His pessimism is depressing:* gloomy outlook, seeing only the gloomy side; despair, hopelessness, discouragement, downheartedness, gloom, gloominess.
Ant. optimism, hopefulness; enthusiasm, cheerfulness.

pessimist n. *A pessimist never expects anything to turn out well:* defeatist, one who sees only the bad side, prophet of doom, gloomy Gus, kill-joy, wet blanket.
Ant. optimist, incurable romantic.

pest n. *mosquitoes and other pests. That child is a real pest!:* troublesome insect, trouble some animal, destructive plant; annoying person, nuisance, bother, annoyance, irritation, vexation.

pester v. *He's always pestering me:* bother, annoy, torment, badger, plague, harass, harry, hector, taunt, nag, vex, irritate, irk, disturb, trouble.

pet n. 1 *Does a dog make a better pet than a cat?:* household animal, house pet. 2 *My younger brother was mother's pet:* favorite, darling, baby, *Slang* apple of one's eye; dear, beloved, loved one, sweetheart. —adj. 3 *my pet project:* favorite, choice, favored, preferred, dearest. —v. 4 *Don't pet the dog:* pat, stroke, caress, fondle.

petition n. 1 *The petition for a new traffic light had 500 names:* formal request, appeal, entreaty, plea; proposal, suit, solicitation; application; prayer, supplication, invocation, imploring. —v. 2 *The condemned man petitioned the governor for clemency:* ask, beg, beseech, entreat, appeal to, request of, plead with, urge, press, seek; pray, supplicate, invoke.

petrified adj. 1 *a piece of petrified wood:* stony, rocklike, hard as a rock, turned to stone. 2 *She was petrified with fear:* paralyzed, frozen, immobilized, transfixed, numb, terror-stricken, *Informal* scared stiff.

petty adj. 1 *Don't bother me with such petty matters:* trivial, trifling, insignificant, unimportant, inconsequential, minor, paltry, slight, small, picayune, piddling, niggling. 2 *It was petty not to accept the apology:* small-minded, narrow-minded, mean, ignoble, ungenerous.
Ant. 1 important, major, consequential,

significant, momentous. 2 broad-minded, large-hearted, magnanimous, generous.

petulant *adj. When he doesn't get his way, he gets petulant:* peevish, irritable, cross, snappish, sullen, sulky, surly, grumpy, grouchy, testy, huffy, irascible, sour, crotchety, ill-tempered.

Ant. pleasant, good-natured, complaisant, gracious.

phantasm *n. Scrooge saw the phantasm of Christmas Past:* phantom, ghost, apparition, vision, specter, spirit, incubus, succubus.

phantom *n. Was it his long-lost sister or only a phantom?:* apparition, specter, spirit, ghost, wraith, phantasm; dream, mirage, chimera, hallucination, illusion, vision.

phase *n.* 1 *an early phase:* stage, period, degree, level, step, point of development. 2 *Examine every phase of the problem:* aspect, facet, feature, side, angle, slant, viewpoint; guise, appearance.

phenomenal *adj. a woman of phenomenal intelligence:* extraordinary, exceptional, outstanding, remarkable, surpassing, uncommon, unusual, unprecedented, unparalleled, stupendous, prodigious, unique, singular, incredible, miraculous, marvelous; spectacular, fantastic, sensational, astonishing, amazing.

Ant. ordinary, common, unexceptional, routine, normal, average.

phenomenon *n.* 1 *Snow is a phenomenon of winter:* occurrence, happening, visible fact, natural event, part of existence, contingency, thing, actuality, incident, episode. 2 *Beethoven was a phenomenon among musicians:* rarity, marvel, miracle, wonder, remarkable person, exceptional thing, sensation.

philanderer *n. Everyone knew he was a philanderer:* trifler, Don Juan, flirt, rake, libertine, womanizer, lothario, adulterer, ladykiller, lecher, woman-chaser, *Slang* wolf, lover boy.

philanthropic Also **philanthropical** *adj. The orphanage is one of her philanthropic causes:* charitable, eleemosynary, benevolent, humanitarian, generous, bounteous, magnanimous, munificent.

philanthropist *n. The philanthropist gave millions to charity:* benefactor of charities, contributor, donor, giver; humanitarian, Good Samaritan.

philanthropy *n. Many organizations benefited from her philanthropy:* charity, charitableness, humanitarianism, benevolence, beneficence, largeheartedness, generosity, munificence.

philistine *n.* 1 *He's too much of a philistine*

to patronize the arts: lowbrow, cultural ignoramus, yahoo; bourgeois, Babbitt. —*adj.* 2 *a philistine remark:* uncultured, uncultivated, uneducated, unenlightened, ignorant; lowbrow, bourgeois; anti-intellectual.

Ant. 1 intellectual, highbrow; *Slang* egghead.

philosopher *n. Plato was a philosopher of ancient Greece:* student of basic truths, seeker of wisdom, truth seeker; wise man, sage, logician, philosophizer, thinker, theorizer.

philosophic, philosophical *adj.* 1 *The problem demands a philosophic approach:* reasonable, logical, rational, judicious, thoughtful, sagacious; theoretical, abstract. 2 *She's very philosophical about her bad luck:* stoic, stoical, resigned, fatalistic, impassive, unemotional, composed, calm, serene, imperturbed, unruffled.

Ant. 1 illogical, irrational, thoughtless; pragmatic. 2 emotional, excited, perturbed, distraught.

philosophy *n.* 1 *The judge pursued philosophy:* study of basic truths, seeking after wisdom; logic, reason, reasoning, thought, thinking, philosophizing, theorizing, ideas. 2 *the philosophy of Bertrand Russell. My philosophy is live and let live:* system of beliefs, beliefs, convictions, conception, doctrine, basic idea, principle; view, viewpoint.

phlegmatic *adj. He was too phlegmatic to relate to other people:* indifferent, apathetic, nonchalant, unemotional, unimpassioned, unresponsive, unconcerned, unexcitable, calm, impassive, stoical; spiritless, listless, languid, lethargic, passive, unfeeling, insensitive.

Ant. emotional, passionate, excited; interested.

phobia *n. She has a phobia about heights:* unreasonable fear, terror, horror, dread, aversion, loathing, apprehension, overwhelming anxiety.

phony Also **phoney** *adj.* 1 *a phony ten-dollar bill:* not genuine, fake, counterfeit, forged, sham, spurious, bogus, mock, pretended; artificial, imitation, synthetic, false, fraudulent, deceptive. —*n.* 2 *This painting isn't a Rembrandt; it's a phony:* fake, sham, fraud, counterfeit, imitation, fraud, hoax, forgery.

Ant. 1 real, authentic, genuine, bona fide. 2 the genuine article, *Slang* the real McCoy.

phrase *n.* 1 *He has a way with a phrase:* expression, words, turn of phrase, word group; remark. 2 *In the words of the old phrase, "Time's a-wasting":* figure of speech, saying, expression, truism, proverb, maxim, aphorism, cliché, platitude, banality, colloquialism, dictum; idiom, locution. —*v.* 3 *The way you phrased the question I couldn't understand it:* express, word, put into words, find words, couch, put, state; say, voice, utter, enunciate, verbalize, articulate.

physical *adj.* 1 *the physical universe:* material, existent, natural, tangible; substantive, solid, real, actual, external. 2 *physical desire:* of the body, corporeal, fleshly, animal, carnal, sensual.
Ant. 1 nonmaterial, intangible. 2 spiritual, moral; intellectual.

physician *n. You'd better see a physician:* doctor, M.D., medical doctor; GP, general practitioner, surgeon, specialist; *Slang* medic, doc.

physiognomy *n. A person's physiognomy was thought to reveal character:* features, outward appearance, countenance, visage; shape, profile, contour, configuration.

picaresque *adj. Don Quixote was a picaresque hero:* roguish, rascally, scampish, roistering, raffish, mischief-loving; adventuresome, daring.

picayune Also **picayunish** *adj. Why quarrel over such a picayune matter?:* trifling, trivial, petty, paltry, insignificant, unimportant, inconsequential, inconsiderable, slight, measly, piddling, small, little.

pick *v.* 1 *Pick the one you want:* select, choose, decide upon, settle upon, single out, elect, opt for. 2 *to pick flowers:* pluck, pull off, pull out; gather, collect, harvest. —*n.* 3 *the pick of the litter:* choice, best, prize, preference, favored one, elite.
Ant. 1 reject, refuse, spurn, scorn. 3 worst.

picket *n.* 1 *One of the pickets in the fence was loose:* stake, palisade, pale, paling; tether, restraint. 2 *The picket warned the troops:* forward lookout, lookout, sentinel, watch, sentry, guard, patrol. 3 *The pickets marched in front of the factory:* striker; protester. —*v.* 4 *The union picketed the plant:* demonstrate against; *(loosely)* strike, walk out, go out.

pickle *n.* 1 *Would you like a pickle with that sandwich?:* pickled cucumber, cucumber pickle; *(variously)* sweet pickle, dill pickle, gherkin, sour pickle, bread-and-butter pickle, mustard pickle. 2 *If the work is late, we'll be in a pickle:* predicament, difficulty, tight spot, plight, jam, quandary, fix, mess, crisis, dilemma.

picture *n.* 1 *This is a picture of the house:* representation, portrayal, illustration, drawing, painting, sketch, study, etching; photograph, photo, snapshot. 2 *There's a good picture at the local theater:* motion picture, film, movie, *Slang* flick. 3 *She's the picture of her mother as a girl:* likeness, image, duplicate, copy, double. 4 *He was the picture of health:* perfect example, model, mirror, exemplification, personification, essence, embodiment. —*v.* 5 *The painter pictured the general sitting on a horse:* portray, represent, depict, illustrate, feature, delineate; paint, draw, sketch; photograph. 6 *Can't you just picture Mother on a roller coaster!:* imagine, see, envision, conceive of, fancy.

picturesque *adj. The view from our cabin is picturesque:* quaint, exotic, colorful, distinctive, interesting; imaginative, charming, artistic.
Ant. commonplace, drab; inartistic.

piddling *adj. The clerk got a piddling raise:* trivial, insignificant, inconsequential, unimportant, picayune, paltry, skimpy, slight, measly, small, little, puny.

piebald *adj. a piebald horse:* dappled, mottled, spotted, speckled; variegated, many-colored, particolored, motley.

piece *n.* 1 *a piece of pork. The glass broke into pieces:* portion, quantity, amount, share, slice, cut, chunk, hunk, lump; pat, bit, fraction; fragment, shard, part, shred, sliver; swatch, length, cutting; component, member, section, segment, division. 2 *This is a foul piece of treachery. The workers are paid by the piece:* instance, example, case, specimen, sample; unit, item, article, thing, entity. 3 *a piece by Chopin. Did you read this piece in today's paper?:* selection, composition, work, creation, study; play, drama, sketch; story, article, essay, review, item.
Ant. 1 all, total, sum, entirety, the whole.

pierce *v.* 1 *The nail pierced the tire:* perforate, puncture, penetrate, make a hole in, bore through, cut through, run through; stick, prick, stab, spear, spike, impale. 2 *Her angry words pierced everyone:* sting, hurt, pain; grieve, distress.

piercing *adj.* 1 *a piercing voice:* shrill, grating, screeching, shrieking, strident; loud, earsplitting, deafening. 2 *a piercing glance:* sharp, keen, penetrating, searching, probing; intense, fierce, furious, caustic, angry, painful, hurtful, agonizing.
Ant. 1, 2 calm, soothing. 1 mellifluous, quiet, low. 2 vague; pleasant, cheering.

piety *n. She expressed her piety by attending church daily:* piousness, religiousness, devoutness, devotion, godliness; reverence, respect, loyalty, dutifulness, humility.
Ant. impiety, sacrilege, ungodliness, irreverence; disrespect.

pigheaded *adj. He's so pigheaded you can't reason with him:* stubborn, obstinate, bullheaded, unyielding, unbending, inflexible, opinionated, obdurate, mulish, insistent.

Ant. complaisant, flexible, open-minded, tractable, amiable.

piker *n. He's a piker when it comes to charity:* cheapskate, pinchpenny, penny pincher, tightwad, skinflint, miser; petty person, niggard.

Ant. big spender, spendthrift, squanderer.

pile¹ *n.* 1 *a pile of dirty clothes:* heap, stack, mass, batch, pyramid, mound; accumulation, collection, assortment, store; quantity, profusion, abundance. —*v.* 2 *Pile the leaves by the tree:* heap, mass, amass, stack, assemble; accumulate, collect, gather.

Ant. 2 scatter, disperse, strew.

pile² *n. The carpet has a thick pile:* nap, shag, fluff; warp.

pile³ *n. Piles were driven into the ground:* piling, support, post, upright, pier, pillar, stanchion.

pilfer *v. He was caught pilfering from the cash register:* steal, thieve, purloin; plagiarize, pirate.

pilgrimage *n.* 1 *to make a pilgrimage to Mecca:* religious journey to a shrine, religious journey, devotional trip, *Islam* hadj, penitential sojourn. 2 *Sailing around the world was quite a pilgrimage:* journey, excursion, trek, long trip, voyage.

pillage *v.* 1 *The barbarians pillaged the town:* plunder, raid, sack, loot, ravage, maraud. —*n.* 2 *The pillage of the troops amounted to millions:* plunder, loot, booty, spoils, stolen goods, filchings; looting, robbery, plundering, sack, piracy.

pillar *n.* 1 *The porch is supported by six pillars:* column, post, upright, support, pile, piling, stanchion; pilaster, obelisk. 2 *a pillar of the community:* mainstay, tower of strength, important person, support, champion.

pilot *n.* 1 *The flying school graduates pilots:* flyer, aviator, airman. 2 *a riverboat pilot:* helmsman, wheelman, steersman, coxswain. —*v.* 3 *It's hard to pilot a boat in rough waters:* steer, be at the helm of, control, manage, handle, navigate; direct, lead, conduct, escort, guide.

pin *n.* 1 *Use a pin to fasten the pattern to the cloth: (variously)* straight pin, common pin; safety pin, diaper pin; hatpin; pushpin. 2 *a diamond pin:* brooch, clasp, clip, stickpin, breast pin. —*v.* 3 *Pin the Tail on the Donkey:* attach with a pin, affix, secure, fasten. 4 *The policeman pinned the thief's arms behind him:* pinion; hold fast, hold down; restrain, bind.

pinch *v.* 1 *She pinched her little brother's arm:* tweak, squeeze, nip; cramp, crimp,

compress, tighten, crush. 2 *Slang The thief pinched her pocketbook:* steal, snatch, swipe, lift, purloin, cop, filch. —*n.* 3 *She gave the boy a playful pinch on the cheek:* tweak, nip, squeeze. 4 *a pinch of salt:* bit, speck, mite, jot, spot, tittle. 5 *the pinch of hunger. I'll help you out in a pinch:* pain, discomfort, hardship, ordeal, trial, affliction, misery; emergency, crisis, predicament, difficulty, jam.

pine *v.* 1 *She pined for her native land:* yearn, long, hanker, sigh, languish; crave, hunger for, thirst after, desire, covet. 2 *She just pined away:* fail in health, decline, weaken, waste away, languish, wither, flag.

pinnacle *n. the pinnacle of a mountain:* highest point, peak, summit, apex, crest, zenith, height, top, acme, crown, cap.

pinpoint *n.* 1 *The car was just a pinpoint in the distance:* dot, spot, speck. —*v.* 2 *to pinpoint the cause of the trouble:* locate, detect, home in on; detail, characterize.

pioneer *n.* 1 *Pioneers settled here in 1870:* first settler, early immigrant, colonist; frontiersman, pioneer. 2 *a pioneer of the auto industry:* leader, trailblazer, forerunner, innovator, developer, founder, founding father, father; predecessor, antecedent, precursor. —*v.* 3 *The Wright brothers pioneered in early aviation:* be a leader, blaze the trail, lead the way, start, establish, found, create, develop.

pious *adj. He's a pious churchgoer:* devout, religious, dedicated, faithful, reverent, reverential; godly, spiritual, holy, divine, saintly, sainted.

Ant. impious, irreverent, irreligious, ungodly.

pipe *n.* 1 *a gas pipe:* tube, conduit; conveyor; main, duct. —*v.* 2 *The birds began piping:* whistle, sing, cheep, peep, trill, warble, twitter, chirp, tweet; play a flute, play a bagpipe.

piquant *adj.* 1 *a piquant sauce:* pungent, spicy, sharp, tangy, zesty, highly seasoned; hot, peppery, strong-flavored; biting, stinging, piercing. 2 *The play sparkled with piquant dialogue:* lively, peppy, sharp, zesty, spirited, scintillating, sparkling, stimulating, animated, provocative; racy, salty, spicy, peppery.

Ant. 1 bland, mild. 2 banal, inane, insipid, tame, uninteresting.

pique *v.* 1 *It piques me not to be consulted:* displease, offend, affront, hurt one's feelings, annoy, irritate, vex, irk, gall, nettle, miff, peeve. 2 *The book piqued my interest:* arouse, kindle, rouse, provoke, excite, stir.

Ant. 1 please, gratify, satisfy. 2 deaden, dull, kill.

pit¹ *n.* 1 *Dig a pit and bury the garbage. The*

wood is full of pits: hole, hollow, hole in the ground, cavity, crater, indentation, concavity, dent, dimple, pock. —*v.* 2 *The metal trivets are pitting the table:* gouge, dent, indent, nick, pock, scratch, scar. 3 *Pit the champion against an unknown:* match, set against, oppose, put in competition; contrast, juxtapose.

Ant. 1 mound, lump, bump, protuberance.

pit² *n. a cherry pit:* seed, stone; kernel.

pitch *v.* 1 *Pitch the tent near the stream:* set up, raise, erect; place, fix, establish, locate, station. 2 *She pitched the ball:* throw, hurl, heave, fling, cast, toss, lob, chuck, sling, fire, propel, shy. 3 *He lost his balance and pitched into the lake:* fall headlong, fall headfirst, fall, topple, tumble. 4 *The boat pitched in the storm:* rock from front to back, toss, plunge, lurch, bob, jolt, jerk. —*n.* 5 *The roof has a steep pitch:* slant, slope, incline, declivity, grade, cant, angle. 6 *The batter hit the pitch:* throw, delivery, heave, toss, lob, fling, chuck. 7 *My voice has a high pitch:* tone, sound; harmonic. 8 *The pitch of the ship threw me off balance:* forward plunge, headlong fall, dip, lurch.

piteous *adj. the piteous cry of a lost child:* pitiable, pitiful, sad, poignant, moving, heart-rending, heartbreaking, woeful, pathetic.

pitfall *n. the pitfalls of a career in politics:* hazard, risk, danger, peril, stumbling block

pithy *adj. The speech was short and pithy:* to the point, meaningful, cogent, forceful, effective, expressive; concise, terse, succinct.
Ant. diffuse, vague; wordy, verbose, rambling.

pitiful *adj.* 1 *the pitiful sobs of a child:* pitiable, piteous, heartrending, heartbreaking, moving, pathetic; sad, plaintive, miserable, forlorn, doleful. 2 *The movie wasn't just bad, it was pitiful!:* contemptible, deserving of scorn, miserable, pitiable, worthless, poor, insignificant, paltry, dreadful, godawful.
Ant. 1 happy, cheerful, merry, joyful. 2 commendable, praiseworthy, laudable; great, grand, glorious.

pitiless *adj. a pitiless tyrant:* merciless, heartless, inhuman, unmerciful, unpitying, unsparing, hard-hearted, cold-blooded, relentless, unrelenting, ruthless, cruel; unmoved, insensitive, uncaring, implacable.
Ant. merciful, softhearted, compassionate, benign, kind; caring.

pittance *n. He lives on a mere pittance:* small amount, trifle, modicum, little, mite; trifling sum.

pity *n.* 1 *The story aroused my pity. It's a pity you didn't finish college:* sympathy, compas-

sion, commiseration; cause for sorrow, regret, sad thing, shame; *Informal* crying shame. 2 *The tyrant showed no pity:* mercy, charity, clemency, leniency, kindliness, humanity, forbearance, lenity, magnanimity. —*v.* 3 *I pity the flood victims:* feel sorry for, have compassion for, commiserate with, sympathize with, feel for, weep for.

Ant. 1 anger, rage, wrath, fury; indifference, apathy. 2 cruelty, brutality, hardheartedness, inhumanity, mercilessness, pitilessness, ruthlessness.

pivot *v.* 1 *The gyroscope pivoted on its stand:* rotate, revolve, wheel, swivel, circle, spin, twirl, turn, whirl, pirouette. 2 *The passage of the bill pivots on the governor's support:* depend, hang, be contingent on, hinge on, revolve around, turn.

pivotal *adj. a pivotal point in my career:* decisive, crucial, critical, determining.

placate *v. No one can placate him:* calm, soothe, pacify, quiet, mollify, assuage.

place *n.* 1 *Is there any place to put this?:* space, spot, niche, point; site, location, position. 2 *This is a good place to shop:* establishment, concern, business, store, shop, company, firm. 3 *He was given an important place in the government:* position, situation, post, appointment, job, office, berth, station, commission, function, rank. 4 *We're having a party at my place:* residence, home, abode, house, dwelling, domicile, habitation, lodgings, quarters, premises; land property. 5 *New York's a nice place to visit. This is the place where the storm hit:* city, town, village; state, county; borough, district, neighborhood, vicinity, area, region, locality, locale, quarter; country, territory. —*v.* 6 *Place the chair in the corner:* put, set, rest, stand, situate, position, plant, deposit, settle, array, locate, ensconce, install; fix, affix, attach; house, lodge. 7 *The employment agency placed her with an insurance firm:* get a job for, find hire, find work for, appoint, assign, install. 8 *I can't place her face:* identify, remember, recognize.
Ant. 6 remove, take away, dislodge, detach.

placid *adj. a placid disposition:* calm, tranquil, peaceful; untroubled, smooth, undisturbed, collected, composed, unexcited, unexcitable, imperturbable; gentle, mild.
Ant. turbulent, agitated; excitable, emotional, impulsive; disturbed, perturbed.

plague *n.* 1 *In the 14th century the plague struck Europe:* bubonic plague, Black Death; epidemic, pandemic, epidemic disease. 2 *The plague of drought swept over the land:* affliction, scourge, calamity, misery,

agony, woe, trouble; evil, curse, bane.
—*v.* 3 *The mistake plagued me for years:*
torment, distress, worry, perturb, persecute,
harass, bother, vex, irk, nettle, harry,
badger; pain, afflict, embarrass, haunt, prey
on one's mind.

plain *adj.* 1 *The figures aren't plain enough
to read:* clear, distinct, legible, discernible;
obvious, apparent, pronounced, striking,
clear-cut. 2 *Please rephrase the question in
plain English:* easily understood, simple,
clear, straightforward, direct, unambiguous, understandable, comprehensible, unequivocal. 3 *The plain truth is that she
doesn't like you:* honest, frank, blunt, candid, sincere, forthright, straight, undisguised, undiluted, naked, bald, bare, unembellished, unvarnished, unadorned. 4 *a
plain blue shirt:* simple, unaffected, unpretentious, unassuming; modest; everyday,
ordinary, average, commonplace; unadorned, undecorated, unornamented, un-
garnished, without frills. 5 *a plain face:*
homely, not beautiful, unhandsome, unattractive; ordinary, not striking. —*n.* 6 *They
crossed the plains in a covered wagon:* prairie, grassland, tableland, plateau, open
country.
Ant. 1 indistinct, vague, blurred, illegible.
2 obscure, abstruse, difficult, ambiguous,
incomprehensible. 3 deceptive, evasive, disguised, veiled. 4 affected, pretentious; orna-
mented, adorned; fancy. 5 beautiful, gorgeous, comely, handsome.

plainly *adv.* 1 *Although wealthy, he dresses
plainly:* simply, unpretentiously, unassum-
ingly, modestly, ordinarily. 2 *It's plainly the
newest house on the block:* clearly, obviously, visibly, strikingly, discernibly, mani-
festly; undeniably, unquestionably, undoubtedly, doubtless, definitely, without
doubt, beyond doubt. 3 *She stated plainly
that she didn't want to go:* clearly, distinctly, explicitly, directly, unmistakably,
unambiguously, unequivocably; frankly,
bluntly, candidly, openly, positively.

plain-spoken *adj. a plain-spoken Yankee
farmer:* frank, direct, open, forthright, sincere, candid.

plaintive *adj. What a plaintive wail!:* sad,
mournful, sorrowful, lamenting, moaning,
melancholy; doleful, woebegone, tearful,
heartrending, rueful, pathetic, piteous, pitiful.

plan *n.* 1 *a plan for renewing the business
district. an architect's plan:* scheme, program, idea, conception, procedure, method,
way, strategy; design, blueprint, sketch, diagram. —*v.* 2 *The entertainment committee
will plan the dance:* organize, devise, make

arrangements, conceive, think out, plot,
contrive, design; form, frame, outline, project. 3 *Do you plan to stay late?:* intend, aim,
purpose, propose.

plant *n.* 1 *Are these bean plants?:* vegetation,
flora, herbage; *(variously)* tree, flower, bush,
shrub, vine, grass. 2 *the workers at the
plant:* factory, shop, works, yard, mill,
foundry; business, establishment. —*v.*
3 *Plant the flowers in April:* put in the
ground, sow seed, set in, set out; transplant.
4 *to plant the love of learning in students:*
implant, instill, engender, inculcate, inspire,
establish.

plastic *adj. Clay is a plastic substance:* easily
molded, shapable, formable, pliable, pliant,
ductile, malleable, flexible, tractable, elastic, supple, soft.
Ant. hard, stiff, inflexible, inelastic.

plate *n.* 1 *Put the plates in the dishwasher:*
dish; serving dish, platter, saucer. 2 *a plate
of stew:* serving, helping, platter, platterful,
portion, dish.

plateau *n. The ranch is in the middle of a
large plateau:* elevated plain, tableland,
mesa; highland, upland.
Ant. valley, ravine; swamp, lowland.

platitude *n. The speech was full of plati-
tudes:* trite remark, stereotyped expression,
cliché, banality, commonplace, truism,
hackneyed saying, old saw, threadbare
phrase.

platoon *n. an infantry platoon:* two or more
squads; *(loosely)* unit, detachment, group,
force, team, crew, band, body.

plaudit *n.* Usually **plaudits** *the plaudits of
the critics:* praise, approval, acclaim, commendation, approbation, kudos, compliment, rave; applause, cheer, cheering, hurrah.
Ant. condemnation, jeer, taunt, hoot, boo,
hiss.

plausible *adj. Is the story plausible?:* believable, probable, credible, convincing, likely,
persuasive, reasonable, rational, feasible,
conceivable, possible, logical.
Ant. unbelievable, improbable, incredible,
unlikely, implausible, unreasonable.

play *n.* 1 *a play by Shakespeare:* drama, stage
play, dramatic piece, dramatic perform-
ance; *(variously)* comedy, tragedy, farce,
melodrama; show. 2 *all work and no play:*
amusement, recreation, entertainment, diversion, fun, pleasure, enjoyment. —*v.*
3 *The children play indoors when it rains:*
engage in games; amuse oneself, have fun,
enjoy oneself; gambol, romp, frisk, sport,
cavort, skylark; trifle, toy. 4 *The teams will*

play Saturday. We played basketball: contend against, compete with, perform in a game; participate in a sport, take part, be on a team. **5** *to play the piano. Who will play Lady Macbeth?:* perform on, perform; act, act out, act the part of, take the part of, personify, enact, represent.

playboy *n. The spoiled son grew into a playboy:* pleasure seeker, party boy, good-time Charlie, profligate, rake, lecher, womanizer, ladies' man, Romeo, Lothario, Casanova, Don Juan.

Ant. ascetic, monk.

player *n.* **1** *a baseball player. Hide-and-seek can be played by many players:* team member, performer, athlete, jock; participant, contender, competitor, contestant, opponent. **2** *the cast of players:* actor, actress, thespian, trouper; performer, entertainer.

playful *adj. Kittens are playful. a playful remark:* full of play, frolicsome, frisky, lively, rollicking, coltish, sportive; not serious, jesting, humorous, capricious, impish, prankish, lighthearted.

Ant. serious, grave.

plea *n.* **1** *a plea for aid:* appeal, entreaty, prayer, suit, petition, supplication, solicitation, beseeching, begging, request. **2** *His plea was that he'd been unavoidably detained:* excuse, defense, argument, justification, apology, alibi.

plead *v. She pleaded with the officer not to give her a ticket:* beg, beseech, implore, entreat, appeal to; importune, enjoin, supplicate, adjure.

pleasant *adj.* **1** *a pleasant day:* agreeable, pleasing, pleasurable, enjoyable, lovely, attractive, inviting, felicitous, good, fine, nice; mild, gentle, soft. **2** *a pleasant young man:* likable, genial, friendly, amiable, cheerful, good-humored, good-natured, sociable, cordial, warm, amicable, polite.

Ant. **1** unpleasant, disagreeable, wretched, distressing, miserable. **2** unlikable, unfriendly, offensive, ill-humored, ill-natured, rude.

pleasantry *n. an exchange of pleasantries:* polite remark, good-natured remark, greeting, quip, jest, witticism, humorous remark.

please *v.* **1** *Good manners please one's elders:* gladden, delight, give pleasure to, make happy, gratify, satisfy, suit, content, elate; charm, enthrall, entrance; amuse, entertain. **2** *She lives as she pleases:* like, wish, choose, desire, want, will, be inclined, elect, prefer.

Ant. **1** displease, offend; sadden, grieve.

pleasing *adj. The movie was pleasing. a pleasing personality:* pleasurable, gratify-

ing, satisfying, enjoyable, amusing, diverting, entertaining; attractive, agreeable, inviting, likable, winning, captivating, charming, friendly, affable, amiable, congenial, genial, good-natured, good-humored, polite.

Ant. displeasing, unpleasant, unattractive, disagreeable, unlikable.

pleasure *n.* **1** *The gift gave the child a great deal of pleasure:* enjoyment, happiness, joy, delight, gratification, cheer, elation, exultation; gaiety, mirth, merriment, jubilation. **2** *All they seek in life is pleasure:* amusement, fun, gratification, diversion, entertainment, recreation, gaiety. **3** *What's your pleasure, coffee or tea?:* desire, choice, wish, will, inclination, preference, selection.

Ant. **1** displeasure, unhappiness, sorrow, sadness; anger, vexation. **2** labor, toil; self-denial, abstinence. **3** necessity, duty, obligation.

plebeian *adj.* **1** *She has plebeian taste in furniture:* common, lowbrow, unrefined, uncultivated, uncultured, commonplace, banal, ordinary, low, lowborn, bourgeois. —*n.* **2** *He may be rich, but at heart he's a plebeian:* common man, commoner, average man, average citizen, one of the masses, bourgeoisie.

Ant. **1** highbrow, refined; upper class, aristocratic, royal, elevated. **2** aristocrat, patrician, noble; intellectual, highbrow.

pledge *n.* **1** *I gave him my pledge I would vote for him:* vow, promise, oath, word, assurance, avowal, troth; agreement, pact, compact, covenant, contract. **2** *The pawnbroker took the camera in pledge for the loan:* security, warranty, guaranty, collateral, surety; pawn. —*v.* **3** *I pledge allegiance to the flag:* promise, vow, swear, bind by an oath, assert, guarantee, warrant, give one's word.

plentiful *adj. a plentiful supply of food:* abundant, profuse, copious, bountiful, bounteous, prolific, ample, plenteous, liberal, generous, large, unsparing, unstinted.

Ant. scant, scanty, sparse, inadequate, insufficient, scarce, skimpy, meager.

plenty *n.* **1** *There's plenty of room for everybody:* abundance, sufficiency, plenitude, good deal, a wealth, enough, lots, worlds, oodles, gobs, scads. **2** *We wish you peace and plenty:* prosperity, well-being, good fortune; riches, wealth, luxury, opulence.

Ant. **1** scarcity, sparsity, dearth, shortage, scantiness, paucity, inadequacy. **2** poverty, hard times.

plethora *n. The potluck supper had a pleth-*

ora of desserts but no meat dishes: excess, surplus, superfluity, surplus, surfeit, overabundance, glut, overage, redundancy.

Ant. shortage, lack, scarcity, deficiency.

pliable *adj.* 1 *Soak the bark to make it pliable:* flexible, easily bendable, pliant, plastic, elastic, springy. 2 *pliable young children:* impressionable, pliant, compliant, receptive, responsive, flexible, easily influenced; manageable, adaptable, yielding, acquiescent, tractable.

Ant. 1 stiff, unbending. 2 stubborn, obstinate, inflexible, unyielding.

plight *n. The plight of the people has not improved:* condition, situation, circumstance, state; poor condition, distressing situation, dangerous circumstances, predicament, dilemma, distress, trouble, difficulty, tribulation; crisis, impasse.

plod *v.* 1 *We plodded through the mud:* trudge, walk heavily, drag, slog, lumber, shuffle, waddle. 2 *The youth plodded along at his lessons:* work slowly, drudge, toil, grind, struggle; persevere, stick with it, *Slang* plug.

plot[1] *n.* 1 *The government uncovered a revolutionary plot:* conspiracy, intrigue, secret plan, evil plan, scheme, machination. 2 *the plot of the novel:* story, story line, tale, narrative. —*v.* 3 *to plot against the king:* conspire, scheme, intrigue, design, contrive, be in collusion. 4 *The navigator plotted the ship's course:* chart, map, compute, calculate, determine; mark, draw, sketch, outline, diagram.

plot[2] *n. Tomatoes will grow easily on this plot:* section, area of ground, patch; lot, tract, field, clearing.

plow *v.* 1 *Plow the field after the last frost:* dig up, turn up, spade, dig, till, break up, furrow, harrow, cultivate. 2 *The ship plowed through the sea:* push, press, plunge, drive, cut, shove, forge.

ploy *n. Her ploy was to get me to invest in her business:* stratagem, ruse, trick, game, maneuver, strategy, tactic, gambit, scheme.

pluck *v.* 1 *Please don't pluck the flowers:* pick, pull out, pull off; pull at, grab, yank, snatch. —*n.* 2 *He showed a lot of pluck by fighting back:* spirit, mettle, courage, valor, boldness, spunk; resolution, determination, resolve, fortitude, doggedness, perseverance, tenacity.

plumb *v. The geologist plumbed the depths of the ocean. She tried to plumb the depths of his mind:* sound, fathom, measure, test; probe, penetrate, gauge, examine.

plummet *v. The hawk plummeted toward the earth:* plunge, fall, fall headlong, drop

straight down, dive, descend abruptly.

Ant. rise, ascend, soar.

plump[1] *adj. She's short and plump:* chubby, pudgy, somewhat fat, fleshy, stout, portly, stocky, rotund.

Ant. slender, slim, lean; thin, skinny, scrawny.

plump[2] *v. The youth plumped down in the chair:* drop, plop, flop, plunk, sprawl, tumble.

plunder *v.* 1 *The invaders plundered the town:* sack, pillage, loot, ransack, raid, rob, ravage. —*n.* 2 *The pirate ship was filled with plunder:* loot, booty, pillage, spoils, prize, *Slang* swag.

plunge *v.* 1 *He plunged the red-hot metal into a bucket of water. The boys plunged into the swimming pool:* dip, thrust, immerse, duck, submerge, submerse; dive, jump, leap, fall headlong, tumble. 2 *The firemen plunged into the building:* rush, dash, run, dart, charge, hurtle, bolt, sprint, scramble, lunge, scurry, tear, shoot, fly, streak, surge; push, press. 3 *The boat plunged in the high seas:* pitch, toss, lurch, heave, reel, rock, roll. —*n.* 4 *The sky diver had a plunge of more than 20,000 feet before his parachute opened:* drop, fall, dive, headlong rush, jump, leap.

Ant. 1 emerge, rise, withdraw, take out. 2 stroll, amble.

plus *adj. Typing isn't a requirement for the job, but would be a plus factor:* additional, extra, added, supplementary; supplemental; helpful, desirable, useful, beneficial, advantageous.

plush *adj. a plush apartment:* sumptuous, luxurious, opulent, deluxe, lavish, fancy, grand, posh, lush, swank, swanky.

Ant. simple, Spartan, austere.

ply *v.* 1 *She plied her shuttles in making lace:* employ, wield, put to use; manipulate, operate, work, handle. 2 *Father still plies his trade as a carpenter:* practice, carry on, follow, labor at, pursue. 3 *Salesmen ply their customers with food and drink. Reporters plied the candidate with questions:* besiege, thrust upon, urge upon, supply persistently, offer repeatedly. 4 *The ship plies the route between Hong Kong and Singapore:* travel regularly, make repeated trips, go back and forth; sail, navigate, run, fly.

pocket *n.* 1 *a shirt pocket. a garment bag with four pockets:* pouchlike part of a garment; compartment, envelope, receptacle, chamber; cavity, hollow. 2 *The prospector found a pocket of silver in the hill:* isolated mass; vein, lode, pit, strip, strain. —*v.* 3 *I pocketed $200 on that deal!:* steal, put into one's pocket, arrogate, help oneself to;

get, obtain, come by, gain, receive. —*adj.*
4 *a pocket camera:* pocket-size, small, compact, little, miniature, diminutive, portable.

pocketbook *n. Is the money in your pocketbook?:* purse, handbag, bag, shoulder bag, clutch; wallet, pocket secretary, notecase, money purse.

pod *n. Remove the peas from the pod:* husk, jacket, hull, shell, sheath, case, seed case, seed vessel, pericarp.

poem *n. Kipling wrote my favorite poem:* verse, rhyme, verse composition; jingle, doggerel; *(variously)* ballad, ode, sonnet, elegy, epic, madrigal, lyric, idyll, limerick.

poignant *adj. The poignant story brought a tear to every eye:* moving, touching, heart-rending, pitiful, pitiable, piteous, pathetic, woeful, lamentable, sad, sorrowful.
Ant. unaffecting, unmoving, unfeeling.

point *n.* 1 *the point of a sword. The light-house is on the northern point of the island:* sharp end, tapered end, tip, nib; projection, protuberance, prominence, promontory. 2 *the freezing point of water:* degree, stage, position, condition, place; limit, mark. 3 *At that point we got up to leave:* instant, moment, time, juncture. 4 *I missed the point of the story:* main idea, purpose, object, gist, essence, pith. 5 *There's no point in arguing:* sense, reason, cause, object, objective, aim, purpose, value, use. 6 *Here's a point you may have overlooked:* item, particular, aspect, feature, quality. 7 *The team won by two points:* score, tally, run, goal. —*v.* 8 *Point the gun at the target:* aim, train, direct; steer, guide, turn, level. 9 *Your conduct points to an ulterior motive:* indicate, suggest, imply, signify, intimate, hint at; portend, foreshadow, presage, bode, argue; demonstrate, prove.

pointed *adj. She made a pointed remark:* pertinent, fitting, telling, penetrating, trenchant, appropriate; piercing, cutting, insinuating.
Ant. pointless, irrelevant, inappropriate.

pointless *adj. Further discussions are pointless:* useless, purposeless, unproductive, unprofitable, unavailing, meaningless, fruitless, futile, worthless, irrational, illogical, preposterous, irrelevant, beside the point.
Ant. useful, profitable, meaningful, fruitful, worthwhile; appropriate, fitting, reasonable, logical.

poise *n. Public speaking requires a lot of poise:* assurance, self-assurance, self-confidence, self-control, presence of mind, aplomb, equanimity, calm, composure.

poison *n.* 1 *Strychnine is a deadly poison:* toxic chemical, harmful chemical, bane;

(loosely) venom, toxin, harmful drug. 2 *Hate is a poison for which there is no antidote:* evil, harm, curse, bane, disease, cancer, malignancy. —*v.* 3 *Tainted food can poison your system. Lucrezia Borgia supposedly poisoned many people:* kill with poison, harm with poison, give poison to; infect, contaminate, make sick, weaken, debilitate. 4 *Industrial wastes are poisoning the atmosphere. Don't allow him to poison your mind:* contaminate, pollute, taint; corrupt, defile, debase.
Ant. 1 antidote. 2 good, benefit.

poisonous *adj. The leaves of some plants are poisonous:* lethal, fatal, toxic, venomous, deadly, baneful.
Ant. beneficial, healthful; harmless, innocuous.

poke *n.* 1 *a poke in the ribs:* jab, thrust, punch, hit, push, prod, nudge, dig, thump. —*v.* 2 *Stop poking me:* prod, jab, dig, push, hit, punch.

police *n.* 1 *Call the police!:* law-enforcement organization, police force, sheriff's office; law-enforcement officers, policemen, troopers, constabulary, police men, men in blue, *Slang* fuzz. —*v.* 2 *Watchmen police the factory at night:* patrol, guard, protect; keep in order, regulate, control. 3 *The soldiers police the parade ground:* clean, clean up, tidy up, pick up trash from, spruce up.

policeman *Fem.* policewoman *n. Ask the policeman for directions:* police officer, officer, officer of the law, law-enforcement officer, cop, *Slang* flatfoot; *(variously)* patrolman, cop on the beat, motorcycle policeman, traffic cop; sheriff, marshal, constable.

policy *n. The store's policy is to give cash refunds. U.S. foreign policy:* practice, procedure, course, system, program, routine, habit, custom, rule, behavior, way, method, principle; plan, strategy, design.

polish *v.* 1 *Polish the silver:* shine, buff, burnish; wax, gloss, varnish, glaze. 2 *She spent several days polishing her speech:* perfect, improve, enhance, round out, touch up, emend, correct. —*n.* 3 *shoe polish:* wax, gloss, varnish, glaze, oil; abrasive, sandpaper, pumice, rouge. 4 *Four years of college gave her considerable polish:* grace, culture, cultivation, refinement, finesse, suavity, urbanity; good manners.
Ant. 1 tarnish, oxidize. 3 remover.

polite *adj.* 1 *What a polite young man!:* courteous, well-mannered, mannerly, well-behaved, respectful, diffident, gentlemanly. 2 *polite society:* refined, cultured, polished, genteel, well-bred, civilized, elegant, fashionable, high, elite, patrician.
Ant. 1 rude, impolite, discourteous, ill-

mannered, unmannerly, impertinent. **2**
unrefined, ill-bred, crude, boorish.

politic *adj. Be politic and don't mention the
time:* tactful, judicious, prudent, circumspect, discreet, diplomatic.
　Ant. rude, tactless, blundering, rash.

politician *n. The mayor is a skilled politician:* politico, political careerist; office
seeker, campaigner, officeholder, public servant, legislator, statesman.

politics *n. pl.* **1** *the history of European politics:* political science, art of government, administration of public affairs, practice of
government; affairs of state, government
policy, statecraft, statesmanship. **2** *an argument about politics:* political views, political matters, party policy, political maneuvers.

poll *n.* **1** *I'll vote as soon as the polls open:*
voting place; voting list; voting, vote, returns, tally, figures. **2** *an independent poll:*
public opinion poll, public survey, sam-
pling, census, canvass; public opinion.
　—v. **3** *We polled the members:* take the vote
of, solicit the vote of, canvass, survey.

pollute *v. Waste products are polluting the
river:* contaminate, befoul, foul, dirty, adulterate, sully, make filthy, defile.
　Ant. purify, clean, cleanse.

pollution *n. air pollution:* contamination,
contaminating, fouling, dirtying, defiling;
uncleanness, adulteration; pollutant, impurity.

pomp *n. The coronation was performed with
great pomp:* stately display, ceremony, solemnity, pageantry, spectacle; splendor,
grandeur, brilliance, flourish.

pompous *adj. a pompous bureaucrat:* self-
important, pretentious, arrogant, patronizing, condescending, overbearing, presumptuous, puffed-up; vain, conceited, egotistic,
supercilious, proud, blustering, swaggering.
　Ant. simple, modest.

pond *n. a duck pond:* small lake, lagoon,
pool.

ponder *v. I pondered the problem for days:*
consider, meditate on, reflect on, think over,
cogitate, ruminate, puzzle over, mull over,
muse, reflect.

ponderous *adj.* **1** *a ponderous package:*
heavy, burdensome, awkward, cumber-
some, unwieldy; massive, bulky, hefty; ungraceful, hulking, lumbering.
　Ant. light, weightless; dainty.

pontifical *adj.* **1** *The Pope donned his pontifical robes:* churchly, priestly, ecclesiastical, clerical, episcopal, apostolic. **2** *He can't
make a simple statement without seeming
pontifical:* pompous, pretentious, conde-

scending, patronizing; overbearing; opinionated, dogmatic.

pool *n.* **1** *Deer often come to drink at the pool:*
pond, lake; puddle. **2** *a car pool:* group, association, combine, coalition, confederation,
cooperative, collective, alliance, union.
　—v. **3** *We pooled our resources:* combine,
merge, share, consolidate, unite, ally.

poor *adj.* **1** *He was so poor, he couldn't afford
the carfare:* poverty-stricken, destitute, impoverished, penniless, moneyless, *Slang*
broke; needy, in need, strapped, *Informal*
hard up. **2** *The land was too poor to produce
crops:* unfertile, infertile, sterile; meager, exhausted, depleted, unproductive. **3** *poor
grades. It was a poor attempt:* inferior,
inadequate, deficient, defective, wanting,
faulty; paltry, wretched, sorry, indifferent,
vain, futile, unprofitable, unworthy. **4** *The
poor man never knew what hit him:* pitiable,
unfortunate, unlucky, pathetic, miserable,
wretched. *—n.* **5** *The state must care for the
poor:* the unfortunate, the needy, the penniless, the destitute, the indigent.
　Ant. **1, 2** rich. **1** affluent, wealthy,
moneyed, well-off. **2** fertile, productive, fecund. **3** worthy, excellent. **5** the rich, the
affluent, the wealthy.

pop *v.* **1** *One of the balloons popped:* explode,
burst; bang, discharge, detonate, crack,
snap. **2** *The magician had rabbits popping
out of the hat:* appear, materialize, issue
forth suddenly.

poppycock *n. Informal Don't tell me you
believe that poppycock!:* balderdash, bunk,
bosh, nonsense, rubbish, hogwash, rot, falderal, twaddle, blather, prattle, tommyrot,
fiddlefaddle, flapdoodle, drivel, baloney.

popular *adj.* **1** *Mary was always popular:*
sought-after, in favor, in demand, accepted;
well-liked, admired; well-known, celebrated, famous. **2** *Taxes are always a popular issue. The movie is back at popular
prices:* public, of the people, democratic;
inexpensive, affordable, cheap. **3** *the popular view on the matter:* current, prevalent,
fashionable; accepted, familiar, conventional, established.
　Ant. **1–3** unpopular. **1** unaccepted; un-
liked. **3** uncommon, unusual, rare, unconventional.

popularity *n. The comedian enjoyed great
popularity:* favor, acceptance, approval,
vogue, fashion, fame, celebrity, renown.

population *n. The population wants lower
taxes:* inhabitants, residents, citizenry, public, citizens; people, populace.

populous *adj. a populous region:* populated,
peopled, crowded, teeming, jammed,
swarming, thronged, thickly settled.

pore v. *We pored over the report:* read, study, examine, scrutinize, inspect, search, review.

pornographic adj. *The book seemed pornographic to me:* obscene, indecent, lewd, salacious, dirty, smutty, filthy, blue.

port n. *The ship arrived in port:* seaport, harbor, dock, pier, wharf, quay, landing; anchorage, mooring; shelter, refuge, haven.

portable adj. *a portable television set:* transportable, movable, haulable, conveyable, liftable; compact, pocket, small; light, manageable.

portal n. Usually **portals** *Many students have passed through these portals:* entrance, entranceway; door, gate, gateway, doorway, entry, threshold, arch.

portend v. *Sales figures portend bad times ahead:* foretell, forecast, augur, bode, prophesy, predict, prognosticate; herald, signify, point to, warn of, forewarn, presage, betoken, denote, suggest.

portent n. *The clouds were portents of rain:* warning, sign, forewarning, boding, foreboding, threat, dire prospect; omen, sign, augury, harbinger.

portentous adj. 1 *The dictator's speech was portentous:* foreboding, threatening, intimidating, ominous, menacing, alarming, frightening; significant, prophetic; unpropitious, inauspicious. 2 *a pianist of portentous talent:* prodigious, stupendous, amazing, astonishing, remarkable, extraordinary, superlative, exceptional. 3 *The book is portentous:* pompous, pretentious, grandiose; bombastic, grandiloquent.

portion n. 1 *A portion of the contract dealt with royalties:* part, section, division, segment, sector; piece, fraction, fragment; measure, quantity. 2 *Her portion of the inheritance was $50,000:* part, division, allotment, share, apportionment, allocation; serving, helping, percentage. 3 *We must accept our portion in life:* fortune, lot, destiny, fate, kismet; God's will. —v. 4 *She portioned out the pie:* divide, distribute, deal out, disperse; separate, split, segment, partition, apportion, allocate.

portly adj. *a portly gentleman:* heavy, fat, corpulent, obese, fleshy, plump, pudgy, full-figured, rotund, stout, stocky, chubby, tubby, endomorphic.
Ant. thin, slender, trim.

portray v. 1 *The artist portrayed her as almost saintly:* depict, describe, picture, delineate; sketch, draw, paint, sculpture, photograph. 2 *Who portrayed King Lear?:* enact, play, characterize; impersonate, pose as, mimic, ape. 3 *The author portrayed his father as a tyrant:* describe, depict, characterize, represent, set forth, delineate, picture.

pose v. 1 *The photographer posed them in front of a fireplace:* position, arrange, group, set, line up. 2 *She always poses at fancy parties:* posture, act self-consciously, act affectedly, show off, give oneself airs. 3 *He posed as a newsman to get in:* pretend to be, pass oneself off as, impersonate. 4 *Allow me to pose a question:* state, put forward, submit, set forth, postulate, advance, present, propose, propound, suggest. —n. 5 *He assumed a stiff pose:* attitude, posture, position, stance, bearing, carriage; mien, air, mannerism.

posh adj. *a posh hotel:* elegant, fancy, refined, deluxe, classy, chic, lavish, luxurious, opulent, swanky, ritzy.
Ant. simple, modest, austere.

position n. 1 *The hill was a perfect position for a home:* place, location, locus, situation, site, station. 2 *The sprinters lined up in a crouching position:* posture, stance, pose, attitude. 3 *The guards were in position at the exits:* at one's station, usual or proper place. 4 *Anyone in my position might have done the same thing:* situation, predicament, condition, state, circumstances, plight. 5 *a woman of high position:* standing, status, station, prominence, eminence, distinction, importance, prestige, consequence, notability; class, place, order. 6 *I held an important position with the company:* job, place, post, capacity, function, role, appointment, assignment, responsibility, commission, office. 7 *What's your position on foreign aid?:* opinion, viewpoint, point of view, stand. —v. 8 *She positioned the shells on the mantle:* put, place, arrange, array, set; pose, establish, stand, fix, situate, locate, lodge, deposit.

positive adj. 1 *He gave a positive identification of the killer:* firm, absolute, decisive, unqualified, definite, definitive, unequivocal, explicit. 2 *She was positive she had seen you:* sure, certain, confident, assured, dead certain, convinced. 3 *He always has positive ideas on policy:* practical, constructive, useful, helpful, serviceable; beneficial, good. 4 *What we need is positive thinking!:* forward-looking, optimistic, progressive, affirmative, cooperative. 5 *Your positive ways made you hard to live with:* dogmatic, opinionated, narrow, overbearing, dictatorial; unchangeable, assertive, self-assured.
Ant. 1 inconclusive, qualified, indefinite. 2 unsure, uncertain. 3 negative; impractical, useless. 4 pessimistic.

positively adv. 1 *She positively identified him as the attacker:* absolutely, unquestionably, indisputably, decidedly, definitely, unmistakably, indubitably; emphatically, categorically, unqualifiedly, affirmatively, confidently, certainly. 2 *It's positively the worst movie I've seen:* definitely, literally, without doubt, assuredly, absolutely.

possess *v.* 1 *They possess eight acres of land:* own, have, hold. 2 *She possesses a beautiful voice:* have, be endowed with, be blest with; command; enjoy. 3 *Nazi Germany possessed most of Europe during World War II:* conquer, vanquish, overrun, control, occupy, take over, acquire. 4 *Richard III was possessed by his wish to be king:* dominate, control, obsess, consume; fixate, mesmerize, dominate; make insane.

possession *n.* 1 *Possession is nine-tenths of the law:* possessing, owning, ownership, proprietorship; occupation, occupancy, control, custody, hold, title, tenancy. 2 *He had few possessions:* belonging, material thing, effect. 3 *These islands were possessions of Spain:* dominion, territory, province, protectorate.

possibility *n.* 1 *What's the possibility of having a sunny weekend?:* chance, likelihood, prospect, probability, odds. 2 *There's always the possibility that I will fail:* chance, eventuality; risk, hazard, gamble, contingency. 3 *That idea has great possibilities:* potentiality, promise, prospects; feasibility, practicability.

possible *adj.* 1 *Here is one possible program:* potential, contingent, conceivable, thinkable, imaginable, hypothetical; reasonable, admissible. 2 *Anything is possible!:* capable of being done, attainable, obtainable, achievable, feasible, conceivable; capable of happening.
   Ant. 1, 2 impossible. 1 inconceivable, unimaginable, improbable; unthinkable, unreasonable. 2 unobtainable, unfeasible.

possibly *adv.* 1 *Possibly we'll meet again:* perhaps, maybe, could be, may be, conceivably, perchance. 2 *She couldn't possibly have left without me:* by any means, in any way, at all, by the remotest chance.

post¹ *n.* 1 *a fence post:* stake, picket, upright, pale, support, column, shaft, pile. —*v.* 2 *He posted the news on the bulletin board:* put up, fasten up; publish, make known, announce, broadcast, circulate, declare, disclose, report, proclaim; inform, notify, advise, apprise, enlighten.

post² *n.* 1 *The policeman was at his post:* place of duty, station; round, beat. 2 *He held an important post with the company:* job, position, office, situation, place, spot, station; assignment, appointment. 3 *The general returned to the post:* military camp, base, headquarters; settlement; trading

post, post exchange. —*v.* 4 *Post two soldiers at each gate:* station, situate, install, place, put, set; camp, settle; locate.

posterior *adj.* 1 *the posterior portion of the house:* rear, back, hindmost, aftermost, hinder, rearward. —*n.* 2 *I slipped and landed on my posterior:* rump, buttocks, backside, behind, seat, bottom; *Slang* butt, fanny, derrière.

posterity *n.* *They preserved her writings for posterity:* future generations, succeeding ages; offspring, descendants, heirs, issue, successors, progeny; young, children.

postpone *v.* *to postpone a meeting:* defer, delay, put off, hold in abeyance, suspend; stay, table, shelve.

postulate *v.* 1 *Some postulate that good exists in everyone:* propose, put forth, submit; assume, take as an axiom, presuppose; conjecture, guess, surmise, theorize, hypothesize, speculate. —*n.* 2 *We believe the postulate that virtue is its own reward:* premise, assumption, fundamental principle, presumption, axiom, theorem, theory, hypothesis.

posture *n.* 1 *These exercises will improve your posture:* stance, carriage, bearing; attitude, mien. 2 *The meeting took on a different posture after that speech:* mood, tone, tenor, aspect, air, attitude; situation, circumstance, predicament.

potent *adj.* 1 *a potent fighter:* powerful, strong, forceful, overpowering, formidable, tough. 2 *a potent speaker:* influential, convincing, persuasive, compelling, impressive; forceful, powerful, dynamic. 3 *Aspirin is a potent drug:* effective, efficacious.
   Ant. 1 impotent, weak; ineffectual. 2 unconvincing, unimpressive.

potentate *n.* *The potentate had three palaces:* ruler, sovereign, *(variously)* sultan, suzerain, monarch, chieftain, mogul, satrap, emperor, prince.

potential *adj.* 1 *potential dangers:* possible, conceivable, latent, concealed, lurking, unapparent; unrealized, dormant; unexerted, unexpressed, implicit. —*n.* Also **potentiality** 2 *You're wasting your potential on this job:* ability, possibilities, capability.

potion *n.* *The potion turned the prince into a frog:* elixir, brew, concoction, dram, tonic, philter, draft, potation, libation.

potpourri *n.* *The meal was a potpourri of many dishes:* medley, mixture, mélange, pastiche, miscellany, hodgepodge, hash, mosaic, patchwork, motley.

pouch *n.* *a leather pouch:* bag, sack, satchel, receptacle, container.

pounce *v.* 1 *The hawk pounced on the mouse:* fall upon, plunge, spring upon, jump at; surprise, take unawares. —*n.* 2 *With one pounce, the leopard killed its prey:* swoop, rush, spring, leap, jump.

pound *v.* 1 *I pounded on the window. The boxer pounded his opponent:* strike, hammer, drum, beat, batter, bang, pummel, thump, thwack, clout, smack, wallop; lambaste, thrash, paste. 2 *My heart pounded:* throb, beat, pulsate, palpitate.

pour *v.* 1 *Pour champagne into the glasses:* let flow, decant; spill, effuse. 2 *Perspiration poured from him:* stream, issue, flow, gush, spout, cascade. 3 *It poured all night:* rain, rain hard, rain cats and dogs, come down in buckets.

pout *v. Stop pouting and do what I tell you:* sulk, make a long face, brood, mope.

poverty *n.* 1 *The family lived in poverty:* privation, need, destitution, indigence, penury, impoverishment, pennilessness, pauperism. 2 *There's a poverty of talent today:* lack, deficiency, insufficiency, shortage, dearth, paucity, scarcity, deficit.
Ant. 1 wealth, affluence, luxury. 2 abundance, overabundance, plethora.

power *n.* 1 *Only humans have the power of speech:* faculty, capability, capacity, competence, aptitude, talent, skill, genius, attribute, qualification, gift, endowment, property, quality. 2 *You could see the power in her hands:* strength, force, might, powerfulness, pressure. 3 *The manager has the power to fire an employee:* right, prerogative, influence, authority, license. 4 *the power behind the throne. The Western powers want peace:* authority, ruler; dominant state, superpower, major nation. —*v.* 6 *Electricity powers our appliances:* energize, activate, operate.
Ant. 1 incapability, incapacity. 2 weakness, impotence, feebleness.

powerful *adj.* 1 *a powerful body:* strong, mighty, potent, robust, sturdy, hardy, brawny, athletic, muscular, herculean. 2 *a powerful speaker:* commanding, authoritative, forceful, energetic, rousing, moving, exciting, effective.

powerless *adj. Samson was powerless after Delilah cut his hair:* helpless, without strength, feeble, incapable, weak, debilitated, immobilized.

practical *adj. Let me give you some practical advice:* useful, sensible, realistic, down-to-earth, serviceable, utilitarian, pragmatic; efficient, businesslike; hardheaded, unsentimental, unromantic, matter-of-fact.
Ant. impractical, theoretical, speculative.

practicable *adj. The idea may not be practicable:* practical, feasible, workable, attainable, doable, possible, achievable, viable,

performable, within the realm of possibility.
Ant. impracticable, impractical, unworkable, unfeasible.

practically *adv. I'm practically finished:* virtually, in effect, nearly, almost, just about, all but, substantially, to all intents and purposes.

practice *n.* 1 *With practice I could speak French fluently:* training, drill, repetition, preparation, exercise, rehearsal. 2 *The new methods did not go into practice:* operation, action, use, effect, execution, performance, exercise, application, play. 3 *It was her practice to rise at dawn:* custom, wont, habit, procedure, rule, routine; process, method, manner, fashion, mode, way; ritual, conduct, observance. 4 *His shady practices got him a prison term:* method, action, deed, maneuver, device. —*v.* 5 *I practiced the piano:* rehearse; drill, train. 6 *Practice what you preach:* perform, do, carry out, follow, put into practice, put into action, apply, use, utilize, live up to, turn to use. 7 *He's practiced dentistry for a year:* work at, engage in, pursue, be engaged in.

pragmatic *adj. a pragmatic solution:* down-to-earth, matter-of-fact, practical, utilitarian, hardheaded, businesslike, sensible, realistic, unidealistic, hard-nosed, unsentimental.
Ant. idealistic, theoretical; romantic, sentimental.

praise *n.* 1 *I have nothing but praise for you:* good words, compliments; approbation, acclaim, congratulation, commendation, laudation; regard, esteem, respect; accolade, plaudit, cheer, hurrah; eulogy, panegyric, tribute, testimonial. —*v.* 2 *The mayor praised us:* commend, laud, acclaim, extol, congratulate, compliment, applaud, eulogize. 3 *Praise the Lord:* worship, celebrate, glorify, exalt; revere, venerate, honor.

praiseworthy *adj. a praiseworthy deed:* worthy, estimable, excellent, fine, exemplary, commendable, admirable, laudable, meritorious.

prank *n. It was a harmless prank:* trick, joke, antic, shenanigan, horseplay, mischief, practical joke, stunt, spoof, tomfoolery.

prattle *n.* 1 *The prattle increased as the crowd grew restless:* gab, babble, blab, twaddle, chitchat; gibbering, jabbering, gabbling. —*v.* 2 *They prattled endlessly:* jabber, chatter, babble, blather, gabble.

pray *v. I pray for your good health:* make devout petition to God, commune with God, address the Lord, offer a prayer, say one's prayers.

prayer *n.* 1 *The priest led the congregation in prayer:* litany, orison, praise, thanksgiving, adoration, worship, glorification. **2** Often **prayers** *You're the answer to my prayers!:* hope, dream, aspiration; request, appeal, plea, petition, solicitation; supplication, invocation; entreaty, suit.

preach *v.* **1** *to preach the word of God:* sermonize, proclaim, discourse, evangelize, homilize, preachify. **2** *Practice what you preach:* advocate, urge, advise, counsel, profess, exhort, hold forth, declare, pronounce, expound, admonish, promulgate, prescribe.

preacher *n. a country preacher:* clergyman, minister, churchman, ecclesiastic, evangelist, reverend, pastor, man of the cloth, parson, vicar, curate, chaplain.

precarious *adj.* **1** *Our situation was precarious:* vulnerable, uncertain, problematical, ticklish, critical, insecure, unreliable, undependable, doubtful, dubious. **2** *a precarious occupation:* hazardous, risky, perilous, unsafe; chancy, unsteady, unstable, shaky; alarming.
Ant. **1** secure, dependable, reliable. **2** safe, steady, stable.

precaution *n. Take every precaution:* safety measure, caution, care, safeguard; forethought, provision, foresight, anticipation, carefulness, wariness.

precede *v. A dance act preceded the star's performance:* go before, come before, take place before; antedate, antecede.

precedence *n. My family takes precedence over my business:* importance, preeminence, predominance, prevalence; priority.

precedent *n. She set a precedent as the first woman executive in the company:* example, pattern, model, guideline, standard, criterion.

preceding *adj. The preceding message was prerecorded:* previous, earlier, prior, foregoing, antecedent, anterior; preexistent.

precept *n. His father gave him a few precepts before he left for college:* maxim, principle, axiom, rule, motto, commandment; law, edict, dictum, decree, regulation, canon.

precious *adj.* **1** *She owned many precious antiques:* costly, dear, expensive, highpriced; valuable, priceless, invaluable; rare, uncommon, choice, exquisite. **2** *A family is a precious blessing:* valuable, cherished, choice, treasured, prized, valued; beloved, adored, sweet, darling, adorable, lovable. **3** *Her precious mannerisms were comical:* excessively nice, dainty, affected, pretentious, overrefined, fastidious, prissy, finicky, fussy, particular.

precipice *n. The precipice has a 50-foot drop:* cliff, cliff edge, ledge, escarpment, bluff, headland, palisade.

precipitate *v.* **1** *The war precipitated inflation:* hasten, bring on, quicken, expedite, speed up, accelerate, advance, spur. **2** *The explosion precipitated tons of rock from the mountain:* throw, hurl, cast, fling, propel, drive, launch, catapult. —*adj.* **3** *to make a precipitate choice:* hurried, hasty, rushed, speedy; headlong, reckless, rash, foolhardy, thoughtless, impetuous, impulsive.

precise *adj. Can't you be more precise?:* exact, specific, strict, definite, explicit, accurate, distinct; careful, painstaking, meticulous, fastidious, particular; finicky, fussy.
Ant. inexact, indefinite, ambiguous, indistinct, vague, nebulous; careless, haphazard.

precision *n. Write with precision:* exactness, preciseness, accuracy, meticulousness, rigor, attention; factualness, truthfulness, fidelity.

preclude *v. Her schedule precludes a visit:* prevent, thwart, stop, check, forestall, deter, debar.
Ant. allow, facilitate, enable.

precocious *adj. a precocious child:* mature, advanced; smart, bright, brilliant, gifted; quick, clever.
Ant. backward, retarded, stupid.

preconception *n. You have this preconception about New Yorkers:* prejudgment, fixed idea, notion, presumption; bias, prejudice.

precursor *n. The damp breeze was the first precursor of the storm:* vanguard, forerunner; harbinger, messenger; usher, herald; predecessor, antecedent; sign, token, omen, portent, warning; symptom.

predestination *n. It was predestination that we met:* fate, fortune, kismet, destiny, providence, God's will, preordination, predetermination.
Ant. accident, chance.

predetermined *adj. The outcome was predetermined:* already settled, foreordained, preplanned, predestined, prearranged, planned, destined, fated.

predicament *n. How'd I ever get into this predicament?:* situation, dilemma, condition, trouble, crisis, difficulty, perplexity, sad plight, strait, quandary, jam, scrape, fix, bind, mess.

predict *v. I predict that you will meet a handsome stranger:* prophesy, forecast, foretell, prognosticate, foresee, divine, anticipate, envision; betoken, presage, augur, omen.

prediction *n. None of her predictions have come true:* prophecy, forecast, prognostication, augury, portent, divination.

predilection *n. I have a predilection for desserts:* preference, predisposition, partiality, proneness, proclivity, propensity, leaning, penchant, bent, inclination, tendency; attraction, love, liking, fondness, fancy, taste, hunger, appetite, relish; prejudice, bias, favor.

Ant. aversion, disinclination, dislike, hatred.

predispose *v. His mother's work as a doctor predisposed him to become one too:* incline, dispose, bias, prejudice, sway, influence, prompt, induce, persuade, encourage; entice, lure.

predominant *adj. English is one of the world's predominant languages:* dominant, important, major, reigning, sovereign, chief, main, leading, supreme, paramount; controlling, authoritative, ruling, influential, ascendant, powerful.

Ant. subordinate, secondary; minor, unimportant, lesser.

preeminent *adj. one of the preeminent surgeons of our day:* foremost, superior, supreme, paramount, consummate; unparalleled, unsurpassed, matchless, peerless, incomparable, best, greatest, dominant, predominant; eminent, renowned, illustrious, famous, famed, celebrated, honored, distinguished.

preempt *v. The President's address preempted an hour of prime TV time:* appropriate, expropriate, arrogate, take, usurp, commandeer.

preface *n. the preface to the book:* foreword, prologue, preamble, introduction, prelude, overture. —*v.* 2 *He prefaced his talk with a humorous story.* begin, introduce, lead into, open, initiate, launch.

Ant. 1 epilogue, postscript. 2 close, end, conclude.

prefer *v.* 1 *I prefer to read mysteries:* choose, like better, fancy, single out, pick out, elect, select, have rather, favor, opt. 2 *Prefer your claim as legal heir:* file, lodge, put forward, set forth, present, bring forward, offer, proffer, tender.

Ant. 1 dislike, reject, eschew.

preference *n.* 1 *Do you have a preference for a particular food?:* partiality, first choice, liking, fancy, predilection, inclination, bent, leaning, predisposition, proclivity, propensity; selection, pick. 2 *College graduates get job preference over high school graduates:* favoring, precedence, advantage, favored treatment, priority.

Ant. 1 dislike, aversion, eschewal.

pregnant *adj.* 1 *She was pregnant:* with young, parturient, gravid, gestating, with child, expecting, in a family way. 2 *The land was pregnant with lush growth:* full, replete, filled, fraught, abounding, teeming, plenteous, rich; prolific, fecund, productive. 3 *He provided many pregnant ideas:* mean-

ingful, important, provocative, significant, weighty, seminal, momentous; suggestive, full of possibilities.

prejudice *n.* 1 *Prejudice often blinds us to the truth:* bias, preconception, slant, prejudgment, predisposition, bigotry; intolerance, unfairness, discrimination, partiality, predilection, favoritism. 2 *Will you be able to judge without prejudice to the defendant?:* impairment, injury, detriment, damage, harm, hurt, disadvantage. —*v.* 3 *He prejudiced the audience with his demagoguery:* influence, sway, bias; predispose. 4 *Our attempted escape prejudiced any hopes for parole:* damage, harm, hurt, injure, spoil.

preliminary *adj. a preliminary hearing:* preparatory, initiatory, preparative, introductory, prefatory, precursory.

Ant. final, concluding; subsequent.

prelude *n.* 1 *Months of training were a prelude to the championship bout:* preliminary, introduction, preparation; opening, beginning, preamble, preface, prologue. 2 *Chopin's preludes:* short instrumental piece; overture, introductory movement.

premature *adj.* 1 *The announcement of victory was premature:* too soon, too early, abortive, overhasty, precipitate. 2 *The crop is too premature to harvest:* unripe, undeveloped, immature, unready; incomplete, embryonic, vestigial; rudimentary.

Ant. 1 timely, opportune; late, overdue. 2 mature, ripe; overripe.

premeditated *adj. premeditated murder:* prearranged, predesigned, plotted, studied, planned; deliberate, conscious, intended, intentional, calculated, contrived.

premise *n.* 1 *My premise was that she was innocent:* hypothesis, basis for reasoning, proposition, argument, postulate, principle, theory; assumption, presumption, supposition, presupposition. 2 *premises The thief is still on the premises:* buildings and grounds, property, site; immediate area, vicinity.

premium *n.* 1 *If you buy now you get a premium:* gift, reward, return; recompense, compensation, payment; incentive, consideration. 2 *Tickets can be bought at a premium:* inflated rate, overpayment, increased value, appreciation. 3 *I put a premium on punctuality:* high value, great stock, priority.

premonition *n. She had a premonition that he had been injured:* forewarning, foreboding, omen, portent, presage, sign, augury, auspice, token, foretoken; presentiment, feeling, hunch.

preoccupy *v. I was too preoccupied to hear*

the bell: engross, occupy, absorb, immerse, take up; fascinate, obsess.

preparation *n.* 1 *We insulated the house in preparation for winter:* anticipation, precaution, prior measure, safeguard, provision, foresight, expectation. 2 *The preparation of the banquet hall took six hours:* readying, preparing. 3 Usually **preparations** *wedding preparations:* plan, arrangement, measure, preliminary. 4 *The druggist suggested a preparation to relieve the ache:* concoction, prescription, mixture, elixir, tincture. 5 *My earlier preparation made me perfect for the job:* experience, training, apprenticeship, instruction, education, guidance, tutelage, teaching, seasoning.

prepare *v.* 1 *We prepared the room for the party:* ready, make ready, get ready, adapt, arrange. 2 *They prepared themselves for the worst:* ready, prime, be resolved, make provision for, provide, be ready; take steps.

preponderance Also **preponderancy** *n. The preponderance of factories made the city ugly:* predominance, prevalence, profusion, domination, majority, dominance, mass, bulk, plurality; excess, abundance, surplus, surfeit, redundance.

preposterous *adj. That's the most preposterous idea I've ever heard:* outrageous, ridiculous, absurd, unthinkable, foolish, silly, imbecilic, asinine, idiotic, stupid, inane, laughable, irrational, unreasonable, bizarre.

prerequisite *adj.* 1 *Algebra is a prerequisite course before taking calculus:* required beforehand, required, mandatory, necessary, imperative, essential; indispensable. —*n.* 2 *Two years' experience is a prerequisite for this job:* requirement, qualification, necessity, requisite, condition, stipulation, demand.

prerogative *n. You have the prerogative of changing your mind:* privilege, right, license, liberty, freedom, advantage, exemption; authorization, legal power; choice, option.

prescribe *v. The bylaws prescribed that membership should be limited. The doctor prescribed rest:* direct, specify, stipulate, dictate, order, command, decree, ordain, proclaim, require, impose, demand; authorize, set, fix; recommend, advocate, urge.

presence *n.* 1 *Your presence at the meeting will help our cause:* attendance; existence, being, substantiality, entity, life. 2 *There's a spy in our presence:* company, midst; circle, group. 3 *She had a certain presence on the stage:* personal appearance, features, aspect, look, figure; charisma, character, vitality; air, manner, bearing, carriage, deportment, demeanor, mien.

present[1] *adj.* 1 *the present state of affairs:* current, existent, existing, contemporary, contemporaneous, prevalent, immediate. 2 *All the students are present:* here, in attendance, not absent; at hand, near, nearby, on hand, nigh; existing. —*n.* 3 *I live in the present:* now, nowadays, here and now, today, this day and age; the time being, the moment.
Ant. 1 past; future. 2 absent. 3 the past, the future.

present[2] *v.* 1 *It is my honor to present you with this token of our esteem:* give, confer, bestow, award, grant, accord, hand over; make a present of, donate, provide, supply; proffer, offer, propose, submit, put forward, tender; render; contribute. 2 *Please present your first witness:* call up, introduce, show, exhibit, display, produce. 3 *I presented my views and then sat down:* state, declare, apprise of, tell, make known, communicate; profess, cite, aver, recount, relate, recite, deliver, read. 4 *Present your bills on the first of the month:* submit, hand in, turn in. —*n.* 5 *birthday presents:* gift; offering, donation, benefaction, largess, bounty.

presentable *adj. Though plainly dressed, the child looked quite presentable:* becoming, proper, fit to be seen, suitable, appropriate, acceptable, passable, respectable.

presentation *n.* 1 *a presentation of an idea:* offering, proposal, proposition, proffering, submission, offer, proffer. 2 *The awards presentation lasted four hours:* show, exhibition, exposition, demonstration, exhibit, display; unfolding, disclosure. 3 *The check was the nicest presentation of all:* gift, present, bestowal, grant, benefaction, bounty.

presently *adv.* 1 *The show will begin presently:* soon, shortly, forthwith, directly, before long, in a while, in a short time. 2 *We are presently reading Shakespeare:* now, at present, at the present time, currently.

preservation *n. the preservation of natural resources:* conservation, saving; safeguarding, safekeeping, protection, maintenance.
Ant. depletion; destruction.

preserve *v.* 1 *We must preserve our natural resources:* keep safe, protect, care for, shield; conserve, save, defend, safeguard, maintain, nurse, foster. 2 *to preserve strawberries: (variously)* can, conserve, put up; freeze, cure, smoke, salt, corn, pickle; dehydrate, dry. —*n.* 3 Often **preserves** *I like peach preserves:* jelly, jam, conserve, compote, marmalade. 4 *a game preserve:* wildlife enclosure, sanctuary, reservation, reserve, refuge, park.

preside *v. Who will preside over the meeting?:* be in authority, hold the chair, chair; direct, conduct, control, govern, administrate, administer, command, supervise, manage, keep order, regulate; overlook, oversee; host, hostess.

president *n.* 1 *The president addressed the nation:* executive officer, chief executive, chief of state, head of government. 2 *the president of the company:* chief officer, chief official, head, executive head, chairman.

press *v.* 1 *Press the "down" button. Press one clove of garlic:* push; depress, push down, push in; compress, mash, crush, reduce, squeeze, cram, jam, stuff, force, strain. 2 *The tailor pressed the trousers:* iron, smooth, flatten. 3 *She pressed the puppy to her bosom:* hold closely, hug, squeeze, fold in one's arms, embrace, clasp. 4 *The problem pressed us for weeks:* trouble, oppress, burden, weigh heavily upon. 5 *He keeps pressing me for money:* beg, implore, urge repeatedly, entreat, enjoin, supplicate, appeal, exhort; dun, beset, urge insistently, prod; insist on, hound, pressure. 6 *The fans pressed around the rock group:* crowd, surge, swarm, throng, mill, gather, flock, cluster, herd, huddle. 7 *I'm pressed for time:* push, rush, hurry, be in short supply of, be hard put. —*n.* 8 *members of the press:* the Fourth Estate, reporters, journalists, newsmen, newspapermen; media, newspapers, periodicals, radio, TV, television, broadcasting, news services. 9 *A press of fans greeted her at the stage door:* crowd, throng, mob, multitude, swarm, host, horde, pack, drove, army, crush. 10 *The press of one-night stands tired the performer:* pressure, stress, obligation, duty; annoyance, bother.

pressing *adj. a pressing need:* urgent, imperative, vital, critical, crucial, essential, indispensable, important; insistent, demanding.
Ant. unnecessary, nonessential, dispensable, unimportant, trivial.

pressure *n.* 1 *The pressure inside the old submarine was almost unendurable:* air pressure, compression, compaction, squeeze; weight, heaviness, gravity, density. 2 *the pressure of responsibility:* strain, tension, difficulty, trouble, trial, load, burden, anxiety, distress. 3 *political pressure:* influence, sway, pull, weight; power, force. 4 *The pressures of business were too much for me:* press, urgency, exigency; demand, requirement.

prestige *n. an author of international prestige:* fame, renown, reputation, prominence, note, repute, mark, notability, distinction,

significance, import, importance, consequence, eminence, honor, respect, esteem.

prestigious *adj. a prestigious university:* distinguished, illustrious, esteemed, honored, respected, notable, famed, prominent, renowned, eminent, acclaimed, celebrated, well-known, important, outstanding.
Ant. unknown, insignificant, unimportant.

presumably *adv. He'll be here next week, presumably:* probably, assumably, likely, in all probability, in all likelihood, ostensibly, apparently.

presume *v.* 1 *Dr. Livingstone, I presume?:* assume, guess, take for granted, take it, believe, think likely, suspect, imagine, fancy; suppose, hypothesize, surmise, gather, deduce. 2 *She presumed to write in her daughter's name:* take leave, take a liberty, make free, venture, make bold, have the audacity.

presumption *n.* 1 *Your presumption was wrong:* assumption, premise, belief, supposition, postulate, speculation, guess, surmise, conjecture; presupposition, prejudgment, preconception. 2 *He had the presumption to insult the ambassador:* audacity, effrontery, arrogance, gall; cheek, nerve; impertinence, insolence, rudeness, presumptuousness; haughtiness, egotism; boldness, daring, forwardness.

presumptuous *adj.* 1 *It was presumptuous to challenge the chess master:* bold, audacious, daring, overconfident; overfamiliar, forward, nervy, brash, brazen, fresh, cocky. 2 *Her presumptuous airs made her disliked:* haughty, proud, snobbish, overbearing, patronizing, pompous, lordly, imperious; disdainful, contemptuous.

pretend *v.* 1 *Let's pretend we're wealthy!:* make believe, take a part, imagine, fancy, suppose; mimic, impersonate, masquerade, playact. 2 *She pretended a headache so she wouldn't have to go:* feign, fake, simulate, imitate, counterfeit, sham.

pretense *n.* 1 *The stage murder was only pretense:* make-believe, fake, hoax; invention, fabrication, imposture, sham, counterfeit; trick, deceit, deception. 2 *By pretense the detective infiltrated the smuggling ring:* deception, subterfuge, guile, pretext; disguise, cover. 3 *Her mannerisms were full of pretense:* show, pretentiousness, showing off, ostentation, display, ostentatiousness, affectedness, affectation, false show.
Ant. 1 reality, fact. 2 truthfulness, honesty. 3 simplicity, sincerity, candor, frankness, openness.

pretentious *adj. a pretentious man. a pretentious monument:* showy, ostentatious, pompous, pedantic, boastful, flaunting, overbearing, affected, presuming, assuming; flashy, ornate, gaudy, garish, overdone; self-glorifying, self-important, smug.

Ant. unpretentious, modest, unaffected, unassuming; plain, simple.

pretext *n. What was your pretext for not coming?:* excuse, alleged reason, pretense, subterfuge; justification, vindication.

pretty *adj.* 1 *What a pretty face!:* attractive, beautiful, lovely, comely, bonny, handsome, good-looking, well-favored; delicate, dainty, graceful; well-proportioned, symmetrical. —*adv.* 2 *It was a pretty good movie:* moderately, adequately, reasonably, fairly, rather, somewhat.

Ant. 1 unattractive, ugly, unsightly.

prevail *v.* 1 *A feeling of anger prevailed:* abound, exist generally, be current, be widespread, be prevalent. 2 *Abstract Expressionism prevailed in the 1950's:* predominate, be prevalent, abound; hold sway, rule, reign. 3 *The better fighter prevailed:* triumph, be victorious, win, win out, succeed, conquer, overcome.

prevailing *adj.* 1 *the prevailing fashion:* current, popular, widespread, prevalent, general, usual, customary, normal, conventional, accustomed; fixed, established, set. 2 *The prevailing color in her apartment is blue:* principal, main, prevalent, dominant, predominant, preponderant.

Ant. 1 dated, out-of-date; unusual, rare, uncommon. 2 minor, subordinate.

prevalent *adj. Pigeons are prevalent in city parks:* numerous, common, frequent, frequently occurring, prevailing, widespread, rife, pervasive, abundant, extensive, rampant, ubiquitous, habitual, usual, normal, conventional, commonplace, customary, popular.

Ant. infrequent, rare, uncommon.

prevent *v. to prevent colds. We prevented him from committing a gross error:* keep from, defend against, fend off, stave off, ward off; block, bar, deter, thwart, frustrate, foil, balk, forestall, avoid, preclude, avert; stop, halt; prohibit, forbid; deflect, draw off, turn away.

Ant. permit, allow, encourage.

prevention *n. Prevention of forest fires is up to you:* avoidance, stoppage, hindrance, inhibition, restraint, preclusion; deterrence, elimination, frustration, thwarting.

previous *adj. Have you had any previous experience?:* prior, preceding, earlier, early; foregoing, foregone, antecedent, former, erstwhile, before; aforesaid, aforementioned.

Ant. subsequent, consequent, ensuing, succeeding.

previously *adv. He stated previously that he would agree:* before, earlier, once, a while back; formerly, in times past, heretofore, earlier on.

prey *n.* 1 *The huge bird flew off with its prey:* quarry, kill; victim; prize. 2 *She was the prey of unscrupulous con men:* victim, dupe, gull. —*v.* 3 *Stronger animals prey upon weaker ones:* feed upon, eat; live off; fasten upon, parasitize.

price *n.* 1 *What's the price of that car?:* cost, face value, amount, charge, fee, rate, expense, outlay; value, worth. —*v.* 2 *The coat was priced at $100:* assess, evaluate, set a price on, appraise, value.

priceless *adj. priceless antiques:* beyond price, invaluable, valuable, precious; irreplaceable, rare; incomparable, peerless; prized, treasured, valued.

Ant. worthless, cheap; common.

pride *n.* 1 *She took great pride in her work:* satisfaction, pleasure, enjoyment, delight, gratification; self-esteem, dignity, self-respect, honor. 2 *He's too full of pride:* self-importance, egoism, egotism, vanity, conceit, self-love, self-glorification, vainglory; immodesty, smugness, self-satisfaction; airs, pretension; swagger, arrogance, haughtiness, superciliousness, imperiousness. —*v.* 3 *She prided herself on being fair:* be proud of, be pleased with, be satisfied with, be gratified at.

Ant. 2 humility, modesty, meekness.

prig *n. That prig never has any fun:* prude, puritan, fuddy-duddy, *Informal* stuffed shirt; pedant, faultfinder, nitpicker.

prim *adj. a prim and proper housekeeper:* particular, fussy, strict, fastidious, straitlaced, puritanical, prudish, prissy, stiff-necked, stuffy.

Ant. careless, loose; informal, casual, easygoing.

primarily *adv. The paintings are primarily landscapes:* chiefly, mainly, principally, mostly, largely, predominantly; first and foremost, essentially, fundamentally, for the most part, basically, in the main, generally.

primary *adj.* 1 *to begin primary negotiations:* first, introductory, beginning, initial, elementary, preparatory. 2 *Your primary duty is bookkeeping:* chief, main, principal, fundamental, basic, key; dominant, leading, greatest, highest, important, necessary, vital, essential. 3 *Love is a primary emotion:* primitive, primordial, primal, primeval; initial, original, prime, beginning, first; basic, fundamental, elementary, elemental, key;

natural, inherent, innate; oldest, earliest.
Ant. 1 secondary, following, subsequent, succeeding. 2 lesser, subordinate, supplemental.

prime *adj.* 1 *the prime suspect:* primary, chief, main, principal, cardinal, leading; ruling, preeminent; greatest, highest, maximal, crowning, paramount, supreme, utmost; unsurpassed, unmatched, best, without peer, peerless; important, necessary, essential, vital. 2 *Only prime foods are served at the hotel:* superior, Grade A, choice, select. 3 *Love is a prime emotion:* basic, fundamental, elementary, elemental; intrinsic, inherent, innate; oldest, earliest, first, original. 4 *Spring is the prime time for planting:* best, preferred, most advantageous, most favored, choice; opportune, propitious, befitting, expedient, auspicious. —*n.* 5 *the prime of life:* peak, perfection, greatest strength; height, zenith, heyday, best days; full flowering, bloom. —*v.* 6 *Her mother primed her for a life on the stage:* prepare, ready, fit, make ready; groom, coach, train, instruct, educate, school, inform, guide, prompt, brief.
Ant. 1 secondary, least important. 2 the worst, third-rate. 4 untimely, unsuitable, inauspicious.

primeval *adj. a primeval forest:* prehistoric, primordial, ancient, primitive, early, aboriginal, ancestral.

primitive *adj.* 1 *Space travel is still in a primitive stage:* early, original, first, primary; beginning, elementary; undeveloped, rudimentary. 2 *He had a primitive style of painting:* unsophisticated, simple, uncomplicated; artless, undeveloped, unlearned. 3 *primitive living conditions:* uncomfortable, inconvenient, crude; bare, Spartan, austere, ascetic.
Ant. 1 advanced, developed. 2 sophisticated. 3 comfortable, elaborate.

primp *v. You primped for hours:* groom oneself, dress fastidiously, preen, groom, prettify, spruce up; make up.

principal *adj.* 1 *I'm the principal stockholder:* chief, leading, foremost, most important, supreme, superior, main, preeminent, dominant, prominent, predominant, outstanding, controlling; primary, prime; fundamental, essential, basic; greatest, ultimate, paramount. —*n.* 2 *The principals were gathered on stage:* star, leading man, leading lady, featured player. 3 *She was sent to the principal's office:* head of a school, headmaster, master, dean, preceptor; person in authority, chief authority, superior. 4 *How much interest will there be on a principal of $5,000?:* original investment,

capital sum, invested sum, fund; money.
Ant. 1 least important, minor, secondary, auxiliary, supplemental.

principally *adv. He is known principally as a pianist:* mostly, primarily, chiefly, mainly, largely, predominantly, for the most part, basically, fundamentally, particularly, especially.

principle *n.* 1 *the principles of psychology:* rule, truth, law, precept, basic, fundamental, theory, rudiment, proposition, element; regulation, canon, code, dictum. 2 *His principles wouldn't allow him to cheat:* belief, article of faith, credo, tenet, creed; dogma, doctrine, religious belief, scruple, way of thinking; teaching, view, attitude, position. 3 *a model of principle:* morality, standards, ethics, honesty, scruples; honor, integrity, righteousness, virtue, morals; conscientiousness.
Ant. 3 immorality, dishonesty; dishonor.

prior *adj. Prior to coming here she was in Paris:* previous, preexisting, preexistent, antecedent, earlier, former; going before, prefatory, preparatory; aforementioned, aforementioned, aforesaid.
Ant. subsequent, following, later.

priority *n. This project has priority over all others:* precedence, preference, urgency, immediacy, preeminence; superiority.

prison *n. He was sent to prison for robbery:* jail, jailhouse, house of detention, penitentiary, penal institution, house of correction, *Slang* jug, clink, slammer, stir, cooler, pokey, pen.

pristine *adj. a pristine mountain stream:* undefiled, unsullied, untouched, unspoiled, untarnished, virginal; uncontaminated, unpolluted, pure, unmarred.
Ant. sullied, defiled, contaminated, spoiled.

private *adj.* 1 *This is private property:* privately owned, personal, exclusive, restricted, closed, limited; not public. 2 *Plans for the takeover were kept private:* confidential, secret, inviolate; undercover, covert, undisclosed, concealed, unrevealed, hidden, under wraps. 3 *a private retreat in the mountains:* secluded, isolated, remote, sequestered, lonely, solitary, unfrequented.
Ant. 1, 2 public. 2 known; disclosed, unconcealed, revealed.

privation *n. The family's privation was pitiable:* need, neediness, want; poverty, indigence, penury, pauperism, destitution; distress, misery, hardship.
Ant. ease, wealth, riches.

privilege *n. It is my privilege to go first:* right, due, entitlement, prerogative; freedom, liberty; power, authority; advantage, favor, boon; honor, pleasure.

privileged *adj. a privileged group of people. Talks between lawyer and client are privileged:* limited, special; exempt, immune, excused; allowed, granted, permitted, sanctioned, empowered, entitled, authorized.

prize *n.* 1 *She won second prize:* award, trophy, medal, medallion, cup; reward, citation, ribbon, decoration; laurels, honors. 2 *As an executive she was a prize:* jewel, gem, treasure, *Slang* humdinger, dandy, pip, peach. *—adj.* 3 *a prize recipe:* honored, winning, award-winning, blue-ribbon. *—v.* 4 *She prized me for my good sense:* value; admire, respect, honor, like, hold in esteem, appreciate; hold dear, treasure, cherish.

probable *adj. He's a probable candidate:* likely, possible, presumable, presumed, expected, supposed; credible, logical, reasonable, plausible, conceivable, believable.

probably *adv. We will probably leave on Sunday:* in all probability, most likely, in all likelihood; presumably, supposedly.

probe *v.* 1 *Scientists probed the causes of the earthquake:* investigate, look into, inspect; study, examine, test; question, inquire; look for, seek, explore, search. *—n.* 2 *The probe into the bribery charges proved futile:* investigation, inspection, exploration, examination, inquiry, study, search, research, analysis, test.

problem *n.* 1 *a math problem. marital problems:* question, query, puzzle, riddle, conundrum; difficulty, disagreement, disputed point. *—adj.* 2 *a problem child. I have problem hair:* unruly, difficult, hard to manage, uncontrollable, unmanageable; intractable, incorrigible.

problematic *adj. The conclusion is problematic:* uncertain, doubtful, questionable, dubious, unsettled, undetermined; enigmatic, perplexing, paradoxical, puzzling. *Ant.* settled, known, undisputed.

procedure *n. a new procedure for liver transplants:* method, way, manner, course, process, technique, approach, methodology, routine.

proceed *v.* 1 *Proceed to the next light, then turn left. Please proceed with your work:* go, move forward, go ahead, move on, go on, continue, progress, advance. 2 *He proceeded to announce his plans:* undertake, begin, commence, start; take action, act, move. 3 *Our destitution proceeded from unwise spending:* result, arise, issue, come, follow, ensue, be caused by, emanate, start, derive, originate, grow, stem. *Ant.* 1 retreat, go backward; stop.

proceedings *n. pl.* 1 *Minutes of the pro-*

ceedings were read: activity, happenings, occurrences, transactions, events, incidents, affairs, matters, actions, goings on, doings. 2 *My lawyer is representing me in the proceedings:* legal action, legal process, lawsuit, suit, litigation, trial, case.

proceeds *n. pl. The proceeds of the bazaar will go to charity:* profit, gain, receipts, gross, net, yield, income, revenue, earnings, money, winnings, take, pickings.

process *n.* 1 *He discovered the answer by a process of elimination:* method, system, manner, practice, procedure, mode; plan, line of action, policy; measure, step, usage, function. 2 *the process of going from childhood to maturity:* procedure, set of changes, proceeding, passage, course, movement, motion, transformation; unfolding; change, progress, progression. *—v.* 3 *to process food:* prepare, treat; convert, alter, transform. 4 *We will process your order at once:* take care of, fill, ship, handle, deal with.

procession *n. The procession moved slowly:* parade, march, caravan, cavalcade, cortege, train, file, rank, column; sequence, course, progression.

proclaim *v. He proclaimed his tonic would cure all ills:* declare, announce, herald, make known, broadcast; assert, affirm, state, profess. *Ant.* suppress, repress, conceal, secrete.

proclivity *n. She has a proclivity for sweets:* propensity, leaning, inclination, disposition, affection, liking, proneness, affinity, tendency, predilection, penchant, bent, bias, prejudice, partiality, predisposition, desire, impulse. *Ant.* dislike, aversion, hatred, loathing, disinclination.

procrastinate *v. Work instead of procrastinating!:* delay, stall, kill time, dilly-dally, dawdle, waste time; put off action, defer, postpone. *Ant.* expedite, hasten, hurry, speed up.

procreate *v. Nature contrived many ways to procreate:* beget, breed, engender, propagate, father, mother, sire, bear, reproduce, multiply, proliferate.

procure *v. to procure provisions for troops:* obtain, acquire, get, secure, lay hands on, attain, achieve, come by; take possession of, gain; effect, bring about, elicit.

prod *v.* 1 *He prodded me in the ribs:* poke, jab; shove, push; quicken, speed, propel. 2 *The teacher tried to prod the students to take more interest:* stir, incite, stimulate, instigate, prompt; rouse, move, encourage, motivate; urge, exhort, goad, spur.

prodigal *adj.* 1 *Your prodigal ways will ruin you:* wasteful, spendthrift, unthrifty, thriftless, overliberal, profligate, extravagant; lavish, excessive; improvident, dissipating, immoderate, wanton. **2** *the prodigal fruits of the earth:* bountiful, profuse, abounding, abundant, plentiful, bounteous, ample; luxuriant, lavish, generous; numerous, countless, innumerable, teeming, myriad, copious. —*n.* **3** *The prodigal had spent a fortune:* spendthrift, squanderer; wastrel, profligate.

Ant. **1** thrifty, frugal, economical, miserly; provident, moderate. **2** scarce, scanty; scant, meager, sparse, limited.

prodigious *adj. Her knowledge was prodigious:* exceptional, rare, singular, extraordinary, uncommon, unique, impressive, striking, noteworthy, renowned; amazing, astounding, astonishing, overwhelming, remarkable, marvelous; enormous, vast, huge, immense, large, monumental, mighty, tremendous.

Ant. ordinary, common, usual; unimpressive, unremarkable.

prodigy *n. a prodigy who could compose music at the age of 5:* gifted child, child genius, young genius, Wunderkind; genius, whiz, marvel, wonder, phenomenon.

produce *v.* **1** *to produce a new synthetic fiber:* make, create, manufacture, construct, fashion, shape, compose, devise, fabricate, frame, form, concoct, develop; bring into being, give birth to, bring into existence. **2** *The land produces enough to feed us:* provide, supply, furnish, give, bear, yield. **3** *Can you produce evidence?:* show, present, advance, cause to appear, manifest, bring forward, display; reveal, divulge, uncover, disclose, discover. **4** *Soft music is supposed to produce a romantic atmosphere:* effect, give rise to, bring about, achieve.

Ant. **3** conceal, hide, withhold. **4** prevent.

production *n.* **1** *the production of transistor radios:* making, producing, manufacture, manufacturing; origination, creation, fabrication. **2** *With the production of an eyewitness, the man was convicted of murder:* introduction, appearance, showing, exhibit, display, materialization, presentation; disclosure, revelation.

productive *adj.* **1** *a very productive firm:* creative, prolific, effectual, efficacious; active, busy, dynamic. **2** *The desert was turned into productive land:* fruitful, fertile, fecund; plentiful, plenteous, copious. **3** *It was not a productive venture:* profitable, remunerative, gainful, worthwhile, moneymaking. **4** *Greed has been productive of many a downfall:* responsible for, bringing about, causing, bringing to pass.

Ant. **1–3** unproductive. **1** inactive; inef-

fectual. **2** unfertile, barren, sterile, unfruitful. **3** unprofitable, ungainful.

profane *adj.* **1** *profane thoughts:* irreverent, blasphemous, ungodly, godless, unbelieving, sacrilegious, irreligious, undevout, heretical, impious, unholy; foul, filthy, vile, wicked, evil, sinful, shameless, unchaste, impure; crude, coarse, vulgar, obscene, lewd. **2** *Both sacred and profane music were played:* secular, nonreligious; lay, temporal, worldly. —*v.* **3** *The infidels profaned the holy shrine:* desecrate, debase, commit sacrilege, blaspheme; offend, outrage, pervert, violate; mock, scorn.

Ant. **1, 2** sacred, religious, spiritual. **1** holy, reverent, clean.

profanity *n. Except for the profanity, I liked the story:* swearing, cursing, cussing, curse words, dirty words, expletives, four-letter words, obscenities, swearwords, oaths; blue language, scatology; blasphemy, irreverence, impiety, ungodliness.

profess *v.* **1** *She professed to be a member of royalty:* claim, allege, lay claim, purport; pass oneself off, simulate, pretend, sham, feign, counterfeit, fake. **2** *He professed that he was, indeed, the robber:* confess, admit, own, acknowledge, affirm, avow, vouch, aver; declare, state, proclaim, announce; assert, tell, say, contend, maintain. **3** *They professed Catholicism:* declare one's faith in, embrace, believe in, practice.

profession *n.* **1** *What profession will you be studying for?:* occupation, line of work, line, business, job, field, specialty, employment, work, vocation, walk of life, career, sphere. **2** *She wanted to work in one of the professions: (variously)* law, medicine, teaching. **3** *a profession of eternal gratitude:* declaration, statement, announcement; acknowledgment, confession, affirmation, avowal; promise, word, word of honor, pledge, vow, assurance; assertion; claim, allegation.

Ant. **1** avocation, hobby. **3** denial.

professional *adj.* **1** *professional athletes:* paid, receiving pay, in business as. **2** *You had better get professional advice:* highly skilled, competent, knowledgeable, practiced, expert, experienced, well-trained. —*n.* **3** *Their house was decorated by a professional:* expert, specialist, authority.

Ant. **1, 3** amateur. **2** incompetent.

professorial *adj. a professorial attitude:* academic, bookish, donnish, pedantic, schoolmasterish, pedagoguish, didactic.

proficient *adj. a proficient typist:* skilled, skillful, capable, competent, able, good, adroit, deft, apt, adept, expert, masterful, efficient, effective; trained, practiced, accomplished, experienced, qualified, professional; talented, gifted.

Ant. unskilled, inept, incompetent, bad, unaccomplished.

profile *n.* 1 *A profile of Washington appears on the U.S. quarter:* outline, contour, delineation, shape, figure; side view, side, half face, silhouette. 2 *John Kennedy wrote* Profiles in Courage: biography, short biography, character sketch.

profit *n.* 1 *Did you make any profit last year?:* gain, return, realization; gross profit; money, income, earnings; proceeds, receipts; compensation, financial reward. 2 *Finishing college will be to your profit:* advantage, benefit, interest, gain, improvement; good, benefaction, boon, service, use, avail, value. —*v.* 3 *Taking those extra courses profited me:* benefit, help, serve, stand in good stead. 4 *You must learn to profit by experience:* make good use of, make the most of, learn from, utilize, use. 5 *We hoped to profit from our investments:* make money, earn, gain.

profitable *adj.* 1 *Selling the property was quite profitable:* gainful, rewarding, yielding profit, paying, moneymaking, remunerative, lucrative, well-paying. 2 *It was a profitable experience:* worthwhile, rewarding, productive, beneficial, useful; valuable.

profligate *adj.* 1 *a profligate playboy:* dissolute, debauched, libertine, dissipated, degenerate, degraded, immoral, wanton, loose, abandoned; corrupt, evil, sinful, immoral, promiscuous, wild, fast, unbridled, licentious, lascivious. 2 *Your profligate ways are depleting your fortune:* wasteful, prodigal, extravagant, lavish, unthrifty, spendthrift, improvident. —*n.* 3 *Don Juan is an archetypal profligate:* reprobate, rake, debauchee, dissipater, libertine, sinner; spendthrift, wastrel, prodigal.

Ant. 1 moral, decent, upright; virtuous, chaste.

profound *adj.* 1 *a profound statement:* deep, thoughtful, wise, sagacious, sage, penetrating, learned, intellectual, educated; knowledgeable, recondite, philosophical; reflective, thoughtful, well-considered, serious; informed, well-informed, knowing. 2 *His death had a profound effect on her:* deep, severe, extreme; thorough, far-reaching, utter, complete, pronounced, decided. 3 *Please accept my profound apologies:* deeply felt, heartfelt, sincere, deep-seated; intense, keen, acute, abject.

Ant. 1 shallow, superficial, stupid, uneducated, thoughtless, uninformed. 2 slight, superficial. 3 insincere.

profuse *adj.* 1 *nature's profuse bounty:* generous, munificent, abundant, bountiful, bounteous, copious, ample, rich, lavish. 2 *Your profuse spending has left you penniless:* wasteful, unthrifty, prodigal, improvident, spendthrift, excessive, lavish, extravagant.

Ant. 1 meager, scanty, sparse, skimpy. 2 thrifty, penny-pinching, moderate.

profusion *n.* *The garden boasted a profusion of flowers:* great amount, great quantity, abundance, plethora, multitude; surfeit, surplus, glut.

progeny *n.* *The castle passed into the hands of the duke's progeny:* descendant, offspring, young, child, children, issue; posterity, race, stock, lineage, line.

program *n.* 1 *Today's program includes a tour of the Statue of Liberty:* schedule, order of events, agenda; card, bill, slate, calendar. 2 *The ushers gave everyone a program:* playbill, list of players, list of selections. 3 *New programs appear in the fall on television:* show, presentation, production.

progress *n.* 1 *We made swift progress:* headway, advance; development, betterment, improvement. 2 *Has the nation's progress been too fast?:* development, growth, rise, promotion. 3 *The play is in progress:* process, development, course, unfolding, action, movement. —*v.* 4 *He progressed within the company and was made a vice-president:* advance, proceed, move ahead, go forward, get ahead, get on. 5 *Have you progressed in your studies?:* advance, improve, become better, make headway; develop, grow, mature.

Ant. 1 regression; loss, failure, decline.

progression *n.* *the progression of events leading up to war:* sequence, succession, order, series, continuation; string, chain, course; progress, advancement, furtherance, advance.

progressive *adj.* 1 *a progressive mayor:* concerned with progress, supporting change; forward-looking, up-to-date; liberal. 2 *It was a progressive disease:* advancing step-by-step, increasingly severe, steadily going on, incremental; spreading, ongoing. —*n.* 3 *The mayor is a progressive:* liberal, reformist; activist; populist.

Ant. 1, 3 reactionary, conservative.

prohibit *v.* 1 *The law prohibits driving over 35 mph on this street:* forbid, disallow, proscribe, deny. 2 *Good manners prohibited us from leaving:* prevent, inhibit, check, limit, hinder, block, curb, hamper, bar; delay, stay, stop, preclude, ban, suppress, restrict, enjoin, restrain.

Ant. 1, 2 permit, let, allow; give permission, authorize; order. 2 direct.

prohibitive Also **prohibitory** *adj. prohibitive costs:* restrictive, forbidding; suppressive, repressive; preventive, hindering, obstructive, disallowing, disqualifying, inadmissible, unacceptable.

project *n.* 1 *My project is to paint the porch:* undertaking, job, task, work, activity, assignment; intention, ambition, aim, objective, goal. —*v.* 2 *Could you project a new plan?:* plan, design, draft, outline, devise, frame, contrive, concoct. 3 *The roof projects over the walk:* extend, jut out, stand out, stick out, protrude, overhang. 4 *Project your voice so that you're heard:* throw, cast; eject, ejaculate, emit, expel, discharge, propel, launch, fire. 5 *He projected sales for the coming year:* forecast, calculate; predetermine.

projection *n.* 1 *The projection provided a foothold:* ledge, shelf, extension, overhang, protuberance; bulge, ridge, bump. 2 *a projection of next year's sales figures:* estimate, estimation, approximation, guess, prediction, forecast.

proletariat *n. The proletariat will determine the outcome of the election:* working class, laboring classes, laborers, rank and file, wage earners; the common people, the masses, the people, populace, the crowd; the multitude; commoners, hoi polloi, lower classes, the herd, the horde, the mob, rabble. **Ant.** upper class, aristocracy, gentry, nobility.

proliferate *v. Rabbits proliferated in Australia:* multiply, increase, reproduce rapidly, breed quickly; procreate, propagate, teem, swarm.

prolific *adj.* 1 *My hamsters were so prolific they soon needed a larger cage:* reproductive, fertile, fruitful, yielding, fecund, procreative, multiplying, germinative; luxuriant, abundant, profuse. 2 *a prolific composer:* very productive, creative. **Ant.** 1 barren, unfruitful, unfertile. 2 unproductive.

prolong *v. We had to prolong our stay:* lengthen, extend, attenuate, draw out; maintain, sustain, continue, perpetuate, drag out. **Ant.** curtail, shorten, abridge, abbreviate.

prominence *n.* 1 *her prominence in the music field:* distinction, importance, eminence, preeminence, fame, renown, prestige, notability, reputation; conspicuousness, significance; greatness, illustriousness; influence, significance. 2 *The doctor could feel a slight prominence on my skull:* projection, extrusion, protuberance, bulge, convexity, swelling, hump, knurl, bump, knob, lump,

node. 3 *a prominence overlooking the sea:* high point, height, promontory, elevation, high place; hill, knoll, rise, mound.

prominent *adj.* 1 *The sign is in a prominent location:* conspicuous, evident, noticeable, apparent, easily seen, obvious, well-marked, pronounced, discernible; glaring, arresting, striking. 2 *He has prominent cheek bones:* jutting out, extended, jutting, protruding, standing out, protuberant, bulging, projecting, convex. 3 *She's a prominent physician:* important, prestigious, preeminent, illustrious, distinguished, respected, well-known, leading, eminent, renowned, celebrated, notable. **Ant.** 1 inconspicuous, unnoticeable. 2 receding, concave, indented. 3 unimportant, undistinguished, unknown.

promiscuous *adj.* 1 *a promiscuous love of food:* indiscriminate, uncritical, undiscriminating, unselective, uncritical, undirected. 2 *a promiscuous life:* wanton, loose, fast, immoral, unchaste, unvirtuous, impure, of easy virtue, immoral, morally loose, incontinent. **Ant.** 1 discriminating, discerning, selective. 2 moral, chaste, virtuous, pure.

promise *n.* 1 *Give me your promise:* word, pledge, word of honor; vow, oath, troth, avowal, covenant, agreement, assurance. 2 *That rookie pitcher is full of promise:* potential, capability, good prospects, cause for hope. —*v.* 3 *I promise never to tell:* give a promise, give one's word of honor, pledge, vow, aver, avow, vouch, assure, agree, be bound, swear. 4 *The skies promise better weather:* indicate, give hope of, lead one to expect, hint of, suggest, betoken, augur.

promising *adj. a promising new writer. a promising start in business:* giving promise, full of promise; favorable, hopeful, reassuring, assuring, encouraging; rising, up-and-coming; inspiriting, bright, cheerful, rosy, optimistic, happy; propitious, auspicious, looking up. **Ant.** unfavorable, unpromising, discouraging.

promontory *n. a promontory overlooking the sea:* headland, hill, high point; point, neck of land, cape, embankment; projection, precipice, cliff, bluff, height.

promote *v.* 1 *He was in town to promote his new book:* publicize, advertise, forward, further, advance, *Slang* push, plug; advocate, foster, support; aid, help, assist, abet. 2 *They promoted her to sergeant:* advance in rank, raise, elevate, upgrade.

promotion *n.* 1 *a promotion to general manager:* advancement in position or rank, elevation, raise, upgrading. 2 *the promotion* *of a new record album:* advertising, advertisement, publicity, fanfare; advancement, furtherance.

Ant. 1 demotion.

prompt *adj.* 1 *Thank you for your prompt attention to the matter:* immediate, quick, punctual, timely, on time; ready, attentive. —*v.* 2 *Whatever prompted you to act in such a way?:* spur, impel, induce, inspire, incite, move, motivate, instigate, cause, occasion; propel, drive, incline, dispose, influence, persuade. 3 *to prompt an onstage actor:* supply with a cue; remind, jog the memory; assist, help out, put words in one's mouth. *Ant.* 1 dilatory, slow, late, tardy. 2 dissuade, deter.

promulgate *v. to promulgate a new theory:* set forth, expound, present, communicate, elucidate; teach, explain; sponsor, foster, promote.

prone *adj.* 1 *I'm prone to giggling:* inclined, susceptible, liable, tending, disposed, predisposed, apt, likely, subject, accustomed, habituated. 2 *He was lying prone on the couch:* flat, face-down, recumbent, reclining, horizontal.

Ant. 1 disinclined. 2 erect, upright; face-up, supine.

pronounce *v.* 1 *to pronounce a word properly:* articulate, speak, say, enunciate, enounce, vocalize, sound, utter. 2 *I now pronounce you man and wife:* declare, proclaim, decree, rule, announce, state; judge, pass judgment.

pronounced *adj. He has a pronounced limp:* decided, distinct, unmistakable, definite, clear-cut, unquestionable; clear, plain, noticeable, obvious, patent, evident, recognizable, visible, manifest.

proof *n.* 1 *Do you have any proof?:* evidence, verification, documentation, substantiation. 2 *Will your theory stand up to proof?:* trial, test, assessment, examination.

prop *n.* 1 *Props kept the wall from collapsing:* support, pillar, buttress, reinforcement, stanchion, stay, brace. —*v.* 2 *They propped the wall with several braces:* support, shore up, hold up, brace, bolster, buttress. 3 *Prop the broom against the chair:* rest, lean, set, stand.

propagate *v.* 1 *All species propagate in order to stay in existence:* multiply, reproduce, proliferate, breed, procreate, increase, generate, engender, beget, give birth; hatch, spawn. 2 *to propagate the teachings of the church:* spread, disseminate, make known, promulgate; publish, publicize, broadcast, make public, proclaim, preach, impart, disperse, sow; instill, implant, inculcate.

propel *v. The bow propels the arrow:* shoot, catapult, eject, impel, drive, push, prod, shove; launch, thrust, send, discharge, project, toss, cast, hurl, pitch, heave, sling.

propensity *n. I have a propensity for candy:* inclination, leaning, proclivity, predilection, liking, partiality, weakness, preference, penchant; attraction, affinity, sympathy, taste, fancy; bent, tendency, predisposition, bias, prejudice.

Ant. disinclination, aversion, dislike, antipathy.

proper *adj.* 1 *the proper way to hold a pencil:* right, correct, appropriate, suitable, fitting, applicable, pertinent, germane, relevant; apropos, fit, apt, meet, orthodox. 2 *proper manners:* decorous, becoming, seemly, befitting, fitting, suitable, fit, acceptable; polite, courteous. 3 *Please go to your proper seats:* own, assigned, respective, particular, specific; distinguishing, peculiar, distinctive, typical, appropriate. 4 *The city proper is half the size of the metropolitan area:* strictly defined, in the limited sense, per se; precise, correct, true.

Ant. 1 wrong, inappropriate, unsuitable, inapt. 2 unseemly, unbecoming, impolite, objectionable, rude.

properly *adv.* 1 *You conducted yourself properly:* in a proper manner, appropriately, suitably, aptly, acceptably; decently, decorously, politely, tastefully. 2 *If you do it properly the first time, you won't have to do it again:* correctly, exactly, right, without error, accurately, precisely, perfectly.

property *n.* 1 *I leave all my property to my son:* belongings, effects, possessions, goods; estate, assets, holdings, chattels. 2 *We bought property in Vermont:* land, real estate, acreage, grounds; territory. 3 *Cheerfulness is one of her many good properties:* quality, aspect, characteristic, trait, feature, attribute; mark, point, badge.

prophecy *n.* 1 *She claimed to have a knack for prophecy:* foretelling the future, prediction, forecasting, soothsaying. 2 *Her prophecies seldom came true:* prediction, forecast, augury, portent; revelation, sign from God.

prophesy *v. The soothsayer prophesied doom:* predict, foretell, presage, forecast, divine, soothsay, foresee, augur.

prophet *Fem.* **prophetess** *n.* 1 *He claimed to be a prophet of the Lord:* revealer of the word of God, proclaimer of holy truth; evangelist, inspired spokesman; intercessor, interpreter, preacher. 2 *Is he really a prophet?:* predictor, foreteller, forecaster, prophesier, soothsayer, oracle, clairvoyant, seer, diviner, augur; crystal gazer, palmist, fortune-teller, geomancer; sorcerer.

propitious adj. a propitious occasion: favorable, fortunate, auspicious, opportune, well-timed; beneficial, fit, suitable, advantageous, promising; happy, benign.
Ant. adverse, harmful, deleterious.

proponent n. a proponent of a new law: advocate, supporter, endorser, champion, spokesman; defender, backer, booster, partisan.

proportion n. 1 The proportion of flour to milk is three to one in this recipe: relationship, ratio, distribution, correspondence. 2 The cost is out of proportion to the true value: proper relation, balance; symmetry, consistency, commensuration, correspondence; harmony, agreement. 3 **proportions** The proportions of the room are enormous: dimensions, size, extent, measurements, area; scope, range, span, spread, width, breadth; amplitude, magnitude. 4 A large proportion of the report was written by me: part, amount; fraction, share, portion; ratio, quota, percentage, measure, degree.
Ant. 2 disproportion, inconsistency, disparity; disagreement, disharmony.

proposal n. 1 a proposal to improve public transportation: recommendation, proposition, plan, program, project, scheme, resolution, design, conception, idea; prospectus, presentation, draft, theory. 2 I've decided to accept their proposal: invitation, proposition, offer, suggestion, motion, bid, presentation; marriage proposition, suit.

propose v. 1 I proposed my neighbor for club membership: recommend, suggest, present, submit, tender, proffer, offer for consideration, put forward, advance, propound. 2 She proposes to move within the month: plan, intend, mean, plot, scheme, venture, expect, aspire, aim, hope. 3 He proposed to her on bended knee: ask for one's hand, affiance; Informal pop the question.

proposition n. 1 The would-be buyer made us an attractive proposition: offer, proposal, offer of terms, deal, bargain. 2 The membership voted on two propositions: proposal, suggestion, recommendation, resolution, plan; issue, question, matter, point.

proprietor n. the hotel's proprietor: landlord, owner, titleholder; possessor, holder.

propriety n. Always conduct yourself with propriety: correctness; courtesy, decorum, good behavior, dignity, good manners, etiquette, gentlemanly or ladylike behavior, respectability, seemliness.
Ant. impropriety, discourtesy, misbehavior, misconduct, bad manners.

prosaic adj. a prosaic remark: dull, unimaginative, vapid, pedestrian, platitudi-

nous, uninteresting, unentertaining, tedious, jejune, trite, common, humdrum, routine.
Ant. exciting, imaginative, fascinating, interesting; unusual, extraordinary.

proscribe v. The church proscribed dissenters: denounce, condemn, censure, disapprove, repudiate; anathematize, outlaw, prohibit, forbid, ban, excommunicate, banish, exile; boycott.
Ant. allow, permit; encourage.

prosecute v. The state is prosecuting him for murder: try, put on trial; bring suit against, prefer charges against.

prospect Usually **prospects** n. 1 The prospects of a treaty aren't good: chances, outlook, likelihood, probability; anticipation, expectation, hope, promise. 2 I delight in the prospect of visiting Quebec: expectation, contemplation, anticipation, expectancy, intention, ambition; plan, design, proposal. 3 The salesman sought new prospects: potential client, potential customer; candidate, possibility. —v. 4 We prospected for gold: explore, seek, search, look for; work a mine.

prospective adj. 1 We are debating a prospective move to the suburbs: future, coming, impending, approaching, to come, forthcoming, eventual; foreseen, expected, looked-for, intended, hoped for. 2 Is she a prospective customer?: likely, possible, potential.

prosper v. The store prospered: thrive, make good, fare well; be successful, flourish, succeed; advance, increase, progress, flower, bear fruit; make one's fortune, grow rich.
Ant. fail, be unsuccessful; grow poor.

prosperity n. We enjoyed our new prosperity: success, well-being, affluence, good fortune; affluence, wealth; bounty opulence, luxury, abundance, plenty.
Ant. want, poverty, indigence, destitution; failure.

prosperous adj. 1 a prosperous businessman: successful, thriving, flourishing; rich, wealthy, affluent, moneyed, well-to-do, well-off. 2 The program got off to a prosperous start: auspicious, propitious, good, favorable, promising, heartening, encouraging, reassuring, pleasing.
Ant. 1 unsuccessful, failing; poor, impoverished. 2 unpropitious, unfortunate, inauspicious, unpromising.

prostitute n. 1 The mayor tried to rid the area of pimps and prostitutes: whore, harlot, slut, hooker, hustler, streetwalker, lady of the night, jade, bawd, tart, trollop, call girl; courtesan. —v. 2 The poet prostituted herself writing greeting card verses: debase, cheapen, sell out, degrade, demean, lower, corrupt, pervert, defile, misuse, misemploy, misdirect, misapply.

prostrate adj. 1 *The prostrate slaves didn't get up until the king left:* lying flat, lying full length, lying face down, stretched out, laid out, prone, recumbent, flat; bowed low, supplicating, beseeching, crouching, on bended knee. 2 *She was prostrate after hiking on that hot day:* overcome, worn out, dead tired, exhausted, spent.

protagonist n. *the protagonist of the play:* hero, heroine, main character, central character, title role, principal, lead, leading man, leading lady.

protect v. *Protect her from harm:* guard, shield, defend, watch over, safeguard, secure; take care of, care for, tend, look after; shelter, harbor, keep, maintain, sustain, save.

Ant. attack, assault, assail; expose.

protection n. 1 *a policeman's protection of the people:* protecting, guarding, safeguard, defense; preservation, safekeeping, guardianship, custody, charge, care, conservation, saving; immunity, safety, security. 2 *protection against the rain:* shield, guard, defense, safeguard, security; barrier, buffer, shelter; asylum, refuge, haven, harbor.

protective adj. 1 *an animal's protective coloration:* protecting, guarding, safeguarding, preventive, shielding, defensive. 2 *I felt protective toward my sister:* sheltering, shielding; watchful, vigilant, heedful, solicitous.

protest n. 1 *The protest was aimed at the government:* demonstration, march, picketing, boycott, sit-in, strike; opposition, dissent, disagreement, dissidence, resistance, demurral, discountenance, remonstrance, remonstration, renunciation, complaint; objection, protestation. —v. 2 *Consumers are protesting higher prices:* complain, express disapproval, cry out, object, take exception; oppose, disapprove, dissent, disagree, deny. 3 *The defendant protested his innocence:* assert, vow, avow, declare, insist, announce, propound, maintain, profess, state, attest, affirm, asseverate, aver, allege, avouch.

Ant. 1 endorsement, agreement, acquiescence, approval. 2 approve, sanction, endorse.

protocol n. *According to protocol, you will be seated to the ambassador's right:* diplomatic code, diplomatic or court etiquette; proprieties, amenities, code of behavior, good form, decorum, formality; manners, usage, customs, conventions, dictates of society.

protract v. *The ceremony was protracted by*

long-winded speeches: prolong, extend, lengthen, draw out, drag out.

Ant. shorten, curtail, condense, abridge.

protrude v. *Nails protruded from the board:* jut out, project, stick out; bulge, swell.

protuberance n. *a painful protuberance on his leg:* bulge, swelling, prominence, projection; knob, bump, hump, knot, lump, node, gnarl; roundness, bow, rising, ridge, welt, weal.

proud adj. 1 *a proud pensioner who accepted no help:* independent, self-sufficient, dignified, honorable, self-respecting; principled, high-minded; reserved, distinguished; august. 2 *I'm so proud of you!:* filled with pride, pleased, gratified, delighted, happy. 3 *a proud, boastful rogue:* conceited, vain, smug, self-satisfied, self-important; prideful, egotistical, vainglorious; pompous, overbearing, arrogant, patronizing, condescending, haughty, snobbish, cocky.

Ant. 1 lowly, ignoble, undignified; servile, cringing, abject. 2 ashamed, displeased, discontented. 3 humble, unassuming, modest, meek, unpresuming, deferential.

prove v. 1 *This document proves her claim:* verify, establish, substantiate, bear out, uphold, sustain, corroborate, authenticate, confirm, affirm, attest, certify, testify to; validate; ascertain, show clearly, demonstrate. 2 *Is there any way to prove the new method?:* test, try, try out, put to the test, verify; check, analyze, examine. 3 *It proved a waste of time:* result in, turn out to be, be found to be, end up, result.

Ant. 1 disprove, refute, negate, contradict, contravert, rebut, discredit.

proverb n. *I live by the proverb, "Waste not, want not":* saying, popular saying, adage, maxim, aphorism, epigram, precept, apothegm, saw, axiom, dictum.

provide v. 1 *Can you provide the information? to provide food for disaster victims:* furnish, give, place at one's disposal, offer, submit, present, impart, render; produce, confer, bestow, donate, contribute, afford, allow, accord, award, deliver, dispense; arm, equip, fit, outfit, supply. 2 *We worked hard to provide for our old age:* prepare, make plans, get ready, arrange, plan; save up, make arrangements, make provision. 3 *The contract provides that you cannot work for another studio:* state, stipulate, specify, require.

Ant. 1 deprive, withhold, refuse, disallow. 2 neglect, overlook.

provident adj. *a provident individual who made careful preparation for the future:* foresighted, well-prepared, farseeing, foreseeing, farsighted; thoughtful, discreet, judicious, circumspect, discerning; cautious, wary, vigilant, careful; ready, prudent; frugal, thrifty, economical, saving.

Ant. improvident, shortsighted; injudicious, unwary, reckless, heedless; imprudent, wasteful.

province *n. British Columbia is a province of Canada:* administrative division, territory, subdivision, department, canton; county, region, area, section, part. **2** *It's within my province to issue authorization:* area, field, sphere, bailiwick, capacity, function, office, domain, authority; responsibility, charge, duty, assignment, role.

provincial *adj.* **1** *The dancers were wearing provincial costumes:* of a province, regional, local. **2** *She had simple provincial manners:* rural, country, countrified, rustic, small-town; unsophisticated; homespun, homely, unrefined. **3** *a provincial distrust of foreigners:* narrow, parochial, insular.

Ant. **2** big-city, citified, urban, polished, refined, smooth; cosmopolitan, sophisticated.

provision *n.* **1** *Provision of shelter was our main concern for the disaster victims:* providing, supplying, furnishing, giving. **2** *provisions Provisions were kept in the storehouse:* supplies, food, eatables, edibles, comestibles, stores, groceries, victuals, viands, provender; feed. **3** *I made provision for their welfare in my will:* arrangement, prearrangement; precaution, preparation, readiness. **4** *the provisions of an agreement:* proviso, requisite, requirement, obligation, stipulation, condition, term, article, clause; restriction, limitation, reservation, qualification.

proviso *n. The house is yours with the proviso that you live in it:* condition, restriction, limitation, qualification, stipulation, requirement; clause, amendment, addition, rider.

provocation *n. She flared up at the smallest provocation:* cause, motivation, incitement, instigation, prodding, stimulation; vexation, irritation, annoyance, aggravation; slight, insult, affront, offense.

provocative *adj.* **1** *The provocative remark started an argument:* provoking, annoying, aggravating, irritating, vexing, irksome. **2** *a provocative look:* seductive, tempting, captivating, intriguing, entrancing, fascinating, beguiling, bewitching, alluring, attractive, sexy; exciting, intoxicating, thrilling, stimulating, arousing, ravishing, inviting.

provoke *v.* **1** *His constant nagging provoked me:* anger, incense, outrage, infuriate, madden, irritate, vex, agitate, annoy, gall, ag-

gravate, irk, exasperate, rile. **2** *The excitement of the game provoked my desire to win:* cause, prompt, incite, inspire, impel, instigate, induce, compel, arouse, stimulate, rouse, stir, animate, move, motivate; bring on, effect, actuate, galvanize, foment, awaken, elicit, fire, quicken, excite, evoke.

Ant. **1** assuage, calm, soothe, mollify, propitiate; please, gratify.

prowess *n.* **1** *a soldier known for prowess:* bravery, valor, heroism, fearlessness, courage, daring; strength, might, power; fortitude, stamina, endurance, mettle, spirit, hardihood. **2** *She had great prowess as a businesswoman:* ability, skill, competence; aptitude, knack, talent, faculty, adeptness, expertness, proficiency.

Ant. **1** cowardice, cowardliness, fear, timidity. **2** incompetence, ineptness.

prowl *v. The cat prowls around the house all night:* stalk, hunt, scavenge, roam, slink, steal, range, lurk.

prudent *adj. a prudent investor:* wise, sensible, careful, judicious, discerning, sagacious, sage, level-headed, well-advised; thoughtful, provident, heedful, cautious, wary, circumspect, shrewd, guarded; prepared, foresighted, discreet, farsighted; frugal, thrifty, economical, sparing.

Ant. imprudent, unwise, irrational; improvident, careless, heedless, reckless, rash; wasteful, extravagant.

prune *v.* **1** *to prune a hedge:* trim, clip, thin, crop, lop. **2** *The editor pruned the manuscript:* reduce, curtail, trim, shorten, cut; abridge, condense, abbreviate.

prurient *adj. The movie will appeal to prurient interests:* lustful, libidinous, lascivious, licentious, lecherous, carnal, lewd.

pry[1] *v. Stop prying into my affairs!:* snoop, poke, butt, nose, stick one's nose in; probe, explore, delve, inquire, search; meddle, interfere, intrude.

pry[2] *v. We pried open the door:* force, prize, lever, jimmy.

pseudonym *n. "Max" was a pseudonym for the French Resistance leader Jean Moulin:* alias, assumed name, false name; cognomen, anonym, pen name, professional name, stage name.

psychic *adj.* **1** *A dream is a psychic event:* mental, psychological; cerebral, intellectual; spiritual. **2** *The medium claimed to have psychic powers:* extrasensory, preternatural, telekinetic, supernatural, occult, mystic; supersensory, telepathic, clairvoyant. *—n.* **3** *She claimed to be a psychic:* clairvoyant, telepathist; prophet, soothsayer, diviner, augur; medium, spiritualist.

pub *n. a London pub: Brit.* public house, tav-

ern, barroom, bar, taproom, saloon, alehouse, beer parlor.

public *adj.* 1 *Public opinion favors tax reform. I'm running for public office:* common,
general, popular, social; political, civic,
civil. 2 *The gardens are public:* open to all
persons, shared, not private or exclusive;
unrestricted, available, accessible, passable;
communal, community-owned. 3 *The investigator made the findings public:* widely
known, disclosed, divulged, open, overt; unabashed, unashamed, plain, frank, obvious,
conspicuous, evident, visible, unconcealed,
exposed, apparent, undisguised, revealed;
observable, discernible, perceivable, in
broad daylight. —*n.* 4 *The museum is open
to the public:* people, everyone, populace,
community, population, citizenry, society,
multitude, masses. 5 *the movie-going public:*
following, attendance, audience, followers,
constituency, supporters.

Ant. 1 private, personal, individual. 2 private, exclusive, restricted; unavailable, inaccessible, closed. 3 secret, unknown, unrevealed.

publicity *n. The movie received much publicity:* public notice, attention, notoriety; pro-
mulgation, advertising, salesmanship, promotion; information, propaganda; build-up,
puffery, *Informal* ballyhoo, hype.

publicize *v. to publicize a new product:* promote, make known, make public, advertise,
proclaim, acclaim, announce, broadcast,
herald, promulgate; *Informal* ballyhoo,
plug, hype.

Ant. keep secret, hush up, conceal, hide.

publish *v.* 1 *The company published her
novel:* print for sale, put to press, issue,
bring out. 2 *Don't publish that—it's off the
record:* print, make public, publicize; disclose, release, give out, air, broadcast, tell,
impart, divulge, disseminate, spread, circulate; proclaim, declare.

Ant. 2 conceal, suppress; withhold, keep
secret.

pucker *v.* 1 *The curtains were puckered at
the top:* draw together, contract; pinch,
crease, purse, compress, squeeze; wrinkle,
crinkle; gather, fold, tuck, pleat. —*n.*
2 *She sewed little puckers in the sweater:*
fold, tuck, gather, pleat; crease, wrinkle,
crinkle.

pudgy Also **podgy** *adj. All that candy has
made him pudgy:* fat, stout, chunky,
chubby, stocky, fleshy, plump, rotund,
tubby, roly-poly.

puerile *adj. Giggling in church is puerile:*
childish, immature, babyish, infantile,

sophomoric, juvenile; inane, ridiculous,
foolish, frivolous, vapid, silly.

Ant. adult, mature.

puff *n.* 1 *puffs of steam:* abrupt emission,
sudden gust, whiff, breath, exhalation,
small cloud, wisp. 2 *Her eye had a slight
puff to it:* swelling, rising, bulge, inflammation, distention, inflation, bow, convexity.
—*v.* 3 *After running the mile, he was huff-
ing and puffing:* breathe hard, be out of
breath, pant, gasp, exhale, blow. 4 *The
dragon puffed fire:* blow in puffs, send forth,
emit, discharge. 5 *He puffed on his pipe:*
draw, suck, inhale; smoke. 6 *The prisoners'
stomachs puffed out from malnutrition:* be
inflated, be distended, swell, expand, extend, distend, stretch, bloat.

puffy *adj. Her face was puffy with bruises:*
swollen, inflated, puffed up, bloated, inflamed, distended.

pugnacious *adj. a pugnacious drunk:* quarrelsome, given to fighting, antagonistic, unfriendly; aggressive, combative, warlike,
hostile, menacing, contentious, belligerent,
bellicose, fractious; disputatious, argumentative.

Ant. peaceful, calm, friendly, conciliatory.

pulchritude *n. a vision of feminine pulchritude:* beauty, prettiness, comeliness, beaute-
ousness, loveliness, fairness.

Ant. homeliness, plainness, ugliness.

pull *v.* 1 *The child pulled a red wagon:* haul,
drag, tug, draw; take in tow, tow. 2 *He
pulled the lifeline:* tug, jerk, grab, yank.
3 *The dentist may have to pull that tooth:*
draw out, remove, withdraw; extract.
4 *Pull over!:* go, move, drive. 5 *She pulled a
back muscle:* strain, stretch, twist, wrench,
sprain. 6 *The fight promoters hoped to pull
record crowds:* draw, attract; lure, entice.
—*n.* 7 *She gave the dog's leash a pull:* tug,
jerk, yank. 8 *I couldn't resist the pull of her
charm:* lure, allure, attraction; influence, enticement, fascination, appeal, allurement;
magnetism.

Ant. 1, 2, 7 push, shove. 3 insert, plant.

pulsate *v. The heart pulsates. She was pul-
sating with excitement:* throb, beat, palpitate, vibrate, reverberate, pound, pulse, undulate, oscillate, quiver, flutter, shake,
shiver, quaver, shudder, tremble; alternate,
ebb and flow.

pulse *n.* 1 *The engine ran with a steady
pulse:* throb, regular beat, rhythm, cadence,
pulsation, palpitation; recurrence, undulation, vibration, oscillation. —*v.* 2 *The veins
in his temple pulsed:* beat, throb, palpitate,
pulsate, vibrate; quiver, shudder, tremble,
oscillate.

pulverize *v. The mill pulverizes grain:* grind,

pound, granulate, powder, mince, crush, crumble, mill, mash.

punch n. 1 *a punch in the mouth:* blow, hit, jab, thrust, clout, thump, box, poke, knock, sock. —v. 2 *I punched the man in the nose:* hit, strike, smite, box, whack, jab, wallop, clout, cuff, sock, paste; baste; pummel, pound, beat.

punctual adj. *Be punctual for your appointments:* on time, not late, in good time, prompt.
Ant. late, tardy.

puncture n. 1 *a puncture in the balloon:* hole, break, rupture, opening, perforation. —v. 2 *She punctured her finger with a needle:* pierce, prick, pink, stick; cut, nick. 3 *Bad reviews punctured the actor's ego:* deflate, depreciate; let down, shoot down.

pundit n. *The pundit wrote a daily column on current affairs:* sage, expert, authority, learned person.

pungent adj. 1 *a pungent sauce:* sharp-tasting, highly flavored, savory, spicy, flavorful, piquant, flavorsome, highly seasoned, peppery, hot; tangy, strong, sharp; acrid, sour, tart, astringent, vinegary, bitter, biting, stinging. 2 *His pungent ridicule made him quite a few enemies:* sharp, piercing, pointed, trenchant, keen, poignant; stinging, biting, caustic, cutting, penetrating, sarcastic, bitter; stirring, provocative, scintillating; sparkling, brilliant, clever.
Ant. 1 bland, mild; flavorless, tasteless. 2 mild, moderate, vapid.

punish v. *Our father punished us for disobeying:* penalize, chastise, discipline, rebuke, reprove, admonish, castigate, chasten, take to task, dress down; avenge, take vengeance on, retaliate; whip, flog, beat.
Ant. excuse, pardon, forgive; praise, laud, reward.

punishment n. *For a punishment, you'll get no allowance for two weeks:* penalty, penalization, retribution; fine, forfeit, redress; discipline, correction, chastisement, castigation, chastening; spanking, whipping, flogging.

puny adj. 1 *an underfed, puny child:* small, undersized, underdeveloped, slight, pint-sized, runty, little, bantam, tiny; weakly, sickly, feeble; thin, fragile, delicate, frail. 2 *What a puny excuse!:* feeble, weak, inadequate, insignificant, slight, inconsiderable, insufficient, meager; unimportant, picayune, paltry, piddling, flimsy, measly.
Ant. 1 large, robust, strong; colossal, gigantic. 2 strong, forceful; important.

pupil n. *a class of 27 pupils:* student learner, schoolgirl, schoolboy, coed; undergraduate,

scholar; initiate, apprentice, trainee, disciple.
Ant. teacher, master.

puppet n. 1 *The children enjoyed the puppets:* animated doll, marionette, manikin; hand puppet. 2 *He's one of the dictator's puppets:* tool, pawn, dupe, instrument; figurehead; hireling, underling, flunky, lackey, henchman.

purchase v. 1 *We purchased a car:* buy, pay for. —n. 2 *We're pleased with our purchase:* acquisition, acquirement. 3 *The rope gave us good purchase for climbing the cliff:* advantage, hold, leverage; footing, foothold, toehold, support.
Ant. 1 sell, dispose of. 2 selling; disposal.

pure adj. 1 *These animals were bred from pure stock. pure oxygen:* unmixed, full-strength, unadulterated, unmodified, unalloyed, unmingled, straight; perfect, faultless, flawless, undefiled, uncorrupted, untainted, unblemished, unmarred; clean, fresh, immaculate, uncontaminated, polluted; disinfected, antiseptic, germfree, sterilized, sterile, sanitary; healthful, wholesome; purebred, thoroughbred, pedigreed, pure-blooded. 2 *It was pure luck that he was home when we called:* mere, sheer, stark; absolute, complete, whole, entire, full, utter, downright, perfect; unqualified, thorough 3 *She was a pure and wholesome girl:* innocent, guiltless, sinless, uncorrupted, moral; virtuous, chaste, undefiled, virgin, virginal, unsullied; unspoiled, spotless, immaculate, untainted, untarnished, unblemished; blameless, above suspicion, true, sincere, guileless, angelic. 4 *the distinction between pure and applied sciences:* theoretical, abstract, hypothetical, conjectural, speculative; fundamental, basic.
Ant. 1, 3 impure. 1 adulterated, mixed, mingled; imperfect, flawed, corrupted, tainted, blemished; unclean, dirty, contaminated; infected, polluted, unsterilized, unhealthful. 3 sinful, corrupt, corrupted, immoral; unvirtuous, unchaste, defiled, sullied; tarnished, blemished, untrue, indecent, filthy. 4 applied, practical.

purely adv. *It's purely a matter of taste:* only, solely, merely, simply, essentially; completely, entirely, totally, wholly.

purge v. 1 *Stalin purged his enemies from the Party:* remove, get rid of, do away with, oust, dismiss, kill, liquidate, eliminate, expel, banish, eradicate, exterminate. 2 *She purged her sins:* wash away, expiate, atone for; obtain absolution, pardon, forgiveness, or remission from. —n. 3 *Stalin conducted a purge of the officer corps:* purging, cleanup, shake-up, purification. 4 *The med-*

icine was an effective purge: laxative, purgative, cathartic, physic, emetic.

puritanical *adj. puritanical censorship:* strict, severe, ascetic, austere, puritan, prim, straitlaced, stuffy, rigid, dogmatic, narrow. *Ant.* permissive, broad-minded, latitudinarian.

purity *n.* 1 *the purity of the air:* pureness, cleanliness, cleanness; fineness; homogeneity, uniformity. 2 *She was a woman of purity and goodness:* guiltlessness, guilelessness, innocence, chastity, virginity, chasteness, virtuousness, virtue, morality; integrity, honesty, honor; simplicity, directness.
Ant. 1, 2 impurity, impureness. 1 contamination, pollution. 2 vice, unchasteness, immorality.

purport *v.* 1 *The scout purported to represent the general:* claim, profess; declare, allege. —*n.* 2 *What is the purport of your visit here?:* meaning, import, significance, implication, reason, intention, purpose, end, aim, object, objective, intent, point; gist, substance, drift, tenor.

purpose *n.* 1 *The purpose of a screen door is to keep flies out:* object, objective, function, point, rationale, intention, intent, raison d'être; reason, aim, design. 2 *My purpose was to become a surgeon:* goal, aim, ambition, aspiration, object, objective, mission, intent, intention, target, plan, motive, design, scheme, project, proposal; desire, wish, hope. 3 *She walked with a stride full of purpose:* resolve, determination, resolution. —*v.* 4 *He purposed to become a surgeon:* intend, mean, resolve, aim, aspire, drive at, design, plan, determine, endeavor, undertake, choose; commit oneself, decide, make up one's mind; contemplate, have a mind to. *Ant.* 3 purposelessness, aimlessness; inconstancy.

purposeful *adj. Every action was purposeful:* deliberate, intentional, calculated, conscious, considered, studied, premeditated; resolute, decided, resolved.
Ant. aimless, purposeless; undecided, undetermined.

purposely *adv. The door was purposely left open:* deliberately, on purpose, intentionally, consciously, calculatedly, expressly, willfully, by design; knowingly, wittingly, voluntarily, consciously.
Ant. accidentally, unintentionally, inadvertently, unknowingly, unwittingly, by chance.

purse *n.* 1 *Keep the money in your purse:* handbag, pocketbook, shoulder bag, clutch,

bag; moneybag, wallet, pouch, sporran. 2 *The purse for the next race is $25,000:* winnings, prize, award; fund, treasury, coffer. —*v.* 3 *She pursed her lips:* pucker, wrinkle, knit; bunch, contract.

pursue *v.* 1 *The police pursued the bank robber:* chase, go after, give chase to, run after; track, trail. 2 *She pursued an acting career:* seek, try for, aspire to, aim for or at, contrive to gain, be determined upon; strive for, labor for, be intent upon, set one's heart upon, be after; engage in, carry on, perform.

push *v.* 1 *Push the button:* press, move. 2 *The celebrity pushed past the reporters:* make one's way, press, struggle, force one's way; shove, elbow, squeeze, worm, wiggle, wedge, shoulder; ram, butt, jostle, fight, forge. 3 *We pushed them to finish quickly:* urge, encourage, egg on, goad, incite, prod, spur, instigate, rouse, inspire, induce, motivate, impel, prompt, stimulate, provoke, move, propel, sway, persuade, exhort; hound, dun, harass, browbeat, badger, harry, coerce, compel, force, drive. 4 *The ads pushed the new product:* promote, publicize, propagandize, advertise, boost; *Informal* hustle, plug. 5 *The child pushed his fingers into the mud:* stick, thrust, drive, shove, stuff, plunge. —*n.* 6 *Give the gate a push:* shove, nudge, prod. 7 *a worker with a lot of push:* energy, vitality, drive, go, get-up-and-go, vigor, ambition, determination. 8 *the army's push into enemy territory:* thrust, advance, incursion, inroad, foray.
Ant. 1 pull, drag, yank; pluck.

put *v.* 1 *Put the milk in the refrigerator:* set, rest, lay, position, deposit. 2 *The sergeant put the soldier to work:* assign, set, employ. 3 *He was put under arrest:* place, bring. 4 *The invading forces put our army on the defensive:* drive, force, throw. 5 *I don't put much faith in her promises:* assign, place, fix, set, lay, attribute, ascribe. 6 *Let me put it this way:* express, phrase, word, state, articulate. 7 *The plan was put to the membership for consideration:* propose, submit, offer, present.
Ant. 1 take, remove, withdraw.

putrefy *v. The meat had begun to putrefy:* rot, decay, decompose, deteriorate, spoil.

putrid *adj. putrid meat:* spoiled, rotten, decomposing, decaying, bad, contaminated, tainted, rancid; rank, foul, stinking.
Ant. clean, uncontaminated, fresh, untainted.

puzzle *v.* 1 *The case puzzled the police:* perplex, nonplus, bewilder, confuse, confound, baffle, mystify, stump. —*n.* 2 *The case was* *a puzzle:* mystery, problem, dilemma, bewilderment, bafflement, mystification, perplexity, enigma, conundrum, riddle.

pygmy *adj. The zoo acquired a pygmy hippopotamus:* dwarf, miniature, diminutive; tiny, small, midget, bantam, undersized.

Q

quack *n.* 1 *Is he a legitimate doctor or a quack?:* pretender, medical impostor, fake doctor, charlatan, quacksalver. *—adj.* 2 *a quack psychiatrist:* fake, fraudulent, phony, sham, counterfeit.

quagmire *n.* 1 *The horses were stuck in the quagmire:* marsh, bog, swamp, fen, morass, mire, slough. 2 *You'll need diplomacy to get out of that quagmire:* predicament, difficulty, critical situation, dilemma, perplexity, quandary, plight, involvement, entanglement, jam, fix, mess.

quail *v. We quailed when the principal entered the room:* blanch, lose courage, take fright, lose heart; recoil, flinch, shy, cower; quake, shudder, tremble.

quaint *adj. We enjoyed the village's quaint customs:* charmingly old-fashioned, picturesque, antique, antiquated; unusual, strange, odd, bizarre, queer, eccentric, peculiar, singular, curious, unique, original, unconventional, uncommon, rare; fanciful, whimsical.
   Ant. modern, current, fashionable; common, usual.

quake *v.* 1 *to quake with fear:* shake, shudder, tremble, shiver, quiver. *—n.* 2 *The quake caused much damage:* earthquake, tremor. 3 *A quake of fear passed through me:* quiver, shiver, shudder, trembling, ripple, spasm, throb.

qualification *n.* 1 *He has the proper qualifications for the job:* requisite, prerequisite, requirement; eligibility, fitness; competency, capability, ability, capacity, faculty, talent, accomplishment, achievement, aptitude, skill, property. 2 *The contract has several qualifications:* limitation, restriction, reservation, stipulation, condition, provision, proviso; exception, exemption; objection; modification.

qualified *adj.* 1 *a qualified veterinarian:* experienced, trained, competent, practiced; eligible, fit, equipped, suited; capable, adept, able, skilled, skillful, expert; certified, licensed, authorized. 2 *She gave a qualified answer:* limited, indefinite, conditional, pro-

visional; hedging, equivocal, ambiguous.
   Ant. 1 inexperienced, untrained, unpracticed.

qualify *v.* 1 *Two years of experience qualified me for a promotion:* make fit, make eligible, train, ground, prepare, ready, equip; license, sanction, empower, authorize, commission; be eligible, measure up, be accepted. 2 *The mayor later qualified her answer:* limit, restrict, circumscribe, narrow; moderate, alter, adjust; temper, soften, mitigate. 3 *Adjectives are words that qualify nouns:* describe, characterize, modify.

quality *n.* 1 *She has a quality of kindness that appeals to everyone:* characteristic, attribute, trait, feature, aspect, property; character, nature, disposition, temperament; qualification, capacity, faculty. 2 *The furniture was of poor quality:* value, worth, caliber, grade, rank, class, merit 3 *a woman of quality:* social status, rank, family, position, high station, standing; eminence, distinction, dignity.
   Ant. 3 low rank, low station.

qualm *n.* 1 *He had no qualms about cheating:* scruple, misgiving, uneasiness, compunction, twinge of conscience, reservation; hesitation, reluctance. 2 *I felt a qualm but never became seasick:* queasiness, faintness, dizzy spell, giddiness, vertigo, nausea.
   Ant. 1 willingness, inclination.

quandary *n. She was in such a quandary she didn't know what to do:* dilemma, difficulty, predicament, strait, fix, entanglement, plight.

quantity *n. a small quantity of sugar:* amount, sum, number; measure; abundance, aggregate; magnitude, greatness, amplitude, expanse; dosage, dose, portion, share, quota, allotment.

quarantine *v. Doctors quarantined the cholera victims:* isolate, confine, segregate, sequester.

quarrel *n.* 1 *Their friendship ended with a quarrel:* dispute, squabble, bickering, argument, spat, tiff, row, falling out; difference, contradiction; disagreement, dissension, contention, discord, controversy; cause for complaint, complaint, objection, bone of contention. —v. 2 *They quarrel constantly:* argue, bicker, wrangle, have words, squabble; differ, dissent, contend, conflict.

Ant. 1 agreement, accord, concord, amity, understanding. 2 agree, concur, consent, assent.

quarrelsome *adj. Overwork can make one quarrelsome:* contentious, bellicose, disputatious, argumentative; antagonistic, disagreeable, contrary, cantankerous, irascible.

Ant. friendly, easygoing, amiable, agreeable.

quarter *n.* 1 *a quarter of the population. This newspaper used to cost a quarter. Payments are due every quarter:* one of four equal parts, fourth part, one-fourth, fourth, 25 percent; 25 cents, quarter dollar; three months. 2 *Rioting broke out in all quarters of the city:* area, place, part, location, locality, locale, district, region, precinct, zone, place, station, domain; direction, point of the compass; side. 3 Usually **quarters** *We must find quarters before nightfall:* lodging, lodgings, housing, place to stay, place to live, shelter, billet. 4 *The army gave no quarter to the enemy:* mercy, pity, clemency; leniency, compassion, humanity, sympathy, indulgence. —v. 5 *I quartered the sandwiches:* cut into quarters, slice four ways, quadrisect. 6 *The visiting diplomat was quartered at the embassy:* furnish with quarters, billet, lodge, house, install, put up; station, post.

quash *v.* 1 *to quash a rebellion:* suppress, put down, crush, quell, squelch, repress; stop, put an end to, extinguish, exterminate; ruin, destroy, wreck, devastate, delete, cancel, expunge, erase, eradicate, dispel. 2 *The court quashed the previous ruling:* set aside, annul, nullify, void, abrogate, declare null and void, invalidate, overrule, override, countermand, revoke, reverse.

quaver *v.* 1 *I quaver when speaking to large audiences:* shake, quiver, shiver, tremble, shudder, quake; wave, wobble, totter, teeter, waver; oscillate, sway, vibrate, pulsate, throb, beat; trill. —n. 2 *His voice had a quaver in it:* tremulous shake, quavering tone, tremor, trembling, quiver, throb, vibration; trill, vibrato, tremolo.

quay *n. The boat was moored at the quay:* landing, wharf, pier, dock, jetty; waterfront, marina.

queasy *adj. I felt queasy after lunch:* sick to the stomach, sickish, nauseated, giddy; nauseating, sickening; uneasy, uncomfortable, uncertain, troubled, upset.

queen *n. the queen of England:* female monarch, empress; *(variously)* princess, czarina, ranee.

queer *adj.* 1 *Her queer way of dressing attracted stares:* strange, odd, unusual, uncommon, peculiar; unconventional, nonconforming, unorthodox, eccentric, extraordinary, exceptional; irrational, unbalanced, crazy, daft; abnormal, unnatural, outlandish, freakish, bizarre, weird, exotic; fantastic, preposterous, absurd, ridiculous, fanciful, capricious; curious, quaint. 2 *He gave some queer answers to the policeman's questions:* suspicious, doubtful, questionable, irregular; *Informal* shady, fishy. 3 *Heights give me a queer feeling:* queasy, slightly ill, faint, dizzy, giddy, light-headed, vertiginous, woozy. —v. 4 *Informal Failing the exam queered his chances of graduating:* ruin, wreck, spoil, thwart; damage, harm, hurt, impair, injure, compromise.

Ant. 1 common, conventional, customary, ordinary, unexceptional, normal; rational, sane. 4 help, aid, boost, enhance.

quell *v.* 1 *The dictator quelled the uprising:* crush, put down, squelch, quash, extinguish; ruin, destroy, stamp out; vanquish, conquer, defeat, overcome, subdue, subjugate, suppress. 2 *The lullaby quelled the baby. Aspirin will quell your headache:* quiet, still, silence, hush, calm, lull, compose, pacify, appease; mitigate, mollify, palliate, allay, alleviate, assuage, ease, soothe; deaden, dull, blunt, stem, abate.

Ant. 1 encourage, foster, foment. 2 agitate, disturb, perturb, annoy, bother.

quench *v.* 1 *Iced tea will quench your thirst:* satisfy, allay, satiate, sate, slake. 2 *The firemen quenched the blaze:* extinguish, put out, stifle, smother; cool, douse; crush, quell, suppress.

querulous *adj. a nagging, querulous man:* complaining, grumbling, peevish, disagreeable, faultfinding, difficult; dissatisfied, discontented, resentful, sour; petulant, crabbed, grouchy, splenetic, irascible, quarrelsome, irritable, cross, cranky, testy.

Ant. uncomplaining, agreeable, good-tempered; contented, cheerful, equable.

query *n.* 1 *Direct all queries to your nearest dealer:* question, inquiry; investigation, examination, quest. —v. 2 *The police queried us on our whereabouts the night of the crime:* ask, question, make inquiry, quiz, interrogate, sound out; investigate, examine. 3 *I query his trustworthiness:* question, doubt, suspect, harbor suspicions, distrust, mistrust, challenge.

quest *n. a quest for truth:* search, pursuit, exploration, hunt, seeking, mission.

question *n.* 1 *Did you ask me a question?:* something asked, request for information, query. 2 *The question was put to a vote:* issue, point in dispute, question at issue, proposal, proposition, motion, subject; uncertainty, doubt, misgiving, controversy. 3 *I'd like to travel more, but there's always the question of money:* problem, difficulty, consideration, matter. —*v.* 4 *Stop questioning me about my personal business!:* ask, query, quiz, interrogate, sound out, *Informal* pump; grill; examine, cross-examine. 5 *I question his abilities:* consider questionable, lack confidence in, doubt, call in question; suspect, distrust, mistrust, disbelieve; challenge, dispute.
Ant. 1, 4 answer, reply. 1 response. 3 solution. 4 respond. 5 trust, believe.

questionable *adj.* 1 *Whether this plan will work is still questionable:* doubtful, debatable, moot, unsure, undecided, unproven, controversial, arguable, disputable. 2 *Your motive was questionable:* dubious, suspicious, shady, *Slang* fishy, suspect, equivocal.
Ant. 1 certain, assured, proven. 2 unimpeachable, aboveboard, proper, legitimate.

quibble *v.* 1 *The children quibbled over who got the bigger piece of cake:* argue, bicker, squabble, hassle; carp, cavil, nitpick, niggle; be evasive, dodge the issue, equivocate. —*n.* 2 *A quibble over exact wording delayed passage of the bill.* trivial objection, cavil, petty distinction, nicety; evasion, equivocation, dodge, subterfuge.

quick *adj.* 1 *After a quick courtship they married:* brief, rapid, fast, abrupt, sudden, precipitate, headlong; fleet, swift, hasty. 2 *She ran with quick steps:* rapid, speedy, fast, brisk, swift, fleet, hasty, hurried; flying, nimble-footed, light-footed; brisk, lively, sprightly, agile, spry, nimble. 3 *a quick mind:* quick-witted, bright, apt, intelligent, smart, clever, acute, keen, astute, sharp, alert, wide-awake, brainy; eager, shrewd, penetrating; facile, dexterous, adroit, deft, adept. 4 *a quick temper:* excitable, impetuous, impulsive, high-strung, impatient; irritable, sharp, snappish, hot-blooded, hot-tempered, irascible, waspish, testy, touchy, temperamental.
Ant. 1–3 slow. 1 long, gradual. 2 deliberate; sluggish, lethargic; heavy. 3 dull, unintelligent, slow-witted; maladroit. 4 calm, restrained, temperate.

quicken *v.* 1 *Can we quicken the preparation of dinner?:* speed, accelerate, expedite, hasten, hurry, precipitate, hustle; propel, drive, rush, dispatch; press, urge, impel. 2 *A good debate quickens one's mind:* excite, stimulate, stir, pique, provoke, spur, goad, rouse, arouse, instigate, galvanize, kindle, incite, inspire, fire; vitalize, vivify, enliven, energize, invigorate, sharpen.
Ant. 1 slow down, slacken, delay, retard. 2 deaden, enervate, dull.

quick-tempered *adj.* *If you're quick-tempered, count to 10 before you speak:* cantankerous, peevish, testy, ill-humored, touchy, waspish, choleric, snappish, cross, cranky, grouchy, irascible, irritable.
Ant. even-tempered, placid, serene.

quick-witted *adj.* *a quick-witted teacher:* keen, perceptive, smart, clever, alert, bright, shrewd, intelligent, sharp, incisive.
Ant. slow-witted, stupid, plodding.

quiet *adj.* 1 *It was so quiet you could hear a pin drop. Why are you so quiet this evening?:* silent, noiseless, soundless, hushed, soft, low, still, calm; reticent, taciturn, reserved, uncommunicative. 2 *My vacation was anything but quiet:* restful, untroubled, calm, serene, tranquil, peaceful, peaceable, placid. 3 *The dog lay quiet at my feet:* inactive, inert, undisturbed, at rest; sleeping, slumbering, dozing, comatose, lethargic; still, motionless, immobile, stock-still; fixed, stationary, immovable. 4 *He was a quiet man who didn't let small things upset him:* gentle, mild, docile, retiring, easygoing, contented; composed, cool-headed, unexcitable, imperturbable, unperturbed, patient; modest, moderate, temperate; unobtrusive, unimpassioned, dispassionate, even tempered. 5 *The quiet decor of the home made you feel at ease:* plain, simple, unostentatious, unassuming, unpretentious; not bright, soft, subdued. —*v.* 6 *The principal tried to quiet the students:* make quiet, silence, still, hush; stifle, muffle. 7 *The aspirin seemed to quiet the headache:* relieve, allay, mitigate, palliate, comfort, soothe, soften, alleviate, mollify, assuage; settle, compose, calm, pacify, tranquilize; dull, blunt, deaden; lessen, decrease, abate, lull, quell, subdue, stay, stop, check, arrest. —*n.* 8 *In the quiet of my room I tried to think things through:* quietness, silence, stillness, hush, quietude; calm, calmness, tranquillity, serenity, peace, peacefulness.
Ant. 1 noisy, talky, verbose, loquacious. 2 excited, troubled, ruffled, agitated, turbulent. 3 active, restless, agitated. 4 violent, excitable, impatient. 5 obtrusive, showy, loud, ostentatious, pretentious; bright. 6 stir, agitate, disturb. 7 worsen, heighten, intensify, increase. 8 noise, din; disturbance, commotion.

quietly *adv.* 1 *Sit quietly:* silently, soundlessly, noiselessly, mutely, softly; inaudibly. 2 *We waited quietly for our mother to return:* calmly, serenely, contentedly; unexcitedly, unperturbedly, placidly, tranquilly, peacefully, pacifically, dispassionately. 3 *She was a quietly capable woman:* unobtrusively, unpretentiously, unostentatiously, modestly, humbly.

quip *n. Dorothy Parker was known for her quips:* clever remark, witty saying, witticism, retort, repartee, wisecrack; banter, badinage, riposte; play on words, wordplay, pun, crack, jest, gibe, raillery, jape.

quirk *n.* 1 *Wearing that silly hat everywhere was a quirk of hers:* peculiarity, oddity, eccentricity, idiosyncrasy, mannerism, affectation, crotchet; foible, whim; aberration, abnormality. 2 *By a quirk of fate the brothers met again:* sudden twist, turn, freak accident.

quit *v.* 1 *We quit smoking:* stop, desist, cease, forswear, discontinue, end, terminate; give up, relinquish; part with, let go; forgo. 2 *He quit the city and moved to the country:* leave, go away from, depart, withdraw, retire from; flee. 3 *You can't quit your job now:* resign, leave a job; renounce reject, disavow, disown, relinquish, give up, abandon, forsake. —*adj.* 4 *I wish I could be quit of these responsibilities!:* released from, free, rid, exempt, absolved, discharged.
   Ant. 1 start, begin; continue, keep on. 2 remain, stay. 3 keep, maintain.

quite *adv.* 1 *The bottle is quite empty:* totally, completely, entirely, wholly, fully, altogether; perfectly, utterly; exactly, precisely; outright, in all respects, throughout; actu-

ally, in fact, really, surely, indeed, truly, certainly, assuredly; absolutely. 2 *That was quite rude:* to a considerable extent, exceedingly, extremely, very, excessively, considerably, highly; hugely, enormously.

quiver *v.* 1 *The building quivered as the explosive went off:* shake slightly, shudder, tremble, shiver, quake, quaver, vibrate, twitch, jump, jerk; palpitate, throb, pulsate; oscillate, wobble, totter. —*n.* 2 *I could tell by the quiver in her lower lip that she was about to cry:* quivering, vibration, tremble, shiver, shudder, shake, tremor, flutter, flicker; quaver; throb, pulsation, palpitation; tic, spasm, twitching.

quiz *v.* 1 *The teacher quizzed the students on history:* question, examine, subject to examination, test; query, ask, inquire of, sound out, interrogate. —*n.* 2 *a history quiz:* test, examination, exam; interrogation, questioning, inquiry.

quizzical *adj.* 1 *a quizzical look:* inquisitive, questioning, puzzled, inquiring, perplexed, searching, curious, baffled. 2 *His quizzical manner angered his teachers:* mocking, teasing, joking, impudent, bantering, arch, coy, derisive, insolent.
   Ant. 1 comprehending, understanding.

quota *n. Each salesman has a quota to sell in each month:* portion, part, share, proportion; allotment, apportionment, allocation, assignment; quantity, measure, ration; minimum.

quotation *n. Her talk was full of quotations from the author's work:* quote, excerpt, citation, extract, passage, selection.

R

rabble *n. The king was disdainful of the rabble:* commoners, proletariat, lower classes, the masses, rank and file, populace, the mob, the great unwashed, riff-raff, hoi polloi, the herd.
   Ant. aristocracy, upper classes, nobility, elite.

race *n.* 1 *a horse race:* competitive trial of speed, contest, competition; heat. 2 *the mayoral race:* campaign, contest, election. —*v.* 3 *Let's race to the corner:* run a race, compete in a race; hasten, hurry, run, rush, hustle, fly, dart, dash, hotfoot it.
   Ant. 3 go slowly, crawl, creep.

racism *n. a country that practices racism:* racial discrimination, racial bias, bigotry, racial prejudice, race hatred, segregation.

racket *n.* 1 *Who's making all that racket?:* loud noise, din, shouting, babel, clamor, clangor, commotion, clatter, uproar, roar; hubbub, tumult, hullabaloo, disturbance. 2 *Loansharking is a racket:* illegitimate enterprise, game, underworld business. 3 *Informal What's your racket?:* business, occupation, line, *Slang* game.
   Ant. 1 quiet, silence; tranquillity, serenity.

racy *adj. It's quite a racy novel:* suggestive, lurid, risqué, bawdy, ribald, off-color, salacious, indecent, immodest, prurient; vulgar, crude, smutty.

radiance Also **radiancy** *n.* 1 *The gems had a subtle radiance:* luster, sparkle, glitter, dazzle, iridescence, gleam, sheen; splendor, resplendence, brightness, brilliancy, brilliance, luminosity, effulgence, refulgence, luminousness. 2 *Her face glowed with radiance:* animation, joy, happiness, rapture.

Ant. 1 dullness, dimness, darkness. 2 sadness, glumness.

radiant *adj.* 1 *The sky was radiant:* shining, bright, sunny, giving off rays of light, luminous, lustrous, glowing, aglow; glittering, gleaming, dazzling, brilliant, sparkling, scintillating, flashing. 2 *a radiant smile:* bright with joy, beaming, glowing, happy, elated, ecstatic, overjoyed, joyous, blissful, rapturous, pleased, delighted.

Ant. 1 dull, dark, dismal, lusterless, gloomy. 2 sad, sorrowful, disconsolate, gloomy, joyless, cheerless.

radiate *v.* 1 *The heater radiated warmth:* emit, give out, circulate, give off, beam, shed, transmit; diffuse, scatter, disperse, spread, disseminate, spread. 2 *Spokes radiate from the hub:* branch out, spread, diverge.

Ant. 1 absorb, soak up. 2 converge, come together, focus, center.

radical *adj.* 1 *Disbanding the congregation seemed a radical step:* severe, extreme, immoderate, drastic, inordinate. 2 *When a society is polarized, the radical Left confronts the radical Right:* extreme, extremist; militant, revolutionary. — *n.* 3 *Is he a radical or merely a liberal?:* revolutionary, extremist, firebrand, freethinker, antiestablishmentarian.

Ant. 1 superficial, negligible, trivial. 2, 3 conservative, moderate. 3 rightwinger, reactionary, conservative, ultraconservative.

rage *n.* 1 *He stamped out of the room in a rage:* violent anger, wrath, frenzy, indignation; fury, choler, vehemence, temper, furor, excitement; resentment, animosity, bitterness, spleen, ire, irritation, pique; passion, rampage, storm, frenzy, ferment, paroxysm. 2 *Big earrings are the rage now:* fashion, vogue, mode, craze, mania, fad, the latest thing, the thing. — *v.* 3 *She raged at his incompetence:* speak with anger, storm, flare up, fly off the handle, lose one's temper, show violent anger, be furious, explode, blow up, fulminate, rant, roar, fume, seethe, boil, rave. 4 *The war raged:* continue violently, go at full force.

Ant. 1 calm, calmness, equanimity; gratification, joy, delight. 3 be pleased, be gratified.

ragged *adj.* 1 *ragged children:* clothed in tatters, wearing worn clothes, dressed in rags, seedy. 2 *an old ragged coat:* worn-out, worn, tattered, shaggy, shabby, torn, rent, threadbare, frayed, battered, shredded, patched. 3 *My nerves were ragged:* overtaxed, strained, aggravated, at the breaking point, run down.

raid *n.* 1 *an enemy raid:* surprise attack, assault, onset, incursion, invasion, sortie, sally, foray. — *v.* 2 *to raid enemy towns:* attack, assault, swoop down on, invade, storm.

rail[1] *n.* 1 *a fence rail:* horizontal support, bar, railing, banister. 2 *to go by rail:* railway, railroad, train.

rail[2] *v.* *She was always railing against the government:* vociferate, inveigh, fulminate, declaim, scold, talk angrily, vituperate, rant, rant and rave, rage; shout abuse, scream.

raillery *n.* *The raillery was good-natured:* jesting, joking, kidding, banter, teasing, japing, badinage, satire, razzing, ribbing, ragging.

rain *n.* 1 *Rain doesn't seem likely today:* precipitation, rainfall, *(variously)* drizzle, sprinkle, cloudburst, thundershower, rainstorm, shower, downpour, deluge. 2 *A rain of pamphlets fell from the plane:* shower, deluge, spate, plethora. — *v.* 3 *It rained all night: (variously)* pour, shower, drizzle, sprinkle, *Slang* come down in buckets, rain cats and dogs. 4 *Black soot rained on the city:* shower, drop; send down. 5 *He rained gifts on his bride:* lavish, shower.

raise *v.* 1 *The carpenter raised the shelf:* erect, put up, elevate, lift. 2 *The building was raised on level ground:* build, set up, construct, erect, put up. 3 *The farmer raises corn. to raise children:* grow, breed, produce, cultivate; develop, nurse, nurture, foster; rear, bring up. 4 *That discussion raised my interest:* excite, stimulate, pique, sharpen, rouse, arouse, awaken, summon up, stir, spark, spur, inspire, boost, kindle. 5 *There's one point I'd like to raise:* put forward, bring up, advance. 6 *The landlord raised my rent:* increase, make higher, inflate, hike. 7 *We're trying to raise funds for the Red Cross:* collect, solicit, obtain, bring in, procure. 8 *The curfew was raised:* lift, end, terminate. — *n.* 9 *We received a raise in salary:* increase, elevation; promotion, advancement.

Ant. 1 lower, let down, drop. 2 raze, demolish. 4 quell, quash, calm, soothe. 6 decrease, reduce. **8** start, begin, establish. **9** decrease, cut; demotion.

rake *n. My uncle was quite a rake:* playboy, libertine, roué; lecher, seducer, womanizer, Don Juan, Lothario, Casanova, rakehell, profligate; rascal, rogue.

rakish *adj.* **1** *a rakish playboy:* loose-living, profligate, lascivious, lecherous, libertine, dissolute, dissipated, immoral, debauched. **2** *He had a rakish walk:* jaunty, sporting, breezy, sauntering, airy, dashing, dapper, sporty, debonair, swaggering.

rally *v.* **1** *to rally the troops:* reassemble, reconvene, reunite; assemble, convene, unite, collect, gather, muster. **2** *My sisters rallied to my side:* come to the aid or support of, rush. **3** *The patient rallied:* recover strength, revive, get better, improve, take a turn for the better. —*n.* **4** *a political rally:* gathering, mass meeting, convention, assembly, assemblage. **5** *The patient's sudden rally surprised the doctors:* recovery, revival, recuperation, renewal of strength, restoration, improvement.

Ant. **1** disband, dissolve, dismiss; disperse. **2** desert, abandon, forsake. **3** get worse, fail. **5** relapse.

ram *v.* **1** *He rammed the stake into the ground:* drive, force, jam, thrust; strike, hit, beat, hammer. **2** *The car rammed into a tree:* slam, crash, smash, run into, butt, bump.

ramble *v.* **1** *We like to ramble around the neighborhood on sunny afternoons:* wander, stroll, amble, saunter, meander, rove, roam. **2** *The road rambles through a thick wood:* meander, zigzag, snake, wind, twist. —*n.* **3** *She likes taking a ramble through the woods:* walk, stroll, saunter.

rambling *adj. a rambling speech:* digressive, discursive, circuitous, diffuse, disjointed. *Ant.* concise, to the point, direct.

rampage *n.* **1** *The gang went on a rampage:* violent spree, bout of violence. —*v.* **2** *The elephants rampaged through the jungle:* storm, rage; go berserk, run riot, run amok.

rampant *adj. Malaria is rampant in some regions:* widespread, rife, unchecked, unrestrained, raging; epidemic, pandemic. *Ant.* restrained, curbed, checked.

rampart *n. the ramparts of the fort:* protective barrier, defensive wall; fortification, barrier, barricade, bulwark, earthwork, breastwork.

ramshackle *adj. an old ramshackle barn:* deteriorating, dilapidated, tumbledown, decrepit, run-down, crumbling; shaky, rickety, flimsy; unsteady, unstable, tottering.

rancor *n. In defeat, he was full of rancor:* resentment, bitterness, ill feeling, ill will,

hostility, antagonism, malevolence, acrimony; hatred, animosity, spite, spitefulness, antipathy, malice, enmity, hate. *Ant.* amity, goodwill, amicability.

random *adj. a random meeting:* chance, unintentional, unplanned, undesigned, unpremeditated, unexpected, accidental; offhand, casual, haphazard, aimless. *Ant.* deliberate, planned, designed, intentional, premeditated.

range *n.* **1** *The company puts out a large range of products:* variety, scope, selection. **2** *Hiring and firing are within the range of my responsibilities:* sphere, field, orbit, domain, province, reach, limit, bounds, purview. **3** *the Rocky Mountain range:* chain of mountains, ridge, sierra, massif. **4** *home on the range:* grazing land, pasture, plains. —*v.* **5** *The children's ages range from three to eighteen:* extend, run, stretch, reach. **6** *I spent the summer ranging the countryside:* rove, wander, roam, explore.

rank[1] *n.* **1** *a product of the lowest rank:* grade, quality, class, order, type, sort. **2** *She had the rank of major:* standing, position, class, status; professional grade, level, classification. **3** *Soldiers stood in ranks for inspection:* line, row, file, column. —*v.* **4** *Buying a boat ranks low on my list of priorities:* be ranked, have place, be classed, stand, rate. **5** *He doesn't rank at the office:* be important, have high status, be respected; hold the highest rank, come first.

rank[2] *adj.* **1** *Rank greenery covered the island:* overgrown, overabundant, luxuriant, lush, dense, profuse, tall, jungly. **2** *Throw all the rank food out:* strong smelling, rancid, foul; spoiled, stale. **3** *It was a rank insult:* utter, absolute, total, complete, sheer, bald, unmitigated, downright, flagrant, arrant, glaring; gross, nasty, scurrilous; outrageous, monstrous, atrocious.

Ant. **1** spare, scanty, sparse. **2** fresh, sweet smelling, unspoiled.

rankle *v. His harsh words rankled:* irritate, gall, chafe, gripe, rile, pique.

ransack *v.* **1** *We ransacked the attic for grandmother's photo album:* rummage through, comb, search, scour. **2** *Vandals ransacked the cathedral:* pillage, sack, vandalize, plunder, loot, rifle, ravage.

rant *v. He ranted about the lack of respect shown him:* harangue, rave, rage, bluster, storm, spout, bellow, yell, explode, scold, fume.

rap *v.* **1** *We rapped at the door, but there was no answer:* tap, drum, knock. **2** *Slang We rapped for several hours:* talk, chat, converse, shoot the breeze. **3** *Informal The critics rapped the new play:* criticize, knock,

Slang pan. —*n.* **4** *We heard a rap at the door:* light blow, knock, tap. **5** *Informal I refuse to take the rap for something you did:* blame, responsibility.

Ant. **3** praise, laud, rave about.

rapacious *adj. His rapacious ways made him wealthy but friendless:* predatory; greedy, avaricious, covetous, grasping; insatiable, voracious, ravenous.

rapid *adj. She made a rapid departure. It was an age of rapid strides in science:* quick, fast, fleet, swift, speedy; hasty, hurried; rushing, accelerated.

Ant. slow, leisurely.

rapidly *adv. She ran rapidly up the stairs:* swiftly, fast, speedily, expeditiously, apace, quickly, at full speed; briskly, hurriedly, hastily.

Ant. slowly, gradually.

rapprochement *n. Diplomats tried to work out a rapprochement between the two nations:* reconciliation, reconcilement, understanding, accord, entente, détente, agreement, conciliation, accommodation, pacification.

rapt *adj.* **1** *a rapt listener:* engrossed, enthralled, absorbed, interested, attentive, intent. **2** *There was a rapt look on his face:* ecstatic, rapturous, enraptured, spellbound, enchanted, charmed, bewitched, captivated, entranced, fascinated, delighted; bemused, dreamy.

Ant. **1** uninterested, disinterested, indifferent; bored.

rapture *n. Seeing her filled me with rapture:* ecstasy, joy, elation, delight, euphoria, bliss.

Ant. unhappiness, sorrow, misery.

rare *adj. Friends like you are rare:* seldom found, scarce, few, few and far between, infrequent, uncommon, unusual, exceptional, unique.

Ant. plentiful, abundant; habitual, regular.

rarely *adv. I rarely studied:* seldom, not often, hardly ever, scarcely ever, infrequently, hardly.

Ant. often, frequently, always, continually.

rascal *n.* **1** *That rascal was always playing practical jokes:* mischievous person, trickster, prankster, scamp, imp, devil, scalawag, rapscallion. **2** *Her husband was something of a rascal:* rake, rogue, reprobate, rakehell, scoundrel, knave, cad.

rash *adj. You were too rash in accepting the offer:* precipitate, hasty, imprudent, injudicious, indiscreet, incautious; reckless, headlong, impulsive, impetuous, adventurous; careless, heedless, thoughtless, unthinking; foolhardy, foolish.

rate *n.* **1** *to read at the rate of 100 words a minute:* speed, pace, tempo. **2** *The rates*

range from $200 to $300 per day: price, charge, fee, dues; levy, tariff. —*v.* **3** *I rate that film one of the best I've ever seen:* classify, class, rank, count, regard, deem.

rather *adv. I was rather surprised:* quite, somewhat, a bit, slightly, in some degree, comparatively, relatively, fairly, moderately, *Informal* sort of, kind of.

ratify *v. A majority is needed to ratify resolutions:* validate, approve, affirm, make good; endorse, support, sanction; authorize, certify, *Informal* okay.

Ant. veto; disapprove, invalidate, repudiate.

ratio *n. The ratio is 2 to 1:* proportional relation, proportion, fixed relation; distribution, apportionment.

ration *n.* **1** *a daily ration:* food share, allotment, apportionment, provision; measure, due. **2 rations** *The fort had rations for two more days:* provisions, stores, food, provender. —*v.* **3** *Will gasoline be rationed?:* apportion, allocate, allot, mete out.

rational *adj.* **1** *a rational plan:* based on reason, sound, reasonable, logical; credible, feasible, plausible. **2** *The doctors found him to be rational:* sane, compos mentis, in one's right mind, lucid, clearheaded, balanced, responsible.

Ant. irrational. **1** unreasonable, unsound. **2** insane.

rationale *n. I don't understand the rationale of the plan:* basis, underlying reason, explanation, logic, foundations, grounds; reasoning, philosophy, key concept.

rationalize *v.* **1** *The boy's parents rationalized his bad behavior:* justify, account for, make allowance for, make excuses for, excuse, explain away. **2** *They were unable to rationalize the appearance of ghosts:* explain, interpret rationally; account for objectively.

rattle *v.* **1** *The engine rattled. The old car rattled down the street:* clatter, clink, clank; jar, shake, bounce. **2** *He rattled on about his ailments:* chatter, gab, prate, blather. **3** *Word of the accident rattled her:* shake, upset, disturb, perturb, agitate, faze, discomfit, fluster, discompose, disconcert, distract; bewilder, confuse. —*n.* **4** *the rattle of the shutters:* clacking, clatter, clang, clank.

Ant. **3** calm, compose, soothe, settle.

raucous *adj. the raucous yelling of the crowd:* harsh, rough, jarring, grating, raspy, hoarse, jangling; discordant, strident, cacophonous, inharmonious, dissonant, blaring, loud, earsplitting; shrill; piercing.

Ant. soft, dulcet, mellow, mellifluous, soothing.

ravage *v. The invaders ravaged the country-*

side: damage, ruin, raze, lay waste, waste, wreck, destroy, devastate, rape, despoil; pillage, plunder, sack, loot, ransack.

rave *v.* 1 *He kept raving until he was led away:* rant, rage; babble, ramble; make delirious utterances. 2 *Father raved when I disobeyed him:* storm, fume, be furious, be mad, be angry, flare up, explode, sputter, bluster, run or go amok. 3 *She raved about the performance:* speak glowingly, gush, wax, expatiate, rhapsodize; rant, carry on. —*n.* 4 *That book has received raves from the critics:* good review, favorable criticism, *Informal* kudos, compliments, praise. —*adj.* 5 *The critics gave rave notices to that play:* laudatory, highly favorable.

Ant. 3 cavil at, deplore. 4 condemnation, disapproval. 5 condemning, bad, disparaging.

ravenous *adj. a ravenous miser. The children were ravenous after the hike:* predatory, rapacious, covetous, greedy, avaricious, grasping, insatiable; hungry, voracious, starved, famished; gluttonous, piggish.

ravine *n. The floodwater rushed through the ravine:* valley, gulch, gorge, *Spanish* arroyo, chasm, gap, canyon, pass, gully.

ravishing *adj. You look ravishing!:* enchanting, alluring, charming, fascinating entrancing, captivating, bewitching; very pleasing, delightful, gorgeous, splendid, beautiful, sensational, *Slang* smashing.

Ant. terrible, awful; disgusting, repulsive.

raw *adj.* 1 *a piece of raw beef:* uncooked, unprepared. 2 *raw materials:* natural, crude, unrefined, unprocessed, not finished, basic. 3 *raw recruits:* untrained, unskilled, unpracticed, unexercised, undrilled, unprepared, inexperienced, uninitiated, unseasoned, untried, untested, undeveloped, untaught; fresh, green, immature, callow. 4 *raw facts:* frank, plain, brutal, unembellished, unvarnished, bare. 5 *a raw wind:* chilly, damp, cold, harsh, nipping, biting, piercing, cutting, freezing; inclement, blustery, windswept.

Ant. 1 cooked, prepared. 2 refined, manufactured, finished. 3 trained, skilled, experienced, professional. 4 embellished, gilded, smoothed over. 5 warm, balmy, sunny, mild.

raze *v. to raze a building:* tear down, pull down, level, knock down, dismantle, wreck, demolish.

reach *v.* 1 *When will we reach Los Angeles? Can you reach his hand?:* arrive at, get to, come to, make, get as far as, set foot in or on, land at, enter; succeed in touching, contact, touch; go to, attain; seize, grasp, se-

cure; get to, come to. 2 *He reached for the phone:* stretch, extend, grab at. 3 *You can reach me at this number:* contact, get, find, get in touch with, communicate with. 4 *The temperature reached the high 90's:* extend, climb, approach, move, amount to, go to, hit. —*n.* 5 *The rope was within reach:* stretch; grab, grasp, clutch.

reaction *n.* 1 *The reaction of iron and oxygen forms rust:* chemical change, chemical transformation; nuclear change. 2 *What was her reaction?:* response, reply, answer, counteraction, reflex.

reactionary *adj.* 1 *reactionary political views:* reversionary, counterrevolutionary, right-wing, conservative. —*n.* 2 *The baron was a reactionary:* conservative, right-winger, counterrevolutionary, rightist.

Ant. 2 radical, liberal, left-winger, leftist.

read *v.* 1 *Do you read me? I can read several languages:* apprehend, understand, construe, comprehend, discern, perceive; translate, interpret, decipher. 2 *I read yesterday's newspaper:* peruse, scan, run the eye over, note, study; pore over. 3 *The actor read the lines well:* utter, speak aloud something written, recite; give a public reading; deliver, present. 4 *The thermometer reads 50 degrees. The invitation read "Open house—come one, come all!":* be worded, say, go; show, indicate.

readily *adv.* 1 *The call to arms was met readily:* promptly, immediately, at once, straightway, quickly, in no time, without delay, speedily; easily, without difficulty, effortlessly, smoothly, with no effort. 2 *She readily accepted our proposal:* willingly, without reluctance, freely, graciously, ungrudgingly.

Ant. 1 slowly, with difficulty. 2 unwillingly, reluctantly.

ready *adj.* 1 *It took us several hours to get the gymnasium ready for the school dance. I'll be ready whenever you need me:* prepared, in readiness, set, equipped; fit, serviceable, in working order; available for use, accessible, present, at hand, handy, on hand, on tap, primed; punctual, speedy, expeditious, equal to, up to; mature, ripe. 2 *I'm always ready to make new friends:* willing, eager, disposed, inclined, prone, predisposed. 3 *We were ready pupils:* prompt in understanding, acquisitive, perceptive, attentive, alert, wide-awake, bright, astute, sharp, acute, keen, cunning, shrewd, quick-witted, clever, resourceful; artful, dexterous, adroit, deft, facile, versatile. 4 *The bank was ready to foreclose:* likely at any time, liable; tending; on the verge of, on the brink of, at the point of, set, just about. —*v.* 5 *The country* *was readied for war:* prepare, put in order, make ready, equip, fit out.

Ant. 1–4 unready. 1 unprepared, unequipped, unfit; unavailable, inaccessible; tardy, late, slow. 2 unwilling, loath, disinclined, indisposed, reluctant, hesitant. 3 slow, plodding.

real *adj.* 1 *real leather:* genuine, actual, authentic, bona fide. 2 *the real evidence:* true, factual, valid, unquestionable, truthful; actual, well-grounded, solid, substantial, substantive, tangible; rightful, legitimate; absolute, positive, certain, unadulterated, unvarnished. 3 *Their love was real:* sincere, unaffected, genuine, unfeigned; true, honest.

Ant. 1–3 unreal, fake, false. 1 imitation, counterfeit. 3 insincere, feigned, faked.

realistic *adj. He was realistic. It was a realistic movie:* pragmatic, down-to-earth; true-to-life, natural, naturalistic, objective, lifelike, graphic, representational, descriptive, depictive; real, authentic, genuine, truthful, faithful.

Ant. unrealistic, impractical, idealistic, romantic.

realize *v.* 1 *I don't think you realize the importance of the speech:* comprehend, apprehend, understand, gather, grasp, get, fathom, appreciate, perceive, penetrate, discern, recognize; conceive, imagine. 2 *I realized my fondest dream:* actualize, fulfill, complete, consummate, bring to pass, effectuate, carry out, execute; discharge, do, produce, perform; attain, get, achieve, accomplish, make good. 3 *She realized very little by selling those stocks:* profit, gain, acquire, clear; make money, accomplish.

really *adv. Did he really say that?:* actually, in fact, truly, truthfully, genuinely; literally, indeed; surely, certainly, veritably, verily, positively, absolutely.

realm *n.* 1 *The realm extended halfway into Asia:* dominion, kingdom, domain, empire, royal domain, monarchy; land, country; nation, state. 2 *That plan is beyond the realm of possibility:* sphere, province, orbit, region, field.

reap *v. to reap a great reward:* gather, glean, harvest, take in, bring in; earn, gain, obtain, acquire, procure, realize, derive, profit, get, win, secure.

Ant. lose, spend.

rear¹ *n.* 1 *Please move to the rear of the bus!:* back, end, tail end, heel, stern, hind part, back part, posterior; after part, area or position behind; rear guard. —*adj.* 2 *The rear end of the car was dented:* back, hindmost, aftermost, after, posterior, rearmost; dorsal; aft.

Ant. 1 front, fore, forepart. 2 front, frontmost, forward, leading.

rear² *v. The boy's aunt reared him:* bring up, raise, care for; train, educate, nurture, foster.

reason *n.* 1 *There was no reason for rudeness:* cause, occasion, grounds, justification, explanation, rationale. 2 *Use the reason that God gave you:* brains, faculties, wit, comprehension, understanding, perception, intelligence, intellect, sense, awareness, discernment, insight. 3 *He won't listen to reason:* common sense, logic, reasoning, appeal to reason, argument, exhortation. 4 *Have you lost your reason?:* rationality, mental balance, sanity, sense, clearheadedness.

Ant. 4 irrationality, insanity.

reasonable *adj.* 1 *Your proposal sounds reasonable:* judicious, sensible, intelligent; logical, rational; sound, credible, plausible, probable, possible, likely; well-grounded, well-founded, justifiable. 2 *Be reasonable in your dealings:* just, fair, impartial, objective, levelheaded; moderate, prudent, intelligent, sensible, wise; not excessive, not extreme, moderate, lenient, equitable; proper, suitable, fitting, legitimate.

Ant. 1 unreasonable, irrational, unsound, impossible.

reasoning *n.* 1 *Her powers of reasoning were formidable:* ratiocination, logic, thought, thinking; deduction, analysis. 2 *Can you understand our reasoning?:* argument, train of thought, rationale, analysis, interpretation, ground, basis.

reassure *v. Reassure children that they have your confidence:* assure, inspire hope in, encourage, uplift, buoy up, cheer; comfort, set one's mind at rest.

Ant. dishearten, discourage, disconcert.

rebel *n.* 1 *The rebels were tried for treason. The film director was a rebel among his peers:* insurgent, insurrectionist, traitor, turncoat; secessionist, seceder, separatist; revolutionist, revolutionary; iconoclast, nonconformist, maverick. —*v.* 2 *The peasants rebelled:* defy authority, rise up, revolt, mutiny. 3 *We rebelled at the idea:* be repelled by, draw back from, flinch, shrink, recoil.

rebellion *n. The troops crushed the rebellion:* insurrection, revolt, insurgency, revolution, mutiny, uprising.

rebellious *adj. The king retaliated against the rebellious earls. rebellious children:* defiant, disobedient, insubordinate, intractable, refractory, recalcitrant, fractious; mutinous, insurgent, revolutionary, unruly, unmanageable, ungovernable, disorderly, alienated.

Ant. patriotic, loyal; dutiful, obedient, subservient.

rebuff *v. Workers rebuffed the plan:* snub, slight, reject, spurn, ignore, disregard, refuse; repel, repulse, decline, *Slang* turn down; check.

Ant. welcome, encourage, accept.

rebuke *v.* 1 *The clerk was rebuked for misplacing the files:* scold, upbraid, reproach, admonish, take to task, reprimand, reprove, remonstrate with, lecture, censure. —*n.* 2 *Father's rebuke came as a surprise:* scolding, reprimand, admonishment, upbraiding, admonition, reproach, reproof, tongue-lashing; disapproval, censure, castigation, berating.

Ant. 1–2 praise. 1 laud, commend, compliment. 2 laudation, commendation, compliment.

rebuttal *n. My rebuttal demolished my opponent's argument:* refutation, rejoinder; confutation, contradiction, retort, counter-argument, disproval, negation, surrejoinder.

recalcitrant *adj. a recalcitrant youth who defied his elders:* stubborn, obstinate; unwilling, headstrong, refractory, willful, contrary, unruly, disobedient, intractable.

Ant. obedient, compliant, submissive, yielding; controllable.

recall *v.* 1 *I don't recall your name:* recollect, remember; recognize, place. —*n.* 2 *Do you have any recall of the accident?:* recollection, memory, remembrance; faculty of memory.

recant *v. She recanted her testimony:* retract, take back, deny, abjure, withdraw, repudiate, disavow, renege, revoke, rescind, disclaim, disown, forswear, repeal, change one's mind.

Ant. affirm, confirm, repeat, validate.

recapitulate *v. The newscaster recapitulated the events:* summarize, recap, sum up; reiterate, recount; repeat, restate, rephrase.

recede *v. The floodwaters have receded:* retreat, go back, regress; abate, ebb, subside; retire, retreat.

Ant. advance, progress.

receipt *n.* 1 *This bill is payable upon receipt:* arrival, receiving, reception, recipience, acquisition, possession. 2 *The clerk asked me to sign a receipt:* written acknowledgment of payment or goods received; voucher, transferral. 3 **receipts** *The receipts exceeded our expectations:* profits, return, gain, proceeds, share; *Slang* take, revenue, income, earnings, payment.

receive *v.* 1 *to receive the best of care:* get, acquire, secure, come by, be in receipt of, obtain, be given. 2 *The prisoners received*

harsh treatment: encounter, meet with, experience, have inflicted on one, be subjected to, undergo, sustain, suffer. 3 *We are not receiving callers today:* be at home to, entertain, admit; welcome, greet, meet. 4 *The book was received favorably by the critics:* regard, accept, approve, adjudge.

recent *adj. in recent times:* new, modern, contemporary, up-to-date, lately made, late; novel, fresh; not long past.

Ant. old-fashioned, old, past.

receptacle *n. Throw your litter in that receptacle:* holder, container, vessel, depository, repository; *(variously)* box, bin, basket, hopper, hamper, compartment, bottle, jar, can, bag, tray.

reception *n.* 1 *I couldn't fathom her cool reception:* act of receiving one, welcome, greeting. 2 *We had a reception for the new ambassador:* affair, social gathering; party, fete.

receptive *adj. Wait until the boss is in a receptive mood:* favorably disposed, open-minded, accessible, approachable, amenable, hospitable, friendly, responsive, interested, susceptible.

Ant. unreceptive, unresponsive, closed-minded, prejudiced, biased.

recess *n.* 1 *a ten-minute recess. the school's winter recess:* suspension of business, intermission, break, respite, rest, hiatus, pause, lull; interlude, interval; holiday, vacation. 2 *The safe was set in a recess of the wall:* indentation, hollow, alcove, nook, niche, slot, pigeonhole, corner, bend. 3 **recesses** *In the recesses of his mind he planned revenge:* inmost part, depths.

reciprocal *adj. Our respect is reciprocal. reciprocal trade agreements:* mutual, common; shared; interdependent, returned, exchanged, equivalent, complementary, bilateral, linked, interrelated, interchangeable.

Ant. unilateral.

reciprocate *v. They've invited us to dinner so many times we must reciprocate:* return, feel, give in return, interchange; respond, return the compliment, act likewise, make return, retaliate.

recital *n.* 1 *a piano recital:* solo musical performance, concert. 2 *His recital of the poem was flawless. Did she give you a recital of her woes?:* recapitulation, narration, recitation, delivery, performance, reciting; narrative, discourse, dissertation; report, description, particulars, account; public reading.

reckless *adj. reckless driving:* incautious, heedless, unheeding, unmindful, careless, irresponsible, mindless, unthinking, neglectful, negligent, unwary, unaware; wild,

reckon · recumbent

daring, precipitate, rash, indiscreet, imprudent, uncircumspect, impulsive, foolhardy, foolish, madcap.

Ant. cautious, careful, responsible.

reckon v. 1 *The wages were reckoned by the number of hours worked:* count, add, add up, total, tally, figure, calculate, compute. 2 *We reckon ourselves fortunate. He reckoned we were only a few miles from the farm:* regard, esteem, consider, deem, think, judge, estimate; count, account, appraise, assess, value; determine, surmise, estimate; decide, guess, speculate. 3 *Informal I reckon you'll feel better soon:* guess, fancy, expect, presume, surmise, suppose, imagine, figure. 4 *I didn't reckon on arriving early:* count, figure, plan, bargain. 5 *I don't know how to reckon with this problem:* deal, cope, handle.

reckoning n. 1 *a reckoning of all accounts:* count, total, tally, adding, summation, calculation, computation; appraisal, estimate, estimation, evaluation, bill, account, charge, tab; settling of an account. 2 *It will be a time of reckoning for us:* judgment, final judgment.

recline v. *She was reclining on a couch:* lie back, lie down, rest, repose; lean, sprawl.

recognition n. 1 *My disguise prevented recognition:* identification, discovery. 2 *Some artists gain recognition after death:* acceptance, acknowledgment, understanding, comprehension, notice.

recognize v. 1 *I didn't recognize you in that disguise:* know, identify, place, make out, discern, pick out. 2 *We recognize your problems:* be aware of, appreciate, understand, comprehend, respect, acknowledge, realize, see, discern, admit, know. 3 *The chair recognizes Mr. Jones:* acknowledge as entitled to speak, give the floor to, yield to, concede to.

Ant. 2, 3 ignore, overlook.

recoil v. 1 *Spiders always made her recoil:* draw back, start, shrink, retreat, blench, quail, flinch, cower, cringe. 2 *The cannon recoiled when it went off:* fly back, spring back, rebound, bound back, jump back, kick.

recollect v. *I can't recollect where we met:* recall, call to mind, remember, place.

recommend v. 1 *The supervisor recommended me for a promotion:* put forward, mention favorably, endorse, advocate, vouch for. 2 *The doctor recommended a change of scenery:* suggest, encourage, propose, advise, prescribe, counsel.

Ant. 2 forbid, discourage.

recommendation n. *It was on your recommendation that we hired her:* commendation, good word, behest, endorsement, reference.

Ant. condemnation, criticism, disapproval.

recompense v. 1 *The company recompensed me for travel expenses:* compensate, remunerate, reimburse, repay. —n. 2 *This money is recompense for the work:* compensation, remuneration, payment; reparation, repayment; return, reward.

reconcile v. 1 *Father was unable to reconcile my brothers:* conciliate, propitiate, restore to friendship, reunite. 2 *A pacifist cannot be reconciled to war:* conciliate, win over, persuade, resign. 3 *We had better reconcile accounts:* settle, set straight, square; harmonize, rectify, adjust, correct.

reconnaissance n. *reconnaissance of enemy territory:* survey, scrutiny, viewing, observation; reconnoitering, scouting, surveillance.

reconsider v. *We begged her to reconsider:* rethink, reexamine, reevaluate, modify, reassess, think over, think better of, revise, amend, correct.

record v. 1 *You should record the lyrics:* write down, put on record, register, transcribe, take down, jot down, make a memorandum of; enter, catalog, list, log; chronicle; register; tape. 2 *A cardiograph records the heartbeat:* register, show, indicate. —n. 3 *a record of births and deaths:* account, report, document, register; file; journal, chronicle, archive, history, proceedings; note, memorandum, memo, jotting. 4 *His employment record has been good:* history, report, account; background, experiences; conduct, performance, career. 5 *to break a world record:* best performance, top performance, unbeaten mark.

Ant. 1 erase, expunge, cancel, delete.

recoup v. *to recoup one's losses:* regain, reacquire, recover, make good.

recover v. 1 *The stolen jewels were recovered:* get back, retrieve, regain, repossess, reclaim, redeem, recapture, win back; restore. 2 *She's recovering from the flu:* regain strength, get well, recuperate, convalesce, improve, heal, mend; revive, revivify, resuscitate, rejuvenate, restore.

Ant. 2 relapse, fail, worsen.

recreation n. *What's your favorite recreation?:* diversion, leisure activity, pastime, play, hobby, sport, entertainment, amusement, avocation; diversion, relaxation.

rectify v. *The accounting error was rectified:* right, set right, correct, adjust, straighten, square; mend, amend, emend, fix, repair, revise; remedy, redress, cure, reform.

recumbent adj. *a recumbent position:* lying down, prone, prostrate, supine, flat,

389

stretched out, horizontal; reclining, leaning. *Ant.* upright, erect, standing, vertical; sitting.

recuperate *v. He's recuperating after heart surgery:* recover, get well, get better, heal, mend, convalesce, regain one's strength, be on the mend.

Ant. fail, sink, worsen.

recur *v.* 1 *If this cheating recurs, you will be expelled:* occur again, repeat; return, come again, reappear; resume, persist, continue. 2 *The good times of my youth recur to me:* come back, return to mind, be remembered.

recurrent *adj. a recurrent dream:* recurring, frequent, periodic, regular, reappearing, repeating.

red *adj.* 1 *She wore red lipstick:* blood-colored; *(variously)* maroon, wine, ruby, vermilion, crimson, cardinal, scarlet, cherry, rose; auburn; pink, coral, flame. 2 *My red cheeks showed my embarrassment:* blushing, reddened, ruddy, flushed, rosy, florid, rubicund; glowing, inflamed, burning.

redeem *v.* 1 *Present this ticket to redeem your ring:* buy back, repurchase; reclaim, recover, retrieve, regain, repossess. 2 *He redeemed his promise:* keep, fulfill, make good; discharge. 3 *She worked weekends to redeem the lost time:* make up for, compensate for, make good, settle; make amends for, recover, regain, retrieve. 4 *to redeem lost souls:* rescue, save, deliver from sin, convert, reform.

Ant. 1 lose, forfeit, give up. 2 break; disregard.

redress *n.* 1 *Redress is obtained when a court grants damages to a victim of fraud:* reparation, compensation, recompense, payment, restitution, rectification, amends, satisfaction. —*v.* 2 *The king redressed past injustices:* correct, set right, rectify, make reparation for, compensate for, make retribution for, make up for; remedy, ease, relieve.

reduce *v.* 1 *to reduce prices:* lessen, diminish, discount, mark down. 2 *You can reduce if you exercise:* lose weight, slim down, diet, slenderize. 3 *The military court reduced the major to captain:* lower in rank, demote, *Slang* bust, lower. 4 *Water reduces the potency of a highball:* minimize, lessen, lower, dilute, blunt, dull, moderate, temper, abate, mitigate, assuage, soften; curb, check, weaken.

Ant. 1, 3, 4 increase. 1 augment, mark up. 2 gain. 3 promote, elevate. 4 heighten, strengthen.

redundant *adj.* 1 *I found the lecture redundant:* repetitious, tautological, pleonastic. 2 *The story doesn't need this redundant*

background material: superfluous, unnecessary, inessential, dispensable, extra, excess.

Ant. 2 necessary, essential, indispensable.

reek *n.* 1 *the reek of garbage:* smell, odor, stink, stench. —*v.* 2 *She reeks of cheap perfume:* smell, be malodorous, stink, smell to high heaven.

reel *v.* 1 *He reeled and grabbed my shoulder:* rock, stagger, totter, teeter, wobble, sway, stumble, lurch, pitch, roll. 2 *Everything started to reel around me:* rotate, whirl, swirl, spin, revolve; feel dizzy, be giddy.

refer *v.* 1 *I was referred to the personnel director:* direct, send. 2 *We referred the proposal to the board of directors:* submit, deliver, transmit, transfer, pass along. 3 *The speaker referred to the book to make a point:* make reference; allude, mention, cite; go, turn, consult.

referee *n.* 1 *The court appointed a referee to settle the claim:* judge, umpire, arbitrator, arbiter, adjudicator, moderator, mediator. —*v.* 2 *I volunteered to referee the match:* umpire, arbitrate, settle, determine, judge, adjudicate, pronounce, judgment; mediate, moderate.

reference *n.* 1 *In her autobiography there's no reference to her brother:* mention, allusion, suggestion, hint, intimation, innuendo, inkling, implication. 2 *He gave her an excellent reference when she resigned:* recommendation, testimonial, endorsement, deposition, good word.

refined *adj.* 1 *a highly refined organic product:* purified, cleansed, clean, clarified. 2 *refined manners:* well-bred, genteel, gentlemanly, ladylike, polite, courteous; discriminating, fastidious, cultured, cultivated, civilized, polished, finished; urbane.

Ant. 1, 2 unrefined. 1 impure, unpurified. 2 ill-bred, coarse, crude, vulgar, ungentlemanly, unladylike, unmannerly.

refinement *n.* 1 *a woman of refinement:* fine sensibilities, cultivation, urbanity, culture, finish, elegance, polish, tastefulness, discrimination, discernment, fastidiousness; gentility, breeding, suavity, urbanity: graciousness, delicacy; politeness, courtesy, good manners, courteousness. 2 *the refinement of crude oil:* purification, cleaning, cleansing, filtration, distillation. 3 *With several refinements your essay would be excellent:* improvement, revision, rectification, amendment; development, enhancement, progression, advancement, step forward.

Ant. 1 vulgarity, crudeness, coarseness, discourtesy.

reflect *v.* 1 *The lake reflected the moon:* mirror, cast back from a surface, give back an image of; copy, imitate, reproduce. 2 *Cow-*

ardice reflects nothing but shame on one's family: cast, bring upon. **3** The book reflected the author's thoughts: show, display, express, exhibit, reveal, disclose, indicate, manifest, set forth, present, demonstrate, represent. **4** Reflect for a moment: think, think carefully, deliberate, reason, ponder, consider, meditate, contemplate, speculate, mull over, cogitate, dwell upon.

Ant. **1** absorb. **3** conceal, hide.

reflection n. **1** a reflection in the mirror: image, mirror image, optical counterpart. **2** We gave much reflection to the problem: thought, deliberation, consideration, attention, thinking, pondering, meditation, musing, study, cogitation. **3** The book included reflections by those involved in the incident: thought, idea, sentiment, impression, view.

reform n. **1** reform of the political system: correction, rectification, reformation, amendment. —v. **2** to reform a political system: change for the better, better, improve, correct, rectify, rehabilitate, remodel, rebuild, remedy, repair; revise, convert, mend, amend; repent, atone, abandon evil conduct, mend one's ways, turn over a new leaf.

refrain v. Refrain from working too much: abstain, restrain oneself, keep oneself, hold off, desist, forbear, forgo, renounce, eschew, avoid, refuse, resist, leave off.

Ant. indulge in; continue, persist.

refresh v. **1** The travelers stopped to refresh themselves: freshen, invigorate, vivify, restore, revive, renew. **2** Please refresh my memory: prompt, prod, jog, stimulate, renew, awaken.

Ant. tire, weary, fatigue.

refreshment n. The hostess served refreshments: food and drink, nourishment, snack; beverage, drink.

refuge n. **1** We took refuge under an awning: shelter, sanctuary, protection. **2** Churches were refuges for the flood victims: haven, retreat, sanctuary, asylum, harbor. **3** Drinking was a refuge from reality: resort, hideout, technique for escaping.

Ant. **1** exposure, danger, threat.

refugee n. The refugees can't return to their homeland: fugitive, exile, escapee, DP, displaced person, evacuee; absconder, runaway.

refund v. **1** The store refunded the overpayment: give back (money), return, pay back, rebate. —n. **2** I returned the merchandise for a refund: rebate, repayment, reimbursement, remittance; amount repaid.

refurbish v. to refurbish an old house: renovate, fix up, remodel, renew, redo, restore, recondition, overhaul; repair, mend.

refusal n. My refusal was final: rejection,

turndown, declining, nonacceptance, nonconsent, unwillingness; regrets; veto.

refuse[1] v. We had to refuse the invitation. They were refused admittance: not accept, decline, say no to, reject, veto, turn down, spurn; forbid, prohibit, disallow, withhold, deny.

Ant. accept, consent to; permit, allow.

refuse[2] n. the refuse at the city dump: rubbish, trash, garbage, waste, junk, litter.

refute v. to refute an accusation: disprove, confute, counter, rebut, answer, contradict, deny.

Ant. prove; support, confirm, corroborate, substantiate.

regain v. You'll never regain your property: recover, retrieve, repossess, get again, get back, retake, reclaim, recapture, recoup, win back.

regal adj. a dancer of regal bearing: royal, kingly, queenly, noble, lordly, proud, kinglike, queenlike; stately, majestic, magnificent, imposing, august.

regard v. **1** I regard that movie highly: consider, look upon, view; think, judge, believe, hold; estimate, rate, value, esteem. —n. **2** He gave little regard to his parents' feelings: thought, consideration, concern, attention, notice, note, observation, heed, mind, care. **3** I have little regard for liars: respect, esteem, admiration, estimation, appreciation. **4** In that regard, at least, we agree: respect, matter, point, subject, aspect, detail.

Ant. **2, 3** disregard, scorn, contempt, disrespect.

regardless adv. It was futile, but I talked to him regardless: nevertheless, nonetheless, notwithstanding, anyway, in spite of everything.

regenerate v. **1** The congregation was spiritually regenerated: reform, rejuvenate, redeem, uplift, enlighten. **2** Good news regenerated our hopes: generate anew, give new life to, revive, renew, reawaken, resuscitate, resurrect, revivify; restore, retrieve.

regime n. The new regime imposed higher taxes: government, rule, reign, administration, dynasty, leadership, command; direction, control, management.

regimentation n. Military life is characterized by strict regimentation: discipline, order, uniformity, regulation, system, method, orthodoxy, regimen, methodization.

region n. a mountainous region: area, territory, space, expanse, tract, country, land, district, neighborhood, zone, province; locality, vicinity; field, sphere, domain, realm.

register n. **1** We signed the hotel register:

record book; ledger, daybook, diary, log, logbook, roll, registry. 2 *The singer's voice had a wide register:* range, scale, compass. —*v.* 3 *The stenographer registered the proceedings:* write down, record, put in writing, note down, take down. 4 *You must register to vote:* enroll, sign up, enlist. 5 *Her face registered disappointment:* show, indicate, exhibit, disclose, manifest, mark, record; portray, express.

regress *v.* 1 *His mind regressed further into the past:* go back, move backward, withdraw, reverse, retrogress, revert, retreat, backslide, recede; relapse, deteriorate. —*n.* 2 *the right of ingress and regress:* return, exit.

Ant. 1 progress, advance; rise, ascend. 2 ingress, entrance.

regret *v.* 1 *I regretted my decision:* be sorry for, feel remorse for, be ashamed of, rue, bemoan, deplore, bewail, mourn, grieve at, lament, reproach oneself for, have second thoughts about. —*n.* 2 *I've never had any regrets over anything I've done:* sorrow, grief, remorse, regretfulness, ruefulness, compunction, contrition, apology, apologies, repentance, disappointment, dissatisfaction, anguish, woe, qualm, reservation, pang of conscience, second thought; self-condemnation, self-reproach; heartache.

Ant. 1 feel happy for, rejoice. 2 satisfaction, contentment.

regrettable *adj. a regrettable situation:* lamentable, pitiable, unhappy, grievous, woeful, unfortunate, deplorable.

Ant. happy, fortunate, lucky.

regular *adj.* 1 *Getting up at dawn is part of our regular routine:* usual, normal, customary, standard, typical, ordinary, common, commonplace, familiar, daily, steady, constant, habitual, undeviating, invariable, unvarying, unchanging, set, fixed, established. 2 *She made regular entries in her diary:* consistent, habitual, frequent, recurrent, recurring, periodic, periodical. 3 *Informal He's a regular guy:* genuine, real, down-to-earth, plain, natural, typical, everyday. 4 *She had regular features:* even, smooth, well-proportioned, fine, symmetrical, well-balanced. —*n.* 5 *He knew all the regulars by their first names:* regular customer, habitué, faithful, loyalist, stalwart.

Ant. 2, 4 irregular. 1 unusual, abnormal, exceptional, rare, uncommon; varied, varying; unmethodical. 2 occasional, infrequent.

regulate *v.* 1 *The officer regulated traffic at the intersection:* control, govern, handle, manage, superintend, supervise, oversee, guide, direct. 2 *Please regulate the sound on*

that radio: adjust, fix, rectify, moderate, modulate.

regulation *n.* 1 *the regulation of room temperature:* adjusting, adjustment, handling, control. 2 *It's against regulations:* rule, decree, direction, statute, dictate, order, command, edict.

rehabilitate *v.* 1 *to rehabilitate juvenile delinquents:* restore to society, resocialize, straighten out, reeducate, set straight; redeem, save. 2 *The old ship was rehabilitated:* renovate, remake, reconstruct, restore, refurbish, recondition.

rehearse *v. The actors rehearsed their parts:* prepare, practice, drill, go over, run through.

reign *n.* 1 *the reign of King John:* regnancy, rule, tenure, regnum; incumbency, government, regime, sovereignty; influence, dominance, supervision. —*v.* 2 *Queen Victoria reigned for over 60 years:* have royal power, wear the crown, occupy the throne, exercise sovereignty; rule, govern, hold authority, hold sway.

reimburse *v. You'll be reimbursed for travel expenses:* pay back, refund, repay, remunerate, pay up, compensate, recompense, make restitution.

rein *n.* 1 Usually **reins** *the horse's reins:* bridle. 2 *Keep a tight rein on expenses:* restraint, check, hold. —*v.* 3 *You must learn to rein in your temper:* control, check, curb, hold back, bridle, restrict, suppress.

reinforce *v. The concrete is reinforced with steel beams:* strengthen, support, bolster, fortify.

Ant. weaken, diminish, lessen.

reiterate *v. Let me reiterate my view:* repeat, resay, iterate, retell, restate; stress, go over and over.

reject *v. The board rejected our ideas:* refuse, say no to, decline, turn down; dismiss, repudiate, rebuff, spurn, deny.

Ant. accept, approve, favor, allow, permit.

rejoice *v. We rejoiced in our good fortune:* be glad, be happy, be pleased, be delighted, be overjoyed, exult, glory, delight, be elated; make merry, celebrate.

Ant. be sad, be unhappy, lament, grieve.

rejoicing *n. The halls were filled with rejoicing:* celebration, festivity, revelry, merrymaking; mirth, merriment, gaiety, jollity, good cheer; happiness, gladness, jubilation, jubilance, joyfulness, delight, pleasure; elation, cheering.

rejoinder *n. Her rejoinder was the perfect squelch:* answer, reply, response, retort, rebuttal, *Slang* comeback, riposte; remonstrance, refutation, repartee, countercharge, counterstatement.

rejuvenate v. *The vacation rejuvenated me:* make youthful again; restore, put new life into, reinvigorate, revive, revitalize, restore. *Ant.* age; tire, weary, fatigue.

relapse v. 1 *He relapsed into his old ways:* fall back, slip back, sink back, turn back, revert, backslide, regress, retrogress, lapse, worsen. —n. 2 *The patient suffered a relapse:* lapse, fall, reversion, turn for the worse, falling back, retrogression, reverse, regression, deterioration, decline, recurrence, worsening.

relate v. 1 *The witness related what he had seen:* tell, recount, give an account of, report, describe, divulge, impart, convey, communicate, state, say, utter. 2 *My remarks related to the topic under discussion:* connect, associate, attach, link, refer, have reference, pertain, concern, be relevant, appertain, apply. 3 *It's unfortunate when a father and son can't relate to each other:* feel close, have rapport, interact well, communicate, feel empathy with. *Ant.* 2 be unconnected, be irrelevant.

relation n. 1 Also **relationship** *There's no relation between our groups:* connection, tie, link, bond, interrelationship, association, affiliation. 2 *He's a distant relation of mine:* relative, kin, kinsman. 3 *Your remarks have no relation to this conversation:* connection, reference, bearing, relevance, concern, pertinence, application. 4 *Her relation of the fairy tale fascinated the youngsters:* narrating, narration, telling, recital, recitation; narrative, account, report, description. *Ant.* 1 dissociation, independence.

relative n. 1 *Most of my relatives were there:* relation, kinsman, kinswoman, kinfolk, kin, kith, kith and kin, people, family, folks, blood relative, flesh and blood. —adj. 2 *We weighed the relative advantages of buying a house and renting an apartment:* comparative, comparable, relational. 3 *The slides were relative to the lecture:* pertinent, appropriate, pertaining, relevant, applicable, germane. *Ant.* 1 stranger. 2 absolute. 3 unconnected, unrelated, irrelevant.

relax v. 1 *Relax and enjoy yourself:* make less tense, calm, soothe; cool off, unwind, unbend, ease up, let up. 2 *The regulations can be relaxed:* make less strict, slacken, loosen, soften, bend, ease. 3 *The doctor told me to relax a month before going back to work:* rest, take it easy, enjoy oneself, vacation, idle, laze, loaf, lie around. *Ant.* 1 tense. 2 tighten, intensify, heighten. 3 work, be active.

relaxation n. 1 *a relaxation of the rules:* loosening, bending, abatement, slackening.

2 *What do you do for relaxation?:* recreation, enjoyment, fun, amusement, entertainment, diversion, pleasure; pastime, avocation, hobby, sport, leisure. *Ant.* 1 tightening, stiffening. 2 work, toil, labor.

release v. 1 *The convict was released from prison:* free, set free, liberate, let out, let go, discharge. 2 *The driver released the brake:* loose, untie, unloose, unfasten, unbind; disengage, detach, extricate. 3 *Don't release this news to the public:* distribute, circulate, present, communicate. —n. 4 *the release of political prisoners:* releasing, liberating, freeing, liberation, setting free, letting go, extrication, dismissal. *Ant.* 1 imprison, incarcerate; hold, keep. 2 fasten, engage. 3 withhold, conceal, hide. 4 imprisonment, incarceration, internment, detention.

relent v. *Father finally relented and let us go camping:* grow lenient, become milder, weaken, soften, unbend, relax, bend, yield, let up, give way, capitulate, have pity, come around.

relentless adj. *a relentless tyrant:* unrelenting, remorseless, implacable, unyielding, inflexible, adamant, harsh, hard, stern, severe, stiff, rigid, rigorous, ruthless, pitiless, merciless. *Ant.* relenting, flexible, compromising; kind, sparing, compassionate, merciful, lenient, softhearted, forgiving.

relevant adj. *The film was relevant to our discussion:* related, pertinent, connected, tied in, associated; germane, material, appropriate, applicable, apropos; apt, suitable, suited, fit, fitting, to the point. *Ant.* irrelevant, unrelated, unconnected; inappropriate, immaterial, extraneous.

reliable adj. *a reliable employee:* dependable, unfailing, faithful, trustworthy, trusty, responsible, conscientious, tried and true. *Ant.* unreliable, undependable, untrustworthy, irresponsible.

reliance n. *I place no reliance on what you say:* trust, confidence, dependence, faith, credence, credit, assurance. *Ant.* distrust; uncertainty.

relief n. 1 *For relief of headaches take aspirin:* easement, alleviation, assuagement, abatement, amelioration, mitigation, reduction; remedy, cure. 2 *Much to my relief, the exam was postponed:* peace of mind, release from anxiety; encouragement, elation. 3 *The poor families survived on relief:* dole, welfare assistance, welfare, public assistance. 4 *Vacationing was a welcome relief from work:* respite, rest, break.

Ant. 1 aggravation, intensification. 2 anxiety, anguish. 4 hardship, burden.

relieve *v.* 1 *The ointment relieved the itching:* ease, lighten, abate, alleviate, assuage, solace, mitigate, mollify, allay, subdue, soothe. 2 *I was relieved to hear you were all right:* reassure, free from fear, comfort, calm, console, solace, cheer, encourage. 3 *Public funds relieved the poverty-stricken families:* aid, help, assist, support. 4 *The general was relieved of his command:* remove, release, let out, replace, free; take the place of.

Ant. 1 increase, intensify, heighten, aggravate. 2 alarm, concern. 3 burden, oppress.

religion *n.* 1 *As she grew old, religion meant more to her. Art was her religion:* belief in God, faith, belief, religious faith, worship, reverence, piety, devoutness, godliness, spirituality; theology, dogma, cult, creed, canon. 2 *the Jewish religion:* system of faith, system of worship; creed, denomination, sect, cult, persuasion, affiliation, church.

Ant. 1 atheism, godlessness, impiety, irreligion, sacrilege, unbelief.

religious *adj.* 1 *religious services:* spiritual, holy, sacred, theological, divine, denominational, devotional. 2 *a religious churchgoer:* devout, spiritual, godly, God-fearing. 3 *She was religious about arriving on time:* conscientious, unswerving, steadfast, undeviating, faithful, scrupulous, fastidious, meticulous, punctilious.

Ant. 1 secular. 2 impious, unfaithful, irreverent, unbelieving, godless; atheistic, agnostic. 3 unreliable, inconstant.

relinquish *v. Edward VIII relinquished his throne:* renounce, repudiate, disclaim, lay aside, shed, cast off, put aside; surrender, cede, give up, hand over, yield; resign, abdicate, quit, withdraw from, leave, vacate, forsake.

Ant. keep, retain, hold, cling to; sustain, maintain.

relish *n.* 1 *a lifelong relish of baseball:* liking, partiality, fondness, love, enjoyment, zest, penchant, propensity, predilection, fancy, taste, appetite. 2 *A hobby gives relish to life:* pleasure, delight, satisfaction, gratification, enjoyment, exuberance, enthusiasm; zest, gusto, spice. —*v.* 3 *I don't relish the idea:* like, fancy, look forward to, dote on, take pleasure in, delight in, rejoice in, enjoy, be pleased with, *Informal* be crazy about.

Ant. 1 dislike, distaste, antipathy. 2 dissatisfaction; distaste. 3 dislike, hate, loathe.

reluctant *adj. He was reluctant to sign the contract:* unwilling, loath, averse, disinclined, indisposed; hesitant.

Ant. eager, keen, desirous, inclined.

rely *v. You can rely on me:* depend, feel sure of, count, bank; believe, place one's trust in.

remain *v.* 1 *Her love remained:* stay, continue, persist, go on, endure, abide, last, survive. 2 *She told the children to remain in the car:* stay, stay behind, wait, stay put; be left, be left behind, be left over.

Ant. 1 die, pass, disappear. 2 go, leave.

remainder *n. $10 is mine, the remainder is yours:* balance, rest, remains, excess, residue, surplus, overage; leftovers, leavings, remaining part, remnant, scourings.

remark *v.* 1 *I remarked on the weather:* observe, say, say in passing, mention, comment. —*n.* 2 *Your remarks hurt her feelings:* commentary, reflection, comment, observation, word. 3 *The movie was not worthy of remark:* consideration, note, notice, attention.

remarkable *adj. remarkable feats of courage:* noteworthy, notable, conspicuous, singular, phenomenal, extraordinary, exceptional, memorable, unforgettable, outstanding; distinguished, striking, impressive.

Ant. ordinary, common, commonplace; mediocre, unexceptional; undistinguished.

remedy *n.* 1 *a remedy for a cold:* cure, medicine, relief, nostrum, medication, treatment, corrective; preventive, panacea, cure-all; help, aid, assistance; redress, rectification. —*v.* 2 *Those pills will remedy your sinus condition. to remedy an injustice:* cure, heal, relieve, ease, alleviate, assuage, ameliorate, soothe, mitigate, mollify; set right, fix, improve, help, aid, repair, mend; correct, rectify, redress, right, amend, emend.

Ant. 1 toxin, poison; disease. 2 aggravate, heighten, intensify, worsen.

remember *v.* 1 *I don't remember her name:* recall, call to mind, recollect; retain the thought of, not forget, bear in mind. 2 *He remembered her in his will:* take note of, recognize; take care of, reward, tip.

Ant. 1 forget. 2 ignore, neglect, overlook.

remind *v. That story reminds me of my childhood:* bring to mind, bring back to, suggest to, awaken memories of.

remiss *adj. He was remiss in his responsibilities:* careless, negligent, lax, undutiful, unmindful, thoughtless; derelict, delinquent; neglectful, forgetful, inattentive, indifferent, uncaring, oblivious, unwatchful.

Ant. careful, dutiful, diligent; neat, meticulous.

remit *v. Please remit the balance due:* pay; make good, discharge; forward, dispatch, transmit.

Ant. withhold.

remnant *n. a remnant of an ancient civiliza-*

tion. A patchwork quilt is made of remnants: remainder, relic, leftover, vestige; piece, bit, scrap, fragment; remains, odds and ends, leavings, residue.

remorse *n. The killer felt no remorse:* regret, regretfulness, rue, ruefulness, guilt, self-reproach, self-reproof, compunction, qualm, pangs of conscience; sorrow, grief, anguish. *Ant.* satisfaction, pride.

remote *adj.* 1 *remote islands:* far, far-off, faraway, distant, far-removed, a long way off; alien, strange, foreign. 2 *a remote part of the forest:* secluded, isolated, solitary, sequestered, out-of-the-way; lonely, quiet. 3 *a remote possibility:* distant, slight, faint, slim; unlikely, doubtful, dubious, implausible. 4 *He seemed remote when we met:* standoffish, aloof, withdrawn, detached. *Ant.* 1 close, near, nearby. 4 attentive, interested, involved.

remove *v.* 1 *Remove those muddy shoes! The rioters were forcibly removed:* take off, doff; take away, dislodge, expel, oust, eject, cart off, take away. 2 *He had the wart removed:* cut away, chop off, cut off, lop off. 3 *They have removed to a warm climate:* move, transfer, transport, transplant; depart, leave, go away, quit, withdraw, retreat, retire. 4 *Bleach removes color:* wipe out, get rid of, take out, erase, extract, eliminate, delete. 5 *He was removed from office:* dismiss, discharge, unseat, oust, eject, fire. *Ant.* 1 put on, don; keep, retain, detain. 3 stay, remain.

remunerate *v. to be remunerated for extra work:* pay, recompense, compensate; satisfy, grant, award. *Ant.* charge, assess, fine.

renaissance *n. a renaissance of interest in science:* rebirth, renewal, renascence, revival, rejuvenation, resurgence, reawakening, reemergence, revitalization, regeneration, restoration, rekindling.

rend *v.* 1 *to rend a piece a cloth. The lightning rent the tree:* rip, tear, split, rupture, cleave, sunder, sever, splinter, fracture, break, crack, shatter. 2 *They rend us with their scorn:* lacerate, afflict, sear, pain, rip, cut, hurt, wound. *Ant.* 1 join, unite, join.

render *v.* 1 *The treatment rendered him healthy again:* cause to be, make, cause to become. 2 *The piano concerto was rendered flawlessly:* do, perform, play, execute, interpret. 3 *to render assistance:* give, present, tender, accord, grant; supply, dispense, dole out, allot. 4 *I was obliged to render back taxes:* pay, remit, make payment of, pay back, requite. 5 *The troops refused to render their position:* give up, yield, surrender,

cede, relinquish, hand over. 6 *The speech was rendered by an interpreter:* translate, construe, interpret. *Ant.* 3 withhold, refuse, retain.

rendezvous *n.* 1 *We have a rendezvous at noon:* agreement to meet, prearranged meeting, date, appointment, engagement; assignation, tryst, tête-à-tête. 2 *The restaurant was our rendezvous:* meeting place, gathering place, haunt, focal point.

rendition *n. a jazz rendition of* Jingle Bells: rendering, translation, interpretation, arrangement, version; reading, performance, portrayal, depiction.

renegade *n.* 1 *He was considered a renegade when he switched sides:* traitor, betrayer, turncoat; recreant, rebel, dissenter, insurgent, mutineer. —*adj.* 2 *The renegade detective became a gangster:* traitorous, mutinous, apostate, recreant, unfaithful.

renege *v. Don't renege on a promise:* break a promise, go back on one's word, back out, withdraw. *Ant.* fulfill, carry out.

renew *v.* 1 *We renewed our old friendship:* begin again, resume, take up again, reestablish, reinstate. 2 *to renew a contract:* extend, continue, prolong, sign again, maintain, retain. 3 *He tried to renew his faith:* revive, rejuvenate, regenerate, reinvigorate, revitalize. 4 *A cleaning renewed the carpet:* restore, revitalize, put back into shape. *Ant.* 1 discontinue, end. 2 discontinue, cancel, let lapse. 4 age, wear out.

renounce *v. She renounced all rights to the throne:* give up, relinquish, abdicate, give up claim to, cede, quit, forgo, eschew, waive; abandon, abnegate, put aside, dismiss; repudiate, abjure, forswear, disavow, disclaim, reject, disown. *Ant.* avow, maintain, uphold, claim; keep, retain, hold.

renovate *v. to renovate an old building:* repair, mend, fix, remake, revamp, modernize, redecorate, restore, refurbish.

renown *n. a musician of renown:* fame, acclaim, repute, reputation, popularity, prominence, note, celebrity; eminence, status, distinction. *Ant.* obscurity; disrepute, disgrace.

renowned *adj. a renowned poet:* celebrated, well-known, popular, famous, famed, notable, noteworthy, noted, prominent, outstanding, acclaimed, eminent, distinguished. *Ant.* obscure, unknown, forgotten, unpopular, undistinguished.

rent[1] *n.* 1 *Rent is due every month:* rental, payment; fee. —*v.* 2 *We rented the cabin:* let, rent out, lease; hire, charter.

rent[2] n. 1 *I tried to sew the rent in my dress:* opening, rip, tear, rift, hole, rupture, fissure, cleft, chink, breach, crack, slit; gash, gap, crevasse; split, fracture. 2 *The opposing factions caused a rent in the club's membership:* breach, break, rift, split, division, schism.

renunciation n. *his renunciation of smoking:* renouncing, rejection, repulsion, spurning, repudiation; denial, disavowal, disclaiming, eschewing, forgoing, abandonment, relinquishment, forswearing, abjuration.
Ant. acceptance, retention.

repair[1] v. 1 *These shoes have to be repaired:* fix, restore, mend, set right, make good, recondition, patch. 2 *I'd like to repair our differences:* remedy, redress, rectify, patch up, mend, amend, emend, correct. —n. 3 *the repair of a broken toy:* repairing, fixing, mending, patching, reconditioning. 4 *Her clothes were in poor repair:* condition, state, shape.
Ant. 1 break, destroy, ruin. 2 aggravate, exacerbate, worsen. 3 destruction, breaking.

repair[2] v. *The ladies repaired to the drawing room:* withdraw, retire, remove, move, betake oneself, go.

repartee n. *a humorist skilled in repartee:* witty reply, witty retort, clever rejoinder, snappy comeback, riposte; badinage, banter.

repay v. *We can never repay your kindness:* pay back, reimburse, reward, make requital, make retribution, give in exchange, return, pay in kind, reciprocate.

repeal v. 1 *Parliament repealed the law:* cancel, abrogate, abolish, annul, nullify, set aside, revoke, rescind. —n. 2 *the repeal of Prohibition:* abrogation, cancellation, abolition, annulment, nullification, voiding, revocation.
Ant. 1 confirm, reestablish; validate. 2 confirmation, reestablishment; validation.

repeat v. 1 *Please repeat the question. Repeat after me:* restate, say again, say over, reiterate; echo, imitate, mimic. 2 *She repeated what she had heard to her mother:* tell, relate, recite, retell, recount, quote, pass on. 3 *The choral society will repeat their program next week:* duplicate, redo, perform again, reproduce. —n. 4 *Today's show was a repeat of yesterday's:* repetition, reiteration, duplication, rerun.

repel v. 1 *We repelled the enemy:* push back, force back, drive back, beat back, repulse, put to flight, drive away; keep off, hold off, ward off, fend off, stave off, resist, foil, frustrate, oppose; check, keep out. 2 *The movie*

repelled me: disgust, revolt, be repugnant to, sicken, nauseate, make one's flesh crawl; offend, alienate.
Ant. 1, 2 attract, draw. 2 please, delight, captivate, entrance.

repellent adj. 1 *This fabric is water-repellent:* repelling, resisting; impermeable, proof. 2 *I find snakes repellent:* repugnant, repulsive, disgusting, nauseating, sickening, abhorrent, offensive, revolting, loathsome.

repent v. *The killer never repented:* regret, deplore, lament; feel remorse, be ashamed, be regretful, reproach oneself; be penitent, be contrite.

repentance n. *repentance for a misspent youth:* remorse, regret, grief, sorrow; self-reproach, self-condemnation, guilt, pangs of conscience; penitence, contrition.
Ant. contentment, satisfaction, gratification.

repetition n. *The play was a repetition of an old plot:* repeat, retelling, recapitulation, restatement, iteration, reiteration.

repetitious adj. *I found the speaker repetitious:* redundant, repetitive, repeated; wordy, prolix.
Ant. concise, succinct, terse.

replace v. 1 *She replaced me as director:* take the place of, fill the place of, succeed, supplant, displace, substitute for. 2 *Replace these books on the shelf:* put back, return, restore.

replenish v. *Our supplies were replenished:* refill, restock, replace, renew, restore.
Ant. empty, drain.

replete adj. *The storeroom was replete with supplies:* filled, abounding, teeming, fraught, well-stocked, loaded, crammed, jam-packed, brimming; stuffed, full.
Ant. empty, bare, barren.

replica n. *We asked the artist for a replica of the portrait:* duplicate, copy, imitation, double, facsimile, reproduction, model.

reply v. 1 *Please reply to the accusation:* answer, respond, rejoin, make rejoinder, retort, counter, react. —n. 2 *Her only reply was an angry stare:* response, answer, retort, rejoinder, reaction; acknowledgment.
Ant. 1 question, demand, ask. 2 request, question; invitation.

report n. 1 *His report of the battle was accurate:* account, description, relation, narration, story, write-up, article, news story. 2 *The messenger brought a secret report:* dispatch, message, communiqué, missive. 3 *The report that he died was false:* information, word, gossip, hearsay, rumor, talk. 4 *the report of cannons:* noise, sound, boom, discharge, detonation, bang, crack. —v.

5 *The newspaper reported the event:* announce, communicate, relate, tell, divulge, disclose, state, recount, describe. 6 *He reported the student for misconduct:* inform against, expose, tell on, complain about. 7 *to report for duty:* present oneself, appear; show up, check in.
Ant. 5 withhold, conceal.

reporter *n. a sports reporter:* journalist, newsman, newspaperman, gentleman of the press, newswoman, newspaperwoman; member of the press, correspondent; announcer, commentator, newscaster.

repose *n.* 1 *a day of repose:* rest, respite, ease, tranquillity, calm, quiet, relaxation, leisure, inactivity. *—v.* 2 *Father reposed in the hammock:* rest, lie, recline; relax, settle; situate, locate.

reprehensible *adj. a reprehensible crime:* unworthy, shameful, disgraceful; heinous, villainous, opprobrious, nefarious, foul, despicable, ignoble, base, vile, wicked, evil; unpardonable, inexcusable, unjustifiable.
Ant. admirable, laudable, commendable, praiseworthy.

represent *v.* 1 *In Morse Code, dots and dashes represent letters:* stand for, symbolize, designate, denote, be the equivalent of, express, indicate, mean, equal, serve as; typify, characterize, betoken. 2 *Her lawyer represented her at the negotiations:* act in place of, be proxy for, be an agent for, be deputy for, speak and act for. 3 *His drawing represented a Parisian café:* portray, depict, show, picture, illustrate, delineate, describe; state, present. 4 *He represented himself as a surgeon:* impersonate, appear as, appear in the guise of, enact, act the part of; pose as.

representative *n.* 1 *The lawyer acted as her representative:* agent, deputy, emissary, envoy, proxy, delegate, proctor, surrogate, spokesman. 2 *Each district sends one representative to Congress:* member of a legislature, legislator, delegate; congressman, congresswoman; assemblyman, assemblywoman. *—adj.* 3 *Is this a representative sample of your work?:* typifying, symbolic, exemplary, typical, characteristic, illustrative, descriptive. 4 *a representative form of government:* representational, republican, democratic, elected, elective; delegated, delegatory.

repress *v. to repress one's feelings:* hold back, check, control, curb, restrain, inhibit, hold in, hold back, suppress, hide, conceal, stifle, smother; pen up, bottle up; quash, quell, subdue.
Ant. let out, release, express.

reprieve *n. He won a last-minute reprieve:*

delay, postponement, remission, suspension, stay; lull, pause.

reprimand *n.* 1 *The motorist received a reprimand from the officer:* sharp reproof, reproval, rebuke, reproach, admonition, admonishment, upbraiding, scolding, remonstrance, castigation, dressing down, berating, chewing out. *—v.* 2 *The teacher reprimanded the class for being noisy:* reprove, rebuke, admonish, reproach, scold, upbraid, rail at, castigate, berate.
Ant. 1 compliment, praise, approval. 2 commend, compliment, praise.

reproach *v.* 1 *He was reproached for his rude behavior:* admonish, reprimand, rebuke, reprove; condemn, stigmatize, revile, scold, upbraid, rail at, castigate, take to task. *—n.* 2 *Her behavior was above reproach:* blame, rebuke, reproof; upbraiding, scolding, remonstrance, criticism. 3 *Bad behavior is a reproach to one's parents:* stigma, taint, blemish, stain, blot, slur; insult, shame, humiliation, embarrassment, disgrace, dishonor, discredit.
Ant. 1 praise, commend, compliment. 2 commendation, compliment, praise. 3 honor, credit.

reprobate *n. Reprobates seldom reform:* profligate, roué, rake, rakehell, voluptuary, wanton, abandoned person; rascal, scamp, rapscallion, rotter; miscreant, sinner, transgressor, evildoer, wrongdoer.
Ant. angel, paragon, saint.

reproduce *v.* 1 *The machine can reproduce a key in two minutes. The bird watcher could reproduce the call of fifty birds:* make a duplicate of, duplicate, replicate, copy; repeat, echo, mirror, reflect; imitate, counterfeit. 2 *Rabbits reproduce quickly:* produce young, produce offspring, procreate, propagate, generate, proliferate; give birth, beget, sire, bring forth, multiply, breed, spawn.

reproduction *n.* 1 *a reproduction of a Greek statue:* copy, duplicate, replica, facsimile; imitation, simulation. 2 *We studied the processes of reproduction in biology class:* generation, propagation, procreation, proliferation, progeneration, breeding.
Ant. 1 original.

reproof *n. He received a reproof for forgetting his manners:* rebuke, reproach, remonstrance, scolding, dressing-down, reprimand, admonition, censure.
Ant. commendation, praise.

reprove *v. Mother reproved her with a stern look:* reproach, rebuke, admonish, reprimand; censure, chasten, scold.
Ant. praise, compliment; encourage.

republic *n. Andorra is a small republic:* republican nation, representative government, popular government, democracy, constitutional government.

repudiate v. 1 *The government repudiated the treaty:* disavow, deny, disclaim, rescind, reverse, revoke, repeal, retract, void, nullify, annul, abrogate, cancel, abolish, dissolve. 2 *We repudiated religion and became atheists:* disown, disavow, reject, cast off, discard, abandon, desert, forsake, renounce.

repugnant adj. *What a repugnant odor!:* repellent, offensive, disgusting, nauseating, sickening, repulsive, foul, nasty, vile, obnoxious, revolting, objectionable, unacceptable, disagreeable, unpleasant; distasteful, odious, hateful, loathsome, detestable, abhorrent, abominable.

Ant. pleasant, desirable, agreeable.

repulse v. 1 *The army repulsed the attacking forces:* repel, throw back, drive back, beat back. 2 *The neighbors repulsed our offers of friendship:* reject, refuse, rebuff, spurn, shun.

Ant. 2 welcome, accept, encourage.

repulsion n. *Spiders fill me with repulsion:* revulsion, repugnance, disgust, distaste, dislike, antipathy, detestation, aversion, loathing, hatred, abhorrence.

repulsive adj. *His table manners are repulsive:* repugnant, repellent, offensive, abhorrent, disgusting, obnoxious, nauseating, nasty, vile, revolting, objectionable, disagreeable, distasteful, loathsome, hateful, detestable, abominable, odious; ugly.

Ant. attractive, agreeable, pleasant.

reputable adj. *a reputable store:* respectable, respected, creditable, trustworthy, held in good repute, esteemed, honored, reliable, of good name.

Ant. disreputable, untrustworthy, shady.

reputation n. *The scandal injured her reputation:* standing, stature, repute, name.

repute n. 1 *a judge of high repute:* respectability; standing, reputation, renown, prominence, regard, esteem. —v. 2 *He was reputed to be a heavy gambler:* consider, regard, hold, deem; believe, think, suppose, reckon, view, say.

request n. 1 *Put in a request for a transfer:* application, solicitation, petition. —v. 2 *Did you request a new desk?:* ask, ask for, apply for; solicit, petition for.

require v. 1 *What do you require to complete the job?:* need, want, lack, desire. 2 *The subpoena requires you to appear in court:* command, charge, enjoin, order, oblige, constrain, compel, direct; bid. 3 *This plan required secrecy:* necessitate, make imperative, entail.

Ant. 1 dispense with, forgo.

requirement n. 1 *Experience is a require-*

ment *for this job:* prerequisite, essential, requisite, must. 2 *The product met all requirements set by the government:* guideline, specification, standard, criterion.

requisite adj. 1 *Past experience is requisite for this job:* required, mandatory, compulsory, obligatory, prerequisite, necessary, essential, imperative, needed, indispensable. —n. 2 *Steady nerves are a requisite for this work:* prerequisite, requirement, necessity, essential, must.

Ant. 1 unnecessary, unessential.

rescind v. *The judge rescinded the lower court's decision:* revoke, reverse, repeal, invalidate, countermand, overrule, override, set aside, void, annul, abrogate, declare null and void, nullify.

Ant. uphold, support; validate.

rescue v. 1 *She rescued three people from the burning building:* save, recover, salvage, extricate, deliver. —n. 2 *The survivor credited his rescue to quick work by the patrol:* rescuing, saving, recovery, liberation, deliverance, freeing, extrication, release.

Ant. 1 abandon. 2 loss, abandonment.

research n. 1 *scholarly research:* inquiry, investigation, search, factfinding, analysis, study, examination, probe, exploration, delving. —v. 2 *to research the cause of a disease:* do research on, study, investigate, conduct an examination on, probe.

resemblance n. *There's no resemblance between the two:* likeness, similarity, affinity, similitude, analogy, correspondence, parallel, congruence.

Ant. dissimilarity, difference.

resemble v. *I resemble my mother:* bear a resemblance to, look like, favor, take after, be like, be similar to, be akin to, parallel.

resent v. *I resent that remark!:* feel anger at, be indignant at, be provoked at, be piqued at, dislike, be offended at, take exception to, take amiss, take offense at, take umbrage at, be jealous of, bear a grudge against.

Ant. like, approve; welcome.

resentment n. *Her words were full of resentment:* indignation, bad feelings, anger, ire, ill will, rancor; acrimony, bitterness, irritation, irritability; wounded pride, umbrage, hurt feelings, displeasure; animosity, animus, malice, vindictiveness, vengefulness, spite; jealousy.

reservation n. 1 *I have no reservation about hiring him:* reluctance, doubt, hesitancy, uncertainty, compunction; qualification, strings, condition, stipulation, provision, proviso. 2 *an army reservation:* reserved land, reserve; preserve, encampment, installation. 3 *We made a reservation* *for dinner:* accommodation, booking, reserved place.

reserve *v.* 1 *It's often wise to reserve judgment. Try to reserve energy:* keep, keep back, withhold, retain, hold; preserve, conserve, save, husband, lay up, store up, amass; delay, put aside, shelve, table. 2 *Call ahead to reserve a room:* set apart, prearrange, engage, book; schedule. —*n.* 3 *Keep $200 as a reserve:* emergency fund, contingency fund, reservoir, savings, nest egg; hoard, stockpile. 4 *A man of reserve shows little emotion:* reticence, aloofness, retiring disposition.

Ant. 1 squander, splurge, waste. 4 sociability, conviviality.

reserved *adj.* 1 *Is this seat reserved?:* kept in reserve, booked, taken, engaged, spoken for. 2 *The English are supposed to be reserved:* reticent, aloof, undemonstrative, restrained, formal, distant, standoffish, unsocial, unsociable, uncommunicative.

Ant. 2 demonstrative, sociable, warm, affable.

reside *v.* 1 *I reside in Salt Lake City. Jim resides at the Grand Hotel:* dwell, live, occupy, inhabit, domicile, have residence, lodge, room. 2 *Does goodness reside in all of us?:* lie, rest, exist, be present, be inherent, be intrinsic.

residence *n. His residence is in the suburbs. I dread taking up residence in a new town:* home, house, lodging, quarters, dwelling, dwelling place, habitation, domicile, abode; stay, sojourn.

resident *n. a resident of Toronto:* inhabitant, resider, dweller; citizen, denizen, local; occupant, lodger.

resign *v.* 1 *He resigned his position in the company:* give up, step down from, quit, relinquish, leave, abdicate. 2 *You must resign yourself to what has happened:* submit, reconcile.

resilient *adj. Rubber is very resilient. He's resilient to trouble:* rebounding, elastic, flexible, springy, supple, rubbery; expansive, rapidly recovering, resistant, irrepressible; hardy, tenacious, adaptable.

Ant. inflexible, stiff, rigid, tense.

resist *v.* 1 *We resisted our attackers. This material resists stains:* fight against, oppose, fight, combat, contest; withstand, hold out against, stand up to, weather, repel, stop, thwart, balk, foil, frustrate. 2 *Try to resist rich foods:* abstain from, refrain from, refuse, reject, turn down.

Ant. 1, 2 give in to, surrender to, submit to. 1 yield, succumb to, capitulate. 2 indulge in.

resistance *n. The proposal met with resist-*

ance: opposition, contention, noncompliance, defiance, rejection, rebuff, refusal, obstruction; insurgency, insurrection.

resolute *adj. a resolute student. a resolute leader:* determined, purposive, steadfast, tenacious, pertinacious, earnest, industrious, assiduous, diligent, persevering, persistent, dogged, untiring, unflagging, indefatigable; unyielding, unwavering, unfaltering, unflinching; inflexible, uncompromising, unswerving, decisive, obstinate, intrepid.

Ant. irresolute, undecided, vacillating, weak.

resolution *n.* 1 *The resolution passed by two votes:* motion, proposition, proposal. 2 *Have you made a New Year's resolution?:* resolve, promise, intent, intention, purpose, design, objective, object, aim, goal. 3 *He lacked the resolution to finish school:* firmness of purpose, persistence, determination, tenacity, resolve, perseverance, earnestness, indefatigability. 4 *I was faced with the resolution of a difficult matter:* solution, resolving, working-out.

resolve *v.* 1 *We resolved to visit Europe:* make up one's mind, determine, decide, intend, set out. 2 *We can resolve the matter to your satisfaction:* settle, solve; explain; determine, settle, decide. —*n.* 3 *It is our resolve never to surrender:* determination, resolution, fixed intention, commitment.

resonant *adj. a resonant voice:* rich, vibrant, sonorous, ringing; stentorian, resounding, reverberant, booming, thunderous.

resort *v.* 1 *Don't resort to violence:* have recourse to, avail oneself of, apply, take up, exercise, make use of, employ, use, utilize. —*n.* 2 *a seaside resort:* holiday retreat, vacation place, tourist spot. 3 *Suicide was the samurai's last resort:* recourse, expedient; avail, hope, chance.

resound *v. Church bells resounded throughout the valley:* peal, ring, sound, reverberate, resonate, tintinnabulate, clang, fill the air, echo.

resource *n.* 1 *The library is a valuable resource to students:* source, recourse, expedient, means of supply. 2 Usually **resources** *We pooled our resources and bought a boat:* wealth, capital, funds, assets, money; revenue, income, collateral.

resourceful *adj. a resourceful teacher:* inventive, creative, imaginative, innovative, original, ingenious; smart, sharp, shrewd, artful; adroit, skillful, able, competent, capable, proficient, enterprising.

Ant. unresourceful, uninventive, uncreative; unskillful, incompetent.

respect *n.* 1 *In that respect, you're perfectly right:* detail, point, particular, matter, circumstance, feature, aspect, regard, sense. **2** *In respect to your request, five dollars is being credited to your account:* relation, regard, reference, connection, bearing. **3** *He had respect for his stepfather:* regard, deference, reverence, esteem, appreciation, admiration; recognition; consideration. **4 respects** *to pay one's respects:* expressions of friendship or esteem, compliments, regards, greetings, remembrances. —*v.* **5** *Respect your elders!:* honor, esteem, revere, venerate, pay deference to; be appreciative of, value, cherish, prize. **6** *They respected the artist's last wishes and burned her letters:* refrain from interfering with, show consideration for, appreciate, honor, comply with, obey, heed, follow, abide by, observe, adhere to, be faithful to.

Ant. **2, 3, 5** disrespect, disregard. **3** contempt, scorn, disdain. **5** scorn, disdain. **6** ignore, disregard, disdain.

respectable *adj.* **1** *My parents are respectable people:* worthy of respect, admirable, worthy, praiseworthy, reputable, honorable, dignified, upright, honest; proper, decent, decorous, correct. **2** *I earn a respectable salary:* ample, sufficient, fairly good, fairly large, considerable, fair, satisfactory, decent, worthy.

Ant. **1** disreputable, dishonorable, ignoble. **2** small, poor, paltry, inadequate.

respectful *adj. Be more respectful!:* deferential, polite, courteous, civil, mannerly, decorous; reverent, reverential; obliging, accommodating.

Ant. disrespectful, impolite, discourteous, rude, uncivil, unmannerly.

respite *n. The workers got a short respite:* rest period, recess, break, breathing spell, pause; lull, letup; reprieve, delay, extension.

respond *v.* **1** *Please respond to the question:* reply, answer, speak up. **2** *to respond to a call for help:* react, reply; recognize, acknowledge.

response *n.* **1** *What's your response to the charges?:* answer, reply; rebuttal; retort, rejoinder, riposte, comeback. **2** *The response to our plan was encouraging:* reaction, impression, acknowledgment, feedback.

Ant. **1** query, question. **2** proposal, proposition.

responsibility *n.* **1** *We accepted responsibility for the mistake:* liability; accountability, answerability, blame, culpability. **2** *Taking care of a family is a big responsibility:* charge, trust, function, task, burden, obligation, duty, order. **3** *I question her responsibility:* dependability, reliability, trustworthiness.

Ant. **3** unreliability, undependability.

responsible *adj.* **1** *Parents are responsible for the welfare of their children:* accountable, liable, answerable, under obligation. **2** *Who's responsible for this mess?:* liable to be called to account, culpable, guilty, at fault. **3** *Betty's a responsible worker:* conscientious, reliable, dependable, trustworthy.

Ant. **1** unaccountable. **3** irresponsible, unreliable, undependable, untrustworthy.

responsive *adj. We should be responsive to others:* alive, susceptible, impressionable, sensitive, sympathetic, compassionate, understanding, receptive, aware of.

Ant. unresponsive, apathetic, insensitive, unsympathetic.

rest¹ *n.* **1** *We took a short rest before dinner:* respite, break, recess, pause, lull, intermission, quiet spell, breathing spell, breather; leisure; sleep, slumber, nap, siesta. **2** *He went to his final rest:* death, the grave, demise, end. **3** *The ball came to a rest:* state of motionlessness, standstill, halt, stop. **4** *The judge put the gavel on a wooden rest:* supporting device, holder, support, prop, base, stand. —*v.* **5** *The hikers rested awhile:* relax, take one's ease, be at ease, take time out, take a breather, pause, let up; loll, repose; sleep, laze, lounge, loaf. **6** *Let the matter rest:* stand, lie, be, remain. **7** *He rested the box on the chair:* set down, deposit, set, place, lay; lean, prop. **8** *Success rests on your cooperation:* be based, depend, rely, hang, hinge; be found, reside, be, exist, lie.

Ant. **1** work, activity, bustle.

rest² *n.* **1** *You may have the rest of the pie:* remains, remainder, remaining part, balance, remnant, residue. —*v.* **2** *Rest easy:* remain, continue to be, keep, stay.

restful *adj.* **1** *a restful vacation:* relaxed, soothing, unagitated, peaceful, tranquil, calm, placid, quiet.

Ant. agitated, disturbing, busy.

restitution *n. Restitution must be made to the victims:* redress, amends, reparation, compensation, recompense, reimbursement, repayment, restoration.

restless *adj.* **1** *I had a restless night. Jimmy's a restless child:* restive, wakeful, sleepless, insomniac, fitful; nervous, jittery, jumpy, fidgety, fretful, highstrung, hyperactive, impatient. **2** *a restless wanderer:* always in motion, never at rest, on the go, on the move.

Ant. **1** restful, quiet, undisturbed.

restore *v.* **1** *to restore order:* bring back, get back, recoup, recover; reinstate, reestablish, reinstall; recreate. **2** *We restored the antique desk:* recondition, rehabilitate, refurbish, renew, renovate. **3** *The medication re-*

stored her: bring back to health, bring round, make well, strengthen; energize, reinvigorate, revitalize, revive, resuscitate, refresh. 4 *I was restored to my former rank:* put back, reinstate, reinstitute, reestablish, reinstall; return.

restrain *v. Restrain your laughter:* keep under control, suppress, contain, withhold, hold back, inhibit, restrict, limit, check, curb, bridle, constrain, hold, prevent, curtail; bind, shackle, fetter, pinion.

restrict *v. Bad weather restricted our activities:* confine, constrain, restrain, suppress, hold back, check, curb, impede, crimp, hamper, obstruct, inhibit, prevent; limit, circumscribe, narrow, constrict.

restriction *n.* 1 *Restriction of the king's powers was necessary:* curbing, limitation, control, restraint, regulation. 2 *It is a club with rigid restrictions on its membership:* rule, regulation, provision, proviso, condition, stipulation, qualification, reservation, requirement.

result *v.* 1 *His lameness resulted from an accident:* arise, ensue, stem, derive, issue, spring. 2 *Her singing lessons resulted in her getting a part in a musical:* culminate, wind up, end up, pan out. —*n.* 3 *What was the result of the medical tests? The fire was the result of carelessness:* finding, decision, verdict, judgment, determination, resolution, solution; consequence, outcome, eventuality, product, outgrowth, fruit.
Ant. 3 cause, antecedent, origin, source, root.

resume *v. Please resume work:* take up again, go on, go on with, proceed, continue, recommence.

résumé *n.* 1 *I wrote a résumé of the first three chapters:* summary, summation, synopsis, digest, précis. 2 *Take a copy of your résumé to the job interview:* work history, curriculum vitae, CV.

resurgence *n. There's been a resurgence of the flu:* revival, appearing again, rising again, rebirth, renewal, rejuvenation, return, reemergence.
Ant. passing away, decline, fading.

retain *v. to retain knowledge:* keep, maintain, keep possession of, possess, absorb, hold; keep in mind, remember.

retaliate *v. He hit me, then I retaliated:* counter, take retribution, return like for like, repay in the same coin, give measure for measure; return, repay, pay back, avenge.

retard *v. Lack of sunlight retards growth:* slow, impede, detain, check; block, obstruct, clog, hamper, hinder, inhibit, arrest; delay.
Ant. speed up, accelerate, expediate, quicken, hasten; advance, further.

reticent *adj. a reticent speaker:* taciturn, quiet, uncommunicative, sparing of words, close-mouthed; restrained, subdued, closed.
Ant. voluble, talkative, expansive.

retinue *n. The queen traveled with a large retinue:* entourage, train, following, attendants, retainers, followers, associates, courtiers.

retire *v.* 1 *For relaxation I retire to an island hideaway:* go away, depart, retreat, withdraw, remove. 2 *I'm tired, so I'll retire now:* go to bed, turn in, go to sleep, lie down to rest, call it a day; *Informal* hit the sack, hit the hay. 3 *He retired from the army:* withdraw, resign, remove from active service.
Ant. 2 get up, arise; wake up, awaken.

retiring *adj. the sister with the retiring manner:* withdrawn, unsocial, quiet; shy, modest, demure, shrinking, meek, sheepish, timid, timorous; unassuming, inconspicuous, unassertive, humble; reserved, self-contained.
Ant. outgoing, gregarious, sociable; bold, brazen, brassy, forward.

retort *v.* 1 *"Same to you!" he retorted:* reply, counter, return, rejoin, rebut; respond, answer, come back with, fire back. —*n.* 2 *Her retort left me with nothing more to say:* sharp reply, pointed answer, rebuttal; quip, rejoinder, witty reply, riposte.

retract *v.* 1 *You should retract that statement:* withdraw, take back, recant, rescind; revoke, repeal, repudiate, disavow, disown, disclaim, abjure, renounce. 2 *The point of this ballpoint pen retracts:* draw back, pull back, peel back, draw in, recede, withdraw, recoil.

retreat *n.* 1 *The general ordered a retreat:* withdrawal, falling back, pulling back, backing out; flight, departure, getaway, escape. 2 *Our retreat from social life was absolute:* withdrawal, retirement, seclusion, solitude, isolation, reclusion. 3 *They spent their honeymoon in a mountain retreat:* place of seclusion, privacy, or refuge; resort, refuge, hideaway, asylum, sanctuary, haven. —*v.* 4 *He retreated from reality:* withdraw, retire, fall back, move back, draw back, back away, recoil, shy away, shrink; depart, go, leave, escape, flee.
Ant. 1 advance, charge. 2 participation. 4 advance, move forward.

retribution *n. There must be retribution for this crime:* retaliation, justice, satisfaction, redress, amends, restitution, reparation, reprisal, penalty, punishment, recompense, vengeance, revenge, just deserts.

retrieve *v. The police retrieved the stolen painting:* recover, regain, get back; fetch, go and get.

retrospect *n. Youth is more enjoyable in retrospect than when one is going through it:* review, retrospection, remembrance, reminiscence, looking backward; reconsideration, hindsight.

return *v.* 1 *When will you return?:* come back, go back; reappear, recur. 2 *The electorate will return their favorite candidate to office:* send back, bring back, put back, restore, reinstate. 3 *Permit me to return the compliment:* repay, give in turn, reciprocate. 4 *The investment returned ten percent a year:* repay, yield, provide, earn, produce, render. —*n.* 5 *We eagerly await your return. Police announced the return of the stolen goods:* returning, coming back, arrival; reinstatement, restoral, recovery, retrieval. 6 *We're headed for the return of rationing:* returning, recurrence, reappearance. 7 *The bonds paid a handsome return:* profit, income, revenue, earnings, proceeds, yield, interest, gain; benefit, compensation, gross, net.

Ant. 1 depart, leave, go away. 4 lose. 5 departure, leaving.

reveal *v. to reveal the facts:* make known, divulge, disclose, impart; unearth, bare, lay bare, bring to light, unmask, expose, uncover, make public; display, show, exhibit. *Ant.* conceal, hide, mask, cover.

revel *v.* 1 *She reveled in her success:* take great pleasure, rejoice, delight, relish; wallow in, bask in. 2 *The villagers reveled far into the night:* make merry, celebrate, carouse, go on a spree; frolic, romp, caper, skylark.

revelation *n.* 1 *He made a startling revelation:* disclosure, divulgence, confession, admission; eyeopener, exposure, exposé; discovery. 2 *revelations of an early Christian mystic:* vision, apocalypse, prophecy, revelatory writing.

Ant. 1 coverup, concealment.

revelry *n. The streets were filled with revelry after the victory:* boisterous festivity, reveling, merrymaking, merriment, celebrating, rejoicing, celebration, celebrating; roistering, spree.

revenge *v.* 1 *I shall revenge this abomination!:* take vengeance for, avenge; wreak vengeance, make reprisal for, retaliate, repay, pay back. —*n.* 2 *We sought revenge for the harm they had done:* vengeance, retaliation, reprisal, retribution.

revenue *n. The harvest produced a sizable revenue:* income, salary, earnings, pay, wages, compensation, profit, return, gains, yield.

reverberate *v. Our voices reverberated in the cave:* carry, echo, resound, ring, vibrate, be reflected, boom, rumble, thunder.

revere *v. We should revere our parents:* honor, venerate, esteem, defer to, look up to, cherish, respect.

Ant. dishonor; despise, scorn, disparage.

reverence *n. We should nurture reverence for learning:* respect, esteem, regard, honor, homage, deference, veneration, admiration, adoration, devotion; devoutness, piety, religiosity.

Ant. irreverence, disrespect, scorn, contempt, dishonor.

reverie *n.* 1 *She sat at the window, deep in reverie:* daydream, dreamy spell, brown study; fantasy, flight of fancy; meditation, woolgathering, musing. 2 *The plan is pure reverie:* fantasy, fancy, castles in the air, wishful thinking.

reverse *adj.* 1 *the reverse side of the page:* reversed, opposite, backward, converse, inverse, inverted, turned over. —*n.* 2 *The answer was the reverse of what we expected:* contrary, opposite, antithesis, counterpart, converse. 3 *On the reverse are lines for your comments:* back, other side. 4 *to suffer a business reverse:* reversal, change for the worse, adversity, setback, disappointment, misfortune, trouble, hard times; frustration, failure, defeat. —*v.* 5 *If you'll reverse the placard you'll see what I mean:* turn over, turn upside down, upend, upturn, turn inside out, invert, transpose. 6 *The umpire never reversed a decision:* change, undo, revoke, rescind, repeal, retract, recant, overrule, override, set aside, countermand, invalidate, nullify, annul, negate.

Ant. 3 obverse, front. 4 advance, success. 6 uphold, stick to.

revert *v. He reverted to his old habits:* go back, return, reverse, turn back, regress, recidivate, retrogress, backslide, lapse, relapse.

review *n.* 1 *The review panned the movie:* critique, criticism, critical piece, evaluation; magazine, journal. 2 *a review of the facts:* examination, reevaluation, reassessment, reconsideration, recapitulation, study, scrutiny, survey. 3 *a military review:* inspection, presentation, display; parade, procession; show, exhibition, exposition, demonstration. —*v.* 5 *Let's review the situation:* look at again, go over again, reevaluate, reexamine, reassess, reconsider, retrace, study; reiterate, recapitulate, summarize, sum up. 6 *The local paper will review the new movie:* critique, criticize, evaluate, report on, comment upon, analyze.

revile *v. She reviled the lazy employee:* scold,

berate, upbraid, bawl out, castigate, vilify, denounce, reproach, rebuke.

Ant. praise, laud, commend.

revise *v. to revise a manuscript:* correct, change, alter, modify, edit, rewrite, amend, blue-pencil, emend, recast, revamp; update.

revive *v.* 1 *The smelling salts revived me:* restore to consciousness; bring back to life, resuscitate. 2 *The lecture revived my interest in volcanology:* bring back to life, rouse again, reawaken, give new life to, refresh, freshen, renew. 3 *The repertory company revived plays from 30 years ago:* bring back into use, produce again, bring back into notice, resurrect.

revoke *v. They revoked my driver's license:* withdraw, take back; negate, annul, nullify, invalidate, void, declare null and void, cancel; repeal, rescind, reverse, retract; overrule, countermand, disallow.

Ant. restore; give, grant, authorize, validate.

revolt *v.* 1 *The army revolted against the government:* rise, rebel, rise up, mutiny. 2 *The movie revolted me:* disgust, repel, repulse, offend, sicken, nauseate, appall, shock. *—n.* 3 *The revolt was put down by the dictator:* rebellion, insurrection, insurgency, uprising, revolution, mutiny.

Ant. 1 support, obey, submit to. 2 attract, delight, please.

revolting *adj. The contest was a revolting spectacle:* disgusting, repulsive, repellent, repugnant, disagreeable, offensive, objectionable, distasteful, obnoxious, nasty, vile, foul, odious, horrid, shocking, appalling, horrible, frightful, dreadful, sickening, nauseating, abhorrent, abominable, loathsome.

Ant. pleasant, agreeable, attractive, delightful, charming.

revolution *n.* 1 *Wagner brought about a revolution in music:* complete change, radical departure, basic reformation, major shift. 2 *the American Revolution: (variously)* revolutionary war, armed struggle, war of national liberation, insurrection, uprising, rising, rebellion, revolt, mutiny, overthrow of an established regime; coup d'état, coup, putsch. 3 *The earth makes one revolution around the sun each year:* revolving, circling, circumvolution, circumrotation; single turn, rotation, gyration.

Ant. 2 counterrevolution, restoration.

revolutionary *adj.* 1 *Revolutionary factions overturned the government:* opposed to the established order, revolutionist, radical, insurgent, rebellious, mutinous; subversive, seditious, dissenting. 2 *a revolutionary idea:* radically innovative, fundamentally different, unprecedented.

Ant. 1 reactionary, counterrevolutionary; loyalist, conservative. 2 old, usual.

revolve *v. The moon revolves around the earth:* go around, circle, rotate, circumrotate, turn, gyrate, wheel, twist, spin.

revulsion *n. a strong feeling of revulsion:* disgust, loathing, repugnance, aversion, distaste, abhorrence, detestation.

Ant. attraction, fascination.

reward *n.* 1 *A large reward is offered for the return of the ring. Eventually evildoers get their just reward:* prize, compensation, recompense, bounty, consideration, premium, bonus; deserts, due, reckoning. *—v.* 2 *I was rewarded with a trip to Spain:* repay, recompense, compensate.

Ant. 1 penalty, fine. 2 punish, penalize.

rhetoric *n.* 1 *Winston Churchill was a master of rhetoric:* art of speaking or writing, rules of composition, verbal communication; elocution, oratory, eloquence, 2 *The speaker used a lot of rhetoric but said nothing of importance:* magniloquence, grandiloquence, figures of speech, hyperbole, empty phrases.

rhythm *n. the rhythm of the music. the rhythm of the seasons:* fluctuation, recurrence, flow, alternation, pattern, meter, measure, accent, beat, pulse, stress, cadence, rhythmic pattern, swing.

ribald *adj. ribald humor:* bawdy, risqué, vulgar, off-color, indecent, earthy, lascivious, licentious, libidinous, racy, wanton, suggestive.

rich *adj.* 1 *I'm not rich but I'm comfortable:* well-to-do, wealthy, affluent, flush, moneyed, prosperous, well-heeled. 2 *rich silks from the Orient:* valuable, precious, opulent, luxurious, sumptuous, splendid, lavish, expensive, fine. 3 *a rich dessert:* heavy, filling, full-bodied; sweet. 4 *The carpets were rich red. His voice was a rich baritone:* intense, lush, deep, vivid; resonant, deep-toned, sonorous, mellow, mellifluous. 5 *rich farmland:* productive, fruitful, fertile, fecund; luxuriant, lush; abundant, abounding.

Ant. 1, 5 poor. 1 impoverished, destitute, penniless, indigent, poverty-stricken. 2 worthless, inexpensive, cheap. 4 weak; high-pitched, tinny. 5 scarce, scanty, meager; unproductive, unfertile, unfruitful, barren.

rickety *adj. a rickety table:* tumbledown, shaky, unsteady, wobbly, tottering, flimsy, broken-down, deteriorated, dilapidated, decrepit; feeble, frail, fragile, wasted.

Ant. sturdy, solid, sound.

rid *v. I want to rid this city of corruption!:* free, purge, clear, eliminate, remove, unburden. *Ant.* burden, encumber.

riddle *n. the riddle of the Sphinx:* mystery, enigma, secret; puzzle, poser, conundrum, puzzler, brain twister, brainteaser.

ride *v.* 1 *to ride a horse:* manage, control, handle. 2 *The bicycle rode roughly on the bumpy road. We rode a motorcycle to the station:* move, move along, travel, progress, journey; transport, drive, carry, support; move along, be supported, be carried.

rider *n. A rider was attached to the will:* additional clause, addition, codicil, supplement, appendage, addendum, attachment.

ridge *n.* 1 *The house is just over that ridge:* hill, rise, crest, hillock, mound, knoll, bank, bluff, promontory. 2 *The potato chips have ridges:* rib, ripple, crinkle, crimp, wrinkle, corrugation, welt, wale.

ridicule *n.* 1 *I was the subject of ridicule:* mockery, sneering, derision, derogation, disparagement, aspersion, scorn, sarcasm, taunt, jeer, gibe, snicker, ribbing, teasing, caricature, burlesque, travesty, lampoonery. —*v.* 2 *His classmates ridiculed him:* make fun of, make sport of, poke fun at, mock, laugh at, sneer at, scoff at, belittle, deride, disparage, taunt, jeer, twit, razz, josh, guy, rib, tease, make sport of, caricature, burlesque, lampoon, parody.

Ant. 1, 2 praise, honor; respect. 1 homage, veneration, deference.

ridiculous *adj. That's the most ridiculous thing I've ever heard!:* absurd, ludicrous, preposterous, asinine, nonsensical, foolish, silly, idiotic, irrational, unreasonable, senseless, outlandish; laughable, comical, funny, droll, amusing; farcical, crazy.

rife *adj.* 1 *The marsh is rife with mosquitos:* teeming, swarming, thick, populous, crowded, packed. 2 *Poverty is rife on the island:* prevalent, general, prevailing, predominant; extensive, universal, widespread, common.

riffraff *n. We refused entry to the riffraff:* mob, herd, masses, rabble, rank and file, the great unwashed.

Ant. gentry, upper crust, high muck-a-mucks.

rifle *v. The burglar rifled the safe:* search and rob, rob, plunder, pillage, ransack, burglarize, loot.

rift *n.* 1 *The blast created a rift in the rock face:* cleft, split, crack, fissure, fracture, break; chink, breach, rent, cut, slit, aperture, gash, rupture; chasm, crevice, gap, fault, crevasse. 2 *There should be no rift between good friends:* division, breach, rupture,

break, breakup; disagreement, quarrel, falling out.

right *adj.* 1 *right behavior:* good, proper, decent, virtuous, fitting, seemly, moral, upright, honest, aboveboard, ethical, honorable, correct. 2 *That's not the right way to do it. the right answer:* valid, allowable, admissible, satisfactory; correct, accurate, free from error; exact, precise, true, factual. 3 *He's not in his right mind:* rational, normal, regular, sane, sound, reasonable. 4 *the right time to act:* most appropriate, suitable, seemly, fitting, proper, desirable, favorable, preferable, opportune, advantageous, ideal. 5 *Who is the right heir?:* actual, genuine, real, authentic; rightful, lawful, legal, legitimate, valid. —*n.* 6 *The prince has the right to the throne. You have the right to remain silent:* just claim, legal title, legal claim, moral claim, justification, due, birthright, inheritance; privilege, prerogative, liberty, power, license, freedom, permission, sanction; authority, legal power, authorization, jurisdiction. 7 *to know right from wrong:* good, virtue, goodness, righteousness, good behavior, good actions, morality, morals; integrity, honor, uprightness, propriety. 8 Often **rights** *He owns the mineral rights to the land:* ownership, deed, proprietorship, warrant, interest. —*adv.* 9 *She went right to the heart of the matter:* directly, promptly, straight, straightaway. 10 *These shoes don't fit right:* correctly, appropriately, suitably, properly, accurately, perfectly; exactly, precisely, just. 11 *Everything came out right in the end:* well, favorably, satisfactorily, O.K. 12 *I'll be right there:* immediately, at once, directly, presently, in a moment. —*v.* 13 *A crane was used to right the statue:* set upright, stand up. 14 *to right injustices:* correct, put right, remedy, redress, make up for, make restitution for.

Ant. 1, 2, 4, 5, 7, 10, 11 wrong. 1 bad, sinful, improper, indecent, immoral; dishonest, unethical, dishonorable; unjust, unfair. 2 incorrect, inaccurate, mistaken, invalid, erroneous, fallacious, false, untruthful. 3 irrational, insane. 4 inappropriate, unsuitable, undesirable, unfavorable, disadvantageous. 5 false, fake, phony, counterfeit, fraudulent; unlawful, illegal, illegitimate. 7 evil, sinfulness, corruption, transgression, iniquity, immorality, impropriety. 9 indirectly, circuitously. 10 incorrectly, improperly; imperfectly. 11 badly, unfavorably, poorly.

righteous *adj. a righteous citizen:* moral, honorable, ethical, honest, upright, just, fair, equitable, good; godly, pious, devout,

God-fearing, religious, reverent; virtuous, incorrupt.

Ant. immoral, bad, evil, wicked, sinful, villainous, dishonest, corrupt, unscrupulous, unprincipled, unjust, unfair; ungodly, irreligious.

rightful *adj. the rightful heir to the throne:* having a right, having a just claim, deserving, right, true, proper, correct, legitimate, legal, lawful, sanctioned, authorized, valid, prescribed, deserved, appropriate, fitting.

Ant. unrightful, improper, illegitimate, illegal, usurping.

rigid *adj.* 1 *Rubber bands are not rigid. Don't be so rigid—relax:* stiff, unyielding, inflexible, unpliant, unbending, inelastic, fixed, set, firm, tense. 2 *a rigid disciplinarian:* strict, stringent, stern, severe, harsh, rigorous, exacting; unrelenting, obdurate, uncompromising, inflexible, unbending, unyielding, firm.

Ant. 1, 2 flexible, yielding. 1 pliant, supple, bending, elastic, plastic. 2 lenient, soft, indulgent.

rigorous *adj.* 1 *rigorous exercise:* demanding, challenging, trying, stern, austere, harsh, exacting, tough, severe, strict, stringent. 2 *rigorous scholarship:* exact, accurate, correct, precise, scrupulous, meticulous.

rile *v. Her haughtiness riled us:* irritate, pique, vex, annoy, irk, provoke, gall, chafe, miff, nettle, aggravate, bother, roil, peeve.

Ant. soothe, calm, pacify, placate.

rim *n. The wheel had an iron rim. the canyon's rim:* edge, outer edge, border, margin, side; brim, verge, brink, lip.

Ant. core, center, hub.

ring¹ *n.* 1 *The dancers formed a ring around the maypole:* circle, perimeter, circumference, loop, circuit, hoop. 2 *The police rounded up a ring of thieves:* gang, band, party, syndicate, combine, league. —*v.* 3 *The lawn was ringed with flowers:* surround, encircle, encompass; enclose, seal off.

ring² *v.* 1 *The bells rang:* sound, resound, reverberate, fill the air, tintinnabulate, chime, peal, clang, knell, toll, jingle, jangle, tinkle; strike. 2 *to ring in the New Year. to ring for service:* announce, make known, broadcast, proclaim, herald; call, signal, buzz. 3 *The arcade rang with gunfire:* reverberate, resound, ring, echo. —*n.* 4 *The ring of bells filled the air:* ringing sound, reverberation, tintinnabulation, chime, peal, clang, ringing, striking, toll, knell, tinkle. 5 *His story had a suspicious ring to it:* quality, sound, tone, aura.

rip *v.* 1 *She ripped the drawing in half:* tear,

rend, rive, cleave. 2 *His shirt ripped at the seam:* tear open, split, burst. —*n.* 3 *Sew that rip in your shirt:* tear, rent, split, cut, slash, rift, slit, gap.

ripe *adj.* 1 *Are the tomatoes ripe?:* fully developed, mature, maturated. 2 *The time is ripe:* come, due; timely; ideal, perfect; prepared, fit, primed, ready.

Ant. 1 unready, immature, green. 2 untimely, unready.

rise *v.* 1 *He rose from the chair. I rise at dawn:* get up, stand, arise; get out of bed. 2 *The people rose against tyranny:* arise, rebel, revolt, mutiny; take up arms, defy; meet, face. 3 *Heat rises. The mountains rise to 2000 feet:* go up, move upward, ascend, climb; mount; soar, tower; extend upward, slope upward. 4 *The temperature kept rising:* increase, become greater, surge, swell, burgeon, become louder. 5 *She quickly rose to a position of importance:* climb, go up, succeed, prosper, thrive, flourish. 6 *Our hopes rose:* soar, surge, grow, improve, lift. —*n.* 7 *Your rise in the company was meteoric:* rising, advance; progress, advancement, headway; growth, climb. 8 *a rise in costs:* increase, upswing; addition, gain, enlargement, expansion, extension.

Ant. 1, 3–7 fall. 1 sit, sit down; lie down, retire. 3–6 sink, descend, drop, plunge. 4 decrease, decline, lessen. 8 decrease, drop, decline, downturn.

risk *n.* 1 *Buying land you've never seen is a risk:* hazard, peril, danger, jeopardy; chance, venture, speculation, gamble, uncertainty. —*v.* 2 *It's senseless to risk other people's lives:* endanger, jeopardize, put in jeopardy, imperil, put in peril. 3 *It's foolish to risk money on a throw of the dice:* take the chance of, run the chance of; venture, hazard, speculate, dare.

risky *adj. Stunt driving is a risky occupation:* hazardous, perilous, dangerous, unsafe, precarious; insecure, venturesome, uncertain, ticklish, chancy.

Ant. safe, sure, secure, certain.

risqué *adj. The risqué story made us blush:* offcolor, improper, ribald, bawdy, indecorous, indecent; indelicate, racy, spicy, suggestive, daring, salacious, vulgar, dirty, smutty.

rite *n. marriage rites. initiation rites:* formal act or procedure, formality, ceremony, ceremonial, liturgy, ritual, service, observance.

ritzy *adj. a ritzy hotel:* chic, elegant, stylish, luxurious, sumptuous; *Slang* classy, swank, high-class, posh, snazzy, spiffy.

Ant. Slang crummy, dumpy, tatty.

rival *n.* 1 *The boxers were rivals in the ring:* competitor, contestant, disputant, con-

road

tender, opponent, adversary, foe, enemy.
—*adj.* 2 *The rival companies tried to outsell
one another:* contending, competing, adversary, opposing. —*v.* 3 *No one can rival her
skill:* equal, match, touch, approach; surpass, outdo.

Ant. 1 ally, friend; associate. 2 allied, noncompeting.

road *n. Drive down this road:* thoroughfare,
boulevard, avenue, street, roadway, parkway, expressway, highway, turnpike, freeway, throughway, byway; trail, lane, path,
way.

roam *v. Troubadors roamed medieval
Europe:* travel, ramble, rove, range, meander, stray, wander, stroll, tramp.

roar *v.* 1 *The lions roared. The crowd roared:*
howl, bellow, bay, growl, cry; thunder,
shout, scream, bawl, yell, clamor. 2 *We
roared at the joke:* laugh loudly, guffaw;
howl. —*n.* 3 *the roar of a wild animal. the
roar of the crowd:* cry, howl, bellow, bay,
growl, grunt, snort; yell, outcry, bawl,
shout, shriek, scream, clamor, boom, uproar, thunder, racket, blare, din, noise.

rob *v. to rob a bank:* hold up, stick up;
(loosely) steal from, burgle, burglarize, ransack, pilfer, loot; swindle, cheat, bilk, fleece,
embezzle.

robber *n. The robber stole three watches:*
thief, bandit, crook; *(variously)* burglar,
stickup man, second-story man, yegg,
embezzler, con man, swindler.

robe *n. Robes are standard apparel in the
Middle East:* gown; *(loosely)* dress, garment, vestment, habit; *(variously)* dressing
gown, bathrobe, housecoat, negligee, lounging robe.

robust *adj. a robust athlete:* hardy, strong,
powerful, mighty, potent; healthy, sound,
hearty, able-bodied; rugged, sturdy, athletic; virile, muscular, brawny, husky,
strapping; vigorous, lusty.

Ant. weak, infirm, sickly, frail, feeble, delicate, fragile, puny.

rock¹ *v.* 1 *The boat rocked on the rough seas:*
sway; toss, roll, pitch, wobble, totter, bob,
quake, shake, undulate, oscillate. 2 *The explosion rocked the valley. The scandal rocked
the community:* shake, jar; upset, stun.
—*n.* 3 *The rock of the cradle quieted the
baby:* rocking, undulation, sway; wobbling,
tottering, shaking.

rock² *n. There are dangerous rocks in the
road:* stone, boulder; *(variously)* crag, cliff,
reef.

rod *n.* 1 *He waved the rod over the hat and a
rabbit appeared:* stick, staff, *(variously)*
wand, baton, scepter, mace; stanchion,
stake, pale. 2 *Spare the rod and spoil the*

child: stick, cudgel; *(variously)* switch,
birch, cane, lash, whip, scourge.

rogue *n. That rogue would sell his own
mother!:* dishonest person, deceiver, fraud,
mountebank, rascal, scoundrel, scamp, rapscallion, good-for-nothing, wretch, knave,
blackguard, villain, bounder, evildoer, miscreant, reprobate, scalawag, scamp.

role *n.* 1 *What role did the actress play?:* character, part, characterization, portrayal, representation, persona, personification; pose,
posture, guise. 2 *In his role as bailiff, he
requested those in the courtroom to rise:*
capacity, function, chore, task, assignment;
job, work.

roll *v.* 1 *Roll the ball to me. Roll over, Fido!:*
turn over and over, turn; revolve, rotate,
gyrate; spin, go round, whirl; wheel, swing,
turn. 2 *The car rolled to a stop. The tide
rolled in:* wheel, coast; flow, swell, billow,
surge. 3 *Roll the yarn before you start knitting:* wind, curl, coil, loop, twist, twirl, furl,
entwine. 4 *The ship rolled on the rough
seas:* rock, undulate, toss, tumble, lurch,
pitch, reel, sway. —*n.* 5 *the roll of the dice.
You'll get used to the roll of the sea:* rolling,
turning, tumble, toss, throw; rocking, tumbling, tossing, undulation. 6 *Archaeologists
found papyrus rolls in the ancient ruins:*
scroll, tube, cylinder, spool, reel. 7 *The
teacher read the roll:* list, inventory, roster,
muster, schedule. 8 *a roll of thunder:* rumble, rumbling, boom, thunder, drumming,
drumbeat, reverberation.

rollicking *adj. We had a rollicking time:* joyous, merry, lighthearted, gleeful, mirthful,
rip-roaring, jolly, jovial, frolicsome, frolicking, playful, romping, gamboling.

Ant. sad, sorrowful, distressing, depressing, mirthless; somber, gloomy.

romance *n.* 1 *She liked to read romances:*
love story; novel, fiction, melodrama.
2 *the romance of Romeo and Juliet:* love
affair, affair of the heart, affair, amour.
4 *the romance of faraway places:* romantic
quality, exoticism, appeal, allure, fascination.

romantic *adj.* 1 *romantic movies:* concerning romance, conducive to romance; idyllic,
sentimental, melodramatic. 2 *They're such
a romantic couple!:* loving, amorous, enamored, fond, devoted. 3 *Don't get carried
away with romantic notions:* high-flown,
idealized, impractical, improbable, rhapsodical; unrealistic, idealistic, imaginary,
dreamy.

Ant. 1–3 unromantic. 1 realistic. 2 unloving, unsentimental, unaffectionate.

Romeo *n. She says Joe is her Romeo:* lover,
Lothario, Don Juan, Casanova, paramour,

beau, boyfriend, wooer, swain, gallant, inamorato, cavalier, sheik.

romp *v. The children romped in the park:* frolic, frisk, rollick, caper, gambol, disport.

room *n.* 1 *the room at the end of the hall:* chamber, compartment; lodging. 2 *We need more room:* space, extent, range, scope, territory, area, elbow room. 3 *There's no room for error here:* provision, leeway, allowance, margin.

roomy *adj. The camper is quite roomy:* spacious, capacious, commodious, sizable, expansive; extensive, large, vast, big.
Ant. small, tiny; cramped, confined.

root[1] *n.* 1 *the root of a flower. Her hair is gray at the roots:* underground part, embedded part, bulb, tubes; radicle, radix; base, lower part, bottom. 2 *Get to the root of the problem:* basic part, basic element, fundamental, essential element, most important part, base, foundation. 3 *The roots of neuroses go back to childhood:* origin, source, spring, derivation, fount, fountain; foundation, basis, starting point, motive, determining condition, reason; inception, beginning, commencement, start. —*v.* 4 *Are you rooted to that spot?:* fix, set, establish; fasten, stick, nail, bind.

root[2] *v. to root for the home team:* cheer, encourage, shout for, boost, pull for.

roster *n. Her name was on the roster of night nurses:* roll, list, listing, slate, record; schedule, agenda, docket.

rostrum *n. The orator stood on the rostrum:* stage, platform, dais, podium, soapbox.

rosy *adj.* 1 *rosy cheeks:* pink, blushing, reddish, reddening, flushed, ruddy, rubicund, glowing, high-colored. 2 *The future is rosy:* rose-colored, hopeful, cheerful, encouraging, promising, full of promise, reassuring, optimistic, bright, auspicious, favorable, propitious.
Ant. 1 pale, pallid. 2 discouraging, unpromising, pessimistic, inauspicious.

rot *v.* 1 *The food rotted:* spoil, go bad, decay, decompose, putrefy, putresce, molder; fall into decay, deteriorate, degenerate. —*n.* 2 *Rot has begun to set in:* rotting, decay, dry rot, decomposition, deterioration, disintegration; putrescence, putrefaction, putridity. 3 *You don't believe that rot, do you?:* nonsense, tommyrot, bosh, bunk, bull, balderdash, poppycock, gobbledygook, twaddle, stuff and nonsense, inanity, absurdity, fiddle-faddle, trash, rubbish, gibberish, blather, folderol.

rotate *v.* 1 *The moon rotates around the earth:* turn around on an axis, go round, turn, revolve, spin, roll, circle, circulate, whirl, gyrate, twirl, swirl, wheel, pirouette,

pivot, swivel. 2 *The guards rotated between day and night shifts:* alternate, change, take turns, interchange.

rotten *adj.* 1 *Don't buy rotten fruit!:* decomposing, decomposed, decaying, decayed, putrid, putrefied, putrescent, moldering, bad, rancid, rank. 2 *What a rotten thing to do!:* dishonest, corrupt, deceitful, faithless, unscrupulous, dishonorable, disgraceful, contemptible, untrustworthy, double-dealing, two-faced, devious, villainous, iniquitous, scurvy, crooked, vicious; immoral, base, unpleasant, nasty, dirty.
Ant. 1 fresh, unspoiled, good. 2 honest, honorable, moral, decent; admirable, commendable; good, wonderful.

rotund *adj.* 1 *A beanbag is generally rotund:* round, globular, bulbous, rounded, spherical, ball-like; ovoid, egg-shaped, curved. 2 *a rotund woman:* plump, fat, obese, corpulent, fleshy, chubby, tubby, pudgy, stout, portly.
Ant. 1 angular, square. 2 thin, slender, slim, lean, skinny, gaunt, scrawny.

roué *n. His reputation as a roué was known to most of the coeds:* rake, libertine, lecher, cad, bounder, profligate, seducer, debauchee, womanizer, rakehell, wanton, playboy, philanderer, Don Juan, Lothario, Casanova; *Slang* wolf, skirt-chaser.

rough *adj.* 1 *Raw wool is a rough material. rough terrain:* coarse, unsmooth, uneven, jagged, ragged, rough-hewn, broken, craggy, unlevel, bumpy, rocky, scraggy; *(variously)* rugged, scratchy, knotty, scaly, scabrous, chapped, gnarled. 2 *Football is a rough game. We sailed in rough seas:* violent, rugged, tough; agitated, turbulent, roiled, tumultuous, stormy, raging. 3 *What rough manners you have!:* boorish, rude, ill-mannered, unmannerly, ungenteel; unpolished, unrefined, inelegant, ungracious, loutish, crusty, gruff, bluff, surly, awkward, clumsy; blunt, brusque, abrupt; coarse, vulgar, indelicate, crude. 4 *The migrant workers had a rough life:* uncomfortable, unluxurious; difficult, unpleasant, tough, rugged, hard, harsh, brutal, severe, difficult, austere. 5 *This is just a rough plan:* not elaborated, unfinished, incomplete, not perfected, imperfect, crude, quick, hasty; vague, sketchy, general, rudimentary, preliminary, approximate, vague, imprecise. 6 *He had a rough voice:* gruff, husky, raspy, rasping, hoarse, grating, harsh.
Ant. 1–4 smooth. 1 regular, level, flat; soft, silky. 2 calm, gentle, tranquil. 3 polite, courteous, gentle, polished, refined, elegant, gracious. 4 comfortable, luxurious, easy,

cushy, plush. **5** elaborate, finished, plush; complete, perfected; detailed, exact, precise.

round *adj.* **1** *Oranges are round:* circular, globular, cylindrical, spherical, spheroid, ball-shaped; elliptical, oval, ovate, ovoid; rounded, curved. **2** *She spoke in round tones:* full, rich, sonorous, resonant, smooth, mellifluent. —*n.* **3** *A round of parties ushered in the New Year:* complete course, circle, series, succession, procession, progression, cycle. **4** Often **rounds** *The nurse made her rounds:* circuit, beat, route. —*v.* **5** *The stagecoach rounded the bend:* travel around, go around, make a circuit. *Ant.* **1** angular, rectangular, square. **2** rough, harsh, hoarse, grating.

roundabout *adj.* *We arrived at the solution in a roundabout way:* indirect, meandering, circuitous, rambling, tortuous, oblique, winding.

rouse *v.* **1** *They had to rouse her from a deep sleep:* awaken, wake, awake, wake up, arouse. **2** *The speaker roused the mob to violence:* excite, animate, incite, stir, provoke, arouse, inflame, move, goad, stimulate, pique, instigate, foment, spur. . *Ant.* **2** soothe, pacify, quell.

rout *n.* **1** *The army suffered a complete rout:* defeat, beating, drubbing, licking, disorderly retreat, dispersal. —*v.* **2** *Joan of Arc routed the English at Orleans:* put to flight, repel, drive off, repulse, chase away, drive away; defeat, vanquish, worst, crush, drub.

route *n.* **1** *Which route do I take to Denver?:* course, itinerary; road, passage. **2** *a mailman's route:* fixed course, beat, round, circuit. —*v.* **3** *Cars were routed around the accident:* direct, ship, dispatch, remit, transmit; detour.

routine *n.* **1** *a daily routine:* regular procedure, practice, custom; method, system, order, technique. —*adj.* **2** *The story has a routine plot:* predictable, unexceptional, customary, conventional, regular, typical, normal, habitual, periodic, ordinary, run-of-the-mill. *Ant.* **2** unusual, different, exceptional, extraordinary.

row[1] *n.* *The soldiers stood in a row:* line; file, tier, queue; series, sequence, succession, rank, chain, column.

row[2] *n.* *We had a small row but quickly made up:* noisy dispute, quarrel, spat, tiff, set-to, difference, squabble, altercation, argument, words, scrape, scrap, fracas; disorder, contretemps.

rowdy *adj.* *rowdy gangs:* boisterous, disorderly, roughneck, unruly, obstreperous. *Ant.* orderly, gentle; mannerly, decorous.

royal *adj.* **1** *the royal family:* regal, sovereign,

monarchal. **2** *They treated us to a royal feast:* fit for a king, regal; majestic, imposing, magnificent, grand, splendid, resplendent, superb; lavish, munificent.

rub *v.* **1** *The wood was rubbed to a glossy finish:* polish, buff, burnish, wipe. **2** *I rubbed my aching legs with liniment:* massage, knead, stroke; finger, manipulate, smear, spread, slather. —*n.* **3** *The masseur gave me a back rub:* rubbing, rubdown, massage, kneading, stroke, stroking. **4** *The plan is good, but how to make it succeed—there's the rub:* hitch, catch, problem, obstacle, trick, thing, difficulty, trouble, dilemma.

rubbish *n.* **1** *Throw the rubbish out:* refuse, trash, garbage, junk, debris, litter. **2** *I don't believe that rubbish:* nonsense, gibberish, balderdash, rot, rigmarole, drivel, bosh, *Informal* flapdoodle, twaddle, blather, idiocy, folderol.

ruddy *adj.* *a ruddy complexion:* rosy, rosy-cheeked, red, reddish, florid, flushed. *Ant.* pale, pallid, wan.

rude *adj.* **1** *Rude behavior will not be tolerated:* discourteous, inconsiderate, uncourteous, uncivil, disrespectful, impolite, impudent, insulting, abusive, impertinent, insolent, saucy, fresh; unmannerly, bad-mannered, ungentlemanly, unladylike, ungracious; indelicate, indecorous, indecent. **2** *We put up a rude shed:* roughly made, crude, roughhewn, makeshift, rough. **3** *Many pride themselves on their rude way of speaking:* blunt, coarse, unrefined, inelegant, unpolished, uncultured, awkward, clumsy; uncouth, vulgar, boorish, loutish, churlish; uneducated, illiterate, rustic. *Ant.* **1** courteous, polite, respectful, mannerly, well-mannered, dignified; decorous, cordial. **2** well-made, finished. **3** refined, elegant, polished, cultured, graceful; educated, literate, urbane, civilized.

rudimentary *adj.* **1** *a rudimentary knowledge of music:* elementary, basic, elemental, primary. **2** *a rudimentary plan:* undeveloped, incomplete, imperfect, simple; immature, primitive. *Ant.* **1** advanced. **2** completely developed, finished, complete, mature.

rue *v.* *I rue the day I met you!:* be sorry for, regret, lament, bemoan, deplore.

ruffle *v.* **1** *The wind ruffled my hair:* muss, dishevel, disorder, disarrange, wrinkle, rumple, roughen, ripple. **2** *The accident ruffled his composure:* disturb, upset, disquiet; perturb, disconcert, discompose; unsettle, agitate, excite, aggravate. —*n.* **3** *The shirt had ruffles on the collar and cuffs:* pleat, flounce, frill, ruff, edging; ripple, wave.

Ant. 1 arrange, smooth. 2 compose, calm, settle.

rugged *adj.* 1 *rugged mountainous territory:* rough, uneven, irregular, craggy, cragged, ridged, jagged, rocky, rock-strewn, bumpy, scraggy. 2 *a rugged face:* furrowed, lined, worn, weathered, weather-beaten; hard-featured, roughhewn, coarse. 3 *a rugged cowboy:* hardy, robust, vigorous, sturdy, stalwart, husky, brawny, muscular, athletic; virile, masculine. 4 *Homesteading is a rugged life:* harsh, tough, difficult, hard, severe, stern, trying, taxing, strenuous, arduous; rude, unrefined, uncultivated; graceless, uncouth.

Ant. 1 smooth, regular, level. 2 smooth, unmarked, delicate. 3 frail, fragile, puny, skinny. 4 gentle, elegant, cultivated.

ruin *n.* 1 **ruins** *the ruins of an ancient Maya temple:* remains, remnants, wreckage. 2 *Military rule was the ruin of the Roman empire:* downfall, fall, undoing, breakdown, ruination, failure, defeat; decay, disintegration, destruction, devastation, doom. *—v.* 3 *The fire ruined the house. The scandal ruined his career:* demolish, destroy, wreck; shatter, devastate, lay waste, ravage; upset, defeat, crush, squash, spoil, end. 4 *The stock market crash ruined many people:* bankrupt, impoverish, pauperize, break.

Ant. 3 build, build up; improve, help, enhance. 4 enrich, profit.

ruinous *adj. The expense was ruinous:* calamitous, disastrous, catastrophic, ravaging, devastating, damaging, destructive, cataclysmic; fatal, deadly.

rule *n.* 1 *You must obey the rules:* law, regulation, order, ordinance, decree, canon, precept, principle; maxim, axiom, adage, doctrine. 2 *Promptness is the rule here:* practice, method, system, routine, custom, policy, normal condition. 3 *There's no set rule for us to follow in this case:* guide, guideline, precedent, criterion, model, precept, formula, prescription; standard, convention. 4 *Queen Victoria's rule lasted 64 years:* reign, regnancy, sovereignty, suzerainty, regime, dominion; control, command, authority, direction, administration, leadership, domination. *—v.* 5 *George III ruled for 60 years:* control, command, govern, direct, administer, manage, run; exercise dominion over, have authority over, reign, lead, head; sway, influence, dominate, prevail. 6 *The jury ruled that I was innocent:* decide, determine, conclude, settle, resolve, find, judge, adjudge; declare, pronounce, decree.

ruler *n.* 1 *King Wenceslaus was a wise ruler:* leader, commander, head of state, *(variously)* president, sovereign, monarch, emperor, king, queen, prince, czar; chief, head, boss. 2 *Use a ruler to measure the width of that cloth:* rule, yardstick, straightedge.

rumble *v.* 1 *The cannon rumbled:* boom, reverberate, resound, roar, thunder. *—n.* 2 *the rumble of cannon in the distance:* roar, thunder, boom, booming; resonance, reverberation, roll; clap, bang.

ruminate *v. We ruminated on the courses of action open to us:* ponder, mull, reflect, think about, meditate, cogitate, contemplate, think over, consider, muse.

rumor *n.* 1 *I don't believe those rumors:* unverified information, report, story, supposition, gossip; hearsay, insinuation, innuendo. *—v.* 2 *It was rumored that she was really a millionaire:* whisper, gossip, intimate, insinuate; spread abroad, bruit about, report.

rump *n. The rider slapped the horse's rump:* hindquarters, rear, posterior, rear end, haunches, buttocks, backside, bottom, croup, seat, behind, stern, derrière.

rumple *v. He rumpled his suit by sleeping in it:* wrinkle, crumple, crease, crinkle, ruffle; disarrange, dishevel, muss, tousle.

rumpus *n. What's all the rumpus about?:* fuss, ado, to-do, disturbance, pother, stir; uproar, tumult, agitation, upheaval, confusion, noise, ruckus.

run *v.* 1 *I've got to run for my bus:* go quickly, move swiftly, race, dart, sprint, dash, hustle, hasten, hurry, scamper, scurry, rush. 2 *The robbers took the money and ran:* leave, take flight, flee, fly, bolt. 3 *The shuttle runs daily from New York to Boston:* go, ply. 4 *to run for mayor:* compete, enter the lists, stand, campaign, make a bid. 5 *The stream runs down the valley:* flow, pour, stream, course, surge, issue. 6 *I ran the car into a ditch:* drive, propel, impel; direct, navigate, maneuver, pilot. 7 *to run a business:* operate, manage, direct, supervise, oversee; head, preside over, boss. 8 *She ran her fingers over the material:* pass, glide. 9 *The escaped prisoners ran the roadblock:* sweep past, break through, penetrate, pierce. 10 *The movie ran for 97 minutes:* elapse, last, endure; proceed, go, continue, advance. 11 *The pond ran dry:* become, get. 12 *How much will the repairs run?:* cost, amount to, total, add up to. 13 *Her red blouse ran in the wash:* bleed, lose color, mingle colors. 14 *Will these hose run?:* come unraveled, separate, ladder. 15 *The prices run from $5 to $200:* vary, extend, be, go. 16 *The ad was run in the paper:* print, publish; display. 17 *She's not afraid to run a risk:*

incur, bring on, court, invite; liable to, be exposed to; encounter, meet, meet with. **18** *The ice cream ran in the warm sun:* dissolve, melt, liquefy. —*n.* **19** *We took a run around the track:* running, trot, canter, gallop, jog, sprint, dash. **20** *Let's take a run upstate for the day:* trip, excursion, journey, voyage, tour, drive, outing. **21** *I'm darning up a run in my old sweater:* unraveled place, *Informal* ladder. **22** *the run of events:* course, passage, flow, progress, movement. **23** *You have the run of my office:* freedom, unrestricted use. **24** *a run of good luck:* series, course, continuance, continuation, duration; period, stretch, streak, spell. **25** *a rabbit run:* enclosure, pen. **26** *We've had nothing exciting—just the usual run of applicants:* class, kind, sort, type. **27** *The run of water down a mountainside increases during spring thaw:* flow, stream, race, course, current. **28** *The home team scored two runs:* point in baseball, score, tally.

Ant. **1** walk, crawl. **2** remain, stay. **10** stop, cease. **18** solidify, congeal. **19** walk, saunter.

rundown *n. Give me a quick rundown of the news:* outline, summary, résumé, synopsis, abstract, précis, brief, review, condensation.

run-down *adj.* **1** *an old, run-down house:* broken-down, dilapidated, deteriorated, rickety, tumbledown, *Slang* beat-up. **2** *Despite her run-down condition she won't see a doctor:* weary, exhausted; frail, feeble, fatigued, sickly.

Ant. **1** renovated, rebuilt, refurbished. **2** fit, robust, sturdy.

run-of-the-mill *adj. The play is run-of-the-mill:* ordinary, commonplace, routine, everyday, mediocre, passable, so-so, undistinguished, humdrum, middling, indifferent.

Ant. superior; unusual, different.

rupture *n.* **1** *a rupture in a water main:* breaking, bursting, break, burst, split, fracture, crack, fissure, rent, cleft. **2** *What caused the rupture between the two friends?:* break, rift, split, breach, schism, separation, disunion; disagreement, falling out, discord. —*v.* **3** *The balloon ruptured:* break, burst, crack, puncture, divide. **4** *What ruptured their friendship?:* disrupt, disunite, divide, break up.

Ant. **2** understanding, agreement. **4** unite, heal, knit.

rural *adj. We left the city for a rural home:* country, pastoral, bucolic, rustic, countrified.

Ant. urban, city, cosmopolitan.

ruse *n. The call was just a ruse to get me out of the way:* stratagem, maneuver, device, contrivance, artifice, subterfuge, trick, hoax, deception, deceit, dodge, feint.

rush *v.* **1** *We've got to rush:* speed, hasten, hie, hurry, run, dash, dart, hustle, scurry. **2** *The operation could not be rushed:* speed up, accelerate, expedite, perform hastily, hurry. **3** *Don't rush me!:* spur, urge, goad, drive; pressure, push, press. **4** *Don't rush into marriage:* go carelessly, act thoughtlessly, leap, plunge. **5** *The children rushed the candy store:* attack suddenly, storm, charge, descend upon. —*n.* **6** *The shoppers made a rush for the bargain counter:* run, dash, sprint. **7** *We have time to eat without rush:* haste, speed, urgency.

Ant. **1** walk, crawl. **2** slow. **7** leisure; dawdling.

rust *n.* **1** *The pipes were full of rust:* corrosion, oxidation; blight. **2** *a lovely shade of rust:* reddish-yellow, reddish-brown, russet, auburn. —*v.* **3** *Exposed iron will rust. His talents had rusted over the years:* corrode, oxidize; decay, decline, deteriorate.

rustic *adj.* **1** *a rustic community:* country, rural, provincial, pastoral, agrarian, bucolic. **2** *rustic manners:* simple, plain, unsophisticated; rough, countrified, unpolished, unrefined, inelegant, uncultured, crude, coarse, boorish; gauche, cloddish. —*n.* **3** *a rustic from the backwoods:* country person, countryman, provincial; bumpkin, hayseed, yokel, clodhopper, rube, hick.

Ant. **1** urban, cosmopolitan. **2** sophisticated, polished, elegant, urbane, citified. **3** sophisticate, cosmopolitan.

rut *n.* **1** *There were deep ruts in the road:* depression, furrow; channel, trough, groove. **2** *You're in a rut!:* fixed way of life, routine, monotonous round, pattern, habit.

ruthless *adj. a ruthless tyrant:* unmerciful, merciless, pitiless, unpitying, unfeeling, heartless, hardhearted, harsh, cruel, unsparing, remorseless, unrelenting; inhuman, vicious, barbarous, savage, ferocious, brutal, coldblooded.

Ant. merciful, compassionate, kind, tenderhearted, humane.

S

Sabbath n. *The seventh day is the Sabbath:* Sabbath day, day of rest, day of worship, Lord's Day.

sabotage n. 1 *The enemy agent was arrested for sabotage:* undermining of a cause, subversion; malicious destruction. —v. 2 *Someone sabotaged our plan:* undermine, conspire against, subvert; damage from within, paralyze, cripple, destroy, disrupt.

saccharine adj. *Saccharine words fail to sway me:* oversweet, cloying, syrupy, sugary, honeyed; maudlin, sentimental, mawkish.

Ant. sharp, sour, acid.

sack¹ n. 1 *A sack of potatoes:* bag; pouch, knapsack, rucksack, haversack, gunnysack. —v. 2 *I got hired to sack grain:* put into a sack, bag.

sack² v. *The invaders sacked the village:* pillage, plunder, loot, ransack, despoil, ravage, raid.

sacrament n. *the sacrament of Holy Communion:* rite, ceremony, liturgy, ceremonial, ministration; pledge, promise, vow, covenant, obligation, plight, affirmation.

sacred adj. 1 *to be buried in sacred ground:* consecrated, hallowed, sanctified, holy. 2 *Salzburg is sacred to Mozart-lovers:* venerable, awe-inspiring, revered. 3 *the sacred books of the Essenes:* religious, ecclesiastical, scriptural, holy, Biblical; hallowed, divinely inspired.

Ant. 1 unconsecrated, profane. 3 profane, secular, lay.

sacrifice n. 1 *The Incas made sacrifices to their gods:* offering, obligation, ritual slaughter. 2 *Parents often make sacrifices for their children:* relinquishment, concession, renunciation. —v. 3 *The ancient Greeks sacrificed lambs before a battle:* make a sacrifice of, offer up, make an offering of. 4 *We decided to sacrifice a trip for a new car:* give up, relinquish, forgo, forfeit, waive, renounce.

sacrilege n. *To fight inside a church is a sacrilege:* profanation, desecration; blasphemy, profanity, profaneness, impiousness, impiety, irreverence, mockery; sin, wickedness.

sad adj. 1 *I was sad when I learned of her death:* unhappy, grieved, grief-stricken; dispirited, downcast, crestfallen, heavy-hearted, disconsolate, desolate, despondent, melancholy, inconsolable, depressed, dejected; blue; distressed, despairing, forlorn, sorrowful, doleful, mournful. 2 *a sad story:* pitiful, touching, pathetic, lamentable. 3 *in sad circumstances:* unfortunate, grave, calamitous, grim, dismal, lamentable, woeful, distressing; taxing, difficult, adverse, troublesome, tragic.

Ant. 1 happy, glad, pleased. 2 happy, amusing. 3 easy, flourishing, successful.

sadden v. *Her sudden departure saddened me:* grieve, depress, dishearten, deject, dispirit, sorrow, aggrieve.

Ant. delight, gladden, please.

safe adj. 1 *The crystal was safe in its casing:* secure, out of danger, safe and sound; unharmed, unhurt, undamaged, unscathed, unscratched. 2 *The streets aren't safe at night:* secure, protected, guarded, invulnerable. 3 *Two weeks to finish the job is a safe estimate:* cautious, prudent, circumspect, conservative, wary; sure, certain. 4 *a safe driver:* careful, not dangerous, cautious; sure, sound, tried and true; harmless, innocuous.

Ant. 1 imperiled; jeopardized, at risk. 2 unsafe, hazardous, perilous. 3 wild, impetuous. 4 unsafe; dangerous.

safeguard n. *safeguards against nuclear holocaust:* defense, protection, shield, bulwark, guard; security, precaution.

sag v. 1 *The mattress sagged in the middle:* droop, slump, bow, decline, give way, settle; sway, list, dip, lean, tilt. 2 *My mother's coat sagged on me:* droop, flop, flap, hang loosely, billow. 3 *Her spirits sagged:* weaken, diminish, decline, flag, tire, fail.

saga n. *a saga of arctic exploration:* narrative, tale, heroic tale, epic, legend, myth, adventure; chronicle, history.

sage n. 1 *The king brought difficult problems to a sage:* wise man, pundit, philosopher, guru. —adj. 2 *He was sage in his judgment:* wise, shrewd, prudent; sensible, sound, sagacious, knowing, astute, intelligent.

Ant. 1 fool. 2 stupid, foolish.

sail n. 1 *We took a sail around the islands:* sailing trip, cruise, voyage, boat ride. —v. 2 *We sailed around the world. The ship sailed at noon:* cruise, go by water, navigate; course, skim, scud, steam; set sail, put to sea, shove off, get under way. **3** *The balloon sailed upward:* float, fly, drift, glide, soar.

sailor *n. The old sailor had worked on many ships:* mariner, seaman, deckhand, seafarer, seafaring man; *Informal* tar, salt, sea dog, *Slang* gob.

saintly *adj. a saintly life:* sainted, godly, holy, blessed, devout, pious, beatific, reverent, religious, spiritual; virtuous, good, upright, moral, righteous, benevolent.

Ant. wicked, sinful, immoral; ungodly.

sake *n. For the sake of your family, don't take risks:* good, benefit, consideration, well-being, welfare; interest, cause, behalf, account; purpose, object.

salary *n. a weekly salary:* compensation, wages, pay, income; remuneration, recompense.

sale *n.* **1** *My agent arranged the sale of the house:* selling, transfer. **2** *a sale of winter coats:* disposal of goods at reduced prices, markdown, reduction, discount; bargain, special.

Ant. **1** purchase, acquisition.

salient *adj. The plan has several salient flaws:* prominent, obvious, conspicuous, noticeable, easily noticed, manifest, flagrant, glaring, pronounced; important, notable, noteworthy.

Ant. inconspicuous, minor, trifling.

sallow *adj. a sallow complexion:* yellowish, yellow, jaundiced, sickly; pale, wan, ashen, pallid, gray.

Ant. ruddy, rosy.

sally *n.* **1** *Joan of Arc was captured during a sally outside the walls:* sortie, thrust, counterattack, foray, raid, attack. **2** *Her quick sally made us laugh:* clever remark, mot, reply, flash of wit, witticism, repartee, badinage, banter, retort, quip.

salon *n.* **1** *the main salon:* large room, drawing room, hall. **2** *a beauty salon:* hairdresser, beauty parlor, establishment.

saloon *n. The temperance league wanted to close the saloon:* bar, tavern, pub, barroom, taproom, beer parlor, alehouse, cocktail lounge, roadhouse, *Slang* ginmill.

salt *n.* **1** *Her wit added a little salt to the conversation:* pungency, piquancy; seasoning, savor, flavor. **2 salt of the earth** best, choice, pick, select. *—adj.* **3** *salt water:* saline, salty, salted, brackish, briny. *—v.* **4** *We salted the meat to preserve it:* cure, brine, marinate, pickle, corn, souse.

salubrious *adj. Regular exercise is salubrious:* healthful, healthy, health-promoting, good for one, salutary, beneficial, wholesome, lifegiving.

Ant. unhealthful, unhealthy, harmful, unwholesome.

salute *v.* **1** *He saluted us heartily:* address, greet, hail, welcome; make obeisance to, bow to, nod to, wave to. **2** *I salute my opponent's courage:* applaud, praise, honor, respect. *—n.* **3** *The hero acknowledged the salutes of the crowd:* expression of goodwill, salutation, greeting, recognition, honor, homage; applause, accolade.

salvage *n.* **1** *the salvage of the Titanic:* recovery, reclamation, retrieval. **2** *The salvage was piled upon the pier:* reclaimed materials, remains, scrap, junk, debris; flotsam and jetsam. *—v.* **3** *We salvaged the cargo from the ship:* save, rescue, retrieve, recover; rehabilitate, restore.

salvation *n.* **1** *Think on your eternal salvation:* redemption, deliverance; election, grace. **2** *Prayer was her salvation:* protection, lifeline, mainstay, rock. **3** *A loan aided in the salvation of his business:* saving, rescue, preservation, salvage; retrieval, reclamation, recovery, survival.

Ant. **1** perdition, damnation, condemnation. **2** downfall. **3** destruction, loss.

salve *n.* **1** *The salve helped her rheumatism:* unguent, ointment, balm, emollient, lotion, liniment, anodyne. *—v.* **2** *My apology seemed to salve his injured feelings:* ease, assuage, alleviate, mitigate, relieve, mollify, calm, pacify.

Ant. **2** exacerbate, inflame, aggravate.

same *adj.* **1** *This is the same dress I wore to the party:* identical, selfsame, very; alike, twin, like, of like kind, similar. **2** *Both houses have the same number of rooms:* corresponding, equivalent, parallel; equal. **3** *You're still the same person I knew ten years ago:* unchanged, invariable, consistent.

Ant. **1–3** different. **1** dissimilar. **3** changed.

sample *n.* **1** *The sketches were samples of her artwork:* representative, specimen, example, illustration, instance, cross section, exemplification. *—v.* **2** *She made us sample her cooking:* judge by a sample, test, partake of, taste, try, experience.

sanctify *v. to sanctify a new church:* bless, consecrate, hallow, make holy, enshrine, exalt, beatify, dedicate; purify, cleanse, absolve; sanction, legitimize, legitimatize, uphold.

Ant. profane, desecrate, defile.

sanctimonious *adj. A true believer doesn't have to be sanctimonious:* make a show of sanctity, affectedly holy, pietistic; self-righteous, holier-than-thou, unctuous; solemn, pretentious, pompous, preachy.

sanction *n.* **1** *We received sanction to proceed:* approval, endorsement, assent, consent, permission, authorization; leave, liberty, license, authority. **2** *political sanctions:* penalty, pressure, punitive measure. —*v.* **3** *Our plan was sanctioned by the directors:* approve, endorse, authorize, legitimate, allow, permit, accept, agree to, favor, ratify, support.
Ant. **1** disapproval, forbiddance, refusal. **2** encouragement. **3** disapprove, reject, ban, prohibit.

sanctuary *n.* **1** *a sanctuary of the Lord:* holy place, consecrated place, house of worship, house of prayer, house of God, church, temple, chapel, shrine; sanctum, sanctum sanctorum. **2** *The storm cellar was a sanctuary against the tornado:* refuge, haven, retreat, safe place; asylum. **3** *a bird sanctuary:* reserve, preserve, park.

sane *adj.* **1** *He was declared sufficiently sane to stand trial:* of sound mind, compos mentis; clearheaded, balanced, rational. **2** *Have a safe and sane holiday!:* reasonable, sensible, judicious, logical.
Ant. **1** insane, non compos mentis, deranged, mad. **2** insane, senseless, stupid.

sanguine *adj.* *to have a sanguine outlook on life:* optimistic, hopeful, confident, cheerful, sunny.
Ant. pessimistic, gloomy, despairing, dispirited, morose.

sanitary *adj.* *The Health Department checks on sanitary conditions. Hospital operating instruments must be sanitary:* healthful, salubrious, healthy, wholesome; sterile, sterilized, clean, germ-free, disease-free, hygienic, disinfected, aseptic, uninfected.
Ant. unhealthy, unwholesome; unsterile.

sanity *n.* *She managed to keep her sanity throughout the ordeal:* soundness of mind, saneness, mental balance; soundness of judgment, reason, rationality, sensibleness, sense, clearheadedness.
Ant. insanity, insaneness, madness, derangement; irrationality.

sap *v.* *The ordeal sapped my energy:* deplete, reduce, rob; weaken, undermine, enervate, enfeeble, exhaust, debilitate, drain.

sarcasm *n.* *His sarcasm hurt her feelings:* ridicule, derision, scorn, mockery, disparagement.
Ant. compliment, praise.

sarcastic *adj.* *She gave a sarcastic reply:* contemptuous, mocking, derisive, taunting; biting, cutting, stinging, mordant, sardonic, scornful, sneering, disparaging.

sardonic *adj.* *He watched his enemies fail with sardonic amusement:* sarcastic, cynical, sneering, mocking, contemptuous, derisive, scornful, biting, taunting, jeering.

Satan *n.* *Satan is the ruler of Hell:* the Devil, the Prince of Darkness, the Evil One, Beelzebub, Lucifer, Mephistopheles, the Foul Fiend, Old Nick, Old Scratch, Moloch, Belial.

satanic *adj.* *the satanic punishments of the damned:* hellish, diabolical, demoniacal, demonic, devilish, fiendish; malicious, malignant, malevolent, wicked, evil, inhuman, heinous, cruel.
Ant. angelic, heavenly, benevolent.

sate *v.* *The huge meal sated our hunger:* satisfy fully, satiate, fill; glut, stuff, surfeit.

satiate *v.* *The meal satiated our need for food:* satisfy, fill, suffice, content; quench, glut, stuff, sate, surfeit; overfill, saturate; sicken, jade, bore, weary.

satire *n.* *The play is full of satire:* comic criticism, parody, takeoff, burlesque, lampoon, travesty, caricature; mockery, ridicule, sarcasm, irony, raillery, banter.

satirical *adj.* *He wrote a satirical piece on the government:* ironically critical, sardonic, sarcastic, ironical; mocking, sneering, biting, scornful, caustic; comic, humorous, tongue-in-cheek.

satisfaction *n.* **1** *I get a good deal of satisfaction from my grandchildren:* pleasure, comfort, gratification, happiness, fulfillment, pride, content, contentment. **2** *We receved satisfaction for the damage:* reimbursement, repayment, compensation, recompense, restitution, remuneration, payment, settlement, quittance; deserts; requital, redress, rectification, justice, amends, correction, answering.
Ant. **1** dissatisfaction, shame, unhappiness, discontent.

satisfactory *adj.* *The actress gave a satisfactory performance:* good enough, competent, adequate, suitable, sufficient, all right, acceptable, passable, OK.
Ant. unsatisfactory, inadequate, bad.

satisfy *v.* **1** *Nothing satisfies her anymore! The water satisfied our thirst:* make content, content, please, mollify, gratify; meet, fill, fulfill, serve, suffice, answer; sate, satiate, quench, appease. **2** *We satisfied all our accounts:* pay off, settle, discharge, clear, pay, repay; reimburse, recompense, compensate, requite. **3** *I'm not satisfied that the plan will succeed:* convince, persuade, assure, reassure.
Ant. **1** dissatisfy, displease, annoy; intensify, worsen. **3** dissuade.

saturate *v.* **1** *Heavy rain saturated the playing field:* soak thoroughly, drench, souse,

douse. 2 *Dust saturated the attic:* fill, permeate, infuse, suffuse, pervade.
Ant. 1 drain, dry.

saucy *adj.* 1 *Her saucy remarks raised eyebrows:* impudent, insolent, impertinent, forward, audacious, bold, brash, brazen, flippant, cheeky, fresh, disrespectful. 2 *a saucy walk:* pert, lively; high-spirited; jaunty, natty.

saunter *v. He sauntered into the house:* walk casually, amble, stroll, traipse; wander, ramble, roam, meander.

savage *adj.* 1 *Her received a savage beating from the thugs:* ferocious, fierce, brutal, barbaric, brutish; cruel, merciless, unmerciful, pitiless, ruthless, relentless. 2 *savage beasts. savage invaders:* untamed, wild, undomesticated, feral; uncivilized, primitive, uncultured; heathenish, barbaric, barbarous. 3 *Savage winds whipped about the mountain:* violent, harsh, rough, rugged. —*n.* 4 *Do you believe in the idea of the noble savage?:* primitive, aborigine, aboriginal, native, barbarian. 5 *Lock that savage up and throw away the key!:* fierce person, brute, fiend, barbarian.
Ant. 1 kind, merciful, gentle. 2 tame, domesticated; civilized, cultured. 3 mild, soft.

save *v.* 1 *The firemen saved the family from the burning building:* rescue, recover, free, deliver, preserve, protect, safeguard; redeem, help. 2 *You'll save electricity by turning off lights:* conserve, preserve, husband, spare. 3 *I'm saving this dress for a special occasion:* set aside, store, reserve, set apart, withhold, hold, keep, conserve, preserve. 4 *Save your voice for tonight's performance:* treat carefully, keep safe, protect, take care of; safeguard, shield, guard. 5 *You must learn to save for the future:* be thrifty, curtail expenses, economize, provide for a rainy day, put by; amass, accumulate, husband.
Ant. 1 endanger, imperil, risk. 2 use, waste. 3 use. 4 expose, risk, endanger. 5 spend, be extravagant.

saving *adj.* 1 *His saving grace was his humor:* redeeming, reclaiming, compensating. 2 *Are you a saving sort of person?:* frugal, thrifty, pennywise, economical, sparing, provident. —*n.* 3 *If you buy now, there's a saving of 20%:* amount saved, reduction in cost, price-cut, markdown. 4 *savings It took all our savings to buy the house:* money laid aside, financial reserve, funds, nest egg.

savior *n.* 1 *Simon Bolivar was the savior of the South American peasants:* protector, champion, defender, preserver, guardian;

rescuer, deliverer, salvation, liberator, emancipator; redeemer. 2 **Saviour** *The birth of the Saviour is celebrated on Christmas:* Christ, the Messiah, Prince of Peace, the Son of God.

savoir faire *n. Diplomats need savoir faire:* social grace, social skill, tact, aplomb; graciousness, finesse, poise, presence, composure, self-possession; polish, suavity, urbanity, worldliness.

savor *n.* 1 *This cake has the savor of nutmeg:* taste, flavor, piquancy, pungency; smell, aroma, odor, scent, fragrance. 2 *His words had the savor of vengeance:* character, nature, quality, property, distinctive feature, peculiarity, trait, aura, gist, spirit. —*v.* 3 *Her sauce savored of garlic:* taste, smell, smack, have a touch, be suggestive. 4 *We savored every bite:* enjoy, relish, take pleasure in, delight in, luxuriate in, appreciate.

savory *adj.* 1 *a savory stew:* tasty, appetizing, mouth-watering; pungent, delectable, delicious, tasteful, toothsome, full-flavored, flavorous. 2 *He wasn't a very savory character:* reputable, respectable, honest; attractive, alluring.
Ant. 1 tasteless, insipid. 2 unsavory, disreputable, shady.

say *v.* 1 *What did she say? What did the telegram say?:* speak, tell, utter, give utterance to, voice, verbalize, vocalize, articulate; express, word, phrase; state, declare, announce; remark, comment, mention; communicate, convey; divulge, repeat, disclose. 2 *The actors said their lines perfectly:* recite, read, speak, deliver, render, perform. 3 *I'd say it's about two o'clock:* guess, suppose, surmise, conjecture, imagine; judge, reason; daresay. 4 *It's been said that he's an impostor:* report, rumor, circulate, bruit, noise abroad, allege, claim, assert, contend, hint, imply, intimate, suggest, insinuate. —*n.* 5 *We should all have a say in the matter:* right to speak, voice, participation; vote; opportunity to speak, expressed opinion.

saying *n. an old saying:* expression, proverb, saw, adage, maxim, truism, aphorism, dictum, motto, epigram.

scale[1] *n.* 1 *A scale of rust covered the steel:* coating, film, skin, lamina, membrane, layer, crust, shell; flake, chip; plate. —*v.* 2 *Scale the old paint from the ceiling:* chip off, flake, scrape, peel.

scale[2] *n.* 1 *What's the scale of that ruler?:* gradation, graduation, calibration, measure. 2 *We were graded on a scale from 1 to 10:* classification, range, series, progression; spread, spectrum, continuum, order. 3 *What is the scale of that map?:* proportion, ratio. 4 *The opera singer could sing in sev-*

eral scales: register, range, octave; key.
—*v.* 5 *to scale a mountain:* climb up, climb
over, go up, ascend, mount, surmount, rise,
progress upward. 6 *to scale wages according to job specifications:* adjust, regulate,
set; vary.

scamp *n. That little scamp has hidden your
glasses:* rascal, scalawag, rogue, scoundrel,
rapscallion, knave, villain, imp, mischief-
maker, tease, prankster.

scamper *v. The children scampered out of
the house:* run, rush, hasten, fly, hurry, race,
sprint, dart, dash, scuttle, scud, scurry,
scoot.

scan *v.* 1 *The lookout scanned the horizon:*
examine, peruse, scour, scrutinize, inspect,
study; search, sweep, survey. 2 *He only
scanned the letter:* read hastily, glance at,
skim. 3 *The English teacher taught the class
how to scan poems:* divide into feet, show
the metrical structure of; analyze.

scandal *n.* 1 *the most famous political scandal in history:* public disgrace, revelation of
misconduct, exposure of wrongdoing; embarrassment, exposé. 2 *She brought scandal
to her family:* dishonor, disgrace, discredit;
shame; smirch, stain, blot, ignominy, oppro-
brium. 3 *I will not listen to this scandal!:*
malicious gossip, slander, aspersion, detraction, disparagement, revilement, vituperation, abuse, evil-speaking.
Ant. 3 honor, esteem, credit.

scandalous *adj.* 1 *scandalous behavior:* disgraceful, shameful, disreputable, highly improper, offensive, shocking, outrageous.
2 *That tabloid is full of scandalous stories:*
slanderous, libelous, scurrilous, defamatory, gossiping.
Ant. 1 proper, decent. 2 praising, laudatory.

scant *adj.* 1 *a scant water supply:* limited,
meager, insufficient, inadequate; small, paltry, sparse. 2 *a scant cupful of water:* not
full, bare, incomplete. 3 *We've been scant of
money:* ill-supplied, in need, short.
Ant. 1 plentiful, profuse, abundant, ample,
adequate. 2 full, overflowing.

scanty *adj. a scanty supply of water:* inadequate, scant, insufficient; meager, sparse,
skimpy, small, modest, paltry.

scar *n.* 1 *He had a scar on his arm. The boat
had scars from hitting the reefs:* mark left
by an old wound, cicatrix, wound, stitch
mark; dent, gash; defect, flaw, blemish.
—*v.* 2 *Falling on the rocks scarred her
arms:* leave a scar on, wound, cut, scratch,
gash, lacerate, mark, bruise.

scarce *adj. Qualified workers were scarce:* in
short supply, scanty, sparse, wanting, insufficient, not abundant; rare, rarely en-

countered, unusual, uncommon; infrequent.
Ant. abundant, plentiful; numerous, common.

scarcely *adj.* 1 *We scarcely had time for
breakfast:* hardly, barely, slightly, just, at
most, no more than, not easily. 2 *He was
scarcely the type of person needed for the
job:* definitely not, certainly not, in no way,
by no means, not at all, not in the least,
hardly, on no account.

scarcity *n.* 1 *a scarcity of supplies:* insufficiency, shortage, scantiness, lack, dearth,
deficiency, want, paucity. 2 *Uranium is expensive because of its scarcity:* rarity, rare-
ness, scarceness, sparsity, uncommonness,
sparseness; fewness.

scare *v.* 1 *The lightning scared the child:* fill
with fear, make afraid, frighten, terrify,
startle, terrorize, horrify, panic, alarm, intimidate, daunt, disconcert, dishearten.
—*n.* 2 *The smell of gas gave me a scare:*
sudden fright, start, sudden terror, alarm,
shock, panic; turn.
Ant. 1 reassure, calm, comfort. 2 calm,
reassurance.

scary *adj. a scary horror movie:* frightening,
terrifying, hair-raising, shocking, disturbing, discomfiting, menacing, alarming,
threatening, fearful.
Ant. reassuring, comforting.

scathing *adj. a scathing criticism of her
essay:* brutal, cutting, scorching, lacerating,
searing, stinging, caustic, vitriolic, biting,
acrimonious, excoriating, savage, ferocious,
sharp, pointed, keen, incisive.
Ant. gentle, considerate, mild.

scatter *v.* 1 *We scattered the seeds over the
yard:* spread loosely, distribute, disperse,
throw, strew, sprinkle, cast, sow; broadcast,
disseminate. 2 *A loud noise scattered the
pigeons:* disperse, flee; dispel, dissipate,
rout, chase away.
Ant. gather, assemble, collect.

scatterbrained *adj. That was a scatterbrained idea:* harebrained, rattlebrained,
birdbrained, emptyheaded, flighty, silly,
zany, stupid; absentminded, forgetful; foolish, foolhardy, rash, heedless, careless, imprudent, frivolous, irresponsible.
Ant. serious, intelligent; prudent; responsible.

scene *n.* 1 *the scene of a crime:* setting, site,
location, locale, locality, whereabouts;
place, spot, position, region. 2 *The setting
of the sun over the lake was a beautiful
scene:* vista, view, vision, sight, panorama,
picture, display, spectacle. 3 *She made a
scene and couldn't be quieted:* display of
temper, embarrassing spectacle, fuss, to-do,
commotion. 4 *The scene of the story is Vic-*

torian England: setting, locale, milieu; backdrop, background, scenery. **5** *We missed the first few scenes of the movie:* episode, part, division, sequence.

scent *n.* **1** *the scent of lemons:* smell, odor, aroma, fragrance, bouquet, essence, perfume. **2** *The fox threw pursuers off the scent:* odor left in passing; trail, track, course, pursuit. —*v.* **3** *We could scent roses in the garden:* smell, sniff, get wind of, detect, recognize, discern; trace, trail, track. **4** *She used lemon juice to scent her hair:* give odor to, perfume, aromatize.

schedule *n.* **1** *What's on the schedule for today?:* list of events, agenda, calendar, program; roll, inventory. **2** *a train schedule:* list, table; timetable. —*v.* **3** *to schedule appointments:* set the time for, slate, fix, plan, book; appoint, set down.

scheme *n.* **1** *a scheme to increase sales:* plan, design, program; method, system, device, procedure, strategy, tactics. **2** *a scheme to overthrow the king:* conspiracy, plot, maneuver; contrivance, connivance; intrigue, machination. **3** *the entire scheme of interstate highways:* arrangement, system, grouping, organization, network. **4** *Follow this scheme to assemble the motor:* schematic diagram, blueprints, outline, layout, drawing; chart, map. —*v.* **5** *They schemed to overthrow the government:* plan secretly, plot, conspire, connive; contrive; study, design; maneuver, intrigue.

scheming *adj. a scheming con man:* conniving, designing, contriving, calculating; Machiavellian, crafty, sly, wily, slippery, cunning, shrewd, tricky, intriguing.

Ant. naive, artless, ingenuous.

scholar *n.* **1** *an eminent scholar:* learned person, sage; academic specialist, intellectual; *Slang* egghead, brain. **2** *Several young scholars enrolled in the course:* pupil, student, learner, matriculant; schoolboy, schoolgirl; bookworm.

Ant. **1** dunce, ignoramus, illiterate.

scholarly *adj. scholarly disputes:* erudite, learned, educated, well-read, academic, intellectual, lettered, literate.

scholarship *n.* **1** *She's renowned for her scholarship:* academic attainments, learning, erudition, education; accurate research, sound academic practice. **2** *He won a scholarship to the university:* aid granted a student, grant, endowment, stipend; assistantship, fellowship.

school *n.* **1** *The children go to school by bus:* place for instruction; academy, lyceum, institute; *(variously)* kindergarten, grade school, high school, college, university, seminary. **2** *a member of the old school. a*

school of thought: order, faction, way of thinking, system, method, style, view; persuasion, doctrine, theory, faith, belief. —*v.* **3** *She was schooled at Harvard:* teach, train, instruct, educate.

scintillating *adj. Conversation at the party was scintillating:* sparkling, lively, animated, ebullient, exuberant, brilliant, dazzling, stimulating, glittering; charming, bright, witty.

Ant. dull, boring, lackluster.

scion *n. the scion of a famous family:* offspring, child, heir, successor, descendant, son, daughter, heiress, progeny, issue.

scoff *v. She scoffed at his attempts to improve himself:* mock, ridicule, deride, poke fun at, laugh at; belittle, taunt, jeer, revile, run down.

Ant. praise, compliment, applaud, cheer.

scold *v.* **1** *Dad scolded me for coming home late:* rebuke, upbraid, reprove, remonstrate with, reprimand, take to task, castigate, censure, berate, rail at. —*n.* **2** *That old scold never has anything nice to say:* constant faultfinder, complainer, nagger; shrew, virago, termagant.

Ant. **1** praise, compliment, applaud.

scope *n.* **1** *an individual of limited scope:* range, vision; application; effect, force, influence, competence, breadth of knowledge, reach, grasp; aim, purpose, goal, ambition. **2** *The scope of the property was enormous:* extent in space, area, span, stretch, spread, extension, compass, reach. **3** *Give your child's creativity a wide scope:* space for movement or activity, free course, rein, latitude, margin, range, room, freedom.

scorch *v. The hot weather scorched the grass:* singe, sear; wither, parch, char, burn.

score *n.* **1** *The score is 2–0. Who made that last score?:* record of points made, tally, count; *(variously)* point, goal, run, basket. **2** *My score on the test was 95:* grade, test result, mark. **3** *The tree trunk had many scores in it:* notch, incision, nick, mark, groove, cut, slash, gash, slit. **4** *"Fourscore and seven years ago . . .":* set of twenty. **5 scores** *Scores of people attended the meetings:* large numbers, multitudes, throngs, hosts, lots, masses, droves, swarms. —*v.* **6** *How many points did we score in the game?:* make, tally, register; pile up, amass. **7** *to score exam papers:* grade, mark, evaluate, judge; keep a tally. **8** *No good scout would score a tree trunk with a knife:* notch, cut, groove. **9** *to score a victory:* achieve, win, register.

scorn *n.* **1** *She regarded me with scorn:* contempt, disdain, haughtiness, arrogance; derision; scoffing, sarcasm, mockery, ridicule. —*v.* 2 *He scorned those who did not follow him into battle. They scorned all attempts at reconciliation:* look down on, hold in contempt, disdain, treat with disdain; spurn, refuse, rebuff, reject; ignore, disregard, have nothing to do with, refuse to listen to; ostracize.

Ant. 1 deference, respect, esteem. 2 esteem, look up to, admire.

scoundrel *n. That scoundrel would sell his own mother!:* villain, rogue, cur, snake in the grass, blackguard, knave, varlet, cad, bounder, rotter; thief, crook, swindler; rascal, scamp, rapscallion, scalawag.

scour¹ *v. to scour the kitchen sink:* scrub, scrape, wash vigorously; abrade, polish, burnish, buff.

scour² *v. We scoured the countryside for antiques:* search through, comb, rummage, range over.

scout *n.* 1 *The scout reported enemy troops were near:* person sent ahead, vanguard, advance guard, advance man, point man, outrider; guide, escort —*v.* 2 *Who scouted for Custer?:* make reconnaissance, reconnoiter, survey, observe.

scowl *v. He scowled when I refused to leave:* frown, glower, lower, glare, give a dirty look.

scramble *v.* 1 *We scrambled for cover:* scurry, rush, race, run. 2 *We had to scramble for a living:* struggle, fight, strive; scrimmage, battle, scrap. 3 *to scramble eggs. to scramble letters so words are unrecognizable:* stir together; mix together, jumble, disarrange, disorganize, disorder. —*n.* 4 *We made a scramble for cover:* rush, race, run. 5 *There was a scramble to recover the football:* scuffle, struggle, tussle, scrimmage.

scrap¹ *n.* 1 *There wasn't a scrap of evidence to convict him. scraps of bread:* small piece, fragment, snippet, trace, particle; bit, speck, atom, molecule, jot, iota, crumb. 2 *The old copper pipes were sold for scrap:* discarded material, reclaimable material, junk; trash, refuse. —*v.* 3 *We decided to scrap the old car:* put in the scrap heap, sell as scrap; discard as worthless, junk, abandon, jettison.

Ant. 3 keep, repair, maintain.

scrap² *Informal n.* 1 *a barroom scrap:* fight, brawl, row; melee, fracas. —*v.* 2 *Those two will scrap at the least provocation!:* fight, quarrel, spat, brawl, come to blows.

scrape *v.* 1 *a machine to scrape floors:* abrade, scour; clean, smooth, plane, buff, burnish. 2 *I scraped my elbow:* graze, abrade, scuff, skin. 3 *Let's scrape up some food:* collect, secure, procure, acquire, ob-

tain, gather, amass. 4 *Don't scrape your fingernail across the blackboard!:* grate, rasp, scratch. 5 *We scraped for years to buy that house:* economize, save, scrimp, stint. —*n.* 6 *How did you get that scrape on your arm?:* abrasion, score, scratch. 7 *Her temper always got her into scrapes:* troublesome situation, predicament, difficulty, dilemma, plight, straits; fight, scuffle, tussle, run-in.

scratch *v.* 1 *The car was only scratched in the accident:* make a mark on, graze, score, scrape; damage slightly. 2 *to scratch one's back:* scrape, rub, dig at; relieve the itching of. 3 *He scratched a match on his boot:* rub, scrape; strike. 4 *Scratch my name from the list:* strike out, cancel, cross out, delete, withdraw, eliminate, remove, exclude, omit, erase, rub out. 5 *to scratch a map in the dirt with a stick:* draw crudely, scrawl, scribble; incise, cut, etch. 6 *Her fingernails scratched against the blackboard:* scrape, grate, rasp. —*n.* 7 *How did you get that scratch on your nose?:* laceration, abrasion, nick.

scrawny *adj. a scrawny scarecrow:* extremely thin, spindly, skinny, spare, lean, sinewy, lank, lanky; bony, gaunt, angular, rawboned; puny, undersized, underweight, stunted, emaciated.

Ant. fat, plump, chubby, brawny.

scream *v.* 1 *She screamed when she saw the snake:* shriek, howl, cry out, wail; screech, yowl, yelp, squeal, bellow, roar. 2 *We screamed for help:* shout, yell, call out, cry out, holler. —*n.* 3 *We heard screams in the night. the scream of sirens:* loud, shrill cry; shriek, outcry, shout, yell; screech, squeal, whine, wail, yelp.

screen *n.* 1 *She changed clothes behind a screen:* partition, room divider, curtain, lattice. 2 *The fog acted as a screen for the smugglers:* concealment, protection, cover, veil, mask, curtain, cloak, mantle; safeguard, defense. 3 *a star of stage and screen:* motion pictures, movies, cinema, the silver screen, films. 4 *Close the screen or the flies will get in:* screen door, window screen, screening; jalousie, lattice. 5 *Put a screen over the drain:* strainer, sifter, filter, grate; web, mesh. —*v.* 6 *Sunglasses will screen your eyes from harmful rays:* shield, shelter, protect, guard; cover, shroud, veil; keep hidden, conceal, keep secret. 7 *to screen applicants:* evaluate, size up, rate, grade; eliminate, weed out; separate, sift, winnow, filter, strain.

scrimp *v. We scrimped for years until the house was paid for:* be sparing, skimp, be frugal, be parsimonious, stint, save, economize.

script *n.* 1 *She has a neat, precise script:*

handwriting, hand, longhand, cursive; penmanship, calligraphy. 2 *Several changes were made in the script:* manuscript, written text; scenario, libretto, score.

Scripture, Holy Scripture *n.* Often the **Scriptures, the Holy Scriptures** *The text for the sermon was a passage from Scripture:* sacred writings, holy writ, the Bible, the Gospels, Old Testament, New Testament, *Informal* The Good Book.

scrub[1] *v.* 1 *Scrub the floors:* rub, scour, swab. —*n.* 2 *She gave the floors a good scrub:* scrubbing, scouring; cleaning.

scrub[2] *n. The land was cleared of scrub:* low trees, brush, brushwood, stunted vegetation.

scrumptious *adj. a scrumptious meal:* delicious, delectable, appetizing, mouth-watering, toothsome, succulent; agreeable, enjoyable, delightful.

scruple *n. He's a greedy person with no scruples:* principle, ethics, moral restraint, compunction, conscience, scrupulousness, care; qualm, hesitation, uncertainty, doubtfulness, squeamishness, fearfulness.

scrupulous *adj. scrupulous accuracy:* having scruples, principled, honest, conscientious, honorable, upright; painstaking, careful, cautious; exact, exacting, precise, meticulous, fastidious, punctilious; dutiful.
Ant. unscrupulous, dishonest, unprincipled; careless, inexact.

scrutinize *v. The building inspector scrutinized the structure:* examine closely, study, peruse, survey; inquire into, investigate, probe.
Ant. disregard, overlook.

scrutiny *n. His testimony was given close scrutiny:* examination, attention, study, investigation, inquiry, inspection, perusal, surveillance.

scuffle *v.* 1 *The boys scuffled in the school corridor:* struggle, fight, scrap, tussle, spar, jostle; *Slang* mix it up. —*n.* 2 *The scuffle in the playground was soon over:* scrap, tussle, row, fight, brawl, fracas; rumpus.

scum *n.* 1 *Don't use the pool until the scum is cleared off:* surface, film, crust, deposit. 2 *the scum of society:* lowest of the low, trash, rubbish, dregs; riffraff, rabble.

scurrilous *adj. scurrilous remarks:* slanderous, derogatory, disparaging, detracting, derisive, contemptuous, insulting; abusive; coarse, gross, churlish, indelicate; vulgar, foulmouthed.
Ant. delicate, refined, polite.

scurry *v.* 1 *The bathers scurried across the hot sand:* move quickly, run with light steps, scamper, scramble, scuttle, rush, speed, hasten, hurry, scoot, skim, race, tear.

—*n.* 2 *We lifted the rock and watched a scurry of insects:* scamper, running; rushing, hurrying, scooting; dispersal, scattering; haste, bustle, confusion.

scuttlebutt *n. There's scuttlebutt that the factory will close:* gossip, rumor, hearsay, talk, prattle, scandal.

sea *n.* 1 *to sail the seas:* ocean, deep, main, the briny deep. 2 *Enormous seas swept over the decks:* wave, swell, roller, breaker. 3 *The manager was deluged with a sea of complaints:* multitude, slew, flood, surge, spate, scads, lots, mass, host, swarm, flock, scores, abundance, profusion.
Ant. 1 land, terra firma.

seacoast *n. a resort on the seacoast:* shore, seashore, coast, seaside, seaboard, coastline, water's edge, shoreline, beach, littoral, lido.

seal *n.* 1 *The document bore the king's seal:* emblem, mark, symbol, distinctive design, insignia, stamp, impression, imprint, brand; signet, imprimatur; hallmark, colophon. 2 *The envelope's seal was torn open:* fastening device, fastener; gummed flap. —*v.* 3 *We sealed our agreement with a handshake:* settle, conclude, make final; fix, establish, confirm, verify, ratify, validate, affirm. 4 *The jars were sealed with paraffin:* secure, fasten; shut.

seam *n.* 1 *Sew the split seams of the shirt:* line of stitches, juncture, joining, junction, joint. 2 *Seams appeared on the dried-up riverbed:* wrinkle, line, furrow, scar; fissure, chink, crevice, rupture, opening, crack, cleft, gap. 3 *The prospectors found a seam of coal:* layer, stratum, vein, lode.

seamy *adj. the seamy side of life:* unpleasant, nasty, disagreeable, sordid, rough, raw, dark, squalid.
Ant. pleasant, nice, wholesome.

sear *v. The flames seared her arm:* burn, scorch, char, singe; cauterize; blister; harden, caseharden, scar.

search *v.* 1 *We searched the attic for the old album:* examine, scrutinize, explore, scour, investigate carefully, look over, inspect, study, survey, check, probe, sift, comb, ransack, rifle, rummage; hunt, cast about, seek, quest. —*n.* 2 *A search of the apartment produced the evidence:* examination, inspection, scrutiny, study, close look, check, investigation, probe, inquiry, exploration; hunt, pursuit, quest.

season *n.* 1 *Spring is my favorite season. Peaches are out of season. the holiday season:* (variously) spring, summer, fall, autumn, winter; appropriate time, peak time, prime; period, term, interval, duration. —*v.* 2 *She seasoned the stew with sage. The* *play was seasoned with humor:* flavor, spice, lace; enliven, color, accent, enhance, embellish, ornament. **3** *The actor was seasoned by years of performing:* improve by experience, train, practice, discipline, drill; mellow, temper; accustom, inure, adapt.

seasoning *n.* **1** *This stew needs more seasoning:* flavoring, spice; condiment, relish, herb. **2** *The pitcher was sent to the minors for a year of seasoning:* training, practice, preparation, maturation; aging; drying.

seat *n.* **1** *Won't you come in and have a seat? to reserve seats at the opera: (variously)* chair, sofa, couch, divan, bench; place, box. **2** *The child received several slaps on his seat:* buttocks, rear end, hindquarters, bottom, haunches, rump, posterior, croup, derriére; backside, behind, *Slang* fanny. **3** *Hollywood is the seat of the film industry:* center, hub, nucleus; heart, core; capital. **4** *The castle was the seat of a noble family:* residence, home, house, dwelling, abode, domicile, quarters; site, location; family seat, ancestral hall. *—v.* **5** *The ushers will not seat latecomers:* show to a seat, provide with a seat; settle, situate.

secede *v. The Southern states seceded from the Union:* withdraw, leave, quit, resign, disaffiliate.

Ant. join, federate.

seclude *v. He secluded himself in order to study:* keep apart, separate, dissociate, place in solitude, isolate, shut off, sequester.

secluded *adj. a secluded cabin. a secluded life:* isolated, sequestered, cloistered; remote, out-of-the-way, solitary, withdrawn, reclusive; hidden from view, closeted.

seclusion *n. The millionaire sought seclusion to avoid interviewers:* isolation, solitude, concealment, retreat, withdrawal, sequestration; sanctuary, asylum, hideaway.

second[1] *adj.* **1** *She was second in her class:* next after the first; runner-up. **2** *They had a second house at the beach:* another, one more, additional. **3** *Every second person was chosen:* alternate, alternating, other. **4** *In beauty, the Rocky Mountains are second to none:* inferior, subordinate, surpassed, exceeded, outdone. *—n.* **5** *He was the second to be chosen:* second one; runner-up. **6** *My second will arrange the duel:* helper, assistant, aid, attendant, lieutenant; representative, deputy, delegate; substitute, alternate, proxy. *—v.* **7** *I second the nomination!:* support, endorse; back, uphold, side with, subscribe to.

second[2] *n. I'll be there in a second!:* moment, minute, instant, jiffy, trice, wink, flash.

secondary *adj.* **1** *secondary schools:* next after the first, second; following, subse-

quent, consequent, resultant. **2** *That problem is secondary:* lesser, inferior, smaller, minor, subordinate, ancillary. **3** *I need a secondary source of income:* other, alternate; subsidiary, auxiliary.

Ant. **1–3** primary, first. **1** preceding. **2** superior, major. **3** original.

second-rate *adj. a second-rate movie:* inferior, mediocre, second-best, inadequate, middling, so-so, undistinguished, pedestrian, fair-to-middling, average; cheap, shabby, low-grade.

Ant. first-class, prize, excellent.

secrecy *n. The plotters were sworn to secrecy. She wrote in secrecy:* secretiveness, silence, confidentiality, covertness, clandestineness, stealth, furtiveness, private, concealment.

secret *adj.* **1** *a secret ballot. a secret room. a secret agent:* private, confidential, unrevealable, unrevealed, undisclosed; hidden, concealed, secluded; undercover, disguised; covert, clandestine, surreptitious; unknown, mysterious. **2** *He's a secret person:* secretive, close-mouthed, tight-lipped. *—n.* **3** *Can you keep a secret?:* confidential information, confidential matter, confidence. **4** *the secrets of the sea:* mystery, enigma, puzzle. **5** *What's your secret for staying fit?:* formula, key, recipe, special method.

Ant. **1** public, revealed, obvious; undisguised; well-known. **2** candid, frank.

secrete *v. The escaped convicts secreted themselves in a cave:* hide, conceal, cache, *Informal* stash.

Ant. reveal, show.

secretive *adj. She was secretive about where she'd been:* unrevealing, uncommunicative, close-mouthed, tight-lipped, silent, mum; reserved, discreet, reticent, private, taciturn; sly, stealthy, furtive, evasive, surreptitious, mysterious, cryptic, enigmatic.

Ant. open, communicative, candid, frank, direct.

sect *n. the Mennonite sect:* religious subgroup, denomination, persuasion, religious creed; faction, splinter group.

section *n.* **1** *grapefruit sections. the middle section of the book:* part, division, segment, portion; installment, increment, measure; chapter, passage. **2** *the residential section of a city:* district, area, region; sector, zone, ward, neighborhood.

sector *n. After World War II, Berlin was divided into four sectors:* administrative division, zone, district; theater, area, sphere of action.

secular *adj. a clergyman who writes secular works:* worldly, profane, mundane, nonspiritual, nonsacred, nonreligious, earthly; lay, nonclerical, nonecclesiastical.

Ant. sacred, divine, spiritual, ecclesiastical.

secure *adj.* 1 *She felt secure only when both doors were locked:* free from danger, free from harm, safe, unthreatened, protected, defended, sheltered, out of danger; easy, at ease, composed, confident. 2 *The citadel was secure:* unattackable, unassailable, impregnable. 3 *His shackles were secure:* firmly fastened; set, fixed, tight. 4 *Your future with the company is secure:* sure, certain, assured, definite. —*v.* 5 *He secured a good location for the business:* obtain, procure, acquire, get, get possession of. 6 *The army secures us from attack:* make safe, safeguard, defend, protect, shelter. 7 *The bank required collateral to secure the loan:* ensure, guarantee. 8 *The boat was secured to the dock:* make fast, fix firmly, fasten.

Ant. 1, 4 insecure. 1 unsafe, endangered, threatened, in danger. 2 vulnerable. 3 loose. 4 unsure, uncertain; precarious. 8 unloose, untie.

security *n.* 1 *My security is of the utmost importance:* freedom from danger, freedom from harm, safety; preservation, maintenance, support, care. 2 *The airport's security requires that every passenger be searched:* defense, safeguards, safety measures, protective devices; police, guards, troops. 3 *The hostages were used by the robbers as security for escape:* assurance, guarantee, surety; pledge, bond, warranty; collateral; deposit. 4 *You can look forward to your future with security:* assurance, confidence, certainty, sureness; trust, peace of mind, reliance, faith.

sedative *adj. phenobarbital's sedative effect:* calming, relaxing, tranquilizing, soporific, narcotic; allaying, alleviating, assuasive, lenitive; anodyne, analgesic.

sedentary *adj. a sedentary job:* sitting, seated, inactive, fixed, stationary; resting, still.

sediment *n. sediment at the bottom of a coffeepot:* settlings, grounds; dregs, remains, residue; dross, debris, waste, slag, sludge.

sedition *n. He was tried for sedition:* mutiny, revolt, insurrection, insurgency, rebellion, subversion, disloyalty; rebelliousness, subversiveness.

Ant. loyalty.

seduce *v. He tried to seduce the actress:* persuade to do wrong, lure, entice, lead astray; corrupt, pervert, dishonor; win over, persuade, charm, tempt, captivate.

Ant. protect; honor; repel, repulse; disgust.

seducer *n. He may be charming but he's a*

seducer: debaucher, cad, roué, womanizer, woman chaser, skirt-chaser, lady-killer, philanderer, Don Juan, Casanova, Lothario, lover-boy.

seductive *adj. a seductive look:* alluring, enticing, tempting, sexy, provocative; attractive, charming, disarming, enchanting, bewitching, beguiling, captivating.

Ant. repulsive, repellent; prim.

see *v.* 1 *Can you see what that sign says? Did anyone see the accident? What you see is what you get!:* make out, discern, distinguish; behold, observe, witness; hold in view, have in sight, notice, look at, regard, spot, catch sight of, sight, glimpse, spy, view, eye, set eyes on. 2 *Do you see what I mean?:* perceive, understand, comprehend, apprehend, appreciate, grasp, fathom, know, realize, be aware of. 3 *I can't see you as a doctor:* visualize, envision, picture, conceive, regard, consider. 4 *Let me see what I can do:* find out, ascertain, discover, determine. 5 *The soldiers saw action:* undergo, experience, go through. 6 *See that you arrive on time!:* make sure, take care, make certain, mind. 7 *Please come to see us. I can see the job applicants tomorrow:* call on, visit; meet, encounter, run into; speak to, consult, confer with; receive, attend to, entertain, listen to, interview. 8 *How long have you two been seeing each other?:* date, court, woo; keep company with. 9 *Maria always sees me to the door:* escort, accompany, attend.

Ant. 1 overlook, ignore. 2 misunderstand, be unaware of.

seed *n.* 1 *to plant marigold seeds:* grain, pit, stone, ovule; seedling. 2 *A good teacher can plant the seeds of knowledge in students:* source, origin, basis, germ, embryo, beginning. —*v.* 3 *I'm seeding my land with grass:* sow with seed, plant. 4 *Seed the cherries:* pit.

seek *v.* 1 *The police seek information as to his whereabouts:* try to find, search for, look for; investigate, examine, pursue, be after, hunt. 2 *to seek fame and fortune. My lawyers are seeking a new trial:* try to obtain, strive for, aim for, aspire to; pursue, be after; request, petition for, call for; solicit, invite. 3 *We sought to change her mind:* try, attempt, endeavor, undertake.

Ant. 1 abandon; avoid, shun.

seem *v. You seem happy:* appear, look, give the impression of being, look like, look as if.

seeming *adj. Her seeming indifference was only an act:* ostensible, apparent, evident, obvious; presumed, supposed.

seemly *adj. to behave in a seemly manner:* suitable, proper, appropriate, fitting, becoming, befitting, acceptable, correct, polite, courteous, decorous, decent.

Ant. unseemly, unbecoming, improper, rude, impolite.

seep *v. Rain seeped through the roof:* leak, ooze, trickle, dribble, drip; suffuse, diffuse, permeate, soak.

seer *n. The seer predicted a long war:* prophet, sage, oracle, soothsayer, astrologer, stargazer, fortuneteller, augur, clairvoyant, sorcerer, sorceress.

seethe *v.* 1 *The water was seething:* boil, bubble, churn, roil; simmer, brew. 2 *She seethed at the criticism:* be agitated, be upset, be irate, be livid, be angry, be indignant, rage, rant, rave, boil, storm, fume, smolder.

segregate *v. If the two groups fight, segregate them:* separate, isolate, divide, disunite; keep apart, set apart, set aside, sort out; quarantine.

Ant. desegregate, integrate.

seize *v.* 1 *He seized my purse and ran. The military junta seized power:* take hold of, take possession of, grab, snatch, pluck, grasp, clutch, embrace; acquire by force; usurp, commandeer; confiscate, appropriate. 2 *She was quick to seize the meaning of my words:* grasp, comprehend, apprehend, understand, catch, glean. 3 *Uncontrollable laughter seized us:* overwhelm, overpower; possess. 4 *The escaped convict was seized:* capture, arrest, apprehend, take into custody, take captive; catch, nab. 5 *Seize every opportunity to succeed:* take advantage of, make use of, utilize.

Ant. 1, 4 let go of, release; free, liberate. 5 waste, pass up.

seizure *n.* 1 *the seizure of a criminal:* act of seizing, taking, grasping; capture, apprehension, arrest; snatching, usurpation; possession, appropriation, confiscation; commandeering, kidnapping. 2 *After his seizure, he needed round-the-clock care:* attack, convulsion, fit, stroke; throe, paroxysm, spell.

seldom *adv. I seldom dance:* rarely, not often, not frequently, infrequently; hardly ever, now and then, sporadically, occasionally, once in a great while.

Ant. often, frequently, always.

select *v.* 1 *I select this one:* choose, pick, pick out, make one's choice; decide for, elect, single out, opt for, prefer. *—adj.* 2 *Only a select few were invited:* choice, picked, privileged, chosen. 3 *a select hotel:* superior, first-rate, first-class, choice, preferred; exclusive.

Ant. 1 reject, refuse, spurn. 2 indiscriminate; random. 3 inferior, second-rate; ordinary, undistinguished.

selection *n.* 1 *I made my selection:* choice, choosing, preference, pick, option. 2 *a selection of winter clothes:* variety, choice, range, option. 3 *The band played a selection of popular tunes:* selected number; collection, medley, miscellany, potpourri.

selective *adj. Learn to be a selective customer:* choosy, choosing carefully, discerning, discriminating, particular, picky.

Ant. unselective, promiscuous, indiscriminate.

self-assured *adj. He was self-assured and bound to succeed:* confident, self-confident; cocky, brash.

Ant. self-doubting, insecure.

self-centered *adj. A self-centered person isn't concerned with the needs of others:* selfish, self-seeking, self-absorbed, self-important; egotistic, egoistic, egocentric; conceited, vain.

self-confidence *n. Repeated failure destroyed her self-confidence:* self-assurance, positive self-image, resolution, spirit; cockiness.

self-consciousness *n. Her self-consciousness made it difficult for her to make friends:* shyness, timidity, bashfulness, diffidence, fearfulness, self-effacement, sheepishness.

Ant. assurance, self-confidence.

self-control *n. Try to maintain self-control when you're angry:* self-discipline, willpower, composure, self-restraint, presence of mind, stability, coolheadedness, poise, unexcitability, imperturbability, patience, temperance, forbearance.

self-esteem *n. You need self-esteem in order to succeed:* pride, self-respect, self-confidence, self-assurance, pride.

Ant. self-effacement, self-loathing, abjectness.

self-evident *adj. The difference is self-evident:* obvious, plain, evident, manifest, apparent, glaring, self-explanatory, explicit.

Ant. doubtful, questionable, arguable.

selfish *adj. A selfish person refuses to share:* self-seeking, self-concerned, self-centered, egocentric; greedy, avaricious, covetous, uncharitable, ungenerous.

Ant. unselfish, selfless, giving; altruistic.

self-reliant *adj. You must learn to be self-reliant:* independent, self-confident, self-sufficient; enterprising, resolute.

self-righteous *adj. Don't give me any of your self-righteous lectures!:* sanctimonious, smug, complacent, pompous, pious, moralizing, pretentious.

self-satisfied *adj. He's so self-satisfied he has no interest in improving:* complacent, smug, overproud, cocksure, self-righteous.

sell *v.* 1 *We sold the house:* give up for a

price, exchange for money; dispose of. **2** *I sell vacuum cleaners:* deal in, trade in, offer for sale; vend, market, peddle, hawk. **3** *We tried to sell her on our plan:* win over, persuade to buy, persuade to accept, convince, prevail upon. **4** *He sold his country for a promise of power:* betray, sell out, deliver up, take a bribe for, play false, deceive.

semblance *n. Let's try to maintain some semblance of order:* outward appearance, aspect, likeness, look, show, pretense.

send *v.* **1** *Send this package by messenger:* cause to go, transport, transmit, dispatch, relay, forward, convey; broadcast, disseminate. **2** *We sent them to the right address:* direct, refer, point the way to, guide, show, lead, head, conduct.

Ant. **1** hold, keep, retain; receive, get.

senior *adj.* **1** *Mr. Gray is a senior officer in this bank:* superior, higher in rank; above, over; of long tenure, veteran; older, elder. —*n.* **2** *My sister is the senior of the two of us:* older, elder. **3** *The vice-president is my senior:* person of higher rank, superior, higher-up, chief, head.

Ant. **1–3** junior. **1** younger, subordinate. **3** subordinate, inferior.

seniority *n. He became committee chairman by virtue of his seniority:* precedence, longer service, tenure; superiority in rank; greater age.

sensation *n.* **1** *I have no sensation in my leg:* feeling, sensitivity, perceptivity, responsiveness. **2** *I have a dizzy sensation:* impression, sense, perception, feeling. **3** *The president's divorce caused a sensation:* public excitement, uproar, stir, commotion; thrill, agitation; cause of excitement; scandal.

sensational *adj.* **1** *a sensational feat of daring:* outstanding, striking, spectacular, extraordinary, exceptional; exciting, thrilling, dramatic; excellent, superb. **2** *She read a sensational novel:* shocking, exaggerated, extravagant, lurid, cheap, scandalous, titillating.

Ant. **1** ordinary, common, everyday, routine.

sense *n.* **1** *the sense of touch:* faculty, function, sensation. **2** *a sense of well-being:* impression, feeling, sensation, realization, awareness, recognition, consciousness. **3** *a keen sense of beauty:* appreciation, understanding, intuition. **4** *She has good sense:* mental ability, judgment, reason, mind, understanding, wisdom, intelligence, reasonableness. **5** *There's no sense in worrying:* value, worth, use, good, point, benefit, purpose. **6** *A sense of impending doom overwhelmed us:* impression, awareness, in-

tuition, premonition, presentiment; aura, atmosphere. **7** *Can you make any sense of this?:* meaning, signification; connotation, denotation, definition. —*v.* **8** *She was quick to sense my difficulty:* grasp, understand, apprehend, comprehend, see, perceive, discern, be aware of, realize, feel; recognize, detect. **9** *We sensed that something was wrong:* have a vague impression, feel, suspect, divine, guess.

Ant. **4** stupidity, folly. **8** misunderstand; overlook, miss.

senseless *adj.* **1** *The blow left me senseless:* unconscious, without sensation, insensible, insensate; comatose, numb; knocked out; stunned. **2** *Quitting your job would be senseless:* useless, meaningless, purposeless; stupid, foolish, foolhardy, silly, nonsensical, irrational, unreasonable, unwise, dumb, illogical, meaningless, pointless.

Ant. **1** conscious. **2** useful, meaningful, worthwhile; sensible, smart, intelligent, wise; sound, logical.

sensibility *n.* **1** *We study the sensibility of plants to light and heat:* ability to perceive, responsiveness, sensitiveness, sensitivity, perception. **2** *He has the sensibility of a painter:* artistic responsiveness, esthetic judgment, refined taste; emotional makeup, temperament.

Ant. **1** insensibility, insensitivity.

sensible *adj.* **1** *a sensible approach to the problem:* sound, intelligent, thoughtful, wise, sagacious; discerning, discriminating, prudent, discreet, judicious, just; well-grounded, logical, rational, reasonable, sane. **2** *There was a sensible antipathy between them:* perceptible, noticeable, discernible; detectable, apparent, evident, obvious.

Ant. **1** unsound, unintelligent, unwise, foolish, senseless; indiscreet, injudicious; illogical, irrational, unreasonable. **2** undetectable, unnoticeable, invisible.

sensitive *adj.* **1** *The tips of the fingers are particularly sensitive:* responsive, perceptive, sentient, sensing. **2** *Don't be so sensitive, I was only joking:* easily affected, easily offended, touchy, thin-skinned, susceptible; perceptive, keen, acute. **3** *The cardiograph is a sensitive machine:* detecting slight change, accurate, precise, exact. **4** *That bruise is still sensitive:* sore, tender, painful.

Ant. **2** tough, thick-skinned, callous.

sensual *adj. sensual pleasures:* erotic, carnal, lustful, licentious, sexy; earthy, fleshly, pleasure-loving, hedonistic.

sentiment *n.* **1** Often **sentiments** *We share the same sentiments:* opinion, attitude, point of view, viewpoint, feeling,

thought, notion, idea. 2 *Resisting sentiment,
she threw out all her old letters:* feeling, emotion, sentimentality, nostalgia, tenderness,
softheartedness, emotionalism.

sentimental *adj.* 1 *sentimental songs:* emotional, mawkish, romantic, melodramatic,
romanticized; *Informal* mushy. 2 *She gets
sentimental when she thinks of her childhood:* emotional, nostalgic; tearful, maudlin.

sentimentality *n. Authors who prolong
death scenes are guilty of sentimentality:*
emotionalism, mawkishness, sentimentalism, pathos, bathos, mush.

sentinel *n. A sentinel stood in front of the
gate:* sentry, guard, lookout, watchman,
picket, scout, guardsman.

separate *v.* 1 *A fence separates the farms.
Separate the orange into sections:* keep
apart, divide, come between, split, partition;
subdivide, detach, sunder, bisect, part.
2 *Separate the white clothes from the dark
clothes before laundering:* set apart, segregate; sort out, remove; distinguish. 3 *We
separated after ten years of marriage. Bear
left when the road separates:* go separate
ways, divorce, split up; branch, diverge,
part, split, bifurcate, fork. 4 *The cake separates easily in one's fingers:* come apart,
break away, break apart; crack, split, crumble. —*adj.* 5 *The offices consisted of four
separate rooms:* not joined, not connected,
detached; not shared, single, individual, distinct, discrete; different, diverse, dissimilar.
6 *The two divisions form separate corporate
entities:* independent, autonomous.

Ant. 1 join, attach, link, unite. 2 combine,
mix, integrate, consolidate. 3 meet, merge.
5 joined, connected; alike, similar. 6 affiliated, interdependent.

separation *n.* 1 *the separation of chaff from
wheat. the separation of church and state:*
separating, division, disjunction, disunion,
disconnection, disengagement, divorce, detachment, disassociation; sorting, removal,
segregation. 2 *Their separation at the station was emotional. A separation appeared
in the dam:* parting, farewell, good-bye; divergence, branching; estrangement, divorce; breach, break, split, schism, gap,
space, opening, distance, interval. 3 *Fifth
Avenue is the separation between the east
and west sides of Manhattan:* partition,
boundary, divider; branching, fork, bifurcation.

sepulcher *n. Thousands of pilgrims visited
the sepulcher of the saint:* tomb, crypt, vault,
ossuary, reliquary; mausoleum, cenotaph.

sequel *n. As a sequel to the story, they met
again 20 years later!:* continuation, follow-
up; subsequent event, aftermath, upshot,

offshoot; epilogue, addendum; culmination;
consequence, result, outcome.

sequence *n. a strange sequence of events:*
progression, order, succession, series;
course, train, string, chain.

serene *adj. She was serene even in emergen-
cies:* calm, tranquil, peaceful, untroubled,
unruffled, unperturbed, placid, composed,
unexcitable, unimpassioned, poised; quiet,
still.

Ant. agitated; excitable.

serenity *n. She wanted a life of serenity:*
calmness, tranquillity, peacefulness, composure, equanimity.

series *n. a series of violent storms:* succession, progression, sequence, order, procession; set, course, chain, string, parade.

serious *adj.* 1 *He had a serious look on his
face:* thoughtful, pensive, grave, solemn,
somber; sedate, staid; grim, sad, dejected,
downcast. 2 *Are you serious about becoming an actor?:* sincere, earnest, not joking,
not trifling, determined, decided, resolved.
3 *Buying a house is a serious matter:* important, consequential, far-reaching, momentous, weighty, crucial; fateful, portentous.
4 *There's been a serious accident:* dangerous, perilous, harmful, critical, severe, bad;
incapacitating, crippling.

Ant. 1 thoughtless, careless; happy, jolly,
frivolous. 2 insincere, joking, trifling.
3 unimportant, insignificant, trivial. 4
slight, minor.

sermon *n.* 1 *The bishop preached the sermon:* speech containing religious instruction, preaching, preachment; exhortation.
2 *Don't give me a sermon on punctuality
just because I'm five minutes late:* lecture,
harangue, tirade; reproof, admonition, rebuke; dressing-down, diatribe.

serpent *n.* 1 *The goddess is shown holding
a serpent:* snake, viper, reptile. 2 *Don't trust
that serpent:* traitor, deceiver, double-
dealer; rogue, snake, snake in the grass;
devil, the Devil, Satan.

serpentine *adj. a serpentine road:* twisting,
winding, meandering, coiling, zigzag,
crooked; mazy, labyrinthine; convoluted,
sinuous; undulating.

servant *n.* 1 *The millionaire had a staff of
servants:* domestic; *(variously)* maid, valet,
cook, butler, hired girl, household help,
help, hired help. 2 *a public servant:* public
employee, public official.

serve *v.* 1 *How may we serve you?:* be of help
to, assist, minister, tend, supply, provide
for, aid, help, further, attend, wait on; take
care of, be of use. 2 *He will serve as mayor.
The convict has to serve the sentence:* work,
act, perform, do duty, hold an office, fill a

post, officiate; go through, carry out, complete. **3** *Dinner will be served now:* provide for customers or guests; supply with food, set food on a table. **4** *This light dinner will serve me:* content, satisfy, suit, suffice, do. **5** *The table will serve as a desk:* act, be of use, be used, function; avail. **6** *The lawyer arrived to serve a writ:* deliver, present, hand over.
Ant. **1** command, order; obstruct, hinder, oppose. **4** be insufficient for; dissatisfy.

service *n.* **1** Sometimes **services** *May I be of service? Your services are no longer required:* labor, effort, ministration, attendance, assistance, help, aid; benefit, advantage, usefulness, use, profit, avail; employment, employ. **2** *Bus service is free in some cities:* use, provision, system, accommodation, facility, utility, convenience. **3** *the health service:* department, agency, bureau. **4** *He was in the service during World War II:* armed forces, military. **5** *There's good money in TV service:* repair, servicing, maintenance. **6** *The service in this restaurant is excellent:* attendance, waiting, accommodation, order-filling. **7** Often **services** *The dentist sent a bill for services:* professional work, treatment. **8** *a church service:* ritual, ceremony, ceremonial, rite, celebration, observance. —*v.* **9** *to service a car:* repair, maintain, adjust, mend. **10** *That power company services the southeast:* supply, serve.

serviceable *adj. The old coat is still serviceable:* usable, useful, utilitarian, functional, effective, operative, workable, practical.

servile *adj.* **1** *a servile attendant:* slavish, submissive, fawning, unctuous, obsequious, truckling, toadying, sycophantic, scraping, groveling. **2** *servile labor:* befitting a slave, menial; abject, slavish, subservient, humble.
Ant. **1** commanding, overbearing, haughty.

servitude *n. to free a slave from servitude:* slavery, serfdom, enthrallment, bondage, subjugation, enslavement; compulsory service, hard labor, imprisonment.
Ant. freedom, emancipation.

session *n.* **1** *Where was the first session of the U.N. General Assembly?:* meeting, sitting, conference, convention, assembly. **2** *to enroll for the spring session:* period, term, semester; round, bout.

set *v.* **1** *Set the package on the table:* put, place, position, lay. **2** *Set the timer for 20 minutes. Set the table:* fix, adjust, regulate, calibrate; prepare, order, arrange, line up, align. **3** *Let the pudding set:* harden, solidify, gel, congeal, thicken. **4** *What time does

the sun set?: sink, pass below the horizon. **5** *I can't set a value on friendship:* place, assign, establish, assess, attach, rate. **6** *Detectives were set at all the exits:* post, station, situate, install, assign. **7** *Let's set the time of the meeting:* decide upon, settle, fix, determine, establish, make. **8** *The play is set in Venice:* locate, represent. **9** *The jeweler set diamonds in the bracelet:* fix, mount, imbed. **10** *The composer set a prayer to music:* fit, arrange, adapt; style. **11** *The hunters set the dogs on the fox:* urge to attack, release, unleash; sic. —*n.* **12** *The set of his chin suggested tenacity:* carriage, bearing, cut, line, profile; firmness, rigidity. **13** *Alice wants a chess set for Christmas:* group, collection, assortment, array, suit, outfit, kit, service. **14** *the fashionable set:* group, crowd, clique, faction, coterie, bunch. **15** *a television set:* apparatus, assembly, machine, complex. **16** *a movie set:* scenery, scene, setting, backdrop; sound stage, studio; locale, location. —*adj.* **17** *We have a set date for Tuesday:* definite, fixed, decided, firm, settled, prearranged, agreed upon. **18** *She has a set routine:* established, usual, customary, accustomed; stock, routine, regular, habitual, familiar. **19** *We're set for the picnic:* arranged; ready, prepared. **20** *I'm set in my ways:* steadfast, immovable, rigid, inflexible.
Ant. **1** remove, lift, pick up. **3** melt, soften. **4** rise. **7** change. **9** remove, extract. **17** tentative, vague. **18** impromptu; irregular. **19** unprepared. **20** flexible, adaptable.

setback *n. After a number of setbacks the business began to show a profit:* reversal, disappointment, misfortune, reverse, adversity, defeat; relapse, regression; failure, mishap.
Ant. advance, gain, success.

settle *v.* **1** *Let's settle on a time for the meeting:* decide, agree, fix, choose, set, determine, establish. **2** *Let's settle matters between us once and for all:* put in order, dispose, arrange; reconcile, resolve, straighten out, rectify, put to rest. **3** *to settle one's account:* pay, discharge, clear, satisfy. **4** *The Pilgrims settled in Massachusetts:* move to, locate, situate; colonize; take root, inhabit, make one's home. **5** *The sedative settled her nerves:* calm, soothe, quiet, compose, allay, pacify. **6** *Bits of cork settled in the wine bottle:* deposit dregs, descend gradually, collect at the bottom, precipitate. **7** *The house is settling:* sink, drop, droop, sag, find one's level. **8** *The bird settled on a branch:* come to rest; land, alight, light.
Ant. **4** wander; emigrate. **5** agitate, excite, roil. **7** rise, ascend.

settlement *n.* 1 *After the settlement of our differences, we became friends:* adjustment, arrangement, reconciliation, resolution, working out. 2 *the first permanent settlement in North America:* colonizing, colonization, community of settlers, colony; encampment, camp, post, outpost; village, hamlet. 3 *the settlement of a debt:* payment, satisfaction, liquidation, discharge, clearing; adjustment, compensation; bequest.

settler *n.* *Early settlers had a difficult life:* homesteader, pioneer, frontiersman; colonist.

sever *v.* 1 *His arm was severed in the accident:* cut in two, cut off, separate, part, amputate, dismember, disconnect, lop off, bisect, cleave, split. 2 *to sever family ties:* discontinue, dissolve, put an end to, terminate, split up, break off, rupture.
Ant. 1 unite, join. 2 keep, maintain.

several *adj.* 1 *We received several replies to our inquiry:* more than two, some, a number of, a few, diverse. 2 *They all had their several duties to perform:* separate, different, distinct, peculiar; individual, respective, own, particular, specific, special, distinctive; assorted, sundry. —*n.* 3 *There are several here that I don't know:* several persons or things, a few, a number.
Ant. 2 joint, combined, communal.

severe *adj.* 1 *severe punishment:* strict, harsh, rigorous, taxing, vigorous; cruel, brutal, merciless, unsparing; drastic. 2 *The general had a severe manner:* serious, stern, dour, strait-laced, grave, sober, grim, somber, austere, forbidding, cold. 3 *a severe storm:* intense, violent, extreme, unrelenting, raging, furious, fierce. 4 *a severe illness:* serious, painful, dangerous, distressing, difficult.
Ant. 1 gentle, lenient, mild, moderate; easy. 2 affable, genial. 3 gentle, mild.

sex *n.* 1 *What sex is the baby?:* gender, sexual classification, sexual identity. 2 *"The birds and the bees" is a euphemism for "sex":* sexuality, generation, reproduction, procreation; sexual urge, libido, Eros; sexual intercourse, lovemaking, coitus, coition, copulation.

sexual *adj.* *the sexual organs. sexual behavior:* genital, generative, reproductive, procreative, venereal, copulatory, sex, coital; marital, conjugal, intimate; erotic, sexy, amatory, sensual, libidinous.

sexy *adj.* *The singer wiggled in a sexy way:* erotic, lewd, voluptuous, provocative, prurient, suggestive, seductive.

shabby *adj.* 1 *shabby clothes. a house grown old and shabby:* worn, ragged, raggy, threadbare, frayed, ratty, tatty; deteriorated, decaying, dilapidated, broken-down, ramshackle, tumbledown, rundown, seedy. 2 *a shabby beggar:* slovenly, ragged, wearing worn clothes, ill-dressed; dirty, scruffy, ratty, tatty. 3 *We received shabby treatment:* unfair; contemptible, ignoble; inferior, ungenerous, poor.
Ant. 1 pristine, new, neat, well-kept. 2 well-dressed, fashionable, chic, dapper. 3 considerate, honorable; generous.

shackle *n.* 1 *Shackles were placed on the prisoner:* fetter, irons, chains, bonds; handcuffs, cuffs, manacle. —*v.* 2 *Shackle the captives:* fetter, chain, manacle, handcuff, cuff, bind. 3 *Lack of money shackled our plans:* restrict, thwart, block, hamper, hobble, hinder, frustrate, foil, limit, curb, check, circumscribe, forestall, deter.
Ant. 2 unshackle, unchain; free. 3 aid, help, foster, further.

shade *n.* *a lighter shade of blue:* hue, tone, tint, color, cast. 2 *There's only a shade of difference between the two:* small degree, trace, tinge, touch, bit, whit, jot, iota, modicum; suggestion, hint.
Ant. 2 great amount, full measure, abundance, heap.

shadow *n.* 1 *beyond the shadow of a doubt:* trace, shade, bit, touch, tinge; suggestion, whisper, hint. 2 *The scandal left a shadow on my reputation:* threat, specter, cloud; dark spot, blight, taint, blot, blemish, smirch, smear, stain. —*v.* 3 *Detectives shadowed the suspect:* follow, tail, trail.

shady *adj.* 1 *It's cooler in the shady part of the yard:* shaded, shadowy. 2 *a shady character:* disreputable, questionable, suspicious, fishy, unethical, dishonest, crooked, devious, underhanded, untrustworthy.
Ant. 1 sunny, unshaded. 2 honest, honorable, ethical, aboveboard, reputable.

shaft *n.* 1 *Grasp the knife by the shaft:* handle, shank, hilt; spindle, trunk, stalk, stem. 2 *The archers sent their shafts through the air: (variously)* arrow, dart, spear, lance. 3 *A shaft of light came through the window:* ray, beam, streak, gleam, patch. 5 *The Washington Monument is a marble shaft:* column, tower, obelisk, pillar, pilaster; minaret, spire, steeple. 6 *a mine shaft. an elevator shaft:* excavation, pit, chasm, well, abyss; duct, vent, flue, conduit.

shaggy *adj.* *a shaggy dog. a shaggy rug:* hairy, long-haired, hirsute, unshorn, bushy, fuzzy, woolly; downy, tufted, nappy, piled.
Ant. short-haired, close-cropped; flatwoven.

shake *v.* 1 *The house shakes when a train goes by. Shake the medicine well:* vibrate, quiver, quake, quaver, totter, wobble, sway, tremble, shudder, shiver, flutter, flicker, jiggle, juggle, jostle; agitate, mix. 2 *Don't shake your fist at me!:* wave, brandish, flourish. 3 *The news shook the town:* disturb, distress, unnerve, perturb; jar, jolt, unsettle, discompose, disquiet, ruffle, frighten; stagger, move, touch, affect, stir. 4 *The thief managed to shake the police:* escape from, get away from, elude; get rid of, rid oneself of, throw off. —*n.* 5 *Give the bottle a couple of shakes:* jiggle, bounce, jounce, flourish. 6 *The shake of the speaker's hands betrayed his nervousness:* trembling, tremble, shaking, shudder, quiver, quivering, quake, quaking, flutter, fluttering, shiver, shivering, jerk, twitch.

Ant. 3 calm, quiet, soothe, reassure. 6 steadiness.

shaky *adj.* 1 *Get down off that shaky ladder:* unsteady, trembling, shaking, quivering, wobbly, tottering, teetery, teetering, unstable; hazardous, precarious; nervous, jumpy, jittery, fidgety. 2 *His determination seems shaky:* wavering, uncertain, unsure, dubious, unreliable, undependable, inconstant, vacillating, faltering, irresolute, hesitant.

sham *n.* 1 *Her illness was a sham to gain sympathy:* fraud, fake, pretense, trick; imitation, counterfeit, forgery, put-on. —*adj.* 2 *The child's sham weeping fooled no one:* feigned, fraudulent, fake, pretended, phony, false, make-believe, put-on; counterfeit, bogus, imitation, artificial, synthetic, simulated, spurious. —*v.* 3 *to sham tears:* pretend, feign, fake, simulate, put on, act, imitate, affect, assume.

Ant. 2 real, genuine, authentic; unfeigned, unpretended.

shame *n.* 1 *The student felt shame at having flunked:* guilt, remorse, embarrassment, mortification, chagrin, shamefacedness. 2 *He brought shame to his family:* disgrace, dishonor, ignominy, humiliation, mortification, disrepute, odium. 3 *The way you act is a shame:* disgrace, scandal, stigma. 4 *What a shame that it rained the day of the picnic:* disappointment, regretful thing, sorrowful happening. —*v.* 5 *The class's behavior shamed the teacher:* embarrass, humiliate, mortify; disgrace, humble.

Ant. 1 pride, glory. 2 honor, credit, glory, esteem. 5 do credit to, make proud.

shamefaced *adj. She was shamefaced after failing the exam:* ashamed, embarrassed, chagrined, mortified, humiliated; sheepish, abashed, blushing, red-faced.

Ant. proud, unashamed, unabashed.

shameful *adj. What a shameful thing to do!:* disgraceful, dishonorable, shameless, contemptible, ignoble, ignominious, shocking,

outrageous, despicable, deplorable, reprehensible; vile, base, mean, low, iniquitous, heinous.

Ant. glorious, noble, praiseworthy, decent, admirable, commendable, meritorious.

shameless *adj.* 1 *a shameless exhibitionist:* without shame, disgraceful, dishonorable; abandoned, dissolute, immodest, wanton, immoral, indecent, indecorous. 2 *He's a shameless liar:* brazen, impudent, brash, boldfaced, barefaced, unblushing, unabashed, unreserved, flagrant.

shape *n.* 1 *The shape of Italy resembles a boot:* outline, contour, figure, silhouette, profile, conformation, configuration; form, build, physique. 2 *Put those files in shape:* order, array, orderly arrangement. 3 *He's in good shape for a man of his age:* condition, physical condition, health, fettle. —*v.* 4 *The potter shaped the clay into a vase:* form, mold, model, fashion, frame; make, create, build, construct, develop.

Ant. 2 disorder, disarray, confusion, chaos.

share *n.* 1 *George's share of the inheritance was $40,000:* part, portion, allotment, apportionment, allowance, quota, percent, percentage, *Informal* cut. —*v.* 2 *Three doctors share the office:* use jointly, receive together. 3 *Share the candy with your brother:* divide and give out, split, apportion; dole, allot, allocate, deal out, measure out, mete out.

sharp *adj.* 1 *a sharp axe. the sharp end of a peg:* keen-edged, fine-edged, fine, razor-sharp; pointed, pointy, piked; edged, cutting. 2 *a sharp drop in temperature. a sharp pain:* sudden, abrupt, precipitous, rapid; distinct, clear; extreme, acute, fierce, violent, keen, severe, intense, drastic, marked, immoderate, inordinate. 3 *a sharp voice:* shrill, piercing, harsh, raucous, strident; high, high-pitched, high-toned. 4 *sharp eyes. a sharp mind:* keen, acute, perceptive, quick; shrewd, astute, clever, alert. 5 *sharp business dealings:* wily, crafty, cunning, sly, artful, calculating, conniving, contriving; unscrupulous, unprincipled, unethical, tricky. 6 *The men exchanged sharp words:* angry, harsh, scathing, unkind, spiteful, bitter, cutting, stinging; cruel, severe, vitriolic, rancorous; abrupt, gruff, brusque, curt. —*adv.* 7 *Look sharp!:* sharply, keenly, acutely, alertly, quickly, closely, attentively. 8 *It's eight o'clock sharp:* promptly, punctually, on the dot, precisely, exactly.

Ant. 1 dull, blunt; rounded. 2 slow, gradual; moderate. 3 soft, mellow, well-modulated, low. 4 dull, slow; unperceptive, uncomprehending. 5 straightforward, aboveboard, guileless, artless; ethical, honest. 6 kind, tender, soothing; friendly, loving.

shatter v. 1 *The plate shattered:* break into pieces, smash; burst, explode, splinter, crumble, pulverize; break, crack, fracture, split. 2 *Bad grades shattered her chances for a scholarship:* destroy, wreck, ruin, devastate, squash, quash, spoil, upset.
Ant. 2 increase, improve, enhance.

sheath n. *a dagger in its sheath:* scabbard; covering, sheathing, wrapper, wrapping, envelope, case, casing; membrane, skin, capsule, pod.

shed v. 1 *Don't shed any tears over that scoundrel. Can anyone shed some light on the situation?:* spill, pour forth, give forth, emit, radiate, exude, discharge, cast, strew, disperse, disseminate. 2 *Trees shed their leaves in autumn. An angora cat sheds more than a Siamese:* cast off, let fall, slough; lose hair; molt.

sheen n. *the sheen of satin:* luster, gloss, shine, glaze, polish, shininess, gleam, shimmer, glossiness, glint, glitter, glister, brightness, radiance, burnish, glow.

sheepish adj. 1 *The sheepish mob followed the leader:* easily led, submissive, passive, docile, tractable, unassertive, obeisant, obedient, servile, subservient. 2 *They offered a sheepish apology:* embarrassed, abashed, shamefaced, ashamed, hangdog, chastened, chagrined, mortified; timorous, fearful, bashful, shy, timid, meek, humble.
Ant. 1 aggressive, strident, assertive, independent; willful; disobedient, intractable. 2 brazen, brash, bold faced, audacious, bold.

sheer adj. 1 *These curtains are too sheer:* transparent, thin, fine, diaphanous, gossamer, gauzy, filmy. 2 *cries of sheer delight:* unmixed, unadulterated, pure, unalloyed; absolute, utter, total, complete, unlimited, unbounded, unrestrained, unmitigated. 3 *The mountain was too sheer to climb:* steep, vertical, perpendicular, abrupt, precipitous.
Ant. 1 opaque; thick, coarse. 2 partial, incomplete; mitigated, qualified, limited. 3 gradual, gentle; horizontal.

sheet n. 1 *A sheet of frost covered the windshield:* coating, coat, layer, covering, blanket, film. 2 *a sheet of paper:* square, rectangle, slab, panel, leaf, piece, plate.

shell n. 1 *a turtle shell. a peanut shell:* carapace; hull, husk, shuck, pod. 2 *Only the shell of the building stood:* framework, skeleton, hulk. 3 *Shells burst over the enemy camp:* artillery shell, cartridge shell; cartridge, bullet, round; cannon shell, bomb. —v. 4 *Please shell some walnuts:* hull, husk, shuck. 5 *Cannons shelled the fort:* fire on, bombard, rain shells on, pound.

shelter n. 1 *The hut was a poor shelter from*

the storm: cover, protection, refuge, haven, asylum, sanctuary. 2 *Most of our money goes for food and shelter:* housing, lodging, quarters, dwelling place, a roof over one's head. —v. 3 *The hut sheltered us from the rain. My ancestors sheltered runaway slaves during the Civil War:* protect, shield, cover; harbor, take in, house, lodge.

shelve v. *The committee decided to shelve the project:* lay aside, put aside, set aside, postpone, put off, defer, table.
Ant. activate, reactivate, revive.

shepherd n. 1 *The shepherd tended the flock:* sheepherder, herder, herdsman. 2 *The Lord is my shepherd:* protector, guardian, defender, keeper, provider. —v. 3 *The guide shepherded the tourists through the Louvre:* tend, herd; guide, lead, direct, show, escort.

shield n. 1 *The sword glanced off the knight's shield:* (variously) buckler, aegis, escutcheon. 2 *The policeman flashed his shield:* badge, emblem, medallion, ensign, insignia. 3 *Dark glasses are a shield against glare:* protection, guard, safeguard, defense; buffer, screen. —v. 4 *The motor is shielded in a shockproof housing:* protect, guard, safeguard, secure, keep safe, shelter; house; screen, cover.
Ant. 3 danger, risk, hazard. 4 expose, lay bare, uncover; endanger, imperil, risk, hazard.

shift v. 1 *Shift the sofa to face the door:* move, transfer; switch, reposition, transpose, change, exchange, interchange. —n. 2 *a shift in the wind:* change, shifting, alteration, modification, deviation, fluctuation; move, switch, veering, swerve.

shiftless adj. *They dismissed the shiftless worker:* lazy, idle, inactive, lackadaisical; slothful, indolent, good-for-nothing.
Ant. ambitious, energetic, industrious.

shifty adj. *a shifty character:* crafty, cunning, wily, scheming, contriving, conniving, sneaky, slippery, tricky, deceitful; untrustworthy, dishonest.
Ant. artless, guileless; reliable, dependable, trustworthy.

shilly-shally v. *Stop shilly-shallying and make up your mind!:* waver, vacillate, procrastinate, hesitate, stall, hem and haw, dillydally.

shimmer v. 1 *A light shimmered in the distance:* glimmer, twinkle, flicker, flash, blink, sparkle, glisten; gleam, glow, shine, beam; quiver, quake, shiver, waver. —n. 2 *the shimmer of a distant star:* twinkle, glimmer, flickering, blinking, glimmering, wavering.

shine v. 1 *The diamond shone brightly:* emit light, reflect light; gleam, glow, beam, spar-

kle, shimmer, glitter, glisten, flash. 2 *Shine the silver:* polish, gloss, buff, burnish, brighten. —*n.* 3 *We saw the shine of the flashlight:* light, illumination, gleam, glow, beam, glare, glint, glitter, glimmer, sparkle, shimmer, twinkle, flash, luminosity, luminousness, incandescence. 4 *Give these shoes a shine:* gloss, luster, sheen, brightness, radiance, brilliance; polish, polishing, shining, waxing, buffing, burnishing.
Ant. 2 dull, darken; tarnish. 4 dullness; tarnish.

shiny *adj. a shiny new penny:* bright, brilliant, shining, gleaming, glistening, shimmering, sparkling, glittering, luminous, radiant, lustrous, glowing, glaring, incandescent; polished, burnished, glossy.

shirk *v. Don't shirk your responsibilities:* avoid, evade, shun, duck, shrink from, dodge, elude, ignore, neglect.
Ant. meet, fulfill, perform, do, honor.

shiver *v.* 1 *to shiver from the cold:* shake, tremble, shudder, quiver, quaver, shimmy, quake. —*n.* 2 *A shiver of fear ran through me:* tremble, shudder, quiver, quaver.

shock[1] *n.* 1 *The shock of the earthquake was felt for miles:* impact, jar, jolt, concussion; blow. 2 *The king's abdication was a shock to the nation:* surprise, unexpected blow, disturbance, consternation, trauma, jolt, jar, start, turn. —*v.* 3 *We were shocked by the news:* surprise, stun, shake, daze, stupefy, jar, jolt, overwhelm, bowl over, give a turn; perturb, dismay, distress, disturb, upset, unsettle, disquiet, disconcert; astonish, astound, startle; appall, horrify, outrage.

shock[2] *n. a shock of hair:* bush, bushy mass, mass, crop, mop, mane, thatch, mat.

shocking *adj.* 1 *shocking news:* surprising, astounding, astonishing, startling, staggering, jarring; disturbing, upsetting, disquieting, unsettling, disconcerting. 2 *Grandmother thought it shocking for girls to wear shorts:* scandalous, disgraceful, outrageous, indecent; appalling; horrifying, terrible, awful, frightful.
Ant. 1, 2 unsurprising, expected; pleasing. 2 decent; good, fine, admirable, praiseworthy, commendable, laudable.

shoddy *adj.* 1 *a shoddy job:* inferior, poor, second-rate, sloppy, slipshod. 2 *Leaving his wife was a shoddy thing to do:* nasty, mean, inconsiderate, low, low-down, base, contemptible.
Ant. 1 excellent, first-rate, good, fine; careful, meticulous, thorough. 2 noble, thoughtful, considerate.

shoot *v.* 1 *The officer shot the mad dog:* hit, wing, nick, plug, riddle; pelt, pepper, shell; kill. 2 *Each archer shot three arrows:* fire,

discharge; hurl, propel, eject, sling, cast, fling, throw, launch, catapult; bombard, shower, rain, pelt. 3 *The horses shot out of the starting gate:* charge, spring, dart, bolt, dash, sweep, spurt, race, speed, fly, tear. —*n.* 4 *New shoots appeared on the bush:* twig, sprout, bud; offshoot.

shop *n.* 1 *a dress shop:* store, retail store, establishment, boutique; market. 2 *He has a woodworking shop in his basement:* workshop, studio, atelier; factory, plant, works. —*v.* 3 *to shop for china:* go shopping for, look, browse; buy, purchase; patronize.

shore[1] *n.* 1 *We spend our weekends at the shore:* coast, seacoast, seaboard; seashore, seaside, waterside, beach. 2 *The ship reached shore:* land, dry land, terra firma.

shore[2] *v. Heavy posts shored the roof:* support, prop, hold up, brace, reinforce, buttress, sustain.

short *adj.* 1 *a short person:* not long; not tall, stubby, small, little, pint-sized, diminutive, pygmy, Lilliputian, dwarfish. 2 *a short vacation. a short speech:* brief, short-lived, quick, fleeting, cursory; concise, terse, succinct, compact; abridged, abbreviated, condensed; curtailed. 3 *The tired clerk was short with the customers:* curt, brusque, abrupt, gruff, impatient, sharp; cross, snappish, ill-tempered, impolite. 4 *The plane had only a short fuel reserve:* low, scanty, scant, sparse, scarce, meager, skimpy, tight, slim; insufficient, deficient, wanting, lacking. —*adv.* 5 *He stopped the car short:* suddenly, abruptly, without warning.
Ant. 1 long; tall, high. 2 long, lengthy, protracted, extended. 3 patient; polite. 4 adequate, sufficient, ample, plentiful, abundant, copious, lavish. 5 slowly, gradually.

shortage *n. a shortage of food:* lack, want, deficiency, shortfall, insufficiency, inadequacy, scant supply, limited amount, scarcity, sparsity, dearth.
Ant. abundance, profusion, copiousness, plethora; surplus, excess.

shortcoming *n. Narrowmindedness is a serious shortcoming:* fault, flaw, defect, blemish, failing, weakness, inadequacy, deficiency, drawback.
Ant. advantage, strength, strong point, virtue.

shorten *v. Can the tailor shorten the coat? Shorten the speech by ten minutes:* make shorter, curtail, trim, clip, pare; abbreviate, cut, condense, contract, reduce, decrease, diminish, lessen.
Ant. lengthen, extend, protract, increase.

shortly *adv. The guests will arrive shortly:*

428

soon, in a short time, in a little while, before long, forthwith.

Ant. later, much later.

shortsighted *adj.* 1 *A shortsighted person needs glasses:* nearsighted, myopic; amblyopic. 2 *It was shortsighted not to plan for the future:* lacking foresight, improvident, imprudent, unthinking, careless, thoughtless, incautious, foolish.

Ant. 1, 2 farsighted. 2 foresighted, prudent, wise.

short-tempered *adj. I'm short-tempered when I'm tired:* irritable, cranky, grouchy; hot-tempered, irascible, testy, snappish, cantankerous, crusty, sharp, peevish, waspish.

shot *n.* 1 *The shots quickly drew the police:* gunfire, report, discharge; volley, salvo, fusillade. 2 *The cannon was out of shot:* ammunition, bullets, projectiles. 3 *The hunter is an excellent shot:* marksman, shooter, rifleman. 4 *the golfer's tee shot. a shot at the basket:* stroke, throw, toss; play, hit, drive. 5 *How about taking a shot at the answer?:* attempt, try, chance, go; guess, surmise; *Informal* crack. 6 *a shot of penicillin:* injection; dose.

shoulder *n.* 1 *The car was parked on the shoulder of the road:* edge, side, rim, margin, verge, border, skirt. —*v.* 2 *We shouldered our way through the crowd:* shove, elbow, push, thrust, jostle, bump. 3 *The oldest child shouldered the burden:* assume, undertake, bear, take, carry.

Ant. 1 middle, center. 3 shirk, shun, avoid, eschew.

shout *v.* 1 *She shouted for help:* cry out, cry, call out, call, yell, holler, scream, shriek, howl, roar, bellow, bawl, clamor, whoop. —*n.* 2 *The shout brought everyone running:* cry, outcry, call, yell, holler, scream, shriek, howl, roar, bellow, yelp; clamor.

shove *v.* 1 *Stop shoving! Shove the chair closer:* push, prod, jostle, elbow, shoulder, nudge; thrust, bump, jolt, propel, impel. —*n.* 2 *Someone gave me a shove:* push, prod, thrust, boost.

show *v.* 1 *Does my slip show?:* be visible, come into view, appear, be noticeable. 2 *The test will show how much we know:* reveal, disclose, manifest, uncover, bare, lay bare, expose, unveil, bring to light; demonstrate, exhibit, display, prove, evince; suggest, intimate, hint at, represent, establish, attest, confirm, bear out. 3 *Show me how this works:* explain, indicate, point out, inform; teach, instruct, demonstrate. 4 *Show the guest into the study:* direct, lead, guide, usher, conduct. 5 *The judge showed leniency to the prisoner:* grant, give, bestow, tender, proffer, impart, dispense, distribute. —*n.* 6 *His face gave no show of fear:* display, demonstration, exhibition, sign, expression, token, evidence, indication, manifestation, revelation, disclosure. 7 *a sidewalk art show:* exhibit, exhibition, exposition, fair; display, demonstration. 8 *The theater has a new show this week:* program, production, entertainment, performance, bill; spectacle, ceremony, pomp. 9 *Her headache was just a show to avoid work. He likes to put on a show of wealth:* display, pretext, pretense, pretension, affectation, pose, sham; impression, appearance, illusion; vaunting, flaunting.

Ant. 1 hide, conceal; be invisible, be unnoticeable. 2 hide, conceal, obscure. 5 withhold, withdraw. 6 hiding, concealing.

shower *n.* 1 *a heavy shower:* brief fall of rain, sprinkle; downpour, cloudburst, torrent, deluge. 2 *His speech was met with a shower of catcalls:* rain, deluge, flood, torrent, stream, rush, profusion, volley, barrage. —*v.* 3 *The lawn sprinkler showered the children:* sprinkle, splash, spray, wet; rain, drizzle. 4 *We showered gifts on her:* lavish, rain, deluge, bombard.

showpiece *n. The sable cape was the showpiece of the fur collection:* masterpiece, masterwork, prize, gem, jewel, classic, treasure.

showy *adj. huge, showy blossoms:* brilliant, striking, ornate, vivid, florid, gaudy, flashy, garish.

Ant. dull, drab, lackluster.

shred *n.* 1 *She tore the paper into shreds:* strip, ribbon, band; fragment, sliver, piece, bit, tatter. 2 *There's not a shred of truth in that story!:* bit, particle, speck, grain, morsel, iota, jot, scrap, atom, whit, scintilla.

shrew *n. Some men perceive assertive women to be shrews:* nag, scold, virago, harridan, termagant.

shrewd *adj.* 1 *Coyotes are shrewd predators:* sly, crafty, cunning, wily, cagey; tricky, shifty, slippery, disingenuous, contriving, designing, scheming, calculating, Machiavellian. 2 *Shrewd investors made a profit:* astute, smart, clever, sharp, acute, keen, canny, discerning, quick-witted, perceptive.

Ant. 1 artless, guileless, ingenuous; naive, unsophisticated. 2 unknowing, slow-witted, shortsighted, careless.

shriek *n.* 1 *shrieks of joy:* cry, outcry, call, yell, yelp; screech, squeal, howl, shout, scream, holler, whoop. —*v.* 2 *I shrieked when I saw the mouse:* cry out, scream, screech, yell, yelp, squeal, holler.

shrill *adj. a shrill voice:* high-pitched, screeching, piercing, strident; loud, blaring, clamorous, raucous.

Ant. soft, mellow, mellifluous, resonant; deep, low.

shrine *n.* 1 *Will to pray at a shrine:* sacred place, consecrated place, sacred tomb; altar, sanctuary, sanctum, chapel, church, temple. 2 *Gettysburg is a national shrine:* honored place, consecrated spot, monument.

shrink *v.* 1 *Will this sweater shrink? A bad harvest caused the farmer's income to shrink:* become smaller, make smaller, make less, lessen, shrivel, shorten, draw together, contract, pucker, condense; decrease, diminish, decline, curtail, reduce, wane, ebb. 2 *The boy shrank from the blow:* draw back, hang back, recoil, cringe, cower, shy, flinch; retreat, withdraw, retire; refuse, balk.

Ant. 1 stretch; increase, grow, expand. 2 meet head on, confront, stand up to.

shrivel *v. The peaches shriveled in the sun:* shrink, dry up, wither, wrinkle, pucker; waste away.

shroud *n.* 1 *A shroud of mystery surrounded the case:* cover, covering, cloak, blanket, veil, mantle, cloud. —*v.* 2 *The negotiations were shrouded in secrecy:* wrap, clothe, swathe, cover, envelop, cloak, veil; hide, conceal.

Ant. 2 uncover, unveil, reveal, expose.

shudder *v.* 1 *to shudder from the cold:* tremble, shake, quiver, quake, shiver; twitch, jerk. —*n.* 2 *She felt a shudder of fear:* trembling, tremor, shiver, quiver, shake, quake, flutter, paroxysm, spasm, throb, pang, twitch, jerk.

shun *v. to shun work. to shun desserts:* avoid, evade, elude, dodge, steer clear of, shy away from, shrink from; eschew, refuse, forgo, reject, disdain.

Ant. welcome, embrace; seek, solicit.

shut *v.* 1 *Shut the door:* close, secure, fasten; draw to, fold. 2 *Shut the cat in the kitchen:* enclose, confine, closet, cage, coop. —*adj.* 3 *Is the window shut?:* closed; fastened, secured, latched, locked; drawn, drawn to.

Ant. 1 open; unfasten, unlock. 2 release, let out. 3 open, opened; unfastened, unlocked.

shy *adj.* 1 *Shy people often dislike parties:* self-conscious, bashful, timid, timorous, meek; reserved, reticent, demure; fearful, apprehensive, anxious, skittish. 2 *The charity drive is $2000 shy of meeting its goal:* short, under, deficient, lacking, wanting, scant, minus. —*v.* 3 *The horse shied:* jump back, draw back, recoil from, swerve, dodge, shrink, cower, flinch.

Ant. 1 forward, brash, brazen, bold, unfrightened. 2 over, ahead, above.

sick *adj.* 1 *I'm too sick to go to work. Are you going to be sick?:* ill, unwell, ailing; laid up,

indisposed, infirm, sickly, invalid, afflicted, unhealthy, poorly; nauseated, throwing up, queasy. 2 *She's sick with worry:* deeply upset, stricken, afflicted, distressed, grieved, heartbroken, miserable, troubled, uneasy, disturbed, perturbed. 3 *I'm sick of the same old routine:* fed up with, tired, bored with; repelled by, revolted by.

Ant. 1 well, fine, healthy, hale and hearty, sound, unimpaired. 2 untroubled, undisturbed, unperturbed, unconcerned, unworried.

sicken *v. The sight of blood sickened him. The captured whale sickened and died:* make sick, make ill, nauseate, turn the stomach, disgust, revolt, repel, horrify, upset, shock; become sick, fall sick, take sick.

Ant. please, delight, gratify.

sickening *adj. a sickening odor:* nauseating; disgusting, vile, horrible, nasty, foul, revolting, repugnant, repulsive, loathsome, distasteful, offensive.

Ant. agreeable, pleasant, pleasing; inviting, attractive.

sickly *adj. a sickly child. Did you notice her sickly complexion?:* ailing, in poor health, unhealthy, sick, ill, unwell, infirm, unsound, weak; pale, wan, ashen, leaden, cadaverous.

sickness *n.* 1 *Chicken pox is a common childhood sickness:* illness, ill health; disease, disorder, ailment, malady, complaint; poor health, sickliness. 2 *Rough seas caused sickness among the passengers:* nausea, vomiting, throwing up.

side *n.* 1 *Stand by my side. both sides of the paper:* flank; surface. 2 *the far side of the room:* boundary, bound, limit, edge, periphery, margin, rim; part, area, section, region, division; half. 3 *Which side will win the election?:* team; group, body, faction, party; alliance, federation. 4 *Look at the problem from both sides:* position, stand, attitude, viewpoint, point of view, view, aspect, angle, slant, facet. —*adj.* 5 *the side yard:* at one side, on one side, lateral, flanking. 6 *He gave her a side glance:* from the side, toward the side, lateral, sideways, sidelong, oblique, indirect. 7 *a side street:* minor, subordinate, lesser, incidental, secondary, subordinate, subsidiary; related, accessory, collateral, allied.

Ant. 1 front, back; top, bottom. 2 middle, center. 5 front, back, rear; top, bottom. 6 direct, headlong. 7 major, main, primary, principal.

sift *v.* 1 *Dust sifted through the window:* sprinkle, scatter; drift, filter. 2 *It's hard to sift the facts from the lies. The jury sifted through the transcripts of the trial:* separate, sort out, sort, distinguish, winnow, screen; study, inspect, examine closely, probe, search, analyze.

sigh v. 1 *He sighed with weariness:* let out one's breath, breathe loudly, moan, groan; whine. 2 *The soldiers sighed for home:* pine, yearn, long; grieve, weep, mourn. —*n.* 3 *a sigh of relief:* deep audible breath; moan, groan.

sight n. 1 *Wearing glasses will aid poor sight:* eyesight, vision. 2 *The car was soon out of sight:* range of vision, field of vision, view. 3 *The sight of land elated the crew:* seeing, vision, appearance, visibility, viewing, view. 4 *The mountain was a sight to behold:* view, spectacle, display, prospect, scene, vista; scenery, place of interest. —*v.* 5 *We sighted a ship on the horizon:* see, observe, glimpse, spot, catch sight of, spy, espy, behold, view.

Ant. 1 blindness.

sign n. 1 *My gift was a sign of love. The dark clouds may be a sign of rain:* symbol, mark, figure, token, evidence, manifestation, emblem, badge; indication, indicator, omen, portent, warning, herald, harbinger, symptom, hint, intimation; characteristic, trait, feature. 2 *a thumbs-up sign:* signal, motion, gesture. 3 *A "for sale" sign was in the window: (variously)* placard, neon sign, signpost, billboard; road sign, street sign. —*v.* 4 *Please sign both copies:* write one's signature, endorse, autograph.

signal n. 1 *Did he give us a signal to go ahead?:* sign, indication, cue; gesture, motion, nod; watchword, password. —*adj.* 2 *a signal light:* indicating, direction, guiding. —*v.* 3 *He signaled us to rise:* motion, gesture, beckon, give a sign to.

significance n. *Do you understand the significance of the findings?:* consequence, importance, import, weight, meaning, implication, relevance, portent, gravity, influence, concern, interest; eminence, prominence, distinction, excellence, value, merit, worth, virtue; sense, drift, intent, intention, aim, object, purpose.

significant adj. 1 *a significant discovery. Does the report give the significant facts?:* consequential, important, substantial, meaningful, material, principal, major, chief, main, vital, critical, serious, influential, considerable, momentous, grave, weighty, noteworthy, notable, eminent, prominent, outstanding, exceptional, signal. 2 *I gave her a significant look:* indicative, expressive, meaningful, suggestive, symbolic, symptomatic, demonstrative; eloquent, telling, knowing.

Ant. 1 insignificant, inconsequential, trivial, unimportant, meaningless.

signify v. *A white flag signifies surrender:* be a sign of, stand for, mean, indicate, represent, connote, convey, express, manifest, evidence, show, declare, announce, communicate, designate, tell; imply, intimate, suggest, hint at, symbolize, betoken, argue; portend, predict, augur, omen, foretell, foreshadow, herald.

silence n. 1 *The silence of the woods. Father's silence indicated disapproval:* quiet, quietness, noiselessness, soundlessness, still, stillness, hush; peace, calm, tranquillity, serenity, placidness; speechlessness, muteness, uncommunicativeness, closemouthedness. —*v.* 2 *She tried to silence the angry crowd:* still, quiet, quieten, hush, calm. 3 *The dictator silenced his opponents by jailing them:* gag, muzzle, suppress, squelch, squash; stifle, check, curb, vanquish, overcome, subdue.

Ant. 1 sound, noise, noisiness, din, roar, clamor; speech, talking, chatter, babel. 2 arouse, rouse, incite, inflame; make louder, amplify.

silent adj. 1 *The cat moved on silent feet. The house was silent:* making no sound, having no sound, soundless, noiseless, quiet, still, hushed, muffled, muted, mute. 2 *The class was silent. the strong, silent type:* not speaking, wordless, mum, speechless, mute, dumb; untalkative, reticent, uncommunicative, closemouthed, taciturn; secretive, discreet. 3 *The two nations have a silent understanding to come to each other's aid if attacked:* tacit, implied, implicit, inferred, unspoken, unsaid, undeclared, unarticulated; unpublished, unwritten; unrevealed, hidden.

Ant. 1 noisy. 2 noisy, vocal, vociferous, talkative, garrulous, loquacious. 3 explicit, declared, announced.

silly adj. 1 *What a silly thing to do!:* foolhardy, senseless, unwise, unwary, ridiculous, pointless; foolish, dumb, stupid, brainless, harebrained, rattlebrained, empty-headed; shallow, fatuous, idiotic, childish, frivolous, giddy. 2 *a silly joke:* ridiculous, nonsensical, preposterous, absurd, farcical, ludicrous, laughable; meaningless, inconsequential.

Ant. 1 sensible, reasonable, smart, astute, clever, intelligent; serious, deep. 2 serious, meaningful, purposeful, consequential.

similar adj. *The two dresses are similar. They have similar political views:* nearly alike, much the same; kindred, akin; like, equivalent, comparable, analogous, close, correspondent, corresponding, correlative, approximate, allied, cognate; matching, duplicate.

Ant. different, dissimilar, unalike, unlike, disparate; opposite, opposed, contrary, antithetical.

similarity *n.* *There's a strong similarity between these two:* resemblance, likeness, correspondence, parallelism, kinship, similitude, sameness, equivalence, agreement, congruity, congruence, harmony, conformance, conformability.

Ant. dissimilarity, difference, unlikeness, dissimilitude, disparity, disagreement.

simmer *v.* 1 *I hear the soup simmering:* boil gently, stew, seethe; bubble, gurgle, burble. 2 *He simmered with anger:* seethe, fume, boil.

simper *v.* *The children simpered behind the teacher's back:* snigger, snicker, smirk, giggle, titter; smile sillily, grin self-consciously.

simple *adj.* 1 *a simple puzzle:* having few parts, not complex, uncomplicated, uninvolved; unsophisticated; basic, elemental, elementary, rudimentary; easy, manageable. 2 *a simple shirt. They led a simple life:* plain, unadorned, undecorated, unembellished, modest, unpretentious; quiet, peaceful, rustic, innocent, guileless, artless, ingenuous. 3 *The simple truth is that no one wants the job:* plain, honest, candid, stark, bare, unadorned, unvarnished, straight, unfeigned, open, blunt, frank, direct, plainspoken, straightforward, out-and-out.

Ant. 1 complex, complicated, involved, intricate, advanced; difficult. 2 fancy, elaborate, ornate, pretentious, ostentatious; busy, hectic, tumultuous. 3 varnished, gilded, artful, guileful, contrived.

simpleton *n.* *Anyone who believes that is a simpleton!:* fool, numskull, dunce, oaf, ignoramus, dolt, ninny, dumbbell, idiot, dummy, imbecile.

simplicity *n.* *He spoke with great simplicity:* obviousness, directness, straightforwardness, plainness, clarity, clearness, purity, austerity, serenity; openness, candor, sincerity, honesty, artlessness, naturalness; innocence, naiveté, unworldliness.

Ant. complexity, elaborateness, ornateness; pretentiousness, affectation, ostentation; sophistication, worldliness; deviousness, insincerity, guile, craftiness, slyness, cunning.

simply *adv.* *The poem is beautiful yet simply expressed:* uncomplicatedly, plainly, directly, straightforwardly, explicitly, clearly, lucidly; modestly, unaffectedly, unpretentiously.

simulate *v.* *She simulated tears to get our sympathy:* feign, put on, pretend, counterfeit, affect, fake, sham; act, play, playact, make believe, imitate, ape, mimic, copy.

simulated *adj.* *The coat is made of simulated leopard skin:* imitation, synthetic, artificial, fabricated, manmade, pretend, make-believe, sham; fake, counterfeit, phony.

Ant. real, authentic, bona fide.

simultaneous *adj.* *The two armies made simultaneous offensives:* occurring at the same time, concurrent, coincident, synchronous, concomitant; coexistent, coexisting, contemporary.

sin *n.* 1 *May God forgive you your sins:* ungodly act, immoral act, irreligious act, sinfulness, iniquity, transgression, trespass; wrong, wrongdoing, evil, evil deed, villainy, vice, misdeed, error. 2 *It's a sin the way he wastes money:* shame, disgrace, scandal. —*v.* 3 *Who has not sinned?:* offend against God, offend against morality, transgress, trespass, err, offend, fall, stray, do wrong, do evil.

Ant. 1 virtue, righteousness, sinlessness, godliness, holiness, good.

sincere *adj.* *my sincere apology:* unfeigned, unaffected, real, honest, genuine, artless, guileless, ingenuous, candid, frank, straightforward, forthright, truthful; earnest, wholehearted, heartfelt, serious, in good faith.

Ant. insincere, feigned, pretended, contrived, affected, deceptive.

sincerely *adv.* *The boy was sincerely sorry:* really, genuinely, honestly, truly, truthfully; earnestly, seriously, wholeheartedly.

Ant. insincerely, falsely, deceptively, untruthfully, deceitfully.

sincerity *n.* *Everyone was touched by the sincerity of her apology:* honesty, genuineness, earnestness, seriousness; candor, openness, frankness, truthfulness, unaffectedness, artlessness, ingenuousness, guilelessness, good faith.

sinful *adj.* *Stealing is sinful:* wicked, evil, unrighteous; unholy, impious, ungodly, irreligious; iniquitous, immoral, wrong, errant.

Ant. sinless, righteous, virtuous, moral, pure, godly.

single *adj.* 1 *Put a single rose in the vase:* one, only one, individual, solitary, lone, sole. 2 *Is he married or single?:* unmarried, unwed; spinster, bachelor, maiden.

Ant. 1 several, some, many, numerous. 2 married, wed, wedded.

singular *adj.* 1 *You have a singular ear for music:* unique, rare, unusual, uncommon, exceptional, extraordinary, unparalleled, matchless, unprecedented, surpassing, superior; remarkable, noteworthy, wonderful,

marvelous. **2** *She has a singular way of talking:* unnatural, odd, strange, peculiar, curious, freakish, bizarre; unconventional, eccentric, atypical, unfamiliar, abnormal, aberrant, unaccountable.
Ant. **1, 2** common, commonplace, ordinary, routine, conventional.

sinister *adj.* **1** *The villain's sinister laugh rang across the stage:* threatening, ominous, menacing, frightening, alarming, disturbing, dismaying; inauspicious, unpropitious, unfavorable, unpromising, adverse. **2** *a sinister plot to take over the country:* wicked, evil, villainous, vile, foul, treacherous, perfidious, malevolent, insidious, rascally; accursed, cursed, diabolical, infernal, hellish, devilish.
Ant. **1** calming, soothing; encouraging, favorable, auspicious, promising, propitious. **2** noble, heroic, honorable.

sink *v.* **1** *The moon sank behind the mountains. The porch sinks a bit in the left corner:* descend, go down, lower, drop, decline, dip, slant, slope, tilt, droop, slump. **2** *The ocean liner sank. The anchor sank to the bottom and held the ship:* descend below the surface, submerse, submerge, go to the bottom, go under; engulf, drown. **3** *Prices sank to an all-time low. The patient's health seemed to sink:* lower, decline, fall, lessen, diminish, drop, shrink, subside; deteriorate, degenerate, worsen, regress, retrogress, wane, ebb, languish, droop, sag. **4** *I never thought he'd sink to cheating:* lower oneself, degrade oneself, debase oneself, stoop, fall, descend.
Ant. **1** rise, ascend, climb; incline. **2** surface, emerge. **3** rise, increase, advance, climb.

sinner *n. The sinner was refused burial in holy ground:* transgressor, evildoer, malefactor, wrongdoer, offender, apostate, trespasser.
Ant. saint, holy person.

sinuous *adj. a sinuous trail up the mountainside:* winding, curving, curved, bending, serpentine, twisted, twisting, coiling, zigzag, meandering, undulating.
Ant. straight, direct.

sip *n. Try a sip of this lemonade:* small mouthful, dram, swallow, drop, soupçon, drink, sample, taste.
Ant. gulp, swig.

sit *v.* **1** *Sit on this chair. The bird sat on the top branch of the tree:* be seated, have a seat; settle, perch, roost; rest. **2** *The trunk still sits in the attic:* situated, be located, be established, be seated, stand, rest, lie; remain, stay. **3** *The state court sits twice a year. Have you ever sat on a jury?:* convene, be in session, assemble, meet, gather, delib-

erate; occupy a place, hold an official position.
Ant. **1** stand; lie. **2** move, remove. **3** adjourn.

site *n. A new school occupies the site of the old armory:* spot, place, ground, position; locale, locality, location, whereabouts, scene, setting.

situate *v. The house must be situated near public transportation:* locate, place, position, put, set, settle, install, house; plant, post.
Ant. move, remove.

situation *n.* **1** *How did you ever get into this situation?:* state of affairs, state, circumstances, condition, status, position; predicament, plight, fix, dilemma. **2** *The situation as sales manager requires a great deal of traveling:* job, position, post, place, office, berth; role, function, duty, work.

size *n.* **1** *The size of the pool is 20 by 40 feet:* dimensions, measurement, extent, amplitude, area, volume, expanse; magnitude, largeness, bulk, mass, scope; content, capacity. **2** *What was the size of the research grant?:* amount, quantity, sum, aggregate, total.

sizzle *v.* **1** *The steak sizzled on the grill:* hiss, sputter, splutter, crackle; fry. *—n.* **2** *We awoke to the sizzle of hot sausages:* hissing, hiss, sputtering.

skeleton *n. the skeleton of the human body. Only the skeleton of the house stood after the fire:* bony framework, bones, frame, underlying structure, hulk, shell.
Ant. skin; exterior, surface.

skeptic Also **sceptic** *n. He's too much of a skeptic to take anything on faith:* doubter, doubting Thomas, scoffer; agnostic, unbeliever, atheist.

skeptical Also **sceptical** *adj. People were skeptical of the theory:* questioning, dubious, doubting, doubtful, unconvinced; disbelieving, unbelieving, cynical.
Ant. convinced, unquestioning, believing; credulous, gullible.

sketch *n.* **1** *the architect's sketch:* drawing, preliminary drawing, rough design. **2** *The committee gave the mayor a sketch of their long report:* outline, brief description, rough account, summary, synopsis. **3** *The actors amused the audience with several impromptu sketches:* skit, vignette, characterization. *—v.* **4** *A sidewalk artist sketched the passersby:* make a quick drawing of, draw, rough out, draft. **5** *The historical article sketched the major events of the decade:* set forth briefly, outline, plot, summarize, map, mark out, portray, chart, rough out.

sketchy *adj. She gave us a sketchy description of the property:* incomplete, cursory, rough, vague, outline, brief, short, skimpy, meager, undetailed; unfinished, preliminary, preparatory.

Ant. complete, full, detailed, in-depth, exact; finished, final.

skill *n.* 1 *The cabinet had been made with great skill:* skillfulness, craft, adroitness, adeptness, expertness, deftness, dexterity, mastery, competence, artistry. 2 *the skill to ski a difficult slope:* ability, capacity, prowess, faculty, facility, proficiency, knowhow, expertise; knack, talent, gift.

Ant. 1 incompetence, ineptness, ineptitude. 2 inability, inexperience.

skillful *adj. a skillful pilot:* able, competent, capable, proficient, qualified, accomplished, professional, masterful, masterly, experienced, veteran; apt, adroit, dexterous, deft, talented, gifted.

Ant. unskilled, inexpert, inept, incompetent, unqualified, unaccomplished; amateurish, unqualified.

skim *v.* 1 *The water skier skimmed over the surface of the lake:* move lightly, glide, sweep, scud, skip, float, sail, fly. 2 *Don't read the report, just skim it:* glance over, scan, flip, thumb through, dip into, leaf through.

Ant. 2 examine carefully, peruse.

skimp *v.* 1 *Don't skimp on the butter:* be sparing of, scrimp, stint, slight, hold back. 2 *By skimping a little we can stick to our budget:* be frugal, economize, cut expenses, scrimp, stint, scrape along.

Ant. 1 lavish, be generous with. 2 be extravagant, squander.

skimpy *adj. a skimpy portion of ice cream:* not large enough, small, smallish, scant, scanty, sparse, meager, modest, slight; inadequate, insufficient.

Ant. large, abundant, profuse, copious, generous, lavish, extravagant, liberal, generous.

skin *n.* 1 *a fair skin. The trappers sold bear skins:* epidermis, body covering; complexion; hide, pelt, coat, fur, fleece. 2 *boiled potatoes in their skins:* peel, rind, hull, shell, pod, jacket, case, casing, sheath, integument, outer coating. —*v.* 3 *The hunter skinned the deer. The boy skinned his knee:* strip the skin from, peel, flay, remove the hide from, lay bare; scrape, bark, abrade.

skinflint *n. That skinflint wouldn't give a nickel to charity:* stingy person, miser, niggardly person, niggard, penny pincher, pinchpenny, tightwad.

Ant. big spender, spendthrift, sport.

skinny *adj. She's skinny but strong:* thin, slender, lean, scrawny, spindly, lanky, wiry, gaunt, skeletal, slight.

Ant. fat, obese, corpulent, plump, chubby, rotund.

skip *v.* 1 *The children skipped down the path:* leap, hop, jump, bob, spring, bounce, bound, flit, gambol, caper, romp. 2 *The autobiography skips the author's childhood:* pass over, omit, leave out, overlook, ignore, neglect, disregard; evade, dodge, shun. 3 *Informal The embezzler tried to skip the country:* leave hurriedly and secretly, escape, flee, make off, abscond, disappear, fly the coop. —*n.* 4 *The ice skater made two little skips and then did a pirouette:* jump, leap, bound, spring, hop, bounce.

Ant. 1 shuffle, lumber, trudge, waddle. 2 include, cover, contain.

skirmish *n. There are skirmishes along the front:* brief fight, clash, engagement, action, firefight; brush, fray, affray, tussle, scuffle.

skittish *adj.* 1 *a skittish horse:* easily startled, easily frightened, fearful, nervous, jumpy, jittery, excitable; restless, restive; fitful, impulsive, flighty, mercurial, volatile, unstable. 2 *Some children are skittish about meeting strangers:* shy, bashful, timid; wary, cautious, chary, leery, guarded, distrustful, suspicious, unsure, reluctant.

Ant. 1 calm, serene, placid, unexcitable.

slab *n. I helped myself to a slab of pie:* thick flat piece, thick slice; hunk, chunk, block; plank, board, slat.

Ant. sliver, splinter, shaving, shred.

slack *adj.* 1 *Keep the reins slack:* loose, lax, limp, not tight, not taut; flexible, flabby, baggy; untied, unfastened. 2 *a slack disciplinarian. He became slack about his appearance:* unexacting, lax, undemanding, soft, permissive; careless, slipshod, neglectful, negligent, dilatory, inattentive, lazy, slothful, indolent, nonchalant, lackadaisical, unthinking, unconcerned, indifferent, heedless. 3 *Business has been slack:* slow, slow-paced, sluggish; not busy, inactive, lethargic, listless, dull, quiet. —*adv.* 4 *The reins fell slack around the horse's shoulders:* limply, loosely, freely, easily; sluggishly, slowly. —*v.* 5 *Slack the rope before trying to untie the knot:* slacken, loosen, loose, untighten, relax, make limp.

Ant. 1 tight, taut, firm; tied, fastened. 2 exacting, demanding, firm, hard; careful, heedful. 3 fast, busy, brisk. 4 tightly, taut. 5 tighten.

slacken *v.* 1 *Wait for the rain to slacken. Don't slacken your efforts:* slack, slack off, slow, slow down, abate, taper off, dwindle, ease, let up, moderate, weaken; relax, reduce, lessen, decrease, diminish. 2 *Don't slacken the reins or the horse may bolt:* loosen, loose, relax, slack, let go limp.

Ant. **1** quicken, increase, accelerate. **2** tighten.

slake *v.* *The lemonade slaked my thirst:* quench, satisfy, sate, satiate, gratify, appease, relieve, mollify, assuage, allay, alleviate, decrease, curb, moderate, ease, mitigate, quell.

Ant. increase, heighten, intensify, aggravate.

slander *n.* **1** *When he called me a thief, I sued him for slander:* defamation, vilification, malicious fabrication, false statement, distortion, misrepresentation. —*v.* **2** *He slandered his opponent's good name:* defame, malign, vilify, smear, sully, soil, besmirch.

slant *v.* **1** *The path slants down to the river:* incline, slope, angle, tilt; lean, list. **2** *The writer slanted the story in favor of the candidate:* bias, prejudice, distort, angle. —*n.* **3** *The floor has a slant:* slope, tilt, rake, incline, pitch. **4** *The play has a political slant:* bias, prejudice, angle, view, viewpoint, leaning.

Ant. **1** straighten, level.

slap *n.* **1** *Her slap left red marks on my arm:* blow, smack, hit, whack, wallop, cuff, clap. **2** *His rudeness was a slap at all of us:* insult, rejection, snub, rebuff. —*v.* **3** *She slapped the child on the arm:* hit, strike, smack, cuff, whack, swat.

slash *v.* **1** *Vandals slashed the paintings:* cut, gash, lacerate, slit, rend, slice. **2** *The shop plans to slash prices:* cut, lower, decrease, reduce, pare. —*n.* **3** *The slash in the painting made it worthless:* stroke, mark, cut, gash, rent, laceration, slit, tear. **4** *a slash in meat costs:* cut, decrease, reduction, drop, lowering.

slaughter *n.* **1** *The attack resulted in a slaughter of the villagers:* massacre, bloodbath, mass murder, killing. —*v.* **2** *The killer slaughtered the entire family:* kill, murder, slay; massacre, destroy, annihilate, exterminate, wipe out.

slave *n.* **1** *There were many slaves in ancient Athens:* serf, vassal, bond servant, bondsman, thrall. **2** *He's a slave to alcohol:* addict, victim. **3** *She's been a slave in that job:* drudge, workhorse, menial, toiler, plodder. —*v.* **4** *Why do you slave at that unfulfilling job?:* drudge, toil, work like a slave.

Ant. **1** master, owner. **3** loafer, idler. **4** loaf, idle.

slavery *n.* **1** *The natives were sold into slavery:* enslavement, bondage, captivity, compulsory service. **2** *She was resigned to the slavery of a dreary job:* drudgery, toil, sweat, labor, grind.

slavish *adj.* **1** *Slavish devotion to another is*

self-destructive: servile, subservient, obsequious, slavelike, submissive. **2** *The painting is a slavish imitation of Van Gogh's style:* strict, exact; unimaginative.

Ant. **1** willful, assertive. **2** imaginative, creative, inventive.

slay *v.* *David slew Goliath:* kill, slaughter, murder; destroy, execute, annihilate, massacre.

sleazy *adj.* **1** *sleazy drug dealers:* disreputable, contemptible, low, dishonorable. **2** *a sleazy old café:* squalid, filthy, run-down, neglected. **3** *sleazy fabric:* flimsy, shoddy; cheap, tacky.

sleek *adj.* **1** *Your hair looks sleek and beautiful:* glossy, shiny, silky, satiny, lustrous. **2** *a sleek gigolo:* smooth, suave, unctuous, oily, slick, ingratiating, fawning.

sleep *n.* **1** *I was awakened from a sound sleep:* slumber, snooze; nap, doze. **2** *She went to her eternal sleep:* death, rest, peace. —*v.* **3** *Everyone slept until dawn:* slumber; nap, snooze, doze.

sleepy *adj.* **1** *I'm too sleepy to watch TV:* drowsy, weary, tired, fatigued, exhausted. **2** *a sleepy village:* quiet, inactive, dull.

Ant. **1** awake, alert. **2** bustling, busy, lively.

slender *adj.* **1** *She admired my slender build:* slim, lean, willowy, skinny, thin, narrow. **2** *Your chance of winning is slender:* slim, slight; small, meager, scant, spare.

Ant. **1** fat, stout, bulky, heavy. **2** considerable, appreciable, strong.

slice *n.* **1** *a slice of pie:* piece, portion, section, cut, segment. —*v.* **2** *Slice the meat thin:* carve, cut, shave; whittle, pare; divide, separate, cut off, sever.

slick *adj.* **1** *A seal's coat is slick:* glossy, sleek, smooth, satiny, shiny. **2** *Be careful not to slip on this slick floor:* slippery; oily, greasy, waxy, glassy. **3** *A slick operator could sell anything:* sly, wily, cunning, tricky, sharp, smooth-talking, fast-talking. —*n.* **4** *an oil slick:* film, coating, coat, scum.

Ant. **1** rough, bumpy, coarse. **3** honest, open.

slide *v.* **1** *The boy likes to slide down the banister:* glide, coast. **2** *The car slid into the ditch:* skid, slip, slither. **3** *The committee let the matter slide:* pass, slip, lapse. —*n.* **4** *Let's take a slide on the toboggan:* coast, glide. **5** *They need a rubber mat at the foot of the slide:* chute, ramp, slope.

slight *adj.* **1** *a slight change in temperature:* small, little, modest, moderate, limited, restricted; unimportant, inappreciable, negligible, tiny. **2** *He's too slight to play football:* slim, slender, frail, thin. —*n.* **3** *I was hurt by*

her slight: snub, insult, cut, rebuff, incivility.
   Ant. 1 considerable, substantial, appreciable. 2 husky, muscular, sturdy.

slim *adj.* 1 *He has a slim figure:* slender, thin, lean, svelte, willowy, skinny. 2 *There's only a slim hope:* slender, faint, remote, slight, small, meager, negligible.
   Ant. 1 chubby, fat; broad. 2 great, considerable.

slink *v. We caught the thief slinking out the back way:* slip, creep, steal, prowl, sneak.

slip[1] *v.* 1 *Slip the shoe on your foot:* slide, glide; put. 2 *She slipped and fell:* skid, slide, lose one's balance. 3 *The years have slipped by:* pass imperceptibly; steal, pass, sneak. 4 *The patient's condition is slipping:* fail, worsen, decline, sink, fall. 5 *He slipped from my grasp:* escape; break away. 6 *How did the news slip out?:* leak, escape, be revealed. —*n.* 7 *She took a bad slip on the icy sidewalk:* skid, slide; fall. 8 *That was an embarrassing slip:* blunder, indiscretion, lapse, error, faux pas. 9 *The slip in the market has been devastating:* drop, fall, decline. 10 *You need a slip under that sheer dress:* petticoat, chemise. 11 *The boat drifted out of the slip:* berth, dock.
   Ant. 4 improve. 9 rise, increase.

slip[2] *n. a slip of paper:* scrap, strip, shred, small piece; receipt, voucher, ticket.

slippery *adj.* 1 *a slippery floor:* slick, smooth; waxy, greasy, oily, glassy. 2 *a slippery character:* shifty, deceitful, untrustworthy, unreliable, treacherous, sneaky, wily, devious, crafty.
   Ant. 2 trustworthy, reliable, dependable.

slipshod *adj. It was put together in a slipshod way:* careless, lax, sloppy; thoughtless, offhand, slovenly.
   Ant. careful, meticulous, exact.

slip-up *n. There was a slip-up in mailing the invitations:* mistake, blunder, error, lapse, oversight, bungle, faux pas; *Slang* goof, foul-up, boo-boo.

slit *n. a slit in the floor:* cut, crevice, gash, incision, slash, crack, fissure.

slobber *v. The baby slobbered:* drivel, slaver, drool, dribble, salivate.

slogan *n. an advertising slogan:* motto, battle cry, catch phrase; byword, watchword, catchword.

slop *v.* 1 *Don't slop water on the floor:* slosh, splash, splatter, spatter, spill. —*n.* 2 *After the flood our rooms were full of slop:* mire, ooze, mud, muck; filth, garbage, waste, refuse.

slope *v.* 1 *The trail slopes down sharply:* slant, angle, pitch, incline, lean, tip, tilt,

bank. —*n.* 2 *a gentle slope:* slant, incline, grade, inclination, descent.
   Ant. 1 flatten, level.

sloppy *adj.* 1 *Heavy rain makes for sloppy roads:* watery, sloshy, muddy, slushy, wet, sodden, swampy, marshy. 2 *a sloppy desk:* messy, untidy, disorderly; soiled, dirty, unclean.
   Ant. 1 dry. 2 neat, tidy, orderly, clean.

sloth *n. Her sloth keeps her from getting ahead:* laziness, lethargy, torpor, indolence, lassitude, listlessness, shiftlessness, languor, sluggishness, idleness.
   Ant. energy, industriousness, activeness, vim, vigor.

slothful *adj. The hot weather made the workers slothful:* lazy, indolent, sluggardly, lax, negligent, sluggish, shiftless, torpid, listless.
   Ant. industrious, energetic, lively.

slouch *v.* 1 *Straighten up and don't slouch!:* droop, slump, stoop, hunch. —*n.* 2 *She'd look taller if it weren't for her slouch:* stoop, slump. 3 *He's no slouch about helping with the dishes:* lazybones, laggard, sluggard, loafer, slacker, shirker.
   Ant. 1 straighten up. 3 go-getter, eager beaver, ball of fire.

slovenly *adj.* 1 *a slovenly room:* messy, sloppy, untidy, dirty, unclean, disorderly, unkempt. 2 *slovenly work:* slipshod, careless, slapdash, indifferent, unconcerned.
   Ant. 1 neat, tidy, orderly. 2 careful, meticulous, precise.

slow *adj.* 1 *a slow runner:* slow-paced, slow-moving; heavy, sluggish, torpid. 2 *The patient made a slow recovery:* long, prolonged, extended, drawn out, protracted, time-consuming. 3 *My rent payments are always slow:* late, behind time, overdue, unpunctual, delayed, belated. 4 *a slow worker:* dawdling, dilatory, procrastinating, laggard, sluggish. 5 *He's slow to take a stand:* hesitant, cautious; halfhearted; indisposed, loath, disinclined, reluctant, averse. 6 *We enjoyed a slow Sunday at home:* leisurely, unhurried, deliberate; inactive, quiet, not lively. 7 *He's too slow for the advanced class:* slow-witted, backward, stupid, obtuse, dense, dumb, dull, unperceptive. —*v.* 8 *The train slowed:* slow down, reduce speed, decelerate; flag, falter. 9 *The strike will slow deliveries:* hold up, retard, check, curb, brake; hinder, impede.
   Ant. 1, 2, 4 fast, quick, speedy. 3 prompt, punctual, on time. 5 eager, enthusiastic. 6 active, busy, lively. 7 quick-witted, smart, bright, intelligent; perceptive. 8, 9 speed up, accelerate. 9 spur, help.

slowdown *n. Business is going through a*

slowdown: slackening, slowing, downturn, decline, flagging, letdown, deceleration.

sludge *n. There was sludge in the bottom of the tank:* mud, mire; dregs, sediment, muck, ooze, slime, slop, slush.

slug *v. The two prizefighters slugged each other brutally:* hit, strike, punch, whack, smite, pound, clout, bat, belt, whale, wallop, sock, bash, batter, lambaste, clobber.

sluggish *adj.* 1 *Hot weather makes me sluggish:* lethargic, listless, languid, spiritless, soporific; lazy, indolent, slothful; lifeless, torpid. 2 *She ran a sluggish race:* slow, unhurried, leisurely, protracted.

Ant. 1 energetic, industrious, animated, lively. 2 rapid, fast, brisk.

slumber *v. I was slumbering soundly:* sleep; doze, snooze, nap.

Ant. be awake.

slump *v.* 1 *He slumped to the pavement:* collapse, fall, drop, sag, tumble. 2 *Her work slumped:* dip, plunge, decline. —*n.* 3 *I could tell from his slump how tired he was:* slouch, droop, sagging posture. 4 *The economy went into a slump:* decline, reverse, setback. *Ant.* 2 improve, increase. 4 rise, upsurge, upturn.

slur *v.* 1 *Don't slur your words:* mumble, mutter, run together, pronounce indistinctly. 2 *She slurred over the criticism:* overlook, skip, disregard, ignore, gloss over, pass over, slight. 3 *Don't slur my reputation!:* blacken, smear, defame, malign, stain, sully. —*n.* 4 *They talked about each other with ugly slurs:* insult, cut, dig, affront. 5 *The rumors cast a slur upon my name:* stain, mark, spot, blemish, taint.

Ant. 1 enunciate. 2 stress, accentuate. 3 praise, laud, compliment. 4 compliment, praise.

slut *n. He called her a slut for dating another man:* slattern, hussy, wanton, strumpet, trollop, wench, tramp, jezebel; whore, harlot, floozy.

sly *adj.* 1 *He won by a sly maneuver:* wily, crafty, cunning, tricky, artful, conniving, sneaky, shrewd, cunning. 2 *She gave me a sly wink:* secret, furtive, private, covert, confidential; mischievous, playful.

smack¹ *v.* 1 *She smacked him with her hand:* slap, smite, hit, whack, spank, strike. —*n.* 2 *He gave the boy a smack on the leg:* slap, blow, buffet, whack, spank, hit, cuff. 3 *a smack on the lips:* loud kiss, buss.

Ant. 1 pet, caress.

smack² *n.* 1 *Add just a smack of cinnamon:* trace, tinge; hint, suggestion, taste, flavor; touch, bit, dash. —*v.* 2 *This cake smacks of rum:* taste; suggest, have a flavor.

small *adj.* 1 *Are you small enough to squeeze through?:* little, tiny, diminutive, under-sized, slight. 2 *a small profit:* meager, scant, modest, not great. 3 *It's only a small problem:* minor, inconsequential, insignificant, trivial, superficial, unimportant, trifling. 4 *Someone with a small mind usually believes the worst:* mean, petty, ignoble, narrow, opinionated, bigoted. 5 *The kitten uttered a small cry:* feeble, weak, fragile, faint.

Ant. 1, 2 large, big, vast, huge, immense, enormous. 3 major, important, significant, vital. 5 strong, powerful; loud, noisy.

small talk *n. She ignored my small talk:* chitchat, prattle, chatter, prattling, gossip, idle talk, table talk.

smart *adj.* 1 *a smart student:* intelligent, bright, sharp, clever, quick, brainy, astute. 2 *smart clothes:* fashionable, chic, elegant, stylish; trim, neat. 3 *They moved at a smart pace:* energetic, vigorous, brisk, quick. —*v.* 4 *Does your hand smart?:* hurt, sting, burn; feel pain, ache. 5 *I smart each time I think of his rudeness:* suffer, wince, flinch, blench.

Ant. 1 dumb, dull, slow, stupid. 2 old-fashioned, dowdy; outmoded. 3 slow.

smash *v.* 1 *I smashed the window with a brick:* shatter, break, disintegrate. 2 *The car smashed into a fence. She smashed him with her fist:* crash, strike, hit, collide with; crack, break; batter, beat, *Slang* bash, clobber. 3 *Our tanks smashed the enemy:* destroy, crush, demolish, shatter. —*n.* 4 *He gave me a smash on the head:* blow, bang, clout, hit. 5 *Informal Her performance was a smash!:* hit, success, sensation, triumph.

Ant. 5 flop, loser, disaster.

smashing *adj. That's a smashing outfit you're wearing:* terrific, sensational, marvelous, wonderful, super, magnificent, superb, extraordinary, fabulous, fantastic, great.

smattering *n. I know a smattering of French:* drop, bit, scrap, small amount, smidgen, snippet, dash, dab, sprinkling.

smear *v.* 1 *He smeared the walls with plaster:* spread, rub, daub, coat, cover. 2 *My clothes are smeared with mud:* stain, smudge, splotch, soil, streak. 3 *Water smeared the ink:* blur, smudge. 4 *You tried to smear my reputation:* soil, stain, tarnish, blacken, besmirch, blemish; malign, slander, denigrate. —*n.* 5 *You have a lipstick smear on your cheek. That's a filthy smear on my good name!:* blotch, smudge, streak, splotch, stain; libel, slander.

smell *v.* 1 *We smelled the stew out in the hallway:* scent, sniff. 2 *The room smells of incense:* have a scent, emit an odor. 3 *This cheese smells!:* reek, stink, be malodorous.

4 *I smell something funny about that plan:* detect, sense, perceive, feel, suspect. —*n.* 5 *What's that smell?:* aroma, scent, odor, fragrance; perfume, bouquet; reek, stink, stench.

smile *n.* 1 *Wipe that smile off your face!:* grin, smirk, simper. —*v.* 2 *We smiled when we heard the good news:* grin, beam, show pleasure; simper, smirk.

smirch *v.* 1 *The floor was smirched with grime:* besmirch, soil, smudge, dirty, stain, smear. 2 *The gossip smirched her good standing in the community:* besmirch, tarnish, stain, smear, sully, soil, blacken; slander, discredit. —*n.* 3 *There's a smirch on your jacket:* stain, smudge, blotch, smear, spot. 4 *The incident was a smirch on my record:* smear, blemish, stain, taint, blot; stigma; dishonor.

smirk *n.* 1 *He gave a smirk when he heard the excuse:* sneer, simper, sarcastic smile, grin, leer. —*v.* 2 *She smirked at my explanation:* sneer; simper; grimace.

smitten *adj.* *I'm smitten with you:* enamored, bewitched, infatuated, enraptured, have a crush (on), taken (with).

smoke *n.* 1 *smoke from the chimney:* sooty vapor; fumes. 2 *I had a smoke after dinner: (variously)* cigar, cigarette, pipe. —*v.* 3 *Is the fireplace smoking?:* fume; give off smoke, billow. 4 *to smoke a cigarette:* puff; light up, *Informal* have a drag.

smolder *v.* 1 *The fireplace smoldered all night:* smoke. 2 *I smoldered for days after our argument:* seethe, rage silently, fume.

smooth *adj.* 1 *a smooth road. smooth skin:* even, flat, level; silky, velvety, sleek. 2 *The changeover in management was smooth:* orderly, harmonious, well-ordered, well-regulated, methodical, uneventful; easy, calm, even, peaceful. 3 *Nothing seems to upset a smooth disposition:* even, calm, steady, serene, placid; pleasant, mild, composed, collected, self-possessed. 4 *a smooth talker:* flattering, ingratiating, glib, facile, suave. 5 *a smooth wine:* mellow, mild. —*v.* 6 *Smooth the plaster:* make even, make level, flatten. 7 *Money smoothed my way to the top:* pave, open; ease; facilitate, help.

Ant. 1 rough, bumpy, uneven, irregular. 2 disorderly, turbulent, troublesome. 4 unpolished, abrasive. 5 harsh, pungent. 7 hamper, hinder.

smother *v.* 1 *The killer smothered the victim:* suffocate, asphyxiate; strangle, choke. 2 *Try to smother the flames with sand:* extinguish, snuff, quench. 3 *They smothered the child with love:* shower, wrap, surround; envelop in. 4 *We tried to smother our laugh-*

ter: hide, suppress, conceal, mask, quash; keep down, choke back.

smudge *n.* 1 *an ink smudge:* smear, blot, stain, spot, mark. —*v.* 2 *She smudged her dress with chalk:* smear, stain, spot, dirty, soil.

Ant. 2 clean, cleanse.

smug *adj.* *He was smug about knowing the answer:* self-satisfied, complacent, self-righteous, superior.

smut *n.* 1 *There is smut on the windowsill:* soot, smudge, dirt, grime. 2 *The police promised to crack down on smut:* pornography; obscenity, scatology, *Slang* porn.

smutty *adj.* 1 *My hands are smutty from the coal:* sooty, dirty, grimy, soiled. 2 *a smutty book:* dirty, lewd, obscene, indecent; filthy, pornographic.

Ant. 1 clean, immaculate.

snack *n.* 1 *Let's have a snack before bed:* refreshment, light repast, bite, light lunch, tidbit. —*v.* 2 *Try not to snack between meals:* nibble, munch, eat, *Slang* nosh.

snag *n.* 1 *Our boat hit a snag in the water:* protrusion, projection; stump. 2 *The project encountered a snag:* hindrance, obstacle, hitch; difficulty, block, stumbling block, impediment, obstruction, barrier. —*v.* 3 *I snagged my stockings on the desk:* tear, rip; catch.

snap *v.* 1 *She snapped her fingers:* crack, click, pop. 2 *Snap the bolt tightly:* latch, catch, lock, secure, clasp; close. 3 *He snapped the stick in two pieces:* break, crack, fracture. 4 *The crab snapped at my toe:* bite, nip, grab. 5 *The cadets snapped to attention:* jumped, clicked. 6 *She snapped at me when I tried to comfort her:* snarl, growl. —*n.* 7 *We could hear the snap of the twigs:* crack, click, pop. 8 *My dress snap is broken:* catch, clasp, fastener. 9 *The dog made a snap at my finger:* nip, bite, grab. 10 *a cold snap:* spell, period. 11 *Beating him at tennis was a snap:* cinch, breeze. —*adj.* 12 *a snap decision:* sudden, hasty, thoughtless, quick, impulsive.

snappish *adj.* *She's always snappish when dinner is late:* peevish, surly, touchy, testy, grouchy, waspish, irascible, cross, ill-natured, petulant, quick-tempered, huffish.

Ant. amiable, good-humored, pleasant.

snappy *adj.* 1 *a snappy new convertible:* classy, smart, sharp, stylish, dapper, spiffy, jaunty. 2 *Get in here and make it snappy!:* fast, quick, hasty, speedy, swift, rapid.

Ant. 1 shabby, tacky. 2 slow, languid.

snare *n.* 1 *We caught a rabbit in the snare:* trap, noose, net. 2 *That advertisement is a snare for inexperienced people:* trap, pitfall, deception, trick, entanglement; lure, bait, decoy, ruse. —v. 3 *to snare rabbits:* capture, ensnare, trap, entrap, catch, seize.

snarl n. 1 *Comb the snarls out of your hair:* tangle, ravel, twist, kink, knot. 2 *These files are in a snarl:* tangle, jumble, mess, chaos, confusion, disorder. —v. 3 *The wind snarled the streamers on the float:* tangle, twist, knot; disorder, jumble, confuse; hinder, clog.

Ant. 2 order. 3 unsnarl, untangle.

snatch v. 1 *The rescuer snatched the boy out of the sea:* grab, seize, grasp; pluck, nab, pull, wrest; catch, take. —n. 2 *We saw only snatches of the show:* part, snippet, fragment, bit, piece.

sneak v. 1 *Let's sneak out the back way:* slip, steal, creep. —n. 2 *Don't trust that sneak:* skulker, lurker, slinker; rascal, knave, bounder, rogue, scoundrel, scamp, miscreant. —adj. 3 *a sneak attack:* surprise, secret, secretive, furtive, surreptitious; sly, underhand.

sneaky adj. *a sneaky trick:* underhand, sly, devious, treacherous, traitorous; secretive, furtive; mean, malicious, vicious.

Ant. open, aboveboard.

sneer v. 1 *He sneered at our attempt to be friendly:* scorn, mock, scoff, rebuff, jeer, deride, disdain, ridicule, belittle. —n. 2 *An ugly sneer was all we got for our trouble:* smirk, scoff, leer.

snicker v. *The children snickered when the teacher tripped:* giggle, titter, simper; snort, cackle.

snide adj. *a snide remark:* sarcastic, nasty, malicious, insinuating; mocking, scoffing, contemptuous.

sniff v. 1 *This cold makes me sniff constantly:* snivel, sniffle; snuff, snort. 2 *Sniff this perfume:* smell, whiff. —n. 3 *Did you get a sniff of that garlic?:* smell, whiff; odor, aroma.

snip v. 1 *Please snip these uneven strands of hair:* clip, cut, crop, lop, trim, prune, shear, bob. —n. 2 *I heard the snip of the scissors:* click, clack, snap. 3 *Will you give me a snip of that material?:* scrap, swatch; bit, fragment, cutting, piece.

snippy adj. *She was quite snippy when I was late:* curt, brusque, rude, impudent, cheeky, saucy, sassy, impertinent, insolent, ill-mannered, smart-alecky, flippant.

Ant. polite, respectful, deferential.

snob n. *He's too much of a snob to mix with us:* elitist, stuck-up person, pretentious person.

snobbish adj. *She's too snobbish to stay at that hotel:* disdainful, condescending, patronizing, overbearing, superior, arrogant, haughty, *Informal* stuck-up, snooty.

Ant. unpretentious, humble.

snort v. 1 *The bull began to snort:* grunt, pant, puff, blow, huff, gasp. 2 *She snorted at our modest plan:* scoff, jeer, sneer. —n. 3 *The pony gave a snort:* grunt, gasp, pant, huff.

snub v. 1 *The rich man snubbed his poor relations:* ignore, disdain, slight, scorn, rebuff; cut, give the cold shoulder. —n. 2 *I was hurt by her snub:* rebuff, slight, cut, repudiation, cold shoulder. —adj. 3 *a snub nose:* short, blunt, stubby.

snug adj. 1 *a snug cabin in the woods:* cozy, comfortable; sheltered, safe, secure. 2 *a snug ship:* tight, neat, well-organized; close, compact. 3 *These shoes are too snug:* tight-fitting, tight, close-fitting, skin-tight.

snuggle v. *The child snuggled in her mother's lap:* nestle, nuzzle, cuddle; enfold, hug.

soak v. 1 *The bedspread is soaking in the dye:* steep, bathe, wet, drench, saturate, immerse. 2 *The snow soaked through my boots:* seep, penetrate, permeate, pervade. 3 *The full impact of the news will soak in later:* penetrate, sink in, be perceived, be absorbed.

soar v. 1 *The bird soared through the air:* wing, glide, float, fly, take wing, go aloft. 2 *Apartment rents soared:* climb, rise, mount, increase swiftly; tower, thrust upward.

Ant. 1 fall, drop. 2 fall, drop, decrease.

sob v. 1 *The child sobbed hysterically:* weep, cry, blubber, whimper, wail. —n. 2 *The sobs of the baby were so sad:* cry, whimper, plaint, wail.

Ant. laugh, chortle.

sober adj. 1 *He was a sober man who seldom smiled:* solemn, serious, somber, grave, sedate. 2 *A funeral is a sober event:* grim, sad, solemn, somber, joyless, sorrowful. 3 *The room colors are sober and depressing:* drab, subdued, dull, somber, dreary. 4 *She gave a sober account of the facts:* realistic, sound, dispassionate, prudent, judicious; level-headed, rational, cool, sane, steady. 5 *He joined Alcoholics Anonymous and has been sober for five years:* temperate, dry, abstemious, not drunk, *Informal* on the wagon.

Ant. 1 frivolous, lighthearted, merry. 2 happy, joyous. 3 light, bright, colorful, lively. 4 frivolous, unrealistic; passionate, injudicious. 5 drunk, intoxicated, inebriated, off the wagon.

sociable adj. *She's very sociable:* gregarious, social, congenial, affable, outgoing, gracious; friendly, cordial, convivial.

Ant. unfriendly, withdrawn, unsociable, stiff, formal.

social adj. 1 *This is just a social call:* friendly, sociable, neighborly. 2 *The ball was the social occasion of the year:* fashionable, smart, stylish.
Ant. 1 business.

society n. 1 *Drug addiction is a major concern of society:* humanity, humankind, mankind, the general public; social order, community. 2 *a literary society:* club, association, organization, circle, alliance, league. 3 *Every important member of society attended:* elite, aristocracy, nobility, gentry, high society, the 400.

sock v. 1 *He socked his opponent in the eye:* hit, strike, box, punch, wallop, smack, smash, belt, clobber. —n. 2 *I'll give you a sock on the jaw:* hit, punch, wallop, smack, blow.

sodden adj. *The field was sodden from the rain:* drenched, saturated, sopping, soaked, soggy, wet through, dripping.
Ant. dry.

soft adj. 1 *a soft mattress:* pliable, pliant, supple, malleable; not hard. 2 *This silk scarf feels so soft:* smooth, sleek, velvety, satiny, downy, furry, silky, silken. 3 *The doorbell is too soft to hear:* subdued, faint, muted, hushed; feeble; gentle. 4 *soft colors. soft rain:* gentle, mild, subdued, tranquil, restful; delicate, pale. 5 *She has a soft spot in her heart for you:* tender, kind, lenient, tolerant, sympathetic, compassionate, pitying; sentimental. 6 *a soft job:* easy; requiring little effort.
Ant. 1 hard, unyielding, stiff, inflexible. 2 rough, coarse, abrasive. 3 loud, noisy. 4 harsh; glaring, bright. 6 difficult, tough.

soften v. 1 *Please soften the music:* lower, subdue, moderate; tone down, make softer, turn down. 2 *She tried to soften the criticism:* lessen, temper, ameliorate, mitigate, cushion, mollify.
Ant. 1 raise, intensify. 2 heighten.

softhearted adj. *She was so softhearted everybody borrowed money from her:* kindhearted, sympathetic, warmhearted, compassionate, generous, forgiving, humane, considerate, indulgent.
Ant. cold, heartless, unforgiving, hardhearted.

softly adv. *He speaks too softly:* quietly, weakly; gently, mildly.
Ant. loud, loudly, blaringly, noisily; harshly.

soggy adj. *The ground is soggy:* soaked, sopping, soppy, saturated, drenched, sodden, dripping, mushy.
Ant. dry.

soil¹ n. 1 *This soil is good for growing things:* ground, earth; loam, humus. 2 *We'll defend our soil:* land, region, country, territory.

soil² v. 1 *She soiled the carpet with her muddy shoes:* dirty, stain, smudge, smear, spot, muddy. 2 *His innuendos soiled my reputation:* blacken, defile, tarnish, debase, stain, sully. —n. 3 *What's that soil on your collar?:* stain, dirt, spot, grime, soot.
Ant. 1 clean, cleanse.

sojourn n. *How long was your sojourn in Tibet?:* visit, stay, stopover, layover, pause, vacation, holiday.

solace n. 1 *We drew solace from the many notes of sympathy:* comfort, consolation, reassurance; help in need. —v. 2 *The minister's words solaced the widow:* console, comfort, cheer, calm, assuage, reassure.
Ant. 1 distress, anxiety, anguish. 2 pain, distress, dishearten.

soldier n. 1 *Our soldiers fought the enemy:* military man, enlisted man, serviceman, warrior, G.I. 2 *He is a soldier for Christ:* militant leader, zealot, follower, partisan, worker, servant.

sole adj. *The hermit is the sole inhabitant of the island:* only, exclusive, lone, solitary, single, exclusive.

solely adv. 1 *The boy was solely at fault for the broken window:* exclusively, alone, singly, single-handedly. 2 *It was solely a case of mistaken identity:* exclusively, purely; uniquely, merely.

solemn adj. 1 *That solemn little girl never smiles:* somber, staid, grave, sedate, sober; quiet. 2 *I made a solemn decision never to drink again:* earnest, serious; determined, sincere, steadfast, absolute. 3 *The inauguration was a solemn event:* formal, dignified, ceremonious, ceremonial, awe-inspiring. 4 *She always wears such solemn clothing:* dark, gloomy, somber, drab, grim, depressing.
Ant. 1 jovial, joyous, lively, merry. 2 frivolous, halfhearted, insincere. 3 informal. 4 bright, colorful.

solicit v. *They solicited our help:* seek, request, ask, appeal for, entreat, plead, endeavor to obtain.

solicitous adj. *He was very solicitous about our problems:* concerned, mindful, regardful, anxious, attentive; eager, zealous, desirous, longing, intense, avid, intent.
Ant. unconcerned, undisturbed; uninterested.

solid adj. 1 *A rock is a solid object:* real, substantial, concrete, tangible; dense, massy, not hollow; hard, firm; solidified. 2 *We couldn't break through the solid line of tanks:* unbroken, impenetrable, impermeable; constant, continuous, uninterrupted.

3 *This old house has a remarkably solid foundation:* firm, strong, well-built, sturdy, rugged, durable, substantial. **4** *The table is solid oak:* pure, unmixed, genuine, thorough, one-hundred-percent, real; complete, unalloyed. **5** *We're solid members of the community:* sound, stable, steady, reliable, dependable, trustworthy; sensible, level-headed, rational. **6** *The city council was solid in its decision:* unanimous, undivided.

Ant. **3** flimsy, shaky, unstable, unsteady. **5** unstable, irresponsible, unreliable. **6** divided, split.

solitary *adj.* **1** *I lead a solitary life:* lone, lonely, lonesome, companionless; isolated, single. **2** *a solitary retreat:* secluded, cloistered, lonely, out-of-the-way, hidden, concealed; desolate, remote, isolated, uninhabited.

Ant. **1** gregarious, sociable, social. **2** busy, well-traveled.

solitude *n.* **1** *the solitude of a hermit's life:* isolation, aloneness, loneliness, solitariness; desolation, seclusion, remoteness. **2** *arctic solitude:* wasteland, wilderness, lonely place.

solution *n.* **1** *the solution of a crime:* solving, resolving, resolution; unraveling. **2** *Have you found a solution yet?:* explanation, answer, key, resolution. **3** *a solution of wine and oil:* emulsion, suspension; mixture, blend.

solve *v.* *to solve a riddle:* resolve, decipher, unravel, find a solution to, find the answer, find the key, figure out, decipher, unriddle.

solvent *adj.* **1** *The business is solvent:* able to pay debts, financially sound. **2** *Sugar is solvent:* dissolvable, dissoluble, soluble. —*n.* **3** *You need a solvent to remove that paint:* dissolving agent, dissolvent.

Ant. bankrupt, broke.

somber *adj.* **1** *a somber day:* drab, gloomy, dark, gray, cheerless, dreary, grim. **2** *His somber voice told us the news was bad:* grim, gloomy, depressing, mournful, funereal, serious, solemn, melancholy.

Ant. **1** cheerful, bright, sunny. **2** cheerful, happy.

song *n.* **1** *The band played our favorite song:* ballad, melody, tune, ditty, number. **2** *the robin's song:* piping, call, musical sound. **3** *I enjoy reading Keats's love songs:* poem, lyric, verse.

sonorous *adj.* **1** *The sonorous clang of cymbals:* resonant, full-toned, deep, vibrant, reverberating, resounding, ringing. **2** *The orator has a sonorous style:* eloquent, florid, flamboyant, grandiose.

Ant. **1** weak, tinny.

soon *adv.* *We hope to leave soon:* directly,

shortly, instantly, pronto, right away, presently, forthwith, before long, without delay, early on, in a little while, any minute.

soothe *v.* **1** *He tried to soothe my rage:* pacify, comfort, calm, moderate, placate, mollify, appease. **2** *The medication soothed the pain:* lessen, alleviate, relieve, ease, mitigate.

Ant. **1** rouse, excite. **2** increase, irritate.

soothsayer *n.* *A soothsayer predicted I would inherit a fortune:* fortune-teller, seer, diviner, prophet.

sophisticated *adj.* **1** *a sophisticated traveler:* seasoned, experienced, worldly, worldly-wise, cosmopolitan. **2** *The play was too sophisticated for them:* intellectual, cultured, cultivated, highbrow; complicated, complex, difficult, subtle, advanced.

Ant. **1** unsophisticated, unseasoned, simple, unworldly. **2** unsophisticated; simple, uncomplicated.

sophomoric *adj.* *sophomoric behavior:* juvenile, childish, infantile, adolescent; puerile, schoolboyish, immature.

Ant. mature, sophisticated, grown-up.

sopping *adj.* *Take off those sopping clothes!:* drenched, wet, saturated, soppy, soaked.

sorcery *n.* *Sorcery turned the girl into a mouse:* witchcraft, witchery, wizardry, black magic, enchantment.

sordid *adj.* **1** *a sordid slum:* filthy, squalid, unclean, dirty. **2** *He led a sordid life:* low, base, depraved, vile, wicked, debauched, degraded, vulgar, disreputable, corrupt.

Ant. **1** clean, pristine. **2** honorable, pure, noble.

sore *adj.* **1** *a sore toe:* painful, tender, aching, sensitive, smarting, irritated; hurting, hurt, bruised. **2** *Losing was a sore disappointment:* sharp, painful, wounding; agonizing, distressing, unbearable. **3** *His heart was sore at the news:* agonized, grieved, distressed, pained. **4** *in sore need:* severe, desperate, critical, grievous, extreme, great. **5** *I'm sore at you for being late:* angry, indignant, irritated, irked, upset. —*n.* **6** *Put some iodine on that sore:* inflammation, wound.

Ant. **1** pain-free. **3** happy, joyous, cheerful. **5** pleased, delighted.

sorely *adv.* *He's sorely in need of advice:* badly, severely, greatly, extremely, desperately, critically.

sorrow *n.* **1** *We felt sorrow at the news:* sadness, unhappiness, woe. **2** *Too many sorrows crushed her spirit:* misfortune, loss, trouble, hardship, affliction, travail. —*v.* **3** *I sorrow for you in your loss:* grieve, weep, lament, despair, mourn; be sad.

Ant. 1 joy, gladness, delight, happiness. 2 happiness, joy. 3 rejoice.

sorry *adj.* 1 *I'm sorry I made you cry:* regretful, contrite, sorrowful, sad, unhappy; remorseful, repentant; melancholy, crestfallen, grieved, unhappy, brokenhearted. 2 *The house is in a sorry mess:* miserable, pitiful, pitiable, deplorable, woeful, pathetic.

Ant. 1 happy, unrepentant; joyous, elated.

sort *n.* 1 *Is this the sort of car you want?:* kind, type; make, brand, species, variety, classification. 2 *Trust him—he's a good sort:* person, individual. —*v.* 3 *Let's sort the names alphabetically:* arrange, group, classify, organize, systematize, order, categorize. 4 *They tried to sort the fakes from the originals:* separate, segregate, sift.

so-so *adj. The movie was so-so:* ordinary, mediocre, fair, passable, middling, tolerable, adequate, bearable, undistinguished, second-rate, indifferent, unexceptional.

soul *n.* 1 *She is gone but her soul lives on:* spirit; vital force. 2 *He loved her with all his soul:* being, spirit; inmost feelings, inner core. 3 *Won't someone help that poor soul?:* person, creature, individual; living being. 4 *I am the soul of honesty:* essence, embodiment, quintessence.

sound[1] *n.* 1 *The sound of rain on the roof:* noise. 2 *I didn't like the sound of her telegram:* drift, tone, tenor, suggestion, implication. 3 *Were you within sound of the explosion?:* range, earshot; hearing distance. —*v.* 4 *The alarm sounded:* make a noise, produce sound, cause to sound. 5 *The bell sounded lunch:* signal, announce. 6 *Her voice sounds happy:* seem, convey a certain impression. 7 *Sound your words more clearly:* pronounce, articulate, enunciate, voice, utter.

sound[2] *adj.* 1 *He's sound again:* robust, sturdy, strong, fit, hardy, healthy. 2 *The old building is surprisingly sound:* undamaged, intact, unmarred; substantial, strong, well-built, sturdy; firm, solid. 3 *She has a sound business:* solid, strong, stable, solvent. 4 *a sound decision:* sensible, solid, reliable, competent, dependable, wise, rational, reasonable, responsible. 5 *I was in a sound sleep:* deep, untroubled. 6 *The officer gave us a sound reprimand:* thorough, thoroughgoing, severe, firm.

Ant. 1–4 unsound. 1 ailing, weak. 3 failing, insolvent, shaky. 4 unreliable, incompetent, rash, irresponsible, frivolous. 5 light.

soupçon *n. I detected a soupçon of garlic in the stew:* trace, dash, suspicion, bit, hint,

vestige, suggestion, whiff, taste, tad, shade, drop, tinge, trifle, jot, touch.

sour *adj.* 1 *These pickles are too sour:* tart, acid, vinegary, tangy, sharp, acerbic, astringent. 2 *Does the milk taste sour?:* spoiled, turned, fermented, rancid, curdled, bad. 3 *She glanced at the noisy child with a sour expression:* disagreeable, nasty, unpleasant, surly, bad-tempered, crabby, jaundiced, dour; petulant, sullen, ill-humored, ill-tempered, cranky, irritable, grouchy. —*v.* 4 *The cream soured:* spoil, ferment, curdle, turn. 5 *A lonely childhood soured him:* embitter, make disagreeable, make unpleasant, jaundice, make cynical, make pessimistic.

Ant. 1 sweet. 2 fresh, unspoiled. 3 sweet, agreeable, pleasant, gracious, good-natured.

source *n.* 1 *What is the source of your strength?:* origin, derivation, basis; antecedent, fountain, fount, spring, wellspring, root, foundation. 2 *the source of a river:* beginning, headwater, head, fount, fountain.

Ant. 1 outcome, result, consequence. 2 mouth.

souse *v.* 1 *The downpour soused us:* wet thoroughly, drench, soak, saturate, douse. —*n.* 2 *Slang He's been a souse all his life:* drunk, drunkard, alcoholic, inebriate, dipsomaniac, boozer, sot, tippler, lush.

Ant. 1 dry. 3 teetotaler, abstainer.

souvenir *n. a vacation souvenir:* memento, reminder, remembrance, relic, keepsake, emblem, trophy.

sovereign *n.* 1 *sovereign of a kingdom:* supreme ruler, monarch; (variously) king, queen, prince, emperor, czar, potentate; crowned head, chief, chieftain, overlord, autocrat, lord. —*adj.* 2 *the queen's sovereign authority:* ruling, supreme, absolute; royal, monarchical, imperial, reigning, regal; kingly, queenly, princely. 3 *Your welfare is my sovereign concern:* principal, chief, foremost, paramount, leading, governing, ruling, supreme, main, uppermost, highest, dominant, major, prime. 4 *a sovereign nation:* self-governing, free, independent, self-directing, self-ruling, autonomous.

Ant. 1 subject. 2 limited, partial. 3 minor, secondary, least.

sovereignty *n.* 1 *the sovereignty of a ruler:* power, dominion, authority, supremacy, control, jurisdiction, predominance, primacy; kingship, lordship; throne, crown. 2 *The United States declared its sovereignty in 1776:* independence, autonomy, self-determination, self-rule, self-government, freedom.

sow v. 1 *Sow the seeds in early spring:* plant, seed, scatter, broadcast, strew, disperse. 2 *Her strange behavior sowed suspicions in our minds:* plant, establish, inject, instill, introduce.

space n. 1 *The rocket was lost in space:* outer space, the void, the firmament, the heavens, sky. 2 *We need more office space:* room, area, territory, expanse, spread, amplitude, reach. 3 *She has a wide space between her teeth:* gap, distance, span, chasm, separation, break, hiatus, interruption, interval, interstice, lacuna, blank. 4 *in the space of an hour:* period, interval, span, duration, term. 5 *Luckily, there was an extra space on the plane:* seat, place, room, berth, spot, accommodation. —v. 6 *Space the paintings evenly on the wall:* place, arrange, organize, distribute, order, range; separate, spread.
Ant. 2 confinement. 3 closure.

spacious adj. *a spacious room:* large, ample, wide, broad, sizable, commodious, capacious, roomy; immense, expansive, extensive, vast, enormous; uncrowded.
Ant. small, cramped, crowded.

span n. 1 *We searched the entire span of the island. The span of human life is short:* distance, breadth, length, dimensions, reach, stretch, scope, range, sweep, area, territory; extent, term, duration, period, interval. 2 *the second span of a bridge:* arch, vault, archway, trestle, wing. —v. 3 *The overpass spans the center of town:* bridge, cross, extend across, vault. 4 *Their friendship spanned a lifetime:* cover, reach over, stretch over; last, endure.

spank v. 1 *Mother spanked him:* paddle, whale, hide, tan; strike, beat, hit, strap, belt, switch, whip, flog, cane, birch. —n. 2 *The spank hurt his hand more than it hurt me:* slap, strike, hit, blow, wallop, belt.

spare v. 1 *The king spared the prisoner:* save from death, refrain from hurting, forgive, have mercy on, let off, reprieve, pardon. 2 *The doctor tried to spare me pain:* safeguard, protect, exempt, guard, shield, shelter, defend; save, relieve. 3 *I can spare some time now:* afford, grant, give, relinquish, forgo, cede. 4 *Spare your energy:* conserve, withhold, hold back, save, hoard, reserve, husband, use frugally, keep. 5 *She never spares the butter when baking:* use frugally, economize on, limit, conserve, skimp on, stint. —adj. 6 *a spare tire. I gave the beggar my spare change:* reserve, extra, auxiliary, supplementary, substitute, supplemental; superfluous, supernumerary, additional, unused, surplus, extraneous, excess, leftover. 7 *The suit hung limply on his spare frame:* lean, bony, scrawny, scraggy, thin,

emaciated, gaunt, skinny; slight, meager, skimpy, scanty, scant.
Ant. 1 punish, condemn, destroy, harm. 2 afflict, expose. 4 squander, use, spend. 5 squander. 7 heavy, plump, large.

sparing adj. *The professor was sparing with praise:* thrifty, economical, frugal, saving; parsimonious, miserly, penurious, stinting, stingy, ungenerous, niggardly, tightfisted; grudging, meager, scanty, scant.
Ant. lavish, profuse, extravagant, generous.

sparkle v. 1 *The diamond ring sparkled:* shine, glitter, glint, glisten, flicker, twinkle, gleam, shimmer, scintillate, flash. —n. 2 *the sparkle of gems:* glint, glitter, twinkle, flicker, shimmer, glimmer, flash; gleam, radiance, glow. 3 *His sparkle made him the life of the party:* liveliness, animation, verve, brilliance, vim; vivacity, exhilaration, exuberance, vitality, spirit; cheerfulness, gaiety, jollity, cheer.
Ant. 2 dullness, flatness. 3 dullness, cheerlessness, drabness, lethargy.

sparse adj. *Sparse trees provide poor shelter:* few, few and far between, thin, thinly distributed, scarce, infrequent; scattered, sporadic; meager, scanty, spare, scant, skimpy.
Ant. plentiful, numerous, dense.

Spartan adj. *to lead a Spartan life:* plain, simple, austere, ascetic, frugal, abstemious, disciplined, restrained, strict, exacting; severe, hard, stringent, self-denying, self-disciplined.
Ant. self-indulgent, luxurious, lavish; undisciplined, unrestrained; soft, easy.

spasm n. 1 *a spasm of pain:* cramp, seizure, crick; twitch, tic, jerk, convulsion, shudder, start, paroxysm; throe, pang. 2 *a spasm of tears:* spell, fit, burst, attack, frenzy, spurt, eruption.

spasmodic adj. *She shows only spasmodic affection:* fitful, intermittent, occasional, periodic, fleeting, sporadic, irregular, inconstant, discontinuous.
Ant. constant, steady, regular.

spat n. 1 *They had a little spat but made up quickly:* disagreement, misunderstanding, quarrel, tiff, dispute, fight, scrap, set-to, squabble, wrangle. —v. 2 *I can't remember what we spatted about:* quarrel, argue, bicker, fight, disagree, squabble.
Ant. 1 agreement, understanding. 2 agree, concur.

speak v. 1 *to speak with an accent:* talk, articulate, vocalize, sound, give utterance; enunciate, pronounce; converse, confer, consult, chat. 2 *She spoke what was in her heart:* express, say, communicate, tell, state, declare, convey, relate, impart, put into

words, give voice to; divulge, reveal, disclose, proclaim, announce, advise, air, report. **3** *Is the governor going to speak at the rally?*: give a speech, deliver an address, lecture; sermonize, preach; expound, orate, hold forth. **4** *His letter spoke of his future plans:* mention, comment, refer, make reference, remark, treat, discuss, deal.
Ant. 2 repress, conceal, suppress.

speaker *n. The senator is the opening speaker:* talker, lecturer, spokesman, spokeswoman, orator, speechmaker.
Ant. listener, audience.

spear *n.* **1** *The spear pierced the lion's heart:* javelin, lance, bolt, shaft. —*v.* **2** *Have you ever speared trout?:* impale, run through; stick, transfix, puncture.

spearhead *n.* **1** *He was the spearhead of the ecology movement:* leader, pioneer, initiator, creator, spokesman, spokeswoman, founder, prime mover, instituter, inaugurator. —*v.* **2** *She spearheaded the political movement:* lead, pioneer, initiate, begin, start, launch, inaugurate, establish, originate, institute, found, develop.

special *adj.* **1** *You'll need a special machine for that:* especial, certain, specific, distinct, specialized, particular; proper. **2** *This is a special day in my life:* out of the ordinary, unusual, uncommon, unique; select, distinctive, rare, singular, extraordinary, distinct, exceptional; important, momentous, signal, outstanding, distinguished, noteworthy, remarkable; personal, individual. **3** *a special friend:* particular, great, outstanding, especial, exceptional; close, fast, good, intimate. —*n.* **4** *Today's special is broiled lamb:* specialty, feature, attraction, highlight; bargain, sale item.
Ant. 1 ordinary, unspecialized. 2 ordinary, undistinctive, unimportant, routine; unexceptional, usual.

specialist *n. She's a specialist in Chinese studies:* expert, authority, master, skilled hand.
Ant. amateur; generalist.

specialty *n.* **1** *Will your specialty be psychology or sociology?:* special field, pursuit, special subject, major; special line of work, profession; faculty, aptitude, bent, talent. **2** *The restaurant's specialty is soup:* special, distinctive product, distinction, earmark, trademark, feature, claim to fame, forte.

species *n. a species of rose:* type, sort, kind, class, category, breed, variety, order, form, subdivision.

specific *adj.* **1** *What is the specific time of arrival? There are two specific questions we must answer:* precise, definite, exact, fixed, specified; clear-cut, concrete, stated, con-

fined, limited, pinned-down, restricted; detailed, minute, relevant, pertinent, pointed, particular. **2** *A specific attribute of the elephant is its long trunk:* especial, distinctive, individual, unique, singular, particular, characteristic, typical, personal. —*n.* **3** Often **specifics** *The specifics of the accident were hazy:* particular, fact, relevant point, detail, circumstance.
Ant. 1 approximate, vague, hazy; general. 2 common, undistinctive, general.

specify *v. Please specify what the job will entail:* detail, indicate, designate, name, stipulate, cite, itemize, particularize, describe, set forth; order.

specimen *n. This is a perfect specimen of an American Beauty rose:* sample, model, representative, example, exemplar, instance, case, exemplification.

specious *adj. specious reasoning:* deceptive, misleading, fallacious, false, invalid, faulty, unsound, unfounded, incorrect, inaccurate, spurious.
Ant. valid, conclusive.

speck *n.* **1** *a speck of dust:* particle, grain, bit; spot, fleck. **2** *I use just a speck of cream in my coffee:* drop, trace, trifle, bit, modicum; whit, mite, scintilla, iota, jot.

spectacle *n.* **1** *The eclipse was a spectacle not to be missed:* marvel, wonder, phenomenon, curiosity; sight. **2** *The performers put on quite a spectacle:* exhibition, presentation, extravaganza, production, exhibit, exposition, display, pageant, parade.

spectacular *adj.* **1** *a spectacular wedding:* magnificent, gorgeous, elaborate, sumptuous, impressive, showy, splendid, opulent, ceremonious, grand, stately; fabulous, marvelous, astounding, overwhelming. **2** *a spectacular rescue:* thrilling, daring, dramatic, sensational. —*n.* **3** *The charity ball was something of a spectacular:* spectacle, elaborate production, extravaganza, gala.
Ant. 1 plain, unimpressive, modest.

spectator *n. Thousands of spectators jammed the stands:* onlooker, viewer, beholder, fan, audience, gallery.
Ant. performer, entertainer.

specter *n. Was there a specter in the deserted house?:* ghost, phantom, spook, spirit, wraith, hobgoblin, sprite, banshee, presence, phantasm.

speculate *v. He speculated about the purpose of life. Scientists speculate about life on other planets:* muse, contemplate, reflect, think, ponder, ruminate; surmise, conjecture, theorize, hazard an opinion, hypothesize; suppose, imagine, fancy, dream.

speech *n.* **1** *We express ourselves through speech and writing:* speaking, oral communication, talking, talk, articulation, utterance, vocalization; conversation, discourse, verbalization, verbal intercourse, chitchat. **2** *The candidate made a moving speech:* address, talk, oration, sermon, lecture, declamation, discourse, appeal, exhortation; soliloquy, monologue. **3** *Her speech is filled with colloquialisms:* style of speaking, manner of speaking, expression, utterance, rhetoric; articulation, pronunciation, enunciation, diction, elocution. **4** *The speech of the islanders is hard to understand:* language, dialect, tongue, idiom.

Ant. **1** muteness, speechlessness; silence.

speed *n.* **1** *He finished the job with amazing speed:* quickness, dispatch, celerity, promptness, alacrity, swiftness, expedition, rapidness, rapidity, haste, hastiness; fleetness, velocity, hurry, rush, acceleration. **2** *the speed of sound:* rate, velocity. —*v.* **3** *The ambulance sped to the hospital:* hurry, rush, hasten, make haste, tear, hurtle, run, race, hie, hustle, dart, dash, hightail. **4** *We'll never get there if he doesn't speed up:* hurry up, hurry, quicken, hasten, accelerate.

Ant. **1** slowness, delay, sluggishness. **3** creep, crawl, dawdle. **4** slow down, slow.

speedy *adj.* *She wished me a speedy recovery:* swift, fast, rapid, hasty, quick, fleet; without delay, early, with dispatch.

Ant. slow, sluggish, lagging; delayed.

spell[1] *n.* **1** *The fairy godmother's spell transformed the pumpkin into a coach:* charm, magic formula, magic, incantation, voodoo, hoodoo, sorcery, witchery, invocation. **2** *She fell under the spell of his charm:* enchantment, fascination, bewitchment, allure, influence.

spell[2] *n.* **1** *The long spell of duty exhausted him:* stretch, turn, period, term, bout, time, course, duration, round, stint. **2** *Just rest for a spell:* while, bit; interval, break, respite, recess, pause. —*v.* **3** *Someone had better spell the night nurse:* relieve, take the place of, take over for, substitute for.

spellbound *adj.* *We were spellbound by the music:* fascinated, transported, enchanted, charmed, enraptured, entranced, enthralled, rapt, bewitched, transfixed, possessed; dumbstruck, awestruck.

Ant. unimpressed, indifferent.

spend *v.* **1** *What did you spend for that lamp?:* pay, pay out, expend, disburse; dispense, allocate, dole, give, *Slang* shell out. **2** *You spend too much energy worrying:* consume, use, employ, expend, squander, waste, dissipate. **3** *I spent myself in the last race:* burn out, drain, use up, exhaust, consume, deplete, wear out. **4** *Let's spend to-*

morrow fishing: occupy, pass, while away, take up, use, fill.

Ant. **1** acquire, get, gain; save, collect, gather. **2, 3** save, conserve.

spendthrift *n.* **1** *I'm a spendthrift and can't save a penny:* wastrel, waster, squanderer, prodigal. —*adj.* **2** *My spendthrift brother pays a fortune for clothes:* extravagant, wasteful, improvident, wastrel, prodigal.

Ant. **1** tightwad, penny pincher, cheapskate. **2** frugal, penny-pinching, stingy.

spent *adj.* *We were completely spent after two weeks of hard labor:* exhausted, weary, wearied, worn out, tired out, ready to drop, fatigued, *Slang* beat.

spew *v.* *The volcano spewed out lava:* disgorge, regurgitate, throw out; cast up, spit out, eject, expel.

sphere *n.* **1** *A ball is a sphere:* globe, ball, spheroid, globule, orb. **2** *Poverty and slums were outside the rich boy's sphere:* domain, realm, range, area, scope, compass, territory, province, bailiwick; experience.

spice *n.* *Pepper is a spice:* seasoning; condiment, flavoring. **2** *He needs a little spice in his life:* zest, excitement, zip, snap.

Ant. **2** boredom, dullness.

spicy *adj.* **1** *spicy food:* pungent, hot, piquant, peppery, fiery, tangy. **2** *That movie is too spicy for the children:* racy, ribald, risqué, scandalous, indelicate, indecent, bawdy, off-color, suggestive.

Ant. **1** bland, tasteless, insipid. **2** proper, prudish.

spill *v.* **1** *Be careful not to spill the coffee. Tears spilled from her eyes:* cause to overflow, slop, slosh; drip, fall, drop, run, flow, overflow, splash; let flow, shed, pour out. **2** *I knew he'd spill the whole story!:* disclose, reveal, tell, *Slang* blab.

spin *v.* **1** *The dancer spun around and around:* twirl, whirl, turn, rotate, revolve, swirl, wheel, pirouette, gyrate. **2** *No one believed that fantastic tale you spun:* tell, narrate, render, relate; concoct, fabricate. —*n.* **3** *Place your bets before the spin of the wheel:* turn, spinning, twirl, roll, rotation.

spine *n.* **1** *He broke his spine in a fall from a horse:* backbone, vertebral column, spinal column, vertebrae. **2** *Hedgehogs protect themselves with their spines:* quill, barb, spur, bristle, prickle; bramble, needle.

spiral *n.* **1** *A coiled spring forms a spiral:* helix, whorl, gyre, coil; curl, curlicue. —*adj.* **2** *a spiral staircase:* helical, corkscrew, spiroid, curled, coiled, whorled; winding, twisting.

spire *n.* **1** *a church spire:* steeple, belfry, turret, tower, bell tower, campanile, shaft.

2 *the spires of mountains:* peak, crest, summit; pinnacle, apex, vertex, tip.

spirit *n.* 1 *They believe the spirit lives on after death:* soul, vital essence; psyche. 2 *The haunted house was filled with spirits:* ghost, spook, apparition, specter, phantom, phantasm, hobgoblin, wraith, banshee, presence; goblin, sprite. 3 *The spirit is willing but the flesh is weak:* will, motivation, resolve, resolution; mind, heart, impulse, urge. 4 *Even the children lacked spirit on that gloomy day:* vigor, vim, zest, liveliness, animation, vitality, verve, vivacity, enthusiasm, energy, drive, zeal, sprightliness, ardor; courage, bravery, dauntlessness, stoutheartedness, daring, backbone, fortitude, boldness, valor, fearlessness. 5 *The spirit of the country is one of disillusionment:* temper, feeling, disposition, frame of mind, mood, humor, tone, tenor, morale, turn of mind. 6 *My father has great family spirit:* allegiance, devotion, loyalty, attachment, bond, feeling. 7 *I feel bound by the spirit as well as the letter of the law:* intention, significance, intent, meaning, essence, purport, substance; sense, purpose, aim.
Ant. 1 body, flesh, materiality. 4 lifelessness, spiritlessness.

spirited *adj. a spirited horse. He gave a spirited reply:* high-spirited, lively, frisky; fiery, courageous, plucky, intrepid, fearless, bold.
Ant. spiritless, dispirited; timid.

spiritual *adj.* 1 *The medium tried to reach someone in the spiritual world:* ghostly, supernatural, supernal, psychic, phantom, incorporeal, immaterial, unearthly, otherworldly, spectral, intangible. 2 *Spiritual beauty outshines physical beauty:* of the soul, inner, innermost; moral. 3 *He devoted himself to a spiritual life:* religious, holy, godly, pious, devotional, divine, ecclesiastical, priestly, sanctified, celestial, heavenly; blessed, hallowed, consecrated.
Ant. 1, 3 physical, earthly, material, corporeal. 2 fleshly, bodily, physical, carnal. 3 temporal, secular, lay, worldly.

spit *v.* 1 *The baby spit applesauce on his bib:* expectorate; spew, eject; slobber, drool, slaver, dribble. 2 *He spat out angry words at his tormentors:* fling, throw, express violently; hiss, shriek. —*n.* 3 *Wipe the spit off the child's chin:* saliva, sputum, spittle, drool.

spite *n.* 1 *He tripped me out of spite:* malice, hatred, vindictiveness, bitterness, ill will, maliciousness, resentment, animosity, malevolence, hostility, antipathy, loathing, grudge, rancor, revengefulness, vengeance, vengefulness; meanness, nastiness. —*v.* 2 *You came late just to spite me!* treat maliciously, annoy, humiliate, mortify, misuse, ill-treat; irk, vex, nettle, irritate.
Ant. 1 kindness, kindliness, benevolence. 2 please, help, assist, support, serve.

spiteful *adj. The story you spread about us was purely spiteful:* malicious, hateful, vicious, malevolent, wicked, hostile, vindictive, rancorous, vengeful, acrimonious.
Ant. loving, affectionate, kind, considerate.

splash *v.* 1 *The diver splashed water all over the sunbathers:* splatter, spatter, slosh, dash, plash. 2 *The children splashed around in the mud:* plunge, paddle, wallow, bathe. 3 *He splashed his shirt with paint:* bespatter, spatter, splatter, sprinkle, splotch, besmirch, soil, stain, daub, smear, streak. 4 *The waves splashed against the rocks:* wash, dash, buffet, toss, break, strike. 5 *The news was splashed across the television screens:* blazon, broadcast. —*n.* 6 *The news made quite a splash around here:* stir, commotion, ado, sensation, uproar; impact, effect.

spleen *n. He vented his spleen on his wife:* bad temper, rancor, spite, peevishness, spitefulness, venom, acrimony, animosity, animus, ill humor, bitterness, enmity, vexation, irritability, anger.
Ant. cheerfulness, good humor, joy.

splendid *adj.* 1 *This is a splendid house:* beautiful, magnificent, superb, gorgeous, resplendent, dazzling, grand, sumptuous, majestic, elegant, imposing, regal, stately. 2 *His reputation as a statesman is splendid:* exalted, lofty, high, august, elevated, illustrious, eminent, distinguished, imposing, preeminent. 3 *That's a splendid painting:* excellent, exceptional, outstanding, brilliant, marvelous, admirable, fine, remarkable, terrific, wonderful.
Ant. 1 plain, tawdry, squalid. 2 inglorious, ignoble, low, ignominious. 3 ordinary, mediocre, unexceptional, unremarkable.

splendor *n.* 1 *the splendor of a smile:* brilliance, dazzle, luster, gleam, sheen, glitter, shine, radiance, luster. 2 *the splendor of a royal wedding. the splendor of the Grand Canyon:* pomp, grandeur, glory, brilliance, beauty, magnificence, opulence, stateliness; sublimity, augustness, nobility; preeminence, renown.
Ant. 1, 2 dullness, drabness. 2 plainness.

splinter *n.* 1 *Pull the splinter out with a tweezer:* sliver, fragment, shiver. —*v.* 2 *The carpenter splintered the wood when he drove in the nail:* sliver, split, shiver, shatter; smash, break up; fly apart, fragment; chip, fracture.

split *v.* 1 *Split the pineapple before peeling it:* divide lengthwise, bisect, halve; cleave, rive, break, crack. **2** *The strike split the union members into factions:* divide, disunite, part, sever, set at odds, sow dissension, alienate; disagree, differ, diverge, part company. **3** *When he bent over, he split his pants. The water pressure split the pipe:* tear, tear asunder, sunder, break, burst, part, rupture, break apart, shiver, splinter, fracture, snap, crack. **4** *The robbers split the loot:* share, divide, divvy up, apportion, portion, allocate, deal, allot, mete, subdivide. —*n.* **5** *Can you mend this split?:* tear, rift, rent, breach, cleft, separation; break, crack, fissure, fracture, opening. **6** *A split in the party could lose us the election:* rupture, breach, disunion, rift, schism, division; quarrel, divorce, disassociation, difference, divergence, disagreement, alienation, estrangement, parting of the ways. —*adj.* **7** *a split seam. a split personality:* torn, severed, rent, ripped; broken, segmented, ruptured, fractured, cracked; divided, separated; dual, twofold; mixed, varied; undecided, ambivalent.

Ant. 1, 2, 3 unite, join. 6 union, merger; agreement. 7 unbroken, sound.

splurge *v.* **1** *Let's splurge and have champagne!:* indulge oneself, be extravagant, live it up, shoot the works. —*n.* **2** *He'll regret that buying splurge when he receives the bills:* indulgence, self-indulgence, binge, spree.

splutter *v.* **1** *She spluttered a nervous apology:* sputter, stammer, stutter, mumble, hem and haw. **2** *The log was spluttering in the fireplace:* spit, hiss, sputter; spew, spray, spatter.

spoil *v.* **1** *I spoiled the soup with too much salt:* ruin, botch, mess up, foul up, bungle, damage, muddle, blemish, flaw; disfigure, mutilate, destroy, harm, injure, deface. **2** *Food spoils quickly without preservatives:* go bad, decay, rot, become tainted, sour, putrefy, decompose, deteriorate, turn. **3** *He spoiled his son by never saying "no":* overindulge, pamper, overgratify; coddle, mollycoddle, baby, humor.

Ant. 1 enhance, improve. 2 preserve, conserve. 3 deprive.

spoils *n. pl. To the victor go the spoils!:* benefits, prizes, loot, booty, plunder, swag, bounty; patronage.

spokesman or **spokeswoman** *n. Through his spokesman the ambassador welcomed us to the embassy:* spokesperson, deputy, delegate, representative; agent, surrogate, proxy.

sponsor *n.* **1** *A large store is the sponsor of the Christmas parade. I need a sponsor for my project:* promoter, financer, backer, advertiser; patron, protector, guarantor, supporter, defender, advocate. —*v.* **2** *Our legislator sponsored the environmental bill:* back, advocate, promote; champion, support, uphold, vouch for.

spontaneous *adj. Her remarks were spontaneous:* unpremeditated, improvised, impulsive, impetuous, ad lib, extemporaneous; natural, unstudied, uncontrived; extempore, impromptu, offhand, voluntary, unplanned, automatic, unhesitating, instinctive.

Ant. premeditated, studied, contrived, planned, calculated.

spoof *n.* **1** *The story was a spoof of Hemingway's style:* parody, takeoff, burlesque, satire, travesty, caricature, joke. —*v.* **2** *The comedian loved to spoof presidents:* satirize, lampoon, parody, caricature.

spook *n. We imagined a spook in the empty house:* apparition, ghost, phantom, haunt, specter, bogey, goblin, hobgoblin, spirit, shadow.

sporadic *adj. We've had sporadic snow this month:* irregular, spotty, scattered, fitful, now and then, occasional, infrequent, intermittent, discontinuous; meager, few, thin, scarce, rare, isolated; haphazard, random.

Ant. continuous, steady, constant.

sport *n.* **1** *Tennis is a popular sport:* athletic pastime, physical activity, game, competition, contest, athletics; diversion, recreation, fun, distraction, entertainment, amusement, play, hobby. **2** *The teasing was only sport:* play, jest, jesting, skylarking, kidding; jollity, gaiety, mirth, hilarity, antics, lark, fun; raillery, ridicule, mockery, scoffing. —*v.* **3** *The colts were sporting in the meadow:* play; caper, gambol, revel, frisk, cavort, frolic, lark, skylark. **4** *He sports an ivory-handled cane:* show off, flourish, carry, bear.

Ant. 1 business, job, work. 3 work, toil.

spot *n.* **1** *There's a spot on your tie:* stain, speck, splotch, smudge, blot, daub, smirch, fleck, speckle; discoloration, blemish. **2** *The dishonorable discharge was a spot on his reputation:* stain, blemish, taint, blot, discredit, stigma, aspersion. **3** *We're going to build on this spot. The swimming hole is a popular spot:* place, locality, locale, location, site, tract, space; region, district, area, quarter, neighborhood. **4** *I'm in a bad spot:* situation, difficulty, plight, dilemma, fix, bind, predicament. —*v.* **5** *Wine spotted the tablecloth:* stain, smudge, smirch, soil, sully, discolor, spatter. **6** *I finally spotted a mailbox:* see, pick out, recognize, light on, discern, detect.

spotless *adj.* **1** *The house was in spotless condition:* clean, unsoiled, unspotted, immaculate, pristine, flawless; unsullied, untarnished, perfect, unblemished. 2 *Her military record was spotless:* perfect, unflawed, flawless, untarnished, unblemished, untainted, unsullied, faultless, clean, unmarred; impeccable, irreproachable.

Ant. 1 filthy, dirty, soiled. 2 tarnished, flawed, marred, blemished.

spotty *adj.* 1 *a spotty complexion from too much sun:* mottled, full of spots, dappled, spotted, freckled, variegated; blotchy, splotchy. 2 *His work is spotty:* uneven, irregular, erratic, variable, capricious, inconstant, unreliable, undependable.

Ant. 1 smooth, clear. 2 even, uniform, constant, dependable.

spout *v.* 1 *The whale spouted. Lava spouted from the volcano:* spurt, discharge, emit forcibly, squirt, issue, spray, pour out, disgorge, vomit, erupt, spew, eject, expel, gush, stream, flow, exude. —*n.* 2 *the spout of a tea kettle:* outlet, vent, mouth, pipe, tube, nozzle, lip, conduit. 4 *a spout of water:* jet, spurt, fountain, gush, spray.

sprawl *v. Don't sprawl at the table:* slouch, stretch out, loll, flop, slump, recline, lounge.

spray[1] *n.* 1 *The spray from the fountain kept us back:* droplets, mist, splash, vapor; shower, burst, discharge.

spray[2] *n. a spray of mistletoe:* sprig, bouquet, shoot, switch, twig, bough, blossom.

spread *v.* 1 *Let's spread the blanket under that tree:* stretch out, open, unfold, unroll, extend. 2 *She spread her toys all over the room:* scatter, strew, sprinkle, distribute, diffuse, disperse; extend, stretch, cover. 3 *The radio spread the news. The fire spread rapidly:* communicate, circulate, disseminate, proclaim, broadcast, make public, report, bruit, noise abroad, publicize, herald, announce, promulgate, diffuse; proliferate, pervade, permeate; overrun, suffuse, advance. 4 *Spread the wax on the floor:* apply, coat, smear, cover, plaster. —*n.* 5 *The spread of the disease frightened the villagers:* spreading, increase, expansion, dispersion, diffusion, dissemination, pervasion, suffusion, proliferation. 6 *The spread of the prairies was breathtaking:* stretch, reach, extent, extension, span, scope, range, breadth, width, compass; expanse, sweep.

Ant. 1 fold, roll up. 2 collect, gather. 3 suppress, conceal, confine; diminish, abate. 5 halting, check, abatement, diminishing.

spree *n. He was hung over after his spree. a buying spree:* carouse, carousal, revel, revelry, bacchanal, orgy, debauch; bout, binge, splurge.

sprightly *adj. He's unusually sprightly*

today: animated, lively, playful, vivacious, sportive, spry, chipper, merry, active, jaunty, breezy, spirited, nimble, energetic.

Ant. lethargic, sluggish, phlegmatic.

spring *v.* 1 *I sprang out of bed when the alarm went off:* leap, bound, rise suddenly, jump, dart, vault, lunge, bounce, start, hop. 2 *Oil wells sprang up all over Texas. Shouts of protest sprang from the crowd:* rise, appear, mushroom, crop out; sprout, burgeon, pop, loom; pour, burst forth, flow, well, surge, rush, break forth, gush, spout, spurt, shoot, emanate. —*n.* 3 *The dancer's high springs dazzled the audience:* jump, leap, saltation, vault, bound, hop, bounce, entrechat. 4 *There's no spring left in this tennis ball:* springiness, elasticity, bounce, resiliency, elastic force, flexibility, stretchability, stretch, recoil. 5 *The spring was too cold for swimming:* small stream, pool, hot spring, waterhole.

Ant. 1 crawl, creep.

sprinkle *v.* 1 *Sprinkle some sugar on the cake:* dust, powder, scatter, strew. 2 *Take your umbrella in case it sprinkles:* shower, rain lightly, drizzle.

sprint *v.* 1 *The player sprinted across the football field:* run, race, dash, tear, whisk, shoot, scamper, dart, rush. —*n.* 2 *She crossed the finish line with a sprint:* dash, burst, spurt, kick.

Ant. 1 stroll, saunter; creep, crawl.

sprout *v. New buds sprouted:* shoot forth, come up, burgeon, grow, come up, bud, bloom, flower, blossom.

spruce *adj. You look spruce in your new suit:* trim, tidy, neat, smart; spick-and-span, well-groomed, kempt.

Ant. sloppy, seedy, shabby.

spry *adj. Dancers are very spry:* lively, sprightly, frisky, lightfooted, active, nimble, brisk, agile; jaunty, sportive, vigorous, energetic.

Ant. doddering, slow, sluggish, lethargic.

spunk *n. Informal It took a lot of spunk to brave that sea:* guts, pluck, spirit, grit; courage, boldness, daring, bravery, mettle, ginger, gumption, backbone, feistiness.

Ant. cowardice, timidity, fear, squeamishness.

spur *n.* 1 *Encouragement is a helpful spur:* stimulus, incitement, inducement, incentive, stimulant, goad, excitant, impetus, instigation, motive, encouragement. —*v.* 2 *Her loving care spurred our recovery:* stimulate, hasten, encourage; goad, prod.

Ant. 1 discouragement, hindrance, curb, deterrent.

spurious *adj. a spurious Rembrandt:* not genuine, fake, counterfeit, sham, imitation, bogus, phony, fraudulent; simulated, feigned, mock, make-believe; false, faulty, specious.

Ant. genuine, real, authentic.

spurn *v. She spurned his love:* reject, turn down, scorn, disdain, refuse, decline, sneer at, scoff at, rebuff.

Ant. welcome, embrace, encourage.

spurt *v.* 1 *Blood spurted from the wound:* spout, jet, gush, issue, burst, spring, stream, flow, pour out, shoot, squirt. 2 *Our horse spurted ahead:* speed, sprint, lunge, tear, spring, dart, dash, rush. —*n.* 3 *A spurt of water came from the hose:* rush, jet, gush, stream, spout, squirt. 4 *I threw the glass in a spurt of anger:* eruption, burst, outbreak, outburst, flash, outpouring, rush, gust.

Ant. 1 drip, ooze. 2 creep, crawl. 3 drip, dribble.

spy *n.* 1 *foreign spies:* espionage agent, secret agent, intelligence agent, operative; agent provocateur; informer. —*v.* 2 *Government agents spied on the enemy submarines:* watch secretly, keep watch, engage in surveillance, reconnoiter; snoop, pry, peep. 3 *The hunter spied a rabbit in the bush:* see, observe, glimpse, spot, catch sight of, sight, make out, detect, notice, find, view, discern.

squabble *v.* 1 *They squabbled over money:* wrangle, quarrel, bicker, dispute, differ, spat; argue, contend. —*n.* 2 *Their squabble was over money:* spat, quarrel, tiff, dispute, difference, disagreement, contention, words, argument, row.

Ant. 1 agree, concur, assent.

squalid *adj. squalid slums:* unclean, foul, dirty, filthy; run-down, tumble-down, dilapidated; degraded, wretched, sordid, miserable, poverty-stricken, abject, mean.

Ant. clean, attractive, tidy.

squalor *n. He lives in unbelievable squalor:* foulness, filth, uncleanness, dirtiness, dirt, uncleanliness; ugliness, sordidness, grubbiness, abjectness, poverty, seediness, dinginess, misery, neglect.

Ant. cleanliness, beauty, splendor, luxury.

squander *v. Don't squander your money on that:* waste, throw away, misspend, fritter away, misuse; lavish, exhaust, spend; consume, deplete.

Ant. save, conserve.

square *n.* 1 *The sides of a square are of equal length:* quadrangle, quadrilateral, box. 2 *a village square:* plaza, green, common. —*v.* 3 *This payment will square my debt:* even, make even, even up, balance; pay off, settle up. 4 *Can you square those crooked pictures?:* align, straighten, make level; plane, smooth. 5 *Be certain your alibi squares with mine:* agree, tally, accord, fit,

conform, match, correspond, jibe, concur. 6 *Did you square your differences with your friend?:* settle, resolve, reconcile, rectify, adjust, set right, patch up, straighten out. —*adj.* 7 *Are you being square with me?:* honest, just, equitable; truthful, candid, straightforward.

Ant. 5 disagree, contradict.

squash *v.* 1 *She sat on my hat and squashed it:* crush, flatten, compress, mash; squeeze, jam, cram, crowd; compact. 2 *to squash all hope of success:* quash, crush, squelch, destroy, annihilate, obliterate.

Ant. 2 promote, enhance, support.

squat *v.* 1 *If you squat behind the table he won't see you:* crouch, sit on the heels; kneel, hunker. —*adj.* 2 *a squat, hairy body:* dumpy, stumpy, stocky, stubby, thickset, square.

Ant. 2 lanky, willowy.

squeak *v. The mouse squeaked. The rusty hinge squeaked:* screech, squeal, shriek; grate, creak; cheep, peep, shrill, chirp, yelp.

squeal *v.* 1 *The puppy squealed when I stepped on its tail:* wail, yelp, cry, whine, shrill, screech, shriek, scream, yell, squeak. 2 *Slang One of the thieves squealed to the police:* inform, turn informer, *Slang* sing.

squeamish *adj. I'm too squeamish to become a surgeon:* easily nauseated, qualmish, easily disgusted, weak-stomached; sick, sickish, queasy; nauseated.

Ant. tough, strong-stomached.

squeeze *v.* 1 *Squeeze the oranges for juice:* press, compress. 2 *I squeezed the orange juice:* extract, press out, wring, wrest, wrench; draw out, withdraw, extricate; compel, coerce. 3 *We all squeezed into the elevator:* crowd, cram, pack, jam, stuff, wedge; compact, consolidate. 4 *Mother squeezed me tightly when I left:* hug, embrace, clasp, clutch, hold. 5 *Can you squeeze through that line of people?:* press, push, force one's way, wedge, elbow, crowd, shove, shoulder, edge. —*n.* 6 *He gave her hand a squeeze:* clasp, grasp, grip, hold, embrace, hug, clutch; pressure, pinch.

squelch *v.* 1 *The army squelched the uprising:* crush, put down, squash, quash, smash, quell; silence, quiet. —*n.* 2 *That was a perfect squelch!:* retort, riposte, crushing reply, put-down.

Ant. 1 incite, provoke.

squirm *v. We squirmed in embarrassment:* twist, contort, wriggle, writhe, wiggle, twitch, pitch, toss; be restless, fidget.

squirt *v.* 1 *The water squirted over everyone:* spray, spurt, shoot, gush, spout, discharge; shower, spatter, splash. —*n.* 2 *the squirt of the watergun:* spray, jet, spurt. 3 *Slang He's* *a little squirt:* insignificant person, punk, piker, runt.

stab v. 1 *The killer stabbed his victim:* jab, pierce, stick, spear, impale, cut, run through, knife, prick. —n. 2 *I felt a sudden stab of pain:* pang, prick, ache, sting, twinge; shiver, thrill, qualm. 3 *Informal Just make a stab at it:* try, attempt, effort, pass; go.

stability n. 1 *to show stability in a crisis:* steadiness, constancy, solidness, soundness, poise, aplomb, balance, reliability, stableness, steadfastness. 2 *I question the stability of the old staircase:* soundness, steadiness, solidness, sturdiness. 3 *The nation has attained political stability:* permanence, fixity, firmness, unchangeableness, durability, continuity.
    Ant. 1 instability, inconstancy, unreliability, irresolution. 2 frailty, unsteadiness, weakness. 3 instability, impermanence, changeableness.

stable adj. 1 *a stable business:* established, durable, sound, secure, solid. 2 *The building has a stable foundation:* sound, sturdy, solid, firm, safe. 3 *a stable government:* fixed, unchanging, steady, abiding, persisting, enduring, constant; uniform, even. 4 *John is a stable employee:* reliable, steady, steadfast, resolute, staunch, loyal, dependable, unwavering, faithful, unfaltering.
    Ant. 1–4 unstable. 1 shaky, unsound. 2 frail, shaky, unsubstantial. 3 shaky, wavering. 4 unreliable, mercurial, erratic.

stack n. 1 *a stack of dirty dishes:* pile, heap, mass, mound; accumulation, aggregation, batch, bundle. —v. 2 *Stack the wood in equal piles:* heap, pile, arrange vertically; bunch, amass, assemble.

stadium n. *a football stadium:* arena, bowl, coliseum, amphitheater, field, hippodrome.

staff n. 1 *He needed his staff to climb the hill:* cane, stick, walking stick, alpenstock, cudgel; scepter. 2 *The flag was raised halfway up the staff:* pole, flagpole, flagstaff; support. 3 *How many are on the hotel staff?:* force, crew, personnel; help, employees, group.

stage n. 1 *the final stage of development:* period, phase, level, step, grade. 2 *The actor almost fell off the stage:* raised platform, *Slang* the boards; rostrum, podium. 3 *Europe was the primary stage for the Second World War:* scene of action, setting, locale, locality, arena, site, position, location, site.

stagger v. 1 *She staggered out of bed:* stumble, sway, wobble, reel, hobble, totter, lurch, waver. 2 *That drink would stagger an ox:* cause to sway, cause to reel, stun, throw off

balance. 3 *The news of his death staggered the country:* stun, jolt, shock, astound, astonish, shake, amaze, dumbfound, unsettle, disconcert, jar, bowl over, stupefy, startle, flabbergast, bewilder, confound. 4 *Stagger the seats so that everyone can see:* arrange in a zigzag order; alternate.
    Ant. 2 steady. 3 steady, stabilize.

stagnant adj. 1 *stagnant water:* still, not flowing, standing, uncirculating; filthy, polluted, slimy. 2 *The resort becomes stagnant when the tourists leave:* inactive, dull, listless, dormant, dead, languid, torpid, slow, lethargic.
    Ant. 1 running, flowing, circulating; clean, pure. 2 lively, busy, thriving.

staid adj. *He's too staid to enjoy parties:* sedate, settled, somber, subdued, serious, dignified, reserved, solemn, stiff, quiet, grave; priggish, prudish, proper.
    Ant. exuberant, jaunty, frivolous, capricious.

stain n. 1 *Will that stain come off your tie?:* spot, discoloration, blemish, blot, smudge, smear, blotch, splotch, taint. 2 *His crime was a stain on his family's good name:* blot, stigma, blemish, taint, flaw, disgrace, slur, dishonor. —v. 3 *The tomato sauce stained the tablecloth:* spot, discolor, blotch, soil, smear, smudge, mar, spoil, mark. 4 *He stained his military record by going AWOL:* blemish, disgrace, tarnish, defile, blacken, debase, stigmatize, sully, spoil, ruin, detract from; discredit.
    Ant. 2 honor, credit. 4 clear, enhance.

stake n. 1 *One of the stakes in the fence is broken:* post, picket, pale, pole, peg, stick; marker. 2 *What is the stake in your poker game?:* money risked, hazard, bet, ante, wager, play; prize, reward, take, winnings, purse, returns. 3 *I have a big stake in the business:* share, investment, risk, interest; personal concern, interest, involvement. —v. 4 *I'd stake my life on his honesty:* bet, wager, hazard, risk, chance, jeopardize, venture. 5 *Informal She offered to stake me to a new coat:* stand, treat; back, finance, subsidize.

stale adj. 1 *These peanuts taste stale. stale air:* flat, not fresh, vapid; musty, close, stagnant. 2 *His writing has become stale:* trite, banal, hackneyed, insipid, flat, vapid, dull, humdrum, unvaried, worn-out, unimaginative, monotonous, uninteresting.
    Ant. 1 fresh. 2 imaginative, varied.

stalemate n. *The negotiators reached a stalemate:* deadlock, impasse, standoff; blockage, standstill.

stalk¹ n. *Hold the flower by its stalk:* stem, shaft, column, trunk, pedicel.

stalk² v. 1 *The mugger stalked his victim:* approach stealthily, pursue quietly, creep up on, sneak up on, track, hunt, prowl, act. 2 *She stalked angrily out of the room:* march, strut, swagger, walk stiffly. 3 *A fear of reprisal stalked us:* haunt, hang over, pervade.

stall n. 1 *a horse stall:* booth, cubicle, compartment, pen, shed. 2 *a newspaper stall:* booth, stand, kiosk. —v. 3 *The horses were stalled in the barn:* confine, pen. 4 *The strike stalled our plans:* stop, halt, arrest, impede, check, block, obstruct, hobble; put off, postpone. 5 *I need your answer—stop stalling!:* delay, put off, postpone, play for time, temporize; be evasive, equivocate.

stalwart adj. 1 *He's young and stalwart:* sturdy, robust, strong, muscular, strapping, hardy, brawny, powerful, rugged, ablebodied, hale, husky. 2 *The stalwart captain refused to desert the ship:* valiant, heroic, intrepid, courageous, stouthearted, indomitable, gallant, brave, valorous, unflinching, staunch. 3 *a stalwart belief in human rights:* unwavering, steadfast, staunch, firm, resolute, constant, unswerving, unflagging, uncompromising, indomitable, unfaltering, unflinching, persistent.
Ant. 1 weak, feeble, frail, puny. 2 cowardly, timorous, fainthearted. 3 faithless, shaky, flagging, deviating, halfhearted.

stamina n. *I don't have the stamina for the trip:* endurance, sturdiness, hardiness, staying power, perseverance.

stamp v. 1 *The horse stamped the ground nervously:* step on, stomp, trample. 2 Usually **stamp out** *They tried to stamp out the fire:* extinguish, put out; crush, put down, squelch. 3 *The soldiers stamped noisily through the town:* tramp, stomp, stride, march. 4 *The bookbinder stamped the leather with a fleur-de-lis:* print, mark, imprint, brand, impress, seal, label. 5 *His wild youth stamped him as the black sheep of the family:* mark, characterize, brand, identify; reveal, betray, exhibit, distinguish, manifest, display, expose, personify. —n. 6 *The cabinet bears the stamp of its maker:* mark, character, seal, brand, hallmark, imprint, identification, official mark, emblem; ratification, endorsement, validation.

stampede n. *Twelve horses were killed in the stampede:* frenzied rush, headlong flight; race, rush, dash.

stand v. 1 *We stood because there were no seats:* be upright, be erect, be on one's feet; rise, rise to one's feet, get up. 2 *Stand the lamp next to the chair:* put, place, set, set upright, raise, rest, put up, erect. 3 *Please stand aside:* step, move, shift, draw. 4 *I*

stand behind the plan 100 percent: support, uphold, argue, champion, be in favor of, commend, sanction, plead for, endorse, countenance, honor, advocate. 5 *The church has stood in the same spot for a hundred years:* be present, be located, be situated, rest, remain, exist, stay; persist, prevail. 6 *The seawall stood against the raging storm:* endure, remain intact, abide, persist, survive, resist destruction, resist decay or change, hold, hold out, last, remain steadfast, bear up, withstand, tolerate, suffer, undergo, brook, face, weather, persevere. 7 *He stands last when it comes to her affection:* be, rank, place. —n. 8 *The army made a valiant stand against the attack:* defense, resistance, effort. 9 *What is the senator's stand on the bill?:* position, policy, opinion, viewpoint, sentiment, standpoint, stance, posture. 10 *Where's the vegetable stand?:* booth, stall, counter, kiosk; tent, pavilion.
Ant. 1 sit, lie, recline. 6 collapse, succumb, yield. 8 retreat, withdrawal.

standard n. 1 *Cars without seat belts do not meet Federal safety standards:* requirement, specification, criterion, guideline, principle; measure, yardstick, ideal. 2 *I carried the standard in the parade:* flag, pennant, banner, streamer, ensign, jack. —adj. 3 *What is the standard size of a twin bed?:* normal, basic, usual, customary, universal, accepted, common, ordinary, typical, regular, stock.
Ant. 3 abnormal, exceptional, unusual.

standing n. 1 *Her standing in the class is high:* rank, position, place, station, grade, status, importance, reputation. 2 *a friendship of ten years' standing:* duration, length of existence, continuance, tenure, time, term, life. —adj. 3 *a standing position:* stand-up, vertical, upright, perpendicular, erect. 4 *standing water:* motionless, still, stationary, not flowing, stagnant. 5 *standing orders:* fixed, continuing, immovable, permanent, perpetual, lasting.
Ant. 3 sitting, reclining, recumbent. 4 flowing, moving, running.

standoffish adj. *We tried to be friendly, but she was standoffish:* unsociable, distant, cool, aloof, reserved, detached, withdrawn, unfriendly.
Ant. friendly, gregarious, affable, extroverted.

staple n. 1 *bread and other staples:* basic item, article of merchandise, commodity, raw material, product. —adj. 2 *Bread is a staple food:* chief, primary, basic, fundamental, essential, key, major, prime, necessary.

star n. 1 **stars** *If the stars are against us, we*

can achieve nothing: fortune, fate, destiny, predestination, the future, portents, omens. 2 *The stars of the movie came to the premiere:* principal actor, principal, lead; popular entertainer, main attraction, headliner, drawing card; great, giant, idol, immortal, celebrity, name, luminary, eminence, notable. —*v.* 3 *The movie stars the director's wife:* present in a leading role, feature; play the lead.

stare *v.* 1 *to stare at celebrities:* gaze intently, fix one's gaze, look intently, gape, gawk, ogle, watch. —*n.* 2 *an icy stare:* glare, look, long glance, glower, gaze; scrutiny, once-over.

stark *adj.* 1 *Stark terror seized the passengers:* downright, utter, plain, sheer, pure, patent, flagrant, absolute, complete, unmitigated, outright, conspicuous, total, out-and-out, unalloyed, consummate. 2 *a stark landscape:* bare, severe, plain, unadorned, barren, austere, empty; forsaken, harsh, bleak, desolate, abandoned, deserted, vacant, forlorn. —*adv.* 3 *The child was stark naked:* absolutely, fully, utterly, wholly, quite, downright, completely, altogether, entirely.

start *v.* 1 *Let's start for Vermont early:* commence, get going, set out, leave, sally forth, depart. 2 *Start the engine:* set in operation, put in motion; ignite, kindle, propel. 3 *He started cooking dinner:* begin, commence, undertake, set about, embark on, take the first step, initiate, take up. 4 *I started the business ten years ago:* initiate, originate, institute, found, establish, launch, set up, institute, begin, inaugurate, create, form, introduce, usher in; propagate, engender. 5 *Suddenly a pedestrian started from between the cars:* spring, bound, jump, burst forth, leap; rush; issue, spurt, gush, erupt, issue, shoot, emerge. —*n.* 6 *the start of a trip:* beginning, outset, commencement, onset, inauguration; inception, birth, origin, genesis, dawn, initiation. 7 *She gave a start:* jump, spasm, jolt, jerk, wince, twitch. 8 *I had a good start over my rivals:* lead, advantage, head start, edge, jump. 9 *Parents give us our start in life:* opening, chance, opportunity.

Ant. 1 delay. 2 stop. 3, 4 end, finish, terminate, stop, cease. 6 end, finish, termination.

startle *v. You startled me:* frighten, surprise, scare, alarm, unnerve, shake, faze, upset, give a turn, unsettle.

Ant. calm, soothe, settle.

starved *adj.* 1 *I'm starved—what's for supper?:* perishing from hunger; hungry, famished. 2 *starved for companionship:* hungry, yearning, longing, craving, languishing; deprived, denied.

Ant. 1 full, gorged. 2 surfeited.

state *n.* 1 *Ice is water in its solid state. What is the financial state of the business?:* condition, position, form, mode, guise, shape, stage, phase, structure, aspect; circumstances, status, situation, plight. 2 *I was disturbed by your depressed state:* condition, attitude, frame of mind, mood, state of mind, spirits, morale. 3 *The prime minister resigned for the good of the state:* nation, republic, commonwealth, country, monarchy, realm, body politic, government. —*adj.* 4 *We attended two state functions this week:* official, governmental. —*v.* 5 *He stated his case. Please state the exact time of arrival:* declare, express, propound, set forth, present, put, explain; report, relate, describe.

stately *adj.* 1 *Mt. Fuji's stately splendor:* impressive, majestic, awesome, imposing, grand, regal, lordly, proud, magnificent, august, noble, royal. 2 *a stately occasion:* formal, ceremonial, dignified; eminent, elegant.

Ant. 1 unimpressive, modest. 2 ordinary, common; informal.

statement *n.* 1 *a flattering statement:* utterance, avowal, pronouncement, assertion, declaration, explanation, testimony; comment, remark, observation, sentence. 2 *a statement of profits and losses:* report, record, account, recitation, recital; bill, invoice, account, reckoning, tab; balance sheet, accounting.

station *n.* 1 *Everyone to your stations!:* assigned place, position, post; location, spot, site. 2 *a railroad station:* terminal, depot. 3 *the police station:* station house; *(variously)* headquarters, precinct station; firehouse. 4 *a first-aid station:* facility, dispensary. 5 *Our station in life is not what it was:* social standing, rank, position, status, place, grade, condition, class; importance, prestige. —*v.* 6 *The army stationed me in West Germany:* assign, post; locate, place, install, ensconce.

stationary *adj.* 1 *a stationary target:* motionless, standing still, standing, immobile; fixed. 2 *Business remained stationary:* constant, unchanged, not changing, steady, stable, fixed, unvarying, unchangeable.

Ant. 1 moving, mobile. 2 varying, changing, volatile, changeable.

stature *n.* 1 *a puny child of small stature:* height, tallness, size. 2 *Such pettiness was surprising in a person of such stature:* standing, position, high station, eminence, prestige, distinction, regard, prominence, importance, reputation.

status *n.* 1 *Jewels symbolize status to some people:* position, rank, grade, degree, caliber, standing, condition; estimation, station, class, place; eminence, distinction, prestige. 2 *What's the status of the peace talks?:* situation, state, condition.

staunch Also **stanch** *adj.* 1 *a staunch supporter:* firm, steadfast, constant, strong, solid, loyal, faithful, resolute, stalwart. 2 *This is a staunch little cabin:* solid, sturdy, well-built, sound. —*v.* 3 *to stanch bleeding:* stop the flow of, check, hold back, stem, impede.
Ant. 1 inconstant, fickle, capricious. 2 jerry-built, flimsy.

stay *v.* 1 *How long did they stay?:* remain, tarry, visit, linger; reside, dwell, abide, sojourn, lodge, room, live. 2 *Stay as sweet as you are!:* keep oneself, endure, continue to be, remain, go on being; persist, persevere, carry on. 3 *She stayed her tears:* restrain, hold back, suppress, withhold, check, keep in, stifle. —*n.* 4 *How long was your stay at the beach?:* sojourn, stop, stopover, halt; visit, vacation. 5 *a stay of execution:* postponement, suspension, delay, deferment, reprieve.
Ant. 1 leave, go, depart. 3 loose, release, express.

steadfast *adj.* 1 *a steadfast course:* steady, fixed, undeviating, direct; unwavering, unflinching, persevering, unfaltering, unflagging. 2 *steadfast faith:* resolute, undaunted, obstinate, tenacious, inflexible, unyielding, uncompromising, unchangeable, unchanging, deep-rooted.
Ant. 1 wavering, flagging, unstable. 2 irresolute, wavering, vacillating, half-hearted, changeable, fickle.

steady *adj.* 1 *Is that stool steady enough to stand on?:* stable, firm. 2 *steady rain:* constant, unremitting, continuous, continuing, persistent, incessant, unending, unceasing, ceaseless; regular, even. 3 *He's a steady visitor:* habitual, constant, frequent, regular, faithful, confirmed. 4 *She's steady in her commitment to her job:* steadfast, constant, unwavering, firm, resolute, staunch, untiring, unfaltering, unflagging, persevering, tenacious, dedicated, devoted, resolute, single-minded; reliable, dependable, careful, conscientious, methodical, stable; level-headed, sure.
Ant. 1 unsteady, shaky. 2 sporadic, intermittent, irregular. 3 infrequent, rare. 4 erratic; undependable, unreliable, irresolute; careless, frivolous.

steal *v.* 1 *Someone stole a painting from the*

museum: purloin, filch, pilfer, lift, snatch; swindle, embezzle, usurp, misappropriate; defraud; copy, crib, plagiarize; appropriate, pocket; *Slang* pinch, swipe, cop. 2 *Try to steal into the room without waking the children:* slip, slide, sneak, creep, slink, skulk, pass unobserved.

stealth *n. a spy known for stealth:* covertness, secrecy, clandestine procedure, secretiveness, furtiveness, sneakiness, stealthiness.

steep[1] *adj. The slope is steep:* close to vertical, sheer, precipitous, abrupt, sharp.
Ant. flat, gentle, gradual.

steep[2] *v. We steeped the cucumbers in brine:* soak, immerse, saturate, brew, souse, impregnate, suffuse, marinate; plunge, drench, imbue, infuse, pervade.

steer *v.* 1 *to steer a ship. to steer a team to victory:* sail, navigate, direct, guide, pilot, run, conduct, govern, supervise, manage, lead. 2 *The ship steered for the open seas:* proceed, head, sail, make, lay a course, aim.

stem[1] *n.* 1 *the stem of a rose:* stalk; *(variously)* trunk, spear, shoot, stock, shank; peduncle, pedicel, petiole, tendril. —*v.* 2 *My back trouble stems from an injury:* come, derive, issue, result, proceed, arise, rise, originate, spring, grow.

stem[2] *v. The government tried to stem inflation:* stop, hold back, curb, stay, restrain, check, arrest, prevent, impede, obstruct, resist, stanch, thwart, stall, halt, block, hinder, deter.
Ant. further, promote, encourage, stimulate.

stench *n. The stench from the sewer is terrible:* stink, bad smell, offensive odor, reek.
Ant. fragrance, aroma, perfume.

step *n.* 1 *He walks with a measured step:* footstep, pace, stride, gait; footfall, tread; footprint, track. 2 *Glazing is the final step in making pottery:* stage, phase, process, measure, proceeding, act, procedure. 3 *The promotion put me three steps from the top:* grade level, stage, rank, rung; degree, point, gradation, notch, span. 4 *One of the back steps needs replacing:* stair, foothold, riser, rung, footing, purchase. —*v.* 5 *Step to the window:* move, walk, pace, tread, stride. 6 *You stepped on my foot:* tread, tramp, trample.

stereotype *n.* 1 *Stereotypes often embody prejudice:* conventional image, received idea, popular preconception, cliché, formula. —*v.* 2 *The newscaster stereotyped him as a "dumb jock":* pigeonhole, typecast, type, categorize, crudely identify.

sterile *adj.* 1 *a sterile operating room:* sterilized, disinfected, free from germs; uncontaminated, sanitary, uninfected, aseptic, antiseptic. **2** *The sterile couple adopted two children:* barren, infertile; unfruitful, infecund, fallow, bare, empty. **3** *The negotiations proved to be sterile:* unproductive, unprofitable, fruitless, ineffective, profitless, unrewarding, ineffectual, bootless, impotent, futile, vain, unavailing.

Ant. **1** unsterile, infected, unsanitary. **2** fertile, prolific, fecund, fruitful. **3** productive, fruitful, effective.

sterling *adj. a sterling example of a good citizen:* noble, high-principled, estimable, meritorious, honorable, worthy, true, superb, admirable, first-rate, superlative; perfect, flawless.

stern *adj.* **1** *a stern supervisor:* severe, strict, hard, unreasonable, despotic, ironhanded, unmerciful, cruel, tyrannical, harsh, austere, grim, rigorous. **2** *She gave me a stern look:* grim, forbidding, unkind, severe, serious, cold, unsympathetic, sharp, stiff, frowning; reproachful, reproving, admonishing.

Ant. **1** permissive, soft, lenient, benign, kind. **2** friendly, kind, amused, warm, sympathetic.

stew *v.* **1** *I stewed the vegetables:* boil slowly, simmer, seethe, steep. **2** *Informal He ignored us as we sat there, stewing:* become irritated, get angry, fume, chafe; worry, agonize, fret, seethe. —*n.* **3** *beef stew:* stewed food, ragout; mixture, miscellany. **4** *Informal She's in a stew over finding a babysitter:* state of worry, mental agitation, fuss, fret, flutter, tizzy, fluster.

stick[1] *n.* **1** *They made a fire of sticks:* branch, switch, twig, fagot. **2** *Grandfather walks with a stick. a policeman's night stick:* cane, staff; baton, wand, rod; club, cudgel, shillelagh, billy, truncheon, bludgeon; pole, shaft, stave, stake, bar, staff, crosier.

stick[2] *v.* **1** *The doctor stuck my arm with a hypodermic needle:* puncture, pierce, stab, jab, prick, poke, spear, spike. **2** *He stuck a needle in my arm:* jab, thrust, poke, insert. **3** *Stick this notice on the bulletin board:* fix, put, place, set, plant, fasten; tack, pin, affix, attach. **4** *Can you stick the pieces back together?:* join; *(variously)* glue, fasten, paste, seal, adhere, cement, fuse, attach, weld, bind. **5** *A bone stuck in my throat:* lodge, catch, snag, be embedded. **6** *The bus stuck fast in the snow:* stall, mire, check, block, immobilize, hold, obstruct, impede, constrain, thwart, hamper, detain, inhibit, bar, stop. **7** *Stick to your ideals:* be true, keep steadily at, hold, be faithful, be constant. **8** *We stuck it out to the end:* endure, abide, stand, bear up under, last, continue, carry

on. **9** *I was stuck over one word in that crossword puzzle:* stymie, stump, bewilder, puzzle, perplex, confuse.

Ant. **3** remove, unfasten. **4** separate, detach, disengage. **6** release, free.

sticky *adj.* **1** *Tar is sticky:* gummy, sticking, adhesive, adherent, gluey, viscid, viscous, clingy, gooey, glutinous, cohesive, mucilaginous. **2** *This sticky weather makes my hair frizz:* clammy, humid, muggy, sultry, damp.

Ant. **1** slick, slippery. **2** dry.

stiff *adj.* **1** *The starch made this shirt too stiff:* rigid, crisp, inelastic. **2** *My back is stiff:* unyielding, tight, resistant, hard to move; unlimber, inflexible, taut, rigid. **3** *a stiff wind:* strong, intense, forceful, powerful, brisk. **4** *We nodded a stiff greeting:* cold, formal, aloof, prim, cool, chilly, constrained, straitlaced, distant. **5** *The acting was stiff:* wooden, graceless, awkward, forced, stilted, labored, unnatural, mannered, artificial. **6** *That's a stiff assignment for a newcomer:* difficult, exacting, tough, hard, rigorous, formidable. **7** *The price is too stiff:* steep, high, excessive, heavy, extravagant. **8** *I don't think the offense deserved such a stiff penalty:* harsh, stern, severe, stringent, drastic, austere, extreme. **9** *The whipped cream is not stiff enough:* thick, firm, solid, solidified, dense, viscid, viscous, clotted.

Ant. **1** soft, yielding, supple, flexible, pliant. **2** supple, limber. **3** gentle, soft. **4** casual, informal, relaxed, warm. **5** natural, unaffected. **6** easy, soft, cushy. **7** moderate. **8** mild, moderate, sparing, merciful. **9** thin, soft, liquid.

stifle *v.* **1** *I'm stifling in this overheated room:* asphyxiate, smother, choke, suffocate, gasp for air, swelter. **2** *She stifled her laughter:* suppress, repress, curb, restrain, smother, muffle, squelch, check, inhibit.

stigma *n. There was no stigma attached to losing:* disgrace, shame, odium, dishonor; blot, blemish, taint.

Ant. glory, honor, distinction.

still *adj.* **1** *The deer stood very still:* motionless, inert, stationary, at rest, unstirring, unmoving, immobile. **2** *The room was still:* silent, hushed, quiet, noiseless, soundless. —*v.* **3** *The wind stilled:* calm, quiet, hush, silence. **4** *Nothing stilled his hunger:* assuage, appease, gratify, pacify; overcome, repress, suppress.

Ant. **1** moving, agitated, restless. **2** noisy, loud.

stilted *adj. The talk was stilted:* stiff, wooden, labored, unnatural, mannered, studied, formal, prim, forced, artificial.

Ant. relaxed, graceful, informal, natural, unforced.

stimulant n. *Tea is a stimulant:* energizer, tonic, bracer, excitant, *Slang* upper.
Ant. depressant, tranquilizer, *Slang* downer.

stimulate v. *Visiting the museum stimulated my interest in art:* incite, arouse, excite, awaken, kindle, fan, rouse, spur, prompt, stir, quicken, activate, initiate, wake, inflame, inspire, sharpen.
Ant. deaden; discourage, dull.

stimulus n. *Nothing is a greater stimulus to pride than success:* incentive, spur, incitement, inducement, goad, encouragement, fillip, motive.
Ant. discouragement, damper.

sting v. 1 *A bee stung him:* prick, pierce, nettle. 2 *The blowing sand stung the back of my legs. My abrupt reply stung her:* burn, pain, hurt, prick, wound; anger, pique, grate, offend, insult, provoke, rile, gnaw, vex, nettle, torment, gall. 3 *My eyes are stinging from the smoke:* burn, smart, tingle. 4 *His smug challenge stung her to action:* impel, incite, provoke, goad, prod, excite, arouse, instigate, spur, quicken, motivate, prompt, move. —n. 5 *The sting of coral can be very painful:* bite, wound, burn; pain, hurt. 6 *I still feel the sting of her bitter words:* wound, pain, hurt, affliction, gall, scourge, vexation.
Ant. 2 soothe; mollify, assuage, calm. 4 delay, hinder, thwart. 6 balm, caress.

stingy adj. 1 *Stingy people won't contribute a cent:* miserly, tight, tightfisted, close, parsimonious, closefisted, niggardly, pennypinching. 2 *a stingy portion:* meager, scanty, scant, sparse, scrimpy, skimpy, small, modest, paltry, piddling, niggardly.
Ant. 1 generous, liberal, open-handed, bountiful, extravagant. 2 large, lavish, huge, profuse, abundant, bountiful.

stint v. 1 *Don't stint in giving to charity:* restrict, reduce, be sparing, restrain, check, curb, hold back, scrimp, be frugal, economize, pinch pennies, be parsimonious. —n. 2 *This is my second stint on the job:* chore, task, duty; period, term, assignment, turn, shift, quota.

stipend n. *The scholarship offers a modest stipend:* income, allowance, salary, compensation, wages, pension, grant.

stipulate v. *Our contract stipulates the completion date:* specify, set forth, state, designate, name, cite, make a point of; pledge, guarantee, provide, allow, assure, warrant.

stir v. 1 *The branches began to stir in the breeze:* move, rustle, shake, shiver, twitch, flutter, quiver. 2 *Stir the sauce:* mix, agitate, blend, mingle, intermix. 3 *The pep talk stirred the team:* rouse, arouse, inspire, excite, inspirit, electrify, vivify, work up, stimulate, fire, enflame, goad, provoke, spur, prod. —n. 4 *She lay awake, listening to the stir of branches above the tent:* stirring, moving, movement, rustle, rustling. 5 *The movie company caused quite a stir in the town:* commotion, tumult, flurry, pother, uproar, to-do.
Ant. 4 stillness, quiet, silence.

stock n. 1 *The shop carries a large stock of wrapping paper:* supply, store, inventory, array, quantity, selection, assortment; cache, accumulation, stockpile, hoard; wares, merchandise, goods. 2 *How much stock do you have in the company?:* shares, capital shares; investment. 3 *We're running low on feed for the stock:* livestock, cattle, domestic animals, herd. 4 *She comes from sturdy peasant stock:* descent, lineage, ancestry, strain, line, breed, parentage, family, heredity, extraction, blood, race, nationality, pedigree; origin, source, forebears. 5 *Grab the rifle by the stock:* haft, shaft, butt. —adj. 6 *Toothpaste is stock merchandise in a drugstore:* standard, basic, regular, staple, routine. —v. 7 *The manager stocked the hotel with plenty of linens:* supply, furnish, equip, provide, fit out.

stocky adj. *One child is stocky and the other is tall and slim:* thickset, short and heavy, husky, chunky, squat, stout, pudgy.
Ant. slim, slender, lanky.

stodgy adj. 1 *Much academic writing is needlessly stodgy:* dull, stuffy, boring, uninteresting, tiresome, dreary, wearisome, monotonous, prosaic. 2 *He's too young to have such a stodgy outlook:* old-fashioned, antiquated, dated, passé; narrow, staid, serious, stuffy.
Ant. 1 exciting, lively, interesting. 2 modern, up-to-date.

stoic n. 1 *The stoic didn't shed a tear at the news:* fatalist, quietist. —adj. 2 *Her stoic attitude helped us to bear the tragedy:* detached, philosophic, impassive, unruffled, unimpassioned, imperturbable, dispassionate.
Ant. 2 undisciplined, excitable, volatile, emotional, passionate.

stomach n. 1 *a protruding stomach:* belly, abdomen, tummy; paunch, midsection, midriff, *Slang* pot, potbelly, breadbasket. 2 *I have no stomach for violent movies:* liking, appetite, disposition, desire, fancy, inclination, taste, relish, hunger, thirst, affinity, leaning, proclivity, partiality, mind, bent, propensity. —v. 3 *The sick man couldn't even stomach liquids:* keep down, retain. 4 *I couldn't stomach the snobbery of some of the guests:* stand, bear, take, endure, suffer, bear with, tolerate, abide, reconcile oneself to, pass over, be patient with. *Ant.* 2 distaste, dislike, disinclination, abhorrence, aversion. 3 regurgitate, vomit. 4 reject, condemn.

stony *adj.* 1 *a stony path:* full of rocks, rocky, pebbly; stonelike, rocklike. 2 *Her tears couldn't move his stony heart:* unfeeling, unsympathetic, cold, hardhearted, coldhearted, merciless, severe, unresponsive, icy, heartless, callous, stern, passionless, unemotional, indifferent, hardened, expressionless, stoical, heartless, pitiless, steely, untouched, unaffected, uncaring.

Ant. 2 sympathetic, softhearted, tenderhearted, compassionate, merciful, kind, friendly.

stoop[1] *v.* 1 *She stooped to pick up a piece of paper:* bend down, lean over. 2 *He stoops from years of carrying heavy objects:* slouch, slump, be bowed, be doubled over. 3 *I can't believe he would stoop to such nonsense:* lower oneself, degrade oneself, sink, descend, fall, condescend, resort, succumb, yield, submit.

Ant. 1 stand erect. 3 rise, ascend.

stoop[2] *n.* We sat on the stoop and chatted for a while: entrance staircase, entranceway, doorstep, porch.

stop *v.* 1 *Stop or I'll shoot! Stop what you're doing. A tourniquet stops heavy bleeding:* halt, stay, stand fast, hold; discontinue, suspend, put an end to, check, arrest, suppress, block, stem, stanch. 2 *The guards stopped him from escaping:* restrain, hinder, prevent, bar, obstruct, preclude, deter, thwart. 3 *She stopped the leak with cement:* plug, close, block, fill, stop up, close up, seal. 4 *The music stopped. The car stopped:* come to an end, cease, discontinue, conclude, finish, be over, terminate, quit, pause, lapse, draw to a close, brake, stall, become inactive, falter, rest. 5 *We stopped at a motel for the night:* stay, rest, lodge, put up; visit, tarry. —*n.* 6 *The strike caused a stop in construction. We put a stop to fighting:* cessation, termination, halt, stoppage, suspension, break, discontinuation, pause, rest, respite, lapse, interruption, intermission, interlude, interval, hiatus; end, ban, curb, block, prohibition. 7 *We made a stop at Mother's on our way to Dallas:* visit, stay, stopover, rest, respite, layover, pause. 8 *I get off at the last stop:* depot, station, terminus, terminal; destination.

Ant. 1 start, begin, commence; continue; originate, inaugurate. 2 assist, expedite, facilitate, further. 3 unplug, open. 4 start, begin, commence; continue, proceed, progress. 6 start, commencement; resumption.

stopgap *adj.* *stopgap measures:* provisional, makeshift, improvised, temporary, substitute, emergency, impromptu, tentative.

Ant. permanent, unalterable.

stoppage *n.* *The explosion caused a stoppage of traffic:* blockage, obstruction, obstacle, barrier; impediment, hindrance, interruption, disruption, curtailment.

store *n.* 1 *a grocery store:* shop, market, mart, supermarket, department store, emporium, establishment. 2 *Our store of fuel is running low:* supply, stock, pile, stockpile, hoard, accumulation, inventory, reserve, reservoir. 3 *We put great store in her advice:* faith, confidence, regard, value, credit, trust, reliance, estimation, esteem. —*v.* 4 *Squirrels store nuts for the winter:* save, stow away, keep, lay aside, put away, deposit, hoard, amass, stockpile, reserve, lay up or by, lay in, accumulate, heap up, cache, stash.

Ant. 3 disbelief, distrust, skepticism. 4 waste, spend, squander.

storehouse *n.* *The harvested grain was taken to the storehouse:* repository, warehouse, depot, depository, store, silo, elevator, granary; bank, treasury, vault.

storm *n.* 1 *The islanders were warned that a storm was coming:* torrent, deluge, rainstorm, cloudburst, downpour; snowstorm, blizzard; windstorm, tempest, gale, blow, hurricane, typhoon, cyclone; tornado, twister. 2 *My criticism produced a storm of anger. The new rule caused a storm on campus:* outburst, eruption, outbreak, burst, explosion; tumult, disturbance, agitation, commotion, turmoil, furor, uproar, upheaval, to-do, hullabaloo. 3 *The enemy took the fort by storm:* sudden attack, violent assault, frontal attack. —*v.* 4 *It stormed so hard that all the electricity went out:* rain heavily, snow heavily, blow violently. 5 *He stormed at the waiter:* rage, rant, rave, complain furiously, fly into a rage, fume, fulminate. 6 *She stormed out of the house:* rush, stamp, stomp, rage, tear, stalk. 7 *Their only hope of victory was to storm the enemy camp at night:* charge, attack, assail, rush, assault, fall upon.

Ant. 1 calm, fair weather. 6 amble, saunter.

stormy *adj.* *stormy weather:* rainy; snowy; windy; turbulent, rough, blustering, tempestuous, blustery, raging, violent, squally.

Ant. mild, calm, fair.

story *n.* 1 *a newspaper story:* report, account; statement, testimony, tidings, article, dispatch, news item, piece. 2 *a collection of short stories:* tale, narrative, romance; fable, yarn, anecdote; plot, legend. 3 *Informal I* *know you're just telling a story!:* lie, white lie, falsehood, fib, fabrication; excuse, alibi.

stout *adj.* 1 *the stout figure of Santa Claus:* fat, corpulent, thickset, portly, rotund, plump, obese, round, pudgy, chubby, stocky. 2 *We need a couple of stout people to move the piano:* sturdy, strapping, strong, husky, stalwart, robust, muscular, able-bodied, brawny.

Ant. 1 lean, skinny, slim, slender, thin. 2 weak, frail, delicate, puny.

stouthearted *adj. The stouthearted survive:* brave, fearless, bold, courageous, dauntless; unflinching, intrepid, undaunted, resolute.

Ant. timid, fearful, cowardly.

straight *adj.* 1 *They cut a straight trail up the mountain:* direct, unbent, unswerving, undeviating, not curved. 2 *Make sure the rearview mirror is straight:* square, even, aligned. 3 *It's hard to get a straight answer from him:* straightforward, honest, candid, forthright, truthful, reliable, frank, clear, accurate. 4 *We've had eight straight days of rain:* unbroken, solid, uninterrupted, continuous, successive, consecutive, ceaseless, unrelieved. 5 *My desk is always straight:* orderly, tidy, neat; arranged, methodical. —*adv.* 6 *Go straight to bed:* directly, immediately, instantly, forthwith; in a straight line, without wandering. 7 *Stand up straight:* straightly, erectly, upright; evenly, on a level, squarely

Ant. 1 curved, crooked, winding, bent, zigzag. 2 crooked, awry. 3 unreliable, confused, ambiguous, qualified, evasive, equivocal. 4 interrupted, discontinuous, nonconsecutive. 5 messy, disorderly, untidy, disarranged. 7 crookedly, unevenly; askew, awry.

straightforward *adj. She gave a straightforward explanation. He's straightforward in his dealings:* open, candid, frank, honest, guileless, plainspoken, forthright; trustworthy, aboveboard, straight, ethical.

Ant. roundabout, devious; unethical, deceitful, unscrupulous, shady.

strain *v.* 1 *If you strain the elastic any more, it will break:* stretch, put under tension, make taut. 2 *The prisoner strained to get away from his captors:* struggle, heave, labor, toil. 3 *The manufacturer strained to get orders out in time. The doctor warned me against straining myself:* drive oneself, exert oneself, press, struggle, overexert, tax, overtax, overdo, bear down. 4 *He strained his Achilles tendon:* pull, sprain, wrench, twist. 5 *Some cooks strain their gravy:* sieve, filter, screen, sift, winnow. —*n.* 6 *Too much strain broke the rope:* stress,

pressure, force, tension. 7 *The strain of keeping awake was painful:* effort, exertion, struggle. 8 *muscle strain:* sprain, pull, wrench, twist. 9 *She was under enormous strain:* tension, pressure, stress.

Ant. 1, 2 relax. 3 idle; pamper, coddle. 7 effortlessness.

strait *n.* 1 *Our boat went aground in the strait:* narrows; channel. 2 Often **straits** *He's in awkward financial straits:* predicament, difficulty, plight, embarrassment, fix.

straitlaced *adj. He's too straitlaced to dance:* puritanical, proper, prudish, prim, rigid, narrow; reserved, inhibited, stiff.

Ant. loose, immoral; relaxed, uninhibited.

strand¹ *v.* 1 *The hurricane stranded the boat on the reef:* run aground, beach, ground; shipwreck. 2 *We were stranded in a strange town:* leave, maroon, desert. —*n.* 3 *We fished along the strand:* shore, coast, seashore, beach, seacoast; bank, riverside.

strand² *n.* 1 *a strand of hair:* filament, fiber, thread; core, rope, string; tress, lock, twist. 2 *a strand of pearls:* string, necklace.

strange *adj.* 1 *His behavior seems strange:* peculiar, odd, unusual, queer, abnormal, curious, singular, uncommon, eccentric, outlandish, unnatural, unconventional, bizarre, unaccountable, freakish, unaccustomed, farfetched. 2 *She felt strange the first few days in Europe:* out of place, ill at ease, uneasy, disoriented, estranged, lost, discomposed, bewildered, foreign, alien, alienated. 3 *This area is strange to me:* unknown, unfamiliar, foreign, alien.

Ant. 1 regular, conventional, normal, commonplace, usual, common, ordinary. 2 at home, at ease. 3 known, familiar.

stranger *n. I was a stranger in town:* unknown person; outsider, newcomer, foreigner, alien.

Ant. friend, acquaintance; native, insider.

strangle *v.* 1 *The killer strangled his victims:* choke, suffocate, stifle, smother, asphyxiate, throttle, garrote. 2 *The dictator's first step was to strangle the free press:* stop, suppress, repress, stifle, throttle, choke off, squelch, quell, extinguish, muzzle, gag.

Ant. 2 encourage, promote, aid, help.

strap *n.* 1 *the strap on a ski boot:* fastening strip, thong, band, tie, cord, belt. —*v.* 2 *Strap the suitcases on top of the car:* lash, tie, bind, truss. 3 *He strapped the boy with a leather belt:* whip, thrash, beat, flog, lash, flail, scourge.

strapping *adj. a strapping lumberjack:* robust, sturdy, husky, muscular, brawny, powerful, strong.

Ant. frail, weak, fragile, puny.

stratagem *n. The general's stratagem was*

successful: maneuver, scheme, plan, plot; trick, intrigue, ruse, artifice, device, deception, deceit, ploy.

strategic *adj.* 1 *a strategic retreat:* tactical, military; calculated, planned, deliberate; clever, cautious, careful, prudent. 2 *Wait for the strategic moment, then strike:* crucial, important, decisive, critical, vital, significant, key, principal.

Ant. 1 nonstrategic; unplanned. 2 unimportant, inconsequential, trifling.

strategy *n.* 1 *The strategy is to wear the enemy down by repeated attacks:* overall plan, grand design, scheme; tactics, policy. 2 *The general is an expert in strategy:* military science, war planning, war policy, art of war.

stray *v.* 1 *The kitten must have strayed from its mother:* go astray, roam, wander, lose one's way. 2 *Her thoughts strayed to her childhood:* wander, drift, digress. —*adj.* 3 *a stray dog:* straying; lost; misplaced. 4 *Only a few stray clouds dotted the sky:* scattered, random.

streak *n.* 1 *You have a streak of paint on your forehead:* long smear, line, stripe, strip, bar, band. 2 *He has a mean streak:* vein, cast, strain, touch. —*v.* 3 *The horse streaked past the finish line:* race, speed, rush, hurtle, tear, zoom, dart, dash, fly.

Ant. 3 creep, crawl.

stream *n.* 1 *The stream is full of trout:* narrow river, brook, creek, rivulet, rill, branch, run, watercourse, tributary. 2 *A stream of water ran off the roof. a stream of traffic. The child kept up a steady stream of talk:* flow, torrent, run, rush, gush, onrush, surge, deluge, flood. —*v.* 3 *Blood streamed from the wound:* flow, pour, run, issue, course, rush, surge, spill, gush, spout, spurt.

street *n.* *The child ran into the street:* road; *(variously)* thoroughfare, roadway, highway, turnpike, expressway, thruway, avenue, boulevard, lane, alley.

strength *n.* 1 *Does he have enough strength to lift these weights? She has great strength of character:* power, vigor, might, muscles, hardiness, force, potency, sturdiness, stamina, endurance, vitality; firmness, toughness, vitality, stoutheartedness. 2 *What is the strength of the enemy army?:* force, number, size. 3 *This medicine has lost its strength:* potency, power, force, effectiveness, efficacy. 4 *Her faith in God is her strength. Math is her strength:* source of power, support, anchor, mainstay, sustenance, succor; forte, strong point.

Ant. 1 weakness, frailness, feebleness. 3 ineffectiveness. 4 frailty, flaw.

strengthen *v. My back strengthened with*

exercise. The new evidence strengthened our case: make stronger, become stronger, grow stronger; reinforce; fortify, buttress, support, sustain; harden, steel, enhance, improve.

Ant. weaken.

strenuous *adj. strenuous exercise:* laborious, taxing, exhausting, physically demanding, arduous, difficult, vigorous; energetic, active, hardworking.

Ant. easy, light, effortless.

stress *n.* 1 *They place too much stress on money:* emphasis, importance, weight, significance, value, prominence, concern, moment. 2 *In the word "sawdust", the stress is on the first syllable:* accent, emphasis, beat. 3 *The limb couldn't bear up under the stress of the heavy snow. The stress of not knowing was too great for her:* strain, tension, anxiety, force, burden, pressure. —*v.* 4 *The speaker stressed the need for better education:* emphasize, accentuate, accent, underscore, underline; insist upon, feature; assert. 5 *Stress the second syllable in "today":* accent, emphasize, accentuate.

Ant. 1 unimportance, insignificance, deemphasis. 5 de-emphasize, underplay, understate; ignore, neglect, pass over.

stretch *v.* 1 *Will this material stretch?:* distend, extend, draw out, protract, expand, elongate; make tense or tight, draw taut, be elastic. 2 *Stretch your hand through the window:* extend, put forth, reach, reach out. 3 *The road stretches across the mountains:* extend, reach, spread, span, traverse. 4 *Let's stretch out on the sand for a while:* lie at full length; sprawl. 5 *The cat stretched and arched its back:* strain the body, draw out the muscles. 6 *I think you have stretched a point there:* exaggerate, strain, overtax, overstrain. —*n.* 7 *He spent a long stretch in jail:* spell, term, duration, period, interval, stint, while. 8 *a stretch of highway:* expanse, spread, tract, distance. 9 *The stretch has gone out of this waistband:* elasticity, elastic quality, resiliency, spring.

Ant. 1 shrink; slacken, contract, condense, compress.

stricken *adj. The stricken animal was put out of its misery:* afflicted; *(variously)* ill, sick, diseased, incapacitated, wounded, injured, hurt.

strict *adj.* 1 *Her strict father insisted she be home by ten:* stern, rigid, severe, authoritarian, rigorous, uncompromising, austere, stringent, unyielding, exacting, inflexible. 2 *The church demands strict loyalty:* perfect, absolute, complete, unerring, conscientious, fastidious, exact, meticulous, scrupulous.

Ant. 1 lenient, indulgent, permissive.

stride v. 1 *He strode out of the house:* march, stalk, lope, step. —n. 2 *She reached the house in two strides:* pace, long step. 3 *We've made tremendous strides toward recovery:* step, advance, advancement, progress, headway, improvement.

strident adj. *a strident voice:* grating, harsh, piercing, jangling, jarring, raucous, shrill, high-pitched, screeching, clashing, cacophonous.

Ant. soft, mellow, mellifluous, soothing.

strife n. *The strife has left its mark on the nation:* conflict, discord, dissension; upheaval, fighting, trouble, unrest, contention, altercation, disturbance, disquiet, struggle, violence, warfare.

Ant. peace, accord, agreement, harmony.

strike v. 1 *He struck me with his fist. Strike the nail as straight as you can:* hit, slug, deal a blow to, bang, box, cuff, slap, club, thump, smash, pound, knock, tap, clap, beat, clout, slam, sock, punch, wallop, pommel, pelt, smite, whack, hammer, clip; thrash, flog, lash, whip, whale, lambaste, scourge, flail. 2 *The enemy struck at dawn:* attack, assail, hit, assault, charge. 3 *The car struck a telephone pole:* hit, dash against, run into, bump into, beat against, collide with. 4 *Heavenly music struck our ears:* reach, fall upon, hit; burst upon. 5 *The lateness of the hour suddenly struck us:* occur to, come to the mind of, dawn upon, reach. 6 *Her enthusiasm struck us favorably:* impress, affect, appear to, seem to. 7 *I struck upon the solution by accident:* hit, come, arrive, light, chance, meet, stumble, find, encounter, come upon, reach, unearth, discover. 8 *The negotiators failed to strike a compromise:* reach, achieve, make, effect, arrange. 9 *The soldiers struck camp:* take down, put away, fold up, take apart. 10 *Strike that statement from the record:* remove, cancel, eliminate, erase, eradicate, delete, cross out. 11 *The clock struck noon:* sound, ring, chime, knell, toll. 12 *A blight struck the crop:* afflict, assault, assail, affect severely, devastate, smite. 13 *The workers struck just before Christmas:* go on strike, walk out. —n. 14 *The strike ended when the wage demands were met:* walkout, work stoppage, labor dispute; protest, boycott.

striking adj. *She bears a striking resemblance to her mother:* remarkable, noteworthy, noticeable, notable, conspicuous, prominent, marked, outstanding, astounding, extraordinary, surprising.

string n. 1 *The string broke:* cord, thread, twine, strand. 2 *a string of pearls:* strand, rope, necklace. 3 *A string of children filed into the house:* procession, file, parade; row,

chain, succession, column, line; sequence, series.

stringent adj. 1 *Stringent laws protect the consumer:* strict, stiff, demanding, rigorous, exacting, inflexible, unbending, uncompromising, unyielding, harsh, severe, stern. 2 *a stringent budget:* tight, close, sparing, spare, frugal.

Ant. 1 flexible, loose; relaxed. 2 lavish, ample, generous.

strip¹ v. 1 *The doctor told him to strip before getting on the scales:* undress, remove one's clothes, disrobe; lay bare, unwrap, uncover. 2 *We had to strip the old paint from the doors:* remove, shave, peel, flay, flake, pull off. 3 *They stripped the prisoners of their dignity:* deprive, rob, divest.

Ant. 1 dress, clothe; cover. 2 apply, put on.

strip² n. *I need two strips of adhesive tape:* length, slip, ribbon, band.

stripe n. 1 *vertical stripes:* band, streak, line, swath, strip, bar, striation. 2 *a sergeant's stripes:* braid; ribbon, emblem, insignia, chevron, bar.

strive v. 1 *A desire to please his parents made him strive to do well:* struggle, try hard, attempt earnestly, exert oneself, take pains, do one's utmost, strain; undertake, endeavor. 2 *The surrounded platoon strove against unbeatable odds:* fight, contend, vie, struggle, battle.

stroke n. 1 *He felled his opponent with one stroke:* blow, punch, chop, whack, swat, sock, wallop. 2 *the stroke of midnight:* striking, tolling, sounding, chime, ringing. 3 *The stroke left him paralyzed:* paralytic stroke, brain hemorrhage; apoplectic fit, apoplexy, seizure. 4 *We outmaneuvered the enemy by a bold stroke. a stroke of fate:* hit, achievement, blow, feat, deed, transaction, coup; piece of luck, chance, fluke, coincidence, accident. —v. 5 *The golfer stroked the ball into the cup:* hit lightly, tap, punch, slap, bat, swat. 6 *She stroked her hair gently:* caress, pat, pet.

stroll v. 1 *We strolled down the avenue:* walk slowly, amble, saunter, wander, ramble, meander. —n. 2 *Will you join us for a stroll?:* walk, amble, ramble, saunter, turn, constitutional.

Ant. 1 run, race, hurry, dash, scurry.

strong adj. 1 *Is the boy strong enough to lift that box? a strong wind:* powerful, forceful, mighty; muscular, stalwart, hardy, brawny, robust, healthy, tough, vigorous, energetic; severe, intense, violent. 2 *a strong competitor:* able, competent, capable, skilled, well-qualified, proficient. 3 *She was strong enough to overcome her handicap:* resourceful, plucky, gritty, stalwart, courageous, tough, resilient, indefatigable. **4** *I offered strong reasons for abandoning the project:* convincing, compelling, forceful, powerful, effective, solid, sound, cogent. **5** *There's a strong similarity between the two:* close, clear, distinct, definite, emphatic, unmistakable. **6** *Those colors are too strong:* bright, bold, vivid, intense, fiery. **7** *Strong religious belief helped them through a bad time:* keen, fervent, intense, deep, deep-seated, ardent, earnest, impassioned, fervid, confirmed. **8** *I like my coffee strong:* highly flavored, tangy, sharp, potent, concentrated, pungent, piquant.

Ant. **1** weak, frail, feeble. **2** unqualified. **4** unconvincing, ineffectual, unsound; mild. **5** slight, vague. **6** faint, dull. **7** shallow, faint. **8** faint, subtle; bland.

stronghold *n.* to attack an enemy *stronghold:* fortified place, fortress, fortification, fort, bulwark, battlement, citadel, bastion, fastness, stockade, blockhouse, rampart.

structure *n.* **1** *A large structure is being erected on the old fairground:* building, construction, edifice. **2** *The structure of the song is very symmetrical:* arrangement, plan, form, makeup, organization, composition, formation, design, pattern.

struggle *v.* **1** *We struggled with the intruder:* battle, fight, combat, contend, compete, vie, tussle, scuffle, brawl, grapple, scrap; clash, argue, oppose, resist. **2** *She had to struggle to meet the deadline:* strain, push, work hard, exert oneself, strive, take pains. —*n.* **3** *The army lost the struggle:* fight, conflict, battle, combat, war, engagement, encounter; altercation, strife, contest. **4** *It was a struggle to stay awake:* strain, grind, trial, labor, long haul, effort.

Ant. **1** surrender, give in, yield, succumb. **4** cinch, sure thing.

strut *v. He strutted into the restaurant:* swagger, walk pompously, sashay.

Ant. slink, sneak.

stub *n.* **1** *a cigarette stub. a pencil stub:* stump, butt, end, fag end, broken remnant, remains. **2** *Keep your ticket stubs:* torn ticket; counterfoil, payment voucher, receipt. —*v.* **3** *I stubbed my toe:* strike accidentally, scrape, bump, knock. **4** *He stubbed out his cigarette:* snuff, crush, tamp out, extinguish.

stubborn *adj. We're too stubborn to give in:* obstinate, unmovable, unyielding, obdurate, tenacious, unbending, refractory, recalcitrant, headstrong, willful, inflexible, mulish, pigheaded, bullheaded, dogged; persistent, resolute, tenacious.

Ant. pliable, flexible; irresolute, yielding, docile, vacillating.

student *n.* **1** *How many students attend the school?:* pupil, learner, scholar, matriculant; undergraduate, schoolgirl, schoolboy, coed; disciple, follower. **2** *A good reporter is a student of human nature:* observer, examiner, reviewer, analyst.

Ant. **1** teacher, professor, instructor.

studied *adj. The studied casualness of the stranger's manner put us on guard:* calculated, deliberate, measured, purposeful, intentional, premeditated.

Ant. spontaneous, impulsive, unplanned.

studious *adj. Good historians are studious:* devoted to study, scholarly, academic, bookish, well-read.

Ant. frivolous; unscholarly.

study *n.* **1** *She never finished her studies:* learning, education, academic work, instruction, reading. **2** *We made a thorough study of the causes of civil disorders:* investigation, inquiry, survey, examination, search, analysis, inspection, exploration, probe. —*v.* **3** *He's studying history:* work at learning, educate oneself, school oneself, pursue knowledge. **4** *The committee will study the plan thoroughly:* delve into, investigate, examine, inquire into, consider, explore, probe, survey, search through, research, read closely, review, scrutinize.

stuff *n.* **1** *Do you have the stuff you need to make the rug? Hope is the stuff that dreams are made of:* material, staple; matter, substance, component, constituent, ingredient. **2** *I left some of my stuff in Mother's attic:* things, effects, gear, belongings, possessions, paraphernalia, tackle. —*v.* **3** *She stuffed the trunk with her summer clothes:* pile, fill, fill up, jam, cram, pad. **4** *She stuffed herself with candy:* gorge, cram, overeat, feed gluttonously, satiate, sate. **5** *Just stuff the laundry into the bag:* load, pack, thrust, jam, cram, crowd, wedge.

Ant. **3, 5** empty, unpack; take out, remove.

stuffing *n.* **1** *He used straw as stuffing for the dolls:* filling, padding, wadding, packing. **2** *I add walnuts to my turkey stuffing:* dressing; forcemeat, farce.

stuffy *adj.* **1** *This room is unbearably stuffy:* close, unventilated, suffocating, stagnant, stifling, sultry, sweltering, airless. **2** *We got a stuffy response from that snob:* smug, pompous, pretentious, self-satisfied, supercilious; cold, reserved, straitlaced; stodgy.

Ant. **1** airy, well-ventilated, cool. **2** modest, unpretentious.

stumble *v.* **1** *She stumbled over a stool:* trip, stagger, pitch forward; fall, lurch, topple. **2** *He stumbled out of the bar:* stagger, reel, totter, sway, hobble, pitch, roll. **3** *The actor stumbled over the lines:* blunder, slip up, make mistakes, falter; botch, bungle. **4** *I stumbled on the answer to the riddle:* happen, fall, blunder, hit, come by chance.

stumbling block *n. The biggest stumbling block to peace is distrust:* obstacle, obstruction, hindrance, barrier, hurdle, snag, block, bar, difficulty, hitch.

Ant. aid, support, encouragement.

stump *n.* **1** *the stump of a pencil:* stub, nubbin, butt, end. **2** *the loud stump of boots on the stairs:* tramping, stomping, footfall. —*v.* **3** *The puzzle stumped me:* mystify, baffle, perplex, foil, bewilder, confound, stymie.

stun *v.* **1** *The blow to his head stunned him:* daze, stagger, stupefy, numb. **2** *Her sudden anger stunned us:* shock, dumbfound, stupefy, amaze, astonish, astound, flabbergast.

stunning *adj. a stunning outfit:* striking, strikingly attractive, beautiful, lovely, exquisite, electrifying.

Ant. ordinary, unremarkable; ugly, drab.

stupefy *v. The fall from the ladder stupefied me:* daze, stun, shock; stagger; amaze, astound, dumbfound, astonish, surprise.

stupendous *adj.* **1** *What a stupendous movie!:* wonderful, marvelous, terrific, great, fabulous, incredible, stunning, amazing. **2** *The stupendous house dwarfed the rest of the neighborhood:* gigantic, huge, mammoth, vast, enormous, tremendous, immense, massive, giant, colossal, big.

Ant. **1** ordinary, unsurprising. **3** small, little, modest, diminutive.

stupid *adj.* **1** *a stupid person:* dumb, brainless, unintelligent, simpleminded, slow-learning, backward, rattlebrained, empty-headed; dimwitted, idiotic, half-witted, imbecilic, moronic. **2** *a stupid decision:* foolish, unwise, reckless, indiscriminating, imprudent, ill-considered, foolhardy, thoughtless, unintelligent, idiotic, silly, senseless, unreasonable, inappropriate; tactless, indiscreet. **3** *a stupid movie:* senseless, meaningless, absurd, pointless, inept, preposterous, purposeless, asinine.

Ant. intelligent. **1** smart, intelligent, bright, clever, sharp. **2** smart, sensible, wise, thoughtful, prudent, reasonable. **3** meaningful, interesting, deep, relevant.

stupor *n.* **1** *The drug caused a state more like a stupor than natural sleep:* stunned condition, near-unconsciousness, insensibility, stupefaction, numbness. **2** *The nation recovered from its stupor:* torpor, apathy, inertia, lethargy, daze.

sturdy *adj.* **1** *We need someone sturdy to push this car:* strong, muscular, rugged, powerful, robust, tough, burly, stalwart, strapping, hardy. **2** *This chair is not sturdy enough to stand on:* solid, substantial, sound, strong, secure, durable, well-constructed, well-made. **3** *She put up a sturdy fight:* brave, courageous, gallant, resolute, stouthearted, plucky, valiant, undaunted, dauntless, doughty, dogged, determined, stubborn.

Ant. weak. **1** frail, feeble. **2** fragile, flimsy. **3** cowardly, fearful, irresolute.

style *n.* **1** *She has a terse writing style:* mode of expression, manner, characteristic tone. **2** *They live in style:* luxury, elegance, comfort, affluence. **3** *He handled the awkward situation with style:* grace, smoothness, polish, class, taste, flair. **4** *Argyle socks are back in style:* fashion, vogue, currency, favor. **5** *Which style of writing paper do you prefer?:* type, kind, sort, pattern, model. —*v.* **6** *He styled my hair in a pageboy:* design, arrange. **7** *She styles herself a revolutionary:* call, name, designate.

Ant. **1** substance, content. **2** squalor, drabness.

stylish *adj. She's a stylish dresser:* fashionable, chic, voguish, modish; in fashion, modern; smart, elegant, dapper, natty.

Ant. unstylish, unfashionable, dowdy.

stymie *v. The riddle stymied us:* stump, mystify, confound, puzzle, baffle, confuse; block, balk, check, thwart, frustrate, obstruct.

suave *adj. He's as suave as a diplomat:* urbane, smooth, polished, gracious, politic, diplomatic, charming, civilized, elegant; smooth tongued, ingratiating.

subconscious *adj. I had only a subconscious awareness of the problem:* half conscious, intuitive, instinctive, dim, dawning.

Ant. conscious, explicit, expressed.

subdue *v.* **1** *The police subdued the rioters:* overcome, quell, put down, overpower, still, defeat, overwhelm, conquer, vanquish. **2** *Her words subdued our fears:* reduce, curb, moderate, palliate, assuage, ease, allay, salve, soothe, slacken, mollify, mitigate, ameliorate, meliorate. **3** *Try to subdue your laughter:* tone down, moderate, quiet down, mute, muffle, soften.

Ant. **2** awaken, quicken, arouse, inflame, agitate. **3** vent, unleash.

subject *n.* **1** *What was the subject of the seminar?:* topic, subject matter, theme, substance, issue, question, concern, business; gist, pith. **2** *The Queen had many loyal subjects:* follower, subordinate; liege, vassal; citizen. —*adj.* **3** *We are subject to the laws of the country:* bound by, owing obedience; subservient, subordinate, answerable, subjected. **4** *The date of our trip is subject to* *change:* dependent upon, conditional upon, contingent on. 5 *He is subject to violent fits of temper:* susceptible, vulnerable, open, liable, prone, disposed, exposed. —*v.* 6 *The hurricane subjected the islanders to devastating floods:* expose, put through, cause to undergo or experience. 7 *Rude behavior subjects one to frequent rebuffs:* make liable, lay open, expose.

Ant. 2 sovereign, ruler. 3 independent of; free, exempt, not liable 5 invulnerable, unsusceptible. 6 exempt, protect.

subjective *adj. My dislike of him is purely subjective:* personal, individual, emotional, individual; partial, partisan, biased, prejudiced, nonobjective.

Ant. objective, impersonal.

sublime *adj.* 1 *the sublime style in the opening chapter of the Book of Genesis:* lofty, exalted, imposing, elevated, noble, majestic, grand, stately, high. 2 *Her performance was sublime:* excellent, splendid, superb, marvelous, wonderful, great, terrific.

Ant. 1 ordinary, everyday, commonplace. 2 poor, bad; ordinary, mediocre.

submerge *v.* 1 *The submarine submerged:* plunge, put or go under water, immerse, submerse, go under, dive. 2 *The raging waters submerged the village:* inundate, flood, engulf, cover, submerse, drown.

Ant. 1 surface, emerge. 2 uncover.

submission *n.* 1 *In a gesture of submission, the serf kissed the king's feet:* submitting, yielding, giving in, surrender, capitulation; submissiveness, obedience, nonresistance, acquiescence, passivity, passiveness, meekness, subservience. 2 *The deadline for submission of entries is June 1st:* handing in, presentation, remittance, submitting, tendering.

Ant. 1 resistance, rebellion, disobedience, defiance.

submissive *adj. Fight for your rights instead of being submissive:* obedient, yielding, meek, humble, mild, deferential, pliant, docile, compliant, acquiescent, passive, capitulating, unassertive, tractable; toadying, obsequious, slavish, servile, fawning, subservient.

Ant. rebellious, disobedient, defiant, assertive, masterful.

submit *v.* 1 *They submitted to our demands:* give in, give up, surrender, yield, bow, resign oneself, capitulate, bend, back down, knuckle under, acquiesce, acknowledge defeat, defer, comply. 2 *He submitted his plan to the city council:* present, tender, put forth, suggest, propose, offer, proffer. 3 *I submit that the prosecution's case is a tissue of lies:* claim, contend, assert, argue.

Ant. 1 resist, withstand, fight, defy. 2 withdraw.

subordinate *adj.* 1 *A private is subordinate to a corporal:* lower in rank, of low rank, inferior, junior; ancillary, auxiliary, subsidiary, secondary; lesser, lower. —*n.* 2 *He treated his subordinates rudely:* person of lower rank, inferior, assistant, junior; help, attendant; servant, underling, lackey, menial.

Ant. 1, 2 superior, senior. 1 higher, primary. 2 chief, supervisor, boss.

subscribe *v.* 1 *We subscribed generously to the new hospital:* pledge money, promise to give, contribute, donate. 2 *Do you subscribe to many magazines?:* have a subscription, receive a periodical by mail. 3 *I don't subscribe to the idea that money brings happiness:* assent, consent; go along with, hold with, support, endorse; believe; follow.

Ant. 3 be opposed, dissent.

subsequent *adj. The first ticket cost $10, but all subsequent ones were $8:* ensuing, consequent, succeeding, following, next, successive.

Ant. previous, preceding.

subservient *adj.* 1 *His subservient attitude makes me wince:* submissive, fawning, obsequious, toadying, servile, ingratiating, sycophantic, bootlicking, cringing, truckling. 2 *A leader's policies should be subservient to the needs of the people:* subordinate, subject, auxiliary, accessory, ancillary.

Ant. 1 domineering, overbearing, assertive, masterful; rebellious. 2 superior.

subside *v.* 1 *As the land subsides, the sea advances:* settle, sink; drop, sag, descend. 2 *My nervousness subsided when the plane landed:* diminish, lessen, abate, decrease, wane, moderate, ebb, recede, ease, shrink, dwindle.

Ant. 1 rise. 2 increase, grow, intensify.

subsidiary *adj.* 1 *In addition to her salary, she receives subsidiary income from investments:* supplementary, supplemental, additional, extra. 2 *He never got beyond a subsidiary position in the firm:* secondary, junior, subordinate, lower, lesser, minor, inferior. —*n.* 3 *That generator is a subsidiary to the main power supply:* auxiliary, addition, supplement, adjunct, accessory. 4 *I work for the corporation's subsidiary:* subsidiary company, affiliate, division, branch.

Ant. 1, 2 primary, principal, main, chief, major. 2 senior, superior.

subsidy *n. The city sought a government subsidy for its arts program:* grant, aid, appropriation, allotment, support.

subsist *v. They subsisted on coconuts and bananas:* live, survive, exist, stay alive, sustain oneself, eke out a living, make ends meet.

Ant. die, perish, starve.

subsistence *n. The few dollars he earned were barely enough for the family's subsistence:* survival, continued existence, maintenance, nourishment, sustenance, support, upkeep; livelihood, living.

substance *n.* 1 *There was a sticky substance on the floor:* material, matter, stuff; ingredient, constituent, element. 2 *Our fears had substance—the house was indeed on fire:* substantiality, reality, actuality; solidity, real content. 3 *The substance of her argument was that we had treated her unfairly:* burden, thrust, main point, essence, import, gist, basic idea, purport; sum and substance, quintessence, sense, force. 4 *I'm not a person of substance:* affluence, property, money, means, wealth, riches.

substantial *adj.* 1 *We had a substantial crop this year:* sizable, considerable, plentiful, large, ample, big, full, abundant. 2 *He has a substantial understanding of economics:* firm, solid, sound. 3 *The banker built herself a substantial home:* big, monumental, massive.

Ant. 1 unsubstantial, poor, meager, small, paltry, scanty. 2 slight, feeble.

substantiate *v. You haven't substantiated your argument:* verify, corroborate, prove, demonstrate, confirm, authenticate, support.

Ant. disprove, refute, discredit.

substitute *n.* 1 *The teacher's ill, so a substitute is teaching today:* alternate, replacement, fill-in, surrogate, standby, understudy, backup. —*v.* 2 *She substituted a fake diamond for the original:* exchange, change, switch. 3 *Her brother substituted as host while her husband was away:* fill in, take over, stand in, act.

subterfuge *n. Why did they resort to this subterfuge?:* scheme, artifice, trick, dodge, deception, evasion, ruse, chicanery, deviousness, duplicity, pretense.

subtle *adj.* 1 *There's a subtle hint of garlic in the sauce:* understated, indirect, delicate, elusive, light, refined, fine. 2 *He has a subtle understanding of the job:* fine, keen, sharp, astute, discriminating, discerning, sophisticated, clever, expert, quick. 3 *I fall for that subtle ploy every time!:* sly, tricky, crafty, wily, cagy, cunning, shrewd, slick, designing, devious, deceptive, shifty, underhand.

Ant. 1 heavy-handed, obvious, direct. 2 undiscerning, undiscriminating, unsophisticated. 3 obvious, artless.

subversive *adj.* 1 *Subversive elements have infiltrated the government:* seditious, traitorous, treasonous, revolutionary, insurgent. —*n.* 2 *The army attempted to eliminate subversives:* traitor, insurrectionary, insurgent, revolutionary.

subvert *v. Radical groups attempted to subvert the peace talks:* upset, disrupt, wreck, undermine, overturn, destroy, spoil.

Ant. support, endorse, encourage, promote.

succeed *v.* 1 *The experiment succeeded. He didn't succeed in getting all the weeds:* be fruitful, turn out successfully, be effective, do well, bear fruit, click, attain a goal, achieve one's aim, triumph, prevail, avail, win. 2 *She finally succeeded as a playwright:* attain fame, prosper, make good, triumph, find fulfillment. 3 *Who will succeed to the throne?:* accede, move up, come next in order, become heir; assume the office of, take over, inherit; follow, come afterward, replace.

Ant. 1, 2 fail, flop. 3 precede.

succeeding *adj. The new law will apply to all succeeding cases:* subsequent, ensuing, consequent, later, following, future.

Ant. preceding, earlier, previous, prior, former.

success *n.* 1 *The school fair was a great success:* happy outcome, triumph, fulfillment; victory, hit. 2 *His success surprised those who remembered him as a poor student:* attainment, prosperity, achievement, advancement, triumph, ascendancy.

Ant. failure, disaster.

successful *adj.* 1 *The plan was successful:* triumphant, effective, efficacious, accomplished, achieved, complete, fruitful, perfect. 2 *a successful businesswoman:* prosperous, flourishing, thriving, well-off, affluent, proven, acknowledged.

Ant. 1, 2 unsuccessful.

succession *n.* 1 *an endless succession of parties:* series, procession, progression, sequence, chain, round, cycle, course. 2 *My succession to the party leadership is in dispute:* taking over, assumption, accession.

successive *adj. She underwent four successive operations in two weeks:* succeeding, ensuing, consecutive; continuous.

succinct *adj. Your comments were succinct:* to the point, terse, brief, direct, concise, compact, short, pithy.

Ant. rambling, circuitous, wordy, verbose, long-winded.

succor *n.* 1 *The volunteers gave succor to the wounded:* help, relief, aid, helping hand, comfort, assistance, support. —*v.* 2 *The vicar was quick to succor those in need:* aid, assist, comfort, help, relieve, sustain, nurture.

succumb *v.* 1 *He succumbed after a long*

illness: die, pass away, expire. **2** *We finally succumbed to her pleading:* give in, yield, submit, accede, capitulate, surrender.

Ant. **1** live, survive. **2** resist, fight.

sucker *n. Only a sucker would buy a used car from them:* dupe, chump; victim, sitting duck, patsy.

sudden *adj. a sudden stop. a sudden decision:* abrupt, quick, immediate, instant, instantaneous; hasty, precipitate, rash; unexpected, unanticipated, unforeseen.

Ant. slow, gradual; deliberate; anticipated, expected.

suddenly *adv. Suddenly the lights went out:* abruptly, all of a sudden, without warning, all at once, unexpectedly, on the spur of the moment, instantly.

Ant. gradually, slowly; deliberately.

sue *v.* **1** *They sued the movers for ruining the furniture:* bring a civil action against, litigate against, prefer a claim against, start a lawsuit against. **2** *The condemned man sued for mercy:* beg, plead, beseech, entreat, appeal, implore, supplicate, petition, pray.

suffer *v.* **1** *Is he suffering much from his injuries?:* feel distress, feel pain, ache, hurt. **2** *My work suffers when I have problems at home:* deteriorate, be impaired, drop off. **3** *One must suffer some bad days:* endure, bear, sustain, go through, undergo; tolerate, bear with, withstand, put up with.

suffering *n. She refused to talk about her family's suffering during the war:* sorrow, distress, travail, heartache, grief, misery, woe, tribulation, anguish, trial; affliction, agony, torment.

Ant. pleasure, joy, happiness.

sufficient *adj. Do we have sufficient fuel for the trip?:* enough, adequate, ample, plenty, abundant, satisfactory.

Ant. insufficient, deficient, inadequate.

suffocate *v. I nearly suffocated in the heat. The murderer suffocated his victims:* choke, smother, asphyxiate, stifle; strangle, throttle, garrote.

suffuse *v. Bright sunlight suffused the room:* overspread, saturate, fill, pervade, permeate.

suggest *v.* **1** *I suggest we leave early. The letter suggested that a new clinic be built:* recommend, advocate, move, urge, advise, propose, counsel, posit, submit, propound, advance. **2** *His restlessness suggested that he wanted to leave:* intimate, hint, imply, indicate.

suggestion *n.* **1** *I followed the suggestion:* advice, prompting, counsel, urging, recommendation, exhortation; pointer, tip. **2** *There's a suggestion of rum in this cake:*

shade, hint, trace, touch, taste, tinge; feeling, intimation.

suggestive *adj.* **1** *This silly old song is suggestive of my youth:* reminiscent, evocative, expressive, allusive, remindful. **2** *His suggestive remarks shocked me:* improper, indelicate, off-color; indecent, lewd, wanton, seductive, sexual, licentious, risqué, racy, bawdy; prurient, provocative.

Ant. **2** delicate, decorous, chaste, clean.

suit *n.* **1** *My new suit doesn't fit well. John wore a clown suit to the party:* set of garments, outfit; jacket and pants, jacket and skirt; clothing, garb, costume, clothes, apparel, habit, habiliment, raiment, trappings, duds, getup, attire, togs. **2** *She responded to her wooer's suit:* courtship, court, wooing, blandishment, attentions, overtures; plea, appeal, solicitation, entreaty, supplication; prayer, petition. *—v.* **3** *The architecture of the house suits the rugged landscape:* conform to, match, befit, fit, correspond to, be proper for, harmonize with, agree with, be appropriate to, accord with, comply with; become. **4** *A later flight suits me even better:* be acceptable to, be convenient to, accommodate, content, oblige; gratify, satisfy, please, gladden.

Ant. **3** disagree with, be inappropriate to. **4** inconvenience, displease, discommode.

suitable *adj. The minister's words were suitable to the sad occasion:* proper, appropriate, meet, fitting, fit, befitting, seemly, right, apt, worthy, apropos, applicable, congruous, relevant, pertinent, germane.

Ant. unsuitable, inappropriate, unbecoming; improper, unfit, unseemly.

suitor *n. She had many suitors in her youth:* beau, boyfriend, young man, admirer, fellow, wooer, swain.

sulk *v. He sulked about not winning:* pout, be sullen, mope, brood, be in a huff, be disgruntled, be resentful, fret, be miffed, chafe, grouch.

sullen *adj.* **1** *a sullen child:* ill-tempered, ill-humored, brooding, out of humor, out of sorts, surly, sulky, resentful, grouchy, sour, morose, peevish, petulant, ill-natured, glum, moody, cross. **2** *This sullen weather is depressing:* gloomy, grim, dismal, somber, funereal, dolorous, doleful, dreary, cheerless, forlorn.

Ant. **1** cheerful, happy, merry, amiable. **2** bright, sunny.

sully *v. They accused me of sullying the family name:* soil, dirty, besmear, stain, spot, blemish, contaminate, defile, corrupt, disgrace, dishonor.

sultry *adj.* **1** *sultry weather:* sweltering, suffocating, stifling, close, stuffy, humid,

muggy. **2** *a sultry glance:* erotic, voluptuous, sexy, sensual, provocative.

sum *n.* **1** *The sum of her achievements is
impressive:* quantity, total, measure, entire
amount, entirety, totality, summation, aggregate, whole; tally. **2** *The sum they demanded for damages was outrageous:*
amount of money, cash, funds.

summarily *adv. The foreman summarily
dismissed the worker:* precipitately, without
delay, on the spot, promptly, with dispatch,
immediately, straightaway, at once, forthwith.

summarize *v. Try to summarize the speech
in a paragraph or two:* capsulize, abstract,
digest, sum up, recapitulate, synopsize, outline.
Ant. expand, flesh out, enlarge on.

summary *n.* **1** *The summary omitted several facts:* digest, concise, statement, brief,
abstract, précis, survey, recapitulation.
—*adj.* **2** *I had time for only a summary
meeting:* short, brief, hasty, succinct, terse,
hurried; perfunctory, token, cursory.
Ant. **2** full, detailed, lengthy.

summit *n. a mountain's summit. She is now
at the summit of her career:* peak, crest,
crown, highest point, apex, vertex, tip,
height, top, pinnacle, zenith, apogee; acme;
crowning point, culmination, climax.
Ant. base, bottom, nadir.

summon *v.* **1** *Summon the police quickly!:*
call for, beckon, send for, muster, activate,
gather. **2** *The state summoned three witnesses:* call, subpoena, serve with a writ.
3 *She had to summon all her strength to
face them again:* call forth, invoke, command, muster, draw on.

sumptuous *adj. a sumptuous meal:* splendid, luxurious, magnificent, grand, regal,
elaborate, lavish, elegant; plush, deluxe,
posh.
Ant. plain, ordinary, cheap.

sundry *adj. We worked at sundry jobs:* various, divers, several, numerous, myriad, diverse, varied, assorted, miscellaneous, different.

sunny *adj.* **1** *a sunny day:* bright, sunlit,
cloudless, clear, brilliant, unclouded, fair,
fine. **2** *a sunny disposition:* amiable, happy,
smiling, cheerful, cheery, lighthearted,
buoyant, optimistic, merry.
Ant. **1** dark, cloudy, overcast, gloomy,
gray. **2** glum, gloomy, dour, unhappy, un-
smiling.

sunrise *n. We got up at sunrise:* dawn,
sunup, daybreak, daylight, break of day.

sunset *n. We met at sunset:* dusk, twilight,
sundown, nightfall, eventide.

super *adj. My new motorcycle is super:* out-

standing, great, extraordinary, superlative,
superior, incomparable, prime, prize, excellent, world-class, unexcelled, nonpareil.
Ant. commonplace, ordinary, mediocre.

superabundance *n. We have a superabundance of tomatoes:* overabundance,
glut, surplus, excess, plethora, superfluity,
oversupply, spate.
Ant. scarcity, lack, shortage, paucity.

superb *adj. His novel was superb:* very fine,
first-rate, excellent, magnificent, admirable,
laudable, praiseworthy, A1, first-class, topnotch; splendid, grand, marvelous, exquisite, elegant, choice, select, breathtaking.
Ant. bad, awful, terrible, second-rate, inferior.

superficial *adj.* **1** *The crack in the table is
only superficial:* on the surface, outer, surface, exterior, skin-deep. **2** *She has only a
superficial understanding of economics:*
shallow, summary, incomplete, cursory,
perfunctory, passing, partial, minimal, surface, nodding, desultory. **3** *He's too superficial to appreciate poetry:* frivolous, shallow, lacking depth, mindless, silly, myopic,
shortsighted, trite.
Ant. **1–3** deep, in-depth, profound. **1** substantial. **2** thorough, complete. **3** serious,
earnest.

superfluous *adj. So many presents are really superfluous:* unnecessary, excessive,
overgenerous, nonessential, inessential; excess, surplus, extra, spare.
Ant. essential, vital, indispensable, required, necessary.

superhuman *adj. superhuman strength:*
superior, transcendent, supernatural, god-
like, herculean, omnipotent, miraculous, su-
pranatural, preternatural, otherworldly, divine.
Ant. mundane, normal, natural, terrestrial.

superintendent *n. the superintendent of
schools:* supervisor, chief administrator; director, head, overseer, proctor, chief; custodian, guardian, foreman, manager, warden.

superior *adj.* **1** *a superior actor:* excellent,
exceptional, fine, notable, incomparable,
distinguished, preeminent, noteworthy,
nonpareil, unrivaled, foremost, first-rate, illustrious, peerless, inimitable, matchless;
deluxe, choice. **2** *Her knowledge of French is
superior to mine:* greater, better, more extensive, more advanced. **3** *His superior
manner makes people resent him:* haughty,
lordly, imperious, condescending, patronizing, snobbish, arrogant. —*n.* **4** *The promotion was approved by my superiors:* senior,
boss, chief, supervisor; leader, higher-up,
better.
Ant. **1** inferior, unexceptional, undistin-

guished, mediocre, ordinary, second-rate. 2 inferior, worse. 4 inferior, subordinate, underling.

superlative *adj. superlative work:* excellent, of the highest order, superior, surpassing, magnificent, preeminent, unsurpassed, expert, surpassing, exquisite, consummate, first-rate; matchless, incomparable, unrivaled, peerless, unequaled, unmatched, unparalleled, nonpareil.

Ant. inferior, poor, undistinguished.

supernatural *adj. The medium claimed to have supernatural powers:* preternatural, otherworldly, occult, mystic, transcendental, unearthly, spiritual, psychic, paranormal, miraculous.

Ant. natural, normal, worldly.

supersede *v. This new drug will supersede all others in the treatment of the disease:* supplant, replace, take the place of, displace, succeed.

supervise *v. Can you supervise a production line?:* superintend, watch over, oversee, look after, preside over, manage, regulate, direct, guide, conduct, administer, head, boss.

supervision *n. My house was built under an architect's supervision:* direction, guidance, control, superintendence, governance, orders, management.

supervisor *n. Only the supervisor can authorize your leave:* overseer, manager, administrator, director, superintendent, foreman, boss, head, chief.

supplant *v. Robots may supplant humans in some industries:* supersede, replace, take the place of, displace.

supple *adj.* 1 *The tubing is supple and fireproof:* pliant, flexible, plastic, bendable, pliable, elastic. 2 *the supple body of a gymnast:* lithe, limber, lissome, graceful. 3 *Her supple nature enables her to accept change:* adaptable, flexible, tractable, compliant, complaisant, yielding, acquiescent.

Ant. 1 stiff, rigid, firm, inflexible. 2 stiff, awkward, graceless.

supplement *n.* 1 *The night courses are a supplement to regular classes:* complement, addition, augmentation, corollary, extra, extension, addendum, adjunct. 2 *The newspaper publishes a special travel supplement twice a year:* section, insert, attachment; appendix, addendum, rider, added part. —*v.* 3 *I supplemented my earnings by taking a night job:* add to, extend, increase, augment.

supplication *n. The supplications of the homeless refugees were pitiful:* entreaty, petition, plea, appeal, beseechment, solicitation; prayer.

supply *v.* 1 *The Red Cross supplied the hos-*

pital with blood: provide, furnish, outfit, stock, equip; contribute, deliver, provision. —*n.* 2 *a daily supply of food:* provisioning, providing, furnishing, allocation; stock; reservoir, reserve, store, quota, provision. 3 Often **supplies** *What supplies will we need for our camp?:* equipment, goods, items, provisions; gear, trappings, accoutrements; foodstuff.

support *v.* 1 *Large beams support the weakened wall:* bear up, hold up; prop, bolster, uphold, brace, sustain, buttress, stay, shore up. 2 *That crate will never support your weight:* sustain, bear, hold. 3 *He has to support his parents:* maintain, provide for, keep, finance, foster. 4 *Her beliefs supported her throughout the tragedy:* help, sustain, succor, comfort, aid, carry, be a source of strength, strengthen. 5 *I support his right to speak out:* defend, back up, champion, uphold, stand up for, stick up for, advocate, sanction, favor, countenance; aid, boost, assist, further. 6 *Your testimony will support my plea of innocence:* verify, confirm, substantiate, corroborate, bear out, vouch for, endorse, guarantee, ratify. —*n.* 7 *One of the roof supports is cracked:* brace, prop, underpinning, post, buttress; pedestal, pillar, column, pilaster, base. 8 *Pat provided support for the children when their father died:* sustenance, maintenance, upkeep, subsistence; comfort, succor, aid, help, strength, encouragement. 9 *The candidate asked for our support:* backing, patronage, aid, help, assistance, espousal, advocacy, involvement.

supporter *n. I'm a supporter of many environmental causes:* backer, upholder, defender, champion, patron, adherent, benefactor, disciple, partisan, advocate, ally, helper, follower.

Ant. adversary, opponent.

suppose *v.* 1 *Suppose you're offered the job—will you accept?:* assume, hypothesize, presume, predicate, posit, consider. 2 *I suppose you're hungry?:* guess, imagine, believe, reckon, take for granted, presume, assume, gather, judge, fancy, conceive, suspect, divine, surmise.

supposition *n. My supposition is that the economy will improve:* presumption, assumption, conjecture, opinion, surmise, guess, belief, theory, view, hypothesis.

Ant. certainty, fact.

suppress *v.* 1 *The government suppressed the rebellion:* put down, crush, subdue, quash, squash, quell. 2 *It was all I could do to suppress my anger:* withhold, stifle, keep back, check, control, smother, restrain, muffle, curb. 3 *He tried to suppress the scandal:* keep secret, conceal, hide.

Ant. 2 let out, unleash, unloose. 3 reveal, uncover, expose.

supremacy *n. The king's supremacy is unquestioned:* preeminence, superiority, primacy, precedence; domination, power, sovereignty, mastery, absolute authority, ascendancy, absolute rule.

supreme *adj.* 1 *The Pope is the supreme leader of the Roman Catholic Church:* sovereign, dominant, uppermost, front-ranking, first, highest, chief, principal, paramount, foremost, all-powerful; commanding, prime, unqualified, absolute, unconditional, unlimited. 2 *supreme skill:* perfect, consummate, nonpareil, peerless, superlative, matchless, unexcelled, incomparable, unsurpassed, unequaled, unparalleled, unmatched, unrivaled; extreme, immeasurable.

sure *adj.* 1 *I'm sure of their loyalty:* confident, assured, fully persuaded, convinced, positive, certain, undoubting. 2 *He's a sure and eager employee:* trustworthy, never-failing, reliable, unfailing, dependable, firm, steady, faithful. 3 *She has a sure eye for color:* unerring, accurate, unfailing, flawless, infallible, dependable, reliable, sound.

Ant. 1, 3 unsure. 1–3 uncertain. 1 unconvinced, doubtful, distrustful. 2 unsteady, inconstant, undependable, unreliable. 3 inaccurate, unreliable.

surely *adv. You surely did well:* for certain, assuredly, without doubt, undoubtedly, certainly, doubtless, unquestionably, definitely, positively, indubitably, emphatically, by all means; without fail, no doubt, to be sure, of course.

surface *n. the surface of a sphere:* outside, face, facade, outer face, exterior; *(variously)* covering, shell, coat, finish, coating, crust, skin.

surfeit *n. There's a surfeit of apples this year:* glut, surplus, excess, overabundance, superfluity, oversupply, surplusage.

Ant. shortage, dearth, lack, paucity, shortfall.

surge *n. A surge of shoppers poured into the store:* wave, swell, torrent, flood, rush.

surly *adj. He's too surly to have many friends:* sullen, irascible, grouchy, discourteous, ill-humored, bad-tempered, testy, crabbed, ill-natured, cross, crusty, uncivil, grumpy, snappish, peevish, churlish, gruff, petulant.

Ant. amiable, gracious, affable, pleasant, friendly, civil.

surmise *v.* 1 *I surmised that she would get the promotion:* conjecture, imagine, guess, suppose, presuppose, think, presume, judge, suspect, theorize, believe, infer, hypothesize, conclude. —*n.* 2 *My surmise is*

that he'll win the election: guess, supposition, conjecture, opinion, speculation, assumption, hypothesis, presumption, belief.

surmount *v.* 1 *How will we surmount that wall?:* get over, scale, climb. 2 *He surmounted his handicap and achieved success:* conquer, defeat, master, overcome, best, triumph over.

surpass *v.* 1 *She surpassed the goal she set for herself:* exceed, go beyond, outdo, top, best, outstrip, beat. 2 *This surpasses any dessert I've ever had:* excel, outdo, be superior to, outshine, overshadow, be better than.

surplus *n.* 1 *The farmers have a potato surplus:* oversupply, superfluity, overage, surplusage, excess, overproduction, glut. —*adj.* 2 *I never have any surplus cash!:* excess, extra, superfluous, leftover, residual.

Ant. 1 deficiency, shortage, insufficiency, paucity, lack.

surprise *v.* 1 *His success surprised us:* astonish, astound, nonplus, startle, amaze, flabbergast, shock, stun, dumbfound, confound. 2 *Mother surprised me raiding the icebox:* catch in the act of, come upon unexpectedly, take unawares, discover. —*n.* 3 *The promotion was a surprise:* something unexpected, bolt out of the blue, revelation. 5 *To my surprise, everyone arrived early:* amazement, wonder, astonishment, wonderment, incredulity, shock.

surrender *v.* 1 *They were the last contingent to surrender:* give up, yield, submit, capitulate, concede, lay down arms. 2 *He surrendered all rights to the property:* give up, abandon, relinquish, renounce, give over, yield, forgo, waive, render, accede, cede, deliver up. —*n.* 3 *Our surrender was delayed:* yielding, capitulation, submission; relinquishment, giving up, delivery; forgoing, renunciation.

Ant. 1 resist, oppose. 2 retain, keep.

surreptitious *adj. a surreptitious meeting:* secret, stealthy, undercover, furtive, clandestine, hidden, covert.

Ant. open, public.

surround *v. A fence surrounds the yard:* encircle, circle, enclose, ring, encompass, girdle, circumscribe.

surroundings *n. pl. It's important to work in friendly surroundings:* environs, conditions; environment, habitat, milieu, setting, ambience, atmosphere.

surveillance *n. The police have us under surveillance:* watch, observation, vigil, scrutiny.

survey *v.* 1 *Let's survey the events leading up to the crime:* review, look over, view; consider, contemplate, examine, inspect, study, scrutinize. 2 *The city engineer surveyed the property to amend the map:* measure, verify the boundaries of, delimit, plot; reconnoiter, observe, scout. —*n.* 3 *a survey of the country's population growth. a public opinion survey:* review, study, comprehensive view, overview, investigation, probe; poll, canvass, analysis.

survival *n.* 1 *an expert at survival in the wilderness:* living, keeping alive, subsistence. 2 *This custom is a survival from Grandmother's day:* carry-over, relic, vestige, continuation, atavism.
Ant. 1 death, extinction, eradication.

survive *v.* 1 *How long can the lost survive in the Arctic? Many early customs survive:* keep alive, subsist, last; live on, persist, endure, continue, exist. 2 *They survived the bombing:* live through, come through alive.
Ant. 1 perish, disappear. 2 succumb to.

susceptible *adj. The rule is susceptible to differing interpretations:* open, prone, subject, vulnerable, receptive to, capable of, sensitive to, disposed to, conducive to, liable to.
Ant. unsusceptible, immune, invulnerable, resistant.

suspect *v.* 1 *He suspected her sincerity:* mistrust, doubt, distrust, have no confidence in, have doubts about, harbor suspicions about, be suspicious of. 2 *We suspect they'll be late:* guess, imagine, conjecture, surmise, hypothesize, believe, theorize, judge, presume, speculate, suppose, think. —*n.* 3 *The suspect is being held at police headquarters:* suspected person, alleged culprit.
Ant. 1 trust, believe. 2 know, be sure, be certain.

suspend *v.* 1 *Suspend the swing from the tree branch:* hang, dangle, append. 2 *I'll suspend judgment until all the facts are in:* put off, postpone, delay, defer, table, reserve, withhold. 3 *They suspended construction during the strike:* discontinue, cease, stop, halt, arrest, interrupt.

suspicion *n. I have a suspicion about his part in this case:* distrust, mistrust; conjecture, idea, surmise, supposition, hypothesis, notion.
Ant. trust, trustfulness.

suspicious *adj.* 1 *Your behavior was suspicious:* open to doubt, questionable, dubious, suspect, doubtful; untrustworthy, shady. 2 *The police are suspicious of my alibi:* inclined to suspect, mistrustful, distrustful, wary, doubting, disbelieving, unbelieving.
Ant. 1, 2 unsuspicious. 1 open, aboveboard. 2 trusting, confident.

sustain *v.* 1 *These four posts sustain the*

entire building: support, bear up, uphold, hold up, underpin, prop. 2 *The company was able to sustain the loss:* bear, brook, endure, abide, stand, withstand, tolerate. 3 *I sustained a terrible head injury:* suffer, undergo, experience. 4 *The runner was able to sustain the same pace for hours:* maintain, keep up, prolong, protract. 5 *The prisoners sustained themselves on bread and water:* nourish, maintain; feed, keep alive.

svelte *adj. Many people want a svelte figure:* slender, slim, thin, lissome, lithe, willowy, sylphlike.
Ant. plump, stocky, pudgy; dumpy, squat.

swagger *v. He swaggered across the room:* strut, stride insolently, swashbuckle, sweep.
Ant. slink, sneak, creep.

swamp *n.* 1 *We saw alligators in the swamp:* marsh, bog, morass, quagmire, bayou, everglade, swampland, slough. —*v.* 2 *The wave swamped our canoe:* sink, engulf, flood, wash over, inundate, envelop, deluge, swallow up. 3 *The senator was swamped with invitations:* overwhelm, flood, besiege, engulf, beset.

swap *v. The boys swapped baseball cards:* trade, exchange, switch.

swarm *n.* 1 *a swarm of locusts. A swarm of fans ran onto the football field:* multitude; drove, throng, horde, mass, herd, host, crowd. —*v.* 2 *The bargain hunters swarmed into the store:* flock, surge, throng, crowd, herd, cluster, rush, mass, stream.

swarthy *adj. He looked swarthy after a month in the Caribbean:* dark-complexioned, dark-skinned, brunet, tawny, brown-skinned, olive-skinned.
Ant. pale, fair, light-complexioned.

swat *v. She swatted the ball for a home run:* hit, smack, knock, strike, smite, wallop, belt, clout, buffet, clobber, sock, slam, bash, whack, slug.

sway *v.* 1 *The boat swayed on the stormy sea:* rock, move to and fro, swing, roll, oscillate, undulate; waver, reel, totter, wobble, stagger. 2 *The cold weather swayed them to go south:* move, influence, prompt, persuade, motivate, lead, induce, dispose, encourage. 3 *I have never swayed in my loyalty:* fluctuate, vacillate, change, shift, waver. —*n.* 4 *The cabinet is completely under the sway of the Prime Minister:* control, rule, domination, command, power, domain, jurisdiction, government, grip, hold; influence, direction.

swear *v.* 1 *The witness swore to tell the truth:* take an oath, vow, vouch, avow, certify, warrant, bear witness, attest, aver, assert, promise. 2 *We swore them to silence:* cause to promise, bind by an oath, pledge. 3 *The boy swears like a trooper:* curse, cuss, use profanity, utter oaths.

sweep *v.* 1 *Sweep up the broken glass:* whisk, gather. 2 *The winner swept past the finish line:* race, dash, rush, dart, scurry, hurry, charge, fly, zoom, swoop, tear. —*n.* 3 *There's a long sweep of empty road before you come to the inn:* stretch, distance, spell. 4 *He cut the rope with one sweep of his machete:* swing, stroke, swoop.

sweetheart *n. Her sweetheart gave her a ring for Christmas:* love, beloved, true love, dear, darling, flame, steady, boyfriend, girl-friend, lover; ladylove; beau, swain, suitor, gentleman friend; fiancé, *(fem.)* fiancée.

swell *v.* 1 *My eye swelled painfully. The guest list swelled to 100 people:* distend, puff up, grow, bulge, inflate, extend; expand, in-crease, lengthen, stretch, widen, burgeon, rise. 2 *The music swelled as the finale approached:* intensify, amplify, heighten, rise, mount, surge. —*adj.* 3 *Informal We had a swell time:* fine, first-rate, good, excellent, super, marvelous, terrific, wonderful, great, delightful, splendid, pleasurable, fabulous, tremendous. —*n.* 4 *The ship scudded along over the swells:* wave, billow; breaker, comber. 5 *The young man imagined himself a swell:* fashion plate, smart dresser, dandy, fop, clotheshorse.
Ant. 1 shrink, contract, constrict. 2 de-crease, diminish, fall, ebb away. 3 horrible, awful, dreadful, lousy, bad.

swift *adj. The thief made a swift exit:* hasty, fast, rapid, fleet, prompt, speedy, brisk, quick.
Ant. slow, sluggish.

swill *v.* 1 *They swilled those drinks down in no time:* guzzle, gulp down, swallow nois-ily, quaff, swig. —*n.* 2 *The farmer fed his pigs swill:* slop; liquid food, mash; garbage, refuse, scraps, leavings.

swindle *v.* 1 *He swindled his kin out of the inheritance:* cheat, defraud, gyp, fleece, cozen, bilk, con, dupe; embezzle. —*n.* 2 *She lost her life's savings in the swindle:* fraud, embezzlement, confidence game, con game, racket.

swindler *n. a police record as a swindler:* embezzler; con man; crook, charlatan, mountebank, gyp, fraud, sharper, cheat.

swing *v.* 1 *The pendulum stopped swinging:* oscillate, sway, rock, undulate, seesaw. 2 *Can you swing us an invitation to the party?:* manage, manipulate, handle, accom-plish, maneuver, pull off, wangle. 3 *He swung round on his heels and walked out:* pivot, rotate, turn, whirl. —*n.* 4 *The swing of the ship made everyone seasick:* swaying,

rocking, pitching, rolling, oscillation. 5 *It takes just one swing of the bat to hit a home run:* sweep, sweeping blow, stroke.

swirl *v. The dancer swirled:* whirl, spin, re-volve, wheel, turn, twirl; rotate, gyrate.

switch *n.* 1 *a hickory switch:* rod, small branch, stick. 2 *a light switch:* actuator, lever, button. 3 *We had to make a switch in our arrangements:* change, alternation, trade, shift. —*v.* 4 *Grandpa switched us when we were disobedient:* whip, birch, lash, cane, tan. 5 *The cow switched its tail:* whisk, jerk, move, swing, lash. 6 *I switched pocket-books with my sister:* exchange, change, trade.

swollen *adj. a swollen eye:* puffed-up, puffy, swelled, distended; bloated, inflated, bulg-ing.
Ant. shrunken, contracted.

swoop *v.* 1 *The sea gull swooped down on the fish:* descend, drop, plunge, sweep down, plummet, dive; spring, pounce, rush. —*n.* 2 *With one swoop the falcon captured its prey:* dive, plunge, drop; pounce, rush.

sword *n. The duelists crossed swords:* blade, steel; *(variously)* saber, rapier, cutlass, foil, scimitar, épée, broadsword.

sycophant *n. The king surrounded himself with sycophants:* toady, flatterer, bootlicker, fawner, flunky, stooge, yes-man, lackey.

sylvan *adj. She loved the sylvan beauty of the country:* forestlike, woodland, wooded, tim-bered, forested.

symbol *n.* 1 *In math, x is the symbol for an unknown quantity:* sign, mark, figure, indi-cation. 2 *The ring is a symbol of love:* em-blem, token, badge; representation, figure.

symbolize *v. The dove symbolizes peace:* stand for, mean, emblematize, represent, per-sonify, connote, denote, signify.

symmetrical *adj. The formal garden is too symmetrical for my taste:* balanced, well-balanced, orderly, regular, well-propor-tioned.
Ant. asymmetrical, unbalanced; disor-derly.

symmetry *n. The snowflake is an example of perfect symmetry:* correspondence of parts, regularity, conformity, balance, pro-portionality, equilibrium, order, parallel-ism, harmony.
Ant. disproportion, disharmony, irregu-larity, disparity.

sympathetic *adj.* 1 *a sympathetic teacher:* sympathizing, compassionate, understand-ing, sensitive; tenderhearted, warmhearted, comforting, humane, kindly, benevolent, benign. 2 *His mother was not sympathetic to his plan:* favorably disposed, agreeable, approving, friendly.

Ant. 1, 2 unsympathetic. 1 coldhearted, insensitive, unpitying, unfeeling.

sympathize *v. I sympathize with the bereaved:* feel compassion for, be sorry for, feel for, have pity for, pity, empathize, feel sympathy for; identify with, grieve with, commiserate with.

sympathy *n.* 1 *There was an instant sympathy between the two:* concord, accord, harmony, congeniality, understanding, rapport, affinity, regard, amity, fellow feeling, friendship. 2 *We felt tremendous sympathy for the orphans:* concern, compassion, commiseration, empathy, grief, sorrow, pity.
Ant. 1 antipathy, hostility, antagonism. 2 pitilessness, indifference, unconcern.

symposium *n. We attended a symposium on ecology:* conference, parley, discussion, panel forum, round table, colloquy, congress, meeting.

symptom *n. A rash is one symptom of scarlet fever:* sign, indication, evidence, token, warning, mark.

syndicate *n. A syndicate is buying up all the stock:* combine, coalition, alliance, league, federation, association, group; trust, cartel, consortium.

synonym *n. "Volume" is a synonym for "book":* equivalent word, parallel word, analogue, equivalent; another name.
Ant. antonym, opposite.

synonymous *adj. "Car" is synonymous with "automobile":* equivalent, similar in meaning, alike, like, same, equal.
Ant. antonymous, opposite in meaning.

synopsis *n. Read a synopsis of the opera before going to it:* outline, summary, précis.

synthetic *adj. synthetic suede:* artificial, manmade, manufactured, ersatz; fake, phony, counterfeit, sham.
Ant. real, authentic, genuine.

system *n.* 1 *the school system. a hi-fi system:* combination of parts, organization, organized entity, overall unit, unit, structure. 2 *Don't wreck your system by lack of sleep!:* constitution, body; organism. 3 *Does the new clerk know the filing system?:* method, procedure, arrangement, scheme, mode of operation, regimen, routine.

systematic *adj.* 1 *You should have a systematic savings program:* planned, organized, systematized, orderly, ordered. 2 *My books are kept in a highly systematic way:* methodical, precise, orderly, well-organized, businesslike, well-regulated, regular.
Ant. 1, 2 unsystematic. 1 haphazard, random. 2 unmethodical, disorderly, disorganized; messy, sloppy.

T

tab *n.* 1 *files with alphabetical tabs:* short strip, flap, projection, lip, tongue. 2 *What's the tab?:* bill, check, cost, price, tally.

table *n.* 1 *Set the table. A clock radio was on the table by the bed: (variously)* eating table, dining room table, kitchen table, breakfast table; stand, end table, coffee table, bedside table, display table. 2 *The math book contained a multiplication table:* list, chart, tabulation; schedule, record, register, roll, roster. *—v.* 3 *The committee tabled the proposal until a later meeting:* lay aside, put aside, postpone, shelve.

tablet *n.* 1 *Each student should have pencils and a tablet:* pad of paper, writing pad, pad. 2 *The statue had a bronze tablet listing the town's war heroes:* plaque, panel, tablature; thin slab. 3 *an aspirin tablet:* lozenge, troche, pellet, bolus.

taboo Also **tabu** *adj.* 1 *Eating pork is taboo in certain religions:* forbidden, banned, prohibited, proscribed, anathema; unacceptable, unthinkable, unmentionable. *—n.* 2 *The Polynesians have a taboo on mentioning certain sacred rites:* religious ban, social ban, ban, prohibition, proscription.
Ant. 1 allowed, permitted, permissible; approved, sanctioned.

tabulate *v. Tabulate the data according to source:* arrange, order, systematize, rank, list, group, organize, sort, categorize, codify, sort out.
Ant. mix, confuse, jumble.

tacit *adj. The neighbors had a tacit agreement not to park in front of each other's houses:* unexpressed, understood, implied, inferred, implicit, wordless, unspoken, unstated.

taciturn *adj. He's so taciturn no one knew whether he enjoyed the party or not:* reserved, reticent, uncommunicative, closemouthed, silent, quiet.

Ant. talkative, loquacious, voluble, garrulous.

tack *n.* 1 *The calendar was held to the wall with tacks:* short nail; *(variously)* thumbtack, carpet tack. 2 *The sailboat's tack to starboard:* zigzag, change, swerve. 3 *If this plan doesn't work, we'll try a new tack:* course of action, approach, method, way. —*v.* 4 *Tack the notice on the bulletin board:* nail, pin; attach, fasten, affix. 5 *Tack on 15% for the tip to the waiter:* add, attach, affix, append. 6 *The ship tacked to starboard:* change course, go about, veer, sheer, zigzag.

Ant. 5 subtract, deduct.

tackle *n.* 1 *fishing tackle:* equipment, gear, paraphernalia, trappings, rigging, accoutrements, implements; instruments. 2 *The policeman nailed the suspect with a flying tackle:* pinioning of the legs. —*v.* 3 *The boys tackled the job of painting the room:* undertake, attempt, try, take on, embark upon, engage in, set about. 4 *The defensive end tackled the ball carrier:* seize and throw down, wrestle to the ground.

Ant. 3 reject, evade, eschew; postpone.

tacky *adj. Did you ever see such a tacky house?:* slovenly, messy, sloppy, disordered, untidy, unkempt; slipshod, shabby, shoddy, frazzled, seedy; cheap, mean, in bad taste.

Ant. 1 neat, orderly; elegant, noble.

tact *n. The hostess showed enormous tact in handling the situation:* diplomacy, delicacy, suavity, finesse, discretion, consideration.

Ant. tactlessness, crudeness, heavy-handedness, indiscretion.

tactful *adj. The tactful suggestion offended no one:* socially adroit, diplomatic, politic, decorous, discreet, delicate, thoughtful.

Ant. tactless, undiplomatic, indiscreet; gauche.

tactic *n. The best tactic is to confess and ask forgiveness:* course of action, plan, stratagem, scheme, policy, approach. 2 Usually **tactics** *The general's brilliant tactics won the battle:* maneuvers, battle arrangements, military operations.

tactless *adj. She made tactless remarks about my sister:* rude, undiplomatic, inconsiderate, insensitive, ham-handed, untactful, boorish, impolitic, indiscreet, gauche.

Ant. tactful, polite, diplomatic, discreet.

tag *n.* 1 *a printed price tag:* label, tab, ticket, slip, marker. —*v.* 2 *The clerks tagged the merchandise for the sale:* label, ticket, mark, identify.

tailor *n.* 1 *A London tailor makes all of Bill's clothes:* garment maker, dressmaker, seamstress, clothier; alteration man, alteration lady. —*v.* 2 *Her clothing is tailored by a*

famous couturier. We can tailor a plan to suit your needs: fashion, make, create, design, devise, shape, construct, produce, fabricate; alter, adapt, change, fit, modify, redo; sew.

taint *n.* 1 *The scandal was a taint on the family's name:* stain, spot, blemish, blot, stigma; defect, fault, imperfection. —*v.* 2 *Rumors of bribery tainted the politician's reputation:* spoil, damage, ruin, sully, stain, soil, tarnish, blemish, mar.

Ant. 2 enhance, elevate, strengthen.

take *v.* 1 *Please take a cookie. Take the rope in your right hand and pull:* get, have, obtain, acquire, secure, avail oneself of, help oneself to; grip, grasp, clutch, clasp, hold, lay hold of, seize, grab, snatch, nab. 2 *The military took control of the government. The thieves took all the money:* seize, grab, usurp, appropriate, misappropriate, capture; steal, purloin, filch. 3 *Take this package to the post office. The teacher took the students on a tour through the art museum:* deliver, carry, bring, bear, convey, transport, transfer; conduct, guide, lead, escort, usher. 4 *My sister has taken a house by the shore for the summer:* buy, purchase; rent, lease, hire, obtain, acquire, get. 5 *If you take 6 from 10, you get 4:* subtract, deduct, take away, remove, eliminate. 6 *We took your silence to mean that you agreed:* interpret, understand, regard, respond to, receive, look on, see, perceive, deem, suppose, believe, consider, ascertain, infer. 7 *Take the doctor's advice:* accept, accede to, agree to, consent to, assent to; heed, follow, mind, obey, observe, resign oneself to. 8 *Becoming a doctor takes years of study. It took all my strength to lift the chair:* require, necessitate, need, demand, call for; use, employ, consume, claim. 9 *She won't take any more insults:* endure, bear, stand, tolerate, suffer, brook, submit to, undergo, put up with. 10 *I take great pleasure in introducing our guest speaker:* feel, have, experience, know; derive, attain, get, draw. 11 *Bill took the blame for the mistake:* accept, assume, undertake, shoulder, draw. 12 *As soon as the medicine takes, the patient should improve:* take effect, begin to work; work, succeed. —*n.* 13 *The fisherman brought home a huge take:* catch, haul. 14 *The day's take came to over $5,000:* proceeds, net; profit, gross.

Ant. 1 give, let go. 2 surrender, give up, return, restore. 5 add. 7 reject, spurn, ignore, dismiss. 11 avoid, evade. 12 fail. 14 loss.

tale *n.* 1 *a tale of intrigue and adventure:* story, narrative, narration; account, report, yarn. 2 *Don't tell tales out of school:* fib, lie, falsehood, untruth, fabrication, falsification; piece of gossip, scandal, rumor.

talent *n. You have a talent for drawing:* special ability, gift, facility, genius, aptitude, knack, bent, flair.

talented *adj. a talented musician:* gifted, accomplished; proficient, competent, capable.

talk *v.* 1 *Can the baby talk yet? We talked for hours:* utter words, speak; converse, bandy words, discuss, chat, chatter, gab, gossip, prattle, babble, rap, jaw. 2 *You'd better talk with a lawyer:* confer, consult, speak; negotiate, parley. 3 *He's talking nonsense!:* utter, speak, say, express; intone, enunciate; state, proclaim, pronounce, declare; preach, pontificate. —*n.* 4 *Let's have a little talk:* conversation, chat, tête-à-tête; discussion, conference, consultation, powwow. 5 *The speaker gave a short, humorous talk:* address, lecture, speech, oration, sermon. 6 *There's been some talk about closing the office:* gossip, rumor, hearsay; report, word. 7 *The kids' hip talk is sometimes hard for adults to follow:* idiom, language, lingo, slang, cant, jargon, argot.

Ant. 1 be silent, be mute; listen.

talkative *adj. The talkative man monopolized the conversation:* loquacious, voluble, effusive, garrulous, talky, gabby, prolix, long-winded, windy, wordy, verbose.

Ant. reticent, taciturn, uncommunicative, close-mouthed, tight-lipped.

talker *n.* 1 *The senator is a marvelous talker:* conversationalist; speaker, lecturer, orator, speechmaker. 2 *She's quite a talker—I couldn't get in a word!:* loquacious person, voluble person, garrulous person, chatterbox, windbag, gabber; gossip, rumormonger, scandalmonger.

tall *adj.* 1 *The boy is four feet tall:* high, in height. 2 *Basketball players are tall. a tall mountain:* of more than average height, long-limbed; high, lofty, towering, soaring, elevated. 3 *a tall tale:* hard to believe, implausible, preposterous, exaggerated, embellished, false.

Ant. 1 wide, broad; long, deep. 2 short, low. 3 believable, credible, plausible, reasonable.

tally *n.* 1 *The final tally was 200 votes for and 150 against:* count, reckoning, mark, score; total, sum. —*v.* 2 *The judges tallied the scores:* record, mark down, register, list; count, add, sum up, total, reckon. 3 *The checkbook stubs don't tally with my bank statement:* match, jibe, square, correspond, agree, accord, concur, harmonize.

tame *adj.* 1 *a tame monkey. Greg is too tame to stand up for his rights:* domesticated, domestic; docile, gentle, mild, tractable, subdued, pliant, meek, timid. 2 *Country life was too tame for the city boy:* unexciting, uninteresting, dull, boring; quiet, serene, tranquil. —*v.* 3 *to tame wild horses. She'd better tame that violent temper:* break, make docile, domesticate, subdue, train; control, conquer, master, govern, restrain, curb, bridle, check.

Ant. 1 wild, untamed, undomesticated; strong-willed. 2 exciting, interesting, stimulating, lively, wild, frenzied.

tamper *v. Did anyone tamper with this lock?:* tinker, meddle, fool around, fiddle, *Informal* mess around, monkey around.

tan *v.* 1 *Fairskinned people don't tan easily:* suntan; brown, bronze. —*adj.* 2 *Marilyn came back from her vacation with tan arms and face:* suntanned, bronzed; sunburned, sunburnt. 3 *tan pants:* light brown, brownish, yellow-brown, beige, tawny, sandy, cinnamon, roan, sorrel, khaki.

tang *n.* 1 *The dressing has too much tang:* taste, flavor, savor, pungency, bite, punch, sharpness, piquancy, spiciness, tartness. 2 *There's a tang of fall in the air:* trace, tinge, hint, touch, suggestion, smack.

tangible *adj.* 1 *A ghost is not a tangible thing:* touchable, material, solid, physical, corporeal, substantial. 2 *We need tangible evidence:* concrete, real, actual, material, verifiable, positive, clear-cut.

Ant. 1 intangible, immaterial, incorporeal.

tangle *v.* 1 *The wind tangled her hair:* twist, snarl, entangle, ravel, knot; disarrange, dishevel, muss, tousle, jumble, disorder. —*n.* 2 *a tangle of vines. The negotiations were in a hopeless tangle:* snarl, knot, entanglement, web, network; labyrinth, maze; fix, impasse.

Ant. 1 untangle, unsnarl, unknot, disentangle.

tank *n. a water tank:* storage tank, vat, container, receptacle; reservoir, cistern, boiler; fish tank, aquarium.

tantalize *v. The speaker tantalized us with tales of buried treasure:* tease, provoke, torment; tempt, titillate, intrigue; fascinate, bewitch, captivate, entice.

Ant. satisfy, gratify, appease.

tantrum *n. The child's tantrums were caused by frustration:* burst of temper, rampage, fit of passion, flare-up, outburst, fit, paroxysm, explosion.

tap[1] *v.* 1 *Rain tapped on the windowpane:* strike lightly, touch lightly, rap, pat, beat softly, drum, peck. —*n.* 2 *I felt a tap on my shoulder:* light strike, gentle blow, touch, stroke, pat, rap, peck.

tap[2] *n.* 1 *the hot-water tap:* faucet, spigot,

stopcock, cock, spout. —v. 2 *The bartender tapped a new keg of beer:* put a tap in, unplug, open the stopcock of; draw liquid from, broach. 3 *The country must tap new sources of energy:* draw upon, use, utilize, exploit, employ.

tardy *adj.* *You'll be tardy if you don't hurry:* late, unpunctual, behind time, overdue.
Ant. punctual, on time, prompt; early.

target *n.* 1 *The arrow hit the target. The organization's target was to double its membership:* mark; objective, object, goal, aim, end, purpose, ambition; design, plan, intent, intention. 2 *He was the target of the practical joke:* butt, goat, victim, dupe.

tariff *n.* 1 *The cigarette tariff has gone up:* duty, input tax, export tax, excise tax, excise, assessment, impost, levy. 2 *The railroads increased their tariff by ten percent:* fare, freightage; *(loosely)* charge, rate, fee, price, cost.

tarnish *v.* 1 *Silver tarnishes easily:* oxidize, corrode, discolor, blacken, lose luster. 2 *The charge of fraud tarnished his reputation:* discredit, degrade, defile, stigmatize, disgrace, taint, stain, sully, spot, blemish, blacken, soil, dirty, dull, dim.
Ant. 1 shine, polish. 2 enhance, glorify, exalt.

tarry *v.* 1 *I mustn't tarry:* linger, dally, remain, stay. 2 *Don't tarry in coming to a decision:* dawdle, delay, wait, take time, procrastinate, stall, hang back.
Ant. 1 leave, go, depart, be off. 2 rush, hurry, hasten.

tart *adj.* 1 *This lemon pie is very tart:* sour, sharp, astringent, acetic, vinegary; tangy, pungent, bitter. 2 *My tart reply offended her:* sharp, caustic, cutting, barbed, biting, acerb, crusty.
Ant. 1 sweet, sugary, saccharine, bland. 2 sweet, kindly, gentle, pleasant, genial, gracious.

task *n.* *household tasks:* chore, job, duty, work, labor, mission, assignment, responsibility, errand, business, undertaking.

taskmaster *n.* *The major was a taskmaster:* martinet, slave driver, disciplinarian, stickler; master, boss, supervisor, superintendent, overseer, foreman, manager.

taste *v.* 1 *Can you taste the mint in the icing? This punch tastes like pineapple juice:* savor, discern; savor of, smack of. 2 *Taste some of this cake:* sample, take a bite of, try, test; drink a little of, take a sip of. 3 *At last we tasted the joys of success:* experience, partake of, undergo, feel, have a foretaste of. —n. 4 *This slaw has a sour taste:* flavor, savor, smack, tang, piquancy. 5 *Have a taste of this pie:* mouthful, bite, bit, sample,

forkful, spoonful; sip, swallow. 6 *Rachel has a taste for sweets:* liking, predilection, propensity, leaning, inclination, penchant, partiality, fondness, craving, desire, fancy, yen, appetite, hunger. 7 *She has marvelous taste in books. The joke showed poor taste:* esthetic judgment, discernment, artistic appreciation; sense of propriety, propriety, correctness, judgment, discrimination, delicacy, decorum.
Ant. 3 miss. 6 distaste, dislike, disinclination, hatred, abhorrence, loathing. 7 tastelessness; impropriety, indelicacy.

tasteful *adj.* *Everyone admired the tasteful decor:* showing good taste, esthetic, artistic, attractive, elegant, refined, cultured, well-chosen, handsome, beautiful, suitable, becoming.
Ant. tasteless, unesthetic, inelegant, ugly, garish, tawdry, unrefined.

tasteless *adj.* 1 *The soup was tasteless:* having no taste, flavorless, without savor, bland, insipid, watery. 2 *a tasteless joke. Her wardrobe seems completely tasteless:* lacking good taste, cheap, common, crude, rude, coarse, crass, gross, uncouth, improper, unseemly, insensitive, indelicate, indecent, indecorous, low, disgusting, distasteful, offensive; gaudy, flashy, garish, inelegant, unrefined, unesthetic.

tasty *adj.* *The stew was quite tasty:* good-tasting, delicious, delectable, toothsome, yummy; savory, flavorful, flavorsome, full-flavored, appetizing.

tatters *n. pl.* *The derelict was in tatters:* shreds, rags; ragged clothing, torn clothes.

tattle *v.* 1 *Teach the child not to tattle:* tell on, inform on, divulge secrets, blab, gossip; *Slang* snitch, rat, squeal; babble, prattle, gabble. —n. 2 *Your conversation is full of tattle:* gossip, prattle, chatter, babble, rumormongering, tittle-tattle, twaddle, loose talk.

tattletale *n.* *Some tattletale got us in trouble:* tattler, talebearer, rumormonger, newsmonger, gossip, telltale, busybody, blabbermouth; *Slang* snitch, fink.

taunt *v.* 1 *The bully taunted the smaller boy:* jeer, mock, tease, rag, twit, guy, sneer at, ridicule, make fun of; torment, provoke, harass. —n. 2 *Her sister's cruel taunts drove the little girl to tears:* jeer, mockery, insult, teasing, ragging, chaffing, gibe, derision, sneer, scoff, ridicule, sarcastic remark, scornful remark, slur.
Ant. 1 flatter, coddle; praise, compliment. 2 humoring, flattering, coddling; praise, compliment.

taut *adj.* 1 *Keep the measuring tape taut:* drawn tight, tight, stretched out full, tense, rigid, inflexible. **2** *The captain runs a taut ship:* well-regulated, orderly, businesslike, well-disciplined, tight.

Ant. **1** slack, loose, relaxed. **2** sloppy, undisciplined.

tavern *n. We stopped at a tavern for ale:* saloon, barroom, taproom, bar, alehouse; restaurant, brasserie, bistro; cocktail lounge; *Brit.* pub, watering hole, grogshop, beer joint.

tawdry *adj. Tawdry clothes won't do for church:* showy, flashy, garish, gaudy, loud, tasteless; vulgar, crass, tacky, cheap, gimcrack.

Ant. tasteful, elegant, refined; simple, plain.

tawny *adj. tawny skin:* tan, bronze, yellowish-brown, light brown, brownish, beige, fawn; dusky, swarthy, olive.

tax *n.* **1** *The French kings used to levy a tax on salt:* payment of money to support a government and its services; *(variously)* income tax, property tax, sales tax, excise tax, luxury tax, inheritance tax, excess profit tax, state tax, county tax, city tax; impost, assessment, excise, levy, tariff, duty, custom, toll. **2** *Racing to make the train was a tax on our nerves:* burden, strain, exertion, drain. —*v.* **3** *The government does not tax certain private foundations:* impose a tax on, assess, levy, exact a duty from. **4** *The child taxed my patience:* overburden, weigh, weight, load; strain, tire, try; drain, exhaust, sap, wear out.

teach *v. to teach French: to teach graduate students:* give instruction in, conduct classes in, give lessons in, be employed as a teacher; give instruction to, conduct class for, give lessons to, instruct, educate, school, tutor, coach; discipline, prepare, inform, enlighten, edify; indoctrinate, inculcate.

Ant. learn, be educated.

teacher *n. The teacher dismissed the class: (variously)* schoolteacher, schoolmaster, master, schoolmistress, schoolmarm, instructor, professor, don, tutor, educator, trainer, coach.

teaching *n.* **1** *She excelled in the teaching of math:* instruction, instructing, schooling, tutoring, tutelage, training, preparation; education, pedagogy; indoctrination, inculcation. **2** *the teachings of Confucius:* precept, doctrine, dogma, principle, tenet.

team *n.* **1** *a team of oxen:* harnessed pair; pair, set, yoke, tandem. **2** *a football team:* sports team, side. **3** *a member of the economic advisory team:* group, unit, staff, band, squad; association, alliance, league, confederation, federation, coalition, party,

force, faction, circle, clique, coterie. —*v.* **4** *Several charities teamed to raise funds for the new hospital:* combine, unite, join together, band together, ally; cooperate.

tear *v.* **1** *Silk stockings tear easily:* rip, rend, split, slit, shred, pull apart, come apart, run, snag. **2** *The thief tore the bag from her hand:* pull, grab, seize, wrench, pluck, snatch, yank. **3** *Political conflict has torn the nation:* divide, disunite, split, splinter, rend, disrupt. **4** *He tore out of the room:* speed, race, rush, hasten, run, bolt, dash, dart, sprint, spurt, shoot, fly, scurry, scoot, scamper, scramble. —*n.* **5** *The house withstood many years of wear and tear:* damage, destruction, ravage, abuse, hard use. **6** *There's a tear in your shirt:* rip, rent, slit, split, hole; gap, break, breach, crack, rift, fissure, rupture, opening.

Ant. **1** mend, sew. **3** unite, solidify. **4** amble, stroll, saunter.

tearful *adj. The lovers bade a tearful farewell:* weeping, teary, crying, lachrymose; mournful, lamenting; weepy, wailing, sobbing, blubbering, whimpering, sniveling.

tease *v. Everyone teased him about his accent. Don't tease that cat or it will scratch you:* taunt, ridicule, mock, chafe, rag, needle, haze, make fun of, josh, laugh at, bait; torment; pester, provoke, bother, harry.

Ant. praise, compliment; humor, flatter; comfort.

technique *n.* **1** *Artists seek to improve techniques:* technical skill, form, style, skillfulness; expertness, proficiency, adroitness. **2** *a new technique for treating diabetes:* procedure, method, way, technology, approach, system.

tedious *adj.* **1** *Cleaning out the basement was a tedious job:* time-consuming, slow; tiring, wearying, fatiguing, exhausting; burdensome, onerous, laborious, dreary, dismal. **2** *a tedious play:* dull, boring, monotonous.

Ant. **1, 2** exhilarating, exciting, interesting. **1** fast, quick; easy.

tedium *n. I couldn't face the tedium of twenty more years at the same job:* monotony, dullness, tediousness, boredom, tiresomeness; drabness, dreariness.

Ant. excitement, interest, fascination, stimulation, exhilaration.

teem *v. Rome teems with tourists in the summer:* swarm, be overrun, overflow, abound, brim, bristle with.

teeter *v. After being hit, the boxer teetered and then fell:* wobble, totter, sway, seesaw, stagger, reel.

teetotaler *n. We are teetotalers but will*

serve guests cocktails: nondrinker, abstainer; prohibitionist, dry. *Ant.* drunk, drunkard, alcoholic, dipsomaniac.

tell *v.* **1** *Tell the truth:* narrate, declare, relate, recount, report, set forth, speak, utter, express, state, say, pronounce, mention, enunciate, apprise, communicate, make known, impart, reveal, divulge, disclose; publish, broadcast, spread abroad, blab, babble, describe, chronicle, write, detail, depict, portray. **2** *Fish lovers find it easy to tell fresh from frozen. Even oldtimers couldn't tell the tornado was coming:* tell apart, distinguish, discern, identify, recognize, perceive, ascertain; predict, forecast, foretell. **3** *Tell the orchestra to begin:* direct, instruct, order, bid, ask, request. **4** *to tell time:* count, count off, enumerate; compute, calculate, reckon, estimate. **5** *Years of dissipation finally told on his health:* take effect, influence, weigh, take a toll on.
Ant. **1** keep quiet, be mute, keep secret, hide, conceal; listen.

telling *adj.* *The court's decision was a telling blow for freedom of the press:* effective, effectual, powerful, forceful, striking, potent, momentous, trenchant, significant, influential, cogent, definitive, decisive, decided, conclusive, solid, important, impressive, consequential.
Ant. ineffective, unimportant, immaterial, insignificant, trivial, inconsequential.

telltale *n.* **1** *Don't rely on that telltale to keep a secret:* talebearer; tattletale, tattler, blabbermouth, gossip, busybody. —*adj.* **2** *There were telltale fingerprints on the cookie jar:* revealing, giveaway, betraying, divulging, disclosing, informative, enlightening.

temerity *n.* *Where does he get the temerity to ask such a personal question?:* audacity, insolence, gall, brazenness, brashness, nerve, cheek, brass, impudence, effrontery, forwardness, impertinence, pushiness, rashness, boldness.
Ant. reserve, reticence, discretion; bashfulness, shyness; timidity.

temper *n.* **1** *The mob was in no temper to listen to reason:* mood, disposition, humor. **2** *She stalked out in a burst of temper:* anger, rage, fury, wrath, ire, irritability, annoyance, vexation, pique, peevishness, indignation. **3** *Don't make me lose my temper!:* good humor, kindly disposition; calmness, composure, equilibrium. —*v.* **4** *a process for tempering steel:* strengthen, harden, toughen, anneal. **5** *Mother tried to temper Father's anger:* soften, moderate, allay, appease, pacify, mitigate, palliate, calm, quiet, soothe.

Ant. **2** good humor, calmness, composure. **4** soften. **5** intensify, heighten, aggravate, increase; stir, rouse, arouse.

temperament *n.* *The child has an easygoing temperament:* disposition, nature, temper, makeup, character, personality, spirit.

temperamental *adj.* *You're as temperamental as an opera star:* high-strung, excitable, moody, thin-skinned, sensitive, explosive, mercurial, volatile, passionate, emotional, hotheaded, tempestuous, turbulent; unpredictable, capricious, fickle, willful, headstrong.
Ant. easygoing, cool-headed, calm, unexcitable, predictable.

temperance *n.* **1** *Use temperance in giving advice to friends:* moderation, forbearance, self-control, self-discipline, restraint, discretion, prudence. **2** *He serves no liquor because he believes in temperance:* teetotalism, abstinence, abstemiousness, prohibition.
Ant. **1, 2** intemperance, immoderation. **1** unrestraint, abandon, wantonness. **2** drinking, alcoholism, dipsomania.

temperate *adj.* **1** *Be more temperate in your eating habits. a temperate personality:* self-restrained, self-controlled, moderate; rational, reasonable; calm, coolheaded, levelheaded, composed, collected, steady. **2** *a temperate climate:* mild, gentle, moderate, clement, pleasant.
Ant. **1, 2** intemperate, immoderate. **1** uncontrolled, abandoned, excessive, extravagant; unreasonable, irrational, temperamental. **2** harsh, severe.

tempest *n.* *A tempest was stirred up by the coach's resignation:* storm, uproar, commotion, furor, upheaval, disturbance, tumult, agitation, hubbub.

tempestuous *adj.* *tempestuous winds. The two candidates had a tempestuous debate:* stormy, turbulent, raging, violent, furious, agitated, tumultuous; passionate, impassioned, emotional, frenzied, overwrought, excited, fiery, hot.
Ant. calm, placid, peaceful; relaxed, serene, tranquil, unemotional.

tempo *n.* *The march was played at too fast a tempo:* speed, pace, time, meter, timing.

temporal *adj.* *The Pope represents spiritual rather than temporal authority:* civil, lay, secular, nonspiritual, nonclerical, nonecclesiastical, profane; worldly, mundane, mortal.
Ant. ecclesiastical, spiritual, sacred, religious, eternal.

temporary *adj.* *The book enjoyed temporary fame:* momentary, brief, impermanent, passing, fleeting, transitory, transient, short-lived, ephemeral, evanescent; provisional, interim.

Ant. lasting, permanent, enduring.

temporize *v. The committee temporized instead of reaching a decision:* delay, hedge, stall, equivocate, hem and haw, waver, vacillate, procrastinate.

Ant. act, decide, proceed.

tempt *v.* 1 *That candy tempts me:* seduce, entice, lure, allure; appeal to, attract, invite, take one's fancy; captivate, bewitch, charm. 2 *Don't tempt fate by driving recklessly:* put to the test, try, risk, provoke.

Ant. 1 repel, repulse, disgust.

temptation *n. Try to resist temptation:* allurement, lure, enticement, attraction, seduction, urge, inducement.

tenacious *adj. He held my hand in a tenacious grip. She was tenacious in her belief:* fast, firm, clinging, set; persevering, persistent, determined, resolute, obstinate, stubborn, inflexible, uncompromising, immovable, unchangeable, unbending, unyielding, adamant, steadfast, staunch, constant.

Ant. loose, lax, slack; irresolute, flexible.

tend¹ *v. Children tend to like cozy corners:* be inclined, be disposed, have a tendency, be apt, be likely, be liable, have an inclination, lean.

tend² *v. Who will tend the garden? A nurse should have experience tending sick people:* attend to, care for, take care of, look after; nurse, nurture, foster, wait on, minister to; supervise, manage, guide.

Ant. neglect, ignore.

tendency *n. He has a tendency to talk too much. Prices are showing an upward tendency:* inclination, disposition, proclivity, proneness, propensity, predisposition, penchant, bent, leaning, impulse; trend, drift, direction, course.

Ant. disinclination, aversion, reluctance, hesitancy.

tender¹ *adj.* 1 *You have a tender heart:* soft, gentle, kind, compassionate, sympathetic, considerate, understanding, thoughtful, caring, softhearted, warmhearted, loving, affectionate, fond. 2 *in tender health:* weak, fragile, frail, feeble, delicate; vulnerable. 3 *She left home at tender age:* young, youthful, underage, immature, inexperienced, callow, green. 4 *The area around the wound is very tender:* sensitive, painful, sore, inflamed.

Ant. 1 hard; mean, cruel, unsympathetic, unkind, uncaring, hardhearted. 2 strong, robust, hale; flourishing, thriving. 3 advanced; full-grown, mature.

tender² *v. May I tender a suggestion?:* pre-

sent, offer, proffer, submit, put forward, volunteer, give, advance, propose, extend.

Ant. withhold; withdraw, retract.

tenderhearted *adj. a tenderhearted man:* sympathetic, compassionate; softhearted, kindhearted, warmhearted, considerate, understanding, responsive, gentle, mild, humane, benign.

Ant. hardhearted, coldhearted, mean, cruel, unsympathetic, inconsiderate.

tenderness *n.* 1 *The tenderness of her touch soothed the child:* softness, gentleness, mildness; kindness, kindliness, loving-kindness, compassion, sympathy; fondness, warmth, affection, love. 2 *The wound's tenderness made walking painful:* sensitivity, soreness, painfulness, smarting.

Ant. 1 hardness, toughness; cruelty, meanness, unkindness, hardheartedness, coldness, harshness.

tenet *n. The tenets of our religion forbid divorce:* belief, doctrine, dogma, creed, credo, canon, teaching; conviction, position, principle, maxim, rule, opinion, ideology.

tense *adj.* 1 *Keep the rope tense:* stretched tight, tight, taut, drawn, rigid, stiff; inflexible, unyielding. 2 *The witness was extremely tense:* nervous, strained, wrought-up, high-strung, uneasy, restless, restive, fidgety, jittery, on edge, excited, agitated; fearful, apprehensive, anxious.

Ant. 1 relaxed, slack, loose, limp. 2 relaxed, calm, cool, collected.

tension *n.* 1 *Too much tension will break the string:* stretching, straining, stress, traction, pressure, exertion; spring, elastic force; tightness, tautness. 2 *We collapsed under the tension of waiting for the news:* strain, stress, anxiety, nervousness, restiveness.

Ant. 1 slack, looseness, laxness. 2 relief, relaxation, calmness, serenity, tranquillity.

tentative *adj. Our plans are still tentative:* not settled, not final, subject to change, provisional, conditional, indefinite, undecided, experimental, trial, temporary, ad interim, proposed.

Ant. final, set, firm, definite, decided.

tenuous *adj. That's a tenuous argument:* weak, flimsy, slight, thin, frail, paltry, unconvincing; halfhearted, uncertain, indefinite.

Ant. strong, solid, valid, substantial.

tenure *n.* 1 *Her tenure of 16 years in office was a record:* term, incumbency, tenancy, occupancy, time, reign, occupation. 2 *After three years the teacher was offered tenure:* permanent status, job security, employment guarantee, permanency.

tepid *adj. This coffee is tepid! Such an accusation demands more than a tepid response:*

lukewarm, warmish; moderate, mild, half-hearted, indifferent, impassive, apathetic, nonchalant, lackadaisical, unenthusiastic.

term n. 1 *A nurse must be familiar with medical terms:* word, phrase, expression, idiom; name, designation, appellation. 2 *The lease is for a term of three years:* span, period, time, duration, course; reign, administration. 3 *What are the terms of the contract?:* stipulation, condition, provision, proviso, clause, item, detail; requirement, requisite. 4 **terms** *I'm on good terms with my employer:* relations, standing, footing, position, circumstance. —v. 5 *The critic termed the picture the worst of the year:* call, name, designate, dub, characterize.

terminal adj. 1 *Main Street is the terminal stop for this bus:* last, final, concluding, end. 2 *a terminal disease:* mortal, fatal, deadly. —n. 3 *a railroad terminal:* station, depot, terminus.
Ant. 1 first, initial.

terminate v. *Let's terminate this meeting. The lease terminates in May:* bring to an end, come to an end, end, conclude, finish, stop, close, discontinue, expire, lapse, run out.
Ant. begin, start, commence; continue, extend.

termination n. *the termination of the meeting:* end, ending, close, closing, conclusion, concluding, finish, windup, cessation, discontinuation, halt.
Ant. beginning, start, commencement, opening, inception.

terrain n. *mountainous terrain:* topography, ground, area, region, territory, countryside; zone, district.

terrible adj. 1 *a terrible storm:* severe, fierce, intense, strong; great, huge, tremendous, inordinate, monstrous, enormous. 2 *a terrible odor:* extremely bad, horrible, horrid, awful, hideous, repulsive, revolting, odious, distasteful, unpleasant, objectionable, intolerable, appalling. 3 *The roar of a lion can be a terrible sound:* alarming, frightening, terrifying, harrowing, horrifying; distressing, upsetting, disturbing.
Ant. 1 mild, moderate, gentle; small, insignificant. 2 wonderful, pleasing, pleasant, delightful; praiseworthy, laudable, commendable. 3 comforting, reassuring, soothing, calming.

terrific adj. 1 *A terrific explosion woke the town:* severe, intense, fierce, extreme, excessive, monstrous, great, enormous, huge, tremendous; frightening, terrifying, fearful, alarming, scary, harrowing, distressing, awful, dreadful, horrifying. 2 *This book is terrific:* great, fine, good, wonderful, superb,

excellent, splendid, marvelous, sensational, fabulous, fantastic, stupendous, smashing, super, extraordinary, remarkable, exceptional.
Ant. 1 mild, moderate, slight, insignificant; comforting, reassuring, calming. 2 bad, terrible, awful, lousy, horrible, dreadful, appalling.

terrify v. *The thunder terrified the child:* fill with terror, frighten, scare, alarm, panic, petrify, daunt, cow, overawe.
Ant. comfort, reassure, hearten, soothe, calm.

territory n. 1 *mountainous territory:* terrain, region, land, area, zone, district, tract, countryside, locale. 2 *The island is a British territory:* domain, realm, province, dominion; state, nation, principality, kingdom, empire; protectorate, dependency, mandate, colony; bailiwick.

terror n. *The idea of a tidal wave caused terror among us:* fear, fright, panic; dread; dismay, trepidation, perturbation, consternation, apprehension, awe.
Ant. security, reassurance, comfort, calm, tranquillity.

terse adj. *a terse statement:* brief and to the point, concise, pithy, succinct, crisp, incisive, pointed, compact; clear, clearcut, unambiguous, trenchant; brief, short, abrupt, curt.
Ant. rambling, verbose, wordy, lengthy, longwinded; vague, ambiguous.

test n. 1 *Chemical tests showed the presence of potassium. a test of the army's offective ness:* analysis, investigation; trial, tryout, probe, check; proof, verification, confirmation, corroboration. 2 *The teacher gives a test every Friday:* examination, exam, quiz. —v. 3 *The teacher will test the class. The company tested the new product before putting it on the market:* quiz, examine; analyze, investigate, try out; verify, confirm, validate.

testament n. 1 *my last will and testament:* final written will; bequest, legacy, settlement. 2 **Testament** *The Apocrypha are Biblical writings belonging to neither Testament:* Old Testament, New Testament; Bible, Scriptures, the Book.

testify v. *She was asked to testify at the trial. His hard work testified to his determination:* bear witness, give evidence, state as fact, declare, affirm; attest, show, indicate, demonstrate, evidence, evince, prove.

testimonial n. 1 *My former employer wrote a glowing testimonial:* recommendation, reference, commendation, endorsement, deposition. 2 *The faculty attended the testimonial for the retiring dean. The statue is a* *testimonial to Daniel Boone:* testimonial dinner; memorial, monument, tribute.

testimony *n.* 1 *The witness's testimony cleared the suspect:* declaration under oath, statement, attestation, avowal, averment; deposition, affidavit. 2 *Winning the scholarship is testimony of her intelligence:* evidence, indication, demonstration, proof, verification, corroboration, confirmation, affirmation.

Ant. 2 denial, disavowal, refutation.

testy *adj. He's in a testy mood:* irritable, ill-humored, quick-tempered, irascible, cross, cranky, grumpy, crabby, snappish, fretful, peevish, petulant, sullen, waspish, cantankerous, contentious, impatient, crusty, faultfinding, sharp-tongued.

Ant. good-natured, good-humored, pleasant, amiable, genial, agreeable, kind, patient.

tether *n.* 1 *The boy kept his pet goat on a tether:* leash, halter; rope, chain. —*v.* 2 *The zoo keeper tethered the monkey:* put on a leash; tie, secure; hobble.

Ant. 2 untether, unleash, untie.

text *n.* 1 *Did you just look at the pictures in the book or did you read the text?:* main body of writing, words, wording, content; textbook, schoolbook. 2 *The preacher took his text from Judges:* sermon, subject, subject matter, theme, topic, thesis, argument; passage, quotation, verse.

textile *n. The fabric will make beautiful clothing:* woven material, fabric, cloth; piece goods, yard goods.

texture *n. Satin has a smooth texture:* weave, composition, structure, grain; feel, touch; fineness, coarseness.

thank *v.* 1 *Don't forget to thank the hostess:* express gratitude to, express appreciation to; be grateful to, bless. —*n.* 2 **thanks** *Let's express our thanks to God:* gratitude, gratefulness, appreciation, thankfulness; grace.

Ant. 2 ingratitude, ungratefulness.

thankful *adj. We were thankful for your help:* full of thanks, grateful, appreciative; obliged, beholden, indebted to.

thankless *adj.* 1 *a thankless task:* unappreciated, unrewarded; unrewarding; useless, profitless, vain, bootless; undesirable, unwelcome, unpleasant, distasteful. 2 *a thankless employer:* ungrateful, ingrate, unappreciative; ungracious, inconsiderate, heedless; critical, faultfinding.

Ant. 1 appreciated, acknowledged, rewarded; rewarding, fruitful, useful; pleasant, agreeable. 2 appreciative, grateful.

thaw *v.* 1 *The ice thawed in the sun:* melt, dissolve, liquefy, soften. 2 *The little girl's*

smile thawed him: make friendly, make sympathetic, make affectionate, make forgiving. —*n.* 3 *a spring thaw:* thawing, melting; first warm weather of spring.

Ant. 1 freeze, solidify, congeal, harden. 3 freeze, frost.

theater *n.* 1 *a small theater off Broadway. Medical students watched the operation from a glass-enclosed theater: (variously)* playhouse; movie theater, movie, cinema, movie house, music hall; amphitheater, arena, lecture hall. 2 *A good production of Hamlet is real theater:* drama, stage entertainment, theatricals, show business; theatricality. 3 *The South Pacific was the theater for much of World War II:* field of operations; site, arena, setting, place.

theatrical *adj.* 1 *the theatrical world:* of the theater, stage, movie, film, entertainment, show-business, *Slang* show-biz; dramatic, thespian. 2 *Your manner is too theatrical:* exaggerated, affected, artificial, stagy, unnatural, mannered; extravagant, showy, grandiloquent, grandiose.

theft *n. He was arrested for theft:* stealing; robbery, burglary, thievery, larceny; filching, pilfering, purloining, shoplifting, hijacking; fraud, swindling, embezzlement.

theme *n.* 1 *Love is a major theme of poetry:* subject, topic, text, motif, thesis, idea, focus, point; argument, proposition, premise. 2 *Each student wrote a theme:* essay, composition, report, commentary, review; thesis, dissertation. 3 *Can you whistle the theme from the overture to* Don Giovanni?: melody, strain, tune, air, motif, leitmotif; theme song.

theology *n. After majoring in theology I taught a course in comparative religion:* divinity; *(variously)* religion; dogma, doctrine, system of belief.

theoretical *adj. That the universe is expanding has been proven and is no longer theoretical:* theoretic, conjectural, hypothetical, suppositional, postulatory; abstract, academic, nonpractical.

Ant. proven, known, verified, established; practical, applied.

theorize *v. Early astronomers theorized that the earth was flat:* hypothesize, conjecture, posit, propose, think, suppose, assume, infer, presume.

theory *n.* 1 *the theory of relativity:* principle, law; science, doctrine, philosophy, ideology. 2 *The scientist's theory is that if matter exists so must antimatter. It's my theory that the dog will find its way home in a day or two:* idea, notion, concept, hypothesis, postulate, conjecture, thesis, speculation, surmise, supposition, guess, thought, opinion, belief, judgment, conclusion, deduction, view.

Ant. 2 practice, application; verification, corroboration, substantiation.

therapy *n. Speech therapy corrected the child's lisp:* treatment, remedial procedure, healing, rehabilitation.

thereafter *adv. On opening day all tickets are 5 dollars, thereafter they'll be 10 dollars:* after that, afterward, afterwards, subsequently, later, from that time on, from then on, thenceforth.

Ant. before, previously.

therefore *adv. The apartment house was being torn down; therefore we had to move:* consequently, so, accordingly, hence, thus, ergo, for which reason.

thereupon *adv. The child murmured "goodnight" and thereupon fell asleep:* then, thereon, forthwith, straightaway, immediately, upon that, at once, without delay.

thesaurus *n. You should keep a thesaurus next to your dictionary:* synonym dictionary, synonymy, dictionary of synonyms and antonyms, synonym finder, word finder.

thesis *n.* 1 *The engineer's thesis was that the machine would double production:* proposition, argument; theory, hypothesis, postulate, notion, conjecture, speculation, surmise, supposition. 2 *Every senior must write a thesis:* dissertation, long essay, research paper, term paper, treatise, formal composition.

thick *adj.* 1 *a good thick sandwich:* fat, deep, wide, broad, bulky. 2 *Thick smoke impeded vision: This gravy is too thick:* dense, heavy, impenetrable; viscous, viscid, gelatinous, glutinous, concentrated, condensed. 3 *He spoke with a thick Scottish brogue:* strong, decided, pronounced, extreme, heavy, intense. 4 *The illness made her speech thick:* inarticulate, indistinct, muffled, fuzzy, blurred. 5 *You're too thick to understand it:* stupid, dumb, dense, obtuse, slow, slow-witted, dull, dull-witted. 6 *Informal The two are as thick as thieves:* close, intimate, chummy, friendly, inseparable, devoted. 7 *The marsh was thick with mosquitoes:* swarming, teeming, profuse, overflowing, crowded; abundant.

Ant. 1, 2 thin. 1 slim, narrow, shallow. 2 light, watery, diluted. 3 slight, faint. 4 distinct, clear. 5 smart, intelligent, sharp, quick-witted. 6 unfriendly, hostile. 7 bare, barren, bereft, empty.

thicken *v.* 1 *Thicken the sauce:* make thick, become thicker, make dense; set, clot, coagulate, condense, jell, jellify. 2 *The mystery*

thickened: become more complicated, intensify, deepen.

Ant. 1 thin, dilute.

thicket *n. The deer hid in the thicket:* thick bushes, bush, undergrowth, underbrush, brush, brake, bracken, copse.

thickheaded *adj. He's too thickheaded to run the business:* stupid, dumb, dim-witted, obtuse, thick, slow-witted.

Ant. bright, smart, intelligent.

thickset *adj.* 1 *The thickset trees hid the sun:* close-set, dense, packed, close. 2 *One child was thickset and the other thin:* stocky, husky, sturdy, chunky, heavyset, stout; squat, tubby, dumpy.

Ant. 1 scattered, sparse. 2 slim, slender; rangy, gangling, lanky.

thickskinned *adj. I'm too thickskinned to take offense at such an insult:* insensitive, insensible, unfeeling, imperturbable, unmovable, impervious, callous, hardened, inured.

Ant. thinskinned, sensitive, feeling, caring; vulnerable.

thief *n. The police arrested the thief:* robber, burglar, bandit, crook; *(variously)* holdup man, pilferer, pursesnatcher, mugger, shoplifter, pickpocket, sneak thief, hijacker; swindler, confidence man, racketeer, embezzler.

thievish *adj.* 1 *Thievish folks are bound to wind up in jail:* thieving, given to stealing, larcenous, light-fingered, sticky-fingered, dishonest. 2 *Their thievish manner aroused the shopkeeper's suspicions:* thieflike, stealthy, furtive, sneaky, sly.

Ant. honest.

thin *adj.* 1 *I was thin for my age. A lightbulb filament is very thin:* lean, slender, slim, skinny, scrawny, emaciated, gaunt, spindly; fine, narrow, threadlike; sheer, transparent. 2 *This gravy is too thin:* watery, runny, diluted. 3 *That's a pretty thin excuse. His hair is getting thin on top:* weak, unsubstantial, feeble, faint, inadequate, insufficient; scant, sparse, spare. —*v.* 4 *Thin the bushes. The traffic begins to thin:* make thin, thin out, prune, reduce, diminish, grow thin. 5 *Thin the paint:* dilute, water, water down.

Ant. 1–3 thick. 1 fat, obese, chubby, rotund, plump, overweight. 2 viscous, concentrated. 3 substantial, solid, forceful; full, dense, plentiful. 4, 5 thicken.

thing *n.* 1 *What's that thing for?:* object, article, gadget, thingamajig, thingamabob, gizmo, doohickey. 2 *The kitten was a cute thing:* creature, living being, person, entity. 3 *What a wonderful thing to do! How are things with you?:* deed, act, feat, action; event, occurrence, eventuality, happening;

matter, affair, transaction, concern, circumstance. **4** *There's just one thing missing to make this perfect:* detail, particular, item, feature, point, aspect. **5** Often **things** *Pack your things and go:* article of clothing, clothing, clothes, possessions, belongings, effects; equipment, gear, paraphernalia.

think *v.* **1** *Think before you act:* use one's mind, reason, reflect, cogitate, deliberate; ponder, contemplate, meditate, ruminate, dwell on. **2** *I think it's going to rain. Mother thinks she'll vacation in Canada:* believe, judge, surmise, presume, conclude, guess, suppose, reckon, expect, speculate; imagine, fancy; intend, propose, plan.

thinking *adj.* **1** *This essay is written for the thinking person:* rational, reasoning, reflective, thoughtful, contemplative, meditative, philosophical; intelligent, studious, educated. **2** *She averted an accident by quick thinking. What is your thinking on the matter?:* thought, brainwork, judgment, deduction; conclusion, belief, view, position, stand, impression; contemplation, meditation, reflection, consideration, study, deliberation, speculation; paying attention, being heedful.

thinskinned *adj.* *Don't be so thinskinned; learn to shake off criticism:* easily offended, sensitive, touchy, irritable, peevish, testy, huffy, sulky, quarrelsome.
Ant. thickskinned, insensitive, callous; sweet-tempered, good-natured.

thirst *n.* **1** *He worked up a tremendous thirst:* need of liquid, dryness in the mouth, thirstiness. **2** *a thirst for knowledge:* desire, craving, hankering, yearning, hunger, appetite, lust, relish. —*v.* **3** *We thirsted for wealth:* desire, covet, crave, yearn, yen, lust, hunger.
Ant. **2** disinterest, apathy; dislike, distaste, aversion. **3** scorn, disdain; dislike, hate, abhor.

thorn *n.* **1** *These bushes have thorns:* spike, barb, prickle. **2** *Ill health was the thorn of his existence:* bane, curse, torment, affliction, infliction, woe, plague, scourge, nuisance, annoyance, vexation; crown of thorns, cross.

thorny *adj.* **1** *This bush is thorny:* full of thorns, prickly, spiny, barbed, spiked. **2** *a thorny problem:* difficult, hard, tough, troublesome, sticky, ticklish, complex, perplexing, complicated, trying, vexatious.
Ant. **2** easy, simple, uncomplicated.

thorough *adj.* **1** *We gave the house a thorough cleaning. a thorough worker:* complete, thoroughgoing, careful, full, painstaking, meticulous, exhaustive, all-inclusive. **2** *The*

entire vacation was thorough pleasure: perfect, pure, utter, sheer, total, absolute, unmitigated, unqualified.
Ant. **1, 2** partial, incomplete. **1** careless, slipshod, lackadaisical. **2** mitigated, qualified, imperfect.

thoroughbred *adj.* **1** *a thoroughbred black Angus:* purebred, pure-blooded, full-blooded, unmixed, pedigreed. —*n.* **2** *Ten thoroughbreds are entered in the Derby:* racehorse; purebred animal.

thoroughfare *n.* *the major thoroughfare of the city:* through street, street, road; avenue, boulevard, parkway, highway, thruway, expressway, turnpike, freeway, interstate, superhighway.
Ant. dead-end street, cul-de-sac; alley, backstreet, sidestreet.

thoroughly *adv.* **1** *Search the house thoroughly:* completely, fully, exhaustively, inclusively, carefully, meticulously. **2** *We had a thoroughly good time:* perfectly, utterly, entirely, totally, completely, uniformly, consistently.
Ant. **1, 2** partially, incompletely. **1** carelessly, sloppily, lackadaisically. **2** imperfectly, somewhat, in part.

thought *n.* **1** *Give the matter careful thought. She was lost in thought:* thinking, mental activity, deliberation, cogitation, consideration, reflection; introspection, meditation, contemplation, rumination, musing, reverie. **2** *What are your thoughts on the matter? an important contribution to scientific thought:* idea, opinion, conclusion, judgment, belief, view, supposition, surmise, sentiment; concept, conception. **3** *It's not the gift, it's the thought that counts. It's our thought to open a branch office next year:* thoughtfulness, consideration, concern, caring, attention; intent, intention, purpose, plan, goal, object, expectation.

thoughtful *adj.* **1** *a thoughtful article on the international situation. Why are you so quiet and thoughtful today?:* serious, probing; contemplative, reflective, meditative, musing, introspective, pensive, wistful. **2** *What a thoughtful gift!:* considerate, kind, attentive, caring, loving.
Ant. **1, 2** thoughtless. **1** shallow, unthinking. **2** inconsiderate, insensitive; cruel, rude, impolite; neglectful.

thoughtfulness *n.* **1** *The problem calls for a lot of thoughtfulness:* thought, thinking, contemplation, reflection, consideration. **2** *We appreciate your thoughtfulness:* consideration, kindness, kindheartedness, solicitousness, attentiveness.

thoughtless *adj.* **1** *a thoughtless mistake:* unthinking, careless, heedless, inattentive,

thoughtlessness

improvident, neglectful; stupid, dumb, foolish, rattlebrained, absent-minded. **2** *Her thoughtless remark offended everyone:* inconsiderate, insensitive, rude, impolite, unkind, indiscreet.
Ant. **1, 2** thoughtful. **1** intelligent, prudent, provident; careful, alert. **2** considerate, sensitive, diplomatic, polite.

thoughtlessness *n.* **1** *The driver's thoughtlessness caused the accident:* carelessness, inattention, inattentiveness, heedlessness, neglect, oversight, recklessness, imprudence. **2** *The son's thoughtlessness hurt the mother's feelings:* lack of consideration, unconcern, insensitivity, unkindness, rudeness, impoliteness.

thrash *v.* **1** *Teachers used to thrash disobedient pupils:* whip, spank, cane, switch, birch, strap; lash, beat, flog, flail; pommel, lambaste. **2** *The child thrashed around so much he fell off the chair:* toss, plunge, wiggle, squirm, writhe, flounce, joggle, jiggle, jerk. **3** *Community leaders met to thrash out mutual problems:* resolve, argue, discuss, solve.

threadbare *adj.* **1** *an old and threadbare sweater:* worn, worn-out, frayed, raveled, shabby, ragged, napless. **2** *The play had a threadbare plot:* hackneyed, banal, clichéd, overfamiliar, stale, commonplace, routine.
Ant. **1** unworn, good as new. **2** novel, fresh, unique, unusual.

threat *n.* **1** *Threats don't scare me:* menacing statement, intimidation; omen, portent, warning sign, foreboding. **2** *The threat of an economic depression hangs over the world:* menace, danger, risk, hazard, peril.
Ant. **1, 2** promise. **1** enticement, reward.

threaten *v.* **1** *The gangster threatened to burn down the store. The foreman threatened the worker with dismissal:* promise harm; menace, intimidate, cow, terrorize; warn, forewarn. **2** *Floodwaters are threatening the town:* menace, endanger, imperil, jeopardize.
Ant. **2** protect, safeguard, guard.

threatening *adj.* **1** *The bully's threatening remarks frightened the child:* menacing, terrorizing, intimidating; warning, forewarning. **2** *Threatening clouds appeared on the horizon:* ominous, menacing, sinister, ill-omened, alarming, forbidding, inauspicious, unpropitious; impending, approaching.

threshold *n.* **1** *Don't just stand there in the threshold, come in!:* doorsill, sill; entranceway, entrance, doorway, door, portal. **2** *We're on the threshold of a great adventure:* brink, verge, edge; beginning, start, commencement, starting point.
Ant. **2** end, conclusion, finish.

throng

thrift *n.* *To save money you must practice thrift now:* economy, frugality, thriftiness, parsimony, parsimoniousness, sparingness.
Ant. extravagance, wastefulness; excess, immoderation.

thrifty *adj.* *He has very thrifty habits:* economical, frugal, parsimonious, economizing, sparing, saving, stingy.
Ant. extravagant, free-spending, prodigal, uneconomical, wasteful.

thrill *n.* **1** *A thrill ran down my spine:* rush of excitement, tingle, quiver, throb, tremble, tremor. **2** *Seeing the pyramids was a real thrill:* thrilling event, adventure, satisfaction, kick; exciting thing. —*v.* **3** *The game thrilled the crowd:* electrify, galvanize, stir, rouse, arouse, stimulate, excite, fire; delight, enrapture, transport.
Ant. **2, 3** bore.

thrilling *adj.* *The story was thrilling:* exciting, stirring, sensational, electrifying, fascinating, absorbing, titillating.
Ant. boring, dull, uninteresting, tedious.

thrive *v.* **1** *The garden seems to thrive on the new fertilizer:* grow vigorously, flourish, wax; bloom, burgeon, fatten. **2** *The new shopping center should thrive:* prosper, succeed, get ahead, grow rich; be fortunate, turn out well.
Ant. **1** languish, die, wither. **2** fail, go bankrupt; be unsuccessful.

thriving *adj.* **1** *We found a thriving stand of berries:* growing fast; blooming, blossoming, flowering; luxuriant, rank, lush. **2** *The store did a thriving business:* flourishing, prospering, successful, succeeding.
Ant. **1** languishing, dying, withering. **2** failing, unsuccessful.

throaty *adj. a throaty voice:* husky, deep, low, base; sonorous, resonant; guttural; thick, gruff, hoarse, rasping.
Ant. high, shrill, squeaky.

throb *v.* **1** *Her heart throbbed with the strain of walking up the hill:* beat, beat fast, pulsate, palpitate, vibrate, flutter, quiver, tremble, shake, twitch, heave. —*n.* **2** *the throb of drums. Her nervousness was shown by a slight throb in her hand:* throbbing, beat, pulsation, palpitation, vibration, reverberation; flutter, fluttering, quiver, quivering, shake, shaking, tremble, trembling, twitch, tremor.

throes *n. pl.* **1** *We're in the throes of moving:* upheaval, disorder, confusion, chaos, tumult, turmoil, disruption. **2** *The woman was in the throes of labor:* pangs, spasms, paroxysms; ordeal, anguish; agony.

throng *n.* **1** *a throng of shoppers:* great number, multitude, crowd, horde, host, army, swarm, flock, pack, crush, flood, deluge.

—*v.* 2 *Spectators thronged the parade route:* crowd, jam, pack; press, surge, stream, huddle, mill; gather, congregate, assemble, collect, cluster, converge.

Ant. 1 smattering, sprinkling, few. 2 disperse, scatter.

throttle *v. That villain ought to be throttled. The dictator throttled news of the atrocities:* choke, strangle, garrote; choke off, block, smother, stifle, silence, gag, stop.

through *Informal* **thru** *adj.* 1 *Dinner was through before 8:* finished, done, completed, concluded; ended, terminated, past. 2 *a through train:* direct, express. —*adv.* 3 *The tunnel is high enough to walk through. Did you read the book through?:* in one side and out the other, from one end to the other; from beginning to end, from first to last, all the way, to the end.

Ant. 1 begun, started. 2 local.

throughout *adv. The factory was painted green throughout. It rained throughout the week:* all over, in every part, everywhere; all the time, all the way through.

Ant. in some places; now and then, some of the time.

throw *v.* 1 *Throw the ball to first base! Throw a sweater over your shoulders:* fling, hurl, toss, cast, pitch, heave, sling, let fly, lob, chuck, shy; propel, impel, launch, project, hurtle; put, place. 2 *The horse threw its rider:* throw off, throw down, unseat; floor. —*n.* 3 *He pitched a ringer with his very first throw:* toss, hurl, fling, cast, pitch, heave, sling, lob, delivery.

Ant. 1, 3 catch.

thrust *v.* 1 *Thrust this under the door. We thrust our way through the crowd:* shove, push, poke, prod, drive, force, ram, jam. 2 *The duelers thrust and parried. She thrust the knife into the meat:* wield a sword, place a sword; stab, pierce, plunge, jab, lunge. —*n.* 3 *The parachute instructor gave the student a hard thrust out the plane's door. The rocket has a million pounds of thrust:* shove, push, poke, prod, boost, impulse; propelling force, impetus, momentum. 4 *With one thrust Saint George killed the dragon:* sword thrust, stab, stroke, lunge, plunge, riposte, swipe. 5 *Napoleon's armies made a thrust into Russia:* military advance, assault, attack, drive, raid, foray, sortie, incursion, strike.

Ant. 1, 3 pull, drag. 2, 4 parry. 5 retreat, withdrawal.

thud *n. The book fell with a thud:* thump, clunk, bang, smack.

thug *n. The two thugs robbed me:* ruffian, hoodlum, hood; (*variously*) gangster, mob-

ster, robber, bandit, killer, murderer, mugger.

thumb *v. He thumbed the address book looking for the number:* flip through, leaf through; handle, finger.

thump *v.* 1 *She thumped her fist on the desk for emphasis:* strike, beat, hit, pound, whack, thwack, bang, buffet, batter, pommel, lambaste, slap, cuff, jab, poke. —*n.* 2 *Did you hear a thump in the attic? A piece of plaster fell and gave me a thump on the head:* clunk, thud, bang; blow, knock, rap, slam, smack, clout, swat, whack, hit.

thunder *n.* 1 *lightning and thunder. the thunder of artillery:* loud rumbling; discharge, thunderbolt, thunderclap; rumbling, clap; explosion, discharge, roar, boom. —*v.* 2 *Applause thundered through the hall:* rumble, reverberate, echo, resound, roll, peal, boom.

thunderstruck *adj. The town was thunderstruck by the scandal:* astounded, astonished, dumbfounded, flabbergasted, agog, agape, awestruck, amazed, surprised.

Ant. unmoved, unexcited, calm.

thus *adv.* 1 *Hold the golf club thus:* in this way, in this manner, like this, like so, so; as follows. 2 *Costs are up, thus prices must rise:* therefore, hence, wherefore, consequently, accordingly, for this reason, ergo.

Ant. 2 but, however, nevertheless.

thwart *v. The barbed wire will thwart an infantry assault:* stop, frustrate, foil, check, hinder; baffle, inhibit, prevent, ward off; cross, oppose.

Ant. encourage, aid, support.

tick *v.* 1 *You can't even hear this clock tick:* click, clack, tap; ticktock; beat, vibrate. 2 *Tick off the items on this list:* check, mark; list, enter, register, chronicle. —*n.* 3 *Is there a tick in the motor?:* ticking noise; ticktock, click, clack, tap; vibration, oscillation. 4 *Put a tick by each item you want to order:* checkmark, check, mark, stroke; notch, nick.

ticket *n.* 1 *I have two tickets to the play. Please show your ticket to the stewardess when you board:* ticket of admission, trip ticket; voucher, coupon, stub. 2 *The driver got a ticket for speeding:* traffic ticket, summons; parking ticket. 3 *The sales ticket says the item is $50:* tag, label, slip, card, sticker. 4 *The governor ran on the Democratic ticket:* list of political candidates, list of nominees, slate, roster; ballot.

tickle *v.* 1 *She tickled the baby under the chin:* stroke lightly, rub lightly, stroke, titillate. 2 *My jaw still tickles from the dentist's injection:* tingle, twitch, itch, sting, throb. 3 *The puppy's antics tickled the children:* amuse, regale, divert, cheer, delight, please, captivate, enthrall, thrill. —*n.* **4** *The little girl laughed when I gave her a tickle:* teasing stroke, tingling rub. **5** *A cough drop can ease that tickle in your throat:* tickling sensation, tingle, twitching sensation, itch, scratchiness, prickle, sting.

ticklish *adj.* **1** *Are you ticklish?:* easily tickled, tickly; tingling, itchy, scratchy. **2** *a ticklish situation:* delicate, awkward, requiring tact, sensitive, uncertain, difficult, complicated, intricate, tricky, knotty, thorny.
Ant. **2** easy, simple.

tide *n.* **1** *The tide left driftwood on the beach:* (*variously*) high tide, ebb tide, neap tide, flood tide, low tide; riptide, undertow; wave, current, flow. **2** *the tide of public opinion:* rise and fall, ebb and flow, wax and wane; drift, current, tendency, movement, direction.

tidy *adj.* **1** *My desk was always tidy. a tidy worker:* neat, orderly, shipshape, in apple pie order; methodical, systematic, organized, careful, businesslike; clean, immaculate, spotless. **2** *a tidy sum of money:* considerable, fairly large, substantial, sizable, goodly, ample. —*v.* **3** *Tidy the living room:* neaten, put in order, straighten, clean up, arrange.
Ant. **1** messy, sloppy, untidy; slovenly, unkempt, unmethodical, unsystematic, careless, slipshod. **2** inconsiderable, unsubstantial, small. **3** mess up, disarrange, disorder.

tie *v.* **1** *Tie the boat to the dock:* bind, fasten, make fast, attach, secure, tether, lash, knot, make a bow. **2** *The United States and Canada are tied by mutual interests:* bind, attach, join, connect, link, ally. **3** *Two teams tied for first place:* draw, come out even; match, divide the honors. —*n.* **4** *Hold back the curtain with a tie:* cord, rope, string, line, cable, band, ribbon, cinch, sash. **5** *Should we wear coats and ties to the party?:* necktie, cravat; bow tie. **6** *The senator is said to have a strong tie with the oil industry:* bond, link, affinity, connection, relation, relationship; kinship, affiliation, shared interest. **7** *The game ended in a tie:* draw; dead heat. **8** *The builder added more ties to the structure:* brace, support, beam, rod, connecting rod; crossbeam.
Ant. **1** untie, unfasten, loose. **2** separate, disunite.

tier *n.* *The cake had three tiers:* row, line, file, level; layer, story, stratum.

tiff *n.* *The couple had a tiff:* petty quarrel, clash, run-in, spat, words, squabble, argument, dispute, disagreement, difference, misunderstanding.

tight *adv., adj.* Also *adv.,* **tightly 1** *This lid is screwed on tight. Make a good tight knot:* firmly, securely, solidly, closely; firm, secure, solid. **2** *Pull the rope tight:* taut, tense, stretched out, rigid, stiff, drawn tight. **3** *This dress fits tight. tight shoes:* too closely, fitting too closely, closefitting, snug, skintight, too small, uncomfortably small, constricted. **4** *The boss has a tight schedule today:* full, crammed, jammed, jampacked; crowded, busy. —*adj.* **5** *The material has a tight weave:* closely constructed, closely fitted, close, dense, compact. **6** *The sergeant maintained tight discipline:* strict, firm, stern, rigid, rigorous, exact, stringent, austere, inflexible, unyielding, uncompromising, harsh. **7** *He's in a tight spot:* difficult, worrisome, tough, onerous, burdensome, trying. **8** *Money is tight around here:* scarce, scant, sparing, skimpy; insufficient, inadequate, deficient. **9** *Informal The mayor won in a tight election:* close, well-matched. **10** *Don't be so tight with your money:* stingy, miserly, tightfisted, close, closefisted, parsimonious, frugal, niggardly, ungenerous, sparing, grudging. **11** *Informal Uncle Lou had too much eggnog and got tight:* drunk, drunken, intoxicated, inebriated, tipsy, plastered, blind, smashed, soused, loaded, pickled, stewed, pie-eyed, juiced, stiff, stoned, zonked.
Ant. **1–3, 5, 6** loose. **1–3** loosely. **2** slack, relaxed, limp. **3** big, too big, loose-fitting. **5** open, porous. **6, 7** easy. **6** lenient, relaxed, unexacting, slack, lax. **8** abundant, plentiful, ample, sufficient. **9** uneven, runaway, landslide. **10** extravagant, squandering, wasteful, lavish; generous, liberal. **11** sober.

tighten *v.* *Tighten the nut on this screw. Tighten the clothesline so it doesn't droop:* make tight, make tighter, fix firmly, fasten, secure; draw tight, make taut, make tense; narrow, squeeze, contract, constrict.
Ant. loosen, loose; slacken.

tightfisted *adj.* *He's too tightfisted to donate to charity:* stingy, parsimonious, niggardly, penny-pinching, tight, penurious, miserly, cheap, closefisted.
Ant. openhanded, generous, liberal, unstinting.

tight-lipped *adj.* *He's tight-lipped about his past:* closemouthed, reticent, discreet, reserved, taciturn, quiet, uncommunicative, untalkative.
Ant. talkative, unreserved, indiscreet.

tightwad *n.* *That tightwad wouldn't give a nickel to charity:* stingy person, skinflint, miser, pinchpenny, cheapskate, piker, Scrooge.

Ant. spendthrift, prodigal, squanderer, big spender.

tilt *v.* 1 *Is the table uneven or does the floor tilt?:* slant, incline, lean, slope; tip, list, cant. —*n.* 2 *The tilt of the roof prevents snow from accumulating:* slope, slant, incline, cant, rake, pitch, grade.

Ant. 1 be even, be plumb, be horizontal.

timber *n.* 1 *Stack the timber near the shed:* wood, lumber, boards, logs. 2 *A wolf howled back in the tall timber:* timberland, wooded land; forest, woods, trees, bush.

timbre *n.* *Her voice had a pleasant timbre:* tone, sound quality, pitch, resonance.

time *n.* 1 *Time and tide stop for no one. It's been a long time since we've seen each other:* the passage of time, duration; period, interval, span of time, elapsed time, spell, while, stretch. 2 Usually **times** *in ancient times:* epoch, era, period, age; season. 3 *The time is 2:30 P.M. It's time to go. At that time grandad was still alive:* particular point in time, appointed time, moment, period, *(variously)* instant, hour, day, week, month, year, season, decade, century, period. 4 *Our allotted time is three score years and ten:* lifetime, years, period, season, generation. 5 *I don't have the time to play golf:* leisure time, spare time, free time, liberty, freedom. 6 *A good time was had by all:* experience, occasion, period, event, episode, incident. 7 *The piece was written in waltz time:* tempo; rhythm, beat, measure. —*v.* 8 *The runner was timed in four minutes flat. The enemy timed their attack perfectly:* clock; choose the time of. 9 *The marchers timed their steps to the drumbeat:* synchronize; keep time.

timeless *adj.* *the timeless reaches of space. Good taste is timeless:* eternal, infinite, unending, endless, everlasting, interminable, perpetual, ceaseless, boundless, continuous; enduring; lasting, durable, permanent, abiding, unchangeable; undying, deathless.

Ant. brief, short, short-lived, passing, fleeting, ephemeral, transitory, impermanent, changing.

timely *adj.* *a timely loan. I'd like to give you some timely advice:* occurring at the right time, well-timed, opportune, convenient, seasonable, prompt, punctual, providential.

Ant. untimely, inopportune, inconvenient, ill-timed.

timid *adj.* *The boy is timid as a mouse:* fainthearted, fearful, afraid, timorous, apprehensive, cowardly, weak-kneed; shy, bashful, sheepish, shrinking, unassuming.

Ant. self-assured, daring, audacious, brave, bold, intrepid, adventuresome;

brash, impudent, insolent, fresh, immodest, shameless.

timidity *n.* *My timidity prevented me from asking her to the dance:* timidness, shyness, lack of self-assurance, faintheartedness, fearfulness, trepidation, cowardice; bashfulness, sheepishness.

Ant. self-assurance, self-confidence, daring, audacity, boldness, courage; brashness, brazenness, impudence, insolence.

tinge *v.* 1 *The ink tinged the water blue. His smile was tinged with cruelty:* color slightly, color, tint, dye, stain; touch, infuse, season, flavor. —*n.* 2 *The wallpaper has just a tinge of orange. The book has a tinge of unpleasantness:* tint, shade, cast, touch, trace, hint; vein, suspicion, flavor, taste.

tingle *v.* 1 *Do your hands tingle in the cold?:* sting, prickle, tickle. —*n.* 2 *A tingle of excitement ran down my back:* prickling, thrill, tremor, flutter, throb, pulsation.

tinkle *v.* 1 *Sleigh bells tinkled in the distance:* ring, jingle, clink, chink, chime, peal, ding. —*n.* 2 *the tinkle of a bell:* ring, jingle, clink, chink, chime, peal, ding, ting-a-ling.

Ant. 1, 2 boom, roar, thunder.

tint *n.* 1 *The blouse was striped in tints of blue:* shade, hue, tone. 2 *There is just a tint of green in the rug:* tinge, trace, hint, suggestion, touch. 3 *hair tint:* dye, coloring. —*v.* 4 *Why not tint your hair red?:* color, dye, tone, tinge.

tiny *n.* *tiny red berries:* small, little, minute, miniature, diminutive, minuscule, microscopic, wee, teeny, teeny-weeny, teensyweensy, itsy-bitsy; undersized, pint-sized, midget, pygmy, dwarfish, Lilliputian, bantam.

Ant. large, big, huge, enormous, immense; oversized, giant, gigantic, colossal.

tip[1] *v.* 1 *The rowboat tipped when I got in:* tilt, slant, incline, lean, list, slope, cant; overturn, upturn, capsize, upend. —*n.* 2 *The tip of the ship caused the dishes to slide across the table:* tipping, tilting, leaning, slanting; slant, incline, tilt, slope, list, pitch, rake, cant.

tip[2] *n.* *The tribe used flint tips on its arrows:* pointed end, tapering end, small end; point, head. 2 *the tip of an iceberg:* top, peak, apex, vertex, acme, zenith, summit, crown, crest, pinnacle, upper part. —*v.* 3 *The baton was tipped with gold:* top, cap, crown; barb, point.

tip[3] *n.* 1 *Many people give service people a tip at Christmas:* gratuity; small reward. 2 *Here's a tip on how to remove stains. The police got a tip that the bank would be robbed tonight:* hint, suggestion, pointer, advice, word to the wise; warning, forewarning, inside information, tip-off. **3** *The golfer gave the ball a tip with a putter:* tap, light blow, pat. —*v.* **4** *Let's tip the waiter generously:* give a gratuity; reward. **5** *The batter just tipped the ball:* tap, hit lightly, stroke, pat.

tippler *n.* *W. C. Fields was quite a tippler:* heavy drinker, habitual drinker, sot, boozer, booze hound, soak, tosspot.

Ant. teetotaler, abstainer, nondrinker.

tipsy *adj.* *Even a little wine can make some people tipsy:* mildly drunk; high, drunk, intoxicated, inebriate, inebriated, tight, plastered, blind, smashed, soused, loaded, pickled, stewed, juiced, stiff, stoned.

Ant. sober.

tirade *n.* *The political candidate let loose a tirade against her opponent:* angry speech, harangue, diatribe, jeremiad, reprimand, scolding, dressing-down; denunciation, condemnation, vilification, invective, vituperation.

Ant. good word, panegyric, laudation, commendation, paean.

tire *v.* **1** *Climbing the hill tired the tourists:* weary, wear out, fatigue, exhaust; make sleepy. **2** *I'm tiring of the same old breakfast every morning. Dealing with bureaucracy would tire anyone:* be bored with, be fed up with, be sick of, lose patience with, lose interest in; irk, annoy.

Ant. **1** refresh; wake up. **2** excite; please.

tired *adj.* *After a full day's work she was tired:* weary, wearied, fatigued, exhausted, worn out, all in; *Slang* beat, pooped, bushed; sleepy, drowsy.

Ant. energetic, peppy, fresh; wide-awake.

tireless *adj.* *The director thanked the committee for its tireless efforts:* untiring, never-tiring; industrious, hard-working, unflagging, unremitting, indefatigable, devoted, unceasing, steadfast, determined, persevering, faithful.

Ant. halfhearted, lackadaisical, sporadic; flagging, faltering.

tiresome *adj.* **1** *Working in the garden all day is very tiresome:* fatiguing, wearying, wearing, tiring, exhausting, tedious. **2** *His constant puns are getting tiresome:* boring, uninteresting, dull, wearisome, tedious; annoying, bothersome, irksome, vexing, trying.

Ant. **1** refreshing; easy. **2** delightful, interesting, stimulating, pleasing.

titillate *v.* *The hint of scandal titillated everyone's curiosity:* excite, tickle, tease, provoke, stimulate, rouse, arouse, attract, whet the appetite.

Ant. allay, quench, quell, still, satisfy, sate.

titillating *adj.* *Boccaccio's* Decameron *is titil-lating and bawdy:* provocative, exciting, alluring; suggestive.

title *n.* **1** *What's the title of the book?:* name; designation, appellation, epithet. **2** *Her title is "Vice President of Marketing Research." She fell in love with the Count because of his title:* rank, occupational rank, position, grade, place; title of nobility, lordly rank, noble birth. **3** *Who owns title to the property?:* legal right, legal possession, ownership; deed, claim. **4** *the heavyweight title:* championship, crown. —*v.* **5** *The youth titled the poem "My Lost Love":* entitle, name, designate, term, dub.

titter *v.* **1** *The audience tittered at the joke:* laugh self-consciously, laugh nervously, giggle, chuckle, snigger, snicker. —*n.* **2** *That little titter of his is annoying:* self-conscious laugh, nervous laugh, giggle, snigger, snicker, simper.

Ant. **1, 2** roar, guffaw.

titular *adj.* *The king was the titular head of state, but the prime minister had the power:* in name only, in title only, so-called, ostensible, nominal.

Ant. actually, in fact.

toady *v.* **1** *He toadies to the teacher:* curry favor, fawn, grovel before, kowtow to. —*n.* **2** *That bunch of toadies won't tell the boss when he's making a mistake:* sycophant, flatterer, fawner, yes-man, bootlicker; servile follower, flunky, stooge.

Ant. **1** defy, stand up to; scorn, disdain. **2** opponent, foe, antagonist.

toast *v.* **1** *Come toast your feet by the fire:* warm, heat, dry. **2** *Toast the bread:* heat until crisp, brown; grill. **3** *Let's toast the bride and groom:* drink in honor of, drink to the health of; honor, celebrate, commemorate.

Ant. **1** cool, chill.

today *n.* **1** *Today is March 22nd. The songs of today aren't as tuneful as when I was young:* the present day, this day; the present age, the present, this epoch, this era, this time, modern times. —*adv.* **2** *Let's go to the beach today. Children get a better education today than in the past:* on this day; nowadays, now, in this day and age, in modern times, during the present age, in this era.

Ant. **1, 2** yesterday; tomorrow.

toddle *v.* *The child is just beginning to toddle:* take short, unsteady steps; walk unsteadily, wobble, waddle.

Ant. stride; run, skip, prance.

togs *n. pl.* *Put on your beach togs:* clothes, clothing, outfit, apparel, attire, duds.

toil *n.* **1** *After much toil the furniture was in the moving van:* hard work, work, labor, effort, exertion, industry, drudgery; hardship, travail. —*v.* 2 *The farmer toiled in the field:* work, labor, drudge, exert oneself.

Ant. 1, 2 play. 1 indolence, idleness, ease. 2 take one's ease, relax.

toilet *n.* *"Half bath" means a room with toilet and sink:* water closet, flush toilet; latrine, lavatory, washroom, rest room; privy, outhouse; facility, commode; *Slang* john, can; men's room, ladies' room.

token *n.* 1 *They gave me a watch as a token of their esteem:* symbol, sign, expression, indication, mark, evidence, manifestation; memento, keepsake, souvenir, remembrance, testimonial. —*adj.* 2 *Employing one woman among fifty men is token recognition of equal rights:* superficial, perfunctory, symbolic, nominal, for show; minimal, sample, vestigial.

tolerable *adj.* 1 *Such behavior is not tolerable:* bearable, endurable, sufferable, acceptable, allowable, permissible. 2 *That restaurant has tolerable food:* fairly good, fair, passable, acceptable, adequate, innocuous, mediocre, average, ordinary, indifferent, so-so.

Ant. 1 intolerable, unbearable, unendurable, unacceptable. 2 excellent, outstanding, superior, noteworthy; awful, terrible, lousy, bad.

tolerance *n.* 1 *Some people have greater tolerance to pain than others:* ability to tolerate, endurance. 2 *Tolerance between the races is a must:* fair treatment, fairness, lack of prejudice, freedom from bigotry; goodwill, brotherly love, fellow feeling; forbearance, patience, compassion, sympathy.

Ant. 1 sensitivity. 2 prejudice, bigotry, bias; ill will, discrimination.

tolerant *adj.* 1 *Can't you be tolerant of other religions?:* understanding, unprejudiced, unbigoted, fair, having goodwill, broadminded; forbearing, patient, compassionate, sympathetic. 2 *The teacher was too tolerant of disobedient behavior:* lenient, permissive, indulgent, forbearing, forgiving, kindhearted, softhearted, sparing.

Ant. 1 intolerant, prejudiced, bigoted, biased, unfair. 2 strict, rigid, harsh, severe, stern, exacting.

tolerate *v.* 1 *I can't tolerate that loud music:* bear, endure, put up with, stand, take, abide, brook, stomach; submit to, undergo. 2 *The school cannot tolerate cheating on exams:* allow, permit, sanction, admit, show mercy toward.

Ant. 2 forbid, prohibit, disallow, proscribe, ban, prevent.

toll *n.* 1 *Each car must pay a toll to cross the bridge:* fee, charge, payment, levy, duty, impost, assessment, tariff, tribute. 2 *The flood took a toll of a hundred lives:* loss, amount of loss, extent of damage, destruction, extinction, sacrifice, penalty; disruption, depletion.

tomb *n.* *Grant's Tomb:* burial chamber, mausoleum, vault, sepulcher, crypt, monument to the dead; resting place, burial place, grave.

tomfoolery *n.* *Stop the tomfoolery!:* foolishness, prankishness, horseplay, high jinks, antics, monkeyshines, nonsense, fooling around.

tomorrow *n.* 1 *Tomorrow is Sunday. Today's youth will be the leaders of tomorrow:* the day after today, the morrow; the future, the next generation. —*adv.* 2 *The county fair starts tomorrow. Tomorrow everyone will be vacationing on the moon:* on the day after today; in the future, in days to come.

Ant. 1, 2 yesterday; today.

tone *n.* 1 *the shrill tone of a factory whistle:* pitch, sound, note; intonation, modulation, inflection, lilt. 2 *The tone of this letter is rather unfriendly:* attitude, mood, spirit, manner, tenor, quality. 3 *a light tone of green:* shade, tint, hue; tinge, cast. —*v.* 4 *Exercise will tone your muscles:* make firm, make supple.

tongue *n.* 1 *Stick out your tongue:* organ of speech, lingua, lingula. 2 *He spoke in a foreign tongue:* language, speech, vocabulary. 3 *the tongue of a shoe:* flap; overhanging strip; shaft.

tonic *n.* *a spring tonic:* restorative, stimulant, invigorant, bracer, refresher, pick-me-up.

tool *n.* 1 *a carpenter's tools:* implement, instrument, device, utensil, contrivance, apparatus, appliance, machine, mechanism. 2 *A good education is a necessary tool for succeeding:* agent, means, instrumentality, medium, vehicle, wherewithal. 3 *The mayor is just a tool of the governor:* instrument, pawn, puppet, dupe, hireling, stooge.

tooth *n.* 1 *The dentist filled the tooth: (variously)* incisor, molar, grinder, cuspid, canine, bicuspid, wisdom tooth; fang, tusk. 2 *Who broke a tooth off this saw?:* serration; *(variously)* point, spoke, tine, spur, barb, cusp, cog.

top *n.* 1 *the top of a hill. the top of the table:* highest point, summit, peak, apex, vertex, pinnacle, acme, zenith; crest, crown, brow; upper surface, upper part. 2 *a bottle top. a box top:* lid, cap, cover, cork, stopper. 3 *She graduated at the top of her class:* highest rank, highest position, head, first place, fore, van, front, place of honor. —*adj.* 4 *the top shelf. The car's top speed is*

120 miles per hour: topmost, highest, uppermost, upper; greatest, best. **5** *the top doctor in the country:* highest-ranking, foremost, best, chief, principal, paramount, preeminent, renowned, noted, notable, celebrated, famous, greatest. —*v.* **6** *Top the strawberries with whipped cream:* put a topping on, put over; crown, cap, cover; complete. **7** *This state tops the nation in per capita income. The swimmer topped the world's record:* be greater than, surpass, exceed, better, best, excel, outdo, outshine, outstrip.

Ant. **1–4** bottom. **1** base, foot, lowest point; underside. **3** foot, end, rear. **4** lowest, lower. **5** inferior, second-rate; unknown. **7** trail, be less than.

topic *n. What will the speaker's topic be?:* subject, subject matter, theme; text, thesis.

topmost *adj. the topmost branch. He reached the topmost echelon of his profession:* top, highest, uppermost; supreme, chief, head, preeminent, leading, foremost, principal, paramount.

topnotch *adj. This book has some topnotch writing in it:* first-rate, outstanding, finest, prime, choice, superior, unparalleled.

Ant. so-so, ordinary, run-of-the-mill, commonplace.

topple *v.* **1** *The vase toppled and broke into smithereens:* tip over, overturn, turn over, upset, fall over; fall, tumble, sprawl. **2** *The rebels toppled the regime:* overthrow, bring down, abolish; defeat, vanquish, overcome.

topsy-turvy *adv.* **1** *We turned the room topsy-turvy looking for the ring:* upside down, inside out, into a confused state. —*adj.* **2** *I've never seen such a topsy-turvy office:* disorderly, disarranged, disorganized, untidy, messy, chaotic; upside-down, reversed.

Ant. **1, 2** right side up. **2** orderly, organized, tidy, neat.

torch *n. The campers lit torches from the campfire:* burning brand, brand, firebrand, flambeau.

torment *v.* **1** *A toothache tormented me all day long. The bully tormented the smaller boys:* cause to suffer, afflict, torture, rack, distress, pain; plague, worry, trouble; annoy, persecute, harass, harrow, vex, nag, pester. —*n.* **2** *Mosquitoes caused the hikers much torment:* suffering, agony, torture, anguish, pain, distress, misery; worry, annoyance, irritation, despair.

Ant. **1, 2** delight, comfort. **1** please, soothe. **2** pleasure, happiness, joy.

torn *adj. a torn shirt:* ripped, rent, split, slit, ruptured; ragged, shredded, unraveled.

torpid *adj. The heat made everyone torpid:* slow-moving, sluggish, inactive, lethargic, lazy, listless, spiritless, languid, languorous, apathetic; sleepy, drowsy.

Ant. active, energetic, vigorous, peppy, lively; wide-awake.

torpor Also **torpidity** *Her torpor may be due to illness:* sluggishness, slow movement, inertia, lethargy, languidness, listlessness, lassitude, languor, apathy; sleepiness, drowsiness.

Ant. energy, vigor, pep, animation, liveliness.

torrent *n.* **1** *The drought was broken by a torrent. The torrent carried the raft far downstream:* heavy rain, downpour, deluge, cloudburst, torrential rain; cascade, waterfall, cataract; current. **2** *He let loose a torrent of curses:* stream, rapid flow, outburst, outpouring, discharge, rain, deluge, flood, volley, barrage, burst, rush.

Ant. **1** shower, sprinkle, drizzle.

torrid *adj.* **1** *a torrid climate:* hot and dry, scorching, parching, sweltering, boiling, burning, broiling, sizzling. **2** *The movie has a torrid love scene:* passionate, impassioned, ardent, fervent, fervid, excited, hot, heated, intense; amorous, erotic, sexy, sexual, lustful.

Ant. **1** cold, cool, chilly. **2** dispassionate, spiritless; mild, apathetic.

tortuous *adj. a tortuous trail. The essay was so long and tortuous I couldn't make sense of it:* winding, twisting, full of curves, circuitous, sinuous, serpentine, meandering, crooked; labyrinthine, convoluted, complicated, involved; roundabout, ambiguous, hard to follow.

Ant. straight, straight as an arrow, beeline, direct; straightforward, simple.

torture *v.* **1** *The secret police tortured the captive:* subject to severe pain; maltreat, abuse. **2** *He was tortured by doubts:* have anxiety, torment, distress, rack, harrow. —*n.* **3** *Waiting for news of the lost girl was sheer torture:* torment, agony, anguish, suffering, distress, pain, ordeal, infliction, cruelty.

Ant. **2** calm, relax; cheer, comfort, solace. **3** pleasure, enjoyment, happiness, joy, delight.

toss *v.* **1** *Children tossed a ball back and forth:* throw, pitch, flip, fling, sling, heave, hurl, cast, lob, propel. **2** *The storm tossed the small boat at its anchor:* pitch, jerk, sway, rock, shake, agitate, roll, joggle. —*n.* **3** *Give the ball a toss:* pitch, throw, heave, fling, sling, hurl, lob. **4** *She gave her head a toss and walked away:* flounce, jerk, shake, flourish.

Ant. **1** catch.

total *n.* **1** *Add up the bill and tell me the total:* sum, sum total, amount, whole, aggregate, totality, entirety. —*adj.* **2** *The total population of the town was only two thousand:* entire, whole, complete, combined, full. **3** *The party was a total success:* complete, utter, perfect, thorough, unconditional, unqualified, unmodified, sheer, out-and-out, *Slang* solid, wholesale. —*v.* **4** *Total the bill:* tote up, add up, add, sum up, reckon; compute, calculate, figure up.
Ant. **2, 3** partial, limited, incomplete. **3** slight, conditional, qualified. **4** subtract, deduct.

totalitarian *adj. a totalitarian country:* fascistic, fascist, autocratic, dictatorial, despotic; tyrannous, tyrannical.
Ant. democratic, republican.

totally *adv. The story is totally false:* completely, utterly, entirely, thoroughly, absolutely, unconditionally, downright, out-and-out.
Ant. partially, in part, slightly, somewhat.

tote *v. Are you going to tote that suitcase all over Europe? The sheriff always toted a gun:* carry, lug; drag, pull, haul; convey, transport.

totter *v. The young child tottered down the street. The vase tottered and fell:* walk unsteadily, stagger, stumble, reel, lurch, falter; wobble, sway, waver, teeter, shake.

touch *v.* **1** *Don't touch the statue:* put a hand against, put a finger against, handle, finger, paw; feel, manipulate, caress, fondle, pet, stroke. **2** *The two buildings touch:* be in contact, meet, be contiguous, abut, converge. **3** *The vegetarian won't touch meat:* use, consume; avail oneself of, resort to, have to do with, be associated with. **4** *The plea touched us deeply:* affect, move, impress; sadden; influence, sway, inspire; thrill, arouse, stir, inflame. **5** *The meeting touched on the problem of costs:* mention, discuss briefly, allude to, refer to, broach, bear upon, concern, pertain to; note, cite. **6** *No one can touch Jeanette as a cook:* compare with, equal, match, rival, come up to, come near. —*n.* **7** *He located the light switch by touch. The slightest touch will bruise the flower:* the sense of touch; feel, feeling; touching, stroke, handling, fingering, pawing, manipulation, caress, fondling. **8** *The baby's skin has such a soft touch:* feel, texture, fineness, surface, quality. **9** *She kept in touch by phone. Dad's out of touch with today's attitudes:* communication, contact; awareness, familiarity, acquaintance, understanding, comprehension, perception. **10** *The salad had a touch of garlic:* trace, tinge, bit, pinch, dash, sprinkling, soupçon,

taste, speck, hint, suggestion, suspicion. **11** *This symphony shows the touch of a master:* technique, deftness, adroitness, hand, manner, method, skill, art, artistry, mastery, finesse, flair, gift, polish, virtuosity; guiding hand, influence.
Ant. **2** separate, diverge. **4** leave unmoved; bore. **5** ignore, disregard, overlook, omit.

touching *adj. The most touching scene in the play:* moving, affecting, stirring; emotional, dramatic; saddening, sad, heartbreaking, heartrending, pitiful, poignant; tender.
Ant. unaffecting, unemotional.

touchstone *n. Her singing remains the touchstone for all later sopranos:* standard, yardstick, measure, criterion, gauge; model, example, guide; benchmark.

touchy *adj.* **1** *Why are you so touchy today?:* sensitive, easily offended, easily hurt, thinskinned; resentful, bitter; irritable, huffy, grumpy, grouchy, cross, testy, crabby, peevish, snappish, petulant, surly. **2** *Negotiations are at a touchy stage:* delicate, requiring diplomacy, sensitive; ticklish, awkward, precarious, difficult.
Ant. **1** insensitive, thickskinned, callous, impervious; good-humored, pleasant, eventempered, in good spirits. **2** noncritical, easy.

tough *adj.* **1** *a tough plastic:* durable, strong, lasting, enduring; firm, resistant, solid, impenetrable, infrangible, leathery. **2** *a tough job. a tough problem:* difficult, hard, laborious, arduous, strenuous, exhausting, onerous, formidable, exacting, troublesome, trying; hard-to-solve, baffling, bewildering, puzzling, perplexing, confusing, complicated, intricate, complex, involved, thorny, knotty, ticklish. **3** *She's a tough teacher. The boss is a tough man to convince:* hard, stern, strict, rigid, exacting, uncompromising; stubborn, obstinate, obdurate, adamant, hardheaded, bullheaded, pigheaded; wily, crafty, canny, cagey. **4** *Tough talk frightens us:* rough, vicious, bloodthirsty, ruthless, mean, cruel, brutal, cold-blooded, heartless, hardhearted, unfeeling, insensitive, pitiless, callous.
Ant. **1, 2** soft. **1** weak, fragile, flimsy. **2, 3** easy. **2** simple. **3** lenient, indulgent, permissive, unexacting; accommodating, acquiescent, complaisant, compliant, flexible. **4** sweet, kind, humane, gentle, softhearted, compassionate, merciful.

toughen *v. Part of athletic training is toughening the body:* strengthen, harden, firm, fortify, inure; stiffen, temper, steel, discipline; accustom, acclimate.
Ant. weaken, enfeeble, enervate.

toupee *n. Toupees cover bald spots:* hairpiece, wig, periwig, peruke; *Slang* carpet, rug.

tour *n.* **1** *a three-week tour of France and Italy:* sightseeing trip, jaunt, excursion, junket. *—v.* **2** *The group is touring Mexico this summer:* visit, travel around, travel through, sightsee in, vacation through.

tousled *adj. tousled hair:* uncombed, mussed, mussed-up, disheveled, unkempt, disordered, rumpled, tangled.
Ant. combed, unmussed, well-kempt, neat, tidy.

tow *v. The car had to be towed to the garage:* haul, drag, draw, pull; hoist, lift.
Ant. push, shove.

tower *n.* **1** *The city hall had a picturesque tower:* tall structure; *(variously)* water tower, clock tower, bell tower, belfry, prison tower, lookout tower; steeple, spire, turret, minaret, skyscraper, column, obelisk; castle, keep. **2** *Throughout the trouble, Joe has been a tower of strength:* pillar, mainstay, bulwark, wellspring, fountainhead. *—v.* **3** *The building towers into the sky. Charlemagne towered above other rulers of his day:* rise high, rise above, ascend, soar, loom; overhang, overshadow, eclipse; surpass, outshine, outdo.

towering *adj.* **1** *the towering hills:* high, tall, lofty, soaring, overhanging, cloud-capped. **2** *a towering musical genius:* surpassing, supreme, transcendent, preeminent, paramount, foremost, principal, dominant, sublime, superior, extraordinary, incomparable, peerless, unequaled, unrivaled, unparalleled, unmatched, matchless.
Ant. **1** low, low-lying, short, squat. **2** lesser, inferior, poor, insignificant; ordinary, commonplace, average, mediocre, run-of-the-mill.

town *n.* **1** *The town has one grade school:* small town, small city; *(loosely)* village, hamlet, burg. **2** *Aunt Edith has a house in town:* municipality, township; city, urban area, population center. **3** *The whole town turned out to welcome the returning heroes:* townspeople, inhabitants, citizenry. **4** *I'm going shopping in town:* main business district, business district, downtown, city center, central city.

toxic *adj. Carbon monoxide is toxic:* poisonous, deadly, fatal, lethal; pernicious, noxious, unhealthy.
Ant. nontoxic, nonpoisonous, nonlethal; healthy.

toy *n.* **1** *A private plane is the millionaire's latest toy:* plaything; trinket, gadget, gimcrack, trifle. *—adj.* **2** *a toy racing car:* for play, for amusement. **3** *toy poodles:* minia-

ture, diminutive, small-scale, small-sized, bantam, midget, pygmy, dwarfed. *—v.* **4** *He's just toying with her affections:* play, trifle, dally, fiddle, amuse oneself with.
Ant. **1** tool, instrument, utensil. **2** real, actual. **3** full-sized.

trace *n.* **1** *These statues are the only traces of a once-great civilization:* sign left behind, sign, indication, evidence, vestige, token, remains; trail, track, footprint. **2** *There was a trace of sadness in her smile. There's a trace of wine in the cake:* tinge, touch, hint, suggestion, flavor; small amount, little bit, bit, jot, drop. *—v.* **3** *Police are trying to trace the missing man:* track down, hunt for, search for, look for, seek. **4** *The book traces the history of modern art:* map, diagram, draw, outline, delineate, describe, depict, mark out.

track *n.* **1** *The garage door is off its track again:* rail, guide rail, parallel rails; train track, streetcar track. **2** *The guide followed the tracks of the elephants:* footprint, mark, sign, spoor; trail. **3** *Try to get off on the right track in your new job:* course, path, route, tack, way. **4** *They sped around the track:* racetrack; running track. *—v.* **5** *The hunters tracked the bear:* follow the track, follow the path, trail, follow, trace.

tract[1] *n. I own a large tract of land in Oregon:* stretch, expanse, zone, area; plot, lot, parcel.

tract[2] *n. Young members of the sect hand out tracts on street corners:* pamphlet, leaflet, brochure, booklet, monograph; treatise, essay.

tractable *adj. a tractable horse:* easy to manage, manageable, easy to control, obedient, trainable, docile, tame, compliant, yielding.
Ant. intractable, unmanageable, uncontrollable, disobedient, wild, unruly.

trade *n.* **1** *Members of the professions used to look down on people in trade:* commerce, buying and selling, business; business transactions, merchandising. **2** *Bricklaying was Father's trade. Jim's a dentist by trade but does fine sculpture, too:* manual occupation, skilled labor, craft, handicraft; occupation, profession, calling, vocation, line of work, business, pursuit, employment. **3** *The boy made a trade of marbles for a kite:* exchange, swap. **4** *The jewelry store caters to an elite trade:* clientele, customers, patrons, buyers, shoppers. *—v.* **5** *I'd love to trade this car for a pickup truck:* exchange, swap, barter. **6** *Germany trades with all European nations:* carry on commerce, do business, buy and sell, deal. **7** *Do you trade at the local store?:* shop, be a customer, patronize, buy, deal.

trader n. a trader in used furs: merchant, dealer, seller, trafficker; tradesperson, salesperson, wholesaler, shopkeeper, retailer, storekeeper.

tradition n. 1 "Fair play" is an old British tradition. a family tradition: handed-down belief, custom, practice, convention, unwritten law. 2 According to tradition, the author of the Iliad and the Odyssey was a blind poet named Homer: legend, folk story, tale, saga; folklore, lore.

Ant. 1 novelty, innovation.

traditional adj. Birthday cakes are a traditional part of birthday parties: customary, typical, habitual, accustomed, fixed, established, acknowledged; old, ancestral, historic.

Ant. new, novel, original, innovative.

traffic n. 1 Traffic is heaviest around noon: vehicular movement; pedestrian movement. 2 The flight to Washington carries a lot of traffic: passengers, travelers, voyagers; (variously) riders, tourists, vacationists, excursionists, commuters; freight. 3 the illegal drug traffic: transportation of goods, trade, dealings, business, commerce, buying and selling; smuggling. 4 The family has never had any traffic with criminals!: dealings, relations, doings, contact, intercourse. —v. 5 trafficking in illegal drugs: trade, deal, buy and sell, carry on commerce; smuggle.

tragedy n. The boy's death was a tragedy. Her life was full of tragedy. The hurricane was a major tragedy: dreadful happening, sad thing, misfortune, affliction; misery, sorrow, grief, heartache, unhappiness, heartbreak; accident, disaster, catastrophe, calamity.

Ant. blessing, boon, good fortune; happiness, joy, bliss.

tragic adj. a tragic accident: dreadful, unfortunate, appalling, heartbreaking, sad, pathetic, deplorable, grievous, woeful, unhappy; awful, frightful, terrible, horrible; disastrous, calamitous, catastrophic, ruinous, devastating, destructive.

Ant. fortunate, happy, felicitous; joyful, lucky.

trail v. 1 The kite's tail trailed in the air: drag, drag behind, tow, draw; dangle, hang down, float, stream, flow. 2 The child trailed along behind. The team trailed by one touchdown: follow, lag behind, bring up the rear; dawdle, poke; be losing, be down. 3 Police trailed the thieves to their hideout: track, trace, follow, tail, hunt. 4 Her voice trailed to a whisper: diminish, dwindle, shrink, subside, fall, grow faint, lessen, decrease. —n. 5 The dogs followed the trail of the fox: track, course, footprints, scent, spoor; sign,

mark, path. 6 Follow the trail to the cabin: path, footpath, beaten track; bridle path.

Ant. 1 push, shove. 2 lead, go before. 4 increase, rise, swell, grow, strengthen.

train n. 1 The train is in the station now. a wagon train: railroad train; subway train, subway, elevated, el; caravan, procession, column. 2 a train of events: series, succession, sequence, progression, chain. 3 The gown had a long train: trailing part, appendage, afterpart. 4 The king is always surrounded by his train: retinue, attendants, escort, followers, entourage, cortege. —v. 5 You should train your dog not to bark. The country needs to train five thousand doctors a year: teach good behavior, teach a habit, domesticate; instruct, teach, educate, school, prepare. 6 The boxer trained for a month before the fight: exercise, get in shape, prepare, practice. 7 The army trained its cannon on the fort: aim, point, direct, level, sight, focus, bring to bear.

trait n. Boldness is one of the traits of a good leader: characteristic, quality, mark, distinguishing mark, hallmark, earmark, attribute.

traitor n. In time of war any traitor will be shot: turncoat, renegade; (variously) mutineer, revolutionary, rebel; betrayer, doublecrosser, Judas, apostate, quisling, fifth columnist.

Ant. patriot, loyalist; true friend.

tramp v. 1 We tramped through the snow: trek, hike, march, trudge, walk, slog. 2 He tramped angrily out of the house. The children tramped on the new plants: stamp, stomp, walk noisily, tread heavily, trample. —n. 3 There's a tramp at the back door asking for a handout: hobo, wandering beggar, panhandler; bum, derelict.

trample v. The cowboy was almost trampled in the stampede. Don't trample the new grass: grind under foot, run over, crush, flatten, squash; step heavily upon, stamp, stomp.

trance n. He seemed to be in a trance and didn't hear me: spell, daze, dazed condition, half-conscious state, hypnotic state, sleepwalking, coma, stupor; daydream, reverie; concentration, abstraction, brown study, woolgathering.

tranquil adj. Mother remained tranquil despite the confusion around her. a tranquil evening: calm, unperturbed, serene, placid, unruffled, unexcited, composed, self-possessed, cool, undisturbed; peaceful, restful, quiet.

Ant. agitated, disturbed, confused, restless; excited, rattled.

tranquillity n. The tranquillity of the coun-

try was heavenly: peace, calm, quiet, serenity, peacefulness, stillness, restfulness, quietude; composure.

Ant. uproar, tumult, commotion.

transact *v. I transact most of my business by phone:* carry on, carry out, conduct, perform, do, execute, handle, accomplish.

transaction *n. We made millions on that transaction:* business dealing, deal, piece of business, venture, enterprise, affair, exchange.

transcend *v.* 1 *That bizarre tale transcends belief:* exceed, go beyond, rise above, surpass, overstep. 2 *Cleopatra's beauty transcended all others':* surpass, be greater than, exceed, outdo, overshadow, outshine, eclipse.

transcendental *adj.* 1 *a transcendental experience:* unworldly, mystical, metaphysical, spiritual, mental, intuitive. 2 *the transcendental beauty of a Beethoven symphony:* extraordinary, unusual, uncommon, superior, unrivaled, peerless, matchless, incomparable, unequaled, unsurpassed, supreme, great, exceeding, surpassing, elevated.

Ant. 1 physical, wordly, empirical. 2 ordinary, common, commonplace, average.

transfer *v.* 1 *Let's transfer these files to the new cabinets. He transferred the ownership of the house to his wife:* move, remove, shift, relocate; convey, carry, bring, send, transport, transmit; consign, turn over, make over, deed, cede. —*n.* 2 *the transfer of the ship's cargo unto the pier:* transferring, transferal, moving, shifting, relocation, relocating, conveying, carrying, bringing, sending, transportation, transporting, transmittal, shipment; consignment, delivering, deeding.

Ant. 1 keep, retain; leave. 2 keeping, retention.

transfix *v.* 1 *The spear fisherman transfixed the bass with his first shot:* impale, skewer, spear, pin. 2 *Magicians transfix children:* rivet, hold rapt, engross, hold, absorb, fascinate, spellbind, mesmerize, hypnotize, captivate, enchant.

transform *v. The caterpillar was transformed into a butterfly. The new owners transformed the old house into a showplace:* change, turn, convert, alter, make over, transmogrify, metamorphose; remodel, remold.

transgression *n. The sinner prayed that his transgressions would be forgiven. Eavesdropping is a transgression on another's privacy:* offense, sin, misdeed, trespass, lapse, iniquity, wrongdoing, immorality, error; infraction, infringement, breach, encroachment; violation, infraction, crime.

Ant. virtue, morality, righteousness, observance, compliance, adherence.

transgressor *n. The preacher warned all transgressors to repent. Transgressors will be fined:* sinner, evildoer, trespasser; offender, lawbreaker, violator, culprit, malefactor, miscreant, felon, criminal.

transient *adj. Youthful beauty is transient:* temporary, transitory, fleeting, brief, momentary, ephemeral, evanescent, unenduring, short-lived.

Ant. permanent, lasting, perpetual, durable, abiding.

transition *n. The transition from rural to urban life is often difficult:* change, changeover, passing, passage, shifting, jump, transformation; progression.

transitory *adj. a transitory feeling:* temporary, fleeting, brief, short-lived, passing, fugitive, not lasting, evanescent, ephemeral.

Ant. long-lived, lasting, persistent, enduring, permanent, abiding, perpetual.

translate *v.* 1 *to translate Chinese into English:* render, convert; decode, decipher. 2 *It's time you translate your beliefs into actions!:* change, turn, transform, convert.

translucent *adj. translucent stained-glass windows:* semitransparent, pellucid, translucid.

Ant. opaque.

transmission *n. to prevent the transmission of secret documents:* transmitting, transfer, transferring, passage, passing, handing over, transmittal, sending, conveyance, dispatch, forwarding, transportation; communication, delivery, broadcast.

transmit *v. to transmit a message:* send, convey, relay, transfer, dispatch, forward, ship, carry, communicate; broadcast, televise.

transparent *adj.* 1 *The water was so transparent we could see the fish clearly:* clear, crystal-clear, lucid, limpid, pellucid, glassy. 2 *Those transparent curtains will never keep the light out:* see-through, thin, sheer, gauzy, translucent, diaphanous. 3 *Her reason for leaving was transparent:* evident, obvious, apparent, perceptible, manifest, visible, patent; unmistakable, unambiguous.

Ant. 1, 2 opaque. 1 muddy, roiled, murky. 3 unapparent, hidden, concealed, invisible; confused, vague, mysterious.

transpire *v.* 1 *After a few days, it transpired that the accident had been more serious than at first supposed:* become known, be discovered, be revealed, come to light. 2 *Informal Be sure to tell us what transpires:* occur, happen, evolve, take place; befall, arise, turn up.

491

transport v. 1 *to transport furniture to a
new apartment:* transfer, move, remove,
convey, carry, take, bring, send, deliver,
fetch, bear, cart, tote; ship, truck, freight.
2 *The beautiful music transported the audience:* carry away, move, thrill, enrapture,
enchant, lift, enthrall, entrance, make ecstatic, captivate, charm, bewitch. —n.
3 *The transport of explosives is a dangerous
business:* transporting, transportation, shipping, conveying, moving, sending, delivery,
carting, trucking. 4 *The transport leaves at
midnight:* vehicle, conveyance; *(variously)*
freighter, cargo ship, freight train, cargo
plane, truck.

transportation n. *The price of the tour includes transportation to and from all air-
ports:* conveyance, transference, transferal,
transport; shipment, transmission, haulage,
cartage, transit.

trap n. 1 *The wolf was caught in a trap:*
(variously) snare, net, pit, pitfall. 2 *Promising a fortune for nothing was just one of the
con man's traps:* ruse, trick, artifice, stratagem, wile, feint, ploy, device; ambush.
—v. 3 *Some cheese helped us trap the
mouse:* entrap, catch, snare; hunt down.
4 *The engineers tried to trap the gas in the
pipes:* seal, stop, lock in, hold back.

trappings n. pl. *The trappings of a king
include his robe, crown, and scepter. The
house was filled with the trappings for a
party:* dress, garb, costume, raiment, attire,
clothing, clothes, apparel, vesture, outfit,
habiliment; gear, accoutrements, paraphernalia, trimmings, effects, things, fittings, ornaments, adornments, decorations, embel-
lishments, adjuncts.

trash n. 1 *Put the trash in the barrel:* litter,
rubbish, refuse, garbage; junk, castoffs.
2 *Don't waste your time reading that trash!:*
worthless writing, worthless talk, junk,
drivel, rot, tripe.
Ant. 1 valuables, treasure.

travail n. 1 *Life is full of travail:* toil, drudgery, hard work, backbreaking work, exer-
tion. 2 *the travails of war:* anguish, suffering, hardship, distress, pain.
Ant. 1 ease, relaxation, loafing. 2 comfort,
pleasure.

travel v. 1 *The ball traveled in a straight line:*
move, proceed, progress, go. 2 *We traveled
to Greece last summer. I like to travel:* take
a trip, journey, tour, visit; pass over, traverse; roam, rove, wander, globetrot.
Ant. 2 stay, remain, settle.

traveler n. *The airport was filled with travelers: (variously)* tourist, journeyer, vacationer, wayfarer, voyager, excursionist,
globetrotter, wanderer, rover.

traverse v. 1 *The hikers had to traverse the
bridge one at a time:* cross, go across, move
along, travel over, move through. 2 *The
highway traverses the business district:*
cross, cross over, span, bridge, intersect,
run through.

travesty n. 1 *The comedian's travesty of the
senator was riotously funny:* ludicrous imitation, burlesque, spoof, takeoff, parody,
caricature, lampoon, mockery, farce. 2 *The
trial was a travesty of justice:* mockery, perversion, sham, disgrace.

treacherous adj. 1 *a treacherous friend:*
traitorous, treasonous, untrustworthy, faithless, falsehearted, unfaithful, disloyal, deceitful, false, perfidious, devious, two-faced.
2 *Ice made the road treacherous:* dangerous, hazardous, unsafe, perilous, precarious.
Ant. 1 loyal, true, faithful, trustworthy.
2 safe.

treachery n. *His treachery was giving information to the enemy:* disloyalty, treason,
betrayal, faithlessness, untrustworthiness,
falseness, deceit, deceitfulness, deception,
perfidy, duplicity, double-dealing, double
cross.

tread v. 1 *Many tourists have trod this same
street to the shrine:* walk, walk along, walk
on, step, trudge along; roam, rove. 2 *The
boys trod on the flowers:* trample, stomp,
stamp, crush under foot. —n. 3 *We heard
father's tread on the steps:* step, footstep,
footfall; walk, gait, stride.

treason n. *In time of war, treason is a crime
punishable by death:* betrayal of one's country, sedition, subversion; rebellion, revolt,
revolution, insurgence, insurrection, mutiny; disloyalty, treachery.
Ant. loyalty, patriotism; faithfulness.

treasure n. 1 *The pirate's treasure was in
the sunken ship:* stored wealth, riches,
hoard, store. 2 *That new clerk is a real treasure:* gem, jewel, paragon, pearl. —v.
3 *We treasured our teacher's good opinion:*
value, cherish, revere, esteem, prize, hold
dear, dote upon.
Ant. 3 scorn, disdain.

treasury n. 1 *How much money is in the
company's treasury?:* repository, depository, storehouse, bank; vault, till, coffer,
safe, strongbox, money box. 2 *The club
treasury was $500:* amount on hand, funds,
bank account.

treat v. 1 *Her parents still treat her like a
child:* act toward, deal with, relate to, consider, look upon; manage, handle. 2 *You'll
need a doctor to treat that wound:* try to
cure, try to heal, doctor, attend, minister to,
prescribe for, remedy. 3 *The book treats the*

problems of economic development: discuss, have as a subject matter, expatiate on, speak about. **4** *Father treated everyone to dinner at a restaurant:* take out, give, *Slang* stand, spring; favor, grant. —*n.* **5** *After days of camping, a hot shower is a real treat:* pleasure, satisfaction, gratification, comfort, delight, joy, thrill. **6** *On Halloween children go from house to house asking for treats:* gift of food, small gift; favor.

treatise *n.* *The doctor wrote a treatise on alcoholism:* detailed article, discourse, essay, thesis, dissertation, study, monograph, paper, tract, report, textbook.

treatment *n.* **1** *The mayor's sensitive treatment of the problem satisfied both sides:* manner of dealing, handling, management, treating, manipulation, conduct; approach, process, procedure. **2** *The doctors decided upon a nonsurgical treatment of the tumor:* medical care, cure, remedy, therapy, doctoring; regimen; application, medication.

trek *n.* **1** *Join us for a trek through the woods:* trip, tramp, hike, outing, march; jaunt, junket, excursion, expedition. —*v.* **2** *We trekked through the woods:* walk, tramp, hike, rove, roam, march, trudge, range, wander, plod; travel, journey.

tremble *v.* *His hands were trembling. The girl's voice trembled:* shake, quiver, shiver, shudder, quake, quaver, waver, flutter, pulsate, palpitate.

tremendous *adj.* **1** *tremendous redwood trees. a tremendous undertaking:* huge, gigantic, immense, colossal, enormous, mammoth, giant, gargantuan; vast, formidable, awesome, major; important, consequential. **2** *Informal The movie was tremendous:* wonderful, excellent, extraordinary, marvelous, fantastic, incredible, great, fabulous, terrific, stupendous.

Ant. **1** small, little, tiny; minor, unimportant. **2** bad, awful, terrible, lousy, second-rate.

tremor *n.* *The tremor in my hands was the only indication of my nervousness:* shaking, shake, trembling, tremble, quiver, quivering, shiver, shivering, shudder, waver, flutter, quavering, pulsation, throb, palpitation, vibration; quake.

trenchant *adj.* **1** *a trenchant analysis of the problem:* clear-cut, incisive, keen, penetrating, well-defined, probing, concise. **2** *Hamlet shows his true feelings in some trenchant asides:* caustic, bitter, sarcastic, acrimonious, acerbic, scathing.

Ant. **1** vague, rambling, disorganized. **2** flattering, complimentary.

trend *n.* *Today's trend is toward less formal clothing:* fashion, style; drift, direction,

movement, flow; leaning, inclination, propensity, proclivity.

trespass *v.* **1** *Don't trespass on this property:* enter unlawfully, intrude; infringe, invade, encroach, impinge. —*n.* **2** *The boat was seized for its trespass into restricted waters:* wrongful entry, unlawful entry; encroachment, intrusion, infringement, invasion. **3** *Forgive us our trespasses:* sin, wrongdoing, evildoing, immorality, iniquity, transgression, error, misdeed, wrong, offense.

Ant. **3** good deed, virtue.

trial *n.* **1** *The trial ended in acquittal for the defendants:* court case, litigation. **2** *The trial of the new plane was delayed by bad weather:* test, testing, test run, tryout, trying; try, attempt, venture, effort. **3** *a life full of trials and tribulations:* hardship, misfortune, trouble, distress, affliction, woe, misery, adversity, ordeal, suffering, wretchedness, anguish, torment, care, heartache.

Ant. **3** ease, comfort, happiness, joy; good fortune, good luck.

tribulation *n.* *Too many tribulations have left them beaten:* affliction, trouble, ordeal, suffering, wretchedness, misfortune, worry, care, hardship, heartache, agony, anguish, pain, adversity; woe, misery, grief, sorrow, unhappiness; ill fortune, bad luck.

Ant. happiness, joy, delight, ease, comfort; good fortune, good luck.

tribunal *n.* *The case was tried before the highest tribunal in the land:* court, forum, judiciary, judges.

tribute *n.* **1** *We must pay tribute to all those who helped make this a free country. The musician gave full tribute to her old teacher:* honor, respect, gratitude, acknowledgment, recognition; praise, compliment, accolade, commendation, laudation, eulogy, panegyric, testimonial, memorial. **2** *The pirates demanded tribute from the captured island:* payment, ransom, bribe, levy, impost, assessment.

Ant. **1** dishonor, disrespect, ingratitude, disdain, scorn.

trick *n.* **1** *Pretending to be hurt is a trick many prizefighters use:* ruse, device, deception, deceit, stratagem, artifice, feint, ploy, hoax; chicanery, subterfuge, contrivance, dodge. **2** *an April Fool's trick:* prank, joke, gag, antic, practical joke, caper. **3** *Can the dog do tricks? Here's a new trick the magician did:* stunt, feat, antic; magic demonstration, sleight of hand, prestidigitation, piece of legerdemain. **4** *There's a trick to making good coffee:* knack, art, skill, technique, secret. —*v.* **5** *Dad tricked Mother into believing he had forgotten her birth-*

day—then surprised her: deceive, hoax, gull, dupe, hoodwink, mislead, bamboozle, bluff; cheat, swindle, flimflam.

trickery *n. The con man obtained that money by trickery:* deceitfulness, deceit, chicanery, duplicity, deviousness, skullduggery, stratagem, wiliness, slipperiness, quackery, pretense, deception.

Ant. honesty, candor, frankness; truth, uprightness.

trickle *v.* 1 *Blood trickled from the wound:* drip, dribble, seep, leak, ooze. —*n.* 2 *Only a trickle of water came out of the pipe:* dribble, drip, seepage, slow stream; little bit, small amount.

Ant. 1 gush, stream, course, pour, spurt. 2 gush, flood, cascade.

tricky *adj.* 1 *Be careful of your opponent, he's tricky:* crafty, cunning, slippery, wily, deceptive, underhanded, shifty, devious. 2 *Working out a compromise will be tricky:* difficult, complicated, touch-and-go.

Ant. 1 straightforward, open, frank, artless, honest, truthful. 2 simple, easy.

trifle *n.* 1 *The lost ring was only a trifle. Don't cry over trifles:* trinket, bauble, gimcrack, knickknack, bagatelle, gewgaw, plaything, toy; triviality, thing of no importance, small matter. 2 *I'll have just a trifle of the dessert:* little, bit, mite, dash, dab, drop, pinch, speck, scrap, jot. —*v.* 3 *He's just trifling with her affections:* deal lightly, amuse oneself, toy, play, dally.

Ant. 2 lot, lots.

trifling *adj. It was a trifling amount:* insignificant, unimportant, inconsequential, trivial, negligible, small, slight, piddling, niggling, inappreciable, paltry.

Ant. significant, consequential, major; considerable, appreciable, large.

trim *v.* 1 *Be sure to trim the rosebushes:* prune, clip, crop, pare, lop, shave, shear, cut. 2 *The seamstress trimmed the dress with red stitching:* decorate, ornament, adorn, deck, bedeck, array, garnish, embellish, beautify, embroider. —*n.* 3 *I'm in fine trim:* shape, condition, form, fettle. 4 *The lace trim on a dress:* trimming, adornment, embellishment, decoration, garnish, ornamentation, border, piping. 5 *My sideburns need a trim:* trimming, cutting, evening-off, clipping, shearing, cropping, pruning, paring. —*adj.* 6 *a trim figure:* lean, slim, sleek, slender, svelte, shapely, well-proportioned; limber, supple, lithe.

trinket *n. We bought a few trinkets as souvenirs:* trifle, bauble, small ornament, bagatelle, gewgaw, gimcrack, knickknack.

trip *n.* 1 *The trip was canceled:* journey, voyage, excursion, outing, tour, jaunt, cruise,

expedition, junket, trek. —*v.* 2 *The boy tripped over a roller skate:* stumble, fall over, miss one's footing, slip, lose one's balance. 3 *The little girl can read easy words but trips on the hard ones. The hard math problem tripped up the student:* make a mistake, err, blunder, slip up, bungle, flounder, flub, muff; cause to make a mistake, throw off; confuse, catch; hoodwink, outfox. 4 *She tripped happily along the path:* skip, step lightly, tread gracefully, flounce, prance, dance, gambol.

trite *adj. The play had a trite plot:* banal, stale, hackneyed, worn-out, stereotyped, clichéd, commonplace, routine, oft-repeated, everyday, common, humdrum, ordinary; silly, frivolous, shallow.

Ant. original, fresh, novel.

triumph *n.* 1 *Her triumph in the race was unexpected. The new opera is a triumph:* victory, win, success; conquest, mastery, ascendancy, superiority, accomplishment, attainment, achievement, *Informal* hit, smash hit, coup. —*v.* 2 *The Allies triumphed in World War II. Justice triumphs in the end:* be victorious, succeed, be successful, win, prevail, conquer, overcome.

Ant. 1 defeat, loss; failure. 2 lose; fail; succumb.

triumphant *adj.* 1 *The triumphant team celebrated its victory:* victorious, winning, successful, conquering, first-place. 2 *The triumphant fans poured onto the field:* rejoicing, celebrating, exultant, jubilant, elated, joyful.

Ant. 1 defeated, beaten, unsuccessful.

trivial *adj. Don't let such trivial things upset you:* trifling, unimportant, inconsequential, petty, piddling, paltry, insignificant, unessential; small, little, meager, niggling; foolish, trite, banal.

Ant. weighty, important, consequential, significant, essential, momentous; considerable, appreciable, substantial.

troop *n.* 1 *a troop of Boy Scouts. A troop of shoppers descended on the store:* band, unit, company; throng, horde, drove, crowd, swarm, army, bunch, gang. 2 **troops** *The nation must keep its troops on alert:* soldiers, soldiery, army, armed force, military force; infantry, fighting men, militia; cavalry, cavalry unit. —*v.* 3 *The children trooped into the yard:* march, file, parade; trudge, tramp.

trophy *n. The winner received a silver trophy:* loving cup, award, medal, prize, citation.

tropical *adj. a tropical climate:* in the tropics, of the tropics; hot and humid, torrid, sultry, sweltering.

Ant. arctic; cold, wintry, cool.

trot *v. We trotted to the corner and back:* jog, walk smartly, step quickly.
Ant. gallop, run; plod.

trouble *v.* 1 *The student's failing grades troubled his parents. May I trouble you for a drink of water?:* distress, worry, upset, dismay, disquiet, perturb, concern, unsettle, oppress, depress; bother, inconvenience, annoy, pester, discommode, put out. 2 *Her arthritis is troubling her again:* bother, afflict; pain, annoy, vex, plague. —*n.* 3 *Her visit has been nothing but trouble. Please take the trouble to read the contract thoroughly:* difficulty, bother, pains, inconvenience, annoyance, irritation, vexation, pother, fuss, stress, struggle; effort, care, attention, exertion. 4 *I'm in trouble:* difficulty, predicament, dilemma, quandary, entanglement, pass, mess, fix, hot water. 5 *a life of toil and trouble:* woe, misery, distress, suffering, affliction, tribulation, hardship, misfortune, adversity, difficulty, grief, sorrow, worry. 6 *Political agitators tried to cause trouble:* unrest, disorder, dissension, commotion, discord, row, disunity, disturbance; dissatisfaction, discontent, strife. 7 *back trouble. car trouble:* ailment, disability, disorder, difficulty; breakdown, malfunction.
Ant. 1, 2 relieve, ease. 1 please, delight. 2 assuage, mollify. 5 pleasure, happiness; ease, comfort; success, good fortune. 6 peace, calm, tranquillity; unity, accord, harmony.

troublesome *adj. a troublesome student. troublesome financial problems:* distressing, worrisome, bothersome, demanding, trying, taxing, disturbing, annoying, vexing, irksome, harassing, pesky, difficult, tough; disobedient, undisciplined; uncontrolled.
Ant. pleasant, pleasing, delightful; obedient, disciplined, accommodating.

trounce *v. Our team trounced opponents:* defeat decisively, win easily over, overwhelm; beat, whip, drub, clobber, lick.

truce *n. The enemy rejected the truce:* temporary halt in fighting, cease-fire, suspension of hostilities, armistice.
Ant. war, hostilities, fighting.

truck *n. The car collided with a truck: (variously)* delivery truck, van; pickup truck, panel truck, eighteen-wheeler, trailer truck.

truckle *v. You never fail to truckle to important people:* ingratiate oneself, fawn, flatter; submit, yield, knuckle under, defer, pander, grovel, curry favor.
Ant. resist, stand up to.

truculent *adj. His truculent nature gets him*

into a lot of scrapes: belligerent, bellicose, aggressive, pugnacious, hostile, fierce, bad-tempered; ill-humored, surly, cross, touchy, peevish, snappish, petulant, ungracious, sulky.
Ant. gentle, kind, diffident, accommodating.

trudge *v. We trudged wearily off the field:* plod, walk, drag, lumber, clump, limp, shamble, march, tramp.
Ant. bound, skip, prance, trot.

true *adj.* 1 *This is a true story:* in accordance with the facts, accurate, correct, right; exact, precise; factual, truthful, faithful. 2 *The table is a true antique:* genuine, authentic, real, valid, bona fide, legitimate, actual. 3 *You've been a true friend:* faithful, loyal, steadfast, devoted, staunch, dependable, reliable. 4 *the true heir to the throne:* rightful, lawful, legitimate, legal, official, proper.
Ant. 1–4 false. 1, 3 untrue. 1 inaccurate, fallacious, nonfactual, fictitious. 2 fake, phony, counterfeit, bogus, spurious, imitation, artificial, synthetic. 3 faithless, disloyal, deceitful, unreliable, inconstant. 4 illegal, unofficial, unlawful, illegitimate.

truly *adv.* 1 *Mozart was truly a brilliant composer:* unquestionably, beyond doubt, indubitably, assuredly, certainly, incontestably, without question, indisputably, absolutely, indeed, really, in truth, in actuality, in fact, surely, positively, definitely, to be sure. 2 *You quoted Hamlet's soliloquy truly:* accurately, correctly, exactly, precisely, literally, factually. 3 *I'm truly sorry:* sincerely, truthfully, honestly, really, genuinely.
Ant. 1 questionably, dubiously. 2 inaccurately, incorrectly, inexactly. 3 insincerely, untruthfully.

truncate *v. Truncate the manuscript by at least half:* shorten, cut, prune, trim, lop, dock, crop, curtail, clip.
Ant. lengthen, elongate, extend.

truss *v.* 1 *Truss the suitcases on top of the car:* tie, secure, strap, bind, make fast, hitch; tie up, bind up, pinion. —*n.* 2 *The bridge was built on steel trusses:* braced framework, brace, support, underpinning, stay, stanchion, beam, girder.
Ant. 1 untie, unbind, unfasten.

trust *n.* 1 *the people's trust in the government:* confidence, faith, belief, credence, reliance, sureness, conviction. 2 *My life is in your trust:* care, custody, guardianship, safekeeping, protection, keeping, charge, hands. 3 *Public office is a public trust:* responsibility, charge, obligation, duty.

—v. 4 *Trust nothing he says:* have faith in, believe, rely on, depend upon; credit, take on faith, take stock in. 5 *I trust the room will be satisfactory:* presume, assume, expect, hope, anticipate, feel sure, contemplate, take for granted.

Ant. 1, 4 mistrust, distrust, doubt. 1 disbelief, misgiving, skepticism. 4 disbelieve, discredit, question.

trusting *adj. You're too trusting:* trustful, believing, unsuspicious; credulous, gullible.

Ant. distrustful, suspicious, skeptical.

trustworthy *adj. Only trustworthy people can be considered for such a position:* responsible, dependable, reliable, trusted; faithful, loyal, true; high-principled, honest, ethical, incorruptible.

Ant. untrustworthy, irresponsible, undependable, unreliable, disreputable; disloyal, treacherous; dishonorable, dishonest.

truth *n.* 1 *I'm not certain of the truth of the story:* facts, reality; truthfulness, veracity, verity, authenticity, fidelity, integrity, faithfulness, accuracy. 2 *Mortality is an unquestioned truth:* fact, proven principle, reality.

Ant. 1, 2 untruth. 1 untruthfulness, falseness, falsity, deceit, dishonesty. 2 fiction, delusion, fallacy.

truthful *adj.* 1 *She's too truthful to lie about anything:* honest, trustworthy, sincere, guileless, artless, candid, frank, open, straightforward, aboveboard. 2 *a truthful account of the incident:* factual, true, honest, accurate, faithful, scrupulous, precise, unvarnished.

Ant. 1, 2 untruthful. 1 lying, deceitful, dishonest, insincere. 2 false, untrue, inaccurate, fictitious, fallacious.

try *v.* 1 *Please try to finish the job by Friday:* attempt, strive, endeavor, make an effort, aim, seek, undertake. 2 *The pilots were eager to try the new plane. Have you tried that new toothpaste?:* test, put to a test, prove; sample, use, avail oneself of. 3 *I wouldn't try water-skiing without a life jacket:* risk, venture, undertake. 4 *The case was tried by the Supreme Court:* hear and decide, adjudicate, adjudge. 5 *The children tried our patience:* strain, tax. —n. 6 *Make a try to succeed on the new job. The contestant has one more try at the answer:* attempt, effort; opportunity, turn, *Informal* shot, go, crack. 7 *Give the new dishwasher a try:* trial, test.

trying *adj. I've had a trying day:* difficult, tough, hard, arduous, taxing, irksome, troublesome, distressing, irritating, vexing, pesky, exasperating, aggravating, harrowing, wearisome, tedious, exhausting.

tryst *n. The lovers arranged a tryst for midnight:* appointment, engagement, rendezvous, date, assignation, meeting, secret meeting.

tuck *v.* 1 *Tuck the scarf into your collar:* stick, insert, thrust, stuff, shove, cram, put. 2 *Tuck this blanket around the children:* wrap snugly, cover snugly, enwrap. —n. 3 *The tailor made the waist smaller by making a tuck:* gather, pleat, pucker.

tuft *n. a tuft of grass. The bird had a beautiful blue tuft:* cluster, bunch, wisp, sheaf, tassel, clump; topknot, crest.

tug *v.* 1 *Tug hard at the handle:* pull, yank, jerk, draw. —n. 2 *Give the drawer a tug:* pull, yank, jerk.

Ant. 1, 2 push, shove.

tumble *v.* 1 *We tumbled down the hill:* fall end over end, fall, roll, topple, go sprawling, stumble. 2 *The temperature tumbled to 30 degrees:* drop, fall, plunge.

Ant. 2 rise, soar, increase.

tumbledown *adj. a tumbledown cabin:* dilapidated, decrepit, rickety, ramshackle, broken-down, falling-down, disintegrating.

tumult *n. The tumult awakened us:* uproar, commotion, hullabaloo, din, disorder, pandemonium, clamor, racket, hubbub; turmoil, upheaval, confusion, bustle, excitement, ado.

Ant. peace, quiet, calm, serenity, tranquillity.

tumultuous *adj. The crowd gave the Governor a tumultuous welcome:* boisterous, raucous, noisy, rowdy; disorderly, unruly, stormy, chaotic.

Ant. quiet, restrained; cool, lukewarm.

tune *n.* 1 *Irving Berlin wrote this tune:* melody, theme, motif; song, air, strain, ditty, number. 2 *The piano is out of tune. The design is in tune with modern architecture:* pitch; agreement, harmony, accord, concord. —v. 3 *The violinist tuned the violin. Please tune the television set to Channel 4:* pitch; adjust.

turbid *n. The landslide left the lake turbid:* unclear, opaque, murky, clouded, stirred up, roiled, muddy; disturbed, agitated, unsettled.

Ant. clear, limpid; calm, placid, smooth.

turbulent *adj. The sea is turbulent tonight. The turbulent meeting ended in a fight:* disturbed, agitated, tumultuous, tempestuous; violent, raging, fierce, stormy, furious; chaotic, disorderly, unruly.

Ant. calm, smooth; quiet, orderly.

turgid *adj.* 1 *The wound was turgid:* swollen, puffed up, puffy. 2 *a writer's turgid prose:*

grandiose, overblown, inflated, pretentious, grandiloquent; ostentatious, showy, florid, flowery.

Ant. 2 simple, concise, succinct, terse.

turmoil *n. The house is in a turmoil:* state of confusion, confusion, disturbance, chaos, disorder; tumult, commotion, uproar, agitation.

Ant. order; peacefulness, calmness.

turn *v.* 1 *The path turns to the left. Turn over or your back will get sunburned:* revolve, rotate, spin, whirl, wheel, roll, swivel, gyrate, pivot; shift, swerve, veer, twist, curve, bend; overturn, invert, reverse. 2 *In the fall the leaves turn red. Military school turned the youth into a leader:* change, change to, become; transform, metamorphose, convert, alter, make. 3 *Everything turns on this last play of the game:* be contingent on, depend, hang, hinge, rest, reside, lie. 4 *Let's turn our attention to the matter at hand:* direct, apply, put; look, go, come. 5 *to turn a phrase:* make skillfully, perform, execute, deliver, accomplish. 6 *He turned his ankle:* wrench, twist, sprain. 7 *How could you turn your child out of the house?:* send, cause to go, discharge; eject, throw. 8 *Don't leave the milk out in the sun or it will turn:* sour, spoil, curdle, ferment, acidify. —*n.* 9 *Give the dial a turn to the left:* rotation, revolution, spin, swing, twirl, whirl, roll, swivel, pivot, gyration, twist. 10 *The patient took a turn for the better:* change, shift, fluctuation; deviation, alteration. 11 *The road is full of turns:* curve, bend, twist, zigzag, winding, arc; loop, coil. 12 *Has each child had a turn?:* opportunity, chance, go, round, attempt, effort; time, shift, spell, period. 13 *One good turn deserves another:* deed, act, action, service. 14 *Let's take a turn in the garden before going to bed:* short walk, walk, stroll. 15 *My, but you gave me a turn!:* shock, start, surprise, scare, fright.

Ant. 2 remain, stay. 7 keep, retain, hold.

turnout *n. There was a huge turnout for the dance:* gathering, crowd, throng, assemblage, assembly, audience.

turpitude *n. He was discharged from the Army for moral turpitude:* wickedness, depravity, immorality, vice, corruption, lewdness, degeneracy, wrongdoing, perversion, defilement, evil, sinfulness.

tussle *v.* 1 *The children tussled over the candy:* scuffle, grapple, fight, brawl, wrestle, battle. —*n.* 2 *He received a black eye in the tussle:* fight, scuffle, scrap, brawl, fracas, fray, melee, conflict.

tutelage *n. I learned to sail under the tutelage of my father:* supervision, guidance,

direction; instruction, training, teaching, coaching, schooling, tutoring.

tutor *n. A tutor helped me prepare for the Spanish exam:* coach, private teacher; instructor, master, teacher, mentor, coach, guru.

Ant. pupil, student, disciple.

twaddle *n. Everyone is tired of listening to twaddle:* idle talk, silly talk, drivel, prattle, tripe, nonsense, tommyrot, rubbish.

twang *n.* 1 *the twang of a guitar:* vibrating sound, vibration, resonance, reverberation. 2 *He speaks with a Midwestern twang:* nasal sound, nasal resonance.

twilight *n.* 1 *Driving at twilight is dangerous:* dusk, gloaming, half-light; nightfall, evening, eve, sundown, sunset, eventide. 2 *The twilight of life:* decline, last phase, ebb.

Ant. 1 dawn, sunrise, daybreak. 2 beginning; peak, height.

twin *adj.* 1 *The twin sisters refused to dress alike:* born as one of a pair, forming a pair. 2 *Twin love seats flanked the fireplace:* paired, matched, identical, duplicate; like, alike. 3 *The plan has a twin purpose:* double, dual, twofold.

twine *n.* 1 *Wrap the bundle with twine:* string, cord, two-strand string, twisted thread. —*v.* 2 *She twined her hair into braids:* intertwine, interlace, weave, entwine, twist, plait, braid; wind, coil.

twinge *n. I had a twinge in my neck:* sudden pain, pain, cramp, spasm, stab, pang, stitch; throb, tingle, twitch.

twinkle *v.* 1 *The lights of the city twinkled far below:* glimmer, shimmer, shine, flicker, flash, sparkle, gleam, glisten, glow, scintillate. —*n.* 2 *the twinkle of a distant star:* glimmer, shimmer, flicker, sparkle, gleam, glow, flare, flash.

twirl *v. The dancers twirled across the stage. to twirl a baton:* spin, whirl, rotate, revolve, gyrate, wheel, pivot, pirouette.

twist *v.* 1 *The girl twisted her hair into a braid. Twist the dial to the left:* wind, twine, intertwine, entwine, interlace, tangle, knot, ravel; coil, curl; rotate, turn, swivel, pivot, whirl, spin. 2 *The road twists to the right:* bend, curve, wind, arc, swing, swerve, veer, curl, snake, zigzag. 3 *Louise twisted her ankle. The boy twisted the toy from his brother's hands:* wrench, turn, sprain; wrest, yank. 4 *His face was twisted in pain:* distort, contort. —*n.* 5 *The prospector carried the gold dust in a twist of paper:* curl, coil, roll, corkscrew, spiral; tangle, knot, kink. 6 *Give the knob a twist:* turn, rotation, spin, whirl. 7 *The road is full of twists:* bend, zigzag, curve, convolution. 8 *An in-*

door picnic—there's a new twist!: change, development, surprise; notion, idea, approach, treatment, way, method.

Ant. 1 untwist, unwind; straighten, uncoil; untangle, unknot.

twitch *v.* 1 *His hands twitched in anger. Stop twitching and sit still!:* jerk, quiver, quaver, shake, tremble; wiggle, squirm, writhe. *—n.* 2 *Is the twitch in my eye noticeable?:* tic, jerk, spasm, quiver, quaver, throb, tremor.

twitter *v.* 1 *The wrens twittered:* chirp, chirrup, cheep, tweet, chatter, peep, warble. *—n.* 2 *The twitter of birds filled the garden:* twittering, chirp, chirping, chirrup, chirruping, cheep, peep.

tycoon *n. a movie tycoon:* magnate, mogul, nabob, captain of industry, entrepreneur, industrialist, *Slang* big shot, bigwig.

type *n.* 1 *a new type of rose:* class, kind, sort, variety, category, order, species, genus, race, family, phylum, division. 2 *a strong, silent type:* typical person, typical thing, example, specimen, model, sample; prototype, archetype.

typical *adj.* 1 *a typical day at the office:* representative, standard, normal, average, stock, regular, usual, ordinary; conventional, orthodox; prototypal, model, exemplary. 2 *That sarcastic reply is typical of him:* characteristic, in keeping, true to type; distinctive, individual.

Ant. 1 atypical, abnormal, unrepresentative, unusual, unique, singular, strange. 2 uncharacteristic, out of keeping.

typify *v. She typifies the healthy American teenager:* personify, represent, exemplify, characterize, embody, epitomize, connote.

tyranny *n. the tyranny of the czar:* despotism, cruel authority, unjust rule; cruelty, harshness, severity, oppression, repression, coercion; absolute rule, iron rule, dictatorship, fascism, totalitarianism.

Ant. humanity, kindness, benevolence; democracy, freedom.

tyrant *n. The American colonies regarded George III as a tyrant:* despot; cruel master, uncompromising superior, taskmaster, martinet, bully; absolute ruler, dictator.

U

ubiquitous *adj. The fog seemed to be ubiquitous:* omnipresent, pervading, pervasive, widespread, allover, everywhere.

ugly *adj.* 1 *One sister is beautiful, the other ugly. What an ugly dress!:* homely, unattractive, unseemly, unbecoming, ill-favored; repulsive, hideous. 2 *His ugly disposition gained him few friends. What an ugly thing to do!:* nasty, quarrelsome, cantankerous, unpleasant, mean, hostile, disagreeable, obnoxious; offensive, dreadful, disgusting, foul, vile, sickening, horrid, horrible, repugnant. 3 *Ugly clouds gathered on the horizon:* forbidding, ominous, threatening, menacing; dangerous, troublesome.

Ant. 1 beautiful, pretty, handsome, lovely, comely, attractive. 2 pleasant, agreeable, personable, likable, friendly; good, nice, sweet. 3 promising, auspicious.

ulterior *adj. an ulterior motive:* hidden, concealed, unrevealed, undisclosed, undivulged; selfish, self-serving, opportunistic.

Ant. obvious, evident, self-evident, plain; altruistic.

ultimate *adj.* 1 *The ultimate cost was over a hundred dollars. Becoming president is his ultimate goal:* final, resulting, definitive, conclusive, crowning, end, eventual, long-range. 2 *An Oscar represents the ultimate accolade for a movie actor:* greatest, utmost, highest, supreme, maximum, extreme.

Ant. 1 initial, beginning. 2 lowest, minimum.

umpire *n.* 1 *A federal umpire will try to settle the labor dispute:* referee, judge; arbiter, arbitrator, mediator, moderator, adjudicator. *—v.* 2 *I umpired the children's baseball game:* referee; judge, arbitrate, mediate, adjudicate, moderate.

unabridged *adj. an unabridged dictionary:* not abridged, full-length, complete, uncut, uncondensed.

Ant. abridged, condensed.

unacceptable *adj. Such behavior is unacceptable:* not acceptable, not allowable, unsatisfactory, unsuitable, unseemly, improper, unwelcome, insupportable.

unaccompanied *adj. She came to the party unaccompanied:* unattended, unescorted, companionless, alone, solitary; *Music* solo, a cappella.

Ant. escorted, accompanied.

unaccountable *adj.* 1 *Many unaccountable things happened in that haunted house:* unexplained, inexplicable, strange, odd, peculiar, incomprehensible, mysterious; unusual, extraordinary. 2 *The driver was held unaccountable for the accident:* not responsible, not liable, blameless, innocent; exempt, immune.

Ant. 1 explainable, explicable; ordinary, normal. 2 accountable, responsible, answerable, liable, blamable.

unaccustomed *adj.* 1 *the unaccustomed sights of Tibet:* unusual, unfamiliar, uncommon, extraordinary, strange, foreign, curious, peculiar, odd, surprising, remarkable; novel, rare. 2 *I was unaccustomed to such luxury:* not used to, unused, not accustomed, unacquainted, inexperienced, unpracticed.

Ant. 1, 2 familiar. 1 ordinary, common, run-of-the-mill. 2 used to, experienced.

unaffected *adj.* 1 *Passersby were unaffected by the beggar's plea:* not affected, not influenced, untouched, unmoved, indifferent to, unconcerned; impervious to, unsympathetic to. 2 *an unaffected manner:* natural, sincere, genuine, simple, wholesome, open, honest, frank, direct, straightforward, open-hearted, undesigning, guileless; innocent, childlike, unsophisticated, unworldly.

Ant. 1, 2 affected. 1 influenced, touched, moved, responsive, concerned, sympathetic. 2 artificial, insincere, pretentious, assumed; devious, scheming, designing; sophisticated, worldly.

unanimous *adj. The members were unanimous in approving the project:* in complete agreement; united, like-minded, of one mind.

Ant. not agreed, discordant, disagreeing.

unapproachable *adj.* 1 *The moat made the castle unapproachable. a stern, unapproachable man:* inaccessible, unreachable, unattainable; aloof, distant, stand-offish, cold, forbidding, intimidating. 2 *Shakespeare's genius is unapproachable:* unequaled, unrivaled, matchless, unparalleled, incomparable, inimitable, unique, nonpareil; supreme, preeminent.

unassuming *adj. Despite her position, she has an unassuming personality:* modest, unpretentious, without airs, unostentatious, natural, plain, unobtrusive, unassertive.

unavailing *adj. Efforts to revive him were unavailing:* futile, unproductive, useless, ineffective, unproductive, ineffectual, fruitless, vain, bootless, unsuccessful.

Ant. effective, useful, productive.

unavoidable *adj. Paying taxes is unavoidable:* inevitable, inescapable, unpreventable; necessary, requisite, compulsory, obligatory, imperative.

unaware *adj. He was unaware of her hostility:* unsuspecting, ignorant, unknowing, unconscious, unapprised, unacquainted.

Ant. aware, conscious, acquainted.

unbalanced *adj.* 1 *The scales are unbalanced. The unbalanced stack of books toppled over:* not balanced, unequal, uneven, unpoised; out of equilibrium, lopsided, leaning, unsteady, unstable. 2 *an unbalanced mind:* mentally disturbed, unsound, deranged, demented, mad; irrational, illogical, unstable, crazed, psychotic, psychopathic, warped.

unbearable *adj. The thought of losing was unbearable:* intolerable, insufferable, unendurable, unthinkable.

unbecoming *adj.* 1 *an unbecoming dress:* unattractive, unappealing, ugly, tasteless, unsightly. 2 *unbecoming conduct:* unsuitable, improper, unsuited, inappropriate, unbefitting, indecorous, unseemly; tasteless, offensive.

unbelieving *adj. The alibi fell on unbelieving ears:* doubting, nonbelieving, skeptical, disbelieving, questioning, incredulous, suspicious, dubious, unconvinced.

Ant. believing, gullible, credulous.

unbending *adj. The captain is an unbending disciplinarian:* rigid, stiff, inflexible, unyielding, severe, firm, strict; obstinate, stubborn, uncompromising.

Ant. soft, easy, flexible, compromising, adaptable.

unbiased *adj. an unbiased jury:* unprejudiced, impartial, neutral, disinterested, open-minded; just, fair, broad-minded, tolerant, unbigoted.

unblemished *adj. an unblemished complexion. an unblemished reputation:* flawless, perfect, immaculate, spotless, pure, unsoiled, unmarred, unsullied.

unbounded *adj. Their joy was unbounded:* boundless, unlimited, unrestrained, unrestricted, absolute, unconstrained, unbridled.

unbroken *adj.* 1 *The eggs remained unbroken: (variously)* uncracked, unshattered, unsmashed, unruptured; whole, intact, complete, entire. 2 *an unbroken series of successes:* continuous, uninterrupted, successive, consecutive; endless, continual.

Ant.1 broken, cracked, smashed, shattered, ruptured. **2** intermittent, interrupted, occasional, disconnected.

unburden v. *I'll unburden you of those packages. The boy unburdened his troubles to me:* relieve, disburden, free, unencumber, disencumber; disclose, confess, reveal, confide.

uncanny adj. **1** *Sherlock Holmes's powers of observation were uncanny:* extraordinary, remarkable, exceptional, astonishing; unbelievable, incredible, marvelous, fantastic, intuitive. **2** *An uncanny silence pervaded the old mansion:* curious, mysterious, strange, unnatural, eerie, spooky.

Ant. **1** average, normal, unexceptional, unremarkable.

uncertain adj. **1** *Where the game will be held is uncertain:* not certain, not sure, unsure; not definite, indefinite, undecided. **2** *The outcome of the election is still uncertain:* indeterminate, unpredictable, not known, undetermined; unclear, doubtful, unsettled, in question, debatable, conjectural. **3** *uncertain weather: uncertain people make poor leaders:* wavering, variable, vacillating, fluctuating, erratic, fitful, irresolute, unsure, hesitant.

Ant. **1, 2** certain, definite. **1** sure, confirmed, decided. **2** predictable, known, clear, settled. **3** firm, resolute, unhesitating.

uncharitable adj. *Scrooge was very uncharitable. He made several uncharitable comments about the musician:* ungenerous, stingy, tight, niggardly, miserly, parsimonious, tightfisted; ungracious, unkind, unfriendly, unsympathetic.

uncivilized adj. **1** *Much of the Roman Empire was uncivilized:* savage, barbaric, barbarous. **2** *What uncivilized manners!:* uncouth, brutish, churlish, rude, boorish, obnoxious, vulgar, uncultivated.

unclad adj. *marble statues of unclad figures:* unclothed, undressed, unrobed, uncovered; nude, naked.

Ant. dressed, clad, clothed, covered.

uncomfortable adj. **1** *These shoes are uncomfortable:* causing discomfort, causing distress, painful, distressful. **2** *I felt uncomfortable with my new classmates:* uneasy, ill at ease, awkward, out of place; edgy, nervous, disquieted, tense; discomfited, troubled, upset.

uncommon adj. **1** *an uncommon occurrence:* unusual, rare, infrequent, unfamiliar, extraordinary, exceptional, unconventional, novel, peculiar, curious. **2** *This rose has an uncommon loveliness:* exceptional, remarkable, outstanding, incomparable, unparal-

leled, notable, extraordinary; superior, matchless, peerless, unmatched.

uncommunicative adj. *She shows her anger by being uncommunicative:* unsociable, reticent, taciturn, close-mouthed, withdrawn, reserved; speechless, silent, quiet, secretive.

Ant. talkative, voluble, loquacious, garrulous, gregarious, expressive.

uncomplimentary adj. *His remarks about you were uncomplimentary:* disapproving, disparaging, unflattering, critical, negative.

uncompromising adj. *a person of uncompromising integrity. If both sides are uncompromising, a strike will result:* firm, strict, rigid, scrupulous; unrelenting, exacting, inflexible, immovable, unbending, unyielding, obdurate.

unconcerned adj. *He seemed unconcerned about the possible danger. Can they be so unconcerned about the child's welfare?:* indifferent, oblivious, insensitive, unaware, nonchalant, uncaring, unsympathetic, unmoved, unresponsive; aloof, cold; untroubled, unperturbed, impervious.

Ant. concerned, mindful, interested, sympathetic, compassionate; anxious, worried, troubled.

unconditional adj. *unconditional surrender:* unqualified, absolute, categorical, complete, utter; downright, outright.

Ant. conditional, provisional, qualified, limited.

unconquerable adj. *an unconquerable fortress:* invincible, undefeatable, insurmountable, invulnerable, impenetrable.

unconscious adj. **1** *The boxer was unconscious for several hours:* without consciousness, senseless, insensate; in a faint, in a coma, comatose, *Informal* out, out cold. **2** *She had an unconscious hostility toward her sister:* unrealized, unsuspecting, unknowing, latent, suppressed.

Ant. **1, 2** conscious. **2** knowing, active.

unconventional adj. *In 1900 automobiles were an unconventional means of transportation. Wearing a football helmet to the movies is unconventional:* uncommon, unusual, unaccustomed, original, unique, irregular; strange, peculiar, odd, outlandish; nonconformist, nonconforming, unorthodox, eccentric, individualistic, bohemian, weird.

uncouth adj. *We were offended by his uncouth manners:* crude, rude, boorish, crass, coarse, gross, uncivil, callow, indelicate, loutish, impolite, ill-bred, ill-mannered, unmannerly, unrefined, uncivilized, uncultivated.

Ant. refined, polite, genteel, well-mannered.

uncover v. 1 *She uncovered her back to get a better tan:* unwrap, undo, unsheathe; undress, disrobe, bare, undrape, unclothe. 2 *A reporter uncovered the plot:* disclose, expose, reveal, lay bare, make known, unmask, unearth.

Ant. 1 cover, wrap, sheathe; dress, clothe. 2 hide, conceal, cloak, suppress.

unctuous adj. *an unctuous and insincere manner:* too smooth, too suave, smug, ingratiating, flattering, sycophantic, obsequious, sanctimonious, oily, slippery, fawning, servile, self-righteous.

Ant. blunt, brusque; open, frank, candid.

uncustomary adj. *He spoke with uncustomary wit:* rare, unaccustomed, uncommon, singular, exceptional; unusual, unexpected, unanticipated; astonishing, incredible.

Ant. normal, customary, usual.

undaunted adj. *We face the future with undaunted spirits:* not discouraged, undismayed, resolute, courageous, unshrinking, valiant, stalwart, intrepid, unflinching, stouthearted, brave, indomitable.

Ant. daunted, discouraged, dismayed, irresolute, cowardly, fearful.

undecided adj. 1 *Our plans are still undecided:* not decided, undetermined, uncertain, unsure, indefinite, unsettled, unresolved, not final, pending, open, tentative. 2 *I'm still undecided about whom to vote for:* unsure, indecisive, of two minds, openminded, fluctuating, wavering, vacillating.

Ant. 1, 2 sure, resolved. 1 decided, determined, certain, definite, settled, final. 2 decisive, certain.

undeniable adj. *an undeniable masterpiece:* unquestionable, indisputable, irrefutable, indubitable, incontrovertible; sure, certain, proven, decisive, conclusive, obvious.

Ant. questionable, debatable, dubious; uncertain, indecisive.

undependable adj. *When it comes to being on time, they're undependable:* not to be depended on, unreliable, untrustworthy, irresponsible, unpredictable; variable, changeable, fickle, capricious.

Ant. dependable, reliable, responsible, predictable.

undercurrent n. 1 *The river has an undercurrent here:* undertow, riptide, crosscurrent. 2 *You could sense the undercurrent of hatred in the room:* underlying attitude, feeling, mood, atmosphere, aura, quality; suggestion, hint, tinge.

underestimate v. *Never underestimate your enemy:* undervalue, underrate, disregard, dismiss, minimize, belittle, depreciate.

Ant. overestimate, overvalue, overrate.

undergo v. *to undergo surgery:* go through, experience; withstand, encounter, endure, sustain, suffer, brave.

Ant. evade, shun, avoid, escape.

underground adj. 1 *The power lines are underground:* buried, belowground, subterranean. 2 *The spy never revealed underground activities:* secret, covert, undercover, clandestine, surreptitious.

underhand Also **underhanded** adj. *He won in an underhand way:* unethical, unscrupulous, unprincipled, devious, sneaky, conniving, crafty; dishonest, crooked.

Ant. open, aboveboard, ethical; legal, honest.

underling n. *The volunteer workers resented being treated like underlings:* menial, flunky, hireling, servant, subordinate, lackey, minion, inferior.

Ant. executive, boss, employer.

undermine v. 1 *The shifting sands undermined the foundation of the beach house:* tunnel under; eat away at, erode, wear away the base of. 2 *He tried to undermine attempts at reform:* subvert, weaken *Informal* torpedo; thwart, foil, neutralize, sabotage.

Ant. 2 reinforce, strengthen, support, forward.

underprivileged adj. *underprivileged children:* disadvantaged, deprived; poor, indigent, impoverished, needy.

Ant. advantaged, privileged, affluent.

underscore v. *Underscore the titles of the books you want. He underscored his words by banging his fist on the table:* underline; stress, emphasize, press home, accent, intensify.

understand v. 1 *We didn't understand what was happening:* comprehend, absorb, make out, fathom, *Informal* get; know, recognize, appreciate, see, perceive, apprehend, realize, grasp. 2 *He understood my letter to be a subtle warning:* interpret, see, read, take. 3 *We understand that you'll be returning next year:* gather, hear, learn, take for granted, assume; appreciate, see the reasons for, accept.

understanding n. 1 *Few people have an understanding of physics:* knowledge, grasp, comprehension, appreciation. 2 *She has great understanding:* sympathy, compassion, appreciation, empathy, sensitivity, insight. 3 *Management has finally reached an understanding with employees:* agreement, pact, concordance, compromise. —adj. 4 *She has understanding parents:* sympathetic, compassionate, responsive, sensitive, tolerant, knowing.

Ant. 1 misunderstanding, incomprehension, ignorance. 2 insensitivity, obtuseness.

4 unsympathetic, uncompassionate, unresponsive, unfeeling, insensitive; strict, stiff.

understudy *n. Her understudy never got a chance to play the role:* stand-by, alternate, substitute, backup.

undertake *v. Who will undertake the job?:* take on, assume, enter upon, tackle, shoulder, commit oneself to, attempt, endeavor, try; commence, begin, start.
Ant. abandon, drop, decline, avoid.

undertaking *n. Building one's own house is a tremendous undertaking:* endeavor, enterprise, project, task, job, commitment, venture.

undertone *n.* 1 *They spoke in undertones:* low tone; whisper, murmur, mumble. 2 *There was an undertone of danger in the air:* undercurrent, feeling, sense, quality, mood, implication, intimation, atmosphere, aura, nuance, suggestion, hint, trace, tinge, scent, flavor.

underweight *adj. The child looks underweight:* gaunt, skinny, scrawny, undernourished, spindly, underfed, emaciated.
Ant. overweight, obese.

underworld *n.* 1 *Most gambling is controlled by the underworld:* criminal element, criminals, organized crime, gangsters, mobsters, *Informal* the mob. 2 *Are sinners doomed to spend eternity in the underworld?:* Hell, Hades, purgatory, limbo, infernal regions.

underwrite *v. Several local businessmen will underwrite the concert season:* subsidize, sponsor, back, support, guarantee; endorse, countersign.

undesirable *adj. an undesirable course of action:* unsavory, offensive, unattractive, objectionable, distasteful, disagreeable, uninviting; unsatisfactory, unacceptable, unsuitable, inadmissible, unwanted, disliked; inappropriate, improper, unbecoming.

undignified *adj. Arriving barefoot was undignified:* lacking dignity, indecorous, inappropriate, unsuitable, inelegant, boorish, unladylike, ungentlemanly, unrefined, improper, tasteless, degrading, shameful, beneath one's dignity.

undisciplined *adj. undisciplined children. The violinist's playing was completely undisciplined:* unrestrained, wayward, obstreperous, uncontrolled; undependable, unreliable, erratic, inconstant, unpredictable; untrained, untaught, unschooled, unpracticed, unfinished.

undisguised *adj. undisguised enthusiasm:* open, unconcealed, unhidden, obvious, evident, unmistakable, manifest, pronounced;

unreserved, wholehearted, complete, thoroughgoing.

undismayed *adj. The Wright brothers were undismayed by their first failures to fly:* not discouraged, not disheartened, undaunted, unabashed; unalarmed, unfrightened, unafraid.

undisputed *adj. Shakespeare's genius is undisputed:* uncontested, not disputed, unchallenged, unquestioned, accepted; indisputable, incontestable, undeniable, admitted, granted, undoubted, irrefutable, beyond question, incontrovertible, acknowledged, unquestionable.

undistinguished *adj. The play was undistinguished:* ordinary, commonplace, mediocre, unexceptional, unremarkable, pedestrian, run-of-the-mill.

undisturbed *adj.* 1 *She remains undisturbed during quarrels:* unruffled, unperturbed, unagitated, unexcited, untroubled, unbothered; composed, tranquil, equable, self-possessed, calm, cool. 2 *Give me an undisturbed hour and I'll finish the work. The papers on the desk must be left undisturbed:* uninterrupted, quiet; untouched, unmoved.
Ant. 1, 2 disturbed. 1 upset, perturbed, agitated, excited, ruffled. 2 interrupted; moved, disordered.

undivided *adj. Give me your undivided attention:* not divided, whole, entire, complete; unanimous, united, unified, unsplit.

undo *v.* 1 *It's impossible to undo the harm you've done:* offset, reverse, cancel, nullify, erase, annul, neutralize, repair, counterbalance, counteract; compensate for, rectify. 2 *Can you undo this knot?:* open, free, unfasten, loose, loosen; *(variously)* disentangle, unknot, unravel, unwrap, unfold, untie, unbind, unlace, disengage, unbutton, unlock, unhook. 3 *The scandal will undo my candidacy:* ruin, destroy, undermine, end, demolish, defeat.
Ant. 1 do, accomplish, realize, manage. 2 fasten, close, tie, knot, button, lock. 3 enhance, help, further.

undoing *n.* 1 *Poor management resulted in the undoing of all we had accomplished:* reversal, cancellation, wiping out, negation, nullification, neutralization, invalidation. 2 *A surprise attack brought about the army's undoing:* ruin, ruination, collapse, downfall, destruction, defeat. 3 *Math was my undoing:* cause of ruin, nemesis, downfall, weakness, Achilles' heel.
Ant. 1 realization, accomplishment, furtherance. 2 victory, success, triumph. 3 strength, strong point, forte.

undoubtedly *adv. You are undoubtedly right:* doubtless, beyond question, without doubt, undeniably, indubitably; certainly, definitely, assuredly, positively, absolutely.

undress v. *The patient undressed in the examination room:* take off one's clothes, disrobe, unclothe, strip; uncover.

Ant. dress, clothe, robe; drape, cover.

undue adj. *You bought that house with undue haste:* excessive, uncalled-for, unwarranted, unnecessary, unjustified, needless; improper, unsuitable, inappropriate, unseemly, indiscreet, unbecoming, objectionable, in bad taste.

Ant. due, proper, suitable, appropriate.

undying adj. *We vowed undying love:* eternal, never-ending, unending, unceasing, unfading, perpetual, everlasting, enduring, abiding, perpetual, permanent, constant, continual, continuing, unrelenting, unfaltering, never-failing; deathless, immortal.

Ant. temporary, impermanent, passing, ephemeral, transitory, transient, fleeting, mortal, dying.

unearth v. **1** *They unearthed a buried pirate chest:* dig up, dredge up, excavate; exhume, disentomb, disinter. **2** *The police have unearthed new information:* discover, uncover, find, ferret out, bring to light, come up with; divulge, disclose, reveal, expose.

Ant. **1** bury. **2** cover up, conceal, hide.

unearthly adj. **1** *an unearthly light in the haunted house:* supernatural, extramundane, ethereal, spectral, ghostly, phantom; incorporeal, disembodied, preternatural, weird, eerie. **2** *What an unearthly time to call!:* strange, unusual, extraordinary, extreme; terrible, horrendous, awful.

Ant. **2** normal, common, ordinary; pleasant, agreeable.

uneasy adj. **1** *I was uneasy about the icy roads:* worried, disturbed, apprehensive, troubled, perturbed. **2** *She felt uneasy with her new in-laws:* ill at ease, awkward, uncomfortable, strained, nervous, on edge, tense, disquieted. **3** *I have an uneasy sensation in my stomach:* upsetting, queasy, unpleasant, uncomfortable, worrying, disquieting.

unemotional adj. *She gave him a quick unemotional greeting:* unfeeling, passionless, indifferent, unresponsive, undemonstrative, cold, cool, remote, reserved, formal.

unemployed adj. *When the factory closed, I was unemployed:* jobless, laid-off, out of work; workless, idle, at leisure, unoccupied.

Ant. working, employed, engaged, busy.

unending adj. *Summer brought an unending series of hot days:* incessant, unceasing, never-ending, perpetual, constant, endless, eternal, permanent, enduring, lasting, ever-

lasting, unremitting, continual, continuous, uninterrupted.

Ant. brief, short, fleeting, momentary, transitory, transient, temporary, passing; sporadic, intermittent.

unenlightened adj. *Some people are unenlightened about sexuality:* uninformed, unknowledgeable, ignorant, unfamiliar with, unlearned, uneducated.

Ant. enlightened, well-informed, knowledgeable, familiar.

unequal adj. **1** *Our salaries are unequal:* not equal, uneven, different, unlike, dissimilar, disparate. **2** *The unequal treatment of minority groups is against the law:* unfair, unjust, not equitable; prejudiced, biased, bigoted.

Ant. **1, 2** equal. **1** even, uniform, alike. **2** fair, just; unprejudiced, unbiased, unbigoted.

unequaled adj. *She grew roses of unequaled beauty:* unsurpassed, unmatched, unparalleled, matchless, incomparable, unrivaled, unexcelled, supreme, paramount, peerless.

unequivocal adj. *My refusal is unequivocal:* decisive, unambiguous, clear, clear-cut, absolute, definite, final; incontestable, indisputable, incontrovertible.

Ant. ambiguous, indecisive, vague, indefinite.

unerring adj. *an unerring ability to spot a fake:* infallible, unfailing, faultless, certain, sure, reliable, constant.

unethical adj. *The lawyer was disbarred for unethical practices:* unprincipled, dishonorable, disreputable, shady, underhand, devious; unfair, unconscionable, dishonest, questionable.

Ant. ethical, principled, honorable, reputable, honest, aboveboard.

uneven adj. **1** *The floor is uneven:* slanted, angled, awry, sloping, tilted; bent, crooked, curved; bumpy, lumpy, jagged. **2** *an uneven fight. The two fighters are uneven in style:* unequal, one-sided, unbalanced, lopsided, ill-matched; dissimilar, different, unlike.

Ant. **1, 2** even. **1** level, flat, straight, smooth. **2** equal, well-balanced; similar, alike.

unexcelled adj. *The beauty of the Taj Mahal is unexcelled:* unsurpassed, supreme, peerless, superior, unequaled, unrivaled, matchless, unmatched, incomparable, unparalleled.

unexpected adj. *an unexpected development:* unanticipated, unlooked-for, unforeseen, unpredicted, startling, astonishing, surprising; undesigned, unplanned, sudden, accidental, unintentional, unintended.

unfailing *adj. He's been an unfailing friend for over twenty years:* dependable, reliable, never-failing, faithful, true, loyal, unwavering, steady, infallible, enduring.

Ant. undependable, unreliable, unfaithful, treacherous, untrue.

unfair *adj. an unfair contest. unfair business practices:* not fair, unjust, not right, inequitable; biased, prejudiced, partisan; unequal, one-sided; unscrupulous, unprincipled, unethical, dishonest, corrupt, dirty, crooked.

unfaithful *adj.* 1 *an unfaithful employee. An unfaithful friend:* disloyal, treacherous, untrustworthy, faithless, falsehearted, deceitful; adulterous, inconstant, untrue, unchaste. 2 *The portrait is unfaithful:* not accurate, inaccurate, erroneous, untrue, false, distorted.

Ant. 1, 2 faithful, true. 1 loyal, trustworthy; constant, chaste. 2 accurate, exact.

unfaltering *adj. He's unfaltering in his belief:* firm, steady, resolute, unwavering, unfailing, steadfast, unswerving, enduring, unflagging, persistent, persevering.

Ant. irresolute, undependable, vacillating.

unfamiliar *adj.* 1 *I'm unfamiliar with classical music:* unacquainted, unconversant, a stranger to, unversed in, ignorant of, inexperienced in, unpracticed in, uninitiated. 2 *This soup has an unfamiliar taste. The artist's name is unfamiliar to most people:* unknown, unusual, strange, curious, novel, exotic, foreign; not well-known, little known.

Ant. 1, 2 familiar. 1 acquainted, well-versed in, knowledgeable, experienced. 2 common, everyday; well-known, known, recognized.

unfavorable *adj. Driving conditions are unfavorable:* not favorable, adverse, poor, unpropitious, inauspicious, bad, disadvantageous, inconvenient, unpromising.

unfinished *adj. The work is still unfinished:* not finished, uncompleted, incomplete, undone, unfulfilled; imperfect, deficient, lacking, wanting, rough, crude.

unfit *adj.* 1 *This water is unfit for drinking:* not fit, unsuited, unsuitable, not suited, inappropriate, not equal to. 2 *He's unfit to run the business:* unqualified, inadequate, incompetent, unprepared, untrained, unskilled, unequipped, ill-equipped, incapable, unready, unequal, unsuited; ineligible.

Ant. 1, 2 fit. 1 suitable, adequate. 2 qualified, competent, capable, able, equipped, prepared; eligible.

unflagging *adj. Her unflagging determina-*

tion is admirable: unfaltering, untiring, tireless, indefatigable, unswerving, steadfast, firm, resolute, undeviating, unwavering, unshaken, indomitable, persevering, constant, firm, staunch, undaunted, enduring, persistent.

Ant. faltering, wavering, flagging, irresolute, half-hearted.

unflinching *adj. unflinching courage:* unshaken, steadfast, unabashed, unfaltering, tenacious, persistent, fearless, indomitable, unhesitating, staunch, stalwart, undaunted, resolute.

Ant. shaken, hesitant, faltering, wavering, irresolute.

unfold *v.* 1 *Unfold the map:* spread out, open up. 2 *The leader began to unfold his plan to his followers:* reveal, make known, disclose, divulge, unveil; set forth, present, tell, explain, describe, recount.

Ant. 1 fold. 2 conceal, hide, keep secret.

unforeseen *adj. an unforeseen snowstorm:* unexpected, unpredicted, unanticipated, unlooked-for, sudden.

Ant. foreseen, expected, anticipated, predicted.

unfortunate *adj. He had an unfortunate career. an unfortunate remark:* unlucky, luckless, hapless, unhappy, ill-fated, unsuccessful, jinxed, unprosperous; regrettable, wretched, sorry, disastrous, woeful, ill-advised, unpropitious, inopportune, untimely, inauspicious.

Ant. fortunate, lucky, happy, felicitous, successful, timely.

unfounded *adj. The rumor proved to be unfounded:* baseless, groundless, without substance, idle; false, untrue, erroneous.

unfriendly *adj. an unfriendly nation. an unfriendly neighbor:* antagonistic, hostile, warlike; disagreeable, unsociable, cold, distant, inhospitable, uncongenial; snobbish, haughty, aloof.

Ant. warm, hospitable, congenial, friendly.

unfruitful *adj. The negotiations were unfruitful:* fruitless, unproductive, unprofitable, unrewarding, unavailing, useless, futile, vain.

Ant. fruitful, productive, useful, rewarding, profitable.

ungainly *adj. I'm too ungainly to be a ballerina:* ungraceful, clumsy, awkward, uncoordinated, stiff, lumbering.

Ant. graceful, lithe, limber, supple.

ungodly *adj.* 1 *His ungodly life was a disgrace to his family:* not religious, godless, impious, blasphemous; wicked, sinful, immoral, depraved, degenerate, dissolute, corrupt, villainous, base, vile. 2 *Informal They* *woke us at an ungodly hour!:* dreadful, awful, horrendous, unacceptable, outrageous, terrible, unreasonable.

Ant. 1 godly, religious, pious, moral, good, virtuous, honorable. 2 acceptable, reasonable.

ungracious *adj. You were most ungracious when we met:* discourteous, rude, ill-mannered, uncivil, churlish, impolite, bad-mannered.

Ant. polite, courteous, gracious.

unguarded *adj.* 1 *an unguarded remark:* indiscreet, imprudent, ill-considered, tactless, careless, unwary; overly candid, too frank. 2 *The unguarded camp was vulnerable to attack:* unprotected, unpatrolled, unwatched; defenseless, undefended.

Ant. 1 discreet, circumspect, cautious. 2 guarded, protected, patrolled, defended.

unhappy *adj.* 1 *Why are you so unhappy?:* not happy, sad, sorrowful, despondent, depressed, dejected, downcast, heavyhearted, gloomy, forlorn, melancholy, dispirited, joyless, crestfallen, woebegone, somber, blue. 2 *Telling the hostess that the pie was "almost perfect" was an unhappy choice of words:* unfortunate, unsuccessful, unwise, imprudent, injudicious, regrettable, infelicitous, poor, bad, unlucky, luckless, inappropriate, awkward.

Ant. 1, 2 happy. 1 cheerful, joyful, joyous, lighthearted, exuberant. 2 fortunate, successful, wise, shrewd, good, wonderful, lucky, favorable; appropriate.

unhealthy *adj.* 1 *He's been unhealthy since childhood:* sickly, sick, infirm, ailing, not well, unwell, in poor health, poorly, unsound; invalid, diseased. 2 *Air pollution is unhealthy:* unhealthful, harmful to health, noxious; hurtful, detrimental, unwholesome, insalubrious. 3 *There's an unhealthy atmosphere of greed throughout the country:* demoralizing, harmful, morally bad, undesirable, destructive, corrupting, contaminating, degrading; hazardous, dangerous, perilous.

Ant. 1–3 healthy. 1 well, sound. 2 healthful, salubrious, wholesome. 3 moral, positive, constructive.

unheralded *adj. an unheralded visitor. The novel is an unheralded masterpiece:* unannounced, unexpected, unanticipated, unforeseen, unlooked-for; unsung, unproclaimed, unrecognized, unpublicized.

unhesitating *adj.* 1 *The sergeant expects unhesitating obedience:* immediate, instantaneous, prompt, without delay. 2 *Their unhesitating support was heartwarming:* unreserved, wholehearted, unflinching, eager.

unholy *adj.* 1 *an unholy alliance between*

gangsters and the police: wicked, evil, ungodly, sinful, depraved, immoral, wicked, heinous, iniquitous, corrupt, dishonest, dishonorable; rotten, base, vile. 2 *The room was an unholy mess:* dreadful, shocking, awful, ungodly, horrendous, outrageous, unreasonable.

Ant. 1 moral, good, virtuous, honest, honorable; godly, religious, pious. 2 pleasant, acceptable, reasonable.

unidentified *adj. The perpetrator of the crime is still unidentified. The cake had a strange unidentified flavor:* unknown, nameless, anonymous, unrecognized; unnamed, unspecified, undesignated, unlabeled.

Ant. known, named, recognized; specified, designated, labeled.

unification *n. the unification of the thirteen American colonies:* uniting, union, consolidation, consolidating, unity, merger, combining, combination, confederation, confederacy, coalition, coalescence, incorporation, amalgamation, fusion.

Ant. separation, division, splitting, disunion.

uniform *n.* 1 *a policeman's uniform:* dress, apparel, attire, costume, garb, array; *(variously)* vestment, habit, livery, regalia, regimentals. —*adj.* 2 *The residents were uniform in their attitude toward strangers:* alike, equal, identical, consistent, consonant, of one mind, conforming, in accord. 3 *The acoustics are uniform throughout the auditorium:* the same, even, unvarying, unvaried, undeviating, unchanging, unaltered, constant, consistent.

Ant. 2, 3 different. 2 unalike, dissimilar, mixed; disagreeing, discordant. 3 uneven, variable, inconsistent, irregular, erratic, deviating.

unify *v. Allegiance to the Crown unifies the British Commonwealth:* unite, combine, join, consolidate, bring together; confederate, federate, incorporate, coalesce, amalgamate, fuse, merge.

Ant. disunite, separate, divide, sever, disband.

unimaginative *adj. Most of the costumes were unimaginative:* uninspired, unoriginal, routine, uncreative, ordinary, prosaic, trite, commonplace, run-of-the-mill, pedestrian, stale, hackneyed, predictable, unexciting, uninteresting, vapid.

Ant. imaginative, original, creative, unusual, different, fanciful.

unimportant *adj. an unimportant job:* not important, inconsequential, insignificant, immaterial, nonessential, negligible, minor, lesser, subordinate, inferior, trivial, trifling, paltry, piddling.

Ant. important, consequential, significant.

uninformed *adj. He was completely uninformed about world affairs:* ignorant, unread, unaware, uninstructed, unknowing, unlearned, unenlightened, uneducated, unconversant.

Ant. informed, knowledgeable, enlightened, well read, educated.

uninhabited *adj. an uninhabited house. an uninhabited island:* unoccupied, unlived in, vacant, empty, untenanted; unpopulated, unpeopled, unsettled, deserted.

Ant. inhabited, occupied; populated, settled.

uninhibited *adj. Only uninhibited people would join a nudist colony. Her uninhibited remarks embarrassed her friends:* unselfconscious, not shy, open; spontaneous, impulsive, impetuous, rash, heedless, unguarded, indiscreet; outspoken, candid, frank, unreserved, straightforward, forthright; reckless, madcap, headstrong, abandoned, free, free-spirited, daring, immodest; unrestrained, unconstrained, unrestricted, unchecked, uncurbed, unbridled, unreined.

Ant. inhibited, self-conscious, shy, bashful, modest; guarded, cautious, careful, discreet; restrained, checked, curbed.

uninspired *adj.* 1 *The audience was left uninspired by the dull speech:* unmoved, unstirred, unimpressed, unaffected, untouched, uninfluenced. 2 *The movie was uninspired:* unimaginative, unoriginal, prosaic, trite, commonplace, stock, pedestrian, hackneyed, predictable, unexciting, uninteresting.

Ant. 1, 2 inspired. 1 moved, stirred, affected, touched, stimulated. 2 imaginative, creative, original, exciting, interesting.

unintelligible *adj. His words were unintelligible:* impossible to understand, incoherent, inarticulate, incomprehensible, illegible; meaningless, baffling, undecipherable.

Ant. intelligible, understandable, coherent, articulate, legible; clear.

unintentional *adj. Any rudeness was unintentional:* accidental, unintended, undesigned, not done purposely, unconscious, inadvertent, unthinking, unwitting.

uninterested *adj. I told him about my trip but he was uninterested:* not interested, not curious, unconcerned, heedless, indifferent; unmindful, listless, uninvolved, uncaring.

Ant. concerned, interested, curious.

uninteresting *adj. Chess strikes me as an uninteresting game:* boring, tiresome, dull,

tedious, uneventful, monotonous, drab, wearisome, insipid, humdrum, vapid, insignificant, ordinary.

uninviting *adj. The house was drab and uninviting:* unappealing, unwelcoming, unalluring, untempting, unattractive, unpleasant, undesirable, disagreeable, distasteful, unappetizing.

union *n.* 1 *The book is a perfect union of humor and seriousness:* combination, mixture, amalgam, amalgamation, joining, blend, merger, unity, uniting, marriage, wedding; fusion, synthesis, unifying, unification. 2 *Representatives from each state hoped to form a more perfect union:* federation, confederation, association, affiliation, alliance, league. 3 *Samuel Gompers was a leader of the cigar-maker's union:* (variously) labor union, trade union, craft union; guild.

Ant. 1 separation, division.

unique *adj. The beauty of the Mona Lisa is unique:* singular, distinctive, one of a kind, incomparable, unrivaled, unparalleled, unequaled, matchless, unmatched, unexcelled, unsurpassed, inimitable, surpassing.

Ant. commonplace, common, ordinary, average, routine, run-of-the-mill.

unit *n.* 1 *The refrigerator needs a new cooling unit. The Hawaiian Islands form one political unit:* part, element, segment, section, component, constituent, member, division; entity, whole, quantity, group, detachment. 2 *A pound is a unit of weight:* measure, measurement, quantity; denomination, entity.

unite *v.* 1 *The school united its music and theater departments:* unify, combine, join, consolidate; confederate, federate, incorporate, coalesce, amalgamate, fuse, merge, couple, blend. 2 *to unite against a tyrant:* join together, join forces, stand together, organize.

Ant. 1 divide, separate, disunite, split, detach.

united *adj.* 1 *The city has a united bus and subway system:* unified, combined, consolidated; incorporated, amalgamated, fused, merged, joined, coupled, blended. 2 *Her parents were united in their insistence that she go to college:* unanimous, of one mind, in agreement.

Ant. 1, 2 divided. 2 split, in disagreement.

unity *n.* 1 *Would national unity be destroyed by stronger state governments? Some Puerto Ricans want unity with the United States while others want complete independence:* oneness, wholeness, entity; unification, consolidation, amalgamation, fusion, merger, joining, federation, confederation, league, union. 2 *The prime minister begged for unity between the warring factions:* accord, peace, harmony, cooperation, unanimity, compatibility.

Ant. 1, 2 disunity. 1 independence, individuality; division, separateness, separation. 2 disagreement, discord, disharmony.

universal *adj. Overpopulation is a universal problem:* worldwide, international, widespread, ubiquitous; general, all-embracing, all-inclusive.

Ant. individual, personal, private, local, parochial, restricted.

unjust *adj. The accusation was unjust:* unfair, wrongful, unjustified, unwarranted, undeserved, unmerited; prejudiced, biased, partisan, unbalanced.

Ant. just, impartial, fair; justified, deserved.

unkempt *adj. The child always looks unkempt:* uncombed, tousled, disheveled, ungroomed; untidy, messy, sloppy, rumpled, disarranged, disordered, slovenly.

Ant. combed, well-groomed, neat, tidy, orderly.

unkind *adj. an unkind remark:* inconsiderate, thoughtless, unfeeling, unsympathetic, insensitive, uncaring, ungracious, uncharitable, ungenerous; mean, nasty, malicious, abusive.

unknown *adj. The poem was written by an unknown author:* anonymous, unidentified, undiscovered, unnamed, nameless, undesignated, undetermined; obscure, unrenowned.

Ant. well-known, celebrated, famous, renowned.

unlawful *adj. Shooting fireworks without a permit is unlawful:* illegal, unauthorized, illicit, unlicensed, against the law, criminal.

Ant. legal, lawful.

unlike *adj. The brothers are completely unlike:* different, unalike, dissimilar, disparate.

Ant. similar, alike, identical.

unlikely *adj.* 1 *He may be right, but it's unlikely:* not likely, improbable, questionable, scarcely conceivable; unpromising, hopeless.

Ant. likely, probable, sure, certain; promising.

unlimited *adj.* 1 *The king has unlimited authority:* limitless, unrestricted, unrestrained, unchecked, uncontrolled; absolute, total, complete, unqualified, all-encompassing, comprehensive. 2 *Life has unlimited possibilities:* endless, limitless, boundless, unbounded, infinite, inexhaustible; vast, immense, huge, immeasurable.

Ant. 1 limited, restricted, constrained; partial. 2 finite, limited; small, little.

unlucky *adj. It was an unlucky day when they met:* ill-fated, hapless, ill-omened, inauspicious, ill-starred, unfortunate, unhappy, star-crossed, jinxed, cursed, luckless, misfortunate.

Ant. happy, auspicious, fortunate.

unmanly *adj.* 1 *The Spartans considered retreat unmanly:* faint-hearted, cowardly, pusillanimous. 2 *The football coach despised ballet as an unmanly pursuit:* effeminate, womanish, sissyish, sissified.

Ant. 1 courageous, brave. 2 masculine, manly, virile.

unmannerly *adj. Who was that unmannerly clod?:* badly behaved, ill-mannered, ill-bred, ungracious, ungentlemanly, unladylike; discourteous, impolite, crude, uncouth, boorish, loutish.

Ant. courteous, polite, gracious, well-bred, mannerly, refined.

unmarried *adj. He remained unmarried:* single, unwed, spouseless, husbandless, wifeless; maiden, spinster; bachelor; divorced, widowed.

Ant. married, wed, *Slang* hitched.

unmask *v. The investigation unmasked the true culprits:* reveal, expose, show, disclose, uncover, discover, unveil, bare, bring to light.

unmatched *adj.* 1 *The necklace is made up of unmatched diamonds:* not matched, unmatching, unlike, differing, not uniform, unequal, dissimilar. 2 *The painting is of unmatched beauty:* matchless, unequaled, unparalleled, peerless, supreme.

Ant. 1 matched, matching, paired, uniform, equal.

unmindful *adj. He's unmindful of his responsibilities:* negligent, derelict, lax, remiss, heedless, unheeding, careless, oblivious, unaware, unconscious, forgetful.

Ant. careful, heedful, aware.

unmistakable *adj. His sincerity was unmistakable:* obvious, evident, manifest, apparent, distinct, conspicuous, undeniable, indisputable, unquestionable.

Ant. vague, faint, unclear.

unmitigated *adj.* 1 *August was a month of unmitigated hot weather:* unrelieved, unalleviated, unabated; persistent, uninterrupted. 2 *He's an unmitigated liar!:* downright, out-and-out, thorough, complete, absolute, unqualified, arrant.

Ant. 1 mitigated, relieved, alleviated, abated, eased; sporadic, intermittent, occasional. 2 partial, incomplete, qualified, limited.

unmoved *adj.* 1 *Mother wants this chair left*

unmoved: not moved, not shifted, left in place. **2** *After debating for hours both sides remained unmoved:* firm, steadfast, unwavering, unswerving, inflexible, undeviating; staunch, determined, resolute, resolved, obstinate, uncompromising, dedicated. **3** *Her sad story left me unmoved:* unaffected, untouched, calm, unstirred, indifferent, undisturbed, unresponsive, unconcerned, uncaring, cold.

Ant. **1** moved, transferred, shifted. **2** wavering, vacillating; flexible, adaptable. **3** moved, touched, stirred, affected, sympathetic.

unnamed *adj. The money was donated from an unnamed source:* anonymous, nameless, undisclosed, unrevealed, unidentified, uncredited, unacknowledged, pseudonymous, undesignated, unspecified, undiscovered.

Ant. known, identified, disclosed.

unnatural *adj.* **1** *an unnatural craving for salty foods:* not natural, abnormal, aberrant, peculiar, freakish, unusual. **2** *Since attending that fancy school she has an unnatural way of talking:* artificial, affected, mannered, stilted, studied, assumed, contrived, phony.

Ant. **1, 2** natural, normal. **1** common, ordinary, typical. **2** unaffected, unpretentious.

unnecessary *adj. Buying the second cake was unnecessary:* not necessary, needless, uncalled-for, dispensable, unessential, unrequired; overmuch, excessive, superfluous.

unnerve *v. Being alone in the woods at night unnerved us:* upset, unsettle, daunt, frighten, scare.

Ant. reassure; steel.

unnoticed *adj.* **1** *The boy slipped out unnoticed:* unseen, unobserved, undiscovered, unperceived; *(variously)* unheard, untasted, not smelled, unfelt. **2** *The lack of dessert went unnoticed:* overlooked, disregarded, unnoted, unheeded.

Ant. **1, 2** noticed. **1** seen, observed, discovered. **2** noted, marked.

unobtrusive *adj. an unobtrusive person:* inconspicuous, unpretentious, modest, humble, unassuming; diffident, reserved, unassertive, retiring.

Ant. conspicuous, prominent, noticeable; pretentious, bold, assertive.

unorganized *adj. These unorganized papers must be sorted:* orderless, unsystematized, unsystematic, random, haphazard, confused, chaotic.

Ant. organized, ordered, systematized, systematic.

unperturbed *adj. Napoleon was unperturbed in the face of defeat:* calm, collected, composed, poised, unruffled, unexcited, unagitated, undisturbed, untroubled, undismayed, coolheaded.

Ant. perturbed, discomposed, upset, disturbed, troubled, dismayed.

unpleasant *adj. an unpleasant taste. an unpleasant man:* disagreeable, nasty, distasteful, offensive; repugnant, obnoxious, objectionable, unlikable, irksome, annoying, vexatious; ill-natured, churlish, ill-humored.

Ant. pleasant, agreeable; likable, goodnatured.

unpredictable *adj. The patient's behavior is unpredictable:* not predictable, not foreseeable, erratic, unstable, uncertain, inconstant, arbitrary, changeable, mercurial, impulsive, capricious, whimsical.

Ant. predictable, constant, undeviating.

unprejudiced *adj. A judge must be unprejudiced:* without prejudice, impartial, objective, unbiased, unbigoted, fair, fairminded, even-handed, uninfluenced, disinterested, open-minded.

Ant. prejudiced, partial, biased, bigoted, unfair.

unpretentious *adj. an unpretentious house:* unassuming, simple, modest, unostentatious, unimposing, humble.

unprincipled *adj. an unprincipled politician:* without principles, unscrupulous, unconscionable, amoral, conscienceless.

unprofessional *adj. unprofessional conduct:* amateurish, unbusinesslike, unworkmanlike; inexperienced, unpracticed, incompetent, sloppy; unethical, negligent.

Ant. professional, businesslike, workmanlike.

unqualified *adj.* **1** *He's completely unqualified for the job:* lacking the qualifications, untrained, uneducated, unskilled, inexperienced, unprepared, ill-equipped. **2** *The play is an unqualified hit:* absolute, total, complete, positive, consummate, utter, downright, thorough, unconditional.

unquestionable *adj. Her integrity is unquestionable:* beyond doubt, undeniable, indisputable, irrefutable, proven, certain, sure, clear, obvious, evident, flawless, faultless, impeccable, irreproachable.

unrealistic *adj. Her plans are unrealistic:* impractical, unreasonable, idealistic, improbable, fanciful, starry-eyed, wild, foolish.

Ant. realistic, sensible, reasonable, practical.

unreasonable *adj.* **1** *It's unreasonable to expect snow in July:* contrary to reason, senseless, irrational, illogical, absurd, farfetched, preposterous, nonsensical. **2** *He's a spoiled, unreasonable young man:* obstinate, headstrong, stubborn, inflexible, unyielding, unbending, pigheaded. **3** *Management considers the union's demands unreasonable:* excessive, extravagant, inordinate, immoderate, unfair, unwarranted, unjustifiable.

Ant. 1–3 reasonable. **1** sensible, logical, plausible, rational. **2** agreeable, open-minded. **3** moderate, restrained, fair, justified, warranted.

unrehearsed *adj. Her talk was unrehearsed:* spontaneous, improvised, extemporaneous, impromptu, off-the-cuff; unplanned, unpremeditated, unprepared, impulsive.

Ant. planned, rehearsed, prepared, studied.

unrelated *adj.* **1** *The two men look alike but are unrelated:* not related, not kin, not kindred; dissimilar, unlike. **2** *Such remarks are unrelated to the matter under discussion:* extraneous, irrelevant, unconnected, nongermane, foreign, unassociated, inapplicable.

Ant. 1, 2 related. **1** kin, akin; similar, like. **2** relevant, pertinent, germane, applicable.

unrelenting *adj. Efforts to find a cure for AIDS are unrelenting:* relentless, unremitting, unrelieved, incessant, ceaseless, unbroken, constant; unswerving, undeviating, unyielding, inflexible, unbending, rigid, adamant, uncompromising, implacable.

unreliable *adj.* **1** *Rumors are always unreliable:* undependable, not to be trusted; questionable, uncertain, fallible. **2** *The new worker was unreliable:* undependable, irresponsible, untrustworthy; changeable, fickle, capricious.

Ant. 1, 2 reliable, dependable. **1** unquestionable, infallible; real, correct, true. **2** responsible, conscientious, trustworthy.

unrepentant *adj. an unrepentant sinner. an unrepentant criminal:* without repenting, uncontrite, not penitent, unexpiated, unatoned; unregenerate, remorseless, hardened, incorrigible.

Ant. repentant, penitent, expiated, atoned; contrite, remorseful.

unresolved *adj. Whether the budget will be increased is still unresolved:* undetermined, unsettled, undecided, unanswered, unsolved; pending, uncertain, speculative.

unrest *n. It was a time of unrest throughout the country:* restlessness, turmoil, ferment, tumult, turbulence, upheaval; discontent, discord, agitation, dissatisfaction, protest, rebellion, disorder, chaos.

Ant. peace, calm, tranquillity.

unrestrained *adj. unrestrained laughter:*
uncontrolled, unrestricted, unchecked, uninhibited, irrepressible, unrepressed, unreserved, unsuppressed, uncurbed, unbridled, ungoverned; unlimited, boundless, inordinate, immoderate, abandoned.

unruly *adj. The child is unruly:* disobedient, obstreperous, willful, unmanageable, ungovernable, undisciplined, uncontrollable, intractable, headstrong, unbridled; rowdy, disorderly, boisterous.

Ant. obedient, well-behaved, well-mannered, manageable, docile, submissive; calm, reserved.

unsatisfactory *adj. The student's work was unsatisfactory:* not satisfactory, unacceptable, unworthy, inept; inadequate, deficient, inferior, poor, unsuitable, inappropriate.

unsavory *adj.* **1** *The food was unsavory:* flat, insipid, tasteless, without savor. **2** *Some people eat sheep's eyes and other unsavory things:* distasteful, unpleasant, unappetizing, unpalatable, nasty, nauseating, disagreeable. **3** *an unsavory reputation:* morally objectionable, bad, tainted.

Ant. 1, 2 savory, appetizing, tasty, agreeable, pleasing. **3** good, moral.

unscathed *adj. He came out of the accident unscathed:* unhurt, uninjured, unharmed, unscratched, untouched, intact.

Ant. hurt, injured, harmed.

unscrupulous *adj. an unscrupulous lawyer:* unprincipled, dishonorable, unethical, immoral, sharp, crooked.

Ant. scrupulous, principled, moral, ethical, honorable, honest.

unseemly *adj. unseemly conduct:* improper, inappropriate, unbecoming, ungentlemanly, unladylike, unsuitable, out of place, undignified, disreputable, tasteless, offensive, distasteful, vulgar, indelicate, incorrect, crude, coarse, rude, discourteous, ill-mannered, boorish, churlish, loutish.

Ant. seemly, proper, appropriate, befitting, becoming, suitable, dignified, tasteful, polite, courteous, mannerly.

unselfish *adj. It was very unselfish of you to help:* selfless, altruistic, generous, munificent, considerate, liberal, open-handed, self-sacrificing, charitable, philanthropic, benevolent, magnanimous.

unsettle *v. The lawyer's questioning unsettled the witness:* perturb, upset, disconcert, confuse, fluster, confound, ruffle, bother, trouble, disturb, agitate, rattle.

unsightly *adj. This room is an unsightly mess:* ugly, unattractive, hideous, obnoxious, offensive, distasteful, repulsive, revolting, sickening.

Ant. attractive, lovely, beautiful, appealing.

unsolicited*adj. an unsolicited gift:* unasked for, unrequested, unsought, unnecessary; voluntary, unforced, spontaneous. *Ant.* requested, sought, solicited.

unsophisticated *adj. an unsophisticated youth:* ingenuous, artless, unworldly, unaffected, unassuming, open, candid, uncontrived; naive, innocent, trusting.

unsound *adj.* 1 *a thin, unsound horse. The doctors judged him to be of unsound mind:* unhealthy, sickly, diseased, crippled, defective, ailing, in poor health, infirm, unfit, invalid; feeble, weak, decrepit; mentally ill, deranged, insane, mad, unbalanced, unhinged. 2 *After the earthquake, the building was unsound:* not solid, shaky, unsteady, weak, unstable; unsafe, hazardous, dangerous, precarious, perilous. 3 *Your reasoning is unsound:* not valid, groundless, weak, fallacious, faulty, incorrect, wrong, illogical, defective, specious, marred, flawed; irrational, foolish, absurd.
Ant. 1–3 sound, strong. 1 healthy, well, fit, in good health, hardy; sane, rational. 2 solid, sturdy; safe, lasting. 3 valid, well-founded, cogent, correct, sensible.

unsparing *adj. She was unsparing of her time:* unstinting, generous, giving, bountiful, munificent, magnanimous, liberal, lavish, abundant, copious, plentiful; unconditional, unqualified.

unspeakable *adj. It was a crime of unspeakable horror:* inexpressible, undescribable, inconceivable, unimaginable, incredible; shocking, fearful, repulsive, repellent, disgusting, loathsome, abhorrent, sickening, revolting, abominable, monstrous.

unspecified *adj. We agreed to meet at some unspecified time in the future:* unnamed, unmentioned, unannounced, undetermined, undesignated, unstipulated; vague, indefinite.

unspoiled *adj.* 1 *The child was charming and unspoiled:* unpampered, not coddled; artless, unaffected, unassuming, unpretentious, open, unself-conscious, unsophisticated, unworldly, uncorrupted. 2 *The wilderness had an unspoiled beauty:* undamaged, unharmed, unimpaired, pristine, perfect; spotless, unmarred, unblemished.

unstable *adj.* 1 *That ladder is too unstable to hold you:* unsteady, unsubstantial, shaky; fragile, frail, weak. 2 *The youth has a very unstable personality:* not constant, changeable, vacillating, shifting, unsteady; erratic, volatile, emotional, mercurial, unpredictable, irrational, insecure, irresponsible.

unsuccessful *adj.* 1 *an unsuccessful attempt:* without success, futile, vain, unavailing, fruitless, unproductive, ineffectual. 2 *No matter what he tried, he was always unsuccessful. an unsuccessful business:* unlucky, unfortunate, thwarted, foiled, baffled; poor, hard up, badly off; unprofitable, unremunerative.
Ant. 1, 2 successful. 1 victorious, winning, triumphant; fruitful, productive, effective. 2 prosperous thriving, flourishing; well-to-do, well-off.

unsuitable *adj. That dress is unsuitable for a wedding:* inappropriate, unbefitting, unfit, unfitting, improper, unsuitable, unbecoming, unseemly, out of keeping, indecorous; unacceptable, inadequate.

unsullied *adj. My reputation is unsullied:* unsoiled, clean, spotless, untainted, untarnished, unblemished, unblackened, uncorrupted, uncontaminated, undefiled.

unsure *adj. She remained unsure about which school to attend:* undecided, unconvinced, uncertain, in a quandary; insecure, unconfident, self-doubting, bashful, shy, timid, reserved.
Ant. self-confident, secure, decisive.

unsurpassed *adj. a poem of unsurpassed beauty:* supreme, consummate, superior, best, peerless, nonpareil, highest, greatest, transcendent, exceptional, unexcelled, incomparable, unparalleled, matchless, unmatched, unequaled, unrivaled.

unsuspecting *adj. The unsuspecting youth was easily cheated:* unsuspicious, unaware; credulous, trusting, overtrustful, gullible, unwary.
Ant. suspicious, cautious, wary.

unswerving *adj. The general had an unswerving devotion to duty:* dedicated, faithful, steadfast, unwavering, undeviating, unflinching, unfaltering, untiring, unflagging, inflexible, uncompromising, resolute, determined, strong, firm, steady.
Ant. wavering, faltering, flagging, irresolute, halfhearted.

unsympathetic *adj. She was unsympathetic about my problem:* unfeeling, indifferent, coldhearted, uncompassionate, uncaring.
Ant. sympathetic, understanding.

untarnished *adj. an untarnished reputation:* spotless, unsoiled, unstained, untainted, unsullied, unblemished, unimpeachable, faultless, flawless, impeccable.
Ant. tarnished, blackened, tainted, sullied, blemished, stained, besmirched, damaged.

unthinkable *adj. To go uninvited would be unthinkable:* out of the question, inconceivable, unimaginable; unjustifiable, unwarranted.

unthinking *adj. an unthinking remark:* thoughtless, inconsiderate, heedless, careless, inadvertent, tactless, insensitive, undiplomatic; mindless, witless, imprudent, negligent.

untidy *adj. an untidy room. untidy people:* messy, disorderly, littered, cluttered, unkempt, chaotic, disarrayed; slovenly, sloppy, disheveled, mussed, rumpled, tousled, bedraggled.

untimely *adj. an untimely visit. an untimely remark:* ill-timed, inconvenient, inopportune; inappropriate, unsuitable, unfitting, unseemly, unbecoming, imprudent, infelicitous.

untiring *adj.* 1 *an untiring runner:* tireless, never tiring, unwearied, fresh. 2 *Your untiring help has been a great blessing:* unflagging, unfaltering, constant, unremitting, unceasing, wholehearted, persevering, staunch, steadfast, resolute, steady, patient, persistent, diligent; devoted, dedicated, earnest.
Ant. 1 tiring, tired, exhausted, fatigued. 2 flagging, wavering, irresolute, fainthearted.

untold *adj.* 1 *The book reveals the hitherto untold story of the incident:* unrevealed, secret, concealed, unknown, suppressed, withheld; unpublished, unreported, undisclosed, unspoken. 2 *The quake left untold thousands homeless:* innumerable, countless, uncounted, numerous; undetermined, incalculable, immeasurable, limitless, endless, infinite.

untroubled *adj. the untroubled days of innocence:* calm, serene, peaceful, tranquil, carefree, easygoing, unbothered, relaxed.
Ant. troubled, disturbed.

untrue *adj.* 1 *That story is untrue:* not true, untruthful, false, fallacious, falsified, made up, fictitious, spurious, fake, fraudulent; incorrect, erroneous, inaccurate. 2 *The queen is believed to be untrue:* unfaithful, faithless, inconstant, adulterous, unchaste; false, perfidious; disloyal.
Ant. 1, 2 true. 1 right, correct, accurate. 2 faithful, constant, chaste, pure, virtuous; loyal, trustworthy, honorable.

untrustworthy *adj. The report is untrustworthy. His friend is untrustworthy:* unreliable, undependable, questionable; unfaithful, disloyal, dishonest, false, untruthful, untrue, devious, deceitful, disreputable, treacherous, irresponsible.

unusual *adj. The shape of this leaf is unusual. a rose of unusual beauty:* singular, rare, exceptional, extraordinary, remarkable, noteworthy; atypical, novel, unique, uncommon, strange, curious, peculiar.
Ant. usual, common, commonplace, ordinary, unremarkable, unexceptional, average, typical, normal.

unvarnished *adj. the unvarnished truth:* plain, frank, bare, naked, candid, honest, straightforward, straight; unembellished, unadorned.

unveil *v.* 1 *The mayor unveiled a new statue in the park:* uncover, unsheathe, uncloak. 2 *The governor unveiled a new tax plan:* disclose, reveal, divulge, make known, announce.
Ant. 1, 2 veil. 1 cover. 2 conceal, hide.

unwarranted *adj. Such criticism was unwarranted:* unjustified, uncalled-for, indefensible, unreasonable, inexcusable, unfounded, groundless.

unwavering *adj. unwavering determination:* unswerving, unfaltering, untiring, unflagging, dedicated, single-minded, unflinching, resolute, determined, steadfast, staunch, strong, firm, persevering, unremitting, persistent, tenacious.

unwelcome *adj.* 1 *Her coolness made us feel unwelcome:* unwanted, rejected, excluded. 2 *an unwelcome task:* disagreeable, unpleasant, distasteful, undesirable, thankless.

unwholesome *adj.* 1 *unwholesome foods:* unhealthy, deleterious, harmful, hurtful, detrimental; noxious, pernicious; dangerous, polluting, contaminating, filthy, foul. 2 *Unwholesome friends lead youth astray:* immoral, corrupting, evil, sinful, wicked, bad, depraved, corrupted, demoralizing.
Ant. 1, 2 wholesome. 1 healthful, healthy, salubrious. 2 moral, edifying.

unwieldy *adj. A heavy ax is too unwieldy for a Boy Scout:* hard to handle, awkward, clumsy, uncomfortable, incommodious, cumbersome, burdensome.

unwilling *adj. I'm unwilling to be transferred:* reluctant, loath, disinclined, unfavorably disposed, averse, against, opposed, resistant, demurring, unenthusiastic.

unwise *adj. Investing all that time would be unwise:* imprudent, improvident, ill-advised, inadvisable, injudicious, unsound, foolish, unintelligent, foolhardy, dumb, stupid.

unwitting *adj. The cab driver became an unwitting accomplice in the bank robbers' getaway:* unknowing, unaware, unintentional, inadvertent; unthinking, unpremeditated, unplanned; unconsenting.
Ant. knowing, voluntary, intentional.

unwonted *adj. He spoke with unwonted*

boldness: unaccustomed, unusual, unfamiliar, rare, uncommon, exceptional.
Ant. accustomed, customary, habitual, typical, usual, normal.

unworldly *adj.* 1 *an unworldly individual:* unsophisticated, naive, innocent, inexperienced; overtrusting, idealistic. 2 *The monk set his mind on unworldly things:* spiritual, holy, sacred, divine, pious, religious, devout, godly, heavenly, transcendental, ethereal, unearthly, immaterial.

unworthy *adj. Such conduct is unworthy:* inappropriate, unbefitting, unfit, improper, unseemly, unsuitable, unacceptable; ignoble, dishonorable, shameful, discreditable, objectionable.
Ant. worthy, honorable, noble, commendable, admirable, praiseworthy; appropriate, fitting, proper.

unwritten *adj. an unwritten law:* unstated, unexpressed, implied, implicit, understood, inferred, tacit, assumed; traditional, customary.

unyielding *adj.* 1 *The mattress was unyielding:* stiff, hard, rigid, unbending, inflexible, unpliable. 2 *He's unyielding in his demands:* unbending, inflexible, unwavering, firm, resolute, determined, uncompromising, unswerving, undeviating, stubborn, obstinate.

upbraid *v. I upbraided him for being late:* reproach, scold, rebuke, reprove, reprimand, censure, chastise, admonish, berate, *Slang* bawl out.
Ant. praise, laud, compliment, command.

upheaval *n.* 1 *The mountain was created by an upheaval millions of years ago: (variously)* upthrust, volcanic eruption, explosion, earthquake, flood; cataclysm, catastrophe. 2 *The war caused an upheaval in many people's lives:* drastic change, disruption, disturbance, tumult, turmoil.

uphill *adj.* 1 *It's an uphill walk:* ascending, rising, upward. 2 *Making a success of the business was an uphill struggle:* difficult, arduous, hard, tough, taxing, toilsome, backbreaking, burdensome.

uphold *v.* 1 *Six pillars upheld the roof:* hold up, support, bear, carry, sustain, brace; elevate, raise. 2 *The President swears to uphold the U. S. Constitution:* support, maintain, preserve, protect, defend; champion, advocate, stand up for; approve, endorse, confirm.

upkeep *n. The upkeep on a big house is ruinous:* maintenance, operating costs; preservation, sustenance, living, support, management.

uplift *v.* 1 *The sermon should uplift your thoughts:* raise, elevate, improve, edify, inspire. —*n.* 2 *Good books can provide moral*

uplift: betterment, elevation, advancement, improvement, enhancement, enrichment, edification.
Ant. 1 degrade, debase. 2 degradation, debasement, lowering.

upper *adj.* 1 *the upper shelves:* top, topmost, high, higher; superior, greater. 2 *He wants to be promoted to the upper ranks:* top, elevated, high, superior, major, important. 3 *She was born in upper Michigan:* northern; inland, further from the sea.

uppermost Also **upmost** *adj.* 1 *The apartment is on the uppermost floor:* highest, top, topmost. 2 *The captain's uppermost concern was the safety of the passengers:* most important, greatest, chief, foremost, major, main, principal, predominant, supreme, leading, prime, primary, first, essential, paramount, highest.
Ant. 1 lowest, bottom. 2 least, last, slightest.

upright *adj.* 1 *We walk in an upright position:* erect, vertical, perpendicular, standing-up. 2 *an upright man:* honest, ethical, honorable, moral, principled, trustworthy, good, just. —*n.* 3 *The porch is supported by uprights:* post, pillar, column, shaft, support, prop, pile, stanchion.
Ant. 1 horizontal, prone, lying down. 2 dishonest, crooked, unethical, dishonorable, unprincipled, untrustworthy, unscrupulous.

uprising *n. Troops quelled the uprising:* rebellion, revolution, revolt, insurrection, insurgence, mutiny; riot, outbreak.

uproar *n. The prime minister's resignation caused an uproar:* state of confusion, clamor, commotion, furor, stir, tumult, turmoil, disturbance, pandemonium.

uproarious *adj.* 1 *an uproarious New Year's Eve party:* full of commotion, tumultuous, riotous, disorderly; raging, stormy, wild, furious; boisterous, noisy, clamorous, loud. 2 *an uproarious comedy:* very funny, hilarious, hysterical, sidesplitting.
Ant. 1 quiet, calm, peaceful, tranquil. 2 sad, tragic, melancholy, gloomy.

uproot *v.* 1 *Uproot the weeds. We must uproot our bad habits:* root out; do away with, cast out, eliminate, exterminate, annihilate. 2 *Floods uprooted many people:* force to move; displace, dislodge.
Ant. 1 plant; establish, form; encourage, further, aid.

upset *v.* 1 *The child upset the glass of milk:* overturn, upend, tip over, topple, turn topsy-turvy, capsize. 2 *Losing the ring upset her:* disturb, distress, trouble, grieve; annoy, bother, worry, perturb, unnerve, discompose, disconcert, agitate, fluster, rattle;

anger, enrage, incense, irk, infuriate, vex. 3 *The rain upset our plans:* change; disorder, confuse, muddle, jumble, mix up. 4 *The home team upset the champions:* defeat a favorite, win against the odds; overthrow. —*adj.* 5 *The upset truck blocked traffic:* overturned, upside-down, upended, upturned, capsized. 6 *The files were so upset no one could find anything:* disorganized, disordered, disorderly, disarranged; chaotic, confused, jumbled, mussed, messy, untidy, topsy-turvy. 7 *Was she upset by my call?:* perturbed, disturbed, distressed, bothered, annoyed, agitated, troubled, worried, grieved, disquieted, unnerved, overwrought, hysterical, angered, enraged, furious, incensed, mad, vexed.

Ant. 1 right. 2 calm, quiet, put at ease, comfort. 3 settle, organize, order, arrange. 6 organized, ordered, orderly; neat, tidy. 7 calmed, quieted, comforted, placated.

upshot *n. The upshot of the matter was that he was asked to resign:* outcome, result, effect, conclusion, final development, consequence; aftermath, aftereffect.

up-to-date *adj. The house has up-to-date features:* modern, up-to-the-minute, contemporary; modish, stylish, trendy.

Ant. out-of-date, passé, dated.

urban *adj urban areas:* city, metropolitan; municipal, civic, heavily populated; citified, cosmopolitan, sophisticated.

urbane *adj. an urbane wit:* suave, elegant, debonair, sophisticated, cosmopolitan, civilized, refined, cultivated, gracious, gallant, genteel.

Ant. crude, coarse, boorish, unrefined, uncultivated, unsophisticated, cloddish, provincial.

urge *v.* 1 *The riders urged their horses up the hill:* drive, goad, prod, spur, push. 2 *She urged members to attend:* beseech, implore, exhort, entreat, request, appeal to, supplicate, importune, press. 3 *The senator urged adoption of the bill:* argue for, advocate, recommend, advise, counsel, champion. —*n.* 4 *We have an urge to visit Africa:* impulse, desire, yearning, craving, hankering, itch, yen, hunger, thirst, passion.

Ant. 1 hinder, hold back, restrain. 2 discourage. 3 oppose.

urgent *adj. The operator said the call was urgent:* pressing, important, requiring immediate attention, compelling, essential, grave, crucial, critical, imperative, necessary, indispensable.

Ant. unnecessary, unimportant, inconsequential, trifling, facetious.

usage *n.* 1 *Usage dictates that the host sit at the head of the table:* custom, tradition, convention, etiquette, practice, good form, normal procedure, habit. 2 *Due to careless usage, the car lasted only two years:* use, treatment, handling; management, control.

use *v.* 1 *Do you know how to use a chain saw? You'll have to use all your strength to open that:* make use of, put to use, operate, employ, work, manipulate, ply, wield; utilize, apply, exercise, exert, resort to, avail oneself of; profit by. 2 *She used all her money for food:* consume, expend, spend; deplete, drain, exhaust; squander, waste. 3 *He complains that she has used him badly:* treat, behave toward, deal with. —*n.* 4 *We've gotten a lot of use from the TV set. The poet is noted for his use of alliteration:* service, serviceability, operation, usefulness, work, function; application, utilization, handling. 5 *What's the use of working so hard? An electronic typewriter would be of great use:* good, value, worth, profit, benefit, advantage, avail; usefulness, service, help.

Ant. 2 save, conserve, preserve. 5 bad, detriment, disadvantage, drawback; obstacle, hindrance.

useful *adj. a useful gadget:* practical, serviceable, functional, utilitarian; helpful, beneficial, worthwhile, effective.

useless *adj. This dull knife is useless. It's useless to speculate what might have been:* of no use, unusable, worthless, unserviceable, unhelpful, ineffectual, impracticable, inadequate, inefficient, incompetent; futile, vain, fruitless, unavailing, unproductive, bootless.

usher *v.* 1 *The mayor ushered the dignitaries through city hall:* escort, guide, show, conduct, convoy, attend, steer, lead. 2 *The rising sun ushered in a new day:* herald, introduce, announce, proclaim; precede, inaugurate, launch.

usual *adj. He spoke with his usual tact. The play had the usual boy-meets-girl plot:* customary, accustomed, expected, familiar, habitual, normal; typical, ordinary, routine, common, commonplace, regular, standard, stock, traditional, conventional, orthodox.

Ant. unusual, uncommon, exceptional, unique, singular, rare, extraordinary, unconventional, unorthodox, novel, fresh.

usurp *v. The duke tried to usurp the throne. He began to usurp his boss's authority:* take unlawfully, steal, appropriate, arrogate; encroach upon, infringe upon.

Ant. give up, surrender, relinquish, renounce.

utilitarian *adj. It's a good utilitarian coat:* useful, practical, serviceable, functional, sensible; usable, beneficial, advantageous.

utilize *v. This machine utilizes solar energy:* use, make use of, employ, put into service, profit by, have recourse to.

utmost Also **uttermost** *adj.* **1** *Secrecy is of the utmost importance:* greatest, maximum, highest; foremost, chief, major, main, principal, predominant, paramount, prime, primary, first, supreme. —*n.* **2** *The ship provided the utmost in luxury:* ultimate, last word, best, acme, zenith, peak.

utopia *n. Retiring to Hawaii is my idea of utopia:* ideal life; perfect place, heaven, paradise, Shangri-la.
Ant. hell, hell on earth.

utter[1] *adj. The house is in utter confusion:* complete, total, absolute, thorough, downright, outright, out-and-out, entire, perfect, unrelieved, unqualified, unmodified, unmitigated.
Ant. moderate, slight, relative, reasonable, limited, qualified.

utter[2] *v. He sat there without uttering a word. Don't utter a word of this to anyone:* speak, say, voice, articulate, vocalize, express; disclose, reveal, divulge, tell; state, proclaim, declare.
Ant. remain silent, keep quiet; keep secret, keep confidential.

utterly *adv. The party was utterly delightful:* thoroughly, entirely, fully, completely, totally, wholly, absolutely, perfectly, extremely.
Ant. partly, partially, somewhat, rather, reasonably, passably.

V

vacancy *n.* **1** *The vacancy between the walls was filled with rubble:* empty space, void, gap, opening, hollow, cavity; emptiness, vacantness. **2** *There's a vacancy on the fifth floor front:* unoccupied place, vacant quarters, room for rent, apartment for rent, house for rent, office for rent, suite for rent. **3** *The personnel department is trying to fill a vacancy:* unfilled position, available job, opening, place.

vacant *adj.* **1** *a vacant apartment:* unoccupied, empty, unused; for rent, for lease, untenanted, tenantless; deserted, uninhabited, abandoned. **2** *He has a great deal of vacant time on his hands:* leisure, unoccupied, free, idle, unemployed. **3** *a vacant stare:* blank, expressionless, uncomprehending; incurious, indifferent, unconcerned, oblivious, apathetic.
Ant. **1, 2** occupied, filled, taken, engaged, full, crowded. **1** rented, leased; inhabited. **2** busy, employed. **3** expressive, comprehending, meaningful, thoughtful; animated, alert, interested, concerned.

vacate *v. We have to vacate these offices:* give up possession of, quit, leave; relinquish, resign, abdicate.
Ant. occupy, take possession of, possess, retain.

vacillate *v.* **1** *He seemed certain yesterday, but today he's vacillating:* waver, be irresolute, hesitate, be doubtful, fluctuate, shilly-shally, hem and haw. **2** *The earthquake caused the house to vacillate:* sway, rock, roll, toss, pitch, oscillate.

vagabond *n. During the depression many became vagabonds:* wanderer, roamer, rover, rambler, wayfarer, itinerant, floater, drifter, nomad; tramp, hobo; vagrant.

vagrant *n. Police kept a close watch on the vagrants:* homeless person; itinerant, floater, wanderer, roamer, rover, vagabond; tramp, hobo; beggar, panhandler.

vague *adj. He was rather vague about his past:* indefinite, inexplicit, unclear, imprecise, undetailed; uncertain, unsettled, undetermined, confused, unsure, fuzzy, hazy, unspecific, unspecified; general, random.
Ant. definite, explicit, precise, specific, detailed.

vain *adj.* **1** *He's very vain about his appearance:* proud, self-satisfied, self-admiring, conceited, vainglorious; pompous, self-important, egotistical, boastful. **2** *The rescuers made a vain attempt to reach the sinking boat:* unsuccessful, unavailing, useless, futile, fruitless, ineffective, profitless; pointless.
Ant. **1** modest, humble; shy, bashful. **2** successful, worthwhile, useful, fruitful, effective.

valedictory *adj.* **1** *The graduation ceremony will end with a valedictory address by the highest-ranking student:* farewell, leave-taking, departing; final, last, conclusive. —*n.* **2** *George Washington's valedictory to* *his troops:* farewell speech; commencement address.

valiant *adj. No knight was more valiant than Sir Lancelot:* courageous, brave, dauntless, intrepid, valorous, bold, fearless, daring, lionhearted, stouthearted; chivalrous, gallant.

Ant. cowardly, craven, afraid, fainthearted.

valid *adj.* 1 *a valid reason for being late. a valid solution to the problem:* acceptable, suitable, proper, applicable, accurate, genuine, sound, well-grounded, well-founded, substantial, realistic, logical, good, compelling. 2 *Such a contract is not valid in this state:* legally binding, legal, lawful, being in effect, legitimate, authentic.

Ant. 1 unacceptable, unsuitable; false, inaccurate; insubstantial, illogical, unrealistic. 2 invalid, void, null, inoperative, illegal, unlawful, unofficial.

validity *n.* 1 *The argument has validity:* soundness, grounds, substance, convincingness, weight; accuracy, truthfulness, authenticity, acceptability, applicability. 2 *The lawyer questioned the validity of the contract:* legality, legal force; authority, authenticity, legitimacy.

Ant. 1 weakness, flaws, inaccuracy. 2 illegality.

valley *n. The town nestled in a valley:* river valley, basin; dell, dale, glade, glen, vale, hollow, dip, ravine, gully, gulch.

Ant. mountain, cliff, butte, ridge, hill, rise.

valor *n. The soldier was decorated for valor:* bravery, courage, heroism, boldness, daring, fortitude.

Ant. cowardice, fear, timidity.

valuable *adj.* 1 *Let me give you some valuable advice:* invaluable, worthwhile, precious, important, priceless, treasured, prized, valued; esteemed, respected; useful, beneficial, helpful, advantageous, profitable, fruitful. 2 *a valuable ring:* costly, expensive, dear, precious, priceless.

Ant. 1 worthless, valueless, unimportant, trivial; useless, pointless, unprofitable, silly, trifling. 2 cheap, inexpensive, worthless.

value *n.* 1 *Mother attaches great value to good manners. A knowledge of marketing is of great value in this job:* merit, worth, importance, significance, esteem, respect, prestige; use, usefulness, benefit, help, advantage, profit. 2 *The ring has a value of $10,000:* worth, monetary worth, face value, market price; cost, charge; appraisal, assessment. 3 **values** *I've never understood his set of values:* ideals, standards, moral code, code of ethics; beliefs. —*v.* 4 *The tax assessor valued the house at $250,000:* assess, assay, appraise, evalu-

ate; count, weigh, judge, reckon, rate. 5 *I value her opinion:* regard highly, prize, respect, treasure, esteem, cherish, revere, appreciate.

Ant. 1 unimportance, insignificance, inferiority; disadvantage, uselessness.

valued *adj. a valued friend:* highly regarded, esteemed, prized, treasured, respected, cherished, revered, appreciated.

vanguard *n.* 1 *The vanguard was sent ahead to clear the woods of enemy snipers:* advance guard, van, front rank, front line, forward troops, foremost division, first line, spearhead. 2 *The vanguard praised the merits of the young painter:* avant-garde, forefront, tastemakers, trendsetters, pacesetters, leaders, trailblazers, innovators.

vanish *v.* 1 *The airplane vanished into the clouds:* disappear, become invisible, be lost to sight, dematerialize. 2 *My anger soon vanished:* disappear, cease, end, die, die out, fade away, evaporate, dissolve.

Ant. 1 appear, loom; materialize. 2 commence, begin, start.

vanity *n.* 1 *There's no excuse for such vanity:* pride, conceit, self-conceit, self-love, self-admiration, self-praise, egotism, vainglory. 2 *The sermon was on the vanity of amassing worldly goods:* worthlessness, uselessness, emptiness, hollowness, folly, futility, delusion.

Ant. 1 self-hate, self-abasement, humility, modesty. 2 value, worth, meaningfulness.

vanquish *v. The army vanquished the rebels:* defeat, conquer, overcome, crush, triumph over, beat, thrash, best, drub, lick, rout, subdue, subjugate, overthrow.

Ant. lose, capitulate, yield, submit.

vapid *adj. a vapid remark:* lifeless, dull, insipid, bland, empty; uninspiring, unsatisfying, colorless, lame, stale, wishy-washy, pointless, meaningless.

Ant. lively, exciting, inspiring, colorful.

vapor *n. A thin coat of vapor was on the windshield:* moisture, mist, dew; haze, fog; steam, smoke, smog.

variable *adj. It was a cloudy day with variable winds:* changeable, changing, shifting, fluctuating, unstable, fitful, fickle, inconstant; unsettled, diverse, uneven, alterable.

Ant. constant, unchanging, steady, invariable, unalterable.

variant *n. The song is a variant of an old folk tune:* variation, different form, modification, alteration, departure.

Ant. origin, pattern, model, source.

variation *n. We need some variation in our daily routine:* variety, change, difference, diversity, modification, departure, variant; discrepancy, divergency, deviation.

Ant. uniformity, sameness, regularity, consistency.

varied *adj. The store carries a varied selection of merchandise:* diversified; diverse, various; assorted, miscellaneous, mixed, heterogeneous, sundry, motley.

Ant. uniform, standardized, homogeneous.

variety *n.* 1 *Variety is the spice of life:* change, diversity, diversification, variation, dissimilarity, nonuniformity. 2 *A variety of objects were on display:* assortment, miscellany, mixture, mélange, multiplicity; hodgepodge, jumble, patchwork, omnium-gatherum. 3 *I like several varieties of apples:* kind, type, sort, classification; class, category, breed, strain, species, genus, division, family.

Ant. 1, 2 sameness, uniformity, homogeneity, standardization.

various *adj.* 1 *We've had various types of cars:* different, sundry, varied, diverse, divers, assorted. 2 *Various people have expressed disagreement with the proposal:* numerous; many, countless, innumerable, myriad; several, some, few.

Ant. 1 same, identical, uniform.

vary *v.* 1 *Let's vary the routine today:* change, alter, diversify, modify. 2 *Television sets vary in price. This marigold varies from the norm in being giant-sized:* differ, be unlike, contrast, fluctuate, alternate; deviate, diverge, depart.

Ant. 1 keep unchanged, standardize. 2 conform, be uniform, be constant, be stable; comply with.

vast *adj. the vast expanse of the Sahara:* extensive, wide, widespread, far-flung, far-reaching, boundless, unbounded, infinite, immeasurable, unlimited, limitless, endless; great, large, big, huge, enormous, prodigious, tremendous, stupendous, gigantic, colossal, titanic; spacious, capacious, voluminous.

Ant. limited, narrow; small, little, modest.

vault[1] *n.* 1 *the vault of the cathedral:* dome, arched roof, arched ceiling, arch; arcade, cupola. 2 *The bank doesn't open its vault until 9 A.M.:* strongroom; wall safe, safe. 3 *The old patrician was buried in the family vault:* burial chamber, mausoleum, crypt, sepulcher, tomb; ossuary, catacomb.

vault[2] *v.* 1 *The boy vaulted the fence:* hurdle, jump, jump over, leap over, spring over, leapfrog, bound; polevault. —*n.* 2 *One vault and I was over the hedge:* jump, leap, spring, bound, hurdle.

vaunt *v. He always vaunts his wealth:* boast about, brag of, gloat over; flaunt, show off, make a display of.

Ant. disparage; conceal, keep quiet about.

veer *v. The car veered to the left:* swerve, wheel, turn, shift, dodge, curve, drift.

vegetation *n. The property was overgrown with vegetation:* plant life, plants, flora; shrubbery, foliage, herbage, leaves, grass, weeds.

vehement *adj. I'm a vehement baseball fan:* ardent, fervent, fervid, intense, fierce, passionate, impassioned, emotional, excited, heated, hotheaded, fiery, enthusiastic, zealous, vigorous, rabid, eager, earnest.

Ant. indifferent, mild, lukewarm, halfhearted, dispassionate.

vehemently *adv. They argued vehemently:* ardently, fervently, intensely, passionately, excitedly, furiously, hotly, strongly, emotionally; enthusiastically, zealously, vigorously, eagerly, earnestly.

Ant. indifferently, feebly, halfheartedly, impassively.

vehicle *n.* 1 *No vehicles are permitted in the park:* conveyance, means of transport, transportation. 2 *Television is a major advertising vehicle:* medium, means, agent, instrument, tool, device.

veil *n.* 1 *A veil of fog covered the valley:* cover, covering, blanket, curtain, screen, mantle. —*v.* 2 *A curtain of smog veiled the sun. The report veiled the facts:* hide, conceal, cover, cloak, mask, screen, envelop; dim; obscure.

Ant. 2 expose, disclose, reveal, divulge; unveil, uncover.

vein *n.* 1 *a vein of coal:* stratum, stria, layer, seam; streak, line, stripe. 3 *The book has a vein of cynicism throughout:* mood, tone, manner, style; character; tendency, inclination, bent, predisposition, propensity, predilection; strain, streak, touch, hint. —*v.* 4 *The dried mud was veined with cracks:* line, streak, mark, marble, stripe, furrow, rib, web.

velocity *n. Some hawks descend with terrific velocity on their prey:* rapidity, swiftness, speed, fleetness; quickness, speediness, celerity, alacrity, expedition.

venal *adj. a venal politician:* bribable, corruptible, corrupt, unprincipled, unscrupulous, dishonest; greedy, rapacious, avaricious, covetous, grasping, mercenary, selfish.

Ant. unbribable, incorruptible, honest; selfless, altruistic.

vendor Also **vender** *n. a hot-dog vendor. The company is the largest vendor of air conditioners in the country:* seller, hawker, peddler, street peddler, huckster; retailer, wholesaler, dealer, merchandiser, supplier; merchant, tradesman.

Ant. buyer, purchaser, customer.

veneer *n.* 1 *The front of the house has a*

stone veneer: facing, façade, outer layer, layer, covering, coat, coating, overlay, sheath, casting, jacket. 2 *Underneath her veneer of haughtiness she's actually very kind:* outward appearance, façade, front, show; mask, pretense.

venerable *adj. a venerable elder of the church:* respected, venerated, revered, esteemed, honored, admired; aged, ancient, hoary.
  Ant. dishonorable, disreputable, dishonored; young, youthful, inexperienced.

venerate *v. He venerated his grandparents:* revere, esteem, respect, honor, admire, idolize, adore, cherish, glorify, treat with deference; worship, hallow.
  Ant. scorn, disdain, dishonor; spurn.

vengeance *n. He swore vengeance for the murder of his brother:* revenge, reprisal, retaliation, retribution; malevolence, ruthlessness.

venial *adj. My sins were venial ones:* forgivable, pardonable, excusable, defensible; slight, minor, trivial, not serious.
  Ant. mortal; unpardonable, unforgivable, inexcusable, indefensible; flagrant.

venom *n.* 1 *The rattlesnake secretes venom through its fangs:* poisonous fluid; toxin. 2 *He spewed out his venom in a series of letters:* hate, hatred, bitterness, ill will, malevolence, maliciousness, malice, animosity, resentment, rancor, spite, spitefulness, acrimony, hostility, enmity, anger, ire.
  Ant. 1 antidote, antitoxin. 2 love, affection, friendliness, kindness, goodwill, benevolence.

venomous *adj.* 1 *Some jellyfish are venomous:* poisonous, noxious, toxic; lethal, deadly, fatal. 2 *Why are some movie reviews so venomous?:* spiteful, malicious, malevolent, resentful, rancorous, hostile, abusive, malign, malignant; caustic, bitter, vicious, cruel.
  Ant. 1 nonpoisonous, nontoxic. 2 friendly, kind, sweet, benevolent, compassionate, magnanimous.

vent *n.* 1 *Smoke poured out of the vent:* opening, outlet, aperture, *(variously)* flue, spout, pipe. 2 *She gave vent to her wrath:* expression, utterance, voice; disclosure, revelation, exposure. —*v.* 3 *This pipe vents smoke from the kitchen:* let out; emit, discharge, release, pour forth, gush, exude, drip, ooze. 4 *He vented his enthusiasm in a series of shouts:* express, communicate, voice, utter, declare; disclose, reveal, divulge.
  Ant. 1 obstruction, closure, stoppage. 3 block, obstruct. 4 suppress, repress, withhold, restrain, check, curb; hide, conceal.

ventilate *v.* 1 *Open the window and ventilate the room:* circulate fresh air, air, air out. 2 *Members are asked not to ventilate club problems:* make widely known, broadcast, circulate, voice, air; discuss, talk about, express.

venture *n.* 1 *Speculating in the commodities market can be a costly venture:* endeavor, undertaking, enterprise, project; adventure, uncertainty. —*v.* 2 *Nothing ventured, nothing gained:* risk, hazard, dare, chance, gamble, wager, undertake, endeavor, attempt, try. 3 *I may venture an opinion:* put forward, offer, proffer, tender, volunteer, hold out. 4 *Don't venture into the jungle without a guide:* travel, go, risk going, plunge.
  Ant. 1 certainty; caution, protection. 2 guarantee; safeguard, protect.

venturesome Also **adventuresome** *adj.* 1 *He's so venturesome he'll try anything:* adventurous, daring, bold, audacious; rash, impulsive, impetuous, reckless; enterprising, ambitious. 2 *Diving for sunken treasure is a venturesome way to make a living:* dangerous, hazardous, risky, perilous, precarious, unsafe; uncertain, insecure, unsure, speculative, ticklish, tricky.
  Ant. 1 cautious, timid, timorous, fearful. 2 safe, certain, sure, reliable, dependable, stable.

veracity *n. I sometimes doubt her veracity:* truthfulness, honesty, integrity, frankness, sincerity, accuracy, verisimilitude.
  Ant. deception, deceit, duplicity, mendacity; lie, falsehood.

verbal *adj. The book gives a good verbal picture of life in China. a verbal agreement:* of words, in words; *(loosely)* oral, spoken, voiced, vocal; unwritten.

verbatim *adv., adj. The witness repeated the conversation verbatim. a verbatim account of what was said:* word for word, exactly, exact, to the letter, literal, literally, faithful, faithfully.

verbiage *n. The speaker bored everyone with verbiage:* wordiness, long-windedness, verbosity, logorrhea, volubility, effusiveness, loquacity.

verbose *adj. The senator is extremely verbose:* wordy, longwinded, voluble, talkative, garrulous, loquacious.
  Ant. terse, concise, succinct.

verdant *adj. the verdant meadows of the park:* green, grassy, leafy, shady; lush, luxuriant.

verdict *n. Has the jury reached a verdict?:* decision, judgment, finding, determination, ruling, adjudication.

verge *n.,* 1 *Guttering was installed around the verge of the roof:* edge, border, margin, rim, skirt, lip; limit, threshold, boundary. —*v.* 2 *The farm verges on the county line:* border, fringe, edge; approach, approximate.

Ant. 1 center, middle, heart, interior.

verify *v. Several witnesses verified his alibi:* confirm, corroborate, substantiate, attest to, prove, establish, sustain; certify, guarantee, testify to, vouch for.

Ant. deny, refute, dispute, contradict, discredit; invalidate.

veritable *adj. She's a veritable gold mine of information:* true, real, genuine, actual, bona fide, absolute, positive.

Ant. supposed, questionable, so-called.

vermin *n. pl.* 1 *The rancher had a rifle to shoot vermin:* varmints, pests. 2 *All sorts of vermin crawled out of the walls of the old house:* pestiferous insects, *(variously)* roaches, lice, fleas, bedbugs, silverfish, centipedes, termites, water bugs.

vernacular *n. I learned formal English but not the vernacular:* common speech, everyday language, slang, colloquial speech, informal speech; lingo, slang, cant, idiom.

Ant. formal speech, educated speech, literary language.

vernal *adj. the vernal equinox. the vernal radiance of her smile:* spring; springlike, fresh, new, green, youthful.

versatile *adj. A handyman has to be versatile. a versatile musician:* having many abilities, many-sided, all-around, multifaceted, many-skilled, handy, adaptable, resourceful; talented, accomplished, proficient, clever, adroit.

Ant. specialized, limited.

verse *n.* 1 *Most of Shakespeare's plays are in verse:* poetry; measure, meter. 2 *The child recited a verse:* little poem, rhyme. 3 *the last verse of the hymn:* stanza, stave, strophe. 4 *a verse from the Book of Job:* Biblical chapter division, passage of Scripture, line of Scripture.

versed *adj. well versed in auto mechanics. The school turns out students versed in the classics:* experienced, practiced, familiar with, acquainted with, conversant with, skilled, skillful, expert, proficient, accomplished, competent, adept; schooled, taught, instructed, well-informed, well-read, learned.

Ant. inexperienced, unpracticed, unfamiliar, unacquainted, unskilled; ignorant, unschooled.

version *n.* 1 *The two men told different versions of the accident:* account, story, interpretation, side. 2 *An up-to-date version of the Romeo and Juliet story:* rendering, adap-

tation, restatement, translation, paraphrase, re-creation.

vertical *adj.* 1 *The cliff rose in a vertical wall from the sea:* perpendicular, upright, sheer. —*n.* 2 *The wall slants 10° from the vertical:* perpendicular, upright position, upright.

Ant. 1, 2 horizontal. 1 slanting, sloping, inclined.

vertigo *n. She felt a touch of vertigo and steadied herself against the wall:* dizziness, lightheadedness, giddiness, unsteadiness, loss of equilibrium; fainting.

verve *n. He played the concerto with tremendous verve:* liveliness, animation, spirit, vivacity, vitality, dash, vigor, energy; gusto, zeal, relish, enthusiasm, eagerness, fervor, passion, fire.

Ant. apathy, lethargy, languor, sluggishness; indifference, spiritlessness, halfheartedness.

very *adv.* 1 *a very large crowd. We were very impressed by her ability:* extremely, exceedingly, especially, unusually, exceptionally, uncommonly, abnormally, terribly, awfully; intensely, deeply, profoundly; definitely, certainly, assuredly, decidedly, emphatically; really, truly, veritably; remarkably, notably, strikingly, markedly, eminently; greatly, vastly, hugely, immensely, tremendously; most, much, quite; completely, totally, entirely, thoroughly, abundantly, surpassingly. 2 *The two friends were born on the very same day:* exactly, precisely; actually, really. —*adj.* 3 *The very thought of eating was repugnant:* mere, sheer, bare, plain, simple, pure. 4 *This is the very thing I was looking for:* precise, exact, specific, particular, perfect, appropriate, suitable, fitting; necessary, essential.

vessel *n.* 1 *The Titanic was an ill-fated vessel:* ship, boat, craft; *(variously)* liner, steamship, steamboat, ocean liner, packet, freighter, tanker, collier, tugboat, barge, scow, houseboat, ferryboat, trawler, whaler, sailboat, cruiser, yacht. 2 *Cook the meat in a large vessel:* receptacle, container; *(variously)* pot, bowl, jug, crock, jar, vase, tub, vat, barrel, keg, cask, butt, caldron; glass, tumbler, cup, mug, carafe, flagon, goblet, beaker, tankard, decanter, flask.

vest *n.* 1 *Is the vest included with the suit?:* waistcoat; *Historical* jerkin, doublet. —*v.* 2 *The bishop was vested with ceremonial robes:* dress, robe, attire, clothe, garb, apparel, array, deck out, fit out, drape. 3 *Most of the authority is vested in the board of directors:* place in control of, put into the hands of.

Ant. 2 divest, strip, disrobe, unclothe.

vested *adj. Each country has vested rights to*

the waters off its shores: permanent, established, fixed, settled, guaranteed, inalienable, absolute.

vestibule *n. I waited in the vestibule:* entrance hall, entrance way, foyer, entry, lobby, antechamber, anteroom, waiting room; hall, hallway, corridor, passage, passageway.

vestige *n. The ring was my last vestige of bygone wealth:* trace, remnant, sign, token, evidence, relic; memento, souvenir.

vestments *n. pl. the king's royal vestments:* ritual garments, official attire, raiment, apparel, dress, garb, costume, outfit, regalia, clothing, clothes, livery, uniform, gear, trappings, accoutrements.

veteran *n.* 1 *The baseball veteran coached young players:* experienced hand, expert, campaigner, *Informal* old-timer, vet. 2 *The American Legion is made up of veterans:* war veteran, ex-serviceman, ex-soldier, *Informal* vet. —*adj.* 3 *a veteran bookkeeper:* experienced, seasoned, long-practiced.
Ant. 1, 3 apprentice, novice, neophyte, tyro. 1 beginner. 2 recruit.

veto *v.* 1 *The president vetoed the proposal:* reject, turn down, deny; negate, nullify, void, forbid, disallow, prohibit. —*n.* 2 *The mayor threatened to use her veto over the proposal:* rejection, refusal, denial, disallowing, prohibition.
Ant. 1 ratify, sign into law, approve, endorse, sanction. 2 ratification, signing, upproval, endorsement, sanction.

vex *v. Nothing vexes me more than your constant criticism:* annoy, irritate, nettle, pique, exasperate, anger, irk, rile, miff, displease; pester, bother, torment, gall, harass, plague; trouble, distress, disturb, upset.
Ant. please, delight, gratify, satisfy; calm, soothe, placate, appease.

viable *adj.* 1 *A fetus is considered viable at six months. No crops are viable in this soil:* capable of independent life, able to live, capable of growing. 2 *Is the plan viable?:* workable, practical, practicable, feasible, usable, applicable, adaptable.
Ant. 1, 2 nonviable. 2 unviable, impractical, unworkable, unusable.

vibrant *adj.* 1 *The leaves were vibrant in the breeze:* fluttering, vibrating, quivering, pulsing. 2 *vibrant colors:* bright, brilliant, vivid, colorful, intense, deep; florid, loud, glowing, shimmering, glittering, luminous, lustrous, radiant. 3 *the vibrant sounds of a violin:* resonant, reverberant, resounding, sonorous, deep-toned; quivering, pealing, ringing. 4 *She was charming and vibrant:* vivacious, lively, vital, animated, spirited;

electrifying, thrilling, energetic, forceful, eager, enthusiastic, ardent, fervent.
Ant. 1 still. 2 dull, drab, pale, soft. 3 shrill, piercing, screeching. 4 listless, sluggish, phlegmatic, spiritless.

vibrate *v. The house vibrates when a truck goes by:* reverberate, quiver, quaver, quake, tremble, flutter, waver; swing, oscillate, undulate, pendulate; palpitate, throb, pulsate, beat, ripple.

vibration *n. When the machinery is running you can feel the vibration in the floor:* tremor, quiver, quivering, quake, quaking, trembling, throbbing.

vicarious *adj. It gave me a vicarious thrill to hear about her trip:* secondhand, indirect, surrogate, sympathetic; imagined, fantasized.
Ant. direct, personal, on-the-spot.

vice *n.* 1 *The police must clean up vice in the city:* sexual immorality, debauchery, depravity, corruption, iniquity, wickedness, wantonness, profligacy, degeneracy, licentiousness. 2 *Gossiping is his only vice:* fault, shortcoming, failing, flaw, imperfection, blemish, defect, frailty, weakness.
Ant. 1 virtue, morality. 2 good point, strong point, gift, talent, forte.

vicinity *n. The store is somewhere in the vicinity of 1st and Main:* proximity, neighborhood, region, area, surroundings, precincts.

vicious *adj.* 1 *a vicious dog. He's in a vicious temper this morning:* ferocious, savage, fierce; dangerous, untamed, predatory, bloodthirsty; cruel, brutal, barbarous, ill-humored, ill-tempered, ill-natured, sullen, surly, churlish. 2 *the most vicious crime of the century:* wicked, evil, atrocious, heinous, monstrous, villainous, fiendish, inhuman, foul, gross, base, vile, terrible, awful, bad, nasty, depraved, abominable, abhorrent, horrid, shocking, diabolical, hellish. 3 *He made up a vicious story about me:* spiteful, malicious, rancorous, mean, nasty, malevolent, venomous, vindictive, hateful.
Ant. 1 tame, friendly, playful, good-humored, good-natured. 2 moral, virtuous, good, noble. 3 kind, kindly, complimentary, laudatory.

victim *n.* 1 *The fire claimed 43 victims:* fatality, dead; casualty, injured, wounded. 2 *One victim was swindled out of her life savings:* quarry, prey, target, dupe, patsy, innocent; butt, scapegoat.
Ant. 2 offender, culprit.

victor *n. The victors won by two points:* winner; champion, medalist, prizewinner; conqueror, vanquisher.

victorious *adj. The victorious team cele-*

brated: winning, triumphant, successful, champion, championship, prizewinning; vanquishing, conquering.

Ant. defeated, beaten, bested, vanquished.

victory *n. Each candidate claimed victory in the election:* triumph, conquest, success, superiority, supremacy, ascendancy.

Ant. defeat, loss, failure.

victuals *n. We laid in enough victuals to last a month:* supplies, stores, provisions, groceries, provender, rations, foodstuffs; food, edibles, comestibles, grub, chow.

vie *v. The two teams are vying for the championship:* compete, contest, contend, struggle, strive, challenge, fight.

Ant. cooperate, share.

view *n.* 1 *The tourists crowded closer to get a view of the painting:* look, glimpse, glance, peek, gaze, sight. 2 *Finally the ship came into view:* range of vision, vision, sight, ken. 3 *What a beautiful view!:* vista, outlook, scene, scenery, panorama, prospect, perspective. 4 *In the mayor's view the budget must be increased:* opinion, notion, feeling, sentiment, attitude, belief, conviction, thought, judgment. —*v.* 5 *Thousands viewed the parade. Have you viewed the stamp collection?:* watch, see, look at, witness, observe, behold, eye, take in, scan, glance at, glimpse; gaze at, survey, inspect, examine, scrutinize, study, pore over. 6 *Experts view the situation with alarm:* regard, consider, perceive, judge.

viewpoint *n. Try to consider food prices from the farmer's viewpoint:* perspective, standpoint, attitude, position, point of view, angle, slant, vantage; opinion, conviction, belief, sentiment.

vigilance *n. Eternal vigilance is the price of liberty:* watchfulness, alertness, attention, heedfulness, heed, concern; carefulness; caution, cautiousness, prudence, forethought.

Ant. negligence, neglect, carelessness, unwariness.

vigilant *adj. The guards must be vigilant:* alert, on the alert, watchful, wide-awake, attentive, heedful, observant; careful, cautious, prudent, guarded, circumspect, wary, chary, on guard.

Ant. negligent, lax, careless, unmindful.

vigor *n.* 1 *She plays with great vigor:* energy, vitality, drive, verve, spirit, vim, pep; strength, force, might, hardiness; haleness, stamina. 2 *He presented his ideas with vigor:* forcefulness, animation, enthusiasm, verve, vim, spirit, liveliness, vivacity; ardor, fervor, zeal, fire, vehemence, intensity, passion.

Ant. 1, 2 lethargy, apathy, torpor. 2 calmness, serenity.

vigorous *adj. The forest ranger was a vigorous man:* energetic, active, dynamic, forceful, vital, spirited, ardent; strong, powerful, sturdy, virile, robust, hale, hardy; bold, assertive, lively.

Ant. lethargic, indolent, torpid; weak, feeble, frail.

vile *adj.* 1 *a vile odor:* disgusting, offensive, revolting, repugnant, repulsive, repellent, nasty, foul, objectionable, abhorrent, loathsome, unpleasant, bad, awful. 2 *a vile crime:* vicious, sordid, base, low, mean, ignoble; wicked, evil, sinful, iniquitous, heinous, abominable, loathsome, ugly, shocking, contemptible, despicable, beastly, villainous, hateful, detestable; immoral, depraved, disgraceful, degrading, humiliating. 3 *There's no excuse for using vile language!:* vulgar, gross, coarse, filthy, smutty, obscene, foulmouthed.

Ant. 1 pleasant, agreeable, attractive, appealing. 2 honorable, noble, sublime, admirable; moral, righteous. 3 polite, delicate, chaste.

village *n. The village has a general store:* small town, hamlet, burg, rural community, burg.

Ant. city, metropolis, metropolitan area.

villain *n. The villain ran off with all my money:* wicked person, scoundrel, rogue, knave, rotter, cad, blackguard, cur; evildoer, malefactor, miscreant, transgressor.

Ant. hero; gentleman.

vim *n.* 1 *How can you be so full of vim early in the morning?:* pep, vigor, energy, vitality, zip, animation, liveliness, vivacity, verve. 2 *The team with the most vim will win:* enthusiasm, spirit, zeal, fervor, ardor, intensity, fire, passion.

Ant. 1, 2 lethargy, apathy, torpor.

vindicate *v.* 1 *The suspect is sure the jury will vindicate him:* exonerate, clear, absolve, acquit, excuse, exculpate. 2 *Her speech vindicated our right to go on strike:* uphold, support, defend, champion, advocate, maintain, assert; justify, corroborate, substantiate.

Ant. 1 blame, accuse, convict. 2 contradict, oppose, refute.

vindictive *adj. He was fired and is vindictive toward his old boss:* vengeful, revengeful, avenging, punitive, retaliative, retaliatory, unforgiving, spiteful, bitter, malicious, malign, malevolent.

Ant. forgiving, relenting, magnanimous.

vintage *n.* 1 *It's a marvelous old lamp of 1890 vintage:* date, period, era, epoch. —*adj.* 2 *This was a vintage year for good*

movies: choice, prime, outstanding, fine, superior, excellent, great, sterling, prize. **3** *a vintage car:* antique; ancient, old, old-fashioned.
Ant. **2** bad, inferior. **3** new, modern.

violate *v.* **1** *The actress violated the terms of her contract:* break, disobey, infringe, contravene, transgress, trespass, encroach upon. **2** *The revolutionaries violated the flag by tearing it down:* profane, desecrate, defile, commit sacrilege, blaspheme, dishonor; abuse, rape, ravish.
Ant. **1, 2** respect, honor. **1** obey, uphold. **2** protect, defend.

violation *n.* *Listening to another's telephone conversation is a violation of privacy:* breach, infringement, infraction, transgression, trespass, encroachment; nonobservance; dishonoring, defilement, desecration, sacrilege.
Ant. compliance, honoring, upholding.

violence *n.* **1** *The violence of the hurricane caused widespread damage:* force, might, power, impact; fury, ferocity, fierceness, intensity. **2** *The violence of the murder shocked everyone:* physical force, brutality, bloodthirstiness, ferocity, ferociousness, savagery.
Ant. **1** mildness, calmness. **2** gentleness, tenderness.

violent *adj.* **1** *a violent earthquake:* forceful, strong, intense, severe, furious, fierce. **2** *a violent temper. The patient became violent:* tempestuous, vehement, fierce, furious, ferocious, fiery, hot, passionate, raging, explosive, uncontrollable, ungovernable, unruly, savage, murderous; wild, insane, maniacal, berserk. **3** *The rebel leader died a violent death:* resulting from the use of force, cruel, brutal.
Ant. **1** mild, weak, feeble. **2** gentle, calm, cool, quiet, serene, tranquil; sane, rational. **3** peaceful.

virgin *n.* **1** *The virgin vowed she would never marry:* maiden, maid; damsel, lass, girl. —*adj.* **2** *a tract of virgin forest. virgin wool:* unused, untouched, unpolluted, unsullied; pure, pristine, undefiled, chaste.

virile *adj.* *a big, virile man:* manly, masculine; vigorous, forceful, masterful, strong, powerful, muscular, robust, hardy, strapping; courageous, brave, stouthearted, bold, fearless, stalwart, valiant; lusty, potent, capable of fathering children.
Ant. effeminate, sissified, unmanly, womanish, feminine; impotent, sterile.

virtual *adj.* *His tender note was a virtual declaration of love:* tacit, implied, indirect, implicit; practical, substantial.
Ant. explicit, direct, expressed.

virtually *adv.* *With the boss out sick, the bookkeeper is virtually in charge:* substantially, practically, in essence, essentially, to all intents and purposes, for the most part, for all practical purposes.

virtue *n.* **1** *Is virtue its own reward?:* moral goodness, morality, goodness, righteousness, uprightness, honor, honesty, integrity, probity. **2** *Honesty is but one of her virtues. Low operating cost is one of the car's virtues:* moral quality, moral principle, strength, principle; benefit, advantage, value, reward, good point. **3** *The queen's virtue is unquestioned:* chastity, virginity, innocence, purity, modesty; good behavior, decency.
Ant. **1** vice, wickedness, evil, sinfulness, immorality, corruption. **2** weakness, weak point, frailty, failing, fault; disadvantage, drawback. **3** promiscuousness, promiscuity.

virtuoso *n.* *a violin virtuoso:* expert, master, master hand, genius, artiste, prodigy.

virtuous *adj.* **1** *He leads a virtuous life:* morally good, moral, good, righteous, upright, honorable, high-principled, exemplary. **2** *Delilah was not a virtuous woman:* chaste, pure, virginal, innocent, continent, unsullied, modest, decent.
Ant. **1** wicked, evil, sinful, immoral, dishonorable, corrupt. **2** unchaste, promiscuous, loose, impure.

virus *n.* *The disease is caused by a virus:* microorganism; (*loosely*) germ, microbe, *Slang* bug.

visage *n.* *She has a cheerful visage:* face, features, countenance; look, aspect, mien, air.

viscera *n. pl.* *Ancient priests foretold the future by examining an animal's viscera:* intestines, bowels, insides, guts, entrails, *Slang* innards.

viscous *adj.* *Molasses is a viscous liquid:* thick, viscid, sticky, syrupy, gummy, glutinous.

visibility *n.* **1** *The orange jacket gave the hunter high visibility:* conspicuousness, prominence, discernibleness, clarity, perceptibility, distinctness. **2** *Because of fog, the visibility is only 200 feet:* range of view, reach of sight; ceiling.

visible *adj.* **1** *The house was visible across the valley:* observable, perceivable, perceptible, discernible, seeable, in sight, in view. **2** *Her dissatisfaction was visible. He had no visible means of support:* plain, manifest, unmistakable, revealed, glaring, patent, conspicuous, marked; obvious, noticeable, evident, apparent.

Ant. 1, 2 invisible, imperceptible, indiscernible, unapparent; hidden, concealed.

vision *n.* 1 *With such poor vision she needs glasses:* eyesight, sight; perception, discernment. 2 *Urban planning requires great vision:* foresight, imagination. 3 *He has a vision of what the business will be like 20 years from now:* mental image, concept, conception, idea, notion; dream, daydream, fantasy, illusion. 4 *The saint saw a vision of the Virgin Mary:* apparition, supernatural appearance, materialization, revelation.

Ant. 1 blindness. 2 hindsight; shortsightedness. 3 reality, fact.

visionary *adj.* 1 *Is "peace on earth" just a visionary idea?:* impractical, idealistic, utopian; unreal, imaginary, insubstantial, illusory, fanciful, unfounded. —*n.* 2 *Columbus was a visionary who made the world accept his dream:* speculative thinker; dreamer, daydreamer, idealist, utopian.

Ant. 1 practical, pragmatic, realistic, hardheaded; real, actual.

visit *v.* 1 *We visited our aunt:* pay a visit to, call on, drop in on, look in on; be a guest of, sojourn at, stay with, go to see. —*n.* 2 *The neighbors dropped in for a short visit:* stay, call; sojourn.

visitor *n. We're entertaining out-of-town visitors:* caller, guest, house guest, company; sojourner, transient; tourist, vacationer, sightseer, traveler.

vista *n. a vista of the distant mountains:* view, scene, picture, perspective, outlook; scenery, landscape, panorama; prospect, vision.

visualize *v. I can't visualize the coat as you describe it:* envision, imagine, picture, conceive of; image, fancy, daydream of.

vital *adj.* 1 *The patient's pulse and other vital signs are weak:* life, living, animate, vivifying; alive, live, existing. 2 *She's one of the most vital people in the organization:* lively, energetic, animated, vibrant, dynamic, vigorous, spirited. 3 *This is the most vital issue before Congress:* important, significant, critical, crucial, urgent, pressing; serious; essential, necessary, indispensable, requisite.

Ant. 2 lethargic, apathetic, phlegmatic, uninvolved. 3 unimportant, insignificant, trivial, trifling; nonessential, unnecessary.

vitality *n. Good nutrition will improve your vitality:* strength; energy, vigor, pep, vim; animation, enthusiasm, vivacity, liveliness, exuberance, zest, zeal, verve.

Ant. lethargy, torpor, listlessness, apathy.

vitriolic *adj. The critic is famous for his vitriolic reviews:* caustic, acid, acerbic, cutting,

biting, scathing, withering; abusive, nasty, sarcastic, sardonic.

Ant. kind, sympathetic, compassionate; mild.

vituperation *n. Her mistake hardly merited so much vituperation:* abuse, invective, scolding, denunciation, revilement, scurrility, castigation, tirade.

Ant. praise, acclaim, flattery.

vivacious *adj. The vivacious girl made a good cheerleader:* lively, buoyant, full of life, animated, effervescent, bubbling, spirited, active; merry, cheerful, cheery, sunny, convivial.

Ant. lifeless, languid, spiritless, lethargic, listless; somber, melancholy, sad.

vivid *adj.* 1 *a vivid red:* bright, intense, brilliant, strong, rich; distinct, conspicuous, garish, loud, florid, colorful; shining, shiny, radiant, luminous, luminescent, glowing, resplendent. 2 *a vivid story. a vivid imagination:* lifelike; true-life, realistic, graphic, descriptive, dramatic, pictorial, moving, stirring; lively, energetic, vigorous. 3 *The tall actress made a vivid impression. The professor has a vivid memory:* striking, strong, powerful, remarkable, impressive; clear, distinct, definite.

Ant. 1–3 dull, pale, drab, vague; weak, faint, dim. 1 pastel; somber. 3 average, unremarkable, routine.

vocabulary *n. the vocabulary of skiing:* lexicon, word stock; language, vernacular, lingo, jargon, argot, cant, slang, dialect, terminology, idiom.

vocal *adj.* 1 *The teacher gives a lot of vocal encouragement:* of the voice; oral, spoken, voiced, vocalized, uttered, articulated. 2 *I prefer symphonies to vocal music:* sung, for singing; lyric, choral, operatic. 3 *She was extremely vocal about the plan:* outspoken, plainspoken, blunt, frank, forthright, candid, direct, voluble.

Ant. 1 written; unspoken, unsaid. 2 instrumental. 3 reserved, reticent.

vocalize *v. It would be better if she vocalized her fears:* put into words, utter, speak, say, express, articulate, air, vent, ventilate.

Ant. suppress, say nothing of, leave unsaid, hush, keep secret.

vocation *n. Nursing is a satisfying vocation:* calling, profession, field, career, line, pursuit, lifework; line of work, occupation, business, trade, job, employment.

Ant. avocation, hobby, leisure pursuit.

vociferous *adj.* 1 *a vociferous group of boys:* loud, shouting, loud-voiced, clamorous, noisy, boisterous. 2 *She was vociferous in criticizing my plan:* strident, blatant; importunate, vehement; vocal, outspoken.

Ant. **1** quiet. **2** reticent, soft-spoken, subdued.

vogue *n.* **1** *Big sunglasses are the vogue this summer:* fashion, style, mode; rage, fad, trend, craze, the latest thing; custom, practice. **2** *That old movie had a great vogue in its day:* popularity, acceptance, currency.

voice *n.* **1** *All that shouting caused him to lose his voice. a deep voice:* vocal sound, speech, power of speech; mode of speaking, tone, intonation, modulation. **2** *Will the club members have a voice in choosing the speakers? the voice of the people:* vote, say, role, part, participation, representation; will, desire, opinion, preference. —*v.* **3** *Some people voice both r's in the word "library":* pronounce, articulate, enunciate, vocalize, utter, speak. **4** *Please voice any objections you have now:* state, express, declare, proclaim, communicate, utter, say, air, vent.
Ant. **1** muteness, speechlessness, voicelessness. **4** keep silent, be quiet; stifle, suppress.

void *adj.* **1** *The book was void of meaning. The street was void of people:* devoid, empty, barren, lacking, wanting; vacant, bare, destitute, clear, free, emptied. **2** *That contract is void:* invalid, not legally binding, not in force, inoperative, null. —*n.* **3** *At one time outer space was believed to be a complete void:* empty space, emptiness, vacuum, vacuity, blank. *v.* **4** *The tanker voided oil from its hold:* discharge, evacuate, empty, emit, eject, purge, pass, exhaust. **5** *Both parties want to void the agreement:* invalidate, revoke, cancel, nullify, annul, repeal, reverse, rescind.
Ant. **1** full, filled, fraught; jammed, packed. **2** valid, binding, enforceable. **5** validate, reiterate, strengthen.

volatile *adj.* **1** *volatile liquids:* evaporating quickly, evaporable, vaporizing, vaporous. **2** *The situation in the Middle East is volatile:* explosive, unstable, unsettled. **3** *Richard is too volatile to stick with one job:* changeable, erratic, unstable, variable, unsteady, fitful, unpredictable, capricious, mercurial, temperamental, moody, reckless, rash.
Ant. **1–3** stable. **3** consistent, steady, dependable, resolute, determined, coolheaded.

volition *n. If you decide to join us it must be of your own volition:* free will, will, choosing, choice, discretion, option.
Ant. coercion, compulsion, duress, force.

volley *n. a volley of shots. a volley of criticism:* salvo, fusillade, barrage, discharge; outburst, burst, shower, outpouring.

volume *n.* **1** *The box has a volume of one hundred cubic feet:* cubic content, capacity; measure, size, dimensions, magnitude, extent, vastness. **2** *The post office handles a tremendous volume of mail:* quantity, mass, amount, aggregate. **3** *a volume of poetry:* book, monograph, quarto, folio; tome. **4** *Please turn down the volume on that radio:* loudness, sound, amplification.

voluminous *adj. He carries on a voluminous correspondence:* of great volume, large, extensive; copious, ample, sizable, massive.
Ant. small, minimal, slight, sparse.

voluntary *adj.* **1** *The hospital is supported by voluntary contributions:* free-will, optional, volunteered, discretionary, noncompulsory, unforced. **2** *Winking is a voluntary muscular action:* deliberate, done consciously, intentional, intended, willed.
Ant. **1** forced, compulsory. **2** involuntary, instinctive, unconscious, automatic.

volunteer *n.* **1** *Students work as volunteers at the hospital:* charity worker, unpaid worker; nonprofessional. **2** *Do volunteers make good soldiers?:* enlistee, recruit. —*adj.* **3** *a volunteer fire department:* of volunteers, by volunteers; voluntary; unpaid, nonprofessional. —*v.* **4** *Three people volunteered to help:* offer willingly, express willingness. **5** *I volunteered the fact that the plan had been tried before:* offer, proffer, tender, present, advance, put forward.
Ant. **2** draftee, conscript. **3** paid, professional. **4** force, coerce, compel.

voluptuary *n. The voluptuary spent his fortune on wine and women:* sensualist, hedonist, pleasure seeker; libertine, debauchee, sybarite, womanizer.
Ant. ascetic, aesthete; abstainer.

voluptuous *adj.* **1** *Velvet has a voluptuous texture:* sensuous, sensual; luxurious, soft, smooth. **2** *The playboy had a voluptuous life:* sensual, pleasure-seeking, pleasure-loving, self-indulgent, hedonistic, sybaritic; erotic, sexual, wanton, carnal, licentious, lascivious.
Ant. **1** rough, coarse. **2** ascetic, abstinent, abstemious, austere, puritanical.

vomit *v.* **1** *In treating some poison cases, force the patient to vomit:* throw up, regurgitate, retch, disgorge, *Informal* puke. **2** *The volcano vomited clouds of smoke:* spew forth, eject, emit, expel, belch forth, discharge, disgorge.

voracious *adj. a voracious appetite:* ravenous, ravenously hungry; insatiable, greedy.
Ant. satiated, sated; delicate, dainty.

vortex *n. The swimmer was caught in the vortex:* whirlpool, maelstrom; whirlwind, cyclone, twister.

vote *n.* **1** *Father's vote usually went to the*

party in power. Do I have a vote on whom to invite?: election choice, ballot, selection; choice, preference, option, decision, judgment, voice, say; ticket. **2** *The vote will be held next Tuesday:* election, plebiscite, referendum, poll. **3** *When did women win the vote?:* right to vote, suffrage, franchise.

vouch *v. I'll vouch for your integrity:* swear to, attest to, affirm, confirm, guarantee, warrant, endorse, certify, authenticate; uphold, maintain.

Ant. refute, repudiate, deny, denounce.

vow *n.* **1** *The couple made their wedding vows. She took her vows as a nun:* solemn promise, pledge, oath, plight, troth, word, word of honor; solemn promise to God, religious pledge. *—v.* **2** *They vowed to love each other throughout eternity. She vowed she would never play tennis again:* promise, pledge, pledge one's word, swear; resolve, declare, assert, affirm; assure, emphasize, stress.

voyage *n.* **1** *The voyage to England took seven days:* sea journey, cruise, passage, crossing, sail. *—v.* **2** *to voyage around the world:* cruise, sail, navigate.

voyager *n. The experienced voyagers already had passports and visas:* traveler, wayfarer, rambler, rover; tourist, sightseer, world traveler, globe-trotter.

vulgar *adj.* **1** *His vulgar manners shocked everyone:* coarse, rude, rough, crude, gross, uncouth, low, base; ill-mannered, boorish, ill-bred. **2** *He told a vulgar joke:* indecent, offensive, obscene, smutty, dirty, filthy; ribald, off-color, risqué. **3** *Is the inscription in Vulgar Latin?:* common, plebeian, proletarian, lowbrow, ordinary.

Ant. **1** elegant, refined, cultivated, polite, delicate. **2** decent, clean. **3** classical, Standard, aristocratic, educated.

vulgarity *n.* **1** *The vulgarity of the movie was shocking:* bad taste, tastelessness, coarseness, crudeness, grossness, indelicacy; indecency, smuttiness, obscenity. **2** *His vulgarity cost him many friends:* ill manners, rudeness, impoliteness, boorishness.

Ant. **1** good taste, decorum, delicacy, decency. **2** good manners, politeness, refinement.

vulnerable *adj. Our army's withdrawal left the city vulnerable. She has always been vulnerable to criticism:* open to attack, defenseless, unprotected, insecure, undefended, unguarded, exposed, susceptible; easily hurt, sensitive, thin-skinned.

Ant. defended, protected, invulnerable, invincible, unassailable; impervious, insensitive.

W

wade *v. It took hours to wade through all that work:* trudge, trek, labor, toil, plod, drudge, plow.

waft *v. The odor of pine wafted through the air:* float, drift, blow, puff.

wag¹ *v.* **1** *He wagged his finger at the child:* move from side to side, move up and down, wave, shake, waggle, wiggle, jiggle, bob, flutter, flicker, flick, wigwag. *—n.* **2** *With a wag of its tail the dog trotted off:* switch, wave, shake, waggle, wiggle, jiggle, bob, flutter, flick, flicker, twitch, wigwag.

wag² *n. Some wag put jello in the toilet:* joker, jokester, jester, clown, comedian, buffoon, wit, humorist, wisecracker, *Slang* card.

wage *n.* **1** *The job pays a good wage:* salary, payment, remuneration, compensation, recompense, earning, income, fee, pay. *—v.* **2** *to wage war:* carry on, conduct, maintain, undertake, engage in, practice.

wager *n.* **1** *I made a wager on the Derby. The most common wager is two dollars:* bet; gamble, hazard. *—v.* **2** *The gambler wagered $100 on each throw of the dice:* bet, venture, hazard, risk, stake; gamble. **3** *I wager he'll be late again:* speculate, guess, hazard an opinion, assume, suppose, presume, imagine, fancy.

waif *n. The waif was left on the steps of the orphanage:* homeless child, foundling; urchin, ragamuffin, gamin, *(fem.)* gamine.

wail *v.* **1** *Citizens wailed over the war victims:* cry, weep, keen, bemoan, moan, lament, bewail; cry out, howl, yell, bawl, caterwaul, whine. *—n.* **2** *A wail went up from the mourners:* mournful cry, wailing, keening, moaning, moan, lament, groan; outcry, howl, yell, whine.

Ant. **1, 2** laugh. **1** rejoice, celebrate. **2** laughter; shout of joy.

waist *n. He's getting a bit thick around the waist:* middle part, middle, midsection, midriff. **2** *The waist should be taken in another inch:* waistline, waistband; shirtwaist, blouse, top.

wait *v.* **1** *You'll have to wait until I finish this work:* bide one's time, remain inactive, tarry, remain ready. **2** *Let the work wait. We waited dinner, hoping you would get here:* be postponed, be put off, be delayed, be tabled, be shelved; delay, stay, postpone, put off. —*n.* **3** *We had a wait of four hours between planes:* delay, suspension, stay, pause, halt, stop, postponement.

waive *v.* **1** *He waived his right to diplomatic immunity:* relinquish, surrender, give up, forbear, forgo, renounce, dispense with. **2** *The judge waived final decision for 60 days:* postpone, defer, put off, shelve, table, stay.
    Ant. **1** claim, demand, insist on, maintain.

waiver *n. She signed a waiver giving up all claims to the property:* relinquishment, disclaimer, renunciation, abandonment.

wake[1] *v.* **1** *She waked her father at six:* awake, awaken, waken, wake up, rouse from sleep. **2** *The newspaper article waked my interest in archaeology:* arouse, rouse, awaken, waken, stimulate, kindle, fire, stir, excite; revive, resuscitate.
    Ant. **2** allay, quell, appease, sate.

wake[2] *n. Seagulls followed in the wake of the ship:* wash, backwash; trail, path, course.

wakeful *adj.* **1** *I was wakeful much of the night:* sleepless, unsleeping, awake, wide-awake, insomniac; restless, astir. **2** *The guards were ever wakeful:* alert, vigilant, watchful, wary, careful, heedful.
    Ant. **1** asleep, sleeping. **2** off-guard, unvigilant, heedless, unwary.

walk *v.* **1** *Let's walk around the lake:* go on foot, stroll, saunter, amble, perambulate, promenade, march, tramp, traipse, trek, trudge, *Informal* foot it. —*n.* **2** *We took a long walk after dinner:* stroll, saunter, constitutional, perambulation, march, trek, hike. **3** *Have you ever noticed her bouncy little walk?:* way of walking, gait, step, stride. **4** *The walk is covered with ice:* walkway, pavement, *(variously)* sidewalk, path, pathway, trail, way, lane.

wall *n. Let's knock out this wall and make the room larger. Two prisoners escaped over the wall:* side of a room, partition, divider; fence, barrier, barricade, rampart.

wallop *v.* **1** *He walloped the child for running away:* hit hard, strike hard, lambaste, clobber, belt, punch, smack, slap, swat, cuff; beat, thrash, pummel, spank, buffet; whip, strap, switch, lash. **2** *The team was wal-* loped in the finals: beat badly, defeat, trounce, rout, clobber, *Slang* lick. —*n.* **3** *The boxer was floored by a wallop to the chin:* hard blow, punch, hit, smack, whack, cuff, belt, slap. swat.

wallow *v.* **1** *Pigs love to wallow:* roll in mud, lie in mud. **2** *Since the inheritance she's been wallowing in luxury:* luxuriate, indulge, revel, live self-indulgently; bask in, relish.

wan *adj.* **1** *He still looks thin and wan:* pale, pallid, white, pasty, colorless, sallow, ashen. **2** *She made a wan smile at the tasteless joke:* weak, feeble, halfhearted, unconvincing, spiritless, lame.
    Ant. **1** ruddy, rosy-cheeked; florid, flushed. **2** spirited, wholehearted.

wand *n. The fairy godmother waved her magic wand:* rod, stick, staff, baton, mace, scepter.

wander *v.* **1** *The college student wandered through Europe during the summer:* roam, ramble, meander, rove, range, prowl; travel, trek. **2** *The stream wanders through the woods:* meander, curve, twist, zigzag; veer.
    Ant. **1** stay, remain, settle.

wanderer *n. Johnny Appleseed spent much of his life as a wanderer:* roamer, rover, rambler, nomad, itinerant; vagrant, vagabond; wayfarer, traveler, globe-trotter, gadabout.
    Ant. homebody, stay-at-home.

wane *v.* **1** *His health began to wane:* fade away, fade, decline, dwindle, weaken, decrease, diminish, subside, abate, ebb, lessen; wither, waste. —*n.* **2** *The 1960's saw the wane of the steamship passenger trade:* fading away, fading, decline, decrease, dwindling, subsiding, abating, ebbing, lessening, weakening, withering, wasting away.
    Ant. **1** rise, increase, strengthen, grow, wax; flourish, thrive. **2** rise, increase, growth, waxing.

want *v.* **1** *I want a big steak:* desire, wish for, crave, fancy, hope for, long for, yearn for, pine for, covet, hanker for, hunger for, thirst for, hunger after. **2** *The FBI wants him for espionage:* seek, search for, hunt; have a warrant for. **3** *This book wants humor:* need, require, lack, be without; be deficient in. **4** *She never wanted for money:* be needy, have a shortage of, be without, lack. —*n.* **5** *Most people have simple wants:* need, necessity, requirement, desire, yearning, craving, wish, demand. **6** *This country has a want of water. In the 1930's many people were reduced to want:* deficiency, lack, scarcity, shortage, dearth, insufficiency, paucity, need; privation, hunger, hard times; poverty, destitution, impoverishment, indigence.

Ant. **1** be sated, be satisfied; have; spurn, loathe, dislike. **6** plenty, abundance, sufficiency, adequacy; wealth, luxury.

wanting *adj. The car was tested for safety and found wanting:* deficient, inadequate, substandard, lacking, insufficient; imperfect, defective; missing, absent.

Ant. adequate, sufficient; perfect.

wanton *adj.* **1** *the wanton destruction of property:* deliberate, willful, malicious, malevolent, unjustified, unprovoked, uncalled-for, senseless, heedless, mindless, irresponsible. **2** *a wanton life:* loose, immoral, dissolute, fast, debauched, promiscuous, unchaste; lewd, lustful, licentious.

war *n.* **1** *the First World War:* state of armed conflict, armed conflict, warfare, hostilities, military operations; fighting, battle, combat. **2** *the war against crime:* fight, struggle, battle, combat, opposition, conflict. —*v.* **3** *The country warred with its neighbors. We must war against poverty:* wage war, make war, be at war, carry on hostilities, battle, fight, combat, contend, struggle, clash, to attack, invade.

Ant. **1** peace, peacetime; neutrality. **2** acceptance, sanction. **3** make peace, call a truce.

ward *n.* **1** *He's running for councilman of our ward:* administrative district, voting district; municipal district, precinct. **2** *The patient was taken to the isolation ward:* section; pavilion. **3** *The orphan became a ward of the state:* charge, dependent; protégé. —*v.* **4** *The boxer fought to ward off his opponent's blows. to ward off bankruptcy:* turn aside, turn away, fend off, stave off, keep at bay, block, repel, beat off, defend against, guard against; avert, prevent, thwart, forestall.

warden *n.* **1** *The prisoner reported to the warden:* chief prison officer, prison superintendent. **2** *a game warden:* keeper, ranger, guard, sentry, watchman, protector, guardian, manager, superintendent, warder.

wardrobe *n.* **1** *I bought a new wardrobe for the cruise:* apparel, clothing, wearing apparel, attire, togs, garments, habiliments. **2** *Better put some mothballs in the hall wardrobe:* clothes closet, clothes cabinet, closet; bureau, chest, cedar chest.

wares *n. pl. The silversmith showed us her wares:* articles for sale, goods for sale, line, merchandise, stock.

warfare *n. Warfare raged along the border:* state of war, war, armed conflict, hostilities, military operation, fighting, battle, combat.

warm *adj.* **1** *a warm, sunny day: The pie was still warm:* moderately hot, somewhat hot, lukewarm, tepid, heated, hot. **2** *warm col-*

ors: bright, sunny, vivid, brilliant, glowing. **3** *The teacher had a warm smile:* loving, warmhearted, affectionate, kind, kindly, kindhearted, tenderhearted, friendly. **4** *The question prompted a warm discussion:* lively, vigorous, animated, fervent, passionate, heated, enthusiastic, spirited, intense, vehement. —*v.* **5** *Warm the soup while I make sandwiches:* heat, warm up, warm over, simmer. **6** *The child's smile warmed his heart:* cheer, make joyful, make happy; arouse affection in, arouse sympathy in, thaw, melt.

Ant. **1–3** cool, cold. **1** chilly, frigid, ice-cold. **2** dull, drab, austere. **3** unfriendly, frigid, aloof, haughty; cruel, hardhearted. **5, 6** chill, freeze.

warmhearted *adj. The warmhearted woman took in the stray cat:* kind, kindly, kindhearted, tenderhearted, sympathetic, compassionate, affectionate, loving.

Ant. unkind, coldhearted, hardhearted.

warmth *n.* **1** *Sit by the warmth of the fire:* warmness, heat, sensation. **2** *Everyone responds to the warmth of a smile:* lovingness, warmheartedness, kindliness, kindness, kindheartedness, tenderness, tenderheartedness; cheerfulness, cheery, joyfulness, cordiality, happiness, friendliness. **3** *He expressed his views with a great deal of warmth:* heat, passion, excitement, spirit, enthusiasm, vehemence, vigor, intensity, animation, zeal, fervor, ardor.

Ant. **1, 2** chill, coldness. **2** sternness, austerity, severity, unfriendliness. **3** apathy, indifference.

warn *v. The spy warned of the imminent attack. I warned you not to buy that car:* alert, forewarn, give warning; caution, apprise, advise, counsel, admonish.

warning *n. The sentry's warning woke the defenders. Didn't you have any warning that the house was being sold?:* warning signal, alarm, signal; forewarning, notice: notification, intimation, sign, apprisal, advice.

warp *v.* **1** *The dampness warped the floorboards:* bend, twist, contort, distort, misshape, deform. **2** *Years of living alone warped his personality:* pervert, twist, distort; misguide, bias, prejudice, mislead.

Ant. **1** straighten, unbend.

warrant *n.* **1** *The police have a search warrant:* authorization, permission, permit; license. —*v.* **2** *Such actions warrant a reprimand:* justify, provide grounds for; permit, authorize, license. **3** *The manufacturer warrants that all parts are new:* guarantee, certify, vouch, pledge, swear, attest, affirm, promise, vow, avow, assert, declare, asseverate, aver.

warranty *n. The vacuum cleaner has a 5-year warranty:* written guarantee; pledge, agreement.

warrior *n. The warriors marched off with Hannibal to the Punic Wars:* soldier, legionnaire, fighting man, man-at-arms, military man; fighter, combatant; veteran, campaigner.

wary *adj. Be wary of new acquaintances:* cautious, careful, guarded, suspicious, chary, watchful, vigilant, on one's guard; discreet, circumspect.
Ant. unwary, unsuspecting; foolhardy, careless, heedless.

wash *v.* 1 *Wash your hands:* clean, cleanse; *(variously)* launder, rinse, scrub, mop, sponge, bathe, shampoo. 2 *You'd better wash that cut with some iodine:* wet, moisten, drench, soak, irrigate, flood, inundate. —*n.* 3 *This bedspread could use a good wash:* washing, cleansing; *(variously)* laundering, mopping, bath, shower, shampoo.

waspish *adj. a waspish character:* testy, huffy, peevish, irritable, petulant, snappish, cranky, crotchety.
Ant. good-natured, agreeable, genial.

waste *v.* 1 *Don't waste time. A badly tuned motor wastes gas:* squander, dissipate, fritter away, expend needlessly, consume extravagantly, misuse, misspend, misapply, misemploy. 2 *Invading armies wasted the countryside:* lay waste, destroy, ruin, devastate, wreck, demolish, despoil, ravage, pillage, plunder, loot, sack, strip. 3 *His strength was wasting away:* fade, dwindle, decline, weaken, decrease, diminish, subside, abate, ebb, wane, wither. —*n.* 4 *industrial waste:* waste material, refuse, garbage, trash, rubbish, debris, litter, sweepings; excrement; offal; leftovers, remainders; scraps, leavings. 5 *The city budget can afford no waste. Such a job is a waste of her talents:* wastefulness, squandering, needless expenditure, useless consumption; misuse, misapplication. 6 *the Arctic wastes:* wasteland, barren expanse, emptiness, void; *(variously)* barren, wilderness, desert region, arid region, tundra, steppe, badlands.
Ant. 1 save, conserve. 2 build, rebuild, restore; protect, defend. 3 strengthen, grow, increase. 5 saving, economy, conservation.

wasteful *adj. It's wasteful to throw out meat bones that could be used for soup:* squandering, prodigal; extravagant, uneconomical, thriftless, unthrifty, improvident.
Ant. economical, thrifty, frugal.

watch *v.* 1 *Watch the magician closely:* look, look on, look at, stare, stare at, gaze at, see, eye, keep an eye on, peer at, ogle; observe,

notice, note, mark, regard, scrutinize, survey. 2 *Watch for an empty seat and grab it:* look out for, be on the lookout, keep an eye out for. 3 *Watch where you're going!:* pay attention, be careful, be on guard, be wary, take heed, be chary. 4 *Who's watching the children?:* look after, keep an eye on, tend, care for, take care of, mind, oversee, superintend; protect, guard. —*n.* 5 *Keep a close watch on him:* eye, surveillance, observance, observation, watchfulness, supervision, notice, vigilance; lookout, guard. 6 *The watch is late making his rounds:* watchman, guard, sentry, patrol, picket.
Ant. 2 overlook, ignore, disregard. 3 be rash, be reckless, be careless. 4 neglect. 5 inattention, disregard, heedlessness.

watchful *adj.* 1 *The hunter kept a watchful eye on the valley:* alert, observant, vigilant, attentive, heedful. 2 *We must be very watchful of expenses:* careful, prudent, cautious, circumspect, wary, guarded, chary.
Ant. 1, 2 careless, inattentive, unmindful. 1 unobservant. 2 rash, reckless, thoughtless.

watchman *n. The watchman caught the prowler:* guard, sentry, sentinel, watch, patrol, foot patrol, patrolman; picket.

water *n.* 1 *Drink six glasses of water a day:* H_2O; drinking water. 2 *The canoeist was out on the water all day:* body of water; *(variously)* sea, ocean, lake, pond, pool, lagoon, river, stream.
Ant. 2 land, dry land, terra firma.

watery *adj.* 1 *What's that watery stain on the wall?:* of water, like water, wet, moist, damp, liquid, fluid, aqueous. 2 *This gravy tastes watery:* thin, diluted, watered, weak, adulterated. 3 *We all had watery eyes in that smoky room:* teary, tearing, tearful, rheumy.

wave *n.* 1 *A big wave swamped the rowboat:* swell, billow, breaker, comber, whitecap, roller; undulation. 2 *radio waves:* pulse, pulsation; vibration. 3 *The captain led the first wave of marines:* moving row, rank, file, line, column. 4 *My hair has a natural wave:* curve, series of curves, curl, coil; winding, spiral, roll, twirl. 5 *There's been a wave of selling on the stock exchange:* surge, rush, deluge, flood; rise, increase. —*v.* 6 *The flag waved in the breeze:* move to and fro, flutter, flap, swing, sway; shake, waver, tremble, quiver; oscillate, vibrate, undulate; brandish, flourish. 7 *The patrolman waved us to a stop:* signal, gesture, gesticulate.

waver *v.* 1 *The palm trees wavered in the breeze:* wave, move to and fro, sway, swing, shake, flutter, flap; tremble, quiver, undulate. 2 *She wavered on the top step and* *nearly fell:* totter, reel; stagger, wobble, sway, weave, careen, falter. 3 *He wavered in his determination:* falter, be irresolute, vacillate, hesitate, vary, fluctuate, sway.

Ant. 3 be resolute, be steadfast, be determined, be decisive.

wavy *adj. a wavy pattern in the sand:* rippling, curved, sinuous, rolling, winding, curvilinear, serpentine, curly, undulating.

wax *v. He waxed enthusiastic over the plan. The moon is always the same size but seems to wax and wane:* grow, become; become larger, enlarge, increase, expand, develop, thrive, become fuller, swell.

Ant. wane, become smaller, diminish, decrease.

way *n.* 1 *It's hard to get used to foreign ways. Being gruff is just his way:* custom, practice, manner, habit, usage, form; behavior, conduct, nature, wont. 2 *What's the best way to make coffee?:* method, means, process, procedure, manner, system, technique. 3 *This is the shortest way to town. Hard work is the way to success:* route, course, road, path, trail, lane, passage; distance. 4 *Make way for the king!:* space, room, room to advance. *—adv.* 5 *Can't you see it way in the distance?:* far, far off, remotely.

waylay *v. Six robbers waylaid the stagecoach:* ambush, lay a trap for; set upon, assail, assault, attack; lure, entrap, ensnare.

wayward *adj. a home for wayward youths:* disobedient, unmanageable, ungovernable, intractable, unruly, insubordinate, rebellious, refractory, troublesome; headstrong, self-willed, willful, obstinate, stubborn.

Ant. obedient, manageable, docile, complaint.

weak *adj.* 1 *The victim was too weak to walk:* lacking strength, weakened, feeble, frail, debilitated; exhausted, spent; shaky, unsteady. 2 *The walls are too weak to hold up the roof:* frail, flimsy, unsubstantial, puny, shaky, unsteady, fragile; breakable, brittle, delicate. 3 *We need strong leaders, not weak ones:* powerless, spineless, cowardly, timorous, irresolute; ineffective, ineffectual, inefficient. 4 *The arguments in favor of the proposal are very weak. The defeat leaves the country in a weak position:* vulnerable, exposed, assailable, unprotected, unguarded, unsafe; untenable, unsupported, unconvincing, lacking. 5 *Don't make the coffee too weak:* watery, thin, diluted, adulterated; tasteless, insipid.

Ant. 1–5 strong. 2–4 sturdy, powerful. 1–3 steady. 1 vigorous, hardy, hale. 2 sound, solid; unbreakable. 3 forceful, aggressive, energetic; firm, bold; capable, effective. 4 solid, sound, forceful, convincing,

valid; impregnable, invulnerable, unassailable, safe, secure. 5 potent.

weaken *v. Lack of food weakened our strength. Public support of the program began to weaken:* make weak, impair, undermine, soften; diminish, lessen, lower, sap, mitigate, moderate; fail, flag, droop, dwindle, wane, fade, abate.

Ant. strengthen, increase, grow, develop, improve, enhance.

weakling *n.* 1 *The young Teddy Roosevelt was a weakling:* physically weak person, frail person, feeble person. 2 *Stand up for your rights; don't be such a weakling:* weak-willed person, coward, sissy, namby-pamby, pantywaist, mouse, *Slang* wimp.

weakness *n.* 1 *His weakness is due to poor nutrition:* feebleness, lack of strength, frailty, debility; shakiness, unsteadiness. 2 *Can't you see the weakness of the argument?:* fault, defect, deficiency, imperfection, unsubstantiality, ineffectiveness, lameness, flimsiness, frailty; vulnerability, susceptibility, unconvincingness. 3 *Jerry has a weakness for sports cars:* passion, fondness, intense liking, penchant, propensity, proclivity, tendency, inclination, proneness, leaning, prejudice, bias, bent, hunger, thirst, appetite.

Ant. 1, 2 strength. 1 vigor, vitality; health, hardiness, sturdiness. 2 force, effectiveness; validity, soundness. 3 dislike, hatred, aversion, horror.

wealth *n.* 1 *Our wealth is estimated at fifty million dollars:* riches, fortune; assets, resources, means, capital, estate, property, goods, chattels. 2 *The family lived in great wealth:* affluence, prosperity; luxury, luxuriousness, opulence. 3 *There is a wealth of detail in the painting:* abundance, profusion, richness, copiousness, fullness, bounty, fund, store, mine.

Ant. 2 poverty, penury, pauperism, destitution, indigence, privation, want, need. 3 want, lack, scarcity, deficiency.

wealthy *adj. a wealthy family:* rich, prosperous, affluent, moneyed, well-to-do, well-off, well-heeled, well-fixed; flush, loaded.

Ant. poor, impoverished, poverty-stricken, destitute, indigent, needy.

weapon *n.* 1 *The army tested a new weapon:* arm, armament, of lethal instrument, deadly weapon. 2 *Reduced spending is our best weapon against inflation:* defense, protection, guard, countermeasure, safeguard; means, measure, resort.

wear *v.* 1 *Are you going to wear blue jeans or a dress?:* dress in, clothe oneself in, put on, don, attire oneself with. 2 *This sweater has worn thin at the elbows:* wear away, wear out; abrade, fray, frazzle, shred; erode, corrode. **3** *The long wait wore everyone out:* exhaust, tire, fatigue, weary, drain; overwork. —*n.* **4** *You can see the wear on the corner of the rug:* worn place, deterioration, disintegration, disrepair, wear and tear; damage.

wearisome *adj. She spent a wearisome afternoon tending the children:* tedious, irksome, tiresome, vexatious, annoying, trying, irritating, bothersome; dreary, boring, dull, monotonous; tiring, exhausting.

Ant. agreeable, pleasant, enjoyable, pleasurable.

weary *adj.* **1** *I'm always weary after work:* tired, exhausted, fatigued, wearied, spent, worn-out, drained, all in, *Slang* beat, bushed; sleepy, drowsy. **2** *I thought that weary speech would never end:* tiring, fatiguing, wearying, tedious; boring, monotonous, tiresome, wearisome, dull. **3** *He's weary of their constant nagging:* tired, sick and tired, annoyed, dispirited, discontented, disgusted; bored, fed up. —*v.* **4** *The long drive wearied the children:* tire, tire out, fatigue, exhaust, wear out.

Ant. **1** refreshed, invigorated; energetic, full of pep. **2** interesting, exciting, amusing. **3** delighted, pleased. **4** refresh, invigorate, revive.

weather *n.* **1** *What's the weather like this morning?:* atmospheric conditions; *(loosely)* climate, temperature. —*v.* **2** *Stack the lumber and let it weather:* dry, season, toughen; bleach; rust, oxidize. **3** *The ship weathered the storm:* withstand, stand; brave, face, confront. —*adj.* **4** *the weather side of the hill:* windward.

weave *v.* **1** *Weave the strings together to make a strong cord:* loom; intertwine, interweave, twist, knit, entwine, braid, lace, plait. **2** *The composer wove three separate melodies into the composition:* interweave, combine, meld, blend, fuse, mingle, incorporate, unify, unite, join, link. **3** *The river weaves through the woods:* zigzag, wind, curve, meander, snake. —*n.* **4** *a herringbone weave:* woven pattern; texture.

Ant. **1** unravel, untwist, disentangle. **2** isolate, separate, divorce.

web *n.* **1** *a spider on its web:* spiderweb; cobweb; snare, trap, webbing, net, netting, mesh. **2** *The story is a web of lies:* network, complex, tangle; maze, labyrinth.

wed *v.* **1** *The couple will be wed in June:* marry, join in marriage, unite in holy wedlock, mate, make one, hitch, tie the knot, espouse. **2** *She is wedded to the idea of equal rights:* attach, commit, dedicate, devote; enamor of, win over. **3** *Try to wed all the*

ideas into one story: blend, combine, unite, meld, weave, link, fuse, merge, incorporate, unify, tie.

Ant. **1, 3** divorce, separate.

wedded *adj.* **1** *The couple had fifty years of wedded bliss:* married, marital. **2** *The fifty states are wedded into one nation:* united, joined, bound, tied, connected, linked; fused, merged, unified, incorporated, blended, melded. **3** *She seems wedded to her career:* devoted, committed, bound, deeply attached, pledged.

Ant. **1, 2** separated, divorced. **1** single, unwed, unmarried.

wedding *n. It was the grandest wedding of the season:* wedding ceremony, marriage ceremony, marriage, nuptials, nuptial rite; wedding anniversary; wedding day.

Ant. separation, divorce.

wedge *n.* **1** *a wedge of cheese:* V-shaped block, chock; pie-shaped piece, chunk. —*v.* **2** *She couldn't wedge another item into the suitcase:* cram, jam, stuff, crowd, ram, squeeze, pack, press.

wedlock *n. They were united in wedlock:* marriage, matrimony, holy matrimony, marriage.

wee *adj. Put a wee bit of liquor in the punch. The elf lived in a wee house in the forest:* tiny, little, minute, scant, scanty, *Informal* teeny; diminutive, miniature, undersized, dwarf, Lilliputian.

Ant. big, large, huge, immense, enormous, gigantic.

weight *n.* **1** *The weight of this car is three thousand pounds:* heaviness, poundage, tonnage, mass. **2** *That package is a heavy weight to carry:* load, burden; stress, strain, pressure. **3** *Tax reform is a matter of great weight:* importance, influence, import, magnitude, significance, consequence, value, consideration, concern. —*v.* **4** *The statue was weighted with a lead base:* add weight to, weigh down, make heavier; ballast. **5** *She's weighted down with many problems:* weigh, weigh down, burden, oppress, encumber, saddle.

Ant. **3** unimportance, insignificance. **4** lighten.

weighty *adj.* **1** *The flatcar held a weighty shipment of ore:* heavy, massive, hefty. **2** *How long has she had this weighty responsibility?:* burdensome, onerous, oppressive, crushing, taxing, arduous, troublesome. **3** *This is a weighty decision:* important, significant, consequential, serious, grave; urgent, crucial, critical, vital, essential.

Ant. **1–3** light, lightweight. **2** easy. **3** unimportant, insignificant, inconsequential, trifling, frivolous.

weird adj. 1 *Weird noises came from the haunted house:* eerie, mysterious, strange, unearthly, spooky, mystic, magical. 2 *She certainly has a weird sense of humor:* odd, queer, eccentric, bizarre, grotesque, abnormal, unconventional, strange, curious, peculiar, unusual, outlandish.

Ant. 1, 2 natural, normal. 2 everyday, routine, common, conventional, orthodox.

welcome n. 1 *The guests received a warm welcome:* greeting, salutation, salute; reception. —v. 2 *The mayor welcomed the visiting dignitaries:* greet, receive, bid welcome, meet; receive with open arms, accept eagerly. —adj. 3 *What a welcome surprise!:* gladly received, wanted, accepted, comfortable; agreeable, delightful, pleasant, pleasing, gratifying, inviting, winning, charming.

Ant. 1 snub, rebuff, cold shoulder. 3 unwelcome, unwanted.

welfare n. 1 *I give you this advice for your own welfare:* well-being, happiness, good, good fortune, success, advantage, benefit, profit. 2 *How long has the family been on welfare?:* relief, public assistance.

well adv. 1 *She's getting along well at college. The reporter can't hear well:* fairly well, satisfactorily, nicely, adequately, acceptably, properly; quite well, successfully, commendably, laudably, advantageously, splendidly. 2 *Dust the room well:* thoroughly, fully, completely, carefully. 3 *We could not refuse her request very well:* properly, rightly, justly, fairly, suitably; readily, easily. 4 *The new play was received well by the critics:* favorably, kindly, approvingly, warmly, sympathetically, enthusiastically. 5 *The bracelet is worth well over a thousand dollars:* considerably, substantially, amply, abundantly. 6 *Do you know the neighbors well?:* intimately, personally. —adj. 7 *The doctor says you'll be well in a few days:* in good health, healthy, strong, sound, hale, hearty. 8 *It's well the children didn't see what happened:* good, right, proper, fitting; fortunate. 9 *All is well with the family:* satisfactory, good, going well, faring well, happy, successful, prosperous, auspicious, favorable, promising.

Ant. 1, 2, 4 badly, poorly. 8, 9 bad. 1 unsatisfactorily, inadequately, unacceptably. 2 carelessly, sloppily, incompletely. 3 unjustly, unfairly, improperly. 4 unfavorably, unkindly, disapprovingly, unsympathetically. 5 somewhat. 7 sick, ill, infirm, ailing. 8 wrong, unfitting, unfortunate. 9 unsatisfactory, going badly, unsuccessful; unfavorable.

well-being n. *I'm concerned for your well-being:* welfare, happiness, good; success, advantage, benefit, fortune, prosperity, comfort; health.

well-bred adj. *The club members all seemed well-bred:* cultivated, refined, genteel, polite, cultured, polished, urbane, civilized, well-mannered, well-brought-up, gentlemanly, ladylike.

Ant. ill-bred, coarse, uncouth.

well-known adj. *She's a well-known chemist:* prominent, famous, noted, outstanding, important, famed, celebrated, eminent, illustrious; notorious, infamous.

Ant. unknown, obscure, unheard-of.

well-off adj. *After years of hard work, he's well-off:* prosperous, moneyed, wealthy, rich, affluent, comfortable, well-fixed, well-to-do.

Ant. broke, needy, penniless, indigent, poor.

welt n. *The blow left a welt on my arm:* ridge, wale, weal, swelling, stripe, streak; lump, bump, mark, contusion.

welter n. 1 *Sort this welter of clothes for the laundry:* jumble, mass, heap, mess, pile, hodgepodge. 2 *It's hard to hear above the welter of street noises:* confusion, tumult, commotion, turmoil, hubbub, racket, bustle.

wend v. *It's time to wend our way home:* direct one's path, move along toward, betake oneself, make.

wet adj. 1 *Take off that wet jacket:* wringing wet, soaked, soaking, drenched, dripping, sodden, sopping, waterlogged, soggy, squishy, moist, damp, dampened; dank, humid, clammy. 2 *Wet weather is predicted for tomorrow:* rainy, showery, stormy. 3 *wet paint:* liquid, liquified, not dry, not dried; not set, not hardened. —n. 4 *Air out the house to get rid of the wet:* wetness, moisture, moistness, dampness, dankness, clamminess, condensation. 5 *Button up your raincoat before going out in the wet:* rain, rainy weather, rainstorm, storm, bad weather, shower; precipitation, water. —v. 6 *Do you wet your hair before combing it?:* moisten, dampen, damp, sprinkle, splash, soak, drench, immerse, submerge, dip, steep; water, irrigate, inundate.

Ant. 1–3, 6 dry. 1 bone-dry. 3 dried; set, hardened. 4 dryness. 5 dry weather.

whack v. 1 *The child whacked the puppy with a rolled-up newspaper:* strike, smack, clout, hit, belt, slug, sock, wallop, slam, smite, pound, baste, slap, cuff, box. —n. 2 *The falling board gave him a whack on the head:* hit, blow, smack, clout, knock, belt, sock, wallop, thump, rap, bang; punch, slap, cuff, box.

wharf n. *The boats unloaded at the wharf:*

pier, dock, quay, marina, landing, landing dock, slip, jetty.

wheedle v. *Mother tried to wheedle me into going to the party:* coax, cajole, flatter, inveigle; charm, beguile, lure, entice, persuade. *Ant.* force, coerce, bully, browbeat.

wheel n. 1 *The refrigerator is mounted on wheels:* roller, caster, drum. 2 *a wheel of cheese:* ring, circle, hoop, round, disk. —v. 3 *Dancers wheeled gracefully on the ballroom floor:* turn, turn round, pivot, rotate, revolve, spin, swivel, whirl; circle, gyrate, swirl, twirl, pirouette.

wheeze v. *Climbing steps made him wheeze:* breathe audibly, breathe with a whistling sound; breathe hard, gasp, puff, pant.

whelp n. 1 *The mother wolf had five whelps:* pup, puppy; cub. 2 *That young whelp needs a good whipping:* whippersnapper, urchin, mischievous boy; youngster, lad, youth, stripling, child, kid.

whet v. 1 *to whet an ax on a grindstone:* hone, grind, strop, sharpen, edge, put an edge on. 2 *The smell of cooking whetted my appetite:* arouse, excite, stir, awaken, kindle, stimulate, pique, provoke, induce, allure, entice, make eager, make keen. *Ant.* 1 dull, blunt. 2 satisfy, sate, satiate; deaden, slake, dampen.

whiff n. 1 *a whiff of air:* breath, puff, slight gust, draft; zephyr, breeze. 2 *There's a whiff of honeysuckle in the air. Did you get a whiff of that cigar?:* faint smell, scent, odor, aroma, bouquet; breath; hint, trace.

whim n. *She caters to his every whim:* fancy, fanciful notion, notion; conceit, eccentricity; urge, impulse.

whimper v. 1 *The child whimpered:* cry softly, sob brokenly, blubber; whine plaintively, snivel, sniffle. —n. 2 *T. S. Eliot wrote that the world will end "not with a bang but a whimper":* sniveling, whine, sobbing, sob.

whimsical adj. *The essay is pleasantly whimsical:* droll, amusing, waggish, fanciful, quaint.

whine v. 1 *The lost child was whining:* cry plaintively, whimper, snivel, mewl. 2 *Don't whine about your difficulties:* complain, grumble, fret, grouse, gripe. —n. 3 *a whine of anguish:* whimper, snivel; wail, moan, cry, sob; murmur, complaint, mutter, grumble.

whip n. 1 *Mule drivers need long whips:* horsewhip, thong, lash, cat-o'-nine-tails, switch, birch, rod. —v. 2 *The boy was whipped for playing hooky:* flog, strap, lash, switch, birch, cane; beat, spank. 3 *The team got whipped in its last game:* trounce, drub, beat decisively, defeat soundly, rout, lick. 4 *The wind whipped through the trees:* lash,

flick; toss about. 5 *The thief whipped the purse from my hand:* snatch, jerk, whisk. 6 *Whip the cream and ladle it on the strawberries:* beat, beat into a froth, whisk.

whir v. 1 *The machine whirred:* drone, hum, buzz, whisper, purr. —n. 2 *the whir of a helicopter:* drone, hum, buzz, whisper, purr.

whirl v. 1 *The propeller began to whirl:* turn, turn round, spin, rotate, revolve; twirl, pivot; gyrate, pirouette, wheel, circle, swirl. 2 *Looking down from that height made my head whirl:* spin, reel; feel dizzy, feel giddy. —n. 3 *the whirl of the dancers:* turning, turn, spin, spinning, rotation, revolving, revolution, twirl, twirling, pivoting, pivot, gyration, pirouette, wheeling, circle, circling, swirling. 4 *Christmas weekend was a whirl of parties:* round, dizzying succession, flurry; dither, state of excitement. 5 *I gave woodworking a whirl:* try, go, attempt, trial, turn, fling, *Slang* crack, stab.

whirlpool n. *The swimmers were warned away from the whirlpool:* maelstrom, vortex; whirl, swirl, eddy.

whirlwind n. 1 *The whirlwind sucked up dust:* dust spout, waterspout; cyclone, twister. —adj. 2 *a whirlwind courtship:* impetuous, headlong, rash, impulsive; short, quick, rapid, swift, hasty. *Ant.* 2 long, lengthy, leisurely; thoughtful, well-considered.

whisk v. 1 *Whisk the lint off your coat:* brush, sweep, flick. 2 *The car whisked past the intersection:* rush, speed, hasten, move quickly; race, shoot, tear, fly, sweep; hurry, scurry, sprint, scoot, dash, bolt, dart. 3 *Whisk the egg whites:* beat, whip. —n. 4 *With a whisk of his napkin the waiter removed the crumbs from the table:* sweep, brush, flick. *Ant.* 2 crawl, creep, inch.

whiskey Also **whisky** n. *Whiskey is distilled from grains:* liquor, hard liquor, spirits, booze; *(variously)* rye, Scotch, Irish, bourbon, vodka, gin, rum.

whisper v. 1 *"I love you," he whispered:* speak softly, utter under the breath; murmur, mutter, sigh, breathe; confide. 2 *People have been whispering about those two for months:* gossip, spread rumor, intimate, hint; reveal, divulge, disclose, tell. 3 *The wind whispered through the pines:* rustle, murmur, sigh; drone, hum, buzz. —n. 4 *Don't talk above a whisper:* undertone, murmur, mutter. 5 *There has never been a whisper about his integrity:* insinuation, innuendo, rumor, gossip; hint, suggestion, inkling. 6 *the whisper of the wind:* rustling sound, rustle, murmur, sigh; drone, hum, purr, buzz.

Ant. **1**, **4** shout, scream, roar, bellow, yell. **3**, **6** roar.

whit *n. Put some mustard on the sandwich, but just a whit:* least bit, speck, mite; dab, drop, dash, pinch, morsel, smidgen, jot, crumb, snip.

Ant. lot, heap, scads.

white *adj.* **1** *Kathy has beautiful white teeth:* ivory-colored, pearly, snow-white, alabaster, milk white, cream-colored. **2** *She turned white with fear:* colorless, pale, pallid, wan, ashen, ashy, pasty; bloodless, gray, leaden. **3** *white hair, a white liquid:* gray, silver, silvery, hoary, grizzled; cloudy, filmy, chalky, milky. **4** *White settlers took the Indians' land:* Caucasian, light-skinned; fair, blond. **5** *a white lie:* harmless, unmalicious, benign, innocent. **6** *My reputation is as white as snow:* pure, spotless, unblemished, unsullied, unstained, unspotted, clean, immaculate; chaste, innocent, virtuous.

Ant. **1** black, jet black, ebony, raven. **2** ruddy, flushed, rosy, red, florid. **3** clear, colorless. **5** malicious, vicious, malevolent. **6** evil, wicked, notorious; black, sullied, stained, tarnished, besmirched.

whiten *v.* **1** *Use a stronger soap to whiten the wash:* make white, make whiter, color white; clean, bleach, blanch, lighten. **2** *She whitened when she heard the bad news:* pale, blanch, turn pallid, turn ashen, turn white.

Ant. **1** blacken; darken, dull. **2** flush, blush.

whittle *v.* **1** *Grandfather whittled whistles from small sticks:* cut away, carve; pare, shave, chip away at. **2** *The company has whittled down its debt:* reduce gradually, lessen, pare, cut, shave, decrease; shorten, curtail, clip.

whiz *v.* **1** *A bullet whizzed by my head:* whistle, swish, whir, whine, hiss, buzz; hum, drone. **2** *Trucks whizzed down the road:* speed, race, shoot, tear, fly, zoom, sweep, whisk, rush; hasten, dash, dart, sprint, bolt. —*n.* **3** *The deer heard the whiz of the arrow and ran:* swish, whistle, whir, whine, hiss, buzz; hum, drone. **4** *Informal She's a whiz at math:* expert, adept, wizard, genius; master, masterhand, skilled hand.

whole *adj.* **1** *The two boys ate a whole pizza:* entire, complete; full, total. **2** *Seals still prefer eating whole fish rather than pieces:* in one piece, entire, undivided, uncut, unbroken; complete, intact, undiminished; uninjured. —*n.* **3** *Buying the house will take the whole of your savings:* entire amount, total, sum total, aggregate; bulk, major part, main part, body; essence, quintessence. **4** *The table and six chairs make up the*

whole: totality, entirety; ensemble, unit, system, assemblage.

Ant. **1** partial, incomplete. **2** divided, cut up, cut, broken. **3**, **4** part, division, portion. **4** component, element, constituent, item.

wholehearted *adj. The plan has my wholehearted support:* sincere, unfeigned, heartfelt, deeply felt, complete, unreserved, earnest, enthusiastic, emphatic.

Ant. halfhearted, lukewarm, perfunctory, unenthusiastic.

wholesome *adj.* **1** *a wholesome diet:* healthful, healthy, nutritious, nourishing, health-giving; sanitary, hygienic. **2** *Hard work in the fresh air gave us a wholesome look:* healthy, hale, sound, well, hardy, vigorous; rosy-cheeked, clear-complexioned. **3** *Wholesome friends won't lead you astray:* morally healthy, moral, honorable, virtuous, upright, decent, pure, clean-minded, clean, innocent, uplifting, ethical, principled, dutiful.

Ant. **1–3** unwholesome. **1** unhealthful, unhealthy, harmful, detrimental; unsanitary, unhygienic. **2** unhealthy, pale, wan, sickly, frail. **3** immoral, dishonorable, evil, evil-minded, wicked, sinful, bad, impure, unethical, unprincipled.

wholly *adv. I'm wholly in agreement:* entirely, completely, fully, totally, utterly, quite, perfectly, thoroughly, altogether.

Ant. partially, incompletely, somewhat.

whoop *n.* **1** *The child let out a bloodcurdling whoop:* shout, yell, scream, cry, holler, shriek, roar, bellow, howl, screech, hollo; outcry; cheer, hurrah. —*v.* **2** *The children whooped with joy:* shout, yell, cry, cry out, holler, shriek, screech, scream, howl, roar, bellow, hoot; cheer, hurrah; hollo.

whore *n. Daniel Defoe's novel* Moll Flanders *tells the story of a whore:* prostitute, hooker, woman of ill fame, woman of ill repute, fallen woman, harlot, bawd, hustler, strumpet, trollop, jade, doxy, woman of easy virtue, demimondaine, demirep, lady of the night, painted lady, tart, streetwalker, chippy, call girl; mistress, kept woman, courtesan, concubine; hussy, slut, wanton, tramp.

Ant. nice girl, good girl, honest woman, lady.

whorl *n. The petals of the flower are arranged in whorls:* spiral, circle, coil, convolution, curl, corkscrew, helix.

wicked *adj.* **1** *Wicked deeds must be repented:* evil, sinful, immoral; bad, iniquitous, reprehensible, vile, foul, base, gross, low; heinous, abominable, atrocious, hellish, fiendish, devilish, villainous, infamous, vicious, malicious, malevolent, evil-minded, shameful, dishonorable, disgraceful, cor-

rupt, depraved, degenerate, monstrous.
2 *Wicked children should be punished:*
naughty, mischievous, knavish, rascally, ill-
behaved. 3 *I have a wicked toothache:* intense, severe, acute, fierce, extreme, bad,
raging, dreadful, troublesome.

Ant. 1 moral, wholesome, upright, righteous, honorable, good, noble, ethical, principled, exemplary. 2 well-behaved, well-
mannered.

wide *adj.* 1 *How wide is this living room?:*
broad; spacious, large. 2 *the wide Arctic
wastes. The group discussed a wide variety
of subjects:* broad, extensive, vast, immense, boundless, far-flung, far-reaching,
far-ranging. 3 *The children's eyes were wide
with excitement. The girl's parents greeted
her with arms wide:* wide open, fully open;
expanded, dilated; extended, distended; out-
stretched, outspread. —*adv.* 4 *Leave the
door wide open:* fully, completely, as far as
possible.

Ant. 1–3 narrow. 1 long; deep. 2 restricted, limited, small. 3 shut, closed, contracted. 4 barely, partially.

widen *v. You ought to widen your circle of
acquaintances:* make wider, broaden, enlarge, expand, extend.

Ant. narrow, reduce, contract.

widespread *adj.* 1 *a widespread flu epidemic:* far-flung, pervasive, far-reaching,
extensive, broad; nationwide, worldwide.
2 *She greeted us with widespread arms:*
wide open, fully extended, outspread.

Ant. 1 localized, restricted, confined, limited. 2 closed.

wield *v.* 1 *The knight wielded a sword:* handle, ply, manage, use, manipulate; brandish,
flourish, wave, swing. 2 *The president
wields tremendous power:* exert, exercise,
employ, apply, display.

wife *n. His wife is a lawyer:* spouse, consort,
marriage partner; better half, helpmate,
mate, *Slang* missus; bride; married woman.
Ant. single woman, miss, spinster, old
maid.

wig *n. The bald man bought a wig. The
woman has a long blond wig for evening:*
toupee, hairpiece; *Slang* carpet, rug; fall,
switch, wiglet.

wiggle *v.* 1 *Can you wiggle your ears? Sit still
and stop wiggling!:* wag, waggle, shake,
twitch, jerk, flutter, quiver; twist, squirm,
writhe, wriggle. —*n.* 2 *The squirrel made a
little wiggle with its tail:* jerk, twitch, wag,
waggle, flutter, shake; squirming, wrig-
gling, writhing.

wild *adj., adv.* 1 *wild horses: A pack of dogs
runs wild in these woods:* untamed, undomesticated, unbroken; feral, savage.

2 *wild blueberries. Strawberries grow wild
on this hill:* uncultivated; without cultivation, naturally. 3 *It's difficult to hike through
this wild country:* untouched by man, uninhabited, uncultivated; rugged, bleak, desolate; wooded, forested, overgrown. 4 *Wild
tribes still inhabit the island:* uncivilized,
primitive, savage. 5 *We ran into wild seas
our third day out. The wind blew wild:* violent, furious, tempestuous, blustery, howling; rough, choppy, turbulent; wildly, violently, furiously. 6 *A group of wild youths
vandalized the school. His wild talk frightened everyone:* unrestrained, disorderly,
lawless, unruly, violent; frantic, frenzied, fa-
natical, rabid, raging, raving, crazed, maniacal, demented. 7 *I took a wild guess at the
answer. Is that another of your wild ideas to
make us rich?:* reckless, rash, uninformed;
illogical, impractical, bizarre, fanciful.
—*n.* the **wild** or **wilds** 8 *The hunter
roamed the wilds for weeks:* wilderness,
bush; barren area, wasteland.

Ant. 1 domesticated, tame, broken. 2 cultivated, planted. 3 inhabited, cultivated.
4 civilized, advanced. 5, 6 calm, mild, gentle, quiet. 6 well-behaved, law-abiding,
peaceful; rational, sane; polite. 7 thoughtful,
realistic, practical, logical.

wilderness *n. a cabin in the wilderness:*
wild, wilds, bush, unsettled area, remote
area; wasteland, barrens, desert, tundra.

wile *n. Often wiles I used all my wiles to get
us tickets:* sly trick, trickery, artifice, subterfuge, contrivance, stratagem, ploy, gambit;
cunning, craftiness, subtlety.

will *n.* 1 *No one stands a chance against his
will. the will to win:* willpower, force of will,
moral courage, self-discipline, strength of
purpose, conviction; determination, resolution, resoluteness; desire. 2 *What is your
will, my lord?:* desire, wish, preference, inclination, pleasure. 3 *Woe to anyone who in-
curs her ill will:* feeling, disposition, attitude.
—*v.* 4 *You can succeed if you will it strongly
enough:* resolve, desire, want, determine
upon. 5 *The deceased willed his estate to his
daughters:* bequeath; endow, bestow, confer, convey at death.

Ant. 1 irresolution, indecision, vacillation.
4 be irresolute, be indecisive, vacillate.

willful *adj.* 1 *It was willful murder:* deliberate, purposeful, intentional, intended,
planned, premeditated, studied, designed.
2 *There's no use arguing with such a willful
person:* stubborn, obstinate, unyielding,
uncompromising, inflexible, determined,
headstrong, intractable, obdurate, closed-
minded, mulish, pigheaded; bullheaded; unruly, ungovernable, undisciplined.

Ant. **1** unintentional, unintended, accidental, involuntary, unplanned. **2** compliant, acquiescent, submissive; obedient, docile.

willing *adj. I'm willing to go if you are:* content, favorably disposed, amenable, agreeable, not averse, game; ready.

Ant. unwilling, averse, disinclined, reluctant.

willowy *adj. Most ballerinas are willowy:* gracefully slender, svelte, sylphlike, long-legged, lithe, lissome, supple, limber, flexible.

wilt *v.* **1** *The roses wilted:* wither, droop, become limp; shrivel, die. **2** *Her strength wilted away. His courage wilted when he saw the enemy:* wither, fade, wane, ebb, sink, dwindle, diminish, decline, weaken, decrease, deteriorate, flag.

wily *adj. He's too wily to be trusted:* devious, sly, cunning, crafty, tricky; scheming, calculating, designing; deceptive, underhand, treacherous, shifty, crooked; shrewd.

Ant. candid, frank, honest, straightforward; artless, guileless.

win *v.* **1** *Our troops will win:* be victorious, triumph, prevail, conquer. **2** *I won my diploma in only three years:* earn, gain, attain, achieve, accomplish, realize, acquire, obtain, receive. **3** *Opponents of the plan must be won over:* convince, persuade, convert, induce, sway, prevail on. —*n.* **4** *Four more wins and we'll clinch the championship:* victory, triumph, success, conquest; winning game, winning contest.

Ant. **1** lose, be defeated, be beaten. **3** alienate, estrange. **4** loss, defeat.

wince *v.* **1** *The boy winced when his father raised his hand:* grimace, make a face, flinch, draw back, recoil, shrink; quail, cower, cringe. —*n.* **2** *She thought with an unpleasant wince of the money she had lost:* grimace, flinch, shudder, recoil, shrinking; quailing, cowering, cringing.

wind¹ *n.* **1** *Is there enough wind to sail a kite?:* air current, breeze, zephyr, draft, gust, blast, whiff, puff. **2** *The wind blew down several trees:* heavy wind, windstorm, gale, blow. **3** *The blow knocked the wind out of him:* breath, air. **4** *If the deer catch wind of us, they'll run. How did you get wind of our plans?:* scent, smell; hint, suggestion, inkling, intimation, clue, information, intelligence, news, knowledge, tidings. **5** *The speech was just a lot of wind:* empty talk, idle talk, boasting, bombast, bluster, braggadocio.

Ant. **1** calm, calmness.

wind² *v.* **1** *The stream winds through the valley:* curve, bend, snake, wend, twist, zig-zag, ramble, wander, meander. **2** *Wind the*

wire around the post: coil, twist, curl, loop, twine, lap, roll, twirl.

windy *adj.* **1** *March is a windy month:* breezy, gusty, blustery; windswept. **2** *a windy speech:* long-winded, wordy, rambling, verbose, garrulous; talkative, loquacious, gabby.

Ant. **1** windless; calm. **2** concise, pithy, succinct, trenchant.

wing *n.* **1** *The bird's wings: an airplane's wings:* pinion, pennon; flap, aileron. **2** *the east wing of the mansion:* section; extension, appendage. **3** *I belong to the radical wing of the party:* faction, segment, group, clique, circle, set. —*v.* **4** *The aircraft winged out over the Atlantic:* fly, soar, zoom; take wing. **5** *The shot winged the escaping convict:* hit in the arm, hit in the wing; wound slightly, graze, nick.

winner *n. He was winner by a knockout:* victor, champion; vanquisher, conqueror, *Slang* champ.

winsome *adj. a winsome child:* charming, engaging, pleasing, attractive, likable, amiable, appealing, delightful, bewitching.

Ant. disagreeable, unpleasant; repulsive.

wintry *adj. The wintry weather didn't end until April:* cold, snowy, icy; chilly, arctic; stormy, bleak, harsh; cheerless, dreary, gloomy.

Ant. summery, sunny, warm, balmy.

wipe *v.* **1** *Wipe your hands. Wipe wax on the scratched surface:* rub lightly; *(variously)* clean, swab, sponge, mop, scrub, scour; rub off; dry; clean off; rub on, apply. **2** *Wipe that grin off your face:* remove, banish, erase, eradicate. —*n.* **3** *It takes more than a wipe or two to clean the oven:* swipe, rub, swab; stroke, brush.

wiry *adj.* **1** *The child has black, wiry hair:* wire-like; stiff, kinky. **2** *The gymnast was a wiry young man:* sinewy, lean, spare, lanky; agile, limber, pliant.

wisdom *n.* **1** *Wisdom sometimes comes with age:* good judgment, sagacity, understanding, profundity, discernment, comprehension. **2** *the wisdom of Plato:* philosophy, teachings, principles.

Ant. **1** folly, foolishness, nonsense, absurdity.

wise¹ *adj. Judges must be wise:* having good judgment, sagacious, sage, understanding, profound, discerning, perceptive, intelligent, knowing, knowledgeable.

Ant. foolish, stupid, silly, unwise.

wise² *n. This will in no wise infringe on anyone's rights:* way, manner, respect.

wish *v.* **1** *I wish to retire next year. We wish you luck:* want, desire, hope, long, crave, yearn, pine, hunger, thirst, yen, aspire; de-

534

sire one to have, want to come about.
—*n.* 2 *Her wish is to visit Rome:* want,
desire, hope, longing, craving, yearning,
yen, aspiration, ambition; hunger, thirst;
whim. 3 *Don't go against the wishes of the
king:* request, command, will, desire. 4 Usually **wishes** *Please accept our good wishes:*
felicitations, congratulations, compliments.

wishful *adj.* 1 *I am still wishful of becoming
a millionaire:* hopeful, desirous, keen on,
eager, bent upon, anxious, ambitious, aspir-
ing; longing, hankering after, yearning.
2 *His talk of going to Harvard is just wishful
thinking:* wistful, fanciful, overoptimistic.

wishy-washy *adj. He's so wishy-washy he
can never make up his mind:* indecisive, irresolute, vacillating, equivocating, wavering, noncommittal; weak, ineffectual, ineffective.
Ant. decisive, resolute.

wistful *adj.* 1 *The child gave a wistful look at
the candy:* desirous, yearning, longing,
craving, hankering, pining. 2 *She has a
wistful look on her face:* pensive, sadly
thoughtful, reflective, musing, introspective; melancholy, forlorn, sad, sorrowful,
woebegone.

wit *n.* 1 *Her speech was full of wit:* cleverness,
humor, drollery, levity, jocularity, funniness, waggery, quickness at repartee; raillery, badinage, banter, joking, witticisms,
quips, jokes, gags. 2 *The speaker is known
as a wit:* witty person, humorist, joker, jokester, wag, gagster, comedian, comic, wisecracker, punster, satirist. 3 *She showed a
great deal of wit in handling the situation:*
intelligence, understanding, perception,
comprehension, judgment, good sense, insight, sagacity, discernment, astuteness,
cleverness, shrewdness, intellect, *Informal*
brains. 4 **wits** *Keep your wits about you
when you're driving:* mind, sanity, composure, mental balance, coolheadedness; mental alertness.
Ant. 1 gravity, solemnity, dullness. 3 foolishness, stupidity, dumbness, obtuseness.

witch *n.* 1 *The witch put an evil spell on the
princess:* devil's consort, sorceress, female
magician; *(loosely)* seeress, prophetess, enchantress. 2 *She's nice but her sister's a
witch:* hag, crone, harridan, battle-ax, beldam; shrew, virago, termagant, scold.

witchcraft *n. She was hanged for practicing
witchcraft:* worship of the Devil, diabolism;
sorcery, wizardry, black magic, black art,
voodoo, voodooism, hoodoo, conjuration,
casting of spells.

withdraw *v.* 1 *He withdrew his hand from
the back of her chair. The knight withdrew
his sword:* remove, take away, take off; ex-

tract, unsheathe. 2 *The waiter withdrew
after serving the meal:* retire, retreat, go
away, move away, leave, depart, absent
oneself. 3 *I withdraw that last statement:*
retract, recant; rescind, recall.
Ant. 1 put on; put in; sheathe. 2 arrive,
come near. 3 introduce, propose, advance;
repeat, reiterate.

withdrawn *adj. The child is so withdrawn
we're concerned about her:* retiring, reserved, uncommunicative, shy, reclusive,
quiet, introverted, unsocial.
Ant. extroverted, outgoing, sociable,
friendly, warm.

wither *v.* 1 *The fruit withered. Frosts withered the leaves:* wilt, shrivel, dry up, fade.
2 *She withered him with one accusing look:*
shame, humiliate, blast, abash, mortify.
Ant. 1 bloom, flower, blossom. 2 praise,
compliment.

withhold *v.* 1 *The company withholds part
of your earnings for income taxes:* hold
back, hold, keep back, keep, retain. 2 *The
witness was withholding information:* conceal, hide, suppress, keep secret.
Ant. 1, 2 give, provide, furnish. 1 grant,
bestow; let go, free. 2 reveal, disclose, divulge.

withstand *v. A politician must be able to
withstand criticism:* stand up to, resist, endure, bear, suffer, tolerate, weather, brave,
defy.

witness *v.* 1 *Did anyone witness the robbery?:* see, observe, view, behold; note,
mark, notice, attend, be present at. 2 *A no-
tary public must witness the signatures:* verify, certify, corroborate, substantiate, document, validate, endorse, sign, countersign,
initial; attest to, confirm, vouch for, testify
to. —*n.* 3 *Were there any witnesses to the
accident?:* eyewitness, onlooker, observer,
spectator, looker-on, beholder. 4 *His worried look is witness to the strain he's under:*
evidence, testimony, proof, confirmation,
corroboration, verification, authentication,
substantiation, documentation.

witty *adj. Mark Twain's writings are both
witty and profound:* amusing, clever, funny,
humorous, quick-witted, comic, jocular,
jocose, mirthful, droll, whimsical.
Ant. serious, somber; sad, melancholy.

wizard *n.* 1 *Merlin was King Arthur's wizard:* sorcerer, magician, conjurer, en-
chanter, medicine man; oracle, seer, soothsayer; necromancer, diviner, clairvoyant.
2 *Informal She's a wizard at math:* genius,
expert, adept, virtuoso, *Slang* whiz.

wobble *v.* 1 *This ladder wobbles when you
stand on it:* sway, teeter, totter, be unsteady; reel, stagger, waver, shake, quake,

shimmy. —*n.* 2 *The left front wheel has a wobble:* sway, swaying, teetering, tottering, unsteadiness, wavering, shake, shaking, shimmy, shimmying.

woe *n. Job's life was full of woe:* suffering, distress, affliction, trouble, misfortune, calamity, adversity, misery, tribulation, wretchedness, torment, agony, sorrow, grief, heartache, anguish, dejection, gloom, worry, despair.

Ant. joy, delight, pleasure, good fortune, happiness, bliss.

woeful *adj.* 1 *The woeful news grieved the nation:* distressing, unhappy, tragic, agonizing, painful, sorrowful, doleful, grievous, sad, heartrending, heartbreaking, depressing, calamitous, disastrous, catastrophic. 2 *I've never seen such a woeful bunch of job applicants:* of poor quality, unpromising, unlikely, awful, hopeless, bad, dreadful, miserable, appalling.

Ant. 1 happy, joyous, joyful, delightful, glad, cheering. 2 promising, excellent, wonderful, fine.

woman *n.* 1 *The woman waited for the bus:* adult female lady; *(variously)* dowager, matron; damsel, maiden, maid. 2 *Woman, like man, deserves political freedom:* womankind, women, females, the female sex. 3 *The queen's women helped her put on the royal robe. A woman comes in twice a week to clean:* handmaiden, chambermaid, female attendant, lady-in-waiting; maid, housekeeper, cleaning woman. 4 *According to the song, she was his woman but he done her wrong:* paramour, lover, mistress, concubine, kept woman; sweetheart, ladylove, beloved, darling, inamorata, girl, girl friend, sweetie; wife.

Ant. 1–4 man. 1 girl.

wonder *v.* 1 *I wonder what she sees in me. Joe says he didn't do it, but I wonder:* be curious about, be inquisitive, speculate, conjecture, question, be doubtful, be uncertain; meditate, ponder, cogitate. 2 *I wonder at her unfailing strength:* marvel, be wonderstruck, stand agog, be awed, be amazed, be dazed, be stunned, be dumbstruck. —*n.* 3 *the seven wonders of the ancient world:* phenomenon, marvel, miracle, rarity, spectacle, sight. 4 *The audience watched in wonder:* amazement, astonishment, wonderment, awe, fascination.

Ant. 1 know, be sure, be certain, comprehend, understand, perceive, see; not care, be uninterested. 2 be unfazed, be unmoved. 3 common occurrence, commonplace. 4 apathy, indifference; boredom.

wonderful *adj.* 1 *The human brain is a wonderful thing:* awe-inspiring, miraculous,

amazing, incredible, phenomenal, fabulous, fantastic, extraordinary, astonishing, astounding, fascinating, striking, spectacular. 2 *We had a wonderful time:* excellent, admirable, marvelous, magnificent, good, fine, great, terrific, first-rate, capital, smashing, super, sensational, fabulous, fantastic, superb, divine.

Ant. 1 ordinary, common, mediocre, paltry. 2 awful, terrible, dreadful, abominable, miserable, horrid, *Slang* lousy.

woo *v.* 1 *Father wooed several girls before marrying Mother:* court, pay court to; pursue, chase. 2 *The mayor knew how to woo the voters:* persuade, solicit, petition, court, appeal to, pursue, cajole, entreat, curry favor with.

wood *n.* 1 *The building was made of wood. Throw more wood on the fire:* lumber, timber, boards, planks; log, firewood, kindling. 2 *Usually* **woods** *a clearing in the woods:* forest, timberland, woodland, wildwood, bush, brush.

wooden *adj.* 1 *a large wooden crate:* wood, frame. 2 *I was amazed at how wooden she was on the dance floor:* stiff, rigid, unbending, inflexible, ungainly, ungraceful. 3 *She gave the stranger a wooden stare:* expressionless, dull, vacant, unemotional, impassive, glassy-eyed.

Ant. 2 lissome, supple, limber, lithe, pliant, graceful. 3 expressive, animated, emotional, fervent.

word *n.* 1 *Let me say a word of thanks:* brief statement, remark, comment, utterance, phrase, pronouncement. 2 *The boss wants to have a word with you:* short talk, chat, brief conversation, discussion, consultation, tête-à-tête, dialogue, discourse. 3 **words** *They had words in the lobby and started to fight in the hall:* angry words, argument, quarrel, dispute, bickering, wrangling, altercation. 4 *She sent word that she had arrived safely. What's the latest word from the war zone?:* message, communication, news, information, report, advice, tidings, intelligence; dispatch, bulletin, communiqué, letter, telegram, telephone call; rumor, gossip, lowdown. 5 *Ed gave me his word he would be here:* assurance, promise, word of honor, pledge; vow, avowal, assertion, declaration. 6 *The troops got the word to move out:* command, order, direction, decree, notice, summons, dictate, edict, mandate; decision, ruling, signal. —*v.* 7 *Try to word the letter in a friendly way:* phrase, put into words, find words for, express.

wording *n. The wording of your report is ambiguous:* phrasing, phraseology, manner of expression, choice of words, language.

wordy *adj. Don't be so wordy:* verbose, long-winded, windy, loquacious, garrulous, talkative, discursive, roundabout; effusive.

Ant. concise, terse, succinct, pithy.

work *n.* 1 *It took a lot of work to make that cabinet:* labor, effort, industry, exertion, toil, endeavor, drudgery, manual labor, elbow grease, sweat. 2 *Cleaning out the files is your work for today:* piece of work, job, task, chore, employment, duty, assignment. 3 *He's looking for work. I decided to make retailing my work:* employment, job; line of work, occupation, profession, business, vocation, line, trade, craft, pursuit. 4 *This painting is one of Matisse's greatest works:* work of art, creation, composition, achievement, piece, product, endeavor; *(variously)* painting, drawing, sculpture, book, opus, symphony, opera, concerto, song, building. 5 *We'll be long remembered for our good works:* deed, act; achievement, feat, exploit, enterprise, transaction. 6 **works** *Every town used to have its own gasworks:* plant, factory, mill, foundry, yard, shop, workshop. 7 **works** *the works of the watch:* internal mechanism, moving parts, insides. —*v.* 8 *He works at the grocery. The mechanic worked for hours to fix the car:* be employed, have a job, be occupied, do business, pursue a vocation; labor, toil, be industrious, apply oneself, endeavor, drudge, slave, sweat. 9 *How does this machine work? It's a good idea, but it won't work. to work a jigsaw puzzle:* operate, function, perform, run, go; be effective, succeed; do, solve, execute, achieve. 10 *Work the dough into a ball:* shape, form, fashion, mold, make, manipulate. 11 *The ship worked its way into the harbor:* progress, move, maneuver. 12 *I can't work miracles!:* bring about, produce, cause, effect; originate, engender.

Ant. 1, 2, 8 play. 1 ease, leisure. 2 recreation, entertainment, fun. 3 unemployment; avocation, hobby. 8 relax, take it easy.

worker *n. The plant employs 500 workers. The charity drive needs more workers to collect funds:* workingman, workingwoman, workman, laborer, laboring man, laboring woman, hired hand, hand; employee, job holder, artisan, craftsman, wage earner, breadwinner; doer, performer, producer, achiever.

Ant. employer; unemployed person, retiree; idler, loafer.

working *n.* 1 *Working takes up about a third of the day:* labor, laboring, toil, industry, drudgery; employment, job, tasks, chores, assignments, business, profession, occupation, duty. 2 *Do you understand the working of a computer?:* operation, action, functioning. —*adj.* 3 *working women:* employed, holding down a job, laboring. 4 *The job requires a working knowledge of Spanish:* usable, useful, practical, effective, operative, functioning.

Ant. 1 play, recreation, fun, entertainment; rest, relaxation, leisure. 3 nonworking, unemployed, jobless; retired, vacationing.

workmanship *n. The chair is a fine example of workmanship:* craftsmanship, handiwork, manual skill, handicraft, handcraft; construction, technique.

world *n.* 1 *China is the largest country in the world. Is there life on other worlds?:* globe, Earth, wide world; planet, heavenly body, celestial object. 2 *We cannot explain many things in the world:* creation, universe, cosmos. 3 *The world must unite in the war on pollution:* mankind, humanity, the human race, humankind, people; everyone, everybody. 4 *The sequoia is the tallest member of the plant world. the world of science:* group, class, division, system, sphere, domain, realm. 5 *It's nice to get away from the world once in a while:* human affairs, society, social intercourse, mundane interests, worldly things. 6 *We're still learning about the ancient world:* era, period, epoch, age, times. 7 *A vacation will do you a world of good:* a great deal, large amount, *Informal* lots.

worldly *adj.* 1 *Worldly things meant nothing to them:* earthly, terrestrial, mundane, temporal, secular, profane; material, mercenary; physical, corporeal, fleshly. 2 *He's too worldly to be shocked by the scandal:* sophisticated, cosmopolitan, urbane, worldly-wise, knowing, experienced.

Ant. 1 spiritual, heavenly, celestial, divine, holy, sacred; ethereal, transcendental, nonmaterial. 2 innocent, naive, unsophisticated.

worn *adj.* 1 *There's a worn place on this jacket:* worn through, worn-down, worn-out, frayed, abraded, threadbare; dilapidated, shabby, weatherbeaten, tumbledown, timeworn; faded. 2 *She looked worn and pale:* exhausted, fatigued, worn-out, weary, wearied, tired, haggard; weak, enfeebled, debilitated; pinched, drawn.

Ant. 1 new. 2 vigorous, peppy, refreshed.

worrisome *adj.* 1 *a worrisome problem:* troublesome, aggravating, annoying, irritating, vexing, trying, irksome, bothersome. 2 *Sue is so worrisome she never has a moment's peace:* anxious, apprehensive, uneasy, despairing, fretful.

Ant. 2 carefree, nonchalant.

worry *v.* 1 *Mother always worries when we stay out late:* be anxious, feel uneasy, be apprehensive, be disturbed, be troubled, be distressed, agonize; fret, despair, be downhearted, be afraid. 2 *Lack of rain is beginning to worry the farmers. Stop worrying me and get to work:* make anxious, make uneasy, disturb, upset, agitate, trouble, distress; harry, badger, hector, pester, vex, plague. —*n*. 3 *The boy caused his parents a lot of worry:* anxiety, uneasiness, apprehension, concern, consternation, dismay; trouble, distress, bother, grief, torment, misery, woe, care, vexation. 4 *Cancellation of the game is our chief worry:* concern, care, problem, dread.

Ant. 2 comfort, soothe, calm, allay. 3 certitude; equanimity, serenity, tranquillity, peace of mind; comfort.

worsen *v. The patient's condition continued to worsen:* decline, deteriorate, slip, slide, take a turn for the worse, degenerate, fail.

Ant. improve, get better.

worship *n*. 1 *The worship of idols is called "idolatry":* adoration, veneration, exaltation, reverence. 2 *Worship is on Sunday at 11 A.M.:* divine service, religious service, devotionals. —*v*. 3 *Each religion worships God in its own way:* pray to, adore, revere, venerate, reverence; glorify, exalt, praise. 4 *He worships his older brother:* idolize, revere, adulate, dote upon, lionize.

Ant. detest, loathe, despise, scorn, disdain.

worth *n*. 1 *A good education is of great worth:* use, usefulness, benefit, value, merit, worthiness, importance. 2 *The appraiser put a worth of a thousand dollars on the ring:* value, price, cost, selling price, going price; valuation, appraisal. 3 *My net worth is over a million dollars:* assets, wealth, resources, holdings.

Ant. 1 uselessness, fruitlessness, worthlessness; drawback, handicap.

worthless *adj. The land proved to be worthless. Joe's idea is worthless:* without value, useless, unusable, unproductive, ineffectual, fruitless, futile, meritless; unimportant, insignificant, trivial, paltry, of no account.

Ant. worthwhile, valuable, profitable, useful, usable, productive, effective, fruitful; important, consequential.

worthwhile *adj. Here's some worthwhile advice. So few movies are worthwhile nowadays:* valuable, worthy, profitable, rewarding, useful, usable, beneficial, good; worth one's time, worth the effort.

Ant. worthless, useless, valueless; unimportant, inconsequential.

worthy *adj*. 1 *a worthy cause. a worthy competitor:* worthwhile, deserving, praise-

worthy, laudable, commendable, admirable, excellent, good, suitable, fitting, befitting, appropriate; honorable, virtuous, moral, ethical, reputable, upright, decent, respectable, honest, reliable, trustworthy. —*n*. 2 *the mayor and other local worthies:* notable, dignitary, leader, official, person of distinction, personage, luminary, pillar of society, *Slang* VIP, bigwig, big shot.

Ant. 1 unworthy, worthless, undeserving; dishonorable, disreputable, dishonest, unethical. 2 nobody.

wound *n*. 1 *He had a wound over his left eye:* laceration, gash, cut, lesion; contusion, bruise. 2 *The argument caused a wound that has never healed:* hurt feelings, trauma, provocation, irritation, vexation, pain, distress, anguish, hurt, injury, damage. —*v*. 3 *The bullet wounded the officer:* lacerate, gash, cut, slash, tear, pierce, bruise; hurt, injure. 4 *His nasty remark really wounded me:* hurt the feelings of, offend, pain, sting, distress, grieve, mortify; harm, damage.

Ant. 3, 4 heal. 4 appease, assuage, comfort.

wrap *v*. 1 *Wrap a bandage around his arm:* enclose, enwrap, bundle, encase; bind, wind, fold. 2 *The valley was wrapped in fog:* clothe, cover, envelop, enclose, swathe, surround, shroud, cloak, hide, conceal. —*n*. 3 *Take a wrap in case the weather turns cool:* (variously) shawl, cloak, cape, stole, mantle, wrapper, scarf; sweater, jacket, coat.

Ant. 1 unwrap, unbind, unwind, undo. 2 uncover, expose, reveal.

wrath *n. I was the object of her wrath:* anger, rage, fury, ire, indignation, rancor, resentment, hostility, animosity, displeasure.

Ant. kindness, friendship, affability, forgiveness.

wreak *v. The hurricane wreaked havoc on the town:* inflict, visit, work, execute, unleash.

wreath *n. The President placed a wreath on the tomb:* garland, laurel, lei, festoon; coronet, crown, chaplet, diadem.

wreck *v*. 1 *The airplane skidded off the runway and wrecked two hangars:* ruin, destroy, demolish, level, raze, smash, shatter, devastate. —*n*. 2 *The owners let the house become a wreck. After the scandal, Henry became a complete wreck:* ruin, mess; sick person, ailing person, debilitated person; derelict, wretch. 3 *The wreck was towed into port for salvage:* shipwrecked vessel, stranded ship; ruins. 4 *Budget cuts mean the wreck of all our plans:* ruin, destruction, devastation, undoing, disruption, upset; crash, crack-up; end, finish, annihilation.

Ant. **1** build, create, construct. **4** salvage, saving.

wrench *v.* **1** *She wrenched the knife from my hand:* twist, wrest, wring, force, pull, jerk, tear, rip. **2** *I wrenched my ankle:* twist, sprain, strain. **3** *Don't wrench the facts:* distort, twist, misrepresent. —*n.* **4** *With one quick wrench he opened the jar:* twist, wring, jerk, pull; tear, rip.

wrest *v.* **1** *He tried to wrest the ball from my grasp:* wrench, twist, wring, take, grab, pull, jerk, tear, rip, force. **2** *to wrest a living from the soil:* obtain, get, gain, attain, make, glean, extract.

Ant. **2** yield, give, furnish, supply.

wrestle *v.* **1** *Mother forbade the boys to wrestle:* engage in wrestling; tussle, scuffle, grapple. **2** *I've been wrestling with this problem for weeks:* struggling, grapple, contend, struggle, labor, battle.

wretch *n.* **1** *The poor wretch was shivering in the doorway:* unfortunate, unhappy person, sufferer. **2** *The miserable wretch deserted his wife and children:* contemptible person, scoundrel, rotter, blackguard, rascal, rogue, knave, swine, cur; *Slang* louse.

wretched *adj.* **1** *The wretched man hadn't eaten in three days. She's been wretched since her child died:* pitiable, pitiful, unfortunate; pathetic, miserable, unhappy, hapless, forlorn, downcast, doleful, despondent, depressed, dejected, abject; brokenhearted, inconsolable, disconsolate, gloomy, despairing, hopeless, sick at heart. **2** *a wretched miser. A wretched meal:* contemptible, despicable, mean, miserable, vile, low, niggardly; worthless, awful, terrible, dreadful, rotten, *Informal* lousy.

Ant. **1** fortunate, enviable, successful, thriving; happy, cheerful, carefree, lighthearted. **2** noble, admirable; excellent, good, wonderful, fine, great.

wring *v.* **1** *Wring the water out of the towel. He wrung my hand in gratitude:* twist, squeeze, press, compress, choke. **2** *Isn't there any way to wring the truth out of you?:* force, coerce, wrest, extract. **3** *Her sad story wrung our hearts:* sadden, grieve, distress, pain, hurt.

Ant. **2** coax, wheedle, cajole, charm. **3** gladden, cheer.

wrinkle[1] *n.* **1** *The shirt didn't have a wrinkle in it:* crinkle, crimp, pucker, furrow, corrugation, fold, gather, pleat; crow's-feet. —*v.* **2** *This dress won't wrinkle:* crease, rumple, crinkle, crumple, pucker, crimp, furrow, gather, pleat.

wrinkle[2] *n.* *A five-wheeled car is a new wrinkle:* trick, device, gimmick; idea, notion, fancy; viewpoint, point of view, slant.

write *v.* **1** *Just write the story exactly as it happened:* be literate; set down, write down, jot down, record, put on paper, put in writing; scribble, scrawl, transcribe, copy, inscribe, dash off, *Informal* author, pen, compose, draft. **2** *Deceit was written all over his face:* be evident, be manifest, be apparent, show, be visible.

Ant. **1** be illiterate; read. **2** hide, conceal, mask, cloak, veil.

writer *n.* **1** *I can print, but I'm still a poor writer:* penman, calligrapher, scribe, copyist, scribbler, scrawler. **2** *Tolstoy is a famous Russian writer. She's a sportswriter for the Tribune:* author, professional writer; *(variously)* novelist, playwright, dramatist, poet, essayist, reporter, journalist, newspaperman, newspaperwoman, correspondent, reviewer, critic, columnist, scriptwriter, screenwriter, television writer, songwriter, librettist, *Informal* hack.

Ant. **2** reader; viewer; listener.

writhe *v.* *The patient was writhing in pain:* twist about, flail, thresh, thrash, jerk, contort, squirm, wiggle, wriggle.

writing *n.* **1** *The actual writing of the report took two days:* writing down, jotting down, composing, drafting, *Informal* authoring; transcribing, copying. **2** *I won't believe it until I see it in writing. Can you read my writing?:* written form, print; handwriting, penmanship, longhand; calligraphy. **3** *The class is studying the writings of 18th-century novelists: (variously)* document, letter, diary, journal, composition, publication, book, work, volume, tome, opus, novel, play, story, poem, essay, article, report, editorial, column, manuscript, script, libretto.

Ant. **1** reading.

wrong *adj.* **1** *Cheating is wrong:* immoral, evil, wicked, sinful, bad, wrongful, dishonest, unethical, dishonorable; unlawful, illegal, crooked, criminal; unfair, unjust, unwarranted, unjustifiable, inexcusable. **2** *a wrong answer:* incorrect, erroneous, untrue, false, inaccurate, mistaken, faulty; inexact, illogical, unsound. **3** *Such dark wallpaper is wrong for a playroom. Did I say the wrong thing?:* improper, incorrect, unsuitable, inappropriate, undesirable, unbecoming, unseemly, unfitting, unbefitting, inapt, unhappy, infelicitous, incongruous. **4** *Something's wrong with the motor:* faulty, amiss, out of order, out of kilter, awry. **5** *Iron the skirt on the wrong side:* inverse, reverse, opposite. —*n.* **6** *to know the difference between right and wrong. We were condemned for our wrongs:* immorality, evil, wickedness, sinfulness, iniquity, unrighteousness, dishonesty, unlawfulness, illegality, unfairness, injustice; immoral act, evil deed, sin, vice, offense, crime, misdeed, wrongdoing, villainy, transgression, trespass. —*adv.* 7 *You guessed wrong:* incorrectly, erroneously, inaccurately, mistakenly. —*v.* 8 *Do you really think I wronged her?:* mistreat, treat unjustly, treat unfairly, dishonor, harm, injure, hurt.

Ant. 1–3, 5–7 right. 1 moral, virtuous, righteous, ethical, honorable, lawful, just, fair; commendable, praiseworthy, worthy, laudable. 2 correct, true, accurate, perfect; logical, sensible. 3 proper, correct, suitable, appropriate, befitting. 6 righteousness,

goodness, honesty, lawfulness, justice, fairness; virtue, good deed. 7 correctly, accurately.

wrongdoer *n. Police apprehended the wrongdoers:* malefactor, perpetrator, miscreant, evildoer, culprit, lawbreaker, transgressor, sinner, trespasser, offender.

wrought *adj. a delicately wrought silver tray:* worked, formed, made, fashioned, crafted, handcrafted, constructed.

wry *adj. He made a wry face to show his disbelief. She made a wry remark:* twisted, contorted, distorted, askew, awry, warped; ironic, cynical, sarcastic, sardonic, satiric, bitter; amusing, droll.

Ant. straight, direct.

X, Y, Z

x-ray *n. The doctor took several x-rays:* roentgenogram, roentgenograph, radiogram, radiograph.

yank *v.* 1 *The boy yanked the flower out of the ground:* pull suddenly, jerk, wrest, tug, snatch, wrench; pull out, pluck, extract. —*n.* 2 *Give the door a good yank:* pull, jerk, tug, wrench.

Ant. 1, 2 push, shove.

yap *v.* 1 *The little dog yapped all night:* bark shrilly, yelp, yip, yawp. 2 *What's he yapping about now?:* talk incessantly, talk foolishly, chatter, jabber, gabble, babble, blather, prattle, rave, gush, blab, gossip, tattle; talk, lecture, scold, complain. —*n.* 3 *The puppy gave a series of yaps:* shrill bark, yelp, yip, yawp.

yard[1] *n. The children are playing in the yard:* grounds; enclosure, compound, confine, close; courtyard, court; garden, lawn.

yard[2] *n.* 1 *two yards of dress material:* three feet, 36 inches, .914 meter; *abbreviation* yd. 2 *The captain threatened to hang the mutineers from the yard:* yardarm, horizontal spar.

yarn *n.* 1 *Buy some yarn and I'll knit you a sweater:* knitting thread, weaving thread. 2 *The old sailor told us yarns about whaling:* tale, story, anecdote, adventure story, narrative.

year *n.* 1 *It's been a good year:* period of 365 days (or in leap year 366 days), 12-month period, 52-week period, period of a planet's revolution around the sun. 2 *years She*

seemed very mature for her years: age, time of life. 3 *years The country went through years of turmoil:* period, time, era, epoch, cycle.

yearn *v. We yearned for peace:* crave, have a strong desire, want, long, hanker, ache, hunger, thirst, wish, languish, pine, sigh, have a fancy for.

Ant. detest, despise, hate, loathe, abhor, be repelled by, recoil from, be revolted by.

yearning *n. I had a yearning to return to Hawaii:* craving, longing, hankering, yen, hunger, thirst, ache, strong desire, wish, want, desire, passion.

yell *v.* 1 *He yelled for help. The crowd yelled at the umpire:* cry out, shout, holler, scream, bellow, roar, howl, shriek, bawl, whoop, yowl, hollo, hoot, screech, squall, yelp, clamor, raise one's voice; cheer, hurrah, huzzah; boo. —*n.* 2 *The child gave a yell of delight. The yells of the crowd drowned out the announcer's voice:* cry, outcry, shout, holler, scream, bellow, roar, howl, shriek, whoop, hoot, screech, squeal, yelp, hollo, clamor; cheer, hurrah, huzzah; boo.

yellow *adj.* 1 *a yellow scarf:* lemon, canary, gold, ocher, saffron; flaxen, straw-colored, blond. 2 *Informal They said I was yellow:* cowardly, pusillanimous, craven, fainthearted, afraid, frightened, *Slang* chicken.

Ant. 2 brave, courageous, fearless, unafraid, lionhearted, *Slang* game.

yelp *n.* 1 *The dog gave a yelp when I stepped on its paw:* sharp cry, yap, howl, yip, bark,

540

squeal. —v. 2 *The girls yelped with glee:* cry shrilly, scream, shriek, screech, squeal, clamor, holler, shout; yap, yip, howl, bark.

yen n. 1 *I had a yen for a big thick steak:* craving, longing, hankering, yearning, hunger, thirst, appetite, aching, desire, wish, passion. —v. 2 *The miner yenned for fresh air and sunlight:* crave, long, hanker, yearn, ache, hunger, thirst, wish, pine, sigh, desire, wish, want, have a passion for.
Ant. 1 loathing, abhorrence, revulsion. 2 detest, despise, hate, loathe, abhor, abominate.

yes adv. 1 *Yes, you are right:* aye, it is so, just so, true, granted, of course, surely, really, truly, to be sure, assuredly, certainly, indeed, undoubtedly, doubtless, positively, precisely, exactly, so be it; affirmatively, in the affirmative. —n. 2 *May we count on your yes?:* affirmative reply, affirmative vote, affirmation, consent, assent, okay, acquiescence, acceptance, agreement, authorization, approval.
Ant. 1, 2 no, nay. 1 not so, untrue, of course not, negatively, in the negative. 2 refusal, rejection, veto.

yield v. 1 *This tree yields apples every year:* bear, bring forth, produce, put forth. 2 *The bond yields 8% a year:* earn, return, generate, pay; provide, furnish, supply, render, give. 3 *Don't yield to temptation:* surrender, give up, give in, give way, capitulate, submit, succumb; accede, acquiesce. 4 *Cars entering the highway must yield the right of way:* relinquish, grant, concede, give up, defer, forgo, waive. 5 *The chair yielded under his weight:* give way, sag, droop, cave in, collapse, break. —n. 6 *Farmers had an exceptionally good yield this year:* harvest, crop; produce, product. 7 *The yield on municipal bonds was 9 3/4%:* interest, dividend, appreciation, return, earnings, proceeds, gain, payment, revenue, premium.
Ant. 3 resist, oppose, combat, repulse, repel. 4 keep, retain, maintain, reserve; appropriate, take, seize.

yoke n. 1 *A yoke held the two wires together:* double harness; coupler, collar, bond, clasp. 2 *It takes a yoke of oxen to pull that wagon:* pair, team, brace, span. —v. 3 *The farmer yoked the oxen to the plow:* couple, double harness; hitch, harness. 4 *The nation's economic growth is yoked to that of its neighbors:* join, unit, couple, link, attach, fasten.
Ant. 3 unyoke, uncouple, unhitch, unharness. 4 separate, divorce.

yokel n. *With modern transportation and communications there are very few yokels anymore:* bumpkin, country bumpkin,

naive rustic, rube, provincial, clod, clodhopper, hayseed, hick, country boy.

yonder adv. *I was born way down yonder in New Orleans:* faraway, far-off, over the hills and faraway; over there, there, thither.
Ant. nearby, close-by; over here, here.

young adj. 1 *You're still young:* youthful, not old; juvenile, infantile, underage, minor; childish, boyish, girlish, puerile, adolescent, teenage; immature, inexperienced; undeveloped, growing, budding. —n. 2 *Both young and old like ice cream:* young persons, young people, children, juveniles, youngsters, kids, youths, teenagers, adolescents. 3 *The mother tiger guards her young fiercely:* baby, child, cub, pup, whelp, kitten; offspring, issue, progeny.
Ant. 1, 2 old, aged. 1 elderly, older, elder, senior, venerable; adult, mature, grown-up; experienced; full-grown. 2 the old, senior citizens, oldster, adults, grownups. 3 parent, progenitor.

youngster n. *The youngsters are both in school:* child, boy, girl, youth, kid, young person; minor, adolescent, juvenile, teenager; offspring, progeny; tot, baby.
Ant. oldster, senior citizen; adult, grownup.

youth n. 1 *I visited South America in my youth:* early life, childhood, boyhood, girlhood, adolescence, growing years, teens, minority, school days, salad days, younger days; youthful condition, youthful appearance. 2 *You have plenty of time yet, you're still a youth:* boy, schoolboy, lad, youngster, child, kid, juvenile, minor, teenager, adolescent, young man. 3 *The TV program is aimed at youth:* young persons, young people, the young, children, boys and girls, youngsters, kids, juveniles, teenagers, adolescents, the rising generation, young men and women.
Ant. 1 old age, later life; adulthood, maturity. 2 man; old man. 3 senior citizens, oldsters; adults, grownups.

youthful adj. *The magician loved youthful audiences. a youthful prank:* young, juvenile, adolescent, teenage; childish, boyish, girlish, immature, sophomoric; young-looking, enthusiastic, fresh, young at heart.
Ant. old, aged, elderly, older, senior; adult, mature, grown-up, old-mannish, old-womanish, old-fashioned.

yowl v. 1 *The cats were yowling on the fence:* howl, bay, caterwaul, yelp, scream, shriek, screech, squeal, bawl, whine. —n. 2 *He let out a yowl when he fell:* howl, wail, yelp, cry, shout, holler, bellow, roar, scream, shriek, screech, squeal, whine, bawl, caterwaul.

zany adj. 1 *I prefer zany comedy to sophisticated humor:* clownish, outlandish, silly, ludicrous, slapstick, wild. —*n.* 2 *Don't be such a zany; be serious for a change:* clown, buffoon, jester, comic, cutup. 3 *That zany ought to be in a circus or an asylum:* eccentric, lunatic, nut, crazy, weirdo.

zeal *n. We began the work with zeal. His political zeal prevented us from having a quiet discussion:* zest, gusto, eagerness, fervor, ardor, enthusiasm, vigor, verve; intensity, intentness, vehemence, fire, passion, fanaticism.
Ant. apathy, indifference, languor, listlessness.

zealot *n.* 1 *It takes a real zealot to be a top-notch car salesman:* believer, enthusiast, partisan, champion, devotee, fan, buff; go-getter, hustler. 2 *Religious zealots wanted everyone to wear sackcloth and ashes:* fanatic, true believer, obsessed person, extremist, crank, crackpot, nut.

zealous *adj. Bill is a zealous worker. The lawyer made a zealous plea for her client:* full of zeal, eager, fervent, fervid, vigorous, ardent, earnest, enthusiastic; intense, fierce, vehement, passionate, impassioned, devoted, industrious; fanatic, raging, raving.
Ant. apathetic, listless, unenthusiastic, dispassionate, passionless, indifferent, lackluster, lackadaisical.

zenith *n. Being elected mayor was the zenith of my political career:* peak, highest point, high point, crowning point, pinnacle, acme, summit, apex, vertex, apogee; maximum, best, culmination, climax.
Ant. nadir; lowest point, low point, depth, worst.

zephyr *n. A zephyr whispered through the trees:* light breeze, gentle wind, breath of air, puff of air; west wind.

zero *n.* 1 *All our efforts added up to zero:* nothing, nothingness, naught, aught; cipher, *Slang* goose egg, zilch, zip; *symbol* 0. —*adj.* 2 *Our chances of making a profit are zero:* nil, nonexistent, no, naught, aught, *Slang* zilch, zip.
Ant. 1 infinity; something, everything. 2 perfect, excellent.

zest *n.* 1 *a zest for adventure:* keen enjoyment, gusto, relish, appetite, zeal, eagerness, enthusiasm, verve, passion; exhilaration, excitement, delight, joy. 2 *The special zest of this soup is due to the saffron:* flavoring, flavor, savor, taste, piquancy, spice.
Ant. 1 weariness, distaste, aversion, repugnance, loathing.

zip *n.* 1 *We heard the zip of a bullet:* hiss, whine, whistle, buzz. 2 *He doesn't have enough zip for the job:* energy, vim, vigor, pep, animation, liveliness, vitality, enthusiasm; drive, force, strength, intensity. —*v.* 3 *Zip down to the store and get a quart of milk:* run, go quickly, dash, dart, rush, hurry, fly. 4 *Better zip your jacket—it's cold outside:* zip up, zipper, close.
Ant. 2 lethargy, languor, sluggishness, listlessness. 3 creep, crawl. 4 unzip.

zone *n. the North Temperate Zone. a residential zone:* region, territory, area, terrain, belt; district, quarter, precinct, ward, sector, section.

zoo *n. We saw the elephants at the zoo:* zoological garden, zoological park; animal farm, menagerie.

zoom *v.* 1 *The car zoomed past us:* speed, race, streak, flash, zip, shoot, fly. 2 *Stock market prices zoomed today:* rise, climb, soar, advance, skyrocket, rocket, ascend, take off.

SYNONYM STUDIES

ability, *n.* ABILITY, FACULTY, TALENT denote power or capacity to do something. ABILITY is the general word for a natural or acquired capacity to do things; it usually implies doing them well: *a leader of great ability; ability in mathematics.* FACULTY denotes a natural or acquired ability for a particular kind of action: *a faculty for putting people at ease.* TALENT usually denotes an exceptional natural ability or aptitude in a particular field: *a talent for music.*

acknowledge, *v.* ACKNOWLEDGE, ADMIT, CONFESS agree in the idea of declaring something to be true. ACKNOWLEDGE implies making a statement reluctantly, often about something previously doubted or denied: *to acknowledge one's mistakes.* ADMIT especially implies acknowledging under pressure: *to admit a charge.* CONFESS usually means stating something formally an admission of wrongdoing or shortcoming: *to confess guilt, to confess an inability to understand.*

adjust, *v.* ADJUST, ADAPT, ALTER imply making necessary or desirable changes, as in position, shape, or the like. To ADJUST is to make a minor change, as to move into proper position for use: *to adjust the eyepiece of a telescope.* To ADAPT is to make a change in character, or to make something useful in a new way: *to adapt a method to a new task.* To ALTER is to change the appearance but not the use: *to alter a suit.*

age, *n.* AGE, EPOCH, ERA, PERIOD all refer to an extent of time. AGE usually implies a considerable extent of time, especially one associated with a dominant personality, influence, characteristic, or institution: *the age of chivalry.* EPOCH and ERA are often used interchangeably to refer to an extent of time characterized by changed conditions and new undertakings: *an era (or epoch) of invention.* EPOCH sometimes refers especially to the beginning of an era: *The steam engine marked a new epoch in technology.* A PERIOD usually has a marked condition or feature: *a period of industrial expansion; the Victorian period.*

agreement, *n.* AGREEMENT, BARGAIN, COMPACT, CONTRACT all suggest an arrangement between two or more parties. AGREEMENT ranges in meaning from a mutual understanding to a binding obligation: *an agreement to meet next week; a tariff agreement.* BARGAIN applies particularly to agreements about buying and selling; it suggests haggling: *We made a bargain that I would do the work if they supplied the materials.* COMPACT applies to treaties or alliances between nations or to solemn personal pledges: *a compact to preserve the peace.* CONTRACT is used especially in law and business for agreements that are legally enforceable: *a contract to sell a house.*

assign, *v.* ASSIGN, ALLOCATE, ALLOT mean to apportion or measure out. To ASSIGN is to distribute available things, designating them to be given to or reserved for specific persons or purposes: *to assign duties.* To ALLOCATE is to earmark or set aside parts of things available or expected in the future, each for a specific purpose: *to allocate income to various types of expenses.* To ALLOT implies making restrictions as to amount, size, purpose, etc., and then apportioning or assigning: *to allot spaces for parking.*

attribute, *v.* ATTRIBUTE, ASCRIBE, IMPUTE mean to assign something to a definite cause or source. Possibly because of an association with *tribute,* ATTRIBUTE often has a complimentary connotation: *to attribute one's success to a friend's encouragement.* ASCRIBE is used in a similar sense, but has a neutral implication: *to ascribe an accident to carelessness.* IMPUTE usually means to attribute something dishonest or discreditable to a person; it implies blame or accusation: *to impute an error to a new employee.*

begin, *v.* BEGIN, COMMENCE, INITIATE, START (when followed by noun or gerund) refer to setting into motion or progress something that continues for some time. BEGIN is the common term: *to begin knitting a sweater.* COMMENCE is a more formal word, often suggesting a more prolonged or elaborate beginning: *to commence proceedings in court.* INITIATE implies an active and often ingenious first act in a new field: *to initiate a new procedure.* START means to make a first move or to set out on a course of action: *to start paving a street.*

bias, *n.* BIAS, PREJUDICE mean a strong inclination of the mind or a preconceived opinion about something or someone. A BIAS may be favorable or unfavorable: *bias in favor of or against an idea.* PREJUDICE implies a preformed judgment even more unreasoning than BIAS, and usually implies an unfavorable opinion: *prejudice against a race.*

bold, *adj.* BOLD, BRAZEN, FORWARD, PRESUMPTUOUS refer to behavior or manners that break the rules of propriety. BOLD suggests shamelessness and immodesty: *a bold stare.* BRAZEN suggests the same, together with a defiant manner: *a brazen liar.* FORWARD implies making oneself unduly prominent or bringing oneself to notice with too much assurance: *The forward young man challenged the speaker.* PRESUMPTUOUS implies overconfidence, or taking too much for granted: *It was presumptuous of her to think she could defeat the champion.*

boundary, *n.* BOUNDARY, BORDER, FRONTIER refer to that which divides one territory or political unit from another. BOUNDARY most often designates a line on a map; it may be a physical feature, such as a river: *Boundaries are shown in red.* BORDER refers to a political or geographic dividing line; it may also refer to the region adjoining the actual line: *crossing the Mexican border.* FRONTIER refers specifically to a border between two countries or the region adjoining this border: *Soldiers guarded the frontier.*

calm, *adj.* CALM, COLLECTED, COMPOSED, COOL imply the absence of agitation. CALM implies an unruffled state in the midst of disturbance all around: *He remained calm throughout the crisis.* COLLECTED implies complete command of one's thoughts, feelings, and behavior, usually as a result of effort: *The witness was remarkably collected during questioning.* COMPOSED implies inner peace and dignified self-possession: *pale but composed.* COOL implies clarity of judgment and absence of strong feeling or excitement: *cool in the face of danger.*

change, *v.* CHANGE, ALTER both mean to make a difference in the state or condition of a thing. To CHANGE is to make a material or radical difference or to substitute one thing for another of the same kind: *to*

change a lock; to change one's plans.* To ALTER is to make some partial change, as in appearance, but usually to preserve the identity: *to alter a garment; to alter a contract.*

character, *n.* CHARACTER, PERSONALITY refer to the sum of the characteristics possessed by a person. CHARACTER refers especially to the moral qualities and ethical standards that make up the inner nature of a person: *a man of sterling character.* PERSONALITY refers particularly to outer characteristics, as wit or charm, that determine the impression that a person makes upon others: *a pleasing personality.*

choice, *n.* CHOICE, ALTERNATIVE, OPTION suggest the power of choosing between things. CHOICE implies the opportunity to choose freely: *His choice for dessert was ice cream.* ALTERNATIVE suggests a chance to choose only one of a limited number of possibilities: *I had the alternative of going to the party or staying home alone.* OPTION emphasizes the right or privilege of choosing: *She had the option of taking the prize money or a gift.*

comfort, *v.* COMFORT, CONSOLE, SOOTHE imply easing sorrow, worry, discomfort, or pain. COMFORT means to lessen someone's grief or distress by giving strength and hope and restoring a cheerful outlook: *to comfort a despairing friend.* CONSOLE, a more formal word, means to make grief or distress seem lighter by means of kindness and thoughtful attentions: *to console a bereaved parent.* SOOTHE means to pacify or calm: *to soothe a crying child.*

concern, *n.* CONCERN, CARE, WORRY connote an uneasy and burdened state of mind. CONCERN implies an anxious sense of interest in or responsibility for something: *concern over a friend's misfortune.* CARE suggests a heaviness of spirit caused by dread, or by the constant pressure of burdensome demands: *Poverty weighed them down with care.* WORRY is a state of agitated uneasiness and restless apprehension: *distracted by worry over investments.*

concise, *adj.* CONCISE, SUCCINCT, TERSE refer to speech or writing that uses few words to say much. CONCISE implies that unnecessary details or verbiage have been eliminated: *a concise summary of a speech.* SUCCINCT suggests clarity of expression as well as brevity: *praised for her succinct statement of the problem.* TERSE suggests brevity combined with wit or polish to produce particularly effective expression; however, it may also suggest brusqueness: *a terse prose style; offended by a terse reply.*

decay, *v.* DECAY, DECOMPOSE, DISINTEGRATE, ROT imply a deterioration or falling away from a sound condition. DECAY implies either entire or partial deterioration by progressive natural changes: *Teeth often decay.* DECOMPOSE suggests the reducing of a substance to its component elements: *Moisture makes some chemical compounds decompose.* DISINTEGRATE emphasizes the breaking up, going to pieces, or wearing away of anything, so that its original wholeness is impaired: *Rocks may disintegrate.* ROT is applied especially to decaying vegetable matter, which may or may not emit offensive odors: *Potatoes can rot.*

decide, *v.* DECIDE, RESOLVE, DETERMINE imply settling something in dispute or doubt. To DECIDE is to make up one's mind after consideration: *I decided to go to the party.* To RESOLVE is to settle conclusively with firmness of purpose: *She resolved to ask for a promotion.* To DETERMINE is to settle after investigation or observation: *It is difficult to determine the best course of action.*

declare, *v.* DECLARE, AFFIRM, ASSERT imply making something known emphatically, openly, or formally. To DECLARE is to make known, sometimes in the face of actual or potential contradiction: *to declare someone the winner of a contest.* To AFFIRM is to make a statement based on one's reputation for knowledge or veracity, or so related to a generally recognized truth that denial is not likely: *to affirm the necessity of high standards.* To ASSERT is to state boldly, usually without other proof than personal authority or conviction: *to assert that the climate is changing.*

decrease, *v.* DECREASE, DIMINISH, DWINDLE, SHRINK imply becoming smaller or less in amount. DECREASE commonly implies a sustained reduction in stages, especially of bulk, size, volume, or quantity, often from some imperceptible cause or inherent process: *The swelling decreased daily.* DIMINISH usually implies the action of some external cause that keeps taking away: *Disease caused the number of troops to diminish steadily.* DWINDLE implies an undesirable reduction by degrees, resulting in attenuation: *His followers dwindled to a mere handful.* SHRINK especially implies contraction through an inherent property under specific conditions: *Many fabrics shrink in hot water.*

defeat, *v.* DEFEAT, CONQUER, OVERCOME, SUBDUE imply gaining victory or control over an opponent. DEFEAT usually means to beat or frustrate in a single contest or conflict: *Confederate forces were defeated at Gettys-*

burg. CONQUER means to finally gain control over by physical, moral, or mental force, usually after long effort: *to conquer poverty; to conquer a nation.* OVERCOME emphasizes perseverance and the surmounting of difficulties: *to overcome opposition; to overcome a bad habit.* SUBDUE means to conquer so completely that resistance is broken: *to subdue a rebellious spirit.*

defect, *n.* DEFECT, BLEMISH, FLAW refer to faults, both literal and figurative, that detract from perfection. DEFECT is the general word for any kind of shortcoming, imperfection, or deficiency, whether hidden or visible: *a birth defect; a defect in a plan.* A BLEMISH is usually a surface defect that mars the appearance; it is also used of a moral fault: *a skin blemish; a blemish on his reputation.* A FLAW is usually a structural defect or weakness that mars the quality or effectiveness: *a flaw in a diamond.*

dwarf, *n.* DWARF, MIDGET, PYGMY are terms for a very small person. A DWARF is someone checked in growth or stunted, or in some way not normally formed. A MIDGET (not in technical use) is someone normally proportioned, but diminutive. A PYGMY is properly a member of one of certain small-sized peoples of Africa and Asia, but the word is often used imprecisely to mean dwarf or midget. DWARF is a term often used to describe very small plants. PYGMY is used to describe very small animals.

effective, *adj.* EFFECTIVE, EFFECTUAL, EFFICACIOUS, EFFICIENT refer to that which produces or is able to produce an effect. EFFECTIVE is applied to something that produces a desired or expected effect, often a lasting one: *an effective speech.* EFFECTUAL usually refers to something that produces a decisive outcome or result: *an effectual settlement.* EFFICACIOUS refers to something capable of achieving a certain end or purpose: *an efficacious remedy.* EFFICIENT, usually used of a person, implies skillful accomplishment of a purpose with little waste of effort: *an efficient manager.*

element, *n.* ELEMENT, COMPONENT, CONSTITUENT, INGREDIENT refer to units that are parts of whole or complete substances, systems, compounds, or mixtures. ELEMENT denotes a fundamental, ultimate part: *the elements of matter; the elements of a problem.* COMPONENT refers to one of a number of separate parts: *Iron and carbon are components of steel.* CONSTITUENT refers to an active and necessary part: *The constituents of a molecule of water are two atoms of hydrogen and one of oxygen.* INGREDIENT is most frequently used in nonscientific contexts to denote any part that is combined into a mixture: *the ingredients of a cake; the ingredients of a successful marriage.*

excuse, *v.* EXCUSE, FORGIVE, PARDON imply being lenient or giving up the wish to punish. EXCUSE means to overlook some (usually) slight offense, because of circumstance, realization that it was unintentional, or the like: *to excuse rudeness.* FORGIVE is applied to excusing more serious offenses; the person wronged not only overlooks the offense but harbors no ill feeling against the offender: *to forgive and forget.* PARDON often applies to an act of leniency or mercy by an official or superior; it usually involves a serious offense or crime: *The governor was asked to pardon the condemned criminal.*

fair, *adj.* FAIR, IMPARTIAL, DISINTERESTED refer to lack of bias in opinions, judgments, etc. FAIR implies the treating of all sides alike, justly and equitably: *a fair compromise.* IMPARTIAL also implies showing no more favor to one side than another, but suggests particularly a judicial consideration of a case: *an impartial judge.* DISINTERESTED implies a fairness arising from lack of desire to obtain a selfish advantage: *a disinterested concern that the best person win.*

false, *adj.* FALSE, SHAM, COUNTERFEIT agree in referring to something that is not genuine. FALSE is used mainly of imitations of concrete objects; it sometimes implies an intent to deceive: *false teeth; false hair.* SHAM is rarely used of concrete objects and usually has the suggestion of intent to deceive: *a sham title; sham tears.* COUNTERFEIT always has the implication of cheating; it is used particularly of spurious imitation of coins and paper money. Figuratively, it means not real, pretended: *counterfeit grief.*

famous, *adj.* FAMOUS, CELEBRATED, RENOWNED, NOTORIOUS refer to someone or something widely known. FAMOUS is the general word for a person or thing that receives wide public notice, usually favorable: *a famous lighthouse.* CELEBRATED refers to a famous person or thing that enjoys wide public praise or honor for merit, services, etc.: *a celebrated poet.* RENOWNED usually implies wider, greater, and more enduring fame and glory: *a renowned hospital.* NOTORIOUS means widely known and discussed because of some bad or evil quality or action: *a notorious criminal.*

fault, *n.* FAULT, FOIBLE, WEAKNESS, FAILING, VICE refer to human shortcomings or imperfections. FAULT refers to any ordinary shortcoming; condemnation is not necessarily implied: *Of his many faults the greatest is vanity.* FOIBLE suggests a weak point that is

slight and often amusing, manifesting itself in eccentricity rather than in wrongdoing: *the foibles of an artist.* WEAKNESS suggests that a person is unable to control a particular impulse or response, and gives way to it: *a weakness for ice cream.* FAILING is particularly applied to humanity at large, suggesting common, often venial, shortcomings: *Procrastination is a common failing.* VICE is the strongest term and designates a habit that is detrimental, immoral, or evil: *to succumb to the vice of compulsive gambling.*

frank, *adj.* FRANK, CANDID, OPEN, OUTSPOKEN imply a freedom and boldness in speaking. FRANK implies a straightforward, almost tactless expression of one's real opinions or sentiments: *He was frank in his rejection of the proposal.* CANDID suggests sincerity, truthfulness, and impartiality: *a candid appraisal of her work.* OPEN implies a lack of reserve or of concealment: *open antagonism.* OUTSPOKEN suggests free and bold expression, even when it is inappropriate: *an outspoken and unnecessary show of disapproval.*

gather, *v.* GATHER, ASSEMBLE, COLLECT, MUSTER, MARSHAL imply bringing or drawing together. GATHER expresses the general idea usually with no implication of arrangement: *to gather seashells.* ASSEMBLE is used of persons, objects, or facts brought together in a specific place or for a specific purpose: *to assemble data for a report.* COLLECT implies purposeful accumulation to form an ordered whole: *to collect evidence.* MUSTER, primarily a military term, suggests thoroughness in the process of collection: *to muster all one's resources.* MARSHAL, another chiefly military term, suggests rigorously ordered, purposeful arrangement: *to marshal facts for effective presentation.*

give, *v.* GIVE, CONFER, GRANT, PRESENT mean that something concrete or abstract is bestowed on one person by another. GIVE is the general word: *to give someone a book.* CONFER usually means to give as an honor or as a favor; it implies courteous and gracious giving: *to confer a medal.* GRANT is usually limited to the idea of acceding to a request or fulfilling an expressed wish; it often involves a formal act or legal procedure: *to grant a prayer; to grant immunity.* PRESENT, a more formal word than GIVE, usually implies a certain ceremony in the giving: *to present an award.*

healthy, *adj.* HEALTHY, HEALTHFUL, WHOLESOME refer to physical, mental, or moral health and well-being. HEALTHY most often applies to what possesses health, but may apply to what promotes health: *a healthy* *child; a healthy climate.* HEALTHFUL is usually applied to something conducive to physical health: *a healthful diet.* WHOLESOME, connoting freshness and purity, applies to something that is physically or morally beneficial: *wholesome food; wholesome entertainment.*

help, *v.* HELP, AID, ASSIST, SUCCOR agree in the idea of furnishing someone with something that is needed. HELP implies furnishing anything that furthers one's efforts or satisfies one's needs: *I helped her plan the concert.* AID and ASSIST, somewhat more formal, imply a furthering or seconding of another's efforts. AID suggests an active helping; ASSIST suggests less need and less help: *to aid the poor; to assist a teacher in the classroom.* To SUCCOR, still more formal and literary, is to give timely help and relief to someone in difficulty or distress: *Succor him in his hour of need.*

idea, *n.* IDEA, THOUGHT, CONCEPTION, NOTION refer to a product of mental activity. IDEA refers to a mental representation that is the product of understanding or creative imagination: *She had an excellent idea for the class reunion.* THOUGHT emphasizes the intellectual processes of reasoning, contemplating, reflecting, or recollecting: *I welcomed his thoughts on the subject.* CONCEPTION suggests imaginative, creative, and somewhat intricate mental activity: *The architect's conception of the building was a glass skyscraper.* NOTION suggests a fleeting, vague, or imperfect thought: *I had only a bare notion of how to proceed.*

importance, *n.* IMPORTANCE, CONSEQUENCE, SIGNIFICANCE, MOMENT refer to something valuable, influential, or worthy of note. IMPORTANCE is the most general of these terms, assigning exceptional value or influence to a person or thing: *the importance of Einstein's discoveries.* CONSEQUENCE may suggest personal distinction, or may suggest importance based on results to be produced: *a woman of consequence in world affairs; an event of great consequence for our future.* SIGNIFICANCE carries the implication of importance not readily or immediately recognized: *The significance of the discovery became clear many years later.* MOMENT, on the other hand, usually refers to immediately apparent, self-evident importance: *an international treaty of great moment.*

join, *v.* JOIN, CONNECT, UNITE imply bringing two or more things together more or less closely. JOIN may refer to a connection or association of any degree of closeness, but often implies direct contact: *to join pieces of wood to form a corner.* CONNECT implies a

joining as by a tie, link, or wire: *to connect two batteries.* UNITE implies a close joining of two or more things, so as to form one: *to unite layers of veneer sheets to form plywood.*

language, *n.* LANGUAGE, DIALECT, JARGON, VERNACULAR refer to patterns of vocabulary, syntax, and usage characteristic of communities of various sizes and types. LANGUAGE is applied to the general pattern of a people or nation: *the English language.* DIALECT is applied to regionally or socially distinct forms or varieties of a language, often forms used by provincial communities that differ from the standard variety: *the Scottish dialect.* JARGON is applied to the specialized language, especially the vocabulary, used by a particular (usually occupational) group within a community or to language considered unintelligible or obscure: *technical jargon.* The VERNACULAR is the natural, everyday pattern of speech, usually on an informal level, used by people indigenous to a community.

legend, *n.* LEGEND, MYTH, FABLE refer to stories handed down from earlier times, often by word of mouth. A LEGEND is a story associated with a people or a nation; it is usually concerned with a real person, place, or event and is popularly believed to have some basis in fact: *the legend of King Arthur.* A MYTH is one of a class of purportedly historical stories that attempt to explain some belief, practice, or natural phenomenon; the characters are usually gods or heroes: *the Greek myth about Demeter.* A FABLE is a fictitious story intended to teach a moral lesson; the characters are usually animals: *the fable about the fox and the grapes.*

liquid, *n.* LIQUID, FLUID agree in referring to matter that is not solid. LIQUID commonly refers to substances, as water, oil, alcohol, and the like, that are neither solids nor gases: *Water ceases to be a liquid when it is frozen or turned to steam.* FLUID is applied to anything that flows, whether liquid or gaseous: *Pipes can carry fluids from place to place.*

list, *n.* LIST, CATALOG, INVENTORY, ROLL imply a meaningful arrangement of items. LIST denotes a series of names, figures, or other items arranged in a row or rows: *a grocery list.* CATALOG adds the idea of an alphabetical or other orderly arranged list of goods or services, usually with descriptive details: *a mail-order catalog.* INVENTORY refers to a detailed, descriptive list of goods or property, made for legal or business purposes: *The company's inventory consists of 2,000* *items.* A ROLL is a list of names of members of a group, often used to check attendance: *The teacher called the roll.*

male, *adj.* MALE, MASCULINE, VIRILE describe men and boys or whatever is culturally attributed to them. MALE classifies individuals on the basis of their genetic makeup or their ability to fertilize an ovum in bisexual reproduction. It contrasts with FEMALE in all uses: *his oldest male relative; the male parts of the flower.* MASCULINE refers to qualities or behavior deemed especially appropriate to or ideally associated with men and boys. In American and Western European culture, this has traditionally included such traits as strength, aggressiveness, and courage: *a firm, masculine handshake; masculine impatience at indecision.* VIRILE implies the muscularity, vigor, and sexual potency of mature manhood: *a swaggering, virile walk.*

meaning, *n.* MEANING, SENSE, SIGNIFICANCE, PURPORT denote that which is expressed or indicated by language or action. MEANING is a general word describing that which is intended to be, or actually is, expressed: *the meaning of a statement.* SENSE often refers to a particular meaning of a word or phrase: *The word "run" has many senses.* SENSE may also be used of meaning that is intelligible or reasonable: *There's no sense in what you say.* SIGNIFICANCE refers to a meaning that is implied rather than expressed: *the significance of a glance.* It may also refer to a meaning the importance of which is not immediately perceived: *We did not grasp the significance of the event until years later.* PURPORT usually refers to the gist or essential meaning of something fairly complicated: *the purport of a theory.*

method, *n.* METHOD, MODE, WAY refer to the manner in which something is done. METHOD implies a fixed procedure, usually following a logical and systematic plan: *the open-hearth method of making steel.* MODE, a more formal word, implies a customary or characteristic manner: *Kangaroos have an unusual mode of carrying their young.* WAY is a general word that may often be substituted for more specific words: *the best way to solve a problem; an attractive way of wearing the hair.*

mistake, *n.* MISTAKE, ERROR, BLUNDER, SLIP refer to an inadvertent deviation from accuracy, correctness, truth, or right conduct. MISTAKE refers to a wrong action, belief, or judgment; it may also suggest an incorrect understanding, perception, or interpretation: *a mistake in arithmetic; It was a mistake to trust them.* ERROR is similar in sense, but may mean a deviation from a moral standard: *I finally saw the error of my ways.* BLUNDER suggests a careless, clumsy, or stupid mistake, often serious: *a tactical blunder.* SLIP refers to a small mistake in speech or writing, or to a minor indiscretion: *I misspelled his name by a slip of the pen.*

noise, *n.* NOISE, CLAMOR, HUBBUB, DIN, RACKET refer to nonmusical or confused sounds. NOISE is a general word that usually refers to loud, harsh, or discordant sounds: *noise from the street.* CLAMOR refers to loud noise, as from shouting or cries, that expresses feelings, desires, or complaints: *the clamor of an angry crowd.* HUBBUB refers to a confused mingling of sounds, usually voices; it may also mean tumult or confused activity: *the hubbub on the floor of the stock exchange.* DIN is a very loud, continuous noise that greatly disturbs or distresses: *the din of a factory.* RACKET refers to a rattling sound or clatter: *to make a racket when doing the dishes.*

oblige, *v.* OBLIGE, ACCOMMODATE imply making a gracious and welcome gesture of some kind. OBLIGE emphasizes the idea of doing a favor (and often of taking some trouble to do it): *to oblige someone with a loan.* ACCOMMODATE emphasizes providing a service or convenience: *to accommodate someone with lodgings and meals.*

oppose, *v.* OPPOSE, RESIST, WITHSTAND imply holding out or acting against something. OPPOSE implies offensive action against the opposite side in a conflict or contest; it may also refer to attempts to thwart displeasing ideas, methods, or the like: *to oppose an enemy; to oppose the passage of a bill.* RESIST suggests defensive action against a threatening force or possibility; it may also refer to an inner struggle in which the will is divided: *to resist an enemy onslaught; hard to resist the chocolate.* WITHSTAND generally implies successful resistance; it stresses the determination and endurance necessary to emerge unharmed: *to withstand public criticism; to withstand a siege.*

pardon, *n.* PARDON, AMNESTY, REPRIEVE refer to the remission or delay of a penalty or punishment for an offense; these terms do not imply absolution from guilt. A PARDON is often granted by a government official; it releases the individual from any punishment due: *The governor granted a pardon to the prisoner.* AMNESTY is usually a general pardon granted to a group of persons for offenses against a government; it often includes an assurance of no further prosecution: *to grant amnesty to the rebels.* A REPRIEVE is a delay of impending punishment, usually for a specific period of time or until a decision can be made as to the possibility of pardon or reduction of sentence: *a last-minute reprieve, allowing the prisoner to file an appeal.*

plentiful, *adj.* PLENTIFUL, AMPLE, ABUNDANT, BOUNTIFUL describe a more than adequate supply of something. PLENTIFUL suggests a large or full quantity: *a plentiful supply of fuel.* AMPLE suggests a quantity that is sufficient for a particular need or purpose: *an auditorium with ample seating for students.* ABUNDANT and BOUNTIFUL both imply a greater degree of plenty: *an abundant rainfall; a bountiful harvest.*

quality, *n.* QUALITY, ATTRIBUTE, PROPERTY refer to a distinguishing feature or characteristic of a person, thing, or group. A QUALITY is an innate or acquired characteristic that, in some particular, determines the nature and behavior of a person or thing; it often refers to a desirable trait: *the qualities of patience and perseverance.* An ATTRIBUTE is a quality that we assign or ascribe to a person or to something personified; it may also mean a fundamental or innate characteristic: *an attribute of God; attributes of a logical mind.* PROPERTY is applied only to a thing; it refers to a principal characteristic that is part of the constitution of a thing and serves to define or describe it: *the physical properties of limestone.*

reluctant, *adj.* RELUCTANT, LOATH, AVERSE describe disinclination toward something. RELUCTANT implies some sort of mental struggle, as between disinclination and sense of duty: *reluctant to expel students.* LOATH describes extreme disinclination: *loath to part from a friend.* AVERSE describes a long-held dislike or unwillingness, though not a particularly strong feeling: *averse to an idea; averse to getting up early.*

revenge, *n.* REVENGE, REPRISAL, RETRIBUTION, VENGEANCE suggest a punishment or injury inflicted in return for one received. REVENGE is the carrying out of a bitter desire to injure another for a wrong done to oneself or to those who are close to oneself: *to plot revenge for a friend's betrayal.* REPRISAL is used specifically in the context of warfare; it means retaliation against an enemy: *The guerrillas expected reprisals for the raid.* RETRIBUTION usually suggests deserved punishment for some evil done: *a just retribution for wickedness.* VENGEANCE is usually vindictive, furious revenge: *He swore vengeance against his enemies.*

scatter, *v.* SCATTER, DISPEL, DISPERSE, DISSIPATE imply separating and driving something away so that its original form disap-

pears. To SCATTER is to separate something tangible into parts at random and drive these in different directions: *The wind scattered leaves all over the lawn.* To DISPEL is to drive away or scatter usually intangible things so that they vanish: *Your explanation has dispelled my doubts.* To DISPERSE is usually to cause a compact or organized tangible body to separate or scatter in different directions, to be reassembled if desired: *Tear gas dispersed the mob.* To DISSIPATE is usually to scatter by dissolving or reducing to small atoms or parts that cannot be reunited: *He dissipated his money and his energy in useless activities.*

speed, *n.* SPEED, VELOCITY, CELERITY refer to swift or energetic movement or operation. SPEED may apply to human or nonhuman activity; it emphasizes the rate in time at which something travels or operates: *the speed of an automobile; the speed of thought.* VELOCITY, a more technical term, is commonly used to refer to high rates of speed, linear or circular: *the velocity of a projectile.* CELERITY, a somewhat literary term, usually refers to human movement or operation, and emphasizes dispatch or economy in an activity: *the celerity of his response.*

stubborn, *adj.* STUBBORN, OBSTINATE, DOGGED, PERSISTENT imply fixity of purpose or condition and resistance to change. STUBBORN and OBSTINATE both imply resistance to advice, entreaty, protest, or force; but STUBBORN implies an innate characteristic and is the term usually used when referring to inanimate things: *a stubborn child; a stubborn lock; an obstinate customer.* DOGGED implies willfulness and tenacity, especially in the face of obstacles: *dogged determination.* PERSISTENT implies having staying or lasting qualities, resoluteness, and perseverance: *persistent questioning.*

talkative, *adj.* TALKATIVE, GARRULOUS, LOQUACIOUS characterize a person who talks a great deal. TALKATIVE is a neutral or mildly unfavorable word for a person who is much inclined to talk, sometimes without significance: *a talkative child.* The GARRULOUS person talks with wearisome persistence, usually about trivial things: *a garrulous cab driver.* A LOQUACIOUS person, intending to be sociable, talks continuously and at length: *a loquacious host.*

theory, *n.* THEORY, HYPOTHESIS are used in non-technical contexts to mean an untested idea or opinion. A THEORY in technical use is a more or less verified or established explanation accounting for known facts or phenomena: *Einstein's theory of relativity.* A HYPOTHESIS is a conjecture put forth as a possible explanation of phenomena or relations, which serves as a basis of argument or experimentation to reach the truth: *This idea is only a hypothesis.*

use, *v.* USE, UTILIZE mean to put something into action or service. USE is a general word referring to the application of something to a given purpose: *to use a telephone.* USE may also imply that the thing is consumed or diminished in the process: *I used all the butter.* When applied to persons, USE implies a selfish or sinister purpose: *He used his friend to advance himself.* UTILIZE, a more formal word, implies practical, profitable, or creative use: *to utilize solar energy to run a machine.*

usual, *adj.* USUAL, CUSTOMARY, HABITUAL refer to something that is familiar because it is commonly met with or observed. USUAL indicates something that is to be expected by reason of previous experience, which shows it to occur more often than not: *There were the usual crowds at the monument.* CUSTOMARY refers to something that accords with prevailing usage or individual practice: *customary courtesies; a customary afternoon nap.* HABITUAL refers to a practice that has become fixed by regular repetition: *a clerk's habitual sales pitch.*

value, *n.* VALUE, WORTH both imply excellence and merit. VALUE is excellence based on desirability, usefulness, or importance; it may be measured in terms of its equivalent in money, goods, or services: *the value of sunlight; the value of a painting.* WORTH usu-

ally implies inherent excellence based on spiritual and moral qualities that command esteem: *Few knew her true worth.*

waver, *v.* WAVER, VACILLATE refer to an inability to decide or to stick to a decision. WAVER usually implies a state of doubt, uncertainty, or fear that prevents one from pursuing a chosen course: *He made plans to move, but wavered at the last minute.* VACILLATE means to go back and forth between choices without reaching a decision, or to make up one's mind and change it again suddenly: *Stop vacillating and set a day.*

woman, *n.* WOMAN, FEMALE, LADY are nouns referring to adult human beings who are biologically female, that is, capable of bearing offspring. WOMAN is the general, neutral term: *a wealthy woman.* In scientific, statistical, and other objective use FEMALE is the neutral contrastive term to MALE: *104 females to every 100 males.* FEMALE is sometimes used disparagingly: *a gossipy female.* LADY in the sense "polite, refined woman" is a term of approval: *We know you will always behave like a lady.*

yearn, *v.* YEARN, LONG, HANKER, PINE all mean to feel a strong desire for something. YEARN stresses the depth and power of the desire: *to yearn to begin a new life.* LONG implies a wholehearted desire for something that is or seems unattainable: *to long to relive one's childhood.* HANKER suggests a restless or incessant craving: *to hanker after fame and fortune.* PINE adds the notion of physical or emotional suffering due to the real or apparent hopelessness of one's desire: *to pine for a lost love.*